A SELECT LIBRARY

OF THE

NICENE AND POST-NICENE FATHERS

OF

THE CHRISTIAN CHURCH

EDITED BY

PHILIP SCHAFF, D.D., LL. D.,

PROFESSOR OF CHURCH HISTORY IN THE UNION THEOLOGICAL SEMINARY, NEW YORK.

IN CONNECTION WITH A NUMBER OF PATRISTIC SCHOLARS OF EUROPE AND AMERICA

VOLUME XI.

SAINT CHRYSOSTOM:

HOMILIES ON THE ACTS OF THE APOSTLES AND
THE EPISTLE TO THE ROMANS

T&T CLARK
EDINBURGH

WM. B. EERDMANS PUBLISHING COMPANY
GRAND RAPIDS, MICHIGAN

British Library Cataloguing in Publication Data

Nicene & Post-Nicene Fathers. — 1st series
1. Fathers of the church
I. Title   II. Schaff, Philip
230′.11   BR60.A62

T&T Clark ISBN 0 567 09400 6

Eerdmans ISBN 0-8028-8109-2

Reprinted, May 1989

PHOTOLITHOPRINTED BY CUSHING - MALLOY, INC.
ANN ARBOR, MICHIGAN, UNITED STATES OF AMERICA

PREFACE TO THE AMERICAN EDITION.

In the preparation of this volume of Chrysostom's Homilies on Acts and Romans, the effort has been to improve the Oxford edition by some changes and corrections, and by the addition of critical and explanatory notes. The translation remains substantially unchanged. Frequent minor changes have, however, been made in phraseology, where it has seemed to me that the sense could thereby be made plainer. Archaic and obsolescent words or expressions have often been replaced by more idiomatic modern language. In Biblical quotations where the translation was an inaccurate rendering of the original, I have substituted either the Revised Version or a translation conformed to the recent critical texts. A considerable number of errors in the English edition have been corrected. The imperfect state of the original text of the Homilies on Acts is a serious embarrassment, alike to translator and editor, in this part of the work. Often the reports of the discourses are in hopeless confusion, and it is impossible to determine confidently the meaning of what has been reported, much less of what the preacher originally said. Happily this remark applies to only a part of the exposition.

The notes which I have added are intended to bring modern criticism into relation with the statements of Chrysostom upon points of special difficulty or importance. Sometimes they are added by way of correction to what is stated in the text. More frequently however, they are intended to present briefly the opinions of critical interpreters upon disputed or doubtful points, and thus to supplement for the modern reader the practical expositions of these books of the New Testament. At other times it has seemed desirable to explain matters which are but lightly touched upon in the text or passed over without explanation or notice. There is frequent occasion to observe how the spiritual insight of the great preacher has led him, in the case of difficult passages, to a right discernment of the same sense which critical exegesis discovers. I trust that these brief annotations, touching upon a great variety of points, may contribute somewhat to the usefulness of the edition.

These notes are distinguished from those of the English editors by having appended to them the initials, G. B. S.

The annotations of the English editors which are so copious upon the Homilies on Acts have been, with trifling exceptions, retained and the references have been, so far as possible, adapted to the American edition. It is obvious, however, that this adaptation could not be perfectly made because but few of the volumes of the American edition of the Homilies had appeared when this volume was prepared for the press. References to English editions of works not yet accessible in an American edition were, of necessity, left unchanged. Some small portions of the work of the English editors which seemed to have no present value have been omitted. It is not improbable that still other omissions might well have been made, but the editor has been slow to follow his own judgment in this particular in dealing with the conscientious and painstaking labors of the Oxford editors.

It will be noticed that the English notes to the Homilies on Romans are few and brief. These have been retained with such adaptations as could be made, and the American editor has added a considerable number of statements of critical opinions, together with such explanations of the course of thought and connections of ideas in difficult passages of the Epistle, as seemed desirable and useful. In the Homilies on Romans the state of the text is such and the work of the translators so well performed, that one is rarely at a loss to perceive the author's meaning; the nature and limitations of his exposition, however, seem to call for occasional supplementing and correction.

The indexes have been carefully revised. Topics which seemed unimportant and texts which are merely quoted or alluded to, without being explained, have often been omitted. By this process of revision the size of the indexes has been considerably reduced. It is hoped that they will be found sufficient to guide those who consult the volume to what is said upon the main themes which find place in it.

GEORGE B. STEVENS.

YALE UNIVERSITY, NEW HAVEN, March, 1889.

THE HOMILIES OF ST. JOHN CHRYSOSTOM,

ARCHBISHOP OF CONSTANTINOPLE,

ON THE

ACTS OF THE APOSTLES,

TRANSLATED, WITH NOTES AND INDICES, BY

REV. J. WALKER, M. A.,

OF BRASENOSE COLLEGE ;

REV. J. SHEPPARD, M. A.,

OF ORIEL COLLEGE, OXFORD ; AND

REV. H. BROWNE, M. A.,

OF CORPUS CHRISTI COLLEGE, CAMBRIDGE.

REVISED, WITH NOTES, BY

GEORGE B. STEVENS, PH.D., D. D.,

PROFESSOR IN YALE UNIVERSITY.

CONTENTS.

PREFACE TO PART I. OF THE OXFORD EDITION.

THE present volume of St. Chrysostom on the Acts of the Apostles has been delayed for some time by the difficulty of fixing the Text. Some farther account of the grounds on which this has been done will be given in the Preface to Part II. (vid. *infra*.) It may suffice for the present to say, that these Homilies appear to have been less carefully reported than usual, and published without a revision by the Author. The printed text was formed for the most part (Erasmus's Latin Version entirely) from a manuscript, said to be of the tenth century, in which these Homilies are given in a very different form, evidently the work of a later hand, and intended to make them read more smoothly. The earlier text, shown to be such by internal evidence, and alone followed in the Catena and all other ancient extracts and compilations, is preserved in other Mss. and appears to have been in general disregarded by former editors, from its difficulty. The Translation was originally made from Savile's Text, by the Rev. J. WALKER, M.A. of Brasenose College, and the Rev. J. SHEPPARD, M.A. of Oriel College, Oxford. The Editors are much indebted to the Rev. H. BROWNE, M.A. of Corpus Christi College, Cambridge, who has restored the Text and corrected the Translation accordingly, the difference being frequently so great as to require a passage to be translated anew. He has likewise undertaken to prepare the Greek Text for publication, and to supply the prefatory matter. Many passages will still be found imperfect and unsatisfactory, but it has been thought better to leave them evidently so, than to resort to uncertain conjectures. A few conjectural emendations, however, have been admitted into the Text, and many more suggested.

C. MARRIOTT.

OXFORD, *Feast of St. James*, 1851.

PREFACE TO PART II. OF THE OXFORD EDITION.

THE manifestly imperfect condition in which these Homilies have come to us may partly be accounted for by the circumstances of the times in which they were preached. It was in the Easter weeks of the third year of his residence at Constantinople as Archbishop, that St. Chrysostom began this course of Sermons; and during all the remaining part of that year (A.D. 400), the Capital of the East was kept in constant trouble and alarm by the revolt of Gainas and the Goths. Moreover, scarcely had the preaching commenced, when the complaints from the Churches of Asia Minor were brought (May, 400) before the Metropolitan See, which business during many months painfully occupied the Archbishop's thoughts, and eventually demanded his presence at Ephesus. Few of St. Chrysostom's Sermons were originally prepared in writing: certainly these were not: and as certainly the text, drawn up by no skilful hand from notes taken during the preaching, can never have been revised by the Preacher himself. This was a serious disadvantage: for these Homilies, if only from the novelty of the subject, stood especially in need of revision. *The Acts of the Apostles*, though read in the churches in the season between Easter and Pentecost, were seldom preached upon; and we find St. Chrysostom complaining in the opening of these Homilies, as also on an earlier occasion at Antioch, that this portion of the Scriptures was not so much read as it ought to be, nay, that there were "many to whom this Book was not even known." (p. 1 and note [1]). Hence it is not surprising, if the Preacher was not always understood; and, in fact, the attentive reader will not unfrequently see reason to suspect, that the scribe (or "reporter,") from whose notes the text was formed, did not rightly apprehend the sense of what he heard. Nor has the transcriber (or "redactor") remedied the defects, whatever they may have been, of the original report. On the contrary, in other ways, of which we shall have to speak presently, he has often perplexed the sense, and sometimes entirely misrepresented the Preacher's meaning.

The earliest mention of our Homilies is by Cassiodorus (A.D. 514), who relates, that with the assistance of friends he caused "the fifty-five Homilies on the Acts, by St. John, Bishop of Constantinople," to be translated into Latin, *Opp.* t. ii. p. 544. This version unfortunately is lost.* In the Canons of the Fifth and Sixth General Councils, St. Chrysostom's view of the Seven Deacons in the Acts is cited at length from Hom. xiv. (p. 91). John of Damascus, *de Fid. Orthod.* iii. 15, (A.D. 730), cites as from the second of these Homilies a passage which appears in the first, being the comment on i. 9. Photius has an entry in the *Bibliotheca* relating to them, but by some mistake the number is given as fifty. Of the *Catena* on the Acts, compiled by a certain Andreas Presbyter of unknown age and country, but not later than the tenth century (for there is a manuscript of that age), a large proportion is taken from St. Chrysostom: and the Commentaries of Œcumenius (990) and Theophylact (1077) are in many places formed from the Catena: as also are the Scholia in Mss. of the Acts. To these may be added the *Florilegium* or *Ecloga*, a compilation the date of which is unknown, but certainly not later than the first half of the eleventh century. The Author of this work seems to have resorted to our Homilies once only (Hom. xix. p 139): but there, he, as all the rest who have been mentioned, used the text which in the notes we call *the old text*, and from which the present Translation is made.

For there is another and a widely different text, by which alone, unfortunately, these Homilies have been known in modern times, except by the few who have had access to Manuscripts. In the National Library at Paris there is (No. 729) a manuscript (in our notes marked E, in Par. Ben. 2, D), which the Parisian Editor describes thus: *Quorum* (of six Mss. on the Acts) *antiquissimus, olim Colb. nunc Reg.* 729, *sæc.* X., *nitide et accurate scriptus, desinit in hom. quinquagesima.* (This is a mistake; it reaches to the end of the 55th.) Of the other Mss. he assigns A. B. C. (No. 725, 6, 7), to the twelfth, fourteenth and thirteenth centuries respectively. These, and a copy in the Library of New College (N), contain the *old text*. Two others D, F, (728, and 73 suppl.) exhibit a text compiled from old and new, and with alterations peculiar to itself. Of the six Parisian Mss. a full collation was made for "the Library of the Fathers:" of N we have at present but a partial collation.

The Ms. E. came into the hands of Erasmus, and from it he made his Latin version, down to the end of Hom. liii. and there for some reason which is not explained he goes off to the other text, of which he has nowhere taken notice in the preceding Homilies. Of this work he says in an Epistle to Tonstal, Bishop of Durham: *Ex Chrysostomo in Acta verteram homilias tres; cujus operæ me pœnituit, cum nihil hic viderem Chrysostomi. Tuo tamen hortatu recepi codicem in manum; sed nihil unquam legi indoctius. Ebrius ac stertens scriberem meliora. Habet frigidos sensiculos nec eos satis commode potest explicare.* In his Preface, however, he considerably abates the severity of this censure, and contents himself with hinting a doubt whether the work be St. Chrysostom's: *quod stylus concisum quiddam et abruptum habeat, id quod a phrasi Chrysostomi videtur alienum: si docti tamen censebunt opus Chrysostomo dignum, libenter hoc ego quicquid est suspicionis ponam.*

Of the Greek text, the *editio princeps*, that of Commelin, professes to be formed from manuscripts *Biblioth. Palatinæ Bavaræ, Augustanæ, Pistorianæ,* of which at present we are unable to give any account. Perhaps Commelin's leading Ms. was of a composite order: such however is his text; for it occasionally deserts E, to which, as a general rule, it closely adheres. This was inconsistent, for the circumstances of the two texts are such, that one or other ought to be followed throughout. There can be no valid reason for alternating between the two: for they are not different reports of the same matter, such that between them one might hope to approximate to the truth: the one is a refashionment of the other, and where it differs, it does so, not because its framer had a more correct report of the Sermons, but because he wished to improve upon the materials which lay before him in the other text.

Commelin's text, in substance, is retained in all the subsequent editions. Savile, from the New College Ms. has corrected words and phrases here and there, but in the main his text is still that of the *editio princeps*. (He describes it as composed from the New College Ms., another belonging to J. A. de Thou (Thuanus), *et tertio non ita pridem excuso in Germania.*) The edition of Morel (which commonly goes under the name of Fronto Ducæus) repeats Commelin, but without Savile's emendations: and the Benedictines (here not Montfaucon), though they profess to have collated the Parisian Mss., have reprinted with but slight improvements,

---

* From the same Cassiodorus there is extant a short work on the Acts under the title *Complexiones Actuum Apostolorum*: but this is merely a brief syllabus of the history, and contains nothing in which we could trace a reference to St. Chrysostom's Exposition.

and with not a few disimprovements, the text of Morel. In the Parisian reprint of the Benedictine Chrysostom (Par. Ben. 2), the Editor has occasionally, but not constantly, recurred to the manuscripts, rarely gives the preference to the text of A. B. C., and constantly assumes the inferiority of those copies, in contents and authenticity as well as in antiquity, to the manuscript (E), which furnished the Latin version of Erasmus, and in substance, as we have explained, the printed text of the original.

Had the Editors collated the manuscript copies of these Homilies—a labor from which they, or those whom they employed, seem to have shrunk—they would probably have reversed their estimate of the relative value of the two recensions. The general superiority of the other text in point of sense and coherence, notwithstanding its frequent abruptness and uncouthness, is too evident to be called in question. Had they also collated the Catena, Œcumenius, Theophylact, and the Scholia, they would have found the external testimony to be coincident with the internal evidence to the higher antiquity as well as greater authenticity of the text which (for the most part unknown) they rejected. It would have been seen that this, besides being, with all its faults, incomparably better, was the older of the two; and that the other could claim no higher antiquity than that of the manuscript (said to be of the tenth century) in which it appears: that it is the work of some scribe, who, offended by the manifest abruptness and ruggedness of the earlier text, set himself to smooth out the difficulties, and to make it read more easily. For this is clearly the true state of the case. With this view, the scribe sometimes alters words and phrases, sometimes transposes: often omits, where he found something that he did not understand, oftener still amplifies, or rather dilutes: and interpolates matter which sometimes is demonstrably borrowed with little disguise from the Catena (see p. 113, note [1]; 279, note [3]; 280, note [2]); or which, when it is his own, is little worth. In short, he has thought more of sound than of sense, and if he could make a passage run smoothly to the ear, has given himself little concern whether St. Chrysostom was likely to have so thought, or so expressed himself. The notes appended to our Translation will abundantly substantiate this censure. To have noted all the variations, either of the printed text, or of E alone, would have been a task as unprofitable as it was wearisome: perhaps as it is, we have given more than enough to vindicate the claims of the older text. If any one desires larger materials for comparison, Erasmus' Latin version, which, except in the two last Homilies, keeps close to E, will show that the text which we represent in our Translation is, with all its imperfections, incomparably the better of the two. Even if it were otherwise and were the alterations not, as they mostly are, disfigurements, but, considered in themselves, decided improvements, still our duty was plain: the text which came to us accredited by all the testimony known to be extant, we were not at liberty to reject in favor of an alien recension, unknown to the Ancients, and, as far as our evidence goes, unheard of before the tenth century. Therefore, in forming the text for this Translation we have entirely dismissed E, except where it has preserved readings which came strictly under the description of "various readings."

But while confining ourselves to that older text, we were not to leave unnoticed its more patent defects and errors. We could not but perceive, that we had before us an unrevised report of St. Chrysostom's Sermons, which, especially in the Expositions, was frequently imperfect—sometimes, indeed, little more than a set of rough notes thrown together, with, apparently, little or no attempt at arrangement. So far as this imperfection was caused by the reporter's negligence or incapacity, there was no remedy: and leaving the matter as we found it, or, at most, inserting in the text the marks of a *lacuna*, we have only ventured, in the notes, to surmise what may have been the general purport of St. Chrysostom's remarks. In other places, where the defects of our sources seemed to be rather chargeable upon the redactor, we have sought to apply a remedy, sometimes, but rarely, by conjectural emendation; very often by inserting portions of sacred text or other connecting matter in [ ], and also by transposing parts which had fallen out of their true order. For it seems that the original transcript from the reporter's notes was defective in these two regards. (1) The reporter would frequently omit to note in his tablets the κείμενον or some other text of Scripture, or would indicate it in the shortest possible way by a word or two at the beginning and ending of the passage, intending to insert it afterwards at his leisure. It appears, however, that in many places this was either not done at all, or done in the wrong place. Hence where the text seemed incurably defective or perplexed, we have often been able to restore coherency by the simple expedient of inserting texts which were omitted, or else, by removing the texts altogether, and redistributing them among the comments. Almost any page of the Translation, especially in the Recapitulations, will illustrate this remark.

(2) It often happens, that the order of the comments both in the first and in the second exposition (or recapitulation), does not follow the order of the texts. Of course the Preacher might be supposed to have sometimes returned upon his own steps, but it was scarcely conceivable that St. Chrysostom should have delivered an Exposition perplexed, as we often found it, by disjointed remarks thrown together without the slightest method. It was necessary therefore to consider whether it might not be possible to educe something like connected exposition, by assuming that the reporter's notes had been transcribed from his tablets in a wrong order. Where it could be seen that one sentence or portion was given as comment on such a verse, another on some other verse, and so on, some clue to the true order was given us in the sequence of the texts

themselves. Even so, the difficulties which beset this part of our task were greater than can be readily estimated by any one who has not tried it. Sometimes the complication resisted all attempts at disentanglement. We are far from supposing that we have done all that might have been done in this way: but it is hoped that the labor which has been bestowed has not been altogether wasted, and that the restoration will carry with it its own evidence. And as in these attempts we have indicated by letters the order in which the trajected parts lie in the manuscripts, the reader in every case has the means of forming his own judgment. In the first seventeen Homilies, we have only now and then resorted to this method: not because it was less needed there, but because we had not then so clearly perceived what was the state of the case, and what was practicable in this way. The eighteenth furnishes a remarkable instance, pp. 116-120. Let any one read it in the order denoted by the letters, i. e. the six parts marked (*a*) consecutively, then the seven parts marked (*b*), inserting in the third of the latter (see p. 116, note [8]), the comment on v. 25, from page 117, ("And they when they had testified," etc., to "when the Samaritans believed,") and he will have the entire "recapitulation" or second exposition of the history of the Samaritans and Simon Magus as it appears in the Mss.—which he will plainly perceive could not have proceeded in that form from St. Chrysostom. The same matter, read as we have arranged it, will be found to form a continuous exposition, not indeed perfect, for the dislocated state into which it had fallen seems to have led to further corruptions on the part of the scribes: but at any rate coherent, and with the parts fitting into each other. Moreover, if the fourteen parts, as here arranged, be numbered 1. 2. 3. etc., it will be seen that the order in which they lie in the Mss. is 1. 3. 5 : 8. 10. 12 : 2. 4. 6 : 14 : 7. 9. 11. 13., whence it seems that the derangement proceeded by some kind of method. The like was often found to be the case in subsequent instances. In p. 229, the trajection is 1. 3. 5. 7. 9. 11. 13 : 2. 4. 6. 8. 10. 12 : i. e., the transcriber missed the alternate portions, and brought them all together at the end. In p. 229 (before the series just noticed), and 260, it is 3. 2. 1., and in 170, 4. 3. 2. 1., i. e. three, and four, parts read in reverse order. In a great number of instances the transposition is only of two parts, 2. 1 : sometimes repeated as in 235, 2. 1., 1 : 2. 1 : 234, 2. 1 : 1 : 2. 1 : 2. 1 : 196, 2. 1 : 1 : 2. 1 : 1 : 2. 1 : 1 : 2. 1. A form of frequent occurrence is 2. 4., 1. 3., as in 188, 220, 225, 247 ; and combined with others as in 213, 2. 4. 1. 3. 2. 1 : in 275, 2. 1 : 1 : 2. 4. 1. 3. and 183, 2. 1 : 1 : 2. 4. 1. 3 : 2. 1. There is the like regularity in the scheme 2. 1. 4. 3., p. 125 ; and 3. 1. 4. 2. p. 216, 301. In the last Homily, which is extremely confused, the trajection seems to yield this very regular scheme, 2. 4. 6. 1. 3. 5 : 1 : 5. 3. 1. 6. 4. 2. In other instances where the trajection is less regular, or does not seem to follow a rule, as in 151, 4. 1. 3. 2 : 152, 3. 2. 4. 1 : 242, 4. 6. 1. 3. 5. 7. 2. 8 : 250, 2. 1. 4. 8. 5. 3. 6. 9. 7. and in 298, 316, 321 (on which three see the notes), the transcriber may have gone wrong on other grounds, and not, as in the generality of instances, from mistaking the order in which the reporter had set the matter on his tablets. The trajections we have attempted to remedy occur mostly in the expository parts. In the *Ethica* it often appeared to us, that the coherency might be greatly improved by transposition, but the evidence of the true order was more precarious here, than where the sequence of the texts furnished a clue ; in these parts, therefore, we have rarely ventured upon applying this remedy.

In these ways it is hoped that something has been done towards presenting these Homilies in a form nearer to that in which they were delivered, than the form in which they are exhibited in the unadulterated manuscripts, much more in the printed editions. The task was arduous, and we are far from supposing that our labors have always been successful ; but at least we have not spared pains and diligence. The Translation was a work only less difficult than the reconstruction of the text. Here again much indulgence is needed on the score of the difficulty of producing a version, which, while it represented the original with its roughnesses and defects, should not be altogether unreadable. We have attempted, however, to give faithfully, though not always literally, the sense, or what seemed to be the sense, of our materials.

As a commentary on *the Acts of the Apostles*, this Work stands alone among the writings of the first ten centuries. The Expositions of St. Clement of Alexandria (in the *Hypotyposes*), of Origen, of Diodorus of Tarsus, and St. Chrysostom's teacher, Theodore of Mopsuestia, as well as of Ammonius and others whose materials are used in the Catena, have perished. Those who are acquainted with the characteristic qualities of St. Chrysostom's exegesis, will perceive here also the same excellencies which mark his other expository works —especially the clear and full exposition of the historical sense, and the exact appreciation of the rhetorical momenta in the discourses of St. Peter, St. Stephen, St. James and St. Paul, as recorded in the Acts. Of the *Ethica* it is perhaps not too much to affirm, that not the most finished work of St. Chrysostom will be found to furnish more of instruction and interesting *matter* (apart from the expression) than will be found in these Homilies, on the religious and moral subjects of which they treat : for example, On the delay of Baptism, On spiritual indolence and excuses derived from the cessation of Miraculous Grace, On the nature and uses of Miracles, On Prayer, On the Study of the Scriptures, On Alms, On Anger and Gentleness, Against Oaths and Swearing, and many others. Nor does any work exhibit a livelier portraiture of the character and life of the great Preacher and Bishop, and of the manners of the times in which his lot was cast.

CONTENTS OF THE HOMILIES.

A COMMENTARY

ON

THE ACTS OF THE APOSTLES,

By ST. JOHN CHRYSOSTOM,

ARCHBISHOP OF CONSTANTINOPLE.[1]

HOMILY I.

ACTS I. 1, 2.

" The former treatise have I made, O Theophilus, concerning all things which Jesus began both to do and to teach, until the day on which, having given charge to the Apostles, whom He had chosen, by the Holy Spirit, He was taken up."

To many persons this Book is so little known, both it and its author, that they are not even aware that there is such a book in existence.[2] For this reason especially I have taken this narrative for my subject, that I may draw to it such as do not know it, and not let such a treasure as this remain hidden out of sight. For indeed it may profit us no less than even the Gospels; so replete is it with Christian wisdom and sound doctrine, especially in what is said concerning the Holy Ghost. Then let us not hastily pass by it, but examine it closely. Thus, the predictions which in the Gospels Christ utters, here we may see these actually come to pass; and

note in the very facts the bright evidence of Truth which shines in them, and the mighty change which is taking place in the disciples now that the Spirit has come upon them. For example, they heard Christ say, " Whoso believeth on Me, the works that I do shall he do also, and greater works than these shall he do " (John xiv. 12) : and again, when He foretold to the disciples, that they should be brought before rulers and kings, and in their synagogues they should scourge them, and that they should suffer grievous things, and overcome all (Matt. x. 18) : and that the Gospel should be preached in all the world (Ib. xxiv. 14) : now all this, how it came to pass exactly as it was said, may be seen in this Book, and more besides, which He told them while yet with them. Here again you will see the Apostles themselves, speeding their way as on wings over land and sea ; and those same men, once so timorous and void of understanding, on the sudden become quite other than they were ; men despising wealth, and raised above glory and passion and concupiscence, and in short all such affections : moreover, what unanimity there is among them now ; nowhere any envying as there was before, nor any of the old hankering after the preëminence, but all virtue brought in them to its last finish, and shining through all, with surpassing lustre, that charity, concerning which the Lord had given so many charges saying, " In this shall all men know that ye are My disciples, if ye love one another." (John xiii. 35.) And then, besides, there are doctrines to be found here, which we could not have known so surely as we now

[1] These Sermons were preached at Constantinople, in the second or third year of St. Chrysostom's archiepiscopate : see Hom. xliv. " Lo, by the grace of God, we also have been by the space of three years, not indeed night and day exhorting you, but often every third, or at least every seventh, day doing this." It appears from Hom. i. that the course began during the weeks of Easter : at which season the Book of Acts was by long established practice read in other Churches (as at Antioch and in Africa), if not at Constantinople. See St. Chrys. *Hom. Cur in Pentecoste Acta legantur*, and St. August. *Tr. in Joann.* vi. 18.

[2] St. Chrys. had made the same complaint at Antioch in the *Homilies* (A. D. 387) *in Principium Actorum*, etc. t. iii. p. 54. " We are about to set before you a strange and new dish. . . . strange, I say, and not strange. Not strange ; for it belongs to the order of Holy Scripture : and yet strange ; because peradventure your ears are not accustomed to such a subject. Certainly, there are many to whom this Book is not even known (πολλοῖς γοῦν τὸ βιβλίον τοῦτο οὐδὲ γνώριμόν ἐστι) and many again think it so plain, that they slight it : thus to some men their knowledge, to some their ignorance, is the cause of their neglect. . . . . We are to enquire then who wrote it, and when, and on what subject : and why it is ordered (νενομοθέτηται) to be read at this festival. For peradventure you do not hear this Book read [at other times] from year's end to year's end."

do, if this Book had not existed, but the very crowning point of our salvation would be hidden, alike for practice of life and for doctrine.

The greater part, however, of this work is occupied with the acts of Paul, who "laboured more abundantly than they all." (1. Cor. xv. 10.) And the reason is, that the author of this Book, that is, the blessed Luke, was his companion : a man, whose high qualities, sufficiently visible in many other instances, are especially shown in his firm adherence to his Teacher, whom he constantly followed.* Thus at a time when all had forsaken him, one gone into Galatia, another into Dalmatia, hear what he says of this disciple : "Only Luke is with me." (2 Tim. iv. 10.) And giving the Corinthians a charge concerning him, he says, "Whose praise is in the Gospel throughout all the Churches." (2 Cor. viii. 18.) Again, when he says, "He was seen of Cephas, then of the twelve," and, "according to the Gospel which ye received" (1 Cor. xv. 5, 1), he means the Gospel of this Luke.† So that there can be no mistake in attributing this work to him : and when I say, to him, I mean, to Christ.[3] And why then did he not relate every thing, seeing he was with Paul to the end? We may answer, that what is here written, was sufficient for those who would attend, and that the sacred writers ever addressed themselves to the matter of immediate importance, whatever it might be at the time : it was no object with them to be writers of books : in fact, there are many things which they have delivered by unwritten tradition. Now while all that is contained in this Book is worthy of admiration, so is especially the way the Apostles have of coming down to the wants of their hearers : a condescension suggested by the Spirit who has so ordered it, that the subject on which they chiefly dwell is that which pertains to Christ as man. For so it is, that while they discourse so much about Christ, they have spoken but little concerning His Godhead : it was mostly of the Manhood that they discoursed, and of the Passion, and the Resurrection, and the Ascension. For the thing required in the first instance was this, that it should be believed that He was risen, and ascended into heaven. As then the point on which Christ himself most insisted was, to have it known that He was come from the Father, so is it this writer's principal object to declare, that Christ was risen from the dead, and was received up into Heaven, and that He went to God, and came from God. For, if the fact of His coming from God were not first believed, much more, with the Resurrection and Ascension added thereto, would the Jews have found the entire doctrine incredible. Wherefore gently and by degrees he leads them on to higher truths. Nay, at Athens Paul even calls Him man simply, without saying more (Acts xvii. 31). For if, when Christ Himself spoke of His equality with the Father, they often attempted to stone Him, and called Him a blasphemer for this reason, it was little to be expected that they would receive this doctrine from the fishermen, and that too, with the Cross coming before it.

But why speak of the Jews, seeing that even the disciples often upon hearing the more sublime doctrines were troubled and offended? Therefore also He told them, "I have many things to say unto you, but ye cannot bear them now." (John xvi. 12.) If those could not, who had been so long time with Him, and had been admitted to so many secrets, and had seen so many wonders, how was it to be expected that men, but newly dragged away from altars, and idols, and sacrifices, and cats, and crocodiles (for such did the Gentiles worship), and from the rest of their evil ways, should all at once receive the more sublime matters of doctrine ? And how in particular should Jews, hearing as they did every day of their lives, and having it ever sounded in their ears, "The Lord thy God is one Lord, and beside Him is none other " (Deut. vi. 4): who also had seen Him hanging nailed on the Cross, nay, had themselves crucified and buried Him, and not seen Him even risen : when they were told that this same person was God and equal with the Father, how should they, of all men, be otherwise than shocked and revolted? Therefore it is that gently and little by little they carry them on, with much consideration and for-

---

* The two reasons which Chrysostom urges for the study of the Acts are also the two chief grounds upon which modern criticism depends for establishing not only the general trustworthiness of the book, but also its authorship by Luke. They are in substance, (1) The continuity of the history as connected with the gospels and, particularly, coincidences of style, matter and diction with the third gospel, and (2) The remarkable undesigned coincidences of statement between the Acts and Pauline Epistles which exclude the possibility of inter-dependence. From Col. i. 11, 14; Philem. 24; 2 Tim. iv. 11, we learn that Luke was a close companion of Paul. In the part of the Book of Acts which treats especially of the work of Paul, the writer frequently refers to himself in the use of the first person plural as an associate of the apostle (vid. xvi, 10 ; xx. 6 sq.; xxi. 1 sq.; xxvii. 1). These considerations demonstrate the fitness of Luke to prepare such a treatise as the Acts and render the supposition of his authorship plausible. When they are combined with those mentioned under (1) and when the dedication of both books to a certain Theophilus is considered, the argument becomes very cogent and complete. —G. B. S.

† The reference in the Text of the expression : "the Gospel which ye received," (1 Cor. xv. 1) to Luke's " gospel " is, of course, groundless. Paul speaks of it as the gospel which he preached unto them. It is " his gospel " as in Rom. ii. 16 ; xvi. 25; Gal. i. 11, etc. The use of εὐαγγέλιον to denote a book is post apostolic.—G. B. S.

[1] Hom. in Princip. Act. p. 54. "First we must see who wrote the Book. . . . whether a man, or God : and if man, let us reject it ; for, " Call no man master upon earth : but if God, let us receive it.""

bearance letting themselves down to their low attainments, themselves the while enjoying in more plentiful measure the grace of the Spirit, and doing greater works in Christ's name than Christ Himself did, that they may at once raise them up from their grovelling apprehensions, and confirm the saying, that Christ was raised from the dead. For this, in fact, is just what this Book is: a Demonstration of the Resurrection :[1]* this being once believed, the rest would come in due course. The subject then and entire scope of this Book, in the main, is just what I have said. And now let us hear the Preface itself.

"The former treatise have I made, O Theophilus, of all that Jesus began both to do and to teach." (v. 1.) Why does he put him in mind of the Gospel? To intimate how strictly he may be depended upon. For at the outset of the former work he says, " It seemed good to me also, having had perfect understanding of all things from the very first, to write unto thee in order." (Luke i. 3.) Neither is he content with his own testimony. but refers the whole matter to the Apostles. saying, " Even as they delivered them unto us, which from the beginning were eyewitnesses and ministers of the word." (Luke, i. 2.) Having then accredited his account in the former instance, he has no need to put forth his credentials afresh for this treatise, seeing his disciple has been once for all satisfied, and by the mention of that former work he has reminded him of the strict reliance to be placed in him for the truth. For if a person has shown himself competent and trustworthy to write of things which he has heard, and moreover has obtained our confidence, much more will he have a right to our confidence when he has composed an account, not of things which he has received from others, but of things which he has seen and heard. For thou didst receive what relates to Christ ; much more wilt thou receive what concerns the Apostles.

What then, (it may be asked), is it a question only of history, with which the Holy Spirit has nothing to do? Not so. For, if "those delivered it unto us, who from the beginning were eyewitnesses and ministers of the word;" then, what he says, is *theirs*. And why did he not say, ' As they who were counted worthy of the Holy Spirit delivered them unto us ;' but " Those who were eyewitnesses?" Because, in matter of belief, the very thing that gives one a right to be believed, is the having learned from eyewitnesses : whereas the other appears to foolish persons mere parade and pretension. And therefore John also speaks thus : " I saw, and bare record that this is the Son of God." (John i. 34.) And Christ expresses Himself in the same way to Nicodemus, while he was dull of apprehension, " We speak that we do know, and testify that we have seen ; and no one receiveth our witness." (Ib. iii. 11.) Accordingly, He gave them leave to rest their testimony in many particulars on the fact of their having seen them, when He said, " And do ye bear witness concerning Me, because ye have been with Me from the beginning." (John xv. 27.) The Apostles themselves also often speak in a similar manner ; " We are witnesses, and the Holy Spirit which God hath given to those that obey Him." (Acts ii. 32) ; and on a subsequent occasion, Peter, still giving assurance of the Resurrection, said, " Seeing we did eat and drink with Him." (Acts x. 41.) For they more readily received the testimony of persons who had been His companions, because the notion of the Spirit was as yet very much beyond them. Therefore John also at that time, in his Gospel, speaking of the blood and water, said, he himself *saw it*, making the fact of his having seen it equivalent, for them, to the highest testimony, although the witness of the Spirit is more certain than the evidence of sight, but not so with unbelievers. Now that Luke was a partaker of the Spirit, is abundantly clear, both from the miracles which even now take place ; and from the fact that in those times even ordinary persons were gifted with the Holy Ghost ; and again from the testimony of Paul, in these words, " Whose praise is in the Gospel " (2 Cor. viii. 18) ; and from the appointment to which he was chosen : for having said this, the Apostle adds, " But also appointed of the Churches to travel with us with this grace which is administered by us."*

Now mark how unassuming he is. He does not say, The former Gospel which I preached, but, " The former treatise have I made ; " accounting the title of Gospel to be too great for him ; although it is on the score

---

[1] *Hom. cur in Pentec. Acta legantur*, t. iii. p. 89. E. "The demonstration of the Resurrection is, the Apostolic miracles : and of the Apostolic miracles this Book is the school."

* The statement that the Acts is a "Demonstration of the Resurrection " has a certain profound truth, but is incorrect if intending to assert that such was the conscious purpose of the author. The resurrection of Jesus is a prominent theme in the Apostolic discourses, but the book is no more designed primarily to prove the resurrection than are the Epistles to the Romans and Corinthians. The immediate purpose of the book is to record the labors and triumphs of the Apostolic Church as supplementary to the narrative of the teaching and work of Jesus (i. 1, 2). The events narrated presuppose the resurrection and would have been impossible without it.— G. B. S.

* Chrys. states too confidently that "the brother" whose praise is referred to in 2 Cor. viii. 18, is Luke. It cannot be determined who this " brother " was. See Meyer *in loco*. Other conjectures are : Barnabas, Mark, Erastus, and an actual brother of Titus.—G. B. S.

of this that the Apostle dignifies him: "Whose praise," he says, "is in the Gospel." But he himself modestly says, "The former treatise have I made—O Theophilus, of all that Jesus began both to do and to teach:" not simply "of all," but from the beginning to the end; "until the day," he says, "in which He was taken up." And yet John says, that it was not possible to write all: for "were they written, I suppose," says he, "that even the world itself could not contain the books written." (John xxi. 25.) How then does the Evangelist here say, "Of all?" He does not say "all," but "of all," as much as to say, "in a summary way, and in the gross;" and "of all that is mainly and pressingly important." Then he tells us in what sense he says *all*, when he adds, "Which Jesus began both to do and to teach;" meaning His miracles and teaching; and not only so, but implying that His doing was also a teaching.

But now consider the benevolent and Apostolic feelings of the writer: that for the sake of a single individual he took such pains as to write for him an entire Gospel. "That thou mightest have," he says, "the certainty of those things, wherein thou hast been instructed." (Luke i. 4.) In truth, he had heard Christ say, "It is not the will of My Father that one of these little ones should perish." (Matt. xviii. 14.) And why did he not make one book of it, to send to one man Theophilus, but has divided it into two subjects? For clearness, and to give the brother a pause for rest. Besides, the two treatises are distinct in their subject-matter.

But consider how Christ accredited his words by His deeds. Thus He saith, "Learn of Me, for I am meek and lowly in heart." (Ib. xi. 29.) He taught men to be poor,[1] * and exhibited this by His actions: "For the Son of Man," He says, "hath not where to lay His head." (Ib. viii. 20.) Again, He charged men to love their enemies; and He taught the same lesson on the Cross, when He prayed for those who were crucifying Him. He said, "If any man will sue thee at the law, and take away thy coat, let him have thy cloak also" (Ib. v. 40): now *He* not only gave His garments, but even His blood.. In

this way He bade others teach. Wherefore Paul also said, "So as ye have us for an ensample." (Philip. iii. 17.) For nothing is more frigid than a teacher who shows his philosophy only in words: this is to act the part not of a teacher, but of a hypocrite. Therefore the Apostles first taught by their conduct, and then by their words; nay rather they had no need of words, when their deeds spoke so loud. Nor is it wrong to speak of Christ's Passion as action, for in suffering all He performed that great and wonderful act, by which He destroyed death, and effected all else that He did for us.

"Until the day in which He was taken up, after that He, through the Holy Spirit, had given commandments unto the Apostles whom He had chosen. After He had given commandments through the Spirit" (v. 2); i. e. they were spiritual words that He spake unto them, nothing human; either this is the meaning, or, that it was by the Spirit that He gave them commandments.† Do you observe in what low terms he still speaks of Christ, as in fact Christ had spoken of Himself? "But if I by the Spirit of God cast out devils" (Matt. xii. 28); for indeed the Holy Ghost wrought in that Temple. Well, what did He command? "Go ye therefore," He says, "make disciples of all the nations, baptizing them into the Name of the Father, and of the Son, and of the Holy Ghost; teaching them to observe all things whatsoever I have commanded you." (Ib. xxviii. 19, 20.) A high encomium this for the Apostles; to have such a charge entrusted to them, I mean, the salvation of the world! words full of the Spirit! And this the writer hints at in the expression, "through the Holy Ghost" (and, "the words which I spake unto you," saith the Lord, "are Spirit") (John vi. 63); thus leading the hearer on to a desire of learning what the commands were, and establishing the authority of the Apostles, seeing it is the words of the Spirit they are about to speak, and the commandments of Christ. "After He had given commandments," he says, "He was taken up." He does not say, 'ascended;' he still speaks as concerning a man. It appears then that He also taught the Disciples after His resurrection, but of this space of time no one has related to us the whole in detail. St. John indeed, as also does the present writer, dwells at greater length on this subject than the others; but none has clearly related every thing (for they hastened to something else); however, we have learnt

---

[1] Ms. C. has οἰκτίρμονας, *merciful;* the rest, ἀκτήμονας, *without possessions,* which is certainly the true reading. Thus in the *Sermon de futuræ Vitæ deliciis,* where Chrys. discourses largely on the harmony of Christ's teaching and actions, he says, Πάλιν ἀκτημοσύνην παιδεύων, ὅρα πῶς διὰ τῶν ἔργων αὐτὴν ἐπιδείκνυται, λέγων, Αἱ ἀλώπεκες, κ. τ. λ.

* "He taught them to be poor." Here we have a tinge of asceticism. Even if we suppose that the beatitude of the poor refers to literal poverty (Luke vi. 20) as well as to poverty in spirit (Matt. v. 3), it is still incorrect to say that Jesus taught his disciples that poverty was in itself a virtue. The ascetic principle is of heathen, not of Christian origin. It is noticeable that Chrys. quotes no passage to sustain his statement.—G. B. S.

† The latter is doubtless the correct interpretation. (So Meyer, Hackett). Cf. Matt. xii. 28; John iii. 34; Luke iv. 1.—G. B. S.

these things through the Apostles, for what they heard, that did they tell. "To whom also He shewed Himself alive." Having first spoken of the Ascension, he adverts to the Resurrection; for since thou hast been told that "He was taken up," therefore, lest thou shouldest suppose Him to have been taken up by others[1], he adds, "To whom He shewed Himself alive." For if He shewed Himself in the greater, surely He did in the minor circumstance. Seest thou, how casually and unperceived he drops by the way the seeds of these great doctrines? *

"Being seen of them during forty days." He was not always with them now, as He was before the Resurrection. For the writer does not say "forty days," but, "during forty days." He came, and again disappeared; by this leading them on to higher conceptions, and no longer permitting them to stand affected towards Him in the same way as before, but taking effectual measures to secure both these objects, that the fact of His Resurrection should be believed, and that He Himself should be ever after apprehended to be greater than man. At the same time, these were two opposite things; for in order to the belief in His Resurrection, much was to be done of a human character, and for the other object, just the reverse. Nevertheless, both results have been effected, each when the fitting time arrived.

But why did He appear not to all, but to the Apostles only? † Because to the many it would have seemed a mere apparition, inasmuch as they understood not the secret of the mystery. For if the disciples themselves were at first incredulous and were troubled, and needed the evidence of actual touch with the hand, and of His eating with them, how would it have fared in all likelihood with the multitude? For this reason therefore by the miracles [wrought by the Apostles] He renders the evidence of His Resurrection unequivocal, so that not only the men of those times—this is what would come of the ocular proof—but also all men thereafter, should be certain of the fact, that He was risen. Upon this ground also we argue with unbelievers. For

if He did not rise again, but remains dead, how did the Apostles perform miracles in His name? But they did not, say you, perform miracles? How then was our religion (ἔθνος) instituted? For this certainly they will not controvert nor impugn what we see with our eyes: so that when they say that no miracles took place, they inflict a worse stab[2] upon themselves. For this would be the greatest of miracles, that without any miracles, the whole world should have eagerly come to be taken in the nets of twelve poor and illiterate men. For not by wealth of money, not by wisdom of words, not by any thing else of this kind, did the fishermen prevail; so that objectors must even against their will acknowledge that there was in these men a Divine power, for no human strength could ever possibly effect such great results. For this He then remained forty days on earth, furnishing in this length of time the sure evidence of their seeing Him in His own proper Person, that they might not suppose that what they saw was a phantom. And not content with this, He added also the evidence of eating with them at their board: as to signify this, the writer adds, "And being at table[3] with them, He commanded." * (v. 4.) And this circumstance the Apostles themselves always put forth as an infallible token of the Resurrection; as where they say, "Who did eat and drink with Him." (Acts x. 41.)

And what did He, when appearing unto them those forty days? Why, He conversed with them, says the writer, "concerning the kingdom of God." (v. 3.) For, since the disciples both had been distressed and troubled at the things which already had taken place, and were about to go forth to encounter great difficulties, He recovered them by His discourses concerning the future. "He commanded them that they should not depart from Jerusalem, but wait for the promise of the Father." (v. 4.) First, He led them out to Galilee, afraid and trembling, in order that they might listen to His words in security. After-

---

[1] i. e. as Œcumenius explains in l. ἵνα μή τις νομίσῃ ἑτέρου δυνάμει τοῦτο γενέσθαι, lest any should suppose this to have been done by the power of another, he adds, to show that it was His own act, To whom also, etc.

* It is more than doubtful whether the mention of the resurrection is introduced (i. 3 sq.) for the purpose of meeting sceptical objections. The writer will rather make it the point of departure for his subsequent narrative. He has mentioned the ascension; the resurrection is the other great event and he will introduce a resumé of the more important circumstances which happened during the period between these two events and which have an important bearing upon the history about to be related.—G. B. S.

† Chrys. seems to overlook the appearance "to above five hundred brethren at once," 1 Cor. xv. 6.—G. B. S.

[2] Περιπείρουσι, Ms. C. and Cat. (see 1 Tim. vi, 9, pierced themselves through with many sorrows), and in this sense Hom. in Matt. 455 B. 463 A. The word is used as here, ibid. 831 C. where several Mss. have πανταχοῦ ἡ πλάνη ἑαυτὴν περιπείρει, for ἑαυτῇ περιπίπτει.

[3] Συναλιζόμενος. In the margin of E. V. "Eating together with them. The Catena here and below, had pr. man. the other reading, συναυλιζόμενος, but corrected in both places. St. Chrys. so takes the word, Hom. in Princip. Act. § 11.767 E. in Joann. 522 D. Œcumen. in l. explains it, τουτέστι κοινωνῶν ἁλῶν, κοινωνῶν τραπέζης, "Partaking of the salt, partaking of the table."

* Chrys. here follows the interpretation which derives συναλιζόμενος (i. 4) from σύν and ἅλς (salt) hence, eating together. So several ancient authorities as Vulgate (convesceus) and even modern, as Meyer. But the preferable derivation is from σύν and ἁλής (crowded). hence to be assembled, to meet with (sc. αὐτοῖς). So Olshausen, Hackett, Lechler, Thayer's Lex. and most modern authorities.—G. B. S.

wards, when they had heard, and had passed forty days with Him, "He commanded them that they should not depart from Jerusalem." Wherefore? Just as when soldiers are to charge a multitude, no one thinks of letting them issue forth until they have armed themselves, or as horses are not suffered to start from the barriers until they have got their charioteer; so Christ did not suffer these to appear in the field before the descent of the Spirit, that they might not be in a condition to be easily defeated and taken captive by the many. Nor was this the only reason, but also there were many in Jerusalem who should believe. And then again that it might not be said, that leaving their own acquaintance, they had gone to make a parade among strangers, therefore among those very men who had put Christ to death do they exhibit the proofs of His Resurrection, among those who had crucified and buried Him, in the very town in which the iniquitous deed had been perpetrated; thereby stopping the mouths of all foreign objectors. For when those even who had crucified Him appear as believers, clearly this proved both the fact of the crucifixion and the iniquity of the deed, and afforded a mighty evidence of the Resurrection. Furthermore, lest the Apostles should say, How shall it be possible for us to live among wicked and bloody men, they so many in number, we so few and contemptible, observe how He does away their fear and distress, by these words, "But wait for the promise of the Father, which ye have heard of Me." (v. 4.) You will say, When had they heard this? When He said, "It is expedient for you that I go away; for if I go not away, the Comforter will not come unto you." (John xvi. 7.) And again, "I will pray the Father, and He shall send you another Comforter, that He may abide with you." (ib. xiv. 16.)

But why did the Holy Ghost come to them, not while Christ was present, nor even immediately after his departure, but, whereas Christ ascended on the fortieth day, the Spirit descended "when the day of Pentecost," that is, the fiftieth, "was fully come?" (Acts ii. 1.) And how was it, if the Spirit had not yet come, that He said, "Receive ye the Holy Ghost?" (John xx. 22.) In order to render them capable and meet for the reception of Him. For if Daniel fainted at the sight of an Angel (Dan. viii. 17), much more would these when about to receive so great a grace. Either this then is to be said, or else that Christ spoke of what was to come, as if come already; as when He said, "Tread ye upon serpents and scorpions, and over all the power of the devil." (Luke x. 19.) But

why had the Holy Ghost not yet come? It was fit that they should first be brought to have a longing desire for that event, and so receive the grace. For this reason Christ Himself departed, and then the Spirit descended. For had He Himself been there, they would not have expected the Spirit so earnestly as they did. On this account neither did He come immediately after Christ's Ascension, but after eight or nine days. It is the same with us also; for our desires towards God are then most raised, when we stand in need. Accordingly, John chose that time to send his disciples to Christ when they were likely to feel their need of Jesus, during his own imprisonment. Besides, it was fit that our nature should be seen in heaven, and that the reconciliation should be perfected, and then the Spirit should come, and the joy should be unalloyed. For, if the Spirit being already come, Christ had then departed, and the Spirit remained; the consolation would not have been so great as it was. For in fact they clung to Him, and could not bear to part with Him; wherefore also to comfort them He said, "It is expedient for you that I go away." (John xvi. 7.) On this account He also waits during those intermediate days, that they might first despond for awhile, and be made, as I said, to feel their need of Him. and then reap a full and unalloyed delight. But if the Spirit were inferior to the Son, the consolation would not have been adequate; and how could He have said, "It is expedient for you?" For this reason the greater matters of teaching were reserved for the Spirit, that the disciples might not imagine Him inferior.

Consider also how necessary He made it for them to abide in Jerusalem, by promising that the Spirit should be granted them. For lest they should again flee away after His Ascension, by this expectation, as by a bond, He keeps them to that spot. But having said, "Wait for the promise of the Father, which ye have heard of Me," He then adds, "For John truly baptized with water, but ye shall be baptized with the Holy Ghost not many days hence." (v. 4, 5.) For now indeed He gives them to see the difference there was betwixt Him and John, plainly, and not as heretofore in obscure hints; for in fact He had spoken very obscurely, when He said, "Notwithstanding, he that is least in the kingdom of heaven is greater than he:" but now He says plainly, "John baptized with water, but ye shall be baptized with the Holy Ghost." (Matt. xi. 11.) And he no longer uses the testimony, but merely adverts to the person of John, reminding the disciples of what he had said, and shows them that they are now become greater than John; seeing they too are to baptize with the Spirit. Again, He did not say, I baptize you with the Holy Ghost, but, "Ye shall be baptized:" teaching us humility. For this was plain enough from the testimony of John, that it was Christ Himself Who should baptize: "He it is that shall baptize you with the Holy Ghost and with fire" (Luke iii. 16.); wherefore also He made mention of John.[1]

The Gospels, then, are a history of what Christ did and said; but the Acts, of what that "other Comforter" said and did. Not but that the Spirit did many things in the Gospels also; even as Christ here in the Acts still works in men as He did in the Gospels: only then the Spirit wrought through the Temple, now through the Apostles: then, He came into the Virgin's womb, and fashioned the Temple; now, into Apostolic souls: then, in the likeness of a dove; now, in the likeness of fire. And wherefore? Showing there the gentleness of the Lord, but here His taking vengeance also, He now puts them in mind of the judgment likewise. For, when need was to forgive, need was there of much gentleness; but now we have obtained the gift, it is henceforth a time for judgment and examination.

But why does Christ say, "Ye shall be baptized," when in fact there was no water in the upper room? Because the more essential part of Baptism is the Spirit, through Whom indeed the water has its operation; in the same manner our Lord also is said to be anointed, not that He had ever been anointed with oil, but because He had received the Spirit. Besides, we do in fact find them receiving a baptism with water [and a baptism with the Spirit], and these at different moments. In our case both take place under one act, but then they were divided. For in the beginning they were baptized by John; since, if harlots and publicans went to that baptism, much rather would they who thereafter were to be baptized by the Holy Ghost. Then, that the Apostles might not say, that they were always having it held out to them in promises (John xiv. 15, 16), (for indeed Christ had already discoursed much to them concerning the Spirit, that they should not imagine It to be an impersonal Energy or Operation, (ἐνέργειαν ἀνυπόστατον) that they might not say this, then, He adds, "not many days hence." And He did not explain when, that they might always watch: but, that it

would soon take place, He told, them, that they might not faint; yet the exact time He refrained from adding, that they might always be vigilant. Nor does He assure them by this alone; I mean, by the shortness of the time, but withal by saying, "The promise which ye have heard of Me." For this is not, saith He, the only time I have told you, but already I have promised what I shall certainly perform. What wonder then that He does not signify the day of the final consummation, when this day which was so near He did not choose to reveal? And with good reason; to the end they may be ever wakeful, and in a state of expectation and earnest heed.

For it cannot, it cannot be, that a man should enjoy the benefit of grace except he watch. Seest thou not what Elias saith to his disciple? "If thou see me when I am taken up" (2 Kings ii. 10), this that thou askest shall be done for thee. Christ also was ever wont to say unto those that came unto Him, "Believest thou?" For if we be not appropriated and made over to the thing given,[2] neither do we greatly feel the benefit. So it was also in the case of Paul; grace did not come to him immediately, but three days intervened, during which he was blind; purified the while, and prepared by fear. For as those who dye the purple first season with other ingredients the cloth that is to receive the dye, that the bloom may not be fleeting;[3] so in this instance God first takes order that the soul shall be thoroughly in earnest, and then pours forth His grace. On this account also, neither did He immediately send the Spirit, but on the fiftieth day. Now if any one ask, why we also do not baptize at that season of Pentecost? we may answer, that grace is the same now as then;[4] but the mind becomes more elevated now, by being prepared through fasting. And the season too of Pentecost furnishes a not unlikely reason. What may that be? Our fathers held Bap-

[2] 'Εὰν γὰρ μὴ οἰκειωθῶμεν πρὸς τὸ διδόμενον. Erasm. *Nisi rei datæ addicti fuerimus.*

[3] Οἱ τὴν ἀλουργίδα βάπτοντες. . . . ἵνα μὴ ἐξίτηλον γένηται τὸ ἄνθος. Comp. *Plat. Republ.* iv. vol. i. p. 289. Stallb. Οὐκοῦν οἶσθα, ἢν δ' ἐγώ, ὅτι οἱ βαφεῖς, ἐπειδὰν βουληθῶσι βάψαι ἔρια ὥστ' εἶναι ἀλούργα, πρῶτον μὲν ἐκλέγονται ἐκ τοσούτων χρωμάτων μίαν φύσιν τὴν τῶν λευκῶν, ἔπειτα προπαρασκευάζουσι οὐκ ὀλίγῃ παρασκευῇ θεραπεύσαντες ὅπως δέξεται ὅτι μάλιστα τὸ ἄνθος, καὶ οὕτω δὴ βάπτουσι.

[4] The question, fully expressed, is, 'Why do we baptize, not at Pentecost, *but on Easter Eve?*' And the answer is, 'Because the lenten fast forms a meet preparation for the reception of baptism. And moreover, there is a reason which weighed with our fathers, in respect of this season of the fifty days, the time of the Church's great festivity. The baptism newly received would restrain the neophytes from giving loose to carnal lusts; having prepared them to keep the feast with a holy and awful gladness.' It should be borne in mind, that these Homilies were commenced during the Πεντηκοστὴ, i. e. the period of fifty days between Easter and Pentecost: at which season the Book of Acts was usually read in the Churches.

tism to be just the proper curb upon evil concupiscence, and a powerful lesson for teaching to be sober-minded even in a time of delights.

As if then we were banquetting with Christ Himself, and partaking of His table, let us do nothing at random, but let us pass our time in fastings, and prayers, and much sobriety of mind. For if a man who is destined to enter upon some temporal government, prepares himself all his life long, and that he may obtain some dignity, lays out his money, spends his time, and submits to endless troubles; what shall we deserve, who draw near to the kingdom of heaven with such negligence, and both show no earnestness before we have received, and after having received are again negligent? Nay, this is the very reason why we are negligent after having received, that we did not watch before we had received. Therefore many, after they have received, immediately have returned to their former vomit, and have become more wicked, and drawn upon themselves a more severe punishment; when having been delivered from their former sins, herein they have more grievously provoked the Judge, that having been delivered from so great a disease, still they did not learn sobriety, but that has happened unto them, which Christ threatened to the paralytic man, saying, "Behold thou art made whole : sin no more, lest a worse thing come unto thee" (John v. 14): and which He also predicted of the Jews, that "the last state shall be worse than the first." (Matt. xii. 45.) For *if*, saith He, showing that by their ingratitude they should bring upon them the worst of evils, "if I had not come, and spoken unto them, they had not had sin" (John xv, 22); so that the guilt of sins committed after these benefits is doubled and quadrupled, in that, after the honour put upon us, we show ourselves ungrateful and wicked. And the Laver of Baptism helps not a whit to procure for us a milder punishment. And consider : a man has gotten grievous sins by committing murder or adultery, or some other crime : *these* were remitted through Baptism. For there is no sin, no impiety, which does not yield and give place to this gift; for the Grace is Divine. A man has again committed adultery and murder ; the former adultery is indeed done away, the murder forgiven, and not brought up again to his charge, "for the gifts and calling of God are without repentance" (Rom. xi. 29); but for those committed after Baptism he suffers a punishment as great as he would if both the former sins were brought up again, and many worse than these. For the guilt is no longer simply equal, but

doubled and tripled.* Look : in proof that the penalty of these sins is greater, hear what St. Paul says : "He that despised Moses' law died without mercy, under two or three witnesses : of how much sorer punishment, suppose ye, shall he be thought worthy, who hath trodden under foot the Son of God, and hath counted the blood of the covenant an unholy thing, and hath done despite unto the Spirit of grace?" (Heb. x. 28, 29.)

Perhaps we have now deterred many from receiving baptism. Not however with this intention have we so spoken, but on purpose that having received it, they may continue in temperance and much moderation. 'But I am afraid,' says one. If thou wert afraid, thou wouldest have received and guarded it. 'Nay,' saith he, 'but this is the very reason why I do not receive it,—that I am frightened.' And art thou not afraid to depart thus? 'God is merciful,' saith he. Receive baptism then, because He is merciful and ready to help. But thou, where to be in earnest is the thing required, dost not allege this mercifulness ; thou thinkest of this only where thou hast a mind to do so. And yet that was the time to resort to God's mercy, and we shall then be surest of obtaining it, when we do our part. For he that has cast the whole matter upon God, and, after his baptism, sins, as being man it is likely, he may, and repents, shall obtain mercy; whereas he that prevaricates with God's mercy, and departs this life with no portion in that grace, shall have his punishment without a word to be said for him. 'But how if he depart,' say you, 'after having had the grace vouchsafed to him?' He will depart empty again of all good works. [1] For it is impossible, yes, it is in my opinion impossible, that the man who upon such hopes dallied with baptism should have effected ought generous and good. And why

* This view, that baptism cleansed from all sin, and that, therefore, sin after baptism was far more heinous and hard to be forgiven, held wide sway in the early church and operated as a powerful motive for the delay of baptism. The reception of the grace of baptism involves this increased liability to deadlier sin. For this reason Tertullian had urged its postponement. "And so according to the circumstances and disposition, and even age, of each individual, the delay of baptism is preferable ; principally, however, in the case of little children." "If any understand the weighty import of baptism, they will fear its reception more than its delay," etc. *De Baptismo,* xviii. Chrys. did not carry the idea to this length.—G. B. S.

[1] Τί οὖν ἂν καταξιωθεὶς φησιν ἀπελεύσεται πάλιν κενὸς κατορθωμάτων, Cod. C, and so A, but with ἀπελεύσῃ In the latter recension this sentence is omitted, and instead of it, we have, Τί δὲ ταῦτα κατὰ τῆς σεαυτοῦ σωτηρίας προβάλλῃ ; 'But why dost thou put forth such pretences against thine own salvation?' Chrys. had just said, ἀπελθὼν ἄμοιρος τῆς χάριτος ἀπαιραίτητον ἕξει τὴν τιμωρίον. The objector (with the usual prevaricating formula, τί οὖν ἐὰν τὸ καὶ τό ; *Hom. in Matt.* 229 D.) says : τί οὖν ἂν καταξιωθείς, sc. τῆς χαριτὸς ἀπέλθῃ ; to which Chrys. answers : Ἀπελεύσεται πάλιν κενὸς κατορθωμάτων : He will depart as empty of good works as he was before his baptism : adding, For it is, I think, utterly impossible that such an one [though he should live ever so long after baptism] would have wrought out his own salvation.

dost thou harbor such fear, and presume upon the uncertain chance of the future? Why not convert this fear into labor and earnestness, and thou shalt be great and admirable? Which is best, to fear or to labor? Suppose some one to have placed thee, having nothing to do, in a tottering house, saying, Look for the decaying roof to fall upon thy head: for perhaps it will fall, perhaps not; but if thou hadst rather it should not, then work and inhabit the more secure apartment: which wouldest thou have rather chosen, that idle condition accompanied with fear, or this labor with confidence? Why then, act now in the same way. For the uncertain future is like a decayed house, ever threatening to fall; but this work, laborious though it be, ensures safety.

Now God forbid that it should happen to us to fall into so great straits as to sin after baptism. However, even if aught such should happen, God is merciful, and has given us many ways of obtaining remission even after this. But just as those who sin after baptism are punished for this reason more severely than the Catechumens, so again, those who know that there are medicines in repentance, and yet will not make use of them, will undergo a more grievous chastisement. For by how much the mercy of God is enlarged, by so much does the punishment increase, if we do not duly profit by that mercy. What sayest thou, O man? When thou wast full of such grievous evils, and given over, suddenly thou becamest a friend, and wast exalted to the highest honor, not by labors of thine own, but by the gift of God: thou didst again return to thy former misconduct; and though thou didst deserve to be sorely punished, nevertheless, God did not turn away, but gave unnumbered opportunities of salvation, whereby thou mayest yet become a friend: yet for all this, thou hast not the will to labor. What forgiveness canst thou deserve henceforth? Will not the Gentiles with good reason deride thee as a worthless drone? For if there be power in that doctrine of yours, say they, what means this multitude of uninitiated persons? If the mysteries be excellent and desirable, let none receive baptism at his last gasp. For that is not the time for giving of mysteries but for making of wills; the time for mysteries is in health of mind and soundness of soul. For, if a man would not prefer to make his will in such a condition; and if he does so make it, he gives a handle for subsequent litigation (and this is the reason why testators premise these words: "Alive, in my senses, and in health, I make this disposal of my property:"), how

should it be possible for a person who is no longer master of his senses to go through the right course of preparation for the sacred mysteries?[1] For if in the affairs of this life, the laws of the world would not permit a man who was not perfectly sound in mind to make a will, although it be in his own affairs that he would lay down the law; how, when thou art receiving instruction concerning the kingdom of heaven, and the unspeakable riches of that world, shall it be possible for thee to learn all clearly, when very likely too thou art beside thyself through the violence of thy malady? And when wilt thou say those words[2] to Christ, in the act of being buried with Him when at the point to depart hence? For indeed both by works and by words must we show our good will towards Him. (Rom. vi. 4.) Now what thou art doing is all one, as if a man should want to be enlisted as a soldier, when the war is just about to break up; or to strip for the contest in the arena, just when the spectators have risen from their seats. For thou hast thine arms given thee, not that thou shouldest straightway depart hence, but that being equipped therewith, thou mayest raise a trophy over the enemy. Let no one think that it is out of season to discourse on this subject, because it is not Lent now. Nay, this it is that vexes me, that ye look to a set time in such matters. Whereas that Eunuch, barbarian as he was and on a journey, yea on the very highway, he did not seek for a set time (Acts viii. 27); no, nor the jailer, though he was in the midst of a set of prisoners, and the teacher he saw before him was a man scourged and in chains, and whom he was still to have in his custody. (ib. xvi. 29.) But here, not being inmates of a jail, nor out on a journey, many are putting off their baptism even to their last breath.

Now if thou still questionest that Christ is God, stand away from the Church: be not here, even as a hearer of the Divine Word, and as one of the catechumens:[3] but if thou art sure of this, and knowest clearly this truth,

---

[1] Μετὰ ἀκριβείας μυσταγωγεῖσθαι: alluding to the κατήχησις μυσταγωγική, i. e. the course of instruction by which the catechumens were prepared for baptism. See the Catechetical Discourses of St. Cyril of Jerusalem.

[2] Τὰ ῥήματα ἐκεῖνα: i. e. not (as Ben seems to interpret) "Buried with Christ;" as if this were part of the form of words put into the mouth of the person to be baptized; but the words, "I renounce thee, O Satan, and all thy angels, and all thy service, and all thy pomp: and I enlist myself with Thee, O Christ." St. Chrysost. Serm. ad pop. Antioch, xxi. p. 244. The words, "buried with Him," serve to show more clearly the absurdity of such delay: "we are 'buried with Christ in His death,' that we may rise again to newness of life, not that we should pass at once from the spiritual burial to the literal."

[3] The catechumens were allowed to be present at the first part of the service (Missa catechumenorum); and were dismissed after the Sermon, before the proper Prayers of the Church, or Missa Fidelium.

why delay? Why shrink back and hesitate? For fear, say you, lest I should sin. But dost thou not fear what is worse, to depart for the next world with such a heavy burden? For it is not equally excusable, not to have gotten a grace set before you, and to have failed in attempting to live uprightly. If thou be called to account, Why didst thou not come for it? what wilt thou answer? In the other case thou mayest allege the burden of thy passions, and the difficulty of a virtuous life: but nothing of the kind here. For here is grace, freely conveying liberty. But thou fearest lest thou shouldest sin? Let this be thy language after Baptism: and then entertain this fear, in order to hold fast the liberty thou hast received; not now, to prevent thy receiving such a gift. Whereas now thou art wary before baptism, and negligent after it. But thou art waiting for Lent: and why? Has that season any advantage? Nay, it was not at the Passover that the Apostles received[1] the grace, but at another season; and then three thousand (Luke says,) and five thousand were baptized: (ch. ii. 41; iv. 4, and ch. x.) and again Cornelius. Let us then not wait for a set time, lest by hesitating and putting off we depart empty, and destitute of so great gifts. What do you suppose is my anguish when I hear that any person has been taken away unbaptized, while I reflect upon the intolerable punishments of that life, the inexorable doom! Again, how I am grieved to behold others drawing near to their last gasp, and not brought to their right mind even then. Hence too it is that scenes take place quite unworthy of this gift. For whereas there ought to be joy, and dancing, and exultation, and wearing of garlands, when another is christened; the wife of the sick man has no sooner heard that the physician has ordered this, than she is overcome with grief, as if it were some dire calamity; she sets up the greatest lamentation, and nothing is heard all over the house but crying and wailing, just as it is when condemned criminals are led away to their doom. The sick man again is then more sorely grieved;

and if he recovers from his illness, is as vexed as if some great harm had been done to him. For since he had not been prepared for a virtuous life, he has no heart for the conflicts which are to follow, and shrinks at the thought of them. Do you see what devices the devil contrives, what shame, what ridicule? Let us rid ourselves of this disgrace; let us live as Christ has enjoined. He gave us Baptism, not that we should receive and depart, but that we should show the fruits of it in our after life. How can one say to him who is departing and broken down, Bear fruit? Hast thou not heard that "the fruit of the Spirit is love, joy, peace?" (Gal. v. 22.) How comes it then that the very contrary takes place here? For the wife stands there mourning, when she ought to rejoice; the children weeping, when they ought to be glad together; the sick man himself lies there in darkness, and surrounded by noise and tumult, when he ought to be keeping high festival; full of exceeding despondency at the thought of leaving his children orphans, his wife a widow, his house desolate. Is this a state in which to draw near unto mysteries? answer me; is this a state in which to approach the sacred table?[2] Are such scenes to be tolerated? Should the Emperor send letters and release the prisoners in the jails, there is joy and gladness: God sends down the Holy Ghost from Heaven to remit not arrears of money, but a whole mass of sins, and do ye all bewail and lament? Why, how grossly unsuitable is this! Not to mention that sometimes it is upon the dead that the water has been poured, and holy mysteries flung upon the ground. However, not we are to blame for this, but men who are so perverse. I exhort you then to leave all, and turn and draw near to Baptism with all alacrity, that having given proof of great earnestness at this present time, we may obtain confidence for that which is to come; whereunto that we may attain, may it be granted unto us all by the grace and mercy of our Lord Jesus Christ, to Whom be glory and power for ever and ever. Amen.

---

[1] Κατηξιώθησαν τῆς χάριτος, as above, p. 8, note [1], τί οὖν ἂν καταξιωθείς;

[2] The Holy Communion, administered immediately after baptism.

HOMILY II.

ACTS I. 6.

"When they therefore were come together, they asked of Him, saying, Lord, wilt Thou at this time restore again the kingdom to Israel?"

WHEN the disciples intend to ask anything, they approach Him together, that by dint of numbers they may abash Him into compliance. They well knew that in what He had said previously, "Of that day knoweth no man" (Matt. xxiv. 36), He had merely declined telling them : therefore they again drew near, and put the question. They would not have put it had they been truly satisfied with that answer. For having heard that they were about to receive the Holy Ghost, they, as being now worthy of instruction, desired to learn. Also they were quite ready for freedom : for they had no mind to address themselves to danger ; what they wished was to breathe freely again ; for they were no light matters that had happened to them, but the utmost peril had impended over them. And without saying any thing to Him of the Holy Ghost, they put this question : "Lord, wilt Thou at this time restore the kingdom to Israel?" They did not ask, when? but whether "at this time." So eager were they for that day. Indeed, to me it appears that they had not any clear notion of the nature of that kingdom ; for the Spirit had not yet instructed them.* And they do not say, When shall these things be? but they approach Him with greater honour, saying, "Wilt Thou at this time restore again the kingdom," as being now already fallen. For there they were still affected towards sensible objects, seeing they were not yet become better than those who were before them ; here they have henceforth high conceptions concerning Christ. Since then their minds are elevated, He also speaks to them in a higher strain. For He no longer tells them, "Of that day not even the Son of Man knoweth" (Mark xiii. 32) ; but He says, "It is not for you to know the times or the seasons which the Father hath put in His own power" (Acts i. 7.) Ye ask things greater than your capacity, He would say. And yet even now they learned things that were much greater than this. And that you may see that this is strictly the case, look how many things I shall enumerate. What, I pray you, was greater than their having learned what they did learn? Thus, they learned that there is a Son of God, and that God has a Son equal with Himself in dignity (John v. 17-20) ; they learned that there will be a resurrection (Matt. xvii. 9) ; that when He ascended He sat on the right hand of God (Luke xxii. 69) ; and what is still more stupendous, that Flesh is seated in heaven, and adored by Angels, and that He will come again (Mark xvi. 19) ; they learned what is to take place in the judgment (Matt. xvi. 27) ; learned that they shall then sit and judge the twelve tribes of Israel (Luke xxi. 27) ; learned that the Jews would be cast out, and in their stead the Gentiles should come in (Matt. xix. 28). For, tell me, which is greater? to learn that a person will reign, or to learn the time when? (Luke xxi. 24). Paul learned "things which it is not lawful for a man to utter" (2 Cor. xii. 4) ; things that were before the world was made, he learned them all. Which is the more difficult, the beginning or the end? Clearly to learn the beginning. This, Moses learned, and the time when, and how long ago : and he enumerates the years. And[1] the wise Solomon saith, "I will make mention of things from the beginning of the world." And that the time is at hand, they do know : as Paul saith, "The Lord is at hand, be careful for nothing." (Phil. iv. 5). These things they knew not [then], and yet He mentions many signs (Matt. ch. xxiv). But, as He has just said, "Not many days hence," wishing them to be vigilant, and did not openly declare the precise moment, so is it here also. However, it is not about the general Consummation that they now ask Him, but, "Wilt Thou at this time," say they, "restore the kingdom to Israel?" And not even this did He re-

---

* The emphatic position of ἐν τῷ χρόνῳ τούτῳ as well as the answer of Jesus shows that the disciples' earnest hope and expectation were that their Lord should, during their life-time, personally organize a kingdom on the basis of the Jewish theocracy. Chrys. is explicit in pointing out their incorrect conception of the kingdom of Christ, but does not here explain the specifically Jewish character of that conception. In the early disciples we behold the constant struggle of the Christian spirit to break away from the forms of Jewish nationalism.—G. B. S.

[1] Cod. C. omits this sentence here, and inserts it below (p. 12), where it is evidently out of place. The passage referred to seems to be Ecclus. 51, 8.

veal to them. They also asked this [about the end of the world] before : and as on that occasion He answered by leading them away from thinking that their deliverance was near, and, on the contrary, cast them into the midst of perils, so likewise on this occasion, but more mildly. For, that they may not imagine themselves to be wronged, and these things to be mere pretences, hear what He says : He immediately gives them that at which they rejoiced : for He adds : " But ye shall receive power, after that the Holy Ghost is come upon you ; and ye shall be witnesses unto Me both in Jerusalem, and in all Judea, and in Samaria, and unto the uttermost part of the earth." (Acts i. 8.) Then, that they may make no more enquiries, straightway He was received up. Thus, just as on the former occasion He had darkened their minds by awe, and by saying, " I know not ; " here also He does so by being taken up. For great was their eagerness on the subject, and they would not have desisted ; and yet it was very necessary that they should not learn this. For tell me,[1] which do the Gentiles most disbelieve ? that there will be a consummation of the world, or that God is become man, and issued from the Virgin ?[2] But I am ashamed of dwelling on this point, as if it were about some difficult matter. Then again, that the disciples might not say, Why dost thou leave the matter in suspense ? He adds, " Which the Father hath put in His own power." And yet He declared the Father's power and His to be one : as in the saying, " For as the Father raiseth up the dead and quickeneth them, even so the Son quickeneth whom He will." (John v. 21.) If where need is to work, Thou actest with the same power as the Father ; where it behooves to know, dost Thou not know with the same power ? Yet certainly to raise up the dead is much greater than to learn the day. If the greater be with power, much more the other.

But just as when we see a child crying, and pertinaciously wishing to get something from us that is not expedient for him, we hide the thing, and show him our empty hands, and say, " See, we have it not : " the like has Christ here done with the Apostles. But as the child, even when we show[3] him [our empty hands], persists with his crying, conscious he has been deceived, and then we leave him, and depart, saying, " Such an one calls me : "

and we give him something else instead, in order to divert him from his desire, telling him it is a much finer thing than the other, and then hasten away ; in like manner Christ acted.* The disciples asked to have something, and He said He had it not. And on the first occasion he frightened them. Then again they asked to have it now : He said He had it not ; and He did not frighten them now, but after having shown[4] [the empty hands], He has done this, and gives them a plausible reason :[5] " Which the Father," He says, " hath put in his own power." What ? Thou not know the things of the Father ! Thou knowest Him, and not what belongs to Him ! And yet Thou hast said, " None knoweth the Father but the Son " (Luke x. 25) ; and, " The Spirit searcheth all things, yea, the deep things of God " (1 Cor. ii. 10) ; and Thou not know this ! But they feared to ask Him again, lest they should hear Him say, " Are ye also without understanding ? " (Matt. xv. 26.) For they feared Him now much more than before. " But ye shall receive power, after that the Holy Ghost is come upon you." As in the former instance He had not answered their question (for it is the part of a teacher to teach not what the disciple chooses, but what is expedient for him to learn), so in this, He tells them beforehand, for this reason, what they ought to know, that they may not be troubled. In truth, they were yet weak. But to inspire them with confidence, He raised up their souls, and concealed what was grievous.

---

* These illustrations, which seem to admit a half deceptive element in our Lord's conversations, are as little justified by the passage in hand as by the character of Jesus. What Jesus promises, viz.: the Holy Spirit, is not promised in order to " divert " the disciples from their desire, but to assure to them a greater blessing than they then knew how to anticipate. The disciples wish a temporal kingdom with personal prerogatives ; Jesus promises them the Spirit of Truth and opens before them the life of spiritual growth and usefulness. The illustration would have been more appropriate, had Chrys. said : " The child persists in his crying, but Jesus quiets him by giving him something far better than he had asked."—G. B. S.

[4] Ἀλλὰ μετὰ τὸ δεῖξαι (as above, καὶ δεικνύντων ἡμῶν, sc. γυμνὰς τὰς χεῖρας), τοῦτο πεποίηκεν, sc. φοβεῖ. The Mss. except C and A, and the Edd. have ὁ before πεποίηκεν, which gives no sense.

[5] Chrys. therefore explains these sayings of our Lord (polemically against the Arians) as οἰκονομία· i. e. the thing said is not objectively true, but the morality of all actions depends on the subjective condition of the προαίρεσις or purpose (παρὰ τὴν τῶν χρωμένων προαίρεσιν γίγνεται φαῦλον ἢ καλὸν, de Sacerdot. i. 8.), so that where this is right and good, a deception is lawful. This lax view of the morality of Truth was very general in the Greek Church : not so in the early Latin Church. See the two Treatises of St. Augustine, De Mendacio (" Lib. of Fathers," Seventeen Short Treatises of St. Aug.) The stricter doctrine however is maintained by St. Basil, who in his shorter Monastic Rule peremptorily condemns all οἰκονομία, and pious fraud (officiosum mendacium) of every description, on the ground that all falsehood is from Satan, John v. 44. and that our Lord has made no distinction between one sort of lying and another. Again, the monk Johannes of Lycopolis in Egypt : " All falsehood is foreign from Christ and Christian men, be it in a small or in a great matter ; yea, though a good end be served by it, it is never to be allowed, for the Saviour hath declared, that all lying is from the Wicked One." Pallad. Hist. Lausiac in Bibl. Patr. t. xiii. p. 965.

---

[1] The connection must be supplied : e. g. It was not that this point of knowledge was too high for them ; for, as has been shown, they knew already, or were soon to know, things much higher than this, and which their hearers would find much harder to believe. For tell me, etc.

[2] Here C. has the sentence : " Also the wise Solomon saith, etc." p. 11, note [1].

[3] Καὶ δεικνύντων ἡμῶν, C. the modern text has μή.

Since he was about to leave them very shortly, therefore in this discourse He says nothing painful. But how? He extols as great the things which would be painful: all but saying, "'Fear not': for ye shall receive power, after that the Holy Ghost is come upon you; and ye shall be witnesses unto Me both in Jerusalem, and in all Judea, and in Samaria." For since he had said, "Go not into the way of the Gentiles, and into any city of the Samaritans enter ye not" (Matt. x. 5), what there He left unsaid, He here adds, "And to the uttermost part of the earth;" and having spoken this, which was more fearful than all the rest, then that they may not again question Him, He held His peace. "And having this said, while they beheld, He was taken up; and a cloud received Him out of their sight" (v. 9). Seest thou that they did preach and fulfil the Gospel? For great was the gift He had bestowed on them. In the very place, He says, where ye are afraid, that is, in Jerusalem, there preach ye first, and afterwards unto the uttermost part of the earth. Then for assurance of what He had said, "While they beheld, He was taken up." Not "while they beheld" did He rise from the dead, but "while they beheld, He was taken up." Inasmuch, however, as the sight of their eyes even here was not all-sufficient; for in the Resurrection they saw the end, but not the beginning, and in the Ascension they saw the beginning, but not the end: because in the former it had been superfluous to have seen the beginning, the Lord Himself Who spake these things being present, and the sepulchre showing clearly that He is not there; but in the latter, they needed to be informed of the sequel by word of others: inasmuch then as their eyes do not suffice to show them the height above, nor to inform them whether He is actually gone up into heaven, or only seemingly into heaven, see then what follows. That it was Jesus Himself they knew from the fact that He had been conversing with them (for had they seen only from a distance, they could not have recognized Him by sight),[1] but that He is taken up into Heaven the Angels themselves inform them. Observe how it is ordered, that not all is done by the Spirit, but the eyes also do their part. But why did "a cloud receive Him?" This too was a sure sign that He went up to Heaven. Not fire, as in the case of Elijah, nor fiery

chariot, but "a cloud received Him;" which was a symbol of Heaven, as the Prophet says;[2] "Who maketh the clouds His chariot" (Ps. civ. 3); it is of the Father Himself that this is said. Therefore he says, "on a cloud;" in the symbol, he would say, of the Divine power, for no other Power is seen to appear on a cloud. For hear again what another Prophet says: "The Lord sitteth upon a light cloud" (Is. xix. 1). For[3] it was while they were listening with great attention to what He was saying, and this in answer to a very interesting question, and with their minds fully aroused and quite awake, that this thing took place. Also on the mount [Sinai] the cloud was because of Him: since Moses also entered into the darkness, but the cloud there was not because of Moses. And He did not merely say, "I go," lest they should again grieve, but He said, "I send the Spirit" (John xvi. 5, 7); and that He was going away into heaven they saw with their eyes. O what a sight they were granted! "And while they looked stedfastly," it is said, "toward heaven, as he went up, behold, two men stood by them in white apparel; which also said, Ye men of Galilee, why stand ye gazing up into heaven? This same Jesus, which is taken up from you into heaven"—they used the expression "This" demonstratively, saying, "this Jesus, which is taken up from you into heaven, shall thus"—demonstratively, "in this way"—"come in like manner as ye have seen Him going into heaven." (v. 10, 11.) Again, the outward appearance is cheering ["in white apparel"]. They were Angels, in the form of men. And they say, "Ye men of Galilee:" they showed themselves to be trusted by the disciples, by saying, "Ye men of Galilee." For this was the meaning: else, what needed they to be told of their country, who knew it well enough? By their appearance also they attracted their regard, and shewed that they were from heaven. But wherefore does not Christ Himself tell them these things, instead of the Angels? He had beforehand told them all things; ["What if ye shall see the Son of Man] going up where He was before?" (John vi. 62).

Moreover the Angels did not say, 'whom you have seen taken up,' but, "going into heaven:" ascension is the word, not assump-

---

[1] Πόρρωθεν γὰρ οὐκ ἐνῆν ἰδόντας γνῶναι; i. e. had they but seen the Ascension from a distance, and not been conversing with the Lord at the moment of His Assumption. Cod. E. transposes the clause to the end of the sentence; meaning that they could not by mere sight have been cognizant of the fact of His ascension *into heaven.*

[2] Ps. civ. 3. ὁ τιθεὶς νέφει τὴν ἐπίβασιν αὐτοῦ; "Who maketh on a cloud His stepping," or, "going."
[3] At first sight it looks as if this sentence were out of place here. But the connection may be thus explained: this circumstance, of the cloud, is not idle, but very significant; and the minds of the disciples were alive to its import, as betokening His Godhead. True, might it not also be said of Moses on the mount Sinai, that a cloud received him out of their sight? For "Moses entered into the darkness," Exod. xx. 21. But the cloud there was because of Him, "where God was," not because of Moses.

tion; the expression "taken up,"[1] belongs to the flesh. For the same reason they say, " He which is taken up from you shall thus come," not, " shall be sent," but, " shall come. He that ascended, the same is he also that descended " (Eph. iv. 10). So again the expression, " a cloud received Him :" for He Himself mounted upon the cloud. Of the expressions, some are adapted to the conceptions of the disciples, some agreeable with the Divine Majesty. Now, as they behold, their conceptions are elevated : He has given them no slight hint of the nature of His second coming. For this, " Shall *thus* come," means, with the body; which thing they desired to hear ; and, that he shall come again to judgment " thus " upon a cloud. " And, behold, two men stood by them." Why is it said, " men ?" Because they had fashioned themselves completely as such, that the beholders might not be overpowered. " Which also said : " their words moreover were calculated for soothing : " Why stand ye gazing up into heaven ? " They would not let them any longer wait there for Him. Here again, these tell what is greater, and leave the less unsaid. That " He will thus come," they say, and that " ye must look for Him from heaven." For the rest, they called them off from that spectacle to their saying, that they might not, because they could not see Him, imagine that He was not ascended, but even while they are conversing, would be present ere they were aware. For if they said on a former occasion, " Whither goest Thou ? " (John xiii. 36) much more would they have said it now. [2]

" Wilt Thou at this time," say they, " restore the kingdom to Israel ? " (Recapitulation). They so well knew his mildness, that after His Passion also they ask Him, " Wilt thou restore ? " And yet He had before said to them, " Ye shall hear of wars and rumors of wars, but the end is not yet," nor shall Jerusalem be taken. But now they ask Him about the kingdom, not about the end. And besides, He does not speak at great length with them after the Resurrection. They ad-dress then this question, as thinking that they themselves would be in high honor, if this should come to pass. But He (for as touching this restoration, that it was not to be, He did not openly declare ; for what needed they to learn this ? hence they do not again ask, " What is the sign of Thy coming, and of the end of the world ? " for they are afraid to say that : but, " Wilt Thou restore the kingdom to Israel ? " for they thought there was such a kingdom), but He, I say, both in parables had shown that the time was not near,* and here where they asked, and He answered thereto, " Ye shall receive power," says He, " when the Holy Ghost is come upon you. Is come upon you," not, " is sent," [to shew the Spirit's coequal Majesty. How then darest thou, O opponent of the Spirit, to call Him a creature [3] ?] " And ye shall be witnesses to Me." He hinted at the Ascension. [" And when he had spoken these things.[4]] Which they had heard before, and He now reminds them of. [" He was taken up."] Already it has been shown, that He went up into heaven. [" And a cloud, etc."] " Clouds and darkness are under His feet," (Ps. xviii. 9; xcvii. 2) saith the Scripture: for this is declared by the expression, " And a cloud received Him :" the Lord of heaven, it means. For as a king is shown by the royal chariot, so was the royal chariot sent for Him. [" Behold, two men, etc.] That they may vent no sorrowful exclamations, and that it might not be with them as it was with Elisha, (2 Kings ii. 12) who, when his master was taken up, rent his mantle. And what say they? " This Jesus, which is taken up from you into heaven, shall thus come." And, " Behold, two men stood by them." (Matt. xviii. 16.) With good reason : for " in the mouth of two witnesses shall every word be established " (Deut. xvii. 6): and these utter the same things. And it is said, that they were " in white apparel." In the same manner as they had already seen an Angel at the sepulchre, who had even told them their own thoughts; so here also an Angel is the preacher of His Ascension ; although indeed the Prophets had frequently foretold it, as well as the Resurrection. [5]

---

[1] i. e. the Angels had before used the phrase of *assumption:* but this does not express the whole matter ; therefore, to show that it is the act of His own Divine power, they now say, *going.* and afterwards express it that He *will come,* not that He will be sent. He ascended, as He descended, by His own Divine power. So again it is said, " A cloud received Him:" but in this He was not passive . as God He stepped upon the cloud: ἐπέβη alluding to the expression in the Psalm above cited, τιθεὶς τὴν ἐπίβασιν.

[2] All the Editions and the Latin Versions connect with this the following sentence: " Much more would they have said now, Dost Thou at this time restore the kingdom to Israel ? " But it is evident, that at this point begins the recapitulation, or renewed exposition. It is in fact a peculiarity of these Discourses, that Chrys. having gone through the exposition of the text, often, as here, goes over the same ground again, usually with some such formula as, " But let us look through what has been said from the beginning."

* The reference here must be to such parables as: " The Sower," " The Leaven," " The Grain of Mustard Seed." (Matt. xiii. 1–43), and the parable of the Growing Seed (Mark iv. 26–29), all of which seem to represent the progress of his truth as a long and slow development. To these might be added such expressions as ἕως τῆς συντελείας τοῦ αἰῶνος (Matt. xxviii. 20) and ἕως ἐσχάτου τῆς γῆς (Acts i. 8).—G. B. S.

[3] This sentence is from the later recension.

[4] The text of these Homilies is often greatly confused by the omission, especially in the recapitulations, of the words on which Chrys. is commenting.

[5] Here Erasmus has followed another reading (of E.), the very reverse in sense ; " And if indeed the Prophets did not foretell this, be not astonished, for it was superfluous to say

Everywhere it is Angels as at the Nativity, "for that which is conceived in her," saith one, "is by the Holy Ghost" (Matt. i. 20): and again to Mary, "Fear not, Mary." (Luke i. 30.) And at the Resurrection: "He is not here; He is risen, and goeth before you." (ib. xxiv. 6.) "Come, and see!" (Matt. xxviii. 6.) And at the Second Coming. For that they may not be utterly in amaze, therefore it is added, "Shall thus come." (ib. xxv. 31.) They recover their breath a little; if indeed He shall come again, if also thus come, and not be unapproachable! And that expression also, that it is "from them" He is taken up, is not idly added. [1] And of the Resurrection indeed Christ Himself bears witness (because of all things this is, next to the Nativity, nay even above the Nativity, the most wonderful: His raising Himself to life again): for, "Destroy," He says, "this Temple, and in three days I [2] will raise it up." (John ii. 19.) "Shall thus come," say they. If any therefore desires to see Christ; if any grieves that he has not seen Him: having this heard, let him show forth an admirable life, and certainly he shall see Him, and shall not be disappointed. For Christ will come with greater glory, though "thus," in this manner, with a body *; and much more wondrous will it be, to see Him descending from heaven. But for what He will come, they do not add.

["Shall thus come," etc.] This is a confirmation of the Resurrection; for if he was taken up with a body, much rather must He have risen again with a body. Where are those who disbelieve the Resurrection? Who are they, I pray? Are they Gentiles, or Christians? for I am ignorant. But no, I know well: they are Gentiles, who also disbelieve the work of Creation. For the two denials go together: the denial that God creates any thing from nothing, and the denial that He raises up what has been buried. But then, being ashamed to be thought such as "know not the power of God" (Matt. xxii. 29), that we may not impute this to them, they allege: We do not say it with this meaning, but because there is no need of the body. Truly it may be seasonably said, "The fool will speak foolishness." (Is. xxxii. 6.) Are

you not ashamed not to grant, that God can create from nothing? If he creates from matter already existing, wherein does He differ from men? But whence, you demand, are evils? Though you should not know whence, ought you for that to introduce another evil in the knowledge of evils? Hereupon two absurdities follow. For if you do not grant, that from things which are not, God made the things which are, much more shall you be ignorant whence are evils: and then, again, you introduce another evil, the affirming that Evil (τὴν κακίαν) is uncreated. Consider now what a thing it is, when you wish to find the source of evils, to be both ignorant of it, and to add another to it. Search after the origin of evils, and do not blaspheme God. And how do I blaspheme? says he. When you make out that evils have a power equal to God's; a power uncreated. For, observe what Paul says; "For the invisible things of Him from the creation of the world are clearly seen, being understood by the things that are made." (Rom. i. 20.) But the devil would have both to be of matter, that there may be nothing left from which we may come to the knowledge of God. For tell me, whether is harder: to [3] take that which is by nature evil (if indeed there be ought such; for I speak upon your principles, since there is no such thing as evil by nature), and make it either good, or even coefficent of good? or, to make of nothing? Whether is easier (I speak of quality); to induce the non-existent quality; or to take the existing quality, and change it into its contrary? where there is no house, to make the house; or where it is utterly destroyed, to make it identically exist again? Why, as this is impossible, so is that: to make a thing into its opposite. Tell me, whether is harder; to make a perfume, or to make filth have the effect of perfume? Say, whether of these is easier (since we subject God to our reasonings: nay, not we, but ye); to form eyes, or to make a blind man to see continuing blind, and yet more sharp-sighted, than one who does see? To make blindness into sight, and deafness into hearing? To me the other seems easier. Say then do

---

any thing individually about this, being necessarily involved in the idea of the resurrection, (τῇ ἀναστάσει συννοουμένης).

[1] In the later recension it is added: "but is declaratory of His love towards them, and of their election, and that He will not leave those whom He has chosen."

[2] John ii. 19; ἐγὼ ἐγερῶ αὐτὸν, Chrys. adding the pronoun for emphasis.

* The emphasis of the οὕτως and ὃν τρόπον is better preserved if we interpret them to mean *visibly*, or with the accompaniment of a cloud, in reference to the νεφέλη (9), rather than merely (as Chrys.) "with a body." They had not raised the question as to his coming with or without a body. What they wanted to know was whether he was coming in such a way that they could recognize him.—G. B. S.

[3] The text in both classes of manuscripts, and in the Edd., needs reformation. The argument is, If good and evil be, as the Manichæans say, both self-subsistent, then evil must subsist for ever. For if, as they affirm, God cannot create out of nothing, neither can He change a thing into its opposite; nay, much less, for this is harder than that. In E. (the text of the Edd.) the reading is, τὸ φύσει κακὸν καλὸν ποιῆσαι (εἰ γε τί ἐστι καθ' ὑμᾶς γὰρ λέγω· φύσει γὰρ οὐδὲν ἐστι ποιῆσαι κακὸν καλοῦ συνεργὸν) ἢ τὸ [οὐκ. A.] ἐξ οὐκ ὄντων : which as usual in this Ms. is an attempt to explain the meaning, but is not what the context requires. in C. A. (the original text) τὸ φύσει κακὸν ποιῆσαι (εἰ γε τί ἐστι· καθ' ὑμᾶς γὰρ λέγω· φύσει γὰρ οὐδὲν ἐστι ποιῆσαι κακὸν ἢ καλὸν κεὶ καλοῦ συνεργὸν) ἢ τὸ [οὐκ. A.] ἐξ οὐκ ὄντων. Read, τὸ φύσει κακὸν (εἰ γε τί ἐστι· καθ' ὑμᾶς γὰρ λέγω· φύσει γὰρ οὐδέν ἐστι κακὸν) ποιῆσαι ἢ καλὸν ἢ καὶ καλοῦ συνεργόν.

you grant God that which is harder, and not grant the easier? But souls also they affirm to be of His substance. Do you see what a number of impieties and absurdities are here! In the first place, wishing to show that evils are from God, they bring in another thing more impious than this, that they are equal with Him in majesty, and God prior in existence to none of them, assigning this great prerogative even to them! In the next place, they affirm evil to be indestructible: for if that which is uncreated can be destroyed, ye see the blasphemy! So that it comes to this, either [1] that nothing is of God, if not these; or that these are God! Thirdly, what I have before spoken of, in this point they defeat themselves, and prepare against themselves fresh indignation. Fourthly, they affirm unordered matter to possess such inherent (ἐπιτηδειότητα) power. Fifthly, that evil is the cause of the goodness of God, and that without this the Good had not been good. Sixthly, they bar against us the ways of attaining unto the knowledge of God. Seventhly, they bring God down into men, yea plants and logs. For if our soul be of the substance of God, but the process of its transmigration into new bodies brings it at last into cucumbers, and melons, and onions, why then the substance of God will pass into cucumbers! And if we say, that the Holy Ghost fashioned the Temple [of our Lord's body] in the Virgin, they laugh us to scorn: and if, that He dwelt in that spiritual Temple, again they laugh; while they themselves are not ashamed to bring down God's substance into cucumbers, and melons, and flies, and caterpillars, and asses, thus excogitating a new fashion of idolatry: for let it not be as the Egyptians have it, "The onion is God;" but let it be, "God in the onion"! Why dost thou shrink from the notion of God's entering into a body? [2] 'It is shocking,' says he. Why then this is much more shocking. But, [3] forsooth, it is not shocking

—how should it be?—this same thing which is so, if it be into us! 'But thy notion is indeed shocking.' Do ye see the filthiness of their impiety?—But why do they not wish the body to be raised? And why do they say the body is evil? By what then, tell me, dost thou know God? by what hast thou the knowledge of existing things? The philosopher too: by means of what is he a philosopher, if the body does nothing towards it? Deaden the senses, and then learn something of the things one needs to know! What would be more foolish than a soul, if from the first it had the senses deadened? If the deadening of but a single part, I mean of the brain, becomes a marring of it altogether; if all the rest should be deadened, what would it be good for? Show me a soul without a body. Do you not hear physicians say, The presence of disease sadly enfeebles the soul? How long will ye put off hanging yourselves? Is the body material? tell me. "To be sure, it is." Then you ought to hate it. Why do you feed, why cherish it? You ought to get quit of this prison. But besides: "God cannot overcome matter, unless he (συμπλακῇ) implicate himself with it: for he cannot issue orders to it (O feebleness!) until he close with it, and (σταθῇ) take his stand (say you) through the whole of it!" And a king indeed does all by commanding; but God, not by commanding the evil! In short, if it were unparticipant of all good, it could not subsist at all. For Evil cannot subsist, unless it lay hold upon somewhat of the accidents of Virtue: so that if it had been heretofore all unmixed with virtue, it would have perished long ago: for such is the condition of evils. Let there be a profligate man, let him put upon himself no restraint whatever, will he live ten days? Let there be

---

[1] Ὥστε ἀνάγκη ἢ μηδὲν τοῦ Θεοῦ εἶναι εἰ μὴ ταῦτα· ἢ καὶ Θεὸν εἶναι. For so it seems the passage should be read, for which the Mss. have ἢ εἰ μὴ ταῦτα, and then in the older text, ἢ καὶ Θεὸν εἶναι, for which the modern recension, D. E. F. and Edd. have ἢ καὶ Θεὸν μὴ εἶναι.

[2] τὴν ἐνσωμάτωσιν τοῦ Θεοῦ. Edd. μετενσωμάτωσιν. But the Manichees affirmed a μετενσωμάτωσιν of the particle of the Divine Substance, the human soul; viz. the more polluted soul transmigrates into other men, and animals (Archelai et Manet. Disput. §. ix. Routh, Rell. Sacc. iv. 161.), but in the last stage of the process of its purgation, into vegetable substances less attached to the earth by roots, such as gourds, etc. in which the Divine particle is self-conscious and intelligent (see the following note), whereas in animal substances it is brutified. In this sense it is said above, ἡ μετενσ. ἐκβαίνει εἰς σικύους κ. τ. λ. What they denied was, an ἐνσωμάτωσις Θεοῦ by Incarnation.

[3] Ἀλλ᾿ οὐκ αἰσχρόν; πῶς γάρ; ὅπερ (om. A.) ἂν εἰς ἡμᾶς γένηται· τὸ δὲ σὸν ὄντως αἰσχρόν. Edd. ἀλλ᾿ οὐκ αἰσχρόν; πῶς; ὅπερ γὰρ ἂν εἰς ἡμᾶς γένηται ὄντως αἰσχρόν. Erasmus; An non hoc turpe est? Quomodo non turpe sit in Deum, quod, si nobis contingat, revera turpe futurum sit? Ben. Quandoquidem

si in nobis fiat, vere turpe est. i. e. For, that same which, if it take place in us, is indeed shocking [how should it not be so in God?]. The exclamation, Εἴδετε συρφετὸν ἀσεβείας! seems to imply either that ὄντως αἰσχρὸν is part of the Manichæan's reply, or that something is omitted. Perhaps the reporter wrote, τὸ δὲ σ. ὄντως αἰσχρόν, meaning σῶμα: "But the body, etc." Ἂν εἰς ἡμᾶς γένηται can hardly be, as taken by Erasm., quod si nobis contingat, i. e. that our substance should migrate into plants, etc. but rather, if it be into us that this (embodying of the Divine Substance) takes place. For illustration of the Manichæan tenets here alluded to, comp. Euod. de Fid. adv. Manich. § 35. (Opp. St. Augustin., Append. t. viii. Ben.) Non Deus Manichæi luctum pateretur de partis suæ abscissione vel amissione; quam partem dicunt quum in fructibus vel in herbis fuerit, id est, in melone. vel beta, vel talibus rebus, et principium suum et medietatem et finem nosse, cum autem ad carnem venerit omnem intelligentiam amittere; ut propterea magister hominibus missus sit, quia stulta in illis facta est pars Dei, etc. "Then the God of the Manichæan would not suffer grief in consequence of the cutting off or loss of part of his substance; which part, they say, if it be in fruits or in herbs, as in the melon or beet or such-like, knows its beginning and middle and end; but when it comes to flesh, loses all intelligence: so that the reason why the Teacher was sent to men was, because in them the particle of God was stultified, etc." And Commonitor, de recip. Manich. Art. 3. (ibid.) ut credatur pars Dei polluta teneri in cucumeribus et melonibus et radiculis et porris et quibusque vilissimis herbulis, etc.

a robber, and devoid of all conscience in his dealings with every one, let him be such even to his fellow-robbers, will he be able to live? Let there be a thief, void of all shame, who knows not what blushing is, but steals openly in public. It is not in the nature of evils to subsist, unless they get some small share at least in good. So that hereupon, according to these men, God gave them their subsistence. Let there be a city of wicked men; will it stand? But let them be wicked, not only with regard to the good, but towards each other. Why, it is impossible such a city should stand. Truly, "professing themselves to be wise, they became fools." (Rom. i. 22.) If bodily substance be evil, then all things visible exist idly, and in vain, both water and earth, and sun, and air; for air is also body, though not solid. It is in point then to say, "The wicked have told me foolish things." (Ps. cxix. 85.) But let not us endure them, let us block up our ears against them. For there is, yea, there is, a resurrection of bodies. This the sepulchre which is at Jerusalem declares, this the pillar[8] to which He was bound, when He was scourged. For, "We did eat and drink with Him," it is said. Let us then believe in the Resurrection, and do things worthy of it, that we may attain to the good things which are to come, through Christ Jesus our Lord, with Whom to the Father, and the Holy Ghost together, be power, honor, now and for ever, world without end. Amen.

HOMILY III.

ACTS I. 12.

"Then returned they unto Jerusalem from the mount called Olivet, which is from Jerusalem a sabbath day's journey.

"THEN returned they," it is said : namely, when they had heard. For they could not have borne it, if the angel had not ($\dot{\nu}\pi\epsilon\rho\dot{\epsilon}\theta\epsilon\tau o$) referred them to another Coming. It seems to me, that it was also on a sabbath-day[1] that these things took place; for he would not thus have specified the distance, saying, "from the mount called Olivet, which is from Jerusalem a sabbath day's journey," unless they were then going on the sabbathday a certain definite distance. "And when they were come in," it says, "they went up into an upper room, where they were making their abode:" so they then remained in Jerusalem after the Resurrection: "both Peter, and James, and John:" no longer is only the latter together with his brother mentioned,[2] but together with Peter the two: "and Andrew, and Philip, and Thomas, Bartholomew, and Matthew, and James (the son) of Alphæus, and Simon Zelotes, and Judas, (the brother) of James." * (v.13.) He has done well to mention the disciples: for since one had betrayed Christ, and another had been unbelieving, he thereby shows that, except the first, all of them were preserved.

"These were all continuing with one accord in prayer together with the women." (v. 14.) For this is a powerful weapon in temptations; and to this they had been trained. ["Continuing with one accord."] Good. ($\kappa\alpha\lambda\tilde{\omega}\varsigma$). Besides, the present temptation directed them to this: for they exceedingly feared the Jews. "With the women," it is said : for he had said that they had followed Him : "and with Mary the mother of Jesus." (Luke xxiii. 55.) How then [is it said, that "that disciple "] took her to his own home" (John xix. 26), at that time? But then the Lord had brought them together again, and so returned.[4] "And

---

the English translators is allowed to stand because it is, probably, the more common one and has many able modern exegetes in its favor among whom are Buttmann, Gram. N. T. Gk. (Eng. Trans.) p. 94. and, more doubtfully, Winer, N. T. Gram. (Eng. Trans., p. 190. It is, however, certain that usage is strongly in favor, of supplying υἱός. The former view identifies this Judas with the author of the Epistle (Jud. i. 1) and is that of our older English Trans. The latter understands this Judas to be the son of an unknown James and is favored by Thayer's *Lex.*, Meyer and the Revised Vs. To me this view seems probably correct.—G. B. S.

[3] τὸ ξύλον ἔνθα προσεδέθη καὶ ἐμαστιγώθη. The ' Pillar of Flagellation ' is exhibited in the Latin Choir of the Church of the Holy Sepulchre.

[4] Πάλιν δὲ συναγαγὼν αὐτοὺς οὕτως κατῆλθεν. So the older text : i. e. When they were scattered every man to his own home, that disciple had taken her εἰς τὰ ἴδια. But after the Resurrection Christ had gathered them together, and *so* (with all assembled) had returned to the usual place or mode of living.

---

[1] This must be taken as a hasty remark, unless (which is not likely) a sabbath extraordinary is meant.
[2] The meaning seems to be, "he is not content to mention only James and John with Peter, but gives the full list of the Apostles.
* The meaning of Ἰούδας Ἰακώβου (i. 13, cf. Luke vi. 16) is a disputed point. Whether the genitive denotes the relation of brother or son has never been decided. The interpretation of

2

with His brethren." (John xvii. 5.) These also were before unbelieving.

"And in those days," it says, "Peter stood up in the midst of the disciples, and said." (v. 15.) Both as being ardent, and as having been put in trust by Christ with the flock, and as having precedence in honor,[1] he always begins the discourse. ("The number of the names together were about an hundred and twenty.) Men and brethren," he says, "this Scripture must needs have been fulfilled, which the Holy Ghost spake before,"[2] [etc.] (v. 16.) Why did he not ask Christ to give him some one in the room of Judas? It is better as it is. For in the first place, they were engaged in other things; secondly, of Christ's presence with them, the greatest proof that could be given was this: as He had chosen when He was among them, so did He now being absent. Now this was no small matter for their consolation. But observe how Peter does everything with the common consent; nothing imperiously. And he does not speak thus without a meaning. But observe how he consoles them concerning what had passed. In fact, what had happened had caused them no small consternation. For if there are many now who canvass this circumstance, what may we suppose they had to say then?

"Men and brethren," says Peter. For if the Lord called them brethren, much more may he. ["Men," he says]: they all being present.[3] See the dignity of the Church, the angelic condition! No distinction there, "neither male nor female." I would that the Churches were such now! None there had his mind full of some worldly matter, none was anxiously thinking about household concerns. Such a benefit are temptations, such the advantage of afflictions!

"This Scripture," says he, "must needs have been fulfilled, which the Holy Ghost spake before." Always he comforts them by the prophecies. So does Christ on all occa-

sions. In the very same way, he shows here that no strange thing had happened, but what had already been foretold. "This Scripture must needs have been fulfilled," he says, "which the Holy Ghost by the mouth of David spake before." He does not say, David, but the Spirit through him. See what kind of doctrine the writer has at the very outset of the book. Do you see, that it was not for nothing that I said in the beginning of this work, that this book is the Polity of the Holy Spirit? "Which the Holy Ghost spake before by the mouth of David." Observe how he appropriates (οἰκειοῦται) him; and that it is an advantage to them, that this was spoken by David, and not by some other Prophet. "Concerning Judas," he says, "which was guide." Here again mark the philosophical temper of the man: how he does not mention him with scorn, nor say, "that wretch," "that miscreant:" but simply states the fact; and does not even say, "who betrayed Him," but does what he can to transfer the guilt to others: nor does he animadvert severely even on these: "Which was guide," he says, "to them that took Jesus." Furthermore, before he declares where David had spoken, he relates what had been the case with Judas, that from the things present he may fetch assurance of the things future, and show that this man had already received his due. "For he was numbered," says he, "with us, and had obtained part of this ministry. Now this man acquired a field out of the reward of iniquity." (v. 17, 18.) He gives his discourse a moral turn, and covertly mentions the cause of the wickedness, because it carried reproof with it.[1] And he does not say, The Jews, but, "this man, acquired" it. For since the minds of weak persons do not attend to things future, as they do to things present, he discourses of the immediate punishment inflicted. "And falling headlong, he burst asunder in the midst." He does well to dilate not upon the sin, but upon the punishment. "And," he says, "all his bowels gushed out." This brought them consolation.[2] "And it was known unto all the dwellers at Jerusalem; insomuch as that field is called in their proper tongue Aceldama, that

---

[1] Προτιμότερος, B. C.: προτιμώμενος A. and Catena: τοῦ χοροῦ πρῶτος, E. D. F. Comp. *Hom. in Matt.* liv. t. ii. 107. "What then saith the mouth of the Apostles, Peter? He, the ever ardent, the coryphæus of the choir of the Apostles."

[2] Chrys. seems to have read on to the end of the chapter. The rest of the citation being omitted in the Mss. the remodeller of the text makes alterations, and adds matter of his own, to make the exposition run smoother. "Why did he not ask Christ, *alone*, to give him some one in the place of Judas? And why of their own selves do they not make the election?" Then instead of βέλτιον γέγονε λοιπὸν πρῶτον μὲν γὰρ, κ. τ. λ. he has, βελτίων λοιπὸν ἢν γεγονὼς ὁ Πέτρος αὐτὸς ἑαυτοῦ, κ. τ. λ. "Peter has now become a better man than he was. So much for this point. But as to their request to have their body filled up not simply, but by revelation, we will mention two reasons; first, "etc.

[3] Edd. "Wherefore he uses this address, they all being present." But the old text has simply πάντων παρόντων, i. e. all, both men and women. Chrys. is commenting on the address ἄνδρες ἀδελφοὶ as including the *women* also who were before said to be present. Comp. *Hom. in Matt.* lxxiii. p. 712, B. on the separation of men and women in the Churches.

[1] λανθανόντως λέγει τὴν αἰτίαν, παιδευτικὴν οὖσαν: i. e. "in speaking of the wages of Judas, he indicates, that the Jews, by whom he was hired, were the authors of the wickedness: but because this carried reproof, he does it covertly, by implication." In the next sentence, he goes on to another point of the exposition, Καὶ οὐ λέγει, κ. τ. λ. i. e. "And observe also, that with the same wise forbearance, he says it not of the Jews, but of Judas, that a piece of ground was all that was gotten by this wickedness: now, in fact, not Judas earned this, but the Jews." The modern text has οὐ λέγει γάρ.

[2] Τοῦτο παραμυθίαν ἐκείνοις ἔφερε. Something seems to be omitted here.

is to say, the field of blood." (v. 19). Now the Jews[1] gave it this name, not on this account, but because of Judas; here, however, Peter makes it to have this reference, and when he brings forward the adversaries as witnesses, both by the fact that they named it, and by saying, "in their proper tongue," this is what he means.

Then after the event, he appositely brings in the Prophet, saying, "For it is written in the Book of Psalms, Let his habitation be desolate, and let no man dwell therein" (v. 20) (Ps. lxix. 25): this is said of the field and the dwelling: "And his bishopric let another take; that is, his office, his priesthood. So that this, he says, is not my counsel, but His who hath foretold these things. For, that he may not seem to be undertaking a great thing, and just such as Christ had done, he adduces the Prophet as a witness. "Wherefore it behooves of these men which have companied with us all the time." (v. 21.) Why does he make it their business too? That the matter might not become an object of strife, and they might not fall into contention about it. For if the Apostles themselves once did this, much more might those. This he ever avoids. Wherefore at the beginning he said, "Men and brethren. It behooves" to choose from among you.[2] He defers the decision to the whole body, thereby both making the elected objects of reverence and himself keeping clear of all invidiousness with regard to the rest. For such occasions always give rise to great evils. Now that some one must needs be appointed, he adduces the prophet as witness: but from among what persons: "Of these," he says, "which have companied with us all the time." To have said, the worthy must present themselves, would have been to insult the others; but now he refers the matter to length of time; for he says not simply, "These who have companied with us," but, "all the time that the Lord Jesus went in and out among us, beginning from the baptism of John unto that same day that He was taken up from us, must one be ordained to be a witness with us of His resurrection" (v. 22): that their college (ὁ χορὸς) might not be left mutilated. Then why did it not rest with Peter to make the election himself: what was the motive? This; that he might not seem to bestow it of favor. And besides, he was not yet

endowed with the spirit. "And they appointed two, Joseph called Barsabus, who was surnamed Justus, and Matthias." (v. 23.) Not he appointed them: but it was he that introduced the proposition to that effect, at the same time pointing out that even this was not his own, but from old time by prophecy; so that he acted as expositor, not as preceptor. "Joseph called Barsabus, who was surnamed Justus." Perhaps both names are given, because there were others of the same name, for among the Apostles also there were several names alike; as James, and James (the son) of Alphæus; Simon Peter, and Simon Zelotes; Judas (the brother) of James, and Judas Iscariot. The appellation, however, may have arisen from a change of life, and very likely also of the moral character.[3] "They appointed two," it is said, "Joseph called Barsabus, who was surnamed Justus, and Matthias. And they prayed, and said, Thou, Lord, which knowest the hearts of all men, show whether of these two thou hast chosen, that he may take part of this ministry and Apostleship, from which Judas by transgression fell, that he might go to his own place." (v. 24, 25.) They do well to mention the sin of Judas, thereby showing that it is a witness they ask to have; not increasing the number, but not suffering it to be diminished. "And they gave forth their lots" (for the spirit was not yet sent), "and the lot fell upon Matthias: and he was numbered with the eleven Apostles." (v. 26.)

"Then," it says, "returned they unto Jerusalem from the mount called Olivet (Recapitulation), ["which[4] is nigh to Jerusalem, at the distance of a sabbath-day's journey:"] so that there was no long way to go, to be a cause of alarm to them while yet trembling and fearful. "And when they were come in, they went up into an upper room." They durst not appear in the town. They also did well to go up into an upper room, as it became less easy to arrest them at once. "And they continued," it is said, "with one accord in prayer." Do

---

[1] Here also Chrys. seems to be imperfectly reported. His meaning may be gathered from what is said further on, in the recapitulation: i. e. in giving the field that name, "because it was the price of blood" (Matt. xxvii. 8), they unconsciously prophesied; for indeed the reward of *their* iniquity was this, that their place became an Aceldama.

[2] So A. B. C. and the Catena. The other text has ἐξ ἡμῶν, which is less apposite.

[3] Ἄλλως δὲ καὶ μεταβολῆς βίου, ἴσως δὲ καὶ προαιρέσεως ἦν ἡ ὀνομασία. i. e. St. Luke gives both the names Joseph (or Joses) and Justus, perhaps for the sake of distinction. The name (as Latin) may have been given in consequence of a change of life (viz. of circumstances), and (as meaning 'the Just') perhaps also from a change of character (προαίρεσις.)—Or, προαίρεσις (βίου) may be opposed to μεταβολὴ βίου and then the meaning would be, that the name may have related to a change, i. e. reformation of life, or perhaps to his original choice or moral purpose of life. But ἴσως δὲ καὶ seems best to suit the former explanation.

[4] This clause of the text is added, though wanting in our Mss. The comment is, ὥστε μηδὲ μακρὰν βαδίζουσιν ὁδὸν φόβον τινὰ γενέσθαι τρέμουσιν ἔτι καὶ δεδοικόσιν αὐτοῖς· i. e. "so that not being a long way for them walking, it was not, etc.," which construction being somewhat obscure, the modern text has, τοῦτό φησιν, ἵνα δείξῃ ὅτι μακρὰν οὐ βαδίζουσιν ὁδὸν, ὡς φόβον τινὰ μὴ γενέσθαι τρέμουσιν ἔτι καὶ δεδοικόσιν αὐτοῖς.

you see how watchful they were? "Continuing in prayer," and "with one accord," as it were with one soul, continuing therein: two things reported in their praise. ["Where [1] they were abiding," etc., to, "And Mary the Mother of Jesus and His brethren."] Now Joseph perhaps was dead: for it is not to be supposed that when the brethren had become believers, Joseph believed not; he who in fact had believed before any. Certain it is that we nowhere find him looking upon Christ as man merely. As where His mother said, ["Thy father and I did seek thee sorrowing." (Luke ii. 48.) And upon another occasion, it was said,] "Thy mother [2] and thy brethren seek thee." (Matt. xiii. 47.) So that Joseph knew this before all others. And to them [the brethren] Christ said, "The world cannot hate you, but Me it hateth. (John vii. 7.)

Again, consider the moderation of James. He it was who received the Bishopric of Jerusalem, and here he says nothing. Mark also the great moderation of the other Apostles, how they concede the throne to him, and no longer dispute with each other. For that Church was as it were in heaven: having nothing to do with this world's affairs: and resplendent not with walls, no, nor with numbers, but with the zeal of them that formed the assembly. They were "about an hundred and twenty," it says. The seventy perhaps whom Christ Himself had chosen, and other of the more earnest-minded disciples, as Joseph and Matthias. (v. 14.) There were women, he says, many, who followed Him. (Mark xv. 41.) ["The number of the names together.] Together [3] " they were on all occasions.

["Men and brethren," etc.] Here is fore-thought for providing a teacher; here was the first who ordained a teacher. He did not say, 'We are sufficient.' So far was he beyond all vain-glory, and he looked to one thing alone. And yet he had the same power to ordain as they all collectively. [4] But well might these things be done in this fashion, through the noble spirit of the man, and because prelacy then was not an affair of dignity, but of provident care for the governed. This neither made the elected to become elated, for it was to dangers that they were called, nor those not elected to make a grievance of it, as if they were disgraced. But things are not done in this fashion now; nay, quite the contrary.—For observe, they were an hundred and twenty, and he asks for one out of the whole body · with good right, as having been put in charge of them: for to him had Christ said, "And when thou art converted, strengthen thy brethren." (Luke xxii. 32, Ben.)

"For he was numbered with us," (πρῶτος τοῦ πράγματος αὐθεντεῖ absent from A. B. C.) says Peter. On this account it behooves to propose another; to be a witness in his place. And see how he imitates his Master, ever discoursing from the Scriptures, and saying nothing as yet concerning Christ; namely, that He had frequently predicted this Himself. Nor does he mention where the Scripture speaks of the treachery of Judas; for instance, "The mouth of the wicked and the mouth of the deceitful are opened against me" (Ps. cix. 1.); but where it speaks only of his punishment; for this was most to their advantage. It shows again the benevolence of the Lord: "For he was numbered with us" (τοῦτο γὰρ αὐτοὺς μάλιστα ὠφέλει· Δείκνυσι πάλιν A. B. C.), he says, "and obtained his lot of this ministry." He calls it everywhere "lot," showing that the whole is from God's grace and election, and reminding them of the old times, inasmuch as God chose him into His own lot or portion, as of old He took the Levites. He also dwells upon the circumstances respecting Judas, showing that the reward of the treachery was made itself the herald of the punishment. For he "acquired," he says, "a field out of the reward of the iniquity." Observe the divine economy

---

[1] Here again, as usual, in the renewed exposition, the text is omitted.

[2] Ἡ μητήρ σου καὶ οἱ ἀδελφοί σου ἐζητοῦμέν σε. A. C. ὁ πατήρ σου κ. τ. λ. B. For ἐζητ. we must read ζητοῦσιν. The passage referred to is Matt. xiii. 47, where however it is not Mary that speaks, but "A certain person said unto Him, Behold, Thy mother and Thy brethren stand without seeking to speak with Thee. In the Homily on that passage, Chrys. interprets that Mary presented herself on that occasion οὐδὲν οὐδέπω περὶ αὐτοῦ μέγα φανταζομένη, "having as yet no high idea of His Person," and that both she and His brethren, ὡς ἀνθρώπῳ προσεῖχον ψιλῷ "looked upon Him as mere man." In the same way he adverts to that incident here, for contrast with the higher faith of Joseph; but as the statement, "His mother said," is not accurate, the modern text substitutes the passage, Luke ii. 48, and reads, ἡ μήτηρ ἔλεγεν, Ἐγὼ καὶ ὁ πατήρ σου ὀδυνώμενοι ἐζητοῦμέν σε. It seems that Chrys. cited this passage also (hence our Mss. have ἐζητοῦμεν for ζητοῦσι), meaning, that it was not Joseph who said this, but Mary.— Œcumenius, however, gives a different turn to this passage of St. Chrys. "And if Joseph had been alive, he too would have been present; especially as he never, like his sons (οἱ ἐξ αὐτοῦ viz. the ἀδελφοὶ), entertained a doubt of the mystery of the Incarnation. But it is manifest that he was long dead; since even on the occasion when, as Jesus was teaching, His kinsfolk demanded to see Him, Joseph was not present. For what says the Gospel? "Thy mother and thy brethren without see : thee;" but not also, Thy father.

[3] Ἐπὶ τὸ αὐτό· a comment on v. 15.

[4] Καίτοιγε ἰσότυπον ἅπασιν εἶχε τὴν κατάστασιν, which Erasm. justly renders, Quanquam habebat jus constituendi por omnibus : i. e. the ordination by St. Peter singly, would have been as valid as the ordination by the whole body. D. F. have καίτοι οὐδὲ, i. e. and yet he possessed a power of ordaining, in which they were not all upon a par with him : which reading is accepted by Morel. Sav. and Ben., and is rendered by the last, Quanquam non pari forma apud omnes ejus vigebat auctoritas. This reading originated in a mistake as to the meaning of the other, as if that asserted only that St. Peter had the same power of ordaining as any of the rest.

in the event. "Of the iniquity," he says. For there are many iniquities, but never was anything more iniquitous than this: so that the affair was one of iniquity. Now not only to those who were present did the event become known, but to all thereafter, so that without meaning or knowing what they were about, they gave it a name; just as Caiaphas had prophesied unconsciously. God compelled them to call the field in Hebrew "Aceldama." (Matt. xxvi. 24.) By this also the evils which were to come upon the Jews were declared: and Peter shows the prophecy to have been so far in part fulfilled, which says, "It had been good for that man if he had not been born." We may with propriety apply this same to the Jews likewise; for if he who was guide suffered thus, much more they. Thus far however Peter says nothing of this. Then, showing that the term, "Aceldama," might well be applied to his fate, he introduces the prophet, saying, "Let his habitation be desolate." For what can be worse desolation than to become a place of burial? And the field may well be called *his*. For he who cast down the price, although others were the buyers, has a right to be himself reckoned owner of a great desolation.[1] This desolation was the prelude to that of the Jews, as will appear on looking closely into the facts. For indeed they destroyed themselves by famine, and killed many, and the city became a burial-place of strangers, of soldiers,[2] for as to those, they would not even have let them be buried, for in fact they were not deemed worthy of sepulture.

"Wherefore of these men which have companied with us," continues Peter. Observe how desirous he is they should be eye-witnesses. It is true indeed that the Spirit would shortly come; and yet great care is shown with regard to this circumstance. "Of these men," he says, "which have companied with us, all the time that the Lord Jesus went in and out among us." He shows that they had dwelt with Christ, not simply been present as disciples. In fact, from the very beginning there were many that then followed Him. Observe, for instance, how this appears in these words: "One of the two which heard John speak, and followed Jesus.—All the time," he says, "that the Lord Jesus went in and out among us, beginning from the baptism of John." (John i. 40.) True! for no one knew what preceded that event, though they did learn it by the Spirit. "Unto that same day that He was taken up from us, must one be ordained to be a witness with us of His resurrection."* He said not, a witness of the rest of his actions, but a witness of the resurrection alone. For indeed that witness had a better right to be believed, who was able to declare, that He Who ate and drank, and was crucified, the same rose again. Wherefore it was needed that he should be a witness, not only of the time preceding this event, nor only of what followed it, and of the miracles; the thing required was, the resurrection. For the other matters were manifest and acknowledged, but the resurrection took place in secret, and was manifest to these only. And they do not say, Angels have told us; but, We have seen.[3] For this it was that was most needful at that time: that they should be men having a right to be believed, because they had seen.

"And they appointed two," it is said.† Why not many? That the feeling of disappointment might not reach further, extending to many. Again, it is not without reason[4] that he puts Matthias last; he would show, that frequently he that is honourable among men, is inferior before God. And they all pray in common saying, "Thou, Lord, which knowest the hearts of all men, show. Thou," not "We." And very seasonably they use the epithet, "heart-knowing:" for by Him Who is this[5] must the choice be made. So confident were they, that assuredly one of them must be appointed. They said not, Choose, but, "Show the chosen one;" knowing that all things were forcordained of God; "Whom

---

[1] κύριος ἐρημώσεως μεγάλης. Something perhaps is wanting between κύρ. and ἐρ. μ. Indeed the text seems to consist of little more than a few rough notes.

[2] Τάφος γέγονεν ἡ πόλις τῶν ξένων, τῶν στρατιωτῶν. In the defective state of the text it is not easy to conjecture what this can mean. Perhaps, alluding to the words in St. Matthew, "a place to bury *strangers* in." St. Chrys. may have explained, that the strangers were not heathen (ἐκείνους γὰρ οὐδ᾽ ἂν εἴασαν ταφῆναι, they would not have allowed such to be buried in or by the Holy City, much less have provided a place of burial for them), but foreign Jews: and if in τάφος γέγονεν ἡ πόλις he alludes to the description in Josephus, B. J. v. 12. 3. and 13. 7. this explanation of the term " strangers " would be the more apposite, as the myriads who perished in the siege were assembled from all parts of the world. The 'soldiers' seem to be the mercenaries on the side of the Jews: five thousand Idumæans are mentioned, B. J. v. 6. 1.

* The requirement for the apostolic office is here clearly indicated. The candidate must have associated with Christ and his apostles during the period from John's baptism to the Lord's ascension, i. e. during His public ministry. The character of the apostolate is also significantly implied in the term μάρτυς τῆς ἀναστάσεως ἀυτοῦ. The resurrection was the great central theme of apostolic teaching and preaching (vid. Acts iv. 2, 33; xvii. 18, 32).—G. B. S.

[3] Here the Edd. have ἡμεῖς· πόθεν δῆλον; ἐξ ὧν θαυματουργοῦμεν. "ourselves: how is this proved? by the miracles we work." C. has not these words, which are not needed, but rather disturb the sense.

† The words of the text (v. 23) Καὶ ἔστησαν δύο are better rendered " put forward " (Rev. Vs.) than "appointed." (A.Y.) The meaning is that the company chose two persons as candidates, leaving the decision between them to the lot.—G. B. S.

[4] Οὐχ ἁπλῶς δὲ προστίθησιν ἐκείνον, D. and E. have οὐχ ἁπλῶς δὲ οὐ προτίθησιν ἐκείνον, according to which the sense would be the same: " Not without reason does he avoid putting Matthias first."

[5] Here the Edd. add, οὐχὶ τῶν ἔξωθεν, "not by those without:" but these words are not found in our Mss. of either text, nor in the Catena.

Thou didst choose: one of these two," say they, "to have his lot in this ministry and apostleship." For there was besides another ministry (διακονία). "And they gave them their lots." For they did not yet consider themselves to be worthy to be informed by some sign.[1] And besides, if in a case where neither prayer was made, nor men of worth were the agents, the casting of lots so much availed, because it was done of a right intention, I mean in the case of Jonah (Jonah i. 7); much more did it here. Thus,[2] did he, the designated, fill up the company, complete the order: but the other candidate was not annoyed; for the apostolic writers would not have concealed [that or any other] failings of their own, seeing they have told of the very chief Apostles, that on other occasions they *had indignation* (Matt. xx. 24; xxvi. 8), and this not once only, but again and again.

Let us then also imitate them. And now I address no longer every one, but those who aim at preferment. If thou believest that the election is with God, be not displeased. (Mark x. 14, 21; xiv. 4.) For it is with Him thou art displeased, and with Him thou art exasperated: it is He who has made the choice; thou doest the very thing that Cain did; because, forsooth, his brother's sacrifice was preferred, he was indignant, when he ought to have felt compunction. However, that is not what I mean here; but this, that God knows how to dispense things for the best. In many cases, thou art in point of disposition more estimable than the other, but not the fit person. Besides, on the other hand, thy life is irreproachable, and thy habits those of a well-nurtured man, but in the Church this is not all that is wanted. Moreover, one man is adapted for one thing, another for another. Do you not observe, how much discourse the holy Scripture has made on this matter? But let me say why it is that the thing has become a subject of competition: it is because we come to the Episcopate not as unto a work of governing and superintending the brethren, but as to a post of dignity and repose. Did you but know that a Bishop is bound to belong to all, to bear the burden of all; that others, if they are angry, are pardoned, but he never; that others, if they sin, have excuses made for them, he has none; you would not be eager

for the dignity, would not run after it. So it is, the Bishop is exposed to the tongues of all, to the criticism of all, whether they be wise or fools. He is harassed with cares every day, nay, every night. He has many to hate him, many to envy him. Talk not to me of those who curry favor with all, of those who desire to sleep, of those who advance to this office as for repose. We have nothing to do with these; we speak of those who watch for your souls, who consider the safety and welfare of those under them before their own. Tell me now: suppose a man has ten children, always living with him, and constantly under his control; yet is he solicitous about them; and a bishop, who has such numbers, not living under the same roof with him, but owing obedience to his authority—what does he not need to be! But he is honored, you will say. With what sort of honor, indeed! Why, the paupers and beggars abuse him openly in the market-place. And why does he not stop their mouths then? Yes, very proper work, this, for a bishop, is it not?[3] Then again, if he do not give to all, the idle and the industrious alike, lo! a thousand complaints on all sides. None is afraid to accuse him, and speak evil of him. In the case of civil governors, fear steps in; with bishops, nothing of the kind. As for the fear of God, it does not influence people, as regards them, in the least degree. Why speak of the anxiety connected with the word and doctrine? the painful work in Ordinations? Either, perhaps, I am a poor wretched incompetent creature, or else, the case is as I say. The soul of a Bishop is for all the world like a vessel in a storm: lashed from every side, by friends, by foes, by one's own people, by strangers. Does not the Emperor rule the whole world, the Bishop a single city? Yet a Bishop's anxieties are as much beyond those of the emperor, as the waters of a river simply moved, by the wind are surpassed in agitation by the swelling and raging sea. And why? because in the one case there are many to lend a hand, for all goes on by law and by rule; but in the other there is none of this, nor is there authority to command; but if one be greatly moved, then he is harsh; if the contrary, then he is cold! And in him these opposites must meet, that he may neither be despised, nor be hated. Besides, the very demands of business preoccupy him: how many is he obliged to offend, whether he will or not! How many to be severe with! I speak not otherwise than it is, but as

---

[1] So, except E. all our Mss. and the Catena: and Morel. Ben. But Sav. and Par. "they did not yet think themselves worthy to make the election by themselves: wherefore they desire to be informed by some sign." An unnecessary alteration; for the *sign* means some miraculous token. So Œcumen.

[2] Mss. and Edd. πολλῷ μᾶλλον ἐνταῦθα ἐπλήρωσε τὸν χορὸν, ἀπήρτισε την τάξιν. The Catena adds ὁ ἀναδεχθεὶς (ἀναδειχθεὶς), which we have adopted.

[3] Edd. Πάνυ γε. Οὐ γὰρ ἐπισκόπου λέγεις ἔργον. Read Πάνυ γε (οὐ γάρ;) ἐπισκ. λέγ. ἔργον.

I find it in my own actual experience. I do not think there are many among Bishops that will be saved, but many more that perish: and the reason is, that it is an affair that requires a great mind. Many are the exigencies which throw a man out of his natural temper; and he had need have a thousand eyes on all sides. Do you not see what a number of qualifications the Bishop must have? to be apt to teach, patient, holding fast the faithful word in doctrine (see 1 Tim. iii. 2–9. Tit. i. 7–9). What trouble and pains does this require! And then, others do wrong, and he bears all the blame. To pass over every thing else: if one soul depart unbaptized, does not this subvert all his own prospect of salvation? The loss of one soul carries with it a penalty which no language can represent. For if the salvation of that soul was of such value, that the Son of God became man, and suffered so much, think how sore a punishment must the losing of it bring! And if in this present life he who is cause of another's destruction is worthy of death, much more in the next world. Do not tell me, that the presbyter is in fault, or the deacon. The guilt of all these comes perforce upon the head of those who ordained them. Let me mention another instance. It chances, that a bishop has inherited from his predecessor a set of persons of indifferent character.[1] What measures is it proper to take in respect of bygone transgressions (for here are two precipices) so as not to let the offender go unpunished, and not to cause scandal to the rest? Must one's first step be to cut him off? There is no actual present ground for that. But is it right to let him go unmarked? Yes, say you; for the fault rests with the bishop who ordained him. Well then? must one refuse to ordain him again, and to raise him to a higher degree of the ministry? That would be to publish it to all men, that he is a person of indifferent character, and so again one would cause scandal in a different way. But is one to promote him to a higher degree? That is much worse.

If then there were only the responsibility of the office itself for people to run after in the episcopate, none would be so quick to accept it. But as things go, we run after this, just as we do after the dignities of the world. That we may have glory with men, we lose ourselves with God. What profit in such honor? How self-evident its nothingness is! When you covet the episcopal rank,[2] put in the other scale, the account to be rendered after this life. Weigh against it, the happiness of a life free from toil, take into account the different measure of the punishment. I mean, that even if you have sinned, but in your own person merely, you will have no such great punishment, nothing like it: but if you have sinned as bishop, you are lost. Remember what Moses endured, what wisdom he displayed, what good deeds he exhibited: but, for committing one sin only,[3] he was bitterly punished; and with good reason; for this fault was attended with injury to the rest. Not in regard that the sin was public, but because it was the sin of a spiritual Ruler (ἱερέως) cf. S.); for in truth we do not pay the same penalty for public and for hidden faults. (Aug in Ps. xcix. 6.) The sin may be the same, but not the (ζημία) harm of it; nay, not the sin itself; for it is not the same thing to sin in secret and unseen, and to sin openly. But the bishop cannot sin unobserved. Well for him if he escape reproach, though he sin not; much less can he think to escape notice, if he do sin. Let him be angry, let him laugh, or let him but dream of a moment's relaxation, many are they that scoff, many that are offended, many that lay down the law, many that bring to mind the former bishops, and abuse the present one; not that they wish to sound the praise of those; no, it is only to carp at him that they bring up the mention of fellow-bishops, of presbyters. Sweet, says the proverb, is war to the inexperienced; but[4] it may rather

---

[1] Συμβαίνει τινὰ κλῆρον διαδέξασθαι ἀνδρῶν μοχθηρῶν. The expression below, ὅτι μοχθηρός τις ἐστι shows that the ἀνδ. μοχθ., 'ill-conditioned men,' are clerks. The offences meant seem to have been before ordination: and the difficulty is, How to deal with a clerk who ought not to have been ordained at all? You cannot cut him off from the order of clergy, there being no present actual delinquency to justify such a step. Then suppose you do not call him to account for the past, on the ground that the bishop who ordained him must be answerable: what are you to do, when this man should in the regular course be advanced to a higher order of the ministry? To refuse to ordain him, would be to publish his unworthiness, and call attention to the scandal of his having been ordained in the first instance: to advance him, would be even worse.

[2] Here the Edd. add ἀντίστησον τὴν γέενναν, "put in the other balance—hell:" which, however, is not found in any of our Mss.

[3] ἵνα ἐν ἁμάρτῃ ἁμάρτημα μόνον, ἐκολάζετο πικρῶς. On this peculiar construction, see Field, Adnotat. in Hom. in Matt. p. 404. E.—In the next sentence St. Chrys. in applying the term ἱερεὺς to Moses, does not mean that Moses was a Priest, but that he held a station similar in some regards to that of Bishops afterwards. Aaron was properly the High Priest, but Moses was a type of Christian Bishops, considered as Chief Pastors and Rulers.

[4] Μᾶλλον δὲ νῦν οὐδὲ μετὰ τὸ ἐκβῆναι δῆλος τοῖς πολλοῖς· οὐ γάρ ἐστιν αὐτοῖς πόλεμος· ἀλλὰ κατὰ τοὺς ποίμενας ἐκείνους, κ. τ. λ. Perhaps Chrys. is not fully reported here. The meaning seems to be: "The proverb, γλυκὺς ὁ πόλεμος ἀπείροις, may well be applied here; it is a fine thing to be a bishop, to those who have not tried it. Little do people think what this war is, before they have entered into it. But in our times, not only πρὸ τοῦ ἐμβῆναι, but even μετὰ τὸ ἐκβῆναι, after a good bishop has gone through with it, the generality of people do not see that there has been any war in the case. We bishops, in their view, are like Ezekiel's shepherds. And no marvel, for many among us are such." The author of the modern text has given a different turn to the sentiment. Here it is: "The same may well be said in the present case; or rather, we do say it before we have entered into the contest; but after we have embarked in it, we become not even visible to the generality. For to us now there is no war, against those who oppress the poor, nor do we endure to battle in defence of the flock; but like those shepherds, etc."

be said now, that even after one has come out of it, people in general have seen nothing of it : for in their eyes it is not war, but like those shepherds in Ezekiel, we slay and devour. (Ezek. xxxiv. 2.) Which of us has it in his power to show that he has taken as much care for the flocks of Christ, as Jacob did for Laban's? (Gen. xxxi. 40.) Which of us can tell of the frost of the night? For talk not to me of vigils, and all that parade.[1] The contrary plainly is the fact. Prefects, and governors (ὕπαρχοι καὶ τοπάρχαι) of provinces, do not enjoy such honour as he that governs the Church. If he enter the palace, who but he is first? If he go to see ladies, or visit the houses of the great, none is preferred to him. The whole state of things is ruined and corrupt. I do not speak thus as wishing to put us bishops to shame, but to repress your hankering after the office. For with what conscience,[2] (even should you succeed in becoming a bishop, having made interest for it either in person or by another), with what eyes will you look the man in the face who worked with you to that end? What will you have to plead for your excuse? For he that unwillingly, by compulsion and not with his own consent, was raised to the office, may have something to say for himself, though for the most part even such an one has no pardon to expect,[3] and yet truly he so far has something to plead in excuse. Think how it fared with Simon Magus. What signifies it that you give not money, if, in place of money, you pay court, you lay many plans, you set engines to work? "Thy money perish with thee!" (Acts viii. 20.) Thus was it said to him, and thus will it be said to these : your canvassing perish with you, because you have thought to purchase the gift of God by human intrigue! But there is none such here? And God forbid there should be! For it is not that I wish any thing of what I have been saying to be applicable to you: but just now the connexion has led us on to these topics. In like manner when we talk against covetousness, we are not preaching at you, no, nor against any one man personally. God grant it may be the case, that these remedies were prepared by us without necessity. The wish of the physician is, that after all his pains, his drugs may be thrown away because not

wanted : and this is just what we desire, that our words may not have been needed, and so have been spoken to the wind, so as to be but words. I am ready to submit to anything, rather than be reduced to the necessity of using this language. But if you like, we are ready to leave off ; only let our silence be without bad effects. No one, I imagine, though he were ever so vainglorious, would wish to make a display of severity, when there is nothing to call for it. I will leave the teaching to you : for that is the best teaching, which teaches by actions.[4] For indeed the best physicians, although the sickness of their patients brings them in fees, would rather their friends were well. And so we too wish all to be well. (2 Cor. xiii. 7.) It is not that we desire to be approved, and you reproved. I would gladly manifest, if it were possible, with my very eyes, the love which I bear to you : for then no one would be able to reproach me, though my language were ever so rough. "For speech of friends, yea, were it insult, can be borne ; "[5] more "faithful are the wounds of a friend, rather than the ready kisses of an enemy. (Prov. xxvii. 6.) There nothing I love more thàn you, no, not even light itself. I would gladly have my eyes put out ten thousand times over, if it were possible by this means to convert your souls ; so much is your salvation dearer to me than light itself. For what profit to me in the rays of the sun, when despondency on your account makes it all thick darkness before my eyes? Light is good when it shines in cheerfulness, to a sorrowful heart it seems even to be a trouble. How true this is, may you never learn by experience! However, if it happen to any of you to fall into sin, just stand by my bedside, when I am laid down to rest and should be asleep ; see[6] whether I am not like a palsied man, like one beside himself, and, in the language of the prophet, "the light of mine eyes, it also is gone from me. (Ps. xxxviii. 10). For where is our hope, if you do not make progress? where our despondency, if you do excellently? I seem to have wings, when I hear any thing good of you. "Fulfil ye my joy." (Phil. ii. 2.) This one thing is the burden of my prayers, that I long for your advancement. But that in which I strive with all is this, that I love you, that I am wrapped up in you, that you are my all, father, mother, brethren, children. Think not then that any

[1] Vigils were celebrated in C.'s time with much pomp. A grand ceremonial of this kind was held in the first year of his episcopate, at the translation of the relics.
[2] Ποίῳ γὰρ συνειδότι ἂν (l. κἂν) γένῃ σπουδάσας ἤ, κ. τ. λ. The meaning is strangely mistaken by the Lat. transl. Erasm. has, Quem enim conscium adibis si vel, etc. Ben. Quo uteris conscio si ambias vel, etc. The ποίοις ὀφθάλμοις following might have shown the meaning, not to mention the ungrammatical rendering of ἂν γένῃ σπουδάσας.
[3] See de Sacerdot. lib. iv. in the opening, where this question is considered at length.

[4] Παραχωρήσω τῆς διδασκαλίας ὑμῖν : I will cede the teaching to you ; let it be yours to teach by your actions, which is the more potent teaching.
[5] Τὰ γὰρ παρὰ φιλῶν λεγόμενα, Κἂν ὕβρις ᾖ, φορητά. Apparently a quotation.
[6] Edd. ἀπυλοίμην εἰ μή· "May I perish if, etc." but none of our Mss. have this word.

thing that has been said was said in a hostile spirit, nay, it is for your amendment. It is written, "A brother assisted by his brother is as a strong city." (Prov. xviii. 19.) Then do not take it in disdain: for neither do I undervalue what you have to say. I should wish even to be set right by you. For all (Edd. 'all we') ye are brethren, and One is our Master: yet even among brothers it is for one to direct, while the others obey. Then disdain it not, but let us do all to the glory of God, for to Him belongs glory for ever and ever. Amen.

HOMILY IV.

ACTS II. 1, 2.

"And when the day of Pentecost was fully come, they were all with one accord in one place. And suddenly there came a sound from heaven."

DOST thou perceive the type? What is this Pentecost? The time when the sickle was to be put to the harvest, and the ingathering was made. See now the reality, when the time was come to put in the sickle of the word: for here, as the sickle, keen-edged, came the Spirit down. For hear the words of Christ: "Lift up your eyes," He said, "and look on the fields, for they are white already to harvest." (John iv. 35.) And again, "The harvest truly is great, but the laborers are few." (Matt. ix. 38.) But as the first-fruits of this harvest, He himself took [our nature], and bore it up on high. Himself first put in the sickle. Therefore[1] also He calls the Word the Seed. "When," it says, "the day of Pentecost was fully come" (Luke viii. 5, 11): that is, when at the Pentecost, while about it, in short.[2] For it was essential that the present events likewise should take place during the feast, that those who had witnessed the crucifixion of Christ, might also behold these. "And suddenly there came a sound from heaven." (v. 2.) Why did this not come to pass without sensible tokens? For this reason. If even when the fact was such, men said, "They are full of new wine," what would they not have said, had it been otherwise? And it is not merely, "there came a sound," but, "from heaven." And the suddenness also startled them, and[3]

brought all together to the spot. "As of a rushing mighty wind:" this betokens the exceeding vehemence of the Spirit. "And it filled all the house:" insomuch that those present both believed, and (Edd. τούτους) in this manner were shown to be worthy. Nor is this all; but what is more awful still, "And there appeared unto them," it says, "cloven tongues like as of fire." (v. 3.) Observe how it is always, "like as;" and rightly: that you may have no gross sensible notions of the Spirit. Also, "as it were of a blast:" therefore it was not a wind. "Like as of fire." For when the Spirit was to be made known to John, then it came upon the head of Christ as in the form of a dove: but now, when a whole multitude was to be converted, it is "like as of fire. And it sat upon each of them." This means, that it remained and rested upon them." For the sitting is significant of settledness and continuance.

Was it upon the twelve that it came? Not so; but upon the hundred and twenty. For Peter would not have quoted to no purpose the testimony of the prophet, saying, "And it shall come to pass in the last days, saith the Lord God, I will pour out of My spirit upon all flesh: and your sons and your daughters shall prophesy, and your young men shall see visions, and your old men shall dream dreams." (Joel ii. 28.) "And they were all filled with the Holy Ghost." (v. 4.) For, that the effect may not be to frighten only, therefore is it both "with the Holy Ghost, and with fire. And began to speak with other tongues, as the Spirit gave them utterance." (Matt. iii. 11.) They receive no other sign, but this first; for it was new to them, and there was no need of any other sign. "And it sat upon each of them," says the writer. Observe now, how there is no longer any occasion for that person to grieve, who was not elected as was Matthias. "And they were all filled," he says; not merely received the grace of the Spirit, but

---

[1] i. e. in reference to the harvest. The modern text has, "therefore He calls this the harvest:" missing the author's meaning, i. e. the allusion to the parable of the sower.
[2] τουτέστι, πρὸς τῇ πεντηκοστῇ περὶ αὐτὴν ὡς εἰπεῖν. Πρὸς, as in the phrase, εἶναι v. γίνεσθαι πρός τινι. Hom. in Matt. 289. B. Field, not. and similarly περὶ as in εἶναι περί τι. Only Œcumen. has preserved the true reading, in his comment πρὸς τῇ π.; περὶ αὐτὴν ἤδη τὴν ἑορτήν. A. B. C. read, πρὸ τῆς πεντηκοστῆς περὶ αὐτὴν ὡς εἰπεῖν: so Cat. but with περὶ for πρὸ. The others, οὐ πρὸ τῆς π., ἀλλὰ περὶ αὐτὴν, ὡς εἰπεῖν.
[3] In the Mss. and Edd. the order of the following sentences is confused. It is here restored by bringing the clause, καὶ πάντας ἐκεῖ συνήγαγεν into what appears to be its proper connection, and supplying the text to the comment πολλὴν τὴν ῥύμην λέγει τοῦ Πνεύματος.

" were filled. And began to speak with other tongues, as the Spirit gave them utterance." It would not have been said, *All*, the Apostles also being there present, unless the rest also were partakers. For were it not so, having above made mention of the Apostles distinctively and by name, he would not now have put them all in one with the rest. For if, where it was only to be mentioned that they were present, he makes mention of the Apostles apart, much more would he have done so in the case here supposed.[1] Observe, how when one is *continuing in prayer*, when one is in charity, then it is that the Spirit draws near. It put them in mind also of another vision : for as fire did He appear also in the bush. "As the Spirit gave them utterance, ἀποφθέγγεσθαι." (Exod. iii. 2.) For the things spoken by them were ἀποφθέγματα, profound utterances. " And," it says, " there were dwelling at Jerusalem Jews, devout men." (v. 5.) The fact of their dwelling there was a sign of piety : that being of so many nations they should have left country, and home, and relations, and be abiding there. For, it says, "There were dwelling at Jerusalem Jews, devout men, out of every nation under heaven. Now when this was noised abroad, the multitude came together, and were confounded. (v. 6.) Since the event had taken place in a house, of course they came together from without. The multitude *was confounded:* was all in commotion. They marvelled ; " Because that every man heard them speak in his own language. And they were amazed," it says, " and marvelled, saying one to another, Behold, are not all these which speak Galileans ?" (v. 7–13.) They immediately turned their eyes towards the Apostles. " And how " (it follows) " hear we every man in our own tongue, wherein we were born ? Parthians, and Medes, and Elamites, and the dwellers in Mesopotamia, and in Judea, and Cappadocia, in Pontus, and Asia, Phrygia, and Pamphylia, in Egypt, and in the parts of Libya about Cyrene :" mark how they run from east to west :[2] "and strangers of Rome, Jews and proselytes, Cretes and Arabians, we do hear them speak in our tongues the wonderful works of God. And they were all amazed, and were in doubt,

saying one to another, What meaneth this ? Others mocking said, These men are full of new wine." O the excessive folly ! O the excessive malignity ! Why it was not even the season for that; for it was Pentecost. For this was what made it worse : that when those were confessing—men that were Jews, that were Romans, that were proselytes, yea perhaps that had crucified Him—yet these, after so great signs, say, " They are full of new wine ! "

But let us look over what has been said from the beginning. (Recapitulation.) " And when the day of Pentecost," etc. " It filled," he says, " the house." That wind πνοὴ was a very pool of water. This betokened the copiousness, as the fire did the vehemence. This nowhere happened in the case of the Prophets : for to uninebriated souls such accesses are not attended with much disturbance ; but " when they have well drunken," then indeed it is as here, but with the Prophets it is otherwise.[3] (Ez. iii. 3.) The roll of a book[4] is given him, and Ezekiel ate what he was about to utter. " And it became in his mouth," is is said, " as honey for sweetness." (And[5] again the hand of God touches the tongue of another Prophet ; but here it is the Holy Ghost Himself : (Jer. i. 9) so equal is He in honor with the Father and the Son.) And again, on the other hand, Ezekiel calls it " Lamentations, and mourning, and woe." (Ez. ii. 10.) To them it might well be in the form of a book ; for they still needed similitudes. Those had to deal with only one nation, and with their own people ; but these with the whole world, and with men whom they never knew. Also Elisha

---

[1] i. e. if the gift descended only upon the Twelve, there would have been specific and distinctive mention of them in this narrative, as there was in the former chapter ; and with much more reason here than there. The writer would not have said merely, They were *all* together : it sat upon each one *of them* : they were *all* filled : if he had meant that the Spirit came only upon the Apostles.

[2] i. e. Mark how the enumeration, " Parthians, and Medes," etc., goes from east to west. This comment having been transposed to the end of v. 12, was misunderstood : and E. has in stead of it, " Do you see how it was, that, as if they had wings, they sped their way through the whole world ? "

[3] Τὰ γὰρ τοιαῦτα νηφουσῶν μὲν ψυχῶν προσπίπτοντα, οὐ πολὺν ἔχει τὸν θόρυβον· ὅταν δὲ μεθύσωσιν τότε μὲν οὕτως, τοῖς προφήταις δὲ ἑτέρως. In the modern text, which here also is followed by Erasm. and Edd. it is, ἀλλὰ τότε μὲν οὕτως ἐκείνοις,·τοῖς προφήταις δὲ ἑτέρως. "But here indeed it is on this wise with them (the disciples), but with the Prophets otherwise.'—The expression "uninebriated " relates to the Old Testament : no such fire there, no mighty rushing wind, no vehement commotion : this comes of " the new wine" of the Spirit ; ὅταν μεθύσωσιν, with allusion to John ii. 10.

[4] So *de Sancta Pentecoste*, Hom. i. t. ii, 465. "Why does Ezekiel receive the gift of prophecy not by the likeness of fire, but by a book, while the Apostles receive the gifts by fire ? For concerning him we read, that one gave him in his mouth a roll of a book, etc.: but concerning the Apostles not so, but " there appeared unto them tongues as of fire." Why is it a book and writing there, here tongue and fire ? Because there the Prophet went his way to accuse sins, and to bewail Jewish calamities : whereas these went forth to consume the sins of the whole world : therefore he received a writing, to call to mind the coming calamities ; these fire, to burn up the sins of the world, and utterly abolish them. For as fire falling among thorns will with ease destroy them, even so the grace of the Spirit consumed the sins of men."

[5] This, which we have marked as parenthesis, seems to be out of its place : it interrupts what is said about Ezekiel, and besides is not relevant to the matter immediately in hand, Ἐνταῦθα δὲ αὐτὸ τὸ Πν. τὸ Ἀ. κ. τ. λ. would come in more suitably after the mention of the fire in the bush, in which God appeared to Moses. And so Œcumenius seems to have taken it. "But it is in the likeness of fire, because the Spirit also is God, and to prove by this also that the Spirit is of one Nature (ὁμοφυὲς) with the Father, Who appears in this manner to Moses at the bush."

receives the grace through the medium of a mantle (2 Kings xiii.); another by oil, as David (1 Sam. xvi. 13); and Moses by fire, as we read of him at the bush. (Exod. iii. 2.) But in the present case it is not so; for the fire itself sat upon them. (But wherefore did the fire not appear so as to fill the house? Because they would have been terrified.) But the story shows, that it is the same here as there.[1] For you are not to stop at this, that "there appeared unto them cloven tongues," but note that they were "of fire." Such a fire as this is able to kindle infinite fuel. Also, it is well said, *Cloven*, for they were from one root; that you may learn, that it was an operation sent from the Comforter.*

But observe how those men also were first shown to be worthy, and then received the Spirit as worthy. Thus, for instance, David:[2] what he did among the sheepfolds, the same he did after his victory and trophy; that it might be shown how simple and absolute was his faith. Again, see Moses despising royalty, and forsaking all, and after forty years taking the lead of the people (Exod. ii. 11); and Samuel occupied there in the temple (1 Sam. iii. 3); Elisha leaving all (1 Kings xix. 21); Ezekiel again, made manifest by what happened thereafter.[3] In this manner, you see, did these also leave all that they had. They learnt also what human infirmity is, by what they suffered; they learnt that it was not in vain they had done these good works. (1 Sam. ix. and xi. 6.) Even Saul, having first obtained witness that he was good, thereafter received the Spirit. But in the same manner as here

did none of them receive. Thus Moses was the greatest of the Prophets, yet he, when others were to receive the Spirit, himself suffered diminution.[4] But here it is not so; but just as fire kindles as many flames as it will, so here the largeness of the Spirit was shown, in that each one received a fountain of the Spirit; as indeed He Himself had foretold, that those who believe in Him, should have "a well of water springing up into everlasting life." (John iv. 14.) And good reason that it should be so. For they did not go forth to argue with Pharaoh, but to wrestle with the devil. But the wonder is this, that when sent they made no objections; they said not, they were "weak in voice, and of a slow tongue." (Exod. iv. 10.) For Moses had taught them better. They said not, they were too young. (Jer. i. 6.) Jeremiah had made them wise. And yet they had heard of many fearful things, and much greater than were theirs of old time; but they feared to object.—And because they were angels of light, and ministers of things above ["Suddenly there came from heaven," etc.] To them of old, no one "from heaven" appears, while they as yet follow after a vocation on earth; but now that Man has gone up on high, the Spirit also descends mightily from on high. "As it were a rushing mighty wind;" making it manifest by this, that nothing shall be able to withstand them, but they shall blow away all adversaries like a heap of dust. "And it filled all the house." The house also was a symbol of the world. "And it sat upon each of them," [etc.] and "the multitude came together, and were confounded." Observe their piety; they pronounce no hasty judgment, but are perplexed: whereas those reckless ones pronounce at once, saying, "These men are full of new wine." Now it was in order that they might have it in their power,[5] in compliance with the Law, to appear thrice in the year in the Temple, that they dwelt there, these "devout men from all nations." Observe here, the writer has no intention of flattering them. For he does not say that they pronounced any opinion: but what? "Now when this was noised abroad, the multitude came together, and were confounded." And well they might be; for they supposed the matter was now coming to an issue against them, on account of the outrage committed against Christ.

---

[1] Ὅτι τοῦτο ἐκεῖνό ἐστι. i. e. The Spirit here given to the disciples, is the same that was given to those: but more intense in operation; therefore it appears not merely under the emblem of cloven tongues, but as tongues of *fire*.

* Chrys. seems to understand by διαμεριζόμεναι (v. 3), divided, distributed among the members of the company, rather than of a cloven form, a forked appearance, as indicating the shape of the fire-like tongues. The former is the preferable interpretation. (So the Rev. Vers. vs. A. V.). The latter view cannot explain the singular verb which follows, ἐκάθισεν.—G. B. S.

[2] ἵνα δειχθῇ αὐτοῦ γυμνὴ ἡ πίστις. Not, *ut palam fieret fides ejus*, Ben. but, *quo ipsius nuda simplexque fides declararetur*," Erasm. The meaning seems to be: David after the victory over Goliath, when the hearts of the people were turned to him, and he might have taken possession of the kingdom to which he was anointed, yet did not seek worldly greatness, but chose rather to suffer persecutions, etc.: as developed in the Homilies *de Davide et Saule*, t. iv. 752. Below, for ἀνατρεφόμενον (" Samuel *brought up* in the temple,") A. has ἀναστρεφόμενον, which we have adopted.

[3] So C. and Cat. B. transposes Elisha and Ezekiel, A. omits the clause. Chrys. elsewhere makes it a special praise of Ezekiel, that he chose rather to accompany his people into captivity, than to remain in his own land: Interp. in Isai. i. t. 1. 2. and *ad Stagyr*. ii. t. ii. 228. In this manner then (he would say here), Ez. " left all," and having thus given proof of his worth, received the gift of prophecy. The modern text reads: " Ezekiel again. And that the case was thus, is manifest from what followed. For indeed these also forsook all that they had. Therefore they then received the Spirit, when they had given proof of their own virtue."—By *these* (οὗτοι) we must understand the Old Test. saints just mentioned. It should rather have been ἐκεῖνοι, but Chrys. is negligent in the use of these pronouns. See *Hom. in Matt*. Field. Adnot. p. 709, B.

[4] Ἠλαττοῦτο. Alluding to Numb. xi. 17. " I will take of the Spirit that is upon thee, and will put it upon them."

[5] Ἵνα δὲ ἐξῇ. (Cat. ἵνα δείξῃ.) Œcumen. ἵνα ἔχωσι, " that they may have it in their power, according to the law of their fathers, to appear thrice in the year, etc." The modern text has, ἐπεὶ ἐξῆν. . . διὰ τοῦτο. " Because it was permitted. . . therefore."

Conscience also agitated their souls, the very blood being yet upon their hands, and every thing alarmed them. "Behold, are not all these which speak Galileans?" For indeed this was confessed. ["And how hear we"] so much did the sound alarm them. ["Every man in our own tongue," etc.] for it found the greater part of the world assembled there. ["Parthians and Medes," etc.] This nerved the Apostles: for, what it was to speak in the Parthian tongue, they knew not but now learnt from what those said. Here is mention made of nations that were hostile to them, Cretans, Arabians, Egyptians, Persians: and that they would conquer them all was here made manifest. But as to their being in those countries, they were there in captivity, many of them: or else, the doctrines of the Law had become disseminated [among] the Gentiles in those countries.[1] So then the testimony comes from all quarters: from citizens, from foreigners, from proselytes. "We do hear them speak in our tongues the wonderful works of God." For it was not only that they spoke (in their tongues), but the things they spoke were wonderful.* Well then might they be in doubt: for never had the like occurred. Observe the ingenuousness of these men. They were amazed and were in doubt, saying, "What meaneth this?" But "others mocking said, 'These men are full of new wine'" (John viii. 48), and therefore mocked. O the effrontery! And what

wonder is it? Since even of the Lord Himself, when casting out devils, they said that He had a devil! For so it is; wherever impudent assurance exists, it has but one object in view, to speak at all hazards, it cares not what; not that the man should say something real and relevant to the matter of discourse, but that he should speak no matter what. ["They are full of new wine."] Quite a thing of course (is no it?),[2] that men in the midst of such dangers, and dreading the worst, and in such despondency, have the courage to utter such things! And observe: since this was unlikely; because they would not have been drinking much [at that early hour], they ascribe the whole matter to the quality (of the wine), and say, "They are full" of it. "But Peter, standing up with the eleven, lifted up his voice, and said unto them." In a former place[3] you saw his provident forethought, here you see his manly courage. For if they were astonished and amazed, was it not as wonderful that he should be able in the midst of such a multitude to find language, he, an unlettered and ignorant man? If a man is troubled when he speaks among friends, much more might he be troubled among enemies and bloodthirsty men. That they are not drunken, he shows immediately by his very voice, that they are not beside themselves, as the soothsayers: and this too, that they were not constrained by some compulsory force. What is meant by, "with the eleven?" They expressed themselves through one common voice, and he was the mouth of all. The eleven stood by as witnesses to what he said. "He lifted up his voice," it is said. That is, he spoke with great confidence, that they might perceive the grace of the Spirit. He who had not endured the questioning of a poor girl, now in the midst of the people, all breathing murder, discourses with such confidence, that this very thing becomes an unquestionable proof of the Resurrection: in the midst of men who could deride and make a joke of such things as these! What effrontery, think you, must go to that! what impiety, what shameless-

---

[1] Ἐκεῖ δὲ ἐν αἰχμαλωσίᾳ ἦσαν πολλοὶ ἢ καὶ ἐκεῖ διέσπαρτο τὰ ἔθνη τὰ τῶν δογμάτων. A. B. C. N. As τὰ τῶν δ taken as apposition to τὰ ἔθνη yields no satisfactory sense, we adopt from the modern text πρὸς before τὰ ἔθνη, and make, as there, τὰ τῶν δ. the nom. to διέσπαρτο. And as in the next sentence Chrys. distinguishes citizens, foreign (Jews), and *proselytes*, and there is no mention of the last, unless it be in the clause ἢ καὶ ἐκεῖ διέσπαρτο, we infer that τὰ τῶν δ. means the Law of Moses. "Or also in those countries (Parthia, Media, etc. in consequence of the dispersion of the Jews) the Law and its religion had been disseminated among the Gentiles. So that from all quarters, etc." Thus it is explained how there came to be present at Jerusalem "devout men" from Parthia and those other countries: there were many Jews there in captivity, and also proselytes of the Law from among the Gentiles.—In the modern text the passage is thus altered: "But, inasmuch as the Jews were in captivity, it is likely that there were then present with them many of the *Gentiles*: ἢ ὅτι καὶ πρὸς τὰ ἔθνη τὰ τῶν δογμάτων ἤδη κατέσπαρτο, καὶ διὰ τοῦτο πολλοὶ καὶ ἐξ αὐτῶν παρῆσαν ἐκεῖ. Or, because τὰ τῶν δ. had become disseminated among the Gentiles also, and therefore many also of them were there present, κατὰ μνημὴν ὧν ἤκουσαν. Here τὰ τῶν δογμάτων is taken to mean 'the doctrines of the Christian Faith:' as Erasmus renders the passage, *Sive quod ad gentes quoque fidei dogmata seminata fuerint, et hanc ob causam complures ex iis aderant ut memorarent quæ audierant.* It can hardly be supposed that St. Chrysostom meant to represent that some of these Parthians, Medes, etc. were Gentiles who had heard in their own country the tidings of the Faith of Christ, and therefore were present at Jerusalem: yet this is what he is made to say in this text.

* It is impossible to gain from this language any clear view of the author's opinion of the gift of tongues. The uncertainty of the text here still further embarrasses the subject. That the narrative means that they received at Pentecost a miraculous gift of speaking foreign languages, is now almost unanimously maintained by modern scholars. The difficult question as to the gift of tongues as referred to in 1 Cor. xiv. should not lead to a weakening or explaining away of such unmistakable expressions as ἑτέραις γλώσσαις (4), ἡμετέραις γλώσσαις (11) and τῇ ἰδίᾳ διαλέκτῳ (6, 8). Cf. Mark xvi. 17.—G.B.S.

[2] Πάνυ γε (οὐ γάρ;) ἄνθρωποι κ. τ. λ. See above, p. 47, note u. and 66, note c. The modern text has, Πάνυ γε· ὅτι ἄνθρωποι κ. τ. λ. Below, "Since this was improbable, therefore, to impose upon the hearers, and show that the men are drunken, they ascribe, etc." But in the old text it is, ὅτι οὐκ ἂν ἐμεθύσθησαν, meaning, "because [so early in the day] they would not have been drinking *much*," (this is the force of the tense μεθυσθῆναι as in John ii. 10) "therefore they ascribe all to the quality (of the wine);" because as Œcumen. says, explaining this remark of Chrys., the fumes of γλεῦκος mount more quickly to the brain, etc. Erasmus, seemingly referring this to μεμεστωμένοι, translates *hebetudini crapulæque rem totam ascribunt*:" Ben. even more strangely, ' *agendi et loquendi modo totum ascribunt.*

[3] Ἐκεῖ: referring to ch. i. as expounded in *Hom.* iii. So Œcumen. in loc. "Ἄνω μὲν τὴν κηδεμονίαν ἐπιδείκνυται, ἐν οἶς τῷ πλήθει ἐπιτρέπει τὴν ἐκλογὴν κ. τ. λ.

ness!¹ For wherever the Holy Spirit is present, He makes men of gold out of men of clay. Look, I pray you, at Peter now: examine well that timid one, and devoid of understanding; as Christ said, "Are ye also yet without understanding?" (Matt. xv. 16) the man, who after that marvellous confession was called "Satan." (Ib. xvi. 23.) Consider also the unanimity of the Apostles. They themselves ceded to him the office of speaking; for it was not necessary that all should speak. "And he lifted up his voice," and spoke out to them with great boldness. Such a thing it is to be a spiritual man! Only let us also bring ourselves into a state meet for the grace from above, and all becomes easy. For as a man of fire falling into the midst of straw would take no harm, but do it to others; not he could take any harm, but they, in assailing him, destroy themselves. For the case here was just as if one carrying hay should attack one bearing fire: even so did the Apostles encounter these their adversaries with great boldness.

For what did it harm them, though they were so great a multitude? Did they not spend all their rage? did they not turn the distress upon themselves? Of all mankind, were ever any so possessed with both rage and terror, as those became possessed? Were they not in an agony, and were dismayed, and trembled? For hear what they say, "Do ye wish to bring this man's blood upon us?" (Acts v. 28.) Did they² (the Apostles) not fight against poverty and hunger: against ignominy and infamy (for they were accounted deceivers): did they not fight³ against ridicule and wrath and mockery?—for in their case the contraries met: some laughed at them, others punished them;—were they not made a mark for the wrathful passions, and for the merriment,⁴ of whole cities? exposed to fac-

tions and conspiracies: to fire, and sword, and wild beasts? Did not war beset them from every quarter, in ten thousand forms? And were they any more affected in their minds by all these things, than they would have been at seeing them in a dream or in a picture?⁵ With bare body they took the field against all the armed, though against them all men had arbitrary power [against them, were]: terrors of rulers, force of arms, in cities and strong walls:⁶ without experience, without skill of the tongue, and in the condition of quite ordinary men, matched against juggling conjurors, against impostors, against the whole throng of sophists, of rhetoricians, of philosophers grown mouldy in the Academy and the walks of the Peripatetics, against all these they fought the battle out. And the man whose occupation had been about lakes, so mastered them, as if it cost him not so much ado as even a contest with dumb fishes: for just as if the opponents he had to outwit were indeed more mute than fishes, so easily did he get the better of them! And Plato, that talked a deal of nonsense in his day, is silent now, while this man utters his voice everywhere; not among his own countrymen alone, but also among Parthians, and Medes, and Elamites, and in India, and in every part of the earth, and to the extremities of the world. Where now is Greece, with her big pretensions? Where the name of Athens? Where the ravings of the philosophers? He of Galilee, he of Bethsaida, he, the uncouth rustic, has overcome them all. Are you not ashamed—confess it—at the very name of the country of him who has defeated you? But if you hear his own name too, and learn that he was called Cephas, much more will you hide your faces. This, this has undone you quite: because you esteem this a reproach, and account glibness of tongue a praise, and want of glibness a disgrace. You have not followed the road you ought to have chosen, but leaving the royal road, so easy, so smooth, you have trodden one rough, and steep, and laborious. And therefore you have not attained unto the kingdom of heaven.

Why then, it is asked, did not Christ exercise His influence upon Plato, and upon Pythagoras? Because the mind of Peter was

---

¹ Here the modern text (Edd.) enlarges by the additions "to account the wonder of the tongues the work of drunkenness? But not a whit did this annoy the Apostles; nor did it make them less bold at hearing such scoffing. By the presence of the Spirit they were now transformed, and were become superior to all bodily considerations."

² The change of subject (from the Jews to the Apostles) is not expressed in the original. To remedy the confusion occasioned by this negligence, the modern text (Edd.) transposes this part: viz. after the sentence ending, "so great a multitude:" it has, "For tell me: did they not fight——in a picture?' 'And then, "What? I pray you; did they not exhaust, etc." Clearly the other is the original order. It is shown, first, how the *Jews* were utterly worsted, and how awfully the whole posture of affairs was reversed for them; and then, how victoriously the preachers of the new Faith maintained their ground against the whole world.

³ Edd. "Were they not subjected to the ridicule and mockery of those present? For in their case both these befel together: for some derided them, others mocked." Which is weak enough; but the original text could not be retained, because on the supposition that all this relates to the Jews *then present*, the mention of "wrath" and "punishment" would be irrelevant.

⁴ Εὐθυμίαις, i. e. "bursts of self-complacent mirth" (e. g. at Athens), opposed to θυμοῖς, "explosions of wrath." Ben.

without specifying the authority, notes a various reading, ἀθυμίαις, which is found in none of the Paris copies, and is quite unmeaning. Edd. μανίαις.

⁵ Ben. interprets: "So unlooked for were these trials, that the Apostles seemed to themselves to be dreaming or beholding these things in a picture." But when the true order of the text is restored, no such far-fetched comment is needed.

⁶ The text is defective here, ἀρχόντων φόβοι, ὅπλων ἰσχύς· πόλεσι καὶ τείχεσιν ὀχυροῖς. The text of the Edd. has: "And the wonder is, that with bare body they took the field against armed men, against rulers having power over them: without experience," etc.

much more philosophical[1] than their minds.
They were in truth children shifted about on
all sides by vain glory; but this man was a
philosopher, one apt to receive grace. If you
laugh at these words, it is no wonder; for
those aforetime laughed, and said, the men
were full of new wine. But afterwards, when
they suffered those bitter calamities, exceeding all others in misery; when they saw their
city falling in ruins, and the fire blazing, and
the walls hurled to the ground, and those manifold frantic horrors, which no one can find
words to express, they did not laugh then.
And you will laugh then, if you have the mind
to laugh, when the time of hell is close at
hand, when the fire is kindled for your souls.
But why do I speak of the future? Shall I
show you. what Peter is, and what Plato, the
philosopher? Let us for the present examine
their respectve habits, let us see what were
the pursuits of each. The one wasted his
time about a set of idle and useless dogmas,
and philosophical, as he says,[2] that we may
learn that the soul of our philosopher becomes a fly.* Most truly said, a fly! not
indeed changed into one, but a fly must have
entered upon possession of the soul which
dwelt in Plato; for what but a fly is worthy of
such ideas! The man was full of irony, and
of jealous feelings against every one else, as
if he made it his ambition to introduce nothing useful, either out of his own head or other
people's. Thus he adopted the metempsy-
chosis from another, and from himself produced the Republic, in which he enacted
those laws full of gross turpitude. Let the
women, he says, be in common, and let the
virgins go naked, and let them wrestle before
the eyes of their lovers, and let there also be
common fathers, and let the children begotten

be common. But with us, not nature makes
common fathers, but the philosophy of Peter
does this; as for that other, it made away
with all paternity.[3] For Plato's system only
tended to make the real father next to unknown, while the false one was introduced.
It plunged the soul into a kind of intoxication
and filthy wallowing. Let all, he says, have
intercourse with the women without fear. The
reason why I do not examine the maxims of
poets, is, that I may not be charged with rip-
ping up fables. And yet I am speaking of
fables much more ridiculous than even those.
Where have the poets devised aught so por-
tentous as this? But (not to enter into the
discussion of his other maxims), what say you
to these—when he equips the females with
arms, and helmets, and greaves, and says that
the human race has no occasion to differ from
the canine! Since dogs, he says, the female
and the male, do just the same things in common, so let the women do the same works as
the men, and let all be turned upside down.
For the devil has always endeavored by their
means[4] to show that our race is not more
honorable than that of brutes; and, in fact,
some have gone to such a pitch of (κενοδοξίας)
absurdity, as to affirm that the irrational
creatures are endued with reason. And see
in how many various ways he has run riot in
the minds of those men! For whereas their
leading men affirmed that our soul passes
into flies, and dogs, and brute creatures;
those who came after them, being ashamed of
this, fell into another kind of turpitude, and
invested the brute creatures with all rational
science, and made out that the creatures—
which were called into existence on our account—are in all respects more honorable
than we! They even attribute to them foreknowledge and piety. The crow, they say,
knows God, and the raven likewise, and they
possess gifts of prophecy, and foretell the
future; there is justice among them, and
polity, and laws. Perhaps you do not credit
the things I am telling you. And well may
you not, nurtured as you have been with
sound doctrine; since also, if a man were fed
with this fare, he would never believe that
there exists a human being who finds pleasure
in eating dung. The dog[5] also among them

---

[1] St. Chrysostom's habitual use of the term philosophy is
thus explained in the index of Mr. Field's edition of the Com.
on St. Matt. "Philosophy, according to the custom of Chrys.
is not Christian piety, not the exercise of any virtue, not a
pious and chaste life, not virtue in general, but that part of
virtue, which consists in subduing the carnal appetites and
affections. Thus to Christian philosophy are to be referred:
forbearance and long suffering; humblemindedness; contempt
of wealth; an austere and monastic life; every other mortifi-
cation (ἀπάθεια). Its contraries are: emulation (ζηλοτυπία, see
below), envy and vainglory, and all other passions."
[2] καὶ φιλόσοφα, φησίν, ἵνα: "And 'philosophical,' forsooth:"
but perhaps it should be καὶ ἐφιλοσόφησεν ἵνα: "this was the
upshot of his philosophizing. Ἡ τοῦ φιλοσόφου ψυχή: "the
soul of the philosopher himself (Α τοῦ διδασκάλου), viz. equally
with the souls of other men, becomes, for instance, a fly," etc.
Comp. infra: "our soul passes into flies and dogs," etc.
and Hom. in Ev. Joann. t. viii. 8. D. "they say that the souls
of men become flies, gnats, shrubs."—Edd. "For what is the
benefit from learning that the soul of the philosopher," etc.
The next sentence (ὄντως μυῖα—οὐκ εἰς μυῖαν μετέπιπτεν (sc. ἡ
ψυχή), ἀλλ' ἐπέβαινε (sc. μυῖα τῇ ἐν Πλατ. οἰκούσῃ) ψυχῇ seems
to mean, 'He talks of the soul becoming a fly: and truly the
soul in Plato might be claimed by a fly:' ἐπέβ. τῇ ψ. as e. g. is
ἐπιβαίνειν τῇ ἐπαρχίᾳ to step into possession of, etc. Ποίας γὰρ
ταῦτα οὐ μυῖας; Edd. ματαιολογίας; adding, Πόθεν δὴ τοιαῦτα
ληρεῖν ἐπεβάλετο; "What could put it into his head to rave in
this fashion?"
* The author's depreciation of Plato contrasts unfavorably
with the more generous estimates of a long line of Church
Fathers from Justin to Augustin.—G. B. S.

[3] Ἐπεὶ ἐκεῖνό γε καὶ ἀνῆρει. Erasmus translates, Quandoquidem et illud quod Plato docuit, sustulit: whence Ben.
Nam illud Platonis hic (Petrus) sustulit: i. e. for Peter's
doctrine (of chastity) has made an end of that lewd dogma of
Plato's. But the following sentence rather implies that the
meaning is as above given.
[4] Δι' αὐτῶν, Ben. per illas, which they seem to refer to
γυναῖκες. Erasm. per illos, which is doubtless right: by
means of the philosophers, as below, ἐν ταῖς ἐκείνων ψυχαῖς.
[5] Καὶ ζηλοῖ παρ αὐτοῖς ὁ κύων κατὰ Πλάτωνα. Edd. have this
after "polity and laws," where it is clearly out of place, whatever it means.

is jealous, according to Plato. But when we tell them that these things are fables, and are full of absurdity, ' You do not enter (ἐνοήσατε) into the higher meaning,' say they. No, we do not enter into this your surpassing nonsense, and may we never do so : for it requires (of course![1]) an excessively profound mind, to inform me, what all this impiety and confusion would be at. Are you talking, senseless men, in the language of crows, as the children are wont (in play)? For you are in very deed children, even as they. But Peter never thought of saying any of these things : he uttered a voice, like a great light shining out in the dark, a voice which scattered the mist and darkness of the whole world. Again, his deportment, how gentle it was, how considerate (ἐπιεικὲς); how far above all vainglory; how he looked towards heaven without all self-elation, and this, even when raising up the dead! But if it had come to be in the power of any one of those senseless people (in mere fantasy of course) to do anything like it, would he not straightway have looked for an altar and a temple to be reared to him, and have wanted to be equal with the gods? since in fact when no such sign is forthcoming, they are forever indulging such fantastic conceits. And what, pray you, is that Minerva of theirs, and Apollo, and Juno? They are different kinds of demons among them. And there is a king of theirs, who thinks fit to die for the mere purpose of being accounted equal with the gods. But not so the men here : no, just the contrary. Hear how they speak on the occasion of the lame man's cure. "Ye men of Israel, why look ye so earnestly on us, as though by our own power or holiness we had made him to walk? (ch. iii. 12.) We also are men of like passions with you. (Ibid. xiv. 14.) But with those, great is the self-elation, great the bragging; all for the sake of men's honors, nothing for the pure love of truth and virtue. (φιλοσοφίας ἕνεκεν.) For where an action is done for glory, all is worthless. For though a man possess all, yet if he have not the mastery over this (lust), he forfeits all claim to true philosophy, he is in bondage to the more tyrannical and shameful passion. Contempt of glory; this it is that is sufficient to teach all that is good, and to banish from the soul every pernicious passion. I exhort you therefore to use the most strenuous endeavors to pluck out this passion by the very roots; by no other means can you have good esteem with God, and draw down upon you the benevolent regard of that Eye which never sleepeth. Wherefore, let us use all earnestness to obtain the enjoyment of that heavenly influence, and thus both escape the trial of present evils, and attain unto the future blessings, through the grace and lovingkindness of our Lord Jesus Christ, with Whom to the Father and the Holy Ghost be glory, power, honor, now and ever, and to all ages. Amen.

HOMILY V.

ACTS II. 14.

"Ye men of Judea, and all ye that dwell at Jerusalem, be this known unto you, and hearken to my words."

["YE men of Judea, and all ye that dwell at Jerusalem,"] whom the writer above described as strangers. Here he directs his discourse to those others, the mockers,[2] and while he seems to reason with those, he sets these right. For indeed it was divinely ordered that "some mocked," that he might have a starting-point for his defence, and by means of that defence, might teach. [" And all ye that dwell in Jerusalem."] It seems they accounted it a high encomium to dwell in Jerusalem too.[3] "Be this," says he, "known unto you, and hearken to my words." In the first instance he made them more disposed

---

[1] Edd. Σφόδρα γε· οὐ γὰρ φρενὸς βαθείας. Read Σφόδρα γε (οὐ γάρ); φρ. β. as above, p. 22, note [1], and 28, note [1].

[2] The ἐκεῖνοι, if the old text be correct, are the mockers, but these are not "the devout men out of every nation under heaven," therefore οὓς ξένους εἶπεν ἀνωτέρω can hardly be meant to refer to the following clause, ἐνταῦθα πρὸς ἐκείνους κ. τ. λ. The omission of the text-words, and the seeming antithesis of ἀνωτέρω and ἐνταῦθα, caused a confusion which the modern text attempts to remedy by transposing τοὺς διαχλ. to the place of τούτους. "Whom the writer above called strangers, to those Peter here directs his speech, and he seems indeed to discourse with those, but corrects the mockers." This just inverts Chrysostom's meaning, which is clear enough from the following context. He says: "The ' dwellers in Jerusalem ' are especially the devout men out of every nation mentioned above, and to instruct these (τούτους) is the real aim of the discourse, which however is addressed in the first instance to the others (ἐκείνους), whose mockery gave occasion to it. St. Peter stands up apparently for the purpose of defending himself and his brethren: but this is in fact quite a secondary object, and the apology becomes a sermon of doctrine."

[3] Καὶ τὸ ἐν Ἰ. οἰκεῖν. Below he explains ἄνδρες Ἰουδαῖοι to mean, " dwellers in Judea: " therefore the καί seems to mean, " to be not only such, but dwellers in Jerusalem also."

to attend to him. "For not as ye[1] suppose," says he, "are these drunken." Do you observe the mildness of his defence? (v. 15.) Although having the greater part of the people on his side, he reasons with those others gently; first he removes the evil surmise, and then he establishes his apology. On this account, therefore, he does not say, "as ye mock," or, "as ye deride," but, "as ye suppose;" wishing to make it appear that they had not said this in earnest, and for the present taxing them with ignorance rather than with malice. "For these are not drunken, as ye suppose, seeing it is but the third hour of the day." And why this? Is it not possible at the third hour to be drunken? But he did not insist upon this to the letter; for there was nothing of the kind about them; the others said it only in mockery.* Hence we learn that on unessential points one must not spend many words. And besides, the sequel is enough to bear him out on this point: so now the discourse is for all in common. "But this is that which was spoken by the prophet Joel, And it shall come to pass in the last days, saith the Lord God. (v. 16. 17. Joel ii. 28.) Nowhere as yet the name of Christ, nor His promise; but the promise is that of the Father. Observe the wisdom: observe the considerate forbearance: (συγκατάβασιν.) He did not pass on to speak at once of the things relating to Christ; that He had promised this after His Crucifixion; truly that would have been to upset all. And yet, you will say, here was sufficient to prove His divinity. True, it was, if believed (and the very point was that it should be believed); but if not believed, it would have caused them to be stoned. "And I will pour out of My Spirit upon all flesh." He offers even to them excellent hopes, if they would have them. And so far, he does not leave it to be regarded as the exclusive advantage of himself and his company; which would have made them be looked upon with an evil eye; thus cutting off all envious feeling. "And your sons shall prophesy." And yet, he says, not yours this achievement, this distinction; the gift has passed over to your children. Himself and his company he calls

their sons, and those [whom he is addressing] he calls his and their fathers. "And your young men shall see visions, and your old men shall dream dreams; and on My servants and on My handmaidens I will pour out in those days of My Spirit; and they shall prophesy." So far he shows that he and his have found favor, in that they had received (καταξιωθέντας) [the Spirit]; not so they whom he is addressing; for that they had crucified [the Lord]. So Christ also, willing to mitigate their wrath, said, "By whom do your sons cast out devils?" (Matt. xii. 27.) He did not say, My disciples; for indeed it seemed a flattering mode of expression. And so Peter also did not say, 'They are not drunk, but speak[2] by the Spirit:' but he takes refuge with the prophet, and under shelter of him, so speaks. As for the accusation [of drunkenness], he cleared himself of that by his own assertion; but for the grace, he fetches the prophet as witness. "I will pour out of My Spirit upon all flesh." ["And your sons," etc.] To some the grace was imparted through dreams, to others it was openly poured forth. For indeed by dreams the prophets saw, and received revelations.

Then he goes on with the prophecy, which has in it also something terrible. "And I will show wonders in heaven above, and signs" ["in the earth beneath"]. (v. 19.) In these words he speaks both of the judgment to come, and of the taking of Jerusalem. "Blood and fire, and vapor of smoke." Observe how he describes the capture. "The sun shall be turned into darkness, and the moon into blood." (v. 20.) This results from the (διαθέσεως) internal affection of the sufferers. It is said, indeed, that many such phenomena actually did occur in the sky, as Josephus attests. At the same time the Apostle strikes fear into them, by reminding them of the darkness which had lately occurred, and leading them to expect things to come. "Before that great and notable day of the Lord come." For be not confident, he means to say, because at present you sin with impunity. For these things are the prelude of a certain great and dreadful day. Do you see how he made their souls to quake and melt within them, and turned their laughter into pleading for acquittal?[3] For if these things are the prelude of that day, it follows that the extreme of danger is impending. But what next? He again lets them take

---

[1] Here our leading Ms. after οὐ γὰρ ὡς ὑμεῖς, has ἀποπληροῦται, φησί, καὶ ὑπολαμβάνεται ὅτι μεθύουσιν. "For not as ye."—It is fulfilled (he says) and it is supposed that they are drunken!" which may have been said by Chrys., but certainly not in this place.

* There is no reason to doubt that the company who witnessed the scenes at Pentecost really supposed the Christians to be intoxicated. To this opinion they were, of course, the more readily inclined because of their prejudice against the new sect. The force of Peter's refutation of the charge of drunkenness: "Seeing it is but the third hour, etc.," lies partly in the fact that 9 A. M. was too early for any such general intoxication, and still more in the fact that the third hour was the first hour of prayer, at which time it would have been sacrilege to drink to excess.—G. B. S.

[2] Here the innovator, again mistaking his author's meaning, as if it were—Peter did not say, "These are not drunk," but what he did say was, "They speak by the Spirit"—finds it necessary to add, Καὶ οὐχ ἁπλῶς, And not merely so, but, etc.

[3] ἀπολογίαν, as in 2 Cor. vii. 11. "Yea, what clearing of yourselves."

breath, adding, "And it shall come to pass, that whosoever shall call upon the name of the Lord, shall be saved." (Rom. x. 13.) This is said concerning Christ, as Paul affirms, but Peter does not venture as yet to reveal this.

Well, let us look over again what has been said. It is well managed, that as against men laughing and mocking, he starts up and begins with, " Be this known unto you all and hearken unto my words." But he begins by saying, " Ye men of Judea." By the expression Ἰουδαῖοι, I take him to mean those that lived in Judea.—And, if you please, let us compare those expressions in the Gospel, that you may learn what a sudden change has taken place in Peter. "A damsel," it is written, "came out unto him, saying, Thou also wast with Jesus of Nazareth." And, says he, " I know not the Man." And being again questioned, " he began to curse and to swear." (Matt. xxvi. 69–72.) But see here his boldness, and his great freedom of speech.—He did not praise those who had said, "We do hear them speak in our tongues the wonderful works of God ; " but by his severity towards those others, he made these more earnest, and at the same time his address is clear from all appearance of adulation. And it is well to remark, on all occasions, however the Apostles may condescend to the level of their hearers (συγκατάβασις), their language is clear from all appearance both of adulation and of insolence : which is a difficult point to manage.

Now that these things should have occurred at " the third hour," was not without cause. For [1] the brightness of this fire is shown at the very time when people are not engaged in their works, nor at dinner ; when it is bright day, when all are in the market-place. Do you observe also the freedom which fills his speech ? "And hearken to my words." •And he added nothing, but, " This," says he, " is that which was spoken by the prophet Joel ; And it shall come to pass in the last days." He shows, in fact, that the consummation is nigh at hand, and the words, " In the last days," have a kind of emphasis. [" I will pour out," etc.] And then, that he may not

seem to limit the privilege to the sons only, he subjoins, " And your old men shall dream dreams." Mark the sequence. First sons ; just as David said, "Instead of thy fathers, were begotten thy sons." (Ps. xlv. 17.) And again Malachi ; "They shall turn the hearts of the fathers to the children. And on my handmaidens, and on my servants." (Mal. iv. 6.) This also is a token of excellence, for we have become His servants, by being freed from sin. And great is the gift, since the grace passes over to the other sex also, not as of old, it was limited to just one or two individuals, as Deborah and Huldah. [2] He did not say that it was the Holy Ghost, neither did he expound the words of the prophet ; but he merely brings in the prophecy to fight its own battle. As yet also he has said nothing about Judas ; and yet it was known to all what a doom and punishment he had undergone ; for nothing was more forcible than to argue with them from prophecy : this was more forcible even than facts. For when Christ performed miracles, they often contradicted Him. But when Christ brought forward the prophet, saying, "The Lord said unto my Lord, Sit Thou on my right hand," they were silent, and " no man," we read, "was able to answer Him a word." (Ps. xc. 1.) And on all occasions He Himself also appealed to the Scriptures ; for instance, " If he called them gods to whom the word of God came." (John x. 35.) And in many places one may find this. On this account here also Peter says, " I will pour out of my spirit upon all flesh ; " that is, upon the Gentiles also. But he does not yet reveal this, nor give interpretations ; indeed, [3] it was better not to do so : (as also this obscure saying, " I will show wonders in heaven above," put them the more in fear because it was obscure.) And it would have been more an offence, had it been interpreted from the very first. Then besides, even as plain, he passes over it, wishing to make them regard it as such. But after all, he does interpret to them anon, when he discourses to them upon the resurrection, and after he has paved the way by his discourse. (infra v. 39.) For [4] since the good things were not sufficient to allure them, [it is added, " And I will show wonders,

---

[1] i. e. The brightness of the miraculous fire appears at a time when there would be many to see it, people not being engaged in their works, nor within their houses at their noontide meal. Œcumenius evidently had the old text before him, for he gives the same sense with the slightest verbal alterations. In the Catena the sense is altered by omission of the negatives. " When people are about their work, when about their dinner, etc. The innovator (followed by Edd.) makes it " For when the brightness of the light is shown, then men are not occupied in the business of dinner (οὐ περὶ ἔργα . . . τὰ περὶ ἄριστον), then the day is cheerful (φαιδρὰ, the brisk and stirring time of day), then all are in the market." By τὸ λαμπρὸν τοῦ φῶτος he seems to mean bright daylight.

[2] Here, after εἰς δευτέραν, C. has Ὀλδὰν (marg. γρ. καὶ Λοβνὰν. οἷον Δεβ. καὶ Λοβνάν. B. after Δεβ. καὶ Ὀλδὰν adds ἢ Λοβνάν) It does not appear who is meant by this Lobna, unless it originates in some strange misconception of 2 Kings xxiii. 31, "daughter of Jeremiah of Libnah," LXX. Θ. Ἰ. ἐκ Λοβνά. Clem. Alex. Str. i. §. 136. has no such name in his list of Old Testament prophetesses.

[3] Edd. "For it was not expedient, because this also was obscure. I will show, etc. For it frightened them more, being obscure. But if he had interpreted, it would even have offended them more."

[4] What follows in the edited text is obscure and perplexed. The original text seems to labor under some defects, besides the omission of the passages commented upon.

etc."]. Yet [1] this has never been fulfilled. For none escaped then [in that former judgment], but now the faithful did escape, in Vespasian's time. And this it is that the Lord speaks of, " Except those days had been shortened, not all flesh should be saved."— [" Blood, and fire, and vapor of smoke."] (Matt. xxiv. 22.) The worst to come first; [2] namely, the inhabitants to be taken, and then the city to be razed and burnt. Then he dwelt upon the metaphor, bringing before the eyes of the hearers the overthrow and the taking. " The sun shall be turned into darkness, and the moon into blood." What means, the moon turned into blood? It denotes the excess of the slaughter. The language is fraught with helpless dismay. (*supra* p. 32.) " And it shall come to pass, every one who shall call upon the name of the Lord shall be saved. Every one," he says : though he be priest (but he does not yet reveal the meaning), though bond, though free. For [3] there is no male nor female in Christ Jesus, no bond, no free. (Gal. iii. 28.) Well may it be so, for all these are but shadow. For if in king's palaces there is no high-born nor low-born, but each appears according to his deeds ; and in art, each is shown by his works ; much more in that school of wisdom ($\phi\iota\lambda o\sigma o\phi\iota\alpha$). " Every one who shall invoke." Invoke : not any how, for it is written, " Not every one that saith unto Me, Lord, Lord : " but with ($\delta\iota\alpha\theta\epsilon$-$\sigma\epsilon\omega\varsigma$) inward earnest affection, with a life more than commonly good, with the confidence which is meet. Thus far, however, he makes the discourse light, by introducing that which relates to faith, and that terrible which relates to the punishment. [4] For in the invocation is the salvation.

What, I pray you, is this you say? Do you talk of salvation for them after the Cross? Bear with me a little. Great is the mercy of God. And this very fact does, no less than the resurrection, prove him to be God, yea, no less than His miracles—the fact that He calls these to Him. For surpassing goodness is, above all things, peculiarly God's own. There-

fore also He says, " None is good save one, that is, God." (Luke xviii. 19.) Only let us not take this goodness for an occasion of negligence. For He also punishes as God. In fact, the very punishments here spoken of, He brought them to pass, even He who said, " Every one who shall call on the name of the Lord, shall be saved." I speak of the fate of Jerusalem ;* that intolerable punishment : of which I will tell you some few of the particulars, useful to us in our contest, both with the Marcionites and many other heretics. For, since they distinguish between Christ a good God, and that evil God [of the Old Testament], let us see who it was that effected these things. The evil God, taking vengeance for Christ? or not so? How then alien to Him? But was it the good God? Nay, but it is demonstrated that both the Father and the Son did these things. The Father in many places ; for instance, when He says in the parable of the vineyard,[5] [" He will miserably destroy those wicked husbandmen " (Matt. xxi. 41); again in the parable of the marriage feast, the King is said] to send His armies (ib. xxii. 7) : and the Son, when He says, " But those Mine enemies, which would not that I should reign over them, bring hither, and slay them before Me." (Luke xix. 27.) * * * .[6] And they sent, saying, We will not have Thee to reign over us. Would you like then to hear the things which actually came to pass? Moreover, Christ Himself also speaks of the future tribulations, than which never any thing more dreadful came to pass ; never any thing more ruthless, my beloved, than the deeds then done! [7] And He Himself declared it. For what could you wish to see more grievous than these? * * *—probed them with their dag-

* It is extremely doubtful if Peter understood by " the great and terrible day of the Lord " (20) the destruction of Jerusalem. (Chrys.) It probably refers to the *Parousia* which is thought of as imminent. The " last days " then would be the days preceding the Messianic age which is to begin at the *Parousia*. This view harmonizes with the Jewish conception and with the Christian expectation that the then existing period ($\alpha i\omega\nu$ $o\hat{\upsilon}\tau o\varsigma$) was soon to pass into a new age ($\alpha i\dot{\omega}\nu$ $\mu\epsilon\lambda\lambda\omega\nu$). The scenes of Pentecost were thought to be the harbingers of this consummation and were so significant both of the joys and woes of the impending crisis, that the bold imagery of the prophet Joel is applied to them. Cf. the prophetic terms in which the destruction of Jerusalem is foretold—an event closely associated with the personal return of our Lord in Matt. xxiv.—G. B. S.
[5] $\dot{\omega}\varsigma$ $\delta\tau\alpha\nu$ $\lambda\epsilon\gamma\eta$ $\epsilon\nu$ $\tau\hat{\omega}$ $\dot{\alpha}\mu\pi\epsilon\lambda\hat{\omega}\nu\iota$ $\pi\epsilon\mu\pi\epsilon\iota\nu$ $\tau\dot{\alpha}$ $\sigma\tau\rho\alpha\tau\epsilon\upsilon\mu\alpha\tau\alpha$ $\alpha\dot{\upsilon}\tauo\hat{\upsilon}$. Chrys. is misreported here, for the sending forth of the armies belongs to the parable of the marriage of the king's son.
[6] Something must have been omitted here: viz. a brief exposition of the parable here referred to. The innovator endeavors to mend the text, by leaving out the following sentence.
[7] $\dot{\Omega}\nu$ $o\dot{\upsilon}\delta\dot{\epsilon}\nu$ $\dot{\omega}\mu\dot{o}\tau\epsilon\rho o\nu$ $\gamma\dot{\epsilon}\gamma o\nu\epsilon\nu$, $\dot{\alpha}\gamma\alpha\pi\eta\tauo\dot{\iota}$, $\tau\hat{\omega}\nu$ $\tau\dot{o}\tau\epsilon$ $\pi\epsilon\pi\rho\alpha\gamma\mu\dot{\epsilon}\nu\omega\nu$ $\pi\rho\alpha\gamma\mu\dot{\alpha}\tau\omega\nu$. This may be explained as a negligent construction, but perhaps some words are omitted. The next sentence, Kα\dot{\iota} $\alpha\dot{\upsilon}\tau\dot{o}\varsigma$ $\dot{\alpha}\pi\epsilon\phi\dot{\eta}\nu\alpha\tauo$ (which phrase is repeated below), refers to Matt. xxiv. 21. " There shall be great tribulation, such as has not been from the beginning of the world to this time."

[1] Something seems wanting here: e. g. as above, " There were signs in heaven, as Josephus relates. This however, in the full sense, has never been fulfilled." And then, a reference to the Babylonian compared with the Roman judgment.
[2] First blood, i. e. the taking and slaughter of the inhabitants: then, fire, etc., i. e. the burning of the city.
[3] As B. has this sentence, which is in fact necessary to the sense, the omission of it in C. A. may be referred to the homœoteleuton, $\dot{\epsilon}\lambda\epsilon\dot{\upsilon}\theta\epsilon\rho o\varsigma$.
[4] $\kappa\alpha\dot{\iota}$ (=$\kappa\alpha\dot{\iota}\pi\epsilon\rho$, or $\epsilon\dot{\iota}$ $\kappa\alpha\dot{\iota}$?) $\phi o\beta\epsilon\rho\dot{o}\nu$ $\tau\dot{o}$ $\tau\hat{\eta}\varsigma$ $\kappa o\lambda\dot{\alpha}\sigma\epsilon\omega\varsigma$. i. e. he alleviates the severity of his discourse by speaking of the effects of faith, at the same time that he shows the fearfulness of the punishment. Edd. $\kappa\alpha\dot{\iota}$ $o\dot{\upsilon}$ $\phi o\beta$. $\kappa\rho\dot{\upsilon}\pi\tau\omega\nu$ $\tau\dot{o}$ $\tau\hat{\eta}\varsigma$ $\kappa o\lambda\dot{\alpha}\sigma\epsilon\omega\varsigma$, i. e. light . . . and not fearful, by withdrawing out of sight what relates to the punishment : which however Ben. renders as if it were $o\dot{\upsilon}$ $\tau\dot{o}$ $\phi o\beta$. And not concealing the fearfulness, etc."

gers!¹—* * * But shall I relate to you the shocking case of the woman, that tragic tale? * * * (Joseph. B. J. vi. 3. 4. Did not the actual events cast all misery into the shade? But shall I tell you of famines and pestilences? One might speak of horrors without number : nature was unknown; law unknown; they outdid wild beasts in ferocity. True, these miseries came by the fate of wars; but because God, because Christ so willed it to be. These facts will apply both against the Marcionites and against those who do not believe that there is a hell: for they are sufficient to silence their impudence. Are not these calamities more severe than the Babylonian?² Are not these sufferings more grievous than the famines of that time? Yes, for ["never was the like from the beginning of the world"] "no, nor ever shall be such." (Matt. xxiv. 21.) And this was Christ's own declaration. In what sense then, think ye, is it said that Christ remitted them their sin?³ Perhaps it seems a commonplace question: but do ye solve it.—It is not possible to show anywhere, even in fiction, any thing like what the reality was here. And had it been a Christian that wrote this history, the matter might be regarded with suspicion: but if he was a Jew, and a Jewish zealot, and after the Gospel, how can the meaning of the facts be otherwise than palpable to all men? For you will see the man, how, everywhere, he always extols the concerns of the Jews.—There is

therefore a hell, O man ! and God is good.— Aye, did you shudder at hearing these horrors? But these, which take place here, are nothing in comparison with what shall be in that world. Once more I am compelled to seem harsh, disagreeable, stern. But what can I do? I am set to this : just as a severe schoolmaster is set to be hated by his scholars: so are we. For would it not be strange indeed, that, while those who have a certain post assigned them by kings do that which is appointed them, however disagreeable the task may be, we, for fear of your censure, should leave our appointed task undone? Another has a different work. Of you, many have it for their work, to show mercy, to act humanely, to be pleasant and agreeable to the persons to whom you are benefactors. But to those to whom we do good, we seem stern and severe, troublesome and disagreeable. For we do good, not by the pleasure we give, but by the pain we inflict. So it is also with the physician : though he indeed is not excessively disagreeable, for the benefit afforded by his art is had immediately; ours hereafter. So again the magistrate is odious to the disorderly and seditious; so the legislator is vexatious to them for whom he makes laws. But not so he that invites to enjoyment, not so he that prepares public festivities and entertainments, and puts all the people in garlands : no, these are men that win acceptance, feasting, as they do, whole cities with all sorts of spectacles; contributing largely, bearing all the cost. And therefore those whom they have treated, requite them for these enjoyments with words of welcome and benediction, with hanging (παραπετάσματα) of tapestries, and a blaze of lamps, and with wreaths, and boughs, and brilliant garments. Whereas, at the sight of the physician, the sick become sad and downcast : at sight of the magistrate, the rioters become subdued : no running riot then, no gambolling, except when he also goes over into their ranks.⁴ Let us see, then, which render the best service to their cities; those who provide these festivities, and banquetings, and expensive entertainments, and manifold rejoicings; or those who restrain all those doings, bearing before them stocks, scourges, executioners, dreaded soldiers, and a voice fraught with much terror : and issuing orders,

---

¹ Ὀβεγίσκοις (dagger-blades, or spear-heads, or spits) αὐτοὺς διέπειραν. In Hom. vi. p. 43. *infra*, we have the phrase τίνες ὀβελίσκοι πεπυρωμένοι διέπειραν σῶμα. It is evident that something is omitted, and no more probable supposition presents itself, than that Chrys. here read out from Josephus or Eusebius the description of the famine among the besieged (which the reporter of the sermon omitted at the time, intending to insert it at his leisure); and that the short sentence in the text is the preacher's own parenthetical explanation of some part of the description. Thus, B. J. vi. 3. 3. speaking of the cruelties practised upon dying wretches suspected of having food concealed about their persons, Josephus says: Ἀλλὰ καὶ τοὺς ἐκπνέοντας οἱ λῃσταὶ διηρεύνων, μήτις ὑπὸ κόλπον ἔχων τροφὴν σκήπτοιτο τὸν θάνατον αὐτῷ. Perhaps ὀβελίσκοις αὐτοὺς διέπειρα is C.'s comment upon διηρεύνων.—Or, in like manner, it may refer to the description in B. J. v. 12. 3. how the λῃσταί, after ransacking the bodies of the dead, tried the edges of their swords upon them, etc. Τάς τε ἀκμὰς τῶν ξιφῶν ἐδοκίμαζον ἐν τοῖς πτώμασι, καὶ τινας τῶν ἐρριμμένων ἔτι ζῶντας διήλαυνον ἐπὶ πείρᾳ τοῦ σιδήρου. Perhaps, however, the expression may be taken in a metaphorical sense as in the phrase above cited: "they pierced themselves (ἑαυτοὺς for αὐτοὺς) as with spits or lancets."

² Against the Marcionites, he says: You say that the God of the Old Testament is a cruel God ; whereas Christ, the good God, is all mildness. Yet was not the Roman judgment upon the Jews inflicted by Him? And was it not beyond comparison more ruthless (ὠμότερον, above) than the Babylonian or any former judgment, inflicted, as you say, by the God of the Old Testament?

³ Πῶς οὖν φατὲ φησίν, i. e. as it is said in the text, "Every one that calleth on the name of the Lord shall be saved." The question is the same as was put in the beginning of this section: "What? do you speak of salvation for them after crucifying the Lord?" And this, when you have shown us how fearfully that sin was visited?" This question, as a very simple one, he leaves the hearers to answer for themselves, by distinguishing between believers and unbelievers, the penitent and the hardened.—The innovator quite alters the sense; "How then say some that Christ remitted them their sin?" which makes the next sentence idle.

⁴ Πλὴν ὅταν κἀκεῖνος εἰς ἐκείνην μεταστῇ τὴν τάξιν. The meaning is obscure: for it may be either, that he is displaced from office (μεταστῆναι, μετάστασις are common in this sense), and makes one of the στασιάζοντες ; or, that he lays aside the magistrate and demeans himself to take part in their excesses. (Τάξις is the expression for the attendants of any high official, and may perhaps be taken in that sense here). Erasmus goes wide of the text: *nec exultant eo quod et ille ad hoc opus ordinatus est* : and so Montf. *nec exultantes quod ille ad hoc officium sit constitutus.*

and making men hang down their heads, and
with the rod dispersing the idlers in the market-
place.   Let us see, I say; these are the disagreeable, those the beloved : let us see where
the gain rests.   (λήλει.) What comes then of
your pleasure-givers ?   A kind of frigid enjoyment, lasting till the evening, and to-morrow
vanished ; mirth ungoverned, words unseemly
and dissolute.   And what of these? Awe,
sobriety, subdued thoughts; reasonableness
of mind, an end of idleness ; a curb on the
passions within ; a wall of defence, next to
God, ¹ against assailants from without.   It is
by means of these we have each our property
but by those ruinous festivities we dissipate it.
Robbers indeed have not invaded it, but
vainglory together with pleasure acts the part
of robber. Each sees the robber carrying off
everything before his eyes, and is delighted
at it !   A new fashion of robbery, this, to
induce people to be glad when one is plundering them ! On the other part, there is nothing
of the kind : but God, as the common Father,
has secured us as by a wall against all [depre-
dators], both seen and unseen. ²   For, " Take
heed," saith He, " that ye do not your alms
before men." (Matt. vi. 1.) The soul learns
from the one, [excess ; ³ from the other] to
flee injustice.   For injustice consists not
merely in grasping at more wealth than belongs to us, but in giving to the belly more
than its needful sustenance, in carrying mirth
beyond its proper bounds, and causing it to
run into frantic excesses.   From the one, it
learns sobriety; from the other, unchastity.
For it is unchastity, not merely to have carnal
intercourse with women, but even to look upon
a woman with unchaste eyes. From the one,
it learns modesty ; from the other, conceited
self-importance.   For, " All things," says the
Apostle, " are lawful for me, but not all things
expedient." (1 Cor. vi. 12.) From the one,
decent behavior; from the other unseemliness.
For, as to the doings in the theatres, I pass
these.   But to let you see that it is not even a
pleasure either, but a grief, show me, but a

single day after the festival, both those who
spent their money in giving it, and those who
were feasted with spectacles : and you shall see
them all looking dejected enough, but most
of all him, your (ἐκεῖνον) famous man that has
spent his money for it. And this is but fair :
for, the day before, he delighted the common
man, and the common man indeed was in high
good humor and enjoyment, and rejoiced indeed in the splendid garment, but then not
having the use of it, and seeing himself stripped
of it, he was grieved and annoyed; and
wanted to be the great man, seeing even his
own enjoyment to be small compared with
his. ⁴   Therefore, the day after, they change
places, and now he, the great man, gets the
larger share in the dejection.

Now if in worldly matters, amusements are
attended with such dissatisfaction, while disagreeable things are so beneficial, much more
does this hold in things spiritual. Why is it
that no one quarrels with the laws, but on the
contrary all account that matter a common
benefit ? For indeed not strangers from some
other quarter, nor enemies of those for whom
the laws are made, came and made these
orders, but the citizens themselves, their
patrons, their benefactors: and this very
thing, the making of laws, is a token of
beneficence and good-will. And yet the laws
are full of punishment and restraint, and there
is no such thing as law without penalty and
coercion.   Then is it not unreasonable, that
while the expositors of those laws are called
deliverers, benefactors, and patrons, we are
considered troublesome and vexatious if we
speak of the laws of God ? When we discourse about hell, then we bring forward
those laws : just as in the affairs of the world,
people urge the laws of murder, highway robbery, and the like, so do we the penal laws:
laws, which not man enacted, but the Only-
Begotten Son of God Himself. Let him that
hath no mercy, He says, be punished (Matt.

---

¹ μετὰ τὸν Θεὸν, omitted in the modern text.
² Hom. in Matt. lxxi. p. 699. C. Chrys. describes κενοδοξία
(vainglory) in almsgiving, as the thief that runs away with the
treasure laid up in heaven. And something of this sort seems
to have been in his thoughts here, where however his meaning
is evidently very imperfectly expressed. The texts cited show
that ἐκεῖ, ἐκεῖθεν, refer to something more than, as above, good
laws and government in general ; for here he speaks of the
Gospel discipline of the inner man. " Where this restraint is,
no dissipation of our temporal or spiritual wealth has place:
for God, as common Father, has raised a wall to keep out all
robbers both seen and unseen, from all our possessions: from
the former He guards us, by law and good government; from
the latter, by the Gospel prohibition of all vainglory : " Take
heed that ye do not your alms," etc.
³ Μανθάνει ψυχὴ ἐντεῦθεν, opp. to ἐκεῖθεν as in the following
sentences: ἐκεῖθεν σωφροσύνην μανθάνει, ἐντεῦθεν ἀκολασίαν—ἐκ.
ἐπιεικειαν, ἐντ. τῦφον—ἐκ. κοσμιότητα, ἐντ. ἀσχημοσύνην. Therefore either something is wanting: e. g. πλεονεξίαν· ἐκεῖθεν, or
for ἐντ. we must read ἐκεῖθεν.

⁴ The old text καὶ ἐβούλετο ἐκεῖνος ὁ ἀναλίσκων καὶ τὴν οἰκείαν
εὐπραγίαν μικρὰν ὁρᾶν πρὸς τὴν ἐκείνου, evidently requires correction, and the emendation assumed in the translation is, καὶ
ἐβ. ἐκεῖνος εἶναι (ὁ ἀναλ. may perhaps be rejected as a gloss) καὶ
τὴν οἰκείαν εὐπρ. μ. ὁρῶν π. τ. ἐκείνου. Thus the whole passage,
from καὶ ὁ μὲν ἰδιώτης, refers to the ἰδ. or person feasted, and
ἐκεῖνος throughout is the entertainer. The edited text has:
Ἐκεῖνος δὲ ὁ ἀναλ. καὶ τὴν οἰκείαν εὐπρ. μικρὰν ὁρᾶν ἐδόκει π. τ.
ἐκείνου· of which Erasm. makes, Ille autem qui sumptus im-
pendit et suam felicitatem parvam cum ea quam ex sumptu
habebat conspicere putabat. But even if this sense lay in the
words, it is not easy to see the connection of the following sentence, Διὰ τοῦτο, etc., Montf. translates, Qui vero sumptus
fecit, suam prae illius felicitate parvam putabat, as if ἐκεῖνος
and ἐκείνου in the same sentence referred to two different and
contrasted persons. The meaning of the passage is, As, on the
day before, the entertainer had τὸ πλέον τῆς εὐθυμίας, it is but
fair that on the following day τὸ πλέον τῆς ἀθυμίας should be
transferred to him. This is expressed by Διὰ τοῦτο τῇ ὑστ.
ἀντιδιδόασιν ἀλλήλοις· which however, Erasmus renders, Ideireo
sequenti die reddunt sibi vestes iterum: Montf. redduntur
vestes. (Perhaps there is an allusion to the legal phrase
ἀντίδοσις. v. Isocrat. περὶ ἀντιδ).

xviii. 23); for such is the import of the parable. Let him that remembereth injuries, pay the last penalty. Let him that is angry without cause, be cast into the fire. Let him that reviles, receive his due in hell. If you think these laws which you hear strange, be not amazed. For if Christ was not intended to make new laws, why did He come? Those other laws are manifest to us; we know that the murderer and adulterer ought to be punished. If then we were meant only to be told the same things over again, where was the need of a heavenly Teacher? Therefore He does not say, Let the adulterer be punished, but, whoso looketh on with unchaste eyes. And where, and when, the man will receive punishment, He there tells us. And not in fine public monuments, nor yet somewhere out of sight, [1] did He deposit His laws; not pillars of brass did He raise up, and engrave letters thereon, but twelve souls raised He up for us, the souls of the Apostles, and in their minds has He by the Spirit inscribed this writing. This cite we to you. If this was authorized to Jews, that none might take refuge in the plea of ignorance, much more is it to us. But should any say, " I do not hear, therefore have no guilt," on this very score he is most liable to punishment. For, were there no teacher, it would be possible to take refuge in this plea; but if there be, it is no longer possible. Thus see how, speaking of Jews, the Lord deprives them of all excuse; " If I had not come and spoken unto them, they had not had sin:" (John xv. 22): and Paul again, " But I say, have they not heard? Nay, but into all the earth went forth their sound." (Rom. x. 18.) For then there is excuse, when there is none to tell the man; but when the watchman sits there, having this as the business of his life, there is excuse no longer. Nay, rather, it was the will of Christ, not that we should look only upon these written pillars, but that we should ourselves be such. But since we have made ourselves unworthy of the writing, at least let us look to those. For just as the pillars threaten others, but are not themselves obnoxious to punishment, nor yet the laws, even so the blessed Apostles. And observe; not in one place only stands this pillar, but its writing is carried round about in all the world. Whether you go among the Indians, you shall hear this: whether into Spain, or to the very ends of the earth, there is none without the hearing, except it be of his own neglect. Then be not offended, but give heed to the things spoken, that ye may be able to lay hold upon the works of virtue, and attain unto the eternal blessings in Christ Jesus our Lord, with Whom to the Father and Holy Ghost together be glory, power, honor, now and ever, world without end. Amen.

HOMILY VI.

ACTS II. 22.

" Ye men of Israel, hear these my words."

["Ye men of Israel"]: it is not for flattery that he uses this term; but, as he has borne hard upon them, he relaxes a little, and puts them in mind of their great ancestor [2] [Israel]. Here again he begins with an introduction, that they may not become excited, now that he is going to make express mention to them of Jesus: for in what preceded, there was no reason why they should be excited, while the Prophet was the subject of discourse: but the name of Jesus would have given offence at the very outset.—And he does not say, " Do as I bid you," but, *Hear;* as being not at all exacting. And observe how he forbears to speak of the high matters, and begins with the very low: " Jesus," he says: and then straightway mentions the place He belonged to, being one which was held in mean estimation: " Jesus of Nazareth": and does not say anything great about Him, nor even such as one would say about a Prophet, so far: " Jesus," he says, " of Nazareth, a man proved (to be) from God among you." Observe; what great matter was this, to say that He was sent from God? [3] For this was the point

---

[1] Εἰς ἀναθήματα οὐδὲ εἰς κρύβδην. The modern text has εἰς ἄξονας οὐδὲ εἰς, κύρβεις, alluding to the peculiar form of tables on which the laws of Athens were written. On critical grounds we retain the reading of the old text, which, as being the more difficult one, is not likely to have been substituted for the other. Οὐκ εἰς ἀναθήματα; "not on public monuments for display." Laws of an Emperor, for instance, engraved on handsome monuments, may be called ἀναθήματα. Οὐδὲ εἰς κρύβδην, (also an unusual expression), 'nor yet where no one would see them.'

[2] τοῦ προπάτορος, A. C. F. D. and Cat. but τοῦ Δαυὶδ εὐκαίρως, B. E. Edd. Œcumenius fell into the same mistake and has τοῦ προπάτορος Δαυίδ. But it is evident that Chrys. is commenting on the address Ἄνδρες Ἰσραηλῖται.

[3] Ὅρα, ποῖον ἦν τοῦτο μέγα, τὸ εἰπεῖν κ. τ. λ. i. e. " He says as yet οὐδὲν μέγα, nothing great, concerning Christ: nothing even that would be great if said of an ordinary Prophet. For,

which on all occasions both He and John and the Apostles were studious to show. Thus, hear John saying: "The same said unto me, On whom thou shalt see the Spirit descending, and abiding on him, this is He." (John i. 33.) But Christ Himself does this to an extreme; Of Myself I am not come, He sent Me. (ib. vii. 28.) And everywhere in the Scriptures this seems the point most studiously insisted upon. Therefore also this holy leader of the blessed company, the lover of Christ, the good shepherd, the man put in trust with the keys of heaven, the man who received the Spiritual Wisdom, when he has first subdued the Jews by fear, and has shown what great things have been vouchsafed to the disciples, and what a right they have to be believed, then first proceeds to speak concerning Him. Only think what boldness it was to say it, in the midst of the murderers— that He is risen! And yet he does not all at once say, He is risen; but what?— "He came," says he, "from God: this is manifest by the signs which "—he does not yet say, Jesus Himself wrought: but what?—"which God wrought by Him in the midst of you." He calls themselves as witnesses. "A man proved (to be sent) from God among you, by miracles and wonders and signs, which God wrought by him in the midst of you, as also ye yourselves know." Then, having fallen upon the mention of that their sacrilegious outrage, observe how he endeavors to quit them of the crime : "Him," he says, "being by the determinate counsel and foreknowledge of God delivered up": (v. 23) [adding however,] "ye have taken, and by wicked hands have crucified and slain:" for though it was predetermined, still they were murderers.[1] ["By the determinate counsel and

foreknowledge of God :"] all but using the same words as Joseph did ; just as he said to his brethren ; "Be not angry one with another by the way : God sent me hither." (Gen. xlv. 5, 24.) It is God's doing. "What of us, then?" (it might be said,) "it was even well done on our part." That they may not say this, therefore it is that he adds, "By wicked hands ye have crucified and slain."* Here then he hints at Judas; while at the same time he shows them that it was not from any strength of theirs, and would not have been, if He had not Himself permitted it : it was God that delivered Him up. He has transferred the evil entire upon the head of Judas, now already parted from them ; for he it was that delivered Him over to them by the kiss. Or, "By wicked hands," refers to the soldiers : for neither is it simply, "Ye have slain," but, By wicked men ye have done this.[2] And observe how everywhere they make it of great importance that the Passion should first be confessed. WHOM GOD RAISED UP (v. 24), says he. This was the great thing; and observe how he sets it in the middle of his discourse : for the former matters had been confessed; both the miracles and the signs and the slaying— "Whom God," says he, "raised up, having loosed the pains of death, because it was not possible that He should be kept in its power." It is something great and sublime that he has hinted at here. For the expression, "It was not possible," even itself is that of one assigning something.[3] It

observe: ποῖον μέγα, what sort of great thing was it, to say that Christ was sent from God?' In the following sentences Chrys. seems to have been scarcely understood by his reporter. His meaning may be thus represented: "And yet, so it is: everywhere in the Scriptures we find examples of this remarkable μείωσις: "Christ was sent from God," seems to be the point most studiously inculcated (τὸ σπουδαζόμενον): nay, we find it carried to the utmost (μεθ᾽ ὑπερβολῆς) in some of Christ's own expressions. And so here: when Peter stands up —he, the leader of the Apostles, the lover of Christ, the good shepherd, the man entrusted with the keys of the kingdom of heaven, the man who has received the deposit of the Wisdom of the Spirit—after he has subdued the audience by the terrors of the coming judgments, has shown that he and his company have received wonderful gifts as foretold by the Prophet, and has made it felt that they have a right to be believed: you may well expect after all this that his first word about Christ will be something great; that he will certainly launch out boldly into the declaration, He is risen! Only think, though, what boldness to say this in the midst of the murderers!—Nothing of the kind. He begins with, "Jesus the Nazarene, a man proved to be from God unto you by signs, etc. which—(He did? no, but) God did by Him, etc. Wait awhile, however: the Orator will say all that needs to be said in due time."

[1] Εἰ γὰρ καὶ ὡρισμένον ἦν, φησὶν, ὅμως ἀνδροφόνοι ἦσαν. B. C. after ἀπαλλ. τοῦ ἐγκλήματος, and before the text. As the sentence so placed seemed to make Chrys. contradict himself, the other Mss. and Edd. before Ben. omit it. Something is want-

ing, which perhaps may be supplied from Œcumen. Ἀλλὰ καὶ ἀπαλλάσσων οὐκ ἀφήσιν αὐτοὺς πάντη τοῦ ἐγκλήματος. Ἐπάγει γὰρ, ὅτι διὰ χειρῶν ἀνόμων ἀνείλετε.

* In v. 23, the preferable reading is διὰ χειρὸς ἀνόμων, "through the hand of lawless men," instead of διὰ χειρῶν ἀνόμων of the Text. Recep. So A, B, C, D, Tisch. W. and H., Lach. Treg. R. V. This reading is also to be preferred in accordance with Bengel's first rule of text-criticism—Lectio difficilior principatum tenet.—G. B. S.

[2] The confusion may be cleared up by supposing that Chrys. here commented upon the words διὰ χειρῶν ἀνόμων as admitting of a double connection: viz.: with ἔκδοτον λαβόντες and with προσπ. ἀνείλετε. In the former, it refers to Judas: while at the same time, it is shown that of themselves they had no power against Him. He was delivered up by the predestination and will of God, by means of the wicked hands of Judas; upon whom (already gone to his doom) the evil is shifted entire. But again, as ἔκδοτον is not put simply and without addition (ἁπλῶς), so neither (οὐδὲ) is ἀνείλετε: but "by wicked hands ye slew," i. e. by the soldiers.

[3] The text seems to be corrupt: καὶ αὐτὸ διδόντος ἐστιν τὶ δείκνυσιν ὅτι. B. omits ἔστιν τί. Perhaps καὶ αὐτὸ is derived from an abbreviation of κρατεῖσθαι αὐτόν: and διδόντος ἐστιν τὶ may be, " is (the expression) of one assigning something." i. e. some special prerogative to Him:" or, possibly, "For the expression, Καθότι οὐκ ἦν δυνατὸν even of itself implies the granting of something (in His case):" viz. as a postulate. E. καὶ αὐτὸν διδόντα ἐμφαίνει κατασχεῖν· καὶ ὅτι, i. e. "that it was even He that gave death the power to hold Him :'" this, which is adopted by Edd. is, however, not a various reading, but only an attempt to restore the passage. Œcumen. gives no assistance: he has only, διὰ δὲ τοῦ, καθότι οὐκ ἦν δυν. αὐτὸν κρατ., τὸ μεγαλεῖον αὐτοῦ παρίστησι, καὶ ὅτι οὐκέτι ἀποθνήσκει. In the next sentence E. and Edd. have: "For by 'pains of death' Scripture is everywhere wont to express 'danger:'" but Œcumen. and Cat. agree with the old reading, ἡ Παλαία. Possibly the meaning of the whole passage may be somewhat as follows. "It is something great and sublime that Peter has darkly hinted in saying, 'it was not possible that HE should

shows that death itself in holding Him had pangs as in travail, and was sore bestead:[*] whereas, by *pains*, or, travail-pangs, *of death*, the Old Testament means danger and disaster: and that He so rose as never more to die. For the assertion, "Seeing that it was not possible that He should be holden of it," means this, that *His* rising was not common to the rest. Then, however, before their thoughts can enter at all into his meaning, he brings David upon them, an authority which sets aside all human reasoning. "For David saith (with reference) to Him." (v. 25.) And observe how, once more, the testimony is lowly. For therefore he begins the citation further up, with the matters of lowlier import: therefore[1] was death not in the number of grievous things [because], says he, "I foresaw the Lord always before my face, that He is on my right hand that I should not be moved:" (v. 25–27) and, "that Thou wilt not leave my soul in hell." Then, having finished the citation from the Prophet, he adds; "Men and brethren." (v. 29.) When he is about to say anything great, he uses this opening address, to rouse and to conciliate them. "Let me be allowed," he says, "to speak freely to you of the patriarch David." Remarkable lowliness, in a case where he was giving no hurt, nor was there any reason why the hearers should be angry. For he did not say, This is not said concerning David, but concerning the Christ. But in another point of view:

by his reverential expression towards the blessed David, he awed them; speaking of an acknowledged fact as if it were a bold thing to say, and therefore begging them to pardon him for saying it. And thereupon his expression is not simply "concerning David," but "concerning the patriarch David, that he is both dead and buried:" he does not also say, "and is not risen again," but in another way (though this too would have been no great thing to say), "And his sepulchre is with us unto this day," he has said whát comes to the same thing. Then—and even so he does not come to the mention of Christ, but what next?—he goes on with his encomium upon David, "Being therefore a prophet, and knowing that with an oath God had sworn unto him." (v. 30.) But this he says, that were it but on account of the honor shown to David, and the descent from him, they may accept what is said concerning Christ's resurrection, as seeing that it would be an injury to the prophecy, and a derogating from (τῆς εἰς αὐτοὺς τιμῆς) their honor, if this were not the fact. "And knowing," he says, "that with an oath God had sworn unto him"—he does not say simply "promised"—"of the fruit of his loins after the flesh to raise up Christ, to seat Him upon his throne." Observe how he has again only hinted at what is sublime. For now that he has soothed them with his expression, he confidently adds this: The prophet [saith it] "of His resurrection, that neither was His soul left in hell, nor did His flesh see corruption." (v. 31.) This again is wonderful: it shows that His resurrection was not like that of other men. For though death laid hold on Him, yet it did not its own work then.—And, as regards the sin, he has spoken of that, covertly and darkly; of the punishment, he forbore to add anything; but that they had slain Him, this he has spoken out; for the rest he now comes to the sign given by God. And when it is once proved, that He, the slain, was just, was dear to God, then, though thou be silent of the punishmnet, be sure that he which did the sin will condemn himself more than ever thou canst condemn him. So then, that he refers all to the Father, is in order that they may receive what is said: and that assertion, "Not possible," he fetches in from the prophecy. Well then, let us again look over what has been said.

"Jesus of Nazareth, a man proved (to be sent) from God unto you." (Recapitulation of v. 22–31): one, of whom, by reason of His works, there can be no doubt; but who, on the contrary, is demonstrated. Thus also Nicodemus said, "No man can do these miracles which Thou doest—By miracles, and

---

be holden of it.' And the very expression καθότι implies that there is something to be thought of (comp. Caten. in l). Then, in the Old. Test., the expression ὠδῖνες θανάτου means pains in which death is the agent; but here they are the pangs inflicted upon death itself, travailing in birth with Christ 'the first-begotten from the dead.' It shows then both that death could not endure to hold Him, and, that Christ being raised from the dead dieth no more. For the assertion, etc. But then, without giving them time to ponder upon the meaning of what he has darkly hinted, he goes off to the Prophet," etc.—On the expression ὠδῖνας λύειν Mr. Field, *Index to Hom. in Matt.* s. v., remarks, that "it is said sometimes of the child-bearing woman herself, as p. 118. B., sometimes of the child born, as p. 375. A., sometimes of the person aiding in the delivery, as Job xxxix, 2. Hence the obscure passage Acts ii, 34 is to be explained. See Theophylact in l."

[*] It is noteworthy that this interpretation of ὠδῖνας τοῦ θανάτου (24) is exactly that of Meyer who explains thus: "Death travailed in birth-throes even until the dead was raised again. With this event these pangs ceased, *they were loosed*; and because *God* had made Christ alive, *God* has loosed the pangs of death." Other interpretations are: (1) The *snares* or *bands* of death, on the ground that ὠδῖνες is used in the lxx. to translate the Hebrew חֶבְלֵי (e. g. Ps. xviii. 5), which has this meaning. So Olsh. (2) That the pains *of Jesus* connected with the whole experience of death are meant. He is popularly conceived as enduring these pains until the resurrection when God loosed them, the conception being that he was under their power and constraint. We prefer this view. So Lechler, Gloag, Hackett.—G. B. S.

[1] i. e. The former part of the passage cited, down to, "Thou wilt not leave my soul in hell," as far as the words go, is no more than David might say in reference to himself, or any other saint: viz. he set God always before his face, etc. therefore (διὰ τοῦτο, referring to v. 26. διὰ τοῦτο εὐφρ.) death was not in the number of things that cause grief. And St. Peter instead of going at once to that in the prophecy which is peculiar to Christ, with wise management begins with what is less exalted, ἅτε εἰσαγωγικωτέρων λόγων δεομένοις, Œcumen.— For διὰ τοῦτο οὐ τῶν λυπούντων ὁ θάνατος, E. and Edd. have ἵνα δείξῃ, ὅτι οὐ . . . "to show that death," etc.

wonders, and signs which God wrought by Him in the midst of you" (John iii. 2) : not secretly. Setting out from facts notorious to those whom he was addressing, he then comes to things hidden. Thereupon [in saying, "By the determinate counsel and foreknowledge of God,"] (v. 23) he shows that it was not because they had the power to do it, and that there was a wisdom and a Divine arrangement in the event, seeing it was from God. He rapidly passes over the unpleasant part, [adding, "Whom God raised up," etc.] (v. 24). For it is always a point of great importance with them to show that He was once dead. Though ye should deny it, says he, (ἐκεῖνοι) those (present) will bear witness to the fact. [" Having loosed the pangs of death."] He that gives Death trouble, may much more give trouble to them that crucified Him : however, nothing of the kind is here said, as that He had power to slay you. Meanwhile,[1] let us also learn thus to hold. For one that is in pain like a woman in travail, does not hold the thing held, and is not active but passive ; and makes haste to cast it off. And it is well said : " For David saith in reference to him" (v. 25); that you may not refer that saying to the Prophet.—[" Therefore being a Prophet, and knowing," etc.] (v. 30, 31.) Do you observe how he now interprets the prophecy, and does not [2] give it bare of comment ? How did He " seat Him upon " David's " throne ?" For the kingdom after the Spirit is in heaven. Observe how, along with the resurrection, he has also declared the kingdom in the fact of His rising again. He shows that the Prophet was under constraint : for the prophecy was concerning Him. Why does he say, not, Concerning His kingdom (it was a great matter), but " Concerning His resurrection ?" And how did He seat Him upon his (David's) throne ? Why, He reigns as King over Jews also, yea, what is much more, over them that crucified Him. " For His flesh saw no corruption." This seems to be less than resurrection, but it is the same thing.

" This Jesus "—observe how he does not call Him otherwise—" hath God raised up ;

whereof all we are witnesses. Being therefore by the right hand of God exalted" (v. 33, 34) : again he takes refuge with the Father, and yet it had been enough to say what precedes : but he knows what a great point this is. Here he has hinted at the Ascension also, and that Christ is in heaven : but neither does he say this openly. " And having received," says he, " the promise of the Holy Ghost." Observe how, in the beginning of his discourse, he does not say that Jesus Himself had sent It, but the Father : now, however, that he has mentioned His signs and the things done to Him by the Jews, and has spoken of His resurrection, he boldly introduces what he has to say about these matters, again adducing themselves as witnesses by both senses : [" He hath shed forth this, which ye do see and hear."] And of the resurrection he has made continual mention, but of their outrageous deed he has spoken once for all. " And having received the promise of the Holy Ghost," This again is great. " The promise," he says ; because [promised] before His Passion. Observe how he now makes it all His [" He hath poured forth this "], covertly making a great point. For if it was He that poured it forth, it is of Him that the Prophet has spoken above, " In the last days I will pour forth of My Spirit on My Servants, and on Mine handmaids, and I will do wonders in the heaven above. (supra, v. 17.) Observe what he secretly puts into it ! But then, because it was a great thing, he again veils it with the expression of " His having received of the Father." He has spoken of the good things fulfilled, of the signs ; has said, that He is king, the point that touched them ; has said, that it is He that gives Spirit. (Arist. Rhet. i. 3.) (For, however much a person may say, if it does not issue in something advantageous, he speaks to no purpose.) Just as John : " The same," says he, " shall baptize you with the Holy Ghost." (Matt. iii. 11.) And it shows that the Cross not only did not make Him less, but rendered Him even more illustrious, seeing that of old God promised it to Him, but now has given it. Or [it may be], " the promise " which He promised to us. He so foreknew it about to be, and has given it to us greater after the resurrection. And, " hath poured it out," he says ; not [3] requiring worthiness : and not

---

[1] τέως μανθάνωμεν καὶ ἡμεῖς οὕτω κατέχειν. As the text stands, this can only mean, " And here by the bye let us also learn how to hold fast Christ ; not to hold Him with pain, like one in travail-pangs, who therefore cannot hold fast, but is in haste to be delivered," etc. But this can hardly have been St. Chrysostom's meaning. Something seems to be omitted after καὶ ἡμεῖς or οὕτω.—Edd. τέως δὲ μανθάνομεν καὶ ἡμεῖς διὰ τῶν εἰρημένων τί ἐστι τὸ κατέχειν. If this is: " What is the meaning of the expression κατέχειν, the emphatic καὶ ἡμεῖς is superfluous; and besides, the word κατέχειν does not occur in the text commented upon. Œcum. and the Catena give no help.

[2] Edd. καὶ γυμνήν τίθησι δηλῶν πῶς. " And gives it bare (of comment), showing." Montf. mistranslates γυμνὴν τιθ, nudam exponat, and notices the old reading (A. B. C.) with the remark, Unus Codex προφ. οὐ γυμνήν. Minus recte. But Chrys. is now commenting on v. 30, 31. " Above, St. Peter gave the prophecy by itself: now he adds his own exposition and reasoning, " Being therefore a Prophet." etc.

[3] Ἐξέχεε, φησίν, οὐκ ἀξίωμα ζητῶν, καὶ οὐχ ἁπλῶς. Edd. Ἐξ., φ. Ἐνταῦθα τὸ ἀξίωμα ἐμφαίνει, καὶ ὅτι οὐχ ἁπλῶς. " Here he intimates the dignity : and that," etc. But the meaning is, " He poured it forth, not requiring merit : i. e. not giving here and there to the most deserving, but as the phrase implies, with unsparing liberality." μετὰ δαψιλείας. N. μεθ' ὑπερβολῆς.

simply gave, but with abundance. Whence[1] does this appear? Henceforth after the mention of His giving the Spirit, he confidently speaks also of His ascension into heaven; and not only so, but again adducing the witness, and reminding them of that Person concerning Whom Christ once spake. (Matt. xxii. 43) "For not David," says he "ascended into the heavens. (v. 34.) Here he no longer speaks in lowly phrase,[2] having the confidence which results from the things said; nor does he say, "Be it permitted me to speak," or the like: "But he saith himself; The Lord said unto my Lord, Sit Thou on My right hand, until I make Thine enemies Thy footstool." Now if He be David's Lord, much more shall they not disdain Him. "Sit thou on My right hand;" he has set the whole matter here; "until I make Thine enemies Thy footstool:" here also he has brought upon them a great terror, just as in the beginning he showed what He does to His friends, what to his enemies. And again, as to the act of subjugation, not to provoke unbelief, he ascribes it to the Father. Since then these are great things that he has uttered, he again brings his discourse down to lowly matters. "Let therefore," he says, "the whole house of Israel know assuredly: i. e. question ye not, nor doubt ye: then also in the tone of command it follows; "that God hath made Him both Lord—" this he says from David—" and Christ," (v. 36), this from the Psalm:[3] For when it would have been rightly concluded, "Let therefore the whole house of Israel know assuredly that" He sitteth on the right hand of God, this, which would have been great, he forbears, and brings in a different matter which is much more humble, and the expression "Hath made;" i. e. hath ordained: so that there is nothing about (οὐσίωσις) communication of substance here, but the expression relates to this which has been mentioned. "Even this Jesus, Whom ye crucified." He does well to end with this, thereby agitating their minds. For when he has shown how great it is, he has then exposed their daring deed, so as to show it to be greater, and to possess them with terror. For men are not so much attracted by benefits as they are chastened by fear.*

But the admirable and great ones, and beloved of God, need none of these motives: men, such as was Paul: not of the kingdom, not of hell, made he account. For this is indeed to love Christ, this to be no hireling, nor to reckon it a matter of trafficking and trading, but to 'be indeed virtuous, and to do all for the love of God. (Rom. ix. 3.) Then what tears does it not deserve, when, owing so large a measure, we do not even like traders seek the kingdom of heaven! He promises us so great things, and not even so is He worthy to be heard? What can come up to this enmity![4] And yet, they are mad after money-making, though it be with enemies, though it be with slaves, though it be with persons most hostile to them, that they come in contact, though it be with persons utterly evil, if only they expect that they shall be enabled by their means to make money, they will do everything, will flatter, and be obsequious, and make themselves slaves, and will esteem them more to be revered than all men, to get some advantage out of them: for the hope of money does not allow them to give a thought to any such considerations as these. But the Kingdom is not so powerful as money is; nay, rather, not in the smallest proportion as powerful. For[5] it is no ordinary Being that promises: but this is greater than even the Kingdom itself that we receive it from such a Giver! But now the case is the same as if a king, wishing, after ten thousand other benefits, to make us his heirs and coheirs with his son [should be despised]: while some captain of a band of robbers, who has done ten thousand wrongs to us and to our parents, and is himself fraught with ten thousand wickednesses, and has utterly marred our honor and our welfare, should, on presenting a single penny,

---

[1] πόθεν τοῦτο; Edd. "Wherefore also to prove this very thing, he adds what follows." The connection is, "He has shed forth. How so? It must be He; for not David ascended," etc.

[2] Here five of our Mss. have μεθ' ὑπερβολῆς, "hyperbolically:" but the reading of E. μεθ' ὑποστολῆς is attested by Œcumen. and the Catena.

[3] i. e. the expression "Lord" is derived from David's, "My Lord:" the expression "Christ," or rather καὶ Χριστὸν ὁ Θεὸς ἐποίησε ἐν, is from the Psalm: meaning perhaps the second Psalm. Edd. have, "this he says from David and from the Psalm," after the text.

* The two Old Test. pp. (Joel ii. 28-32; Ps. xvi. 8-11) which occur in this chapter are quoted from the lxx., the former freely, the latter with great exactness. The following peculiarities of phraseology are noticeable in the first passage. (1) "In the last days," more definite expression for the Heb. and lxx. "afterward." (2) The partitive expression: "I will pour out of my Spirit," is after the lxx. vs. the original which reads: "I will pour out my spirit." (3) The phrases: "saith God" and "they shall prophesy" (17, 18) are added to both Heb. and lxx. (4) "Vapor" is from lxx. for Heb. "columns." (5) If we read καὶ ἐπιφάνη at the end of v. 20 (as Mey., W. and H.) it is from the lxx. an inaccurate trans. of Hebrew for "fearful," occasioned by misunderstanding on the part of the Seventy of the derivation of the Heb. word. The second pp. follows the lxx. exactly and in several deviations from the original.—G. B. S.

[4] Alluding to the Psalm above cited, "Until I make Thine enemies Thy footstool."

[5] In the modern text the connection is supplied, and the thought expanded. "And yet neither is it any ordinary being that promises it: but One who is beyond comparison greater than the Kingdom itself. Now when the promise is a Kingdom, and God the Giver thereof, it is a great thing, the very receiving from such a Giver.

receive our worship. God promises a King-dom, and is despised : the Devil helps us to hell, and he is honored ! Here God, there Devil. But let us see the difference of the tasks enjoined. For if there were none of these considerations in the case : if it were not, here God, there Devil ; not, here one helping to a kingdom, there to a hell : the nature itself of the tasks enjoined were suffi-cient to induce us to comply with the former. For what does each enjoin ? The one,[1] the things which make glorious ; the other, the things which put to shame : one, the things which involve in ten thousand calamities and disgraces ; the other, the things which have with them abundant refreshment. For look : the one saith, " Learn ye of Me, for I am meek and lowly of heart, and ye shall find rest unto your souls." (Matt. xi. 29) : the other saith, Be thou savage, and ungentle, and passionate, and wrathful, and more a wild beast than a man. Let us see which is more useful, which, I pray you, more profitable. " Speak not of this," say you.[2] * * * But consider that he is the devil : above all indeed, if that be shown : there is need also to undergo toils, and, on the other hand, the prize of victory will be greater. For not he that enjoins easy tasks is the kind (κηδεμὼν) benefactor, but he that enjoins what is for our good. Since fathers also enjoin disagreeable tasks ; but for this[3] they are fathers : and so again do masters to slaves : but kidnappers and destroyers (λυμεῶνες) on the other hand, do

just the reverse. And[4] yet that the commands of Christ are attended with a pleasure, is manifest from that saying. For to what sort do you take the passionate man to belong, and to what the forbearing and meek ? Does not the soul of the (ἐκείνου) one[5] seem to be in a kind of solitary retreat, enjoying exceed-ing quiet ; while that of (τούτου) the other is like a market-place and tumult and the midst of cities, where great is the clamor of those going out, the noise of camels, mules, asses : of men shouting loud to those that meet them, that they may not be trodden under foot : and again, of silver-beaters, of braziers, of men thrusting and pushing this way and that and some overborne, some overbearing ? But the soul of (τούτου) the former is like some mountain-top, with its delicate air, its pure sunshine, its limpid gushing fountains, its multitude of charming flowers, while the vernal meads and gardens put on their plumage of shrubs and flowers, and glance with rilling waters : and if any sound is heard there, it is sweet, and calculated to affect the ear with a sense of much delight. For either the warbling birds perch on the outermost spray of the branching trees, and cicadas, nightingales and swallows, blended in one harmony, perform a kind of concerted music ; or the zephyr gently stirring the leaves, draws whistling tones from pines and firs, resem-bling oft the notes of the swan : and roses, violets, and other flowers, gently swayed, and (κυανίζοντα) dark-dimpling, show like a sea just rippled over with gentle undulations. Nay, many are the images one might find. Thus, when one looks at the roses, one shall fancy that he beholds in them the rainbow ; in the violets a waving sea ; in the lilies, the sky. But[6] not by the spectacle alone, and the beholding, does such an one then cause delight : but also in the very body of him that looks to the meadow, rather it refreshes him, and causes him to breathe freely, so that he thinks himself more in heaven than on

---

[1] In the original the pronouns are ἐκείνος (God), οὗτος (the Devil ; for which however our Mss. have οὐ τὰ and αὐτὰ)· then inversely, ἐκείνος (the Devil), οὗτος (God). The modern text reduces the antithesis to regularity by transposing the first and second clause, with ἐκείνος, οὗτος, in each member. Mr. Field, however, *Hom. in Matt.* 709 B. not. has remarked, that St. Chrys. is negligent in his use of these pronouns, and this passage may be added to those cited.

[2] Ἴδωμεν τί χρησιμώτερον, τί δαὶ (δὲ, A. N.) ὠφελιμώτερον. (Here N. adds: Μὴ τοῦτο δῶμεν τί χρησιμώτερον· τὶ δὲ ὠφελιμώ-τερον;) Μὴ τοῦτο φησὶν εἴπῃς· ἀλλ᾽ ἐννόησον ὅτι διάβολός ἐστιν· μάλιστα μὲν ἂν ἐκείνο δειχθῇ· δεῖ καὶ πόνους ὑποστῆναι καὶ πάλιν, κ. τ. λ. The addition in N. is perhaps the result of uninten-tional repetition. If meant for emendation, it supposes an antithesis of χρησ. and ὠφελιμώτερον : " let us grant which is more serviceable (to others) : but (the question is) which is more profitable (to one's self)." This, however, is not what the context requires. Rather it seems that something is omitted after εἴπῃς : e. g. ἀλλ᾽ ἴδωμεν τί εὐκολώτερον, " But let us see which is more easy." In the following sentence, it is not clear whether μάλιστα μὲν belongs to δεῖ καὶ π. ὑ. "of course, if the former appear to be the case, it is necessary," etc. or, to the preceding clause, as in the translation: "above all (con-sider that it is the devil who gives the bidding), if that appear to be the case (i. e. that it is the easier of the two) : it is need-ful," etc.—Edd. " But not only this, but bethink you that he indeed is the devil : for above all if that be shown, again the prize of victory shall be greater."

[3] διὰ τοῦτο, i. e. by enjoining τὰ συμφέροντα, although φορτικὰ, are fathers and masters shown to be truly such, whereas kid-nappers who steal away children, seduce them by promising pleasure, and λυμεῶνες, masters who ruin their servants, let them have their own way.—Morel. Ben. Ἐκεῖνοι δὲ ἀνδραπ. καὶ λυμ. καὶ πάντα τὰ ἐνάντια : " but the others are kidnappers and destroyers, and all that is contrary (to fathers and masters)." Savil. as above.

[4] Πλὴν ὅτι καὶ ἡδονὴν ἔχει, δῆλον ἐκεῖθεν. We have supplied the interpretation in the translation. Ἐκεῖθεν, i. e. from that saying, " Come unto Me." etc. D. has ἐντεῦθεν· i. e. " is man-ifest from the following consideration."

[5] Here is another instance of the negligent use of the pro-nouns ἐκείνος and οὗτος noticed above (note [1]). In the modern text this is altered, besides other changes intended as im-provements upon the ornate description following. We have retained the original text throughout.

[6] Οὐ τῇ θέᾳ δὲ μόνον οὐδὲ τῇ ὄψει τέρπει (Sav. τέρποιτο ἄν) τότε ὁ τοιοῦτος, ἀλλὰ καὶ (ἐν B. C.) τῷ σώματι αὐτῷ τοῦ πρὸς τὸν λειμ-ῶνα ὁρῶντος, (τοῦ π. τ. λ. ὁ. om. Sav. with full stop at αὐτῷ.) ἐκεῖνον (γὰρ add. B. Sav.) μᾶλλον ἀνίησι κ. τ. λ. Savile's read-ing, adopted by Ben. rests on the sole authority of the New College Ms. and is manifestly a correction, as the Paris Editor remarks. (This Ms. has the clause τοῦ . . . . ὁρῶντος, but dotted for correction or omission, and the γὰρ is added by a later hand.) But the passage seems to be incurably corrupt, and only so much of the sense can be guessed at, that the de-light is said not only to affect the eye, but to be felt through the whole frame of the beholder.

earth. There is withal a sound of a different kind, when water from the mountain-steep, borne by its own force through ravines, gently plashes over its pebbly bed with lulling noise, and so relaxes our frame with the pleasurable sensations, as quickly to draw over our eyes the soft languor of slumber. You have heard the description with pleasure: perhaps also it has made you enamored of solitude. But sweeter far than this solitude is the soul * * of the long-suffering. For it was not for the sake of describing a meadow, nor for the sake of making a display of language, that we have broached this similitude : but the object was, that, seeing how great is the delight of the long suffering, and how, by converse with a long suffering man, one would be far more both delighted and benefited, than by frequenting such spots, ye may follow after such men. For when not even a breath of violence proceeds from such a soul, but mild and engaging words, then indeed does that gentle softness of the zephyr find its counterpart : entreaties also, devoid of all arrogance, but forming the resemblance to those winged warblers,—how is not this far better? For not the body is fanned by the soft breeze of speech; no, it refreshes our souls [1] heated and glowing. A physician, by ever so great attention, could not so speedily rid a man of the fever, as a patient man would cool, by the breath of his own words, a person who was passionate and burning with wrath. And why do I speak of a physician? Not even iron, made red-hot and dipped into water, so quickly parts with its heat, as does the passionate man when he comes in contact with the soul of the long-suffering. But as, if it chance that singing birds find their way into the market, they go for nothing there, just so is it with our precepts when they light upon souls addicted to wrathful passions. Assuredly, sweeter is gentleness than bitterness and frowardness. —Well, but the one was God's bidding, the other the devil's. Do you see that it was not for nothing that I said, even if there were no devil or God in the case, the things enjoined would be enough in themselves to (ἀποστῆσαι) revolt us? For the one is both agreeable to himself, and serviceable to others, the other displeasing to himself, and hurtful to others. Nothing is more unpleasant than a man in a passion, nothing more noisome, more odious, more shocking,

as also nothing more pleasing than one who knows not what it is to be in a passion. Better dwell with a wild beast than with a passionate man. For the beast, when once tamed, abides by its law ; but the man, no matter how often you have tamed him, again turns wild, unless [2] however he should of himself settle down into some such habit (of gentleness). For as a bright sunny day and winter with all its gloom, so are the soul of the angry and that of the gentle. However, let us at present look not to the mischievous consequences resulting to others, but to those which affect the persons themselves : though indeed it is also no slight mischief (to one's self) to cause ill to another: for the present, however, let that be the consideration. What executioner with his lash can so lacerate the ribs, what red-hot lancets (ὀβελίσκοι) ever so pierced the body, what madness can so dispossess a man of his natural reason, as anger and rage do,? I know many instances of persons engendering diseases by giving loose to anger : and the worst of fevers are precisely these. But if they so injure the body, think of the soul ! For do not argue that you do not see the mischief, but rather consider, if that which is the recipient of the malignant passion is so hurt, what must be the hurt sustained by that which engenders it ! Many have lost their eyes, many have fallen into most grievous disease. Yet he that bears bravely, shall endure all things easily. But, however, both such are the troublesome tasks the devil enjoins, and the wages he assigns us for these is hell. He is both devil and foe to our salvation, and we rather do his bidding than Christ's, Saviour as He is, and Benefactor and Defender, and speaking as He does such words, which are both sweeter, and more reverend, and more profitable and beneficial, and are both to ourselves and to those who live in our company the greatest of blessings. Nothing worse than anger, my beloved, nothing worse than unseasonable wrath. It will not have any long delay ; it is a quick, sharp passion. Many a time has a mere word been blurted out in anger, which needs for its curing a whole lifetime, and a deed been done which was the ruin of the man for life. For the worst of it is this, that in a little moment, and by one act, and by a single word, full oft has it cast us out from the possession of eternal good, and brought

---

[1] ἀλλὰ ψυχὰς ἀνίησιν θερμαινομένη καὶ ζέουσα. (θέουσα A.) The latter words, "heated and glowing," as manifestly unsuitable to αὖρα are omitted in the modern text. They seem to be a fragment of a sentence describing the heat of fever, or of passion.

[2] πλὴν εἰ μὴ εἰς ἕξιν ἑαυτόν τινα τοιαύτην καταστήσειε. Edd. ἅπαξ εἰς ἕξιν . . . . καταστήσας : "having settled himself down into some such habit." But the old reading is preferable. "You may pacify him again and again, but the fit is subdued for the time, not the temper changed. There will be a fresh outbreak by and bye, unless indeed by self-discipline (ἑαυτὸν κατ.) he bring himself into a habit," etc.

to nought a world of pains. Wherefore I beseech you to do all you can to curb this savage beast. Thus far, however, I have spoken concerning meekness and wrath; if one should take in hand to treat of other opposites, as covetousness and the mad passion for glory, contrasted with contempt of wealth and of glory; intemperance with sobriety; envy with benevolence; and to marshal them each against its opposite, then one would know how great the difference.

Behold how from the very things enjoined it is plainly shown, that the one master is God, the other the devil! Why then, let us do God's bidding, and not cast ourselves into bottomless pits; but while there is time, let us wash off all that defiles the soul, that we may attain unto the eternal blessings, through the grace and mercy of our Lord Jesus Christ, with Whom to the Father and Holy Ghost together be glory, power, honor, now and ever, and world without end. Amen.

HOMILY VII.

ACTS II. 37.

"Now when they heard these words (E. V. 'this,') they were pricked in their heart, and said unto Peter and to the rest of the Apostles, Men and brethren, what shall we do?"

Do you see what a great thing gentleness is? More than any vehemence, it pricks our hearts, inflicts a keener wound. For as in the case of bodies which have become callous, the man that strikes upon them does not affect the sense so powerfully, but if he first mollify them and make them tender, then he pierces them effectually; so in this instance also, it is necessary first to mollify. But that which softens, is not wrath, not vehement accusation, not personal abuse; it is gentleness. The former indeed rather aggravate the callousness, this last alone removes it. If then you are desirous to reprove any delinquent, approach him with all possible mildness. For see here; he gently reminds them of the outrages they have committed, adding no comment; he declares the gift of God, he goes on to speak of the grace which bore testimony to the event, and so draws out his discourse to a still greater length. So they stood in awe of the gentleness of Peter, in that he, speaking to men who had crucified his Master, and breathed murder against himself and his companions, discoursed to them in the character of an affectionate father and teacher. Not merely were they persuaded; they even condemned themselves, they came to a sense of their past behavior. For he gave no room for their anger to be roused, and darken their judgment, but by means of humility he dispersed, as it were, the mist and darkness of their indignation, and then pointed out to them the daring outrage they had committed. For so it is; when we say of ourselves that we are injured, the opposite party endeavor to prove that they

have not done the injury; but when we say, we have not been injured, but have rather done the wrong, the others take the contrary line. If, therefore, you wish to place your enemy (εἰς ἀγῶνα) in the wrong, beware of accusing him; nay (ἀγώνισαι), plead for him, he will be sure to find himself guilty. There is a natural spirit of opposition in man. Such was the conduct of Peter. He did not accuse them harshly; on the contrary, he almost endeavored to plead for them, as far as was possible. And this was the very reason that he penetrated into their souls. You will ask, where is the proof that they were pricked? In their own words; for what say they? "Men and brethren, what shall we do?" Whom they had called deceivers, they call "brethren:" not that hereby they put themselves on an equality with them, but rather by way of attracting their brotherly affection and kindness: and besides,[1] because the Apostles had deigned to call them by this title. And, say they, "What shall we do?" They did not straightway say, Well then, we repent; but they surrendered themselves to the disciples. Just as a person on the point of shipwreck, upon seeing the pilot, or in sickness the physician, would put all into his hands, and do his bidding in everything; so have these also confessed that they are in extreme peril, and destitute of all hope of salvation. They did not say, How shall we be saved? but, "What shall we do?" Here again Peter, though the question is put to all, is the man to answer. "Repent," says he, "and be bap-

---

[1] This is strangely rendered by Ben. *At alioquin, postquam illos sic appellare dignati fuerant, et dixerant.* Erasmus rightly, *Et aliter: quoniam illi eos primum ita appellare dignati fuerunt.* Œcumen. "And because Peter in the beginning of his discourse had so addressed them, hence they themselves had a handle for so addressing the Apostles."

tized every one of you, in the name of Jesus Christ." (v. 38.) He does not yet say, Believe, but, "Be baptized every one of you." For [1] this they received in baptism. Then he speaks of the gain; "For the remission of sins, and ye shall receive the gift of the Holy Ghost." If you are to receive a gift, if baptism conveys remission, why delay? He next gives a persuasive turn to his address, adding, "For the promise is unto you" (v. 39): for he had spoken of a promise above. "And to your children," he says: the gift is greater, when these are to be heirs of the blessings. "And to all," he continues, "that are afar off:" if to those that are afar off, much more to you that are near: "even as many as the Lord our God shall call." Observe the time he takes for saying, "To those that are afar off." It is when he finds them conciliated and self-accusing. For when the soul pronounces sentence against itself, no longer can it feel envy. "And with many other words did he testify, and exhort, saying." (v. 40.) Observe how, throughout, the writer studies brevity, and how free he is from ambition and display. "He testified and exhorted, saying." This is the perfection of teaching, comprising something of fear and something of love. "Save yourselves from this untoward generation." He says nothing of the future, all is about the present, by which indeed men are chiefly swayed; he shows that the Gospel releases from present [2] evils as well. "Then they that gladly received his word were baptized; and the same day there were added unto them about three thousand souls." (v. 41.) Think you not this cheered the Apostles more than the miracle? "And they continued steadfastly and with one accord in the Apostles' doctrine and fellowship." * (v. 42.) Here are two virtues, perseverance and concord. "In the Apostles' doctrine," he says: for they again taught

them; "and fellowship, and in breaking of bread, and in prayer." All in common, all with perseverance. "And fear came upon every soul" (v. 43): of those that believed. For they did not despise the Apostles, like common men, nor did they fix their regard on that which was visible merely. Verily, their thoughts were kindled into a glow. [3] And as Peter had before spoken much, and declared the promises, and the things to come, well might they be beside themselves with fear. The wonders also bore witness to the words: "Many wonders and signs were done by the Apostles." As was the case with Christ; first there were signs, then teaching, then wonders; so was it now. "And all that believed were together, and had all things common." (v. 44.) Consider what an advance was here immediately! For the fellowship was not only in prayers, nor in doctrine alone, but also in (πολιτεία) social relations. "And sold their possessions and goods, and parted them to all men, as every man had need." See what fear was wrought in them! "And they parted them," he says, showing the (τὸ οἰκονομικὸν) wise management: "As every man had need." Not recklessly, like some philosophers among the Greeks, of whom some gave up their land, others cast into the sea great quantities of money; but this was no contempt of riches, but only folly and madness. For universally the devil has made it his endeavor to disparage the creatures of God, as if it were impossible to make good use of riches. "And continuing daily with one accord in the temple" (v. 46), they enjoyed the benefit of teaching. Consider how these Jews did nothing else great or small, than assiduously attend at the temple. For, as having become more earnest, they had increased devotion also to the place. For the Apostles did not for the present pluck them away from this object, for fear of injuring them. "And breaking bread from house to house, did take their portion of food with gladness and singleness of heart, praising God, and having favor with all the people." (v. 47.) It seems to me that in mentioning "bread," he here signifies fasting and hard life; for they "took their portion of food," not of dainty fare. "With gladness," he says. Seest thou that not the dainty fare, but the (τροφῆς οὐ τρυφῆς) food made the enjoyment. For they that fare daintily are under punishment and pain; but not so these. Do you see that the words of Peter contain this also, namely, the regulation of life? ["And single-

[1] Τοῦτο γὰρ ἐν τῷ βαπτίσματι παρέλαβον. St. Chrysostom cannot mean to say that they received the gift of faith in baptism, not having it before: (see Mark xvi. 16, Acts viii. 37.) But the meaning seems to be, with allusion to the *traditio symboli* in baptism, "He does not as yet say, "Believe:" the question, "Dost thou believe?" would be put to them in their baptism, when the Creed was delivered to them. So that the injunction "Believe" is in fact included in the "Be baptized."

[2] We adopt the reading of A. N. The other Mss. have καὶ τῶν παρόντων καὶ τῶν μελλόντων ἀπαλλάττει κακῶν, "both from present and from future evils." Below, v. 42, ὁμοθυμαδὸν, which Chrys. seems to have had in his copy, was probably derived into this verse after προσκαρτ. from προσκαρτ. ὁμοθ. v. 46.

* The exact force of κοινωνία here has been much disputed. By many it is thought to mean *communication* (to the needy) in the having all things common (κοινά), Ols., Lechler, et al. By others it is understood to refer to the Lord's Supper, but against this view is the fact that κοινωνία did not become a name for the sacrament until the third or fourth century. Others render: *fellowship* understanding either the participation in common meals (ἀγάπαι) or the enjoyment of mutual sympathy, helpfulness and encouragement—the fellowship of Christian friendship. So Bengel, Mey., Hack., Gloag. This view is the preferable one.—G. B. S.

[3] Of our Mss. N. E. have the true reading, πεπύρωτο, which is attested by the Catena: the rest, πεπώρωτο "were hardened."

ness of heart."] For no gladness can exist where there is no simplicity. How had they "favor with all the people?" On account of their alms deeds. For do not look to the fact, that the chief priests for envy and spite rose up against them, but rather consider that "they had favor with the people."—"And the Lord added to the Church daily (ἐπὶ τὸ αὐτό) [together] such as should be saved.—And [1] all that believed were together." Once more, the unanimity, the charity, which is the cause of all good things!*

["Now when they heard this," etc. "Then Peter said unto them," etc.] (Recapitulation, v. 37.) What had been said was not enough. For those sayings indeed were sufficient to bring them to faith; but these are to show what things the believer behooves to do. And he said not, In the Cross, but, "In the name of Jesus Christ let every one of you be baptized." (v. 38.) And he does not put them continually in mind of the Cross, that he may not seem to reproach them, but he says simply, "Repent: and why? That we may be punished? No: "And let each of you be baptized in the name of Jesus Christ, for the remission of sins." And yet quite other is the law of this world's tribunals: but in the case of the Gospel proclamation (κηρύγματος); when the delinquent has confessed, then is he saved! Observe how Peter does not instantly hurry over this, but he specifies also the conditions, and adds, "Ye shall receive the gift of the Holy Ghost;" an assertion accredited by the fact, that the Apostles themselves had received that gift. ["For the promise," etc.] (v. 39.) "The promise," i. e. the gift of the Holy Ghost.[2] So far, he speaks of the easy

part, and that which has with it a great gift; and then he leads them to practice : for it will be to them a ground of earnestness, to have tasted already of those so great blessings ["and with many other words did he testify," etc.] (v. 40). Since, however, the hearer would desire to learn what was the sum and, substance of these further words, he tells us this : ["Saying, save yourselves from this untoward generation."] ["They then, that gladly received his words," etc.] (v. 41) they approved of what had been said, although fraught with terror, and after their assent given, proceed at once to baptism.[3] "And they continued" it is written, "steadfastly in the doctrine" (or, "teaching") "of the Apostles" (v. 42): for it was not for one day, no nor for two or three days that they were under teaching as being persons who had gone over to a different course of life. [4] ["And they continued with one accord in the Apostles' doctrine," etc.] The expression is not, ὁμοῦ "together," but ὁμοθυμαδὸν, "with one accord;" ("and daily," he says [afterwards], "they were continuing with one accord in the temple,") ʔ. e. with one soul. [5] And here again in his conciseness, he does not relate the teaching given; for as young children, the Apostles nourished them with spiritual food. "And fear came upon every soul" (v. 43): clearly, of those, as well, who did not believe; namely, upon seeing so great a change all at once effected, and besides in consequence of the miracles. ["And all that believed were together, and had all things in common," etc.] (v. 44.) They are all become angels on a sudden; all of them continuing in prayer and hearing, they saw that spiritual things are *common*, and no one there has more than other, and they speedily came together (ἐπὶ τὸ αὐτὸ), to the same thing in common, even to the imparting to all.[6] "And all the believing" (v. 44), it says,

---

[1] This citation from v. 44. is not misplaced: it refers to the words ἐπὶ τὸ αὐτὸ with which in Chrysostom's copy and many considerable authorities, this verse ended. ('Ο Κύριος προσε. τ. σως. καθ᾽ ἡμέραν ἐπὶ τὸ αὐτό. Πέτρος δὲ καὶ Ἰ. ἀνέβαινον κ. τ. λ. Lachm.)—In the opening of the next paragraph, the modern text has: "And with many other words he testified. This he says, showing that what had been said," etc. But it is evident that the recapitulation begins here, with v. 37. and τὰ λεχθέντα, and ἐκεῖνα, mean the preceding discourse, v. 14-36.; ταῦτα, not "the many other words," v. 40. but, "Repent and be baptized."

* The main lines of the picture which Luke here draws of the Apostolic community are: (1) Constant teaching and exhortation on the part of the Apostles. (2) Christian fellowship, with prayer and the regular observance of the Lord's Supper. (3) The doing of miracles. (4) The contribution of all to the common fund—not all at once, but gradually and as' occasion required—as the imperfects and καθότι ἄν τις χρείαν εἶχεν (v. 44) show. (5) The confident hope and exultant joy with which the work of the new kingdom was carried forward in the conviction that the gospel was for all (v. 39). The πᾶσιν τοῖς εἰς μακράν must, we think, refer to the heathen (Calv., Beng., Lech., De W., Lange, Alf., Hack., Gl.) and not merely to distant members of the Jewish nation (Baumg., Mey.).—G. B. S.

[2] In the old text (Mss. and Catena) after τῶν πλειόνων λόγων τὸ κεφάλαιον comes the clause τοῦτό ἐστι, φησὶν, ἡ δωρεὰ τοῦ Ἀ. Πν. where it is clearly misplaced: for τὸ εὔκολον κ. τ. λ. is, "Be baptized, and ye shall receive," etc., and τότε ἐπὶ τὸν βίον ἄγει refers to v. 40.: "And with many other words," of which πλειόνων λόγων the κεφάλαιον is, "Save yourselves," etc. Hence the clause must belong to v. 39. and accordingly the Catena gives the whole passage from Ἀξιόπιστος ὁ λόγος to ἐπὶ τὸ βαπτ. ἐξέρχονται. as the comment on v. 38, 39. We have re-

stored the proper order, and supplied the omitted citations.— The modern text after τὸ κεφάλαιον, has καὶ τοῦτο προστίθησι, δεικνὺς, ὅτι ἡ δωρεὰ τοῦ Ἀ. Πν. "Since the hearer, etc. this also he adds, showing that it is the gift of the Holy Ghost."— But the "hearer" is the person hearing or reading the narrative.

[3] Here E. strangely inserts the formula of recapitulation, Ἀλλ᾽ ἴδωμεν ἄνωθεν τὰ λεγόμενα : received by Sav., Ben. but bracketted by Morel.

[4] Here the Mss. have: "And fear came," etc., v. 43, with its comment, which we have restored to its proper place.

[5] Οὐχὶ ὁμοῦ δὲ, ἀλλ᾽ ὁμοθυμαδὸν ἦσαν· "καθ᾽ ἡμέραν τε φησὶν, προσκαρτ. ὁμοθυμ. ἐν τῷ ἱερῷ," τουτέστι, μιᾷ ψυχῇ. B. C. F. D. St. Chrys. here returns to v. 42. in which he read in his copy the word ὁμοθυμαδόν. Commenting on that expression, he refers to v. 46 (as his remark on that verse above was that they were taught, τῆς διδασκαλίας ἀπέλαυον, in the Temple). Or perhaps this clause may have been added by the scribe, because he did not find προσκαρτ. ὁμοθ. in v. 42, but did find it in v. 46.—E. "But he says not ὁμοῦ, but ὁμοθ since it is possible to be ὁμοῦ yet not ὁμοθ., when people are divided in opinion. And with words he exhorted. And here again," etc. So Edd.

[6] Ἐπὶ τοῦτο, ἐπὶ τὸ πᾶσι μεταδοῦναι B. C. D. F. N. Cat. on v. 46, but on v. 45, Cat. has ἐπὶ τὸ αὐτὸ, which is doubtless the true reading : for which the innovator, not understanding it, has ἐπὶ τὸ τὰ αὐτῶν πᾶσι διαδοῦναι. On ἐπὶ τὸ αὐτὸ compare the comment on ch. iv. 32. in Hom. xi. §. 1.

were ἐπὶ τὸ αὐτὸ: and to see that this does not mean that they were together in place, observe what follows [" And had all things common"]. " All," it says : not one with the exception of another. This was an angelic commonwealth, not to call anything of theirs their own. Forthwith the root of evils was cut out. By what they did, they showed what they had heard : this was that which he said, " Save yourselves from this untoward generation."— " And daily continuing with one accord in the temple." (v. 46.) Since they are become three thousand, they take them abroad now : and [1] withal, the boldness imparted by the Spirit being great : and daily they went up as to a sacred place, as frequently we find Peter aud John doing this : for at present they disturbed none of the Jewish observances. And this honor too passed over to the place ; the eating in the house. In what house ? In the Temple.[2] Observe the increase of piety. They cast away their riches, and rejoiced, and had great gladness, for greater were the riches they received without labor (ἄπονα Cat. al. ἀγαθά). None reproached, none envied, none grudged; no pride, no contempt was there. As children they did indeed account themselves to be under teaching : as new born babes, such was their disposition. Yet why use this faint image ? If you remember how it was when God shook our city with an earthquake, how subdued all men were. (Infra, Hom. xli. § 2.) Such was the case then with those converts. No knavery, no villany then : such is the effect of fear, of affliction ! No[3] talk of " mine " and " thine " then. Hence gladness waited at their table ; no one seemed to eat of his own, or of another's ;— I grant this may seem a riddle. Neither did they consider their brethren's property foreign to themselves ; it was[4] the property of a Master ; nor again deemed they aught their own, all was the brethren's. The poor man knew no shame, the rich no haughtiness. This is gladness. The latter deemed himself the obliged and fortunate party ; the others felt themselves as honored herein, and closely were they bound together. For indeed, because

when people make doles of money, there are apt to be insults, pride, grudging ; therefore says the Apostle, " Not grudgingly, or of necessity."—(2 Cor. ix. 7.) [" With gladness and simplicity of heart," etc.] See of how many things he bears witness to them ! Genuine faith, upright conduct, perseverance in hearing, in prayers, in singleness, in cheerfulness. [" Praising God."] (v. 47.) Two things there were which might deject them ; their abstemious living, and the loss of their property. Yet on both these accounts did they rejoice. [" And having favor with all the people."] For who but must love men of this character, as common fathers ? They conceived no malice toward each other ; they committed all to the grace of God. [" With all the people."] Fear there was none ; yea, though they had taken their position in the midst of dangers. [5] By singleness, however, he denotes their entire virtue, far surpassing their contempt of riches, their abstinence, and their preseverance in prayer. For thus also they offered pure praise to God : this is to praise God. But observe also here how they immediately obtain their reward. " Having favor with all the people." They were engaging, and highly beloved. For who would not prize and admire their simplicity of character ; who would not be linked to one in whom was nothing underhand ? To whom too does salvation belong, but to these ? To whom those great marvels ? Was it not to shepherds that the Gospel was first preached ? and to Joseph, [6] being a man of simple mind, insomuch that he did not let a suspicion of adultery frighten him into doing wrong ? Did not God elect rustics, those artless men ? For it is written, " Blessed is every simple soul." (Prov. xi. 25.) And again, " He that walketh simply, walketh surely." (Prov. x. 9.) " True," you will say, " but prudence also is needed." Why, what is simplicity, I pray you, but prudence ? For when you suspect no evil, neither can you fabricate any : when you have no annoyances, neither can you remember injuries. Has any one insulted you ? You were not pained. Has any one reviled you? You were nothing hurt. Has he envied you ? Still you had no hurt. Simplicity is a high road to true philosophy. None so beautiful in soul as the simple. For as in regard of personal appearance, he that is sullen, and downcast, and reserved (σύννους), even if he

---

[1] ἄμα τῆς τούτων (N. and Cat. τοῦ Πνεύματος) παρρησίας (παρουσίας B.) πολλῆς οὔσης, καθ' ἡμέραν τε κ. τ. λ. B. C. D. F. N. Cat. We have adopted the reading preserved by N. and the Catena.—E. and Edd. " Who also with boldness, seeing there was great boldness now, daily went up and continued in the Temple."

[2] καὶ αὐτὴ (l. αὕτη δὲ ἡ τιμὴ εἰς τὸν τόπον διέβαινε τὸ ἐν τῷ οἴκῳ ἐσθίειν· ποίῳ οἴκῳ ; ἐν τῷ ἱερῷ B. C. D. F. Cat. This " eating in the house " refers to the clause κλῶντες τε κατ' οἶκον ἄρτον. If the passage be sound, Chrys. here represents that the Temple was honored by the breaking of bread (the Holy Eucharist ?), there—Edd. from E. καὶ αὐτὴ δὲ ἡ εἰς τὸν τόπον τιμὴ διέβαινε πρὸς τὸν τοῦ ἱεροῦ Δεσπότην· " And the honor itself paid to the place passed over to the Lord of the Temple."

[3] Edd. add, τὸ ψυχρὸν ῥῆμα, " That cold expression."

[4] Δεσποτικὰ, i. e. of Christ their common Master. But Erasm. Erant enim ut dominorum, and so Ben.

---

[5] καὶ ταῦτα ἐν μέσοις κινδύνοις ἐμβεβληκότων αὐτῶν. Erasm. omits the two last words: Ben. in media pericula conjectis. The meaning is: " Not even in the midst of dangers, which they themselves had boldly charged, or, invaded."

[6] Although he speaks below of Joseph the Patriarch, it seems that the husband of Mary is meant here.

be good-looking, loses much of his beauty; while he that relaxes his countenance, and gently smiles, enhances his good looks ; so in respect of the soul, he that is reserved, if he have ten thousand good points, disfigures them; but the frank and simple, just the reverse. A man of this last description may be safely made a friend, and when at variance easily reconciled. No need of guards and outposts, no need of chains and fetters with such an one; but great is his own freedom, and that of those who associate with him. But what, you will say, will such a man do if he fall among wicked people ? God, Who has commanded us to be simple-minded, will stretch out His hand. What was more guileless than David? What more wicked than Saul ? Yet who triumphed? Again, in Joseph's case ; did not he in simplicity approach his master's wife, she him with wicked art ? Yet what, I pray, was he the worse ? Furthermore, what more simple than was Abel ? what more malicious than Cain ? And Joseph again, had he not dealt artlessly with his brethren ? Was not this the cause of his eminence, that he spoke out unsuspiciously, while they received his word sin malice ? He declared once and again his dreams unreservedly ; and then again he set off to them carrying provisions ; he used no caution ; he committed all to God : nay, the more they held him in the light of an enemy, the more did he treat them as brothers. God had power not to have suffered him to fall into their hands; but that the wonder might be made manifest, how, though they do their worst, he shall be higher than they : though the blow do come upon him, it comes from another, not from himself. On the contrary, the wicked man strikes himself first, and none other than himself. "For[1] alone," it is said, "shall he bear his troubles." (Prov. ix. 12.) Ever in him the soul is full of dejection, his thoughts being ever entangled : whether he must hear aught or say aught, he does all with complaints, with accusation. Far, very far from such do friendship and harmony make their abode : but fightings are there, and enmities, and all unpleasantness. They that are such suspect even themselves. To these not even sleep is sweet, nor anything else. And have they a wife also, lo, they are enemies and at war with all : what endless jealousies, what unceasing fear ! Aye, the wicked, πονηρὸς has his name from πονεῖν, "to have trouble." And, indeed, thus the Scripture is ever calling "wickedness" by the name of labor ; as, for

instance, "Under his tongue is toil and labor ;" and again, "In the midst of them is toil and labor." (Ps. x. 7 ; xc. 10; and lv. 11.)

Now if any one should wonder, whence those who had at first been of this last class, now are so different, let him learn that affliction was the cause, affliction, that schoolmistress of heavenly wisdom, that mother of piety. When riches were done away with, wickedness also disappeared. True, say you, for this is the very thing I am asking about; but whence comes all the wickedness there is now ? How is it that it came into the minds of those three thousand and five thousand straightway, to choose virtue, and that they simultaneously became Christian philosophers, whereas now hardly one is to be found ? how was it that they then were in such harmony ? What was it, that made them resolute and active? What was it that so suddenly inflamed them ? The reason is, that they drew near with much piety ; that honors were not so sought after as they are now ; that they transferred their thoughts to things future, and looked for nothing of things present. This is the sign of an ardent mind, to encounter perils ; this was their idea of Christianity. We take a different view, we seek our comfort here. The result is, that we shall not even obtain this, when the time is come. "What are we to do ?" asked those men. We, just the contrary—"What shall we do?" What behooved to be done, they did. We, quite the reverse.[2] Those men condemned themselves, despaired of saving themselves. This is what made them such as they were. They knew what a gift they had received. But how can you become like them, when you do everything in an opposite spirit ? They heard, and were forthwith baptized. They did not speak those cold words which we do now, nor did they contrive delays (p. 47, note 3); and yet they had heard all the requirements : but that word, "Save yourselves from this generation," made them to be not sluggish ; rather they welcomed the exhortation ; and that they did welcome it, they proved by their deeds, they showed what

---

[1] Μόνος γὰρ, φησὶν, ἀντλήσει τὰ κακά. A. omits this and the next clause: E. substitutes, "so is he even to himself an enemy. Of such an one the soul is," etc. so Edd.

[2] We adopt the reading preserved by A. N. (what is also contained in the modern text with additions meant for explanation.) "Τί ποιήσωμεν ;" ἠρώτων ἐκεῖνοι. Ἡμεῖς δὲ τὸ ἐναντίον· Τί ποιήσομεν ; ῞Απερ ἔδει γενέσθαι ἐποίουν. Ἡμεῖς δε τοὐναντίον. The modern text, after ἠρ. ἐκεῖνοι, inserts, ἀπογινώσκοντες ἑαυτῶν· "despairing of themselves:" and, after the second question, λέγομεν, ἐπιδεικνύμενοι πρὸς τοὺς παρόντας, καὶ μέγα φρονοῦντες ἐφ᾽ ἑαυτοῖς· "Say (we), showing off ourselves to those present, and thinking great things of ourselves." B. C. omit, perhaps by oversight, the clauses between, Τί ποιήσωμεν (B. τί ποιήσομεν); and, ῞Απερ ἔδει. In the following sentences, the force of the verbs κατέγνωσαν, ἀπέγνωσαν, ἔγνωσαν might be rendered thus: "They knew themselves guilty, knew that in them was no power to save themselves—knew what a gift they received."

manner of men they were. They entered· at once the lists, and took off the coat ; whereas we do enter, but we intend to fight with our coat on. This is the cause that our antagonist has so little trouble, for we get entangled in our own movements, and are continually thrown down. We do precisely the same thing as he who, having [1] to cope with a man frantic, breathing fire ; and seeing him, a professed wrestler, covered with dust, tawny, stripped, clotted with dirt from the sand and sun, and running down with sweat and oil and dirt ; himself, smelling of perfumes, should put on his silken garments, and his gold shoes, and his robe hanging down to his heels, and his golden trinkets on the head, and so descend into the arena, and grapple with him. Such a one will not only be impeded, but being taken up with the sole idea of not staining or rending his fine clothes, will tumble at the very first onset, and withal will suffer that which he chiefly dreaded, the damage of those his fond delights. The time for the contest is come, and say, are you putting on your silks ? It is the time of exercise, the hour of the race, and are you adorning yourself as for a procession ? Look not to outward things, but to the inward. For by the thoughts about these things the soul is hampered on all sides, as if by strong cords, so that she cannot let you raise a hand, or contend against the adversary ; and makes you soft and effeminate. One may think himself, even when released from all these ties, well off, to be enabled to conquer that impure power. And on this account Christ too did not allow the parting with riches alone to suffice, but what saith He ? " Sell whatsoever thou hast, and give to the poor, and come and follow Me." (Mark x. 21.) Now if, even when we cast away our riches, we are not yet in a safe position, but stand still in need of some further art and close practice ; much more, if we retain them, shall we fail to achieve great things, and, instead thereof, become a laughing-stock to the spectators, and to the evil one himself. For even though there were no devil, though there were none to wrestle with us, yet ten thousand roads on all sides lead the lover of money to hell. Where now are they who ask why the devil was made (διατί ὁ δ. γέγονεν;) ? Behold here the devil has no hand in the work, we do it all ourselves. Of a truth they of the hills might have a right to speak thus, who after they had given proof of their temperance, their contempt of wealth and disregard of all such things, have

infinitely preferred to abandon father, and houses, and·lands, and wife, and children. Yet, they are the last to speak so : but the men who at no time ought to say it, these do say it. Those are indeed wrestlings with the devil ; these he does not think worth entering into. You will say, But it is the devil who instils this same covetousness. Well, flee from it, do not harbor it, O man. Suppose now, you see one flinging out filth from some upper story, and at the same time a person seeing it thrown out, yet standing there and receiving it all on his head : you not only do not pity him, but you are angry, and tell him it serves him right ; and, " Do not be a fool," everyone cries out to him, and lays the blame not so much on the other for shooting out the filth, as on him for letting it come on him. But now, you know that covetousness is of the devil ; you know that it is the cause of ten thousand evils ; you see him flinging out, like filth, his noisome imaginations ; and do you not see that you are receiving on your bare head his nastiness, when it needed but to turn aside a little to escape it altogether ? Just as our man by shifting his position would have escaped ; so, do you refuse to admit such imaginations, ward off the lust. And how am I to do this ? you will ask. Were you a Gentile, and had eyes for things present alone, the matter perhaps might be one of considerable difficulty, and yet even the Gentiles have achieved as much ; but you—a man in expectation of heaven and heavenly bliss—and you to ask, " How am I to repel bad thoughts ? " Were I saying the contrary, then you might doubt : did I say, covet riches, " How shall I covet riches," you might answer, " seeing such things as I do ? " Tell me, if gold and precious stones were set before you, and I were to say, Desire lead, would there not be reason for hesitation ? For you would say, How can I ? But if I said, Do not desire it ; this had been plainer to understand. I do not marvel at those who despise, but at those who despise not riches. This is the character of a soul exceeding full of stupidity, no better than flies and gnats, a soul crawling upon the earth, wallowing in filth, destitute of all high ideas. What is it you say ? Are you destined to inherit eternal life ; and do you say, how shall I despise the present life for the future ? What, can the things be put in competition ?[2] You are to receive a royal vest ; and say you, How shall I despise these rags ? You are going to be led into the king's

---

[1] πρὸς ἄνδρα μαινόμενον ἔχων, πῦρ πνέοντα. E. F. D. and Edd. omit these words.

[2] μὴ γὰρ ἀμφηρισϑὰ τὰ πράγματο ; Erasm. negligently, *non sunt æque amabiles illæ res:* Ben. *num res sunt mutuo comparabiles ?*

palace; and do you say, How shall I despise this present hovel? Of a truth, we ourselves are to blame in every point, we who do not choose to let ourselves be stirred up ever so little. For the willing have succeeded, and that with great zeal and facility. Would that you might be persuaded by our exhortation, and succeed too, and become imitators of those who have been successful, through the grace and mercy of our Lord Jesus Christ, with Whom to the Father and the Holy Ghost together be glory, and power, and honor, now and ever, and world without end. Amen.

HOMILY VIII.

ACTS III. 1.

"Now Peter and John went up together into the temple, at the hour of prayer, being the ninth hour."

EVERYWHERE we find these two Apostles in great harmony together. "To him Simon Peter beckoned." (John xiii. 24.) These two also "came together to the sepulchre. (Ib. xx. 3 *et seq.*) And concerning John, Peter said unto Christ, "And what shall this man do?" (Ib. xxi. 21.) Now as for the other miracles, the writer of this book omits them; but he mentions the miracle by which they were all [1] put in commotion. Observe again that they do not come to them purposely; so clear were they of ambition, so closely did they imitate their Master. Why now did they go up to the temple? Did they still live as Jews? No, but for expediency (χρησίμως).* A miraculous sign again takes place, which both confirms the converts, and draws over the rest; and such, as they were a sign for having wrought. [2] The disease was in the nature of the man, and baffled the art of medicine. He had been forty years lame (ch. iv. 20), as the writer says afterwards, and no one during all that time had cured him. And the most obstinate diseases are those which are born with men. It was a great calamity, insomuch that even to provide for himself his necessary sustenance was impossible for him.

The man was conspicuous both from the place, and from his malady. Hear how the matter is related. "And a certain man, lame from his mother's womb, was carried, whom they laid daily at the gate of the temple which is called Beautiful, to ask alms of them that entered into the temple." (v. 2.) He sought to receive alms, and he did not know who the men were. "Who seeing Peter and John about to go into the temple, asked an alms. And Peter, fastening his eyes upon him, with John, said, Look on us." (v. 3, 4.) Yet, not even so were the man's thoughts elevated, but he persisted in his importunity. For such is poverty; upon a refusal, it compels people still to persist. Let this put us to shame who fall back in our prayers. But observe, I pray you, Peter's gentleness: for he said, "Look on us." So truly did their very bearing, of itself, betoken their character. "And he gave heed unto them, expecting to receive something of them. Then Peter said, Silver and gold have I none; but such as I have I give thee." (v. 5, 6.) He did not say, I give thee something much better than silver or gold: but what? "In the name of Jesus Christ of Nazareth, rise up and walk. And he took him by the right hand, and lifted him up." (v. 7.) Such was also the way of Christ. Often He healed by word, often by an act, often also He stretched forth the hand, where men were somewhat weak in faith, that the cure might not appear to be spontaneous. "And he took him by the right hand, and lifted him up." This act made manifest the Resurrection, for it was an image of the Resurrection. "And immediately his feet and ankle bones received strength. And he leaping up stood, and walked." (v. 8.) Perhaps it was by way of trying himself that he put it thus to further proof, whether perchance the thing done might not be to no purpose. His feet were weak; it was not that he had lost them.

---

[1] Œcumen. has preserved the true reading: ἀφ' οὗ πάντες ἐκινήθησαν. Mss. and Cat. ἐκίνησεν. (N. in the margin, by a later hand, ἐνίκησε.) E. and Edd. ὁ δὲ πολλὴν εἶχε τὴν ἔκπληξιν καὶ πάντας ἐξένισε, τοῦτο λέγει.

* There is no evidence that Peter and John attended upon the Jewish worship simply "for expediency." There is much to the contrary. The early Christians had no idea of ceasing to be Jews. Peter at this time supposed it to be necessary for the Gentile converts to be circumcised (Gal. ii.). It was incident to the gradual separation of Christianity from Judaism that those who had been zealous adherents of the latter should suppose that its forms were still to be the moulds of the new system. They were not for this reason less honestly and genuinely Christian, but had not yet apprehended the principle of Christian liberty as Paul afterward expounded it. The point of difficulty was not so much the entrance of the Gentiles into the Kingdom of God as the question whether they should enter through the gate of Judaism.—G. B. S.

[2] καὶ οἷον σημεῖον ἦσαν ποιήσαντες. E. "And a miracle such as they had not yet wrought." So Edd.

Some say that he did not even know how to walk. [1] "And entered with them into the temple." Of a truth it was marvellous. The Apostles do not urge him ; but of his own accord he follows, by the act of following pointing out his benefactors. "And leaping and praising God ;" not admiring them, but God that wrought by them. The man was grateful.

["Now [2] Peter and John went up together into the temple," etc.] You observe how they continued in prayer. "The ninth hour :" there they prayed together. ["And a certain man," etc.] The man was in the act of being carried at that instant. ["Whom they laid daily :"] (his bearers carried him away :) ["at the gate," etc.] just when people went into the temple. And that you may not suppose that they carried him for some other purpose, but that it was in order that he might receive alms, hear what the writer says : "so that he might receive alms of those entering into the temple." (Recapitulation of vv. 1-8.) And this is the reason why he also makes mention of the places, to give evidence of what he relates. "And how was it," you may ask, "that they did not present him to Christ ?" Perhaps they were certain unbelieving men, that haunted the temple, as in fact neither did they present him to the Apostles, when they saw them entering, after having done such great miracles. "He asked," it is written, "to receive an alms." (v. 3.) Their bearing marked them as certain devout and righteous men. ["And Peter fastening his eyes upon him, with John, said," etc.] (v. 4, 5.) And observe how John is everywhere silent, while Peter makes excuse for him also ; "Silver and gold," he says, "have I none." (v. 6.) He does not say, I have none here, as we are wont to speak, but absolutely, I have none. "What then ?" he might say, "do you take no notice of me, your suppliant ?" Not so, but of what I have, receive thou. Do you remark how unassuming Peter is, how he makes no display even to the object of his beneficence ? ["In the name," etc. "And he took him by the hand," etc.] (v. 7.) And the mouth and the hand did all. Such [3] sort of persons were the Jews ; lame, and the right

thing being to ask for health, these same ask for money, grovelling on the ground : for this it was that they beset the temple—to get money. What then does Peter ? He did not despise him ; he did not look about for some rich subject ; he did not say, If the miracle is not done to some great one (εἰς ἐκεῖνον), nothing great is done : he did not look for some honor from him, no, nor heal him in the presence of people ; for the man was at the entrance, not where the multitude were, that is, within. But Peter sought no such object ; nor upon entering did he proclaim the matter : no, it was by his bearing that he attracted the lame man to ask. And the wonder is, that he believed so readily. For those who are set free from diseases of long standing, hardly believe their very eyesight. Once healed, he remains with the Apostles, giving thanks to God. "And he entered," it is said, "with them into the temple, walking, and leaping, and praising God." (v. 8.) Observe how restless he is, in the eagerness of his delight, at the same time shutting the mouths of the Jews. Also, that he leaped, was to prevent the suspicion of hypocrisy ; for after all, this was beyond the possibility of deception. For if previously he was totally unable to walk, even when hunger pressed hard (and indeed he would not have chosen to share with his bearers the proceeds of his begging, if he had been able to manage for himself), this holds still more in the present case. And how should he have feigned in behalf of those who had given him no alms ? But the man was grateful, even after his recovery. And thus on either side his faith is shown, both by his thankfulness, and by the recent event.

He was so [4] well known to all, that "they recognized him. And all the people," it says, "saw him walking and praising God ; and they recognized (ἐπεγίνωσκον) that it was he which sat for alms at the Beautiful gate of the temple." (v. 9.) It is well said, "they recognized," inasmuch as he was one unknown now by reason of what had happened : for we use this term with regard to objects, which we find a difficulty in recognizing. ["And they were filled with wonder and amazement at

---

[1] Œcumen. "That he leaped was either because he was incredulous of what had happened, or, by way of trying his power of stepping more surely and firmly, or, the man did not know how to walk."

[2] E. and Edd. "But let us look over again what has been said. 'They went up,' he says, 'at the hour of prayer, the 'ninth hour.' Perhaps just at that time they carried and laid the lame man, when people," etc. In the old text the clause αὐτὸν βαστάζοντες ἀπήνεγκαν (which should be οἱ βαστ. αὐτὸν) seems meant to explain καθ᾽ ἡμέραν : they bore him daily, and the same persons carried him away.

[3] E. and Edd. τοιοῦτοί τινες ἦσαν καὶ Ἰουδαῖοι (for οἱ Ἰ.) χωλεύοντες . . . οἱ δὲ (for αὐτοί) μᾶλλον χρήματα αἰτοῦσι . . . οἱ καὶ διὰ τοῦτο . . . "Such sort of people were also [the] Jews, being lame (i e. like many beggars among ourselves): even

when they have only to ask for health, yet they rather ask for money . . . who even for this reason beset the temple," etc. But the meaning seems rather to be : "See here an emblem of the Jews. Lame, and needing but," etc.

[4] οὕτω πᾶσι γνώριμος ἦν ὅτι ἐπεγίνωσκον, A. B. C. D. F. Sav. Morel. Ben. But Commelin. and Ed. Par. Ben. 2. after Erasm. adopt the reading of E. οὐ μὴν πᾶσι γνώριμος ἦν ὅθεν καὶ : because of the following comment on ἐπεγίνωσκον. But the meaning is: They were all acquainted with him (it could not be otherwise): but seeing him walking and leaping, they found it difficult to believe that it was he, and yet they could not doubt it. This is well denoted by ἐπεγίνωσκον : for we use this word, ἐπὶ τῶν μόλις γνωριζομένων : strange as it was, they were satisfied that it was he, the man whom they all knew so well.

that which had happened unto him."] Needs must it be believed that [1] the name of Christ remits sins, seeing it produces even such effects as this. ("And as he held Peter and John, all the people came together at the porch that is called Solomon's, greatly wondering." (v. 11.) From his good feelings and love towards the Apostles, the lame man would not leave them; perhaps he was thanking them openly, and praising them. "And all the people," it is said, "ran together unto them. And when Peter saw them, he answered." (v. 12.) Again it is he who acts, and addresses the people.

And in the former instance, it was the circumstance of the tongues that aroused them to hearing, now it was this miracle; then, he took occasion to speak from their accusations : now, from their supposition. Let us then consider, in what this address differs from the former, and in what it agrees with that. The former was held in a house, before any one has come over, and before they themselves have wrought anything; this, when all are wondering, and the healed man is standing by; when none doubt, as in the other case, where some said "These men are full of new wine." (Acts xii. 13.) At the one, he was surrounded by all the Apostles as he spoke; but at this, he has John alone; for by this time he is bold, and become more energetic. Such is the nature of virtue; once started, it advances, and never stops. Observe also how it was divinely ordered, that the miracle should take place in the temple, that others also might wax bold, while the Apostles work, not in holes (εἰς καταδύσεις) and corners, and in secret : though not in the interior of the temple either, where the greater number were. How then, I pray you, was it believed? The man himself who was healed proclaimed the benefit. For there was no reason why he should lie, nor why he should have joined a different set of people. [2] Either then it was because of the spaciousness of the place, that he there wrought the miracle, or because the spot was retired. And observe the event. They went up for one object, and they accomplished another. Thus also did Cornelius : he prayed and fasted [3] * * *. But hitherto they

always call Him, "of Nazareth." "In the name of Jesus Christ of Nazareth," said Peter, *walk*. For in the first instance, the thing required was, that He should be believed in.

Let us not, I pray you, give over at the beginning of the story : [4] and if one has named some particular achievement of virtue, and then has dropped it for awhile, let us begin over again. If we get into the right mood (ἐν ἕξει), we shall soon arrive at the end, soon reach the summit. For earnestness, it is said, begets earnestness, and dulness begets dulness. He who has effected some little reformation, thereby receives encouragement to approach greater things, and thence again to go on something more than that; and just as it is with fire, the more wood it lays hold on, the more vehement it becomes, so likewise zeal, the more pious reflections it kindles, the more effectually is it armed against their opposites. As, for example : There are set in us, like so many thorns, perjury, falsehood hypocrisy, deceit, dishonesty, abusiveness, scoffing, buffoonery, indecency, scurrility; again under another head, covetousness, rapacity, injustice, calumny, insidiousness; again, wicked lust, uncleanness, lewdness, fornication, adultery; again, envy, emulation, anger, wrath, rancor, revenge, blasphemy, and numberless others. If we effect a reformation in the first instances, not only in them will the success have been achieved, but through them in the following cases also. For reason has then gained more strength to overthrow those other vices. For instance, if he, who has frequently sworn, once extirpates that satanic habit, he has not only gained this point, but a habit of piety in other respects will have been brought in. For no one, I suppose, averse to swearing would easily consent to do any other wicked act; he will feel a reverence for the virtue already acquired. Just as the man who wears a beautiful robe, will blush to roll himself in the mire; so is it also here. From this beginning he will come to learn not to be angry, not to strike, not to insult. For if once he has come right in little matters, the whole affair is done. Often, however, something of this sort takes place, that a person has once reformed, and then again through carelessness falls back into the old sins but too readily, so that the case becomes irremediable. For instance, we have

---

[1] Ἔδει πιστευθῆναι διότι, B. C. δι ὅτι A. This seems to be the comment on the remaining clause of v. 10, which we have supplied: but the meaning is obscure. The modern text has ἔδει γοῦν π. ὅτι.

[2] οὐδὲ γὰρ ἂν ἐψεύσατο, οὐδ᾽ ἂν ἐπ᾽ ἄλλους τινὰς ἦλθεν. It is not clear who are the ἄλλοι τινὲς : and something is wanting. In fact, this part of the Homily is very defective. The next sentence seems to refer to the mention of the porch called Solomon's, but evidently supposes something preceding: e. g. "The miracle was performed at the Beautiful Gate, beside which was the Porch called Solomon's."

[3] E. and Edd. Κορνήλιος ἄλλα νηστεύων ηὔχετο, καὶ ἄλλα ὁρᾷ. "Cornelius prayed with fasting, for one object: and sees a vision of something other than he thought for."

[4] It can hardly be imagined that St. Chrysostom's meaning is correctly reported here. Ἐν ἀρχῇ τοῦ διηγήματος, can only mean, In the beginning of the narrative (of this miracle). It seems that the case of this man, who at first lies at the gate of the temple, unable to stir, and in the end, enters with the Apostles walking and leaping and praising God, furnished the theme for the ethical part of the discourse. "There is the like cure for our souls: let us not give over for want of success in the first attempt, but begin again after every failure."

made it a law to ourselves not to swear; we have got on well, for some three, or even four days; after that being hard put to it, we scattered away the whole of our collected gain; we then fall into indolence and reckless-ness. Still it is not right to give over; one must set to work zealously again. For it is said, he that has built up a house, and then sees his building pulled down, will have less spirit for building again. Yes, but for all this, one must not be dispirited, but must once more set to work zealously.

Let us then lay down daily laws for our-selves. For a time let us begin with the easier. Let us retrench all that superfluity of paths, and put a bridle on our tongues; let no one swear by God. Here is no outlay, here is no fatigue, here is no cost of time. It is sufficient to will, and all is done. It is a matter of habit. I beseech and entreat you, let us contribute thus much of zeal. Tell me, if I had bid you contribute your money, would not each one of you readily cast in according to his ability? If you saw me in extreme danger, would you not, if it had been possible, have cut off your own flesh to give me? Well, I am in danger now, and in great dan-ger, such indeed that, were I withal confined to a dungeon, or had I received ten thousand stripes, or were a convict in the mines, I could not suffer more. Reach me then the hand. Consider how great is the danger, that I should not have been able to reform this which is least: I say "least" in regard to the labor required. What shall I have to say hereafter, when thus called to account? "Why did you not remonstrate? why did you not enjoin? why did you not lay the law be-fore them? why did you not check the diso-bedient?" It will not be enough for me to say, that I did admonish. It will be answered, "You ought to have used more vehement rebuke; since Eli also admonished." (1 Sam. ii. 24.) But God forbid I should compare you with Eli's sons. Indeed, he did admonish them and say, "Nay, my sons, do not so; evil is the report that I hear of you." (1 Sam. iii. 13.) But subsequently the Scripture saith, that he did not admonish his sons: since he did not admonish them severely, or with threats. For is it not strange indeed, that in the synagogues of the Jews the laws are in such force, and whatever the teacher enjoins is performed; while here we are thus despised and rejected? It is not my own glory that I care for (my glory is your good report), but it is for your salvation. Every day we lift up our voice, and shout in your ears. But there is none to hear. Still we take no strong measures. I fear we shall have to give an

account at the coming Day of this excessive and unseasonable leniency.

Wherefore, with a loud and clear voice, I proclaim to all and testify, that those who are notorious for this transgression, who utter words which come "of the evil one," (Matt. v. 37.) (for such is swearing,) shall not step over the threshold of the Church. Let this present month be the time allowed you for reforming in this matter. Talk not to me, "Necessity of business compels me to use oaths, else people do not believe me." To begin with this, retrench those oaths which come merely of habit. I know many will laugh, but it is better to be laughed at now, than wept for hereafter. They will laugh, who are mad. For who, I ask, in his right mind would laugh at the keeping of the command-ment? But suppose they do; why, it will not be at us, but at Christ, that such men will laugh. You shudder at the word! I knew you would. Now if this law were of my mak-ing, at me would be the laughing; but if Another be the Lawgiver, the jeering passes over to Him. Yes, and Christ was once spit upon, and smitten with the palm, smitten upon the face. Now also He bears with this, and it is no wonder (οὐδὲν ἀπεικὸς)! For this, hell is prepared; for this, the worm that dieth not. Behold, again I say and testify; let him laugh that will, let him scoff that listeth. Hereunto are we set, to be laughed at and mocked, to suffer all things. We are "the offscouring" (1 Cor. iv. 13) of the world, as blessed Paul says. If any man refuse to conform to this order, that man I, by my word, as with a trumpet's blast, do prohibit to set foot over the Church's threshold, be he prince, be he even the crowned head. Either depose me from this station, or if I am to remain, ex-pose me not to danger. I cannot bear to ascend this throne, without effecting some great reformation. For if this be impossible, it is better to stand below. Nothing more wretched than a ruler who does his people no good. Do exert yourselves, and attend to this, I entreat you; and let us strive, and of a surety more will come of it. Fast, entreat God (and we will do the same with you) that this pernicious habit may be eradicated. It is no great matter, [1] to become teachers to the world; no small honor to have it said everywhere, that really in this city there is not a man that swears. If this come to pass,

---

[1] Οὐδὲν μέγα ἐστὶ γεν. διδασκ. τῆς οἰκ. Οὐ μικρὸν κ. τ. λ. The passage is manifestly corrupt, and the Mss. lend no assistance. Ben. conjecturally, *Nihil majus est quam esse doctores orbis: nec parum*, etc. Ed. Par. Ben. 2. *Fortasse*, οὐκοῦν μέγα. But it is more likely that something is wanting, e. g. "It is no great matter [to be free from the vice of swearing. But to set an example to others would be a great thing], to be teachers herein of the whole world," etc.

you will receive the reward not only of your own good works; indeed what I am to you, this you will become to the world. Assuredly others also will emulate you; assuredly you will be a candle set upon a candlestick.

And is this, you will say, the whole matter? No, this is not all, but this is a beginning of other virtues. He who swears not, will certainly attain unto piety in other respects, whether he will or not, by dint of self-respect and awe. But you will urge that most men do not keep to it, but fall away. Well, better one man that doeth the will of the Lord, than ten thousand transgressors. In fact, hereby is everything subverted, everything turned upside down, I mean, because after the fashion of the Theatre we desire numbers, not a select number. For what indeed will a multitude be able to profit? Would you learn that it is the saints, not the numbers, which make the multitude? Lead out to war ten hundred thousand men, and one saint, and let us see who achieves the most? Joshua the son of Nun went out to war, and alone achieved all; the rest were of no use. [1] Wouldest thou see, beloved, that the great multitude, when it does not the will of God, is no better than a thing of naught? I wish indeed, and desire, and with pleasure would be torn in pieces, to adorn the Church with a multitude, yea, but a select multitude; yet if this be impossible, that the few should be select, is my desire. Do you not see, that it is better to possess one precious stone, than ten thousand farthing pieces? Do you not see that it is better to have the eye sound, than to be loaded with flesh, and yet deprived of sight? Do you not see that it is better to

have one healthy sheep, than ten thousand with the murrain; that fine children, though few, are better than many children diseased withal; that in the Kingdom there will be few, but in hell many? What have I to do with a multitude? what profit therein? None. Rather they are a plague to the rest. It is as if one who had the option of ten healthy persons of ten thousand sick folks, should take to himself the latter in addition to the ten. The many who do nothing well, will avail us only for punishment hereafter, and disgrace for the time being. For no one will urge it as a point in our favor that we are many; we shall be blamed for being unprofitable. In fact, this is what men always tell us, when we say, We are many; "aye, but bad," they answer.

Behold again: I give warning, and proclaim with a loud voice, let no one think it a laughing matter: I will exclude and prohibit the disobedient; and as long as I sit on this throne, I will give up not one of its rights. If any one depose me from it, then I am no longer responsible; as long as I am responsible, I cannot disregard them; on account not of my own punishment, but of your salvation. For I do exceedingly long for your salvation. To advance it, I endure pain and vexation. But yield your obedience, that both here and hereafter you may receive a plentiful reward, and that we may in common reap eternal blessings; through the grace and mercy of the only-begotten Son of God; to Whom with the Father and the Holy Ghost be glory, power, and honor, now and ever, world without end. Amen.

HOMILY IX.

ACTS III. 12.

" And when Peter saw it, he answered unto the people, Ye men of Israel, why marvel ye at this, or why look ye so earnestly on us, as though by our own power or holiness we have made this man to walk?"

THERE is greater freedom of speech in this harangue, than in the former. Not that he was afraid on the former occasion, but the persons whom he addressed there, being jesters and scoffers, would not have borne it.

Hence in the beginning of that address he also bespeaks their attention by his preamble; "Be this known unto you, and hearken to my words." (ch. ii. 14.) But here there is no need of this management. (κατασκευῆς.) For his hearers were not in a state of indifference. The miracle had aroused them all; they were even full of fear and amazement. Wherefore also there was no need of beginning at that point, but rather with a different topic; by which, in fact, he powerfully conciliated them, namely, by rejecting the glory which was to

---

[1] Ἀλλὰ ποῦ θέλεις ἰδεῖν. ἀγαπητὲ, ὅτι ὁ πολὺς ὄχλος κ. τ. λ. The modern text, Ὁ πολὺς ὄχλος, ἀγαπητὲ, κ. τ. λ.

be had from them. For nothing is so advantageous, and so likely to pacify the hearers, as to say nothing about one's self of an honorable nature, but, on the contrary, to obviate all surmise of wishing to do so. And, in truth, much more did they increase their glory by despising glory, and showing that what had just taken place was no human act, but a Divine work; and that it was their part to join with the beholders in admiration, rather than to receive it from them. Do you see how clear of all ambition he is, and how he repels the honor paid to him? In the same manner also did the ancient fathers; for instance, Daniel said, "Not for any wisdom that is in me." (Dan. ii. 30.) And again Joseph, "Do not interpretations belong to God?" (Gen. xi. 8.) And David, "When the lion and the bear came, in the name of the Lord I rent them with my hands." (1 Sam. xvii. 34.) And so likewise here the Apostles, "Why look ye so earnestly on us, as though by our own power or holiness we had made this man to walk?" (v. 13.) Nay, not even this;[1] for not by our own merit did we draw down the Divine influence. "The God of Abraham, and of Isaac, and of Jacob, the God of our fathers." See how assiduously he thrusts himself (εἰσωθεῖ) upon the fathers of old, lest he should appear to be introducing a new doctrine. In the former address he appealed to the patriarch David, here he appeals to Abraham and the rest. "Hath glorified His Servant[2] Jesus." Again a lowly expression, like as in the opening address.

But at this point he proceeds to enlarge upon the outrage, and exalts the heinousness of the deed, no longer, as before, throwing a veil over it. This he does, wishing to work upon them more powerfully. For the more he proved them accountable, the better his purpose were effected. "Hath glorified," he says, 'His Servant Jesus, Whom ye delivered up, and denied Him in the presence of Pilate, when he was determined to let him go." The charge is twofold: Pilate was desirous to let Him go; you would not, when he was willing.

"But ye denied the Holy One and the Just, and desired a murderer to be granted unto you; and killed the Prince (or Author) of Life: Whom God hath raised from the dead; whereof we are witnesses." (v. 14, 15.) Ye desired a robber instead of Him. He shows the great aggravation of the act. As he has them under his hand, he now strikes hard. "The Prince of Life," he says. In these words he establishes the doctrine of the Resurrection. "Whom God hath raised from the dead." (ch. ii. 26.) "Whence doth this appear?" He no longer refers to the Prophets, but to himself, inasmuch as now he has a right to be believed. Before, when he affirmed that He was risen, he adduced the testimony of David; now, having said it, he alleges the College of Apostles. "Whereof we are witnesses, he says.

"And His name, through faith in His name, hath made this man strong, whom ye see and know: yea, the faith which is by Him hath given him this perfect soundness in the presence of you all." Seeking to declare the matter (ζητῶν τὸ πρᾶγμα εἰπεῖν), he straightway brings forward the sign: "In the presence," he says, "of you all." As he had borne hard upon them, and had shown that He Whom they crucified had risen, again he relaxes, by giving them the power of repentance; "And now, brethren, I wot that through ignorance ye did it, as did also your rulers." (v. 17.) This is one ground of excuse. The second[3] is of a different kind. As Joseph speaks to his brethren, "God did send me before you (Gen. xlv. 5); what in the former speech he had briefly said, in the words, "Him, being delivered by the determinate counsel and foreknowledge of God, ye have taken,"—this he here enlarges upon: "But what God before had showed by the mouth of all His Prophets, that His Christ should suffer, He hath so fulfilled." (v. 18.) At the same time showing, that it was not of their doing, if this be proved, that it took place after God's counsel. He alludes to those words with which they had reviled Him on the Cross, namely "Let Him deliver Him, if He will have Him; for He said, I am the Son of God. If[4] He trust in God, let Him now come down from the cross." (Matt. xxvii. 42, 43.) O foolish men, were these idle words? It must needs so come to pass, and the prophets bear witness

---

[1] 'Αλλ' οὐδὲ τοῦτο· οὐ γὰρ, κ. τ. λ. This seems to refer to εὐσεβείᾳ· "but not by our holiness any more than by our own power." The modern text: Οὐδὲ τοῦτο ἡμέτερον, φησίν· οὐ γὰρ, κ. τ. λ. "Not even this is our own, he says; for not," etc.

[2] or, Child, τὸν παῖδα. Œcumen. seems to have considered this as a lowly title, for he says: "And of Christ he speaks lowly, τῷ προσθεῖναι, τὸν Παῖδα." But to this remark he adds, "For that which in itself is glorified, can receive no addition of glory."—Below, καθὼς ἐν τῷ προοιμίῳ may refer to the prefatory matter (after the citation from Joel) of the sermon in ch. ii.: see below, in the Recapitulation, whence we might here supply, ἀνωτέρω ἔλεγεν, "Ἰησοῦν τὸν Ναζ. κ. τ. λ." "As in the opening address [above, he said: 'Jesus of Nazareth, a man approved of God,' etc.]." Or, "like as in the opening words of this discourse he speaks in lowly manner of themselves." Œcumen. "He still keeps to lowlier matters, both as to themselves, and as to Christ. As to themselves, in saying that not by their own power they wrought the miracle. As to Christ," etc.

[3] ἡ δευτέρα ἑτέρα, A. B. C. (N. om. ἡ) Cat. Namely, the first, "Ye did it ignorantly, as did also your rulers." The second, "It was ordered by the counsel of God:" as below, "And he puts this by way of apology," etc. The Edd. have adopted the absurd innovation, "'Through ignorance ye did it:' this is one ground of excuse: the second is, 'As did also your rulers:'" E. F. D.

[4] Εἰ πέποιθεν, A. C. F. D. N. Cat. and νῦν after καταβ. om. C. F. D. N. Cat.

thereunto. Therefore if He descended not, it
it was for no weakness of His own that He
did not come down, but for very power. And
Peter puts this by way of apology for the Jews,
hoping that they may also close with what he
says. "He hath so fulfilled," he says. Do
you see now how he refers everything to that
source? "Repent ye therefore," he says,
"and be converted." He does not add,
"from your sins;" but, "that your sins,
may be blotted out," means the same thing.
And then he adds the gain: "So shall the
times of refreshing come from the presence of
the Lord." (v.1 9.) This betokens them in a
sad state, brought low by many wars.¹ For it is
to the case of one on fire, and craving comfort, that the expression applies. And see
now how he advances. In his first sermon,
he but slightly hinted at the resurrection, and
Christ's sitting in heaven; but here he also
speaks of His visible advent. "And He shall
send Jesus the Christ ordained² (for you),
"Whom the heaven must (i. e. must of necessity) receive, until the times of the restitution
of all things." The reason why He does
not now come is clear. "Which God hath
spoken," he continues, "by the mouth³ of
His holy prophets since the world began.
For Moses truly said unto the fathers, A
Prophet shall the Lord your God raise up
unto you of your brethren, like unto me; him
shall ye hear in all things whatsoever he shall
say unto you." Before, he had spoken of
David, here he speaks of Moses. "Of all
things," he says, "which He hath spoken."
But he does not say, "which Christ," but,
"which God hath spoken⁴ by the mouth of all
His holy prophets since the world began."
(v. 20, 21.) Then he betakes him to the
ground of credibility, saying, "A Prophet shall
the Lord your God raise up unto you of your

brethren, like unto me; Him shall ye hear in
all things." And then the greatness of the
punishment: "And it shall come to pass, that
every soul which will not hear that Prophet,
shall be destroyed from among the people.
Yea, and all the prophets, from Samuel and
those that follow, after, as many as have spoken
have likewise foretold of these days." (v. 23, 24.)
He has done well to set the distinction here.
For whenever he says anything great, he appeals to them of old. And he found a text
which contained both truths; just as in the
other discourse he said, "Until He put His
foes under His feet." (ch. ii. 35.) The remarkable circumstance is, that the two things
stand together; that is, subjection and disobedience, and the punishment. "Like unto
me," he says. Then why are ye alarmed?
"Ye are the children of the prophets" (v. 25):
so that to you they spake, and for your sakes
have all these things come to pass. For as
they deemed that through their outrage they
had become alienated (and indeed there is no
parity of reason, that He Who now is crucified, should now cherish them as His own), he
proves to them that both the one and the
other are in accordance with prophecy. "Ye
are the children," he says, "of the Prophets,
and of the covenant which God made with
our fathers, saying unto Abraham, 'And in
thy seed shall all the kindreds of the earth be
blessed.' Unto you first," he continues,
"God having raised up His Son (τὸν Παῖδα) sent
Him." "To others indeed also, but to you first
who crucified Him." "To bless you," he adds,
"in turning away every one of you from his
iniquities." (v. 26.)

Now let us consider again more minutely
what has been read out. (Recapitulation.)
In the first place, he establishes the point that
the miracle was performed by them⁵; saying,
"Why marvel ye?" And he will not let the
assertion be disbelieved: and to give it more
weight, he anticipates their judgment. "Why
look ye," he says, "so earnestly on us, as though
by our own power or holiness we had made
this man to walk?" (v. 12.) If this troubles
and confounds you, learn Who was the Doer,
and be not amazed. And observe how on all
occasions when he refers to God, and says
that all things are from Him, then he fearlessly chides them: as above where he said,

¹ Πολέμοις attested by Cat. and Œc. but A. has πόνοις, E.
and Edd. κακοῖς. In the following sentence, Πρὸς γὰρ τὸν
καυσούμενον καὶ παραμυθίαν ἐπιζητοῦντα οὗτος ἂν ἁρμόσειεν ὁ
λόγος, B. and Œc. read κλαυσόμενον, C. F. D. N. κλαυσούμενον,
("to him that shall weep,") A. κανσάμενον, Cat. καυσούμενον,
the true reading. The scribes did not perceive that Chr. is
commenting on the word ἀναψύξεως, "refrigeration," as implying a condition of burning: hence the alteration, κλαυσόμενον, or in the "Doric" form (Aristoph.) κλαυσούμενον. E. and
Edd. Διὸ καὶ οὗτως εἶπεν εἰδὼς ὅτι πρὸς τὸν πάσχοντα καὶ παραμυθ.
ζητοῦντα κ. τ. λ. "Wherefore also he speaks thus, knowing
that it is to the case of one who is suffering," etc.—In the text
here commented upon, ὅπως ἂν ἔλθωσι καιροὶ ἀναψ., E. V.
makes ὅπως ἂν temporal, "When the times of refreshing," etc.
But here and elsewhere in the N. T. Matt. vi. 5; Luke ii. 35;
Acts xv. 17; Rom. iii. 4; the correct usage is observed, according to which, ὅπως ἂν is nearly equivalent to "so (shall);" i. e.
"that (ὅπως) they may come, as in the event of your repentance (ἂν) they certainly shall." And so Chrys. took the passage: Εἶτα τὸ κέρδος ἐπάγει· "Ὅπως ἂν κ. τ. λ. "Then he adds
the gain: So shall the times," etc.
² τὸν προκεχειρισμένον. Other Mss. of N. T. read προκεκηρυ-
γμένον, whence Vulg. E. V. "which was before preached."
³ E. V. has "all," and so some Mss. πάντων, and St. Chrys.
gives it a little further on.
⁴ Instead of this clause, "by the mouth," etc. the Edd. have
from E. "Still by keeping the matter in the shade, drawing
them on the more to faith by gentle degrees."

⁵ Τέως κατασκευάζει ὅτι αὐτοὶ ἐποίησαν τὸ θαῦμα. i. e. "by
saying, Why marvel ye? he makes this good at the very outset: You see that a miracle has been wrought, and by us (as
the instruments), not by some other man (this is the force of
the αὐτοὶ here). This he will not allow them to doubt for a
moment: he forestalls their judgment on the matter: you see
that it is done by us, and you are inclined to think it was by
our own power or holiness," etc. There is no need to insert
the negative, ὅτι οὐκ αὐτοὶ: Erasm. and Ben. Lat.

" A man approved of God among you." (ch. ii. 22.) And on all occasions he reminds them of the outrage they had committed, in order that the fact of the Resurrection may be established. But here he also subjoins something else; for he no more says, "of Nazareth," but what? "The God of our fathers hath glorified His Servant Jesus." (v. 13.) Observe also the modesty. He reproached them not, neither did he say at once, "Believe then now: behold, a man that has been forty years lame, has been raised up through the name of Jesus Christ." This he did not say, for it would have excited opposition. On the contrary, he begins by commending them for admiring the deed, and again calls them after their ancestor: "Ye men of Israel." Moreover, he does not say, It was Jesus that healed him: but, "The God of our fathers hath glorified," etc. But then, lest they should say, How can this stand to reason—that God should glorify the transgressor? therefore he reminds them of the judgment before Pilate, showing that, would they but consider, He was no transgressor; else Pilate had not wished to release Him. And he does not say, "when Pilate was desirous," but, "was determined to let Him go." "But ye denied the Holy One," etc. (v. 13, 14.) Him who had killed others, ye asked to be released; Him Who quickeneth them that are killed, ye did not wish to have! And that they might not ask again, How should it be that God now glorifies Him, when before He gave no assistance? he brings forward the prophets, testifying that so it behooved to be. "But those things which God before had showed," etc., (*infra* v. 18.) Then, lest they should suppose that God's dispensation was their own apology, first he reproves them. Moreover, that the denying Him "to Pilate's face," was no ordinary thing; seeing that he wished to release Him. And that ye cannot deny this, the man who was asked in preference to Him is witness against you. This also is part of a deep dispensation. Here it shows their shamelessness and effrontery; that a Gentile, one who saw Him for the first time, should have discharged Him, though he had heard nothing striking; while they who had been brought up among His miracles, have done the very opposite! For, as he has said, "When he (Pilate) had determined to let Him go," that it may not be imagined that he did this of favor, we read, "And he said, It is a custom with you to release one prisoner: will ye therefore that I release unto you this man? (Matt. xxvii. 15.) "But ye denied the Holy One and the Just." (Mark xv. 6.) He does not say, "Ye delivered up;" but everywhere, "Ye

denied." For, said they, "We have no king but Cæsar." (John xix. 15.) And he does not say only, Ye did not beg off the innocent, and, "Ye denied" Him; but, "Ye slew" Him. While they were hardened, he refrained from such language; but when their minds are most moved, then he strikes home, now that they are in a condition to feel it. For just as when men are drunk we say nothing to them, but when they are sober, and are recovered from their intoxication then we chide them; thus did Peter: when they were able to understand his words, then he also sharpened his tongue, alleging against them many charges; that, Whom God had glorified, they had delivered up; Whom Pilate would have acquitted they denied to his face; that they preferred the robber before Him.

Observe again how he speaks covertly concerning Christ's power, showing that He raised Himself: just as in his first discourse he had said, "Because it was not possible that He should be holden of it" (ch. ii. 24), so here he says, "And killed the Prince of Life." (v. 15.) It follows that the Life He had was not from another. The prince (or author) of evil would be he that first brought forth evil; the prince or author of murder, he who first originated murder; so also the Prince (or Author) of Life must be He Who has Life from Himself.* "Whom God raised up," he continues: and now that he has uttered this, he adds, "And his name, upon faith in his name, hath made this man strong, whom ye see and know; yea, the faith which is by Him hath given Him this perfect soundness. [The faith which is by Him ἡ δι' αὐτοῦ πίστις.] And[1] yet it was ἡ εἰς αὐτὸν πίστις, "the faith which is in Him" (as its object) that did all. For the Apostles did not say, "By the name," but, "In the name," and it was in Him (εἰς αὐτὸν) that the man believed. But they did not yet make bold to use the expression, "The faith which is in Him." For, that the phrase "By Him" should not be too low, observe that after saying, "Upon the faith of His name," he adds, "His name hath made him strong," and then it is that he says, "Yea, the faith which is by Him hath given him this perfect soundness." Observe how he implies, that in

---

* Peter sharpens his accusation of them by the following contrasts: (1) This healing at which you wonder is to the glory of *Christ*, not of us. (2) *God* has glorified whom *you* have betrayed and denied. (3) This you did though Pilate himself would have released him. (4) You preferred to kill the *holy and just one* and let a *murderer* go free. (5) You sought to put to *death* the Author of *Life*. Vv. 12-15.—G. B. S.

[1] The meaning of the following passage is plain enough, but the innovator has so altered it as to make it unintelligible. Yet the Edd. adopt his reading (E. D. F.) without notice of the other and genuine reading. "And yet if it was ἡ εἰς αὐτὸν πίστις that did all, and that (ὅτι) it was εἰς αὐτὸν that the man believed, why did (Peter) say, not Διὰ τοῦ ὀνόματος, but Ἐν τῷ ὀνόματι? Because they did not yet," etc.

the καὶ ἐκεῖνο former expression also "Whom God raised up," he did but condescend to their low attainments. For that Person needed not Another's help for His rising again, Whose Name raised up a lame man, being all one as dead. Mark how on all occasions he adduces their own testimony. Thus above, he said, "As ye yourselves also know;" and, "In the midst of you:" and here again, "Whom ye see and know: in the presence of you all." (ch. ii. 22.) And yet that it was, "In His name," they knew not: but they did know that the man was lame, that he stands there whole. [1] They that had wrought the deed themselves confessed, that it was not by their own power, but by that of Christ. And had this assertion been unfounded, had they not been truly persuaded themselves that Christ had risen again, they would not have sought to establish the honor of a dead man instead of their own, especially while the eyes of the multitude were upon them. Then, when their minds were alarmed, immediately he encourages them, by the appellation of Brethren, "And now, brethren, I wot, etc." For in the former discourse he foretold [2] nothing, but only says concerning Christ, "Therefore let all the house of Israel know assuredly:" here he adds an admonition. There he waited till the people spoke: here, he knew how much they had already effected, and that the present assembly was better disposed toward them. "That through ignorance ye did it." And yet the circumstances mentioned above were not to be put to the score of ignorance. To choose the robber, to reject Him Who had been adjudged to be acquitted, to desire even to destroy Him—how should this be referred to ignorance? Nevertheless, he gives them liberty to deny it, and to change their mind about what had happened. "Now this indeed, that you put to death the innocent, ye knew: but that you were killing "the Prince of Life," this, belike, ye did not know." And he exculpated not them alone, but also the chief contrivers of the evil, "ye and your rulers:" for doubtless it would have roused their opposition, had he gone off into accusation. For the evil-doer, when you accuse him of some wickedness that he has done, in his endeavor to exonerate himself, grows more vehement. And he no longer says, "Ye crucified," "Ye killed," but, "Ye did it;" leading them to seek for pardon. If those rulers did it through ignorance, much more did these present.* "But these things which God before had showed," etc. (v. 18.) But it is remarkable, that both in the first and in the second discourse, speaking to the same effect, that is, in the former, "By the determinate counsel and foreknowledge of God;" and in this, "God before had showed that Christ should suffer;" in neither does he adduce any particular text in proof. The fact is, that each one of such passages is accompanied with many accusations, and with mention of the punishment in store for them [as]; "I will deliver up," says one, "the wicked in requital for His grave, and the rich in return for His death." (Is. liii. 9.) And again, * * * "Those things," he says, "which God before had showed by the mouth of all His prophets, that Christ should suffer, He hath so fulfilled." It shows the greatness of that "counsel," [3] in that all spoke of it, and not one only. It does not follow, because the event was through ignorance, that it took place irrespectively of God's ordinance. See how great is the Wisdom of God, when it uses the wickedness of others to bring about that which must be. "He hath fulfilled," he says: that they may not imagine that anything at all is wanting; for whatsoever Christ must needs suffer, has been fulfilled. But do not think, that, because the Prophets said this, and because ye did it through ignorance, this sufficeth to your exculpation. However, he does not express himself thus, but in milder terms says, "Repent ye therefore." (v. 19.) "Why? For [4] either it was through ignorance, or by the dispensation of God." "That your sins may be blotted out." I do not mean the crimes committed at the Crucifixion; perhaps they were through ignorance; but so that your other sins may be blotted out: this [5] only. "So shall the times of refreshing come unto

---

[1] E. has ὅτι ὑγιὴς ἕστηκεν after οὐκ ᾔδεσαν instead of after τοῦτο ᾔδεσαν. So Commel. Erasm. Ed. Par. Hence D. F. have it in both places, and so Morel. Ben. All these omit ὅτι before ἐν τῷ ὄν. "And yet in His name they knew not that he stands whole: but this they knew, that he was lame, (that he stands whole)." Savile alone has retained the genuine reading.

[2] οὐδὲν προεῖπεν, A. B. C. N. i. e. foretold nothing concerning them. Edd. οὐδὲν περὶ ἑαυτῶν εἶπεν, "said nothing concerning (the hearers) themselves."

* There is one extenuating circumstance: they did it in ignorance (Cf. Luk. xxiii. 34; 1. Cor. ii. 8 ; Acts xiii. 27). This fact forms the transition-point to the presentation of a different side of the death of Jesus. It was their crime, but it was also God's plan. They did it from motives of blindness and hate, but God designed it for their salvation. So that Peter, in effect, says: There is hope for you although you have slain the Lord, for his sacrificial death is the ground of salvation. To this view of the death of Christ he now appeals as basis of hope and a motive to repentance (οὖν v. 19).—G. B. S.

[3] μεγάλην δείκνυσι τὴν βουλήν, meaning the determinate counsel of God above spoken of. Above, after καὶ πάλιν, some other citation is wanting, in illustration of his remark that the prophecies of the Passion are all accompanied with denunciations of punishment.

[4] ἢ γὰρ κατὰ ἄγνοιαν, ἢ κατὰ οἰκονομίαν. Edd. omit this interlocution, Sav. notes it in the margin. "Repent ye therefore." Why repent? for either it was through ignorance, or it was predestinated. (Nevertheless, you must repent, to the blotting out of your sins, etc.)

[5] τοῦτο μόνον, B. C. N. "this is all:" i. e. no more than this: he does not impute that one great sin to them, in all its heinousness; he only speaks of their sins in general. A. and the other Mss. omit these words.

you." Here he speaks of the Resurrection, obscurely.* For those are indeed times of refreshing, which Paul also looked for, when he said, "We that are in this tabernacle do groan, being burthened." (2 Cor. v. 4.) Then to prove that Christ is the cause of the days of refreshing, he says, "And He shall send Jesus Christ, which before was for you ordained." (v. 20.) He said not, "That your sin may be blotted out," but, "your sins;" for he hints at that sin also. "He shall send." And whence?[1] "Whom the heaven must receive." (v. 21.) Still ["must "] "receive?" And why not simply, Whom the heaven hath received? This, as if discoursing of old times: so, he says, it is divinely ordered, so it is settled: not a word yet of His eternal subsistence.—"For Moses indeed said unto the fathers, A Prophet shall the Lord raise up for you:" "Him shall ye hear in all things that He shall speak unto you:" and having said, "All things which God hath spoken by the mouth of all His holy Prophets," (v. 22) now indeed he brings in Christ Himself. For, if He predicted many things and it is necessary to hear Him, one would not be wrong in saying that the Prophets have spoken these things. But, besides, he wishes to show that the Prophets did predict the same things. And, if any one will look closely into the matter, he will find these things spoken in the Old Testament, obscurely indeed, but nevertheless spoken. "Who was purposely designed," says he : in Whom[2] there is nothing novel. Here he also alarms them, by the thought that much remains to be ful-

filled. But if so, how says he, "Hath fulfilled?" (v. 18.) The things which it was necessary "that Christ should suffer," are fulfilled : the things which must come to pass, not yet. "A prophet shall the Lord God raise up for you from among your brethren, like unto me." This would most conciliate them. Do you observe the sprinkling of low matters and high, side by side,—that He Who was to go up into the heavens should be like unto Moses? And yet it was a great thing too. For in fact He was not simply like unto Moses,[3] if so be that "every soul which will not hear shall be destroyed." And one might mention numberless other things which show that He was not like unto Moses; so that it is a mighty text that he has handled. "God shall raise Him up unto you," says Moses, "from among your brethren," etc. : consequently Moses himself threatens those that should not hear. "Yea, and all the prophets," etc. : all this[4] is calculated to attract- "Yea, and all the prophets," says the Apostle. "from Samuel." He refrains from enumer, ating them singly, not to make his discourse too long; but having alleged that decisive testimony of Moses, he passes by the rest. "Ye," he says, "are the children of the Prophets, and of the covenant which God made." (v. 25) "Children of the covenant;" that is, heirs. For lest they should think that they received this offer from the favor of Peter, he shows, that of old it was due to them, in order that they may the rather believe that such also is the will of God. "Unto you first," he continues, "God having raised up His Son Jesus, sent Him." (v. 26.) He does not say simply, "Unto you He sent His Son," but also, after the resurrection, and when He had been crucified. For that they may not suppose that he himself granted them this favor, and not the Father, he says, "To bless you." For if He is your Brother, and blesses you, the affair is a promise. "Unto you first." That is, so far are you from having no share in these blessings, that He would have you become moreover promoters and authors of them to others. For[5] you are not

---

* The reference is hardly to the resurrection, but to the *Parousia.* To the hope of this event, always viewed as imminent, all the expressions: "times of refreshing," " times of restitution " and " these days" (vv. 19-24) undoubtedly refer. So Olshansen, Meyer, Alford, Hackett, Gloag, Lechler and most recent critics.—G. B. S.

[1] The modern text; "Saying this. he does not declare, Whence, but only adds," etc.—Ἀκμὴν δεξασθαι. Ben. *Utique suscipere.* Erasm. *adhuc accipere.* It means, Is this still to take place, that he should say ὃν δεῖ δεξασθαι, as if the event were yet future? And the answer is, " He speaks in reference to former times, i. e. from that point of view. (So Œcumen. in loc. τὸ δεῖ ἀντὶ τοῦ ἔδει.) And then as to the necessity ; this δεῖ is not meant in respect of Christ's Divine Nature (for of that he forbears to speak), but the meaning is, So it is ordered," etc. The report, however, is very defective, especially in what follows. He is commenting upon the words, "Until the time of restitution (or making good) of all that God spake," etc. πάντων ὧν ἐλάλησεν ὁ Θεὸς, which expression he compares with what is said of the Prophet like unto Moses, πάντων ὅσα ἂν λαλήσῃ. Christ is that Prophet: and what He spake, the Prophets, obscurely indeed, spake before. He adds, that St. Peter's mention of the yet future fulfilment of all that the Prophets have spoken is calculated also to alarm the hearers. See the further comment on these verses at the end of the recapitulation.

[2] Οὐ οὐδὲν νεώτερον. Meaning perhaps, that as Christ was from the first designed for the Jews, the Gospel is no novelty, as if nothing had been heard of such a Saviour before. E. D. F. ὥστε οὐδὲν νεώτερον, which is placed before the citation τὸν προκεχ.—Below, A. B. C. N. Ἐπλήρωσεν ἃ ἔδει παθεῖν ; Ἐπληρώθη ἃ δεῖ γενέσθαι ἐχρῆν οὐδέπω, which is manifestly corrupt. We restore it thus: Ἐπλήρωσεν; Ἃ ἔδει παθεῖν ἐπληρώθη, ἃ δὲ γενέσθαι ἐχρῆν οὐδέπω. The modern text: Ἐπλήρωσεν ἃ ἔδει παθεῖν ; Ἐπλήρωσεν, εἶπεν, οὐκ ἐπληρώθη· δεικνυς ὅτι ἃ μὲν ἐχρῆν παθεῖν, ἐπλήρωσεν· ἃ δὲ (δέοι add. F. D.) γενέσθαι λείπεται ἔτι, οὐδέπω.

[3] C. N. Οὐ γὰρ δὴ κατὰ Μωσέα ἦν, εἰ γὰρ πᾶς ὁ μὴ ἀκ. ἐξολοθρευθήσεται, μυρία δὲ εἶπεν τὰ δεικνύντα ὅτι οὐκ ἐστι κατὰ Μωσέα. B. omits οὐ γὰρ . . . . ἦν, inadvertently passing from ἦν· οὐ γὰρ to the subsequent ἦν· εἰ γάρ. A. omits the words μυρία . . . . ὅτι, which disturb the sense of the passage. In the translation we have rejected the second γάρ. For εἶπεν, Sav. marg. gives εἴποι τις ἄν, which we have adopted. The modern text substitutes τὸ, καὶ, ἔσται for εἰ γάρ, and inserts καὶ ἄλλα after μυρία δέ.

[4] Ταῦτα ὅλα ἐπαγωγὰ is strangely rendered by Ben. *hæc omnia adjecta sunt.* But this is the comment, not upon the threatening in v. 23, but upon the matters contained in the following verses, 24-26.

[5] Μὴ γὰρ ὡς ἀπερριμμένοι διακεῖσθε, B. N. οὐκοῦν μὴ γὰρ, A. πάλιν μὴ γὰρ, C. μὴ οὖν, F. D. καὶ γὰρ, Cat. οὐκοῦν μὴ. E. and Edd., which also add at the end of the sentence, ἢ ἀποβεβλημένοι, where the other Mss. have, Πάλιν ἢ ἀνάστασις, as comment on ἀναστήσας.

to feel like castaways. "Having raised up": again, the Resurrection. "In turning away," he says, "every one of you from his iniquities." In this way He blesses you: not in a general way. And what kind of blessing is this? A great one. For of course not the turning a man away from his iniquities is itself sufficient to remit them also. And if it is not sufficient to remit, how should it be to confer a blessing? For it is not to be supposed that the transgressor becomes forthwith also blessed; he is simply released from his sins. But this, [1] "Like unto me," would no wise apply. "Hear ye Him," he says; and not this alone, but he adds, "And it shall come to pass, that every soul, which will not hear that Prophet, shall be destroyed from among the people." When he has shown them that they had sinned, and has imparted forgiveness to them, and promised good things, then indeed, then he says, "Moses also says the same thing." What sort of connection is this: "Until the times of the restitution;" and then to introduce Moses, saying, that [2] all that Christ said shall come to pass? Then also, on the other hand, he says, as matter of encomium (so that for this reason also ye ought to obey): "Ye are the children of the prophets and of the covenant:" i. e. heirs. Then why do you stand affected towards that which is your own, as if it were another's? True, you have done deeds worthy of condemnation; still you may yet obtain pardon. Having said this, with reason he is now able to say, "Unto you God sent his Son Jesus to bless you." He says not, To save you, but what is greater; that the crucified Jesus blessed His crucifiers.

Let us then also imitate Him. Let us cast out that spirit of murder and enmity. It is not enough not to retaliate (for even in the Old Dispensation this was exemplified); but let us do all as we would for bosom-friends, as we would for ourselves so for those who have injured us. We are followers of Him, we are His disciples, who after being crucified, sets everything in action in behalf of his murderers, and sends out His Apostles to this end.

And yet we have often suffered justly; but those acted not only unjustly, but impiously; for He was their Benefactor, He had done no evil, and they crucified Him. And for what reason? For the sake of their reputation. But He Himself made them objects of reverence. "The scribes and the pharisees sit in Moses' seat; all therefore whatsoever they bid you observe, that do ye, but after their works do ye not." (Matt. xxiii. 2.) And again in another place, "Go thy way, show thyself to the priest." (ib. viii. 4.) Besides, when He might have destroyed them, He saves them. Let us then imitate Him, and let no one be an enemy, no one a foe, except to the devil.

Not a little does the habit of not swearing contribute to this end: I mean to the not giving way to wrath: [3] and by not giving way to wrath, we shall not have an enemy either. Lop off the oaths of a man, and you have clipt the wings of his anger, you have smothered all his passion. Swearing, it is said, is as the wind to wrath. Lower the sails; no need of sails, when there is no wind. If then we do not clamor, and do not swear, we have cut the sinews of passion. And if you doubt this, just put it to experiment. Impose it as a law upon the passionate man that he shall never swear, and you will have no necessity of preaching moderation to him. So the whole business is finished. For [4] even though you do not forswear yourselves [yet], by swearing at all, do you not know in what absurd consequences you involve yourselves —binding yourselves to an absolute necessity and as with a cord, and putting yourselves to all manner of shifts, as men studying how to

---

[1] Τὸ δὲ, Ὡς ἐμὲ οὐδαμοῦ λόγον ἂν ἔχοι. He had before said, that in the very description of "the Prophet like unto Moses," it is shown that He is more than like Moses: for instance, "Every soul which will not hear," etc. would not apply to Moses. Having finished the description, he now adds, You see that the ὡς ἐμὲ nowhere holds as the whole account of the matter: to be raised up (from the dead) and sent to bless, and this by turning every one from his iniquities, is not to be simply such as Moses. The modern text adds, "Unless it be taken in regard of the manner of legislation:" i. e. Christ is like unto Moses considered as Deliverer and Lawgiver, not in any other respect.

[2] E. and Edd. "that they shall hear all things which Christ shall say: and this not in a general way, but with a fearful menace? It is a powerful connection, for it shows that for this reason also they ought to obey Him. What means it, "Children of the Prophets," etc.

[3] λέγω δὴ τὸ μὴ ὀργίζεσθαι, as the explanation of εἰς τοῦτο. The other text confuses the meaning by substituting καὶ τὸ μὴ ὀργ. "Not to swear, and not to be angry, is a great help to this." Which increases the "intricacy" of which Ben. complains in the following passage, where oaths are first said to be the wings of wrath, and then are compared to the wind filling the sails. Here instead of, ὥσπερ γὰρ πνεῦμα τῆς ὀργῆς ὁ ὅρκος, φησὶν, ἐστί, (cited as an apothegm), the modern text gives, ὥσπερ γὰρ πν. ἡ ὀργὴ καὶ ὁ ὅρκος ἐστί. "For wrath and swearing is as a wind." The imagery is incongruous: oaths, the wings of wrath: oaths the wind, and wrath (apparently) the sails: but the alterations do not mend the sense.

[4] κἂν γὰρ μὴ ἐπιορκῆτε, ὀμνύντες ὅλως οὐκ ἴστε. The modern text, καὶ οὔτε ἐπιορκήσετε, οὔτε ὁμόσεσθε ὅλως. Οὐκ ἴστε. Which does not suit the context. "Make it a law with the passionate man, never to swear . . . . The whole affair is finished, and you will neither perjure yourselves, nor swear at all." He seems to be speaking of oaths and imprecations, by which a man in the heat of passion binds himself to do or suffer some dreadful thing. "Suppose you do not perjure yourself, yet think of the misery you entail upon yourself: you must either study all sorts of expedients to deliver your soul, or, since that cannot be without perjury, you must spend your life in misery, etc. and curse your wrath."—'Ανάγκη τινὶ καὶ δεσμῷ, with comma preceding: so Sav. but A. B. C. ἀνάγκη nom. preceded by a full stop: "For needs must you, binding yourselves as with a cord," etc: and so the modern text, with other alterations (adopted by Sav.) which are meant to simplify the construction, but do not affect the sense. Below, Ἐπειδὴ γὰρ ἠκούσατε, καὶ τὸ πλέον ὑμῖν κατώρθωται. Ben makes this a sentence by itself, Quia enim audistis, magna pars rei a vobis perfecta est. Savile connects it with the following, φέρε δὴ κ. τ. λ. See p. 53, where he alludes to some who laughed at him, perhaps even on the spot.

rescue their soul from an evil which there is no escaping, or, failing of that, obliged [by that self-imposed necessity] to spend your life thenceforth in vexation, in quarrels, and to curse your wrath? But all is in vain, and to no purpose. Threaten, be peremptory (διόρισαι), do all, whatever it be, without swearing ; [so]: it is in your power to reverse (ἀναλῦσαι) both what you have said and what you have done, if you have the mind. Thus on the present day I must needs speak more gently to you. For since ye have heard me, and the greater part of the reformation is achieved by you, now then let us see for what purpose the taking of oaths was introduced, and why allowed to be. In relating to you their first origin, and when they were conceived, and how, and by whom we shall give you this account in requital for your obedience. For it is fit that he who has made his practice right, should be taught the philosophy of the matter, but he who is not yet doing the right, is not worthy to be told the history.

They made many covenants in Abraham's time, and slew victims, and offered sacrifices, and as yet oaths were not. Whence then did they come in? When evil increased, when all was confusion, upside down, when men had turned aside to idolatry: then it was, then, when men appeared no longer worthy to be believed, that they called God as witness, as if thereby giving an adequate surety for what they said. Such in fact is the Oath: it is a security where men's principles cannot be trusted.[1] So that in the indictment of the swearer the first charge is this,—that he is not to be trusted without a surety, and a great surety too : for such is the exceeding faithlessness, that they ask not man as surety, but will needs have God! Secondly, the same charge lies against him who receives the oath : that, in a question of compact, he must drag in God for warranty, and refuse to be satisfied unless he get Him. O the excessive stupidity, the insolence of such conduct! Thou, a worm, earth and dust, and ashes, and vapor, to drag in thy Lord as thy surety, and to compel the other to drag Him in likewise! Tell me, if your servants were disputing with each other, and exchanging[2] assurances with each other, and the fellow-servant should declare that for his part he would not be satisfied till he had their common master given him for surety, would he not have stripes given him without number, and be made to know that the master is for other purposes, and not to be put to any

such use as this? Why do I speak of a fellow-servant?[3] For should he choose any respectable person, would not that person consider it an affront? But I do not wish to do this, say you.[4] Well : then do not compel the other to do so either : since where men only are in question, this is done—if your party says, " I give such an one as my surety," you do not allow him. " What then," say you, " am I to lose what I have given?" I am not speaking of this ; but that you allow him to insult God. For which reason greater shall be the inevitable punishment to him who forces the oath upon another, than to him who takes it : the same holds with regard to him who gives an oath when no one asks him. And what makes it worse, is, that every one is ready to swear, for one farthing, for some petty item, for his own injustice. All this may be said, when there is no perjury ; but if perjury follow in the train, both he that imposes and he that takes the oath have turned everything upside down. " But there are some things," you will say, " which are unknown." Well take these into account, and do nothing negligently ; but, if you do act negligently, take the loss to yourself as your punishment. It is better to be the loser thus, than in a very different way. For tell me—you force a man to take an oath, with what expectation? That he will forswear himself? But this is utter insanity ; and the judgment will fall upon your own head ; better you should lose your money, than he be lost. Why act thus to your own detriment, and to the insulting of God? This is the spirit of a wild beast, and of an impious man. But you do this in the expectation that he will not forswear himself? Then trust him without the oath. " Nay, there are many," you reply, " who in the absence of an oath would presume to defraud ; but, once the oath taken, would refrain." You deceive yourself, man. A man having once learnt to steal, and to wrong his neighbor, will presume full oft to trample upon his oath ; if on the contrary he shrinks from swearing, he will much more shrink from injustice. " But he is influenced against his will." Well then, he deserves pardon.

But why am I speaking of this kind of oaths, while I pass over those in the market-place? For as regards these last, you can urge none

---

[1] Τοῦτο γὰρ ὅρκος ἐστὶ, τρόπων ἀπιστουμένων ἐγγύη.
[2] πιστουμένων ἑαυτοὺς, A. B. C. N. as in the phrase πιστοῦσθαί τινα (ὅρκῳ), " to secure a person's good faith by oath." Edd. ἀπιστουμένων ἑαυτοῖς, " being objects of distrust to each other."

[3] ὁμόδουλον. So the Mss. but we should have expected δεσπότην, " the master."
[4] 'Αλλ' ἐγὼ οὐ βούλομαι, φησί. " I do not wish [so to insult God].—Then do not oblige the other to do so: [nay, do not suffer him :] just as, should he pretend to name as his surety some person with whom he has no right to take such a liberty, σὺ οὐκ ἀνέχῃ you would not allow him." That this is the meaning, is shown by what follows: ὅτι τὸν Θεὸν ὑβρίσαι ἀνέχῃ· " he insults God, and you suffer him to do it."

of these pleas. For ten farthings you there have swearing and forswearing. In fact, because the thunderbolt does not actually fall from heaven, because all things are not overthrown, you stand holding God in your bonds : to get a few vegetables, a pair of shoes, for a little matter of money, calling Him to witness. What is the meaning of this? Do not let us imagine, that because we are not punished, therefore we do not sin; this comes of God's mercy; not of our merit. Let your oath be an imprecation upon your own child, upon your own self : say, "Else let the hangman lash my ribs." But you dare not. Is God less valuable than thy ribs? is He less precious than thy pate? Say "Else let me be struck blind." But no. Christ so spares us, that He will not let us swear even by our own head; and yet we so little spare the honor of God, that on all occasions we must drag Him in! Ye know not what God is, and with what sort of lips he behooves to be invoked. Why, when we speak of any man of eminent worth, we say, "First wash your mouth, and then make mention of him :" and yet, that precious Name which is above every name, the Name which is marvellous in all the earth, the Name which devils hear and tremble, we haul about as we list! Oh! the force of habit! thereby has that Name become cheap. No doubt, if you impose on any one the necessity of coming into the sacred edifice to take his oath there, you feel that you have made the oath an awful one. And yet how is it that it seems awful in this way, but because we have been in the habit of using that at random, but not this? For ought not a shudder of awe to be felt when God is but named? But now, whereas among the Jews His Name was held to be so reverend, that it was written upon plates, and none was allowed to wear the characters except the high-priest alone : we bandy about His Name like any ordinary word. If simply to name God was not allowed to all; to call Him to witness, what audacity is it! nay, what madness! For if need were (rather than this) to fling away all that you have, ought you not readily to part with all? Behold, I solemnly declare and testify; reform these oaths of the forum, these superfluous oaths,[1] and bring to me all those who

wish to take them. Behold, in the presence of this assembly, I charge those who are set apart for the tending of the Houses of Prayer, I exhort and issue this order to them, that no person be allowed to take such oaths at his own discretion : or rather, that none be allowed to swear in any other way, but that the person be brought to me, whosoever he be, since even for these matters less will not serve but they must needs come before us, just as if one had to do with little children. May there be no occasion! It is a shame in some things still to need to be taught. Do you dare to touch the Holy Table, being a person unbaptized? No, but what is still worse, you the baptized dare to lay your hand upon the Holy Table, which not even all ordained persons are allowed to touch, and so to take your oath. Now you would not go and lay your hand upon the head of your child,[2] and yet do you touch the Table, and not shudder, not feel afraid? Bring these men to me; I will judge, and send them away rejoicing, both the one and the other.[3] Do what you choose; I lay it down as a law that there be no swearing at all. What hope of salvation, while we thus make all to have been done in vain? Is this the end of your bills, and your bonds, that you should sacrifice your own soul? What gain do you get so great as the loss? Has he forsworn himself? You have undone both him and yourself. But has he not? even so still you have undone (both), by forcing him to transgress the commandment.[4] Let us cast out this disease from the soul : at any rate let us drive it out of the forum, out of our shops, out of our other work-places; our profits will but be the greater. Do not imagine that the success of your worldly plans is to be ensured by transgressions of the Divine laws. "But he refuses to trust me," say you; and in fact I have sometimes heard this said

No, it stands there that we may lose sins, not that we may bind them. But do thou, if nothing else, at least reverence the very Volume which thou holdest forth to the other to swear by: the very Gospel which thou, taking in thine hands, biddest the other make oath thereby.—open it, read what Christ there saith concerning oaths, and shudder, and desist."
—Here, he forbids the sacristans to admit persons for any such purpose. "Let such be brought to me, since I must needs be the person to be troubled with these things, as if you were little children, needing to be taught such a simple matter as this."

[2] i. e. to take an oath by the head of your child. So in the *Tract. de Virgin.* t. i. 309 D. it is remarked, that "men of rude and dull minds, who do not scruple to swear by God in great matters and small, and break their oath without remorse, would not for a moment think of swearing by the head of their children: although the perjury is more heinous, and the penalty more dreadful, in the former than in the latter case, yet they feel this oath more binding than that."

[3] καὶ χαίροντας ἑκατέρους ἀποπέμψω. i. e. "both of them glad (to be rid of the quarrel) :" unless it is a threat, in the form of an ironical antiphrasis. In a law-suit one party comes off rejoicing (χαίρων): here let both exult—if they can.

[4] Matt. v. 34. "Swear not at all :" which St. Chrysostom (as the surest remedy) would enforce literally, and without any exception.

[1] Τοὺς περιττοὺς, καὶ πάντας ἐμοὶ ἀγάγετε. E. and Edd. for τοὺς περιττοὺς καὶ have τοὺς δὲ μὴ πειθομένους. The following passage relates to a practice of swearing by touching, the Sacred Volume on the Holy Table. Against this custom he inveighs in one of his Sermons *ad Pop. Antioch.* xv. §. 5. (t. ii. 158. E.) "What art thou doing, O man? On the Holy Table, and where Christ lies sacrificed, there sacrificest thou thy brother? . . . . sacrificest him in the midst of the Church, and that, with the death to come, the death which dieth not? Was the Church made for this, that we should come there to take oaths? No, but that we should pray there. Does the Table stand there, that we should make men swear thereby?

by some : " Unless I swear oaths without number, the man will not trust me." Yes, and for this you may thank yourself, because you are so off-hand with your oaths. For were it not so, but on the contrary were it clear to all men that you do not swear, take my word for it, you would be more readily believed upon your mere nod, than those are who swallow oaths by thousands. For look now : which do you more readily believe ? me who do not swear, or those that do swear ? "Yes," say you, "but then you are ruler and bishop." Then suppose I prove to you that it is not only for that reason ? Answer me with truth, I beseech you ; were I in the habit of perpetually swearing, would my office stand me in that stead ? Not a whit. Do you see that it is not for this reason ? And what do you gain at all ? Answer me that. Paul endured hunger ; do you then also choose to hunger rather than to transgress one of the commandments of God. Why are you so unbelieving ? Here are you, ready to do and suffer all things for the sake of not swearing : and shall not He reward you ? Shall He, Who sustains day by day both takers and breakers of oaths, give you over to hunger, when you have obeyed Him ? Let all men see, that of those who assemble in this Church not one is a swearer. By this also let us become manifest, and not by our creed alone ; let us have this mark also to distinguish us both from the Gentiles and from all men. Let us receive it as a seal from heaven, that we may everywhere be seen to be the King's own flock. By our mouth and tongue let us be known, in the first place, just as the barbarians are by theirs : even as those who speak Greek are distinguished from barbarians, so let us be known. Answer me : the birds which are said to be parrots, how are they known to be parrots ? is it not by speaking like men ? Let us then be known by speaking like the Apostles ; by speaking like the Angels. If any one bid you swear tell him, "Christ has spoken, and I do not swear." This is enough to make a way for all virtue to come in. It is a gate to religion, a high road leading to the philosophy of piety ; [1] a kind of training-school. These things let us observe, that we may obtain also the future blessings, through the grace and mercy of our Lord Jesus Christ, to Whom with the Father and the Holy Ghost together be glory, power and honor, now and ever, world without end. Amen.

HOMILY X.

ACTS IV. 1.

" And as they spake unto the people, there came unto them the priests, and the captain of the temple. "

ERE yet they had time to take breath after their first trials, straightway they enter into others. And observe how the events are disposed. First, they were all mocked together ; this was no small trial : secondly, they enter into dangers. And these two things do not take place in immediate succession ; but when first the Apostles have won admiration by their two discourses, and after that have performed a notable miracle, thereupon it is that, after they are waxen bold, through God's disposal, they enter the lists. But I wish you to consider, how those same persons, who in the case of Christ must need look out for one to deliver Him up to them, now with their own hands arrest the Apostles, having become more audacious and more impudent since the Crucifixion. In truth, sin, while it is yet struggling to the birth, is attended with some sense of shame ; but when once fully born, it makes those more shameless who practise it. " And the captain of the temple," it is said. The object again was to attach a public criminality to what was doing, and not to prosecute it as the act of private individuals : such in fact was constantly their plan of proceeding.

" Being grieved that they taught the people." (v. 2.) Not merely because they taught, but because they declared, not alone that Christ Himself was risen from the dead, but moreover, that we through Him do rise again. " Because they taught the people, and preached through Jesus the resurrection of the dead." So mighty was His Resurrection, that to others also He is the cause of a resurrection.* " And they laid hands on

---

[1] A. B. C. N. Sav. Ben. Ὁδὸς ἐπὶ φιλοσοφίαν εὐλαβείας εἰσάγουσα· (N. ἄγουσα·) παλαίστρα τίς ἐστι. E. F. D. omit εὐλαβείας, and so Commel. Morel. It would be better transferred (as remarked by Ed. Par.) to the next clause: " a training-school for piety."

* It is more likely that καταγγέλλειν ἐν τῷ Ἰησοῦ τὴν ἀνάστασιν κ. τ. λ. means " to declare in (the case of) Jesus the resurrection," i. e. that the reference is specifically to the resurrection of Jesus instead of (as Chrys.) to the resurrection generally.—G. B. S.

them, and put them in hold unto the next day; for it was now eventide. (v. 3.) What impudence! They [1] feared not the multitude; for this also the captain of the temple was with them: they had their hands still reeking with the blood of the former victim. "For it was now eventide," it is said. It was with the wish to abate their spirit that those men did this, and guarded them; but the delay only served to make the Apostles more intrepid. And consider who these are who are arrested. They are the chiefs of the Apostles, who are now become a pattern to the rest, that they should no longer crave each other's support, nor want to be together. "Howbeit, many having heard the word, believed; and the number of the men was about five thousand."(v. 4.) How was this? Did they see them in honor? Did they not behold them put in bonds? How then did they believe? Do you see the evident efficacy? And yet even those that believed already might well have become weaker. But no, it is no longer so: for Peter's sermon had laid the seed deep into them, and had taken a hold upon their understandings. Therefore were [their enemies] incensed, that they did not fear them, that they made no account of their present troubles. For, say they, if He that was crucified effects such great things, and makes the lame to walk, we fear not these men either.[2] This again is of God's ordering. For those who now believe were more numerous than the former. Therefore it was that in their presence they bound the Apostles, to make them also more fearful. But the reverse took place. And they examine them not before the people, but privately, that the hearers may not profit by their boldness.

"And it came to pass on the morrow, that their rulers, and elders, and scribes, and Annas the High Priest, and Caiaphas, and John, and Alexander, and as many as were of the kindred of the High Priest, were gathered together at Jersualem." (v. 5, 6.) For now

along with the other evils (of the times [3]), the Law was no longer observed. And again they set off the business with the form of a tribunal, to constitute them guilty by their iniquitous sentence. "And when they had set them in the midst, they asked, By what power, or by what name, have ye done this?" (v. 7.) And yet they knew it well; for it was because they were "grieved that they preached through Jesus the resurrection" that they arrested them. Then for what purpose do they question them? They expected the numbers present would make them recant, and thought by this means to have put all right again. Observe then what they say: "And by what name have ye done this? Then Peter, filled with the Holy Ghost, said unto them." (v. 8.) And now, I pray you, call to mind Christ's saying; "When they deliver you up unto the synagogues, take ye no thought how or what thing ye shall speak; for it is the Spirit of your Father which speaketh in you. (Luke xii. 11, 14.) So that it was a mighty Power they enjoyed. What then says Peter? "Ye rulers of the people, and elders of Israel." Mark the Christian wisdom of the man; how full of confidence it is: he utters not a word of insult, but says with respect, "Ye rulers of the people, and elders of Israel, if we be this day called to account of the good deed done to the impotent man." He takes them in hand right valiantly; by the opening of his speech he exposes [4] them, and reminds them of the former things: that it is for a work of beneficence they are calling them to account. As if he had said, "In all fairness we ought to have been crowned for this deed, and proclaimed benefactors; but since "we are even put upon our trial for a good deed done to an impotent man," not a rich man, not powerful, not noble—and yet who would feel envy in a case like this?" It is a most forcible (ἀπαγγελία, al. ἐπαγγελία) way of putting the case; and he shows that they are piercing their own selves:—"By what means this man is made whole: be it known unto you all, and to all the people Israel; that by the Name of Jesus Christ of Nazareth:"—this is what would vex them most. For this was that which Christ had

[1] So A. C. N. Cat. but B. omits οὐκ. Edd. "They had their hands still reeking with the blood of their former victim, and they were not chilled (ἐνάρκων), but again laid them upon others, to fill them with fresh blood. Or perhaps also they feared them as having now become a multitude, and for this reason the captain," etc. But the statement, οὐκ ἔδεισαν τὸ πλῆθος is explained in the Recapitulation: they led Christ to trial immediately, for fear of the multitude; but not so here.
[2] C. D. E. F. Εἰ γὰρ ὁ σταυρωθεὶς, φησὶ τοιαῦτα ἐργάζεται, καὶ τὸν χωλὸν ἀνέστησέν, οὐ φοβούμεθα οὐδὲ τούτους. A. B. N. ἐργάζεται, οὐδὲ τούτους φοβούμεθα· τὸν χωλὸν ἀνέστησε, and so Cat. which however has ἔστησαν. The meaning is obscure, especially the emphatic οὐδὲ τούτους: but perhaps it may be explained: "He was crucified; they did their worst to Him, to how little purpose! therefore neither need we fear these men, what they can do to us." But the report is otherwise so defective and confused, that perhaps what Chrys. actually said here was meant of the priests: "We were able to crucify the Master, therefore we do not fear these common men, His followers, though, as they say, it is He that does these works, that made the lame man walk."

[3] Something is wanting here: perhaps a remark on the mention of Annas as the high-priest, whereas elsewhere Caiaphas appears to have been high-priest shortly before.
[4] ἀπὸ τοῦ προοιμίου διεκωμῴδησεν, i. e. "You, the rulers of the people, and elders of Israel,—to make it a crime," etc. For this, which is the reading of the other Mss. and the Catena, E. alone has καὶ διεκωδώνισε, μᾶλλον δὲ αὐτοὺς καὶ ἀνέμνησεν κ. τ. λ. "And he rung them, nay, rather also reminded them," etc. Διακωδωνίζειν is a word elsewhere used by St. Chrys., and would suit the passage very well, either as "he put their unsoundness to the proof (like false metal, or cracked earthenware)," or "he sounded an alarm in their ears:" but the other is equally suitable, and better accredited here. Below, Ἐπειδὴ δὲ καὶ κρινόμεθα κ. τ. λ.—Cat. ἐπεὶ δέ. Edd. νῦν δέ.

told the disciples, "What ye hear in the ear, that preach ye upon the housetops.—That in the name of Jesus Christ," he says, "of Nazareth, Whom ye crucified, Whom God raised from the dead, even by Him doth this man stand here before you whole." (v. 10). (Matt. x. 27.) Think not, he says that we conceal the country, or the nature of the death. "Whom ye crucified, Whom God raised from the dead, even by Him doth this man stand before you whole." Again the death, again the resurrection. "This is the stone," he says, "which was set at nought of you builders, which is become the head of the corner." (v. 11.) He reminds them also of a saying which was enough to frighten them. For it had been said, "Whosoever shall fall on this stone, shall be broken; but on whomsoever it shall fall, it will grind him to powder. (Matt. xxi. 44.)—Neither is there salvation in any other, (v. 12.) Peter says. What wounds, think you, must these words inflict on them! "For there is none other name," he continues, "under heaven given among men, whereby we must be saved." Here he utters also lofty words. For when[1] the object is, not to carry some point successfully, but only to show boldness, he does not spare; for he was not afraid of striking too deep. Nor does he say simply, "By another;" but, "Neither is there salvation in any other: that is, He is able to save us. In this way he subdued their threatening.

"Now when they saw the boldness of Peter and John, and perceived that they were unlearned and ignorant men, they marvelled and they took knowledge of them, that they had been with Jesus." (v. 13.) The two unlearned men beat down with their rhetoric them and the chief priests. For it was not they that spake, but the grace of the Spirit. "And beholding the man which was healed standing with them, they could say nothing against it." (v. 14.) Great was the boldness of the man; that even in the judgment-hall he has not left them. For had they said that the fact was not so, there was he to refute them. "But when they had commanded them to go aside out of the council, they conferred among themselves, saying, What are we to do to these men?" (v. 15.) See the difficulty they are in, and how the fear of men again does everything. As in the case of Christ, they were not able (as the saying is) to undo what is

done,[2] nor to cast it into the shade, but for all their hindering, the Faith did but gain ground the more; so was it now. "What shall we do?" O the folly! to suppose that those who had tasted of the conflict, would now take fright at it: to expect, impotent as their efforts had proved in the beginning, to effect something new, after such a specimen of oratory as had been exhibited! The more they wished to hinder, the more the business grew upon their hands. But what say they? "For that indeed a notable miracle hath been done by them is manifest to all them that dwell in Jerusalem; and we cannot deny it. But that it spread no further among the people, let us straightly threaten them, that they speak henceforth to no man in this name. And they called them, and commanded them not to speak at all, nor teach, in the name of Jesus." (v. 16–18.) See what effrontery is shown by these, and what greatness of mind by the Apostles. "But Peter and John answered and said unto them, Whether it be right in the sight of God to hearken unto you more than unto God, judge ye. For we cannot but speak the things which we have seen and heard. So when they had further threatened them, they let them go, finding nothing how they might punish them, because of the people." (v. 19–21.) The miracles shut their mouths: they would not so much as let them finish their speech, but cut them short in the middle, most insolently. "For all men glorified God for that which was done. For the man was above forty years old, on whom this miracle of healing was showed." (v. 22.) But let us look over what has been said from the beginning.

"And as they spake unto the people, etc. Being grieved that they taught the people, and preached through Jesus the resurrection of the dead." (Recapitulation, v. 1, 2.) So[3] then at first they did all for the sake of man's opinion (or glory): but now another motive was added: that they should not be thought guilty of murder, as they said subsequently, "Do ye wish to bring this man's blood on us?" (ch. v. 28.) O the folly! Persuaded that He was risen, and having received this proof of it,[4] they expected that He Whom death could not hold, could be cast into the shade by their machinations! What

---

[1] Ὅταν γὰρ μὴ ᾖ τι κατορθῶσαι. Quando enim non est aliquid præclare agendum. Ben. Non est corrigendum aliquid, Erasm. But see the comment in the recapitulation. "Where need was to teach, they allege prophecies; where to show boldness, they affirm peremptorily." κατορθῶσαι, "to carry their point," "to come off in the right;" viz. here, to convince by argument.

[2] ἀνατρέψαι (φησὶν) τὸ γενόμενον οὐκ ἔνι, A. B. C. Cat. A proverbial expression. Edd. ἀνατρέψαι τὸ γενόμενον οὐκ ἰσχυσαν, "Since then they had not power to undo," etc.

[3] We have supplied the text, instead of which C. inserts, "What shall we do to these men?" adopted by E. and Edd. Below, after the text 5. 28. E. inserts the latter part of v. 17. "Let us straitly threaten them," etc.

[4] All our Mss. and Cat. πεισθέντος ὅτι ἀνέστη, καὶ τοῦτο (A. C. N. τούτου, Cat. τὸ) τεκμ. λαβ., ὅτι ἐστὶ Θεός, except that B. reads ὅτι ἂν ἔστη Θεός. Hence we read, ὅτι ἀνέστη. The repetition of these words may have led to the alteration.

can match the folly of this!¹ Such is the nature of wickedness : it has no eyes for anything, but on all occasions it is thrown into perturbation. Finding themselves overborne, they felt like persons who have been outwitted : as is the case with people who have been forestalled and made a sport of in some matter. And yet² they everywhere affirmed that it was God that raised Him : but³ it was "in the Name of Jesus" that they spake ; showing that Jesus was risen. "Through Jesus, the resurrection of the dead" : for they themselves also held a resurrection : a cold and puerile doctrine, indeed, but still they held it. Why this alone, was it not sufficient to induce them to do nothing to them—I mean, that the disciples with such boldness bore themselves in the way they did ? Say, wherefore, O Jew, dost thou disbelieve ? Thou oughtest to have attended to the sign done, and to the words, not to the evil disposition of the many. "By their teaching the people."⁴ For already they were in ill repute with them by reason of what they had done to Christ ; so that they were rather increasing their own obloquy. "And they laid hands on them, and put them in hold until the morrow ; for it was now eventide." (v. 3.) In the case of Christ, however, they did not so ; but having taken Him at midnight, they immediately led him away, and made no delay, being exceedingly in fear of the multitude : whereas in the case of the Apostles here, they were bold. And they no more take them to Pilate, being ashamed and blushing at the thought of the former affair, lest they should also be taken to task for that.

"And it came to pass on the morrow, that their rulers, and elders, and scribes, were gathered together at Jerusalem." (v. 5.) Again in Jerusalem : and there it is that men's blood is poured out; no reverence for their city either ; "And Annas, and Caiaphas," etc. (v. 6.) "And Annas," it says, "and Caiaphas." His maid-servant it was that questioned Peter, and he could not bear it : in his house it was that Peter denied, when Another was in bonds there : but now, when he has come into the midst of them all, see how he speaks ! "By what name have ye done this ?" Why dost thou not speak it, what it is, but keepest that out of sight ? "By what name have ye done this ?" (v. 7.) And yet he affirmed, It was not we that did it. "Ye rulers of the people," etc. (v. 8.) Observe his wisdom : he does not say outright, "In the Name of Jesus we did it," but how ? "In His Name this man"—He does not say, "was made whole by us;" but—"doth stand here before you whole." And again, "If we be examined concerning the good deed done to the impotent man." (v. 9.) He hits them hard, that they are always making a crime of such acts, finding fault with works of beneficence done to men : and he reminds them of their former doings, that they run to do murder, and not only so, but make a crime of doing good deeds. Do you observe too (in point of rhetoric) with what dignity they express themselves ?⁵ Even in the use of words they were becoming expert by practice, and henceforth they were not to be beaten down.* "Be it known unto you all," etc. (v. 10.) Whereby he shows them that they rather do, in spite of themselves, preach Christ ; themselves extol the doctrine, by their examining and questioning. O exceeding boldness—"Whom ye crucified ! Whom God raised up"—this is bolder still ! Think not that we hide what there is to be ashamed of. He says this all but tauntingly : and not merely says it, but dwells upon the matter. "This," says he, "is the Stone which was set at naught by you builders ;" and then he goes on to teach them, saying in addition, "Which is made the head of the corner" (v. 11.); that is to say, that the Stone is indeed approved ! Great was the boldness they now had, in consequence of the miracle. And when there was need to teach, observe how they speak and allege many prophecies ; but when the point was to use boldness of speech, then they only speak peremptorily. Thus "Neither," says he, "is there any other name under heaven given among men whereby we must be

---

¹ The modern text adds, "And marvel not that they again attempt what had been vainly essayed before."
² Καὶ μὴν ἄνω καὶ κάτω ἔλεγον. E. F. D. for the sake of connection insert διὰ τοῦτο before ἔλεγον, adopted in Edd.
³ The same Mss. and Edd. "And that in the Name of Jesus, this man stands before you whole." And below : "And besides, they themselves held, etc. . . . : but now they disbelieve and are troubled, taking counsel to do something to them." Again, after "the wickedness of the many :"—"And pray why do they not deliver them up to the Romans ? Already they were," etc. All these variations are due to the innovator, who did not perceive that the recapitulation began at the place marked above.
⁴ The modern text inserts Καὶ τί δήποτε οὐ παραδιδόασιν αὐτοὺς Ῥωμαίοις ; "And why do they not deliver them over to the Romans ? Already they were," etc. And after ὥστε μᾶλλον ἑαυτοὺς ἐκάκιζον, the same adds, ὑπερτιθέμενοι τὴν αὐτῶν ἔνδειξιν· and below, "But concerning these, they neither were bold, nor yet do they take them to Pilate."

⁵ πῶς ἔχει καὶ τὸ βαρὺ τὰ ῥήματα ; καὶ ἐν τούτοις ἐγυμνάζοντο. i. e. "how their words have the rhetorical quality of τὸ βαρύ—grave and dignified impressiveness. Even in these, i. e. in the use of words," etc.
* Chrys. rightly remarks upon the great boldness and force of Peter's answer to the Sanhedrin (8–12). The εἰ ἀνακρινόμεθα, κ. τ. λ. (9) is ironical: "If for doing a good deed a man must make answer." Then follow the bold declarations which are almost of the nature of a challenge (10) "Be it known to you all," etc., and the assertion that it was in the name which they despised—the "Nazarene"—that the miracle had been wrought and all this is pointed by the contrast: "Ye crucified" but "God raised" and the charge of opposition to the divine plan in that they had rejected the stone which God had made the head of the corner.—G. B. S.

saved." (v. 12.) It is manifest to all, he says, because not to us alone was that Name given; he cites even themselves as witnesses. For, since they asked, "In what name did ye it?" "In Christ's," says he: "there is none other name. How is it that ye ask? On all hands this is palpable. "For there exists not another name under heaven, whereby we must be saved." This is the language of a soul which has renounced (κατεγνωκυίας) this present life. His exceeding out-spokenness proves here, that when he speaks in lowly terms of Christ, he does it not of fear, but of wise forbearance (συγκαταβαίνων): but now that it was the fitting time, he speaks not in lowly terms: by this very thing intending to strike dismay into them. Behold another miracle not less than the former. "And beholding the boldness of Peter and John," etc. "And they took knowledge of them that they had been with Jesus." (v. 13.) Not without a meaning has the Evangelist set down this passage; but in saying, "they recognized them that they had been with Jesus," he means, in His Passion: for only these were [with Him] at that time, and then indeed they had seen them humble, dejected: and this it was that most surprised them: the greatness of the change. For in fact Annas and Caiaphas with their company were there, and these men also had stood by Him, and their boldness now amazed them. "And beholding the boldness." For[1] not only their words; their very bearing showed it; that they should stand there so intrepidly to be tried in a cause like this, and with uttermost peril impending over them! Not only by their words, but by their gesture also, and their look and voice, and, in short, by everything about them, they manifested the boldness with which they confronted the people. From the things they uttered, they marvelled, perhaps: "that they were unlearned and common men:" for one may be unlearned, yet not a common or private man, and a common man, yet not unlearned. "Having perceived," it says. Whence? From[2] what they said? Peter

does not draw out long speeches, but then by his very manner and method (τῆς ἀπαγγελίας καὶ τῆς συνθήκης) he declares his confidence. "And they recognized them that they had been with Jesus." Which circumstance made them believe that it was from Him they had learned these things, and that they did all in the character of His disciples.* But not less than the voice of these, the miracle uttered a voice of its own: and that sign itself stopped their mouths. "And beholding the man," etc.] So that they would have been peremptory (ἐπέσκηψαν) with them, if the man had not been with them. "We cannot deny it." So that they would have denied it, if the thing had not been so: if the testimony had not been that of the people in general. "But that it spread no further among the people." (v. 17.) And yet it was palpable to all men! But such is the nature of wickedness: everywhere it is shamed. "Let us straitly threaten them." What sayest thou? Threaten? And expect ye to stop the preaching? And[3] yet all beginnings are hard and trying. Ye slew the Master, and did not stop it: and now, if ye threaten, do ye expect to turn us back? The imprisonment did not prevail with us to speak submissively, and shall ye prevail? "And they called them, and commanded them," etc. (v. 18, 19.) It[4] had been much better for them to let them go. "And Peter and John answered and said unto them, Whether it be right in the sight of God to hearken unto you more than unto God, judge ye." When the terror was abated (for that command was tantamount to their being dismissed), then also the Apostles speak more mildly: so far were they from

---

Here and in what follows we have endeavored to restore the proper order. In the Mss. in consequence, as it seems, of a confusion between the two clauses, οὐ δυνάμεθα ἀρνήσασθαι, and οὐ δυνάμεθα γὰρ . . . μὴ λαλεῖν, the order of the comments is deranged: viz. "So that they would—been with them." "And they recognized—stopped their mouths:" "'Whether it be right—judge ye.' When the terror—mere bravery. 'Whether it be right,' he says, and, 'We cannot deny it.' So that they would—better to let them go. 'Whether it be right—more than unto God.' Here by God—His Resurrection."

* The author seems to give two different interpretations of the statement: "They recognized them that they had been with Jesus." (1) They perceived that these were the men whom they had before seen in company with Jesus. (2) They saw that their words and acts betokened association with Jesus. It is evident that the former only is meant in this place.—G. B. S.

[1] Οὐ γὰρ τὰ ῥήματα μόνον, καὶ τὰ σχήματα ἐδείκνυντο τὸ ἀφρον-τίστως ἑστάναι περὶ τοιούτων κρινομένους. A. C. but the former has ἐδείκνυον, N. ἐδείκνυ. Our other Mss. have, οὐ γὰρ τοῖς ῥήμασι μόνον ἐδείκνυντο ἀφροντιστοῦντες π. τ. κρινόμενοι: which is only an attempt to make the passage grammatical. The comment is on the word θεωροῦντες: they beheld the boldness, for not words only, their gestures also, declared it.—Below, τὴν παρρησίαν ἐνέφαινον τὴν κατὰ τοῦ λαοῦ. Ἐξ ὧν ἐφθέγγοντο ἐθαύ-μαζον ἴσως. Edd. τὴν παρρ. ἐνέφαινον ἐπὶ τοῦ λαοῦ ἐξ ὧν ἐφθέγ-γοντο. Ἐθαύμαζον δὲ ἴσως.

[2] ἀφ᾽ ὧν ἔλεγον; Edd. and Erasm. take this affirmatively: but this can hardly be the Author's meaning; as he has just said that "from the things they uttered, they marvelled" that the speakers should be illiterate and common men. Something perhaps is wanting: e. g. "Not from the matter, but from the dialect, or from the brevity and abruptness of Peter's style, or, from the appearance of the men.—In the Mss. the next sentence is, ὥστε ἐπέσκηψαν ἂν αὐτοῖς, Extrema auctoritate mandassent iis, Erasm. Acrius in eos egissent, Ben.

[3] Καίτοι πανταχοῦ αἱ ἀρχαὶ δειναὶ καὶ δύσκολοι. "If at the beginning you failed, how can you expect to succeed now? for the beginning being always the hardest part of any difficult undertaking, if you could not stop it then, much less afterwards." The modern text unnecessarily alters it to οὔπω π. αἱ ἀ. χαλεπαί τε καὶ δυσκ.

[4] Πολλῷ μᾶλλον αὐτοῖς βέλτιον ἦν αὐτοὺς ἀφεῖναι. N. has a colon at αὐτοῖς, which perhaps is better; then the first clause may be the comment on τὸ καθόλου μὴ φθέγγεσθαι: "not to speak at all: much more to them. It had been better to dismiss them (at once)." For this sentence E. alone has, Πάνυ γε, τοὺς οὐδὲν ὑμᾶς ἡγουμένους καὶ ἀπειλοῦντας: "Aye, men who make nothing of you for all your threatening:" which is adopted by Edd.

mere bravery: "Whether¹ it be right," says he: and "We cannot [but speak]. Whether it be right in the sight of God to obey you rather than God." (v. 20.) Here [by "God"] they mean Christ, for he it was that commanded them. And once more they confirm the fact of His Resurrection. "For we cannot but speak the things we have seen and heard:" so that we are witnesses who have a right to be believed. "So when they had further threatened them." (v. 21.) Again they threatened in vain. "They let them go, finding nothing how they might punish them, because of the people: for all men glorified God for that which was done." So then the people glorified God, but these endeavored to destroy them: such fighters against God were they! Whereby they made them more conspicuous and illustrious. "For My strength," it is said, "is made perfect in weakness." (2 Cor. xii. 9.)

Already these as martyrs have borne testimony: set in the battle against all, they said, "We cannot but speak the things we have seen and heard." If the things we speak be false, reprehend them; if true, why hinderest thou? Such is philosophy! Those, in perplexity, these in gladness: those covered with exceeding shame, these doing all with boldness: those in fear, these in confidence. For who, I would ask, were the frightened? those who said, "That it spread no further among people," or these who said, "we cannot but speak the things we have seen and heard?" And these had a delight, a freedom of speech, a joy surpassing all; those a despondency, a shame, a fear; for they feared the people. But these were not afraid of those; on the contrary, while these spake what they would, those did not what they would. Which were in chains and dangers? was it not these last?

Let us then hold fast to virtue; let not these words end only in delight, and in a certain elevation of the spirits. This is not the theatre, for singers (κιθαρῳδῶν), and tragedians, and musicians (κιθαριστῶν), where the fruit consists only in the enjoyment and where the enjoyment itself passes with the passing day. Nay, would that it were enjoyment alone, and not mischief also with the enjoyment! But so it is: each man carries home with him much of what he has witnessed there, sticking to him like the infection of a plague: and one indeed, of the younger sort, having culled such snatches of song here and there of those

satanic plays,² as he could fix in his memory, goes singing them about the house: while another, a senior, and forsooth too staid for such levity, does not this indeed, but what is there spoken, both the preachments and the very words, he remembers it all; and another again, some filthy and absurd ditty. From this place you depart, taking nothing with you.—We have laid down a law—nay, not we: God forbid! for it is said, "Call no man your master upon the earth" (Matt. xxiii. 8); Christ has laid down a law that none should swear. Now, say, what has been done with regard to this law? For I will not cease speaking of it; "lest," as the Apostle saith, "if I come again, I must not spare." (2 Cor. xiii. 2.) I ask then, have you laid the matter to heart? have you thought of it seriously? have you been in earnest about it, or must we again take up the same subject? Nay, rather, whether you have or not, we will resume it, that you may think seriously about it, or, if you have laid it to heart, may again do this the more surely, and exhort others also. With what then, I pray you, with what shall we begin? Shall it be with the Old Testament? For indeed this also is to our shame, that the precepts of the Law, which we ought to surpass, we do not even thus observe! For we ought not to be hearing such matters as these: these are precepts adapted to the poor Jewish level (τῆς Ἰουδαϊκῆς εὐτελείας): we ought to be hearing those counsels of perfection; "Cast away thy property, stand courageously, and give up thy life in behalf of the Gospel, scorn all the goods of earth, have nothing in common with this present life; if any wrong thee, do him good; if any defraud thee, bless him; if any revile thee, show him honor; be above everything." (S. Ambros. de Off. i. 2.) These and such as these are what we ought to be hearing. But here are we discoursing about swearing; and our case is just the same as if, when a person ought to be a philosopher, one should take him away from the great masters, and set him to spell syllables letter by letter! Just think now what a disgrace it would be for a man having a flowing beard, and with staff in hand, and cope on shoulders,³ to go to school with chil-

---

¹ E. and Edd. "That a notable miracle is done, we cannot deny:" and below "Here they say, of God, for, 'of Christ.' Do you see how that is fulfilled which He said unto them, 'Behold I send you as sheep in the midst of wolves; fear them not.' Then once more they confirm," etc. For τοῦ Θεοῦ, A. B. have τοῦ Χριστοῦ.

² The various readings are ᾀσμάτων for δραμάτων, and μέρη for μέλη. Below, τῶν δὲ ἐκεῖσε λεγομένων καὶ κηρυγμάτων καὶ ῥημάτων μέμνηται πάντων. The mod. omits καὶ κηρ. The meaning is, "He cannot carry away in his memory the preaching which he hears in Church: but the preachments (proclamations) which he hears in the theatre he remembers, every word."

³ A description of the attire of a philosopher. Lucian mentions the long beard and the staff, but as the vestment, the τριβώνιον or tritum pallium. The ἐξωμὶς elsewhere denotes (in opposition to ἐπωμὶς) a tunic without sleeves, forming part of the dress of old men, and slaves, and also used in comedy. Here it seems to mean a cope, perhaps (Doun. ap. Savil.), the original of the academic hood, caputium.

dren, and be set the same tasks with them: would it not be above measure ridiculous? And yet the ridicule which belongs to us is even greater. For not as the difference between philosophy and the spelling-lesson, so is that between the Jewish polity and ours: no indeed, but as the difference between angels and men. Say now, if one could fetch down an angel from heaven, and should bid him stand here and listen to our preaching, as one whose duty it is to conform himself thereto, would it not be shameful and preposterous? But if to be yet, like children, under teaching about these things be ridiculous; what must it be, not even to attend to these things: how great the condemnation, how great the shame! To be Christians still, and to have to learn that it is not right to swear! However, let us put up with that, lest we incur even worse ridicule.

Well, then, let us speak to you to-day from the Old Testament. What does it tell us? "Accustom not thy mouth to swearing; neither use thyself to the naming of the Holy One." And why? "For as a servant that is continually beaten shall not be without a blue mark, so he that sweareth." (Ecclus. xxiii. 10.) See the discernment of this wise man. He did not say, "Accustom not to swearing" thy mind, but "thy mouth"; because being altogether an affair of the mouth, thus it is easily remedied. For at last it becomes a habit without intention; as for instance, there are many who entering the public baths, as soon as they have passed the threshold, cross (Hom. in 1 Cor. xi. 7) themselves (σφραγί-ζονται).[1] This the hand has got to do, without any one's bidding, by force of habit. Again, at the lighting of a candle, often when the mind is intent on something else, the hand makes the sign. In the same way also the mouth, without concurrence of the mind, articulates the word, from mere habit, and the whole affair is in the tongue. "Neither use thyself," he says, "to the naming of the Holy One. For as a servant that is continually beaten shall not be without a blue mark, so he that sweareth." He speaks not here of false oaths, but he cuts down all oaths, and to them also assigns their punishment. Why then, swearing is a sin. For such in truth is the soul; full of all these ulcers, all these scars. But you do not see them? Yes, this is the mischief of it; and yet you might see if you wished; for God has given you eyes. With eyes of this kind did the Prophet see, when he said, "My wounds stink, and are corrupt, because of my foolishness." (Ps. xxxviii. 5.) We have despised God, we have hated that good Name, we have trodden Christ under foot, we have lost all reverence, none names the Name of God with honor. Yet if you love any one, even at his name you start to your feet; but God you thus continually invoke, and make nothing of it. Call upon Him for the benefit of your enemy; call upon Him for the salvation of your own soul; then he will be present, then you will delight Him; whereas now you provoke Him to anger. Call upon Him as Stephen did; "Lord," he said, "lay not this sin to their charge." (ch. vii. 59.) Call upon Him as did the wife of Elkanah, with tears and sobs, and prayers. (1 Sam. i. 10.) I prevent you not, rather I earnestly exhort you to it. Call upon him as Moses called upon Him, yea, cried, interceding for those[2] who had driven him into banishment. For you to make mention at random of any person of consideration, is taken as an insult: and do you bandy God about in your talk, in season, out of season? I do not want to hinder you from keeping God always in your mind: nay, this I even desire and pray for, only that you should do this, so as to honor Him. Great good would this have done us, if we had called upon God only when we ought, and for what we ought. And why, I would ask, were such miracles wrought in the Apostles' times, and not in ours? And yet it is the same God, the same Name. But no, the case is not the same. For then they called upon Him only for those objects which I have mentioned; whereas we call upon Him not for these, but quite other purposes.—If a man refuse to believe you, and that is why you swear, say to him, "Believe me:" however, if you will needs make oath, swear by yourself. I say this, not to set up a law against Christ's law; God forbid; for it is said, "Let your yea be yea, and your nay, nay (Matt. v. 37): but by way of coming down to your present level, that I may more easily lead you to the practice of this commandment, and divert you from this tyrannical habit. How many who have done well in other respects, have been undone by these practices! Shall I tell you why it was permitted the ancients to take oaths? (for to

---

[1] Tertull. de Corona militum. "Ad omnem progressum atque promotum, ad omnem aditum et exitum, ad calceatum, ad lavacra, ad mensas, ad lumina, ad cubilia, ad sedilia, quæcunque nos conversatio exercet, frontem crucis signaculo terimus."

[2] ὑπὲρ τῶν φυγαδευσάντων αὐτόν. When the "intercession" of Moses is spoken of, it is natural to suppose that the reference is to Exod. xxxii. 11 ff. But Sav. and Ben. refer this to Num. xii. 13, perhaps because of ἐβόα (LXX. ἐβόησε). But the addition, "for those who had driven him into banishment," does not suit the latter and less memorable occasion: for Miriam and Aaron did but "speak against Moses," not attempt to banish or expel him. More fully expressed, the meaning may be, "For a people who began by making him a fugitive, Ex. ii. 15, Acts vii. 29, and now had put the finishing stroke to their ingratitude." Comp. Ex. xvii. 4; Num. xiv. 10, 13, etc.

take false oaths, was not permitted to them either.) Because they swore by idols. But are you not ashamed to rest in laws, by which they in their infirmity were led on to something better? It is true, when I take a Gentile in hand, I do not immediately lay this injunction upon him, but in the first place I exhort him to know Christ; but if the believer, who has both learnt Him and heard Him, must needs crave the same forbearance with the Gentile, what is the use, what the gain (of his Christianity?)—But the habit is strong, and you cannot detach yourself from it? Well then, since the tyranny of habit is so great, transfer it into another channel. And how is this to be done? you will ask. What I have said often, I say also now; let there be many monitors (λογισταί), let there be many examiners and censors (ἐξετασταὶ, δοκιμασταί). Say, if you chance to put on your[1] mantle inside out, you allow your servant to correct your mistake, and are ashamed to learn of him, although there is much to be ashamed of in this; and here when you are getting hurt to your soul, are you ashamed to be taught better by another? You suffer your menial to put your dress in order, and to fasten your shoes, and will you not endure him that would put your soul in order? Let even your menial, your child, your wife, your friend, your kinsman, your neighbor, be your teachers on this point. For as when a wild beast is hunted down from all sides, it is impossible for it to escape; so he that has so many to watch him, so many to reprove him, who is liable to be struck at from all sides, cannot help being on his guard. The first day he will find it hard to put up with, and the second, and the third; but after that it will come easier, and, the fourth passed, there will not even be anything to do. Make the experiment, if you doubt me; take it into consideration, I beseech you. It is not a trifling matter to be wrong in, nor yet to come right in; on both sides it is great for evil and for good. May the good be effected, through the grace and loving-mercy of our Lord Jesus Christ, to Whom with the Father and the Holy Ghost be glory, power, and honor, now and ever, world without end. Amen.

HOMILY XI.

ACTS IV. 23.

"And being let go, they went to their own company, and reported all that the chief priests and elders had said unto them."

NOT for their own glory did they tell the tale—how should such be their motive?—but what they displayed was the proofs therein exhibited of the grace of Christ. All that their adversaries had said, this they told; their own part, it is likely, they omitted: this made the hearers all the more courageous. What then? These again flee to the true Succor, to the Alliance invincible, and again, "with one accord. And when they heard that," it is said, "with one accord they lifted up their voice to God, and said:" (v. 24) and with great earnestness, for it is no prayer made at random. Observe with what exquisite propriety their prayers are framed: thus, when they besought to be shown who was meet for the Apostleship, they said, "Thou, Lord, which knowest the heart of all men, show:" (ch. i. 24) for it was a subject for Prescience there: but here, where the thing needed was that the mouths of their adversaries should be stopped, they speak of lordship; wherefore they begin thus: Lord, "(Δέσποτα) the God that madest heaven and earth, and the sea, and all that in them is: Who,[2] by the Holy Ghost through the mouth of Thy servant, David our father, didst say, Why did the heathen rage, and the people imagine vain things? The kings of the earth stood up, and the rulers were gathered together against the Lord, and against His Christ." (v. 24–26.) It is to sue God, as one may say upon His own covenants, that they thus produce this prophecy: and at the same time to comfort themselves with the thought, that in vain are all the imaginations of their foes. This then is what they say: Bring those words into accomplishment, and show that they "imagine vain things.—For of a truth," they proceed, "there were gathered together in this city, against Thy holy Child Jesus, (Παῖδα) Whom Thou hast anointed, both Herod, and Pontius

---

[1] ἂν μὲν τὸν βίρρον ἐναλλὰξ περιβάλῃ. A. N. βίρον. B. C. βίον (the word βίρρος, birrhus having perhaps become obsolete). Mod. τὴν ἐσθῆτα.

[2] The various readings are: ὁ τοῦ πατρὸς ἡμῶν διὰ Πνεύματος Ἁγίου στόματος Δ. παιδός σου, A. N. τοῦ π. ἡμῶν, om. C. ὁ ἐκ στόματος τοῦ π. ἡμῶν Δ. καὶ παιδός σου, B. ὁ διὰ στόμ. Δ. τοῦ παιδὸς σου, D. F. τοῦ, om. E.

Pilate, together with the Gentiles and the people of Israel, for to do whatsoever Thy hand and Thy counsel determined before to be done. And now, Lord, behold their threatenings." (v. 27–29.) Observe their largeness of mind (φιλοσοφίαν). These are not words of imprecation. In saying, "their threatenings," they do not mean this or that thing specifically threatened, but only in general, the fact of their threatening, perhaps, as being formidable. In fact, the writer is concise in his narrative. And observe, they do not say, "Crush them, cast them down;" but what? "And grant unto Thy servants, that with all boldness they may speak Thy word." Let us also learn thus to pray. And yet how full of wrath one would be, when fallen among men intent upon killing him, and making threats to that effect? how full of animosity? But not so these saints. "By stretching forth Thine hand to heal, and that signs and wonders may be done by the Name of Thy holy Child Jesus." (v. 30.) If in that Name the mighty deeds are wrought, great will be the boldness.

"And when they had prayed, the place was shaken where they were assembled together." (v. 31.) This was the proof that they were heard, and of His visitation. "And they were all filled with the Holy Ghost." What means, "They were filled?" It means, They were inflamed; and the Gift burned up within them. "And they spake the word of God with boldness. And the multitude of them that believed were of one heart and of one soul." (v. 32.) Do you see that together with the grace of God they also contributed their part? For everywhere it ought to be well observed, that together with the grace of God they do their part likewise. Just as Peter said above, "Silver and gold have I none"; and again, that "they were all [1] together." (ch. iii. 6.) But in this place, having mentioned that they were heard, the sacred writer proceeds to speak also of them, what virtue they showed. Moreover, he is just about to enter upon the narrative of Sapphira and Ananias, and with a view to show the detestable conduct of that pair, he first discourses of the noble behavior of the rest. Now say, did their love beget their poverty, or the poverty the love? In my opinion, the love begat the poverty, and then the poverty drew tight the cords of love. For observe what he says: "They were all of one heart and of one soul."

Behold,[2] heart and soul are what make the "together." "Neither said any of them that aught of the things which he possessed was his own; but they had all things common. And with great power the Apostles rendered their testimony (ἀπεδίδουν) of the resurrection." (v. 33.) The phrase betokens them to be as persons put in trust with a deposit: he speaks of it as a debt or obligation: that is, their testimony they with boldness did render, or pay off, to all. "And great grace was upon them all. Neither was there any among them that lacked." (v. 34.) Their feeling was just as if they were under the paternal roof, all for awhile [3] sharing alike. It is not to be said, that though indeed they maintained the rest, yet they did it with the feeling that the means whereof they maintained them were still their own. No, the admirable circumstance is this, that they first alienated their property, and so maintained the rest, on purpose that the maintenance might not come as of their own private means, but as of the common property. "For as many as were possessors of lands or houses sold them, and brought the price of the things that were sold, and laid them down at the Apostles' feet; and distribution was made unto every man according as he had need." (v. 35.) A great mark of honor this, that "they laid them at the Apostles' feet. And Joses, who by the Apostles was surnamed Barnabas, ('which is, being interpreted, The son of consolation.')" (v. 36.) I do not think that this is the same with the companion of Matthias; for that person was also called Justus and [Barsabas, but this, Joses and] "Barnabas" ["son of consolation"]. I suppose he also received the name from his virtue, as being qualified and suited for this duty. "A Levite, and of the country of Cyprus by birth." Observe on all occasions how the writer indicates the breaking up of the Law. But how was he also a "Cyprian by birth?" Because they then even removed to other countries, and still were called Levites. "Having land, sold it, and brought the price, and laid it at the Apostles' feet.[4]"

Let us now look over again what has been said. ["And being let go, they went to their own company, and reported all that the chief priests and elders had said unto them."] (Recapitulation, v. 23.) See the unostentatious

---

[1] Ἐπὶ τὸ αὐτὸ, At the same, as interpreted in a former Homily, vii. §. 2. For the next sentence, E. has Πάλιν ἐνταῦθα δηλῶν τὸ αὐτὸ λέγει, ὅτι τοῦ πλήθους, κ. τ. λ. "Here again explaining the 'τὸ αὐτὸ,'" etc.—It is in allusion to the same expression that he says a little further on, Ἰδοὺ καρδία καὶ ψυχὴ τὸ αὐτό.

[2] i. e. the ἐπὶ τὸ αὐτὸ is not local, but moral, the union of all believers in one heart and soul: q. d. "Do not object that it is impossible for all believers to be together now."

[3] The Catena has preserved the true reading, τέως, for which A. C. N. have ἅτε ὡς, B. F. D. ἅτε. E. substitutes υἱοί.

[4] A. B. C. N. τῶν Ἀποστόλων. ὅρα τὸ ἄτυφον. Ἰδωμεν λοιπὸν ἄνωθεν τὰ εἰρημένα. Καὶ τῶν Ἀποστόλων τὴν φιλοσοφίαν. The clause ὅρα τὸ ἄτυφον is to be restored to its place after the second τῶν Ἀποστόλων, as in the modern text, ὅρα τῶν Ἀ. τὸ ἄ. καὶ τὴν φ.

conduct of the Apostles, and their largeness of mind. They did not go about boasting, and say, "How we served (ἀπεχρησάμεθα) the priests!" nor were they ambitious of honor: but, we read, "they came unto their own company. Observe how they do not cast themselves upon temptations, but when the temptations present themselves, with courage endure them. Had it been some other of the disciples, perhaps, emboldened by the countenance of the multitude, he might have insulted, might have vented ever so many harsh expressions. But not so these true philosophers; they do all with mildness and with gentleness. "And when they heard that, we read, with one accord they lifted up their voice to God. (v. 24.) That shout proceeded from delight and great emotion. Such indeed are the prayers which do their work, prayers replete with true philosophy, prayers offered up for such objects, by such persons, on such occasions, in such a manner; whereas all others are abominable and profane. "Lord, Thou the God that madest heaven and earth, the sea, and all that in them is." Observe how they say nothing idle, no old wives' talk and fables, but speak of His power. Just as Christ Himself said to the Jews, "If I by the Spirit of God do cast out devils: behold the Father also speaks by the Spirit. For what saith it? "Lord, the God Who,[1] by the Holy Ghost, through the mouth of our father Thy servant David didst say, Why did the nations rage?" (v. 25.) Scripture is wont thus to speak of one as of many. "For of a truth, Lord, against Thy Holy Child Jesus, Whom Thou didst anoint,[2] both Herod and Pontius Pilate, etc. (v. 27.) Observe how, even in prayer, they circumstantially describe the Passion, and refer all to God.—That is, Not they had power to do this: but Thou didst it all, Thou[3] that didst permit, that dost call to account,

and yet didst bring to accomplishment, Thou the All-skilful and Wise, that didst serve Thee of Thine enemies for Thine own pleasure. (v. 28.) "For to do whatever Thy hand," etc. Here they discourse of His exceeding Skill and Wisdom and Power. So then, as enemies they came together, and with murderous purpose, and as opposing themselves, but they did what things Thou wouldest: ' For to do," as it is said, "whatsoever Thy hand and Thy purpose determined before to be done." What means, "Thy hand?" Here he seems to me to denote[4] one and the same thing by power and purpose, meaning that for Thee it is enough but to will: for it is not by power that one determines. "Whatsoever Thy hand," etc. i. e. Whatsoever Thou didst ordain: either this is the meaning, or, that by His hand He did effect. "And now, Lord, regard their threatenings." (v. 29.) As at that time, it is said, they "imagined vain things," so "now," grant that their imaginations may be in vain: i. e. let not their threatenings come into accomplishment. And this they said not because they would themselves deprecate any hardship, but for the preaching's sake. For they do not say, "and deliver us out of dangers;" but what? "And grant unto Thy servants, that with all boldness they may speak Thy word." Thou Who didst bring to pass the former designs, bring these also to accomplishment. Observe,[5] how they affirm God to be the Author of their confidence; and how they ask all for God's sake, nothing for their own glory or ambition. They promise for their own part, that they will not be dismayed; but they pray that signs may be wrought "by stretching forth Thy hand to heal, and that signs and wonders may be done:" (v. 30) for without these, however great the zeal they showed, they would be striving to no purpose. God assented to their prayer, and manifested this, by shaking the place. For "when they had prayed," it is said, "the place was shaken. (v. 31.) And wherefore this was done, hear from the prophet, when he says, "He looketh on the earth, and maketh it to tremble. (Ps.

---

[1] Against the Arians, who from such texts as Matt. xii. 28, inferred the inferiority of the Son, Chrys. says, "Observe, the Father Himself is here said to speak by the Holy Ghost." This is lost in the modern text, which substitutes Σωτὴρ for Πατήρ. The text is given in our Mss. with these variations. Comp. note a. A. C. Δεσποτα ὁ Θεὸς (ὁ Cat.) τοῦ πατρὸς ἡμῶν (ὁ N.) διὰ Πν. Ἀ στόματος Δ. B. Δεσπ. ὁ Θ. τῶν πάτρων ἡμῶν ὁ διὰ Πν. Ἀ διὰ στομ. Δ. E. F. D. Δεσπ. ὁ Θ. ὁ διὰ στομ. Δ. omitting διὰ Πν. Ἀ., but recognizing this clause in the comment. "Observe how they say nothing idle, but speak of His power only: or rather, just as Christ said to the Jews, If I by the Spirit of God do speak, so these also say, 'By the Holy Ghost.' Behold, the Saviour also speaks by the Spirit. And hear what it is that they say, 'Lord, the God Who by the mouth of David,'" etc.
[2] In the Mss. this clause of v. 27, with the following comment, ὅρα πῶς, κ. τ. λ. is set in the midst of the comment on v. 29; viz. before the sentence which (in the old text) also begins with ὅρα πῶς. It is certainly misplaced there. See note [5].—Διαιροῦσι τὸ πάθος seems to refer to the mention of Herod and Pontius Pilate.
[3] ὁ ἐπιτρέψας, ὁ καὶ ἐγκαλῶν καὶ εἰς πέρας ἀγαγών. The meaning seems to be, that though permitting, He calls to account, and though holding men responsible, yet brought it to pass. The modern text omits ὁ καὶ ἐγκαλῶν, and adds εἰργάσω at the end.

[4] τὸ αὐτὸ λέγειν τὴν δύναμιν καὶ βουλήν. i. e. "hand" means "power," and "hand" (or, power) and "purpose," or, "will" here make one notion, "Thy will which is also power," for to Thee to will is to prevail: not two notions, for we do not say that power determines, but only the will.—The Edd. however, adopt from E. τὴν χεῖρα for τὸ αὐτὸ, which spoils the sense. "By the hand he means the power and the purpose."—Below, B. C. have ὅτι τῇ χειρὶ διέταττεν (A. omits the clause), we retain from E. F. D. διέπραττεν.—Œcum. "The hand and the counsel mean the same thing: for where there is power, there is no need of counsel. What Thou didst order from the beginning is done."
[5] Here the Mss. insert, Ὃν ἔχρισας, φησίν. Ὅρα πῶς, κ. τ. λ. "Observe how, even in prayer, they circumstantially describe the Passion, and refer all to God," etc. And then: "Observe how they ask all," etc. See note [2].—Here for the latter ὅρα or ὁρᾷς πῶς of the old text, E. has εἶδες πῶς.

civ. 32.) For by this He made it manifest that He is present to their prayers. And again, another prophet saith, "The earth was shaken, and did tremble at the presence of the Lord." (Ps. xviii. 7 ; lxviii, 8.) And God did this, both to make it more awful, and to lead them on to a courageous trust. "And they were all filled with the Holy Ghost, and they spake the word of God with boldness." They[1] gained increased boldness. As it was the beginning (of their work), and they had besought a sensible sign for their persuasion (πρὸς τὸ πεισθῆναι αὐτούς)—but after this we nowhere find the like happening—therefore great was the encouragement they received. In fact, they had no means of proving that He was risen, save by miraculous signs. So that it was not only their own assurance (ἀσφαλείαν) that they sought : but that they might not be put to shame, but that they might speak with boldness. "The place was shaken," and that made them all the more unshaken. For this is sometimes a token of wrath, sometimes of favor and providence, but on the present occasion, of wrath. For[2] in those times it took place in an unusual manner. Thus, at the Crucifixion, the earth was shaken : and the Lord Himself says, "Then there shall be famines, and pestilences, and earthquakes in divers places. (Matt. xxiv. 7.) But then the wrath of which it was a sign was against the adversaries : as for the disciples, it filled them with the Spirit. Observe, even the Apostles, after the prayer, are "filled with the Holy Ghost." "And[3] the multitudes of them that believed," etc. (v. 32.) Great, you perceive, is the virtue of this thing, seeing their was need of this (grace) even in that company. For this is the foundation of all that is good, this of which he now for the second time makes mention, exhorting all men to the contempt of riches : "Neither[4] said any of them that aught of the things he possessed was his own," "but they had all things common." For that this was in consequence not merely of the miraculous signs, but of their own purpose, is manifest by the case of Sapphira and Ananias. "And with great power gave the Apostles witness," etc. (v. 33.) Not in word, but with power the Apostles exhibited their testimony of the Resurrection : just as Paul saith, "And my preaching was not with persuasive words of human wisdom, but with manifestation of the Spirit and of power." And it is not merely, With power, but, "With great power." (1 Cor. ii. 4.) "And great grace," it says, "was upon them all ; for neither was there any among them that lacked. (v. 34.) This is why the grace (was upon them all,) for that "there was none that lacked : " that is, from the exceeding ardor of the givers, none was in want. For they did not give in part, and in part reserve : nor yet in giving all, give it as their own. And they lived moreover in great abundance : they removed all inequality from among them, and made a goodly order. "For as many as were possessors," etc. And with great respect they did this : for they did not presume to give into their hands, nor did they ostentatiously present, but brought to the Apostles' feet. To them they left it to be the dispensers, made them the owners, that thenceforth all should be defrayed as from common, not from private, property.*

the reference to ch. ii. 44), has, Saying above (v. 32), Neither said any of them," etc., and here (v. 34), "Neither was there any among them that lacked." So Edd.

* The strong expressions of Chrys. concerning the community of goods at Jerusalem are quite different from the guarded and limiting statements of most modern commentators who seem bent upon showing that it was only a case of remarkable liberality, e. g. Hackett *in loco :* "Common in the use of their property, not necessarily in their possession of it." Our author's statements agree better with the New Test. notices on the subject. The main facts are these. (1) There was a real and general community of property. The statements in Acts on this point are clear and strong : καὶ εἶχον ἅπαντα κοινά (ii. 44) ; They were selling and distributing their real and personal property—τὰ κτήματα καὶ τὰς ὑπάρξεις (ii. 45). Nor did any one say that anything of his possessions was his own, ἀλλ ἦν αὐτοῖς ἅπαντα κοινά, (iv. 32) ; "As many as (ὅσοι) were possessors of lands or houses," sold them, brought the money and distribution was made to the needs of each (iv. 34, 35). This is more than distinguished liberality or mere prevailing willingness to give. (2) This peculiar phenomenon was connected with the habit of living together as a group or family, on the part of the Jerusalem Christians (i. 13 ; ii. 42-44). It was an evidence that they were peculiarly one in heart and soul, that no member of this closely-knit community was allowed to suffer while others could supply him (iv. 32-34). (3) The arrangement was purely voluntary. There was no law or demand in the case. Ananias and Sapphira (v. 1-11) were not punished for contributing to the common treasury only a part of the price of the land but as verse 4 clearly shows, for falsely presenting it *as the whole.* Yet the fact that they wished to have it thought that they had brought all seems to show that to bring all was customary and expected. (4) This community of goods was both local and temporary. It seems to have been confined to Jerusalem. There is no allusion to it in the Epistles. It sprang out of the ardor of brotherly love in the early years of the Christian community at Jerusalem and in view of the special needs of many of its members. The special poverty of the church at Jerusalem which made contributions from other churches necessary, may have resulted in part, as Meyer suggests, from the working

[1] Edd. καὶ εἰς παρρησίαν πλείονα ἀλείφων, as the conclusion of the preceding sentence before the (omitted) text. "And anointing them (as wrestlers) unto greater boldness." Then, "For since it was the beginning (of their work), they besought also a sensible sign in order that they might be believed (πρὸς τὸ πιστευθῆναι αὐτούς, but after this, etc.). Great was the encouragement they thus received from their prayer. And with good reason they crave the grace of signs, for they had no other means," etc.

[2] Ἐπεὶ τότε ξένως γέγονεν. Καὶ γὰρ ὅτε ἐσταυρώθη, ἐσαλεύθη ἡ γῆ. Edd. Ἐπὶ δὲ τοῦ σωτηρίου πάθους ξένως καὶ παρὰ φύσιν γέγονε· καὶ γὰρ τότε πᾶσα ἐσαλεύθη ἡ γῆ. "But at the Passion of our Saviour it happened in an unusual manner and preternaturally : for then all the earth was shaken." Instead of the next sentence, "And the Lord Himself," etc. E. has, "to the intent the power of Him that was crucified everywhere be known, and that the Sufferer was God, and not simply man. But further : although it was a token of wrath, yet was it of His wrath against the adversaries," etc., but Edd. follow the old text here.

[3] A. B. C. omit the text : D. F. Edd. insert from v. 33, 34. "And great grace was upon them all, neither was there any among them that lacked : " E. "And with great power, etc. and great grace," etc. Τοῦ πράγματος ἡ δύναμις, i. e. of the having all things common, as below, p. 163. C. has πνεύματος, which Savile adopts.

[4] The innovator. mistaking the meaning of τὸ δεύτερον (viz

This was also a help to them against vain-glory. If this were done now, we should live more pleasant lives, both rich and poor, nor would it be more pleasant to the poor than to the rich themselves. And if you please, let us now for awhile depict it in words, and derive at least this pleasure from it, since you have no mind for it in your actions. For at any rate this is evident, even from the facts which took place then, that by selling their possessions they did not come to be in need, but made them rich that were in need. However, let us now depict this state of things in words, and let all sell their possessions, and bring them into the common stock—in words, I mean : let none be excited, rich or poor. How much gold think you would be collected? For my part, I conjecture—for of course it is not possible to speak exactly—that supposing all here, men and women, to empty out their whole property, lands, possessions, houses,—for I will not speak of slaves, since at that time there was no such thing, but doubtless such as were slaves they sat at liberty,—perhaps ten hundred thousand pounds weight of gold would be the amount collected : nay, twice or thrice as much. For consider ; at what number of "*juga*"[1] (yokes) is our city rated? How many (of the population) shall we say are Christians? shall we say an hundred thousand, and the rest Greeks and Jews? Then what thousands (of pounds) of gold would be collected! And what is the number of poor? I do not think more than fifty thousand. Then to feed that number daily, what abundance there would be! And yet if the food were received in common, all taking their meals together, it would require no such great outlay after all. But, you will ask, what should we do after the money was spent? And do you think it ever could be spent? Would not the grace of God be ten thousand fold greater? Would not the grace of God be indeed richly poured out? Nay, should

we not make it a heaven upon earth? If, where the numbers were three thousand and five thousand, the doing of this thing had such splendid success, and none of them complained of poverty, how much more glorious would this be in so vast a multitude? And even of those that are without, who would not contribute?—But, to show that it is the living separately that is expensive and causes poverty, let there be a house in which are ten children : and the wife and the man, let the one work at her wool, the other bring his earnings from his outdoor occupation : now tell me, in which way would these spend most? by taking their meals together and occupying one house, or by living separately? Of course, by living separately. For if the ten children must live apart, they would need ten several rooms, ten tables, ten attendants, and the income otherwise in proportion. Is it not for this very reason, that where there is a great number of servants, they have all one table, that the expense may not be so great? For so it is, division always makes diminution, concord and agreement make increase. The dwellers in the monasteries live just as the faithful did then : now did ever any of these die of hunger? was ever any of them not provided for with plenty of everything? Now, it seems, people are more afraid of this than of falling into a boundless and bottomless deep. But if we had made actual trial of this,[2] then indeed we should boldly venture upon this plan (τοῦ πράγματος). What grace too, think you, would there not be! For if at that time, when there was no believer but only the three thousand and the five thousand : when all, throughout the world, were enemies, when they could nowhere look for comfort, they yet boldly entered upon this plan with such success ; how much more would this be the case now, when by the grace of God there are believers everywhere throughout the world? What Gentile would be left? For my part, I think there would not be one ; we should so attract all, and draw them to us? But yet if we do but make[3] fair progress, I trust in God that even this shall be realized. Only do as I say, and let us successfully achieve things in their regular order ; if God grant life,

of this plan. (5) The custom can hardly be explained apart from the expectation of the nearness of the *Parousia*. In the Thessalonian church all labor for self-support was upon the point of ceasing for the same reason. 1 Thess. iii. 10, sq.—G. B. S.

[1] εἰς πόσον ἰούγων ἀριθμὸν συντείνει : The word here used perplexed the scribes of later times when it had become obso-lete, and N. has ἰούλων, B. ἰούγγων, C. ὅγγων (sic), only A. ex corr. ἰούγων. The innovator substitutes μιγάδων and συντελεῖ. The meaning is, At what number of *juga* is our city assessed to the imperial tributes? Justinian *Novell.* xvii. c. 8. pre-scribes that the imperial πράκτορες, *exactores*, shall be com-pelled to insert in their returns (ἀποχαί) the exact quantity " of *zygocephala* or *juga* or *jugalia* or whatever else be the term used in different localities :" τὸ πόσον τῶν ζυγοκεφάλων ἢ ἰο ὑγων ἢ ἰουγαλίων, ἢ ὅπως δήποτε ἂν αὐτὰ κατὰ χώραν καλοίεν. See Du Fresne *Gloss.* s. vv. It seems that each holding of land was rated or assessed at so many *juga* or yokes of oxen ; moreover the term *jugum* is equivalent to a measure of land, as Varro remarks that land is measured in some places by *juga*, in others by *jugera*.

[2] i. e. People now are more afraid of this (the cenobitical way of life, than they are of launching into the sea of this world's temptations : whereas if we had made trial of this, we should boldly venture upon the practice so happily adopted by the first Christians. (τοῦ πράγματος as above, p. 73, note 3.)

[3] Ἐὰν ὁδῷ προβαίνωμεν. B. unnecessarily inserts ταύτῃ, which Ben. adopts. "*Si hac via progrediamur.*" Ὁδῷ προ-βαίνειν (or ὁδῷ βαδίζειν) is a common phrase in St. Chrys. Ap-plied to persons, it means "to be fairly started and getting on :" to things, "to be in train," as in Hom. i. ὁδῷ καὶ τὰ ἄλλα προύβαινεν, "the rest would follow in course."

I trust that we shall soon bring you over to this way of life.

In the first place, as regards that law about swearing : accomplish that ; establish it firmly : and let him that has kept it make known him that has not, and call him to account withal, and rebuke him sternly. For the *supra*, Hom. viii.) appointed time (ἡ προθεσμία, is at hand, and I am holding inquisition in the matter, and him that is found guilty I will banish and exclude. But God forbid that any such should be found among us ; rather may it appear, that all have strictly kept this spiritual watchword. And as in war it is by the watchword that friends and strangers are shown, so let it be now ; for indeed now also we are engaged in a war ; that we may know our brethren that are properly such. For what a good thing it is that we should have this to be our cognizance both here and in a foreign land ! What a weapon this, against the very head of the devil ! A mouth that cannot swear will soon both engage God in prayers, and smite the devil a deadly blow. A mouth that cannot swear will also be incapable of using insulting language. Cast out this fire from your tongue, as you would from a house : this fire, drag it out. Give your tongue a little rest : make the sore less virulent. Yea, I beseech you, do this, that I may go on to set you another lesson : for as long as this is not rightly done, I dare not pass on to any other. Let this lesson be got perfectly, and you shall have a consciousness of the achievement, and then I will introduce you to other laws, or rather not I, but Christ. Implant in your soul this good thing, and by little and little ye shall be a paradise of God, far better than that paradise of old. No serpent among you, no deadly tree, nor any such thing. Fix this habit deep. If this be done, not ye only that are present shall be benefitted, but all that are in all the world ; and not they alone, but those that are to succeed hereafter. For a good habit having once entered, and being kept by all, will be handed on to long ages, and no circumstances shall be able to erase it. If he that gathered sticks on the sabbath was stoned,—the man that is doing a far more heinous work than that gathering, the man that is amassing a load of sins, for such is the multitude of oaths, what shall he undergo ? what shall he not have to endure ? You will receive great assistance from God, if this be well achieved by you. If I were to say, Be not abusive, immediately you will plead to me your indignation ; should I say, Be not envious, you will urge some other excuse. But in this case you have nothing of the kind to say. On which account I began with the easy precepts, which indeed is also the uniform practice in all arts. And

thus one comes to the higher duties, by learning first those which are easier far. How easy it is you will see, when by the grace of God having succeeded in this, you shall receive another precept.

Put it in my power to speak out boldly, in the presence both of Gentiles and of Jews, and, above all, of God. Yea, I entreat you by the love, by the pangs wherewith I have travailed for your birth, " my little children." I will not add what follows, " of whom I travail in birth again ; " nor will I say, " until Christ be formed in you." (Gal. iv. 19). For I am persuaded, that Christ has been formed in you. Other language I will use towards you ; " My brethren, dearly beloved and longed for, my joy and my crown." (Phil. iv. 1.) Believe me that I shall use no other language. If at this moment there were placed upon my head ten thousand richly-jewelled royal crowns, they could not give me the joy which I feel at your growth in holiness ; or rather, I do not think the monarch himself has such a joy, as that wherewith I joy over you. Let him have come home, victorious over all the nations at war with him, let him have won many other crowns besides the crown of his right ; and receive other diadems as tokens of his victory : I do not think he would joy over his trophies, as I joy over your soul's progress. For I exult, as if I had a thousand crowns on my head ; and well may I rejoice. For if by the grace of God you achieve this good habit, you will have gained a thousand battles far more difficult than his ; by wrestling and fighting with malicious demons, and fiendish spirits, with the tongue, not with sword, but by the will. For consider how much is gained, if so be that you do succeed ! You have eradicated, first, a heinous habit ; secondly, an evil conceit, the source of all evil, namely, the opinion that the thing is indifferent and can do no hurt ; thirdly, wrath ; fourthly, covetousness ; for all these are the offspring of swearing. Nay, hence you will acquire a sure footing in the way to all other virtues. For as when children learn their letters, they learn not them alone, but by means of them are gradually taught to read ; so shall it be with you. That evil conceit will no longer deceive you, you will not say, This is indifferent ; you will no longer speak by mere habit, but will manfully stand against all, so that having perfected in all parts that virtue which is after God, you may reap eternal blessings, through the grace and loving-kindness of His Only-Begotten Son, to Whom with the Father and the Holy Ghost be glory, power and honor, now and ever, world without end. Amen.

HOMILY XII.

ACTS IV. 36, 37.

"And Joses, who by the Apostles was surnamed Barnabas (which is, being interpreted, The son of consolation), a Levite, and of the country of Cyprus, having land, sold it, and brought the money, and laid it at the Apostles' feet."

THE writer is now about to relate the affair of Ananias and Sapphira, and in order to show that the man's sin was of the worst description, he first mentions him who performed the virtuous deed; that, there being so great a multitude all doing the same, so great grace, so great miracles, he, taught by none of these, but blinded by covetousness, brought destruction upon his own head. "Having land,—meaning that this was all he possessed,—sold it, and brought the money, and laid it at the Apostles' feet. But a certain man named Ananias, with Sapphira his wife, sold a possession, and kept back part of the price, his wife also being privy to it, and brought a certain part, and laid it at the Apostles' feet." (ch. v. 1, 2.) The aggravating circumstance was, that the sin was concerted, and none other saw what was done. How came it into the mind of this hapless wretch to commit this crime? "But Peter said, Ananias, why hath Satan filled thine heart to lie to the Holy Ghost, and to keep back part of the price of the land?" (v. 3.) Observe even in this, a great miracle performed, greater far than the former. "Whiles it remained," say she, "was it not thine own? and after it was sold, was it not in thine own power?" (v. 4.) That is, "Was there any obligation and force? do we constrain you against your will?" "Why hast thou conceived this thing in thine heart? thou hast not lied unto men, but unto God. And Ananias hearing these words fell down, and gave up the ghost." (v. 5.) This miracle is greater than that of the lame man, in respect of the death inflicted, and the knowing what was in the thought of the heart, even what was done in secret.* "And great fear came on all them that heard these things.

And the young men arose, and wound him up, and carried him out, and buried him. And it was about the space of three hours after, when his wife, not knowing what was done, came in. And Peter answered unto her, Tell me whether ye sold the land for so much?" (v. 6–8.) The woman he would fain save, for the man had been the author of the sin: therefore he gives her time to clear herself, and opportunity for repentance, saying, "Tell me whether ye sold the land for so much? And she said, Yea, for so much. Then Peter said unto her, How is it that ye have agreed together to tempt the Holy Ghost? Behold, the feet of them which have buried thy husband are at the door, and shall carry thee out. Then she fell down straightway at his feet, and yielded up the ghost; and the young men came in, and found her dead, and, carrying her forth, buried her by her husband. And great fear came upon all the Church, and upon as many as heard these things." (v. 9–11.)

After this fear had come upon them, he wrought more miracles; both Peter and the rest; "And by the hands of the Apostles were many signs and wonders wrought among the people; and they were all with one accord in Solomon's porch. And of the rest durst no man join himself to them," i. e. to the Apostles; "but the people magnified them," i. e. the Jewish people. If[1] "no man durst join himself unto them," the Apostles, "there were," however, "the more added unto the Lord, believers, multitudes both of men and of women, insomuch that they brought out into the streets their impotent folk, and laid them upon couches and beds, that at the least the shadow of Peter passing by might overshadow some of them." (v. 12–15.) For Peter was the

---

* Chrys. evidently regards the death of Ananias and Sapphira as a miracle wrought by Peter (so Meyer). All that the narrative states is that Peter disclosed the sin of Ananias and foretold the fate of his wife (Lechler). The middle position seems preferable: Peter acted as the instrument of God, the agent of the divine retribution. His will acted in conscious harmony with the divine purpose of which it was the organ (so Gloag).—G. B. S.

[1] Εἰ οὐδεὶς ἐτόλμα κολλᾶσθαι αὐτοῖς τ. ἀποστ. For εἰ, which is the reading of A., and seems to be the true reading, B. C. N. have ἤ. The passage is corrupt, but the sense may be restored by inserting the words of the sacred text as above: i. e. To them, the Apostles, none durst join himself, but believers were the more added to the Lord, etc. Then ὁ γὰρ Πέτρος κ. τ. λ. falls into its natural place as the comment on Πέτρου κἂν ἡ σκία. But with the other reading, ἤ, the sense may be completed as below, p. 78, viz. " or, no man durst," etc., [so that they were allowed to remain undisturbed in Solomon's porch.] The modern text, after " the people magnified them," substitutes: Εἰκότως· καὶ γὰρ ὁ Π. κ. τ. λ. "With reason. For indeed Peter was henceforth terrible, inflicting punishment, exposing even the thoughts of the mind : to whom also they gave more heed by reason of the miracle," etc.

wonderful one, and he to whom they more gave heed both because of his public harangue, the first and the second and the third, and because of the miracle; for he it was that wrought the miracle, the first, the second, the third: for the present miracle was twofold: first, the convicting the thoughts of the heart, and next the inflicting of death at his word of command. "That at the least the shadow of Peter passing by," etc. This had not occurred in the history of Christ; but see here what He had told them actually coming to pass, that "they which believe on Me, the works that I do shall they do also; and greater works than these shall they do." (John xiv. 12.) "There came also a multitude out of the cities round about unto Jerusalem, bringing sick folks, and them that were vexed with unclean spirits; and they were healed every one." (v. 16.)

And now I would have you observe the way in which their whole life is interwoven. First, there was despondency on account of Christ taken from them, and then came joy because of the Spirit descending upon them; again, dejection because of the scoffers, and then joy in the result of their own apology. And here again we find both dejection and gladness. In that they were become conspicuous, and that God made revelations to them, there was gladness: in that they had cut off some of their own company, there was sadness. Once more: again there is gladness upon their success, and again sadness by reason of the High Priest. And so it will be seen to be the case throughout. And the same will be found to hold in the case of the ancient saints likewise.—But let us look over again what has been said.

"They sold them," it is written, "and brought the prices, and laid them down at the Apostles' feet." (Recapitulation. iv, 34-37.) See, my beloved brethren, how instead of leaving the Apostles to sell, they themselves sold, and presented the prices to them. "But[1] a certain man named Ananias," etc. (v. 1.) This history touches Bishops too, and very forcibly. And the wife of Ananias was privy to the thing done: therefore he examines her. But perhaps some one will say that he dealt very harshly with her. What do you mean? What harshness? If for gathering sticks a man is to be stoned, much rather ought he for sacrilege; for this money was become sacred. He that has chosen to sell his goods

and distribute them, and then withdraws them, is guilty of sacrilege. But if he is sacrilegious, who resumes from his own, much more he who takes from what is not his own. And do not think that because the consequence is not now the same, the crime will go unpunished. Do you see that this is the charge brought against Ananias, that having made the money sacred, he afterwards secreted it? Couldest thou not, said Peter, after selling thy land, use the proceeds as thine own? Wast thou forbidden? Wherefore after thou hadst promised it? See how at the very beginning, the devil made his attack; in the very midst of such signs and wonders, how this man was hardened! Something of the same kind had happened upon a time in the Old Testament. The son of Charmi coveted the devoted thing: for observe there also what vengeance ensues upon the sin. Sacrilege, beloved, is a most grievous crime, insulting, and full of contempt. We neither obliged thee to sell, the Apostle says, nor to give thy money when thou hadst sold; of thine own free choice thou didst it; why hast thou then stolen from the sacred treasury? "Why," he says, "hath Satan filled thine heart?" (v. 3.) Well, if Satan did the thing, why is the man made guilty of it? For admitting the influence of the devil, and being filled with it. You will say, they ought to have corrected him. But he would not have received correction; for he that has seen such things as he had seen, and is none the better, would certainly be none the better for anything else that could be done; the matter was not one to be simply passed over: like a gangrene, it must be cut out, that it might not infect the rest of the body. As it is, both the man himself is benefitted in regard that he is not left to advance further in wickedness, and the rest, in that they are made more earnest; otherwise the contrary would have ensued. In the next place, Peter proves him guilty, and shows that the deed was not hidden from him, and then pronounces the sentence. But wherefore, upon what purpose hast thou done this? Didst thou wish to keep it? Thou oughtest to have kept it all along, and never to have professed to give it. The sacrilege, beloved, is a grievous one. For another, it may be, coveted what was not his own: but it was at thy discretion to keep what was thine own. Why then didst thou first make it sacred, and then take it? Out of excessive contempt hast thou done this. The deed does not admit of pardon, it is past pleading for.—Therefore let it be no stumbling-block to any, if at present also there are sacrilegious persons. If there were such persons then, much more now, when evils are

---

[1] The modern text inserts here: "But not so Ananias: he secretes a part of the price of the field which he sold: wherefore also he is punished as one who did not manage his business rightly, and who was convicted of stealing what was his own."

many. But let us "rebuke them before all,
that others also may fear." (1 Tim. v. 20.)
Judas was sacrilegious, but it was no stumbling-block to the disciples. Do you see
how many evils spring from love of money?
"And great fear, it is said, came on all them
that heard these things." (v. 5.) That man
was punished, and others profited thereby.
Not without cause. And yet, signs had been
wrought before: true, but there was not such
a sense of fear. So true is that saying,
"The Lord is known by executing judgments."
(Ps. ix. 16.) The same thing had occurred
in the case of the Ark: Uzzah was punished
and fear came upon the rest. (2 Sam. vi. 7.)
But in that instance the king through fear
removed from him the Ark; but here the
disciples became more earnestly heedful.
["And it was about the space of three hours
after, when his wife, not knowing what was
done, came in," etc.] (v.7.) But observe how
Peter, instead of sending for her, waited till
she entered; and how none of the others
durst carry out the intelligence. Such the
teacher's awfulness, such the disciples' reverence, such the obedience! "An interval of
three hours,"—and yet the woman did not
hear of it, and none of those present reported
it, although there was time enough for it to
be noised abroad; but they were afraid. This
circumstance the Evangelist relates with
wonder even, when he says, "Not knowing
what was done, came in." "And Peter
answered unto her," etc. (v. 8.) And yet she
might have perceived even from this that
Peter knew the secret. For why, having
questioned none other, does he question you?
Was it not clear that he asked because he
knew? But so great was her hardness, it
would not let her attempt to evade the guilt;
and with great confidence she replied; for
she thought she was speaking only to a man.
The aggravation of the sin was, that they committed it as with one soul, just as upon a
settled compact between them. "How is it
that ye have agreed together," he said, "to
tempt the Spirit of the Lord? behold, the feet
of them which have buried thy husband are at
the door." (v. 9.) First he makes her learn
the sin, and then shows that she will justly
suffer the same punishment with her husband,
since she has committed the same wickedness:
"And they shall carry thee out. And she fell
down straightway at his feet," for she was
standing near him, and yielded up the ghost."
(v. 10.) So entirely by their own act had they
invited upon themselves the vengeance! Who
after that would not be struck with awe? who
would not fear the Apostle? who would not marvel? who not be afraid? "And they were with

one accord, all of them in Solomon's porch," (v.
12) no longer in a house, but having occupied
the very Temple, they there passed their
time! No longer they guarded themselves
against touching the unclean; nay, without
scruple they handled the dead. And observe
how, while to their own people they are severe,
against the aliens they do not exercise their
power. "But[1] the people," he says, "magnified them." (v. 13.) And as he had mentioned their being "in Solomon's porch," that
you may not wonder how the multitude allowed
this, he tells us that they did not dare even to
approach them: for "no man," he says, "durst
join himself unto them." "But believers
were the more added unto the Lord, multitudes
both of men and women: insomuch that they
brought forth the sick into the streets, and
laid them on beds and couches, that at the
least the shadow of Peter passing by might
overshadow some of them." (v. 14, 15.)
Great faith, surpassing what had been shown
in the case of Christ. How comes this? Because Christ declared: "And greater works
than these shall he do, because I go unto My
Father." (John xiv. 12.) And these things
the people do, while the Apostles remain there,
and are not moving about from place to place:
also from other places they were all bringing
[their sick] on beds and couches: and from
all quarters accrued to them fresh tribute of
wonder; from them that believed, from them
that were healed, from him that was punished;
from their boldness of speech towards those
(their adversaries), from the virtuous behavior of the believers: for certainly the effect
produced was not owing to the miracles only.
For though the Apostles themselves modestly
ascribe it all to this cause, declaring that they
did these things in the name of Christ, yet
at the same time the life and noble conduct
of the men helped to produce this effect.
"And believers were more added unto the
Lord, multitudes both of men and women."
Observe, how he now no longer tells the
number of them that believe; at such a rate
was the faith making way even to an immense
multitude, and so widely was the Resurrection
proclaimed. So then "the people magnified
them:" but they were now no longer lightly
to be despised as once they were: for in a
little moment, at a single turn of the scale,
such have been the effects produced by the
fisherman and by the publican! Earth was
become a heaven, for manner of life, for
boldness of speech, for wonders, for all besides; like Angels were they looked upon with

[1] Edd. from E., omitting this and the following sentence,
insert v. 14, 15, and below, John xiv. 12, both of which are
wanting in the old text.

wonder: all unconcerued for ridicule, for threats, for perils: compassionate [1] were they, and beneficent; some of them they succoured with money, and some with words, and some with healing of their bodies and of their souls; no kind of healing ($\pi\tilde{\alpha}\nu$ $\epsilon\tilde{\iota}\delta o\varsigma$ $\iota\alpha\tau\rho\epsilon\iota\alpha\varsigma$) but they accomplished.

Peter all but pleads for himself, when at the point to inflict the punishment, and at the same time gives a lesson to the rest. For because the act would seem exceeding stern, therefore it is that he does so much [2] in the case. * In respect of the woman also the process of judgment was terrible. But [3] see how many evils grow out of the sacrilege: covetousness, contempt of God, impiety; and upon these too he pleaded for himself before the assembly, in that he did not immediately proceed to punishment, but first exposed the sin. None groaned, none lamented, all were terrified. For as their faith increased, the signs also were multiplied, and great was the fear among their own company: for the things which are from without do not so militate ($\pi o\lambda\epsilon\upsilon\epsilon\tilde{\iota}$) against our peace, as do the acts of our own people. If we be firmly joined together, no [4] warfare will be hard: but the mischief would be the being divided and broken up. Now they went about in the public place: with boldness they attacked even the market, and in the midst of enemies they prevailed, and that saying was fulfilled, "Be Thou Ruler in the midst among Thine enemies." (Ps. cx. 2.) This was a greater miracle, that they, arrested, cast into prison, should do such acts as these!

If those for lying suffered such things, what shall not the perjured suffer? Because she simply affirmed, "Yea, for so much," ye see what she suffered. Bethink you then; they that swear and forswear themselves, of what should they be worthy? It [5] comes in opportunely to-day even from the Old Testament to show you the heinousness of perjury. "There was," it says, "a flying sickle, ten cubits in breadth." (Zech. v. 2.) The "flying" betokens the swift advent of the vengeance which pursues oaths; that it is many cubits in length and breadth, signifies the force and magnitude of the woes; that it comes flying "from heaven," is to show that the vengeance comes from the judgment-seat on high: that it is in the form of a "sickle," denotes the inevitableness of the doom: for just as the sickle, where it comes and has hooked the neck, is not drawn back with nothing but itself, but with the head reaped off, even so the vengeance which comes upon the swearers is severe, and will not desist until it have completed its work. But if we swear and escape, let us not be confident; this is but to our woe. For what think ye? How many, since Ananias and Sapphira, have dared the same with them? How is it then, say you, that they have not met with the same fate? Not because it was allowed in them, but because they are reserved for a greater punishment. For those who often sin and are not punished, have greater reason to fear and dread than if they were punished. For the vengeance is increased for them by their present impunity and the long-suffering of God. Then let us not look to this, that we are not punished; but let us consider whether we have not sinned: if sinning we are not punished, we have the more reason to tremble. Say, if you have a slave, and you only threaten him, and do not beat him; when is he most in fear, when most inclined to run away? Is it not when you only threaten him? And hence we advise each other not to be continually using

---

[1] Edd. from E. "But not only for this reason, but because, being exceedingly humane and beneficent, they succored some with money, some with healing of their bodies. Why hath Satan filled thine heart? Peter," etc.

[2] E. Edd. "therefore both in the case of the man himself, and in that of the wife, he makes the judgment terrible."

* Our author touches upon the difficulty which has so often been found in this narrative on account of the apparent disproportion of the penalty to the offence. But it is to be remembered that: (1) The narrative presents the sin as the most heinous—lying to God—trying to deceive the Holy Spirit whose organs the Apostles were. It was a deliberate conspiracy for this purpose. (2) These persons were members of the church who professed to possess and should have possessed the Holy Spirit. Instead they had been overcome by a Satanic principle which here makes its manifestation in pride and hypocrisy. The selfishness of the deed is the more grievous because of the great piety and sacrifice of the act which was counterfeited. Pride is the greater evil, the higher the virtue which it simulates. (3) Such a retributive miracle, besides being just in itself, may have been specially necessary in this early stage of the church's life to warn against deception and fraud and to emphasize the principles of honor in the early church. "So terrible was this judgment in order to guard the first operations of the Holy Spirit" (Neander).—G. B. S.

[3] Edd. from E. "Now if, their sin being inexcusable, he had not inflicted such punishment on them both, what contempt of God would thence have arisen! And that this was the reason, is evident from the fact, that he did not immediately," etc.

[4] E. Edd. "There will be none to war upon us: just as, if we be put asunder one from another, on the contrary all will set upon us. Hence it was that they henceforth were of good courage, and with boldness attacked," etc.

[5] $E\tilde{\upsilon}\kappa\alpha\iota\rho o\nu$ $\kappa\alpha\tilde{\iota}$ $\dot{\alpha}\pi\dot{o}$ $\tau\tilde{\eta}\varsigma$ $\Pi\alpha\lambda\alpha\iota\tilde{\alpha}\varsigma$ $\delta\epsilon\tilde{\iota}\xi\alpha\iota$ τo $\chi\alpha\lambda\epsilon\pi\dot{o}\nu$ $\tau\tilde{\eta}\varsigma$ $\epsilon\pi\iota o\rho\kappa\iota\alpha\varsigma$ $\tau\eta\mu\epsilon\rho o\nu$. Meaning perhaps that this had occurred in one of the Scripture Lessons for the day. Below, $K\alpha\theta\dot{\alpha}\pi\epsilon\rho$ $\gamma\dot{\alpha}\rho$ $\delta\rho\epsilon\pi\alpha\nu o\nu$ $\ddot{o}\pi o\upsilon\pi\epsilon\rho$ $\ddot{\alpha}\nu$ $\dot{\epsilon}\mu\pi\dot{\epsilon}\sigma\eta$ $o\dot{\upsilon}\kappa$ $\ddot{\alpha}\nu$ $\kappa\alpha\theta'$ $\dot{\epsilon}\alpha\upsilon\tau\dot{o}$ $\dot{\alpha}\nu\epsilon\lambda\kappa\upsilon\sigma\theta\epsilon\tilde{\iota}\nu$ $\mu\dot{o}\nu o\nu$, $\dot{\alpha}\lambda\lambda\dot{\alpha}$ $\kappa\alpha\tilde{\iota}$ $\dot{\alpha}\pi o\tau\epsilon\mu\nu o\mu\dot{\epsilon}\nu\eta\varsigma$ $\tau\tilde{\eta}\varsigma$ $\kappa\epsilon\phi\alpha\lambda\tilde{\eta}\varsigma$. So A. B. N. Savil. and C., which last however has $\dot{\alpha}\pi\dot{o}$ for $\dot{\alpha}\pi o\tau\epsilon\mu\iota\nu o\mu\dot{\epsilon}\nu\eta\varsigma$. Hales ap. Sav. suggests, that $\dot{\alpha}\pi o\tau\epsilon\mu\nu$. $\tau\tilde{\eta}\varsigma$ $\kappa\epsilon\phi$. ought to be rejected: it is better however to supply $\epsilon\iota\varsigma$ $\tau\rho\dot{\alpha}\chi\eta\lambda o\nu$ before $\dot{\epsilon}\mu\pi\dot{\epsilon}\sigma\eta$ as in the translation. The meaning is explained in Serm. ad. Pop. Antioch. xv. t. ii. 158. D. "A flying sword, one might manage to escape from, $\delta\rho\epsilon\pi\dot{\alpha}\nu\eta\nu$ $\delta\dot{\epsilon}$ $\epsilon\dot{\iota}\varsigma$ $\tau\dot{o}\nu$ $\tau\rho\dot{\alpha}\chi\eta\lambda o\nu$ $\dot{\epsilon}\mu\pi\epsilon\sigma o\tilde{\upsilon}\sigma\alpha\nu$ $\kappa\alpha\tilde{\iota}$ $\dot{\alpha}\nu\tau\iota$ $\sigma\chi o\iota\nu\iota o\upsilon$ $\gamma\epsilon\nu o\mu\dot{\epsilon}\nu\eta\nu$, $o\dot{\upsilon}\delta\epsilon\iota\varsigma$ $\ddot{\alpha}\nu$ $\delta\iota\alpha\phi\upsilon\gamma o\iota$, but from a sickle darted round the neck and catching it as a halter would, there can be no escape." Hence it appears that the innovator has quite mistaken the Author's meaning. He reads, $K\alpha\theta\dot{\alpha}\pi\epsilon\rho$ $\gamma\dot{\alpha}\rho$ $\delta\rho\epsilon\pi\alpha\nu o\nu$ $\epsilon\dot{\iota}\varsigma$ $\tau\rho\dot{\alpha}\chi\eta\lambda o\nu$ $\dot{\epsilon}\mu\pi\epsilon\sigma\dot{o}\nu$ $o\dot{\upsilon}\kappa$ $\ddot{\alpha}\nu$ $\kappa\alpha\theta'$ $\dot{\epsilon}\alpha\upsilon\tau\dot{o}$ $\dot{\alpha}\nu\epsilon\lambda\kappa\upsilon\sigma\theta\epsilon\tilde{\iota}\nu$, $\mu\dot{\epsilon}\nu\epsilon\iota$ $\delta\dot{\epsilon}$ $\pi\tilde{\omega}\varsigma$ $\ddot{\epsilon}\tau\iota$ $\kappa\alpha\tilde{\iota}$ $\dot{\alpha}\pi o\tau\epsilon\mu\nu o\mu\dot{\epsilon}\nu\eta\varsigma$ $\tau\tilde{\eta}\varsigma$ $\kappa\epsilon\phi\alpha\lambda\tilde{\eta}\varsigma$: i. e. "having cut off one head, it still remains, that it may cut off more:" which is irrelevant to the matter in hand. viz. how. $\tau\dot{o}$ $\delta\rho\epsilon\pi\alpha\nu o\epsilon\iota\delta\dot{\epsilon}\varsigma$ denotes $\tau\dot{o}$ $\dot{\alpha}\phi\upsilon\kappa\tau o\nu$ $\tau\tilde{\eta}\varsigma$ $\tau\iota\mu\omega\rho\iota\alpha\varsigma$. Of the Edd. Savile alone retains the old and genuine reading. Montf. strangely remarks, "Savilianam lectionem esse Morelliana quam sequimur obscuriorem."

threats, thereby choosing rather to agitate the mind by the terror, and lacerating it worse than with blows. For in the one instance the punishment is momentary, but in the other it is perpetual. If then no one feels the stroke of the sickle, do not look to this, but rather let each consider whether he commits such sins. Many like things are done now as were done before the Flood, yet no flood has been sent: because there is a hell threatened, and vengeance. Many sin as the people did in Sodom, yet no rain of fire has been poured down; because a river of fire is prepared. Many go the lengths of Pharaoh; yet they have not fared like Pharaoh, they have not been drowned in a Red Sea: for the sea that awaits them, is the sea of the bottomless pit, where the punishment is not accompanied with insensibility, where there is no suffocation to end all, but in ever lengthened torture, in burning, in strangling, they are consumed there. Many have offended like the Israelites, but no serpents have devoured them: there awaits them the worm that never dieth. Many have been like Gehazi, yet they have not been struck with leprosy: for instead of leprosy, it remains for them to be cut asunder, and numbered among the hypocrites. Many have both sworn and forsworn; but if they have indeed escaped, let us not be confident: the gnashing of teeth awaits them. Yea, here too they will suffer many grievous woes, though, it may be, not immediately, but after further transgressions, that the vengeance may be the greater; for even we often set out at first with small sins, and then through great offences lose all. Therefore when you see anything happening to you, call to mind that particular sin of yours. The sons of Jacob are an example of this. Remember Joseph's brothers; they had sold their brother, they had even attempted to slay him; nay, they had slain him, as far as inclination went; they had deceived and grieved the old man; they suffered nothing. After many years they are brought into extreme peril, and now they are put in remembrance of this their sin. Exceeding wisely is this circumstance brought in. Hear what they say: "We are verily guilty concerning our brother." (Gen. xlii. 21.) In this manner then do thou also, when anything happens, say, We are verily guilty, because we have not obeyed Christ; because we have sworn; my much swearing, and my false swearing, has fallen upon my own head. Confess thou; since they also confessed, and were saved. For what though the punishment follow not immediately? Since Ahab also did not immediately after his sin in the matter of Naboth suffer that vengeance which he yet at last suffered. (1 Kings xxi. 19.) And what is the reason of this? God sets thee a time, in which to wash thyself clean; but if thou persist, at last He will send down the vengeance. You have seen the fate of liars. Consider what is the fate of false swearers, consider, and desist. It is impossible a swearer should not forswear himself, whether he will or not; and no perjurer can be saved. One false oath sufficeth to finish all, to draw down upon us the whole measure of vengeance. Let us then take heed to ourselves, that we may escape the punishment due to this offence, and be deemed worthy of the loving kindness of God, through the grace and mercies of His only-begotten Son, with Whom to the Father and the Holy Ghost be glory, power, and honor, now and ever, and world without end. Amen.

HOMILY XIII.

ACTS V. 17, 18.

"Then having risen up, the high-priest and they that were with him (which is the sect of the Sadducees) were filled with indignation, and laid their hands on the Apostles, and put them in the common prison."

"Having risen up," that is, being[1] roused, being excited at the things taking place, "the high-priest and they which were with him (which is the sect of the Sadducees) were

F. Edd. "Nothing more reckless than wickedness, nothing more audacious. Having learned by experience the courage of these men, from the attempts they had made before, they nevertheless attempt, and again come to the attack. What means it, 'And having risen up, the high-priest and they that were with him?' He was roused, it says, being excited at what had taken place. 'And laid their hands on the Apostles, and put them in the common prison.' Now they assault them more vigorously: but did not forthwith, etc. And whence is it manifest that they assaulted them more vigorously? From their putting them in the common prison. Again they are involved in danger, and again they experience succor from God. And in what manner, hear from what follows."

[1] Œcumenius has in part preserved the true reading, τ. ἐ. διεγερθεὶς, κινηθεὶς, ἐπὶ τοῖς γινομένοις [text omitted] σφοδρότερον αὐτοῖς ἐπιτίθεται. A. B. C. Cat. τ. ἐ., διηγέρθη, κινηθεὶς ἐπὶ τοῖς γεν. "Καὶ ἐθ. αὐτοὺς ἐν τ. δ." Νῦν σφοδρ. αὐτοῖς ἐπιτίθενται. And again after πράους ἔσεσθαι,—Καὶ σφοδρ. ἐπιτίθενται (Cat. ἐπιτίθεται)· ἔθεντο αὐτοὺς, φ., ἐν τ. δ. Ἄγγελος δὲ κ. τ. λ.—E. D.

filled with indignation, and laid their hands on the Apostles:" they now assault them more vigorously : "and put them in the common prison ;" but did not forthwith bring them to trial, because they expected them again to be softened down. " But the Angel of the Lord opened the prison doors, and brought them forth, and said, Go, stand and speak·in the temple to the people all the words of this life." "And when they heard that, they entered into the temple early in the morning, and taught." (v. 19-21.) This was done both for the encouragement of the disciples, and for the benefit and instruction of the others. And observe how the proceeding in the present instance is just the same as in what Christ Himself did. Namely, in His miracles though He does not let men see them in the act of being wrought, He furnishes the means whereby they may be apprised of the things wrought : thus, in His Resurrection, He did not let them see how He rose : in the water made wine, the guests do not see it done, for they have been drinking much, and the discernment He leaves to others. Just so in the present case, they do not see them in the act of being brought forth, but the proofs from which they might gather what had been done, they do see. And it was by night that the Angel put them forth. Why was this ? Because[1] in this way they were more believed than they would have been in the other: so, people

would not even have had occasion to put the question : they would not in some other way have believed. So it was in the old times, in the case of Nebuchadnezzar : he saw them praising God in the furnace, and then indeed he was put in amazement. (Dan. iii. 24.) Whereas then these priests ought as their first question to have asked, How came ye out ? instead of this, as if nothing had happened, they ask, " Did we not straitly charge you not to speak ? " (v. 28.) And observe, by report of others they are apprised of all the circumstances : they see the prison remaining closed with safety, and the guards standing before the doors.[2] A twofold security this ; as was the case at the sepulchre, where was both the seal, and the men to watch. See how they fought against God ! Say, was this of man's doing, that happened to them ? Who led them forth, when the doors were shut ? How came they out, with the keepers standing before the door ? Verily they must be mad or drunken to talk so. Here are men, whom neither prison, nor bonds, nor closed doors, had been able to keep in ; and yet they expect to overpower them : such is their childish folly ! Their officers come and confess what has taken place, as if on purpose to debar them from all show of reason. Do you mark how there is miracle upon miracle, differing in kind, some wrought by them, others on them, and these more illustrious than the others ? "And when they heard that, they entered into the temple early in the morning, and taught. But the high-priest came, and they that were with him, and called the council together, and all the senate of the children of Israel, and sent to the prison to have them brought. But when the officers came, and found them not in the prison, they returned, and told, saying, The prison truly found we shut with all safety, and the keepers standing without before the doors : but when we had opened, we found no man within. Now when the high-priest and the captain of the temple and the chief priests heard these things, they doubted of them whereunto this would grow." (v. 21-25.) It[3] is well ordered that the information was not brought to them at once, but they are first utterly at a loss what to think, that when they have considered it well and seen that there is a Divine Power in the case, then they may learn the whole state of the case. " Then came one, and told them, say-

---

[1] Ὅτι οὕτω μᾶλλον ἢ ἐκείνως ἐπιστεύθησαν· οὕτω καὶ οὐκ ἂν ἐπὶ τὸ ἐρωτῆσαι ἦλθον, οὐκ ἂν ἑτέρως ἐπίστευσαν. If it be meant that the Apostles were more believed because the miracle itself was not seen, than they would have been if the Angel had brought them out in open day, this may be understood in a sense which St. Chrys. expresses elsewhere, viz. with reference to the nature of faith : "in the latter case there could have been no room for doubt; people would have been forced to acknowledge the claims of the Apostles." Thus Hom. vi. in 1 Cor. "Put the case that Christ should come this moment with all the Angels, reveal Himself as God, and all be subject unto Him : would not the heathen believe? But will this be counted unto the heathen for faith? No : this were no faith ; for a compulsory power from without—the visible appearance —would have effected this. There is no free choice in the matter : οὐκ ἔστι τὸ πρᾶγμα προαιρέσεως." But then the next sentence ought to be, Ἐκείνως γὰρ οὐδ' ἂν ἐπὶ τὸ ἐρ. ἦλθον· εἰ δὲ οὐχ οὕτως, οὐκ ἂν ἑτέρως ἐπ., or to that effect.—Perhaps, however, the meaning is rather : "It was so plain to common sense that a miracle must have been wrought, that had the Angel brought them out in the sight of all men (οὕτω), they could not have been more believed than they had a right to be as the case was (ἐκείνως). Had the miracle been performed openly (οὕτω), people would have had no occasion even to ask, How is this? And they who, as it was, were not brought to ask such a question, would certainly not have believed under any other circumstances. So in the Old Testament, Nebuchadnezzar, when he sees the Holy Men praising God in the furnace, is brought to ask in amazement, Did we not cast three men, etc.: but these priests are so hardened, that instead of asking as they ought to have done, How came ye out? they only ask, as if nothing had happened, Did we not straitly charge you, etc. And observe, they have no excuse for their wilful apathy : for they have had a full report of the circumstances from the officers: the prison shut, the guards at their posts." If this be the meaning, we must replace οὐκ ἂν or οὐδ' ἂν in the sentence ὅτι οὕτω μᾶλλον κ. τ. λ. But the text is too corrupt to be restored by any simple emendation.—Edd. "Because in this way, etc. especially as they would not have been brought to ask the question, nor yet in another case would they themselves have believed ;" ἄλλως τε καὶ ὅτι οὐκ ἂν, and οὔτε μὴν ἑτέρως ἂν καὶ αὐτοὶ ἐπίστευσαν.

[2] Here the Mss. insert v. 21-23, inconveniently; for it interrupts the connection. Chrys. here deviates from his usual method, not following the narrative point by point, but reflecting first upon the conduct of the priests. Of course it is to be understood, that the whole text, at least to v. 28, had been first read out.

[3] In the Mss. this comment is placed before v. 24.

6

ing, Behold, the men whom ye put in prison are standing in the temple, and teaching the people. Then went the captain with the other officers, and brought them without violence : for they feared the multitude, lest they should have been stoned." (v. 25, 26.) O the folly of the men ! "They feared," saith he, "the multitude." Why, how had the multitude helped the Apostles ? When they ought to have feared that God Who was continually delivering them like winged creatures out of their power, instead of that, "they feared the multitude ! "And the high-priest," shameless, reckless, senseless, "asked them, saying, Did not we straitly command you that ye should not teach in this name ? and, behold, ye have filled Jerusalem with your doctrine, and intend to bring this man's blood upon us." (v. 27, 28.) What then (say the Apostles)? Again with mildness they address them ; and yet they might have said, "Who are ye, that ye countermand God ? " But what do they say ? Again in the way of exhortation and advice, and with much mildness, they make answer. "Then Peter and the other Apostles answered and said, We ought to obey God rather than men." (v. 29.) High magnanimity ! He shows them too that they are fighting against God.[1] For, he says, Whom ye killed, Him hath God raised up. "The God of our fathers raised up Jesus, Whom ye slew and hanged on a tree. Him hath God exalted with His right hand to be a Prince and a Saviour, for to give repentance to Israel, and forgiveness of sins." (v. 30, 31.) And again they refer the whole to the Father, that He should not seem to be alien to the Father. "And hath exalted," saith He, "with his right hand." He affirms not merely the Resurrection, but the Exaltation also. "For to give repentance to Israel." Observe here as before the gain (to them) : observe the perfection of doctrine conveyed in the form of apology. "And we are witnesses of these things." (v. 32.) Great boldness of speech ! And the ground of their credibility : "And so is also the Holy Ghost, Whom God hath given to them that obey Him." Do you observe that they allege not only the Spirits testimony ? And they said not, "Whom He hath given " to us, but, "to them that obey Him : therein alike showing their own unassuming temper, and intimating the greatness of the gift, and showing the hearers that it was possible for them also to receive the Spirit. See, how these people were instructed both by deeds and by words, and yet they paid no

heed, that their condemnation might be just. For to this end did God suffer the Apostles to be brought to trial, that both their adversaries might be instructed, and all might learn, and that the Apostles might be invigorated to boldness of speech. "And they hearing that, were cut to the heart." (v. 33.) The [2] others (on a former occasion) "when they heard these things were pricked ; " here they were cut (as with a saw) (διεπρίοντο) "and desired to slay them." (ch. ii. 37.)

But it is necessary now to look over again what we have read. "But the angel of the Lord by night opened the prison doors, and brought them forth, and said, Go, stand and speak in the temple to the people all the words of this life. Brought [3] them forth." (Recapitulation, v. 19, 20.) He did not bring them away to benefit themselves thereby, but, "Stand," he says, "and speak in the temple to the people." But if the guards had put them out, as those thought, they would have fled, that is, supposing they had been induced to come out : and if those had put them forth, they would not have stood in the temple, but would have absconded. No one is so void of sense, as not at once to see this. "Did we not straitly charge you ? " (v. 28.) Well, if they undertook to obey you, ye do well to call them to account : but if even at the very time they told you they would not obey, what account have you to call them to, what defence is there for them to make ? "And behold ye have filled Jerusalem with your doctrine, and intend to bring this man's blood upon us." * Mark the inconsistency of the

<hr>

[1] Here A. B. C. N. insert v. 29 omitted above by the two first. The following sentence, omitted here by D. E. F. and inserted after v. 31, is there repeated by A. B. C.

[2] E. Edd. "Observe the excess of their wickedness. When they ought to have been struck with alarm at what they heard, here they are cut (to the heart), and take counsel in their temerity (βουλεύονται εἰκῇ) to slay (them)." The innovator did not perceive the reference to ii. 37 in οἱ ἄλλοι "ταῦτα ἀκούσαντες κατενύγησαν."

[3] E. and Edd. "'Having brought them forth.' He does not himself bring them away, but lets them go : that in this way also their intrepidity might be known ; which also they showed, in that by night they entered into the temple and taught." In the following sentence perhaps the purport of what St. Chrys. said was, that "if, as the priests supposed, the guards had let them out, the guards themselves would have absconded, and the Apostles would not have stood in the temple, but would have escaped." Εἰ γε πεισθέντες may have been said of the guards, "if they had been bribed or otherwise induced to let them out ; " but all the Mss. have εἰ γε π. ἐξῆλθον, in the sense, "supposing, which is not likely, that the Apostles had been induced to come forth at the request of the guards." Savile gives this clause to the latter part, beginning as E. and Edd. with μᾶλλον δὲ εἰ ἐξέβ. for καὶ εἰ ἐξέβ. "Supposing they had been induced to come out, or rather if those had put them out : " Ben. refers it to what precedes ; "they would have fled, if they had come out at their request : nay, if those had put them out," etc.

* The meaning of the council's statement : "Ye intend to bring this man's blood upon us" (28) probably is : You would cause an insurrection against us and thus be avenged for the crucifixion of Jesus (Meyer) : others take it to mean : You would carry the idea that we had murdered an innocent man in crucifying Jesus (Hackett). The strong language of Peter in reply (29) which seems to imply : We cannot help consequences ; we must obey God in our preaching and healing, favors the former view. The confusion of the text of Chrys. here (see note *in loco*) makes his view on this point uncertain. —G. B. S.

accusations, and the exceeding folly. They want to make it appear now, that the dispositions of the Jews[1] are sanguinary, as if they were doing these things not for the truth's sake, but in the wish to be revenged. And for this reason too the Apostles do not answer them with defiance (θρασέως): for they were teachers. And yet where is the man, who, with a whole city to back him, and endowed with so great grace, would not have spoken and uttered something big? But not so did these: for they were not angered; no, they pitied these men, and wept over them, and marked in what way they might free them from their error and wrath. And they no longer say to them, "Judge ye:" (ch. iv. 19) but they simply affirm, saying, "Whom God raised up, Him do we preach: it is by the will of God that these things are done." They said not, Did not we tell you even then, that "we cannot but speak the things which we have seen and heard?" (ib. 20.) for they are not contentious for glory; but they repeat again the same story,—the Cross, the Resurrection. And they tell not, wherefore He was crucified—that it was for our sakes: but they hint at this indeed, but not openly as yet, wishing to terrify them awhile. And yet what sort of rhetoric is here? None at all,[2] but everywhere it is still the Passion, and the Resurrection and the Ascension, and the end wherefore: "The God of our fathers raised up Jesus," etc. (v. 30, 31.) And yet what improbable assertions are these! Very improbable, no doubt; but for all that, not rulers, not people, had a word to say against them: but those had their mouths stopped, and these received the teaching. "And we," saith he, "are witnesses of these things." (v. 32.)   Of what things? Of His having promised forgiveness and repentance: for the Resurrection indeed was acknowledged, now. But that He giveth forgiveness, both we are witnesses, and "so is the Holy Ghost," Who would not have come down, unless sins had been first remitted: so that this is an indisputable proof. "When they heard that, they were cut" (to the heart), "and took counsel to slay them." (v. 33.)   Hearest thou of the

forgiveness of sins, O wretched man, and that God doth not demand punishment, and dost thou wish to slay them? What wickedness was this! And yet, either they ought to have convicted them of lying, or if they could not do that, to have believed: but if they did not choose to believe, yet they ought not to slay them. For what was there deserving of death? Such was their intoxication, they did not even see what had taken place. Observe, how everywhere the Apostles, when they have made mention of the crime, add the mention of forgiveness; showing, that while what had been done was worthy of death, that which was given was proffered to them as to benefactors! In what other way could any one have persuaded them?

"Then stood up the high-priest," etc. As[3] men in high repute, these (the Apostles) were about to take their place near to the Prophets. The Sadducees were they that were most sore on the subject of the Resurrection. But perchance some one will say: Why, what man, endowed with such gifts as the Apostles were, would not have been great? But consider,[4] I pray you, how, before that they were endowed with the grace, "they were continuing steadfastly with one accord in prayer" (ch. i. 14), and depending on the aid from above. And dost thou, my beloved, hope for the kingdom of heaven, yet endurest naught? And hast thou received the Spirit, yet sufferest not such things, nor encounterest perils? But they, before they had breathing-time from their former dangers, were again led into others. And even this too, that there is no arrogance, no conceit, how great a good

<hr>

[1] φονικὰς λοιπὸν βούλονται δεῖξαι τὰς προαιρέσεις τῶν Ἰουδαίων. As the latter part of the sentence, ὡς οὐ δι' ἀλήθειαν ταῦτα ποιούντων ἀλλ' ἀμύνασθαι βουλομένων, seems inapplicable to the Jews, and to be meant for the Apostles, it may be conjectured that the true reading is τῶν Ἀποστόλων· "that the Apostles were bent upon having blood." But all the Mss. have τῶν Ἰουδαίων, and the sense so far is satisfactory: viz. They want to make it appear now indeed what bloody-minded men the Jews are: now, not when Christ was crucified.

[2] The modern text: "So artlessly did they preach the Gospel of life. But when he says, 'He hath exalted,' he states for what purpose, namely, 'to give repentance' he adds, 'to Israel, and remission of sins.' But, it will be said, these things seemed incredible. How say you? And why not rather credible. seeing that neither rulers," etc.

[3] Here begins a second recapitulation or rather gleaning, partly of matter not touched upon before, partly of further remarks on what has been said.—Ὡς εὐδοκιμοῦντες ἐγγὺς τῶν προφητῶν ἔμελλον ἵστασθαι· This relates to v. 13-16, as the reason why they were "filled with indignation." The innovator (E. F. D. Edd.) not perceiving this, alters ὡς εὐδοκιμοῦντες to ἢ ὡς εὐδοκιμοῦντας, which he joins to the former sentence, "How else could any one have persuaded them than (by treating them) as persons in high repute?" and adds, "And mark their malignity: they set on them the Sadducees who were most sore on the subject of the Resurrection: but they got nothing by their wickedness. But perchance," etc.

[4] St. Chrysostom frequently contends against the common excuse, "We cannot attain to the holiness of the first Christians, because there are no miracles now." Thus, he urges, Hom. in Matt. xlvi., that it was not their miracles that made the saints, both of the Old and of the New Testament, great and admirable, but their virtues: without which, no miracles would have availed for themselves or others: that if they wrought miracles, it was after they, by their noble qualities and admirable lives had attracted the Divine grace: for miracles proceed from a holy life, and this is also their goal: only he that lives a holy life receives this grace; and he that receives it, receives it only that he may amend the life of others. . . Let no man therefore wait for miracles. It afflicts the evil spirit when he is expelled from the body, much more when he sees the soul set free from sin: for in this lies Satan's great power, and to destroy this, Christ died. In expelling this from thyself, thou hast performed a miracle greater than all miracles. This is not my doctrine; it is the doctrine of the Apostle Paul. 1 Cor. xii. 31, the "more excellent way" is not miracles, but Charity, the root of all good. If we practise this we need no miracles; and if we practise not from miracles we shall get no good.

it is! To converse with mildness, what a gain it is! For not all that they did was the immediate work of grace, but there are many marks of their own zeal as well. That the gifts of grace shine forth in them, this was from their own diligence. See, for instance, from the very beginning, how careful Peter is; how sober and vigilant: how they that believed cast away their riches, had no private property, continued in prayer, showed that they were of one mind, passed their time in fastings. What grace, I ask (alone), did all this? Therefore it is that He brings the evidence home to them through their own officers. Just as in the case of Christ, it was their officers who said, "Never man spake as this Man speaketh." (John vii. 46.) These[1] (proofs) are more apt to be believed than the Resurrection.—Observe also the moderation shown by (the rulers) themselves, and how they give way. "The high-priest asked them, saying," etc. (v. 27): here he reasons with them, forsooth, in a moderate tone; for he was frightened: indeed to hinder was what he desired rather than to kill, since that he cannot do: and with the view to rouse them all, and show them the extreme danger they are in, "And intend," says he (to the Apostles), "to bring this man's blood upon us." Dost thou still take Him to be but *man?* He wants to make it appear that the injunction was necessary for their own safety. But mark what (Peter) says: "Him hath God exalted with His right hand to be a Prince and a Saviour, for to give repentance to Israel, and forgiveness of sins." (v. 31.) Here he forbears to mention the Gentiles, not to give them a handle against him. "And they desired," it says, "to slay them." (v. 33.) See again these in perplexity, these in pain: but those in quiet and cheerfulness and delight. It is not merely, They were grieved, but "They were cut" (to the heart). Truly this makes good that proverb, "Evil do, evil fare:" as we may see in this case. Here were these men in bonds, set at the bar of judgment, and the men that sit in judgment upon them were in distress and helpless perplexity. For as he who strikes a blow upon the adamant, gets the shock of the blow himself, so it was with these men. But they saw that not only was their boldness of speech not stopped, but rather their preaching increased the more, and that they discoursed without a thought of fear, and afforded them no handles against them.

Let us imitate these, my beloved: let us be undaunted in all our dangers. There is nothing dreadful to him that fears God; but all that is dreadful is for others. For when a man is delivered from his passions, and regards all present things as a shadow, say, from whom shall he suffer anything dreadful? whom shall he have to fear? whom shall he need plead to? Let us flee to this Rock which cannot be shaken. If any one were to build for us a city, and throw up a wall around it, and remove us to a land uninhabited, where there were none to disturb us, and there supply us with abundance of everything, and not suffer us to have aught to trouble us with anybody, he would not set us in such perfect safety, as Christ hath done now. Be it a city made of brass, if you will, surrounded on all sides with a wall, lofty and impregnable, let there be no enemy near it; let it have land plentiful and rich, let there be added abundance of other things, let the citizens too be mild and gentle, and no evil-doer there, neither robber, nor thief,' no informer, no court of justice, but merely agreements (συναλλάγματα); and let us dwell in this city: not even thus would it be possible to live in security. Wherefore? Because there could not but be differences with servants, with wives, with children, to be a groundwork of much discomfort. But here was nothing of the kind; for here was nothing at all to pain them or cause any discomfort. Nay, what is more wonderful to say, the very things which are thought to cause discomfort, became matter of all joy and gladness. For tell me, what was there for them to be annoyed at? what to take amiss? Shall we cite a particular case for comparison with them? Well, let there be one of consular dignity, let him be possessed of much wealth, let him dwell in the imperial city, let him have no troublesome business with anybody, but only live in delight, and have nothing else but this to do, seated at the very summit of wealth and honor and power: and let us set against him a Peter, in bonds if you will, in evils without number: and we shall find that he is the man that lives the most delightfully. For when there is such excess of joy, as to be delighted when in bonds, think what must be the greatness of that joy! For like as those who are high in office, whatsoever evils may happen, are not sensible of them, but continue in enjoyment: so did these the more rejoice on account of these very evils. For it is impossible, impossible in words to express how great pleasure falls to their lot, who suffer for Christ's sake: for they rejoice in their sufferings, rather than in their good things. Whoso

---

[1] ταῦτα τῆς ἀναστάσεως πιστότερα. E. omits this, and inserts ἀπήγγειλαν ὑποστρέψαντες ἅπερ εἶδον. "They reported on their return just what they had seen:" so Edd. except Savile, who retains the reading of E. and adds to it as above (from N.)

loves Christ, knows what I say.—But what as regards safety? And who, I ask, if he were ever so rich, could have escaped so many perils, going about among so many different nations, for the sole purpose [1] of bringing about a reformation in their manner of life? For it was just as if by royal mandate that they carried all before them, nay, far more easily, for never mandate could have been so effectual, as their words were. For the royal edict compels by necessity, but these drew men willingly and spontaneously, yea, and with hearts above measure thankful. What royal edict, I ask, would ever have persuaded men to part with all their property and their lives; to despise ·home, country, kindred, yea, even self-preservation? Yet the voices of fishermen and tent-makers availed for this. So that they were both happy, and more powerful and strong than all others. "Yes," say you, "those of course were, for they wrought miracles." (*supra*, p. 83, note 4.) But I ask, what miracles did those who believed work, the three thousand, and the five thousand; and yet these, we read, passed their time in gladness? And well they might: for that which is the groundwork of all discomforts, the possession of riches, was done away with. For that, that, I say, was ever the cause both of wars and fighting, and grief, and discomfort, and all evils: the thing which makes life full of labor and troubles, it is that. And indeed it would be found that many more rich than poor have reason to be sad. If any think this is not true, their notion is derived not from the nature of the things, but from their own fancy. And if the rich do enjoy some sort of pleasure, this is not to be wondered at: for even those who are covered all over with the itch, have a good deal of pleasure. For that the rich are for all the world like these, and their mind affected in the same sort, is plain from this circumstance. Their cares annoy them, and they choose to be engrossed with them for the sake of the momentary pleasure: while those who are free from these affections, are in health and without discomfort. Whether is more pleasant, I ask, whether of the two more safe? To have to take thought only for a single loaf of bread and suit of clothes, or for an immense family, both slaves and freemen, not having care about himself (only)? For as this man has his fears for himself, so have you for those who depend on your own person. Why, [2] I pray you, does poverty seem a thing

to be shunned? Just in the same way as other good things are, in the judgment of many, things to be deprecated. "Yes," say you, "but it is not that those good things are subjects for deprecation, but that they are hard of attainment." Well, so is poverty, not a thing to be deprecated, but hard of attainment: so that if one could bear it, there would be no reason to deprecate it. For how is it that the Apostles did not deprecate it? how is it that many even choose it, and so far from deprecating, even run to it? For that which is really a thing to be deprecated, cannot be an object of choice save to madmen. But if it be the men of philosophic and elevated minds that betake themselves to this, as to a safe and salubrious retreat, no wonder if to the rest it wears a different appearance. For, in truth, the rich man seems to me to be just like a city, unwalled, situated in a plain, inviting assailants from all sides: but poverty, a secure fortress, strong as brass can make it, and the way up to it difficult. "And yet," say you, "the fact is just the reverse: for these are they, who are often dragged into courts of law, these are they who are overborne and ill-treated." No: not the poor, as poor, but those who being poor want to be rich. But I am not speaking of them, but of such as make it their study to live in poverty. For say, how comes it that nobody ever drags the brethren of the hills into courts of law? and yet if it be to be poor is to be a mark for oppression, those ought most of all to be dragged thither, since they are poorer than all others. How comes it that nobody drags the common mendicants into the law-courts? Because they are come to the extreme of poverty. How is it that none does violence to them, none lays vexatious informations against them? Because they abide in a stronghold too safe for that. How many think it a condition hard to struggle against, poverty, I mean, and begging! What then, I ask, is it a good thing to beg? "It is good, if there be comfort," say you; "if there be one to give: it is a life so free from trouble and reverses, as every one knows." But I do not mean to commend this; God forbid! what I advise is the not aiming at riches.

For say, whom would you rather call blessed? those who find themselves at home with virtue, (ἐπιτηδείους πρὸς ἀρετήν) or those who stand aloof? Of course, those who are near. Say then, which of the two is the man to learn anything that is profitable, and to shine in the true wisdom? the former, or the latter? The first, all must see. If you doubt it, satisfy yourself in this way. Fetch hither from the market-place any of the poor wretches there;

---

[1] ἔθνεσι τοσούτοις ὁμιλῶν ὑπὲρ μεταστάσεως πολιτείας μόνης.

[2] Edd. "And why," you will ask, "is poverty thought a thing to be fled from!" Why, because other good things are, in the judgment of many, things to be fled from, not because they are to be deprecated, but because hard of attainment.

let him be a cripple, lame, maimed : and then produce some other person, comely of aspect, strong in body, full of life and vigor in every part, overflowing with riches : let him be of illustrious birth, and possessed of great power. Then let us bring both these into the school of philosophy : which of them, I ask, is more likely to receive the things taught ? The first precept, at the outset, "Be lowly and moderate" (for this is Christ's command) : which will be most able to fulfil it, this one or the other ? "Blessed are they that mourn" (Matt. v. 4) : which will most receive this saying ? "Blessed are the lowly :" which will most listen to this ? "Blessed are the pure in heart. Blessed are they which do hunger and thirst after righteousness. Blessed are they which are persecuted for righteousness' sake" (ib. 8, 6, 10). Which will with ease receive these sayings ? And, if you will, let us apply to all of them these rules, and see how they will fit. Is not the one inflamed and swollen all over, while the other is ever lowly minded and subdued in his whole bearing ? It is quite plain. Yes, and there is a saying to that effect among those that are without : "(I was) a slave,[1] Epictetus by name, a cripple in body, for poverty a very Irus, and a friend of the Immortals." For how, I would ask, can it be otherwise, but that the soul of the rich must teem with evils ; folly, vainglory, numberless lusts, anger and passion, covetousness, iniquity, and what not ? So that even for philosophy, the former is more congenially (ἐπιτηδεία) disposed than the latter. By all means seek to ascertain which is the more pleasant : for this I see is the point everywhere discussed, whether such an one has the more enjoyable way of life. And yet even as regards this, we need not be in doubt ; for to be near to health, is also to have much enjoyment. But whether of the two, I would ask, is best disposed (ἐπιτήδειος) to the matter now in hand, that which we will needs carry into accomplishment—our law, I mean—the poor man or the rich ? Whether of them will be apt to swear ? The man who has children to be provoked with, the man who has his covenants with innumerable parties, or the man who is concerned to apply for just a loaf of bread or a garment ? This man has not even need of oaths, should he wish, but always lives free from cares of business ; nay, more, it is often seen that he who is disciplined to swear not at all, will also despise riches ; and one shall see in his whole behav-

ior his ways all branching off from this one good habit, and leading to meekness, to contempt of riches, to piety, to subduedness of soul, to compunction of heart. Then let us not be indolent, my beloved, but let us again show great earnestness : they who have succeeded, that they may keep the success achieved, that they be not easily caught by the receding wave, nor the refluent tide carry them back again [they[2] too who are yet behindhand, that they may be raised up again, and strive to make up that which is wanting. And meanwhile let those who have succeeded, help those who have not been able to do the same] : and by reaching out their hands, as they would to men struggling in the deep water, receive them into the haven of no-swearing (ἀνωμοσίας). For it is indeed a haven of safety, to swear not at all : whatever storms burst upon us, to be in no danger of sinking there : be it anger, be it insult, be it passion, be it what it may, the soul is stayed securely ; yea, though one have vented some chance word or other that ought not, and had been better not, to be spoken, yet he has laid himself under no necessity, no law. (Supra, Hom. ix. § 5. ad. Pop. Ant. viii. § 3.) See what Herod did for his oath's sake : he cut off the head of the Fore-runner. "But because of his oaths," it says, "and because of them which sat at meat with him" (Mark vi. 26), he cut off the head of the Prophet. Think what the tribes had to suffer for their oath in the matter of the tribe of Benjamin (Judges xxi. 5-10) : what Saul had to suffer for his oath (1 Sam. xiv. 24, etc.). For Saul indeed perjured himself, but Herod did what was even worse than perjury, he committed murder. Joshua again—you know how it fared with him, for his oath in the matter of the Gibeonites. (Joshua, ch. ix.) For it is indeed a snare of Satan, this swearing. Let us burst[3] the cords ; let us bring ourselves into a condition in which it will be easy (not to

---

[1] The Epigram is preserved in the Palatine Anthology, 7. 676.

Δοῦλος Ἐπίκτητος γενόμην, καὶ σώματι πηρὸς,
καὶ πενίαν Ἴρος, καὶ φίλος ἀθανάτοις.

But our Mss. except E., for Ἴρος have ἱερὸς, "sacred."

[2] Something is wanting in the old text to complete the sense : the matter in the brackets is supplied from E. D. F. Below, the same have : "to swear not at all : a haven, that one be not drowned by the storm bursting. For though wrath, though (sense of) insult, though passion boil over, yea though anything, be what it may, the soul is in security, so that it will not even utter aught that should not be spoken : for one has laid himself," etc.

[3] Διαρρήξωμεν τὰ σχοινία· ἐν εὐκολίᾳ καταστήσωμεν ἑαυτοὺς πάσης ἀπορίας ἀπαλλαγῶμεν καὶ τῆς σατανικῆς παγίδος. i. e. "The cords of this snare are, the ties of worldly business in the possession or pursuit of wealth : there is a condition, as was said above, in which it is full easy not to swear ; let us bring ourselves into that condition : all that makes us say, 'We cannot help swearing,' (πάσης ἀπορίας), let us have done with it, and break loose from the snare of the devil." The exhortation connects both parts of the "Morale"—the commendation of voluntary poverty, and the invective against swearing. In the modern text (E. F. D. Edd.) this is lost sight of : it reads : διαρρ. τὰ σχ. καὶ ἐν εὐκ. καταστήσομεν (al. -σωμεν) πάσης φυλακῆς· ἀπαλλαγῶμεν τῆς σατ. παγ. "Let us burst the cords, and we shall bring ourselves into a facility of all watchfulness : let us break loose," etc.

swear); let us break loose from every entanglement, and from this snare of Satan. Let us fear the command of the Lord : let us settle ourselves in the best of habits : that, making progress, and having achieved this and the rest of the commandments, we may obtain those good things which are promised to them that love Him, through the grace and loving-kindness of our Lord Jesus Christ, with Whom to the Father and the Holy Ghost together be glory, power, and honor, now and ever, and world without end. Amen.

HOMILY XIV.

ACTS V. 34.

"Then stood there up one in the council, a Pharisee, named Gamaliel, a doctor of the law, had in reputation among all the people, and commanded the men to be put forth a little space."

THIS Gamaliel was Paul's teacher. And one may well wonder, how, being so right-minded in his judgment, and withal learned in the law, he did not yet believe. But it cannot be that he should have continued in unbelief to the end.[1] Indeed it appears plainly from the words he here speaks. He "commanded," it says, "to put the men forth a little space [and said unto them.]" Observe how judiciously he frames his speech, and how he immediately at the very outset puts them in fear. And that he may not be suspected of taking their part, he addresses them as if he and they were of the same opinion, and does not use much vehemence, but as speaking to men intoxicated through passion, he thus expresses himself : " Ye men of Israel, take heed to yourselves what ye intend to do as touching these men." (v. 35.) Do not, he would say, go to work rashly and in a hurry. " For before these days rose up Theudas, boasting himself to be somebody : to whom a number of men, about four hundred, joined themselves : who was slain ; and all, as many as obeyed him, were scattered, and brought to naught." (v. 36.) By examples he teaches them prudence ; and, by way of encouragement, mentions last the man who seduced the greatest number. Now before he gives the examples, he says, "Take heed to yourselves ; " but when he has cited them, then he declares his opinion, and says, "Refrain from these men." For, says he,

"there rose up Judas of Galilee in the days of the taxing, and drew away much people after him : he also perished ; and all, even as many as obeyed him, were dispersed. And now I say unto you, Refrain from these men, and let them alone : for if this council or this work be of men, it will come to naught. But if it be of God, ye cannot overthrow them." (al. *it*) (v. 37-39.) Then[2] what is there, he would say, to hinder you to be overthrown? For, says he (take heed), "lest haply ye be found even to fight against God." He would dissuade them both by the consideration that the thing is impossible, and because it is not for their good. And he does not say by whom these people were destroyed, but that there they "were scattered," and their confederacy fell away to nothing. For if, says he, it be of man, what needs any ado on your part ? but if it be of God, for all your ado you will not be able to overcome it. The argument is unanswerable. " And they were persuaded by him." (v. 40.) How were they persuaded ? So as not to slay them, but merely to scourge. For, it says, "And when they had called the Apostles, and beaten them, they commanded that they should not speak in the name of Jesus, and let them go." See after what great works they are scourged ! And again their teaching became more extended : for they taught at home and in the temple, " And they departed from the presence of the council, rejoicing that they were counted worthy to suffer shame for His name. And daily in the temple, and in every house, they ceased not to teach and preach Jesus Christ. (v. 41, 42.) And in those days, when the number of the disciples was multiplied, there arose a murmuring of the Hellenists against the Hebrews, because their widows were neglected in the daily

---

[1] In the Clementine *Recogn.* i. 65, Gamaliel is spoken of as having been early a Christian in secret. Lucian the Presbyter A.D. 415, writes an account of the discovery in consequence of a vision in which Gamaliel himself appeared to him, of the reliques of St. Stephen, together with those of Nicodemus and Gamaliel. See note on St. Augustin *Comm. on St. John*, p. 1048. Photius, *Cod.* 171, p. 199 read in a work of Eustratius how Gamaliel was baptized by St. Peter and St. John. (According to the Jewish tradition, Wolf. *Bibl. Hebr.* ii. 882. he died President of the Sanhedrim, eighteen years after the fall of Jerusalem.)

[2] The modern text: " As if he had said, Forbear; and it these men came together of themselves, nothing will hinder them also to be overthrown." C. reads ἡμᾶς, " What to hinder us ? " Catena, as above.

ministration." (ch. vi. 1.) Not absolutely in those immediate days; for it is the custom of Scripture to speak of things next about to happen, as taking place in immediate succession. But by "Hellenists" I suppose he means those who spoke Greek ["against the Hebrews"]: for[1] they did not use the Greek language. Behold another trial! observe how from within and from without there are warrings, from the very first! "Then," it says, "the twelve called the multitude of the disciples unto them, and said, It is not reason that we should leave the word of God, and serve tables." (v. 2.) Well said: for the needful must give precedence to the more needful. But see, how straightway they both take thought for these (inferior matters), and yet do not neglect the preaching. "Because their widows were overlooked:" for those (the Hebrews) were treated as the persons of greater consequence (αἰδεσιμώτεροι). "Wherefore, brethren, look ye out among you seven men of honest report, full of the Holy Ghost and wisdom, whom we may appoint over this business. But we will give ourselves continually to prayer, and to the ministry of the word. And the saying pleased the whole multitude: and they chose Stephen, a man full of faith and of the Holy Ghost (v. 3-5.) so were the others also full of faith;[2] not to have the same things happening as in the case of Judas, as in the case of Ananias and Sapphira—" and Philip, and Prochoras, and Nicanor, and Timon, and Parmenas, and Nicolas a proselyte of Antioch: whom they set before the Apostles: and when they had prayed, they laid their hands on them. And the word of God increased; and the number of the disciples multiplied in Jerusalem greatly; and a great company of the priests were obedient to the faith. (v. 5-7.)

But[3] let us look over again what has been spoken. "Ye men of Israel take heed to yourselves." (Recapitulation, v. 35.) See here, I pray you, how mildly Gamaliel reasons, and how he says but a few words to them, and does not recount ancient histories, although he might have done so, but more recent instances, which are most powerful to produce belief. With this view he throws out a hint himself, saying, "For before these days" (v. 36): meaning, not many days before. Now had he at once said, "Let these men go," both himself would have fallen into suspicion, and his speech would not have been so effective: but after the examples, it acquired its own proper force. And he mentions not one instance, but a second also: "for," saith the Scripture, "in the mouth of two witnesses" (Matt. xviii. 16): and yet he had it in his power to mention even three. "Refrain from these men." (v. 38.) See how mild his manner is, and his speech not long, but concise, and his mention even of those (impostors) how free from passion: "And all, as many as obeyed him, were scattered." And[4] for all this he does not blaspheme Christ. They heard him, all these unbelievers, heard him, these Jews. ["For if this council or this work be of men, it will come to naught."] Well then, since it did not come to nought, it is not of men. ["But if it be of God, ye cannot overthrow it."] (v. 39.) Once more he checks them by the impossibility and the inexpediency of the thing, saying, "Lest haply ye be found even to fight against God."* And he does not say, If Christ be God; but the work (itself) declares (this). He does not pronounce upon it, either that, it is "of men," or that it is "of God;" but he leaves the proof to the future. "They were persuaded [by him]." (v. 40.) Then why, it may be asked, do ye scourge them? Such was the incontrovertible justness of his speech, they could not look it in the face; nevertheless, they sated their own animosity; and again they expected to terrify them in this way. By the fact also of his saying these things not in the presence of the Apostles, he gained a hearing more than he would otherwise have done; and then the suavity of his discourse and the justness of what was said, helped to persuade them. In fact, this man all but preached the Gospel.

---

[1] οὔτε γὰρ ἑλληνιστὶ διελέγοντο. So A. B. C. N. but Cat. οὗτοι, and E. D. F. add Ἐβραῖοι ὄντες. "For these used the Greek language, being Hebrews." There is no need to adopt this reading: the comment seems to belong to the words, against the Hebrews: viz. "they murmured against them, seeing they were overlooked, etc., for neither could these Hebrews converse with them in the Greek language."

[2] ἄρα (Cat. ὅρα) καὶ ἐκεῖνοι πλήρεις πίστεως ἦσαν (E. D. F. add οὓς καὶ ἐξελέξαντο). ἵνα μὴ τὰ αὐτὰ κ. τ. λ. The meaning seems to be: "If Stephen was a man full of faith, so were the others: (they were careful to choose only such,): in order that," etc.

[3] Omitted in the old text: supplied by E.—Below, E. omits, "for. saith the Scripture, in the mouth of two witnesses:" and amplifies the rest, adding, "even a third, superabundantly: both showing how well he himself speaks, and leading them away from their sanguinary purpose."

[4] Edd. from E. "Saying this, he speaks nothing blasphemous against Christ, but what he most wishes, he effects. 'If,' says he, 'it be of men, it will come to naught.' Here he seems to me to put it to them by way of syllogism, and to say: Consequently, since it has not come to naught, it is not of man. 'Lest haply ye be found even to fight against God.' This he said to check them," etc.—Below, ἀλλὰ τὸ ἔργον τοῦτο δηλοῖ, might be rendered, "but he is declaring this work" (viz. "if this work be of men," etc.): the modern text, τὸ γὰρ ἔργον τοῦτο ἐδήλου.

* Meyer finds in the expression of Gamaliel (38, 39): "if it be of men—ἐὰν ᾖ ἐξ ἀνθρώπων" and "if it is of God—εἰ δὲ ἐκ θεοῦ ἐστίν" an indication that he leaned to the latter opinion. While this distinction is grammatically valid it can scarcely be justified as intentional. Gamaliel, although tolerant toward Christianity, as the Pharisaic party in general were at this time, was not a Christian in secret, but an orthodox Jew. His advice was politic even from a Jewish point of view. He saw, as the more bitter party did not, that this sort of opposition would only serve to rouse all the energy and perseverance of the Christian disciples and thus indirectly tend to the increase and spread of their doctrines among the people.—G. B. S.

"[1] Ye were persuaded," one may say, "that ye had not. strength to overthrow it. Wherefore did ye not believe?" Such is the witness borne even by enemies. There it is four hundred, there, four thousand: and here the first movers were twelve. Let not the number which added itself affright you. (ch. ii. 41; iv. 4.) He might also have mentioned another instance, that of the Egyptian, but what he has spoken is fully sufficient. And he closes his speech with an alarming topic: "Lest haply," etc. And he does not pronounce upon it, lest he should seem to be pleading their cause; but he reasons by way of syllogism from the issue of the matter. And he does not venture to pronounce that it is not of men, nor yet that it is of God; for had he said that it was of God. they would have gainsaid him: but had he said that it was of men, they would again have taken prompt measures. Therefore he bids them wait for the end, saying, "Refrain," But they once more threaten knowing indeed that they avail nothing, but doing after their manner. Such is the nature of wickedness: it attempts even impossibilities.—"And after this man rose up Judas," etc. These things Josephus relates in detail. (*Ant.* xx. 8; ib. v. 2; xviii. 1. *B. J.* ii. 8. 1.) But what a great thing it was that he ventured to affirm: that it was of God, when in the sequel it received its proof from the events! Great boldness of speech, great freedom from all respect of persons! [2] And he does not say, "But if ye do not overthrow it, it is of God;" but, "If it be of God, it will not be overthrown." "And to him they agreed." (v. 40.) They reverenced the high character of the man. "And they departed from the presence of the council, rejoicing that they were counted worthy to suffer shame for the name of Christ." (v. 41.) What miracles so wonderful as this? Nowhere is the like of this recorded of the old saints: for Jeremiah indeed was scourged for the word of God, and they threatened Elijah, and the rest: but in this case, even by this very thing, and not only by their miracles, these showed forth the power of God. He does not say, that they were not pained, but that though pained they rejoiced. How does this appear?

From their boldness afterwards: they were so instant still, even after their beatings, in preaching the word. "But in the temple," it says, "and in every house, they ceased not to teach and preach Jesus Christ." (v. 42.) "And in those days"—when these things were done, when there were scourgings, when there were threatenings, when the disciples were multiplying—also, it says, "there arose a murmuring." (ch. vi. 1.) And this comes of the multitude: for it is impossible to have strict order in a multitude. "There arose a murmuring," etc. to,—"And [3] a great company of the priests were obedient to the faith.—There arose murmuring against the Hebrews"—for that description of people seemed to be more honorable—"because their widows were neglected in the daily ministration." * (v. 1-7.) So then there was a daily ministration for the widows. And observe how he calls it a "ministration" (διακονία), and not directly alms: extolling by this at once the doers, and those to whom it was done. "Were neglected." This did not arise from malice, but perhaps from the carelessness of the multitude. And therefore he brought it forward openly, for this was no small evil. Observe, how even in the beginning the evils came not only from without, but also from within. For you must not look to this only, that it was set to rights, but observe that it was a great evil that it existed.† "Then the twelve," etc. (v. 2.) Do you observe [4] how outward concerns succeed to inward? They do not act at their own discre-

---

[1] E. F. D. and Edd. (except Savile) add, μᾶλλον δὲ μονονουχὶ τοιαῦτα δικαιολογούμενος πρὸς αὐτοὺς ἀποτείνεται. "Or rather he all but with just remonstrance thus expostulates with them: "Ye were persuaded," etc. Below, Ἐκεῖ τετρακόσιοι, ἐκεῖ τετρακισχίλιοι· καὶ ὧδε κ. τ. λ. But the mention of the four thousand, here referred to the second instance (Judas of Galilee), is in fact derived from the case of the Egyptian, ch. xxi. 38, being the third instance which "he might have cited." Accordingly the modern text substitutes, "There four hundred stood up, and after this a great multitude."

[2] E. and Edd. omit the following sentence, substituting the first two clauses of v. 40 and after "the character of the man," add, "wherefore also they desist from their purpose of killing the Apostles. and having only scourged they dismiss them."

[3] Standing here by itself. this last clause of v, 7 is quite out of its place. It is best explained as marking the conclusion of the text v. 1-7 here again read out. In the old text it is followed by the comment, Ἐκεῖνο γὰρ τὸ γένος ἐδόκει τιμιώτερον εἶναι· as if "this description of people" meant the priests: and then, "And there arose," it says, "a murmuring," v. 1. We have restored the comment to its proper place.—The innovator adds as comment on v. 7: Τοῦτο αἰνιττομένου ἐστὶ καὶ δεικνύντος ὅτι ἀφ' ὧν ὁ κατὰ Χριστοῦ θάνατος ἐσκευάσθη, πολλοὶ ἀπὸ τούτων πιστεύουσιν. "This is by way of hint, to show that of those very persons, by whose machinations the sentence of death against Christ was procured, of those same many believe. "There arose," it says, "a murmuring," etc. And so Edd.

* The murmuring arose from the "Hellenists" who are not mentioned by Chrys. (probably because of a defect of the text). These Hellenists are distinguished from the "Hebrews" and were probably Greek-speaking Jews resident in Jerusalem who had become Christians and who are here distinguished by their language from the great mass of the Jewish Christians who spoke the vernacular.—G. B. S.

† The neglect here referred to was doubtless, as Chrys. says, unintentional (vs. Meyer) and arose from the increasing difficulties of administering the affairs of so large a society as the Christian community at Jerusalem had now become, on the plan of a common treasury. The narrative gives the impression that the complaint was not unfounded. It is not unlikely that the natural jealousy between the Greek and Palestinian Jews may have sharpened the sense of neglect. This is the first record of dissension in the Christian Church. We may note thus early the conditions which tended to develop a Jewish and a Gentile party in the church; the germs of dissenting sects of Ebionites and Gnostics which developed into so many dangerous and harmful forms in the apostolic, and especially in the post-apostolic age.—G. B. S.

[4] Ὁρᾷς τὰ ἔξω διαδεχόμενα τὰ ἔσω; E. omits this and so Edd. The antithesis here seems to be, not, as before, of evils from without and from within the Church; but of the concerns of the body and of the soul.

tion, but plead for themselves to the congregation. So ought it to be done now. "It is not reason," says he, "that we should leave the word of God, and serve tables." First he puts to them the unreasonableness of the thing; that it is not possible for both things to be done with the same attention: just as when they were about to ordain Matthias, they first show the necessity of the thing, that one was deficient, and there must needs be twelve. And so here they showed the necessity; and they did it not sooner, but waited till the murmuring arose; nor, on the other hand, did they suffer this to spread far. And, lo! they leave the decision to them: those who pleased all, those who of all were honestly reputed, them they present : [1] not now twelve, but "seven, full of the Spirit and of wisdom : well reported of" for their conversation. (v. 3.) Now when Matthias was to be presented, it was said, "Therefore must one of these men which have companied with us all the time" (ch. i. 21) : but not so here : for the case was not alike. And they do not now put it to the lot; they might indeed themselves have made the election, as moved by the Spirit : but nevertheless, they desire the testimony of the people. The fixing the number, and the ordaining them, and for this kind of business, rested with them: but the choice of the men they make over to the people, that they might not seem to act from favor : just as God also leaves it to Moses to choose as elders those whom he knew. (Num. xi. 16.) "And of wisdom." For indeed there needs much wisdom in such ministrations. For think not, because he hath not the word committed unto him, that such an one has no need of wisdom : he does need it, and much too. "But we," saith he, "will give ourselves continually to prayer, and to the ministry of the word." (v. 4.) Again they plead for themselves, beginning and ending with this. "Will give ourselves continually," he saith. For so it behooved, not just to do the mere acts, or in any chance way, but to be continually doing them. "And the saying," we are told, "pleased the whole multitude." (v. 5. 6.) This too was worthy of their wisdom. All approved of what was said, so sensible was it. "And they chose," it says (again it is the people (αὐτοί) that choose,) "Stephen, a man full of faith and of the Holy Ghost, and Philip, and Prochorus, and Nicanor, and Timon, and Parmenas, and Nicolas a proselyte of Antioch : whom they set before the Apostles : and when they had

prayed, they laid their hands on them." They separated them from the multitude, and it is the people (αὐτοί) that draw them, not the Apostles that lead them. Observe how he avoids all that is superfluous : he does not tell in what way it was done, but that they were ordained (ἐχειροτονήθησαν) with prayer : for this is the meaning of χειροτονία, (i. e. "putting forth the hand,") or ordination : the hand of the man is laid upon (the person,) but the whole work is of God, and it is His hand which toucheth the head of the one ordained, if he be duly ordained. "And the word of God," it says, "increased : and the number of the disciples multiplied." (v. 7.) It is not for nothing that he says this: it shows how great is the virtue of alms and good order. And as he is about in the sequel to enlarge (αὐξειν) upon the affair of Stephen, he puts first the causes which led to it. "And many," he says, "of the priests were obedient to the faith." For [2] since they perceived such to be the mind of their ruler and teacher, they put the matter to the test of facts.—It is also a subject for wonder, how it was that the multitude was not divided in its choice of the men, and how it was that the Apostles were not rejected by them. But what sort of rank these bore, and what sort of office they received, this is what we need to learn. Was it that of Deacons? And yet this is not the case in the Churches. But [3] is it to the Presbyters that

---

[1] E. D. F. Morel. Ben. omit this sentence, and go on with, "Now when Matthias," etc. Savile: And a very good decision this is. And they present seven, not now twelve, full," etc.

[2] Ἐπειδὴ γὰρ εἶδον τὸν ἄρχοντα καὶ διδάσκαλον τοιαῦτα ἀποφηνάμενον, ἀπὸ τῶν ἔργων λοιπὸν τὴν πεῖραν ἐλάμβανον. Meaning, perhaps, that these priests, acting upon the counsel of Gamaliel, put the question to the test of facts and experience, and learned that it was of God.—In the next sentence, a covert censure seems to be implied : q. d. "Would it be so now? Would there not be parties and factions in the choosing of the men? Would not the Bishop's overture be rejected, were he to propose a plan for ridding himself of the like distracting demands upon his time?

[3] ἀλλὰ τῶν πρεσβυτέρων ἐστὶν ἡ οἰκονομία; interrogatively (so in Conc. Quinisext. Can. xvi., see below), this in the Edd. this is put affirmatively; Ben. Sed presbyterorum erat œconomia. Atqui nullus adhuc erat episcopus. Erasm. Sed presbyterorum est hæc dispensatio, tametsi nullus adhuc esset episcopus." But to say that the οἰκονομία, i. e. stewardship and management of Church funds (in Chrysostom's time), was vested in the presbyters, would be contrary to facts. Therefore we take it interrogatively : the answer not expressed, being, "No: it belongs to the Bishops." Perhaps, however, the passage may be restored thus ; Ἀλλὰ τῶν πρεσβυτέρων ; Ἀλλὰ τῶν ἐπισκόπων (or Οὐδὲ τῶν πρεσβ.) ἐστὶν ἡ οἰκ. Καίτοι κ. τ. λ. "Well, was it that of presbyters? Nay, this stewardship belongs to Bishops. (Or, No, neither does it belong to presbyters.) And yet," etc.—The following sentence. "Ὅθεν οὔτε διακόνων οὔτε πρεσβυτέρων οἶμαι(Cat. om.)τὸ ὄνομα εἶναι δῆλον καὶ φανερόν, as the text stands, might seem to mean, " Whence I think that neither of deacons nor of presbyters is the name clearly and manifestly expressed:" i. e. "there is no express and clear mention in this narrative either of deacons or of presbyters; and I account for this circumstance by the fact, that there were no Bishops." Ben. Unde puto nec diaconorum nec presbyterorum tunc fuisse nomen admissum nec manifestum. But transposing οἶμαι and εἶναι, or indeed even as the words stand, we get the sense expressed in the translation, which is more suitable. So Erasmus : Unde neque diaconorum neque presbyterorum nomen esse opinor quod clarum ac manifestum. St. Chrys. says, "Their appellation and office is neither deacons nor presbyters: they were ordained upon a special emergency."—It seems to have been commonly held in earlier times, that Acts vi. 1-6 is the history of the first institution of the Diaconate. Thus the Council of Nicocæsarea ordains (A.D. 314) that in each city, however large, the number of deacons according to the Canon ought to

the management belongs? And yet at present there was no Bishop, but the Apostles only. Whence I think it clearly and manifestly follows, that neither Deacons nor Presbyters is their designation: but it was for this particular purpose that they were ordained.* And this business was not simply handed over to them without further ceremony, but the Apostles prayed over them, that power might be given to them. But observe, I pray you, if there were need of seven men for this, great in proportion must have been the sums of money that flowed in, great in proportion also the number of widows. So then the prayers were not made in an off-hand way, but with much deliberate attention: and this office, [1] as well as preaching, was thus brought to good effect;

be seven, and for proof appeals to this history, πεισθήσῃ δὲ ἀπὸ τῆς βίβλου τῶν πράξεων. In the third century, Cornelius *Ep. ad Fab.* ap. Eus. *H. E.* vi. 43 states, that the clergy of Rome consisted of one Bishop, forty-six presbyters, seven deacons, etc. (Accordingly St. Jerome, *Ep.* 146 *al.* 101 *ad Evang.* remarks: *Diaconos paucitas honorabiles facit.* Comp. Sozomen. vii. 19.) But the rule which assigned to each Bishop seven deacons, neither more nor less, was not always followed in large cities, as appears even from the Canon above cited: how greatly that number was exceeded in later times, may be seen in the *Novellæ* of Justinian, when it is enacted (iii. c. l.) that the number of deacons in the metropolitan Church at Constantinople should be a hundred. The Council or Councils commonly called the fifth and sixth General (Conc. Quinisextum, or Trullanum,) held under the same Emperor, A.D. 692, sanctioned this departure from the earlier rule, in the following Canon (xvi). "Whereas the Book of Acts relates that seven deacons were appointed by the Apostles, and the Council of Neocæsarea in its Canons determines'that "The number of deacons in each city," etc. (as above): we, having applied the sense of the Fathers to the Apostolic text, find that the said history relates not to the deacons who minister in the mysteries, but to the service of tables, etc.: the history in the Acts being as follows, "And in those days," etc. (Acts vi. 1-6.) The doctor of the Church, John Chrysostom, expounding the same, thus speaks: "It is a subject for wonder . . . . neither deacons nor presbyters is their designation," (as above.) Hereupon therefore do we also publish, that the aforesaid seven deacons be not taken to mean those which minister in the mysteries, as in the doctrine above rehearsed: but that these are they which were charged with the service of the common need of the people then gathered together; albeit herein these be unto us a pattern of humane and diligent attendance on them that be in necessity.

* There is no sufficient ground to doubt that this narrative describes the formation of the diaconate which we find existing later in the apostolic age (Phil. i. 1; 1 Tim. iii. 8–12). Although the word διάκονος does not here occur, we have the corresponding verb διακονεῖν and abstract noun διακονία (1, 2). The chief grounds of this opinion are: (1) the substantial identity of the duties here described and those of the later diaconate; (2) the almost universal testimony of patristic tradition to their identity: (3) the continuance for centuries of the number seven in the diaconate of churches (like that at Rome) where more than seven would naturally be required, out of deference to the apostolic mode. See Lightfoot, *Com. on Philippians*, pp. 187–9.—G. B. S.

[1] καὶ τοῦτο, ὥσπερ τὸ κήρυγμα, οὕτως ἡγνίετο—τοῦτο, the "serving of tables" itself: οὕτως, by this arrangement. Τὰ γὰρ πλείω ταύταις ἡνυον· the more time the Apostles had for prayer, the better for the Church: so much depended on their prayers. Therefore the plan was every way beneficial: οὕτω τὰ πνευματικὰ ἐπελέγοντο, (Erasm. adnumerabantur, Ben. præferebantur, but the meaning is, "they chose to themselves,") οὕτω καὶ ἀποδημίας ἐστέλλοντο, οὕτως ἐνεχειρίσθησαν οὗτοι τὸν λόγον· "by this arrangement, the Apostles were free to give their undivided attention to spiritual matters; to leave Jerusalem, if need were, on journeys to distant places: by this arrangement, in short, the Word was their proper charge—not secular matters, such as Bishops are now burdened with, in addition to their proper duties," Comp. note 1, p. 90. He adds: The writer, indeed, does not say all this, nor extol the devotion with which the Apostles gave themselves up to their work, and how beneficial the arrangement proved: but it is said, "It is not reason," etc. Moses had set the example in this regard: and in token of their concern for the poor, observe the charge which they afterwards gave to Paul and Barnabas, to "remember the poor."

for what they did, they effected mostly by the means of these (their prayers.) Thus they were enabled to give their attention to things spiritual; thus were these also free to undertake long journeys; thus were these put in trust with the word. But the writer does not say this, nor extol them, but that it was "not reason" that they should leave the work given to them. Thus they had been taught by Moses's example not to undertake the management of everything by themselves. (Num. xi. 14.) "Only," it is said, "that we should remember the poor." (Gal. ii. 10.) And [2] how did they bring these forward? They fasted. "Look you out seven men," etc. (v. 3.) It is not simply, spiritual men, but, "full of the Spirit and of wisdom, "for it needed very great superiority of mind (φιλοσοφίας) to bear the complainings of widows. For what profits it, that the dispenser of alms steal not, if nevertheless he waste all, or be harsh and easily provoked? "And they chose Stephen, a man full of faith and of the Holy Ghost." (v. 5.) And in this regard Philip also was admirable: for it is of him that the writer says: "And we entered into the house of Philip the Evangelist, which was one of the seven; and abode with him."—(ch. xxi. 8.) Dost thou mark how matters are ordered quite otherwise than after the matter of men? "And the number of disciples was multiplied in Jerusalem." (v. 7.) In Jerusalem the multitude increased. Wonderful, where Christ was slain, there the preaching increased! And not only was it not the case that some were offended then in the manner of Ananias, but the awe became even greater: while these are scourged, those threatening, those tempting the Spirit, those murmuring. But I would have thee remark under what circumstances the multitude increased: after these trials, then it was that the multitude increased, and not before. Mark also how great the mercy of God. Of those chief-priests, of the very men who had indignation and sore displeasure and so cried out and said, "He saved others, Himself He cannot save;" of these same, "Many," it says, "were obedient unto the faith." (Matt. xxvii. 42.)

[2] Πῶς δὲ προῆγον τούτους; Ἐνήστευον. Edd. from E., "But how they also brought these forward, learn thou. They fasted, they continued in prayer. This ought also to be done now."—As there is no mention of fasting in Acts vi. 1–6 perhaps this refers to 'the history xiii. 2, 3 of the mission of Paul and Barnabas, to which he has just alluded.—Below, καὶ ταύτῃ δὲ θαυμαστὸς ἦν ὁ Φ. The clause to which this refers is misplaced in the old text, viz. before the sentence, "In Jerusalem," etc. where E. and Edd. restore the proper clause of v. 7 καὶ ἐπληθύνετο, κ. τ. λ. The connection is: "The Apostles desired seven men full of the Holy Ghost and of wisdom:" and such was Stephen, "a man full of faith and of the Holy Ghost:" such doubtless were the others likewise; (supra, p. 88) certainly Philip was eminent in this regard, for [besides the history of his preaching at Samaria, ch. viii.] he is afterwards conspicuous in the history as Philip the Evangelist.

Him therefore let us also imitate. He received them, and did not cast them out. So let us requite those our enemies, who have wrought us even numberless ills. Whatever good thing we may have, let us impart to them: let us not pass them by, in our acts of beneficence. For if we ought, by suffering ill, to sate their rage, much more, by doing them good: for this is a less thing than the other. For it is not all alike, to do good to an enemy, and to be willing to suffer greater wrongs than he wishes (to inflict): [1] from the one we shall come on to the other. This is the dignity of Christ's disciples. Those crucified Him, when He had come for the very purpose of doing them good; His disciples they scourged; and after all this, He admits them to the same honor with His disciples, making them equally partakers of His gifts. I beseech you, let us be imitators of Christ: in this regard it is possible to imitate Him: this makes a man like unto God: this is more than human. Let us hold fast to Mercy: she is the schoolmistress and teacher of that higher Wisdom. He that has learnt to show mercy to the distressed, will learn also not to resent injuries; he that has learnt this, will be able to do good even to his enemies. Let us learn to feel for the ills our neighbors suffer, and we shall learn to endure the ills they inflict. Let us ask the person himself who ill-treats us, whether he does not condemn himself? would he not be glad to show a nobler spirit (φιλοσοφεῖν)? must he not own that his behavior is nothing but passion, that it is little-minded, pitiful? would he not like to be of those who are wronged and are silent, and not of those who do wrong, and are beside themselves with passion? can he go away not admiring the patient sufferer? Do not imagine that this makes men despicable. Nothing makes men so despicable, as insolent and injurious behavior: nothing makes men so respectable, as endurance under insolence and injury. For the one is a ruffian, the other a philosopher; the one is less than man, the other is equal to angels. For though he be inferior to the wrong-doer, yet, for all that, he has the power, if he had the mind, to be revenged. And besides, the one is pitied by all, the other hated. What then? The former will be much the better of the two: for everybody will treat the one as a madman, the other as a man of sense.

He [2] cannot speak of him in evil sort: yea, thou fearest, says one, lest perchance he be not such (as thou wouldest represent). Best that thou speak not evil in thy thought even; next, that thou speak it not to another. Pray not thou to God against this man: if thou hear him evil-spoken of, take his part: say, It was passion that spoke such words, not the man; say, It was anger, not my friend: his madness, not his heart. Thus let us account of each offence. Wait not for the fire to be kindled, but check it before it comes to that: do not exasperate the savage beast, rather do not suffer it to become exasperated: for thou wilt no longer be able to check it, if once the flame be kindled. For what has the man called thee? "Thou fool and simpleton." And which then is liable to the name? the called, or the caller? For the one, be he ever so wise, gets the character of being a fool: but the other, even if he be a simpleton, gets credit for being wise, and of philosophic temper. Say, which is the simpleton? he who alleges against another what is untrue, or he who even under such treatment is unmoved? For if it be the mark of true philosophy to be unmoved however moved; to fall into a passion when none moves to anger—what folly is it! I say not yet, how sore a manner of punishment is in store for those who utter such reproaches and revilings against their neighbor. But how? has he called thee "a low fellow and low-born, a sorry creature and of sorry extraction?" Again he has turned the taunt against himself. For the other will appear worthy and respectable, but he a sorry creature indeed: for to cast up such things, that is to say, meanness of birth, as a disgrace, is little-minded indeed: while the other will be thought a great and admirable character, because he thinks nothing of such a taunt, and is no more affected by it than if he were told [3] that he had about him any other ordinary

---

[1] καὶ μείζονα θελῆσαι παθεῖν ἢ βούλεσθαι: so all our Mss. Erasm. "*Et majora voluisse pati, vel velle.*" Ben. *Et majora velle pati.*" But the meaning is, "To be ready to suffer greater wrongs than an enemy chooses to inflict:" alluding to Matt. v. 39-41. Comp. *Hom.* xviii. *in Matt.* p. 238. D. τὸ καὶ παρασχεῖν ἑαυτὸν εἰς τὸ παθεῖν κακῶς· . . . τὸ καὶ πλέον παρασχεῖν ἢ ἐκεῖνος βούλεται ὁ ποιήσας. If for βούλεσθαι we read βούλεται, the sense is clearer: ἢ βούλεσθαι, "than that he should wish it," is somewhat abrupt.

[2] Οὐ δύναται εἰπεῖν αὐτὸν κακῶς· καὶ δέδοικας μήπως ουκ ἦν, φησίν, τοιοῦτος. Here and in the following sentences we seem to have a string of apothegms from heathen moralists: τὰ ἔξωθεν εἰρημένα, as he says below. But in this sentence the text appears to be corrupt, and the Mss. lend no real assistance for the reading adopted by Edd. from E. F. D. is quite meant for restoration: viz. "Therefore, when any would compel thee to speak evil of some person (κακηγορῆσαί τινα, Sav. marg. ἀπεχθῶς πρός τινα ἔχειν) say to him, 'I cannot speak evil of him: for I fear lest perchance he were not (ἦν, Sav. εἴη) such.'"—A. as usual in cases of difficulty, omits the passage as unintelligible. Whether φησὶν denotes a citation or an interlocution, and whether ἦν is the first or the third person, must be left doubtful; but the words might be rendered, "Lest perchance I, says he, (i. e. the person attacked) be not such." Below, μὴ ἐντύχῃς κατὰ τούτου τῷ Θεῷ is strangely rendered by Erasm. *Ne in hoc cum Deo pugnes: "Lest herein thou fight against God."

[3] ὅτι ἔχοι τι τῶν ἄλλων τῶν ἀδιαφόρων. E. D. F. Edd. διαφέρον "something about him, better than other men." Below, for ἐννοήσαντα γὰρ "for when one has considered," Edd. have ἐννοήσαντας δὲ καὶ, "but when you consider also:" i. e. "but if the case be not so," etc. In fact something is wanting: for the case here supposed is that the charge is true: the person has been guilty of some immorality, which the other publicly exposes.

and quite indifferent circumstance. But does he call thee "adulterer," and such like? At this thou mayest even laugh: for, when the conscience is not smitten, there can be no occasion for wrath. * * For when one has considered what bad and disgraceful disclosures he makes, still for all that, there is no need to grieve. He has but laid bare now, what everybody must be apprised of by and bye: meanwhile, as regards himself, he has shown all men that he is not to be trusted, for that he knows not how to screen his neighbor's faults: he has disgraced himself more than he has the other; has stopped up against himself every harbor: has made terrible to himself the bar at which he must hereafter be tried. For not the person (whose secrets are betrayed) will be the object of everybody's aversion, but he, who where he ought not to have raised the veil, has stripped off the clothes. But speak thou nothing of the secrets thou knowest: hold thou thy peace if thou wouldest bear off the good fame. For not only wilt thou overthrow what has been spoken, and hide it: but thou wilt also bring about another capital result: thou wilt stop sentence being given against thyself. Does somebody speak evil of thee? Say thou: "Had he known all, he would not have spoken only thus much."—So you admire what has been said, and are delighted with it? Aye, but you must follow it. For when we tell you all [1] these maxims of the heathen moralists, it is not because Scripture does not contain hundreds of such sayings, but because these are of more force to put you to the blush. As in fact Scripture itself is wont to use this appeal to our sense of shame; for instance, when it says, "Do ye even as the heathen." (Jer. xxxv. 3.) And the prophet Jeremiah brought forward into public view the children of Rechab, how they would not consent to violate the command of their father.—Miriam and her company spake evil of Moses, and he immediately begged them off from their punishment; nay, would not so much as let it be known that his cause was avenged. (Num. ch. xii.) But not so we: on the contrary, this is what we most desire; to have all men know that they have not passed unpunished. How long shall we breathe of the earth?—One party cannot make a fight. Pluck the madmen from both sides, you will exasperate them the more: but pluck from right or from left, and you have quenched the passion. The striker, if he has to do with one who will not put up with blows, is the more set on: but if with one who yields, he is the sooner unnerved, and his blow is spent upon himself. For no practised pugilist so unnerves the strength of his antagonist, as does a man who being injuriously treated makes no return. For the other only goes off ashamed, and condemned, first by his own conscience, and secondly by all the lookers on. And there is a proverb too, which says, that "to honor another, is to honor one's self": therefore also to abuse another is to abuse one's self. None, I repeat, will be able to harm us, unless we harm ourselves; nor will any make me poor, unless I make myself such. For come, let us look at it in this way. Suppose that I have a beggarly soul, and let all lavish all their substance upon me, what of that? So long as the soul is not changed, it is all in vain. Suppose I have a noble soul, and let all men take from me my substance: what of that? So long as you do not make the soul beggarly, no harm is done. Suppose my life be impure, and let all men say just the contrary of me: what of that? For though they say it, yet they do not judge thus of me in their heart. Again, suppose my life be pure, and let all say of me just the reverse: and what of that? For in their own conscience they will condemn themselves: since they are not persuaded of what they say. Just as we ought not to admit the praise, so neither the criminations. And why say I these things? None will ever be able to plot against us, nor lay us under any evil charge, if we choose (that they shall not). For how now, I ask you? Let him drag me into a court of justice, let him lay vexatious informations, let him, if you will, have the very soul out of me: and what of that? for a little while, undeservedly to suffer these things, what does it signify? "Well,[2] but this," say you, "is of itself an evil." Well, but of itself this is a good, to suffer undeservedly. What? would you have the suffering to be deserved? Let me mention again a piece of philosophy, from one of the sages. A certain person, says the story, had been put to death. And one of the sage's disciples said to him, "Woe is me, that he should have suffered unjustly!" The other

---

[1] τὰ λεγόμενα συνάγομεν, B. C. N. omitting ἔξωθεν, which Sav. supplies. A. E. D. F. Ben. τὰ ἔξωθεν εἰρημένα λέγομεν.— Below, for καθὼς τὰ ἔθνη (φησὶν) ποιήσατε, which is not found in Scripture, E. Edd. have, Οὐχὶ καὶ οἱ ἐθνικοὶ τὸ αὐτὸ ποιοῦσιν; Matt. v. 47.

[2] Τοῦτο μὲν οὖν αὐτὸ κακὸν, φησίν. Αὐτὸ μὲν οὖν τοῦτο καλὸν τὸ μὴ κατ' ἀξίαν παθεῖν. Morel. from E. κακὸν for καλὸν: which supposes it to be put interrogatively: "this thing itself an evil, say you?"—The philosopher, whose apothegm is here referred to, is Socrates: of whom Diog. Laert. in Vit. relates: "His wife having said, Thou art unjustly put to death: σὺ δὲ, ἔφη, δικαίως ἐβούλου; wouldst thou rather it were justly?" But Xenophon, in Apol. relates a similar answer made to Apollodorus, "a simple-minded but affectionate disciple of Socrates. This, said he, O Socrates, is what hurts me most, that I see thee unjustly put to death. And he, stroking the head of his disciple, replied: And wouldest thou, my friend, rather see me justly than unjustly put to death?" Down. ap. Sav.

turned upon him, "Why, how now?" said he, "would you have had him justly suffer?" (Socrates ap. Diog. Laert. and Xen. *Mem*. Socr.) John also, was not he unjustly put to death? Which then do you rather pity: them that justly suffer death, or [him?[1] Do you not count them miserable, while] him you even admire? Then what is a man injured, when from death itself he has got great gain, not merely no hurt? If indeed the man had been immortal, and this made him mortal, no doubt it would be a hurt: but if he be mortal, and in the course of nature must expect death a little later, and his enemy has but expedited his death, and glory with it, what is the harm? Let us but have our soul in good order, and there will be no harm from without. But thou art not in a condition of glory? And what of that? That which is true of wealth, the same holds for glory: if I be magnanimous (μεγαλοπρεπής), I shall need none; if vainglorious, the more I get, the more I shall want. In this way shall I most become illustrious, and obtain greater glory; namely, if I despise glory. Knowing these things, let us be thankful to Him Who hath freely given us such a life, and let us ensue it unto His glory; for to Him belongs the glory, forever. Amen.

HOMILY XV.

ACTS VI. 8.

"And Stephen, full of faith and power, did great wonders and miracles among the people."

SEE how even among the seven one was preëminent, and won the first prize. For though the ordination was common to him and them, yet he drew upon himself greater grace. And observe, how he wrought no (signs and wonders) before this time, but only when he became publicly known; to show that grace alone is not sufficient, but there must be ordination also; so that there was a further access of the Spirit. For if they were full of the Spirit, it was of that which is from the Laver of Baptism. "Then there arose certain of them of the synagogue." (v. 9.) Again he uses the phrase of "rising up" (ἀνάστασιν, Hom. xiii. p. 81), to denote their exasperation and wrath. Here we have a great multitude. And observe the difference in the form of accusation: for since Gamaliel had stopped them from finding fault on the former plea, they bring in another charge. "And there rose up, it says, certain of them of the synagogue of those who are called (τῶν λεγομένων. Edd. τῆς λεγομένης) Libertines, and of the Cyrenians and Alexandrians, and of them of Cilicia and Asia, disputing with Stephen. And they were not able to resist the wisdom and the spirit by which he spake. Then they suborned men, which said, We have heard him speak blasphemous words against Moses, and against God." (v. 9–12.) That they may establish the charge, the phrase is, "he speaks against God, and against Moses." And with this object too they disputed, that they might force him to say somewhat. But he now discoursed more openly, and perhaps spoke of the cessation of the Divine Law: or, spoke it not, but hinted as much: since had he spoken plainly, there had been no need of suborned men, nor yet of false witnesses.* The synagogues were diverse: [to wit, "Of the Libertines"]: "of the Cyrenians, i. e. those in the parts beyond Alexandria ["of the Alexandrians," etc.]. There also they seem to have had synagogues according to their different nations; for many stayed behind there, that they might not be obliged to be continually travelling. The Libertines perhaps were freedmen of the Romans. As there were many foreigners dwelling there, so they had their synagogues, where the Law was to be read. "Disputing with Stephen." Observe him, not taking upon him to teach, but forced to do so. The miracles once more brought him into ill-will; but when he overcame in argument, it was false-witness! For they did not wish to kill

---

[1] We supply this from the modern text, which, however, has τὸν οὐχ οὕτως; But ἐκεῖνον is better, as this will account for the omission. Our Mss. have: τοὺς δικαίως ἀποθανόντας, ἢ ἐκεῖνον καὶ θαυμάζεις

* The accusations against Stephen were probably true in part and false in part. He had doubtless spoken against Jewish legalism and narrowness and had perhaps shown the bearing of O. T. prophecy and of Jesus' doctrine of fulfilment upon the fate of the Jewish system. The charge that he had spoken "against Moses" had, then, a certain verbal truth which made its moral falseness all the more subtle. The perversion of his words was due in part to their utter incapacity to apprehend Christianity as the fulfilment of their own religion which necessarily involved the passing away of the latter, and partly from their bitter jealousy and hatred of the Christian "sect" and the determination to find some excuse to bring against it all the legal and social forces of the whole Jewish people. In his preaching Stephen had doubtless sought to set forth the distinctive character of Christianity as a religion historically founded in Judaism, but not to be limited and bound by its forms. He but developed germs of truth found in the teaching of Jesus concerning the Sabbath, ceremonial purifications, etc. He was the forerunner of Paul, who brought upon himself the same accusations (Acts xviii. 13; xxi. 21).—G. B. S.

intolerable to them. "They could not resist, etc.: then they suborned men." Everywhere out of hand, but by means of a sentence, that they might hurt their reputation also: and leaving those (the Apostles), they attack these (the disciples), thinking in this way to terrify those also. They say not, "he speaketh," but, "he ceaseth not to speak. And they stirred up the people, and the elders, and the scribes, and came upon him, and caught him, and brought him to the council, and set up false witnesses, which said, This man ceaseth not to speak blasphemous words against this holy place, and the law." (v. 12, 13.) "Ceaseth not," say they, as if he made this his business. "For we have heard him say that this Jesus of Nazareth shall destroy this place, and shall change the customs which Moses delivered us." (v. 14.) "Jesus," they say, "the Nazarene," as a term of reproach, "shall destroy this place, and shall change the customs." This is also what they said about Christ. "Thou that destroyest this Temple." (Matt. xxvii. 40.) For great was their veneration for the Temple (as indeed they had chosen to leave their own country (μετοικεῖν) in order to be near it) and for the name of Moses. The charge is twofold. If[1] He "shall change the customs," He will also introduce others instead: observe how the charge is a bitter one, and fraught with perils. "And all that sat in the council, looking steadfastly on him, saw his face as it had been the face of an angel." (v. 15.) So possible is it even for one in a lower degree to shine. For what, I ask, had this man less than the Apostles? He lacked not miracles, and great was the boldness he exhibited.[2]— "They saw his face," it is said, "as it had been the face of an angel." (Ex. xxxiv. 30.) For this was his grace, this was the glory of Moses. God made him thus gracious (ἐπίχαριν) of visage, now that he was about to say somewhat, thus at once by his very look to awe them. For there are, yes, there are faces full-fraught with spiritual grace, lovely to them that love, awful to haters and enemies. It mentions also the reason, why they suffered his oration.—"Then," it proceeds, "said the high-priest, Are these things so?" (ch. vii. 1.) Observe, the question is put with mildness, that he may effect some great mischief. For this reason Stephen too begins his speech in a tone of gentleness, and says, "Men, brethren, and fathers,

hearken; The God of glory appeared unto our father Abraham, when he was in Mesopotamia, before he dwelt in Charran." (v. 2.) Immediately at the outset he overthrows their conceit, and makes it appear by what he says, that the temple is nothing, that the customs are nothing either, without their suspecting his drift: also that they shall not overcome the preaching; and that from powerless (ἀμηχάνων) things God evermore contrives Him powerful (εὐμήχανα) instruments. Mark then how these threads make the texture of the whole speech: and moreover that having evermore enjoyed exceeding goodness, they still requited their Benefactor with the opposite conduct, and that they are now attempting impossibilities. "The God of glory appeared unto our father Abraham, when he was in Mesopotamia, before he came into Charran." Both the temple was not, and sacrifice was not, and yet a vision of God was vouchsafed to Abraham, and yet had he Persians[3] for his ancestors, and was in a strange land. And he does well at the beginning of his speech to call Him, "the God of glory:" seeing that He hath made them that are without honor to be glorious. "Because" (says he) "it was He that made them glorious, He will make us also." Observe how he leads them away from things of the body, from the place, in the first instance, as the place was in question. "The God of glory," says he: implying again, that He needs not the glory which comes from us, which comes by the Temple: for Himself is the Fountain thereof. Think not, he would say, in this way to glorify Him. "And from thy kindred." How[4] then saith the Scripture, that Abraham's father was willing to go out? Hence we learn, that it was in consequence of Abraham's vision, that his father was moved to join in the migration. (Gen. xi. 31.) "And said unto him, Get thee out of thy country, and from thy kindred, and come into a land which I shall show thee." (v. 3.) It shows how far these men are from being children of Abraham, how obedient he was. "And[5] from thy kindred." Uncomfortable (φορτικὰ) reflections, both, that he endured the labors, while ye reap the fruits, and that all your ancestors were in evil case. "Then came he out of the land of the Chaldæans, and dwelt in Charran: and from thence, when

---

[1] E. "And observe how the charge is twofold. 'Shall destroy,' say they, 'the place,' and, 'shall change the customs. And not only twofold, but bitter," etc. So Edd. but Savil. adds, "and shall introduce others instead."

[2] A. B. C. N. Οὐχὶ σημείων ἐδεήθη, καὶ (A. B. οὐ) πολλὴν ἐπεδείξατο τὴν παρρησίαν. Cat. has πολλῶν for σημείων, and reads it affirmatively. Edd. οὐχὶ σημεῖα εἰργάσατο; οὐ (D. F. καὶ) πολλὴν κ. τ. λ. Perhaps the passage may be restored thus: "Did he not work miracles—though he needed not many—and show great boldness?"

[3] Chrys. commonly denotes the oriental nations, generally, by the name, "Persians." Ben.

[4] Edd. from E. "And how, it may be asked, doth the Scripture say this concerning Abraham's father? Because it does not trouble itself about matters that are not very essential. What was useful for us to learn, this only it has taught us, that in consequence of his son's vision, he went out with him: the rest it leaves untold, by reason that he died soon after settling in Charran. 'Get thee out of thy kindred.' Here he shows that these men," etc.

[5] E. Edd. "but these disobedient: or rather, we learn from what he does, as he was bidden, that he endured," etc.

his father was dead, He removed him into this land, wherein ye now dwell. And He gave him none inheritance in it, no, not so much as to set his foot on." (v. 4, 5.) See how he raises their thoughts away from (their possession of) the land. [1] For if He said (that, He will give : clearly [all came from him], and nothing from themselves. For he came, having left both kindred and country. Wherefore then did He not give it to him? Truly it was a figure of another land. "And He promised to give it to him." Do you perceive, that he does not merely resume the thread of his discourse? " He gave him not," says he; " and He promised ; and to his seed after him, when as yet he had no child." Again, what God can do: that out of impossibilities, He doeth all; For here is a man in Persia, so far away, and this man God saith He will make lord of Palestine. But let us look back to what was said before.

Whence, I pray you, did that grace bloom upon the countenance of Stephen? (Recapitulation.) The writer gives him this report above, that he was " full of faith." (ch. vi. 8.) For it is possible to have a grace that does not consist in works of healing: " For to one is given the grace of the Spirit (1 Cor. xii. 8, 9) in such and such wise (τοιῶσδε). But here, it seems to me, it says that he was also gracious to look at: "They saw his face as it had been the face of an angel." "Full of faith and of power": (v. 15) which is also the character given of Barnabas " he was a good man, full of faith and of the Holy Ghost." (ch. xi. 24.) Whence we learn that the sincere and innocent are, above all others, the [2] men to be saved, and that these same are also more gracious. "Then they suborned men, which said, We have heard him speak blasphemous words." (v. 11.) In the case of the Apostles they were annoyed that they preached the Resurrection, and that much people flowed unto them : but in this case, that they were getting their diseases healed. (ch. iv. 2.) The things for which they ought to give thanks, they made matter of blame: O the madness! The men who

overcame them by works, they expected to overcome by words! It is just what they did in the case of Christ, and always they forced them to words. For they were ashamed to seize them without more ado, having nothing to charge them with. And observe, not the persons themselves who bring them to judgment bear witness against them; for they would have been refuted : but they simply hire others, that it may not seem to be an act of mere violence. It is all of a piece with their proceeding in the case of Christ. And observe the power of the preaching, that, though they are not only scourged but stoned, it still prevails : not [3] only, private individuals as they are, dragged to the bar, but assailed from all quarters : and, their enemies themselves being witnesses, not only were these worsted, but " they were not able " even " to resist " (v. 10), though they were exceeding shameless : so mightily did it overthrow them, for all that they could do with their preposterous figments (as the saying that He had a devil—He that cast out devils!). For the battle was not man's, but God's against men. And there were many combined together; and not only they in Jerusalem, but others as well. (v. 9.) For " we have heard him," say they, "speaking blasphemous words against Moses and against God." (v. 11.) O ye shameless ones! Ye work blasphemous deeds, and think nothing of it. This is why Moses is added—because the things of God were no great concern to them ; and it is ever and always Moses that they make mention of: "This Moses, which brought us out." (ch. vii. 40.) "And they stirred up the people." (v. 12.) Fickleness [4] of the multitude! And yet how could a man who was a blasphemer have so succeeded? How could a blasphemer work such miracles among the people? But the undisciplined multitude made them strong who had

---

[1] A. C. N. Εἰ γὰρ εἶπεν, δώσει, δῆλον ὅτι, καὶ οὐδὲν παρ αὐτῶν Cat. Οὐ γὰρ κ. τ. λ. B. Οὐ γὰρ εἶπεν, δώσει, ἀλλ᾽, Οὐκ ἔδωκε, δῆλον ὅτι τὰ παρ ἐκείνου, καὶ οὐδὲν παρ αὐτῶν. So E. D. F. Edd. except that for δῆλον ὅτι τὰ these have δηλῶν ὅτι πάντα. The meaning seems to be: "They boasted of their possession of the land, as the token of God's favor to themselves. See how Stephen will not allow them to rest in this conceit. Abraham was ' the friend of God,' yet to him ' He gave none inheritance,' etc. True ' He promised to give it ': but if God said (that) ' He will give it (spoke of giving it at some future time); this very circumstance shows that the Jews had it from Abraham, in consequence of God's favor to him; not as deserved by themselves."

[2] τοὺς σωζομένους. Edd. from E. τοὺς θαυμαζομένους, "they that are admired."—Below, all our Mss. and the Catena have Ἐπὶ μὲν τῶν ἀποστόλων ἔλεγον, "In the case of the Apostles, they said." We read, conjecturally, ἤλγουν.

[3] C. N. have οὐχὶ ἰδιωτῶν ὄντων ἀλλὰ καὶ ἐλαυνομένων πάντοθεν: B. F. D. E. Edd. οὐδὲ ἐς δικαστήριον ἀγομένων, ἀλλὰ καὶ ἐλ. π. In the translation we assume the full reading to be, οὐχὶ, ἰδιωτῶν ὄντων, ἐς δ. ἀγομένων, ἀλλὰ καὶ ἐ. π. In the next sentence E. alone (followed by Edd.) has the unnecessary alteration, Ἐντεῦθεν καὶ ψευδομαρτυρούντων αὐτῶν, οὐ μόνον οὐκ ἐκράτουν, ἀλλ᾽ κ. τ. λ. A. οὐχὶ ἰδ. ὄντων ἀλλὰ καὶ ῥητόρων, οὐ μόνον [οὐχ ?] ἡττῶντο, ἀλλὰ καὶ [κατά?] κράτος ἐνίκων, καίτοι κ. τ. λ. i. e. [" their adversaries "] being not private individuals, but public speakers too, they not only were [not] worsted, but mightily conquered: [so that ' they were not able to resist '] though," etc.—Below, for πλάττοντας A. E. πράττοντας C. we read πράττοντας καὶ πλάττοντας : after which, Edd. have (from E. alone) : "As also in the case of Christ: who did everything to compass His death: insomuch that it became manifest to all men that the battle," etc. And, instead of the next sentence ; " And mark what say the false-witnesses, who were got up by those who murderously dragged Him before the council : 'We have heard,' " etc.

[4] τὸ εὐρίπιστον τοῦ ὄχλου. Edd. add ἀνερεθίζοντες, "irritating the fickle-minded multitude." Below, for Ἀλλ᾽ ὁ ὄχλος ὁ ἄτακτος κ, τ, λ., A. has Ἀλλ᾽ οὐχ ὁ ὄχλος ταῦτα ἀλλ᾽ οἱ γραμματεῖς. Ἡμεῖς ἀκ. κ. τ. λ. "But not the multitude (said) this, but the scribes: We have heard," etc. Edd. from E., "But such is envy: it makes them demented whom it possesses, so that they do not so much as consider the meaning of the words they utter."

the worst of it (in argument).—This was what most annoyed them. "We have heard him," they say, "speaking blasphemous words against Moses and against God" (v. 13): and again, "This man ceaseth not to speak blasphemous words against this holy place and the law," and with an addition, "the customs" "which Moses delivered to us" (v. 14); Moses, not God. Upon the supposition of a design to overturn their manner of life (πολιτείας), they accused him of impiety also. But to show that it was not in the nature of such a man to speak such things, and harshly ["Then all," it says, "which were in the council, looking steadfastly upon him, saw his face, as it had been the face of an angel"] (v. 15): so mild was he even in countenance. For, in cases where persons were not falsely accused, Scripture mentions nothing of this kind: but as in this case it was all false accusation, with reason does God rectify it by the very look of the man. For the Apostles indeed were not falsely accused, but were forbidden: but this man is falsely accused: and therefore before all else his countenance pleads for him. This abashed even the priest. "And he said," etc. (ch. vii. 1.) He shows here, that the promise was made before the Place, before Circumcision, before Sacrifice, before the Temple, and that it was not of their merit that these received either Circumcision or Law, but that the land was the reward of obedience alone. Moreover, that neither on the giving of circumcision does the promise receive its fulfilment. Also, that these were figures, and (so was) both the leaving his country at God's command—not [1] against the law (for home and country is where God shall lead): "Then came he out," it says, "of the land of the Chaldeans" (v. 4): —and that if one look closely into the matter, the Jews are of Persian origin: and that, without miracles, one must do as God bids, whatever hardships be the consequence; since the Patriarch left both the grave of his father and all that he had, in obedience to God's command. But if Abraham's father was not allowed to take part with him in the privilege of migrating to Palestine, because he was unworthy: much more shall the children (be excluded at last), for all that they may have gone a good distance on the way. "And He promised," it says, "to give it to him, and to his seed after him." (v. 5.) Herein is shown the greatness both of God's goodness and of Abraham's faith. For the expression, "when

as yet he had no child," does show his obedience and faith. "Promised to give it to him and to his seed." And yet the events showed the contrary: namely, after he came, he had not "so much as to set his foot on," had not a child; which very things were contrary to his faith.

These things having seen, let us likewise, whatever God shall promise, receive the same, however contrary may be the events. And yet in our case, they are not contrary, but very suitable. For where the promises are, there, when the contraries turn out, they are really contrary; but in our case it is just the reverse: for He has told us that we should have tribulation here, but our rest there. Why do we confound the times? Why do we turn things upside down? Say, art thou afflicted, and livest in poverty, and in dejection? Be not troubled: for it were worth being troubled at, wert thou destined to be afflicted in that world: as for this present affliction, it is the cause of rest. "This sickness," saith He, "is not unto death." (John xi. 4.) That affliction is punishment: this, schooling and correction. It is a contest, this life present: if so, to fight is our business now: it is war and battle. In war one does not seek to have rest, in war one does not seek to have dainty living, one is not anxious about riches, one's care is not about a wife then: one thing only he looks at, how he may overcome his foes. Be this our care likewise: if we overcome, and return with the victory, God will give us all things. Be this alone our study, how we may overcome the devil: though after all it is not our own study that does it, but God's grace does the whole business. Be it our one study, how we may attract His grace, how we may draw to ourselves that assistance. "If God be for us, who can be against us?" (Rom. viii. 31.) Let us make one thing our study; that He be not our enemy, that He turn not away from us.

Not the being afflicted is an evil; the evil is, to sin. This is the sore affliction, however we may pass our days in luxury:—not to speak of the life to come, it is so even in this life present. Think how our conscience is stung with remorse, and whether this is not worse than any kind of torture! I should like to put the question searchingly to those who live in evil ways (ἐν κακοῖς), whether they never come to reflect upon their own sins, whether they do not tremble, and are in fear and anguish, whether they do not think those blessed who live in abstinence, them of the mountains, them of the strict rule? (τοὺς ἐν πολλῇ φιλοσοφίᾳ.) Dost thou wish to find rest in the life to come? Suffer affliction in this life

---

[1] οὐ παρὰ τὸν νόμον. For this, E. alone has καὶ συγγένειαν, and instead of the text, "Then came he out," etc. καὶ τὸ κληρονομίαν ἐνταῦθα μὴ λαβεῖν: so Morel. Ben. Savile retains the reading of E., but adds οὐ παρὰ τὸν νόμον after συγγένειαν.

for Christ's sake: there is nothing equal to this rest. The Apostles rejoiced when scourged. Paul gives this exhortation, saying, "Rejoice in the Lord." (Philip. iv. 4.) And how can there be rejoicing, where there are bonds, where there are tortures, where there are courts of justice? There, most of all, is rejoicing. But[1] say, how can there be rejoicing, where these are not? For he who is conscious of no evil, will have a sort of exceeding delight, insomuch that in what degree you speak of tribulation, in the same you tell of his delight. The soldier who has received numberless wounds and is come home again, will he not return with exceeding delight, with his wounds[2] as his title for speaking up boldly, and as evidence of his glory and renown? And thou, if thou be able to exclaim as Paul does, "I bear the marks of Jesus" (Gal. vi. 17), wilt be able to become great and glorious and renowned. "But there is no persecution." Make thy stand against glory: and should any one speak anything against thee, fear not to be evil-spoken of for Christ's sake: make thy stand against the tyranny of pride, against the fighting of anger, against the torment of concupiscence. These also are "marks,"[3] these also are torments. For, I ask, what is the worst in tortures? Is it not, that the soul is pained, and is on fire? For in the other case, the body too has its share: but in this, the whole belongs to the soul. On the soul alone comes all the smart, when one is angry, when one is envious, whatever else of this kind one does, or rather suffers. For, in fact, it is not action, but passion, not a doing, but a suffering—to be angered, to feel envy: therefore indeed they are called passions (or sufferings) (πάθη, *perturbationes*) of the soul, yea wounds, and bruises. For it is indeed a suffering, and worse than suffering. Bethink you, ye that are angry, that ye do such things in "passion," in a state of suffering. Therefore he who is not angry suffers not. Do you mark that not he who is abused is the sufferer, but he that abuses, as I said above? For that he is a sufferer, is plain in the first place from the very fact, that such a thing is called by this name of passion: and it is also plain from the (effects on the) body: for these are the affections (πάθη) [or "sufferings," as we call them] engendered by anger, viz. dimness

of vision, insanity, and numberless others. "But he insulted my boy," say you; "but [he called him] clown."[4] Deem it not weakness thy not doing the same thing thyself. For, I ask you, was it well done? You will not say that: then leave that undone which being done were not well done. I know what passions are engendered in such cases. "But," say you, "how if he despise me, how if he say it again?" Show him that he is in the wrong: rebuke him, entreat him: by meekness anger is put down: go and expostulate with him. For though in cases of wrong done to ourselves it is right not to do even this, yet it is quite necessary to do it in behalf of others. Do not look on it as an insult to yourself that your boy has been insulted: annoyed you may be for his sake, yet not as if you were insulted: for it does not follow because your boy has been ill-treated, that you are disgraced, but he is disgraced that did the ill. Quench (thine anger) that sharp sword: let it lie in its scabbard. If we have it unsheathed, we shall be apt to use it even when the time is not proper, being drawn on by it: but if it be hidden, though a necessity should arise, yet, while we seek it in order[5] to draw it, the anger will be quenched. Christ would not have us be angry on his account: (hear what He saith to Peter: "Put up again thy sword into the sheath:") (Matt. xxvi. 52) and art thou angry on account of a boy? Teach thy boy also to be philosophical: tell him thy own sufferings: imitate (herein) thy Teacher. (Matt. xxvi. 52.) When they too (His disciples) were about to be treated with dishonor, He said not, "I will avenge you:" but, "to Me also," saith He, "they have done the same: bear it nobly, for ye are not better than I." These words too do thou speak to thy son and thy boy: "Thou art not better than thy master." But these words of philosophy are counted as the talk of a widow woman. Alas! that it is not in the power of words to bring it home to people in the way that it is possible to be taught it by actual experience! And that you may learn this; stand between two combatants, take part with the wronged, not with the wrong-doers

---

[1] E. F. D. Edd. "And how there may be rejoicing where these are, learn (thus). He who in nothing is conscious of evil," etc.

[2] παρρησίας ὑπόθεσιν ἔχων τὰ τραύματα. Ben "*argumentum audaciae*." Erasm. "*testimonium libertatis*."

[3] στίγματα, i. e. "the marks of Jesus may be gained in these encounters also, and the spirit of a confessor may be exhibited under these tortures likewise.

[4] ἀλλὰ τὸν ἀγροῖκον. Edd. from E., ἀλλὰ τὸν οἰκέτην: which is idle, for it appears below that the παῖς here is a servant. We supply ἐκάλεσε or εἶπεν: and indeed ἂν πάλιν εἴπῃ below shows that the insult spoken of was some contumelious speech.—Also before Μὴ νομίσῃς, something needs to be supplied, e. g. Μὴ σὺ μιμήσῃ τοῦτον, "Do not thou imitate him." And perhaps indeed τὸν ἀγρ. may belong to this: "He insulted my boy." But do not thou imitate the rude, uncivil man: deem it not, etc.

[5] ὡς ζητοῦμεν σκεπάσαι. A. B. C. The other Mss. omit the clause, and Edd. except Savile who reads from N. οὐ ζητοῦμεν αὐτὴν σπάσαι, "we do not seek to draw it." We adopt σπάσαι.—Below, E. F. D. Edd. τοῦ Δεσπότου, "thy Master's sufferings," for σαυτοῦ, which the context shows to be the true reading.

[that you may learn]¹ whether you shall not see the victory on your side, whether you shall not get splendid crowns.—See, how God is insulted, and how He answers ; how gently, "Where," saith He, "is Abel thy brother ?" and what saith the other : " Am I my brother's keeper ?" (Gen. vi. 9.) What could be more contumacious than this ? Would any one have heard it (patiently) even from a son? and if from a brother, would he not have thought such conduct an insult ? What then ? See how again God gently answers, "The voice of thy brother's blood," saith He "crieth unto Me." "But God," it will be said, "is superior to wrath." Yes, but for this reason the Son of God came down, that He might make thee a God as far as human power can go. "But I cannot," says one, "seeing I am man." Well then, let us give you men for instances. And do not suppose I speak of Paul or of Peter : no, but of some of inferior sort, yea, very much lower down. Eli's menial insulted Hannah, saying, " Put away thy wine from thee." (1 Sam. i. 14.) What could be more insulting than this ? What then said she? "I am a woman of a hard lot."² Indeed, there is nothing equal to affliction : she is the mother of true philosophy. But this same woman, though she has her rival, insulted her not : but what does she ? She takes refuge with God, and in her prayer does not even make mention of her, nor say, "Avenge me, for such an one reproaches me :" so magnanimous was that woman (let us men be ashamed) :—and yet ye know, that there is nothing like jealousy. The publican, when insulted by the Pharisee, insulted not in return, though, had he wished it, he might have done so : but he bore it like a philosopher, saying, "Be merciful to me a sinner." (Luke xviii. 13.) Mephibosheth,³ having been accused and calumniated by his servant, neither said, nor did, any evil to him, not even in the presence of the king himself. (2 Sam. xix. 26.) Shall I tell you even of a harlot, what philosophic magnanimity she showed? Hear Christ saying, as she was wiping His feet with her hair, "The publicans and harlots go into the kingdom before you." (Matt. xxi. 31.) Do you see her standing, and taking courage, and washing away her own sins? Observe, how she was not angry even

with the Pharisee, when reproached by him : "for had He known," says he, "that this woman is a sinner, He would not have suffered her (Luke vii. 39) : and how she said not to him, "What then ? Say, art thou pure from sins?" but felt more, wept more, and let fall hotter tears. But if women and publicans and harlots play the philosopher, and that before grace (i. e. of Baptism), what pardon can they deserve, who, after so great grace, fight, and worry, and kick one another, worse than beasts? Nothing is more base than passion, nothing more disgraceful, nothing more frightful, nothing more odious, nothing more hurtful. These things I say, not only in order that towards men we may be gentle, but also if a wife be a talker, that thou mayest bear it : let thy wife be to thee a school for training and exercise (παλαίστρα καὶ γυμνάσιον) For how can it but be absurd, to submit to exercises which yield no profit, where we afflict the body, but not to practise exercises at home, which, even before the contest, present to us a crown? Does thy wife abuse thee? Do not thou become a woman : to be abusive is womanly : it is a disease of the soul, an inferiority. Think not that it is unworthy of thee, when thy wife abuses thee. Unworthy it is, when thou art abusive, but she bears patiently (φιλοσοφῇ) : then dost thou act unseemly, then art thou disgraced : but if, having been abused, thou bear it, great is the proof of thy strength. I do not say this, to induce wives to be abusive : God forbid : but only in case it should so happen at the instance of Satan. It is the part of men that are strong, to bear the weak. And if thy servant contradict thee, bear it philosophically : not what he deserves to have said to him, do thou say or do, but that which it behooves thee both to do and to say. Never insult a girl by uttering some foul word against her : never call thy servant, scoundrel (μιαρὸν) : not he is disgraced, but thou. It is not possible to be master of one's self, being in a passion. Like a sea rolling mountains high, it is all hurly-burly : or even as a pure fountain, when mire is cast into it, becomes muddied, and all is in turmoil. You may beat him, you may rend his coat to rags, but it is you that sustain the greater damage : for to him the blow is on the body and the garment, but to you on the soul. It is your own soul that you have cut open ; it is there that you have inflicted a wound : you have flung your own charioteer from his horses, you have got him dragging along the ground upon his back. And it is all one, as if one driver being in a passion with another, should choose to be thus dragged along. You may rebuke, you may chide, you may do whatever

---

¹ ἂν μὴ παρὰ σαυτῷ τὰ νικητήρια ἴδῃς ἂν μὴ λαμπροὺς λάβῃς στεφάνους. This depends on ἵνα μάθῃς at the beginning of the sentence. Erasmus wrongly, " Si non videas:" Ben. " Si non videbis."
² γυνὴ ἐν σκληρᾷ ἡμέρα εἰμὶ, Chrys. γυνὴ ἡ σκληρὰ ἡμερὰ (or ἡμέρα) LXX.
³ Memphibaal, Chrys. here and Synops. Sacr. Script. t. vi. 349. and Theodoret Quæst. 31, in lib. 2. Reg. Μεμφιβοσθέ, LXX. Elsewhere he is called Meribbaal, 1 Chron. viii. 34. So Jerubbaal, Judg. vi. 32. Jerubbesheth, 2 Sam. xi. 21. Memphibaal is compounded of the two forms. Ben.

if be, only let it be without wrath and passion. For if he who rebukes is physician to him who offends, how can he heal another, when he has first hurt himself, when he does not heal himself? Say, if a physician should go to heal another person, does he first wound his own hand, first blind his own eyes, and so set about healing that other? God forbid. So also, however thou rebuke, however thou chide, let thine eyes see clearly. Do not make thy mind muddy, else how shall the cure be wrought? It is not possible to be in the same tranquillity, being in a passion, and being free from passion. Why dost thou first overturn thy master from his seat, and then discourse with him as he lies sprawling on the 'ground? Seest thou not the judges, how, when about to hold the assize, they seat themselves upon the bench, in their becoming attire? Thus do thou likewise dress thy soul with the judicial robe (which is gentleness). "But he will not be afraid of me," say you. He will be the more afraid. In the other case, though you speak justly, your servant will impute it to passion: but if you do it with gentleness, he will condemn himself: and, what is of the first importance, God will accept thee, and thus thou wilt be able to attain unto the eternal blessings, through the grace and loving-kindness of our Lord Jesus Christ, with Whom to the Father together with the Holy Spirit be glory, dominion, and honor, now and ever, and world without end. Amen.

HOMILY XVI.

ACTS VII. 6, 7.

"And God spake on this wise, That his seed should sojourn in a strange land; and that they should bring them into bondage, and entreat them evil four hundred years. And the nation to whom they shall be in bondage will I judge, said God: and after that shall they come forth, and serve Me in this place."

SEE, what a number of years the Promise has been given, and the manner of the Promise, and nowhere sacrifice, nowhere circumcision! He here shows, how God Himself suffered them to be afflicted, not[1] that He had anything to lay to their charge. "And they shall bring them into bondage," etc. But nevertheless, they did not these things with impunity. "And the nation to whom they shall be in bondage I will judge, said God." For,[2] to show that they are not to go by this, in estimating who are pious (by reason of their saying, "He trusted in God, let Him deliver Him,") (Matt. xxvii. 43).—He, the Same that promised, He that gave the land, first permits the evils. So also now, though He has promised a Kingdom, yet He suffers us to be exercised in temptations. If here the freedom was not to be till after four hundred years, what wonder, with regard to the Kingdom? Yet He performed it, and lapse of time availed not to falsify His word. More-over, it was no ordinary bondage they underwent.* And the matter does not terminate solely in the punishment of those (their oppressors); but they themselves also, He saith, shall enjoy a mighty salvation. Here he reminds them too of the benefit which they enjoyed. "And he gave him the covenant of circumcision: and so he begat Isaac." Here he lets himself down to lower matters. "And circumcised him on the eighth day: and Isaac (begat) Jacob, and Jacob the twelve patriarchs." (v. 8).—Here[3] he seems to hint now at the type. "And the patriarchs moved with envy, sold Joseph into Egypt." (v. 9.) Here again, the type of Christ.† Though they had no fault to find with him, and though he came on purpose to bring them their food, they thus ill-treated him. Still here again the promise, though it is a long while first, receives its fulfilment. "And God was with him"—this also is for them—"and delivered

---

* The relation of v. 6 and 7 to v. 5 is, as Chrys. intimates, to show that the apparent incongruity between the promise of God to give the land to Abraham and his seed, and the fact that Abraham never personally possessed the land, was not accidental nor did it involve the failure of the divine promise. Accompanying the promise were divine assurances (Gen. xv. 13, 14) that a period of bondage and oppression was to precede the occupation of the land which was to be the inheritance of the nation.—G. B. S.

[3] E. Edd. omit this sentence: and below for "Here again," etc. the same substitute: "This happened also in the case of Christ: for indeed Joseph is a type of Him: wherefore also he narrates the history at large, hinting (at this meaning)."

† If it be too strong language to say, with Chrys., that Joseph is set forth here as a "type of Christ," it is clear that the narrative of his ill-treatment by his brethren, subsequent exaltation and his return of good for evil to those who had sold him into bondage, is meant to suggest that their treatment of Jesus had been similar.—G. B. S.

---

[1] καίτοι οὐδὲν ἔχων αὐτοῖς ἐγκαλεῖν. A. B. C. N. Cat.—E. F. D. Edd. omit this clause, and read: "to be afflicted: and that they did not," etc. So Edd.

[2] Ἵνα γὰρ μὴ τούτῳ (Cat. τούτων, A. C. N. τοῦτο B. om.) νομίσωσιν εὐσεβεῖς (N. εὐσεβεῖν) εἶναι, διὰ τὸ λέγειν κ. τ. λ. The wording of the passage is not strictly grammatical, but the sense seems to be as expressed above.—E. D. F. omit this sentence, and substitute, "Seest thou?" So Edd.

him out of all his afflictions." (v. 10). He shows that unknowingly they helped to fulfil the prophecy, and that they were themselves the cause, and that the evils recoiled on their own selves. "And gave him favor and wisdom in the sight of Pharaoh king of Egypt, Gave him favor," in the eyes of a barbarian, to him, the slave, the captive: his brethren sold him, this (barbarian) honored him. "Now there came a dearth over all the land of Egypt and Canaan, and great affliction: and our fathers found no sustenance. But when Jacob heard that there was corn in Egypt, he sent out our fathers first. And at the second time Joseph was made known to his brethren." (v. 11-13). They came down to buy, and had to depend upon him for everything. What then did he? ["He made himself known to his brethren:"] not to this point only did he carry his friendliness; he also made them known to Pharaoh, and brought them down into the land. "And Joseph's kindred was made known unto Pharaoh. Then sent Joseph, and called his father Jacob to him, and all his kindred, threescore and fifteen souls. So Jacob went down into Egypt, and died, he, and our fathers, and were carried over into Sychem, and laid in the sepulchre that Abraham bought for a sum of money of the sons of Emmor the father of Sychem. But when the time of the promise drew nigh, which God had sworn to Abraham, the people grew and multiplied in Egypt, till another king arose, which knew not Joseph. (v. 13-18). Then again, fresh disappointment (ἀνελπιστία): first, famine, but they came through that: secondly, the falling into the hands of their enemy: thirdly, the being destroyed by the king. Then (to show) God's fulness of ways and means (εὐμήχανον), "In which time," it says, "Moses was born, and was exceeding fair." (v. 20.) If the former circumstance was wonderful, that Joseph was sold by his brethren, here again is another circumstance more wonderful still, that the king "nourished" the very person who was to overthrow his dominion, being himself the person that was to perish. Do you observe all along a figurative enacting, so to say, of the resurrection of the dead? But it is not the same thing for God himself to do a thing, and for a thing to come to pass in connection with man's purpose (προαίρεσις). For these things indeed were in connection with man's purpose ['but the Resurrection by itself, in-

dependently.]—"And he was mighty," it says, "in word and in deed" (v. 22): he that was to have died. Then again he shows how ungrateful they were to their benefactor. For, just as in the former instance, they were saved by the injured Joseph, so here again they were saved by another injured person, I mean, Moses. "And when he was full forty years old," etc. For[2] what though they killed him not actually? In intention they did kill, as did the others in the former case. There, they sold out of their own into a strange land: here, they drive from one strange land into another strange land: in the former case, one in the act of bringing them food; in this, one in the act of giving them good counsel'; one to whom, under God, the man was indebted for his life! Mark how it shows (the truth of) that saying of Gamaliel's, "If it be of God, ye cannot overthrow it." (ch. v. 39.) See the plotted-against eventually becoming the authors of salvation to those plotting against them: [3] the people, plotting against itself, and itself plotted against by others; and for all this, saved! A famine, and it did not consume them: nor was this all: but they were saved by means of the very person, whom they had expected to be destroyed (by their means). A royal edict, and it did not consume them: nay then most did their number increase, when he was dead "who knew" them. Their own Saviour they wished to kill, but for all that, they had not power to do it. Do you observe, that by the means whereby the devil tried to bring to naught the promise of God, by those very means it was advanced?

"And God spake on this wise," etc. (Recapitulation, v. 6, 7.) This[4] is suitable to be said here also: that God is rich in ways and means to bring us up from hence. For this above all showed the riches of God's resources, that in its very reverses (ἀποστροφῇ) the nation increased, while enslaved, while evil-

clause, ὁ ὀφείλων ἀποθανεῖν: and for Εἶτα πάλιν, have, "This he says, by way of showing both him (Moses) as saviour, and these ungrateful to their benefactor."

[2] Τί γὰρ εἰ μὴ ἀνεῖλον αὐτὸν τῷ πράγματι; τῷ λόγῳ ἀνεῖλον ὥσπερ κἀκεῖνοι. N. and Catena read ἀνεῖλεν, both times, as if the Compiler understood the passage in the sense of a preceding comment extracted from S. Clem. Alex. Strom. "φασὶ δὲ οἱ μυσταὶ λόγῳ μόνῳ ἀνελεῖν τὸν Αἰγύπτιον: the initiated say that Moses struck the Egyptian dead by a word, as in the Acts Peter is related to have done in the case of Ananias," etc. But Chrys. nowhere thus interprets the fact, and the context, ὥσπερ κἀκεῖνοι, is against this view.—Below, δἰ ὃν ἔζη μετὰ Θεὸν: i. e. the Hebrew whom Moses saved, v. 24, who is here supposed to be one of the parties in the strife mentioned in v. 26. This however not being clear, A., as usual omits: and the innovator, assuming the passage to be corrupt, substitutes, δἰ ὧν ἔσονται μετὰ Θεοῦ, giving them counsel by means of which they shall be with God." So Edd.: only Sav. notes in the margin the genuine reading of the other Mss. and Cat.

[3] E. "But do thou, observing this, stand amazed at the riches of God's wisdom and resources: for, had those not been plotted against, these had not been saved." So Edd.

[4] Τοῦτο καὶ ἐνταῦθα ἁρμόττει εἰπεῖν. Edd. from E. only, τοῦτο καὶ αὐτοὺς ἥρμοττε τότε εἰπεῖν: "This was also suitable for them to say at that time." It was not perceived that the recapitulation begins here. See note [5], p. 102.

[1] ἡ δὲ ἀνάστασις καθ᾽ ἑαυτήν. This clause is found in the Catena alone. Something seems to be required as the antithesis to the preceding clause, ταῦτα μὲν γὰρ μετὰ προαιρ. ἀνθρ. ἦν—for which E. Edd. have ταῦτα γοῦν οὐκ ἀπὸ προαιρ. ἀνθρ. ἦν. "These things however did not come of man's purpose."—At the end of the next sentence, Edd. (with E. alone) omit the

entreated, and sought to be exterminated. And this is the greatness of the Promise. For had it increased in its own land, it had not been so wonderful. And besides, it was not for a short time, either, that they were in the strange land : but for four hundred years. Hence we learn [1] a (great lesson) of philosophic endurance (φιλοσοφίαν) :—they did not treat them as masters use slaves, but as enemies and tyrants—and he foretold that they should be set in great liberty : for this is the meaning of that expression, "They shall serve (Me) : and they shall come up hither again" (ἐνταῦθα ἐπανελεύσονται) ; and with impunity.[2]— And observe, how, while he seems to concede something to circumcision, he in fact allows it nothing (v. 8) ; since the Promise was before it, and it followed after.—"And the patriarchs," he says, "moved with envy. (v. 9.) Where it does no harm, he humors (χαρίζεται) them : [3] for they prided themselves much on these also.—[4] And he shows, that the saints were not exempt from tribulation, but that in their very tribulations they obtained help. And that these persons did themselves help to bring about the results, who wished to cut short these same (afflictions) : just as these made Joseph the more glorious : just as the king did Moses, by ordering the children to be killed : since had he not ordered, this would not have been : just as also that (Hebrew) drives Moses into exile, that there he may have the Vision, having become worthy. Thus also him who was sold for a slave, makes He to reign as king there, where he was thought to be a slave. Thus also does Christ in His death give proof of His power : thus also does He there reign as king where they sold Him. "And gave him favor and wisdom," etc. (v. 10.) This [5] was not only by way of honor, but that he should have confidence in his own power. "And he made him governor over Egypt and all his house." "Now there came a dearth," etc. On account of famine—such preparations is he making—"with threescore and fifteen souls,"

he says, "Jacob went down into Egypt, and died, he and our fathers, and were carried over into Sychem, and laid in the sepulchre that Abraham bought for a sum of money from the sons of Emmor the father of Sychem.* (v. 11-16). It shows, that they were not masters even to the extent of a burying-place. "But when the time of the promise drew nigh, which God had sworn to Abraham, the people grew and multiplied in Egypt, till another king arose, which knew not Joseph" (v. 17, 18). Observe, that it is not during the four hundred years that He multiplies them, but (only) when the end was about to draw nigh. And yet already four hundred years were passed, nay more, in Egypt. But this is the wonder of it. "The same dealt subtly with our kindred, and evil-entreated our fathers, that they should cast out their young children, to the end they might not live." (v. 19.) "Dealt subtly : " he hints at their not liking to exterminate them openly : "that they should cast out their young children," it says. "In which time Moses was born and was exceeding fair." (v. 20.) This is the wonder, that he who is to be their champion, is born, neither after nor before, these things, but in the very midst of the storm (θυμῷ). "And was nourished up in his father's house three months." But when man's help was despaired of, and they cast him forth, then did God's benefit shine forth conspicuous. "And when he was cast out, Pharaoh's daughter took him up, and nourished him for her own son." (v. 21.) Not a word of Temple, not a word of Sacrifice, while all these Providences are taking place. And he was nourished in a barbarian house. "And Moses was learned in all the wisdom of the Egyptians, and was mighty in words and in deeds." (v. 22.) "Was trained," both [6] in discipline and in letters. "And when he was full forty years old." (v. 23.) Forty years he was there, and was not found out from his being circumcised. Observe, how, being in safety, they overlook their own interests, both he and Joseph, in order that they may save others : "And when he was full forty years old, it came into his heart to visit his brethren the children of Israel. And seeing one of them suffer wrong, he defended him, and avenged him that was oppressed,

[1] Edd. from E. D. F. "how they exhibited a great (example of) philosophy."

[2] Edd. (from E. alone) καὶ οὐκ ἀτιμωρητὶ, "not unavenged (upon their enemies)." But the meaning is, "Their enemies shall not be able to be avenged of them."

[3] E. D. F. insert for explanation, πατριάρχας δέ φησι τοὺς προγόνους· "he calls their ancestors, patriarchs." This is the "humoring" spoken of above: in C.'s time, "patriarch" had become a title of honor.

[4] Edd. from E. "But they not only did not loose (the afflictions), but even coöperated with those afflicting them, when they ought rather to have cut through them (the afflictions)."

[5] Morel. Ben. with E. D. F. omit this clause: Savile transposes it. "But as this (Joseph) reigns there as king where they sold him, so does Christ in His death," etc.—In the next sentence, τοῦτο seems to refer to the description in Gen. xli. 42, 43, of the distinctions conferred upon Joseph, which perhaps Chrys. cited.—After this sentence, Edd. have (from E. only) the formula of recapitulation, 'Αλλ' ἴδωμεν κ. τ. λ., which is quite misplaced.—Below, A. and the mod. t. insert Ὅρα, before διὰ λιμὸν οἷα κατασκευάζει.

* The reading of τοῦ Συχέμ (T. R.), doubtless meaning the "father of Sychem" (Gen. xxxiii. 19), is replaced by Tisch., W. and H. (after א. B. C.) with ἐν Συχέμ, making Συχέμ the name of the place just mentioned—not of the person referred to in the O. T. The Vulgate renders filii Sichem thus coming into collision with the O. T. l. c.—G. B. S.

[6] καὶ παιδείᾳ καὶ γράμμασιν, as the comment on ἐπαιδεύθη v. 22, which must be supplied. Cat. has, καὶ παιδεία καὶ γράμματα. E. omits the clause, and substitutes, as the beginning of the next sentence, Ἐμοὶ θαυμάζειν ἐπέρχεται πῶς. "To me it occurs to wonder how he could be forty years," etc. So Edd.

and smote the Egyptian : for he supposed his brethren would have understood how that God by his hand would deliver them : but they understood not." (v. 23-25.)—See how up to this point he is not yet offensive to them ; how they listened to him while he said all this. And "his face," we read, "was as the face of an angel" (ch. vi. 15).—" For he supposed," etc. And yet it was by deeds that his championship was shown ; what intelligence was there need of here ? but still for all this "they understood not. And the next day he showed himself unto them as they strove, and would have set them at one again, saying, Sirs, ye are brethren ; why do ye wrong one to another ?" (v. 26-28.) Do you mark with what mildness he addresses them ? He who had shown his wrath in the case of the other, shows his gentleness[1] in his own case. "But he that did his neighbor wrong thrust him away, saying, Who made thee a ruler and a judge over us ? Wilt thou kill me, as thou didst the Egyptian yesterday ?" Mark ; the very words which they said to Christ : "Who made Thee ruler and judge over us ?" So habitual a thing was it for Jews to wrong (their benefactors) when in the act of receiving benefits ! And again, mark the atrocious baseness : (μιαρίαν al. μοχθηρίαν, Sav. marg.) "As thou didst the Egyptian' yesterday ! Then fled Moses at this saying, and was a stranger in the land of Midian, where he begat two sons." (v. 29.) But neither did flight extinguish the plan of Providence, as neither did death (i. e. the death of Christ).

"And when forty years were expired, there appeared to him in the wilderness of mount Sinai an angel of the Lord in a flame of fire in a bush." (v. 30.) Do you mark that it is not hindered by lapse of time ? For when he was an exile, when a stranger, when he had now passed much time in a foreign land, so as to have two sons, when he no longer expected to return, then does the Angel appear to him. The Son of God he calls an Angel, as also he calls Him man. (Appears) in the desert, not in a temple. See how many miracles are taking place, and no word of Temple, no word of Sacrifice. And here also not simply in the desert, but in the bush. "When Moses saw it, he wondered at the sight : and as he drew near to behold it, the voice of the Lord came unto him." (v. 31.) Lo ! he was

deemed worthy of the Voice also. "I am the God of thy fathers, the God of Abraham, and the God of Isaac, and the God of Jacob." (v. 32, 33.) Lo ![2] how He shows that He is none other than "the God of Abraham, and the God of Isaac, and the God of Jacob "—He, "the Angel of the Great Counsel." (Is. ix. 6. LXX. "Wonderful, Counsellor," E. V.) Here he shows what great loving-kindness God herein exhibits. "Then Moses trembled, and durst not behold. Then said the Lord to him, Put off thy shoes from thy feet ; for the place where thou standest is holy ground." Not a word of Temple, and the place is holy through the appearance and operation of Christ. Far more wonderful this than the place which is in the Holy of Holies : for there God is nowhere said to have appeared in this manner, nor Moses to have thus trembled. And then the greatness of His tender care. "I have seen, I have seen the affliction of My people which is in Egypt, and I have heard their groaning, and am come down to deliver them. And now come, I will send thee into Egypt." (v. 34.) See, how he shows, that both by kindnesses, and by chastisements, and by miracles, God was drawing them to Him : but they were still the same. That God is everywhere present, they learned.

Hearing these things, let us in our afflictions flee to Him. "And their groaning," saith He, "I have heard :" not[3] simply, "because of their calamities." But if any should ask, Why then did He suffer them to be evil entreated there ? Why, in the first place, to every just man his sufferings are the causes of his rewards. And in the next place, as to why He afflicted them : it was to show His power, that He can (do all), and not only so, but that He may also train them. Observe in fact ; when they were in the desert, then they "waxed fat, they grew thick, they spread out in breadth, they kicked" (Deut. xxxii. 15) : and ever and always ease was an evil. Therefore also from the beginning He said to Adam : "In the sweat of thy face thou shalt eat thy bread." (Gen. iii. 19.) Also[4] (it was) in order that having come out of much suffering into rest, they might give thanks to God. For affliction is a great good. For hear the Prophet saying, "It is good for me, that Thou

---

[1] ἐφ' ἑαυτοῦ, B. C. F. D. N. but A. E. Edd. ἐπὶ τούτου "in the case of this man." So perhaps Œcumen. ἐπιεικῶς νῦν τῷ ἀδικοῦντι προσφέρεται.—Below, E. Edd. "With the same spirit they appear to say the same with reference to Christ, ' We have no king but Cæsar.' Thus was it ever habitual to the Jews to act, even when receiving benefits. Do you mark their madness ? Him who was to save them, they accuse, by saying, ' As thou,' " etc.

[2] So A. B. N. Cat. (in C. the sentence Ἰδου—Ἰακὼβ is omitted by an oversight caused by the homœoteleuton Ἰακώβ.) Edd. "Not only does he here show that the Angel which appeared unto him was the Angel of the Great Counsel, but he shows also what loving-kindness God exhibits by this manifestation."
[3] i. e. "I have heard their groaning :" not simply ("I have come down) because of their calamities." The expression, "I have heard" denotes His ready sympathy.—But the modern text: "He does not simply say, ' I have heard ;' but because of their calamities."
[4] Edd. from E. "Therefore in order that having come out of much affliction into rest, they may not be insolent, he permits them to be afflicted."

hast humbled me." (Ps. cxix. 71.) But if to great and wonderful men affliction be a great (good), much more to us. And, if you will, let us examine into the nature of affliction as it is in itself. Let there be some person rejoicing exceedingly, and gay, and giving a loose to jollity : what more unseemly, what more senseless than this ? Let there be one sorrowing and dejected : what more truly philosophic than this ? For, "It is better," we read, "to go into the house of mourning, than into the house of laughter." (Eccles. vii. 2.) But, likely enough, you[1] do not like the saying, and want to evade it. Let us however see, what sort of man Adam was in Paradise, and what he was afterwards : what sort of man Cain was before, and what he was afterwards. The soul does not stand fast in its proper place, but, like as by a running tide, (ῥεύματος, Edd. πνεύματος, "wind") is raised and buoyed up by pleasure, having no steadfastness ; facile in making professions, prompt at promising ; the thoughts all in restless commotion : laughter ill-timed, causeless hilarity, idle clatter of unmeaning talk. And why speak of others ? Let us take in hand some one of the saints, and let us see what he was while in pleasure, what again, when in distress. Shall we look at David himself ? When he was in pleasure and rejoicing, from his many trophies, from his victory, from his crowns, from his luxurious living, from his confidence, see what sort of things he said and did : "But I said in my prosperity," says he, "I shall never be moved." (Ps. xxx. 6.) But when he has come to be in affliction, hear what he says : "And if He say to me, I have no mind for thee ; lo ! here am I, let Him do that which is pleasing in His sight." (2 Sam. xv. 26.) What can be more truly philosophic than these words? "Whatsoever may be pleasing to God," saith he, "so let it be." And again he said to Saul : "If the Lord stirreth thee up against me, may thy sacrifice be acceptable." (1 Sam. xxvi. 19.) And then too, being in affliction, he spared even his enemies : but afterwards, not friends even, nor those who had done him no injury. Again, Jacob when he was in affliction, said : "If the Lord will give me bread to eat, and raiment to put on." (Gen. xxviii. 20.) As also the son of Noah did nothing of the kind erewhile ; but when he was no longer afraid for his safety, you hear how wanton he became. (ib. ix. 22.) Hezekiah too, when he was in affliction, see what things he did in order to his deliverance ; he put on sackcloth, and such like ; but when he was in pleasure, he fell through the haughtiness of his heart. (2 Kings ch. xix. 20.) For, saith the Scripture, "When thou hast eaten, and drunk, and art filled, take heed to thyself." (Deut. vi. 11, 12.) For perilous, as on a precipice's brink, is the post of affluence. "Take heed," saith he, "to thyself." When the Israelites were afflicted, they became all the more increased in number : but when He left them to themselves, then they all went to ruin. And why speak of examples from the ancients ? In our own times, let us see, if you please, is it not the case, that when the most are in good case, they become puffed up, hostile to everybody, passionate, while the power is with them : but if it be taken away, they are gentle, lowly (and as) human beings, are brought to a consciousness of their own natural condition. Therefore the Scripture saith, "Pride hath holden them unto the end : their iniquity shall go forth as from fatness." (Ps. lxxiii. 6. LXX.)

Now these things I have spoken, that we should not make enjoyment every way our object. How then does Paul say, "Rejoice alway?" He does not say simply, "Rejoice," but he adds, "in the Lord." (Phil. iv. 4.) This is the greatest joy, such as the Apostles rejoiced withal ; the joy of which prisons, and scourges, and persecutions, and evil report, and all painful things, are the source, and the root, and the occasion ; whence also it comes to a happy issue. But that of the world, on the contrary, begins with sweets and ends in bitters. Neither do I forbid to rejoice in the Lord, nay, I earnestly exhort to this. The Apostles were scourged, and they rejoiced : were bound, and they gave thanks : were stoned, and they preached. This is the joy I also would have : from nothing bodily has it its origin, but from spiritual things. It is not possible for him who joys after the fashion of the world, to rejoice also after a godly sort : for every one who joys after the world's fashion, has his joy in riches, in luxury, in honor, in power, in arrogance : but he who rejoices after the mind of God, has his joy in dishonor for God's sake, in poverty, in want, in fasting, in humbleness of mind. Seest thou, how opposite are the grounds (of joy) ? To go without joy here, is to be without grief also : and to be without grief here, is to go without pleasure too. And in truth these are the things which produce real joy, since the others have the name only of joy, but they altogether consist of pain. What misery the arrogant man endures ! How is he cut short (διακόπτεται) in the midst of his arrogance, bespeaking for

---

[1] διακρούεσθε τὰ λεγόμενα. Edd. διαμωκᾶσθε, " make a mock at."—Below all the Mss. agree in οἷος ἦν ὁ Κάϊν πρὸ τούτου. Either the text is corrupt, or something is needed for explanation.

himself numberless insults, much hatred, great enmity, exceeding spite, and many an evil eye! Whether it be that he is insulted by greater men, he grieves: or that he cannot make his stand against everybody, he is mortified. Whereas the humble man lives in much enjoyment: expecting honor from none, if he receive honor, he is pleased, but if not, he is not grieved. He takes it contentedly that he is honored; but[1] above all, none dishonors him. Now not to seek honor, and yet to be honored—great must be the enjoyment of this. But in the other, it is just the reverse: he seeks honor, and is not honored. And the pleasure that the honor gives is not the same to him who seeks it, as it is to him who seeks it not. The one, however much he receives, thinks he has received nothing: the other, though you give him ever so little, takes it as though he had received all. Then again, he who lives in affluence and luxury has numberless affairs of business, and let his revenues flow in to him ever so easily, and, as it were, from full fountains, yet he fears the evils arising from luxurious living, and the uncertainty of the future: but the other is always in a state of security and enjoyment, having accustomed himself to scantiness of diet. For he does not so bemoan himself at not partaking of a sumptuous board, as he luxuriates in not fearing the uncertainty of the future. But the evils arising from luxurious living, how many and great they are, none can be ignorant: it is necessary, however, to mention them now. Twofold the war, in the body, and in the soul: twofold the storm: twofold the diseases; not only in this respect, but because they are both incurable, and bring with them great calamities. Not so, frugality: but here is twofold health, twofold the benefits. "Sleep of health," we read, "is in moderate eating." (Ecclus. xxxi. 20.) For everywhere, that which keeps measure is pleasant, that which is beyond measure, ceases to please. For say now: on a little spark put a great pile of fagots, and you will no longer see the fire shining, but much disagreeable smoke. On a very strong and large man lay a burden which exceeds his strength, and you will see him with his burden lying prostrate on the ground. Embark too large a freight in your vessel, and you have ensured a grievous shipwreck. Just

so it is here. For just as in overladen ships, great is the tumult of the sailors, the pilot, the man at the prow, and the passengers, while they cast into the sea the things above deck, and things below; so here too, with their vomitings upwards, and their purgings downwards, they mar their constitutions, and destroy themselves. And what is the most shameful of all, the mouth is made to do the office of the nether parts, and that becomes the more shameful member. But if to the mouth the disgrace be such, think what must it be in the soul! For indeed there it is all mist, all storm, all darkness, great the uproar of the thoughts, at being so thronged and crushed, the soul itself crying out at the abuse done to it: all[2] (the parts and faculties) complaining of one another, beseeching, entreating, that the filth may be discharged somewhere. And after it is flung out, still the turmoil is not at an end; but then comes fever and diseases. "And how comes it," say you, "that one may see these luxurious livers, in goodly plight, riding on horseback? What idle talk is this," say you, "to tell us of diseases? It is I that am diseased, I that am racked, I that am disgusting, while I have nothing to eat." Ah me! for one may well lament at such words. But the sufferers with the gout, the men that are carried on litters, the men that are swathed with bandages, from what class of people, I ask you, shall we see these? And indeed, were it not that they would deem it an insult, and think my words opprobrious, I would before now have addressed them even by name. "But there are some of them, who are in good health as well." Because they give themselves not merely to luxurious living, but also to labors. Else show me a man, who does nothing whatever but fatten himself, free from pain as he lies there, without an anxious thought. For though a host of physicians without number came together, they would not be able to rescue him from his diseases. It is not in the nature of things. For I will hold you a medical discourse. Of the matters sent down into the belly, not all becomes nourishment; since even in the food itself, not all is nutritive, but part of it in the process of digestion passes into stool, part is turned into nourishment. If then in the process of digestion the operation is perfect, this is the result, and each finds its proper place; the wholesome and

---

[1] μάλιστα δὲ οὐδεὶς αὐτὸν ἀτιμάζει. Savile justly retains this sentence from the old text. Montf. rejects it, as supsrfluous, and disturbing the sense. Downe ap. Sav. proposes ὅτι οὐκ ἠτιμάσθη: "non ambit honorem, sed bene secum actum putat si nulla affectus sit ignominia." But in the old text there is no ἀλλὰ before ἀγαπᾷ: and the meaning is not, "he thinks himself well off," etc., nor as Ben., "he rejoices that," etc., but, "he is content not to be honored; knowing this at any rate, that nobody can dishonor him."

[2] E. Edd. "Thence also the gormandizers (γαστριζόμενοι) themselves complain of one another, are in ill humor, haste to be rid of the filth within. Still, even after it is cast out," etc. And below:—"fever and diseases. 'Yes,' say you, 'they are sick and are disgusting; it is waste of words to tell us all this, and make a catalogue of diseases: for it is I that am diseased, etc, .. while these luxurious livers one may see in good plight, sleek, merry, riding on horseback.'"

useful part betakes itself to its appropriate place, while that which is superfluous and useless, withdraws itself, and passes off. But if it be in too great quantity, then even the nutritive part of it becomes hurtful. And, to speak by way of example, in order that my meaning may be clearer to you : in wheat, part is fine flour, part meal, part bran : now if the mill be able to grind (what is put in), it separates all these : but if you put in too much, all becomes mixed up together. Wine again, if it go through its proper process of formation, and under due influence of the seasons, then, whereas at first all is mixed together, anon part settles into lees, part rises into scum, part remains for enjoyment to those that use it, and this is the good part, and will not readily undergo any change. But what they call "nourishment," is neither wine, nor lees, while all are mixed up together. —The same may be seen in the river,¹ when its waters make a whirling flood. As at such time we see the fishes floating at top, dead, their eyes first blinded by the muddy slime : so is it with us. For when gormandizing, like

a flood of rain, has drenched the inward parts, it puts all in a whirl, and makes that the faculties (λογισμοί), healthy till then and living in a pure element, drift lifeless on the surface. Since then by all these examples we have shown how great the mischief is, let us cease to count these men happy for that, for which we ought to think them wretched, and to bemoan ourselves for that, for which we ought to count ourselves happy, and let us welcome sufficiency with a contented mind. Or do you not hear even what physicians tell you, that "want is the mother of health ?" But what I say is, that want is mother, not of bodily health, but also of that of the soul. These things Paul also, that physician indeed, cries aloud ; when he says, "Having food and raiment, let us therewith be content." (1 Tim. vi. 8.) Let us therefore do as he bids us, that so, being in sound health, we may perform the work that we ought to do, in Christ Jesus our Lord, with Whom to the Father and the Holy Ghost together be glory, dominion, honor, now and ever, world without end. Amen.

HOMILY XVII.

ACTS VII. 35.

"This Moses whom they refused, saying, Who made thee a ruler and a judge over us? the same did God send to be a ruler and a deliverer by the hand of the Angel which appeared to him in the bush."

THIS is very suitable to the matter in hand. "This Moses," he says. "This," the man who had been in danger of losing his life; the man who had been set at naught by them ; "this" the man whom they had declined ; "this" same, God having raised up, sent unto them. "Whom they refused, saying, Who made thee a ruler?" just as they themselves (the hearers) said, "We have no king, but Cæsar." (John xix. 15.) He here shows also, that what was then done, was done by Christ. "The same did God send by the hand of the Angel," who said unto him, "I am the God of Abraham." "This" same Moses, he says,—and observe how he points to his renown—"this" same Moses, he says, "brought them out, after that he had showed wonders and signs in the land of Egypt, and

in the Red sea, and in the wilderness forty years. This is that Moses, which said unto the children of Israel, A prophet shall the Lord your God raise up unto you of your brethren, like unto me" (v. 36, 37): set at naught like me. Him, likewise, Herod wished to kill, and in Egypt He found preservation ; just as it was with the former, even when He was a babe, He was aimed at for destruction. "This is he, that was in the Church in the wilderness with the Angel which spake to him in the mount Sina, and with our fathers : who received the lively oracles to give unto us." (v. 38.) Again no mention of temple, none of sacrifice. "With the Angel," it says, "he received the lively oracles to give unto the fathers." It shows, that he not only wrought miracles, but also gave a law, as Christ did. Just as Christ first works miracles, and then legislates : so did Moses. But they did not hear him, keeping their disobedience, even after the miracles : "To whom," he says, "our fathers would not obey :" (v. 39) after the wonders done in those forty years. And not only so, but just the contrary : "but thrust him from them, and in their hearts turned back again into Egypt. Saying unto Aaron, Make us gods to go before us; for as for this Moses, which brought us out of the land of Egypt, we wot not what is become of him. And they made a calf in those days, and offered sacrifice unto the idol, and rejoiced in the works of their own hands. Then God turned, and gave them up to worship the host of heaven; as it is written in the book of the Prophets, O ye house of Israel, have ye offered to me slain beasts and sacrifices by the space of forty years in the wilderness? Yea, ye took up the tabernacle of Moloch, and the star of your god Remphan, figures which ye made to worship them: and I will carry you away beyond Babylon." (v. 40, 43.) The expression, " gave them up," means, He suffered. "Our fathers had the tabernacle of witness in the wilderness, as he had appointed, speaking unto Moses, that he should make it according to the fashion he had seen." (v. 44.) Even when there was a Tabernacle, yet there were no sacrifices. "Did ye offer unto Me slain beasts and sacrifices?" (Amos v. 25.) There was "the tabernacle of witness," and yet it profited them nothing, but they were consumed. But neither before, nor afterwards, did the miracles profit them aught. "Which also, our fathers that came after brought in." Seest thou, how the holy place is there wherever God may be? For to this end also he says, "in the wilderness," to compare place with place. Then the benefit (conferred upon them): And our fathers that came after brought it in with Jesus into the possession of the Gentiles, whom God drave out before the face of our fathers, unto the days of David; who found favor before God, and desired to find a tabernacle for the God of Jacob. (v. 45, 46.) David "desired to find favor:" and he builded not, he, the wonderful, the great; but the castaway, Solomon. " But Solomon," it says, "built Him an house. Howbeit the Most High dwelleth not in (places) made with hands. (v. 47-50.) This was shown indeed already by what had been before said: but it is shown also by the voice of a prophet; "What house will ye build for Me? saith the Lord God. As saith the prophet, Heaven is my throne, and earth is my footstool: what house will ye build for me? saith the Lord: or what is the place of my rest? Hath not my hand made all these things?" (Is. lxvi. 1, 2.)

Marvel not, he says, if they on whom Christ confers His benefits refuse His kingdom, seeing in the case of Moses it was just the same. (Recapitulation). " He brought them out;" and rescued them not in a general way, but

also while they were in the wilderness. " Wonders and signs," etc. (v. 35-50.) Do you mark that they themselves (Stephen's hearers) are concerned in those old miracles also? "This is that Moses:" (v. 37) he, that conversed with God; he, that had been saved out of situations so strange and wonderful; he, that wrought so great works, and had so great power. ["Which said unto the children of Israel, A prophet," etc.] He shows, that the prophecy must by all means be fulfilled, and that Moses is not opposed to Him. [1] "This is he that was in the Church in the wilderness, and, that said unto the children of Israel." (v. 38.) Do you mark that thence comes the root, and that "salvation is from the Jews?" (John iv. 22.) "With the Angel," it says, "which spake unto him." (Rom. xi. 16.) Lo, again he affirms that it was He (Christ) that gave the Law, seeing Moses was with "Him" in the Church in the wilderness.* And here he puts them in mind of a great marvel, of the things done in the Mount : "Who received living oracles to give unto us." On all occasions Moses is wonderful, and (so) when need was to legislate. What means the expression, "Living oracles" (λόγια)? Those, whereof the end was shown by words (διὰ λόγων) : in other words, he means the prophecies.† Then follows the charge, in the first instance, against the patriarchs [after], the "signs and wonders," after the receiving of the "lively oracles : To whom," he says, " our fathers would not obey." (v. 39.) But concerning those, Ezekiel says that they are not "living;" as when he says, " And I gave you statutes that are not good." (Ezek. xx. 25.) It is with reference to those that he says, "Living. But thrust him from them, and in their hearts turned back to Egypt"— the place where they groaned, where they

---

[1] Here the innovator, not perceiving that the renewed exposition began above, inserts the formula Ἀλλ᾽ ἴδωμεν ἄνωθεν τὰ εἰρημένα, and then has: " This, it says, is Moses, which said, A Prophet, etc. To this, I suppose, Christ refers, when He says, ' Salvation is of the Jews,' hinting at Himself. This is he that was in the wilderness, with the Angel that spake unto him. Lo, again he shows, that it was He," etc. So Edd.

* The meaning of v. 38 is that Moses became (γενόμενος) a mediator between God (represented by the Angel) and the people. Cf. Gal. iii. 19 where the law is said to have been "ordained through angels, by the hand of a mediator" (Moses). No mention is made of angels as revealers of the law in Exodus xix. the first mention of angels in connection with the giving of the law being in a highly poetic passage in Moses' benediction, Deut. xxxiii. 2. (Even here the Heb. text is uncertain. Cf. the lxx. *in loco*). The function of angels in the giving of the law has a prominent place in later Jewish theology as opposed to the action of mere human ministers. The New Testament notices on the subject reflect this later phase of thought (Cf. Acts vii. 53 ; Heb. ii. 2). See Lightfoot on Gal. ii. 19.—G. B. S.

† By λόγια ζῶντα are meant living oracles in the sense of operative, effectual, as Jesus affirmed his words to be ' spirit and life " (John vi. 63). They contain vital truth. The law was indeed "weak" (Rom. viii. 3) but it was so "through the flesh," i. e. human sinfulness. It was not inherently weak but was so relatively to the great power of sin in man which needed to be overcome.—G. B. S.

cried, whence they called upon God. "And said unto Aaron, Make us gods which shall go before us." (v. 40.) O the folly! "Make," say they; "that they may go before us." Whither? "Into Egypt."* See how hard they were to tear away from the customs of Egypt! What sayest thou? What, not wait for him that brought thee out, but flee the benefit, and deny the Benefactor? And mark how insulting they are: "For as for this Moses," they say:—"which brought us out of the land of Egypt" nowhere the name of God: instead of that, they ascribed all to Moses. Where[1] they ought to give thanks (to God), they bring Moses forward: where it was, to do as the Law bade them, they no longer make account of Moses. "We know not what is become of him." And yet he told them that he was going up to receive the Law: and they had not patience to wait forty days. "Make us gods"—they[2] did not say, "a God."—And yet one may well wonder at this, that they do not even know.—"And they made a calf in those days, and offered sacrifices unto the idol, and rejoiced in the works of their own hands" (v. 41): for which they ought to have hid their faces. What wonder that ye know not Christ, seeing ye knew not Moses, and God Who was manifested by such wonders? But they not only knew Him not: they also insulted in another way, by their idol making. "Then God turned, and gave them up to worship the host of heaven." (v. 42.) Hence these same "customs" date their origin, hence the sacrifices: they were themselves the first that made sacrifices to their idols! For that is why it is marked,[3] "They

made a calf in Horeb, and offered sacrifices to the idol:" seeing that, before this the name of sacrifice is nowhere mentioned, but only lively ordinances, and "lively oracles. And rejoiced"—that is the reason for the feasts. (Exod. xxxii. 5, 6.) "As it is written in the Book of the Prophets"—and observe, he does not cite the text without a purpose, but shows by it that there is no need of sacrifices; saying: "Did ye offer slain beasts and sacrifice to Me?"—He lays an emphasis on this word (to Me?). "Ye cannot say that it was from sacrificing to Me, that ye proceeded to sacrifice to them:—"by the space of forty years:" and this too, "in the wilderness," where He had most signally shown Himself their Protector. "Yea, ye took up the tabernacle of Moloch, and the star of your god Remphan: images which ye made to worship them.† The cause of sacrifices! "And I will carry you away beyond Babylon." (v. 43.) Even the captivity, an impeachment of their wickedness! "But a Tabernacle," say you, "there was (the Tabernacle) 'of Witness.'" (v. 44.) (Yes,) this is why it was: that they should

---

* It is not probable that this passage (v. 39, 40) means that the people proposed to return to Egypt (as Chrys.). In the O. T. the constant representation is that the golden calf (or bull) was worshipped as the image of the divinity who had *led them out of Egypt* (Ex. xxxii. 4; 1 Kings xii. 28). It seems clearly implied in Ezek. xx. 7, 8, 24, that the Israelites while in Egypt had been much addicted to the idolatry of the country. The meaning here is that, being discouraged and disappointed on account of Moses' continued absence in the mount, they were ready to transfer their allegiance from Jehovah to some of the divinities to whose worship they had previously been accustomed. The worship of cattle was especially common, as of Apis at Memphis and Mnevis at Heliopolis.—G. B. S.

[1] Ἔνθα μὲν εὐχαριστεῖν ἔδει, A. B. C. D. F., but N. and Cat. ἀχαριστεῖν.—E. Καὶ ἔνθα μὲν αὐτοὺς ἀχαριστεῖν ἦν. Edd. εὐχ.

[2] This clause, omitted by A. B. C., is preserved by N. and the Catena. The calf was one, yet they called it Gods: on which St. Chrys. remarks elsewhere, that they added polytheism to idolatry.—The next sentence may perhaps be completed thus: "that they did not even know that there is One God."—Edd. from E. F. D. "So frantic are they, that they know not what they say."

[3] διὰ γὰρ τοῦτο ἐπισημαίνεται. The meaning is: Stephen was accused of speaking against "the customs,"—sacrifices, temple, feasts, etc. Therefore he significantly points to that critical conjuncture from which these "customs" date their introduction: namely, the Provocation at Horeb. Prior to that, he tells of "living oracles," life-giving precepts: after it, and as its consequence, sacrifices, etc., those statutes which were not good, and ordinances by which a man shall not live, as God says by Ezekiel. Not a word of sacrifice till then: and the first mention is, of the sacrifices offered to the calf. In like manner, "they rejoiced," the people ate and drank, and rose up to play:" and in consequence of this, the feasts were prescribed: καὶ εὐφραίνοντο, φησιν· διὰ τοῦτο καὶ ἑορταί.—'Επισημαίνεται

might be rendered, "he marks," "puts a mark upon it" (so the innovator, who substitutes, τοῦτο καὶ Δαυὶδ ἐπισημαινόμενος λέγει): we take it passively, "there is a mark set over it—it is emphatically denoted." In the active, the verb taken intransitively means "to betoken or announce itself," "make its first appearance."—In the Treatise *adv. Judæos*, iv. §. 6. tom. i. 624, C. St. Chrysostom gives this account of the legal sacrifices: "To what purpose unto Me is the multitude of your sacrifices? etc. (Isaiah i., 11, ff.) Do ye hear how it is most plainly declared, that God did not from the first require these at your hands? Had He required them, He would have obliged those famous saints who were before the Law to observe this practice. 'Then wherefore has He permitted it now?' In condescension to your infirmity. As a physician in his treatment of a delirious patient, etc.: thus did God likewise. For seeing them so frantic in their lust for sacrifices, that they were ready, unless they got them, to desert to idols; nay not only ready, but that they had already deserted, thereupon He permitted sacrifices. And that this is the reason, is clear from the order of events. After the feast which they made to the demons, then it was that He permitted sacrifices: all but saying: 'Ye are mad, and will needs sacrifice: well then, at any rate sacrifice to Me.'"—(What follows may serve to illustrate the brief remark a little further on, Καὶ ἡ αἰχμαλωσία κατηγορία τῆς κακίας.) "But even this, He did not permit to continue to the end, but by a most wise method, withdrew them from it... For He did not permit it to be done in any place of the whole world, but in Jerusalem only. Anon, when for a short time they had sacrificed, he destroyed the city. Had He openly said, Desist, they, such was their insane passion for sacrificing, would not readily have complied. But now perforce, the place being taken away, He secretly withdrew them from their frenzy." So here: "Even the captivity impeaches the wickedness (which was the cause of the permission of sacrifice.")

† Our passage here follows the lxx. which speaks of Moloch and Remphan. The terms in the original (vid. R. V.: Amos v. 25–27) are "Siccuth" and "Chiun." It is a disputed point whether these are in the prophecy names of divinities or whether they mean respectively "tabernacle" and "shrine" (or image). The difficulty lies in the ambiguity of the Hebrew text. The name Moloch being akin to the Hebrew word for king (מלך), confusion might easily arise. The N. T. text varies from the lxx. only in adding the word προσκυνεῖν (43) to lay emphasis upon the charge of idolatry, and in replacing Damascus by Babylon (43), an interpretation from the standpoint of subsequent history. The statement of our text that the Israelites fell into the worship of these divinities *in the wilderness* rests upon extra-Pentateuchal tradition, derived, perhaps, from such prohibitions of Moloch-worship and similar idolatries as are found in Lev. xviii. 21, and Deut. xviii. 10. The charge in the prophecy of Amos is a general one referring to the frequent lapses of the people into image-worship down to his own time.—G. B. S.

have God for Witness: this was all. "According to the fashion," it says, "that was shown thee on the mount:" so[1] that on the mount was the Original. And this Tabernacle, moreover, "in the wilderness," was carried about, and not locally fixed. And he calls it, "Tabernacle of witness:" i. e. (for witness) of the miracles, of the statutes.* This is the reason why both it and those (the fathers) had no Temple. "As He had appointed, that spake unto Moses, that he should make it according to the fashion that he had seen." Again, it was none other than He (Christ) that gave the fashion itself. "Until the days of David" (v. 45): and there was no temple! And yet the Gentiles also had been driven out: for that is why he mentions this: "Whom God drave out," he says, "before the face of our fathers. Whom He drave out," he says: and even then, no Temple! And so many wonders, and no mention of a Temple! So that, although first there is a Tabernacle, yet nowhere a Temple. "Until the days of David," he says: even David, and no Temple! "And he sought to find favor before God" (v. 46): and built not:—so far was the Temple from being a great matter! "But Solomon built Him an house." (v. 47.) They thought Solomon was great: but that he was not better than his father, nay not even equal to him, is manifest. "Howbeit the Most High dwelleth not in temples made with hands; as saith the prophet, Heaven is My throne, and earth is My footstool." (v. 48, 49.) Nay, not even these are worthy of God, forasmuch as they are made, seeing they are creatures, the works of His hand. See how he leads them on by little and little (showing) that not even these are to be mentioned. And again the prophecy says openly, "What house will ye build Me?" etc. (v. 50.)

What is the reason that at this point he speaks in the tone of invective (καταφορικῶς)? Great was his boldness of speech, when at the point to die: for in fact I think he knew that this was the case. "Ye stiffnecked," he says, "and uncircumcised in heart and ears." This also is from the prophets: nothing is of himself. "Ye do always resist the Holy Ghost: as your fathers did, so do ye." (v.

51.) When it was not His will that sacrifices should be, ye sacrifice: when it is His will, then again ye do not sacrifice: when He would not give you commandments, ye drew them to you: when ye got them, ye neglected them. Again, when the Temple stood, ye worshipped idols: when it is His will to be worshipped without a Temple, ye do the opposite. Observe, he says not, "Ye resist God," but, "the Spirit:" so far was he from knowing any difference between Them. And, what is greater: "As your fathers did," he says, "so do ye." Thus also did Christ (reproach them), forasmuch as they were always boasting much of their fathers. "Which of the prophets have not your fathers persecuted? and they have slain them which showed before of the coming of the Just One:" he still says, "the Just One," wishing to check them: "of Whom ye have been now the betrayers and murderers" —two charges he lays against them[2]— "who have received the Law by the disposition of Angels, and have not kept it." (v. 52.) How, "By the disposition of Angels?" Some say (The Law), disposed by Angels; or, put into his hand by the Angel Who appeared to him in the bush; for was He man? No wonder that He[3] who wrought those works, should also have wrought these.† "Ye slew them who preached of Him." much more Himself. He shows them disobedient both to God, and to Angels, and the Prophets, and the Spirit, and to all: as also Scripture saith elsewhere: "Lord, they have slain Thy Prophets, and thrown down Thine altars." (1 Kings xix. 10.) They, then, stand up for the Law, and say, "He blasphemeth against Moses:" he shows, therefore, that it is they who blaspheme, and that (their blasphemy is not only against Moses, but) against God; shows that "they" from the very beginning have been doing this: that "they" have themselves destroyed their "customs," that there is no need of these: that while accusing him, and saying that he opposed Moses, they themselves were opposing the Spirit: and not merely opposing, but with murder added to it:

---

[2] E. F. D. Edd. add, "that they knew (Him) not, and that they murdered (Him):" but the meaning is, that they betrayed, and that they murdered: or, as below, Their fathers slew the Prophets, and they, Him Whom they preached.

[3] τὸν ἐκεῖνα ποιήσαντα, A. B. C. N. Cat. i. e. that Christ, Who, as the Angel, did those works, etc. The modern text τοὺς ἐκ. ποιήσαντας: that those who did those wickednesses, etc.: and so Œc. seems to have taken it: "If ye killed them who preached Him to come, no wonder that ye kill Me," etc.—Below, for Οἱ τοίνυν ἀντιποιοῦνται τοῦ νόμου, καὶ ἔλεγον, A. B. N. (N. corrected οὗτοι νῦν) have Οὐ τοίνυν κ. τ. λ. and A. λέγοντες: "Therefore they claim not the Law (on their side), saying," etc.

† Ἀγγέλων (53) cannot refer (as Chrys.) to the Jehovah-angel of the bush. It refers to angels as the mediators in the giving of the law, an idea which appears in the lxx., the N. T. elsewhere (Gal. iii. 19; Heb. ii. 2) and is prominent in later Jewish theology (Cf. Josephus, Ant. XV. v. 3) Vid. note *, p. 107.— G. B. S.

---

[1] ὥστε ἐν τῷ ὄρει ἡ ὑπογραφὴ γέγονε. In the following sentences, there are numerous variations in Edd. from the old text, but they do not materially affect the sense, and certainly do not improve it.

* The expression here used—ἡ σκηνὴ τοῦ μαρτυρίου is the constant but inexact lxx. translation of אֹהֶל מוֹעֵד "tent of meeting"—i. e. the tent where God met the people. From a misunderstanding of the etymology of מוֹעֵד (it being taken from עוּד to witness, instead of from יָעַד to assemble) it was translated by μαρτυρίου—a rendering which has occasioned frequent misunderstanding. Μαρτυρίου is rightly used in the lxx. to render עֵדֻת (from עוּד) in Exod. xxv. 22; Num. ix. 15.— G. B. S.

and that they had their enmity all along from the very beginning. Seest thou, that he shows them to be acting in opposition both to Moses and to all others, and not keeping the Law? And yet Moses had said, "A Prophet shall the Lord raise up unto you : and the rest also told of this (Christ) that He would come : and the prophet again said, "What house will ye build Me?" and again, "Did ye offer to Me slain beasts and sacrifices" those "forty years?" (Deut. xviii. 18.)

Such is the boldness of speech of a man bearing the Cross. Let us then also imitate this : though it be not a time of war, yet it is always the time for boldness of speech. For, "I spake," says one, "in Thy testimonies before kings, and was not ashamed." (Ps. cxix. 46.) If we chance to be among heathens, let us thus stop their mouths, without wrath, without harshness. (Comp. Hom. in 1 Cor. iv. § 6; xxxiii. § 4, 5; Col. xi. § 2.) For if we do it with wrath, it no longer seems to be the boldness (of one who is confident of his cause,) but passion : but if with gentleness, this is boldness indeed. For [1] in one and the same thing success and failure cannot possibly go together. The boldness is a success : the anger is a failure. Therefore, if we are to have boldness, we must be clean from wrath, that none may impute our words to that. No matter how just your words may be, when you speak with anger, you ruin all : no matter how boldly you speak, how fairly reprove, or what not. See this man, how free from passion as he discourses to them! For he did not abuse them : he did but remind them of the words of the Prophets. For, to show you that it was not anger, at the very moment he was suffering evil at their hands, he prayed, saying, "Lay not to their charge this sin." So far was he from speaking these words in anger; no, he spake in grief and sorrow for their sakes. As indeed this is why it speaks of his appearance, that "they saw his face as it had been the face of an angel," on purpose that they might believe. Let us then be clean from wrath. The Holy Spirit dwelleth not where wrath is : cursed is the wrathful. It cannot be that aught wholesome should approach, where wrath goes forth. For as in a storm at sea, great is the tumult, loud the clamor, and then would be no time for lessons of wisdom (φιλοσοφεῖν) : so neither in wrath. If the soul is to be in a condition either to say, or to be disciplined to, aught of philosophy, it must first be in the haven. Seest thou not how, when we wish to converse on matters of serious im-

port, we look out for places free from noise, where all is stillness, all calm, that we may not be put out and discomposed? But if noise from without discomposes, much more disturbance from within. Whether one pray, to no purpose does he pray "with wrath and disputings:" (1 Tim. ii. 8) whether he speak, he will only make himself ridiculous : whether he hold his peace, so again it will be even then : whether he eat, he is hurt even then : whether he drink, or whether he drink not; whether he sit, or stand, or walk; whether he sleep : for even in their dreams such fancies haunt them. For what is there in such men that is not disagreeable? Eyes unsightly, mouth distorted, limbs agitated and swollen, tongue foul and sparing no man, mind distraught, gestures uncomely : much to disgust. Mark the eyes of demoniacs, and those of drunkards and madmen; in what do they differ from each other? Is not the whole madness? For what though it be but for the moment? The madman too is possessed for the moment : but what is worse than this? And they are not ashamed at that excuse; "I knew not (saith one) what I said." And how came it that thou didst not know this, thou the rational man, thou that hast the gift of reason, on purpose that thou mayest not act the part of the creatures without reason, just like a wild horse, hurried away by rage and passion? In truth, the very excuse is criminal. For thou oughtest to have known what thou saidst. "It was the passion," say you, "that spoke the words, not I." How should it be that? For passion has no power, except it get it from you. You might as well say, "It was my hand that inflicted the wounds, not I." What occasion, think you, most needs wrath? would you not say, war and battle? But even then, if anything is done with wrath, the whole is spoiled and undone. For of all men, those who fight had best not be enraged : of all men, those had best not be enraged, who want to hurt (τοὺς ὑβρίζοντας). And how is it possible to fight then? you will ask. With reason, with self-command (ἐπιεικείᾳ) : since fighting is, to stand in opposition. Seest thou not that even these (common) wars are regulated by definite law, and order, and times? For wrath is nothing but an irrational impulse : and an irrational creature cannot possibly perform aught rational. For instance, the man here spoke such words, and did it without passion. And Elias said, "How long will ye halt on both your knees?" (1 Kings xviii. 21) and spake it not in passion. And Phinees slew, and did it without passion. For passion suffers not a man to see, but, just as in a night-battle, it leads him, with eyes blind-

[1] Οὐ γὰρ δύναται ὁμοῦ καὶ κατὰ ταὐτὸν (κατ' αὐτὸν A. C. and N. originally) καὶ κατόρθωμα εἶναι καὶ ἐλάττωμα. Ἡ παρρησία, κατόρθωμα· ὁ θυμὸς, ἐλάττωμα.

folded and ears stopped up, where it will. Then let us rid ourselves of this demon, at its first beginning let us quell it, let us put the sign of the Cross on our breast, as it were a curb. Wrath is a shameless dog: but let it learn to hear the law. If there be in a sheep-fold a dog so savage as not to obey the command of the shepherd, nor to know his voice, all is lost and ruined. He is kept along with the sheep: but if he makes a meal on the sheep, he is useless, and is put to death. If he has learnt to obey thee, feed thy dog: he is useful when it is against the wolves, against robbers, and against the captain of the robbers that he barks, not against the sheep, not against friends. If he does not obey he ruins all: if he learns not to mind thee, he destroys all. The mildness in thee let not wrath consume, but let it guard it, and feed it up. And it will guard it, that it may feed in much security, if it destroy wicked and evil thoughts, if it chase away the devil from every side. So is gentleness preserved, when evil works are nowhere admitted: so we become worthy of respect, when we learn not to be shameless. For nothing renders a man so shameless, as an evil conscience. Why are harlots without shame? Why are virgins shamefaced? Is it not from their sin that the former, from their chastity that the latter, are such? For nothing makes a person so shameless, as sin. "And yet on the contrary," say you, "it puts to shame." Yes; him who condemns himself: but him that is past blushing, it renders even more reckless: for desperation makes daring. For "the wicked," saith the Scripture, "when he is come into the depths of evils, despiseth." (Prov. xviii. 3.) But he that is shameless, will also be reckless, and he that is reckless, will be daring. See in what way gentleness is destroyed, when evil thoughts gnaw at it. This is why there is such a dog, barking mightily: we have also sling and stone (ye know what I mean): we have also spear and enclosure and cattle-fold: let us guard our thoughts unhurt. If the dog be gentle (σαίνῃ) with the sheep, but savage against those without, and keep vigilant watch, this is the excellence of a dog: and, be he ever so famished, not to devour the sheep; be he ever so full, not to spare the wolves. Such too is anger meant to be: however provoked, not to forsake gentleness; however at quiet, to be on the alert against evil thoughts: to acknowledge the friend, and not for any beating forsake him, and for all his caressing, to fly at the intruder. The devil uses caressing full oft: let[1] the dog

know at sight that he is an intruder. So also let us caress (σαίνωμεν) Virtue, though she put us to pain, and show our aversion to Vice, though she give us pleasure. Let us not be worse than the dogs, which, even when whipped and throttled, do not desert their master: but if[2] the stranger also feed them, even so they do hurt. There are times when anger is useful; but this is when it barks against strangers. What means it, "Whosoever is angry with his brother without a cause?" (Matt. v. 22.) It means, Stand not up in thine own quarrel, neither avenge thyself: if thou see another suffering deadly wrong, stretch out thy hand to help him. This is no longer passion, when thou art clear of all feeling for thyself alone. David had gotten Saul into his power, and was not moved by passion, did not thrust the spear into him, the enemy he had in his power; but took his revenge upon the Devil. (1 Sam. xxvi. 7.) Moses, when he saw a stranger doing an injury, even slew him (Exod. ii. 22): but when one of his own people, he did not so: them that were brethren he would have reconciled; the others not so. That "most meek" (Num. xii. 3) Moses, as Scripture witnesseth of him, see how he was roused! But not so, we: on the contrary, where we ought to show meekness, no wild beast so fierce as we: but where we ought to be roused, none so dull and sluggish. (Hom. vi. de laud. Pauli, ad fin.) On no occasion do we use our faculties to the purpose they were meant for: and therefore it is that our life is spent to no purpose. For even in the case of implements; if one use them, one instead of other, all is spoilt: if one take his sword, and then, where he should use it and cut with it, uses only his hand, he does no good: again, where he should use his hand, by taking the sword in hand he spoils all. In like manner also the physician, if where he ought to cut, he cuts not, and where he ought not, he does cut, mars all. Wherefore, I beseech you, let us use the thing (τῷ πράγματι) at its proper time. The proper

---

[1] Edd. from E. Σαίνει ὁ διάβολος πολλάκις ὡς ὁ κύων, ἀλλὰ γνώτω πᾶς ὅτι. "The devil fawns full oft as the dog, but let every man know that," etc. A. B. C. N. ὡς ὁ κύων, εἰδέτω

[(ἰδέτω C.) ὅτι. We restore the true reading by omitting ὡς. "The dog" is anger: the devil σαίνει, not as the dog, but upon the dog, as the ἀλλότριος in the preceding sentence. "Let our faithful watch-dog see at once that he is an intruder." In the following sentence the image is so far incongruous, as σαίνωμεν here has a different reference: viz. "as the dog fawns upon the friend though beaten, so let us," etc.

[2] ἂν δὲ αὐτοὺς καὶ τρέφῃ ὁ ἀλλότριος καὶ οὕτω βλάπτουσιν (A. βλάψουσιν). The antithesis seems to require the sense to be, "While, if the stranger even feed them, for all that, they do him a mischief." But the words τρέφῃ and βλάπτουσιν are scarcely suitable in the sense, τροφὴν διδῷ and λυμαίνονται. Edd. have from E. alone, πῶς οὐ μᾶλλον βλάψουσιν; in the sense, "If however the stranger (not merely caresses but) also (regularly) feeds them, how shall they not do more hurt (than good)?" i. e. "If the devil be suffered to pamper our anger, that which should have been our safeguard will prove a bane to us."—Perhaps this is the sense intended in the old reading; but if so, καὶ οὕτω is unsuitable.

time for anger is never, where we move in our own quarrel : but if it is our duty to correct others, then is the time to use it, that we may by force deliver others. (*Hom. in Matt.* xvi. § 7.) So shall we both be like unto God, always keeping a spirit free from wrath, and

shall attain unto the good things that are to come, through the grace and loving-kindness of our Lord Jesus Christ, with whom, to the Father and the Holy Ghost together, be glory, dominion, and honor, now and evermore, world without end. Amen.

HOMILY XVIII.

ACTS VII. 54.

"When they heard these things, they were cut to "the heart, and they gnashed on him with their teeth.".

SEE,[1] once more, the wrong-doers in trouble. Just as the Jews are perplexed, saying, "What are we to do with these men?" so these also are "cut to the heart." (ch. iv. 16.) And yet it was he that had good right to be incensed, who, having done no wrong, was treated like a criminal, and was spitefully calumniated. But the calumniators had the worst of it in the end. So true is that saying, which I am ever repeating, "Ill to do, is ill to fare." And yet he (in his charges against them) resorted to no calumny, but proved (what he said). So sure are we, when we are shamefully borne down in a matter wherein we have a clear conscience, to be none the worse for it.—"If[2] they desired," say you, "to kill him, how was it that they did not take occasion, out of what he said, that they might kill him?" They would fain have a fair-seeming plea to put upon their outrage. "Well then, was not the insulting them a fair plea?" It was not his doing, if they were insulted : it was the Prophet's accusation of them. And besides, they did not wish it to look as if they killed him because of what he had said against them —just as they acted in the case of Christ ; no,

but for impiety: now[3] this word of his was the expression of piety. Wherefore, as they attempted, besides killing him, to hurt his reputation also, "they were cut to the heart." For they were afraid lest he should on the contrary become an object of even greater reverence. Therefore, just what they did in Christ's case, the same they do here also. For as He said, "Ye shall see the Son of Man sitting on the right hand of God" (Matt. xxvi. 64), and they, calling it blasphemy, "ran upon Him ;" just so was it here. There, they "rent their garments;" here, they "stopped their ears. But he, being full of the Holy Ghost, looked up steadfastly into heaven, and saw the glory of God, and Jesus standing on the right hand of God, and said, Behold I see the heavens opened, and the Son of Man standing on the right hand of God. Then they cried out with a loud voice, and stopped their ears, and ran upon him with one accord, and cast him out of the city, and stoned him." (v. 55–58.) And yet, if he lied, they ought to have thought him beside himself, and to have let him go.—But he wished to bring them over, "and said, Behold," etc., for, since he had spoken of Christ's death, and had said nothing of His resurrection, he would fain add this doctrine also. "Standing at the right hand of God." And in this manner He appeared to him :[4] that, were it but so, the Jews

---

[1] In our Mss. the Homily opens abruptly with the question, Πῶς οὐκ ἔλαβον ἐκ τῶν εἰρημένων ἀφορμὴν εἰς τὸ [μὴ Cat.] ἀνελεῖν αὐτόν ; which is left unanswered, till some way further on. See note [2].—Montf. notes, "Unus, εἰς τὸ μὴ ἀνελεῖν." But this reading does not appear in any of our Mss. though the Catena has it. Edd. from E, have; "How it was that they did not take occasion from what he had said to kill him, but are still mad, and seek an accusation, one may well wonder. So ever in trouble are the wrong-doers. Just then as the chief priests, in their perplexity, said," etc. F. D. adopting part of this addition, "but are still mad, and seek an accusation. See, once more," etc.

[2] οὐδὲν πάσχομεν. Καὶ ἐβούλοντο, φησὶν (om. D. F.) ἀνελεῖν αὐτόν. (as if these words were part of the sacred text. Then) Πρόφασιν ('Αλλὰ πρόφ. D. F.) ἤθελον εὔλογον κ. τ. λ. A. B. C. D. F. The modern text substitutes, Ἐβούλοντο μὲν οὖν ἀνελεῖν· ἀλλ' οὐ ποιοῦσι τοῦτο, αἰτίαν θέλοντες εὔλογον κ. τ. λ.—Œcumenius, however, begins his comment thus: Εἰ ἐβούλοντο ἀνελεῖν, πῶς οὐκ ἀνεῖλον εὐθέως τότε ; Ὅτι πρόφασιν εὔλογον κ. τ. λ. Hence we restore the true reading, and the proper order. Namely, for Καὶ we read Εἰ, and transpose to this place, as part of the interlocution, the question πῶς οὐκ ἔλαβον—; So, the φησίν is explained, the question is followed by its answer, and there is no abruptness.

[3] τοῦτο δὲ εὐσεβείας ἦν τὸ ῥῆμα. i. e. all that Stephen had spoken in accusation of their wickedness, especially v. 51-53, was the language of piety, of a devout man zealous for the honor of God: they could not say, "This is impious;" and they were waiting to catch at something which might enable them to cry out, "He blasphemeth:" and, disappointed of this, they were cut to the heart.—Below Ben. retains (from E. alone) μὴ πάλιν καινόν τι περὶ αὐτὸν ἄλλο γένηται, though Savile had restored the genuine reading μὴ πάλιν αἰδεσιμώτερος γένηται. They had desired to injure his reputation for sanctity, and now feared that his speech would have the opposite result.

[4] Edd. from E. οὕτω δὲ αὐτῷ λέγει φανῆναι, ὥς που διέξεισιν, ἵνα κἂν οὕτω δέξωνται τὸν λόγον. "And Stephen describes Christ as appearing to Him in this manner, as one somewhere relates at large, in order that," etc.: meaning, that he might have said "sitting at the right hand," but forbears to do this, because it was offensive to the Jews, and accordingly τέως περὶ τῆς ἀναστάσεως κινεῖ λόγον, καὶ φησιν αὐτὸν ἵστασθαι. The clause ὥς που διέξεισιν seems to have been intended by the in-

might receive Him : for since the (idea of His) sitting (at the right hand of God) was offensive to them, for the present he brings forward only what relates to His Resurrection. This is the reason also why his face was glorified. For God, being merciful, desired to make their machinations the means of recalling them unto Himself. And see, how many signs are wrought! "And cast him out of the city, and stoned him." Here again, "without the city," and even in death, Confession and Preaching. (Heb. xiii. 21.) "And the witnesses laid down their clothes at a young man's feet, whose name was Saul. And they stoned Stephen, calling[1] upon God, and saying, Lord Jesus, receive my spirit." (v. 59.) This is meant to show them that he is not perishing, and to teach them. "And he knelt down, and cried with a loud voice, Lord, lay not this sin to their charge." (v. 60.) To clear himself, and show that neither were his former words prompted by passion, he says, "Lord" "lay not this sin to their charge" : wishing also even in this way to win them over. For to show that he forgave their wrath and rage in murdering him, and that his own soul was free from all passion, was the way to make his saying to be favorably received.

"And Saul was consenting unto his death." Hereupon arises a persecution, and it becomes a great one. "And at that time there was a great persecution against the Church which was at Jerusalem. And they were all scattered abroad throughout the regions of Judea and Samaria, except the Apostles." (ch. viii. 1.) Mark how once more God permits temptations to arise ; mark, and well observe, how the events are ordered by Divine Providence. They were admired because of the signs : being scourged, they were none the worse for it : (some) were ordained in the matter of the widows[2] : the word increased : once more, God

permits a great hindrance to arise. And a persecution of no ordinary kind ["and they were all scattered," etc.]; for they feared their enemies, now become more daring : and at the same time it is shown that they were but men, these that were afraid, that fled. For, that thou mayest not say after these things that[3] by grace alone they effected (what they did), they were also persecuted, and themselves became more timorous, while their adversaries were more daring. "And were all scattered abroad," it says, "except the Apostles." But this was divinely ordered, so that they should no longer all sit there in Jerusalem. "And devout men," it says, "carried Stephen to his burial, and made great lamentation over him." (v. 2.) If they were "devout," why did they "make great lamentation over him?" They were not yet perfect. The man was gracious and amiable : this also shows that they were men—not their fear alone, but their grief and lamentation. Who would not have wept to see that mild, that lamb-like person stoned, and lying dead?* Fit eulogy to be spoken over his grave has the Evangelist recorded, in this one speech, "Lay not this sin to their charge."—"And made," he says, "great lamentation over him."—But let us look over again what has been said.

He[4] mentions the cause of his (angelic) appearance (Recapitulation, vii 54 ; viii. 2.); "But he, being full of the Holy Ghost, looked up steadfastly into heaven, and saw the glory of God, and Jesus standing on the right hand of God." And when he said, "I see the heavens opened, they stopped their ears, and ran upon him with one accord." (v. 56, 57.) And yet in what respect are these things deserving of accusation? "Upon him," the man who has wrought such miracles, the man who has prevailed over all in speech, the man who can hold such discourse ! As if they had got the very thing they wanted, they straightway give full scope to their rage. "And the witnesses," he says, "laid down their clothes

---

novator, not as part of the text, but as a gloss, "as is somewhere shown at large." But what Chrys. says is, that Christ was pleased to appear in this attitude to Stephen for the sake of the Jews, in order, etc.—Hom. vi. *in Ascens.* (Cat. in l,) he says, "Why standing, and not sitting? To show that He is in act to succor His martyr. For thus it is said also of the Father, 'Stand up, O God, and, Now will I stand up, saith the Lord, I will set him in safety.' "—Below, Διὰ τοῦτο κ. τ. λ. Comp. de Mundi Creat. Hom. ii. t. vi. 447. C. "Why did He cause the face of Stephen to shine? Because he was to be stoned as a blasphemer for saying 'Behold,' etc., therefore God, forestalling this, crowned his face with angelic beauty, to show those thankless ones, that if he were a blasphemer, he would not have been thus glorified." But E. (Edd.) ἀπὸ τούτου στοχάζομαι δεδόξ. "I conjecture that it was from this vision (Erasm. from this time: Ben. hence) that his face was glorified." In the next sentence, Edd. from E. δι ὧν ἐπεβουλεύοντο ἐκείνοι, δι αὐτῶν ἐβούλετο αὐτούς ἐκκαλέσασθαι, εἰ καὶ μηδὲν πλέον ἐγένετο. Καὶ ἐκβαλόντες κ. τ. λ. "by means of the very machinations wherewith those were assailed He desired to call (the doers) themselves to Himself, even if nothing more had been done."

[1] A. E. N. Cat. omit the τὸν Θεόν.

[2] κατέστησαν ἐπὶ τῶν χηρῶν, A. C. N. Sav. χειρῶν, Cat. χωρῶν, B. D. E. F. Morel. Ben. *versati sunt in regionibus,* Erasm. *constituti sunt per regiones,* Ben.

[3] ὅτι τῇ χάριτι μόνον κατώρθουν. Or, "that by grace they only succeeded," i. e. always, without failure.

* Chrys. seems to assume that ἄνδρες εὐλαβεῖς refers to Christian men, a view that has been taken by some modern expositors (as Ewald and DeWette). It is better to understand by the term. pious Jews who were favorably disposed to Christianity (So Meyer, Olshausen, Lechler, Lange, Gloag, Hackett). The usage of εὐλαβής in the N. T. favors this view as it is applied to devout persons who were not Christians (vid. ii. 5 ; Luke ii. 25) in every case, except in xxii. 12 when it refers to Ananias, a Christian, but is used in describing him in a legal point of view : εὐλαβὴς κατὰ τὸν νόμον. Moreover, if Christians had been meant, they would not probably have been designated by so vague a term, but, as uniformly, would have been called *disciples* or *brethren.* The burial of Stephen by devout Jews recalls the burial of Jesus by Joseph of Arimathæa and Nicodemus (John xix. 38, 39).—G. B. S.

[4] Τὴν αἰτίαν τῆς ὄψεως φησίν. B. C. Sav. marg. meaning, That his face was as the face of an angel was caused by the glory of Christ which he now beholds. The modern text omits this, having said the same thing above in the words ἀπὸ τούτου, see note 4, p. 112.

at the feet of a young man, whose name was
Saul. (v. 58.) Observe how particularly he
relates what concerns Paul, to show thee that
the Power which wrought in him was of God.
But after all these things, not only did he not
believe, but also aimed at Him with a thousand hands: for this is why it says, "And
Saul was consenting unto his death."—And
this blessed man does not simply pray, but
does it with earnestness: "having kneeled
down." Mark his divine death! So long[1]
only the Lord permitted the soul to remain in
him "And having said this, he fell asleep."
(v. 60.)—"And they were all scattered abroad
throughout the region of Judea and Samaria.
(ch. viii. 1.) And now without scruple they
had intercourse with Samaria, whereas it had
been said to them, "Go not into the way
of the Gentiles" "and into any city of the
Samaritans enter ye not." (Matt. x. 5.)
"Except the Apostles," it says: they, in this
way also, wishing to win the Jews,—but not
to leave the city,—and to be the means of in-
spiring others with boldness.

"As for Saul, he made havoc of the
Church, entering into every house, and haling men and women committed them to
prison." (v. 3.) Great was his frenzy: that
he was alone, that he even entered into houses:
for indeed he was ready to give his life for the
Law. "Haling," it says, "men and women:"
mark both the confidence, and the violence,
and the frenzy. All that fell into his hands,
he put to all manner of ill-treatment: for in
consequence of the recent murder, he was
become more daring. "Therefore they that
were scattered abroad went everywhere
preaching the word. Then Philip went down
to the city of Samaria, and preached Christ
unto them. And the people with one accord
gave heed unto those things which Philip
spake, hearing and seeing the miracles which
he did. For unclean spirits, crying with loud
voice, came out of many that were possessed
with them: and many taken with palsies, and
that were lame, were healed. And there was
great joy in that city. But there was a certain man, called Simon, which beforetime in
the same city used sorcery, and bewitched the

people of Samaria." (v. 4–9.) Observe[2]
another trial, this affair of Simon. "Giving
out," it says, "that he was himself some great
one. To whom they all gave heed, from the
least to the greatest, saying, This man is the
great power of God. And to him they had
regard, because that of long time he had bewitched them with sorceries. But when they
believed Philip preaching the things concerning the kingdom of God, and the name of
Jesus Christ, they were baptized, both men
and women. Then Simon himself believed
also: and when he was baptized, he continued
with Philip, and wondered, beholding the
miracles and signs which were done. Now
when the Apostles which were at Jerusalem
heard that Samaria had received the word of
God, they sent unto them Peter and John:
who, when they were come down, prayed for
them, that they might receive the Holy
Ghost." (v. 10–15.) And (yet) great signs
had been done: how then had they not
received the Spirit? They had received the
Spirit, namely, of remission of sins: but the
Spirit of miracles they had not received.
"For as yet He was fallen upon none of
them: only they were baptized in the name
of the Lord Jesus. Then laid they their
hands on them, and they received the Holy
Ghost." (v. 16, 17.) For, to show that this
was the case, and that it was the Spirit of
miracles they had not received, observe how,
having seen the result, Simon came and asked
for this. "And when Simon saw that through
laying on of the Apostles' hands the Holy
Ghost was given, he offered them money, saying. Give me also this power, that on whomsoever I lay hands, he may receive the Holy
Ghost." (v. 18, 19.)

"The[3] persecution," say you, "gained

[1] Ben. after Morel. from E. without notice of the true reading (A. B. C. N. Cat.), received by Savile, has: Ὅθεν θεῖος
αὐτοῦ καὶ ὁ θάνατος γέγονε. Μεχρὶ γὰρ τούτου συγκεχώρητο ταῖς
ψυχαῖς ἐν τῷ ᾅδῃ εἶναι. (The latter part is adopted also by D.
F.) "Whence also his death became divine. For until this
time it had been granted to the souls to be in Hades." This
comment is derived from St. Cyril. Al. from whom the Catena cites: "Since we are justified by faith in Him . . . .
He hath wrought a new thing for us, τὸ μηκέτι μὲν εἰς ᾅδου
τρέχειν τὰς τῶν σωμάτων ἀπαλλαττομένας ψυχὰς καθὰ καὶ πρωήν,
πέμπεσθαι δὲ μᾶλλον εἰς χεῖρας Θεοῦ ζῶντος: that our souls, on
their deliverance from our bodies, no longer as aforetime
haste into Hades, but are conveyed into the hands of the Living God. And knowing this, Saint Stephen said, "Lord Jesus
receive my spirit." Œcumen. repeats this, almost in the same
words.

[2] In the old text, v. 4–10, are given continuously, and v.
11–19; between them the brief comments which we have restored to their proper places, viz. here and after v. 15: and
after v. 19, the comment which we have placed after v. 17. In
the modern text, the first comment (omitting λέγων εἶναι κ. τ. λ.)
is placed after v. 10; in the second, the words, καὶ σημεῖα
μεγάλα ἐγένετο, are omitted; the rest is given after v. 19.
[3] The modern text E. F. D. Edd. "But although the persecution then most gained strength, nevertheless God again
delivered them, ἐπιτείχισας αὐτοῖς τὰ σημεῖα. Stephen's death,
however, did not quench their rage, nay, increased it rather,
wherefore also the teachers, etc. But observe again how
good things take their turn with them, and how they are in
joy. 'For there was great joy,' it says, 'in that city. And
yet there had also been 'great lamentation.' Thus is God
ever wont to do, and to temper things grievous with things
joyful, that He may be more held in admiration. But of a
long time had this disease been upon Simon; wherefore not
even thus is he rid of it." But in the genuine text, (A. B. C.
N. Cat. ad. v. 15–17, and 3, 4.) the subject to ἐξείλετο and
ἐπετείχισε is not Θεὸς, but διωγμὸς: and the persons delivered
are not the disciples, but the Samaritans, described as προκατε-
χόμενοι, viz. under the influence of Simon's sorceries. In the
last sentence, the meaning is entirely mistaken: for the νόσημα
is the infatuation of the Samaritans, not the wickedness of
Simon.—Ἐπετείχισε γὰρ αὐτοῖς τὰ σημεῖα can hardly be rendered
without an awkward periphrasis: ἐπιτειχ. τί τινι, a phrase frequently used by St. Chrys., means to raise up something
against a person as an ἐπιτείχισμα, (as Decelea in Attica
against the Athenians in the Peloponnesian war:) see Mr.
Field's Index to Hom. in Matt.

strength." True, but at that very time to men possessed before (by a hostile power) it brought deliverance. For it planted the miracles, like a stronghold, in the heart of the enemy's' country.—Not even the death of Stephen quenched their rage, nay, increased it rather: it scattered wide the teachers, so that the greater became the discipleship.— "And there was joy." And yet there had been "great lamentation:" true; but mark again the good—"Of a long time" was the malady, but this man brought them deliverance.—And how came he to baptize Simon also? Just as Christ chose Judas.—And "beholding the signs" which he did, forasmuch as the others did not receive the (power of working) signs, he durst not ask for it.— How was it then that they did not strike him dead, as they did Ananias and Sapphira? Because even in the old times, he that gathered sticks (on the sabbath-day) was put to death as a warning to others (Num. xv. 32) and in no other instance did any suffer the same fate. So too on the present occasion, "Peter said to him, Thy money perish, because thou hast imagined that the gift of God is to be purchased with money."—(v. 20.) Why had not these received the Holy Ghost, when baptized? Either because Philip kept this honor for the Apostles; or, because he had not this gift (to impart); or, he was one of the Seven: which is rather to be said. Whence, I take it, this Philip was one of the Seven, the second of them, next to Stephen, but he of the Eunuch one of the Apostles.[1]

But observe; those went not forth: it was Providentially ordered that these should go forth and those be lacking, because of the Holy Ghost: for they had received power to work miracles, but not also to impart the Spirit to others: this was the prerogative of the Apostles. And observe (how they sent) the chief ones: not any others, but Peter [and John[2]]. "And when Simon," it says, "saw that through laying on of the Apostles' hands the Holy Ghost was given." He would not have said, "And having seen,"[3] unless there had been some sensible manifestation.* "Then laid they their hands on them," etc. Just as Paul also did, when they spake with tongues. (ch. xix. 6.) Observe the execrable conduct of Simon. "He offered money," with what object? And yet he did not see Peter doing this for money. And it was not of ignorance that he acted thus; it was because he would tempt them, because he wished to get matter of accusation against them. And therefore also Peter says, "Thou hast no part nor lot in this matter, for thine heart is not right before God "because thou hast thought," etc. (v. 21.) Once more he brings to light what was in the thoughts, because Simon thought to escape detection. "Repent therefore of this thy wickedness, and pray God, if perhaps the thought of thine heart may be forgiven thee. For I perceive that thou art in the gall of bitterness, and in the bond of iniquity. Then answered Simon, and said, Pray ye to the Lord for me, that none of these things which ye have spoken come upon me." (v. 22-24.) Even this[4] he did only formally, as words of course, when

<hr/>

[1] So A. B. C. N. Cat. Of the Edd., Savile alone retains this clause, the rest follow the mod. text, which rejects it. And indeed it can hardly be doubted, that St. Chrys. himself would have' expunged, or altered this statement, had he revised these Homilies: for in the next Hom. he shows that the Philip of vv. 26 ff. was certainly not the Apostle, but probably one of the seven deacons. The fact seems to be, that having had no occasion until now to discuss this question, he had assumed (as others had done before him) that the Philip of the Eunuch's history was the Apostle of that name: thus in *Hom. ad Gen.* xxxv. § 2 (delivered but a few years before), he takes this for granted. Here, however, he perceives that the Philip who preached at Samaria could not be the Apostle: but at present he is still under the impression, that the person by whom the Eunuch was converted was St. Philip the Apostle, and accordingly speaks as in the text. "This Philip, I take it, was one of the Seven; he of the story of the Eunuch was one of the Apostles." Of course it was impossible on a review of the circumstances to rest in this conclusion; and in the very beginning of the next Homily he tacitly revokes the notion here advanced, and points out how the command, "Arise, and go to the south," must have been addressed to Philip in Samaria (the deacon), and not Philip the Apostle in Jerusalem. (See the note there.) The early writers frequently confound the Philip of this chapter (the deacon and evangelist, Acts xxi. 9, with the Apostle: Polycrates *ap. Eus. H. E.* iii. 30, and v. 24, (see Vales and Heinichen on the former passage.) *Const. Apol.* vi. 7. S. Clementine *Strom.* iii. p. 192. Comp. St. Augustin *Serm.* 266. § 5.—S. Isadore of Pelusium, Ep. 448, in reply to a correspondent who was not satisfied with his statement (Ep. 447), that "Philip who baptized the Eunuch and catechized Simon was not the Apostle, but one of the Seven," and requested proof from Scripture ('Επειδὴ καὶ μαρτυρίαν ζητεῖς γραφικήν . . . . Ἐπειδὴ πολλῶν ἀποδεξέων ἐρᾷς,) bids him observe, ch. viii. 1. that the Apostles remained at Jerusalem: that Philip the Apostle would have been competent to impart the gift of the Spirit: and further suggests, that Philip the deacon, fleeing from the persecution, was on his way through Samaria to Cæsarea his native place, (where we afterwards find him

xxi. 9), when these events befell, viz. the preaching, etc., at Samaria, and the conversion of the Eunuch.—In the next sentence, ἐκεῖνοι (i. e. the Apostles) οὐκ ἐξῆεσαν· ᾠκονομήθη τούτους (i. e. Philip the deacon and others) ἐξελθεῖν· καὶ ἐκείνους (the Apostles) ὑστερῆσαι: "should come after," or rather, "should be lacking, be behindhand, not be forthcoming (at the time):" but Cat. καὶ ἐκείνους ἑτέρως, "and those (the Apostles) otherwise."—The modern text, after "next to Stephen," proceeds thus: "Wherefore also, when baptizing, he did not impart the Spirit to the baptized, for neither had he authority to do so, since the gift belonged only to the Twelve. But observe; those went not forth; it was Providentially ordered that these should go forth, οἱ καὶ ὑστέρουν τῆς χάριτος διὰ τὸ μήπω λαβεῖν Πν. ῾Α., who were deficient in the grace because they had not yet received the Holy Ghost. For they received power, etc. Consequently, this was the prerogative of the Apostles."

[2] Καὶ ὅρα τοὺς κορυφαίους. οὐκ ἄλλους τινὰς ἀλλὰ Πέτρον. B. C. D. F. N. Cat. but A. adds, seemingly from a marginal gloss, καὶ 'Ιωάννην μὴν, "and John, however," E. (Edd.) ὅθεν καὶ τοὺς κορ. οὐκ ἄλλους τινὰς ἔστιν ἰδεῖν τοῦτο ποιοῦντας. " Whence also the leaders, not any others, are to be seen doing this."

[3] Οὐκ ἂν δὲ εἶπεν, A. B. D. F. οὐκ ἂν δίδοται τότε εἶπεν, C. οὐκ ἂν εἶδεν, Cat. Sav. marg. ἴδεν N. Read, οὐκ ἂν " ἰδὼν δὲ " εἶπεν. —E. οὐκ ἂν οὕτως εἶπεν.

* Chrys. appropriately remarks that the word ἰδὼν (18) implies that there were visible manifestations connected with the gifts of the Spirit here spoken of. This would seem to show that when it said (16) that the Holy Spirit had not fallen upon any of the Samaritans, that the ordinary influences of the Spirit which accompany conversion, were not referred to, but some special and miraculous endowments such as the gift of tongues, and of prophecy and perhaps of miracles were meant. —G. B. S.

[4] Καὶ τοῦτο ἀφοσιώσει (μόνον add. D. F.) ἐποίει, δεὸν κλαῦσαι καὶ πενθῆσαι. Cat. ἀφοσιωμένος, l. ἀφοσιουμένως, "as a mere formal ceremony *ominis causa*."

he ought to have wept and mourned as a penitent. "If perchance it may be forgiven thee." Not as though it would not have been pardoned, had he wept, but this is the manner of the Prophet also, to denounce absolutely, (ἀπαγορεύειν) and not to say, "Howbeit, if thou do this, thy sin shall be forgiven," but that in any wise the punishment shall take effect.

(a) "Therefore they that were scattered abroad, went everywhere, preaching the word." But[1] I would have thee admire how even in a season of calamity they neglected not the preaching. "Hearing and seeing the miracles which he did." (Recapitulation, v. 4–6.) Just as in the case of Moses by contrast (with the magicians) the miracles were evident miracles, so here also. There was magic, and so these signs were manifest. (b) "For unclean spirits came out of many that were possessed with them" (v. 7); for this was a manifest miracle :—not as the magicians did : for the other (Simon), it is likely, bound (men with spells) ;—"and many," it says, "that were palsied and lame were healed." There was no deceit here : for it needed but that they should walk and work. "And to him they all gave heed, saying, This (man) is the Power of God." (v. 10.) And that was fulfilled which was spoken by Christ, "There shall come false Christs and false Prophets in My name."—(Matt. xxiv. 24.) "And to him they had regard, because that of long time he had bewitched them with sorceries." (v. 11.) (a) And yet there ought to have been not one demoniac there, seeing that of a long time he had been bewitching them with sorceries :· but if there were many demoniacs, many palsied, these pretences were not truth. But Philip here by his word also won them over, discoursing concerning the kingdom of Christ. (v. 12.) "And Simon," it says, "being baptized, continued with Philip (v. 13) : not for faith's sake, but in order that he might become such (as he). (b) But why did they not correct him instantly? They were content with his condemning himself. For

this too belonged to their work of teaching (τῆς διδασκαλίας). But[2] when he had not power to resist, he plays the hypocrite, just as did the magicians, who said, "This is the finger of God." And indeed that he might not be driven away again, therefore he "continued with Philip," and did not part from him. "And when the Apostles which were at Jerusalem," etc. (v. 13, 14.) See how many things are brought about by God's Providence through the death of Stephen! (a) "But they," it says, "having come down, prayed for them that they might receive the Holy Ghost : for as yet He was fallen upon none of them. Then laid they their hands upon them, and they received the Holy Ghost." (v. 15–17.) Seest thou that it was not to be done in any ordinary manner, but it needed great power to give the Holy Ghost? For it is not all one, to obtain remission of sins, and to receive such a power. (b) By degrees it is, that those receive the gift. It was a twofold sign : both the giving to those, and the not giving to this man.[3] Whereas then this man ought, on the contrary, to have asked to receive the Holy Ghost, he, because he cared not for this, asks power to give It to others. And yet those received not this power to give : but this man wished to be more illustrious than Philip, he being among the disciples! (a) "He offered them money." (v. 18, 19.) What? had he seen the others doing this? had he seen Philip? Did he imagine they did not know with what mind he came to them? (b) "Thy money with thee to perdition" (v. 20) : since thou hast not used it as it ought to be used. These are not words of imprecation, but of chastisement. "To thee," he says, be it (to thee) : being snch. As if one should say, Let it perish along with thy purpose. Hast thou so mean conceptions of the gift of God, that thou hast imagined it to be altogether a thing of man? It is not this. (a) Wherefore also Peter well calls the affair a gift : "Thou hast thought that the gift of God may be purchased with money." Dost thou observe how on all occasions they are clean from money ? "For thine heart is not right in the sight of God." (v. 21.) Dost thou see how he does all of malice ? To be simple, however, was the thing needed. (b) For had it been done with simplicity,[4] he would have even wel-

---

[1] What follows, to the end of the Exposition, has by some accident fallen into strange confusion. In the Translation we have endeavored to restore the proper order. In the first place it should be observed, that the portion beginning Οἱ μὲν διαμαρτυράμενοι, p. 148. D. Ben and ending at ὅτε πρῶτον ἐπίστευσαν, p. 149. A. consisting of about 20 lines, is interchanged with the portion of about 25 lines, beginning Δεὸν οὖν τοῦτον, and ending ἐκεῖ τοῦ ἀποστόλου, p. 149. C. These being restored to their proper order, which is evident from the contents of the two portions, we have, to the end of the Recapitulation, two portions, dividing at οὐκ ἰσχυσεν ἐλεῖν τοὺς ἀποστόλους (ἐξίσατο,) p. 148. B. the former beginning with the exposition of v. 4, the second with v. 7, and both ending at v. 24. These, it may be supposed, are two several and successive expositions. But it will be seen on comparing them, that each in itself is often abrupt and ♦incomplete, and that their parts fit into each other in a way which can hardly be accidental. It may also be remarked, that the length of each is the same ; each containing about 46 lines. We have marked the order of the Mss. and Edd. by the letters a, b, prefixed to the several parts.

[2] This sentence alone seems still to be out of its place. Ἐπειδὴ δὲ ἀντιστῆναι οὐκ ἰσχυσεν κ. τ. λ. might be very fitly inserted in the passage below, ending οὐκ ἰσχ. ἐλεῖν τ. ἀπ. which is otherwise mutilated : see the note there.
[3] Between this and the following sentence the Mss. and Edd. give the exposition of v. 25.
[4] Εἰ γὰρ μετὰ ἀφελείας ἐγίνετο, καὶ κἂν F.) ἀπεδέξατο (ἀπεδέξαντο C. F.) αὐτοῦ τὴν προθυμίαν. B. C. F. The preceding sentence from (a) is καὶ μὴν ἀφελῆ ἔδει εἶναι. The connection

comed his willing mind. Seest thou that to have mean conceptions of great things is to sin doubly? Accordingly, two things he bids him: "Repent and pray, if haply the thought of thine heart may be forgiven thee." (v. 22.) Seest thou it was a wicked thought he had entertained? Therefore he says, "If haply it may be forgiven thee:" because he knew him to be incorrigible. (a) "For I perceive that thou art in the gall of bitterness, and in the bond of iniquity." (v. 23.) Words of exceeding wrath! But otherwise he did not punish him: that faith may not thereafter be of compulsion; that the matter may not seem to be carried ruthlessly; that he may introduce the subject of repentance: or also, because it suffices for correction to have convicted him, to have told him what was in his heart, to have brought him to confess himself overcome (ὅτι ἑάλω). For that he says, "Pray ye for me," is a confession that he has done wrong. Observe him,[1] what a miscreant he is; when he was convicted, then he believed: when again he was convicted, then he became humble.* "Seeing [2] his miracles," ["he was amazed," and came over.] He thought to be able to escape detection: he thought the thing was an art: but when he had not power to defeat (ἑλεῖν) the Apostles, * * *. (b) Again, he fears the multitude, and is afraid to deny it; and yet he might have said, "I did not know: I did it in simplicity: but he was struck with dismay, first by the former circumstance, that he was overcome (ὅτι ἑάλω), by the miracles and secondly by this, that his thoughts are made manifest.

being lost, this passage was not understood, and A. omits it, B. F. N. read ἀσφάλειας, and E. D. substitute, "If however he had come (προσῆλθεν) as he ought to have come, he would have been received, he would not like a pest have been driven away."

[1] Ὅρα αὐτὸν μιαρὸν ὄντα. The modern text (Edd.) alters the sense: ὅρα πῶς, καίτοι μιαρὸς ὤν, ὅμως. See how, miscreant though he is, nevertheless, etc."

* Simon believed (13) only in an intellectual sense, being impressed with wonder, rather than convinced of sin. So, now, it is fear of calamity and penalty, not repentance, which leads him to ask the apostles to pray for him.—G. B. S.

[2] Θεωρῶν αὐτοῦ τὰ σημεῖα, ἐνόμιζε δύνασθαι λανθάνειν· ἐνόμιζε τεχνην εἶναι τὸ πρᾶγμα· ἐπειδὴ δὲ οὐκ ἴσχυσεν ἰδεῖν (Sav. marg. ἑλεῖν) τοὺς ἀποστόλους, ἐξίστατο καὶ προσῆλθεν. A. B. C. This, which is the conclusion of (a), is both corrupt and defective. He is enlarging upon the μιαρία of Simon's conduct, as shown in the preceding ὅτε ἠλέγχθη . . . . ὅτε πάλιν ἠλέγχθη: comp. the following sentence. It looks as if the sentence ἐπειδὴ δὲ ἀντιστῆναι οὐκ ἴσχυσεν κ. τ. λ. must belong to this place. The reading ἑλεῖν τ. ἀπ. is probably the true one: ὅτι ἑάλω is twice said of Simon. Perhaps the passage may be restored somewhat thus: "Seeing his miracles, he was amazed, and came over." He thought to escape detection, he thought the thing was an art: but when he had not power to resist, he plays the hypocrite, as the magicians did, who said, "This is the finger of God. Having seen the Apostles," (hence the reading ἰδεῖν τ. ἀπ.) how by laying on of hands, etc. ; again he thought it was an art, he thought to purchase it with money: but when he was not able to defeat the Apostles (as it was said above, "he wished to get matter of accusation against them,") again he plays the hypocrite, and says, "Pray ye for me, etc."—Edd. from E. "Seeing signs wrought he was amazed, showing that all was a lie (on his part). It is not said, Προσῆλθεν, but, Ἐξίστατο. And why did he not do the former at once? He thought to be able, etc. ἐπειδὴ δὲ οὐκ ἴσχυσε λαθεῖν τ. ἀπ., προσῆλθεν."

Therefore he now takes himself a long way off, to Rome, thinking the Apostle would not soon come there.

"And they, when they had testified, and preached the word of the Lord, returned to Jerusalem. (v. 25.) "Testified," probably because of him (Simon), that they may not be deceived; that thenceforth they may be safe. "Having preached," it says, "the word of the Lord, they returned to Jerusalem." Why do they go thither again where was the tyranny of the bad, where were those most bent upon killing them? Just as generals do in wars, they occupy that part of the scene of war which is most distressed. "And preached the Gospel in many villages of the Samaritans." Observe them again, how they do not (προηγουμένως) of set purpose come to Samaria, but driven by stress of persecution, just as it was in the case of Christ; and how when the Apostles go thither, it is to men now believers, no longer Samaritans. "But when the Apostles," it says, "which were at Jerusalem heard this, they sent unto them Peter and John. Sent" them, again, to rid them of magic. And [3] besides, (the Lord) had given them a pattern at the time when the Samaritans believed. "And in many villages," it says, "of the Samaritans, they preached the Gospel." (John iv. 39.) Observe how actively employed even their journeys were, how they do nothing without a purpose.†

Such travels should we also make. And why do I speak of travels? Many possess villages and lands, and give themselves no concern, nor make any account of this. That baths may be provided, their revenues increased, courts and buildings erected, for this they take plenty of pains: but for the husbandry of souls, not so. When you see thorns—answer me—you cut them up, you burn, you utterly destroy them, to rid your land of the hurt thence arising. And seest thou the laborers themselves overrun with thorns, and dost not cut them up, and art thou not afraid of the Owner Who shall call

[3] ἄλλως δέ, καὶ τύπον αὐτοῖς ἐδεδώκει τοτε, ὅτε οἱ Σαμαρεῖται ἐπίστευσαν. A. B. D. F. Sav. marg. But C. "to rid them of magic, to put them in mind of the doctrine which they learned from Christ when first they believed:" which reading is adopted by E. and Edd.

† The preaching of Philip in Samaria was the first Gentile mission, for the Samaritans were a mixed people and were regarded as heathen by the Jews. An interesting concatenation of events took its rise in the bold preaching of Stephen. On the one side there proceeded from this the increased opposition of the Jewish nation and the sad calamity of the preacher's own death, but on the other there flowed from this opposition and the persecution which was consequent upon it great benefit. The Christians were indeed scattered abroad by ill-treatment, but with them went the gospel message, and the great work of heathen missions dated directly back to the martyrdom of Stephen. Christian history furnishes no more impressive illustration of the saying of Tertullian: "The blood of martyrs is seed."—G. B. S.

thee to account? For ought not each individual believer to build a Church, to get a Teacher, to coöperate (συναί· ρεσθαι) (with him), to make this above all his object, that all may be Christians? Say, how is it likely thy laborer should be a Christian, when he sees thee so regardless of his salvation? Thou canst not work miracles, and so convert (πεῖσαι) him. By the means which are in thy power, convert him; by kindness, by good offices, by gentleness, by courting (κολακεία) him, by all other means. Market-places, indeed, and baths, the most do provide; but no Churches: nay, sooner everything than this! Wherefore I beseech and implore, as a favor I entreat, yea as a law I lay it down, that there be no estate to be seen destitute of a Church.[1] Tell not me, There is one hard by; there is one in the neighboring properties; the expense is great, the income not great. If thou have anything to expend upon the poor, expend it there: better there than here. Maintain a Teacher, maintain a Deacon, and a sacerdotal body complete. As by a bride, whether a wife whom thou takest, or a daughter whom thou givest in marriage,[2] so act by the Church: give her a dowry. So shall thy estate be filled with blessing. For what shall not be there of all that is good? Is it a small thing, tell me, that thy wine-press

should be blessed;[3] a small thing, tell me, that of thy fruits God is the first to taste, and that the first fruits are there (with Him)? And then even for the peace of the laboring people this is profitable. Then as one whom they must respect, there will be the presbyter among them and this will contribute to the security of the estate. There will be constant prayers there through thee[4] (infra, note 1, p. 119) hymns and Communions through thee; the Oblation on each Lord's Day. For only consider what a praise it will be, that, whereas others have built splendid tombs, to have it said hereafter: "Such a one built this," thou hast reared Churches! Bethink thee that even until the coming of Christ thou shalt have thy reward, who hast reared up the altars of God.

Suppose an Emperor had ordered thee to build an house that he might lodge there, wouldest thou not have done everything to please him? And here now it is a palace of Christ, the Church which thou buildest. Look not at the cost, but calculate the profit. Thy people yonder cultivate thy field: cultivate thou their souls: they bring to thee thy fruits, raise thou them to heaven. He that makes the beginning is the cause of all the rest: and thou wilt be the cause that the people are brought under Christian teaching (κατηχουμένων) both there, and in the neighboring estates. Your baths do but make the peasants less hardy, your taverns give them a taste for luxury, and yet you provide these for credit's sake. Your markets and fairs, (πανηγύρεις) on the other hand, promote[5] covetousness. But think now what a thing it would be to see a presbyter, the moving picture of Abraham, gray-headed, girded up, digging and working with his own hands? What more pleasant than such a field! Their virtue thrives. No intemperance there, nay, it is driven away: no drunkenness and wantonness, nay, it is cast out: no vanity, nay, it is extinguished. All benevolent tempers shine out the brighter through the simplicity of

---

[1] In St. Chrysostom's time, little had been done for the conversion and instruction of the peasantry: hence in the latter half of the fourth century *paganus* came to be as synonymous with "heathen." Even Christian proprietors neglected their duty in this regard, while they improved their properties, and swelled their revenues by great oppression of their tenants and laborers: see *Hom. in Matt.* xliii., lxi. and at the same time often connived at the practice of the old idolatries, for the sake of the dues accruing to them from the Temples which still remained. Thus Zeno of Verona, *Serm.* xv. p. 120, complains: *In prædiis vestris fumantia undique sola fana non nostis, quæ, si vera dicenda sunt, dissimulanda subtiliter custoditis. Jus templorum ne quis vobis eripiat, quotidie litigatis.* The Christianity which was outwardly professed in the country parts was often for want of Churches and Clergy little more than nominal: and the heathen orator Libanius, in his *Oratio pro Templis,* addressed to the Emperor Theodosius, perhaps did not greatly exaggerate in the following description: "When you are told, that through this proceeding on your part (viz. the destruction of the Temples and suppression of the sacrifices) many are become Christians, you must not forget to distinguish between show and reality. They are not a whit changed from what they were before: they only say they are so. They resort indeed to the public acts of religion, and mingle themselves with the general body of Christians. But when they have made a show of praying, they invoke either none, or the Gods."—Moreover, the country clergy were often themselves ill-taught and needing instruction. Thus *Hom. in Col.* (t. xi. p. 392) delivered at Constantinople, Chrys. says: "How much instruction is needed by your brethren in the country, and by their teachers (καὶ τοὺς ἐκείνων διδασκάλους)!" Which perhaps was the result of a law passed A.D. 398, *Cod. Theodos.* xvi. tit. 2 l. 33 which enacted, that the clergy for the Churches founded on estates, or in villages, should be ordained from no other estate or village, but that to which the Church pertained: and of these a certain number, at the discretion of the bishop, according to the extent of the village, etc.—On the other hand, Chrys. "on the Statues," Or, xix. t. ii. p. 189 dwells with much delight on the virtues and patriarchal simplicity of the rural clergy in Syria, and the Christian attainments of their people.

[2] Ὡσανεὶ γυναῖκα ἀγαγὼν ἢ νυμφην, ἢ θυγατέρα, τῇ Ἐκκλ. οὕτω διάκεισο. Before θυγ., A. B. F. N. insert καὶ, E. alone δοὺς, and so Edd. Perhaps we may read ὡσανεὶ νύμφῃ, ἢ γυν. ἀγ., ἢ δοὺς θυγ.

[3] "The first-fruits of corn and of grapes, or wine were presented as oblations at the Altar, and the elements for the Holy Eucharist thence taken. See *Can. Apost.* ii. *Cod. Afr.* c. 37. *Concil. Trull.* c. 28. In a Sermon of St. Chrys. on the Ascension, this peculiar usage is mentioned, that a handful of ears of corn in the beginning of harvest was brought to the Church, words of benediction spoken over them, and so the whole field was considered as blessed. Ὅπερ γίνεται ἐπὶ τῶν πεδίων τῶν σταχυηφόρων, ὀλίγους τις στάχυας λαβὼν, καὶ μικρὸν δράγμα ποιήσας καὶ προσενεγκὼν τῷ Θεῷ, διὰ τοῦ μικροῦ πᾶσαν τὴν ἄρουραν εὐλογεῖ· οὕτω καὶ ὁ Χριστὸς κ. τ. λ. (t. ii. 450. C.)" Neander.

[4] διὰ σέ. Erasm. *propter te,* Ben. *pro te,* but this would be ὑπὲρ σοῦ, as below where this benefit is mentioned, ὑπὲρ τοῦ κεκτημένου.

[5] αἴτιαι πλεονεξίας. Edd. from E. ἰταμούς· τὰ δὲ ἐνταῦθα πᾶν τοὐναντίον. "make them forward and impudent. But here all is just the reverse.' Below, ὡς εἰκόνα βαδίζοντα τοῦ Ἀβρ. in the sense above expressed, as if it had been βαδίζουσαν. E. has εἰς for ὡς, "walking after the likeness:" and Sav. marg, εἰς οἶκον βαδ. μετὰ τὸν Ἀβρ. "walking into his house after (the manner of) Abraham."

manners. How pleasant to go forth and enter into the House of God, and to know that one built it himself: to fling himself on his back in his litter, and [1] after the bodily benefit of his pleasant airing, be present both at the evening and the morning hymns, have the priest as a guest at his table, in associating with him enjoy his benediction, see others also coming thither! This is a wall for his field, this its security. This is the field of which it is said, "The smell of a full field which the Lord hath blessed." (Gen. xxvii. 27.) If, even without this, the country is pleasant, because it is so quiet, so free from distraction of business, what will it not be when this is added to it? The country with a Church is like the Paradise of God. No clamor there, no turmoil, no enemies at variance, no heresies: there you shall see all friends, holding the same doctrines in common. The very quiet shall lead thee to higher views, and receiving thee thus prepared by philosophy, the presbyter shall give thee an excellent cure. For here, whatever we may speak, the noise of the market drives it all out: but there, what thou shalt hear, thou wilt keep fixed in thy mind. Thou wilt be quite another man in the country through him: and moreover to the people there he will be director, he will watch over them both by his presence and by his influence in forming their manners. And what, I ask, would be the cost? Make for a beginning a small house (ἐν τάξει ναοῦ) to serve as temple. Thy successor will build a porch, his successor will make other additions, and the whole shall be put to thy account. Thou givest little, and receivest the reward for the whole. At any rate, make a beginning: lay a foundation. Exhort one another, vie one with another in this matter. But now, where there is straw

and grain and such like to be stored, you make no difficulty of building: but for a place where the fruits of souls may be gathered in, we bestow not a thought; and the people are forced to go miles and miles, and to make long journeys, that they may get to Church! Think, how good it is, when with all quietness the priest presents himself in the Church, that he may draw near unto God, and say prayers for the village, day by day, and for its owner! Say, is it a small matter, that even in the Holy Oblations evermore thy name is included in the prayers, and that for the village day by day prayers are made unto God?—How greatly this profits thee for all else! It chances [2] that certain (great) persons dwell in the neighborhood, and have overseers: now to thee, being poor, one of them will not deign even to pay a visit: but the presbyter, it is likely, he will invite, and make him sit at his table. How much good results from this! The village will in the first place be free from all evil suspicion. None will charge it with murder, with theft: none will suspect anything of the kind.—They have also another comfort, if sickness befall, if death.—Then again the friendships formed there by people as they go side by side (to and from the Church) are not struck up at random and promiscuously: and the meetings there are far more pleasant than those which take place in marts and fairs. The people themselves also will be more respectable, because of their presbyter. How is it you hear that Jerusalem was had in honor in the old times above all other cities? Why was this? Because of the then prevailing religion. Therefore it is that where God is honored, there is nothing evil: as, on the contrary, where He is not honored, there is nothing good. It will be great security both with God and with men. Only, I beseech you, that ye be not remiss: only may you put your hand to this work. For if he who brings out "the precious from the vile," shall be "as the mouth of God" (Jer. xv. 19); he who benefits and recovers so many souls, both that now are and that shall be even until the coming of

---

[1] καὶ ῥῖψαι ἑαυτὸν ὕπτιον καὶ μετὰ τὴν αἰώραν τὴν σωματικὴν καὶ λυχνικοῖς καὶ ἑωθινοῖς ὕμνοις παραγενέσθαι. This passage has perplexed scribes and editors. Αἰώρα " a swing, swinging bed, hammock," or, as here, "litter," or rather, "a swinging in such a conveyance: after the swinging motion in his litter, pleasant and healthful for the body." The meaning is: "without fatigue, lying at his ease on his back, he is borne to Church in his litter, and after this wholesome enjoyment for the body, gets good for his soul, in attending at evening and morning prayer. Ben. seipsumque projicere supinum, et post illam corpoream quietem: as if it related to taking rest in his bed, which is inconsistent with the scope of the description. Erasmus, et quiescere "in villa" securum, et habere "deambulationem" servientem corpori, "to sleep securely 'in his villa," and to 'take a walk' which is good for the body." Neander simply, und sich niederzuwerfen, "to prostrate himself," (viz. on entering the Church)—overlooking both ὕπτιον and αἰώραν σωμ. Of the Mss., A., for καὶ ῥῖψαι κ. τ. λ. substitutes, καὶ μετὰ τροφὴν σωμ. "and after taking food for the body." C. ex corr. gives ἑῶαν for αἰώραν, F. ὥραν, Sav. marg. "ὥραν al. ἑῶαν:" both unmeaning: N. ωραν with two letters erased before it; and B. καὶ μετὰ τὴν ἐνάτην ὥραν τῆς σωματικῆς μεταλαβεῖν τροφῆς καὶ ἐν λυχν., "and after the ninth hour to partake of the food for the body, and to attend at evening and morning hymns:" quæ lectio non spernenda videtur,' Ben. On the contrary, it is both needless and unsuitable, for the repast is mentioned afterwards. The "hymns" are the ψαλμὸς ἐπιλύχνιος s. λυχνικός, ad incensum lucernæ, which was Psalm cxli. ψαλμὸς ἑωθινὸς, Psalm lxiii. St. Chrysost. in Psalm cxl. and Constit. Apost. ii. 59, viii. 37.

[2] Συμβαίνει τινὰς ἐκ γειτόνων οἰκεῖν καὶ ἐπιτρόπους ἔχειν. Sav. marg. λέγειν. The meaning is not clearly expressed, but it seems to be this; "It chances that some important personage has an estate in your neighborhood, and occasionally resides there. His overseer informs him of your Church: he sends for your presbyter, invites him to his table, gains from him such information about your village, as he would never have acquired otherwise; for he thinks it beneath him even to call upon you. In this way, however, he learns that yours is a well-ordered village: and should any crime be committed in that part of the country by unknown persons, no suspicion even will light upon your people; no troublesome inquisition will be held, no fine or penalty levied on your estate." The v. l. λέγειν cannot be the true reading, but something of this sort must be supplied: οἱ καὶ λέγουσιν αὐτῷ. It seems also that something is wanting between τινὰς and ἐκ γειτ. e. g. τινὰς ἐκ τῶν δυνατωτέρων ἐκ γειτ. οἰκεῖν.

Christ, what favor shall not that person reap from God! Raise thou a garrison against the devil: for that is what the Church is. Thence as from headquarters let the hands go forth to work: first let the people hold them up for prayers, and then go their way to work. So shall there be vigor of body; so shall the tillage be abundant; so shall all evil be kept aloof. It is not possible to represent in words the pleasure thence arising, until it be realized. Look not to this, that it brings in no revenue: if [1] thou do it at all in this spirit, then do it not at all; if thou account not the revenue thou gettest thence greater than from the whole estate beside; if thou be not thus affected, then let it alone; if thou do not account this work to stand thee more in stead than any work beside. What can be greater than this revenue, the gathering in of souls into the threshing-floor which is in heaven! Alas, ye know not how much it is, to gain souls! Hear what Christ says to Peter, "Feed My sheep." (John xxi. 15–17.) If, seeing the emperor's sheep, or herd of horses, by reason of having no fold or stable, exposed to depredation, thou wert to take them in hand, and build a fold or stables, or also provide a shepherd or herdsman to take charge

of them, what would not the emperor do for thee in return? Now, thou gatherest the flock of Christ, and puttest a shepherd over them, and thinkest thou it is no great gain thou art earning? But, if for offending even one, a man shall incur so great a punishment, how can he that saves so many, ever be punished? What sin will he have thenceforth? for, though he have it, does not this blot it out? From the punishment threatened to him that offends, learn the reward of him that saves. Were not the salvation of even one soul a matter of great importance, to offend would not move God to so great anger. Knowing these things, let us apply ourselves forthwith to this spiritual work. And let each invite me, and we will together help to the best of our ability. If there be three joint-owners, let them do it by each bearing his part: if but one, he will induce the others also that are near. Only be earnest to effect this, I beseech you, that in every way being well-pleasing unto God, we may attain unto the eternal blessings, by the grace and mercy of our Lord Jesus Christ, with Whom to the Father and the Holy Ghost together be glory, dominion, and honor, now and ever world without end. Amen.

HOMILY XIX.

ACTS VIII. 26, 27.

"And the Angel of the Lord spake unto Philip, saying, Arise and go toward the south unto the way that goeth down from Jerusalem unto Gaza, which is desert. And he arose and went."

IT seems to me, this [2] (Philip) was one of the seven; for from Jerusalem he would not have gone southwards, but to the north; but from Samaria it was "towards the south. The same is desert:" so that there is no fear of an attack from the Jews. And he did not ask, Wherefore? but "arose and went. And, behold," it says, "a man of Ethiopia, an eunuch of great authority under Candace, queen of the Ethiopians, who had the charge of all her treasure, and had come to Jerusa-

lem for to worship, was returning, and sitting in his chariot read Esaias the prophet." (v. 27, 28.) High encomiums for the man, that he, residing in Ethiopia and beset with so much business, and when there was no festival going on, and living in that superstitious city, came "to Jerusalem for to worship." Great also is his studiousness, that even "sitting in his chariot he read. [3] And," it says, "the Spirit said unto Philip, Go near, and join thyself to this chariot. And Philip ran thither to him, and heard him reading the prophet Esaias, and said, Understandest thou

---

[1] ὅλως εἰ οὕτω ποιεῖς μὴ ποιήσῃς. Ben. *Si omnino id facias, ne facias tamen.* Neander, *Wenn du so handelst, wirst du nichts thun,* as if it were οὐ ποιήσεις.

[2] So all the Mss. and the Catena; except E. which having already made Chrys. affirm that Philip was one of the seven, *supra,* p. 115, and note [1], gives a different turn to this passage. "It seems to me, that he received this command while in Samaria: because from Jerusalem one does not go southward, but to the north: but from Samaria it is to the south." An unnecessary comment; for it would hardly occur to any reader of the Acts to suppose that Philip had returned to Jerusalem.

[3] "Behold, an eunuch (comp. p. 122, note [4]), a barbarian—both circumstances calculated to make him indisposed to study—add to this, his dignified station and opulence: the very circumstance of his being on a journey, and riding in a chariot: for to a person travelling in this way, it is not easy to attend to reading, but on the contrary very troublesome: yet his strong desire and earnestness set aside all these hindrances," etc. *Hom. in Gen.* xxxv. § 1. Throughout the exposition of the history of the eunuch there given (t. iv. p. 350-352) he is called a barbarian: so in the tenth of the "Eleven Homilies," § 5, t. xii. 393, 394, he is called a "barbarian," and "alien," ἀλλόφυλος, but also "a Jew:" ἀλλ' οὐχ ὁ βάρβαρος τότε ἐκεῖνος ταῦτα εἶπε (viz. excuses for delaying baptism) καὶ ταῦτα Ἰουδαῖος ὢν κ. τ. λ. i.e. as Matthäi explains in l., "a Jewish proselyte." —Both expositions should be compared with this in the text.

what thou readest? And he said, How can I, except some man should guide me?" (v. 29-31.) Observe again his piety; that though he did not understand, he read, and then after reading, examines. "And he desired Philip that he would come up and sit with him. The place of the Scripture which he read was this, He was led as a sheep to the slaughter; and like a lamb dumb before his shearer, so opened He not His mouth: in His humiliation His judgment was taken away: and who shall declare His generation? for His life is taken from the earth. And the eunuch answered Philip, and said, I pray thee, of whom speaketh the prophet this? of himself, or of some other man? Then Philip opened his mouth, and began at the same Scripture, and preached unto him Jesus." (v. 32-35.) Observe how it is Providentially ordered. First he reads and does not understand; then he reads the very text in which was the Passion and the Resurrection and the Gift. "And as they went on their way, they came unto a certain water: and the eunuch said, See, here is water; what doth hinder me to be baptized?" (v. 36.) Mark the eager desire, mark [1] the exact knowledge. "And he commanded the chariot to stand still: and they went down both into the water, both Philip and the eunuch; and he baptized him. And when they were come up out of the water, the Spirit of the Lord caught away Philip, that the eunuch saw him no more: and he went on his way rejoicing." (v. 38, 39.) But why did the Spirit of the Lord bear him away? (Hereby) the occurrence was shown to be more wonderful. Even then, the eunuch did not know him. Consequently this was done, that Philip might afterwards be a subject of wonder to him. [2] "For," it says, "he went on his way rejoicing. But Philip was found at Azotus: and passing through he preached in all the cities, till he came to Cæsarea." (v. 40.) This (Philip, therefore) was one of the seven; for there in fact he is afterwards found at Cæsarea. It was well and expedient therefore that the Spirit caught Philip away; else the eunuch would have desired to go with him, [3] and Philip would have

grieved him by declining to comply with his request, the time being not yet come. (a) But [4] at the same time here was an encouraging assurance for them that they shall also prevail over the heathen: for [5] indeed the high character (τὸ ἀξιόπιστον) of the (first) believers was enough to move them. If however the eunuch had stayed there, what fault could have been found? [But he knew him not]: for this is why it says, "he went on his way rejoicing:" so that had he known him, he would not have been (so) delighted.

"And the Angel of the Lord," etc. (Recapitulation, v. 26.) (b) See Angels assisting the preaching, and not themselves preaching, but calling these (to the work). But the wonderful nature of the occurrence is shown also by this: that what of old was rare, and hardly done, here takes place with ease, [6] and see with what frequency! (c) "An eunuch," it says, "a man of great authority, under Candace, queen of the Ethiopians." * (v. 27.) For there women bore rule of old, and this was the law among them. Philip did not yet know for whose sake he had come into the desert: (d) but [7] what was there to hinder his learning all (these particulars) accurately, while in the chariot? "Was reading the prophet Esaias." (v. 28.) For the road was desert, and there was no display in the matter. Observe also at what time: in the most violent heat (of the day). (e) "And the Spirit said

the meaning seems to be as above expressed, not, "would have desired Philip to go with him."

[4] What follows is confused in the Mss. and Edd., by transposition of the portions of text here marked a, b; and c, d: the order in the Mss. being b, a, d. c, e.

[5] Καὶ γὰρ τὸ τῶν πιστευόντων ἀξιόπιστον ἱκανὸν αὐτοὺς ἆραι· εἰ δὲ ἐπέμεινεν (B. ἐπέμενον) ἐκεῖ, ποῖον τὸ ἔγκλημα; Meaning, perhaps, that the character and station of such converts as the eunuch would weigh much with their countrymen (τοὺς ἀλλοφύλους). Though if the eunuch had stayed behind in Judea, who could have blamed him?—The modern text: "——sufficient to persuade the learners to be roused up themselves also to the same zeal.

[6] εὐχερῶς, ὅρα μεθ' ὅσης ἀφθονίας. Cat. The Mss. omit εὐχερῶς. He means, angelic manifestations.

* It is probable that this eunuch was an Ethiopian by birth and a Jewish proselyte. It was customary for such foreign proselytes, as well as for Jewish non-residents, to go up to Jerusalem to worship. Others suppose him to have been a Jew, resident in Ethiopia; but he is designated as "an Ethiopian." The fact that those in his condition were not admitted to full standing in the congregation of Israel (Deut. xxiii. 1) is not a sufficient reason for the opinion of Meyer that this man must have been an uncircumcised heathen—a "proselyte of the gate," since he could occupy the same relation as native Jews in his condition. Ethiopia lay to the S. of Egypt and Candace was queen of Meroë, the northern portion of the country. Eunuchs not only served as keepers of the harem but sometimes, as here, as royal treasurers.—G. B. S.

[7] τί δὲ ἐκώλυσεν πάντα αὐτὸν ἀκριβῶς μαθεῖν καὶ ἐν τῷ ὀχήματι ὄντα; καὶ γὰρ ἔρημος ἦν καὶ οὐκ ἦν τὸ πρᾶγμα ἐπίδειξις. We conjecture the first clause to be meant as the answer to an objection: How should Philip know all these particulars? It may indeed relate to the eunuch's accurate knowledge (ἀκρίβεια) above mentioned, note [1]. The latter part, however, seems to belong to v. 28 to which the Catena refers the mention of the χαλεπώτατον καῦμα.—Edd. (from E. alone), "Pray what hindered, say you, that he should learn all, even when in the chariot, and especially in the chariot? Because the matter was not one of display. But let us look over again what has been read. And behold," etc.

[1] ἀκρίβειαν. Below, ὁρᾷς ὅτι τὰ δόγματα ἀπηρτισμένα εἶχε. The 37th verse (Philip's answer and the Eunuch's confession) seems to have been absent from St. Chrysostom' copy (unless indeed it is implied in the passage just cited). It is found in Laud's Gr. and Lat. copy of the Acts, part is cited by St. Irenæus, p. 196. and part by St. Cypr. p. 318, but unknown to the other ancient authorities.

[2] ὥστε οὖν ὕστερον αὐτὸν θαυμασθῆναι, τοῦτο ἐγένετο: i.e. as below, the eunuch saw that it was the work of God: it was done in order that he might not think ὅτι ἄνθρωπός ἐστιν ἁπλῶς. —Edd. from E. " Why, it may be asked, did the Spirit of the Lord carry Philip away? Because he was to pass through other cities, and to preach the Gospel. Consequently this was done, etc. that he might not think what had happened to him was of man, but of God."

[3] συναπελθεῖν (Œc. συμπαρελθεῖν) αὐτῷ. As there is no αὐτὸν,

unto him." (v. 29.) Not now the Angel[1] but the Spirit urges him. Why is this? "Then," the vision took place, in grosser form, through the Angel, for this is for them that are more of the body, but the Spirit is for the more spiritual. And how did He speak to him? Of course, suggested it to him. Why does not the Angel appear to the other, and bring him to Philip? Because it is likely he would not have been persuaded, but rather terrified. Observe the wisdom of Philip: he did not accuse him, not say, "I know these things exactly:" did not pay court to him, and say, "Blessed art thou that readest." But mark his speech, how far it is from harshness alike and from adulation; the speech rather of a kind and friendly man. "Understandest thou what thou readest?" (v. 30.) For it was needful that he should himself ask,. himself have a longing desire. He plainly intimates, that he knows that the other knew nothing: and says, "Understandest thou what thou readest?" at the same time he shows him that great was the treasure that lay therein. It tells well also, that the eunuch looked not to the outward appearance (σχῆμα) (of the man), said not, "Who art thou?" did not chide, not give himself airs, not say that he did know. On the contrary, he confesses his ignorance: wherefore also he learns. He shows his hurt to the physician: sees at a glance, that he both knows the matter, and is willing to teach. Look[2] how free he is from haughtiness; the outward appearance announced nothing splendid. So desirous was he of learning, and gave heed to his words; and that saying, "He that seeketh, findeth," (Matt. vii. 8.) was fulfilled in him. "And," it says, "he besought Philip, that he would come up and sit with him." (v. 31.) Do you mark the eagerness, the longing desire? But should any say he ought to have waited for Philip (to speak), (the answer is), he does not

know what is the matter: he could not in the least tell what the other was going to say to him, but supposed merely that he was about to receive some (lesson of) prophecy. And moreover, this was more respectful, that he did not draw him into his chariot, but besought him. "And Philip," we have read, "ran to him, and heard him reading;" even the fact of his running, showed[3] that he wished to say (something). "And the place," it says, "of the Scripture which he read was this: As a sheep He was led to the slaughter." * (v. 32.) And this circumstance, also, is a token of his elevated mind, (φιλοσοφίας) that he had in hand this prophet, who is more sublime than all others. Philip does not relate matters to him just as it might happen, but quietly: nay, does not say anything until he is questioned. Both in the former instance he prayed him, and so he does now, saying, "I pray thee of whom speaketh the prophet this?" That[4] he should at all know either that the Prophets speak in different ways about different persons, or that they speak of themselves in another person—the question betokens a very thoughtful mind. † Let us be put to shame, both poor and rich, by this eunuch. Then, it says, "they came to a certain water, and he said, Lo, here is water." (v. 36.) Again, of his own accord he requests, saying, "What doth hinder me to be baptized?" And see again his modesty: he does not say, Baptize me, neither does he hold his peace; but he utters somewhat midway betwixt strong desire and reverent fear, saying, "What doth hinder me?" . Do you observe

---

[1] ἁρπάζει: but this, derived from v. 39 is not the right word here.—This, with the clause immediately preceding in the Mss., is thus altered by the innovator (E. Edd.): "So little did P. know (οὕτως οὐκ ᾔδει Φ.) for whose sake he was come into the desert: because also (ὅτι καὶ, F. D. ὅθεν) not now an Angel, but the Spirit bears him away. But the eunuch sees none of these things, being as yet not fully initiated (ἀτελὴς, imperfectus Ben.); or because also these things are not for the more bodily, but for the more spiritual: nor indeed does he learn the things which Philip is fully taught (ἐκδιδάσκεται)."

[2] Ἴδετε (ἴδε B.) τὸ (τὸν N.) ἄτυφον· οὐδὲν λαμπρὸν ἐπεφέρετο σχῆμα. Read τὸ σχῆμα.—E. D. F. Edd., Εἶδε and οὐδὲ γὰρ. Vidit illum esse a fastu alienum: neque enim splendidum gestabat vestitum. Ben. and similarly Erasm. as if the meaning were, "the eunuch saw there was no pride in Philip, for he had no splendid clothing." But it is the eunuch in whom this (τὸ ἄτυφον) is praised, (see below, § 4 init.) that he did not disdain Philip for the meanness of his appearance: comp. Hom. in Gen. xxxv. § 2. "For when the Apostle (supra, p. 115, note [1]) had said, "Knowest thou," and came up to him in mean attire (μετὰ εὐτελοῦς σχήματος), the eunuch did not take it amiss, was not indignant, did not think himself insulted . . . . but he, the man in great authority, the barbarian, the man riding in a chariot, besought him, the person of mean appearance, who might for his dress have easily been despised, to come up and sit with him," etc.

[3] ἐδείκνυ βουλόμενον εἰπεῖν. This seems meant to explain why the eunuch at once besought Philip to come up into the chariot: his running showed that he wished to say something.—E. Edd. "was a sign of his wishing to speak, and the reading (a sign) of his studiousness. For he was reading at a time when the sun makes the heat more violent."

* The rendering of ἡ δὲ περιοχὴ τῆς γραφῆς given in the text (A. V.) is also that of the R. V. Another interpretation is preferred by many scholars: "the content of the Scripture" (γραφὴ being used in the limited sense of the particular passage in question). This view harmonizes with the derivation of περιοχή (περι-έχειν) meaning an enclosure, or that which is enclosed. Γραφή is also used in the limited sense in v. 35 (So, Meyer, Hackett, and Thayer's Lex.)

[4] *Η (Ν. om. Cat. τὸ) ὅλως εἰδέναι ὅτι ἄλλως καὶ (om. C.) περὶ ἄλλων λέγουσιν οἱ προφῆται, ἢ ὅτι κ. τ. λ. A. B. C. Cat. We read, τὸ ὅλως εἰδέναι ἢ . . . . But the modern text: "It seems to me that he knew not that the prophets speak of other persons: or if not this, he was ignorant that they discourse concerning themselves in another person;" omitting the last clause, σφόδρα ἐπεσκεμμένου (Cat. περιεσκεμμένη) ἡ ἐρώτησις.—In the next sentence B. has retained the true reading, ἐκτομίαν, for which the rest have ταμίαν. N. ταμιείαν.

† The eunuch must have heard much said about Jesus at Jerusalem for he had been crucified but five or six years before. In this time of persecution and excitement, discussions would be rife concerning the Christian interpretation of prophecy. The eunuch seems to have heard two theories concerning the prophecies (e. g. Is. liii.) relating to the "Servant of Jehovah," one that the prophet was speaking of the Messiah (whom the Christians asserted Jesus to be) and the other that the prophet spoke concerning himself in these prophecies, an opinion not wholly abandoned in modern times. The eunuch's sudden conversion presupposes prolonged consideration of the claims of Jesus to be the Messiah and a keen interest in religious truth.—G. B. S.

that he has the doctrines (of faith) perfect?
For indeed the Prophet had the whole, In-
carnation, Passion, Resurrection, Ascension,
Judgment to come. And if he shows exceeding earnestness of desire, do not marvel.
Be ashamed, all ye as many as are unbaptized.
"And," it says, "he commanded the chariot
to stand still." (v. 38.) He spoke, and gave
the order at the same moment, before hearing
(Philip's answer). "And when they were
come up out of the water, the Spirit of the
Lord caught away Philip;" (v. 39) in order
that the occurrence might be shown to be of
God; that he might not consider it to be
merely man. "And he went," it says, "on
his way rejoicing." (P. 121, note 2.) This
hints, that he would have been grieved had he
known: for the greatness of his joy, having
had the Spirit also vouchsafed to him, he did
not even see things present—"But Philip
was found at Azotus." (v. 40.) Great was the
gain to Philip also:—that which he heard concerning the Prophets, concerning Habakkuk.
concerning Ezekiel, and the rest, he saw done
in his own person. (Bel. & Dr. v. 36; Ez. iii.
12.) Thence it appears that he went a long
distance, seeing he "was found at Azotus."
(The Spirit) set him there, where he was
thenceforth to preach: "And passing through,
he preached in all the cities, until he came to
Cæsarea."

"And Saul, yet breathing out threatenings
and slaughter against the disciples of the
Lord, went unto the high priest, and desired
of him letters to Damascus to the synagogues, that if he found any of this way,
whether they were men or women, he might
bring them bound unto Jerusalem." (ch. ix.
1, 2.) He fitly mentions Paul's zeal, and
shows that in the very midst of his zeal he is
drawn. "Yet breathing out threatenings
and slaughter," and not yet sated with the
murder of Stephen, he was not yet glutted
with the persecution of the Church, and the
dispersion. Lo, this was fulfilled which was
spoken by Christ, that "they which kill you
shall think they offer worship to God."
(John xvi. 2.) He then in this wise did it,
not as the Jews: God forbid! For that he
did it through zeal, is manifest from his going
abroad even to strange cities: whereas they
would not have cared even for those in Jerusalem; they were for one thing only, to enjoy
honor. But why went he to Damascus?
It was a great city, a royal city: he was
afraid lest that should be preoccupied. And
observe his strong desire and ardor (and),
how strictly according to the Law he went to
work: he goes not to the governor, but "to
the priest. That if he found any of this

way:" for so the believers were called, probably because of their taking the direct way
that leads to heaven. And why did he not
receive authority to have them punished
there, but brings them to Jerusalem! He
did these things here with more authority.
And mark on what a peril he casts himself.
He [1] was not afraid lest he should take any
harm, but (yet) he took others also with him,
"that if," it says, "he found any of this way,
whether they were men or women"—Oh, the
ruthlessness!—"he might bring them bound."
By this journey of his, he wished to show
them all (how he would act): so far were
they from being earnest in this matter.
Observe him also casting (people) into prison
before this. The others therefore did not
prevail: but this man did prevail, by reason
of his ardent mind. "And as he journeyed,
he came near Damascus: and suddenly there
shined round about him a light from heaven:
and he fell to the earth, and heard a voice
saying unto him, Saul, Saul, why persecutest
thou Me?" (v. 3, 4.) Why not in Jerusalem? why not in Damascus? That there
might be no opening for different persons
to relate the occurrence in different ways, but
that he alone should be the authentic narrator (ἀξιόπιστος), he that [2] went for this purpose.
In fact, he says this [both in his oration on
the stairs], and when pleading before Agrippa.
"Fell to the earth": (ch. xxii. 6: xxvi. 12)
for excess of light is wont to shock, because

---

[1] Edd. " on what danger casting himself, still even so he is
afraid lest he should suffer some harm. This is the reason
why he takes others with him, probably to rid himself of his
fear: or also, because they were many against whom he was
going, he takes many, in order that the more boldly, whomsoever he should find, both men and women," etc. Just the
opposite to C.'s meaning: viz. " It is not to be supposed, because he took many with him, that he had any fears for himself: he was above all such regards. The fact is, he wished
to show them all (both the Jews at Jerusalem, and the companions of his journey), how they ought to act:" διὰ τῆς ὁδοῦ
πᾶσιν αὐτοῖς δεῖξαι ἐβούλετο. C. however has πᾶσιν αὐτοῦ,
N. πᾶσιν αὐτούς, meaning: "by means of his journey, he
wished to show them (the Christians bound) to all." Perhaps
the true reading is αὐτοῦ τὴν προθυμίαν, or the like. E. D. F.
Edd. " Especially as by means of the journey he wished to
show them all (πᾶσιν αὐτοῖς), that all depended on him (αὐτοῦ
τὸ πᾶν ὄν).

[2] ὁ διὰ τοῦτο ἀπιών· i. e. who would have a right to be believed, because it was known that he left Jerusalem for the
purpose of persecuting. Had it taken place in Jerusalem or in
Damascus, some would have given one account of the matter,
some another—as, in the case of our Lord, when the voice
came to Him from heaven at Jerusalem, "some said it thundered, some that an Angel spake to Him," (so Chrys. explains
below, p. 125)—but, happening in the way it did, the person
most interested in it, and who by this very thing was caused
to take so momentous a step, was the authentic narrator; i. e.
the story was to come from him, as the only competent authority: ἀλλ' αὐτὸς ἀξιόπιστος ἦν διηγούμενος (so Cat.; C., ἦν
διηγήσασθαι· the other Mss. ἠδιηγούμενος) ὁ διὰ τοῦτο ἀπιών·
Infra, p. 125, οὗτος δὲ ἀξιόπιστος ἦν ἀπαγγέλλων μᾶλλον τὰ
ἑαυτοῦ.—In the next sentence, Τοῦτο γοῦν λέγει, καὶ πρὸς
Ἀγρίππαν ἀπολογούμενος, something seems wanting before καί,
as supplied in the translation: but also both before and
after these words: e. g. For the men which were with him,
heard not the voice, and were amazed and overpowered. In
fact, he says this in his oration on the stairs, "They heard not
the voice of Him that spake to me," and when pleading before
Agrippa, he says, "And when we were all fallen to the
ground, I heard a voice." etc.

the eyes have their measure : it is said also that excess of sound makes people deaf and stunned (as in a fit) (ἀποπλῆγας). But [1] him it only blinded, and extinguished his passion by fear, so that he should hear what was spoken. "Saul, Saul," saith He, "why persecutest thou me?" And He tells him nothing : does not say, Believe, nor anything whatever of the kind : but expostulates with him, all but saying, What wrong, great or small, hast thou suffered from Me, that thou doest these things? "And he said, Who art Thou, Lord?" (v. 5) thus in the first place confessing himself His servant. "And the Lord said, I am Jesus, whom thou persecutest:" think not thy warring is with men. [2] And they which were with him heard the voice of Paul, but saw no person to whom he answered —for (the Lord) suffered them to be hearers of what was less important. Had they heard the other Voice, they would not have believed; but perceiving Paul answering (some person), they marvelled. "But arise, and go into the city, and it shall be told thee what thou must do." (v. 6.) Observe, how He does not immediately add all, but first softens his mind. In the same way He called the disciples also a second time. [3] "It shall be told thee," etc.: He gives him good hopes, and (intimates) that he shall recover his sight also. "And the men which journeyed with him stood speechless, hearing a voice, but seeing no man. And Saul arose from the earth; and when his eyes were opened, he saw no man : but they led him by the hand, and brought him into Damascus" (v. 7, 8):— the spoils of the devil (τὰ σκεύη αὐτοῦ), "his goods" (Matt. xiii. 29), as from some city, yea, some metropolis which has been taken. And

the wonder of it is, the enemies and foes themselves brought him in, in the sight of all! "And for three days he neither did eat nor drink, being blinded." (v. 9.) What could equal this? To compensate the discouragement in the matter of Stephen, here is encourment, in the bringing in of Paul : though that sadness had its consolation in the fact of Stephen's making such an end, yet it also received this further consolation : moreover, the bringing in of the villages of the Samaritans afforded very great comfort.—But why did this take place not at the very first, but after these things? That it might be shown that Christ was indeed risen. This furious assailant of Christ, the man who would not believe in His death and resurrection, the persecutor of His disciples, how should this man have become a believer, had not the power of His resurrection been great indeed? Be it so, that the other Apostles favored (His pretensions [4]): what say you to this man? Why then not immediately after His resurrection? That his hostility might be more clearly shown as open war. The man who is so frantic as even to shed blood and cast men into prisons, all at once believes! It was not enough that he had never been in Christ's company : the believers must be warred upon by him with vehement hostility : he left to none the possibility of going beyond him in fury : none of them all could be so violent. But when he was blinded, [5] then he saw the proofs of His sovereignty and loving kindness : then he answers, "Lord, what wilt Thou have me to do?" that none may say that he played the hypocrite, he that was even eager for blood, and went to the priests, and flung himself upon such dangers, in persecuting and bringing to punishment even them that were in foreign parts—under these circumstances he now acknowledges His sovereignty. And why was he shone upon by that light not within the city, but before it? The many would not have believed, since

---

[1] Ἀλλὰ τοῦτον μόνον ἐπήρωσε· may be rendered, They all saw the light, but it blinded only Paul:—or, Him however it only blinded, did not cast him into insensibility, but left him otherwise in possession of his faculties.

[2] The remainder of the verse and the first part of v. 6 to πρὸς αὐτὸν, were absent from Chrysostom's copy (and Cat. Œc. Theoph.) as from Codd. A. B. C. (of New Test.) and Laud's Gr. and Lat. of Acts: but the last have the clause, σκληρόν σοι π. κ. λ. after διώκεις, v. 4. St. Hil. omits the clause durum est, etc. but has, tremens et pavens, etc.—"The voice of Paul:" Didymus in Cat. gives this as Chrysostom's solution of the seeming contradiction between this statement and that of St. Paul in xxii. 9. "In the first narrative, they heard Paul's voice, saying, Who art thou, Lord? But saw no man save Paul: in the second, they saw the light, but did not hear the voice of the Lord.'

[3] οὔτω καὶ τοὺς μαθητὰς ἐκάλεσεν ἐκ δευτέρου (Cat. and Sav. marg. join ἐκ δ. to the next sentence). The meaning is: As here, there is an interval between the conversion of Saul, and Christ's announcement of the purpose for which he was called (which in Acts xxvi. 15, 16 are put together as if all was said at the same time), so in the case of the disciples, Andrew, John, and Simon, there was a first call, related in John i.; then after a while, Christ called them a second time, (see Hom. in Matt. xiv. § 2) namely, to be fishers of men, Matt. iv. In both cases there was an interval, during which he and they were prepared for the further revelation of His will concerning them. The mod. t. (E. Edd.) omits this clause, and substitutes, καὶ δι ὧν παρακελεύεται αὐτὸν ποιεῖν παραχρῆμα κ. τ. λ. "And by what He bids him do, straightway gives him," etc.

[4] Ἔστω ἐκείνοι αὐτῷ ἐχαρίζοντο. Hom. in illud, Saulus adhuc spirans, etc. § 5, t. iii. p. 105. "But shameless objectors may say (of Peter), that because he was Christ's disciple, because he had been partaker at His table, had been with Him three years, had been under His teaching, had been deluded and cajoled by Him (ἐκολακεύθη ὑπ' αὐτοῦ ἀπατηθείς), therefore it is that he preaches His resurrection: but when thou seest Paul, a man who knew Him not, had never heard Him, had never been under His teaching: a man, who even after His crucifixion makes war upon Him, puts to death them that believe in Him, throws all into confusion and disorder, when thou seest him suddenly converted, and in his toils for the Gospel outstripping the friends of Christ; what plea canst thou then have for thine effrontery, in disbelieving the word of the Resurrection?"

[5] Ἐπειδὴ δὲ ἐπληρώθη (ἐπληροφορήθη, A. om., Cat. ἐπηρώθη, E. D. F. Edd.) τῆς δεσποτείας αὐτοῦ τὰ τεκμήρια καὶ τῆς φιλανθρωπίας τότε ἀποκρίνεται (for τ. ἀ. E. D. F. Edd. γνωρίζει, Cat. εἶδεν)· ἵνα (γὰρ add B.) μή τις εἴπη ὅτι ὑπεκρίνετο, ὁ καὶ αἱμάτων ἐπιθυμῶν κ. τ. λ. (ἢ καὶ ἵνα μή τις . . . ὑπεκρ. Πῶς γὰρ ὁ καὶ αἱμ. ἐπ. κ. τ. λ. E. D. F. Edd.) We read Ἐπειδὴ δὲ ἐπηρώθη, . . . τῆς φ. εἶδε. Τότε ἀπ. Κύριε, κ. τ. λ. ἵνα λὴ κ. τ. λ.

even there (at Jerusalem when the people heard the voice which came from above, they said that "it thundered" (John xii. 29, *supra*, note [2], p. 123) ; but this man was authority enough in reporting what was his own affair. And bound he was brought in, though not with bonds upon him : and they drew him, who had expected to draw the others. "And he eat not, neither drank :" he condemned himself for the past, he confessed, prayed, besought God. But should any say, This was the effect of compulsion : (we answer) The same thing happened to Elymas : then how came it that he was not changed? (ch. xiii. *de Laud. Pauli Hom.* iv. § 1, t. ii. p. 491.) What (evidence) could be more compulsory than the earthquake at the Resurrection, the report of the soldiers, the other miracles, the seeing Himself risen? But these things do not compel (belief) they are calculated to teach (it) (οὐκ ἀναγκαστικὰ ἀλλὰ διδακτικά). Why did not the Jews believe when they were told of these things? That he spoke truth was manifest: for he would not have been changed, had this not happened ; so that all were bound to believe. He was not inferior to them that preached the Resurrection, and was more credible, by being all at once converted. He had no intercourse with any of the believers; it was at Damascus that he was converted, or rather before he came to Damascus that this happened to him. I ask the Jew: Say, by what was Paul converted? He saw so many signs, and was not converted : his teacher (Gamaliel, *supra*, p. 87, note [1]) was converted, and he remained unconverted. Who convinced him—and not only convinced, but all at once inspired him with such ardent zeal? Wherefore was it, that he wished even to go into hell itself [1] for Christ's sake? The truth of the facts is manifest.

But, as I said, for the present let us take shame to ourselves (when we think of) the eunuch, both in his baptism and his reading. Do ye mark how he was in a station of great authority, how he was in possession of wealth, and even on his journey allowed himself no rest? What must he have been at home, in his leisure hours, this man who rested not even on his travels? What must he have been at night? Ye that are in stations of dignity, hear : imitate his freedom from

pride, [2] (*de Lazaro, Conc.* iii. § 3, t. i. p. 748. c) his piety. Though about to return home, he did not say to himself : "I am going back to my country, there let me receive baptism ;" those cold words which most men use! No need had he of signs, no need of miracles: from the Prophet merely, he believed. (*b*) But [3] why is it (so ordered) that he sees (Philip) not before he goes to Jerusalem, but after he has been there? It was not meet that he should see the Apostles under persecution. Because [4] he was yet weak, the Prophet was not easy; (but yet the Prophet) catechized him. For even now, if any of you would apply himself to the study of the Prophets, he would need no miracles. And, if

<hr/>

[1] Διά τι καὶ εἰς γεένναν ηὔξατο ἀπελθεῖν ὑπὲρ τοῦ Χριστοῦ ; The modern text substitutes, "that he wished even to be accursed (Rom. ix. 2.) for Christ," See Hom. xvi. ad Rom. in l. But Chrys. elsewhere uses as strong expressions as he does here. Hom. ii. in 2 Thess. § 4 οὐδὲ τὴν πεῖραν τῆς γεέννης ἡγεῖτό τι εἶναι διὰ τὸν τοῦ Χριστοῦ πόθον. And, διὰ τὸν τοῦ Χ. πόθον, καταδέχεται καὶ εἰς γεένναν ἐμπεσεῖν καὶ τῆς βασιλείας ἐκπεσεῖν, (cited in the *Ecloga de Laud. Paul.* t. xii. p. 659, E.)

[2] τὸ ἄτυφον, above, p. 122, [2]. Comp. x. § 5. of the Eleven Homilies, t. xii. p. 393. "Admire how this man, barbarian as he was, and alien, and liable to be puffed up with his great authority, demeaned himself towards a man, poor, beggarly, unknown, whom until then he had never set eyes on. . . . If our rulers now, believers though they be, and taught to be humble-minded, and with nothing of the barbarian about them, meeting in the public place, I do not say an unknown stranger, but one whom they know, would be in no great hurry to give him a seat beside him (in their carriage), how came this man to condescend so much to a perfect stranger—for I will not cease to insist upon this—a stranger, I say, one whom he had never seen, a mean-looking person, apt to be despised for his appearance, as to bid him mount and sit beside him? Yet this he did, and to his tongue committed his salvation, and endured to put himself in the position of a learner; yea, beseeches, intreats, supplicates, saying, 'I pray thee, of whom saith the Prophet this?' and receives with profound attention what he says. And not only so, but having received, he was not remiss, did not put off, did not say, 'Let me get back to my own country, let me see my friends, my family, my kinsfolk'—which is what many Christians say now-a-days when called to baptism: 'let me get to my country, let me see my wife, let me see my children with my other kinsfolk: with them present, and making holiday with me, so will I enjoy the benefit of baptism, so partake of the Grace.' But not these words spake he, the barbarian: Jew as he was, and trained to make strict account of places, especially with (the Law) ever sounding in his ears the duty of observing the Place, insomuch that he had gone a long journey to Jerusalem, on purpose that he might worship in the place which God commanded: and behold, all at once casting away all that he had been used to in this regard, and relinquishing this strict observance of place, no sooner is the discourse finished, and he sees a fountain by the roadside, than he says, 'See, here is water, what doth hinder me to be baptized?'"

[3] The letters (*a*) (*b*) denote the order of the two parts in Mss. and Edd.

[4] διὰ τὸ ἀσθενὲς ἔτι. Edd. give this to the preceding sentence, and then: Οὐδὲ πρότερον οὕτως ἦν ἰεύκολον, ὡς ὅτε ὁ προφήτης αὐτὸν κατήχησεν : "nor was it so easy before, as (it was) when the Prophet had catechized him :" which is irrelevant to the question : for Philip might have found him engaged in the same study then as afterwards. The old text has: οὐκ ἦν εὔκολος, ὁ προφήτης γὰρ αὐτὸν κατήχησεν, but A. rightly omits γὰρ. Something is wanting ; e. g. either, "until Philip catechized him," or rather, "but yet the prophet catechized him." What follows is much confused in the Mss. By "the prophecy itself" Chrys. probably means more than the two verses given in the Acts, viz. Isai. liii. 7-12.—"It is likely he had heard that He had been crucified," so C. D. F. (i. e. as appears further on, the eunuch when at Jerusalem had heard of the Crucifixion, had seen the rent in the rocks, etc., another reason why it was fit that he should have first visited Jerusalem:) but B., "Perhaps he had *not* heard:" and E. Edd., "Hence he learnt." After "taken from the earth," C. alone has, καὶ τὰ ἄλλα ὅσ' (sic) ἁμαρτίαν οὐκ ἐποίησεν, the others. ὅτι ἁμ. οὐκ ἐπ. after which Savile alone adds, "nor was guile found in His mouth." After ἐσταυρώθη something is wanting, e. g. νῦν δὲ ἔμαθεν or κατηχήθη. In καὶ τὰ ἄλλα there seems to be a reference to the sequel in "the prophecy itself," viz. "and the rest which may be read in Isaiah, as that He did no sin," etc.—A., as usual, omits the whole passage: E. refashions it thus: "Hence He learnt that He was crucified, that His life is taken away from the earth, that He did no sin, that He prevailed to save others also, that His generation is not to be declared, that the rocks were rent, that the veil was torn, that dead men were raised from the tombs: or rather, all these things Philip told him." etc. so Edd.

you please, let us take in hand the prophecy itself. " He was led as a sheep to the slaughter; and like a lamb dumb before his shearer, so opened He not His mouth: in His humiliation His judgment was taken away: and who shall declare His generation? for His life is taken from the earth. * (v. 22, 23.) It is likely he had heard that He was crucified, [and now he learns], that " His life is taken away from the earth," and the rest: that " He did no sin, nor deceit in His mouth:" that He prevailed to save others also: [and] who He is, Whose generation is unutterable. It is likely he had seen the riven rocks there (on the spot), and (had heard) how the veil was rent, and how there was darkness, and so forth: and all these things Philip mentioned, merely taking his text from the Prophet. It is a great thing, this reading of the Scriptures! That was fulfilled which was spoken by Moses, " Sitting, lying down, rising up, and walking, remember the Lord thy God." (Deut. vi. 7.) For the roads, especially when they are lonely, give us opportunity for reflection, there being none to disturb us. Both this man is on the road, and Paul on the road: howbeit the latter no man draws, but Christ alone. This was too great a work for the Apostles: and, greater still, in that, the Apostles being at Jerusalem, and no person of authority at Damascus, he nevertheless returned thence converted: yet those at Damascus knew that he did not come from Jerusalem converted, for he brought letters, that he might put the believers in bonds. Like a consummate Physician, when the fever was at its height, Christ brought help to him: for it was needful that he should

be quelled in the midst of his frenzy. For then most of all would he be brought down, and condemn himself as one guilty of dreadful audacity. (a) For these things Paul deplores himself, saying, " Howbeit for this cause I obtained mercy, that in me first Jesus Christ might show all His long suffering. (1 Tim. i. 13–16.) Verily one has reason to admire this eunuch. He did not see Christ, he saw no miracle: he beheld Jerusalem standing yet entire (συνεστῶτα): he believed Philip. How came he to behave thus? His soul was earnest (μεμεριμνημένη). Yet the thief (on the cross) had seen miracles: the wise men had seen a star; but this man, nothing of the kind. So great a thing is the careful reading of the Scriptures! What of Paul then! did he not study the law? But he, it seems to me, was specially reserved, for the purpose which I have already mentioned by anticipation, because Christ would fain draw to Himself the Jews by inducements from every quarter. For had they been in their right mind, nothing was so likely to do them good as this; for this, more than miracles and all else, was calculated to attract them: as, [2] on the other hand, nothing is so apt to prove a stumbling block to men of duller minds. See then how, after the Apostle, we have God also doing miracles. They accused the Apostles after these [miracles of theirs]; they cast them into prison: see thereupon God doing the miracles. For instance, the bringing them out of prison, was His miracle: the bringing Philip, His miracle: the bringing Paul over, was His.— Observe in what way Paul is honored, in what way the eunuch. There, Christ appears, probably because of his hardness, and because Ananias [3] would not (else) have been persuaded. Conversant with these wonders, let us show ourselves worthy. But many in these times, even when they come to church, do not know what is read; whereas the eunuch, even in public (ἐπ' ἀγορᾶς) and riding in his chariot, applied himself to the reading of the Scriptures. Not so you: none takes the Bible in hand: nay, everything rather than the Bible.

Say, what are the Scriptures for? For as much as in you lies, it is all undone. What is

---

* In the quotation the N. T. follows the LXX. (Is. liii: 7, 8), which but imperfectly renders the original. The meaning is obscure in Hebrew, but the best rendering is probably that of the R. V. which renders v. 8 thus: " By oppression and judgment he was taken away; and as for his generation, who *among them* considered that he was cut off out of the land of the living?" for which the LXX. and N. T. have: "In his humiliation his judgment was taken away: His generation who shall declare, for his life is taken from the earth." It is almost useless to inquire what the LXX. translators could have meant by this rendering. Concerning the meaning of the first clause, there are four theories: (1) The judgment announced by His enemies was taken away, i. e., annulled by God (Bengel, Lechler). (2) His judicial power was taken away during his humiliation, i. e., he did not appear as men's judge (Humphrey). (3) His judgment (punishment) was taken away, i. e., ended—by death (Meyer, Robinson). (4) The judgment due him—the rights of justice—was withheld by his enemies (Gloag, Hackett).
The latter part of the LXX. trans.: "who shall declare," etc., has been understood in the following ways: (1) Who shall declare his divine Sonship?—the reference being to the "eternal generation" of the Son (the Patristic view). (2) Who shall declare the number of his spiritual seed, i. e., predict the extent of his kingdom? (the Reformers). (3) Who shall declare the wickedness of his contemporaries, for he was put to death (Meyer, De Wette, Lechler, Alford, Gloag). This interp. assigns to the word "generation," the same meaning which the R. V. gives to it in the original passage and is the preferable view. It should be admitted that this is a probable theory of what the LXX. ought to have meant by the words which they used; that they did consciously mean this is far less certain.—G. B. S.

[1] ὥσπερ οὖν οὐδὲν οὕτω σκανδαλίζειν εἴωθε τοὺς παχυτέρους: i.e. Saul's conversion would have weighed with the Jews εἰ νοῦν εἶχον, but it was a great stumbling-block to them as παχυτέροι: " as indeed nothing is so apt to prove a stumbling-block to men of duller minds," as this is—viz. the sudden conversion of one of their own party to the opposite side.
[2] καὶ ὅτι οὐκ ἂν ἐπείσθη Ἀνανίας, A. B. C. But Edd. omit Ananias: " because he (Paul) would not otherwise have been persuaded." In the next sentence, C. F. have Ἐντρεφόμενοι, " nurtured." B. ἐντρυφῶντες, " luxuriating:" A. E. D. Edd. ἐνστρεφόμενοι.

the Church for? Tie up[1] the Bibles: perhaps the judgment would not be such, not such the punishment: if one were to bury them in dung, that he might not hear them, he would not so insult them as you do now. For say, what is the insult there? That the man has buried them. And what here? That we do not hear them. Say, when is a person most insulted—when he is silent, and one makes no answer, or, when he does speak (and is unheeded)? So that the insult is greater in the present case, when He does speak and thou wilt not hear: greater the contempt. "Speak not to us" (Is. xxx. 10), we read, they said of old to the Prophets: but ye do worse, saying, Speak:[2] we will not do. For there they turned them away that they should not even speak, as feeling that from the voice itself they got some sort of awe and obligation; whereas you, in the excess of your contempt, do not even this. Believe me, if you stopped our[3] mouths by putting your hands over them, the insult would not be so great as it is now. For say, whether shows greater contempt, he that hears, even when hindering by this action, or, he that will not even hear? Say—if we shall look at it as a case of an insult offered—suppose one person to check the party insulting him, and to stop his mouth, as being hurt by the insults, and another person to show no concern, but pretend not even to hear them: whether will show most contempt? Would you not say the latter? For the former shows that he feels himself hit: the latter all but stops the mouth of God. Did ye shudder at what was said? Why, the mouth by which God speaks, is the mouth of God. Just as our mouth is the mouth of our soul, though the soul has no mouth, so the mouth of the Prophets is the mouth of God. Hear, and shudder. There, common (to the whole congregation) stands the deacon crying aloud, and saying, "Let us attend to the reading." It is the common voice of the whole Church, the voice which he utters, and yet none does attend. After him begins the Reader, "The Prophecy of Esaias," and still none attends, although Prophecy has nothing of man in it. Then

after this, he says, "Thus saith the Lord,[4] and still none attends. Then after this punishments and vengeances, and still even then none attends. But what is the common excuse? "It is always the same things over again." This it is most of all, that ruins you. Suppose you knew the things, even so you certainly ought not to turn away: since in the theatres also, is it not always the same things acted over again, and still you take no disgust? How dare you talk about "the same things," you who know not so much as the names of the Prophets? Are you not ashamed to say, that this is why you do not listen, because it is "the same things over again," while you do not know the names of those who are read, and this, though always hearing the same things? You have yourself confessed that the same things are said. Were I to say this as a reason for finding fault with you, you would need to have recourse to quite a different excuse, instead of this which is the very thing you find fault with.—Do not you exhort your son? Now if he should say, "Always the same things!" would not you count it an insult? It would be time enough to talk of "the same things," when we both knew the things, and exhibited them in our practice. Or rather, even then, the reading of them would not be superfluous. What equal to Timothy? tell me that: and yet to him says Paul, "Give attention to reading, to exhortation. (Tim. iv. 13.) For it is not possible, I say not possible, ever to exhaust the mind of the Scriptures. It is a well which has no bottom. "I said," saith the Preacher, "I am become wise:[5] and then it departed from me."— (Eccles. vii. 24.) Shall I show you that the things are not "the same?" How many persons, do you suppose, have spoken upon the Gospels? And yet all have spoken in a way which was new and fresh. For the more one dwells on them, the more insight does he get, the more does he behold the pure light. Look, what a number of things I am going to speak of:— say, what is narrative? what is prophecy? what is parable? what is type? what is allegory? what is symbol? what are Gospels? Answer me only to this one point, which is

---

[1] δῆσον. i.e. tie them up, and keep them shut. E. Edd. κατά-χωσον, "Bury." Below, for καὶ μὴ ἀκούει αὐτῶν, we read ἵνα μή. C. however has ἀκούει, which may imply that the sentence should be joined to the preceding one, οὐ τοιαύτη κόλασις, εἴ τις καταχώσειεν αὐτὰ ἐν κόπρῳ, καὶ εἰ μὴ ἀκούει αὐτῶν: "not such the punishment, were one to bury, etc., as it is if he refuse to hear them."

[2] All the Mss. and Edd. Μὴ λαλεῖτε, "Speak not." But the context plainly requires the sense. "Speak on, if you will: we will not do what you bid us:" though it should rather be, Οὐκ ἀκούσομεν.

[3] E. ὑμῖν, "your mouths," so Edd. except Sav. and below, ὁ ἀκούων καὶ μὴ πειθόμενος μειζόνως καταφρονεῖ, where the old text has, ὁ ἀκούων μεις. κατ. καὶ διὰ τούτου κωλύων, "by this," viz. by putting his hand on the speaker's mouth.

[4] When the Deacon had ordered silence by proclaiming, if need were, several times, Προσέχωμεν! the Reader commenced the Lesson, if from the Old Testament or the Gospels, with the formula, Τάδε λέγει Κύριος, "Thus saith the Lord:" (for the Epistles, with, "Dearly beloved Brethren.") See Hom. in 2 Thess. iii. § 4, p. 527. D.

[5] Εἶπον, ἐσοφίσθην, φησί, καὶ τότε ἀπέστη ἀπ' ἐμοῦ. Ben. rendering the passage with Erasmus, "Deceptus sum, et tunc recessit a me," remarks, "I do not see how this agrees with what precedes." The Paris Editor, "Novi. inquiunt. et tum mihi effluxit," as if it were a proverb. In the LXX. it is, Εἶπα, σοφισθήσομαι, καὶ αὕτη ἐμακρύνθη ἀπ' ἐμοῦ. E. V. "I said I will be wise, but it was far from me."

plain : why are they called Gospels, "good tidings?" And yet ye have often heard that good news ought to have nothing sad in it: yet this "good news" has abundance of sadness in it. "Their fire," it saith, "shall never be quenched : their worm shall not die:" (Mark ix. 44.) "Shall appoint his portion," it saith, "with the hypocrites," with them that are "cut asunder : then shall He say, I know you not: Depart from Me, ye that work iniquity." (Matt. xxiv. 51; vii. 23.) Surely, [1] we do not deceive ourselves, when we imagine that we tell you in your own mother-tongue (Ἑλληνιστί) these good tidings? *You* look downcast; *you* are stunned; you are struck all of a heap, unable to hold up your heads. "Good news" should have nothing in it of a duty to be done, but rather should counsel what is good: whereas these "Gospels" have endless duties to be done. And again, to mention other things, as for instance, Except a man hate father and mother, he is not worthy of Me" (Luke xiv, 26): and "I am not come to bring peace upon earth, but a sword" (Matt. x. 34; Luke xii. 51): and "In the world ye shall have tribulation— John xvi. 33.) excellent [2] good tidings these, are they not! For good news is such as this—"You shall have this and that good thing:" as in common life men say one to another, "What shall I have for my good news? Your father is coming, or, your mother:" he does not say, "You must do this or that."—Again, tell me, how do the Gospels differ from the Prophets? Why are not the Prophecies also called Gospels,

good tidings? For they tell the same things : for instance, "The lame shall leap as an hart." (Is. xxxv. 6.) "The Lord shall give the word to them that preach the Gospel" (Ps. lxviii. 11): and, "A new heaven and a new earth." (Is. lxv. 17.) Why are not those also called Gospels? But if, while you do not so much as know what "Gospels" mean, you so despise the reading of the Scriptures, what shall I say to you?— Let me speak of something else. Why four Gospels? why not, ten? why not twenty? If "many have taken in hand to set forth a narrative" (Luke i. 1), why not one person? Why they that were disciples (i. e. Apostles)? why they that were not disciples? But why any Scriptures at all? And yet, on the contrary, the Old Testament says, "I will give you a New Testament." (Jer. xxxi. 31.) Where are they that say, "Always the same things?" If ye knew these, that, though a man should live thousands of years, they are not "the same things," ye would not say this. Believe me, I will not tell you the answers to any of these questions; not in private, not in public : only, if any find them out, I will nod assent. For this is the way we have made you good-for-nothing, by always telling you the things ready to your hands, and not refusing when we ought. Look, you have questions enough: consider them, tell me the reasons. Why Gospels? Why not Prophecies? Why duties, to be done, in the Gospels? If one is at a loss, let another seek the answer, and contribute each to the others from what he has : but now we will hold our peace. For if what has been spoken has done you no good, much less would it, should we add more. We only pour water into a vessel full of holes. And the punishment too is all the greater for you. Therefore, we will hold our peace. Which that we may not have to do, it rests with yourselves. For if we shall see your diligence, perhaps we will again speak, that both ye may be more approved, and we may rejoice over you, in all things giving glory to the God and Father of our Lord Jesus Christ : to Him be glory and dominion now and ever, and world without end. Amen.

---

[1] Ἄρα μὴ ἀπατῶμεν ἑαυτούς, νομίζοντες ταῦτα ἑλληνιστὶ ὑμῖν λέγειν; Mss. and Edd., ἄρα μὴ without the interrogation. Ben. "*Igitur ne decipiamus nosmetipsos hæc Græco more dici.*" The meaning seems to be, "When we tell you these things as εὐαγγέλια, do we deceive ourselves in thinking that we are speaking Greek—that we are using the term aright?— Yet to judge from your looks, one may see that they are anything but εὐαγγέλια to you. Ὑμεῖς κατηφεῖτε, ὑμεῖς κεκώφωσθε· ἀπόπληκτοι τυγχάνετε κάτω κύπτοντες." The innovator (E. Edd.) quite alters the meaning, as if it were, "You look as indifferent as if it were no concern of yours;" viz. "Or, have you nothing to do with these things? But you are struck deaf (κεκώφωσθε), and as if you were in a fit, hang down your heads."—Below, for καὶ πάλιν ἕτερα ἐρῶ, οἷον, the same have, οἷαπέρ ἐστι καὶ τὰ τοιαῦτα, such as are also these."

[2] Edd. Καλά γε· οὐ γὰρ ταῦτα εὐαγγέλια: read Καλῦγε (οὐγάρ;) ταῦτα εὐαγγέλια. In the next sentence, Τί μοι τῶν εὐαγγελίων; Ben. "*Quid mihi est evangeliorum.*"

HOMILY XX.

ACTS IX. 10, 12.

" And there was a certain disciple at Damascus, named Ananias; and to him said the Lord in a vision, Ananias. And he said, Behold, I am here, Lord. And the Lord said unto him, Arise, and go into the street which is called Straight, and inquire in the house of Judas for one called Saul, of Tarsus: for, behold, he prayeth, and hath seen in a vision a man named Ananias coming in, and putting his hand on him, that he might receive his sight."

WHAT may be the reason that He neither drew any one of high authority and importance, nor caused such to be forthcoming for the purpose of instructing Paul?[1] It was, because it was not meet that he should be induced by men, but only by Christ Himself: as in fact this man taught him nothing, but merely baptized him; for, as soon as baptized (φωτισθείς), he was to draw upon himself the grace of the Spirit, by his zeal and exceeding earnestness. And that Ananias was no very distinguished person, is plain. For, " the Lord," it says, " spake unto him in a vision, and Ananias answered and said, Lord, I have heard by many of this man, how much evil he hath done to Thy saints at Jerusalem." (v. 13.) For if he spoke in objection to Him, much more would he have done so, had He sent an Angel. And this is why, in the former instance, neither is Philip told what the matter is; but he sees the Angel, and then the Spirit bids him go near to the chariot. But observe here how the Lord relieves him of his fear: " He is blind," saith He, " and prayeth, and art thou afraid?" In the same way Moses also is afraid: so that the words betokened that he was afraid, and shrunk from the task, not that he did not believe. He said, " I have heard from many concerning this man." What sayest thou? God speaketh, and thou hesitatest? They did not yet well know the power of Christ. " And here he hath authority from the chief priests to bind all that call on Thy name." (v. 14.) How was that known? It is likely that they, being in fear,

made minute enquiries. He does not say this, as thinking that Christ does not know the fact, but, " such being the case, how," says he, " can these things be?" As in fact those (in the Gospel) say, " Who can be saved?"— (Mark x. 26.) This is done, in order that Paul may believe him that shall come to him: " he hath seen in a vision:" it hath showed him beforehand: " he prayeth," saith (the Lord): fear not. And observe, He speaks not to him of the success achieved: teaching us not to speak of our achievements. And,[2] though He saw him afraid, for all this He said it not. " Thou shalt not be disbelieved:" " he hath seen," saith He, " in a vision a man (named) Ananias:" for this is why it was " in a vision," namely, because he was blind. And not even the exceeding wonderfulness of the thing took possession of the disciple's mind, so greatly was he afraid But observe: Paul being blind, in this way He restored to sight. " But the Lord said unto him, Go thy way: for he is a chosen vessel unto Me, to bear My name before the Gentiles, and kings, and the children of Israel: for I will show him how great things he must suffer for My name's sake." (v. 15, 16.) " Not only," saith He, " shall he be a believer, but even a teacher, and great boldness shall he show: ' before Gentiles and kings'—such shall be the spread of the doctrine!—that just as He astonished (him) by the former, so He may (startle him even more) by the latter.[3] " And Ananias went, and entered into the house, and laid his hands upon him, and said, Brother

---

[1] Œcumen. adds from some other source, " but Ananias who was one of the Seventy:" and afterwards, " And this Ananias was a deacon, as Paul himself testifies in the Canons:" the latter from Ammonius the Presbyter, in the Catena.—Below, Καὶ ὅτι (Cat., Ὅτι γὰρ)οὐ τῶν σφόδρα ἐπισήμων ἦν, δῆλον, C. comp. p. 279. But Edd. " But that Ananias also was one of the very distinguished persons, is plain both from what (the Lord) reveals and says to him, and from what he himself says in answer: Lord, I have heard," etc.'

[2] Καὶ φοβούμενον ἰδὼν, οὐδὲ οὕτως εἶπεν. Οὐκ ἀπιστηθήσῃ. The mod. t. prefixes Μᾶλλον δὲ, and adds, ἀλλά τι ; Ἀναστὰς πορεύθητι. " Nay, even seeing him afraid, even then He said not, Thou shalt not be disbelieved: (Erasm. negligently, Be not unbelieving:) but what? Arise," etc. So Morel. Sav. but Ben. puts a full stop at ἰδών: as if the meaning were, " because He would teach us," etc.: or rather, because He also saw him to be afraid. Nor did He speak thus. Thou shalt not," etc. But the full stop should be placed at εἶπεν: " nay, though he saw him afraid, He did not tell him what had happened to Paul—the victory He had won over this adversary. But only, Fear not to be disbelieved for he hath seen," etc.

[3] ἵνα ὥσπερ ἐξέπληττεν τούτῳ, οὕτω κἀκεῖνο. (Sav. marg. τοῦτο, κἀκεῖνο.) " That as He (Christ) astonished (Ananias) by the one, so He may by the other." τούτῳ, by the announcement of Saul as a believer; ἐκείνῳ, by that of his becoming a preacher, and before Gentiles and kings. (Chrys. is negligent in his use of the pronouns οὗτος and ἐκεῖνος.) Or it may be, " that as he (Saul) astonished (men) by his conversion, so by his wonderful boldness as a preacher.—E. Edd. omit this, and substitute, " as to prevail over all nations and kings."

9

Saul"—he straightway addresses him as a friend by that name—"Jesus, Who appeared unto thee in the way in which thou camest"— and yet Christ had not told him this, but he learnt it from the Spirit—"hath sent me unto thee, that thou mayest receive thy sight, and be filled with the Holy Ghost." (v. 17.) As he said this, he laid his hands upon him. "And immediately there fell from his eyes as it had been scales." (v. 18.) Some say this was a sign of his blindness. Why did he not blind his eyes (entirely)? This was more wonderful, that, with his eyes open, he did not see: (v. 8) which was just his case in respect of the Law, until[1] the Name of Jesus was put on him. "And he received sight forthwith, and, arose, and was baptized. And having taken food, he recovered strength." (v. 19.) He was faint, therefore, both from his journey and from his fear; both from hunger, and from dejection of mind. Wishing therefore to deepen his dejection, He made the man blind until the coming of Ananias: and, that he might not imagine the blindness to be (only) fancy, this is the reason of the scales. He needed no other teaching: that which had befallen was made teaching (to him). "And he was with the disciples which were at Damascus certain days. And straightway in the synagogues he preached Jesus,[2] that He is the Son of God." (v. 20.) See, straightway he was a teacher in the synagogues. He was not a ashamed of the change, was not afraid while the very things in which he was glorious aforetime, the same he destroyed. Even[3] from his first appearance on the stage here was a man, death-dealing, ready for deeds of blood: seest thou what a manifest sign (was here)? And with this very thing, he put all in fear: for, said they, Hither also is he come for this very thing. "But all that heard him were amazed, and said: Is not this he that destroyed them which called on this name in Jerusalem, and came hither for that intent, that he might bring them bound unto the chief priests? But Saul increased the more in strength, and

confounded the Jews which dwelt at Damascus, proving that this is very Christ." (v. 21, 22.) As one learned in the Law, he stopped their mouths, and suffered them not to speak. They thought they were rid of disputation in such matters, in getting rid of Stephen, and they found another, more vehement than Stephen.*

(Recapitulation.) But let us look at what relates to Ananias.[4] The Lord said not to him, Converse with him, and catechize him. For if, when He said, "He prayeth, and hath seen a man laying his hands upon him." (v. 11, 12.) He did not persuade him, much less had He said this. So that he shall not disbelieve thee, "he hath seen in a vision." Observe how in the former instance neither is Philip told all immediately. Fear not, He saith: "for this man is a chosen vessel for Me. (v. 15.) He more than sufficiently released him of his fear, if the case be so that this man shall be so zealous in our cause, as even to

---

* The narratives given by Paul himself of his conversion in Acts xxii. and xxvi. as well as allusion to the subjects in his epistles, present some harmonistic difficulties, which have, however, been greatly exaggerated by a criticism which is unfavorable to the historical character of the Acts. The constant factors in all the accounts are: the light from heaven, the voice of Jesus and Saul's answer, and the solemn charge commissioning Saul to bear the name of Christ to the Gentiles. In Acts xxvi. the interview with Ananias is omitted; in chap. xxii. it is narrated, but the occasion of Ananias' going to Saul is not given; in chap. ix. the Lord is represented as speaking to him and bidding him go, and it is affirmed that at the same time Saul has a vision of his coming. In xxii. the address of Ananias is considerably more extended than in ix. Some minor points of difference have been noted, as: in ix. 7 it is said that Saul's companions heard the voice but saw no one, while in xxii. 9, it is said that they saw the light but heard not the voice of Him who spoke. The discrepancy is resolved by many by translating ἤκουσαν (xxii. 9) "understood"—an admissable sense (so, Lechler, Hackett, Lange). It is certainly an unwarranted criticism which rejects the common matter of the various narratives upon the ground of such incidental variations in the traditions in which a great and mysterious experience has been preserved.—G. B. S.

[4] Σκεῦος δὲ καλεῖται δικαίως· δεικνύντος τοῦ λόγου ὅτι οὐκ ἔστι φυσικὴ ἡ κακία· σκεῦος, φησίν, ἐκλογῆς· τὸ δόκιμον γὰρ ἐκλεγόμεθα. A. B. C. N. i. e. "Justly is he called a σκεῦος, for he is well-fitted for the work of Christ by his energy and earnestness. These need but to be turned to the right objects. It is contrary to right reason to say, that evil is a physical quality or essence, and therefore unchangeable. (See this argued Hom. lix. in Matt. p. 596.) A fit implement, therefore, and of no common kind: a σκεῦος ἐκλογῆς, of all others to be chosen, because of its approved suitableness for the purpose." Thus St. Chrysostom constantly interprets this expression. Hom. xviii. in Rom. § 6 t. ix. 638. "When the stars were created, the Angels admired: but this man Christ Himself admired, saying, A chosen vessel is this man to Me!" Comm. in c. l. Gal. § 9, t. x. 674 "Called me by His grace. Yet God saith, that He called Him, because of his virtue, (διὰ τὴν ἀρετήν,) saying, A chosen vessel, etc.: i. e. fit to do service, and do a great work . . But Paul himself everywhere ascribes it all to grace." Hom. iii. in 1 Tim. § 1, t. xi. 562. "God, foreknowing what he would be before he began to preach, saith, A chosen vessel, etc. For as they who in war bear the royal standard, the labarum as we call it, have need of much skill and bravery not to deliver it into the enemy's hands, so they that bear the name of Christ," etc. And de Compunct. ad Demetr. lib. i. § 9, t. i 138. "Since grace will have our part, (τὰ παρ' ἡμῶν ζητεῖ,) therefore some it follows and abides with, from some it departs, and to the rest it never even reaches. And to show that God first examined well the bent of the will (προαίρεσις,) and thereupon gave the grace before this blessed man had done aught wonderful, hear what the Lord saith of him: A chosen vessel," etc.—The modern text: "And having said Σκεῦος, so as to show that the evil in him (ἡ κακία αὐτοῦ) is not physical, He adds, ἐκλογῆς, to declare that he is also approved; for," etc.—Œcumen. δεικνύσιν ὅτι οὐκ ἔστι φυσικὴ ἡ κακία αὐτῷ, "The Lord shows that vice is not natural to him."

---

[1] "But when was the name of Jesus put upon Paul, that he should recover his sight? Here is either something wrong in the text, or we must say that Ananias put the name of Jesus on Paul, when, having laid his hands on him, he told him that it was Jesus from whom he should receive his sight." Ben.,— who surely must have overlooked the clause ὅπερ ἔπαθεν ἐπὶ τοῦ νόμου, to which these words belong.—Above, Τινές φασι τῆς πηρώσεως εἶναι τοῦτο σημεῖον, the meaning is, that this falling off the scales, etc., is an emblem of his mental blindness, and of his recovery therefrom, The innovator, not understanding this, alters it to, ταύτας τινές φασι τῆς π. αὐτοῦ εἶναι αἰτίας. "Some say that these were the cause of his blindness:" which is accepted by Edd.—And below, "lest any should imagine," etc., where τις, E. bracketted by Sav., adopted by the other Edd. is due to the same hand.

[2] For Ἰησοῦν (the reading accredited by the leading authorities in v. 20) here and in the second exposition, E. alone has Χριστὸν (with text recept.) adopted by Edd.

[3] Καὶ εὐθέως ἐκ προοιμίων, θανατῶν ὁ ἄνθρωπος ἦν viz. ch. vii. 58. C. has θανάτων, for which A. conjecturally substitutes θαυμαστός.

suffer many things. And justly he is called "a vessel" (or, instrument)—for reason shows that evil is not a physical quality : "a vessel of election" (or, chosen instrument), He saith ; for we choose that which is approved. And let not any imagine, that (Ananias) speaks in unbelief of what was told him, as imagining that Christ was deceived : far from it ! but affrighted and trembling, he did not even attend to what was said, at hearing the name of Paul. Moreover, the Lord does not tell that He has blinded him : at the mention of his name fear had prepossessed his soul : "see," he says, "to whom Thou art betraying me: 'and hither for this very purpose is he come, to bind all that call upon Thy Name.' I fear, lest he take me to Jerusalem : why dost Thou cast me into the mouth of the lion ? " He is terrified, even while he speaks these words ; that from every quarter we may learn the energetic character (ἀρετήν) of the man. For that these things should be spoken by Jews, were nothing wonderful : but that these (the believers) are so terrified, it is a most mighty proof of the power of God. Both the fear is shown, and the obedience greater after the fear. For there was indeed need of strength. Since He says, "a vessel of election," that thou mayest not imagine that God is to do all, He adds, "to bear My Name before Gentiles and kings, and the children of Israel. Ananias has heard what he most desired—that against the Jews also he will take his stand : this above all gave him courage. "For I," saith He, "will show him how great things he must suffer for My Name's sake." At the same time also this is said by way of putting Ananias to the blush : If he, that was so frantic, shall suffer all things, and thou not willing even to baptize him ! "It is well," saith he : "let him continue blind " (this[1] is why he says these words) : "he is blind : why dost Thou at all bid me open his eyes, that he may bind (men) again ? " Fear not the future : for that opening of his eyes he will use not against you, but for you (with reference to that saying, "That he may receive his sight" (v. 12), these words are spoken) : for not only will he do you no harm, but he "will suffer many things." And what is wonderful indeed is,

[2] that he shall first know "how great things he shall suffer," and then shall take the field against the perils.—"Brother Saul, the Lord Jesus "—he saith not, "Who made thee blind," but, "Who appeared with thee in the way, hath sent me unto thee that thou mayest receive thy sight " (v. 17) : observe this man also, how he utters nothing boastful, but just as Peter said in the case of the lame man, "Why look ye on us, as though by our own power or holiness we had made him to walk," (ch. iii. 12) so here also he saith, "Jesus, Who appeared unto thee.'' (b) Or, [3] (he saith it) that the other may believe : and he saith not, He that was crucified, the Son of God, He that doeth wonders : but what ? " He that appeared unto thee :" (speaking) from what the other knew : as Christ also added no more, neither said, I am Jesus, the Crucified, the Risen : but what ? " Whom thou persecutest." Ananias said not, "The persecuted," that he may not seem as it were to rave over him (ἐπενθουσίαν), to deride him, "Who appeared unto thee in the way :" and yet He did not (visibly) appear, but was seen by the things done. And immediately he added, wishing to draw a veil over the accusation : "That thou mayest receive thy sight." I came not to reprove the past, but to bestow the gift : "that thou mayest receive thy sight, and be filled with the Holy Ghost." (a) With hands laid on, he spake these words. " And immediately there fell from his eyes," etc. (v. 18) : a double blindness is removed.—And why saith it, "Having taken food, he was strengthened ? " (v. 19.) Because they that are in such case become relaxed : he had no heart to partake of food before, until he obtained the mighty gifts. (c) It seems to me, that both Paul and Cornelius, at the very instant when the words were spoken, received the Spirit. And yet (in this case) the giver was no great one. So true is it, that there was naught of man's in the things done, nor aught was done by man, but God was present, the Doer of these things. And at the same time (the Lord) both teaches him to think modestly of himself, in that He does not bring him to the Apostles who were so admired, and shows that there is nothing of man here. He was not filled, however, with the Spirit which works signs : that in this way also his faith might be shown ; for he

---

[1] διὰ τοῦτο ταῦτα λέγει· i. e. Ananias' objection, (v. 13) in fact comes to this : this was the feeling which prompted his words. The innovator substitutes, διὰ τοῦτο νῦν ἥμερος, ὅτι . . "therefore is he now gentle, because he is blind : " E. Edd.—The meaning is ; "In saying, 'I will show him how much he shall suffer,' etc. the Lord rebukes Ananias' reluctance to baptize him, and restore his sight : his answer, 'Lord, I have heard,' etc. was in fact as good as saying, Let him remain blind, it is better so." The parenthetic, πρὸς τὸ, Ἵνα ἀναβλέψῃ, ταῦτα εἴρηται, looks like a marginal note of one who did not perceive the connection.—E. makes it, "To that saying, 'That he may receive his sight,' let this be added."

[2] Καὶ τὸ δὴ θαυμαστὸν ὅτι πρότερον πείσεται, καὶ τότε. So all our Mss. (Cat. τὸ πρ.) We conjecture the true reading to be, ὅτι πρότερον εἴσεται· "he shall first know," viz. "how many things he must suffer," etc. v. 16.

[3] In the Mss. and Edd. the portions here marked b, a, c, occur in the order a, b, c. The clause ἢ ὥστε πιστεῦσαι ἐκεῖνον being thus thrown out of its connection, perplexed the scribes : Cat. omits ἢ, "until he obtained the mighty gifts, so that he (ἐκεῖνον, Ananias ?) believed." A. E. F. D. reject the clause altogether. N. ὥστε καὶ π. ἐ.

wrought no miracles. "And straightway," it says, "in the synagogues he preached Jesus" —(v. 20) not that He is risen—not this: no, nor that He liveth: but what? immediately he strictly expounded the doctrine— "that this is the Son of God. And all that heard him were amazed," etc. (v. 21.) They were reduced to utter incredulity. And yet they ought not to have wondered only, but to worship and reverence. "Is not this he," etc. He had not merely been a persecutor, but "destroyed them which called on this Name" —they did not say, "on Jesus;" for hatred, they could not bear even to hear His name— and what is more marvellous still, "and came hither for this purpose," etc. "We cannot say, that he associated with the Apostles before." See by how many (witnesses) he is confessed to have been of the number of the enemies! But Paul not only was not confounded by these things, nor hid his face for shame, but "increased the more in strength, and confounded the Jews" (v. 22), i. e. put them to silence, left them nothing to say for themselves, "proving, that this is very Christ." "Teaching," it says: for this man was a teacher.

"And after that many days were fulfilled, the Jews took counsel to kill him."* (v. 23.) The Jews again resort to that valid argument (ισχυρὸν συλλογισμόν) of theirs, not now seeking false-accusers and false-witnesses; they cannot wait for these now: but what do they? They set about it by themselves. For as they see the affair on the increase, they do not even use the form of a trial. "But their laying await was known of Saul. And they watched the gates day and night to kill him." (v. 24.) For this was more intolerable to them than the miracles which had taken place—than the five thousand, the three thousand, than everything, in short. And observe him, how he is delivered, not by (miraculous) grace, but by man's wisdom— not as the apostles were—(ἐκεῖνοι, ch. v. 19) that thou mayest learn the energetic (ἀρετὴν) character of the man, how he shines even without miracles. "Then the disciples took him by night," that the affair might not be suspected, "and let him down by the wall in

a basket." † (v. 25.) What then? having escaped such a danger, does he flee? By no means, but goes where he kindled them to greater rage.

(Recapitulation, v. 20, 21.) "And straightway in the synagogues he preached Jesus" —for he was accurate in the faith—"that this is the Son of God. But all that heard him were amazed," etc., for indeed it was incredible. "But Saul increased," etc. Therefore " after many days" this happens: viz. the Jews "took counsel to kill him. And their laying await was known of Saul." (v. 22–24.) What does this mean? It is likely that for awhile he did not choose to depart thence, though many, perhaps, besought him; but when he learnt it, then he permitted his disciples: for he had disciples immediately. "Then the disciples," etc. (v. 25.) Of this occurrence he says: "The ethnarch of Aretas the king kept the city of the Damascenes with a garrison, desiring to apprehend me." (2. Cor. xi. 32.) But observe the Writer here,[1] that he does not tell the story ambitiously, and so as to show what an important person Paul was, saying, "For they stirred up the king," and so forth: but only, "Then the disciples took him by night, and let him down by the wall—in a basket:" for they sent him out alone, and none with him. And it was well they did this: the consequence being, that he showed himself to the Apostles in Jerusalem. Now they sent him out, as bound to provide for his safety by flight: but he did just the contrary—he leaped into the midst of those who were mad against him. This it is to be on fire, this to be fervent indeed! From that day forth he knew all the commands which the Apostles had heard: "Except a man take up his cross, and follow Me." (Matt. x. 38.) The very fact that he had been slower to come than the rest made him more zealous: for "to whom much is forgiven" (Luke vii. 47) the same will love more, so that the later he came, the more he

---

* It is noticeable that in chap. xxii. 17, Paul is reported as connecting his going to Jerusalem directly with the narrative of his conversion, while in Gal. i. 16, 17 he states that it was not until three years after his conversion that he went up to Jerusalem. The various notices can only be matched together on the view that the coming to Jerusalem mentioned in ix. 26 was the same as that of Gal. i. 18, and that this occurred about three years after his conversion. The ἡμέραι ἱκαναί of v. 23 must therefore include the time spent in Arabia (Gal. i. 17), after which Paul must have returned to Damascus, before going up to Jerusalem. In this way the narratives can be harmonized without admitting a contradiction (as Baur, Zeller, De Wette); it is probable, however, that Luke did not know of the visit to Arabia, but connected Paul's going to Jerusalem closely with his conversion.—G. B. S.

† The best textual authorities (A. B. C. ℵ,) and critics (Tisch. W. and H., Lechler, Meyer, Gloag) here read: "his (Saul's) disciples," So R. V. . . . The reference is to the band of converts whom he had been successful in winning at Damascus. In Paul's own narrative of his escape from Damascus (2 Cor. xi. 33) he states more specifically that he was let down "through a window, through the wall." This may have been either through the window of a house overhanging the wall, or through a window in the face of some portion of the wall (Cf. Josh. ii. 15; 1 Sam. xix. 12).—G. B. S.

[1] τοῦτον: Edd. τὸν εὐαγγελιστὴν: and below from E. alone, "ἀλλὰ μόνον ὅτι ἐπήγειραν τὸν βασιλέα, not speaking ambitiously, and making Paul illustrious, but only (saying) that they stirred up the king." But he does not say it, and his not saying it is the very thing which Chrys. commends: ἀλλ' ὅρα τοῦτον οὐ φιλοτίμως λέγοντα, οὐδὲ λαμπρὸν δεικνύντα τὸν Π., "Ἐπήγειρα γάρ," φησιν, "τὸν βασιλέα." The φησὶν here is put hypothetically, "as if he had said," or "when he might have said." The sentence, however, requires something to complete it, such as we have added in the translation.

loved : * * *[1] and having done ten thousand wrongs, he thought he could never do enough to cast the former deeds into the shade. "Proving" (v. 22), it says : i. e. with mildness teaching. And observe, they did not say to him, Thou art he that destroyed : why art thou changed ? for they were ashamed : but they said it to themselves. For he would have said to them, This very thing ought to teach you, as in fact he does thus plead in his speech before Agrippa. Let us imitate this, man : let us bear our souls in our hands ready to confront all dangers.—(That he fled from Damascus) this was no cowardice :[2] he preserved himself for the preaching. Had he been a coward, he would not have gone to Jerusalem, would not immediately have commenced teaching : he would have abated somewhat of his vehemence : for he had been taught by the fate of Stephen. He was no coward, but he was also prudent (οἰκονομικός) (in husbanding himself). Wherefore he thought it no great thing to die for the Gospel's sake, unless he should do this to great advantage : willing not even to see Christ, Whom most of all he longed to see, while the work of his stewardship among men was not yet complete. (Phil. i. 23, 24). Such ought to be the soul of a Christian. From[3] his first appearance from the very outset, the character of Paul declared itself : nay even before this, even in the things which he did "not according to knowledge" (Rom. x. 2), it was not by man's reasoning that he was moved to act as he did.[4] For if, so long afterwards, he was content not to depart, much more at the beginning of his trading voyage, when he had but just left the harbor ! Many things Christ leaves to be done by (ordinary) human wisdom, that we may learn that (his disciples) were men, that it was not all everywhere to be done by grace : for otherwise they would have been mere motionless logs : but in many things they managed matters themselves.— This is not less than martyrdom,—to shrink from no suffering for the sake of the salvation of the many. Nothing so delights God. Again will I repeat what I have often said : and I repeat it, because I do exceedingly

desire it : as Christ also did the same, when discoursing concerning forgiveness : "When ye pray, forgive if ye have aught against any man :" (Mark xi. 25.) and again to Peter He said, "I say not unto thee, Forgive until seven times, but until seventy-times seven." (Matt. xviii. 22.) And Himself in fact forgives the transgressions against Him. So do we also, because we know that this is the very goal of Christianity, continually discourse thereof. Nothing is more frigid than a Christian, who cares not for the salvation of others. Thou canst not here plead poverty : for she that cast down the two mites, shall be thine accuser. (Luke xxi. 1.) And Peter said, "Silver and gold have I none." (Acts iii. 6.) And Paul was so poor, that he was often hungered, and wanted necessary food. Thou canst not plead lowness of birth : for they too were ignoble men, and of ignoble parents. Thou canst not allege want of education : for they too were "unlearned men." (Acts iv. 13.) Even if thou be a slave therefore and a runaway slave, thou canst perform thy part : for such was Onesimus : yet see to what Paul calls him, and to how great honor he advances him : "that he may communicate with me," he says, "in my bonds." (Philem. v. 13.) Thou canst not plead infirmity : for such was Timothy, having often infirmities ; for, says the apostle, "Use a little wine for thy stomach's sake, and thine often infirmities." (1 Tim. v. 23.) Every one can profit his neighbor, if he will fulfil his part. See ye not the unfruitful trees, how strong they are, how fair, how large also, and smooth, and of great height ? But if we had a garden ; we should much rather have pomegranates, or fruitful olive trees : for the others are for delight to the eye, not for profit, which in them is but small. Such are those men who only consider their own interest : nay, not such even since these persons are fit only for burning : whereas those trees are useful both for building and for the safety of those within. Such too were those Virgins, chaste indeed, and decent, and modest, but profitable to none (Matt. xxv. : 1) wherefore they are burned. Such are they who have not nourished Christ. For observe that none of those are charged with particular sins of their own, with fornication, for instance, or with perjury ; in short, with no sin but the having been of no use to another. Such was he who buried his talent, showing indeed a blameless life, but not being useful to another. (ib. 25.) How can such an one be a Christian ? Say, if the leaven being mixed up with the flour did not change the whole into its own nature, would

---

[1] 'Αλλ' ἔνεδρα (N. ἔνεδρα) ἐποίει τὸν πρῶτον χρόνον, καὶ μυρία ἠδικηκὼς, οὐδὲν ἡγεῖτο ἱκανὸν, κ. τ. λ. So all our Mss. except E. If ἔνεδρα be not corrupt, it seems to be used in a sense unknown to the Lexicons.—Edd. from E. "Therefore it is that he so pillories (στηλιτεύων) his former life, and brands (στίζων) himself repeatedly, and thinks nothing enough," etc.
[2] *Hom.* xxv. *in 2 Cor.* p. 615. *Hom. v. de Laud. S. Pauli,* t. ii. 501.
[3] *Hom.* xxvi. *in 2 Cor.* p. 617, B.
[4] Μᾶλλον δὲ καὶ πρὸ τούτου, καὶ ἐν οἷς οὐ κατὰ γνῶσιν ἐποίει, οὐκ (B. οὐδὲ, A. om. ἀνθρωπίνῳ κινούμενος λογισμῷ διεπράττετο. i. e. "Even as a persecutor, he was not swayed by common worldly considerations." The mod. t. (Edd.) perverts the Author's meaning : " —— nay even before this. For in the things, etc. he was moved by man's reasoning to act as he did."

such a thing be leaven? Again, if a perfume shed no sweet odor on those who approach it, could we call it a perfume? Say not, " It is impossible for me to induce others (to become Christians)"—for if thou art a Christian, it is impossible but that it should be so. For as the natural properties of things cannot be gainsaid, so it is here: the thing is part of the very nature of the Christian. Do not insult God. To say, that the sun cannot shine, would be to insult Him: to say that a Christian cannot do good, is to insult God, and call Him a liar. For it is easier for the sun not to give heat, nor to shine, than for the Christian not to send forth light: it is easier for the light to be darkness, than for this to be so. Tell me not that it is impossible: the contrary is the impossible. Do not insult God. If we once get our own affairs in a right state, the other will certainly follow as a natural and necessary consequence. It is not possible for the light of a Christian to be hid; not possible for a lamp so conspicuous

as that to be concealed. Let us not be careless. For, as the profit from virtue reaches both to ourselves, and to those who are benefited by it: so from vice there is a twofold loss, reaching both to ourselves, and to those who are injured by it. Let there be (if you will) some private man, who has suffered numberless ills from some one, and let no one take his part, yet let that man still return good offices; what teaching so mighty as this? What words, or what exhortations could equal it? What wrath were it not enough to extinguish and soften? Knowing therefore these things, let us hold fast to virtue, as knowing that it is not possible to be saved otherwise, than by passing through this present life in doing these good works, that we may also obtain the good things which are to come, through the grace and mercy of our Lord Jesus Christ, with Whom to the Father together with the Holy Spirit be glory, might, honor, now and ever, world without end. Amen.

HOMILY XXI.

ACTS IX. 26, 27.

" And when Saul was come to Jerusalem, he assayed to join himself to the disciples: but they were all afraid of him, and believed not that he was a disciple. But Barnabas took him, and brought him to the Apostles, and declared unto them how he had seen the Lord in the way."

ONE may well be much at a loss here to understand how it is that, whereas in the Epistle to the Galatians Paul says, " I went not to Jerusalem," but " into Arabia" and " to Damascus," and, " After three years I went up to Jerusalem," and " to see Peter" (Gal. i. 17), (ἱστορῆσαι Cat.) here the writer says the contrary. (There, Paul says,) " And none of the Apostles saw I; but here, it is said (Barnabas), brought him to the Apostles."—Well, then, either (Paul) means, " I went not up with intent to refer or attach myself to them (ἀναθέσθαι)—for what saith he? " I referred not myself, neither went I to Jerusalem to those who were Apostles before me : "[1] or else, that the laying

await for him in Damascus was after his return from Arabia;[2] or else, again, that the visit to Jerusalem was after he came from Arabia. Certainly of his own accord he went not to the Apostles, but " assayed to join himself unto the disciples "—as being[3] a teacher, not a disciple—" I went not," he says, " for this purpose, that I should go to those who were Apostles before me : certainly, I learnt nothing from them." Or,[4] he does not speak

---

[1] St. Chrysostom's exposition cannot be correctly reported here. Perhaps what he did say, was in substance as follows: " but I went into Arabia, and returned again unto Damascus: whence we learn, that the plot against him at Damascus was after his return from Arabia, and then the visit (to Jerusalem), after the escape from Damascus. Certainly of his own accord he went not to the Apostles," etc.—(So far, the first hypothesis, viz. that the visit, Acts ix. and the visit in Gal. are one and the same. Then) " or else, Paul does not mean *this* visit (viz. after the flight from Damascus), but passes it by, so that the order

(in his narration) is as follows: I went to Arabia, then to Damascus, then viz., at some time during the residence in Damascus, to Jerusalem (to see Peter), then to Syria, i. e. back to Damascus: whereas, had he related matters fully, it should have been, that he went into Arabia, thence to Damascus, then to Jerusalem to see Peter, thence to Damascus again, then again to Jerusalem after the escape from D., thence to Cæsarea."
[2] For ἢ εἰ μὴ τοῦτο, E. gives (as emendation) εἶτα πάλιν, and ἐκεῖθεν for ἀπὸ Ἀραβίας, but retains the ἢ εἰ μὴ τοῦτο of the preceding clause, which equally needs correction.
[3] E. F. D. Edd. " As *not* being a teacher, but a disciple:" the reading of A. B. C. N. is attested by Cat. Œc. but below it is said that he joined himself to the disciples, ἅτε μαθητὴν ὄντα, *Infra*, note [1], p. 135.
[4] Here should begin the alternative to the former hypothesis (beginning ἢ τοίνυν τοῦτο φησίν) perhaps, with ἤ, εἰ μὴ τοῦτο. Cat. has ἀπῆλθον. ἦλθον, which we adopt, as the mention of *Syria* shows that the narrative in Gal. i. 17-21, is referred to; the subject therefore of λέγει, ἀφίησιν is Paul, and ταύτην means the visit in Acts ix. The next sentence, for ἢ εἰ μὴ τοῦτο πάλιν κ. τ. λ. requires to be remodelled as above, e. g. δέον λέγειν ὅτι ἐξ Ἀραβίας εἰς Δαμ. ὑποστρέψας, ἀνῆλθεν εἰς Ἱεροσόλυμα, εἶτα εἰς Δαμ. ἀπῆλθε πάλιν, εἶτα πάλιν εἰς Ἱεροσ., εἶτα ἐξεπέμφθη εἰς Καισαρείαν. The reporter, or redactor, seems to have intended a recital of St. Paul's movements before as well as after his conversion: viz. (from Tarsus) he went up to

of this visit, but passes it by, so that the order is, "I went into Arabia, then I came to Damascus, then to Jerusalem, then to Syria:" or else, again, that he went up to Jerusalem, then was sent to Damascus, then to Arabia, then again to Damascus, then to Cæsarea. Also, the visit "after fourteen years," probably, was when he brought up the [alms to the] brethren together with Barnabas : (Gal. ii. 1) or else he means a different occasion. (Acts xi. 30.) For the Historian for conciseness, often omits incidents, and condenses the times. Observe how unambitious the writer is, and how he does not even relate (related in c. xxii. 17-21) that vision, but passes it by. "He assayed," it says, "to join himself to the disciples. And they were afraid of him." By this again is shown the ardor of Paul's character : not (only) from the mouth of Ananias, and of those who wondered at him there, but also of those in Jerusalem : "they believed not that he was a disciple :" for truly that was beyond all human expectation.† He¹ was no longer a wild beast, but a man mild and gentle! And observe how he does

not go to the Apostles, such is his forbearance, but to the disciples, as being a disciple. He was not thought worthy of credit. "But Barnabas"—"Son of Consolation" is his appellation, whence also he makes himself easy of access to the man : for " he was a kind man" (ch. xi. 24), exceedingly, and this is proved both by the present instance, and in the affair of John (Mark)—"having taken him, brought him to the Apostles, and related to them how he had seen the Lord in the way."² (xv. 39.) It is likely that at Damascus also he had heard all about him : whence *he* was not afraid but the others were, for he was a man whose glance inspired fear. "How," it says, "he had seen the Lord in the way, and that He had spoken unto him, and how in Damascus he had spoken boldly in the name of the Lord. And he was with them coming in and going out at Jerusalem, and speaking boldly in the name of Jesus" (v. 28) : these things were demonstrative of the former, and by his acts he made good what was spoken of him. "And he spake, and disputed with the Hellenists." (v. 29.) So then the disciples were afraid of him, and the Apostles did not trust him ; by this therefore he relieves them of their fear. "With the Hellenists :" he means those who used the Greek tongue : and this he did, very wisely ; for those others, those profound Hebrews had no mind even to see him. "But they," it says, "went about to slay him :" a token, this, of his energy, and triumphant victory, and of their exceeding annoyance at what had happened. Thereupon, fearing lest the issue should be the same as in the case of Stephen, they sent him to Cæsarea. For it says, "When the brethren were aware of this, they brought him down to Cæsarea, and sent him forth to Tarsus" (v. 30), at the same time to preach, and likely to be more in safety, as being in his own country. But observe, I pray you, how far it is from being the

---

Jerusalem, then was sent (by the high-priest) to Damascus: then (after his conversion) went into Arabia (the mod. substitutes, Syria): then returned to Damascus: then (omitting all the rest) to Cæsarea.—In the *Comment. on Gal.* i. t. x. 675, D. Chrys. expounds thus: "Whereas he says, 'I went not up,' this also may be said, that he went not up at the outset of his preaching, and, when he did, it was not for the purpose of learning.

* Chrys. here confuses the visits of Paul to Jerusalem. That mentioned in Acts xi. 30, was the second visit, when he went to carry the gift of alms to the poor. The visit mentioned in Gal. ii. 1, synchronizes with Acts xv. 1, sq., when Paul went to attend the Apostolic council.—G. B. S.

† The incredulity of the Christians at Jerusalem concerning the genuineness of Saul's conversion is difficult to understand, especially since they must have heard of the miraculous manner of it. It can, however, more readily be conceived of if, as we suppose, the three years absence from the city had intervened, and during this period, Saul had been unheard of. The impression might have gone abroad that he had fallen back into his old Jewish life. Certainly the persecution which the Christians at Jerusalem had suffered at his hands would incline them to be incredulous concerning his conversion, unless there were positive proof of it. When it is said (27) that Barnabas brought Paul " to the apostles" in Jerusalem, we must hold this statement subject to the modification made in Paul's own statement (Gal. i. 18) that during this visit he saw, of the apostles, only Peter and James, the Lord's brother. These may have been the only apostles then in the city, for Paul's stay was but for fifteen days. The purpose of this visit was to see Peter (Gal. i. 18).—G. B. S.

¹ A. B. C. ἐκεῖνο. Βαρνάβας δὲ ἄνθρωπος ἐπιεικὴς καὶ ἥμερος ἦν καὶ ὅρα κ. τ. λ. Cat. ἐκεῖ. Βαρνάβας ἄνθρωπος ἐπιεικὴς ἦν· καὶ ὅρα. The epithet ἥμερος, "tamed," was felt to be unsuitable to Barnabas, hence Cat. omits it, Œc. substitutes (from below) καὶ χρηστὸς σφόδρα. The mod. t. transposes the clause to the comment on v. 27. The fact seems to be, that Βαρνάβας δὲ is out of its place, and that ἄνθρ. ἐπ. καὶ ἥμ. is a description of Saul's present bearing contrasted with his former character: and that the sentence should begin with ἐκεῖνο, somewhat in this way: οὐ γὰρ ἦν ὄντως προσδοκίας ἀνθρωπίνης. Ἐκεῖνο e. g. τὸ θηρίον, that raging wild-beast, now was a man, mild and gentle.—Below, all the Mss. have ἅτε μαθητὴν ὄντα, which is not easily reconciled with the former passage (note c). There it is represented, that he assayed to join himself to the disciples as being a teacher, and not a disciple; here, that he did this as being a disciple, and διὰ τὸ μετριάζειν. Œc. combines this with the former statement : "he went not to the Apostles, but assayed," etc., μετριάζων, ἅτε διδ. ὢν, καὶ οὐ μαθ., where Henten. renders, *modeste de se sentiens* "*quum tamen*" *præceptor esset et non discipulus*: rather, forbearing to put himself forward as he might have done, seeing he was himself a teacher, etc. The Catena has the διὰ τὸ μετριάζειν after ἀπιόντα, and again after ὄντα. Hence the true reading may be, καὶ ὅρα αὐτὸν οὐ πρὸς τ. ἀπ. ἀπιόντα, ἀλλὰ πρὸς τοὺς μαθητάς· οὐχ ἅτε μαθητὴν ὄντα, ἀλλὰ διὰ τὸ μετριάζειν.

² 'A. B. C. (and Cat.) give the text, "But Barnabas—in the way," continuously, and then the comments all strung together. Also the clause "it is likely—about him " is placed last, after γοργὸς ἦν ὁ ἀνήρ. This expression (Cat. adds γὰρ) may denote either the quick, keen glance of Paul's eye, or the terror with which he was regarded—"to them the man had a terrible look with him."—The modern text: "'But Barnabas—in the way.' This Barnabas was a mild and gentle sort of man. 'Son of Consolation' is the meaning of his name: whence also he became a friend to Paul. And that he was exceedingly kind and accessible, is proved both from the matter in hand, and from the affair of John. Whence *he* is not afraid, but relates 'how he had seen,' etc.—' in the name of the Lord Jesus.' For it is likely, etc. Wherefore also ταῦτα ἐκείνων κατασκευαστικὰ ποιῶν, διὰ τῶν ἔργων ἐβεβαίωσε τὰ λεχθέντα." In the original text it is simply Ταῦτα ἐκείνων κατασκευαστικά, καὶ διὰ τῶν ἔργων ἐβεβαίωσε τὰ λεχθέντα, which being put before v. 28, would mean, that the conduct of Paul "in Damascus," the πῶς ἐπαρρησ., evidenced the truth of what he said, about the Lord's appearing to him in the way. Hence in the mod. text: "wherefore Barnabas making the latter prove the former, confirmed by (Paul's) deeds the things told of him." (But Ben., *Ideo hæc ad illa præparant, dum ille operibus dicta confirmat. Erasm., Ideo et hæc præparatoria facit operibus confirmans ea quæ dicta erant.*) We have transposed the clause, as comment on v. 28.

case that everything is done by (miraculous) grace; how, on the contrary, God does in many things leave them to manage for themselves by their own wisdom and in a human way; so [1] to cut off the excuse of idle people: for if it was so in the case of Paul, much more in theirs.[*] "Then, it says, "the Church throughout all Judea and Galilee and Samaria had peace (they), being edified, and walking in the fear of the Lord, and abounded in the comfort of the Holy Ghost."[2] (v. 31.) He is about to relate that Peter goes down (from Jerusalem), therefore that you may not impute this to fear, he first says this. For while there was persecution, he was in Jerusalem, but when the affairs of the Church are everywhere in security, then it is that he leaves Jerusalem. See how fervent and energetic he is! For he did not think, because there was peace, therefore there was no need of his presence. Paul [3] departed, and there was peace: there is no war nor disturbance. Them, they respected most, as having often stood by them, and as being held in admiration by the multitude: but him, they despised, and were more savage against him. See, how great a war, and immediately, peace! See what that war effected. It dispersed the peace-makers. In Samaria, Simon was put to shame: in Judea, the affair of Sapphira took place. Not that, because there was peace, therefore matters became relaxed, but such was the peace as also to need exhortation. "And it came to pass, as Peter passed throughout all quarters, he came down also to the saints which dwelt at Lydda."

(v. 32.) Like the commander of an army, he went about, inspecting the ranks, what part was compact, what in good order, what needed his presence. See how on all occasions he goes about, foremost. When an Apostle was to be chosen, he was the foremost: when the Jews were to be told, that these were "not drunken," when the lame man was to be healed, when harangues to be made, he is before the rest: when the rulers were to be spoken to, he was the man; when Ananias, he (ch. i. 15; ii. 15; iii. 4–12; iv. 8; v. 3–15.): when healings were wrought by the shadow, still it was he. And look: where there was danger, he was the man, and where good [4] management (was needed); but where all is calm, there they act all in common, and he demands no greater honor (than the others). When need was to work miracles, he starts forward, and here again he is the man to labor and toil. "And there he found a certain man named Æneas, which had kept his bed eight years, and was sick of the palsy. And Peter said unto him, Æneas, Jesus Christ maketh thee whole: arise, and make thy bed. And he arose immediately." (v. 33–34.) And why did he not wait for the man's faith, and ask if he wished to be healed? In the first place, the miracle served for exhortation to many: hear then how great the gain. "And all that dwelt at Lydda and Saron saw him, and turned to the Lord." (v. 35.) For the man was notable. "Arise, and make thy bed:" he does well to give a proof of the miracle: for they not only released men of their diseases, but in giving the health they gave the strength also. Moreover, at that time they had given no proofs of their power, so that the man could not reasonably have been required to show his faith, as neither in the case of the lame man did they demand it. (ch. iii. 6.) As therefore Christ in the beginning of His miracles did not demand faith, so neither did these. For in Jerusalem indeed, as was but reasonable, the faith of the parties was first shown; "they brought out their sick into the streets, but as Peter passed by, his shadow at least might fall upon some of them" (ch. v. 15); for many miracles had been wrought there; but here this is the first that occurs. For of the miracles, some were wrought for the purpose of drawing others (to faith); some for the comfort of them that believed. "Now there was at Joppa a certain disciple named Tabi-

---

[1] This and the next clause are transposed in the Mss. so that ἐπ’ αὐτῶν would mean "in the case of the brethren."

[*] The reason given in v. 30 for Paul's leaving Jerusalem is, that he was in danger of being slain by his opponents; that assigned by himself in xxii. 17, 18 is a revelation of the Lord given to him when in a trance in the temple, warning him that Jerusalem would not receive his message, and charging him to go unto the Gentiles. The two explanations have a common element in the opposition of the Jews and Hellenists at Jerusalem to Paul and their rejection of his message. "Paul, notwithstanding the opposition and machinations of the Jews, may have felt desirous to remain: he had a warm heart toward his brethren according to the flesh; he was eager for their conversion; and it required a revelation from Christ himself to cause him to comply with the importunity of his friends and to depart. Luke mentions the external reason; Paul the internal motive." (Gloag.)—G. B. S.

[2] A. B. C. of N. T. and vulg. Hieron. have the singular throughout; and so Cat. in l. Edd. from E. the plural throughout: our other Mss. οἰκοδομούμενοι and πορευόμενοι (F. D. περισσευόμενοι), "they being edified," etc., in apposition with Ἐκκλησία.

[3] i. e. "If Paul had remained there would not have been peace and quiet." It is doubtful, as the text stands, whether the subject to ἡδοῦντο is, the Jewish believers, or, the adversaries: and κατεφρόνουν, ἠγρίαινον seem inconsistent as predicated of the same persons. Perhaps what Chrys. said is not fully reported, and the text may be completed thus: (comp. p. 304,) "there is no war from without, nor disturbance within. For the Jewish believers respected the Apostles, as having often stood by them, and the unbelievers durst not attack them as being had in admiration by the people: but as for Paul, the one party—viz. the zealous Jewish believers, 'the profound Hebrews,' despised him, while the others—viz. the unbelievers were more savage against him." Edd. (from E. alone). "And why, you may ask, does he this, and 'passes through' when there is peace, and after Paul's departure, i. e. why does Peter delay his journey until Paul is gone, and all is quiet? Because them they most respected, as having," etc.

[4] Καὶ ἔνθα οἰκονομία· ἔνθα δὲ, κ. τ. λ. It does not appear what οἰκονομία can be intended, unless it be the order taken for the appointment of the deacons, but this was the act of all the Apostles, vi. 2. Hence perhaps the reading should be: ἔνθα δὲ οἰκονομία, καὶ ἔνθα. . . . "But where management (or regulation) only is concerned, and where all is peace," etc.

tha, which by interpretation is called Dorcas : this woman was full of good works and alms-deeds which she did. And it came to pass in those days, that she was sick, and died : whom when they had washed, they laid her in an upper chamber. And forasmuch as Lydda was nigh to Joppa, and the disciples had heard that Peter was there, they sent unto him two men, desiring him that he would not delay to come to them." (v. 36–38). Why did they wait till she was dead? Why was not Peter solicited (ἐσκύλη) before this? So right-minded (φιλοσοφοῦντες) were they, they did not think it proper to trouble (σκύλλειν) the Disciples about such matters, and to take them away from the preaching : as indeed this is why it mentions that the place was near, seeing[1] they asked this as a thing beside his mark, and not now in the regular course. " Not to delay to come unto them :" for she was a disciple. And Peter arose, and went with them. And when he was come, they led him into the upper chamber." (v. 39.) They do not beseech, but leave it to him to give her life (σωτηρίαν.) See[2] what a cheering inducement to alms is here ! "And all the widows," it says, "stood round him weeping, and showing the coats and garments which Dorcas had made while she was with them." Peter went into the apartment, as one who took it calmly, but see what an accession came of it! It is not without a meaning that the Writer has informed us of the woman's name, but to show that the name she bore (φερώνυμος ἦν) matched her character; as active and wakeful was she as an antelope. For in many instances there is a Providence in the giving of names, as we have often told you. " She was full," it says, " of good works : " not only of alms, but " of good works," first, and then of this good work in particular. " Which," it says, " Dorcas made while she was with them." Great humility ! Not as we do ; but they were all together in common, and in company with them she made these things and worked. " But Peter put them all forth, and kneeled down, and prayed ;

and turning him to the body said, Tabitha, arise. And she opened her eyes : and when she saw Peter, she sat up." (v. 40.) Why does he put them all out ? That he may not be confused nor disturbed by their weeping. "And having knelt down, he prayed." Observe the intentness of his prayer. " And[3] he gave her his hand." (v. 41.) So did Christ to· the daughter of Jairus : " And (says the Evangelist) having taken her by the hand." Mark severally, first the life, then the strength brought into her, the one by the word, the other by his hand—"And he gave her his hand, and lifted her up, and when he had called the saints and widows, presented her alive :" to some for comfort, because they received back their sister, and because they saw the miracle, and for kindly support (προστασίαν) to others. "And it was known throughout all Joppa ; and many believed in the Lord. And it came to pass, that he tarried many days in Joppa with one Simon a tanner." (v. 42–43.) Mark the unassuming conduct, mark the moderation of Peter, how he does not make his abode with this lady, or some other person of distinction, but with a tanner : by all his acts leading men to humility, neither suffering the mean to be ashamed, nor the great to be elated ! " Many days ; "[4] for they needed his instruction, who had believed through the miracles.—Let us look then again at what has been said.

" Assayed," it says, " to join himself to the disciples." (Recapitulation, v. 26.) He did not come up to them unabashed, but with a subdued manner. " Disciples "[5] they were all called at that time by reason of their great virtue, for there was the likeness of the disciples plainly to be seen. " But they were all afraid of him." See how they feared the dangers, how the alarm was yet at its height in them. " But Barnabas," etc. (v. 27.)—it seems to me that Barnabas was of old a friend of his—"and related," etc. : observe how Paul says nothing of all this himself : nor would he have brought it forward to the others, had he not been compelled to do so. "And he was with them, coming in and going out at Jerusalem, and speaking boldly in the name of the Lord Jesus." (v. 28, 29.) This gave them all confidence. " But they

---

[1] εἶπον (ἤπου, B.) ἐν τάξει παρέργου τοῦτο ἤτουν (ἦν, C.), προηγουμένως δὲ οὐκ ἔτι, μαθήτρια γὰρ ἦν. A. B. C. Cat. But Edd. ὥστε δεῖξαι ὅτι ἐν κ. τ. λ. and μαθήτρια γὰρ ἦν before προηγ. Œcum. ἐν τάξει γὰρ παρ. τοῦτο ἤτουν, μαθ. γὰρ ἦν, omitting προηγ. δὲ οὐκέτι.—" If the place had not been near, they would not have made the request : for it was asking him to put himself out of his way, to do this over and above, and not in the regular course."—This is a hint to the hearers that they should show the like forbearance and discretion, in not giving their Bishop unnecessary trouble.
[2] Ὁρᾷς ἐλεημοσύνης πόση γίνεται προτροπή. Edd. from E,, "Thus is here fulfilled the saying, 'Alms delivereth from death. And all the widows,' " etc. Below, for Εἰς τὴν οἰκίαν εἰσήει ὁ Πέτρος ὡς φιλοσοφῶν· ὁρα δὲ πόση ἡ ἐπίδοσις γέγονεν : the same have, " Where she was laid out dead, they take Peter, τάχα οἰόμενοι πρὸς φιλοσοφίαν αὐτῷ τι χαρίζεσθαι, perhaps thinking to give him a subject for elevated thought. Seest thou," etc.—The meaning seems to be, " Peter went to see the dead body, expecting no miracle, but only as one who could bear such sights, and would teach others to do so : but see what a mighty additional boon came of it ! "

[3] In the Mss. Καὶ κρατήσας, φησί, τῆς χειρός. Ὅρα (E. Edd. Ἐνταῦθα δείκνυσι) κατὰ μέρος κ. τ. λ. But the passage cited is from Luke viii. 52, καὶ κρατήσας τῆς χειρὸς αὐτῆς, ἐφώνησε κ. τ .λ. to which, and probably to the ἐκβαλὼν ἔξω πάντας there preceding, St. Chrys. here referred.
[4] Edd. from E. ὃς καὶ διὰ τοῦτο ἔκρινε διελθεῖν, ἐπείδη τῆς αὐτοῦ διδασκαλίας ἐδέοντο οἱ πιστεύσαντες. " Who also for this reason judged it right to make this circuit, because those who had believed needed his instruction."
[5] The modern text : " He calls by the name of 'disciples' even those who were not included in the company of the twelve (Apostles), because they were all called disciples," etc.

went about to slay him: which when the brethren knew," etc. (v. 30.) Do you observe how both there (at Damascus), and here, the rest take care for him, and provide for him the means of departure, and that we nowhere find him thus far receiving (direct supernatural) aid from God? So the energy of his character is betokened. "To Cæsarea, and sent him forth to Tarsus:" so that, I suppose, he did not continue his journey by land, but sailed the rest of it. And this (departure) is Providentially ordered, that he might preach there also: and so likewise were the plots against him ordered by God's Providence, and his coming to Jerusalem, that the story about him might no longer be disbelieved. For there he was "speaking boldly," it says, "in the name of the Lord Jesus; and he spake and disputed against the Hellenists; and again, "he was with them coming in and going out.—So[1] the Church throughout all Judea and Galilee and Samaria had peace" —i. e. it increased: and peace with itself, that peace which is peace indeed: for the war from without would have done them no harm —"they being edified, and walking in the fear of the Lord, and abounded in the consolation of the Holy Ghost." And the spirit consoled them both by the miracles and by the works, and independently of these in the person of each individual. "And it came to pass, etc. And Peter said unto him, Eneas," etc. (v. 32–34.)[2] But before discourse, before exhortations, he says to the lame man himself, "Jesus Christ maketh thee whole." This word he believed in any wise, and was made whole. Observe how unassuming he is: for he said not, "In the Name," but[3] rather as a sign he narrates the miracle itself, and speaks as its Evangelist. "And having seen him," it says, "all that dwelt in Lydda,

and Saron, turned unto the Lord.—Now there was at Joppa," etc. (v. 35, 36.) Observe everywhere the signs taking place. But let us so believe them, as if we were now beholding them. It is not simply said, that Tabitha died, but that she died, having been in a state of weakness. And (yet) they did not call Peter until she died; then "they sent and told him not to delay to come unto them." Observe, they send and call him by others. And he comes: he did not think it a piece of disrespect, to be summoned by two men: for, it says, "they sent two men unto him." —Affliction, my beloved, is a great thing, and rivets our souls together. Not a word of wailing there, nor of mourning. See[4] how thoroughly matters are cleansed! "Having washed her," it says, "they laid her in an upper chamber:" that is, they did all (that was right) for the dead body. Then Peter having come, "knelt down, and prayed; and turning him to the body, said, Tabitha, arise." (v. 40.) They did not perform all their miracles with the same ease. But this was profitable for them: for truly God took thought not only for the salvation of others, but for their own. He that healed so many by his very shadow, how is it that he now has to do so much first? There are cases also in which the faith of the applicants coöperated. This is the first dead person that he raises. Observe how he, as it were, awakes her out of sleep: first she opened her eyes: then upon seeing (Peter) she sat up: then from his hand she received strength. "And it was known throughout all Joppa, and many believed in the Lord." (v. 42.) Mark the gain, mark the fruit, that it was not for display. Indeed, this is why he puts them all out, imitating his Master in this also.

[5] For where tears are—or rather, where miracles are, there tears ought not to be; not where such a mystery is celebrating. Hear, I beseech you: although somewhat of the like kind does not take place now, yet in the case of our dead likewise, a great mystery is cele-

---

[1] Here the modern text has: "And the Churches had peace, being edified, and walking in the fear of the Lord:" i. e. they increased, and (had peace), peace as it is in itself, the true peace, εἰρήνην αὐτὴν δήπου πρὸς ἑαυτήν, τὴν ὄντως εἰρήνην." (The singular ἡ Ἐκκλ. being altered to the plural, the reference in πρὸς ἑαυτήν was not perceived.) "With good reason. For the war from without exceedingly afflicted them. 'And were filled with the consolation of the Holy Ghost.'" See p. 136, note [3].

[2] Something must be supplied: e. g. "He did not wait for Eneas to ask, or to show his faith," as above, p. 301.—Edd. from E. "'And it came to pass—maketh thee whole.' It is not the word of one making a display, but of confidence that the thing shall be. And it does very much seem to me, that the sick man believed this word, and was made whole. That Peter is unassuming, is clear from what follows. For he said not, In the Name of Jesus, but rather as a miracle he narrates it. 'And they that dwelt at Lydda saw, and turned unto the Lord.' It was not for nothing that I said, that the miracles were wrought in order to persuade and comfort. 'But in Joppa—and died.' Do you mark the miracles everywhere taking place? It is not merely said, etc. Wherefore also they do not call Peter until she was dead. 'And having heard, (that Peter was there) the disciples sent," etc.

[3] 'Αλλ' ὡς σημεῖον μᾶλλον αὐτὸ (αὐτὸς B.) διηγεῖται καὶ εὐαγγελίζεται: "he speaks not in the form of command or promise, but of narration: he relates it, Evangelist-like, as a fact."

[4] Ὅρα πῶς διακαθαίρεται τὰ πράγματα (omitted in E. D. F. Edd.): i. e. how the Gospel has purged away all excess of mourning, and all noisy demonstrations of grief. St. Chrys. frequently inveighs against the heathenish customs of mourning for the dead, which were still practised—such as the hiring of heathen mourning-women: Hom. in Matt. xxxi. p. 207. A. "I confess to you, I am ashamed when I see the troops of women tearing their hair, gashing their flesh, as they move through the market—and this under the very eyes of the heathen." Conc. in Laz. v. t. i. p. 765 D. where the Christian mode of interment is described; viz. the procession of clergy with psalms and hymns of praise, lighted tapers, etc. comp. Hom. iv. in Heb. (ii. 15.)

[5] Ἔνθα γὰρ δάκρυα, μᾶλλον δὲ ἔνθα θαύματα, οὐ δεῖ δάκρυα παρεῖναι· ἔνθα τοιοῦτον μυστήριον τελεῖται. It seems, he was going to say, "Where tears are, it is no fit time for miracles," but corrects himself, for put in that way the proposition was not true. The innovator weakly substitutes, "For where tears are, such a mystery ought not to be performed: or rather, where miracles are, there tears ought not to be."

brating. Say,[1] if as we sit together, the Emperor were to send and invite some one of us to the palace, would it be right, I ask, to weep and mourn? Angels are present, commissioned from heaven and come from thence, sent from the King Himself to call their fellow servant, and say, dost thou weep? Knowest thou not what a mystery it is that is taking place, how awful, how dread, and worthy indeed of hymns and lauds? Wouldest thou learn, that thou mayest know, that this is no time for tears? For it is a very great mystery of the Wisdom of God. As if leaving her dwelling, the soul goes forth, speeding on her way to her own Lord, and dost thou mourn? Why then, thou shouldst do this on the birth of a child: for this in fact is also a birth, and a better than that. For here she goes forth to a very different light, is loosed as from a prison-house, comes off as from a contest. "Yes," say you, "it is all very well to say this,[2] in the case of those of whose salvation we are assured." Then, what ails thee, O man, that even in the case of such, thou dost not take it in this way? Say, what canst thou have to condemn in the little child? Why dost thou mourn for it? What in the newly baptized? for he too is brought into the same condition: why dost thou mourn for him? For as the sun arises clear and bright, so the soul, leaving the body with a pure conscience, shines joyously. Not such the spectacle of Emperor as he comes in state to take possession of the city (ἐπιβαίνοντα πόλεως), not such the hush of awe, as when the soul having quitted the body is departing in company with Angels. Think what the soul must then be! in what amazement, what wonder, what delight! Why mournest thou? Answer me.—But it is only in the case of sinners thou doest this? Would that it were so, and I would not forbid your mournings, would that this were the object! This lamentation were Apostolic, this were after the pattern of the Lord; for even Jesus wept over Jerusalem. I would that your mournings were discriminated by this rule. But when thou speakest the words of one[3] that would call back (the

dead), and speakest of thy long intimacy and his beneficence, it is but for this thou mournest (not because he was a sinner), thou dost but pretend to say it. Mourn, bewail the sinner, and I too will give a loose to tears; I, more than thou, the greater the punishment to which he is liable as such: I too will lament, with such an object. But not thou alone must lament him that is such; the whole city must do the same, and all that meet you on the way, as men bewail them that are led to be put to death. For this is a death indeed, an evil death, the death of sinners. But (with you) all is clean reversed. Such lamentation marks a lofty mind, and conveys much instruction; the other marks a littleness of soul. If we all lamented with this sort of lamentation, we should amend the persons themselves while yet living. For as, if it rested with thee to apply medicines which would prevent that bodily death, thou wouldest use them, just so now, if *this* death were the death thou lamentest, thou wouldest prevent its taking place, both in thyself and in him. Whereas now our behavior is a perfect riddle; that having it in our power to hinder its coming, we let it take place, and mourn over it when it has come. Worthy indeed of lamentations are they (when we consider), what time as they shall stand before the judgment seat of Christ, what words they shall then hear, what they shall suffer! To no purpose have these men lived: nay, not to no purpose, but to evil purpose! Of them too it may be fitly said, " It were good for them had they never been born." (Mark xiv. 21.) For what profit is it, I ask, to have spent so much time to the hurt of his own person? Had it been spent only to no purpose, were not that, I ask you, punishment enough! If one who has been an hired servant twenty years were to find that he has had all his labor in vain, would he not weep and lament, and think himself the most miserable of men? Why, here is a man who has lost all the labor of a whole life: not one day has he lived for himself, but to luxury, to debauchery, to covetousness, to sin, to the devil. Then, say, shall we not bewail this man? shall we not try to snatch him from his perils? For it is, yes, it is possible, if we will, to mitigate his punishment, if we make continual prayers for him, if for him we give alms. However unworthy

---

[1] The rest of the Hom. is given in the *Florilegium* or *Eclogæ*, in t. xii. ecl. xlv.—the only instance in which these Homilies have been employed in that compilation. Its author wrote the old text: it does not appear that any of his various readings were derived from the modern text.

[2] ἐπὶ τῶν εὐδοκίμων: i. e. those who are certainly not reprobates (οὐκ ἀδοκίμων). In the next sentence, E. Edd. καὶ τί πρὸς σὲ, ἄνθρωπε; σὺ γὰρ οὐδὲ ἐπὶ τῶν εὐδοκ. τοῦτο ποιεῖς. Ben. *Et quid hoc ad te, o homo? tu enim erga probos hoc non agis.* *Erasm. tu enim neque apud probatissimos hoc agis.* The other Mss. and Ecl. τί οὖν . . . ὅτι.

[3] Ὅταν δὲ ἀνακαλούμενος ῥήματα λέγῃς καὶ συνήθειαν καὶ προστασίαν, so Mss. and Edd. but Ecl. ἀνακαλουμένου, which we adopt. To the same purport, but more fully, *Hom.* xii. in 1 Cor. p. 392. (and Ecl. xlv.) " If when some (friend) were taken into the palace and crowned, thou shouldest bewail and lament, I should not call thee the friend of him that is crowned,

but very much his hater and enemy. 'But now, say you, I do not bewail him, but myself.' But neither is this the part of a friend, that for thine own sake thou wouldest have him still in the contest, etc. 'But I know not where he is gone.' How knowest thou not, answer me? For whether he lived rightly or otherwise, it is plain where he will go. 'Why, this is the very reason why I do bewail—because he departed a sinner.' This is mere pretence. If this were the reason of thy lamenting him that is gone, thou oughtest while he was alive to have amended him, and formed his manners," etc.

he may be, God will yield to our importunity. For if [1] Paul showed mercy on one (who had no claims on his mercy), and for the sake of others spared one (whom he would not have spared), much more is it right for us to do this. By means of his substance, by means of thine own, by what means thou wilt, aid him: pour in oil, nay rather, water. Has he no alms-deeds of his own to exhibit? Let him have at least those of his kindred. Has he none done by himself? At least let him have those which are done for him, that his wife may with confidence beg him off in that day, having paid down the ransom for him. The more sins he has to answer for, the greater need has he of alms, not only for this reason, but because the alms has not the same virtue now, but far less: for it is not all one to have done it himself, and to have another do it for him; therefore, the virtue being less, let us by quantity make it the greatest. Let us not busy ourselves about monuments, not about memorials. This is the greatest memorial: set widows to stand around him. Tell them his name: bid them all make for him their prayers, their supplications: this will overcome God: though it have not been done by the man himself, yet because of him another is the author of the almsgiving. Even this pertains to the mercy of God: "widows standing around and weeping" know how to rescue, not indeed from the present death, but from that which is to come. Many have profited even by the alms done by others on their behalf: for even if they have not got perfect (deliverance), at least they have found some comfort thence. If it be not so, how are children saved? And yet there, the children themselves contribute nothing, but their parents do all: and often have women had

their children given them, though the children themselves contributed nothing. Many are the ways God gives us to be saved, only let us not be negligent.

How then if one be poor? say you. Again I say, the greatness of the alms is not estimated by the quantity given, but by the purpose. Only give not less than thine ability, and thou hast paid all. How then, say you, if he be desolate and a stranger, and have none to care for him? And why is it that he has none, I ask you? In this very thing thou sufferest thy desert, that thou hast none to be thus thy friend, thus virtuous. This is so ordered on purpose that, though we be not ourselves virtuous, we may study to have virtuous companions and friends—both wife, and son, and friend—as reaping some good even through them, a slight gain indeed, but yet a gain. If thou make it thy chief object not to marry a rich wife,[2] but to have a devout wife, and a religious daughter, thou shalt gain this consolation; if thou study to have thy son not rich but devout, thou shalt also gain this consolation. If thou make these thine objects then wilt thyself be such as they. This also is part of virtue, to choose such friends, and such a wife and children. Not in vain are the oblations made for the departed, not in vain the prayers, not in vain the almsdeeds: all those things hath the Spirit ordered, [3] wishing us to be benefited one by the other. See: he is benefited, thou art benefited: because of him, thou hast despised wealth, being set on to do some generous act: both thou art the means of salvation to him, and he to thee the occasion of thine almsgiving. Doubt not that he shall get some good thereby. It is not for nothing that the Deacon cries, "For them that are fallen asleep in Christ, and for them that make the memorials for them." It is not the Deacon that utters this voice, but the Holy Ghost: I speak of the Gift. What sayest thou? There is the Sacrifice in hand, and all things laid out duly ordered: Angels are there present, Archangels, the Son of God is there: all stand with such awe, and in the general silence those stand by, crying aloud:

---

[1] Εἰ γὰρ Παῦλος ἕτερον ἠλέησε, καὶ δι᾽ ἄλλους ἄλλων (Ecl. ἄλλον) ἐφείσατο, πολλῷ μᾶλλον ἡμᾶς τοῦτο δεῖ ποιεῖν. But E. Edd. Εἰ διὰ Παῦλον ἑτέρους διέσωσε, καὶ δι᾽ ἄλλους ἄλλων φείδεται, πῶς οὐχὶ καὶ δι᾽ ἡμᾶς τὸ αὐτὸ τοῦτο ἐργάσεται; "If (God) for Paul's sake saved others, and for some men's sake spares other men, how shall He not for our sakes do this same thing?" In Hom. xli. in 1 Cor. p. 393. B. Chrys. uses for illustration Job's sacrifice for his sons, and adds, "For God is wont to grant favors to others in behalf of others, ἑτέροις ὑπὲρ ἑτέρων χαρίζεσθαι. And this Paul showed, saying, Ἵνα ἐν πολλῷ προσώπῳ, κ. τ. λ. 2 Cor. i. 11." But here the reference seems to be to 2 Cor. ii. 10, "To whom ye forgive anything, I forgive also; for if I forgave anything, to whom I forgave it, 'for your sakes' forgave I it in the person of Christ."—St. Chrysostom constantly teaches, as here, that the souls of the departed are aided by the prayers, alms. and Eucharistic oblations of the living, Hom. xli. in 1 Cor. u. s. "Even if he did depart a sinner, . . . we ought to succor him, in such sort as may be (ὡς ἂν οἷόν τε ᾖ), not by tears, but by prayers and supplications, and alms and oblations. For not idly have these things been devised, nor to no purpose do we make mention of the departed in the Divine Mysteries, and for them draw near, beseeching the Lamb Which lieth there, Which taketh away the sins of the world, but in order that some consolation may thence come to them. Nor in vain does he that stands beside the altar, while the dread Mysteries are celebrating, cry out, "For all that sleep in Christ, and for them that make the memorials for them.'" See also Hom. iii. ad Phil. p. 217, 218. Comp. St. Cyrill. Hier. Catech. Mystag. v. § 9, St. Augustin, Serm. 172.

[2] εὐλαβῆ γυναῖκα καὶ θυγάτριον ἀγαγέσθαι σεμνόν. A. B. C. In the Edd. καὶ θυγ. σεμνόν, is transposed after μὴ πλουτοῦντα υἱὸν καταλιπεῖν ἀλλ᾽ εὐλαβῆ· and so in the Ecl. which however retains ἀγ, between θυγ. and σεμνόν. In the old text, wife and daughter are mentioned first, as the persons most apt to perform these offices of religion: in ἀγαγέσθαι there is a zeugma; "to take to wife, and to have wife and daughter, etc."

[3] Hom. iii. in Phil. ad fin. Οὐκ εἰκῇ ταῦτα ἐνομοθετήθη ὑπὸ τῶν ἀποστόλων κ. τ. λ. "Not idly were these things enacted by the Apostles, that in the dread mysteries there is mention made of the departed; they know that to them great is the gain which accrues, great the benefit. For when the whole congregation stands there, all lifting up their hands, the sacerdotal body (πλήρωμα ἱερατικὸν), and the dread sacrifice is laid out, how shall we fail to prevail with God, in supplicating for these?"

and thinkest thou that what is done, is done in vain? Then is not the rest also all in vain, both the oblations made for the Church, and those for the priests, and for the whole body? God forbid! but all is done with faith. What thinkest thou of the oblation made for the martyrs, of the calling made in that hour, martyrs though they be, yet even "for martyrs?"[1] It is a great honor to be named in the presence of the Lord, when that memorial is celebrating, the dread Sacrifice, the unutterable mysteries. For just as, so long as the Emperor is seated, is the time for the petitioner to effect what he wishes to effect, but when he is risen, say what he will, it is all in vain, so at that time, while the celebration of the mysteries is going on, it is for all men the greatest honor to be held worthy of mention. For look: then is declared the dread mystery, that God gave Himself for the world: along with that mystery he seasonably puts Him in mind of them that have sinned. For as when the celebration of Emperors' victories is in progress, then, as many as had their part in the victory receive their meed of praise, while at the same time as many as are in bonds are set at liberty in honor of the occasion; but when the occasion is past, he that did not obtain this favor then, no longer gets any: so is it here likewise: this is the time of celebration of a victory. For, saith it, "so often as ye eat this bread, ye do show forth the Lord's death." Then let us not approach indifferently, nor imagine that these things are done in any ordinary sort. But it is in another sense[2] that we make mention of martyrs, and this, for assurance that the Lord is not dead: and this, for a sign that death has received its death's blow, that death itself is dead. Knowing these things, let us devise what consolations we can for the departed, instead of tears, instead of laments, instead of tombs, our alms, our prayers, our oblations, that both they and we may attain unto the promised blessings, by the grace and loving-kindness of His only-begotten Son our Lord Jesus Christ, with Whom to the Father and the Holy Ghost together be glory, dominion, honor, now and ever, world without end. Amen.

HOMILY XXII.

ACTS X. 1-4.

"There was a certain man in Cæsarea called Cornelius, a centurion of the band called the Italian band, a devout man, and one that feared God with all his house, which gave much alms to the people, and prayed to God alway. He saw in a vision evidently about the ninth hour of the day an angel of God coming in to him, and saying unto him, Cornelius. And when he looked on him, he was afraid, and said, What is it, Lord? And he said unto him, Thy prayers and thine alms are come up for a memorial before God."

THIS man is not a Jew, nor of those under the Law, but he had already forestalled our manner of life.* Observe, thus far, two persons, both of high rank, receiving the faith, the eunuch at Gaza and this man; and the pains taken on behalf of these men. But do not imagine that this was because of their high rank: God forbid! it was because of their piety. For that the Scripture mentions their

---

[1] Τί οἴει τὸ ὑπὲρ μαρτύρων προσφέρεσθαι, τὸ κληθῆναι ἐν ἐκείνῃ τῇ ὥρᾳ κἂν μάρτυρες ὧσι, κἂν (καὶ A. ὑπὲρ μαρτύρων; There is no reason to suppose (as Neander, *Der Heilige Johannes Chrysostomus*, t. ii. p. 162) that the words κἂν μάρτυρες κ. τ. λ. are part of the Liturgy: the meaning is, Think what a great thing it is to be mentioned in that Prayer of Oblation; to be mentioned as the martyrs are mentioned, for of them also, martyrs though they be, the same form of expression is used, ὑπὲρ μαρτύρων.—In the Liturgy of St. Chrysostom the words are, Ἔτι προσφέρομεν σοι τὴν λογικὴν ταύτην λατρείαν ὑπὲρ τῶν ἐν πίστει ἀναπαυομένων προπατόρων, πατέρων, πατριαρχῶν, προφητῶν, ἀποστόλων, κηρύκων, εὐαγγελιστῶν, μαρτύρων κ. τ. λ. See St. Augustin, *Hom. on St John*, p. 842, note a.

* The conversion of Cornelius marks an important step in the progress of the gospel. Hitherto Christianity had been confined to Jews, Hellenists, and that mixed people—the Samaritans (unless, as is improbable, the Ethiopian chamberlain formed an exception). Now a beginning was made of receiving the Gentiles, and in connection with that apostle to whom Christ had committed a certain leadership and privilege of opening the doors to the Kingdom (ch. Acts xv. 7). The narrative is one of the important notices in the N. T. concerning the gradual realization of Christ's command to make disciples of all nations, and shows, so far as it relates to Peter, with how great difficulty the most enlightened of the early Christians conceived of Christianity becoming free from the forms of Judaism. Cornelius was doubtless a Roman who had become dissatisfied with the idolatrous religion of his people and who had been attracted by the influences of the Jewish religion to the worship of the true God. There is no evidence, however, that he was a proselyte to the Jewish religion. He could not have failed to hear of Jesus and his disciples. Probably Philip, the deacon, was at this time residing in Cæsarea and Peter had been preaching and working miracles in the neighboring towns. It is not unlikely that the vision which he had, appealed to thoughts and convictions concerning the gospel which had been growing stronger in his own mind. To the vision of Cornelius, that of Peter forms the complement. They symbolize the great facts that while God in his providence was preparing his apostles for the larger truth of Christianity for the world, he was also preparing the Gentile world for the reception of the gospel. It is noticeable that the three centurions who appear in the N. T. are favorably mentioned. (Matt. viii. 10: xxviii. 54, and this passage).—G. B. S.

[2] i. e. not to intercede on their behalf, but for commemoration of Christ's victory over death, achieved in Himself and in them. The Eucharist is, so to say, Christ's ἐπινίκια, in which the Martyrs are eulogized as sharers of His triumph (and this is our commemoration of truth), and the prisoners are set at liberty (and in this sense we name our dead).

dignified stations, is to show the greatness of their piety; since it is more wonderful when a person being in a position of wealth and power is such as these were. What makes the praise of the former is, his undertaking so long a journey, and this when there was no (festival) season to require it,[1] and his reading on his road, and while riding in his chariot, and his beseeching Philip, and numberless other points: and the great praise of the latter is, that he makes alms and prayers, and is a just man, holding such a command. The reason why the writer describes the man so fully, is, that none may say that the Scripture history relates falsehoods: "Cornelius," he says, "a centurion of the band called the Italian band." (v. 1.) A "band," σπεῖρα, is what we now call a "numerous."[2] "A devout man," he says, "and one that feared God with all his house" (v. 2): that you may not imagine that it is because of his high station that these things are done.—When Paul was to be brought over, there is no angel, but the Lord Himself: and He does not send him to some great one, but to a very ordinary person:[3] but here, on the contrary, He brings the chief Apostle (to these Gentiles), not sends them to him: herein condescending to their weakness, and knowing how such persons need to be treated. As indeed on many occasions we find Christ Himself hasting (to such), as being more infirm. Or (it may be) because (Cornelius) was not able himself to leave his home. But here again is a high commendation of alms, just as was there given by means of Tabitha. "A devout man," it says, "and one that feared God with all his house." Let us hear this, whoever of us neglect them of our own house, whereas this man was careful of his soldiers also. "And that gave alms," it says, "to all the people." Both his doctrines and his life were right. "He saw in a vision evidently, about the ninth hour of the day, an angel of God coming in to him, and saying unto him, Cornelius." (v. 3.) Why does he see the angel? This also was in order to the full assurance of Peter, or rather, not of him, but of the others, the weaker ones. "At the ninth hour," when he was released from his cares and was at quiet, when he was engaged in prayers and compunction. "And when he looked on him, he was afraid." (v. 4.) Observe how what the angel speaks he does not speak immediately, but first rouses and elevates his mind. At the sight, there was fear, but a fear in moderation, just so far as served to fix his attention. Then also the words relieved him of his fear. The fear roused him: the praise mitigated what was unpleasant in the fear. "Thy prayers," saith he, "and thine alms are come up for a memorial before God. And now send men to Joppa, and call for one Simon, whose surname is Peter. (v. 5.) Lest they should come to a different person, he designates the man not only by his surname, but by the place. "And the same," saith he, "is lodging with one Simon a tanner, who hath his house by the seaside." (v. 6.) Do you mark how the Apostles, for love of solitude and quiet, affected the retired quarters of the cities? "With one Simon a tanner:" how then if it chanced that there was another? Behold, there is another token, his dwelling by the seaside. All three tokens could not possibly coincide (elsewhere). He does not tell for what purpose, that he may not take off the intense desire, but he leaves him to an eager and longing expectation of what he shall hear. "And[4] when the Angel which spake unto Cornelius was departed, he called two of his household servants, and a devout soldier of them that waited on him continually; and when he had declared all these things unto them, he sent them to Joppa." (v. 7, 8.) Do you see, that it is not without a purpose that the writer says this? (it shows) that those also "who waited on him continually" were such as he. "And when he had declared the whole matter unto them:" observe the unassuming character of the man: for he does not say, Call Peter to me: but, in order also to induce him to come, he declared the whole matter:—this was so ordered by Providence;—for he did not choose to use the authority of his rank to fetch Peter to him; therefore "he declared the matter;" such was the moderation of the man: and yet no great notion was to be formed of one lodging with a tanner. "And

---

[1] καὶ τὸ, μηδὲ καιροῦ καλοῦντος. As above xix. p. 120, note [2], Chrys. remarks, that there was no festival which required the presence of the eunuch at Jerusalem. Probably he was led to this by the circumstance, that the incident of the eunuch occurs after the Martyrdom of St. Stephen and the Conversion of St. Paul, i.e. according to the Church Calendar, between the 26th of December and the 25th of January.

[2] "Σπεῖρα and cohors in Polyb. differ. The Greeks call the cohort λόχος, it contained about five hundred men. Polyb. vi. καὶ μὲν μέρος ἕκαστον ἐκάλεσε καὶ τάγμα καὶ σπεῖραν καὶ σημεῖον. Casaubon: Ac singulas partes appellant ordinem, manipulum, signum." Downe ap. Sav.

[3] ἀλλὰ πρὸς εὐτελῆ. The innovator (E. Edd.) having made Chrys. say above, Hom. xx. § 1, that Ananias was a man of note, here alters the text to: "But the Lord Himself appears: neither does He send him to some one of the Twelve, but to Ananias." Below καὶ οὐκ αὐτοὺς πέμπει πρὸς αὐτὸν: meaning, it seems, Cornelius and his house. The same hand substitutes (for explanation of the plural, αὐτῶν τῇ ἀσθενείᾳ), "as He did Philip to the eunuch, condescending to their infirmity." And in the following sentence; "Since Christ Himself is often seen going to them that are ill, and in their own persons unable to come to Him."

[4] The clause οὗτος λαλήσει σοι τί σε δεῖ ποιεῖν is not recognized by Chrys., nor by the leading authorities. See infra. p. 145, note [6].

on the morrow, as they journeyed, and drew nigh to the city" v. 9.—observe how the Spirit connects the times: no sooner than this, and no later, He causes this to take place—"Peter about the sixth hour went up upon the housetop to pray:" that is, privately and quietly, as in an upper chamber. "And he became very hungry, and would have eaten; but while they made ready, there fell upon him a trance." (v. 10.) What means this expression,[1] ἔκστασις, "trance?" Rather, there was presented to him a kind of spiritual view (θεωρία): the soul, so to say, was caused to be out of the body (ἐξέστη). "And saw heaven opened, and, knit at the four corners, a certain vessel descending unto him, as it had been a great sheet, and let down to the earth: wherein were all manner of fourfooted beasts of the earth, and wild beasts, and creeping things, and fowls of the air. And there came a voice to him, Rise, Peter; kill, and eat. But Peter said, Not so, Lord; for I have never eaten anything that is common or unclean. And the voice spake unto him again the second time, What God hath cleansed, that call not thou common. This was done thrice: and the vessel was received up again into heaven." (v. 11-16.) What is this? It is a symbol of the whole world. The[2] man was uncircumcised: and —for he had nothing in common with the Jews—they would all accuse him as a transgressor: "thou wentest in to men uncircumcised, and didst eat with them: (ch. xi. 3)." this[3] was a thing altogether offensive to them: observe then what is providentially managed. He himself also says, "I have never eaten:" not being himself afraid—far be the thought from us—but it is so contrived by the Spirit, in order that he may have it to say in answer to those accusing him, that he did object: for it was altogether necessary for them to observe the Law. He was in the act of being sent to the Gentiles: therefore that these also may not accuse him, see how many things are contrived (by the Providence of God). For, that it may not seem to be a mere fancy, "this was done thrice. I[4] said," saith he, "Not so, Lord, for I have never eaten aught common or unclean.—And the voice came unto him, What God hath cleansed, that call not thou common." (ch.

---

[1] τί ἐστιν ἔκστασις. Because the word also, and more commonly, means the being beside one's self, amazed, or stupefied by excess of grief, Chrys. explains that it denotes the being rapt out of the bodily consciousness: it was not that Peter was out of his mind, but his soul out of his body. (St. Augustin, *Serm.* 266, § 6, "*orantis mens alienata est; sed ab infimis ad superua; non ut deviaret, sed ut videret.*") Comp. *Exp. in Psa.* 115. t. v. p. 312, D. "In Gen. ii. 21. the ἔκστασις which fell upon Adam denotes a kind of insensibility, for ἔκστ. means τὸ ἔξω ἑαυτοῦ γενέσθαι: and in Acts x. 10 it denotes κάρον τινα καὶ τὸ ἔξω αἰσθήσεως γενέσθαι: and everywhere ἔκστασις implies this. It comes, either by the act of God: or because the excess of calamity causes a kind of stupor, κάρος. For calamity likewise is wont to occasion ἔκστ. and κάρος." Didymus (or some other author) in the Catena: "They that have chosen to be disciples of frantic women, I mean, they of Phrygia (the Montanists), affirm that the Prophets, when possessed by the Holy Ghost, were not in a condition to be strictly cognizant of their own thoughts, being borne away from themselves at the instant of prophesying. And they think to confirm their error by this Scripture, which says, that Peter ἐξεστακέναι. But let these silly ones, these indeed frantic persons, know that this is a word of many significations. It denotes the amazement of wonder: and the being wrapt above sensible objects, led on to spiritual things: and the being beside one's self (παρακόπτειν)—which is not be said either of Peter, or of the Prophets. Nay Peter, in his trance, was strictly cognizant, so as to report what he had seen and heard, and to be sensible of what the things shown were symbolical. The same is to be said of all the Prophets—that their consciousness kept pace with the things presented to their view." Comp. on this subject, *S. Epiphan. adv. Hæres. Montan.* 2. ὅσα γὰρ οἱ προφῆται εἰρήκασι μετὰ συνέσεως παρακολουθοῦντες ἐφθέγγοντο. Euseb. H. E. v. 17. relates that Miltiades wrote a treatise περὶ τοῦ μὴ δεῖν προφήτην ἐν ἐκστάσει λαλεῖν. See also *S. Heironym. Præf. in Esai.* "*Neque vero ut Montanus cum insanis fœminis somniat, prophetæ in ecstasi locuti sunt, ut nescirent quid loquerentur, et cum alios erudirent, ipsi ignorarent quid dicerent.*" *Id. Præm. in Nahum. Præf. in Abac.* and, on the difference between the heathen μάντις and the divinely inspired Prophet, St. Chrysost. *Hom.* xxix. *in* 1 *Cor.* p. 259, C. τοῦτο γὰρ μάντεως ἴδιον, τὸ ἐξεστηκέναι κ. τ. λ. and *Expos. in Psa.* xliv. p. 161. .C.—The clause τέσσαρσιν ἀρχαῖς δεδεμένον, before σκεῦός τι, (A. B. C.) agrees with the Lat. ot S. Hilar. p. 750. "*exquatuor principiis ligatum vas quoddam,*" etc.

[2] St. Chrysostom's exposition, as we gather it from this and the following Homily, seems to be in substance as follows: St. Peter was not ignorant of nor averse to, the counsel of God in respect of the free admission of the Gentiles. He did not need instruction on this point for himself, and the vision was not so much intended for his instruction or assurance, as for reproof to the Jewish believers who were not yet enlightened in this mystery. (Even the token which was given in the descent of the Holy Ghost on Cornelius before baptism, was for them, not for him.) He needed but a command to act upon it without hesitation. But because this would certainly be regarded as a flagrant offence by the weaker brethren, for their sakes this symbolical lesson is given: and the circumstances are so contrived (οἰκονομεῖται) as to silence their objections. It is so ordered, that the matter of accusation is put by them in this form, "Thou didst go in to men uncircumcised, and didst eat with them." Had they said, "Thou didst baptize such," St. Peter could not have alleged that he did it reluctantly: but to the charge of unclean eating he had his answer: "I did object; I said, not so, Lord, for nothing common or unclean," etc. This carried with it his exculpation from the whole matter of offence: for they would apply it thus—"he baptized these Gentiles, but not without objecting to the command; not until his reluctance was overruled," though in fact St. Peter had no such reluctance.

[3] Τοῦτο πάνυ αὐτοῖς προσίστατο (B. and Sav. marg. παρίστατο) *Erasm. Et hoc illis valde frequens erat. Ben. Et illis admodum cordi erat.* But Hom. xxiv. 2. ἵνα μὴ προστῇ (προσστῇ) αὐτοῖς, Ben. remarks that προσίστασθαι in the sense "offendere" is frequent in St. Chrysostom. It properly applies to food against which the stomach rises: "to raise the gorge, to be nauseous, disgusting, offensive." See Field *Annotat. in Hom. ad Matt.* p. 319. B.—Τοῦτο, i. e. the going in to men uncircumcised, and eating with them. Comp. *Hom.* li. *in Matt.* p. 317. (Am. ed.) "Such was the strict observance in respect of meats, that, even after the Resurrection, Peter said, 'Not so, Lord,' etc. For though 'he said this for the sake of others, and so as to leave himself a justification against those who should accuse him, and that he may show that he did object,' (ὅτι καὶ ἀντεῖπον), and for all this, the point was not conceded to him, still it shows how much was made of this matter."

[4] Here besides the clause, "this was done thrice," something is wanting: e. g. "And observe how Peter relates the matter, and justifies himself," viz. in xi. 8. "I said," saith he, "Not so, Lord, for nothing common or unclean hath ever entered my mouth." Here for εἶπον, B. has εἶπεν, which is adopted by the modern text, in which the whole passage is refashioned thus: "Since then they would all accuse him as a transgressor, and this was altogether offensive to them, of necessity it is managed (οἶκον.) that he says, "I never ate:" not being himself afraid, God forbid! but, as I said, being managed (οἰκονομούμενος) by the Spirit, that he may have a justification to those accusing him, namely, that he did object: for they made a great point of keeping the Law. He was sent to the Gentiles: therefore, that these also may not have to accuse him, as I said before, these things are contrived, or also, that it may not seem to be a fancy, 'he said, Not so, Lord,'" etc.

XI. 8, with x. 14.) It seems indeed to be spoken to him, but the whole is meant for the Jews. For if the teacher is rebuked, much more these.* The earth then, this is what the linen sheet denotes, and the wild beasts in it, are they of the Gentiles, and the command, "Kill and eat," denotes that he must go to them also; and that this thing is thrice done, denotes baptism. "What God hath cleansed," saith it, "call not thou common." Great daring! Wherefore[1] did he object? That none may say that God was proving him, as in the case of Abraham, this is why he says, "Not so, Lord," etc. not gainsaying—just as to Philip also He said, "How many loaves have ye?" Not to learn, but tempting, or "proving him."[2] And yet it was the same

* Peter's vision fitly represents the divine lesson concerning the destination of the gospel and the manner of its progress. None of the apostles doubted that Christianity was for the Gentiles: the great question was, whether it was to be preached to them through the medium of Judaism. Should it still be held within Jewish forms? Should circumcision and observance of the Mosaic law be required? This was a great practical question in the days of transition from Judaism to Christianity. Later Paul became the champion of the idea that it was to be cut loose from the Jewish system. Peter and James came but slowly to this idea. The destruction of Jerusalem and the fall of the Jewish state brought the question to a decisive settlement. Apart from this, however, the Pauline type of teaching on this point constantly gained ground and influence. The vision of Peter takes its place in the gradual development of the idea that Christianity was free from the law—an idea on which he seems after this to have held a somewhat uncertain and vacillating position, so that Paul "resisted him to the face" for his declining to eat with the Gentiles on account of the presence of certain delegates from Jerusalem—a practice in which he had, before their coming, engaged (Gal. ii. 11, 12). It is not strange that perplexing questions arose concerning the relations of the new system to the old at this time. The general line of procedure was settled by the apostolic conference at Jerusalem (Acts xv., Gal. i., ii.) and was substantially determined by the apostle Paul. While as matter of fact, the Church has always followed the lead of Paul in this matter, the most diverse views still prevail among Christians as to the relation, theoretically considered, of Christianity to Judaism and the Old Testament Scriptures.—G. B. S.

[1] St. Chrys. seems here to be controverting a different exposition. He will not allow that the vision was meant for instruction to St. Peter, as if he were in ignorance up to this time of the counsel of God concerning the Gentiles. Let it not be said, that like as God did tempt Abraham, so He was putting Peter to the proof whether he would obey the call to the Gentiles, as if Peter understood the vision in that sense. Had he so understood the command, "Kill and eat," he would not have objected; for he could not be either ignorant or unwilling. But he did not so understand it, and his objection was solely to the matter of eating. And as he needed not the lesson (it was intended for others): so neither did God need to learn his willingness. When God tempts, or proves, it is not to learn something that He did not know before; as, when Christ said to Philip, "Whence shall we buy bread that these may eat? this He said tempting, or, proving him, for He Himself knew what He would do." He put that question to Philip that he might the more admire the greatness of the miracle which he was about to work. (see note [2].) But nothing of the kind can be said here; the case is not parallel: the command to baptize the Gentiles would not surprise Peter; he expected no less from the beginning.—His objection, then, was to the thing itself, the command, "kill and eat." And no wonder, for the same Lord had in the Law strictly commanded to distinguish between clean and unclean, while there in the sheet were animals of all sorts indiscriminately.

[2] Hom. xlii. in Ev. Joann. § 2. "What meaneth, Tempting, or, proving him? was He ignorant what would be said by him? This cannot be said, . . . We may learn the meaning from the Old Testament. For there also it is said, After these things God did tempt Abraham, etc, He did not say this in order to learn by the proof whether he would obey or not—how should it be so? for He knoweth all things before they come into existence: but on both occasions it is spoken after the manner of men. As, when it is said, He searcheth the hearts of men, it indicates the search, not of ignorance, but of perfect knowl-

(Lord) that had discoursed above (in the Law) concerning things clean and unclean. But in that sheet were also "all the four-footed beasts of the earth:" the clean with the unclean. And[3] for all this, he knew not what it meant. "Now while Peter doubted in himself what this vision which he had seen should mean, behold, the men which were sent from Cornelius had made enquiry for Simon's house, and stood before the gate, and called, and asked whether Simon, which was surnamed Peter, were lodged there.— But while Peter," it says, "doubted in himself" (v. 17, 18), the men come at the right moment to solve his doubt: just as (the Lord) suffered Joseph first to be perturbed in mind, and then sends the Angel: for the soul with ease accepts the solution, when it has first been in perplexity. His perplexity neither lasts long (when it did occur), nor (did it occur) before this, but just at the moment when they "asked whether he were lodging there. While Peter thought on the vision, the Spirit said unto him, Behold, three men seek thee. Arise therefore, and get thee down, and go with them, doubting nothing: for I have sent them." (supra, p. 142, and 145, note [7]; v. 19, 20.) And this again is a plea for Peter in answer to the disciples, that he did doubt, and was instructed to doubt nothing. "For I," saith He, "have sent them." Great is the authority of the Spirit! What God doth, this the Spirit is said to do. Not so the Angel, but having first said, "Thy prayers and thine alms have ascended, for a memorial before God," to show that he is sent from thence, then he adds, "And now send men," etc.: the Spirit not so, but, "For I have sent them." Then Peter went down to the men which were sent unto him from Cornelius; and said, Behold, I am he whom

edge; so when it is said, He tempted, tried, or proved, it means no other than that He perfectly knew.—Or, it may mean, that He made the person more approved: as Abraham there, so Philip by this question, leading him into the sure knowledge of the sign:" i. e. bringing more home to his mind the greatness of the miracle, by leading him in the first place to estimate the utter inadequacy of the means.

[3] Either this refers to the clause, "This was done thrice,' etc., which should be inserted; or, the connection may be—This very circumstance of the clean and unclean being together in the sheet (as in the Ark), might have led him to an apprehension of the thing symbolized, viz., that he was not commanded to "kill and eat" the unclean with the clean (by the same Lord who of old had commanded a distinction of meats), but that the time was come to baptize all nations without respect of persons. But, obvious as it may seem, St. Peter was still ignorant what it meant: as the Writer adds, And while Peter was at a loss to know what the vision should mean, etc.—In E. (Edd.) the whole passage from "that this is thrice done, denotes baptism," is refashioned thus: "'Not so, Lord, for I have never eaten aught common or unclean.' And why, it may be asked, did he object? That none may say that God was tempting him, as in the case of Abraham, when he was ordered to offer up his son as a sacrifice: as in the case of Philip, when he was asked by Christ, How many loaves have ye? not that he may learn, did He so ask, but proving him. And yet in the Law Moses had distinctly enjoined concerning clean and unclean, both of land and sea; and yet for all this he knew not."

ye seek: what is the cause wherefore ye are come? And they said, Cornelius the centurion, a just man, and one that feareth God and of good report among all the nation of the Jews, was warned from God by an holy angel to send for thee into his house, and to hear words of thee." (v. 21, 22.) They speak his praises, so as to persuade him that an Angel has in fact appeared unto him. "Then called he them in,"[1] (b) that they may suffer no harm, " and lodged them : " thenceforth he without scruple takes his meals with them. "And on the morrow Peter went away with them, and certain brethren from Cæsarea accompanied him. And the morrow after, they entered into Cæsarea." (v. 23, 24.) The man was a person of note, and it was in a city of note that he then was.

(a) But let us look over again what has been said. "There was a certain man in Cæsarea," etc. (Recapitulation, v. 1, 2.) Observe with whom the beginning of the Gentiles is made—with "a devout man," and one proved to be worthy by his works. For if, though the case be so, they are still offended, if this had not been the case, what would not have been the consequence ! But[2] mark the greatness of the assurance. (c) To this end[3] all is done (in the way it is done), and the affair takes its beginning from Judea. (d) "He saw in a vision, evidently," etc. (v. 3). It was not in his sleep that the Angel appeared to him, but while he was awake, in the daytime, "about the ninth hour. He[4] saw an Angel of God coming in unto him, and saying unto him, Cornelius. And when he looked on him, he was afraid." So occupied was he with himself. Implying, that it was in consequence of the Angel's calling him by a voice that he saw him ; as, had he not called him, he would not have seen him: so taken up was he with the act in which he was en-

gaged.[5] But the Angel says to him, "Thy prayers and thine alms are come up for a memorial before God, and now send men to Joppa, and call for one Simon, who is called Peter." (v. 5.) So far, he signified that the sending for him would be for good consequences, but in what way good, he did not intimate. [6] So, neither does Peter relate the whole matter, but everywhere, the narratives are in part only, for the purpose of making the hearers apply their minds to what is said. "Send and call for Simon : " in like manner the Angel only calls Philip. "And[7] as they went on their journey, and drew nigh to the city " (v. 9): in order that Peter should not be in perplexity too long. "Peter went up upon the housetop," etc. Observe, that not even his hunger forced him to have recourse to the sheet. "Rise, Peter," saith the Voice, " kill and eat." (v. 13.) Probably he was on his knees when he saw the vision. —To me[8] it seems that this also denotes the Gospel (or, "the Preaching"). That the thing taking place was of God (the circumstances made evident, namely), both that he sees it (descending) from above, and that he is in a trance ; and, that the voice comes from thence, and the thrice confessing that the creatures there were unclean, and its coming from thence, and being drawn back thither (all this), is a mighty token of the cleanness (imparted to them).—But why is this done ?

---

[1] The letters a, b, c, d, denote the order of the parts in the old text. But C. has the formula of recapitulation, both in the beginning of (a), and again in (d), before the verse, " And the Angel said," etc.: E. D. F. Edd. retain it only in the latter place.

[2] 'Αλλ' ὅρα πόση ἀσφάλεια, i. e. how it is made infallibly certain, that it was the purpose of God to admit the Gentiles without circumcision. It might indeed be inserted in (b), after συνδιαιτᾶται : " he has no scruples—but mark the greatness of the assurance he has received." In the modern text, the connection is, " He called them in, and lodged them. See what security : (Θέα πόση ἀσφάλεια) in order that they should take no harm, he calls them in, and thenceforth without scruple," etc. i. e. " how sure he feels that he is doing right in receiving them : with what assuredness of mind he does this." But Sav. "See what security for them, in order that they should take no harm."

[3] Διὰ τοῦτο πάντα γίνεται, A. B. C. N. Cat. But Edd. Διὸ καὶ ἐπ' αὐτῷ πάντα ὁμοῦ οἰκονομεῖται : " wherefore both in his person at once all the circumstances are providentially ordered, and " etc.

[4] Here after the clause, οὕτως ἑαυτῷ προσεῖχεν (meaning, as afterwards explained, that he did not notice the Angel until he spoke), A. B. C. have, Λέγει δὲ ὁ ἄγγελος κ. τ. λ. Edd. 'Αλλ' ἴδωμεν ἀνωθεν τὰ εἰρημένα. Καὶ εἶπεν ὁ ἄγγελος κ. τ. λ.

[5] The old text : " And thy prayers, saith he. So far," etc. Edd. "And send for Simon, who is called Peter. So far," etc."

[6] The text is defective here. He seems to be commenting upon the variations of the different narratives : viz. the writer himself v. 6. mentions only the command to send for Peter. (p. 142, note [4].) The messengers v. 22 add, " And to hear words of thee." Cornelius, v. 32, " who, when he cometh, shall speak unto thee." St. Peter 11, 14, " who shall tell thee words, whereby thou and all thy house shall be saved." " On the other hand," he says, " neither does Peter, though he is more full on this point, relate all that the Angel said, but gives only the substance." See the comment on 11, 14.

[7] The modern text, omitting this clause, and the comment, inserts the rest of the verse, " Peter went up," etc.: and has below, But that Peter may not be in perplexity too long, he hears a voice saying, " Rise, Peter, kill and eat." But the meaning is, The Spirit caused the vision to take place when they were near the city, that Peter might not be too long in doubt : as above, on the same clause, " Observe how the Spirit connects the times," etc.

[8] 'Εμοὶ δοκεῖ καὶ (om. A. B.) τὸ (om. Cat.) κήρυγμα τοῦτο εἶναι (om. Cat.) 'Ότι θεῖον ἦν τὸ γινόμενον τό τε ἄνωθεν ἰδεῖν, τό τε ἐν ἐκστάσει γενέσθαι. (Here δηλοῖ, δείκνυσιν, or the like, must be supplied. Œcumen. Δείκνυται δὲ ὅτι θεῖον κ. τ. λ. In the modern text the wording is slightly altered, but the sense is the same. In the latter part, for ὅτι ἀκαθαρτὰ ἦν ἐκεῖ, Œcumen. has ἐκεῖνα: the modern text substitutes καὶ τὸ τρὶς τοῦτο γενέσθαι, καὶ τὸ οὐρανὸν ἀνεωχθῆναι, καὶ τὸ ἐκεῖθεν κ. τ. λ. and at the end, τοῦ θεῖον εἶναι τὸ πρᾶγμα for καθαρότητος.— Above, he had said that the sheet was a symbol of the world; now he adds, that the command " Kill and eat" denotes the Gospel, to be preached universally: that the descent of the sheet from heaven, and the circumstance of Peter's being in a spiritual trance, shows that the thing was of God—not a φαντασία. Again: that it is all done thrice, denotes baptism: thrice the Voice says, Kill and eat: thrice Peter confesses that the creatures are unclean: thrice it is declared that God hath cleansed them: nay, thrice these unclean creatures are let down from heaven, and drawn up thither again: a mighty proof that they are now clean, and of the Kingdom of Heaven.

10

For[1] the sake of those thereafter, to whom he is about to relate it. For to himself it had been said, "Go not into the way of the Gentiles." (Matt. x. 5.) * * For if Paul needed both (to give) circumcision, and (to offer) sacrifice, much more (was some assurance needed) then, in the beginning of the Preaching, while they were as yet weaker. (Acts xvi. 3 ; xxi. 16.)—Observe[2] too how he did not at once receive them. For, it says, they "called, and asked, whether Simon, which was surnamed Peter, were lodging there." (v. 18.) As it was a mean looking house, they asked below, they inquired[3] of the neighbors. "And while Peter thought, the Spirit said unto him, Arise, get thee down, and go, nothing doubting, for I have sent them." (v. 19, 20.) And he does not say, For to this end did the vision appear unto thee ; but, "I have sent them." Then Peter went down" (v. 21)—this is the way the Spirit must be obeyed, without demanding reasons. For it is sufficient for all assurance to be told by Him, This do, this believe : nothing more (is needed)—"Then Peter went down, and said, Behold, I am he whom ye seek :[4] what is the cause wherefore ye are come ?" He saw a

soldier, saw a man : [5] it was not that he was afraid, on the contrary, having first confessed that he was the person whom they sought, then he asks for the cause (of their coming) ; that it may not be supposed that the reason of his asking the cause, was, that he wished to hide himself : (he asks it) in order, that if it be immediately urgent, he may also go forth with them, but if not, may receive them as guests. "And[6] they said, etc. into his house." (v. 22.) This he had ordered them. Do not think he has done this out of contempt : not as of contempt has he sent, but so he was ordered. "And Cornelius was waiting for them, and had called together his kinsmen and near friends." (v. 24.) It was right that his kinsmen and friends should be gathered to him. But being there present,[4] they would have heard from him (what had happened).

See how great the virtue of alms, both in the former discourse, and here ! There, it delivered from death temporal; here, from death eternal; and opened the gates of heaven. Such are the pains taken for the bringing of Cornelius to the faith, that both an angel is sent, and the Spirit works, and the chief of the Apostles is fetched to him, and such a vision is shown, and, in short, nothing is left undone. How many centurions were there not besides, and tribunes, and kings, and none of them obtained what this man did ! Hear, all ye that are in military commands, all ye that stand beside kings. "A just man," it says, "fearing God ; devout (v. 2, and 22) ; and what is more[7] than all, with all his house. Not as we (who) : that our servants may be afraid of us, do everything, but not that they may be devout. And[8] over the domestics too, so * *. Not

---

[1] It was remarked above, that St. Chrysostom's exposition proceeds upon the assumption, that St. Peter did not need the instruction for himself. Here the reporter has not fully expressed his meaning: which should be to this effect. "Since it had been said at the outset to Peter and the other Apostles, 'Go not into the way of the Gentiles,' though after the Resurrection they were commanded to 'baptize all nations,' it is no marvel that the less enlightened brethren needed some strong assurance on this behalf. And if at a later time, we find Paul, to conciliate the Jewish believers, causing Timothy to be circumcised and himself offering sacrifice, much more was some condescension to their infirmity needed now."—Didymus in the Catena puts the question, "How was it that Peter needed a revelation in the matter of Cornelius, when the Lord after his Resurrection had expressly ordered to 'baptize all the nations ?' or how came it that the Apostles in Jerusalem, having heard of the affair of Cornelius, disputed with Peter?" To which he answers: "Peter did undoubtedly need the revelation; for he knew not that the distinction of circumcision and uncircumcision was to cease: knew not for certain that the Lord meant the Gentiles to be baptized apart from the visible worship under the Law, unlil the Lord manifested this mystery to him, convincing him both by the emblem of the sheet, and by the faith and grace of the Holy Spirit given to the Gentiles, that in Christ Jesus there is no distinction of Jew and Greek: of which thing because the Apostles at Jerusalem were ignorant, therefore they contended with Peter, until they also learnt the hidden riches of God's mercy over all mankind." St. Cyril, Alex., also, c. Julian. (ibid.) explains, that "Peter was fain to dwell in the Jewish customs, and, in a manner, was loath to go on to the better, because he was overawed by the types: therefore he is corrected by this vision."

[2] E. D. F. Edd. omit this clause, see note x: and A. B. for οὐδέ . . . ἐδέξατο have οὐδὲν . . . ἐδείξατο, which is evidently corrupt. "Neither did he at once receive these Gentiles: not until the Spirit expressly commanded him."

[3] So Cat. and the Mss. except E., which has οὐ τοὺς γείτονας ἠρώτων, and so Œcumen. But the meaning seems to be, that not expecting to find so mean a house, and thinking they might have come wrong, they asked below, in the street, i. e. inquired of the neighbors.

[4] Here Edd. from E. have, "Wherefore did he not receive them immediately, but asks this question?" but D. F. insert it as above, Ὅρα πῶς οὐκ εὐθέως αὐτοὺς ἐδέξατο, with the addition, ἀλλὰ πυνθάνεται. In the next sentence: A. B. C. Cat. εἶδεν στρατιώτην, εἶδεν ἄνθρωπον· i. e. Saw a soldier, saw him, as he would have seen any common man, without fear. For this, D. F. have εἶδε στρατιώτας ἀνθρώπους. E. Edd. εἶδε στρατιώτας ὄντας τοὺς ἐπιστάντας.—Below, for καὶ ζητήσας A. B. C. Cat. which the other Mss. omit, we correct, ὃν ἐξήτησαν.

[5] In the old text, the last words of the citation, v. 22. εἰς τὸν οἶκον αὐτοῦ, the rest being lost, are joined on to ἵνα ξενίσῃ : Cat. εἰς τὸν οἶκον αὐτούς. Edd. from E. D. F. "But why do they say, 'Sends for thee into his house?' Because he had given them this order. And perhaps also, by way of apology, they as good as say, Do not find fault (μηδὲν καταγνῷς·) not as of contempt has he sent, etc." In A. B. C. Cat. μὴ καταφρονήσῃς, for which Sav. marg. has ὡς ἂν εἴποιεν, μὴ καταφρ., is corrupt: perhaps it should be μὴ νομίσῃς, ὅτι κατεφρόνησέ σε· οὐχ ὡς κ. τ. λ.

[6] ἀλλ' (A. καὶ) ἐκεῖ πάροντος αὐτοῦ ἤκουσαν ἂν (A. ταῦτα ἀκούειν). We read, πάροντες, and conjecture the meaning to be, But they being there present, would have heard from Cornelius an account of all that had happened to him. Edd. from E. D. F. Ἄλλως δὲ καὶ ἐκεῖ πάροντες μᾶλλον αὐτοῦ ἤκουσαν ἂν. "And besides by being there present they would the more hear him (Peter)," what he had to say.

[7] The modern text: "and what is greater, that he was such with all his house. So intent was he, and so set upon this, that he not only well ordered his own affairs, but also over his household (ἐπὶ τῆς οἰκετείας) he did the same. For not as we, who," etc.

[8] A. B. καὶ ἐπὶ τῆς οἰκετείας δὲ οὕτως. Ἀλλ' οὗτος οὐχ οὕτως, ἀλλὰ μετὰ τῆς οἰκίας ἁπάσης. ὥσπερ γὰρ κ. τ. λ. C. καὶ ἐπὶ τ. οἰκ. δὲ οὐκέτι κακῶς, ἀλλὰ δικαίως· ὥσπερ γὰρ κ. τ. λ. Below, the modern text has, "he feared God with all his house, as being the common father, not only of all who were with him, but also of the soldiers under him." In the next sentence, Ὅρα δὲ τί φησιν καὶ αὐτός, the meaning seems to be, "Observe what is said of him by the soldier whom Cornelius sent: 'A just man,

so this man; but he was "one that feared God with all his house" (v. 2), for he was as the common father of those with him, and of all the others (under his command.) But observe what (the soldier) says himself. For, fearing * *, he adds this also: "well reported of by all the nation." For what if he was uncircumcised? Nay, but those give him a good report. Nothing like alms: great is the virtue of this practice, when the alms is poured forth from pure stores; for it is like a fountain discharging mud, when it issues from unjust stores, but when from just gains, it is as a limpid and pure stream in a paradise, sweet to the sight, sweet to the touch, both light and cool, when given in the noon-day heat. Such is alms. Beside this fountain, not poplars and pines, nor cypresses, but other plants than these, and far better, of goodly stature: friendship with God, praise with men, glory to Godward, good-will from all; blotting out of sins, great boldness, contempt of wealth. This is the fountain by which the plant of love is nourished: for nothing is so wont to nourish love, as the being merciful: it makes its branches to lift themselves on high. This fountain is better than that in Paradise (Gen. ii. 10); a fountain, not dividing into four heads, but reaching unto Heaven itself: this gives birth to that river "which springeth up into eternal life" (John iv. 14): on this let Death light, and like a spark it is extinguished by the fountain: such, wherever it drops, are the mighty blessings it causes. This quenches, even as a spark, the river of fire: this so strangles that worm, as naught else can do. (Mark ix. 44.) He that has this, shall not gnash his teeth. Of the water of this, let there be dropped upon the chains, and it dissolves them: let it but touch the firebrands,[1] it quenches all.—A fountain does not give out streams for a while and anon run dry,—else must it be no more a fountain,—but ever gushes: so let our fountain give out more copiously of the streams of mercy (in alms). This cheers him that receives: this is alms, to give out not only a copious, but a perennial, stream. If thou wouldest that God rain down His mercy upon thee as from fountains, have thou also a fountain. And[2] yet there is no comparison (between God's fountain and thine): for if thou open the mouths of this fountain, such are the mouths of God's Fountain as to surpass every abyss. God does but seek to get an opportunity on our part, and pours forth from His storehouses His blessings. When He expends, when He lavishes, then is He rich, then is He affluent. Large is the mouth of that fountain: pure and limpid its water. If thou stop not up the fountain here, neither wilt thou stop up that fountain.—Let no unfruitful tree stand beside it, that it may not waste its spray. Hast thou wealth? Plant not poplars there: for such is luxury: it consumes much, and shows nothing for it in itself, but spoils the fruit. Plant not a pine-tree—such is wantonness in apparel, beautiful only to the sight, and useful for nothing—nor yet a fir-tree, nor any other of such trees as consume indeed, but are in no sort useful. Set it thick with young shoots: plant all that is fruitful, in the hands of the poor, all that thou wilt. Nothing richer than this ground. Though small the reach of the hand, yet the tree it plants starts up to heaven and stands firm. This it is to plant. For that which is planted on the earth will perish, though not now, at any rate a hundred years hence. Thou plantest many trees, of which thou shalt not enjoy the fruit, but ere thou canst enjoy it, death comes upon thee. This tree will give thee its fruit then, when thou art dead.—If thou plant, plant not in the maw of gluttony, that the fruit end not in the draught-house: but plant thou in the pinched belly, that the fruit may start up to heaven. Refresh the straightened soul of the poor, lest thou pinch thine own roomy soul.—See you not, that the plants which are overmuch watered at the root decay, but grow when watered in moderation? Thus also drench not thou thine own belly, that the root of the tree decay not: water that which is thirsty, that it may bear fruit. If thou water in moderation, the sun will not wither them, but if in excess, then it withers them: such is the nature of the sun. In all things, excess is bad; wherefore let us cut it off, that we also may obtain the things we ask for.—Fountains, it is said, rise on the most elevated spots. Let us be elevated in soul, and our alms will flow with a rapid stream: the elevated soul cannot but be merciful, and the merciful cannot but be elevated. For he that despises

---

and one that feareth God:' and then—for fearing (lest Peter should refuse to come to him, as being a Gentile) he adds this —'and well reported of by all the nation of the Jews." Edd. from E. alone: "But hear also what they say besides: for of necessity that is added, 'Well reported of by all the nation,' that none may say, What, if he was uncircumcised? Even those, saith he, give him a good report. Why then, there is nothing like alms; or rather great is the virtue of this thing, when," etc.

[1] καὶ εἰς τὰς λαμπάδας (E. Edd., καμίνους) ἄψηται (ἐμπέσῃ, E. D. F. Edd.) In the next sentence, Αὕτη ἡ πηγή κ. τ. λ. the pronoun must be omitted.—E. D. F., Edd., "As therefore the fountain in Paradise (or, in a garden) does not give out streams," etc.

[2] Καίτοιγε οὐδὲν ἴσον. Ἂν γὰρ σὺ ταύτης κ. τ. λ.—Edd., Οὐδὲν ταύτης ἴσον. Ἂν σὺ ταύτης κ. τ. λ. "Nothing like this fountain. If then," etc.—Below, Ὅταν ἀναλίσκῃ, ὅταν δαπανᾷ, κ. τ. λ. in itself, may perhaps be better referred to the giver of alms: "when (one) expends, when one lavishes (alms)," etc. but in that case the connection is obscure.

wealth, is higher than the root of evils.—
Fountains are oftenest found in solitary
places: let us withdraw our soul from the
crowd, and alms will gush out with us. Fountains, the more they are cleaned, the more
copiously they flow: so with us, the more we
spend, the more all good grows.—He that has
a fountain, has nothing to fear: then neither
let us be afraid. For indeed this fountain is
serviceable to us for drink, for irrigation, for
building, for everything. Nothing better than
this draught: it is not possible for this to
inebriate. Better to possess such a fountain,
than to have fountains running with gold.
Better than all gold-bearing soil is the soul

which bears this gold. For it advances us,
not into these earthly palaces, but into those
above. The gold becomes an ornament to
the Church of God. Of this gold is wrought
"the sword of the Spirit (Eph. vi. 17), the
sword by which the dragon is beheaded.
From this fountain come the precious stones
which are on the King's head. Then let us
not neglect so great wealth, but contribute
our alms with largeness, that we may be
found worthy of the mercy of God, by the
grace and tender compassion of His only begotten Son, with Whom to the Father and
Holy Ghost together be glory, dominion, honor,
now and ever, world without end. Amen.

HOMILY XXIII.

ACTS X. 23, 24.

"Then called he them in, and lodged them. And
on the morrow Peter went away with them, and
certain brethren from Joppa accompanied him.
And the morrow after they entered into Cæsarea.
And Cornelius waited for them, and had called
together his kinsmen and near friends."

"HE called them in, and lodged them."
Good, that first he gives the men friendly
treatment, after the fatigue of their journey,
and makes them at home with him; "and on
the morrow," sets out with them." And
certain accompany him: this too as Providence ordered it, that they should be witnesses afterwards when Peter would need to
justify himself. "And Cornelius was waiting
for them, and had called together his kinsmen and near friends." This is the part of a
friend, this the part of a devout man, that
where such blessings are concerned, he takes
care that his near friends shall be made partakers of all. Of course (his "near" friends),
those in whom he had ever full confidence;
fearing, with such an interest at stake, to
entrust the matter to others. In my opinion,
it was by Cornelius himself that both friends
and kinsmen had been brought to a better
mind. "And as Peter was coming in, Cornelius met him, and fell down at his feet, and
worshipped him." (v. 25.) This, both to
teach the others, and by way of giving thanks
to God, and showing his own humility:
thereby making it plain, that though he had
been commanded, yet in himself he had great
piety. What then did Peter? "But Peter
took him up, saying, Stand up; I myself also
am a man." (v. 26.) Do you mark how,

before all else (the Apostles) teach them this
lesson, not to think great things of them?
"And as he talked with him, he went in, and
found many that were come together. And
he said unto them, Ye know how that it is an
unlawful thing for a man that is a Jew to keep
company, or come unto one of another
nation; but God hath showed me that I
should not call any man common or unclean."
(v. 27, 28.) Observe, he straightway speaks of
the mercy of God, and points out to them that
it is a great grace that God has shown them.
Observe also how while he utters great things,
at the same time he speaks modestly. For he
does not say, We, being men who do not
deign to keep company with any (such), have
come to you: but what says he? "Ye know"
—God commanded this [1]—"that it is against
law to keep company with, or come unto, one
of another nation." Then he goes on to say,
"And to me God has shown"—this he says,
that none may account the thanks due to him
—"that I should call no man"—that it may
not look like obsequiousness to him, "no
human being," says he—"common or unclean."* (v. 29.) "Wherefore also"—that

---

[1] So Mss. and Edd. but the clause ὁ Θεὸς τοῦτο ἐκέλευσε
might be better transferred, in the sense, "It is only in obedience to God's command that I come to you." Below, Εἶτα
ἵνα μηδεὶς αὐτῷ τὴν χάριν ἔχῃ (A. B. C. D. F. Cat.) ἐπάγει
(om. C.) τί φησίν; (A. B. C. but Cat. for ἐπάγει τί φησίν; has,
ταῦτα φησίν·) Καὶ ἐμοὶ κ. τ. λ. We read, Εἶτα ἐπάγει, Καὶ
ἐμοὶ ἔδειξεν ὁ Θεὸς (ἵνα μηδεὶς αὐτῷ τὴν χάριν ἔχῃ ταῦτα φησὶν)
μηδένα κ. τ. λ.

* By saying "it is not lawful," Peter does not refer to any
specific command in the Mosaic law forbidding intercourse
with Gentiles. The separateness of the Jewish people from
the heathen world had, indeed, its basis in the Levitical system, especially in the regulations concerning ceremonial cleanness. Still the Jews had constant commercial relations with

they may not think the affair a breach of the law on his part, nor (Cornelius) suppose that because he was in a station of command, therfore he had complied, but that they may ascribe all to God,—" wherefore also I came without gainsaying as soon as I was sent for:" (though) not only to keep company, but even to come unto (him) was not permitted. "I ask therefore, for what intent ye have sent for me." Already Peter had heard the whole matter from the soldiers also, but he wishes them first to confess, and to make them amenable to the Faith. What then does Cornelius? He does not say, Why, did not the soldiers tell thee? but observe again, how humbly he speaks. For he says, "From the fourth day I was fasting until this hour; and at the ninth hour I prayed in my house, and, behold, a man stood before me in bright clothing, and said, Cornelius, thy prayer is heard, and thine alms are come up for a memorial before God. And at the ninth hour," he says, "I was praying." (v. 30, 31.) It seems to me, that this man had also fixed for himself set times of a life under stricter rule, and on certain days.[1] For this is why

he says, "From the fourth day." * See how great a thing prayer is! When he advanced in piety, then the Angel appears to him. "From the fourth day:" i. e. of the week; not "four days ago." For, "on the morrow Peter went away with them, and on the morrow after they entered into Cæsarea:" this is one day: and the day on which the persons sent came (to Joppa) one day: and on the third (the Angel) appeared: so that there are two days after that on which (Cornelius) had been praying. "And, behold, a man stood before me in bright clothing:" he does not say, an Angel, so unassuming is he: "and said, Cornelius, thy prayer is heard, and thine alms are had in remembrance in the sight of God. Send therefore to Joppa, and call hither Simon, whose surname is Peter: he is lodged in the house of one Simon a tanner by the seaside: who, when he cometh, shall speak unto thee. Immediately therefore I sent to thee; and thou hast well done that thou art come. Now therefore are we all here present before God, to hear all things that are commanded thee of God." (v. 31–33.) (b) See [2] what faith, what piety! He

---

other nations. Peter here refers, no doubt, to the customary and traditional exclusiveness of his nation which had become a social as well as a religious trait, and which had been extended far beyond the purport of the Mosaic requirements, which had for their end the preservation of the truth and purity of the religion of the nation. This exclusive and jealous spirit is frequently reflected in the N. T. and contemporaneous literature. The Jewish Christians accuse Peter (Acts xi. 3) of eating with the uncircumcised. On another occasion, the prejudices of his kinsmen and friends intimidated him and constrained him to break off his custom of associating with the Gentile Christians at meals (Gal. ii. 11 sq.). "Moses," says Josephus, " does not allow those who come to us without living according to our laws to be admitted into communion with us " (Contra Apion. ii. 29). Tacitus accuses the Jews of harboring " the bitterest animosity against all other nations" (Hist. v. 5) and Juvenal says that they will not point out the way except to those of their own religion, and that they will " conduct those only to the fountain inquired after who are circumcised " (Sat. xiv. 103). How great was the lesson then, which Peter had been taught in the vision! It is not strange that it was only gradually learned and practised.—G. B. S.

[1] Καὶ ἔν τισιν ἡμέραις· so all the Mss. with Cat. (ἔν τισιν ἡμ.) and Œcum. If the text be not corrupt, Chrys. must be understood to interpret ἀπὸ τετάρτης ἡμ. of the "fourth day of the week:" i. e. Cornelius had anticipated, among other pious observances, this practice also, viz. of the Wednesday fast. Otherwise, there is no intelligible connection for the following words, Διὰ γὰρ τοῦτο εἶπεν, Ἀπὸ τετάρτης ἡμέρας. This, he says, was an advance in piety: and then it was that the Angel appeared to him. Then he proceeds to argue, that that it is not "four days ago," for the time does not amount to that number of days: the day on which Peter arrived was not the fourth, but between that and the day on which Cornelius prayed, there are but two entire days. It seems that this must be St. Chrysostom's meaning, though it is obscured by mistakes of the scribes. B. C. αὕτη μία ἡμέρα· καὶ ἦν ἦλθον μία· καὶ τῇ τρίτη ἐφάνη· ὡς εἶναι δευτέραν μεθ' ἥν προσηύξατο. (A. omits the passage.) E. D. F. Edd. αὕτη μία ἡμέρα· καὶ ἦν ἀπῆλθον οἱ πεμφθέντες, μία· καὶ ἦν ἦλθον, μία· καὶ τῇ τετάρτῃ ἐφάνη· ὡς εἶναι δευτέραν μεθ' ἥν προσηύξατο. Cat. and Œc. agree with E. D. F. in supplying the clause omitted in B. C., to which however they add παρὰ Κορνηλίου· they have also τετάρτῃ ἐφάνη, but for the last clause they read, ὡσεὶ τρίτην ὥραν μεθ' ἥν προσηύξατο. But the sense intended by Chrys. should be: "This, the day (on which they left Joppa), is one day (before the day on which Cornelius is speaking): and the day on which the messengers from Cornelius came, one day; (therefore the second day before that on which Cornelius is speaking:) and on the third day (previous) the Angel appeared: so that, exclusively of the day on which Cornelius is speaking, and that on which Cornelius prayed, there are two days." This sense will be satisfied by

reading, αὕτη μία ἡμέρα· καὶ ἦν ἦλθον οἱ πεμφθέντες παρὰ Κορνηλίου, μία· καὶ τῇ τρίτῃ ἐφάνη· ὥστε εἶναι δυὸ ἡμέρας μεθ' ἥν προσηύξατο. The scribes, mistaking both the drift and the method of the calculation, supposed αὕτη ἡμ. to mean " the day of Peter's arrival:" but the day before that was the day on which they came away (ἀπῆλθον) from Joppa, and on the previous day the messengers arrived (ἦλθον), and on the day before that, which is therefore the fourth, the Angel appeared: hence they insert the words καὶ ἦν ἀπῆλθον . . . μία, in order to make out the calculation, i. e. to verify the day of the Vision as the fourth day before that on which Cornelius is speaking. So Cat. Œc. and E. D. F. But B. C. retain the original reading, and only mistake the abbreviated form ὥστε εἶναι β' ἡμ., i. e. δυὸ ἡμέρας, as if it meant "the second day," δευτέραν ἡμέραν· which reading, though unintelligible, was retained by the later Editors. But what Chrys. means to say, is, that, not reckoning the day of the vision and the day of the meeting, there are two whole days: therefore the day of the vision was not "the fourth day hence;" consequently, that it means "the fourth day of the week." This hasty and ill considered interpretation of the expression ἀπὸ τετάρτης ἡμέρας, was suggested by the circumstance that the rule was to fast on the dies stationum, τετράς and προσάββατον, to "the ninth hour:" so that the practical scope of the interpretation may be of this kind: "See how this man, Gentile as he was, had forestalled our rule of discipline: he fasted on the fourth day of the week, and to the ninth hour of the day: and see how God was pleased to approve of his piety, by sending the Angel to him on that day, and at that hour. But you who know the rule, and why it is prescribed, do not obey it," etc.—On the Dies Stationum, see Tertull. de Jejun. l. where in defence of the Montanists, who extended the fast beyond the ninth hour, (or 3 p. m.) he says: Arguunt nos quod stationes plerumque in vesperam producamus: ib. 10. Æque stationes nostras ut indignas, quasdam vero et in serum constitutas, novitatis nomine incusant, hoc quoque munus et ex arbitrio obeundum esse dicentes, et non ultra nonam detinendum, suo scilicet more : i. e. the Catholics maintained, that the fast on these days ought not to be compulsory, nor to be prolonged beyond the ninth hour. Epiphan. Expos. Fid. §. 22. δι ὅλου μὲν τοῦ ἔτους ἡ νηστεία φυλάττεται ἐν τῇ αὐτῇ ἁγία καθολικῇ ἐκκλησίᾳ, φημὶ δὲ τετράδι καὶ προσαββάτῳ ἕως ὥρας ἐννάτης.

* It is wholly improbable that ἀπὸ τετάρτης ἡμέρας refers to the fourth day of the week, as Chrys. supposes. The meaning is that, four days ago (reckoning from the time when he was speaking) he was praying (" observing the ninth hour of prayer ") until the time of day at which he was now saying these words to Peter. There is still less ground for Chrysostom's interpretation if with Lechler, Tischendorf, and Westcott and Hort νηστεύων be omitted from the text.—G. B. S.

[2] The letters a, b, c, d, mark the order of these portions in B. C. At the end of (a) the clause, "We are present," etc. is

knew that it was no word of man that Peter spake, when he said, "God hath shown me." Then says the man, "We are present to hear all things that are commanded thee of the Lord. (a) Therefore it was that Peter asked, "For what intent have ye sent for me?" on purpose that he might so speak these very words. (d) "Then Peter opened his mouth, and said, Of a truth I perceive that God is no respecter of persons: but in every nation he that feareth Him, and worketh righteousness, is acceptable to him." (v. 34, 35.) That is, be he uncircumcised or circumcised. (c) This also Paul declaring, saith, "For there is no respect of persons with God." * (Rom. ii. 11.) (e) What then? (it may be asked) is the man yonder in Persia acceptable to Him? If he be worthy, in this regard he is acceptable, that it should be granted him to be brought unto faith (τῷ καταξιωθῆναι τῆς πίστεως). The Eunuch from Ethiopia He overlooked not. "What shall one say then of the religious men who have been overlooked?" It is not the case, that any (such) ever was overlooked. But what he says is to this effect, that God rejects no man.† "In every nation, he that feareth God and worketh righteousness:" (by righteousness) he means, all virtue. Mark, how he subdues all elation of mind in him. That (the Jews) may not seem to be in the condition of persons cast off (he adds), "The word

which He sent unto the children of Israel, preaching peace by Jesus Christ: He is Lord of all (v. 36): this he says also for the sake of those present (of the Jews), that He may persuade them also: this is why he forces Cornelius to speak. "He," saith he, "is Lord of all." But observe at the very outset, "The word," says he, "which He sent unto the children of Israel;" he gives them the preëminence. Then he adduces (these Gentiles) themselves as witnesses: "ye know," says he, "the matter which came to pass throughout all Judea, beginning at Galilee—then he confirms it from this also—"after the baptism which John preached (v. 37)—("even Jesus of Nazareth, how God anointed Him with the Holy Ghost and with power." (v. 38.) He does not mean, Ye know Jesus, for they did not know Him, but he speaks of the things done by Him: ‡ "Who went about doing good, and healing all that were oppressed of the devil: by this [1] he shows that many cases of lost senses or paralyzed limbs are the devil's work, and a wrench given to the body by him: as also Christ said. "For God was with Him." Again, lowly terms. "And we are witnesses of all things which He did, both in the country of the Jews, and in Jerusalem" (v. 39): both "we," saith he, and ye. Then the Passion, and the reason why they do not believe: "Whom also they slew, and hanged on a tree. Him God raised up the third day, and showed Him openly; not to all the people, but unto witnesses chosen before of God, even to us, who did eat and drink with Him after He rose from the dead. (v. 40, 41.) This is a proof of the Resurrection. "And he commanded us to preach unto the people, and to testify that it is He which was ordained of God to be the Judge of quick and dead." (v. 42.) This is great. Then he adduces the testimony from the Prophets: "To Him give all the prophets witness, that through His name, whosoever believeth in Him shall receive remission of sins. (v. 43.)

---

repeated. In A the order is, a, d, the rest being omitted: in the modern text, a, d, c, b : and the text, "Now therefore are we all present," etc. between (c) and (b).—With the interpretation of δεκτὸς comp. Severianus of Gabala in the Catena on x. 4, οὐκ εἶπεν ἐν παντὶ ἔθνει ὁ ποιῶν δικαιοσύνην σώζεται, ἀλλὰ δεκτός ἐστιν, τουτέστιν, ἄξιος γίνεται τοῦ δεχθῆναι. And St. Chrys. Hom. viii. in 1 Cor. C. δεκτὸς αὐτῷ ἐστι· τουτέστι, καλεῖ καὶ ἐπισπᾶται αὐτὸν πρὸς τὴν ἀλήθειαν. Paul is cited as an instance: persecutor as he was, "yet, because he led a blameless life, and did not these things of human passion, he was both accepted and far outwent all. But if some one should say, ' How is it that such an one, the Greek, kind as he is and good and humane, continues in error?' I answer, that he has a fault of a different kind, vainglory or sluggishness of mind, or not being in earnest about his salvation, but thinking that all the circumstances of his life are mere chance-medley and haphazard. But by ' him that worketh righteousness,' Peter means, him that is blameless in all things (comp. infra p. 151.) . . . . . . ' How is it then,' you will say, ' that impure persons have been accounted worthy to have the Gospel preached to them (κατηξιώθησαν τοῦ κηρύγματος)?' Because they were willing and desirous. For some, even which are in error, He draws, when they become cleansed from their vices; and others coming of their own accord, He repulses not: many also have inherited their piety from their ancestors."

* The word προσωπολήμπτης —"respector of persons"— (personarum acceptor, Vulg.) is a term founded upon the phrase, λαμβάνειν πρόσωπον, an imitation of the Hebrew פָּנִים נָשָׂא, to accept the person, the presence; to have a favorable or partial regard to the outward appearance,—as opposed to פָּנִים הֵשִׁיב, to turn away the face (of the petitioner) i. e. to deny him favor or acceptance (1 Kgs. ii. 16, 17, 20 ; 2 Chron. vi. 42 ; cf. Gen. xxxii. 21 ; 1 Kgs. v. i.)—G. B. S.

† The pertinent comments of Dr. Gloag may here be fitly introduced (v. 35): "Peter is here speaking of the admissibility of the Gentiles into the Church of Christ; and he here asserts that there is no natural obstacle in the way of any one who fears God and works righteousness ; that there is now no barrier such as circumcision, no external hindrance, but that all are equally acceptable to God. As Meyer well puts it, δεκτὸς αὐτῷ ἐστίν indicates the capability in relation to God to become a Christian, but not the capability to be saved without Christ; or, as Bengel observes, non indifferentissimus religionum, sed indifferentia nationum hic asseritur." (Gloag, Com. in loco).—G. B. S.

‡ There is no sufficient reason for the statement of Chrys. that those to whom Peter spoke did not know Jesus. It is meant that they were acquainted with the chief facts of his life. Grammatically Ἰησοῦν must be construed as the object (resumed in another form) of ὑμεῖς οἴδατε (37). Residents in Cæsarea must have heard of Jesus' teaching and miracles, during his lifetime on earth. Moreover, the apostles had taught in the neighboring cities and wrought miracles, and probably Philip had been for some little time residing and laboring in Cæsarea itself (Acts viii. 40).—G. B. S.

[1] Ἐντεῦθεν δείκνυσι πολλὰς πηρώσεις διαβολικὰς καὶ διαστροφὴν (B., διαστροφὰς) σώματος (Cat., σωμάτων) ὑπ' ἐκείνου γενομένας. The term πήρωσις here includes loss of sight, speech, hearing, palsied or withered limbs. "He shows that these are diabolical, and that they are a violent wrenching, or distortion, of the body from its proper condition, caused by him." The sense requires either διαστροφὰς or γενομένην. The next sentence, ὥσπερ καὶ ὁ Χριστὸς ἔλεγεν, omitted by Edd., though, except E., all the Mss. and Cat. have it, may refer to such expressions as that in Luke xiii. 16. Or, it may be in its proper place after the following clause, "For God was with Him:" again, a lowly expression: just as Christ spake: "for My Father is with Me."

This is a proof of that which was about to be: this is the reason why he here cites the Prophets.

But let us look over again what relates to Cornelius. (Recapitulation.) He sent, it it says, to Joppa to fetch Peter. "He was waiting for him," etc; see how fully he believed that Peter would certainly come: (*b*) "and¹ fell down at his feet, and worshipped him." (v. 24, 25.) (*a*) Mark how on every side it is shown how worthy he is! (So) the Eunuch there desired Philip to come up and sit in the chariot (ch. viii. 31), although not knowing who he was, upon no other introduction (ἐπαγγελίας) than that given by the Prophet. But here Cornelius fell at his feet. (*c*) "Stand up, I myself also am a man." (v. 26.) Observe how free from adulation his speech is on all occasions, and how full of humility. "And conversing with him, he came in." (*a*) (v. 27.) Conversing about what? I suppose saying these words: "I myself also am a man." (*e*) Do you mark (Peter's) unassuming temper? He himself also shows that his coming is God's doing: "Ye know that it is unlawful for a man that is a Jew," etc. (v. 28.) And why did he not speak of the linen sheet? Observe Peter's freedom from all vainglory: but, that he is sent of God, this indeed he mentions; of the manner in which he was sent, he speaks not at present; when the need has arisen, seeing he had said, "Ye know that it is unlawful for a man that is a Jew to keep company with, or to come unto, one of another nation," he simply adds, "but to me God hath shown," etc. There is nothing of vainglory here. "All ye," he says, "know." He makes their knowledge stand surety for him. But Cornelius says, "We are present before God to hear all things that are commanded thee of the Lord" (v. 33): not, Before man, but, "Before God." This is the way one ought to attend to God's servants. Do you see his awakened mind? do you see how worthy he was of all these things? "And Peter," it says, "opened his mouth, and said, Of a truth I perceive that God is no respecter of persons." (v. 34.) This he said also by way of justifying himself with the Jews then present. For, being at the point to commit the Word to these (Gentiles), he first puts this by way of apology. What then? Was He "a respecter of persons" beforetime? God forbid! For beforetime likewise it was just the same: "Every one,"

as he saith, "that feareth Him, and worketh righteousness, would be acceptable to Him." As when Paul saith, "For when the Gentiles which have not the Law, do by nature the things of the Law." (Rom. ii. 14.) "That feareth God and worketh righteousness:" he assumes² both doctrine and manner of life: is "accepted with Him;" for, if He did not overlook the Magi, nor the Ethiopian, nor the thief, nor the harlot, much more them that work righteousness, and are willing, shall He in anywise not overlook. "What say you then to this, that there are likely persons (ἐπιεικεῖς), men of mild disposition, and yet they will not believe?" (Above, p. 149, note ².) Lo, you have yourself named the cause: they will not. But besides the likely person he here speaks of is not this sort of man, but the man "that worketh righteousness:" that is, the man who in all points is virtuous and irreproachable, when he has the fear of God as he ought to have it. But whether a person be such, God only knows. See how this man was acceptable: see how, as soon as he heard, he was persuaded. "Yes, and now too," say you, "every one would be persuaded, be who he may." But the signs that are now, are much greater than those, and more wonderful.—Then Peter commences his teaching, and reserves for the Jews the privilege of their birth. "The³ word," he says, "which He sent unto the children of Israel, preaching peace (v. 36), not bringing judgment. He is sent to the Jews also: yet for all this He did not spare them. "Preaching peace through Jesus Christ. He is Lord of all." First he discourses of His being Lord and in exceeding elevated terms, seeing he had to deal with a soul more than commonly elevated, and that took all in with ardor. Then he proves how He was Lord of all, from the things which He achieved "throughout all Judea. For ye know," saith he, "the matter which came to pass throughout all Judea:" and, what is the wonderful part of it, "beginning at Galilee: after the baptism which John preached." (v. 37.) First he speaks of His success, and then again he says concerning Him, "Jesus of Nazareth." Why, what a stumbling-block, this

---

¹ The letters denote the order of the parts in the Mss. and Edd.

² καὶ δόγμα τίθησι (E. Edd. εἰσάγει) καὶ πολίτειαν. i. e. "it is assumed, or the case is put, that the person has the right doctrine, of the One True God (that feareth God), and that he is of a right conversation (that worketh righteousness.)"

³ In the Mss. and Edd. the order is confused. In the old text: "The word—Lord of all. First he discourses—with ardor. Yet for all this He did not spare them. Then he proves how He is Lord of all. Which He sent, preaching good tidings, not bringing judgment. [3.] He is sent from God to the Jews. Then He shows this withal from the things which He achieved," etc. So, with verbal alterations, the modern text, except that it omits the clause, οὐ μὴν οὐδὲ οὕτως ἐφείσατο.

birthplace! "How[1] God anointed Him with the Holy Ghost and with power. (v. 38.) Then again the proof—how does that appear? —from the good that He did. "Who went about doing good, and healing all that were oppressed of the devil:" and the greatness of the power shown when He overcomes the devil; and the cause, "Because God was with Him." Therefore also the Jews spake thus: "We know that Thou art a teacher come from God: for none can do these miracles except God be with him." (John iii. 2.) Then, when he has shown that He was sent from God, he next speaks of this, that He was slain: that thou mayest not imagine[2] aught absurd. Seest thou how far they are from hiding the Cross out of view, nay, that together with the other circumstances they put also the manner? "Whom also," it says, "they slew by hanging on a tree. And gave Him," it is added, "to be made manifest not to all the people, but to witnesses before ordained of God, even unto us:" and yet it was (Christ) Himself that elected them; but this also he refers to God. "To the before-ordained," he says, "even to us, who did eat and drink with Him after that He was risen from the dead. (v. 39, 41.) See whence he fetches his assurance of the resurrection. What is the reason that being risen he did no sign, but only ate and drank? Because the Resurrection itself was a great sign, and of this nothing was so much[3] a sign as the eating and drinking. "To testify," saith he—in a manner calculated to alarm— that they may not have it in their power to fall back upon the excuse of ignorance: and he does not say, "that He is the Son of God," but, what would most alarm them, "that it is He which is ordained of God, to be the Judge of quick and dead." (v. 42.) "To him give all the Prophets witness," etc. (v. 43.) When by the terror he has agitated them, then he brings in the pardon, not spoken from himself but from the Prophets. And what is terrifying is from him, what is mild from the Prophets.

All ye that have received this forgiveness, all ye to whom it has been vouchsafed to attain unto faith, learn, I beseech you, the greatness of the Gift, and study not to be in-

solent to your Benefactor. For we obtained forgiveness, not that we should become worse, but to make us far better and more excellent. Let none say that God is the cause of our evil doings, in that He did not punish, nor take vengeance. If (as it is said) a ruler having taken a murderer, lets him go, say, is he (not)[4] judged to be the cause of the murders afterwards committed? See then, how we expose God to the tongues of the wicked. For what do they not say, what leave unuttered? "(God) Himself," say they, "allowed them; for he ought to have punished them as they deserved, not to honor them, nor crown them, nor admit them to the foremost privileges, but to punish and take vengeance upon them: but he that, instead of this, honors them, has made them to be such as they are." Do not, I beseech and implore you, do not let any man utter such speech as far as we are concerned. Better to be buried ten thousand times over, than that God through us should be so spoken of! The Jews, we read, said to (Christ) Himself, "Thou that destroyest the Temple, and in three days buildest it up, come down from the Cross" (Matt. xxvii. 40): and again, "If Thou be the Son of God:" but the reproaches here are more grievous than those, that[5] through us He should be called a teacher of wickedness! Let us cause the very opposite to be said, by having our conversation worthy of Him that calleth us, and (worthily) approaching to the baptism of adoption. For great indeed is the might of baptism (φωτίσματος): it makes them quite other men than they were, that partake of the gift; it does not let the men be men

---

[1] Here also the order in the Mss. is confused. "Again proof. How God—with power. Whence does this appear? who went about—of the devil. Then from the good that He did, and the greatness," etc. The modern text has the same order, and the alterations do not affect the sense.

[2] Perhaps it should be φαντασθῇ, "that he (Cornelius) may not imagine," etc., therefore he mentions first the Divine Mission, then the Crucifixion.

[3] ταύτης δὲ οὐδὲν οὕτω σημεῖον μεῖζον ἦν, ὡς τὸ φαγεῖν καὶ πιεῖν. Cat. rightly omits μεῖζον ἦν. E. Edd. οὕτως εἰς ἀπόδειξιν μεῖζον, ὡς.

[4] The original reporter seems to have misunderstood what was said. If εἰπέ μοι be retained, we must read οὐχὶ αὐτὸς. The sense is, "Take heed lest any lay the blame of your evil doings upon God. For you know what would be said of a magistrate who should let a murderer go unpunished; that he would be held responsible for all the murders that may be afterwards done by that man, or in consequence of his impunity. Dread lest through your misconduct God be thus blasphemed." But—as if Chrysostom's meaning had been, Since God's purpose in forgiving us our sins was, that we should lead more virtuous and holy lives, therefore let none presume to say that God, by forgiving us, is the cause of the evil doings of which we are afterwards guilty"—the modern text (E. D. F. Edd.) goes on thus: "For say, if a magistrate, etc. is he judged to be the cause of the murders thereafter committed? By no means. And how is it that we ourselves, while, by the things we dare to do, we expose God to be insulted by godless tongues, do not fear and shudder? For what," etc.

[5] E. D. F. Edd. "Therefore, that it may not be possible for Him through us to be called, etc., and lest by the very fact of His being thus blasphemed; we ourselves become liable to the punishment thereof ('For through you,' it is written, 'My Name is blasphemed among the Gentiles,') let us cause the very opposite to be said, by having our conversation worthy of Him that calleth us, and (worthily) approaching to the baptism of adoption. For great indeed," etc. In C. it is: "teacher of wickedness. For great indeed," etc. B. "teacher of wickedness. For great indeed," etc. But the genuineness of the latter clauses, ἀξίως τοῦ καλοῦντος πολιτευόμενοι καὶ τῷ τῆς υἱοθεσίας προσιόντες βαπτίσματι, which are also needed by the following context, is attested by A. which retains them; for this Ms. abridges much, but never borrows from the modern text.

(and nothing more). Make thou the Gentile (τὸν Ἕλληνα), to believe that great is the might of the Spirit, that it has new-moulded, that it has fashioned thee anew. Why waitest thou for the last gasp, like a runaway slave, like a malefactor, as though it were not thy duty to live unto God? Why dost thou stand affected to Him, as if thou hadst in Him a ruthless, cruel Master? What can be more heartless (ψυχρότερον), what more miserable, than those who make that the time to receive baptism? God made thee a friend, and vouchsafed thee all His good things, that thou mayest act the part of a friend. Suppose you had done some man the greatest of wrongs, had insulted him, and brought upon him disgraces without end, suppose you had fallen into the hands of the person wronged, and he, in return for all this, had honored you, made you partaker of all that he had, and in the assembly of his friends, of those in whose presence he was in sulted, had crowned you, and declared that he would hold you as his own begotten son, and then straightway had died: say, would you not have bewailed him? would you not have deemed his death a calamity? would you not have said, Would that he were alive, that I might have it in my power to make the fit return, that I might requite him, that I might show myself not base to my benefactor? So then, where it is but man, this is how you would act; and where it is God, are you eager to be gone, that you may not requite your benefactor for so great gifts? Nay rather, choose the time for coming to Him so that you shall have it in your power to requite Him like for like. True, [1] say you, but I cannot keep (the gift). Has God commanded impossibilities? Hence it is that all is clean reversed, hence that, all the world over, every thing is marred—because nobody makes it his mark to live after God. Thus those who are yet Catechumens, because they make this their object, (how they may defer baptism to the last,) give themselves no concern about leading an upright life: and those who have been baptized (φωτισθέντες), whether it be because they received it as children, or whether it be that having received it in sickness, and afterwards recovered (ἀνενεγκόντες), they had no hearty desire to live on (to the glory of God), so it is, that neither do these make an earnest business of it: nay, even such as received it in health, have little enough to show of any good impression, and warmly affected for the time, these also presently let the fire go out. Why do you flee? why do you tremble? what is it you are afraid of? You do not mean to say that you are not permitted to follow your business? I do not part you from your wife! No, it is from fornication that I bar you. I do not debar you from the enjoyment of your wealth? No, but from covetousness and rapacity. I do not oblige you to empty out all your coffers? No, but to give some small matter according to your means to them that lack, your superfluities to their need, and not even this unrewarded. We do not urge you to fast? We do but forbid you to besot yourselves with drunkenness and gormandizing. The things we would retrench are but the very things which bring you disgrace; things which even here, on this side of hell-fire, you yourselves confess to be things to be shunned and hated. We do not forbid you to be glad and to rejoice? Nay, only rejoice not with a disgraceful and unbecoming merriment. What is it you dread, why are you afraid, why do you tremble? Where marriage is, where enjoyment of wealth, where food in moderation, what matter of sin is there in these things? And yet, they that are without enjoin the opposites to these, and are obeyed. For they demand not according to thy means, but they say, Thou must give thus much: and if thou allege poverty, they will [2] make no account of that. Not so Christ: Give, saith He, of what thou hast, and I inscribe thee in the first rank. Again those say, If thou wilt distinguish thyself, forsake father, mother, kindred, friends, and keep close attendance on the Palace, laboring, toiling, slaving, distracted, suffering miseries without number. Not so Christ; but keep thou, saith He, at home with thy wife, with thy children, and as for thy daily occupations reform and regulate them on the plan of leading a peaceable life, free from cares and from perils. True, say you, but the other promises wealth. Aye, but Christ a kingdom, and more, He promises wealth also with it. For, "Seek ye," saith

<hr/>

[1] Here all the Mss. have Τί φεύγεις; τί τρέμεις; τί δέδοικας; (Edd. omit the two latter clauses,) which, being out of place here, and required below, we have transposed to the beginning of the set of questions Μὴ γὰρ οὐκ ἔνι κ. τ. λ.—Below, he laments that the Catechumens, while delaying their baptism, if possible, to their dying hour, think themselves no way concerned to lead a virtuous life: of the baptism he distinguishes three classes: 1. those who received the sacrament in infancy; 2. those who were baptized in sickness and fear of death, but afterwards recovered: both which sorts, he says, are alike careless (the former because baptized in unconscious infancy), the latter because they did not think to survive, and had no hearty desire to live to the glory of God; 3. those baptized in mature age, and in health; and these also, if at the time their affections were kindled, soon let the flame go out.

[2] οὐδὲν προσποιήσονται, meaning perhaps, "they will pretend to make no account of that: they will say that that makes no difference." Edd. from E. only, οὐδὲ οὕτως ἀφίστανται, "they do not desist for all that."—Below: καὶ αὐτὰ ταῦτα διάπλαττεκαὶ ῥύθμιζε: i. e. Christ does not require you to abandon your calling in life, but these same occupations and duties of your station He bids you to mould and bring into entire conformity with His commandments:—τὸν ἀπράγμονα βίον ζῆν καὶ ἀκίνδυνον: something is wanting, the sense being, "making it your object (not to obtain distinction, wealth, etc. but) to lead a quiet life in godliness and honesty." Savile reads ζῆθι.

He, "the kingdom of Heaven, and all these things shall be added unto you" (Matt. vi. 33) : throwing in,[1] by way of additional boon, what the other holds out as the main thing : and the Psalmist says, he has "never seen the righteous forsaken, nor his seed begging their bread." (Ps. xxxvii. 25.) Let us set about practising virtue, let us make a beginning; let us only lay hold on it, and you shall see what the good will be. For surely in these (worldly) objects you do not succeed so without labor, that you should be so faint-hearted for these (higher) objects—that[2] you should say, Those are to be had without labor, these only with toil. Nay,—what need to tell you what is the true state of the case ?—those are had only with greater labor. Let us not recoil from the Divine Mysteries, I beseech you. Look not at this, that one who was baptized before thee, has turned out ill, and has fallen from his hope : since among soldiers also we see some not doing their duty by the service, while we see others distinguishing themselves, and we do not look only at the idle ones, but we emulate these, the men who are successful. But besides, consider how many, after their baptism, have of men become angels! Fear the uncertainty of the future. "As a thief in the night," so death comes : and not merely as a thief, but while we sleep it sets upon us, and carries us off while we are idling. To this end has God made the future uncertain, that we may spend our time in the practice of virtue, because of the uncertainty of expectation. But He is merciful, say you. How long shall we hear this senseless, ridiculous talk? *I* affirm not only that God is merciful, but that nothing can be more merciful than He, and that He orders all things concerning us for our good. How many all their life do you see afflicted with the worst form of leprosy! (ἐν ἐλέφαντι διάγοντας, "Elephantiasis,") how many blind from their earliest youth even to old age! others who have lost their eyesight, others in poverty, others in bonds, others again in the mines, others entombed (καταχωσθέντας) together, others (slaughtered) in wars! These things say you, do not look like mercy. Say, could He not have prevented these things had He wished, yet He permits them? True, say you.

Say, those who are blind from their infancy, why are they so? I will not tell you, until you promise me to receive baptism, and, being baptized, to live aright. It is not right to give you the solution of these questions. The preaching is not meant just for amusement. For even if I solve this, on the back of this follows another question : of such questions there is a bottomless deep. Therefore[3] do not get into a habit of looking to have them solved for you : else we shall never stop questioning. For look, if I solve this, I do but lead the way to question upon question, numberless as the snowflakes. So that this is what we learn, rather to raise questions, not to solve the questions that are raised. For even if we do solve them, we have not solved them altogether, but (only) as far as man's reasoning goes. The proper solution of such questions is faith : the knowing that God does all things justly and mercifully and for the best : that to comprehend the reason of them is impossible. This is the one solution, and another better than this exists not. For say, what is the use of having a question solved? This, that one needs no longer to make a question of the thing which is solved. And if thou get thyself to believe this, that all things are ordered by the Providence of God, Who, for reasons known to Himself, permits some things and actively works others, thou art rid of the need of questioning, and hast gotten the gain of the solution. But let us come back to our subject. Do you not see such numbers of men suffering chastisements? God (say you) permits these things to be. Make the right use of the health of the body, in order to the health of the soul. But you will say, What is the use to me of labors and toil, when it is in my power to get quit of all (my sins) without labor? In the first place, this is not certain. It may happen, that a person not only does not get quit of his sins without labor, but that he departs hence with all his sins upon him. However, even if this were certain, still your argument is not to be tolerated. He has drawn thee to the contests : the golden arms lie there. When you ought to take them, and to handle them, you wish to be ingloriously saved, and to do no good work! Say, if war broke out, and the Emperor were here, and you saw some charging into the midst of the phalanxes of the enemy, hewing them down, dealing wounds by thousands, others thrusting (with the sword's

---

[1] Καὶ ἐπὶ προσθήκης μέρει, ἃ προηγουμένως ἐκεῖνος· καὶ οὐκ εἶδεν, φησί, δίκαιον κ. τ. λ. The modern text (E. D. F. Edd.) inverts the meaning: Καὶ ἐκεῖνος μὲν οὐδὲ ἐν προσθήκης μέρει, οὗτος δὲ καὶ προηγουμένως. "And the former does not even by way of additional boon (hold out this), the latter (Christ) as the main thing." Adding, "I have been young, saith (the Psalmist), for indeed I am become old : and I never saw," etc.

[2] E. D. F. Edd. "'Yes,' say you, 'those (are to be had) without labor, these with labor.' Away with (such talk): it is not, no it is not so, but if one must say the truth, those (objects) are more yoked with toils, and are achieved with greater toil : but these, if we choose, easily."

[3] Ὥστε μὴ πρὸς τοῦτο ἐθίζετε ἑαυτοὺς, πρὸς τὸ λύσιν ζητεῖν. A. B. C. Sav. But the modern text has μόνον for πρὸς τοῦτο, and adds ἀλλὰ καὶ πρὸς τὸ μὴ ζητεῖν· "therefore accustom yourselves not only to seek the solution (of the questions), but also not to raise the questions."—Below : ὥστε τοῦτο μανθάνομεν (so A. D. F. Sav. the rest, μανθάνωμεν) μᾶλλον ζητεῖν, οὐχὶ (Edd. ἢ) τὰ ζητηθέντα λύειν.

point), others bounding (now here, now there), others dashing on horseback, and these praised by the Emperor, admired, applauded, crowned : others on the contrary thinking themselves well off if they take no harm, and keeping in the hindmost ranks, and sitting idly there; then after the close of the war, the former sort summoned, honored with the greatest gifts, their names proclaimed by the heralds : while of the latter, not even the name becomes known, and their reward of the good obtained is only that they are safe : which sort would you wish to belong to? Why, if you were made of stone, if you were more stupid even than senseless and lifeless things, would you not ten thousand times rather belong to the former ? Yea, I beseech and implore you. For if need were to fall fighting, ought you not eagerly to choose this ? See you not how it is with them that have fallen in the wars, how illustrious they are, how glorious ? And yet they die a death, after which there is no getting honor from the emperor. But in that other war, there is nothing of the kind, but thou shalt in any wise be presented with thy scars. Which scars, even without persecutions, may it be granted all us to have to exhibit, through Jesus Christ our Lord, with Whom to the Father and the Holy Ghost together be glory, dominion, honor, now and ever, and world without end. Amen.

HOMILY XXIV.

ACTS X. 44, 46.

" While Peter yet spake these words, the Holy Ghost fell on all them which heard the word. And they of the circumcision which believed were astonished, as many as came with Peter, because that on the Gentiles also was poured out the gift of the Holy Ghost. For they heard them speak with tongues, and magnify God."

OBSERVE God's providential management. He does not suffer the speech to be finished, nor the baptism to take place upon a command of Peter, but, when He has made it evident how admirable their state of mind is, and a beginning is made of the work of teaching, and they have believed that assuredly baptism is the remission of sins, then forthwith comes the Spirit upon them. Now this is done by God's so disposing it as to provide for Peter a mighty ground of justification.* And it is not simply that the Spirit came upon them, but, "they spake with tongues :" which was the thing that astonished those who had come to-gether. They altogether disliked the matter, wherefore it is that the whole is of God; and as for Peter, it may almost be said, that he is present only to be taught[1] (with them) the lesson, that they must take the Gentiles in hand, and that they themselves are the persons by whom this must be done. For whereas after all these great events, still both in Cæsarea and in Jerusalem a questioning is made about it, how would it have been if these (tokens) had not gone step by step with the progress of the affair ? Therefore it is that this is carried to a sort of excess.[2] Peter seizes his advantage, and see the plea he makes of it. " Can any man forbid water, that these should not be baptized, which have received the Holy Ghost as well as we ? " (v. 47.) Mark the issue to which he brings it; how he has been travailing to bring this forth. So (entirely) was he of this mind ! " Can any one, he asks, " forbid water ? " It is the language, we may almost say, of one triumphantly pressing his advantage (ἐπεμβαίνοντος)

---

* This is the only instance in the Acts in which the Holy Spirit is said to be given anterior to baptism (cf. xix. 5, 6) which was generally accompanied by the laying on of hands by the apostles. A special reason is observable here which greatly diminishes the force of Baur's objections to the historicity of the narrative drawn from this exceptional order of events, viz: the marked receptivity of Cornelius and his company. Perhaps it was intended by divine providence to signalize this bringing in of the first fruits of the Gentiles by showing how little the gifts of grace are conditioned upon outward rites. Some critics suppose that this gift of the Spirit before baptism was granted to impress Peter with the idea of the admissibility of the Gentiles, but this seems unnecessary, as he had been taught this lesson already by the vision and had distinctly avowed his conviction (v. 35). Chrysostom's exposition is in the line of the latter interpretation; he forcibly calls this gift of the Spirit an ἀπολογία μεγάλη for Peter. The principle which Bengel lays down in his comments—*liberum gratia habet ordinem*—together with the special significance of the occasion is a sufficient explanation of the apparently exceptional manner of the bestowment of the Spirit here.—G. B. S.

[1] καὶ ὁ Πέτρος σχεδὸν ἁπλῶς πάρεστι παιδευόμενος. Erasm. *fere simpliciter adest ut discat.* Not meaning that St. Peter needed to be taught (see above p. 146, note [1]), but that —such is the οἰκονομία for his exculpation—it is made to appear as if he needed the lesson and was now taught it, and had his misapprehensions rectified in common with them. Ben., entirely mistaking the meaning, has *quasi fortuito adest docens.*

[2] Καὶ διὰ τοῦτο μεθ᾽ ὑπερβολῆς γίνεται. Erasm. *Idcirco hæc cum excellentia quadam fiebant.* Ben. *Ideo hæc modo singulari fiunt.* But the meaning is, " There is a lavish array of Divine interpositions. The mission of the Angel to Cornelius, Peter's vision, the command given by the Spirit, above all, the gift of the Holy Ghost and the speaking with tongues before the baptism. This last was in itself an unanswerable declaration of the will of God, and sufficed for the Apostle's justification. The others are ἐκ περιουσίας, arguments *ex abundanti.*"

against such as would forbid, such as should say that this ought not to be. The whole thing, he says, is complete, the most essential part of the business, the baptism with which we were baptized. " And he commanded them to be baptized in the name of Jesus Christ." (v. 48.) After he has cleared himself, then, and not before, he commands them to be baptized: teaching them by the facts themselves. Such was the dislike the Jews had to it! Therefore it is that he first clears himself, although the very facts cry aloud, and then gives the command. " Then prayed they him "—well might they do so—" to tarry certain days:" and with a good courage thenceforth he does tarry.

" And the Apostles and brethren that were in Judea heard that the Gentiles had also received the word of God. And when Peter was come up to Jerusalem, they that were of the circumcision contended with hìm, saying, Thou wentest in to men uncircumcised, and didst eat with them." (ch. xi. 1–3.) After such great things, " they of the circumcision contended:" not the Apostles; God forbid! It means, they took no small offence.* And see what they allege. They do not say, Why didst thou preach? but, Why didst thou eat with them? But Peter, not stopping to notice this frigid objection—for frigid indeed it is— takes his stand (ίσταται) on that great argument, If they had the Spirit Itself given them, how could one refuse to give them the baptism? But how came it that in the case of the Samaritans this did not happen, but, on the contrary, neither before their baptism nor after it was there any controversy, and there they did not take it amiss, nay, as soon as they heard of it, sent the Apostles for this very purpose? (ch. viii. 14.) True, but neither in the present case is this the thing they complain of; for they knew that it was of Divine Grace: what they say is, Why didst thou eat with them? Besides, the difference[1] is not so great for Samaritans as it is for Gentiles. Moreover, it is so managed (as part of the Divine plan) that he is accused in this

way: on purpose that they may learn: for Peter, without some cause given, would not have related the vision. But observe his freedom from all elation and vainglory. For it says, " But Peter rehearsed the matter from the beginning, and expounded it by order unto them, saying, I was in the city of Joppa, praying:" he does not say why, nor on what occasion: " and in a trance I saw a vision, a certain vessel descend, as it had been a great sheet, let down from heaven by four corners; and it came even to me (v. 4, 5): upon the which when I had fastened mine eyes, I considered, and saw fourfooted beasts of the earth, and wild beasts, and creeping things, and fowls of the air. And I heard a voice saying unto me, Arise, Peter; slay and eat." (v. 6, 7.) As much as to say, This of itself was enough to have persuaded me—my having seen the linen sheet: but moreover a Voice was added. " But I said, Not so, Lord: for nothing common or unclean hath at any time entered into my mouth." (v. 8.) Do you mark? " I did my part," says he: " I said, that I have never eaten aught common or unclean:" with reference to this that they said, " Thou wentest in, and didst eat with them." But this he does not say to Cornelius: for there was no need to mention it to him. " But the voice answered me again from heaven, What God hath cleansed, that call not thou common. And this was done three times: and all were drawn up again into heaven." (v. 9, 10.) The essential points were those[2] (that ensued at Cæsarea); but by these he prepares the way for them. Observe how he justifies himself (by reasons), and forbears to use his authority as teacher. For the more mildly he expresses himself, the more tractable he makes them. " At no time," says he, " has aught common or unclean entered into my mouth.— And, behold—this too was part of his defence —three men stood at the house in which I was, sent to me from Cæsarea. And the Spirit bade me go with them, nothing doubting." (v. 11, 12.) Do you mark that it is to the Spirit the enacting of laws belongs! " And these also accompanied me "—nothing can be more lowly, when he alleges the brethren for witnesses!—" these six men, and we entered into the man's house: and he showed us how he had seen an angel in his house, which stood and said unto him, Send men to Joppa, and call for Simon, whose surname is Peter; who shall tell thee words, whereby thou

---

* Some critics (as Meyer, Olshausen) have affirmed the opposite of what Chrys. states, in regard to the οἱ ἐκ περιτομῆς. He excludes the apostles from this category; they would include them. The οἱ ἐκ περιτομῆς, however, seem to have been a special class of Christians in the mind of the writer. In expressing the fact that the Church learned of the reception of the Gentiles, the " apostles and brethren" are named, but when the narrative advances to the thought of the *contention* against Peter on account of it, a new term is chosen; the writer could not allow the same subject to stand for the verb διεκρίνοντο, but chooses another term—οἱ ἐκ περιτομῆς. The two subjects, then, can hardly be identical. The phrase more probably denotes judaizing Christians, i. e. those who gave special prominence to the Law and the necessity of circumcision (So Lechler, Gloag, Alford).—G. B. S.

[1] ῎Αλλως δὲ οὐ τοσοῦτον τὸ διάφορον Σαμαρειτῶν καὶ ἐθνῶν. Edd. (from E. alone,) for οὐ τοσοῦτον have πολὺ καὶ ἄπειρον, " great and infinite the difference between Samaritans and Gentiles."

[2] A. B. C. (after v. 11. which we have removed), Ἐκεῖνα ἀναγκαῖα ἦν (read τὰ ἀν.) ἀλλὰ διὰ τούτων αὐτὰ κατασκευάζει. By ἐκεῖνα he means, what we have heard above, what happened at Cæsarea. The modern text (Edd.): " What points were essential, he relates, but of the rest he is silent: or rather by these he confirms them also, καὶ αὐτὰ κατασκευάζει."

and all thy house shall be saved." (v. 13, 14.) And he does not mention the words spoken by the Angel to Cornelius, "Thy prayers and thine alms are come up for a memorial before God, that he may not disgust them; but what says he? "He shall tell thee words, whereby thou and all thy house shall be saved:" with good reason this is added.[1] Also he says nothing of the man's fitness (ἐπιεικές). "The Spirit," he might say, "having sent (me), God having commanded, on the one part having summoned (me) through the Angel, on the other urging (me) on, and solving my doubt about the things, what was I to do?" He says none of these things, however: but makes his strong point of what happened last, which even in itself was an incontrovertible argument. "And as I began to speak," etc. (v. 15.) Then why did not this happen alone? Of superabundance (ἐκ περιουσίας) this is wrought by God, that it might be shown that the beginning too was not from the Apostle. But had he set out of his own motion, without any of these things having taken place, they would have been very much hurt: so[2] that from the beginning he disposes their minds in his favor * * : saying to them, "Who have received the Holy Ghost even as we." And not content with this, he reminds them also of the words of the Lord: "Then remembered I the word of the Lord, how that he said, John indeed baptized with water; but ye shall be baptized with the Holy Ghost." (v. 16.) He means, that no new thing has happened, but just what the Lord foretold. "But[3] there was no need to baptize?" (Comp. p. 158.) But the baptism was completed already. And he does not say, I ordered them to be baptized: but what says he? "Forasmuch then as God gave them the like gift as He did unto us, who believed on the Lord Jesus Christ; what was I, that I could withstand God?" (v. 17.) He shows that he had himself done nothing: for the very thing which we have obtained, he says, that same did those men

receive. That he may more effectually stop their mouths, therefore he says, "The like gift." Do you perceive how he does not allow them to have less: when they believed, says he, the same gift did God give unto them, as He did to us who believed on the Lord, and Himself cleanses them. And he does not say, To you, but to us. Why do you feel aggrieved, when we[4] call them partakers (with us?) "When they heard these things, they held their peace, and glorified God, saying, Then hath God also to the Gentiles granted repentance unto life." (v. 18.) Do you mark that it all came of Peter's discourse, by his admirably skilful way of relating the facts? They glorified God that He had given repentance to themselves (καὶ αὐτοῖς) also: they were humbled by these words. Hence was the door of faith opened thenceforth to the Gentiles. But, if you please, let us look over again what has been said.

"While Peter yet spake," etc. (Recapitulation.) He does not say that Peter was astonished, but, "They of the circumcision:" since he knew what was in preparation. And yet they ought to have marvelled at this, how they themselves had believed. When they heard that they had believed, they were not astonished, but when God gave them the Spirit. Then[5] "answered Peter and said," etc. (v. 47.) And therefore it is that he says, "God hath shown that I should not call common or unclean any human being." (v. 28.) He knew this from the first, and plans his discourse beforehand (with a view to it). Gentiles? What Gentiles henceforth? They were no longer Gentiles, the Truth being come. It is nothing wonderful, he says, if before the act of baptism they received the Spirit: in our own case this same happened. Peter shows that not as the rest either were they baptized, but in a much better way. This is the reason why the thing takes place in this manner, that they may have nothing to say, but even in this way may account them equal with themselves. "And they besought him," it says, "to tarry certain days." (v. 48.) "And the Apostles and brethren, etc. And they of the circumcision contended with him." (ch. xi. 1. 2.) Do you remark how they were

---

[1] τοῦτο εἰκότως πρόσκειται. i. e. though this was not mentioned before (see above, p. 145. note [6]) with good reason it is added here: viz. for Peter's justification. Edd. from E. "that he may not disgust them: but what had nothing great in it, 'He shall speak,' etc. Do you mark how for this reason I mentioned before, he hastens on?" But the saying, "He shall speak," etc. was great, even greater than that which he omits: but this was not necessary, the other (Chrys. means) made a strong point for Peter's defence, and therefore is added.

[2] ἄνωθεν αὐτῶν τὴν διανοίαν οἰκειοῖ, viz. by letting them see how all along it was not his doing. Then before λέγων πρὸς αὐτούς, something is wanting: e. g. "Which done, he urges most effectively, 'Who have received,'" etc.

[3] E. D. F. Edd. "But there was no need to baptize, it may be said, for the baptism was complete, when the Spirit fell upon them.' Therefore he does not say, I first ordered them to be baptized, but what? 'Can any man forbid water that these should not be baptized?' By this showing that he did nothing himself. What therefore we have obtained, those received."

[4] ὅταν ἡμεῖς αὐτοὺς κοινωνοὺς λέγωμεν; "when we put them on a level with us the Apostles and first disciples, in regard that they received the Spirit in the same manner as we received, and as the rest of you did not?"

[5] τότε ὁ Π. ὕστερον ἐξίσταται· καὶ διὰ τοῦτο τοῦτο φησίν. "But when God gave them the Spirit, then Peter afterwards is astonished," etc. This is evidently corrupt. Τότε ὁ Π.seems to be part of the text v. 46. τότε ἀπεκρίθη ὁ Π. For ὕστερον ἐξίσταται we may perhaps restore, καὶ πρὸς τοῦτο ὁ Π. ὕστερον ἵσταται. "On this Peter afterwards insists (as above, p. 156), and with a view to this he says (before), 'God hath shown me,'" etc. The innovator substitutes: "When Peter expounded to them his trance, saying, 'God hath shown me,'" etc. So Edd.

not kindly disposed towards him? Saying Thou wentest in to men uncircumcised, and didst eat with them." (v. 3.) Do you note what zeal they had for the Law? Not Peter's authority abashed them, not the signs which had taken place, not the success achieved, what a thing it was, the Gentiles having "received the word;" but they contended about those petty things. For if none of those (signs) had taken place, was not the success (itself) enough?[1] But not so does Peter frame his defence: for he was wise, or rather it was not his wisdom, but the Spirit that spake the words. And by the matter of his defence, he shows that in no one point was he the author, but in every point God, and upon Him he casts the whole. "The trance," he says—"it was He that caused me to fall into it, for "I was in Joppa," etc.: the vessel—it was He that showed it; I objected: again, He spake, and even then I did not hear: the Spirit commanded me to go, and even then though I went, I did not run: I told that God had sent me, and after these things, even then I did not baptize, but again God did the whole. God baptized them, not I." And he does not say, Was it not right then to add the water? but, implying that nothing was lacking, "What was I, that I should withstand God?" What a defence is here! For he does not say, Then knowing these things, hold your peace; but what? He stands their attack, and to their impeachment he pleads—"What was I, to be able to hinder God?" It was not possible for me to hinder—a forcible plea indeed, and such as might well put them to shame. Whence being at last afraid, "they held their peace and glorified God."

In like manner ought we also to glorify God for the good things which befall our neighbors, only[2] not in the way that the rest of the newly-baptized are insulted, when they see others receiving baptism, and immediately departing this life. It is right to glorify God, even though all be saved: and as for thee, if thou be willing, thou hast received a greater gift (than they): I do not mean in respect of the baptism, for the gift there is the same for him as for thee, but in regard that thou hast received a set time for winning distinction. The other put on the robe, and was not suffered to exhibit himself therewith in the procession, whereas to thee, God hath given full opportunity to use thine arms for the right purpose, thereby to make proof of them. The other goes his way, having only the reward of his faith: thou standest in the course, both able to obtain an abundant recompense for thy works, and to show thyself as much more glorious than he, as the sun is than the smallest star, as the general, nay rather as the Emperor himself, than the lowest soldier. Then blame thyself, or rather not blame, but correct: for it is not enough to blame thyself; it is in thy power to contend afresh. Hast thou been thrown? hast thou taken grievous hurt? Stand up, recover thyself: thou art still in the course, the meeting (θέατρον) is not yet broken up. Do you not see how many that have been thrown in the wrestling have afterwards resumed the combat? Only do not willingly come by thy fall. Dost thou count him a happy man for departing this life? Much rather count thyself happy. Was he released of his sins? But thou, if thou wilt, shalt not only wash away thy sins, but shalt also have achievements (of good works), which in his case is not possible. It is in our power to recover ourselves. Great are the medicinal virtues (φάρμακα) of repentance: let none despair of himself. That man truly deserves to be despaired of, who despairs of himself; that man has no more salvation, nor any hopes. It is not the having fallen into a depth of evils, it is the lying there when fallen, that is dreadful, it is not the having come into such a condition, it is the making light of it that is impious. The very thing that ought to make thee earnest, say, is it this that makes thee reckless? Having received so many wounds, hast thou fallen back? Of the soul, there

---

[1] Εἰ γὰρ μηδὲν τούτων ἦν, οὐκ ἦρκει τὸ κατόρθωμα; Of the Edd. only Savile puts this, as it ought to be, interrogatively: Ben. renders, *non sat fuisset præstitum.*

[2] μόνον μὴ καθάπερ οἱ λοιποὶ τῶν νεοφωτίστων ἐπηρεάζονται, ὅταν ἄλλους ὁρῶσι φωτισθέντας, καὶ εὐθὺς ἀπιόντας. Δοξάζειν δεῖ τὸν Θεόν, κἂν πάντες σωθῶσιν· καὶ σὺ ἐὰν θέλῃς κ. τ. λ. Above Hom. i. p. 20, it is said, "the sick man" having received baptism in the prospect of death, "if he recovers, is as vexed" because of his baptism "as if some great harm had happened to him." And so it might have been said here, "not (to feel) as some of the newly-baptized (are apt to do, who) are annoyed (or aggrieved, ἐπηρεάζονται), when they see others" etc.: i. e. who, seeing such cases, think themselves ill used that they were not allowed to defer their baptism to the last moment, but were forced upon the alternative either of leading a strict life, or of forfeiting the grace of baptism. But the assertion οἱ λοιποὶ τῶν νεοφ. is too sweeping, and the word ἐπηρεάζονται is scarcely suitable to this sense: it should rather have been δεινοπαθοῦσιν or ἀναξιοπαθοῦσιν. The meaning, not fully expressed, is: "only not, like as the rest of the newly-baptized are insulted, taunted or jeered (by some), when they see others," etc.: i. e. it is right to glorify God, only not to imagine that God is glorified by those who, exulting in the safety of their friends who received baptism at the point of death, taunt the rest of the newly baptized, saying, "See, these men are safe: they are baptized to some purpose: while you have received the gift, only to be in danger of losing it."—He adds,

"It is right to glorify God, though all be saved"—though that were the case with all except yourself, that they passed at once from baptism to that world, with the gift unimpaired, and no more in danger to be lost. "And as for you, if you will, you have received a greater gift," than they: etc.—For ἐπηρεάζονται, A. has ἐπηρεάζουσιν: and this is adopted by the innovator, who alters the passage thus (E. Edd.): "to glorify God, ἀλλ' οὐκ ἐπηρεάζειν (adopted by F. D.) καθάπερ οἱ πολλοὶ τῶν νεοφωτ. ἐπηρεάζουσιν, when they see, etc. It is right to glorify God, καὶ ὅτι μένειν οὐ συγχωρεῖ· Ὥστε καὶ σὺ ἐὰν θέλῃς κ. τ. λ. (Erasm. *et non insultare:* Ben. *non autem insultare illis.*)

can be no incurable wound; for the body, there are many such, but none for the soul: and yet for those we cease not in our endeavors to cure them, while for these we are supine. Seest thou not the thief (on the cross), in how short a time he achieved (his salvation)? Seest thou not the Martyrs, in how short a time they accomplished the whole work? "But martyrdom is not to be had nowadays." True, but there are contests to be had, as I have often told you, if we had the mind. "For they that wish," says the Apostle, "to live godly in Christ Jesus, shall suffer persecution." (2 Tim. iii. 12.) They that live godly are always undergoing persecution, if not from men, at any rate from evil spirits, which is a more grievous persecution. Yes, and it is in consequence, first and foremost, of ease and comfort, that those who are not vigilant undergo this. Or, thinkest thou it is a trifling persecution to be living at ease? This is more grievous than all, this is worse than persecution. For, like a running flux, ease makes the soul languid (χαυνοῖ): and as summer and winter, so persecution and ease. But to show you that this is the worse persecution, listen: it induces sleep in the soul, an excessive yawning and drowsiness, it stirs up the passions on every side, it arms pride, it arms pleasure, it arms anger, envy, vainglory, jealousy. But in time of persecution none of these is able to make a disturbance; but fear, entering in, and plying the lash vigorously, as one does to a barking dog, will not let any of these passions so much as attempt to give tongue. Who shall be able in time of persecution to indulge in vainglory? Who to live in pleasure? Not one: but there is much trembling and fear, making a great calm, composing the harbor into stillness, filling the soul with awe. I have heard from our fathers (for in our own time God grant it may not happen, since we are bidden not to ask for temptation), that in the persecution of old time one might see men that were indeed Christian. None of them cared for money, none for wife, none for children, nor home, nor country: the one great concern with all was to save their lives (or, souls). There were they hiding, some in tombs and sepulchres, some in deserts: yes tender and dainty women too, fighting all the while with constant hunger. Then think whether any longing for sumptuous and dainty living at all came into the mind of a woman, while in hiding beside a coffin (παρὰ λάρνακι), and waiting for her maid-servant to bring her meal, and trembling lest she should be taken, and lying in her terror as in a furnace: was she even aware that there ever

was such a thing as dainty living, that such things as dress and ornaments exist at all (ὅτι κόσμος ὅλως ἐστίν)? Seest thou that now is the persecution, with our passions, like wild beasts, setting upon us on every side? Now is the trying persecution, both in this regard, and especially if it is not even thought to be persecution at all. For this (persecution) has also this evil in it, that being war, it is thought to be peace, so that we do not even arm ourselves against it, so that we do not even rise: no one fears, no one trembles. But if ye do not believe me, ask the heathen, the persecutors, at what time was the conduct of the Christians more strict, at what time were they all more proved? Few indeed had they then become in number, but rich in virtue. For say, what profit is it, that there should be hay in plenty, when there might be precious stones? The amount consists not in the sum of numbers, but in the proved worth. Elias was one: yet the whole world was not worth so much as he. And yet the world consists of myriads: but they are no myriads, when they do not even come up to that one. "Better[1] is one that doeth the will of God, than ten thousand who are transgressors:" for the ten thousands have not yet reached to the one. "Desire not a multitude of unprofitable children." (Ecclus. xvi. 1.) Such bring more blasphemy against God, than if they were not Christians. What need have I of a multitude? It is (only) more food for the fire. This one might see even in the body, that better is moderate food with health, than a (fatted) calf with damage. This is more food than the other: this is food, but that is disease. This too one may see in war: that better are ten expert and brave men, than ten thousand of no experience. These latter, besides that they do no work, hinder also those that do work. The same too one may see to be the case in a ship, viz. that better are two experienced mariners, than ever so great a number of unskilful ones: for these will sink the ship. These things I say, not as looking with an evil eye upon your numbers, but wishing that all of you should be approved men, and not trust in your numbers. Many more in number are they who go down into hell: but greater than it is the Kingdom, however few it contain. As the sand of the sea was the

---

[1] κρείσσων εἷς ποιῶν τὸ θέλημα Κυρίου, ἢ μύριοι παράνομοι. St. Chrys. repeatedly cites this, and almost in the same words, as a text of Scripture, and the Edd. refer it to Ecclus. xvi. 3, but there it is, κρείσσων γὰρ εἷς ἢ χίλιοι (with no various reading), and here the following words, οἱ (B. εἰ) γὰρ μύριοι πρὸς τὸν (τὸ, B. F. ἕνα οὐδέπω ἔφθασαν, seem to be meant as part of the citation. For these E. Edd. substitute, Τοῦτο καί τις σοφὸς αἰνιττόμενος οὕτω πως φησί. Savile adopts both, but reads οὐ γὰρ μύριοι.

multitude of the people (Israel) yet one man saved them. Moses was but one, and yet he availed more than they all: Joshua was one and he was enabled to do more than the six hundred thousand. Let us not make this our study merely, that (the people) may be many, but rather, that they may be excellent; when this shall have been effected, then will that other follow also. No one wishes at the outset to make a spacious house, but he first makes it strong and sure, then spacious: no one lays the foundations so that he may be laughed at. Let us first aim at this, and then at the other. Where this is, that also will be easy: but where this is not, the other, though it be, is to no profit. For if there be those who are able to shine in the Church, there will soon be also numbers: but where these are not, the numbers will never be good for anything. How many, suppose you, may there be in our city who are likely to be saved (τοὺς σωζομένους)? It is disagreeable, what I am going to say, but I will say it nevertheless. Among all these myriads, there are not to be found one hundred likely to be saved: nay, even as to these, I question it. For think, what wickedness there is in the young, what supineness in the aged! None[1] makes it his duty to look after his own boy, none is moved by anything to be seen in his elder, to be emulous of imitating such an one. The patterns are defaced, and therefore it is that neither do the young become admirable in conduct. Tell me not, "We are a goodly multitude:" this is the speech of men who talk without thought or feeling (ψυχρῶν.) In the concerns of men indeed, this might be said with some show of reason: but where God is concerned, (to say this with regard to Him) as having need of us,[2] can never be allowed. Nay, let me tell you, even in the former case, this is a senseless speech (ψυχρόν). Listen. A person that has a great number of domestics, if they be a corrupt set what a wretched time will he have of it! For him who has none, the hardship, it seems, amounts to this, that he is not waited on: but where a person has bad servants, the evil is, that he is ruining himself withal, and the damage is greater (the more there are of them.) For it is far worse than having to be one's own servant, to have to fight with others, and take up a (continual) warfare. These things I say, that none may admire the

Church because of its numbers, but that we may study to make the multitude proof-worthy; that each may be earnest for his own share of the duty—not for his friends only, nor his kindred as I am always saying, nor for his neighbors, but that he may attract the strangers also. For example, Prayer is going on; there they lie (on bended knees), all the young, stupidly unconcerned (ψυχροί), (yes,) and old too:[3] filthy nuisances rather than young men; giggling, laughing outright, talking—for I have heard even this going on—and jeering one another as they lie along on their knees: and there stand you, young man or elder: rebuke them, if you see them (behaving thus): if any will not refrain, chide him more severely: call the deacon, threaten, do what is in your power to do: and if he dare do anything to you, assuredly you shall have all to help you. For who is so irrational, as, when he sees you chiding for such conduct, and them chidden not to take your part? Depart, having received your reward from the Prayer.—In a master's house, we count those his best-disposed servants, who cannot bear to see any part of his furniture in disorder. Answer me; if at home you should see the silver plate lie tossed out of doors, though it is not your business, you will pick it up and bring it into the house: if you see a garment flung out of its place, though you have not the care of it, though you be at enmity with him whose business it is, yet, out of good-will to the master, will you not put it right? So in the present case. These are part of the furniture: if you see them lying about in disorder, put them to rights: apply to me, I do not refuse the trouble: inform me, make the offender known to me: it is not possible for me to see all: excuse me (in this). See, what wickedness overspreads the whole world! Said I without reason that we are (no better than) so much hay (disorderly as) a troubled sea? I am not talking of those (young people), that they behave thus; (what I complain of, is) that such a sleepy indifference possesses those who come in here, that they do not even correct this misbehavior. Again I see others stand talking while Prayer is going on; while the more consistent[4] of them (do this)

---

[1] Οὐδεὶς τὴν ἐπιμέλειαν ἔχει τοῦ παιδὸς τοῦ ἑαυτοῦ· οὐδεὶς ἔχει ζῆλον πρὸς πρεσβύτην ἰδὼν μιμήσασθαι. i. e. "The young are neglected by their own parents and masters, and elsewhere they see no good example of the old to move them to virtue."

[2] Ἐπὶ δὲ τοῦ Θεοῦ τοῦ δεομένου ἡμῶν, οὐκ ἔτι. So A. B. C. The modern text, τοῦ οὐδ.

[3] πάντες νέοι ψυχροὶ καὶ γέροντες. The last word must be corrupt, for he is speaking only of the young: perhaps it should be γέμοντες with some genitive, e. g. "full of folly," or "evil thoughts." Then, καθάρματα μᾶλλον ἢ νέοι, more fit to be swept away from the floor as filthy litter than to be regarded as young men. But κάθαρμα, in the sense derived from the heathen ritual, has no equivalent in our language: it means, what remains of the sacrifice used for lustration or atonement, which as having taken into itself the uncleanness or the guilt which was to be removed, was regarded with the utmost abhorrence.

[4] οἱ δὲ ἐπιεικέστεροι αὐτῶν. Erasm., Et quidam ex illis, adhuc meliores scilicet. Ben. alios modestiores scilicet.

not only during the Prayer, but even when the Priest is giving the Benediction. O, horror! When shall there be salvation? when shall it be possible for us to propitiate God?—Soldiers[1] go to their diversion, and you shall see them, all keeping time in the dance, and nothing done negligently, but, just as in embroidery and painting, from the well-ordered arrangement in each individual part of the composition, there results at once an exceeding harmony and good keeping, so it is here: we have one shield, one head, all of us (in common): and if but some casual point be deranged by negligence, the whole is deranged and is spoilt, and the good order of the many is defeated by the disorder of the one part. And, fearful indeed to think of, here you come, not to a diversion, not to act in a dance, and yet you stand disorderly. Know you not that you are standing in company with angels? with them you chant, with them sing hymns, and do you stand laughing? Is it not wonderful that a thunderbolt is not launched not only at those (who behave thus), but at us? For such behavior might well be visited with the thunderbolt. The Emperor is present, is reviewing the army: and do

you, even with His eyes upon you, stand laughing, and endure to see another laughing? How long are we to go on chiding, how long complaining? Ought not such to be treated as very pests and nuisances; as abandoned, worthless reprobates, fraught with innumerable mischiefs, to be driven away from the Church? When will these forebear laughing, who laugh in the hour of the dread Mystery (ἐν ὥρᾳ φρίκης)? when refrain from their trifling, who talk at the instant of the Benediction? Have they no sense of shame before those who are present? have they no fear of God? Are our own idle thoughts not enough for us, is it not enough that in our prayers we rove hither and thither, but laughter also must needs intrude, and bursts of merriment? Is it a theatrical amusement, what is done here? Aye, but, methinks, it is the theatres that do this: to the theatres we owe it that the most of you so refuse to be curbed by us, and to be reformed. What we build up here, is thrown down there: and not only so, but the hearers themselves cannot help being filled with other filthinesses besides: so that the case is just the same as if one should want to clean out a place with a fountain above it discharging mire; for however much you may clean out, more runs in. So it is here. For when we clean people out, as they come here from the theatres with their filthiness, thither they go again, and take in a larger stock of filthiness, as if they lived for the purpose of only giving us trouble, and then come back to us, laden with ordure, in their manners, in their movements, in their words, in their laughter, in their idleness. Then once more we begin shovelling it out afresh, as if we had to do this only on purpose that, having sent them away clean, we may again see them clogging themselves with filth. Therefore I solemnly protest to you, the sound members, that this will be to you judgment and condemnation, and I give you over to God from this time forth, if any having seen a person behaving disorderly, if any having seen any person talking, especially in that part (of the Service), shall not inform against him, not bring him round (to a better behavior). To do this is better than prayer. Leave thy prayer and rebuke him, that thou mayst both do him good, and thyself get profit, and so we may be enabled all to be saved and to attain unto the Kingdom of Heaven, through the grace and loving-kindness of our Lord Jesus Christ, with Whom to the Father and the Holy Ghost together be glory, dominion, honor, now and ever, and world without end. Amen.

But the irony is not of this kind, and the word here has its proper sense: "men whose conduct is more of a piece, the more consistent of them." Some stand and talk during the prayers, yet kneel and are silent for the Benediction: but these make no such inconsistent pretence: they do not commit this absurdity at least.—Comp. *Hom.* i. *in Oziam*, § 4, t. vi. p. 101. "A grievous disease prevails in the Church: when we have purposed to hold converse with God, and are in the act of sending up the doxology to Him, we interrupt our business, and each takes his neighbor aside to talk with him about his domestic concerns, about the goings on in the agora, the public, the theatre, the army: how this was well managed, that neglected: what is the strong point, and what the weak point in this or that business: in short, about all sorts of public and private matters they talk here with one another. Is this pardonable? When a man speaks with the earthly sovereign, he speaks only on the subjects the sovereign chooses to speak and put questions about, and if against the will of the sovereign he should presume to start any other subject, he would bring upon himself the severest punishment. And you, who are speaking with the King of kings, to Whom the angels minister with dread reverence, do you leave your converse with Him to talk about mire, and dust, and spiders—for that is what earthly things are? But you say, the public affairs are in such a bad way, and there is much to talk of and much to be anxious about. And whose fault is that? They say, The blunders of our rulers are the cause. No, not the blunders of our rulers, but our sins: the punishment of our faults. It is these have ruined all, have brought upon us all our sufferings, wars, and defeats. Therefore if we had an Abraham, a Moses, a David, a Solomon, for our ruler, yea, the most righteous of men, it would signify nothing as far as the cause of all our evils is concerned . . . And if we have one of the most iniquitous of men, a blundering ill-managing person for our ruler, it is our own folly and wickedness that has brought this upon us, it is the punishment of our sins. Therefore let each when he comes here think of his own sins, and not complain of others." *Hom.* ix. *in* 1 *Tim.* he complains of the women talking in Church.

[1] The illustration is taken from some kind of shield dance, which formed one of the amusements of the camp, skilfully executed by a large body of soldiers. The innovator, (E. D. F. Edd.) not understanding the allusion, substitutes: "If you go to a diversion, you will see all keeping time in the dance, and nothing done negligently. As therefore in a well-harmonized and curiously wrought lyre, one well sounding symphony results from the orderly arrangement severally of the component parts, so here there ought to result from all one symphonious harmony. For we are become one Church, we count as members, 'fitly joined together' of one Head, we all make one Body: if any carnal point be done negligently, the whole, etc. Thus the good order," etc.

HOMILY XXV.

ACTS XI. 19.

"Now they which were scattered abroad upon the persecution that rose about Stephen travelled as far as Phenice, and Cyprus, and Antioch, preaching the word to none but unto the Jews only."

THE persecution turned out to be no slight benefit, as "to them that love God all things work together for good." (Rom. viii. 28.) If they had made it their express study how best to establish the Church, they would have done no other thing than this—they dispersed the teachers.* Mark in what quarters the preaching was extended. "They travelled," it says, "as far as Phenice and Cyprus and Antioch; to none however did they preach the word but to Jews only." Dost thou mark with what wise purposes of Providence so much was done in the case of Cornelius? This serves both to justify Christ, and to impeach the Jews. When Stephen was slain, when Paul was twice in danger, when the Apostles were scourged, then the Gentiles received the word, then the Samaritans. Which Paul also declares: "To you it was necessary that the Word of God should first be spoken; but since ye thrust it from you, and judge yourselves unworthy, lo, we turn unto the Gentiles." (ch. xiii. 46.) Accordingly they went about, preaching to Gentiles also. "But some of them were men of Cyprus and Cyrene, who, when they were come to Antioch, spake unto the Greeks, preaching the Lord Jesus:" (v. 20.) for it is likely both that they could now speak Greek, and that there were such men in Antioch.† "And the hand of the Lord," it says, "was with them," that is, they wrought miracles; "and a great number believed, and turned unto the Lord." (v. 21.) Do you mark why now also there was need of miracles (namely) that they might believe? "Then tidings of these things came unto the ears of the church which was in Jerusalem: and they sent forth Barnabas, that he should go as far as Antioch." (v. 22.) What may be the reason that, when such a city received the word, they did not come themselves? Because of the Jews. But they send Barnabas. However, it is no small part of the providential management even so that Paul comes to be there. It is both natural, and it is wisely ordered, that they are averse to him, and (so) that Voice of the Gospel, that Trumpet of heaven, is not shut up in Jerusalem. Do you mark how on all occasions, Christ turns their ill dispositions to needful account and for the benefit of the Church? Of their hatred to the man, He availed Himself for the building up of the Church. But observe this holy man—Barnabas, I mean—how he looked not to his own interests, but hasted to Tarsus. "Who, when he came, and had seen the grace of God, was glad, and exhorted them all, that with purpose of heart, they would cleave unto the Lord. For he was a good man, and full of the Holy Ghost, and of faith: and much people was added unto the Lord." (v. 23, 24.) He was a very kind man, and single-hearted, and considerate (συγγνωμονικός). "Then departed Barnabas to Tarsus, for to seek Saul." (v. 25.) He came to the athletic wrestler, the general (fit to lead armies),

---

* The narrative beginning with xi. 19, may be considered as a resumption of viii. 4, sq. where the preaching of Philip in Samaria is referred to the persecution at Jerusalem as its occasion. The dispersion of the disciples now becomes the means of a great extension of the Gospel and the founding of the first Gentile Church (at Antioch in Syria). This is the third great movement in the spread of early Christianity. The order is: (1) The preaching of Philip in Samaria, (2) The conversion of Cornelius and his company—the first Gentile additions to the church. (3) This mission which resulted in the founding of the church at Antioch. But at this time Divine Providence was preparing an agent who was destined soon to enter upon his great life work as the Christian missionary to the Gentile world, to prove the chief means of spreading the gospel throughout the Roman world—this was the former persecutor Saul, now transformed into the great apostle to the Gentiles. The conversion of Cornelius must have occurred about eight years after the ascension of Jesus. During this time the church had continued Jewish. But in this very period the conditions were preparing for the extension of Christianity to the Gentile world. Stephen had caught glimpses of the largeness of God's truth and purposes. Peter had learned that God is no respecter of persons. The mother church at Jerusalem now finds that God's grace has outrun all their former conception of its scope; consecrated and able men like Barnabas and Paul are rising up to labor in the line of the more comprehensive conception of Christianity's method and purpose which is now dawning upon the consciousness of the church.—G. B. S.

† While the textual evidence for the reading Ἑλληνιστάς (v. 20.) predominates over that for the reading Ἕλληνας (A. C.), yet the latter is the reading adopted by Meyer, Tischendorf, and most critics (not so, W. and H.) on grounds of internal evidence, such as: (1) That they should preach to Hellenists—men of Jewish nationality residing out of Judea—would be nothing noteworthy, since they had long been received into the Christian community. (2) The contrast between vv. 19 and 20 would be greatly weakened, if not lost, on the supposition that Hellenistic Jews were meant. If this view is correct, they now preached to the Greeks, the uncircumcised heathen, and the Antioch Church was founded and its reception into Christian fellowship approved by the mother church at Jerusalem. Antioch now became an important centre of Christian work, second only to Jerusalem. Here Paul labored a year, and from Antioch he went forth to his three great missionary journeys. —G. B. S.

the champion of single combat, the lion—I am at a loss for words, say what I will—the hunting-dog, killer of lions, bull of strength, lamp of brightness, mouth sufficing for a world. "And when he had found him, he brought him to Antioch." (v. 26.) Verily this is the reason why it was there they were appointed to be called Christians, because Paul there spent so long time! "And it came to pass, that a whole year they assembled themselves with the Church, and taught much people. And the disciples were first called Christians at Antioch."* No small matter of praise to that city! This is enough to make it a match for all, that for so long a time it had the benefit of that mouth, it first, and before all others: wherefore also it was there in the first place that men were accounted worthy of that name. Do you observe the benefit resulting (to that city) from Paul, to what a height that name, like a standard (σημεῖον), exalted it? Where three thousand, where five thousand, believed, where so great a multitude, nothing of the sort took place, but they were called "they[1] of the way:" here they were called Christians. "And in these days came prophets from Jerusalem unto Antioch." (v. 27.) It was need that the fruit of alms should also be planted there. And see how of necessity (ἀναγκαίως) (it comes about that) none of the men of note becomes their teacher. They got for their teachers, men of Cyprus, and Cyrene, and Paul—though he indeed surpassed (the Apostles) themselves—since Paul also had for teachers Ananias and Barnabas. But[2] here of necessity (this was the case). "And there stood up one of them named

Agabus, and signified by the spirit that there would be great dearth throughout the world, which also came to pass in the days of Claudius Cæsar." (v. 28.) "By the Spirit," it says: for; that they may not imagine that this was the reason why the famine came, (namely) because Christianity was come in, because the demons were departed, the Holy Ghost foretells it: this, however, was nothing wonderful, for in fact Christ predicted it. Not this was the reason, else this must have been the case from the beginning: but it was because of the evils done to the Apostles— and God had borne long with them ; but, when they pressed upon them, a great famine ensues, betokening to the Jews the coming woes. "If it was because of them, in any wise it ought to have stopped (there), when it did exist. What harm had the Gentiles done, that they should have their share in the evils? They ought rather to have been marked as approved (εὐδοκιμῆσαι), because they were doing their part, were slaying, punishing, taking vengeance, persecuting on every side. And mark also at what time the famine comes: precisely when the Gentiles were thenceforth added to the Church. But if, as you say, it was because of the evils (done by the Jews), these ought to have been exempted." How so? Christ, forestalling this objection, said, "Ye shall have tribulation." (John xvi. 33.) (It is) just as if you should say, They ought not to have been scourged either. "Then the disciples, every man according to his ability, determined to send relief unto the brethren which dwelt in Judea." (v. 29.) Mark how the famine becomes to them the means of salvation, an occasion of alms-giving, a harbinger of many blessing. And (so it might have been) to you, one may say, if you were so minded, but ye would not. But it is predicted, that they might be prepared beforehand for almsgiving. "Unto the brethren which dwelt in Judæa;" for they were enduring great hardships, but before this, they were not suffering from famine. "Which also they did, and sent it to the elders by the hands of Barnabas and Saul." (v. 30.) Do you mark

* The name Christians was probably given by the Gentiles. The word appears but twice, besides here, in the N. T. (Acts xxvi. 8; 1 Pet. iv. 16), and in both cases it is implied that the name was a name applied to the disciples of Jesus by others. The Jews could hardly have originated the name since Christ was to them the Greek equivalent for their sacred name Messiah, and from that word they would not have formed a name for the hated sect. The Jews called them rather Nazarenes (Acts xxiv. 5). The Romans seem to have misunderstood the origin of the name, as Tacitus says: *Auctor nominis ejus (Christiani) Christus*, as if *Christus* was an appellative instead of a title.—G. B. S.

[1] ἀλλ' οἱ τῆς ὁδοῦ μόνον ἤκουον, so Cat. Œcum. which we adopt. A. B. C. ἀλλ' ὅτι, the modern text ἀλλ' ἔτι.

[2] ἀναγκαίως δὲ ἐνταῦθα, as above πῶς ἀναγκαίως. But in the Mss. part of the text v. 28. being transposed, it reads "But here of necessity he says there will be a great dearth," etc.— Below, Εἰ δὶ αὐτοὺς ἦν, πάντως ἔδει καὶ ὄντα παύσασθαι. Τὶ ἠδίκησαν Ἕλληνες, ἵνα καὶ αὐτοὶ τῶν κακῶν μετέχωσιν; εὐδοκιμῆσαι γὰρ αὐτοὺς μᾶλλον ἐχρῆν, ὅτι τὸ αὐτῶν ἐποίουν, κ. τ. λ. Ἀλλ' εἰ διὰ τὰ κακά, φησίν, κ. τ. λ. So the old text in Mss. and Cat. The meaning is obscure, but on the whole it seems most probable that all this is an interlocution of an objector. "If as you say, it was because of the Jews, assuredly it ought, even when it was there, to have ceased (and not gone on to the rest of the world). What harm had the Gentiles done, that they should share in the punishment? Why, they ought rather to have been distinguished by special marks of the Divine favor, because they were doing their part (in executing God's judgments upon the Jews), were slaying, punishing, etc. Observe, too, the time when this visitation first came—precisely when the Gen-les were added to the Church. Whereas if, as you say, it was because of the evils the Jews inflicted upon the believers, these (the believers, Jews and Gentiles) ought to

have been exempted," etc. The modern text has: "But even if (ἀλλ' εἰ καὶ) it were because of them, yet because of the rest (διὰ τοὺς ἄλλους) it ought, even when it was, to have ceased. For what harm had the Gentiles done, that even they, having done no harm, should have their share of the evils? But if not because of the Jews verily they ought rather to have been even marked as objects of favor," etc. Perhaps this was intended to mean: "Suppose it was inflicted by the demons, the Gods of the heathen, because of the Christians, why were the Gentiles included? And as for the Jews, if it was not, as I say, sent by God because of their wickedness, but as the heathen say, was a token of the anger of their Gods because of the new religion, why assuredly the Jews ought to have been marked objects of favor because they were doing all they could to exterminate the faith." But if so, it does not appear how the next sentence, was understood, "And observe at what time," etc.

them, that no sooner do they believe than they bring forth fruit, not only for their own, but for those afar off? And Barnabas is sent and Saul, to minister (the same.) Of this occasion (Ἐνταῦθα) he says (to the Galatians), "And James, Cephas, and John gave to me and Barnabas the right hands of fellowship, only" (they would) "that we should remember the poor." (Gal. ii. 9.) James was yet living.[1]

"Now they which were scattered abroad upon the persecution," etc. (Recapitulation.) Do you mark how even in the tribulation instead of falling to lamentations and tears, as we do, they give themselves up to a great and good work? "Travelled as far as Phenice, and Cyprus, and Antioch," and there with more security preached the word. "And some of them, which were men of Cyprus and Cyrene," etc. (v. 20.) And they did not say, "(What), we, Cyrenians and Cyprians, to attack this splendid and great city!" but trusting in the grace of God, they applied themselves to the work of teaching, nor did these (Gentiles) themselves think scorn to learn anything of them. Mark how by small means all is brought about: mark the preaching how it spreads: mark those in Jerusalem, having like care for all, holding the whole world as one house. "They heard that Samaria had received the word, and " (ch. viii. 14) to Samaria they send the Apostles: they heard what had befallen at Antioch, and to Antioch they send Barnabas: they also send again, and (these) prophets. For the distance was great, and it was not meet the Apostles at present should separate from thence, that they might not be thought to be fugitives, and to have fled from their own people. But then, almost precisely, is the time of their parting from Jerusalem, when the state (of the Jews) was shown to be past remedy, when the war was close at hand, and they must needs perish: when the sen-

tence was made absolute. For, until Paul went to Rome, the Apostles were there (at Jerusalem). But they depart, not because afraid of the war—how should it be so?— seeing those they went to, were those that should bring the war : and moreover the war breaks out only after the Apostles were dead. For of them (the Apostles) says, "The wrath is come upon them unto the end." (1 Thess. ii. 16.) The more insignificant the persons, the more illustrious the grace, working great results by small means.—"And [2] he exhorted them to cleave unto the Lord, for he was a good man." (v. 23, 24.) By "good man," I take it, he means one that is kind, (χρηστὸν) sincere, exceedingly desirous of the salvation of his neighbors—"for he was a good man, and full of the Holy Ghost and of faith. To [3] cleave unto the Lord with purpose of heart " (this is said) : with encomium and praise. "And much people was added unto the Lord:" for like rich land this city received the word, and brought forth much fruit. "Then departed Barnabas to Tarsus," etc. (v. 25.) But why did he take him off from Tarsus and bring him here? Not without good reason ; for here were both good hopes, and a greater city, and a great body of people. See how grace works all, not [4] Paul: by small means the affair was taking its commencement. When it is become difficult the Apostles take it up. Why did they not before this seen Barnabas? Because they had enough to do (ἠσχόληντο) with Jerusalem. Again they justified themselves [5] to the Jews, that the Gentiles were receiving (προσελάμβανε) the word, even without enjoying so great attention. There is about to be a questioning : therefore the affair of Cornelius forestalled it. Then indeed they say, "That we to the Gentiles, and they to the Circumcision." (Gal. ii. 9.) Observe, henceforth the very stress of the famine introduces the fellowship on the part of the Gentiles, namely, from the alms. For they receive the offerings sent from them.

---

[1] Ἔτι Ἰάκωβος ἔζη. So, except E., all our Mss.—Ben. finds it strange that this clause is added in some Mss. "For what is it to the matter in hand, that James was yet living? And which James? For James the brother of John is mentioned presently afterwards, as slain with the sword: and James the brother of the Lord, Bishop of Jerusalem, is repeatedly mentioned as living, in the subsequent history. Then for what purpose should it be noticed here that he was alive? And yet why the copyists should add this clause, is not easy to see." The copyists are not in fault. St. Chrys. (not fully reported) is identifying this visit to Jerusalem with the visit mentioned in Gal. ii. The mention there made (v. 9) of James, whom at the moment he takes to be James the brother of John (especially as he is named with Cephas and John), leads him to remark, "James was yet alive:" i. e. when Paul and Barnabas went up with the alms, and when this conference ensued. (Acts xi.) A similar inadvertency with respect to St. Philip has been noted above, p. 115, note [1]—E. substitutes τοσοῦτον ὠφέλει ὁ λιμός. and connects the following sentence with this by reading Καὶ ὅρα αὐτοὺς, where the rest have Ὁρᾷς αὐτοὺς, as if the θλῖψις here spoken of was the famine: which however had not yet begun. Hence Ben. Et vide illos ex fame, etc. In like manner the innovator has mistaken the connection below. See note [1], p. 165. In fact. the Recapitulation begins here.

[2] Here Edd. from E. insert the formula of recapitulation, ἀλλ' ἴδωμεν κ. τ. λ.

[3] Edd. from E.: "Wherefore also with purpose of heart he exhorted all: that is, with encomium and praise:" as if τῇ προθέσει τῆς καρδίας belonged to παρεκάλει, in the sense, " with heartfelt earnestness he exhorted."

[4] οὐ Παῦλον· διὰ μικρῶν ἀρχὴν τὸ πρᾶγμα ἐλάμβανε. C. omits Παῦλον· διὰ, D. om. οὐ Παῦλον. Edd. from E., " not Paul: and how by the small means, the affair took its beginning, but when it became conspicuous, then they sent Barnabas. And why did they not send him before this? They took much forethought for their own people, and did not wish the Jews to accuse them because they received the Gentiles: and yet because of their inevitably mixing with them, since there was some questioning about to arise, the matters relating to Cornelius forestalled (this). Then indeed they say," etc.

[5] The meaning seems to be, that they let the preaching to the Gentiles take its course at first ; and were enabled to say to the Jews, " See, the Gentiles receive the word without encouragement from us: καὶ οὐ τοσαύτης ἀπολαύοντα ἐπιμελείας."

" Now [1] they which were scattered abroad," etc. (v. 19) and not as we who pass our time in lamentations and tears, in our calamities ; but with more fearlessness they passed their time, as having got to a distance from those hindering them, and as being among men not afraid of the Jews : which also helped. And they came to Cyprus, where they had the sea between them, and greater freedom from anxiety : so [2] they made no account of the fear of men, but (still) they gave the precedence to the regard of the Law : " they spake to Jews only. But there were in Antioch certain men of Cyprus and Cyrene : " these, of all others, least cared for the Jews : " who spake unto the Greeks, preaching the Lord Jesus." (v. 20.) Probably it was because of their not knowing Hebrew, that they called them Greeks. And " when " Barnabas, it says, " came and had seen the grace of God," —not the diligence of men—" he exhorted them to cleave unto the Lord " (v. 23) : and by this he converted more. " And much people was added unto the Lord." Why do they not write to Paul, but send Barnabas ? They They did not yet know the virtue of the man : but it is providentially ordered that Barnabas should come. As there was a multitude, and none to hinder, well might the faith grow, and above all because they had no trials to undergo. Paul also preaches, and is no longer compelled to flee. And it is well ordered, that not they speak of the famine, but the prophets. The men of Antioch also did not take it amiss that they sent not the Apostles, but were content with their teachers : so fervent were they all for the word. They did not wait for the famine to come, but before this they sent : " according as each had the ability." And observe, among the Apostles, others are put in charge with this trust, but here Paul and Barnabas. For this was no small order (οἰκονομία) of Providence. Besides, it was the beginning, and it was not fit they should be offended.

" As each had the ability, they sent." But now, none does this, although there is a famine more grievous than that. For the cases are not alike, for (all) to bear the calamity in common, and, while all (the rest) abound, for the poorer to be famishing. And the expression shows that the givers also were poor, for, it says, " as each of them had the means." A twofold famine, even as the abundance is twofold : a severe famine, a famine not of hearing the word of the Lord, but of being nourished by alms. [3] Then, both the poor in Judea enjoyed the benefit, and so did those in Antioch who gave their money ; yea, these more than those : but now, both we and the poor are famishing : they being in lack of necessary sustenance, and we in luxurious living, [4] lacking the mercy of God. But this is a food, than which nothing can be more necessary. This is not a food, from which one has to undergo the evils of repletion : not a food, of which the most part ends in the draught. (ἀφεδρῶνα.) Nothing more beauteous, nothing more healthful, than a soul nurtured by this food : it is set high above all disease, all pestilence, all indigestion and distemper : none shall be able to overcome it, (ἐλεῖν) but just as, if one's body were made of adamant, no iron, nor anything else, would have power to hurt it, even so when the soul is firmly compact by almsgiving, nothing at all shall be able to overcome it. For say, what shall spoil this ? Shall poverty ? It cannot be, for it is laid up in the royal treasuries. But shall robber and housebreaker ? Nay, those are walls which none shall be able to break through. But shall the worm ? Nay, this treasure is set far above the reach of this mischief also. But shall envy and the evil eye ? Nay, neither by these can it be overcome. But shall false accusations and plottings of evil ? No, neither shall this be, for safe as in an asylum is this treasure. But it were a shame should I make it appear as if the advantages which belong to almsgiving were only these (the absence of these evils), and not (the presence of) their opposites. For in truth it is not merely that it is secure from ill-will ; it also gets abundant blessing from those whom it benefits. For as the cruel and unmerciful not only have for enemies those whom they have injured, but those also who are not themselves hurt, partake the grief and join in the accusation : so those that have done great good have not only those who are benefited, but those also who are not

---

[1] The matter contained in this second recapitulation looks as if it were derived from a different, and in part fuller, report. The innovator as above (note [1], p. 164) connects it with the preceding : " they receive the offerings sent from them; who also, not as we," etc.

[2] Καὶ οὐκ ἐλάλουν τὸν λόγον εἰ μὴ Ἰουδαίοις μόνοις· οὕτως τὸν μὲν τῶν ἀνθρώπων φόβον οὐδὲν ἡγοῦντο· τὸν δὲ τοῦ νόμου προετίμων. Ἰουδαίοις μόνοις ἐλάλουν. For προετίμων, A. B. προυετίμουν. The passage is corrupt, but the sense is sufficiently plain, and is thus expressed by E. Edd. " Which thing itself helped not a little. But they came also to Cyprus, where was great fearlessness (ἀδεὲς), and greater freedom from anxiety. ' But to none,' it says, ' did they speak the word save to Jews only.' Not because of the fear of men, of which they made no account, did they this thing : " but keeping the law, and still bearing them, καὶ αὐτοὺς ἔτι διαβαστάζοντες."—Below, v. 23, Edd. from E, " Perhaps by praising the multitude and receiving them, by this he converted more : as above, μετὰ ἐγκωμίου καὶ ἐπαίνου.

[3] He means, There is no lack of wealth, no lack of hearing the word of God : this is the ἀφθονία διπλῆ. Yet many poor around us are famishing, and the rich who might aid them, starve their own souls, by their neglect of almsgiving : διπλοῦς λιμός.

[4] ἡμεῖς δὲ ἐν σπατάλῃ τοῦ ἐλέους ὄντες τοῦ Θεοῦ. Read ἡμεῖς δὲ (ἐν σπατάλῃ ὄντες), τοῦ ἐλέους τοῦ Θεοῦ, sc. ἀποροῦντες. The mod. text substitutes σπάνει for σπατάλῃ.

themselves affected, to speak their praises. Again (that), it is secure from the attacks of the evil-disposed, and robbers, and house-breakers—what, is this all the good, or is it this—that besides the not suffering diminution, it grows also and increases into multitude? What more shameful than Nebuchadnezzar, what more foul, what more iniquitous? The man was impious; after tokens and signs without number he refused to come to his senses (ανενεγκεῖν), but cast the servants of God into a furnace : and (yet) after these doings, he worshipped. What then said the Prophet? "Wherefore," saith he, "O king let my counsel be acceptable unto thee, ransom (λύτρωσαι) thy sins by alms, and thine iniquities by mercies to the poor : peradventure there shall be pardon for thy transgressions." (Dan. iii. 27.) In so speaking, he said it not doubting, nay, with entire confidence, but wishing to put him in greater fear, and to make a stronger necessity of doing these things. For if he had spoken it as a thing unquestionable, the king would have been more supine : just as it is with us, we then most urge some person (whom we wish to persuade), when [1] they say to us, "Exhort such an one," and do not add, "he will be sure to hear," but only, "peradventure he will hear :" for by leaving it doubtful, the fear is made greater, and urges him the more. This is the reason why the Prophet did not make the thing certain to him. What sayest thou? For so great impieties shall there be pardon? Yes. There is no sin, which alms cannot cleanse, none, which alms cannot quench : all sin is beneath this : it is a medicine adapted for every wound. What worse than a publican? The very matter (ὑπόθεσις) (of his occupation) is altogether one of injustice : and yet Zaccheus washed away all these (sins). Mark how even Christ shows this, by the care taken to have a purse, and to bear the contributions put into it. And Paul also says, "Only that we remember the poor" (Gal. ii. 10) : and everywhere the Scripture has much discourse concerning this matter. "The ransom," it saith, "of a man's soul is his own wealth" (Prov. 13, 8) : and with reason : for, saith (Christ), "if thou wouldest be perfect, sell what thou hast, and give to the poor, and come, follow Me." (Matt. xix. 21.) This may well be part of perfection. But alms

may be done not only by money, but by acts. For example : one may kindly stand (προστῆναι) by a person (to succor and defend him), one may reach to him a helping hand : the service rendered (προστασία) by acts has often done more good even than money. Let us set to work all the different kinds of alms-giving. Can you do alms by money? Be not slack. Can you by good offices? Say not, Because I have no money, this is nothing. This is a very great point : look upon it as if you had given gold. Can you do it by kind attentions (θεραπείας)? Do this also. For instance, if you be a physician, (give) your skill : for this also is a great matter. Can you by counsel? This (service) is much greater than all : this (alms) is better than all, or it is also more, by how much the gain it has is greater. For in so doing you put away not starvation, but a grievous death. (ch. iii. 6 ; vi. 4.) With such alms the Apostles above measure abounded : therefore it was that the distribution of money they put into the hands of those after them, themselves exhibiting the (mercy) shown by words. Or is it, think you, a small alms, to a lost, castaway soul, a soul in uttermost jeopardy, possessed by a burning fever (πυρώσεως), to be able to rid it of its disease? For example, do you see one possessed by love of money? Pity the man. Is he in danger of suffocation? Quench his fire. "What if he will not be persuaded?" Do your part, and be not remiss. Have you seen him in bonds?—for wealth is indeed bonds. (Matt. xxv. 35 ff.) Go to him, visit him, console him, try to release him of his bonds. If he refuse, he shall bear the blame himself. Have you seen him naked, and a stranger? —for he is indeed naked, and a stranger to heaven. Bring him to your own inn, clothe him with the garment of virtue, give him the city which is in heaven. "What if I myself be naked?" say you. Clothe also yourself first : if you know that you are naked, assuredly you know that you need to be clothed ; if you know what sort of nakedness this is.[2] What numbers of women now wear silken apparel but are indeed naked of the garments of virtue! Let their husbands clothe these women. "But they will not admit those garments; they choose to have these." Then do this also first : induce them to have a longing for those garments : show them that they are naked : speak to them of judgment to

---

[1] καθάπερ καὶ ἡμεῖς τότε μάλιστα ἀθοῦμέν τινας, ὅταν λέγωσιν ἡμῖν . . . καὶ μὴ ἐπαγάγωμεν, A. B. C. We read τινα, and ἐπαγάγωσιν. "When people bid us exhort some person, adding, Peradventure he will hear, not, He will certainly hear, we are then most urgent in our endeavor to persuade him." The mod. text ὅταν λέγωμεν. i. e. "When we would induce some persons to exhort some one, we the more effectually urge them to do so, when we say, Peradventure he will hear," etc. The sense would be improved by reading ἡμᾶς . . ὠθοῦσί τινες, "persons then most urge us, when they say," etc.

[2] εἰ ταύτης (mod. text adds μόνον) τῆς γυμνότητος ἐπίστασαι τὸν τρόπον: which might also be taken with the following sentence, If you know what sort of nakedness this is (why then, only think) what numbers of women, etc. A. has πόσαι οὖν. The mod. text adds, δυνήσῃ γνῶναι ῥαδίως καὶ τὴν αὐτῆς καταστολήν. "If you know the sort of nakedness this is, you will easily be able to know the (manner of) clothing it."

come : answer me,[1] what is the clothing we shall need there ? But if ye will bear with me, I also will show you this nakedness. He that is naked, when it is cold, shrinks and shudders, and stands there cowering, and with his arms folded : but in summer heat, not so. If then I shall prove to you that your rich men, and rich women, the more they put on, the more naked they are, do not take it amiss. How then, I ask you, when we raise the subject of hell-fire, and of the torments there ? Do not these shrink and shudder more than those naked ones ? Do they not bitterly groan and condemn themselves ? What ? when they come to this or that man, and say to him, Pray for me, do they not speak the same words as those (naked wretches) ? Now indeed, after all that we can say, the nakedness is not yet apparent : but it will be plain enough there. How, and in what way ? When these silken garments and precious stones shall have perished, and it shall be only by the garments of virtue and of vice that all men are shown, when the poor shall be clad with exceeding glory, but the rich, naked and in disgraceful sort, shall be haled away to their punishments. What more naked (Edd. " more dainty ") than that rich man who arrayed himself in purple ? What poorer than Lazarus ? Then which, of them uttered the words of beggars ? which of them was in abundance ? Say, if one should deck his house with abundance of tapestry hangings, and himself sit naked within, what were the benefit ? So it is in the case of these women. Truly, the house of the soul, the body I mean, they hang round with plenty of garments : but the mistress of the house sits naked within. Lend me the eyes of the soul, and I will show you the soul's nakedness. For what is the garment of the soul ? Virtue, of course. And what its nakedness ? Vice. For just as, if one were to strip any decent person, that person would be ashamed, and would shrink and cower out of sight ; just so the soul, if we wish to see it, the soul which has not these garments, blushes for shame. How many women, think you, at this moment feel ashamed, and would fain sink to the very depth, as if seeking some sort of curtain, or screen, that they may not hear these words ? But those who have no evil conscience, are exhilarated, rejoice, find delight, and gayly deck themselves (ἐγκαλλωπίζονται) with the things said. Hear concerning that blessed Thekla,[2] how, that she might see Paul, she gave even her gold : and thou wilt not give even a farthing that thou mayest see Christ : thou admirest what she did, but dost not emulate her. Hearest thou not that " Blessed are the merciful, for they shall obtain mercy ? " (Matt. v. 7.) What is the gain of your costly garments ? how long shall we continue agape for this attire ? Let us put on the glory of Christ : let us array ourselves with that beauty, that both here we may be praised, and there attain unto the eternal good things, by the grace and mercy of our Lord Jesus Christ, with Whom, to the Father and the Holy Ghost together, be glory, dominion, honor, now and ever, world without end. Amen.

---

[1] E Edd. ' Say, We need other (garments) there, not these.'' —Below, θερους δε, ουκ ετι: i. e. cold, not heat, makes the naked body shudder: not cold, but hell-fire, the naked soul.

[2] In the " Acts of Paul and Thekla," Grab. Spicileg. Patr. t. i. p. 95. reprinted with a translation by Jeremiah Jones, *On the Canon of the N. T.*, vol. ii. p. 353 ff. the incident is thus related (ch. ii.): " When the proconsul heard this, he ordered Paul to be bound, and to be put in prison . . . . . But Thekla in the night taking off her earrings, gave them to the turnkey, and he opened for her the doors, and let her in: and having given to the keeper of the prison a silver mirror, she was admitted unto Paul, and having sat at his feet, heard from him the mighty works of God." The earliest notice of this work occurs in Tertull. *de Bapt.* c. 17: Thekla is mentioned, or her history referred to, by other ancient writers, as St. Greg. Naz., Sulpic. Severus, St. Augustin; see Jones u. s. p. 387 ff. A Homily in her praise ascribed to St. Chrysostom, t. ii. p. 749, is justly placed by Savile among the ἀμφιβαλλόμενα.

HOMILY XXVI.

ACTS XII. 1, 2.

" Now at that time Herod the King stretched forth his hands to vex certain of the Church. And he killed James the brother of John with the sword. And because he saw it pleased the Jews, he proceeded further to take Peter also. Then were the days of unleavened bread. "

" At that time," of course meaning the time immediately following : for [1] this is the custom of Scripture. And he well says that Herod "the king" (did this) : this was not he of Christ's time. Lo, a different sort of trial— and mark what I said in the beginning, how things are blended, how rest and trouble alternate in the whole texture of the history —not now the Jews, nor the Sanhedrim, but the king. Greater the power, the warfare more severe, the more it was done to obtain favor with the Jews. "And," it says, "he slew James the brother of John with the sword : " (taking him) at random and without selection. But, should any raise a question, why God permitted this, we shall say, that it was for the sake of these (Jews) themselves : thereby, first, convincing them, that even when slain (the Apostles) prevail, just as it was in the case of Stephen : secondly, giving them opportunity, after satiating their rage, to recover from their madness ; thirdly, show- ing them that it was by His permission this was done. "And when he saw," it says, "that it pleased the Jews, he proceeded further to seize Peter also. O excessive wickedness ! On whose behalf was it, that he gratified them by doing murders thus with- out plan or reason ? "And it was the day of unleavened bread." Again, the idle pre- ciseness of the Jews : to kill indeed they

forbade not, but [2] at such a time they did such things ! "Whom having arrested, he put in ward, having delivered him to four quater- nions of soldiers." (v. 4.) This was done both of rage, and of fear. "He slew," it says, "James the brother of John with the sword." Do you mark their courage ? For, that none may say that without danger or fear of danger they brave death, as being sure of God's delivering them, therefore he permits some to be put to death, and chief men too, Stephen and James, thereby convincing their slayers themselves, that not even these things make them fall away, and hinder them. "Peter therefore was kept in prison : but prayer was made without ceasing of the Church unto God for him." (v. 5.) For the contest was now for life and death : both the slaying of the one made them fearful, and the casting of the other into prison. "And when Herod would have brought him forth, the same night Peter was sleeping between two soldiers, bound with two chains ; and the keepers before the door kept the prison. And, behold, the angel of the Lord came upon him, and a light shined in the prison : and he smote Peter on the side, and raised him up, saying, Arise up quickly. And his chains fell off from his hands." (v. 6, 7.) In that night He delivered him. "And a light shined in the prison," that [3] he might not deem it fancy : and none saw the light, but he only. For if, notwithstanding this was done, he thought it a fancy, because of its unex- pectedness ; if this had not been, much more would he have thought this : so [4] prepared was he for death. For his having waited there many days and not being saved caused this. Why then, say you, did He not suffer him to fall into the hands of Herod, [5] and then deliver him ? Because that would have brought people into astonishment, whereas

---

[1] The modern text (E. D. F. Edd.) "But here it is said in this sense, elsewhere in a different sense. For when Matthew says, ' In those days cometh John preaching,' he speaks it not as meaning the days immediately following, but ' those' in which the things he relates were about to take place. For it is the custom of Scripture to use this mode of speech, and at one time to expound in their sequence the things successively taking place, at another to relate as in immediate succession the things about to take place afterwards. ` And he well says that Herod the king did this, for this was not he of Christ's time: " as if Chrys. meant, He does right to call him king, for this was not the tetrarch of the Gospel history. But this is merely a parenthetic remark: the point to which the καλῶς λέγει refers is this—that the persecution is now raised by a king, not by the Jews: " he does well to designate Herod as the king, thereby showing that the trial here was of a different kind, more severe, as the power wielded against them was greater."

[2] ἐν δὲ καιρῷ τοιούτῳ τοιαῦτα ἔπραττον. So Mss. and Edd. But the Catena has ἐν δὲ καιρῷ τοιούτῳ πράττειν οὐκ ἤθελον. "They had no objection to killing, but they had rather not do it at such a time."

[3] This seems more suitable to the clause, "And his chains fell off from his hands: but see below in the recapitulation, p. 170.

[4] i. e. so unexpected was it, so entirely had he made up his mind that he was to be put to death, that he thought it all a dream.

[5] i. e. on the morrow, to be led out to execution, and then and there deliver him.

this was credible :¹ and they would not even
have been thought human beings. But in the
case of Stephen, what did He not do? Did
He not show them his face as it had been the
face of an angel? But what in short did He
leave undone here also? "And the angel
said to him, Gird thyself, and bind on thy
sandals." (v. 8.) Here again it shows, that
it was not done of craft : for one that is in
haste and wishes to break out (of prison), is
not so particular as to take his sandals, and
gird himself. "And he did so And he
said unto him, Put on thy cloak, and follow
me. And he went out, and followed him ;
and wist not that it was true which was
done by the Angel; but thought he saw a
vision. When they were past the first and
the second ward, they came unto the iron gate
that leadeth unto the city; which opened to
them of its own accord." (v. 9, 10.) Behold, a second miracle. "And they went
out, and passed on through one street; and
forthwith the angel departed from him. And
when Peter was come to himself, he said,
Now I know of a surety, that the Lord hath
sent His Angel, and hath delivered me out of
the hand of Herod, and from all the expectation of the people of the Jews." (v. 10, 11.)
When the angel departed, then Peter understood : "Now I perceive," says he, not then.
But why is this so, and why is Peter not sensible of the things taking place, although he
had already experienced a like deliverance,
when all were released? (ch. v. 18.) (The
Lord) would have the pleasure come to him
all at once, and that he should first be at
liberty, and then be sensible of what had
happened. The circumstance also of the
chains having fallen off from his hands, is a
strong argument of his not having fled.²
"And when he had considered the thing, he
came to the house of Mary the mother of
John, whose surname was Mark ; where many
were gathered together praying." (v. 12.)
Observe how Peter does not immediately
withdraw, but first brings the good tidings to
his friends. "And as Peter knocked at the
door of the gate, a damsel came to hearken,
named Rhoda. And when she knew Peter's
voice, she opened not the gate for gladness,"
—Mark even the servant-girls, how full of

piety they are,—"but ran in, and told how
Peter stood before the gate." (v. 13-15.) But
they, though it was so, shook their heads
(incredulously) : "And they said unto her,
Thou art mad. But she constantly affirmed
that it was even so. And they said, It is
his angel. "But Peter continued knocking :
and when they had opened the door, and saw
him, they were astonished. But he, beckoning unto them with the hand to hold their
peace, declared unto them how the Lord had
brought him out of the prison. And he said,
Go show these things unto James, and to the
brethren. And he departed, and went into
another place." (v. 16, 17.) But let us review the order of the narrative.

(Recapitulation.) "At that time," it says,
"Herod the king stretched forth his hands to
afflict certain of the Church." (v. 1.) Like a
wild beast, he attacked all indiscriminately
and without consideration. This is what
Christ said : "My cup indeed ye shall drink,
and with the baptism wherewith I am baptized,
shall ye be baptized." (Mark x. 39.)   (b)
"And³ he killed James the brother of John."
(v. 2.) For there was also another James,
the brother of the Lord : therefore to distinguish him, he says, "The brother of John." *
Do you mark that the sum of affairs rested in
these three, especially Peter and James? (a)
And how was it he did not kill Peter immediately? It mentions the reason : "it was the
day of unleavened bread :" and he wished
rather to make a display (ἐκπομπεῦσαι) with the
killing of him. "And when he saw it pleased
the Jews." (v. 3.) For their own part, they
now in consequence of Gamaliel's advice,
abstained from bloodshedding : and besides,
did not even invent accusations ; but by
means of others they compassed the same
results. (c) This (counsel of Gamaliel's)
above all was their condemnation : for the
preaching was shown to be no longer a thing

---

¹ τοῦτο δὲ πιστὸν ἐγένετο. That would have astonished :
this was calculated to obtain belief. E. D. F. Edd. τοῦτο δὲ
ὑπὲρ αὐτῶν ἐγένετο. "But this was done for their sakes for they
would not have been counted human beings, if he had done
all after the manner of God, εἰ θεοπρεπῶς πάντα ἐποίει."
² In the old text this sentence and the next are transposed.
The mod. text has restored the true order, but for ἡδονὴν has
ἀπαλλαγὴν, "his deliverance to come to him all at once."—
The connection may be thus supplied, "When he came to himself, he found himself there at large, and with his hands no
longer chained. And this circumstance again is a strong evidence that he had not fled."

³ The order in Mss. and Edd. is a, b, c. Αὕτη, in the beginning of (c) evidently refers to τῆς παραινέσεως τῆς Γαμ. in (a).
* James the brother of John was the son of Zebedee, commonly called the "elder" James. He was the first of the
apostles to suffer martyrdom. The other James, called "the
Lord's brother" (Gal. i, 19.) mentioned in v. 17 (cf. Acts xv.
13 ; xxi. 18) was the Bishop of Jerusalem, a man of much importance and influence in the apostolic church, whom Paul
reckons among the "pillars" (Gal. ii. 9). Chrys. gives no
opinion here concerning him. Three views have prevailed in
the church : (1) that he was the same as the apostle, James
the son of Alphæus and is called the "brother" of Jesus in
the loose sense of that word in which it is taken as equivalent
to "relative." (2) That he was the son of Joseph by a former
marriage. (3) That he was the son of Joseph and Mary—the
real brother of Jesus and is called an apostle in Gal. i. 19, in
the more comprehensive sense which that word acquired according to which it was applied also to Paul and Barnabas
(Acts xiv. 14). This view seems to me the correct one. There
were also other brothers (Matt.xii. 46 ; xiii. 55, 56) Joses, Simon
and Judas, and sisters who are not personally named. Chrys.
seems to have held view (2) in his earlier writings, but to have
adopted view (1), following Jerome. (Cf. Lightfoot on Galatians, pp. 289, 290).—G. B. S.

of men. " He proceeded further to kill Peter also." (ch. v. 8.) In very deed was that fulfilled, " We are accounted as sheep for the slaughter." (Psa. xliv. 13.) " Seeing," it says, " it was a pleasing thing to the Jews." (Rom. viii. 36.) A pleasing thing, bloodshed, and unrighteous bloodshed, wickedness, impiety ! [1] He ministered to their senseless (ἀτόποις) lusts : for, whereas he ought to have done the contrary, to check their rage, he made them more eager, as if he were an executioner, and not a physician to their diseased minds. (And this) though he had numberless warnings in the case of both his grandfather and his father Herod, how the former in consequence of his putting the children to death suffered the greatest calamities, and the latter by slaying John raised up against himself a grievous war. But [2] as they thought * * He feared lest Peter, in consequence of the slaying of James, should withdraw ; and wishing to have him in safe keeping, he put him in prison : " and delivered him to four quaternions of soldiers " (v. 4) : the stricter the custody, the more wondrous the display. " Peter therefore was kept in prison." (v. 5.) But this was all the better for Peter, who was thereby made more approved, and evinced his own manly courage. And it says, " there was earnest prayer making." It was the prayer of (filial) affection : it was for a father they asked, a father mild. " There was," it says, " earnest prayer." Hear how they were affected to their teachers. No factions, no perturbation : [3] but they betook them to prayer, to that alliance which is indeed invincible, to this they betook them for refuge. They did not say, " What ? I, poor insignificant creature that I am, to pray for him ! " for, as they acted of love, they did not give these things a thought. And observe, it was during the feast, that (their enemies) brought these trials upon them, that their worth might be the more approved. " And when Herod," etc. (v. 6.) See Peter sleeping, and not in distress or fear ! That same night, after which he was to be brought forth, he slept, having cast all upon God. " Between two soldiers, bound with two

chains." (comp. 1 Pet. v. 7.) Mark, how strict the ward ! " And says, Arise." (v. 7.) The guards were asleep with him, and therefore perceived nothing of what was happening. " And a light shined." What was the light for ? In order that Peter might see as well as hear, and not imagine it to be all fancy. And the command, " Arise quickly, [4] " that he may not be remiss. He also · smote him ; so deeply did he sleep. (a) " Rise," says he, " quickly : " this is not to hurry him (θορυβοῦντος) but to persuade him not to delay. (c) " And " immediately " his chains fell off from his hands." (b) How ? answer me : where are the heretics ?—let them answer. " And the Angel said unto him," etc. (v. 8) by this also convincing him that it is no fancy : to this end he bids him gird himself and put on his shoes, that he may shake off his sleep, and know that it is real. (a) (e) " And he wist not that it was true that was done by the Angel, but thought he saw a vision " (v. 9) : (e) well he might, by reason of the excessive greatness (ὑπερβολὴν) of the things taking place. Do you mark what a thing it is for a miracle to be excessive (ὑπερβολὴ σημείου) ? how it amazes (ἐκπλήττει) the beholder ? how it will not let the thing be believed ? [5] For if Peter " thought he saw a vision," though he had girded himself and put on his shoes, what would have been the case with another ? " And," it says, " when they had passed the first and the second ward, they came to the iron gate, which opened unto them of its own accord " (v. 10) : and yet the things that had happened within (the prison) were more marvellous : but this was now more after the manner of man. " And having gone out, they went along one street and immediately (all ' until ') the Angel departed from him." (v. 11.) When there was no hindrance, then the Angel departed. For Peter would not have gone along (προῆλθεν), there being so many hindrances. " And when he came to himself ; " for in very truth, it was indeed an amazement (ἔκπληξις). " Now," saith he, " I know "—now, not then, when I was in the

---

[1] A. B. C. κακία, ἀσέβεια. Cat , φονος ἄδικος κακίας ; ἀσέβεια ταῖς κ. τ. λ. Mod. text substitutes for these two words, Πολλὴ ἡ ἄνοια τοῦ Ἡρώδου.

[2] Καθὼς δὲ ᾤοντο A. B. C. Either this is out of its place, or the sentence is incomplete. The mod. text substitutes, " And when he had apprehended him, he put him in prison."

[3] οὐκ ἐστασίασαν, οὐκ ἐθορυβήθησαν : alluding perhaps to the factious and turbulent proceedings, which in his time often ensued when a Bishop was removed or at the point of death. But possibly ἔστασ. is corrupt.—Below, Τοῦτο δὲ ἦν ὑπὲρ Πέτρου, etc. the meaning seems to be, " That Herod was permitted to do this, and that Peter was delivered into his hands, not withdrawing upon the death of James, was all the better for Peter : it gave fresh proof of his worth, it showed how courageous he was in himself, independently of supernatural aid.'

[4] A. B. C. Cat. καὶ τὸ " ἐν τάχει," ὥστε μὴ ῥαθυμῆσαι· καὶ ἔπληξεν αὐτόν· (C. καὶ ἔκπληξις ἦν εἰς αὐτόν) οὕτω βαθέως ἐκάθευδεν. Perhaps C. has preserved the true reading, see on v. 11. If so, it should be transposed with the part marked (a), viz. " —by the Angel : and it was an amazement to him, so deeply did he sleep : but he thought he saw a vision." The letters as usual denote the order of parts in the Mss. Before (b), the clause, " And he passed the first and second ward," is inserted. It is not easy to see what can be the reference of the question, Πῶς; ποῦ εἰσιν οἱ αἱρετικοί; it can hardly be meant for the mention of the sandals and cloak, v. 8, for the persons who objected to the Christians, that, according to Christ's command, they ought to have no shoes, nor two coats, etc. were not heretics, but heathens : see Hom. in illud, Salutate Prisc. et Aq. t. iii. 181. and Hom. ix. in Philip. t. xi. 272 (the latter cited in the Catena here).

[5] A. B. C. Cat. ἀπιστηθῆναι, " be disbelieved ? " But this is evidently corrupt.

prison,—" that the Lord hath sent His Angel, and hath delivered me out of the hand of Herod and from all the expectation of the people of the Jews. And when he had considered " (v. 12), it says : viz. where he was, or, that he must not without more ado depart but requite his Benefactor : " he came to the house of Mary the mother of John." Who is this John ? Probably[1] he that was always with them : for this is why he adds his distinctive name (τὸ παράσημον), " whose surname was Mark." But observe, " praying " in the night, how much they got by it : what a good thing affliction is ; how wakeful it made them ! Do you see how great the gain resulting from the death of Stephen ? do you see how great the benefit accruing from this imprisonment ? For it is not by taking vengeance upon those who wronged them that God shows the greatness of the Gospel : but in the wrong-doers themselves,[2] without any harm happening to those, he shows what a mighty thing the afflictions in themselves are, that we may not seek in any wise deliverance from them, nor the avenging of our wrongs. And mark how the very servant-girls were henceforth upon an equality with them. " For joy," it says, " she opened not." (v. 13, 14.) This too is well done, that they likewise may not be amazed by seeing him at once, and that they may be incredulous, and their minds may be exercised. " But ran in," etc. just as we are wont to do, she was eager to be herself the bringer of the good tidings, for good news it was indeed. " And they said unto her, Thou art mad : but she constantly affirmed that it was even so : then said they, It is his Angel." (v. 15.) This is a truth, that each man has an Angel.* And what would the Angel ?[3] It was from the time (of night) that they surmised this. But when he " continued knocking, and when they had opened, and

saw him, they were astonished. But he beckoning to them with his hand " (v. 16, 17), made them keep quiet, to hear all that had happened to him. He was now an object of more affectionate desire to the disciples, not only in consequence of his being saved, but by his sudden coming in upon them and straightway departing. Now, both his friends learn all clearly; and the aliens also learn, if they had a mind, but they had not. The same thing happened in the case of Christ. " Tell these things," he says, " to James, and to the brethren." How free from all vainglory ! Nor did he say, Make known these things to people everywhere, but, " to the brethren. And he withdrew to another place : " for he did not tempt God, nor fling himself into temptation : since, when they were commanded to do this, then they did it. " Go," it was said, " speak in the temple to the people." (ch. v. 20.) But this the Angel said not (here) ; on the contrary, by silently removing him and bringing him by night, he gave him free permission to withdraw—and this too is done, that we may learn that many things are providentially brought about after the manner of men—so that he should not again fall into peril.—For that they may not say, " It was his Angel,"[4] after he was gone, they say this first, and then they see himself overthrowing their notion of the matter. Had it been the Angel, he would have knocked at the door, and not have retired to another place. And[5] what followed in the day, make them sure.

" So Peter was kept in the prison," etc. (v. 5.) They, being at large, were at prayer : he, bound, was in sleep. " And he wist not that it was true." (v. 9.) If he thought it was true that was happening, he would have been astonished, he would not have remembered[6] (all the circumstances) : but now, seeming to be in a dream, he was free from perturbation. " When," it says, " they were past the first and the second ward "—see also how strong the guard was—" they came unto the iron gate." (v. 10.) " Now know I that the Lord hath sent His Angel." (v. 11.) Why is not this effected by themselves?[7] (I answer,) By this also the Lord honors them,

---

[1] ἴσως ἐκεῖνος ὁ ἀεὶ αὐτοῖς συνών. Œcumen. may have read οὐκ ἐκεῖνος, for he has, ἵνα δείξῃ ὅτι οὐ τοῦ ἀεὶ συνόντος αὐτοῖς Ἰωάννου τὴν μήτερα φησίν : " to show that he does not mean the mother of John (the Apostle) who was always with them, he adds his distinctive name."

[2] ἐν αὐτοῖς τοῖς ἀδικοῦσιν. Perhaps it may mean, He brings it home to the conviction of the wrong-doers themselves, etc. Ἐκείνων, i. e. the enemies. But ἀδικουμένοις would suit the meaning better than ἀδικοῦσιν, and then ἐκείνων would be right : otherwise it should be αὐτῶν.

* The interpretation of Chrys. regarding the idea of the company assembled in Mary's house expressed by : " It is his angel," is doubtless correct. Others interpret : " It is his messenger "—a messenger sent by Peter to them, but it is said that Rhoda recognized Peter's voice (14). Others understand angel in the sense of spirit—a view which is not sanctioned by linguistic usage. Their idea was that Peter's guardian angel who had taken on his form and appearance was before the door. The belief in guardian angels attending individuals was common in later Jewish theology as well as in the Greek and Roman religions. It was doubtless stimulated in the early church by the saying of Jesus concerning children: " In heaven their angels do always behold the face of my Father who is in heaven " (Matt. xviii. 10), which seems to sanction the idea (cf. Heb. i. 14).—G. B. S.

[3] καὶ τί βούλεται ὁ ἄγγελος ; A. B. C. Cat. The mod. text substitutes, " And whence did it come into their minds at that time to surmise that it was an Angel ? "

[4] i. e. It was so ordered (ᾠκονόμητο) that the notion of its being his Angel came into their minds before they saw him, in order that it might not be possible for them to think this after he was gone.

[5] Πιστοῦται δὲ αὐτοὺς καὶ τὸ ἐν ἡμέρα γενόμενον. i. e. " When it was day there was no small stir among the soldiers," etc. v. 18. The innovator, not perceiving the meaning, substitutes καὶ τὸ μὴ ἐν ἡμέρα γενέσθαι, " And its not happening by day, confirms their belief."

[6] ἐμνημόνευσεν. i. e. astonishment would have deprived him of the power of remembering, and afterwards relating the circumstances, v. 17.

[7] Here, and on former occasion, v. 19. Hence the plural δι' εαυτῶν.

that by the ministry of His Angels he rescues them. Then why was it not so in the case of Paul? There with good reason, because the jailer was to be converted, whereas here, it was only that the Apostle should be released. (ch. xvi. 25.) And God disposes all things in divers ways. And there too, it is beautiful, that Paul sings hymns, while here Peter was asleep. "And when he had considered, he came to the house of Mary," etc. (v. 12.) Then let us not hide God's marvels, but for our own good let us study to display these abroad for the edifying of the others. For as he deserves to be admired for choosing to be put into bonds, so is he worthy of more admiration, that he withdrew not until he had reported all to his friends. "And he said, Tell James and the brethren." (v. 17.) That they may rejoice: that they may not be anxious. Through these[1] those learn, not those through him: such thought had he for the humbler part!—

Truly, nothing better than affliction not above measure (σνμμέτρον). What think you must have been their state of mind—how full of delight! Where now are those women, who sleep the whole night through? Where are those men, who do not even turn themselves in their bed? Seest thou the watchful soul? With women, and children, and maidservants, they sang hymns to God, made purer than the sky by affliction. But now, if we see a little danger, we fall back. Nothing ever was more splendid than that Church. Let us imitate these, let us emulate them. Not for this was the night made, that we should sleep all through it and be idle. To this bear witness the artisans, the carriers, and the merchants (to this), the Church of God rising up in the midst of the night. Rise thou up also, and behold the quire of the stars, the deep silence, the profound repose: contemplate with awe the order (οἰκονομίαν) of thy Master's household. Then is thy soul purer: it is lighter, and subtler, and soaring disengaged: the darkness itself, the profound silence, are sufficient to lead thee to compunction. And if also thou look to the heavens studded with its stars, as with ten thousand eyes,[2] if thou bethink thee that all those multitudes who in the daytime are shouting, laughing, frisking, leaping, wronging, grasping, threatening, inflicting wrongs without number,

lie all one as dead, thou wilt condemn all the self-willedness of man. Sleep hath invaded and defeated (ἤλεγξεν) nature: it is the image of death, the image of the end of all things. If[3] thou (look out of window and) lean over into the street, thou wilt not hear even a sound: if thou look into the house, thou wilt see all lying as it were in a tomb. All this is enough to arouse the soul, and lead it to reflect on the end of all things.

Here indeed my discourse is for both men and women. Bend thy knees, send forth groans, beseech thy Master to be merciful: He is more moved by prayers in the night, when thou makest the time for rest a time for mourning. Remember what words that king uttered: "I have been weary with my groaning: every night will I wash my bed, I will water my couch with my tears." (Ps. vi. 6.) However delicate a liver thou mayest be, thou art not more delicate than he: however rich thou mayest be, thou art not richer than David. And again the same Psalmist saith, "At midnight I rose to give thanks unto Thee for the judgments of Thy righteousness." (Ps. cxix. 62.) No vainglory then intrudes upon thee: how can it, when all are sleeping, and not looking at thee? Then neither sloth nor drowsiness invades thee: how can they, when thy soul is aroused by such great things? After such vigils come sweet slumbers and wondrous revelations. Do this, thou also the man, not the woman only. Let the house be a Church, consisting of men and women. For think not because thou art the only man, or because she is the only woman there, that this is any hindrance. "For where two," He saith, "are gathered together in My Name, there am I in the midst of them." (Matt. xviii. 20.) Where Christ is in the midst, there is a great multitude. Where Christ is, there needs must Angels be, needs must Archangels also and the other Powers be there. Then ye are not alone, seeing ye have Him Who is Lord of all. Hear again the prophet also saying, "Better is one that doeth the will of the Lord, than ten thousand transgressors." (comp. Ecclus. xvi. 3.) Nothing more weak than a multitude of unrighteous men, nothing more strong than one man who lives according to the law of God. If thou hast children wake up them also, and let thy house altogether become a Church through the night: but if they be tender, and cannot endure the watching, let them stay for the first or second prayer, and then send them to rest: only stir up thyself,

---

[1] διὰ τούτων (the persons assembled in the house of Mary) ἐκεῖνοι (James and the brethren), οὐκ ἐκεῖνοι διὰ τούτου. This is corrupt, but the meaning is, James and the more important of the brethren learn the particulars through these inferior persons, not these through those, but through Peter himself. Mod. text, ἵνα διὰ τούτων ἐκεῖνοι μανθάνωσιν, οὐκ αὐτοὶ δὲ ἐκείνων.

[2] Mod. text adds, "thou wilt enjoy all pleasure, being led forthwith to reflect on the Creator.

[3] Ἂν διακύψῃς εἰς τὸν στενωπόν. The στενωποί, angiportus or vici are the lanes or alleys in the quarters formed by intersection of the broad streets, πλατεῖαι.

establish thyself in the habit. Nothing is better than that storehouse which receives such prayers as these. Hear the Prophet speaking: "If I remembered Thee upon my bed, I thought upon Thee in the dawn of the morning." (Ps. lxiii. 7.) But you will say: I have labored much during the day, and I cannot. Mere pretext this and subterfuge. For however much thou hast labored, thou wilt not toil like the smith, who lets fall such a heavy hammer from a great height upon the (metal flying off in) sparks, and takes in the smoke with his whole body: and yet at this work he spends the greater part of the night. Ye know also how the women, if there is need for us to go into the country, or to go forth unto a vigil, watch through the whole night. Then have thou also a spiritual forge, to fashion there not pots or cauldrons, but thine own soul, which is far better than either coppersmith or goldsmith can fashion. Thy soul, waxen old in sins, cast thou into the smelting-furnace of confession: let fall the hammer from on high: that is, the condemnation of thy words (τῶν ῥημάτων τὴν κατάγνωσιν): light up the fire of the Spirit. Thou hast a far mightier craft (than theirs). Thou art beating into shape not vessels of gold, but the soul, which is more precious than all gold, even as the smith hammers out his vessel. For it is no material vessel that thou art working at, but thou art freeing thy soul from all imaginations belonging to this life. Let a lamp be by thy side, not that one which we burn, but that which the prophet had, when he said, "Thy law is a lamp unto my feet." (Ps. cxix. 105.) Bring thy soul to a red heat, by prayer: when thou seest it hot enough, draw it out, and mould it into what shape thou wilt. Believe me, not fire so effectual to burn off rust, as night prayer to remove the rust of our sins. Let the night-watchers, if no one else, shame us. They, by man's law, go their rounds in the cold, shouting loudly, and walking through lanes (στενωπῶν) and alleys, oftentimes drenched with rain and (all) congealed with cold, for thee and for thy safety, and the protection of thy property. There is he taking such care for thy property, while thou takest none even for thy soul. And yet I do not make thee go thy rounds in the open air like him, nor shout loudly and rend thy sides: but in thy closet itself, or in thy bedchamber, bend thy knees, and entreat thy Lord. Why did Christ Himself pass a whole night on the mountain? Was it not, that He might be an ensample to us? Then is it that the plants respire, in the night, I mean: and then also does the soul take in the dew even more than they. What the sun has parched by day becomes cool again at night. More refreshing than all dew, the tears of the night descend upon our lusts and upon all heat and fever of the soul, and do not let it be affected in any such way. But if it do not enjoy the benefit of that dew, it will be burnt up in the daytime. But God forbid (it should be so [1])! Rather, may we all, being refreshed, and enjoying the mercy of God, be freed from the burden of our sins, through the grace and mercy of our Lord Jesus Christ, with Whom to the Father together with the Holy Spirit be glory, might, honor, now and ever, world without end. Amen.

HOMILY XXVII.

ACTS XII. 18, 19.

"Now as soon as it was day, there was no small stir among the soldiers, what was become of Peter. And when Herod had sought for him, and found him not, he examined the keepers, and commanded that they should be put to death. And he went down from Judea to Cæsarea, and there abode."

SOME persons, it is likely, are at a loss how to explain it, that God should quietly look on while (His) champions [2] are put to death, and now again the soldiers on account of Peter: and yet it was possible for Him after (delivering) Peter to rescue them also. But it was not yet the time of judgment, so as to render to each according to his deserts. And besides, it was not Peter that put them into his hands. For the thing that most annoyed him was the being mocked; just as in the case of his grandfather when he was deceived by the wise men, that was what made him

---

[1] Mod. text ἀλλὰ μὴ γένοιτο μηδένα ὑμῶν ὑπέκκαυμα τοῦ πυρὸς ἐκείνου γενέσθαι: "God forbid that any of you should become the fuel of that fire."

[2] περιεῖδεν τοὺς ἀθλητὰς ἀπολλυμένους: i. e. those (as St. Stephen, St. James) engaged in contending for the heavenly prize. The mod. t. substitutes, "Many are quite at a loss, how

God could quietly look on while his children (or servants? τοὺς παῖδας, Ben. infantes) were put to death because of Him, and now again," etc. After this sentence, the same inserts from the recapitulation: "But—if the Angel," etc. to . . . . . "why did He not rescue him? and besides"—

(feel) cut to the heart—the being (eluded and) made ridiculous. [1] "And having put them to the question," it says, "he ordered them to be led away to execution." (Matt. ii. 16.) And yet he had heard from them—for he had put them to the question—both that the chains had been left, and that he had taken his sandals, and that until that night he was with them. "Having put them to the question:" but what did they conceal? [2] Why then did they not themselves also flee? "He ordered them to be led away to execution:" and yet he ought to have marvelled, ought to have been astonished at this. The consequence is, by the death of these men (the thing), is made manifest to all : both his wickedness is exposed to view, and (it is made clear that) the wonder (is) of God. "And he went down from Judea to Cæsarea, and there abode : and Herod was highly displeased with them of Tyre and Sidon : but they came with one accord to him, and, having made Blastus the king's chamberlain their friend, desired peace ; because their country was nourished by the king's country. And upon a set day Herod, arrayed in royal apparel, sat upon his throne, and made an oration unto them. And the people gave a shout, saying, 'It is the voice of a god, and not of a man,' And immediately the angel of the Lord smote him, because he gave not God the glory : and he was eaten of worms, and gave up the ghost." (v. xx. 23.) * * But see how (the writer) here does not hide these things. [3] Why does he mention this history? Say, what has it to do with the Gospel, that Herod is incensed with the Tyrians and Sidonians? It is not a small matter, even this, how immediately justice seized him ; although not because of Peter, but because of his arrogant speaking. And yet, it may be said, if those shouted, what is that to him? Because he accepted the acclamation, because he accounted himself to be worthy of the adoration. Through him those most receive a lesson, who so thoughtlessly flattered him (al. οἱ κολακεύοντες). Observe again, while both parties deserve

punishment, this man is punished. For this is not the time of judgment, but He punishes him that had most to answer for, leaving the others to profit by this man's fate.* "And the word of God," it says, "grew," i. e. in consequence of this, " and multiplied." (v. 24.) Do you mark God's providential management? "But Barnabas and Saul returned from Jerusalem, when they had fulfilled their ministry, and took with them John, whose surname was Mark." (v. 25.) "Now there were in the Church that was at Antioch, certain prophets and teachers; as Barnabas, and Simeon that was called Niger, and Lucius of Cyrene, and Manaën, which had been brought up with Herod the tetrarch, and Saul."† (ch. xiii. 1.) He still mentions Barnabas first : for Paul was not yet famous, he had not yet wrought any sign. "As they ministered to the Lord, and fasted, the Holy Ghost said, Separate Me Barnabas and Saul for the work whereunto I have called them. And when they had fasted and prayed, and laid their hands on them, they sent them away." (v. 2, 3.) What means, " Ministering?" Preaching. "Separate for Me," it says, "Barnabas and Saul." What means, "Separate for Me?" For the work, for the Apostleship. See again by what persons he is ordained (γυμνοτέρα. Cat. σεμνοτέρα, "more awful.") By Lucius the Cyrenean and Manaën, or rather, by the Spirit. The less the persons, the more palpable the grace. He is ordained henceforth to Apostleship, so as to preach with authority. How then does he himself say, "Not from men, nor by man?" [4]

---

* Josephus' narrative of the death of Herod (*Ant*. xix. 8, 2) is of peculiar interest here on account of its substantial agreement with that of Luke. The following points of agreement may be noted: (1) The place was Cæsarea. (2) He was attacked by disease in a public assembly when, arrayed in gorgeous apparel, he received the impious flatteries of the people. (3) His disease and death were a penalty for accepting the flattery of those who accorded to him divine honors. Thus the main outlines are the same. Josephus introduces some historical notices, such as that the occasion was a celebration in honor of the Emperor Claudius, which are wanting in Luke. He also relates that after receiving the people's flattery, Herod observed an owl perched on a rope above him, which he interpreted at once as an omen of the fate which soon befell him. The supernatural element—" an angel smote him "—is wanting in Josephus. The Jewish historian is less specific in describing the disease which he speaks of as violent pains in the bowels and adds that after the attack, Herod lingered five days and died in the fifty-fourth year of his age and the seventh of his reign.—G. B. S.

† At this point (ch. xiii.) begins the second part of the Book of Acts which has chiefly to do with the missionary labors of Paul. It is a reasonable supposition that the previous chapters rest upon different documents from those which follow. From chapter xvi. onward occur the so-called " we " passages (e. g. xvi. 10; xx, 6. xxi. 1 ; xxvii. 1) in which the writer, identifying himself with his narratives, indicates that he writes from personal knowledge and experience. The appointment of Barnabas and Saul at Antioch for missionary service, marked an epoch in the history of the early church and practically settled the questions relating to the admission of the Gentiles to the Christian community.—G. B. S.

[1] μᾶλλον αὐτὸν ἐποίει διαπρίεσθαι (as in ch. vii. 54, cut to the heart with passion) καὶ καταγέλαστον εἶναι. The last words are either misplaced, or something is wanting ; perhaps (after διαπρίεσθαι), τὸ διακρούεσθαι καὶ καταγέλαστον εἶναι.

[2] i. e. what was to be drawn from them by the torture ? Had they let him out, they would have contrived appearances, or would themselves have fled. But the reporter's notes of what St. Chrys. said, seem to be very defective, and the arrangement much confused.

[3] ἀλλ' ὅρα πῶς οὗτος οὐ κρύπτει ταῦτα. In the recapitulation (see note [3], p. 175) he says, that the death of Herod was regarded as a judgment for his having slain James and the soldiers. Here, it seems, he must have said something to that effect; then, " but observe how St. Luke does not conceal the true' state of the case, viz. that he was punished not for this, but for the sin which he proceeds to mention." We have transposed the text v. 20-23. Mss. and Edd. place it before οὐ μικρὸν οὐδὲ τοῦτό ἐστιν, thus separating these words from their connection with the preceding question,

[4] Mss. and Edd. δι ἀνθρώπων, but the singular is implied below in οὐχ ὑπὸ τοῦδε. In the old text, B. C. Cat. " Not from men nor by men ? Because not man called nor brought him over : that is, neither by men ; therefore he says, that he was not sent (B., I was not sent) by this," etc. The mod. text " Not from men neither by men. The one, not from men, he uses to

(Gal. i. 1.) Because it was not man that called or brought him over : this is why he says, "Not from men. Neither by man," that is, that he was not sent by this (man), but by the Spirit. Wherefore also (the writer) thus proceeds : " So they, being sent forth by the Holy Ghost, departed unto Seleucia; and from thence they sailed to Cyprus. " (v. 4.) But let us look over again what has been said.

(Recapitulation.) "And when it was day," etc. (v. 18.) For[1] if the Angel had brought out the soldiers also, along with Peter, it would have been thought a case of flight. Then why, you may ask, was it not otherwise managed? Why, where is the harm? Now, if we see that they who have suffered unjustly, take no harm, we shall not raise these questions. For why do you not say the same of James? Why did not (God) rescue him? "There was no small stir among the soldiers." So (clearly) had they perceived nothing (of what had happened). Lo, I take up the plea in their defence. The chains were there, and the keepers within, and the prison shut, no-where a wall broken through, all told the same tale : the man had been carried off :[2] why dost thou condemn them? Had they wished to let him off, they would have done it before, or would have gone out with him. "But he gave them money?" (ch. iii. 6.) And how should he, who had not to give even to a poor man, have the means to give to these? And then neither had the chains been broken, nor were they loosed. He ought to have seen, that the thing was of God, and no work of man. "And he went down from Judea to Cæsarea, and there abode. And Herod was highly displeased with them of Tyre and Sidon," etc. (v. 19.) He is now going to mention (a matter of) his-tory: this is the reason why he adds the names, that it may be shown how he keeps to the truth in all things. "And," it says, "hav-ing made Blastus the king's chamberlain their friend, they desired peace; because their country was nourished by the king's country." (v. 20, 21.) For probably there was a famine. "And on a set day," etc. (Joseph. Ant. xix.) Josephus also says this, that he fell into a lingering disease. Now the gener-

ality were not aware of this,[3] but the Apostle sets it down : yet at the same time their igno-rance was an advantage, in regard that they imputed what befell (Agrippa) to his putting James and the soldiers to death. Observe, when he slew the Apostle, he did nothing of this sort but when (he slew) these; in fact he knew not what to say about it :[4] as being at a loss, then, and feeling ashamed, "he went down from Judea to Cæsarea." I suppose it was also to bring those (men of Tyre and Sidon) to apologize, that he withdrew (from Jerusalem): for with those he was incensed, while paying such court to these. See how vainglorious the man is : meaning to confer the boon upon them, he makes an harangue. But Josephus says, that he was also arrayed in a splendid robe made of silver. Observe both what flatterers those were, and what a high spirit was shown by the Apostles : the man whom the whole nation so courted, the same they held in contempt. (v. 24.) But observe again a great refreshing granted to them, and the numberless benefits accruing from the vengeance inflicted upon him. But if this man, because it was said to him, " It is the voice of God and not of a man (v. 22) although he said nothing himself, suffered such things: much more should Christ, had He not Himself been God (have suffered) for saying always as He did, "These words of mine are not Mine " (John xiv. 10; xviii. 36) and, "Angels minister to Me," and such like. But that man ended His life by a shameful and miserable death, and thenceforth no more is seen of him. And observe him also, easily talked over even by Blastus, like a poor creature, soon incensed and again pacified, and on all occasions a slave of the populace, with nothing free and independent about him. But mark also the authority of the Holy Ghost : "As they min-istered to the Lord, and fasted, the Holy Ghost said, Separate Me Barnabas and Saul." (ch. xiii. 2.) What being would have dared, if not of the same authority, to say this? "Separate," etc. But this is done,

---

[3] i. e. of the circumstances related v. 22, 23.—Below, πλὴν ἀλλὰ καὶ ἡ ἄγνοια ὠφέλει, i. e. to the believers : and yet, as he says above, the writer does not conceal the facts: see note [3], p. 174.

[4] Mss. and Edd. οὐδὲν τοιοῦτον εἰργάσατο· ὅτε δὲ τούτους, λοιπὸν ἐν ἀφασίᾳ ἦν : what this means, is very obscure, only the last clause seems to be explained by the following, ἄτε οὖν ἠπορηκὼς καὶ αἰσχυνόμενος, i. e. not knowing what to think of it, he withdrew from Jerusalem. Ben. quando illos, nihil dicebat. Erasm., et quando alios, nihil de illis traditur.—Below, Ἐμοὶ δοκεῖ καὶ ἐκείνους πρὸς τὴν ἀπολογίαν ἐνάγων ἀπαγαγεῖν ὠργίζετο γὰρ ἐκείνοις, τουτους οὕτω θεραπεύων. By ἐκείνους, ἐκείνοις, he means the Tyrians and Sidonians : ἀπαγ-αγεῖν. sc. ἑαυτόν, to have withdrawn himself from Jerusalem, to Cæsarea, nearer to Tyre and Sidon. The innovator substi-tutes, Ἐμοὶ δοκεῖ καὶ ἐκείνους ἀπαγαγεῖν βουλόμενος, πρὸς ἀπολογίαν ἦλθε τούτων· ὠργίζετο γὰρ κ. τ. λ. which Ben. renders Mihi videtur, cum illos abducere vellet, ad hos venisse ut sese purgaret.

---

show that not man, etc.: and the other, neither by men, that he was not sent by this (man), but by the Spirit. Wherefore," etc.

[1] Here he further answers the question raised in the opening of the discourse. The mod. text transposes it to that place, beginning the recapitulation with, " 'And when it was day there was no small stir among the soldiers because of Peter, and having put the keepers to the question. he ordered them to be led away to execution.' So senseless was he, οὕτως οὐκ ᾔσθετο, that he even sets about punishing them unjustly." The latter clause is added by the innovator. For ᾔσθετο Cat. has preserved the true reading, ᾔσθοντο.

[2] ἀνάρπαστος ὁ ἄνθρωπος γέγονε. Ben. homo ille raptus non est.

that they may not keep together among themselves. The Spirit saw that they had greater power, and were able to be sufficient for many. And how did He speak to them? Probably by prophets: therefore the writer premises, that there were prophets also. And they were fasting and ministering: that thou mayest learn that there was need of great sobriety. In Antioch he is ordained, where he preaches. Why did He not say, Separate for the Lord, but, "For me?" It shows that He is of one authority and power. "And when they had fasted," etc. Seest thou what a great thing fasting is? "So they being sent forth by the Holy Ghost:" it shows that the Spirit did all.

A great, yes a great good is fasting: it is circumscribed by no limits. When need was to ordain, then they fast: and to them while fasting, the Spirit spake. Thus much only do I enjoin: (I say) not fast, but abstain from luxury. Let us seek meats to nourish, not things to ruin us; seek meats for food, not occasions of diseases, of diseases both of soul and body: seek food which hath comfort, not luxury which is full of discomfort: the one is luxury, the other mischief; the one is pleasure, the other pain; the one is agreeable to nature, the other contrary to nature. For say, if one should give thee hemlock juice to drink, would it not be against nature? if one should give thee logs and stones, wouldest thou not reject them? Of course, for they are against nature. Well, and so is luxury. For just as in a city, under an invasion of enemies when there has been siege and tumult, great is the uproar, so is it in the soul, under invasion of wine and luxury. "Who hath woe? who hath tumults? who hath discomforts and babblings? Are they not they that tarry long at the wine? Whose are bloodshot eyes?" (Prov. xxiii. 29, 30,) But yet, say what we will, we shall not bring off those who give themselves up to luxury, unless [1] we bring into conflict therewith a different affection. And first, let us address ourselves to the women. Nothing uglier than a woman given to luxury, nothing uglier than a woman given to drink. The bloom of her complexion is faded: the calm and mild expression of the eyes is rendered turbid, as when a cloud intercepts the rays of the sunshine. It is a vulgar, (ἀνελεύθερον) slave-like, thoroughly low-lived habit. How disgusting is a woman when from her breath you catch sour whiffs of fetid wine: a woman belching, giving out a fume (χυμὸν) of decomposing meats; herself weighed down, unable to keep upright; her face flushed with an unnatural red; yawning incessantly, and everything swimming in a mist before her eyes! But not such, she that abstains from luxurious living: no (this abstinence makes her look) a more beautiful, well-bred (σωφρονεστέρα) woman. For even to the body, the composure of the soul imparts a beauty of its own. Do not imagine that the impression of beauty results only from the bodily features. Give me a handsome girl, but turbulent (τεταραγμένην), loquacious, railing, given to drink, extravagant, (and tell me) if she is not worse-looking than any ugly woman? But if she were bashful, if she would hold her peace, if she learnt to blush, if to speak modestly (συμμέτρως), if to find time for fastings; her beauty would be twice as great, her freshness would be heightened, her look more engaging, fraught with modesty and good breeding (σωφροσίνης καὶ κοσμιότητος). Now then, shall we speak of men? What can be uglier than a man in drink? He is an object of ridicule to his servants, of ridicule to his enemies, of pity to his friends; deserving condemnation without end: a wild beast rather than a human being; for to devour much food is proper to panther, and lion, and bear. No wonder (that they do so), for those creatures have not a reasonable soul. And yet even they, if they be gorged with food more than they need, and beyond the measure appointed them by nature, get their whole body ruined by it: how much more we? Therefore hath God contracted our stomach into a small compass; therefore hath He marked out a small measure of sustenance, that He may instruct us to attend to the soul.

Let us consider our very make, and we shall see there is in us but one little part that has this operation—for our mouth and tongue are meant for singing hymns, our throat for voice—therefore the very necessity of nature has tied us down, that we may not, even involuntarily, get into much trouble (πραγματείαν) (in this way). Since, if indeed luxurious living had not its pains, nor sickness and infirmities, it might be tolerated: but as the case is, He hath stinted thee by restrictions of nature, that even if thou wish to exceed, thou mayest not be able to do so. Is not pleasure thine object, beloved? This thou shalt find from moderation. Is not health? This too thou shalt so gain. Is not easiness of mind? This too. Is not freedom? is not vigor and good habit of body, is not sobriety and alertness of mind? (All these thou shalt find); so entirely are all good things there, while in the

---

[1] οὐκ ἀποστήσομεν . . . ἂν μὴ ἕτερον ἀντιστήσωμεν πάθος (Mod. text πρὸς ἔτ. and τὸ πάθος), i. e. unless, as Solomon does in the last clause of the text cited, we set against this lust a different affection, viz. vanity, especially female vanity, regard to personal appearance. Hence that last clause might be better transposed to the end of this sentence.

other are the contraries to these, discomfort, distemper, disease, embarrassment—waste of substance (ἀνελευθερία). Then how comes it, you will ask, that we all run eagerly after this? It comes of disease. For say, what is it that makes the sick man hanker after the thing that does him harm? Is not this very hankering a part of his disease? Why is it that the lame man does not walk upright? This very thing, does it come of his being lazy, and not choosing to go to the physician? For there are some things, in which the pleasure they bring with them is temporary, but lasting the punishment: others just the contrary, in which the endurance is for a time, the pleasure perpetual. He, therefore, that has so little solidity and strength of purpose as not to slight present sweets for future, is soon overcome. Say, how came Esau to be overcome? how came he to prefer the present pleasure to the future honor? Through want of solidity and firmness of character. (Gen. xxv. 33.) And this fault itself, say you, whence comes it? Of our ownselves: and it is plain from this consideration. When we have the mind, we do rouse ourselves, and become capable of endurance. Certain it is, if at any time necessity comes upon us, nay, often only from a spirit of emulation, we get to see clearly what is useful for us. When therefore thou art about to indulge in luxury, consider how brief the pleasure, consider the loss—for loss it is indeed to spend so much money to one's own hurt—the diseases, the infirmities: and despise luxury. How many shall I enumerate who have suffered evils from indulgence? Noah was drunken, and was exposed in his nakedness, and see what evils came of this. (Gen. ix. 20.) Esau through greediness abandoned his birthright, and was set upon fratricide. The people of Israel "sat down to eat and to drink, and rose up to play." (Ex. xxxii. 6.) Therefore saith the Scripture, "When thou hast eaten and drunken, remember the Lord thy God." (Deut. vi. 12.) For they fell over a precipice, in falling into luxury. "The widow," he saith, "that liveth in pleasure, is dead while she liveth" (1 Tim. v. 6): and again, "The beloved waxed sleek, grew thick, and kicked" (Deut. xxxii. 15): and again the Apostle, "Make not provision for the flesh, to fulfil the lusts thereof." (Rom. xiii. 14.) I am not enacting as a law that there shall be fasting, for indeed there is no one who would listen; but I am doing away with daintiness, I am cutting off luxury for the sake of your own profit: for like a winter torrent, luxury overthrows all: there is nothing to stop its course: it casts out from a kingdom: what is the gain of it (τί τὸ πλέον)? Would you enjoy

a (real) luxury? Give to the poor; invite Christ, so that even after the table is removed, you may still have this luxury to enjoy. For now, indeed, you have it not, and no wonder: but then you will have it. Would you taste a (real) luxury? Nourish your soul, give to her of that food to which she is used: do not kill her by starvation.—It is the time for war, the time for contest: and do you sit enjoying yourself? Do you not see even those who wield sceptres, how they live frugally while abroad on their campaigns? "We wrestle not against flesh and blood" (Eph. vi. 12); and are you fattening yourself when about to wrestle? The adversary stands grinding his teeth, and are you giving a loose to jollity, and devoting yourself to the table? I know that I speak these things in vain, yet not (in vain) for all. "He that hath ears to hear, let him hear." (Luke viii. 8.) Christ is pining through hunger, and are you frittering yourself away (διασπῇς) with gluttony? Two inconsistencies (Δύο ἀμετρίαι). For what evil does not luxury cause? It is contrary to itself: so that I know not how it gets its name: but just as that is called glory, which is (really) infamy, and that riches, which in truth is poverty, so the name of luxury is given to that which in reality is nauseousness. Do we intend ourselves for the shambles, that we so fatten ourselves? Why cater for the worm that it may have a sumptuous larder? Why make more of their humors (ἰχῶρας)? Why store up in yourself sources of sweat and rank smelling? Why make yourself useless for everything? Do you wish your eye to be strong? Get your body well strung? For in musical strings, that which is coarse and not refined, is not fit to produce musical tones, but that which has been well scraped, stretches well, and vibrates with full harmony. Why do you bury the soul alive? why make the wall about it thicker? Why increase the reek and the cloud, with fumes like a mist steaming up from all sides? If none other, let the wrestlers teach you, that the more spare the body, the stronger it is: and (then) also the soul is more vigorous. In fact, it is like charioteer and horse. But there you see, just as in the case of men giving themselves to luxury, and making themselves plump, so the plump horses are unwieldy, and give the driver much ado. One may think one's self (ἀγαπητὸν) well off, even with a horse obedient to the rein and well-limbed, to be able to carry off the prize: but when the driver is forced to drag the horse along, and when the horse falls, though he goad him ever so much, he cannot make him get up, be he ever so skilful himself, he will be deprived of the victory. Then let us

12

not endure to see our soul wronged because of the body, but let us make the soul herself more clear-sighted, let us make her wing light, her bonds looser: let us feed her with 'discourse, with frugality, (feeding) the body only so much that it may be healthy, that it may be vigorous, that it may rejoice and not be in pain : that having in this sort well ordered our concerns, we may be enabled to lay hold upon the highest virtue, and to attain unto the eternal good things by the grace and loving-kindness of our Lord Jesus Christ, with Whom, to the Father and Holy Ghost together, be glory, dominion, honor, now and ever, world without end. Amen.

HOMILY XXVIII.

ACTS XIII. 4, 5.

" So they, being sent forth by the Holy Ghost, departed unto Seleucia; and from thence they sailed to Cyprus. And when they were at Salamis, they preached the word of God in the synagogues of the Jews: and they had also John to their minister."

As soon as they were ordained they went forth, and hasted to Cyprus, that being a place where was no ill-design hatching against them, and where moreover the Word had been sown already. In Antioch there were (teachers) enough, and Phœnice too was near to Palestine; but Cyprus not so. However, you are not to make a question of the why and wherefore, when it is the Spirit that directs their movements : for they were not only ordained by the Spirit, but sent forth by Him likewise. "And when they were come to Salamis, they preached the word of God in the synagogues of the Jews." Do you mark how they make a point of preaching the word to them first, not to make them more contentious ? * The persons mentioned before " spake to none but to Jews only " (ch. xi. 19), and so here they betook them to the synagogues. "And when they had gone through the isle unto Paphos, they found a certain sorcerer, a false prophet, a Jew, whose name was Bar-jesus : which was with the deputy of the country, Sergius Paulus, a prudent man : who called for Barnabas and Saul, and desired to hear the word of God. But Elymas the sorcerer (for so is his name by interpretation) withstood them, seeking to turn away the deputy from the faith." (v. 6-8.) Again a Jew sorcerer, as was Simon. And observe this man, how, while they preached to the others, he did not take it much amiss, but only when they approached the proconsul. And then in respect of the proconsul the wonder is, that although prepossessed by the man's sorcery, he was nevertheless willing to hear the Apostles. So it was with the Samaritans : and from the competition (συγκρίσεως) the victory appears, the sorcery being worsted. Everywhere, vainglory and love of power are a (fruitful) source of evils ! "But Saul, who is also Paul,"—(v. 9) here his name is changed at the same time that he is ordained, as it was in Peter's case,†—"filled with the Holy Ghost, looked upon him, and said, O full of all guile and all villany, thou child of the devil :" (v. 10) and observe, this is not abuse, but accusation : for so ought forward, impudent people to be rebuked "thou enemy of all righteousness ; " here he lays bare what was in the thoughts of the man, while under pretext of saving he was ruining the proconsul : " wilt thou not cease," he says, " to pervert the ways of the Lord ? " (He says it) both confidently (αξιοπίστως), It is not with us thou art warring, nor art thou fighting (with us), but " the ways of the Lord " thou art perverting, and with praise (of these, he adds) " the

---

* That Barnabas and Saul preached first to the Jews for the reason mentioned by Chrysostom is wholly improbable. The mission to the Gentiles entrusted to them never cancelled, in their minds, their obligation to the Jews as having in the plan of God an economic precedence. Paul not only maintained throughout his life an ardent love and longing for his people (Rom. ix.) and a confident hope of their conversion (Rom. xi.), but regarded them as still the people of privilege, on the principle: " To the Jew first, and also to the Greek." (Rom. i. 16.) This view, together with the fact that they were Jews, constitutes a sufficient explanation for their resort to the synagogues. Additional reasons may be found in the fact that in the synagogues might be found those who were religiously inclined—of both Jewish and Gentile nationality—and who were therefore most susceptible to the influence of Christian truth, and in the fact that the freedom of speech in the synagogue-service offered the most favorable opportunity to expound the Gospel.—G. B. S.

† Chrysostom here hints at the most probable explanation of the change of name in the Acts from Saul to Paul, although that change is not strictly simultaneous with his ordination which occurred at Antioch (v. 3), whereas the first use of the name " Paul " is in connection with his labors at Paphos, after he had preached for a time in Salamis. It seems probable that, as in so many cases, Paul, a Hellenist, had two names, in Hebrew Saul, and in Greek Paul, and that now when he enters distinctively upon his mission to the Gentiles, his Gentile name comes into exclusive use. (So, among recent critics, De Wette, Lechler, Alford, Neander, Gloag.) Other opinions are: (1) that he took the name Paul—signifying little—out of modesty (Augustin); (2) that he was named Paul, either by himself (Jerome), by his fellow-Christians (Meyer) or by the proconsul (Ewald), in honor of the conversion of Sergius Paulus. —G. B. S.

right" ways. "And now, behold, the hand of the Lord is upon thee, and thou shalt be blind." (v. 11.) It was the sign by which he was himself converted, and by this he would fain convert this man. As also that expression, "for a season," puts it not as an act of punishing, but as meant for his conversion: had it been for punishment, he would have made him lastingly blind, but now it is not so, but "for a season" (and this), that he may gain the proconsul. For, as he was prepossessed by the sorcery, it was well to teach him a lesson by this infliction (and the sorcerer also), in the same way as the magicians (in Egypt) were taught by the boils.* (Ex. ix. 11.) "And immediately there fell on him a mist and a darkness: and he went about seeking some to lead him by the hand. Then the deputy, when he saw what was done, believed, being astonished at the doctrine of the Lord." (v. 12.) But observe, how they do not linger there, as (they might have been tempted to do) now that the proconsul was a believer, nor are enervated by being courted and honored, but immediately keep on with their work, and set out for the country on the opposite coast. "Now when Paul and his company loosed from Paphos, they came to Perga in Pamphylia; and John departing from them returned to Jerusalem. But when they departed from Perga, they came to Antioch in Pisidia, and went into the synagogue on the sabbath day, and sat down." (v. 13, 14.) And here again they entered the synagogues, in the character of Jews, that they might not be treated as enemies, and be driven away: and in this way they carried the whole matter successfully. "And after the reading of the Law and the Prophets, the rulers of the synagogue sent unto them, saying, Ye men and brethren, if ye have any word of exhortation for the people, say on." (v. 15.) From this point, we learn the history of Paul's doings, as in what was said above we have learned not a little about Peter. But let us review what has been said.

(Recapitulation.) "And when they were come to Salamis," the metropolis of Cyprus, "they preached the word of God." (v. 5.) They had spent a year in Antioch: it behooved that they should go hither also (to Cyprus) and not sit permanently where they were (the converts in Cyprus): needed greater teachers. See too how they remain no time in Seleucia, knowing that (the people there) might have reaped much benefit from the neighboring city (of Antioch): but they hasten on to the more pressing duties. When they came to the metropolis of the island, they were earnest to disabuse (διορθῶσαι) the proconsul. But that it is no flattery that (the writer) says, "he was with the proconsul, a prudent man" (v. 7), you may learn from the facts; for he needed not many discourses, and himself wished to hear them. And[1] he mentions also the names. * * * Observe, how he said nothing to the sorcerer, until he gave him an occasion: but they only "preached the word of the Lord." Since (though Elymas) saw the rest attending to them, he looked only to this one object, that the proconsul might not be won over. Why did not (Paul) perform some other miracle? Because there was none equal to this, the taking the enemy captive. And observe, he first impeaches, and then punishes, him. He shows how justly the man deserved to suffer, by his saying, "O full of all deceit" (v. 10): ("full of all,") he says: nothing wanting to the full measure: and he well says, of all "deceit," for the man was playing the part of a hypocrite.—"Child of the devil," because he was doing his work: "enemy of all righteousness," since this (which they preached) was the whole of righteousness (though at the same time): I suppose in these words he reproves his manner of life. His words were not prompted by anger, and to show this, the writer premises, "filled with the Holy Ghost," that is, with His operation. "And now behold the hand of the Lord is upon thee." (v. 11.) It was not vengeance then, but healing: for it is as though he said: "It is not I that do it, but the hand of God." Mark how unassuming! No "light,"[2] as in the case of Paul, "shone round about him." (ch. ix. 3.) "Thou shalt be blind," he says, "not seeing the sun for a season," that he may give him opportunity for repentance: for we nowhere find them wishing to be made conspicuous by the more stern (exercise of their authority), even though it was against enemies that this was put forth: in respect of those of their own body (they used severity),

---

* It can hardly be meant that the smiting of Elymas with blindness was not a judicial infliction *to himself*; but that the proconsul should see it rather on its merciful side as being only ἄχρι καιροῦ. The Hebraistic use of Χεὶρ Κυρίου clearly implies a divine judgment upon Elymas as does the whole force of the narrative.—G. B. S.

[1] Καὶ τὰ ὀνόματα δὲ λέγει· ἐπειδὴ προσφάτως ἔγραφον· ὅρα κ. τ. λ. A. B. C. N. Cat. It is not clear whether this relates to the two names, Barjesus and Elymas, (if so we might read ἔγραφεν, "since he wrote just before, (whose name was Barjesus, but now Elymas, for so is his name interpreted,") or to the change of the Apostle's name, "Then Saul, who is also called Paul," (and then perhaps the sense of the latter clause may be, Since the change of name was recent: ἐπειδὴ προσφάτως μετεγράφη or the like.) The mod. text substitutes, "But he also recites the names of the cities: showing that since they had but recently received the word, there was need (for them) to be confirmed, to continue in the faith: for which reason also they frequently visited them."

[2] Mod. text omits this sentence. The connection is: Paul inflicts this blindness upon him, not in vengeance, but in order to his conversion, remembering how the Lord Himself had dealt with him on the way to Damascus. But it was not here, as then—no "light shown round about him from heaven."

and with good reason, but in dealing with those without, not so; that (the obedience of faith) might not seem to be matter of compulsion and fear. It is a proof of his blindness, his "seeking some to lead him by the hand." (ch. v. 1. ff.) And[1] the proconsul sees the blindness inflicted, "and when he saw what was done, he believed:" and both alone believed not merely this, but, "being astonished at the doctrine of the Lord" (v. 12): he saw that these things were not mere words, nor trickery. Mark how he loved to receive instruction from his teachers, though he was in a station of so high authority. And (Paul) said not to the sorcerer, "Wilt thou not cease to pervert" the proconsul?[2] What may be the reason of John's going back from them? For "John," it says, "departing from them returned to Jerusalem" (v. 13): (he does it) because they are undertaking a still longer journey: and yet he was their attendant, and as for the danger, they incurred it (not he).— Again, when they were come to Perga, they hastily passed by the other cities, for they were in haste to the metropolis, Antioch. And observe how concise the historian is. "They sat down in the synagogue," he says, and, "on the sabbath day" (v. 14, 15): that they might prepare the way beforehand for the Word. And they do not speak first, but when invited: since as strangers, they called upon them to do so. Had they not .waited, there would have been no discourse. Here for the first time we have Paul preaching. And observe his prudence: where the word was already sown, he passes on: but where there was none (to preach), he makes a stay: as he himself writes: "Yea, so have I strived to preach the Gospel, not where Christ was named." (Rom. xv. 20.) Great courage this also. Truly, from the very outset, a wonderful man! crucified, ready for all encounters (παρατεταγμένος), he knew how great grace he had obtained, and he brought to it zeal equivalent. He was not angry with John: for this was not for him:[3] but he kept to the work, he quailed not, he was unappalled, when shut up in the midst of a host. Observe how

wisely it is ordered that Paul should not preach at Jerusalem: the very hearing that he is become a believer, this of itself is enough for them; for him to preach, they never would have endured, such was their hatred of him: so he departs far away, where he was not known. But[4] it is well done, that "they entered the synagogue on the sabbath day" when all were collected together. "And after the reading of the Law and the Prophets, the rulers of the synagogue sent unto them, saying, Ye men and brethren, if ye have any word or exhortation for the people, say on." (v. 15.) Behold how they do this without grudging, but no longer after this. If ye did wish this (really), there was more need to exhort.

He first convicted the sorcerer (and showed), what he was; and that he was such, the sign showed: "thou shalt be blind, not seeing the sun" this was a sign of the blindness of his soul: "for a season" (v. 11): he says, to bring him to repentance. But, oh that love of rule! oh, that lust of vainglory! how it does overturn and ruin everything; makes people stand up against their own, against each other's salvation; renders them blind indeed, and dark, insomuch that they have even to seek for some to lead them by the hand! Oh that they did even this, oh that they did seek were it but some to lead them by the hand! But no, they no longer endure this, they take the whole matter into their own hands. (This vice) will let no man see: like a mist and thick darkness it spreads itself over them, not letting any see through it. What pleas shall we have to offer, we who for one evil affection, overcome another evil affection (supra p. 176), but not for the fear of God! For example, many who are both lewd and covetous, have for their niggardliness put a bridle upon their lust, while other such, on the contrary, have for pleasure's sake, despised riches. Again, those who are both the one and the other, have by the lust of vainglory overcome both, lavishing their money unsparingly, and practising temperance to no (good) purpose; others again, who are exceedingly vainglorious, have despised that evil affection, submitting to many vile disgraces for the sake of their amours, or for the sake of their money: others again, that they may satiate their anger, have chosen to suffer losses without end, and

---

[1] Καὶ (Εἶτα mod.) (ὁρᾷ C. N. Cat.) τὴν πήρωσιν (Cat. πύρωσιν) ὁ ἀνθ. καὶ (om. Cat.) μόνος ἐπίστευσεν (mod. εὐθὺς πιστεύει). The reading in Cat. is meant for emendation: "And mark the fervor (or kindling, viz. of the proconsul's mind): the proc. alone believed" etc.

[2] Mod. text adds, "but, the ways of the Lord, which is more: that he may not seem to pay court."

[3] οὐ γὰρ τούτου ἦν. "Down. renders it non enim iræ deditus erat, he was not the man for this (anger): or perhaps, For he (John) was not his, not associated by him, but by Barnabas." Ben. But the meaning should rather be, "So great a work was not for him (Mark); he was not equal to it." The connection is of this kind: "Paul knew how great grace had been bestowed on him, and on his own part he brought corresponding zeal. When Mark withdrew, Paul was not angry with him, knowing that the like grace was not bestowed on him, therefore neither could there be the like σπουδὴ on his part."

[4] In Mss. and Edd. this portion, to the end of the paragraph, is placed after the part relating to Elymas, "He first convicted," etc. and immediately before the Morale, as if the occasion of the invective against φιλαρχία and κενοδοξία were furnished by the conduct of the rulers of the synagogue: but see above, p. 178, in the expos. of v. 8, πανταχοῦ ἡ κενοδοξία καὶ ἡ φιλαρχία αἴτιαι τῶν κακῶν, and below, the allusion to the blindness of Elymas.

care for none of them, provided only they may work their own will. And yet, what passion can do with us, the fear of God is impotent to effect! Why speak I of passion? What shame before men can do with us, the fear of God has not the strength to effect! Many are the things we do right and wrong, from a feeling of shame before men; but God we fear not. How many have been shamed by regard to the opinions of men into flinging away money! How many have mistakenly made it a point of honor to give themselves up to the service of their friends (only), to their hurt! How many from respect for their friendships have been shamed into number-less wrong acts! Since then both passion and regard for the opinion of men are able to put us upon doing wrong things and right, it is idle to say, "we cannot:" we can, if we have the mind: and we ought to have the mind. Why canst not thou overcome the love of glory, when others do overcome it, having the same soul as thou, and the same body; bearing the same form, and living the same life? Think of God, think of the glory that is from above: weigh against that the things present, and thou wilt quickly recoil from this worldly glory. If at all events thou covet glory, covet that which is glory, indeed. What kind of glory is it, when it begets in-famy? What kind of glory, when it compels one to desire the honor of those who are in-ferior, and stands in need of that? Real honor is the gaining the esteem of those who are greater than one's self. If at all events thou art enamoured of glory, be thou rather enamoured of that which comes from God. If enamoured of that glory thou despisest this world's glory, thou shalt see how ignoble this is: but so long as thou seest not that glory, neither wilt thou be able to see this, how foul it is, how ridiculous. For as those who are under the spell of some wicked, hideously ugly woman, so long as they are in love with her, cannot see her ill-favoredness, because their passion spreads a darkness over their judgment: so is it here also: so long as we are possessed with the passion, we cannot perceive what a thing it is. How then might we be rid of it? Think of those who (for the sake of glory) have spent countless sums, and now are none the better for it:[1] think of the

dead, what glory they got, and (now) this glory is nowhere abiding, but all perished and come to naught: bethink thee how it is only a name, and has nothing real in it. For say, what is glory? give me some definition. "The being admired by all," you will say. With justice, or also not with justice? For if it be not with justice, this is not admiration, but crimination (κατηγορία), and flattery, and misrepresentation (διαβολή). But if you say, With justice, why that is impossible: for in the populace there are no right judgments; those that minister to their lusts, those are the persons they admire. And if you would (see the proof of this), mark those who give away their substance to the harlots, to the charioteers, to the dancers. But you will say, we do not mean these, but those who are just and upright, and able to do great and noble good acts. Would that they wished it, and they soon would do good: but as things are, they do nothing of the kind. Who, I ask you, now praises the just and upright man? Nay, it is just the contrary. Could anything be more preposterous than for a just man, when doing any such good act, to seek glory of the many —as if an artist of consummate skill, employed upon an Emperor's portrait, should wish to have the praises of the ignorant! Moreover, a man who looks for honor from men, will soon enough desist from the acts which virtue enjoins. If he will needs be gaping for their praises, he will do just what they wish, not what himself wishes. What then would I advise you? You must look only to God, to the praise that is from Him, perform all things which are pleasing to Him, and go after the good things (that are with Him), not be gaping for anything that is of man: for this mars both fasting and prayer and alms-giving, and makes all our good deeds void. Which that it be not our case, let us flee this passion. To one thing alone let us look, to the praise which is from God, to the being accepted of Him, to the commendation from our common Master; that, having passed through our present life virtuously, we may obtain the promised blessings together with them that love Him, through the grace and mercy of our Lord Jesus Christ, with whom to the Father, together with the Holy Ghost, be glory, might, honor, now and ever, world without end. Amen.

---

[1] καὶ οὐδὲν ἀπ' αὐτῆς καρπουμένους, i. e. reaping no fruit from it (the glory which they sought here) where they are now. Mod. text οὐδὲν ἀπ' αὐτῶν καρπωσαμένους: "reaped no fruit, while here, from their money which they squandered"—mis-taking the meaning of the passage, which is, "They got what they sought, but where is it now?"

HOMILY XXIX.

ACTS XIII. 16, 17.

" Then Paul stood up, and beckoning with his hand said, Men of Israel, and ye that fear God, give audience. The God of this people of Israel chose our fathers, and exalted the people when they dwelt as strangers in the land of Egypt, and with an high arm brought He them out of it."

BEHOLD Barnabas giving place to Paul—how should it be otherwise ?—to him whom he brought from Tarsus ; just as we find John on all occasions giving way to Peter : and yet Barnabas was more looked up to than Paul : true, but they had an eye only to the common advantage. " Then Paul stood up," it says ;—this[1] was a custom of the Jews—" and beckoned with his hand." And see how he prepares the way beforehand for his discourse : having first praised them, and showed his great regard for them in the words, " ye that fear God," he so begins his discourse. And he says not, Ye proselytes, since it was a term of disadvantage.[2] " The God of this people chose our fathers : and the people "—See, he calls God Himself *their* God peculiarly, Who is the common God of men ; and shows how great from the first were His benefits, just as Stephen does. This they do to teach them, that now also God has acted after the same custom, in sending His own Son ; (Luke xx. 13) : as (Christ) Himself (does) in the parable of the vineyard—" And the people," he says, " He exalted when it sojourned in the land of Egypt "—and yet the contrary was the case :[3] true, but they increased in numbers ; moreover, the miracles were wrought on their account : " and with an high arm brought He them out of it." Of these things (the wonders) which were done in Egypt, the prophets

are continually making mention. And observe, how he passes over the times of their calamities, and nowhere brings forward their faults, but only God's kindness, leaving those for themselves to think over. " And about the time of forty years suffered He their manners in the wilderness." (v. 18.) Then the settlement. " And when he had destroyed seven nations in the land of Canaan, He divided their land to them by lot." (v. 19.) And the time was long ; four hundred and fifty years. " And after that He gave unto them judges about the space of four hundred and fifty years, until Samuel the prophet."* (v. 20.) Here he shows that God varied His dispensations towards them (at divers times). " And afterward they desired a king : " and (still) not a word of their ingratitude, but throughout he speaks of the kindness of God. " And God gave unto them Saul the son of Cis, a man of the tribe of Benjamin, by the space of forty years." (v. 21.) " And when he had removed him, He raised up unto them David to be their king : to whom also He gave testimony, and said, I have found David the son of Jesse, a man after Mine own heart, which shall fulfil all My will. Of this man's seed hath God according to His promise raised unto Israel a Saviour, Jesus." (v. 22, 23.) This was no small thing that Christ should be from David. Then John bears witness to this : " When John had first preached before His coming the baptism of repentance to all the people of Israel. And as John fulfilled his course, he said, Whom think ye that

---

[1] i. e. for one of the congregation to expound or preach : or perhaps rather, to preach standing, not sitting, as Christian bishops did for their sermons. We have transposed the comment to its proper place.—Mod. text adds, " Wherefore he too in accordance with this discourses to them."

[2] ὅπερ ἦν συμφορᾶς ὄνομα, in regard that a proselyte might be deemed inferior to a Jew of genuine descent, "a Hebrew of the Hebrews."

[3] καὶ μὴν τοὐναντίον γέγονεν. Here also we have transposed the comment to the clause to which it belongs. In the Edd. it comes after " And with a high arm," etc. whence Ben. mistaking its reference says, " i. e., if I mistake not, God brought them out of Egypt, that he might bring them into the Land of Promise : but, for their wickedness, the contrary befell ; for the greatest part of them perished in the wilderness." It plainly refers to ὕψωσεν—i. e. how is it said, that He exalted them in Egypt, where, on the contrary, they were brought low ? This is true—but He did exalt them by increasing them into a great multitude, and by the miracles which He wrought on their behalf.

* Upon the reading of the T. R. (A. V.) the period of the Judges is here stated to have been 450 years. This agrees with the chronology of the book of Judges and of Josephus, but conflicts with 1 Kings vi. 1 where we are told that " in the four hundred and eightieth year after the children of Israel were come out of the land of Egypt, in the fourth year of Solomon's reign over Israel, he began to build the house of the Lord." This would give but 331 years for the period of the Judges. It is the view of many critics that Paul has here followed a different chronology from that of 1 Kings which was also in use among the Jews and was followed by Josephus (so Meyer.) But if the reading of Tischendorf, Lechler, and Westcott and Hort (R. V.) is adopted—and it is sustained by A. B. C. א—the difficulty, so far as Acts xiii. 21 is concerned, disappears. This reading places μετὰ ταῦτα after ὡς ἔτεσιν sq. and inserts a period after πεντήκοντα. Then the translation would be, " He gave them their land for an inheritance for about four hundred and fifty years. And after these things He gave them judges," etc. On this reading the 450 years is the period of their inheritance, approximately stated, up to the time of the judges. The point from which Paul reckoned is not stated and is uncertain. This is the preferable reading and explanation.—G. B. S.

I am? I am not He. But, behold, there cometh one after me, whose shoes of His feet I am not worthy to loose." (v. 24, 25.) And John too not merely bears witness (to the fact), but (does it in such sort that) when men were bringing the glory to him, he declines it: for it is one thing (not to affect) an honor which nobody thinks of offering; and another, to reject it when all men are ready to give it, and not only to reject it, but to do so with such humility. "Men and brethren, children of the stock of Abraham, and whosoever among you feareth God, to you is the word of this salvation sent. For they that dwell at Jerusalem, and their rulers, because they knew Him not, nor yet the voices of the prophets which are read every sabbath day, they have fulfilled them in condemning Him. And though they found no cause of death in Him, yet desired they Pilate that He should be slain." (v. 26–28.) On all occasions we find them making a great point of showing this, that the blessing is peculiarly theirs, that they may not flee (from Christ), as thinking they had nothing to do with Him, because they had crucified Him. "Because they knew Him not," he says: so that the sin was one of ignorance. See how he gently makes an apology even on behalf of those (crucifiers). And not only this: but he adds also, that thus it must needs be. And[1] how so? "By condemning Him, they fulfilled the voices of the prophets." Then again from the Scriptures. "And when they had fulfilled all that was written of Him, they took Him down from the tree, and laid Him in a sepulchre. But God raised Him from the dead. And He was seen many days of them which came up with Him from Galilee to Jerusalem, who are His witnesses unto the people—"(v. 29–31) that He rose again. "And we declare unto you glad tidings, how that the promise which was made unto the fathers, God hath fulfilled the same unto us their children, in that He hath raised up Jesus again; as it is also written in the second Psalm, Thou art My Son, this day have I begotten Thee. And as concerning that He raised Him up from the dead, now no more to return to corruption, He said on this wise, I will give you the sure mercies of David. Wherefore he saith also in another Psalm, Thou shalt not suffer Thine Holy One to see corruption. For David, after he had served his own generation by the will of God,

fell on sleep, and was laid unto his fathers, and saw corruption: but He, Whom God raised again, saw no corruption. Be it known unto you therefore, men and brethren, that through this Man is preached unto you the forgiveness of sins: and by Him all that believe are justified from all things, from which ye could not be justified by the law of Moses." (v. 32–39.) Observe[2] how Paul here is more vehement in his discourse: we nowhere find Peter saying this. Then too he adds the terrifying words: "Beware therefore, lest that come upon you, which is spoken of in the prophets; Behold, ye despisers, and wonder, and perish: for I work a work in your days, a work which ye shall in no wise believe, though a man declare it unto you." (v. 40, 41.)

(a) Observe[3] how he twines (the thread of) his discourse (alternately) from things present, from the prophets. Thus, "from[4] (this man's) seed according to the promise"—(v. 23): (c) the name of David was dear to them; well then, is it not (a thing to be desired) that a son of his, he says, should be their king?—(b) then he adduces John: then again the prophets, where he says, "By condemning they fulfilled," and again, "All that was written:" then the Apostles as witnesses of the Resurrection: then David bearing witness. For neither the Old Testament proofs seemed so cogent when taken by themselves as they are in this way, nor yet the latter testimonies apart from the former: wherefore he makes them mutually confirm each other. "Men and brethren," etc. (v. 26.) For since they were possessed by fear, as having slain Him, and conscience made them aliens (the Apostles), discourse not with them as unto Christicides, neither as putting into their hands a good which was not theirs, but one peculiarly their own. (d) "For they that dwell at Jerusalem, and their rulers:" as

---

[1] Καὶ πόθεν ὅτι ἀνέστη φησι καὶ μάρτυρες εἰσιν. Εἶτα πάλιν ἀπὸ τῶν γραφῶν, followed by v. 29–37. We read, καὶ πόθεν; ὅτι τὰς φωνὰς τῶν προφ., κρίναντες τοῦτον ἐπλήρωσαν. Εἶτα πάλιν ἀπὸ τ. γρ. v. 29–31, ending, καὶ μάρτυρες αὐτοῦ εἰσιν πρὸς τὸν λαὸν ὅτι ἀνέστη. The mod. text "And that no man may say, And whence is this manifest that He rose again? He says that (word), And are His witnesses. Then again He presses them from the Scriptures, v. 29–37."

[2] This comment, which in the Mss. and Edd. is inserted after v. 37, refers to the following verses 38, 39, i. e. to what is there said of the insufficiency of the Law for justification: we have therefore transposed it.
[3] In the old text the parts lie in the order here shown by the letters a, b, etc. The confusion may be explained by the scribe's copying in the wrong order from the four pages of his tablets: viz. in the first place, in the order 1, 3, 2, 4: then 2, 4, 1, 3: and lastly, 2, 1. In the modern text, a different arrangement is attempted by which all is thrown into worse confusion. Thus it was not perceived that Chrys. having in a cursory way read through v. 24–41, begins his exposition in detail with the remark of the Apostle's passing and repassing from the Old to the New Test. and vice versa, viz. alleging first the Promise, then John, then the Prophets, then the Apostles, then David and Isaiah, v. 24–34; then comments upon the matters contained in these and the following verses, and then as usual goes over the whole again in a second exposition. Now the innovator makes the recapitulation begin immediately after (a), commencing it at v. 26, and collecting the comments in this order: v. 26–32: v. 24–36: v. 17–41
[4] The transposition of the part (c), makes this read in the Mss. and Edd. as if it were parallel with ἀπὸ τῶν παρόντων (i. e. New Testament facts), ἀπὸ τῶν Προφητῶν (Old Testament testimonies).

much as to say, not ye, but they :* and again, apologizing even for those, " Because they knew Him not, and the voices of the Prophets which are read every sabbath day, in condemning Him, they fulfilled them." A great charge it is against them that they continually hearing heeded not. But no marvel : for what was said above concerning Egypt and the wilderness, was enough to show their ingratitude. And observe how this Apostle also, as one moved by the Spirit Himself,[1] continually preaches the Passion, the Burial. (g) " Having taken Him down from the tree." Observe, what a great point they make of this. He speaks of the manner of His death. Moreover they bring Pilate (conspicuously) forward, that (the fact of) the Passion may be proved by the mention of the tribunal (by which he was condemned), but at the same time, for the greater impeachment of those (His crucifiers), seeing they delivered Him up to an alien. And he does not say, They made a complaint (against Him), (ἐνέτυχον, al. ἐντυγχάνει) but, " They desired, though having found no cause of death " (in Him), " that He should be slain. (e) Who appeared," he says, " for many days to them that came up with Him from Galilee to Jerusalem." (Rom. xi. 2.) Instead of[2] * * he says, " Who are His witnesses unto the people," to wit, " The men which came up with Him from Galilee to Jerusalem." Then he produces David and Esaias bearing witness. " The faithful (mercies)," the abiding (mercies), those which never perish. (h) Paul loved them exceedingly. And observe, he does not enlarge on the ingratitude of the fathers, but puts before *them* what they must fear. For Stephen indeed with good reason does this, seeing he was about to be put to death, not teaching them ; and showing them, that the Law is even now on the point of being abolished : (ch. vii.) but not so Paul; he does but threaten and put them in fear. (f) And he does not dwell long on these,[3] as taking it for

granted that the word is of course believed ; nor enlarge upon the greatness of their punishment, and assail that which they affectionately love, by showing the Law about to be cast out : but dwells upon that which is for their good (telling them), that great shall be the blessings for them being obedient, and great the evils being disobedient.

But let us look over again what has been said. " Ye men of Israel," etc. (v. 16–21.) The Promise then, he says, the fathers received ; ye, the reality. (j) And observe, he nowhere mentions right deeds of theirs, but (only) benefits on God's part : " He chose : Exalted : Suffered their manners : " these are no matters of praise to them : " They asked, He gave." But David he does praise (and him) only, because from him the Christ was to come. " I have found David, the son of Jesse, a man after Mine own heart, which shall fulfil all My will." (v. 22.) (i) Observe also, it is with praise (that he says of him), " David after that he had served the will of God : " just as Peter—seeing it was then the beginning of the Gospel—making mention of him, said, " Let it be permitted me to speak freely of the patriarch David." (ch. ii. 29.) Also, he does not say, Died, but, " was added to his fathers. (k) Of this man's seed," etc. " When John," he says, " had first preached before His entry "—by *entry* he means the Incarnation—" the baptism of repentance to all the people of Israel." (v. 23–25.) Thus also John, writing his Gospel, continually has recourse to him : for his name was much thought of in all parts of the world. And observe, he does not say it " Of this man's seed," etc. from himself, but brings John's testimony.

" Men and brethren, children of the stock of Abraham "—he also calls them after their father—" unto you was the word of this salvation sent." (v. 26.) Here the expression, " Unto you," does not mean, Unto (you) Jews, but it gives them a right to sever themselves from those who dared that murder. And what he adds, shows this plainly. " For," he says, " they that dwell at Jerusalem, because they know Him not." (v. 27.) And how, you will say, could they be ignorant, with John to tell them ? What marvel, seeing they were so, with the prophets continually crying aloud to them ? Then follows another charge :

---

* It is probable that Chrys. has pointed out the true connection of thought as established by γὰρ (27). " The word of this salvation is sent unto you (of the dispersion) on the ground that the Jews at Jerusalem have rejected it." (So Meyer, Gloag.) The more common explanation is : The word is sent unto you because the Jews have fulfilled the prophecies which spoke of the rejection of the Messiah and have thus proved that He is the Messiah. (De Wette, Hackett, Lechler.) —G. B. S.

[1] i. e. Though not one of the original witnesses. v. 31, yet, being one who has been moved or raised up, κεκινημένον, by the Spirit of Christ Himself, he preaches as they did, insisting much on the Passion, etc.

[2] Ἀντὶ τοῦ, Οἱ ἄνδρες οἱ συναναβάντες κ. τ. λ. Perhaps the sense may be supplied thus : Ἀντὶ τοῦ, Οὐ πάντες ἡμεῖς ἐσμὲν μάρτυρες, ii. 32, οὗ ἡμεῖς μάρτ. ἐσμὲν, iii. 15. Instead of saying as Peter does, " Whereof we are witnesses."

[3] Καὶ οὐκ ἐγχρονίζει τούτοις, as in the recapitulation on v. 40, 41. καὶ ὅρα, τραχὺ ὂν πῶς ὑποτέμνεται. Hence it is clear that τούτοις refers not to " the sure mercies of David," as in Mss. and Edd. (end of e), but to the threats and terrors (end of h). Below, for ἀλλ' ἐπιτείνει τὴν κόλασιν the sense of ἐπιτείνει (not as Ben. *minatur*, but *intentat*, " makes much of, aggravates,

dwells upon the greatness of)", and the whole scope of the passage, require us to read οὐδὲ. Then, καὶ μετέρχεται with the negative extending to the whole clause, " and (like Stephen) assail that which is dear to them, (viz. their preëminence as Jews,) by showing the Law on the point of being cast out : " then, ἀλλὰ (so we restore for καὶ) τῷ συμφ. ἐνδιατρ., but dwells, etc.

"And having found no cause of death in Him:" in which ignorance had nothing to do. For let us put the case, that they did not hold Him to be the Christ: why did they also kill Him? And "they desired of Pilate, he says, that He should be slain." (v. 28.) "And when they had fulfilled all that was written of Him." (v. 29.) Observe what a point he makes of showing that the (whole) thing was a (Divine) Dispensation. See,[1] by saying what did they persuade men? (By telling them) that He was crucified? Why, what could be less persuasive than this? That He was buried— by them to whom it was promised that He should be salvation? that He who was buried forgives sins, yea, more than the Law (has power to do)? And (observe), he does not say, From which ye would not, but, "from which ye could not be justified by the Law of Moses." (v. 39.) "Every one," he says: be who he may. For those (ordinances) are of no use, unless there be some benefit (accruing therefrom.) This is why he brings in forgiveness later: and shows it to be greater, when, the thing being (otherwise) impossible, yet this is effected. "Who are His witnesses," he says, "unto the people"—the people that slew Him. Who would never have been so, were they not strengthened by a Divine Power: for they would never have borne such witness to blood-thirsty men, to the very persons that killed Him. But, "He hath raised up Jesus again: This day," he says, "I have begotten thee."* (v. 33.) Aye, upon this the rest follows of course. Why did he not allege some text by which they would be persuaded that forgiveness of sins is by Him? Because the great point with them was to show, in the first place, that He was risen: this being acknowledged, the other was unquestionable. "Through this man," nay more, by Him, "is remission of sins." (v. 38.) And besides, he wished to bring them to a longing desire of this great thing. Well then, His death was not dereliction, but fulfilling of Prophecy.—For the rest, he puts them in mind of historical facts, wherein they through ignorance suffered evils without number. And this he hints in the conclusion, saying, "Look, ye despisers, and behold." And observe how, this being harsh, he cuts it short. Let not that, he says, come upon you, which was spoken for the others, that "I work a work which ye shall in no wise believe, though one declare it unto you." (v. 41.) Marvel not that it seems incredible: this very thing was foretold from the first— (that it would not be believed). "Behold, ye despisers," as regards those who disbelieve in the Resurrection.

This too might with reason be said to us:[2] "Behold ye despisers." For the Church indeed is in very evil case, although ye think her affairs to be in peace. For the mischief of it is, that while we labor under so many evils, we do not even know that we have any. "What sayest thou? We are in possession of our Churches, our Church property, and all the rest, the services are held, the congregation comes to Church every day."[3] True, but one is not to judge of the state of a Church from these things. From what then? Whether there be piety, whether we return home with profit each day, whether reaping some fruit, be it much or little, whether we do it not merely of routine and for the formal acquittance of a duty (ἀφοσιούμενοι). Who has become a better man by attending (daily) service for a whole month? That is the point: otherwise the very thing which seems to bespeak a flourishing condition (of the Church,) does in fact bespeak an ill condition, when all this is done, and nothing comes of it. Would to God (that were all), that nothing comes of it: but indeed, as things are, it turns out even for the worse. What fruit do ye get from your services? Surely if you were getting any profit by them, ye ought to have been long leading the life of true wisdom (τῆς φιλοσοφίας), with so many Prophets twice in every week discoursing to you, so many Apostles, and Evangelists, all setting forth the doctrines of salvation, and placing before you with much exactness that which can form the character aright. The soldier by going to

---

[1] Edd. "But let us hear τί καὶ λέγοντες οἱ Ἀπόστ. ἔπεισαν, ὅτι ἐσταυρώθη, by saying what, by what announcement, the Apostles persuaded (men) that He was crucified." For τί τούτου ἀπιθ. B. has τὸ τ. ά. "(yea), what is more incredible still." Both clauses must be read interrogatively, The scope of the whole passage (which is obscure in the original) is, the supreme importance of the article of the Resurrection, Leave that out, and see what the preaching of the Apostles would have been; how it would have been received.

* The reading: "In the *Second* Psalm" is the best attested and is followed by the T. R., R. V. and Wescott and Hort. Πρώτῳ is found in D. and is supported by the Fathers. It is the more difficult reading and for this reason is preferred by Tischendorf, Lachmann, Meyer, Alford and Gloag. If it is correct, we must suppose that what we now call the first psalm was considered introductory and that our second psalm was counted as the first. In some Heb. Mss. this order actually occurs. The reading δευτέρῳ, however, is better supported. The expression: "this day have I begotten thee" refers evidently to the resurrection of Christ. (Cf. Heb. i. 5; Rom. i. 4.) The resurrection is conceived as the solemn inauguration of Christ into his office as theocratic king represented under the figure of begetting.—G. B. S.

[2] We have transposed this clause from before, "Behold," etc. preceding.
[3] Mod. text needlessly adds, Καὶ καταφρονοῦμεν; "And do we make light of these things?"

his drill, becomes more perfect in his tactics: the wrestler by frequenting the gymnastic ground becomes more skilful in wrestling: the physician by attending on his teacher becomes more accurate, and knows more, and learns more: and thou—what hast thou gained? I speak not to those who have been members of the Church only a year, but to those who from their earliest age have been attending the services. Think you that to be religious is to be constant in Church-going (παραβάλλειν τῇ συνάξει)? This is nothing, unless we reap some fruit for ourselves: if (from the gathering together in Church) we do not gather (συνάγωμεν) something for ourselves, it were better to remain at home. For our forefathers built the Churches for us, not just to bring us together from our private houses and show us one to another: since this could have been done also in a marketplace, and in baths, and in a public procession:—but to bring together learners and teachers, and make the one better by means of the other. With us it has all become mere customary routine, and formal discharge of a duty: a thing we are used to; that is all. Easter comes, and then great the stir, great the hubbub, and crowding of— I had rather not call them human beings, for their behavior is not commonly human. Easter goes, the tumult abates, but then the quiet which succeeds is again fruitless of good. "Vigils, and holy hymn-singing."— And what is got by these? Nay, it is all the worse. Many do so merely out of vanity. Think how sick at heart it must make me, to see it all like (so much water) poured into a cask with holes in it! But ye will assuredly say to me, We know the Scriptures. And what of that? If ye exemplify the Scriptures by your works, that is the gain, that the profit. The Church is a dyer's vat: if time after time perpetually ye go hence without receiving any dye, what is the use of coming here continually? Why, the mischief is all the greater. Who (of you) has added ought to the customary practices he received from his fathers? For example: such an one has a custom of observing the memorial of his mother, or his wife, or his child: this he does whether he be told or whether he be not told by us, drawn to it by force of habit and conscience. Does this displease thee, you ask? God forbid: on the contrary, I am glad of it with all my heart: only, I would wish that he had gained some fruit also from our discoursing, and that the effect which habit has, were also the effect as re-

gards us [1] (your teachers)—the superinducing of another habit. Else why do I weary myself in vain, and talk uselessly, if ye are to remain in the same state, if the Church services work no good in you? Nay, you will say, we pray. And what of that? "Not every one that saith unto Me, Lord, Lord, shall enter into the Kingdom of heaven; but he that doeth the will of My Father which is in heaven." (Matt. vii. 21.) Many a time have I determined to hold my peace, seeing no benefit accruing to you from my words; or perhaps there does accrue some, but I, through insatiableness and strong desire, am affected in the same way as those that are mad after riches. For just as they, however much they may get, think they have nothing; so I, because I ardently desire your salvation, until I see you to have made good progress, think nothing done, because of my exceeding eager desire that you should arrive at the very summit. I would that this were the case, and that my eagerness were in fault, not your sloth: but I fear I conjecture but too rightly. For ye must needs be persuaded, that if any benefit had arisen in all this length of time, we ought ere now to have done speaking. In such case, there were no need to you of words, since both in those already spoken there had been enough said for you, [2] and you would be yourselves able to correct others. But the fact, that there is still a necessity of our discoursing to you, only shows, that matters with you are not in a state of high perfection. Then what would we have to be brought about? for one must not merely find fault. I beseech and entreat you not to think it enough to have invaded [3] the Church, but that ye also withdraw hence, having taken somewhat, some medicine, for the curing of your own maladies: and, if not from us, at any rate from the Scriptures, ye have the remedies suitable for each. For instance, is any passionate? Let him attend to the Scripture-readings, and he will of a surety find such either in history or exhortation. In exhortation, when it is said, "The sway of his fury is his destruction" (Ecclus. i. 22); and, "A passionate man is not seemly" (Prov. xi. 25); and such like: and

---

[1] Τοῦτο καὶ ἐφ' ἡμῶν γενέσθαι, ἑτέραν ἐπεισαχθῆναι συνήθειαν. Morel. Ben. ἀφ' ἡμῶν. "By our means," idque unum probandum, Ed. Par. but ἐφ' ἡμῶν is not as he renders it, in nobis: the meaning is, "where habit works, this is the effect (in the case of habit): I wish it were so in the case of us (where we work)."

[2] Mod. text "Having been so sufficiently spoken, that ye are able to correct others, εἴγε ἀπόντων ὠφέλειά τις ὑμῖν προσεγίνετο, since in their absence some benefit accrued to you."

[3] ὅπως εἰς 'Εκκλησίαν ἐμβάλητε, ἀλλ' ὅπως τι καὶ λαβόντες ἀναχωρῆτε. (Above we had the phrase παραβάλλειν τῇ συνάξει.) Here the metaphor is taken from an invading army, So below, p. 188, μὴ ἐμβάλῃς εἰς ἀγοράν.

again, "A man full of words shall not prosper" (Ps. cxl. 11); and Christ again, "He that is angry with his brother without a cause (Matt. v. 22); and again the Prophet, "Be ye angry, and sin not" (Ps. iv. 4); and, "Cursed be their anger, for it was fierce." (Gen. xlix. 7.) And in histories, as when thou hearest of Pharaoh filled with much wrath, and the Assyrian. Again, is any one taken captive by love of money? let him hear, that "There is not a more wicked thing than a covetous man: for this man setteth even his own soul for sale (Ecclus. ix. 9); and how Christ saith, "Ye cannot serve God and mammon" (Matt. vi. 24); and the Apostle, that "the love of money is a root of all evils" (1 Tim. vi. 10); and the Prophet, "If riches flow in, set not your heart upon them" (Ps. lxii. 10); and many other like sayings. And from the histories thou hearest of Gehazi, Judas, the chief scribes, and that "gifts blind the eyes of the wise." (Exod. xxiii. 8 and Deut. xvi. 19.) Is another proud? Let him hear, that "God resisteth the proud" (James iv. 6); and, "Pride is the beginning of sin" (Ecclus. x. 14) and, "Every one that hath a high heart, is impure before the Lord." (Prov. xvi. 5.) And in the histories, the devil, and all the rest. In a word, since it is impossible to recount all, let each choose out from the Divine Scriptures the remedies for his own hurts. So wash out, if not the whole at once, a part at any rate, part to-day, and part to-morrow, and then the whole. And with regard to repentance too, and confession, and almsgiving, and justice also, and temperance, and all other things, thou wilt find many examples. "For all these things," says the Apostle, "were written for our admonition." (1 Cor. x. 11.) If then Scripture in all its discoursing is for our admonition, let us attend to it as we ought. Why do we deceive ourselves in vain? I fear it may be said of us also, that "our days have fallen short in vanity, and our years with haste." (Ps. lxxvii. 33.) Who from hearing us has given up the theatres? Who has given up his covetousness? Who has become more ready for almsgiving? I would wish to know this, not for the sake of vainglory, but that I may be inspirited to more zeal, seeing the fruit of my labors to be clearly evident. But as things now are, how shall I put my hand to the work, when I see that for all the rain of doctrine pouring down upon you shower after shower, still our crops remain at the same measure, and the plants have waxed none the higher? Anon the time of threshing is at hand (and)

He with the fan. I fear me, lest it be all stubble: I fear, lest we be all cast into the furnace. The summer is past, the winter is come: we sit, both young and old, taken captive by our own evil passions. Tell not me, I do not commit fornication: for what art thou the better, if though thou be no fornicator thou art covetous? It matters not to the sparrow caught in the snare that he is not held tight in every part, but only by the foot: he is a lost bird for all that; in the snare he is, and it profits him not that he has his wings free, so long as his foot is held tight. Just so, thou art caught, not by fornication, but by love of money: but caught thou art nevertheless; and the point is, not *how* thou art caught, but *that* thou art caught. Let not the young man say, I am no money-lover: well, but perchance thou art a fornicator: and then again what art thou the better? For the fact is, it is not possible for all the passions to set upon us at one and the same time of life: they are divided and marked off, and that, through the mercy of God, that they may not by assailing us all at once become insuperable, and so our wrestling with them be made more difficult. What wretched inertness it shows, not to be able to conquer our passions even when taken one by one, but to be defeated at each several period of our life, and to take credit to ourselves for those which (let us alone) not in consequence of our own hearty endeavors, but merely because, by reason of the time of life, they are dormant? Look at the chariot-drivers, do you not see how exceedingly careful and strict they are with themselves in their training-practice, their labors, their diet, and all the rest, that they may not be thrown down from their chariots, and dragged along (by the reins)?—See what a thing art is. Often even a strong man cannot master a single horse: but a mere boy who has learnt the art shall often take the pair in hand, and with ease lead them and drive them where he will. Nay, in India it is said that a huge monster of an elephant shall yield to a stripling of fifteen, who manages him with the utmost ease. To what purpose have I said all this? To show that, if by dint of study and practice we can throttle into submission (ἀγχομεν) even elephants and wild horses, much more the passions within us. Whence is it that throughout life we continually fail (in every encounter)? We have never practised this art: never in a time of leisure when there is no contest, talked over with ourselves what shall be useful for us. We are never to be seen in our place on the chariot, until the• time for the contest is actually come. Hence the ridiculous figure we make there. Have I not often said, Let us practise ourselves upon those of our own family before the time of trial? With our servants (παῖδας) at home we are often exasperated, let us there quell our anger, that in our intercourse with our friends we may come to have it easily under control. And so, in the case of all the other passions, if we practised ourselves beforehand, we should not make a ridiculous figure in the contests themselves. But now we have our implements and our exercises and our trainings for other things, for arts and feats of the palæstra, but for virtue nothing of the sort. The husbandman would not venture to meddle with a vine, unless he had first been practised in the culture of it: nor the pilot to sit by the helm, unless he had first practised himself well at it: but we, in all respects unpractised, wish for the first prizes! It were good to be silent, good to have no communication with any man in act or word, until we were able to charm (κατεπᾴδειν) the wild beast that is within us. The wild beast, I say: for indeed is it not worse than the attack of any wild beast, when wrath and lust make war upon us? Beware of invading the market-place (Μὴ ἐμβάλῃς εἰς ἀγοράν) with these beasts, until thou have got the muzzle well upon their mouths, until thou have tamed and made them tractable. Those who lead about their tame lions in the market-place, do you not see what a gain they make of it, what admiration they get, because in the irrational beast they have succeeded in producing such tameness—but, should the lion suddenly take a savage fit, how he scares all the people out of the market-place, and then both the man that leads him about is himself in danger, and if there be loss of life to others, it is his doing? Well then do thou also first tame thy lion, and so lead him about, not for the purpose of receiving money, but that thou mayest acquire a gain, to which there is none equal. For there is nothing equal to gentleness, which both to those that possess it, and to those who are its objects, is exceeding useful. This then let us follow after, that having kept in the way of virtue, and with all diligence finished our course therein, we may be enabled to attain unto the good things eternal, through the grace and mercy of our Lord Jesus Christ, with Whom to the Father and the Holy Ghost together be glory, might, honor, now and ever, world without end. Amen.

HOMILY XXX.

ACTS XIII. 42.

"And as they were going out (text rec. 'from the syn. of the Jews,') they besought (the Gentiles) that these words might be spoken unto them on the following sabbath."

Do you mark Paul's wisdom? He not only gained admiration at the time, but put into them a longing desire for a second hearing, while in what he said he dropped some seeds (εἰπών τινα σπέρματα) as it were, and forbore to solve (the questions raised), or to follow out the subject to its conclusion, his plan being to interest them and engage their good-will to himself,[1] and not make (people) listless and indifferent by casting all at once into the minds of those (who first heard him). He told them the fact, that "through this Man is remission of sins announced unto you," but the how, he did not declare. "And when the congregation was broken up, many of the Jews and worshipping proselytes followed Paul and Barnabas"—after this point he puts Paul first[2]—"who, speaking unto them, persuaded them to continue in the grace of God." (v. 43.) Do you observe the eagerness, how great it is? They "followed" them, it says. Why did they not baptize them immediately? It was not the proper time: there was need to persuade them in order to their steadfast abiding therein. "And the next sabbath day came almost the whole city together to hear the word of God." (v. 44.) "But when the Jews saw the multitudes, they were filled with envy, and contradicted the things spoken by Paul, contradicting and blaspheming." (v. 45.) See malice wounded in wounding others: this

[1] Mss. and Edd. ἀπάρτισαι καὶ οἰκειῶσαι ἑαυτῷ. The Catena has preserved the true reading ἀναρτῆσαι. in the sense, to make them hang upon (him for further communications).— Below, τῷ πάντα ἀθρόον εἰς τὰς ἐκείνων ῥῖψαι ψυχάς, the ἐκείνων distinguishes the first hearers from the people generally: if he had spoken all at once to those, the consequence would have been χαυνοτέρους ἐργάσασθαι, not that "nearly the whole city" should assemble on the following sabbath.

[2] Edd. from E. F. αὐτὸς ἑαυτοῦ instead of τοῦ Παύλου. We have restored the comments to their proper clauses in the Scripture text.

made the Apostles more conspicuous—the contradiction which those offered. In the first instance then they of their own accord besought them to speak (and now they opposed them) : " contradicting," it says, " and blaspheming." O recklessness ! " Then Paul and Barnabas waxed bold, and said, It was necessary that the word of God should first have been spoken to you : but seeing ye put it from you, and judge yourselves unworthy of everlasting life, lo, we turn to the Gentiles." (v. 46.) Do you mark how by their contentious behavior they the more extended the preaching, and (how the Apostles here) gave themselves the more to the Gentiles, having (by this very thing) pleaded their justification, and made themselves clear of all blame with their own people (at Jerusalem)? (c) See 1 how by their " envy " they bring about great things, other (than they looked for): they brought it about that the Apostles spake out boldly, and came to the Gentiles ! For this is why he says, " And speaking out boldly, Paul and Barnabas said." They were to go out to the Gentiles : but observe the boldness coming with measure : 2 for if Peter pleaded in his justification, much more these needed a plea, none having called them there. (ch. xi. 4.) But by saying " To you first," he showed that to those also it was their duty (to preach), and in saying " Necessary," he showed that it was necessary to be preached to them also. " But since ye turn away from it "—he does not say, " Woe unto you," and " Ye are punished," but " We turn unto the Gentiles." With great gentleness is the boldness fraught ! (a) Also he does not say, " Ye are unworthy," but " Have judged yourselves unworthy. Lo, we turn unto the Gentiles. For so hath the Lord commanded us, saying, I have sent thee to be a light of the Gentiles, that thou shouldest be for salvation unto the ends of the earth." (v. 47.) For that the Gentiles might not be hurt at hearing this, as 3 if the case were so that, had the Jews been in earnest, they themselves would not have obtained the blessings, therefore he brings in the prophecy, saying, " A light of the Gentiles," and, " for salvation unto the ends of the earth. And hearing " (this) " the Gentiles " (v. 48)—this, while it was more

cheering to them, seeing the case was this, that whereas those were of right to hear first, they themselves enjoy the blessing, was at the same time more stinging to those—" and the Gentiles," it says, " hearing " (this) " were glad, and glorified the word of the Lord : and believed, as many as were ordained unto eternal life " : i. e., set apart for God.* Observe how he shows the speediness of the benefit : " And the word of the Lord was borne through all the region," (v. 49) διεφέρετο, 4 instead of διεκομίζετο, " was carried or conveyed through (it)." (d) " But the Jews stirred up the devout and honorable women, and the chief men of the city, and raised persecution against Paul and Barnabas, and expelled them out of their coasts." (v. 50.) " The devout women," (b) 5 instead of the proselyte-women. They did not stop at " envy," but added deeds also. (e) Do you see what they effected by their opposing the preaching? to what dishonor they brought these (" honorable women ")? " But they shook off the dust of their feet against them, and came unto Iconium." (v. 51.) Here now they used that terrible sign, which Christ enjoined, " If any receive you not, shake off the dust from your feet " (Matt. x. 14; Mark vi. 11); but these did it upon no light ground, but because they were driven away by them. This was no hurt to the disciples ; on the contrary, they the more continued in the word : "And the disciples were filled with joy, and with the Holy Ghost " (v. 32) for the suffering of the teacher does not check his boldness, but makes the disciple more courageous.

" And it came to pass in Iconium, that they went both together into the synagogue of the Jews." (ch. xiv. 1.) Again they entered into the synagogues. See how far they were from

* The expression : " As many as were ordained to eternal life believed," has been both minimized and exaggerated. Chrys. points the way to its correct interpretation in saying : " set apart for God " and adding later : " not in regard of necessity." The writer is by no means seeking to define a doctrine of the divine plan in its bearing upon human self-determination, but pointing out a historical sequence. Those who became believers were as truly so in God's plan as they are so in fact. The passage says nothing of the relation of God's ordainment to the believer's choice. It is an example of the Pauline type of thought which grounds salvation upon the eternal purpose of God. Whoever are saved in fact, were saved in God's purpose. If as matter of fact they are saved on condition of faith and not through the enforcement of a *decretum absolutum*, then it is certain that their salvation as foreseen in God's purpose does not exclude their self-determination and personal acceptance.—G. B. S.

<hr>

1 The order of the exposition in the Mss. and Edd. marked by the letters a, b, etc. is much confused, but not irremediably. The matter falls into suitable connection, when the parts are taken in the order c, a, d, b.

2 ἀλλ' ὅρα τὴν παρρησίαν μετὰ μέτρου γινομένην. A. μετὰ τὸ μέτρον. Mod. text μέτρῳ. If this be not corrupt, it may be explained by the clause at the end of c, πολλῆς ἐπιεικείας ἡ παρρ. γέμουσα, but then the connection with the following εἰ γὰρ Πέτρος κ. τ. λ. is obscure. Perhaps from A. we may restore μετὰ τὸ Πέτρου : " the boldness coming to them after the affair of Peter."

3 ὡς ἐκ τῆς ἐκείνων σπουδῆς μὴ (om. A. B.) τυγχάνοντα τῶν ἀγαθῶν.

4 διεφέρετο, was published, E. V. διαφέρειν ἀγγελίας, " to bear tidings," and διαφέρεται ὁ λόγος, " the saying is bruited," are classical, but perhaps the expression was not familiar to Chrysostom's hearers.

5 Ἀντὶ τοῦ, οὐκ ἔστησαν μεχρὶ τοῦ ζήλου. As in the Mss. this clause follows that at the end of a, ἀντὶ τοῦ, διεκομίζετο, the ἀντὶ τοῦ may be only an accidental repetition. At the end of this clause, the Mss. have ὅρα πάλιν πῶς (om. A. C. Cat.) διωκόμενοι, and then, πῶς (C. Cat.) ἕτερα κατασκ. (beginning of c.) The former clause, as the conclusion of b, may be completed with " they extend the preaching," or the like. But probably διωκόμενοι is due to the scribes, who seem to have understood by ζήλου here the zeal of the Apostles, not the envy of the Jews. v. 45.

becoming more timid! Having said, "We turn unto the Gentiles," nevertheless [1] (by going into the synagogues) they superabundantly fortify their own justification (with their Jewish brethren). "So that," it says, "a great multitude both of Jews and Greeks believed." For it is likely they discoursed as to Greeks also. "But the unbelieving Jews stirred up the Gentiles, and made their minds evil affected against the brethren." (v. 2.) Together (with themselves) now they took to stirring up the Gentiles too, as not being themselves sufficient. Then why did the Apostles not go forth thence? Why, they were not driven away, only attacked. "Long time therefore abode they speaking boldly in the Lord, which gave testimony unto the word of His grace, and granted signs and wonders to be done by their hands." (v. 3.) This caused their boldness; or rather, of their boldness indeed their own hearty good-will was the cause—therefore it is that for a long while they work no signs—while the conversion of the hearers was (the effect) of the signs,[2] though their boldness also contributed somewhat. "But the multitude of the city was divided: and part held with the Jews, and part with the Apostles." (v. 4.) No small matter this dividing. And this was what the Lord said, "I am not come to bring peace, but a sword." (Matt. x. 34.) "And when there was an assault made both of the Gentiles, and also of the Jews with their rulers, to use them despitefully, and to stone them, they were ware of it, and fled unto Lystra and Derbe, cities of Lycaonia, and unto the region that lieth round about: and there they preached the Gospel." (v. 5-7.) Again, as if they purposely wished to extend the preaching after it was increased, they once more sent them out. See on all occasions the persecutions working great good, and defeating the persecutors, and making the persecuted illustrious. For having come to Lystra, he works a great miracle, by raising the lame man.[3] "And there sat a certain man at Lys-

tra, impotent in his feet, being a cripple from his mother's womb, who never had walked: the same heard Paul speak: who steadfastly beholding him, and perceiving that he had faith to be healed, said with a loud voice"— why with a loud voice? that the multitude should believe—"Stand upright on thy feet." (v. 8, 9.) But observe, he gave heed, it says, to the things spoken by Paul.[4] Do you mark the elevation of the man's mind (φιλοσοφίαν)? He was nothing defeated (παρεβλάβη) by his lameness for earnestness of hearing. "Who fixing his eyes upon him, and perceiving," it says, "that he had faith to be made whole." He was already predisposed in purpose of mind.[5] And yet in the case of the others, it was the reverse: for first receiving healing in their bodies, they were then taken in hand for cure of their souls, but this man not so. It seems to me, that Paul saw into his soul. "And he leaped," it says, "and walked." (v. 10.) It was a proof of his perfect cure, the leaping. "And when the people saw what Paul had done, they lifted up their voices, saying in the speech of Lycaonia, The gods are come down to us in the likeness of men. And they called Barnabas, Jupiter; and Paul, Mercurius, because he was the chief speaker. Then the priest of Jupiter, which was before their city, brought oxen and garlands unto the gates, and would have done sacrifice with the people. (v. 11-13.) But this purpose was not yet manifest, for they spake in their own tongue, saying, "The gods in the likeness of men are come down to us:" therefore the Apostle said nothing to them as yet. But when they saw the garlands, then they went out, and rent their garments, "Which when the Apostles, Barnabas and Paul, heard of, they rent their clothes, and ran in among the people, crying out, and saying, Sirs, why do ye these things? We also are men of like passions with you." (v. 14, 15.) See how on all occasions they are clean from the lust of glory, not only not coveting, but even repudiating it when offered: just as Peter also said, "Why gaze ye on us, as though by our own power or holiness we had made him to walk" (ch. iii. 12)? so these also say the same. And Joseph also said of the dreams, "Is not their interpretation of God?" (Gen. lx. 8.) And Daniel in like manner, "And to me also, not through the wisdom that is in me was it revealed." (Dan. ii. 30.) And Paul everywhere says this, as

---

[1] ἐκ πολλῆς περιουσίας ὅμως ἀναιροῦσιν αὐτῶν τὴν ἀπολογίαν. The sense is evidently as above, but ἀναιρ. will hardly bear this meaning, and perhaps was substituted for some other word by the copyist, who took it to mean, "They leave the Jews no excuse."—The connection is, It was not because they were less bold than when they said, "We turn unto the Gentiles," that they still went to the Jews first : but *ex abundanti* they enabled themselves to say to their brethren at Jerusalem, We did not seek the Gentiles, until repulsed by the Jews.

[2] τῶν σημείων ἦν. A. has σημείον ἦν. In the preceding clause, C., μεχρὶ πολλοῦ σημεῖα ποιοῦσι, the rest οὐ ποιοῦσι. The antithesis τὴν μὲν (om. A.) παρρησίαν . . . . τὸ δὲ πιστεύσαι must be rendered as above : not as Ben. *immo fiduciam addebat ipsorum alacritas. . . . Quod autem auditores crederent inter signa reputandum.*

[3] Here all the Mss. have καὶ μεγάλῃ τῇ φωνῇ (to which mod. text adds καὶ πῶς, ἄκουε.) then the text 8, 9, 10, followed by Διὰ τί, μεγ. τῇ φ. and so all the Edd. But in fact that clause is only the reporter's abbreviation of the Scripture text, καὶ [ἐν Λύστροις. . . . το] μεγάλῃ τῇ φωνῇ, followed by its comment.

[4] Mod. text adds, τοῦτο γάρ ἐστι τὸ ἤκουσεν.—Below παρεβλάβη is an expression taken from the foot-race : this was a race in which his lameness was no hindrance.

[5] Ἤδη ᾠκείωτο τὴν προαίρεσιν. Strangely rendered by Erasmus, *Jam præelectione assumptus familiariter erat*, and Ben. *Jam præelectionem in familiaritatem assumserat.*

when he says, "And for these things who is sufficient? Not that we are sufficient of ourselves to think (aught) as of ourselves, but our sufficiency is of God." (2 Cor. ii. 16; iii. 5.) But let us look over again what has been said.

(Recapitulation.) "And when they were gone out," etc. (v. 42). Not merely were the multitudes drawn to them, but how? they besought to have the same words spoken to them again, and by their actions they showed their earnestness. "Now when the congregation," etc. (v. 43.) See the Apostles on all occasions exhorting, not merely accepting men, nor courting them, but, "speaking unto them," it says, "they persuaded them to continue in the grace of God. But when the Jews," etc. (v. 45.) Why did they not contradict before this? Do you observe who on all occasions they were moved by passion? And they not only contradicted, but blasphemed also. For indeed malice stops at nothing. But see what boldness of speech! "It was necessary," he says, "that the word should have been spoken first to you, but since ye put it from you,"— (v. 46) it[1] is not put as affronting (though) it is in fact what they did in the case of the prophets: "Talk not to us," said they, "with talk"—(Is. xxx. 10): "but since ye put it from you"— it, he saith, not us: for the affront on your part is not to us. For that none may take it as an expression of their piety (that he says,) "Ye judge not yourselves worthy," therefore he first says, "Ye put it from you," and then, "We turn unto the Gentiles." The expression is full of gentleness. He does not say, We abandon you, but so that it is possible—he would say—that we may also turn hither again: and this too is not the

consequence of the affront from you, "for so hath (the Lord) commanded us."—(v. 47.) "Then why have ye not done this?"[2] It was indeed needful that the Gentiles should hear, and this not before you: it is your own doing, the "before you." "For so hath the Lord commanded us: I have set thee for a light of the Gentiles, that thou shouldest be for salvation," i. e. for knowledge which is unto salvation, and not merely of the Gentiles, but of all men, "unto the ends of the earth—As many as were ordained unto eternal life" (v. 48.): this is also a proof, that their having received these Gentiles was agreeable with the mind of God. But "ordained," not in regard of necessity: "whom He foreknew," saith the Apostle, "He did predestinate." (Rom. viii. 29.) "And the word of the Lord," etc. (v. 49.) No longer in the city (only) were (their doctrines) disseminated, but also in the (whole) region. For when they of the Gentiles had heard it, they also after a little while came over. "But the Jews stirred up the devout women, and raised persecution"—observe even of what is done by the women, they are the authors—"and cast them," it says, "out of their coasts" (v. 50), not from the city merely. Then, what is more terrible, "they shook off the dust of their feet against them, and came unto Iconium. But the disciples, it says, were filled with joy, and with the Holy Ghost." (v. 51, 52.) The teachers were suffering persecution, and the disciples rejoiced.

"And so spake, that a great multitude," etc. (ch. xiv. 1.) Do you mark the nature of the Gospel, the great virtue it has? "Made their minds evil-affected," it says, "against the brethren:" (v. 2.) i. e. slandered the Apostles, raised numberless accusations against them: (these people, being simple,[3] they "made evil-affected," disposed them to act a malignant part. And see how on all occasions he refers all to God. "Long time," he says, "abode they speaking boldly in the Lord, which gave testimony unto the word of His grace." (v. 3.) Think not this (expression, "Gave testimony,") hath aught derogatory[4] (to the Lord's Divine Majesty): "Who witnessed," it is said, "before Pontius Pilate." (1 Tim. vi. 13.) Then the boldness—"and granted signs and wonders to be done by their hands." Here he speaks

---

[1] οὐδὲν ὑβριστικόν, ὃ δὴ καὶ ἐπὶ τῶν προφ. ἐποίουν. The meaning appears from the context to be: he speaks throughout with much ἐπιεικεία. When he says ἀπωθεῖσθε, he does not upbraid them with this as ὕβρις, a personal outrage to himself and Barnabas, though in fact he might have done so, being just what their fathers did to the prophets: but he does not say, Ye repulse us, for the affront is not to us. And he says it to show that in what he is going to say, "Ye judge yourselves not worthy of eternal life," he does not mean that they do this of humility. In short, he says it not by way of complaint, but to justify what he adds, "Lo, we turn to the Gentiles."

[2] Mod. text omits this clause, which we take as an interlocution: q. d. "If the Lord ordered you to go to the Gentiles, why did ye not do this in the first instance?" In the next sentence, A. C. καὶ τοῦτο οὐ παρ᾽ ἡμῶν παρ᾽ ὑμῶν δὲ γέγονε τὸ, πρὸ ὑμῶν (B., with accidental omission, καὶ τοῦτο πρὸ ὑμῶν. Οὕτω γάρ), meaning, "And this is not our doing, but yours, the 'before you:'" i. e. the Gentiles hearing the word before you. But Cat., καὶ τοῦτο οὐ πρὸ ὑμῶν, παρ᾽ ὑμῶν δὲ κ. τ. λ. (attested by the mutilated reading in B.) which we have expressed in the translation.—The mod. text has πλὴν τοῦτο οὐ παρ᾽ ἡμῶν, παρ᾽ ὑμῶν δὲ γέγονε τὸ πρὸ ὑμῶν ὀφείλον: which Ben. takes to be corrupt, but leaves in the text, only adopting in the translation τὸ παρ᾽ ἡμῶν ὀφείλον, which interpres legisse videtur. Downe ap. Sav. proposes τὸ πρὸ τούτων ὑμῖν ὀφειλόμενον vel ὀφείλον. Sed præstare videtur lectio quam propono, quamque secutus est vetus Interpres Latinus, Ben. forgetting that the Latin version is Erasmus's (Veruntamen hoc non ex nobis facimus. A vobis autem factum est, quod a nobis oportebat, Erasm.) and was made from E. which has no such reading here. Ed. Par. Ben. 2. expresses the sense of E. thus, 'Quod nos oporteat ante vos gentes erudire,' it is your doing that it is become our duty to teach the Gentiles before you.

[3] ἀπλάστους ὄντας (i. e. the Gentiles who would otherwise have received the Apostles) κακούργως διέθηκαν, evidently the interpretation of ἐκάκωσαν: not evil-treated the Apostles, etc.

[4] Μὴ τοῦτο ἐλαττώσεως εἶναι νομίσῃς. The innovator (Edd.), mistaking the meaning, connects this and the following clauses thus: "For when they said, ὅτε γὰρ ἔλεγον, 'Which witnessed,'' saith it, ''before Pontius P., then the (His?) boldness was shown, but here he speaks concerning the people:'' what he meant is not easy to see, nor does it much matter. Below, ἐνταῦθα περὶ τοῦ λαοῦ φησιν, i. e. the παρρησία is in reference to their own nation (Israel): they spake boldly to the Gentiles, fearless of the reproaches of the Jews.

it as concerning their own nation. " And the multitude of the city," etc. (v. 4, 5.) Accordingly they did not wait for it, but saw the intention of attacking them,* and fled, on no occasion kindling their wrath,[1] " to the cities of Lycaonia, Lystra, and Derbe, and the adjacent region." (v. 6.) They went away into the country, not into the cities only.—Observe both the simplicity of the Gentiles, and the malignity of the Jews. By their actions they showed that they were worthy to hear: they so honored them from the miracles only. The one sort honored them as gods, the other persecuted them as pestilent fellows : and (those) not only did not take offence at the preaching, but what say they ? "The gods, in the likeness of men, are come down to us; but the Jews were offended. "And they called Barnabas, Jupiter; and Paul, Mercurius." (v. 11, 12.) I suppose Barnabas was a man of dignified appearance also. Here was a new sort of trial, from immoderate zeal, and no small one : but hence also is shown the virtue of the Apostles, (and) how on all occasions they ascribe all to God.

Let us imitate them : let us think nothing our own, seeing even faith itself is not our own, but more God's (than ours).[2] " For by grace are ye saved through faith; and this," saith he, " not of ourselves ; it is the gift of God." (Eph. ii. 8.) Then let us not think great things of ourselves, nor be puffed up, being as we are, men, dust and ashes, smoke and shadow. For say, Why dost thou think great things of thyself ? Hast thou given alms, and lavished thy substance? And what of that? Think, what if God had chosen not to make thee rich ? think of them that are impoverished, or rather, think how many have given (not their substance only, but) their bodies moreover, and after their numberless sacrifices, have[3] felt still that they were miserable creatures !

Thou gavest for thyself, Christ (not for Himself, but) for thee : thou didst but pay a debt, Christ owed thee not.—See the uncertainty of the future, and " be not high-minded, but fear" (Rom. xi. 20); do not lessen thy virtue by boastfulness. Wouldest thou do something truly great ? Never let a surmise of thy attainments as great enter thy mind. But thou art a virgin ? So were those in (the Gospel) virgins, but they got no benefit from their virginity, because of their cruelty and inhumanity.[4] (Matt. xxv. 12.) Nothing like humility : this is mother, and root, and nurse, and foundation, and bond of all good things : without this we are abominable, and execrable, and polluted. For say—let there be some man raising the dead, and healing the lame, and cleansing the lepers, but with[5] proud self-complacency: than this there can be nothing more execrable, nothing more impious, nothing more detestable. Account nothing to be of thyself. Hast thou utterance and grace of teaching ? Do not for this account thyself to have aught more than other men. For this cause especially thou oughtest to be humbled, because thou hast been vouchsafed more abundant gifts. For he to whom more was forgiven, will love more (Luke vii. 47) : if so,[6] then oughtest thou to be humbled also, for that God having passed by others, took notice of thee. Fear thou because of this: for often this is a cause of destruction to thee, if thou be not watchful. Why thinkest thou great things of thyself ? Because thou teachest by words ? But this is easy, to philosophize in words : teach me by thy life : that is the best teaching. Sayest thou that it is right to be moderate, and dost thou make a long speech about this thing, and play the orator, pouring forth thy eloquence without a check ? But " better than thou is he " shall one say to thee, " who teaches me this by his deeds "—for not so much are those lessons wont to be fixed in the mind which consist in words, as those which teach by things : since if thou hast not the deed, thou not only hast not profited him by thy words, but hast even hurt him the more—" better thou wert silent." Wherefore ? " Because the thing thou proposest to me is impossible : for I consider, that if thou who hast so much to say about it,

---

* It seems clear from the fact that the apostles are said to have been aware (v. 6) of what the Jews had done against them, that the word ὁρμή (v. 5) can hardly mean an "assault" (A. V.) or even "onset" (R. V.) in the sense of any open violence. There would be no propriety in Luke adding that they became aware of an attack upon them. Ὁρμή must have here the sense of *appetitus animi*—a strong movement of mind, an intention to attack them—"Trieb," "Drang." (Meyer.) The word occurs in but one other passage (Jas. iii. 4) where the ὁρμή of the pilot is spoken of as directing the ship, evidently, meaning the "purpose " or "intention." (So Trench, Gloag, Meyer, Lechler, Alford.)—G. B. S.

[1] οὐδαμοῦ τὸν θυμὸν αὐτῶν ἐκκαίοντες (restored to its fitting-place after κατέφυγον), i. e. as on all occasions we find them forbearing to kindle the wrath of their enemies, so here, seeing the intended assault, they fled. Mod. text ἔνθα οὐδαμοῦ and ἐκκαίειν ἦν, "fled to Derbe," etc. where (the enemies) had nowhere power to let their wrath blaze against them : so that they went away into the country-parts, etc.

[2] So the order must be restored instead of, καὶ τοῦτό φησι διὰ πίστεως οὐκ ἐξ ἡμῶν ἀλλὰ τὸ πλέον τοῦ Θεοῦ· Θεοῦ γὰρ φησι τὸ δῶρον. The mod. text, "And that it is not ours, but the more (part) God's : " hear Paul saying, "And this not of ourselves, it is the gift of God : " omitting διὰ πίστεως, which is essential to the sense.—Perhaps we may read, καὶ τοῦτο, φησί, τὸ "διὰ π."

[3] ἑαυτοὺς ἐταλάνισαν, " not as thou, ἑαυτοὺς ἐμακάρισαν."

[4] διὰ τὴν ὠμότητα καὶ τὴν ἀπανθρωπίαν. A strong expression, but so in the *Homily on the Parable of the Virgins*, Matt. p. 751, Am. Ed. p. 470, he interprets that the oil is charity (almsgiving), and that even virgins, lacking this, " are cast out with the harlots:" " καὶ τὸν ἀπάνθρωπον καὶ τὸν ἀνελεήμονα ἵστησι μετʼ αὐτῶν (sc. τῶν πόρνων).

[5] μετὰ ἀπονοίας, so Hom. XXXI. p. 196, οὐκ ἀπενοήθησαν, "they did not bear themselves proudly."

[6] οὐκοῦν καὶ ταπεινοῦσθαι χρή. "if he to whom most is forgiven, loveth most, so ought he to whom more is given, to humble himself more."

succeedest not in this, much more am I excusable." For this cause the Prophet says, "But unto the sinner said God. Why declarest thou My statutes?" (Ps. lx. 16.) For this is a worse mischief, when one who teaches well in words, impugns the teaching by his deeds. This has been the cause of many evils in the Churches. Wherefore pardon me, I beseech you, that my discourse dwells long on this evil affection (πάθει). Many take a deal of pains to be able to stand up in public, and make a long speech: and if they get applause from the multitude, it is to them as if they gained the very kingdom (of heaven): but if silence follows the close of their speech, it is worse than hell itself, the dejection that falls upon their spirits from the silence! This has turned the Churches upside down, because both *you* desire not to hear a discourse calculated to lead you to compunction, but one that may delight you from the sound and composition of the words, as though you were listening to singers and minstrels (κιθαρῳδῶν καὶ κιθαριστῶν, *supra* p. 68): and *we* too act a preposterous and pitiable part in being led by your lusts, when we ought to root them out. And [1] so it is just as if the father of a poor cold-blooded child (already, more delicate than it ought to be, should, although it is so feeble, give it cake and cold (drink) and whatever only pleases the child, and take no account of what might do it good; and then, being reproved by the physicians, should excuse himself by saying, "What can I do? I cannot bear to see the child crying." Thou poor, wretched creature, thou betrayer! for I cannot call such a one a father: how much better were it for thee, by paining him for a short time, to restore him to health forever, than to make this short-lived pleasure the foundation of a lasting sorrow? Just such is our case, when we idly busy ourselves about beautiful expressions, and the composition and harmony of our sentences, in order that we may please, not profit: (when) we make it our aim to be admired, not to instruct; to delight, not prick to the heart; to be applauded and depart with praise, not to correct men's manners! Believe me, I speak not other than I feel—when as I discourse I hear myself applauded, at the moment indeed I feel it as a man (for why

should I not own the truth?): I am delighted, and give way to the pleasurable feeling: but when I get home, and bethink me that those who applauded received no benefit from my discourse, but that whatever benefit they ought to have got, they lost it while applauding and praising, I am in pain, and groan, and weep, and feel as if I had spoken all in vain. I say to myself: "What profit comes to me from my labors, while the hearers do not choose to benefit by what they hear from us?" Nay, often have I thought to make a rule which should prevent all applauding, and persuade you to listen with silence and becoming orderliness. But bear with me, I beseech you, and be persuaded by me, and, if it seem good to you, let us even now establish this rule, that no hearer be permitted to applaud in the midst of any person's discourse, but if he will needs admire, let him admire in silence: there is none to prevent him: and let all his study and eager desire be set upon the receiving the things spoken.—What means that noise again?[2] I am laying down a rule against this very thing, and you have not the forbearance even to hear me!—Many will be the good effects of this regulation: it will be a discipline of philosophy. Even the heathen philosophers—we hear of their discoursing, and nowhere do we find that noisy applause accompanied their words: we hear of the Apostles, making public speeches, and yet nowhere do the accounts add, that in the midst of their speeches the hearers interrupted the speakers with loud expressions of approbation. A great gain will this be to us. But let us establish this rule: in quiet let us all hear, and speak the whole (of what we have to say). For if indeed it were the case that we departed retaining what we had heard, what I insist upon is, that even so the praise is not beneficial[3]—but not to go too much into particulars (on this point); let none tax me with rudeness—but since nothing is gained by it, nay, it is even mischievous, let us loose the hindrance, let us put a stop to the boundings, let us retrench the gambollings of the soul. Christ spoke publicly on the Mount: yet no one said aught, until He had finished His discourse. I do not rob those who wish to be applauded: on the contrary, I make them to

---

[1] καὶ ταὐτὸν γίνεται, οἷον ἄν εἰ τις πατὴρ ψυχροῦ (mod. text om.) καὶ πέρα τοῦ δέοντος μαλθακοῦ παιδίου κ. τ. λ. πλακοῦντα ἐπιδῷ καὶ ψυχρὸν καὶ ὅσα τέρπει μόνον κ. τ. λ. Erasmus translates loosely, *videns puerum, quem supra modum tenere amat, ægrotum, illi frigida et quæcumque oblectant, porrigat.* Ben., *si pater nimis molli puero, etsi infirmanti, frigidam placentam et quæ solum oblectant porrigat.* If the text be not corrupt, πέρα τοῦ δ. μαλθ. may mean, "brought up more tenderly than need be although ill," and ψυχροῦ, "silly." But the ψυχρὸν following may rather imply the physical sense as above expressed: the child is a poor creature, with no warmth or life in it, yet the father instead of warm and nourishing food, gives it cake and cold drink, etc.

[2] Διὰ τί ἐκροτήσατε; even now while he was protesting against this evil custom, derived from the theatres, some of the hearers could not refrain from expressing their approbation by applause.—Comp. *de Sacerdot.* lib. v. init. *Hom.* xv. *in Rom.* fin, *Hom.* vii. *in Laz.* § I. xvii. *in Matt.* § 7.

[3] μάλιστα μὲν οὐδὲ οὕτω χρήσιμος ὁ ἔπαινος. i. e. as appears from the context, "to the preacher:" it does him no good, it is even a harm, both by hindering him (κώλυμα) and by elating his mind (σκιρτήματα καὶ πηδήματα τῆς ψυχῆς). In the intermediate clause, ἀλλ' οὐκ ἄν ἠκριβολογησάμην, μὴ μέ τις ἀγροικίας γραφέτω, the meaning implied seems to be—"as it would be easy to show, were it not ungracious to point out to you how little your praise is worth."

be more admired. It is far better that one's hearer, having listened in silence, should by his memory throughout all time applaud, both at home and abroad, than that having lost all he should return home empty, not possessed of that which was the subject of his applauses. For how shall the hearer be otherwise than ridiculous? Nay, he will be deemed a flatterer, and his praises no better than irony, when he declares that the teacher spoke beautifully, but what he said, this he cannot tell. This has all the appearance of adulation. For when indeed one has been hearing minstrels and players, it is no wonder if such be the case with him, seeing he knows not how to utter the strain in the same manner: but where the matter is not an exhibition of song or of voice, but the drift and purport of thoughts and wise reflection (φιλοσοφίας), and it is easy for every one to tell and report what was said, how can he but deserve the accusation, who cannot tell what the matter was for which he praised the speaker? Nothing so becomes a Church as silence and good order. Noise belongs to theatres, and baths, and public processions, and market-places: but where doctrines, and such doctrines, are the subject of teaching, there should be stillness, and quiet, and calm reflection, and a haven of much repose (φιλοσοφία καὶ πολὺς ὁ λιμήν). These things I beseech and entreat: for I go about in quest of ways [1] by which I shall be enabled to profit your souls. And no small way I take this to be: it will profit not you only, but us also. So shall we not be carried away with pride (ἐκτραχηλίζεσθαι), not be tempted to love praises and honor, not be led to speak those things which delight, but those which profit: so shall we lay the whole stress of our time and diligence not upon arts of composition and beauties of expression, but upon the matter and meaning of the thoughts. Go into a painter's study, and you will observe how silent all is there. Then so ought it to be here: for here too we are employed in painting portraits, royal portraits (every one of them), none of any private man, by means [2] of the colors of virtue—How now? Applauding again? This is a reform not easy, but (only) by reason of long habit, to be effected —The pencil moreover is the tongue, and the Artist the Holy Spirit. Say, during the celebration of the Mysteries, is there any noise? any disturbance? when we are baptizing (βαπτιζώμεθα), when we are doing all the other acts? Is not all Nature decked (as it were) with stillness and silence? [3] Over all the face of heaven is scattered this charm (of repose). —On this account are we evil spoken of even among the Gentiles, as though we did all for display and ostentation. But if this be prevented, the love of the chief seats also will be extinguished. It is sufficient, if any one be enamoured of praise, that he should obtain it after having been heard, when all is gathered in. [4] Yea, I beseech you, let us establish this rule, that doing all things according to God's will, we may be found worthy of the mercy which is from Him, through the grace and compassion of His only begotten Son our Lord Jesus Christ, with Whom to the Father together with the Holy Spirit be glory, dominion, honor, now and ever, world without end. Amen.

---

[1] Περίειμι γὰρ τούτους ζητῶν. Read τρόπους. Mod. text adds πάντας εἰδέναι to the former sentence, and here II. γὰρ καὶ αὐτὸς τρόπους παντοίους ἐπιζητῶν.

[2] διὰ τῶν χρωμάτων τῆς ἀρετῆς. Erasm. and Ben. ungrammatically, *propter* (*ob*) *coloris virtutem;* as meaning that such is the virtue or value of the colors, that they are fit to be employed only on imperial portraits. But the connection is plainly this: "the colors are the hues of virtue, the pencil is the tongue, the Artist the Holy Spirit." In the next sentence the old text has: οὐκ εὔκολον τοῦτο ἀλλὰ τὸ μὴ πολλῇ συνηθείᾳ κατορθωθῆναι, which is corrupt, unless indeed it may be construed, "but (it is) the not being, by reason of long habit, successfully achieved: i. e. it only shows that I have not, such is the force of long habit, succeeded in carrying my point." The mod. text Οὐκ εὐκ. τὸ πρᾶγμα δοκεῖ, καὶ τοῦτο οὐ φύσει ἀλλὰ τῷ συνηθείᾳ πολλῇ μήπω κατορθοῦν αὐτὸ μεμαθηκέναι. "It seems to be no easy matter, this: and this, not naturally, but by reason that from long habit you have not yet learnt to effect this reformation."

[3] οὐκ ἡσυχία καὶ σιγῇ (Mss. ἡσυχία καὶ σιγῇ) τὰ πάντα κεκόσμηται (mod. text κατέχει). We alter the punctuation, and understand by τὰ πάντα not "all the proceedings in Church," but "all nature."

[4] ὅταν πάντα συλλέγῃ, when all (that he has spoken) is gathered in by diligent attention of the hearers. Mod. text ὅταν τοὺς καρποὺς συλλέγῃ, "when he collects the fruits."

HOMILY XXXI.

ACTS XIV. 14, 15.

" Which when the Apostles, Barnabas and Paul, heard of, they rent their clothes, and ran in among the people, crying out, and saying, Sirs, why do ye these things? We also are men of like passions with you, and preach unto you that ye should turn from these vanities unto the living God, which made heaven, and earth, and the sea, and all things that are therein."

MARK the vehemence with which all this is done by the Apostles: " rent their clothes, ran in, cried out," all from strong affection of the soul, revolted[1] by the things that were done. For it was a grief, indeed a grief inconsolable, that they should needs be thought gods, and introduce idolatry, the very thing which they came to destroy! This also was a contrivance of the devil—but he did not prevail.[2] But what say they? " We also are men of like passions with you." At the very outset they overthrew the evil. They said not simply, " Men," but " As ye." Then, that they may not seem to honor the gods, hear what they add : " Preaching unto you, that ye should turn from these vanities unto the living God, Who made heaven, the sea, and all things that are therein." Observe how they nowhere mention things invisible.[3] (b) For[4] they had

learnt that one should study not so much to say somewhat worthy of God, as to say what is profitable for the hearers. (a) What then? if He be Maker of all things, why does He not also attend to these things by His Providence ?—" Who in times past suffered all nations to walk in their own ways " (v. 16)— but wherefore He suffered them, this he does not say, for at present he keeps to the matter of immediate importance, nowhere bringing in the name of Christ. Observe, he does not wish to swell the accusation against them, but [5] rather that they themselves should refer all to God. " Nevertheless, He left not Himself without witness, in that He did good, giving you rain from heaven, and fruitful seasons, filling your hearts with food and gladness." (v. 17.) (c) See how covertly he puts the accusation "in that He did good," etc. And yet if God did this, He could not have " let them alone ; " on the contrary, they ought to be punished, for that, enjoying so great benefits, they had not acknowledged Him, not even as their feeder.* " From heaven," he says, " giving you rain." Thus also David said, " From the fruit of their corn and wine and oil were they made to abound " (Ps. iv. 7), and in many places speaking of

---

[1] A. B. C. Cat. ἀποστρεφομένης Mod. text ἀποστρεφόμενοι, and adds καὶ πένθους σημεῖα ποιοῦντες, and so Œcumen.

[2] A. B. C. ἀλλ' οὐχ ἡσύχασαν. The true reading is preserved by Cat. ἀλλ' οὐκ ἴσχυσεν. Mod. text ἀλλ' οὐχ ἡσυχάζουσιν.

[3] All our Mss. τῶν προφητῶν. From the recapitulation we restore τῶν ἀοράτων. The meaning may be, He abstains from the mention of things invisible, because he would recall them from their polythesim, therefore avoids whatever would seem to favor the notion of inferior gods. With the restoration ἀοράτων we obtain a suitable connection for the part b, both grammatically (in respect of the plur. ἔμαθον), and in respect of the sense : they spoke only of things visible, for they had learned not always to speak according to the dignity of the subject, but according to the needs of the hearers. In the next sentence (a) in A. B. C. τί οὖν ; εἰ πάντων ἐστὶ δημιουργός, διὰ τί μὴ καὶ εἰς ταῦτα προνοεῖ; we may understand by εἰς ταῦτα "the nations of the world, or their doings : " but the sense perhaps might be improved by supplying εἰς after εἰ, and restoring εἰς for εἰς. Perhaps also ταῦτα is a corruption of πάντα. " If One be the Maker of all, why not One also direct all by His Providence : " i. e. if One Creator, why not One Providence? Why imagine a number of inferior Providences ?—Mod. text " nowhere mentioning the Prophets, nor, saying for what reason, being Maker of all, He left the Gentiles independent, τὰ ἔθνη ἀφῆκεν αὐτόνομα."

[4] From this point to the end of the recapitulation the matter required to be rearranged. The letters show the sequence of the parts in the old text : in the mod. text a partial restoration of the order has been attempted. The " method " of the derangement explains itself thus—the true order being denoted by the figures 1, 2, 3, etc. we have two portions transposed into the order, 2, 1 ; (a, b) : then four portions taken alternately in the order 1, 3, 2, 4. (c to f) : then again two portions in the order 2, 1, (g, h) : then again four portions in the alternate order 1. 3, 2, 4, (i to m) : and lastly, two in the order 2, 1.

[5] ἀλλὰ μᾶλλον ἐπὶ τὸν Θεὸν τὸ πᾶν ἄγειν αὐτοὺς ἐκείνους, A. B. C. As v. 17, " Nevertheless," etc. is placed in the Mss. before " Observe, he does not wish," etc. the intention is that τὸ πᾶν should refer to the contents of that verse : " he does not say this to increase their culpability, but he wishes them to refer all to God." But then ἐκείνους is idle, accordingly mod. text substitutes παιδεύει. We have removed the text v. 17. to the end of this sentence, so that its comment is (c) ὅρα πῶς λανθανόντως κ. τ. λ., and ὅρα οὐ βούλεται κ. τ. λ. will belong to v. 16, and τὸ πᾶν will refer to their ignorance and walking in their own ways.—So Cat. seems to take it, reading ἄγειν ἢ αὐτοὺς ἐκείνους, viz. he rather refers the whole to God, than to those (the heathen) themselves.

* There was doubtless something polemic in the words of vv. 16, 17 inasmuch as the apostle ascribes to the " living God " alone the blessings which the heathen were wont to attribute to their divinities. The language has also a conciliatory element. Their guilt is mitigated, no doubt, by their limited light, but by no means removed, because God had given them evidences of his goodness and power in the return of seasons and harvests. The thought is closely akin to that in the address at Athens (xvii. 23-31) where God is said to have overlooked the times of the ignorance of the heathen, and to that of Rom. i. 18-32 ; ii. 14, 15, where emphasis is laid upon the revelation of God to the heathen world which renders their sinful lives without excuse. The three passages combined yield the following ideas : (1) God has revealed Himself to the heathen in nature and conscience. (2) This revelation is sufficient to found responsibility. (3) As obedience to this inner law would merit God's approval (Rom. ii. 14), so disobedience to it would merit his displeasure. (4) As matter of fact the Gentiles have not followed the light which they had and thus they have wickedly brought upon themselves the wrath of God and the penalties of his moral law.—G. B. S.

Creation, he brings forward these benefits: and Jeremiah mentions first Creation, then Providence (shown) by the rains, so that the Apostle here discourses as taught from those Scriptures. "Filling," he says, "with food and gladness." (Jer. v. 24.) With large liberality (φιλοτιμίας) the food is given, not merely for a frugal sufficiency, nor stinted by the need. "And saying these things, they scarcely stopped the multitudes" (v. 18)—indeed by this very thing they gained most admiration—"from sacrificing to them." Do you observe that this was the point with them to put an end to that madness? "But there came," it says, "certain Jews from Antioch and Iconium" (v. 19).—Indeed children of the devil, that not in their own cities only, but also beyond them, they did these things, and as much made it their study to make an end of the preaching, as the Apostles were in earnest to establish it!—"and having persuaded the multitude and stoned Paul, they dragged him out of the city." (e) So then, the Gentiles regarded them as gods, but these "dragged" him, "out of the city, supposing he had been dead. Having persuaded the multitude"—for it is not likely that all thus reverenced them. In the very city in which they received this reverence, in the same were they thus terribly ill treated. And this also profited the beholders. "Lest any man," he says, "should think of me above that which he seeth me to be, or that he heareth aught from me." (v. 20.)—"Howbeit as the disciples stood round about him, he rose up and came into the city." (d) Here is fulfilled that saying, "My grace is sufficient for thee, for My strength is made perfect in weakness." (2 Cor. xii. 9.) Greater this than the raising of the lame man! (f) "Came into the city." Do you mark the zeal, do you mark how fervent he [1] is, how set on fire! He came into the city itself again: for proof that if on any occasion he did retire, it was because he had sown the word, and because it was not right to inflame their wrath. (h) Then they went over all the cities in which they had been in danger. "And on the morrow," it says, "he went forth with Barnabas to Derbe. And when they had preached the Gospel to that city, and had taught many, they returned again to Lystra, and to Iconium, and Antioch, confirming the souls of the disciples, and exhorting them to continue in the faith, and that we must through much tribulation enter into the kingdom of God." (v. 21, 22.) This

they said, this they showed. But it is purposely so done, not only by [2] the Apostles, but by the disciples also, that they may learn from the very outset both the might of the preaching, and that they must themselves also suffer such things, that they may stand nobly, not idly gaping for the miracles, but much more (ready) for the trials. Therefore also the Apostle himself said, "Having the same conflict which ye saw in me and heard." (Phil. i. 30.) Persecutions succeeded to persecutions: wars, fightings, stonings. (g) These things, not less than the miracles, both made them more illustrious, and prepared for them a greater rejoicing. The Scripture nowhere says that they returned rejoicing because they had done miracles, but (it does say that they rejoiced), that "they were counted worthy for that Name to suffer shame." (ch. v. 41.) And this they were taught of Christ, saying, "Rejoice not that the devils obey you." (Luke x. 20.) For the joy indeed and without alloy is this, to suffer aught for Christ's sake. (i) "And that through much tribulation:" what sort of cheering (προτροπή) is this? how did they persuade them, by telling them at the outset of tribulations? Then also another consolation.[3] "And when they had appointed for them elders in every Church,* and had prayed with fasting, they commended them to the Lord, on whom they believed. (v. 23.) Do you mark Paul's ardor?—Then other consolation: "Commended them," it says, "to the Lord. And after they had passed throughout Pisidia, they came to Pamphylia. And when they had preached the word in Perga, they went down into Attalia (v. 24, 25): (l) and thence sailed to Antioch, from whence they

---

[2] οὐ διὰ τῶν ἀποστόλων κ. τ. λ. so all our Mss. The sense rather requires διὰ τοὺς ἀπ. or ἕνεκα τῶν ἀπ. " for the sake of the Apostles," etc.

[3] παραμυθία. i, e. by the ordination of elders, as explained below in the recap. "but there they needed πολλῆς παραμυθίας, and especially they of the Gentiles, who behooved to be taught much."— The θερμότης of Paul, shown in his zeal for the establishment of the Gospel among the Gentiles : see below at the end of the recap. Then, εἶτα ἄλλη παραμυθία, if it be not an accidental repetition of the clause before v. 23. must be referred to the clause. "They commended them to the Lord," which it follows in the Mss.

* The appointment of elders in every church (which the apostles visited on this journey) is made by Paul and Barnabas. Meyer supposes that the apostles only superintended the popular choice by the church itself. The word employed (χειροτονέω), meaning to stretch forth the hand, as in voting would seem especially appropriate to the idea of a popular election, but the participle here employed (χειροτονήσαντες) has not the church but Paul and Barnabas for its subject. It seems necessary, therefore, to take it in the general and derived sense—to elect—to choose. There were several elders for each church as there had been several for each synagogue, the model for the constitution of the early churches. They were also called bishops (ἐπίσκοποι). These with the deacons were the only church officers. (Phil. i. 1.) Their duty was to be leaders, teachers, and rulers in the churches. They were at once pastors, teachers and rulers. Their functions were coördinate. No one of them was above the others in any particular church. Each church had several co-pastors, teachers or bishops.—G. B. S.

---

[1] B. and mod. text have πόθον " his affection," C. and Cat. om, A. " his zeal, fervent and set on fire." Below, for κατεσπαρκέναι, mod. text βούλεσθαι σπείραι, " because he wished to sow the word (elsewhere)."

had been recommended to the grace of God for the work which they fulfilled." (v. 26.) Why do they come back to Antioch? To report what had taken place yonder. And besides, there is a great purpose of Providence concerned: for it was needful that they should thenceforth preach with boldness to the Gentiles. They come therefore, reporting these things, that they may be able to know them: and it is providentially ordered, that just then came those who forbade to keep company with the Gentiles in order that from Jerusalem they might obtain great encouragement, and so go their ways with boldness. And besides, it shows that in their temper there was nothing of self-will: for they come, at the same time showing their boldness, in that without the authority of those (at Jerusalem) they had preached to the Gentiles, and their obedience, in that they refer the matter to them: for they were not made arrogant, as (ἀπενοήθησαν) having achieved so great successes. "Whence," it says, "they had been recommended to the grace of God for the work which they had fulfilled." And yet moreover the Spirit had said, "Separate Me Barnabas and Saul for the work whereunto I have called them." (ch. xiii. 2.) "And when they were come, and had gathered the Church together, they rehearsed all that God had done with them, and how He had opened the door of faith unto the Gentiles. And there they abode long time with the disciples." (v. 27, 28.) For the city being great had need of teachers.—But let us look over again what has been said.

(Recapitulation.) "Which when the Apostles," etc. (v. 14). First by the sight they checked them, by rending their garments. This did Joshua the son of Nun upon the occasion of the defeat of the people. Then think not that this action was unworthy of them: for such was the eagerness, they would not otherwise have restrained it, would not otherwise have quenched the conflagration (πύραν). Therefore when need is to do something that is fit to be done, let us not decline it. For if even after all this they hardly persuaded them, if they had not acted thus, what might have been the consequence? For if they had not done thus, they would have been thought to make a show of humility (ταπεινοφρονεῖν), and to be all the more desirous of the honor. And observe their language, how in rebuking it is moderated, alike full of wonder and of rebuke. This above all it was that hindered them, the saying, "Preaching unto you to turn from these vanities unto God." (v. 15.) We are men indeed, they say, but greater

than these: for these are dead things. Mark how they not only subvert (the false), but teach (the true), saying nothing about things invisible—"Who made," say they, "heaven and earth, and the sea, and all things that are therein. Who in times past," etc. (v. 16, 17.) He names as witnesses even the years (in their courses).[1] "And there came thither certain Jews," etc. (v. 19.) O that Jewish madness! Among a people that had so honored the Apostles, they had the hardihood to come, and to stone Paul. "And they dragged him out of the city," being afraid of those (others),—"Supposing he had been dead." (k) "Howbeit," etc. "and came into the city." (v. 20.) For that the spirits of the disciples might not be downcast because they who were accounted gods suffered such treatment, they came in unto them and discoursed. "Then on the morrow," etc. And observe, first he goes forth to Derbe, and then comes back to Lystra and Iconium and Antioch, (v. 21) giving way to them while their passions are roused, but when they have ceased, then attacking them again. Do you mark, that it was not by (supernatural) grace that they managed all that they did, but by their own diligence? "Confirming," it says "the souls of the disciples:" ἐπιστηρίζοντες, "further establishing;" so that they were established, but they added more thereto. "And that we must," etc. (v. 22): they foretold (this), that they might not be offended. "And when they had appointed for them," etc. Again the ordinations accompanied with fastings: and again fasting, that purifying of our souls. (m) "And having prayed," it says, "with fastings, they commended them unto the Lord" (v. 23): they taught them to fast also in their trials. (o) Why did they not make elders in Cyprus nor in Samaria? Because the latter was near to Jerusalem, the former to Antioch, and the word was strong there; whereas in those parts they needed much consolation, especially they of the Gentiles, who behooved to have much instruction. "And when they were come," etc. (v. 27.) They came, teaching them that with good reason had they been ordained by the Spirit. (n) They said not what they themselves, but "what God had done with them." It seems to me, that they mean their trials. It was not for nothing that they come here, nor

---

[1] τοὺς ἐνιαυτούς. Cat. τοὺς ἐνιαυσιαίους ὑετούς, "the yearly rains."—Below, our Mss. have, "And out of the city," being afraid of those, O the madness! "they dragged him," etc. (ὦ τῆς μανίας! repeated from above).—Mod. text But "out of the city they dragged" (him). perhaps being afraid of him, ἐκεῖνον.

to rest, but providentially guided by the Spirit, to the end that the preaching to the Gentiles might be firmly established. (p) And mark Paul's ardor. He does not ask whether it be right to speak to Gentiles, but he straightway speaks: therefore it is that he says, "I did not refer myself to flesh and blood." (Gal. i. 16.)

For it is indeed[1] a great thing, a great, a generous soul (like this)! How many have since believed, and none of them all has shone like him! What we want is earnestness, exceeding ardor, a soul ready to encounter death. Else is it not possible to attain unto the Kingdom, not being crucified. Let us not deceive ourselves. For if in war it is impossible to come off safe while living daintily, and trafficking, and huckstering and idling, much more in this war. Or think ye not that it is a war worse than all others? (Infra, p. 204, note [1].) "For we wrestle not," he says, "against flesh and blood." (Eph. vi. 12.) Since even while taking our meals and walking, and bathing, the enemy is present with us, and knows no time of truce, except that of sleep only: nay, often even then he carries on the war, injecting into us unclean thoughts, and making us lewd by means of dreams. We watch not, we do not rouse ourselves up, do not look to the multitude of the forces opposed to us, do not reflect, that this very thing constitutes the greatest misfortune—that though surrounded by so great wars, we live daintily as in time of peace. Believe me, worse than Paul suffered may have to be suffered now. Those enemies wounded him with stones: there is a wounding with words, even worse than stones. What then must we do? The same that he did: he did not hate those who cast stones at him, but after they had dragged him out, he entered again into their city, to be a benefactor to those who had done him such wrongs. If thou also endurest him who harshly insults thee, and has done thee wrongs, then hast thou too been stoned. Say not, "I have done him no injury." For what injury had Paul done, that he should be stoned? He was announcing a Kingdom, he was bringing men away from error, and bringing them to God: benefits these, worthy of crowns, worthy of proclamation by voice of herald, worthy of a thousand good things—not of stones. And yet (far from resenting)

he did[2] just the contrary. For this is the splendid victory. "And they dragged him," (v. 19) it says, These too they often drag: but be not thou angry; on the contrary, preach thou the word with gentleness. Hath one insulted thee? Hold thy peace, and bless if thou canst, and thou also hast preached the word, hast given a lesson of gentleness, a lesson of meekness. I know that many do not so smart under wounds, as they do under the blow which is inflicted by words: as indeed the one wound the body receives the other the soul. But let us not smart, or rather feeling the smart let us endure. Do you not see the pugilists, how, with their heads sorely battered, they bite their teeth into their lips, and so bear their smarts kindly? No need to grind the teeth, no need to bite (the lips). Remember thy Master, and by the remembrance thou hast at once applied the remedy. Remember Paul: reflect that thou, the beaten hast conquered, and he the beater, is defeated; and by this hast thou cured the whole. It[3] is the turning of the scale a moment and thou hast achieved the whole: be not hurried away, do not even move, thou hast extinguished the whole (fire). Great[4] eloquence of persuasion there is in suffering aught for Christ: thou preachest not the word of faith, but thou preachest the word of patience (φιλοσοφίας). But, you will say, the more he sees my gentleness, the more he sets upon me. Is it for this then that thou art pained, that he increases thy rewards the more? "But[5] this is the way," you say, "to make him unbearable." This is mere pretext of thine own littleness of mind: on the contrary, the other is the way to make him unbearable, namely, that thou avenge thyself. If God had known, that through forbearance of revenge, the unjust became unbearable, He would not have done[6] this Himself: on the contrary, He would have said, Avenge thyself: but He knew, that other than this is the more likely way to do good. Make not thou a law contary to God: do as He bids thee. Thou art not kinder than He that made us. He hath said, "Bear to be

<hr>

[1] Μέγα γὰρ ὄντως μεγάλη ψυχὴ γενναία: for this, which is evidently meant as eulogy of St Paul. the mod. text substitutes Μέγα ὄντως ἀγαθὸν ἡ θλίψις: καὶ μεγάλης ψυχῆς καὶ γενναίας κατόρθωμα. "A great benefit indeed is affliction, and an achievement of a great and generous soul."

[2] ἀλλ' ὅμως τἀναντία ἐποίει. But A. ἔπαθεν, mod. text ἔπασχεν, "the treatment he received was just the opposite to these (honors)."

[3] τοὺς ὀδόντας ἐνδάκνουσιν. Erasm. dentibus studentes, ἐνδακόντες mod. text for which, as "gnashing the teeth" does not suit the context, Ben. gives dentes excussi.

[4] ῥοπή ἐστι, καὶ τὸ πᾶν κατώρθωσας εὐθέως, μὴ συναρπαγῇς μηδὲ κινηθῇς. Mod. text ῥοπή ἐστι, "be not hurried, and thou," etc; μὴ κιν., "do not move, and," etc.—Below μεγάλη παραμυθία. meaning either consolation to the beholders, or rather as below, a soothing of the excited passions of the opponent.

[5] 'Αλλ' ἄχρηστος γίνεται: i. e. "It is bad for himself that he should go unpunished: so he becomes good for nothing."

[6] ἐποίησεν: i. e. "He would not Himself have exercised this forbearance. Mod. text ἐπέταξεν, "He would not have enjoined this."

wronged:" thou sayest, "I requite wrong for wrong, that he may not become unbearable." Hast thou then more care for him than God has? Such talk is mere passion and ill temper, arrogance and setting up laws against God's laws. For even if the man were hurt (by our forbearance), would it not be our duty to obey? When God orders anything, let us not make a contrary law. "A submissive answer," we read, turneth away wrath" (Prov. xvi. 1): not an answer of opposition. If it profits thee, it profits him also: but if it hurts thee who art to set him right, how much more will it hurt him? "Physician, heal thyself." Hath one spoken ill of thee? Commend him thou. Hath he reviled thee? Praise him thou. Hath he plotted against thee? Do him a kindness. Requite him with the contrary things, if at least thou at all carest for his salvation, and wish not thou to revenge thine own suffering. And yet, you will say, though he has often met with long-suffering from me, he has become worse. This is not thine affair, but his. Wilt thou learn what wrongs God suffered? They threw down His altars, and slew His prophets (1 Kings xix. 10), yet He endured it all. Could He not have launched a thunderbolt from above? Nay, when He had sent His prophets, and they killed them, then He sent His Son (Matt. xxi. 37), when they wrought greater impieties, then He sent them greater benefits. And thou too, if thou seest one exasperated, then yield the more: since this madness has greater need of soothing (παραμθίας). The more grievous his abuse of thee, the more meekness does he need from thee: and even as a gale [1] when it blows strong, then it requires yielding to, so also he who is in a passion. When the wild beast is most savage, then we all flee: so also should we flee from him that is angry. Think not that this is an honor to him: for is it an honor we show to the wild beast, and to madmen, when we turn aside out of their way? By no means: it is a dishonor and a scorn: or rather not dishonor and scorn, but compassion and humanity. Seest thou not how the sailors, when the wind blows violently, take down their sails, that the vessel may not sink? how, when the horses have run away with the driver, he only leads them into the (open) plain, and does not pull against them that he may not voluntarily exhaust his strength? This do thou also. Wrath is a

fire, it is a quick flame needing fuel: do not supply food to the fire, and thou hast soon extinguished the evil. Anger has no power of itself; there must be another to feed it. For thee there is no excuse. He is possessed with madness, and knows not what he does; but when thou, seeing what he is, fallest into the same evils, and art not brought to thy right senses by the sight, what excuse can there be for thee? If coming to a feast thou see at the very outset of the feast some one drunken and acting unseemly, would not he, who after seeing him makes himself drunk, be much more inexcusable? Just so it is here. Do we think it any excuse to say, I was not the first to begin? This is against us, that even the sight of the other in that condition did not bring us to our right senses. It is just as if one should say, "I did not murder him first." For this very thing makes thee deserving of punishment, that even upon the warning of such a spectacle thou didst not restrain thyself. If thou shouldest see the drunken man in the act of vomiting, retching, bursting, his eyes strained, filling the table with his filthiness, everybody hurrying out of his way, and then shouldest fall into the same state thyself, wouldest thou not be more hateful? Like him is he that is in a passion: more than he who vomits, he has his veins distended, his eyes inflamed, his bowels racked; he vomits forth words far more filthy than that food; all crude what he utters, nothing duly digested, for his passion will not let it be. But as in that case excess of fumes (χυμων), making an uproar in the stomach, often rejects all its contents; so here, excess of heat, making a tumult in the soul suffers him not to conceal what it were right to leave unsaid, but things fit and unfit to be spoken, he says all alike, not putting the hearers but himself to shame. As then we get out of the way of those that vomit, so let us from those who are angry. Let us cast dust upon their vomit: By doing what? [2] By holding our peace: let us call the dogs to eat up the vomit. I know that ye are disgusted at hearing this: but I wish you to feel this same disgust when ye see these things take place, and not to be pleased at the thing. The abusive man is filthier than the dog that returneth to its own vomit. For if indeed having vomited once he were done with it, he would not be like that dog: but if he vomits the same things again, it is plain that he does so from having eaten

---

[1] All our Mss. καὶ καθάπερ πυρετὸς ὅταν σφοδρὸν πνεύσῃ, and this the Edd. retain without remark. We restore πνεῦμα, or ἄνεμος . . . σφόδρα. Between πνεῦμα and ἄνεμος as an interlinear correction arose the absurd reading πυρετός.

[2] In the mod. text τί ποιοῦντες; is placed before Κόνιν επιβ, and σιγῶντες is connected with τοὺς κυνας καλῶμεν: " by holding our peace let us call the dogs," etc.

the same again. What then is more abominable than such an one? What filthier than that mouth which chews such food? And yet this is a work of nature, but the other not; or rather both the one and the other are contrary to nature. How? Since it is not according to nature to be causelessly abusive, but against nature: he speaks nothing then like a man, but part as beast, part as madman. As then the disease of the body is contrary to nature, so also is this. And to show that it is contrary to nature, if he shall continue in it, he will perish by little and little: but if he continue in that which is natural, he will not perish. I had rather sit at table with a man who eats dirt, than with one who speaks such words. See ye not the swine devouring dung? So also do these. For what is more stinking than the words which abusive men utter? It is their study to speak nothing wholesome, nothing pure, but whatever is base, whatever is unseemly, that they study both to do and say: and what is worse, they think to disgrace others, while they in fact are disgracing themselves. For that it is themselves they disgrace is plain. For, leaving out of the question those who speak lies (in their railings), say it be some notorious harlot, or even from the stage some other (abandoned creature), and let that person be having a fight with some other person: then let the latter cast this up to the former (what she or he is), and the former retort upon the latter the same reproach: which of them is most damaged by the words? For[1] the former is but called what in fact he or she is, which is not the case with the other: so that the first gets nothing more in the way of shame (than there was before), while to the other there accrues a great accession of disgrace. But again, let there be some hidden actions (mod. text εἰργασμένα " which have been done"), and let only the person abusing know of them: then, holding his peace until now, let him openly parade (ἐκπομπευέτω) the reproach: even so, he himself is more disgraced than the other. How? by making himself the herald of the wickedness, so[2] getting for himself either the

imputation of not being privy to any such thing, or the character of one not fit to be trusted. And you shall see all men forthwith accuse him: "If indeed he had been privy to a murder being done, he ought to have revealed it all:" and so they regard him with aversion as not human even, they hate him, they say he is a wild beast, fierce and cruel: while the other they pardon much rather than him. For we do not so much hate those that have wounds, as those that compel one to uncover and show them. Thus that man has not only disgraced the other, but himself as well and his hearers, and the common nature of men: he has wounded the hearer, done no good. For this reason Paul says: "If there be any word that is good for edifying, that it may minister grace unto the hearers." (Eph. iv. 29.) Let us get a tongue speaking only good things, that we may be lovely and amiable. But indeed, everything is come to that pitch of wickedness, that many boast of the very things, for which they should hide their faces. For the threats of the many are of this kind: "thou canst not bear my tongue," say they. Words, these, worthy only of a woman, of an abandoned drunken old hag, one of those that are dragged (to punishment)[3] in the forum, a procuress. Nothing more shameful than these words, nothing more unmanly, more womanlike, than to have your strength in the tongue, and to think great things of yourself because you can rail, just like the fellows in processions, like the buffoons, parasites, and flatterers. Swine they are rather than men, who pride themselves upon this. Whereas you should (sooner) have buried yourself, and if another gave you this character, should recoil from the charge as odious and unmanly, instead of that you have made yourself the herald of (your own) disgrace (ὕβρεων). But you will not be able to hurt him you speak ill of. Wherefore I beseech you, considering how the wickedness is come to such a height, that many boast of it, let us return to our senses, let us recover those who are thus mad, let us take away these councils[4] out of the city, let us make

[1] In the original the sense is perplexed by the negligent use of the demonstr. οὗτος and ἐκεῖνος, supra p. 42. The meaning is: "B. (the second person mentioned) says to A. (suppose a πόρνη περιφανής), "You are so and so," such being the fact: she retorts with a like reproach, which is not true: whether is most damaged (ὕβρισται)? Not she, for being what the other calls her she is just where she was before. The disgrace is to him; and that, not from her words, for they do not fit: but from his own indecent railing: so that he thinking to disgrace her has more disgraced himself. He is more disgraced by calling the other the thing that she is, than ...; being called by her the thing that he is not."

[2] ἀσυνειδησίας ἄπιστον δόξαν λαβών: which being unintelligi-

ble, must be restored by replacing ἡ before ασυν. and before ἀπίστου (so mod. text rightly for ἄπιστον). "He gets the δόξα either of ἀσυνειδ. in which case he is a foul calumniator, or of an ἄπιστος:" which latter in the way in which it is put supra Hom. xiv. p. 193: "as regards himself, he has shown all men that he is not to be trusted, as not knowing how to screen his neighbor's faults."

[3] τῶν ἐπ' ἀγορᾶς συρομένων, not as Ben. eorum qui forum frequentant: but, "one of those old hags, bawds, and the like, whom for their crimes you may see dragged by the officers to punishment, and screaming out their foul-mouthed railings."

[4] ταῦτα ἐκ τῆς πόλεως τὰ συνέδρια. So all our Mss.: perhaps ταύτας——τὰς συνηθείας.

our tongue gracious, let us rid it of all evil speaking, that being clean from sins, we may be able to draw down upon us the good-will from above, and to have mercy vouchsafed unto us from God, through the grace and compassion of His only-begotten Son, with Whom to the Father, together with the Holy Spirit, be glory, might, honor, now and ever, world without end.   Amen.

HOMILY XXXII.

ACTS XV. 1.

"And certain men which came down from Judea taught the brethren, and said, Except ye be circumcised after the manner of Moses, ye cannot be saved."

MARK [1] how at every step of the right progress in respect of the Gentiles, the beginning is brought in as matter of necessity. Before this (Peter) being found fault with, justified himself, and said all that he said in the tone of apology, which was what made his words acceptable : then, the Jews having turned away, upon this (Paul) came to the Gentiles. Here again, seeing another extravagance coming in, upon this (the apostle) enacts the law. For as it is likely that they, as being taught of God, discoursed to all indifferently, this moved to jealousy them of the Jews (who had believed). And they did not merely speak of circumcision, but they said, Ye cannot even be saved. Whereas the very opposite to this was the case, that receiving circumcision they could not be saved. Do you mark how closely the trials succeed each other, from within, from without? It is well ordered too, that this happens when Paul is present, that he may answer them. "When therefore Paul and Barnabas had no small dissension and disputation with them, they determined that Paul and Barnabas, and certain other of them, should go up to Jerusalem unto the apostles and elders about this question." (v. 2.) And Paul does not say, What? Have I not a right to be believed after so many signs? but he complied for their sakes. "And being brought on their way by the

Church, they passed through Phenice and Samaria, declaring the conversion of the Gentiles : and they caused great joy unto all the brethren." (v. 3.) And observe, the consequence is that all the Samaritans also, learn what has come to the Gentiles : and they rejoiced. "And when they were come to Jerusalem, they were received of the Church, and of the apostles and elders, and they declared all things that God had done with them." (v. 4.) See what a providence is here ! "But there rose up certain of the sect of the Pharisees which believed, saying, That it was needful to circumcise them, and to command them to keep the law of Moses. And the apostles and elders came together to consider of this matter. And when there had been much disputing, Peter rose up and said unto them, Men and brethren, ye know how that of old days God made choice among us, that the Gentiles by my mouth should hear the word of the Gospel, and believe." (v. 5–7.) Observe Peter from the first standing aloof (κεχωρισμένον) from the affair, and even to this time judaizing.   And yet (says he) " ye know." (ch. x. 45 ; xi, 2.) Perhaps those were present who of old found fault with him in the matter of Cornelius, and went in with him (on that occasion): for this reason he brings them forward as witnesses. "From old days," he says, "did choose among you." What means, " Among you ? " Either, in Palestine, or, you being present. "By my mouth." Observe how he shows that it was God speaking by him, and no human utterance. "And God, that knoweth the hearts, gave testimony unto them : " he refers them to the spiritual testimony : "by giving them the Holy Ghost even as unto us." (v. 8.) Everywhere he puts the Gentiles upon a thorough equality. "And put no difference between us and them, having purified their hearts by faith." (v. 9.) From faith alone, he says, they obtained the same gifts. This is also meant as a lesson to those (objectors) ; this is able to teach even them

---

[1] Ὅρα πανταχοῦ τῆς εἰς τὰ ἔθνη διορθώσεως (the putting things right, the introduction of the right and proper course : mod. text μεταβάσεως) ἀναγκαίαν τὴν ἀρχὴν εἰσαγομένην. Mod. text ἀπ᾿ αὐτῶν εἴσαγ. which Ben. renders, vide ubique transitum ad Gentes necessario a Judæis inductum. But the meaning is : "Throughout, it is so ordered by the Providence of God, that the Apostles do not seem to act spontaneously in this matter, but to be led by the force of circumstances." The persons (Peter, Paul, James) are not specified, the sense being : First, upon fault being found, there is apologizing and self-justifying : then, upon the Jews' open aversion, the preaching comes to the Gentiles : now, upon a new emergency, a law is enacted.—In the next sentence, B. C. διαφόρως: A. and mod. text ἀδιαφόρως, which we retain.

that faith only is needed, not works nor circumcision. For indeed they do not say all this only by way of apology for the Gentiles, but to teach (the Jewish believers) also to abandon the Law. However, at present this is not said. "Now therefore why tempt ye God, to put a yoke upon the neck of the disciples?" (v. 10.) What means, "Tempt ye God?" As if He had not power to save by faith. Consequently, it proceeds from a want of faith, this bringing in the Law. Then he shows that they themselves were nothing benefited by it, and he turns the whole (stress of his speech) against the Law, not against them, and (so) cuts short the accusation of them: "which neither our fathers nor we were able to bear. But we believe that through the grace of the Lord Jesus we shall be saved, even as they." (v. 11.) How full of power these words! The same that Paul says at large in the Epistle to the Romans, the same says Peter here. "For if Abraham," says (Paul), "was justified by works, he hath whereof to glory, but not before God." (Rom. iv. 2.) Do you perceive that all this is more a lesson for them than apology for the Gentiles? However, if he had spoken this without a plea for speaking, he [1] would have been suspected: an occasion having offered, he lays hold of it, and speaks out fearlessly. See on all occasions how the designs of their foes are made to work with them. If those had not stirred the question, these things would not have been spoken, nor what follows.*

(Recapitulation.) (b) But [2] let us look more closely at what has been said. "And certain men," etc. In Jerusalem, then, there were not any believers from among the Gentiles: but in Antioch of course there were. Therefore [3] there came down certain yet laboring under this disease of the love of rule, and wishing to have those of the Gentiles attached to them. And yet Paul, though he too was learned in the Law, was not thus affected. "When therefore Paul and Barnabas had no small disputation with them," etc. (v. 2.) But when he returned from thence, the doctrine also became more exact. For if they at Jerusalem enjoin no such thing, much more these (have no right to do so). "And being brought on their way," etc, "they caused no small joy to the brethren." (v. 3.) Do you mark, as many as are not enamoured of rule, rejoiced in their believing? It was no ambitious feeling that prompted their recitals, neither was it for display, but in justification of the preaching to the Gentiles. (v. 4.) Thus they say nothing of what had happened in the matter of the Jews.[4] "But there arose up certain of the sect of the Pharisees which believed," etc. (v. 5.) (a) But even if they would needs bring over the Gentiles to their side, they learn that neither must the Apostles overlook it.[5] "And the Apostles and elders," etc. (v. 6.) "Among us," he says, "God chose:" and "from old days:" long ago, he says, not now. And [6] this too is no small point—at a time when Jews believed, not turned away (from the Gospel). "Among us;" an argument from the place: "of old days," from the time. And that expression, "Chose:" just as in their own case [7] he says not, (so) willed it, but,

---

[1] Mod. text ἴσως οὐδαμῶς ὕποπτος ἦν, "perhaps he would *not* have been any way suspected."

* With Luke's narrative of the Apostolic council at Jerusalem should be compared Paul's (Gal. ii.) which gives additional particulars. The conference marked an epoch in the history of the church. Here came into decisive conflict two opposing tendencies—the Pharisaic tendency which insisted that the Gentiles must enter the Kingdom through the door of the law, and the catholic spirit which. following the principles of Stephen's apology and appreciating the revelations made to Peter, insisted that adherence to the Mosaic law was not only unnecessary, but was positively inconsistent with the freedom and completeness of Christ's salvation. The decree of the council was, no doubt, of great service in checking the Judaizing tendencies of the early church. It was in the line of this decree that the work of Paul was done, as the champion of catholic Christianity. The chief points to be noted in v. 1–12 are: (1) The representatives of the narrower Jewish view came to Antioch on purpose to antagonize the work of Paul and Barnabas among the Gentiles (v. 1). (2) They took the extreme position that salvation depended on circumcision and caused great anxiety and debate among the Gentile Christians regarding their relations to the Mosaic law (v. 2). (3) The Apostles and messengers who were sent to appeal the question to the leaders of the mother church at Jerusalem answered their objections by the *fact* of the Gentiles' conversion (v. 3–5). (4) Peter's position was now clear and pronounced. This is implied even in his subsequent conduct at Antioch whence he withdrew from the Gentiles (Gal. ii. 11 sq.) which Paul represents as an *inconsistency*. (5) Peter's view is first given both on account of his prominence among the Apostles and because he had been the first to bear the gospel to the Gentiles.—G. B. S.

[2] In the Mss. and Edd. the part marked (b) is transposed to the beginning (c) of the remarks introductory to the morale, so that the Recapitulation (announced by mod. text at the end of the first sentence of (a) is split into two halves and the latter given first. In the old text the two parts (b) (c) make the entire Recapitulation, so that it is by no means ἀκριβέστερον.

[3] Mod. text "Therefore they depart (thither) and stay no short time there (ch. xiv. 28). 'But there arose certain of the Pharisees (v. 5) yet laboring under the disease," etc.

[4] τῶν εἰς τοὺς Ἰουδαίους συμβεβηκότων: i. e. of the dispute about circumcision, see below p. 203, note [7]. The first sentence of (c) "Great effrontery (this) of the Pharisees," etc., would come in suitably here, but it is required for introduction of the sentence which follows it, "But see the Apostles," etc.

[5] Here mod. text has the formula, Ἀλλ' ἴδωμεν ἄνωθεν τὰ εἰρημένα.

[6] Καὶ τοῦτο δὲ οὐ μικρόν, Ἰουδαίων πιστευόντων καὶ τούτων οὐκ ἀποστραφέντων, ἀπὸ τοῦ τόπου, ἀπὸ τοῦ καιροῦ. Mod. text substitutes the sense of the latter words: δύο τούτοις ὁ λέγει πιστοῦται, τῷ καιρῷ καὶ τῷ τόπῳ: but for the former, οὐ μικρὸν δὲ τὸ καὶ Ἰουδαίων πιστευόντων τοῦτο ἀποστραφῆναι, *quod etiam Judæis credentibus hoc avertatur*. Ben. We reject τούτων, which disturbs the sense. He says: "Long ago—therefore why raise this question now, which was settled in those early days, when Jews received the faith, not rejected it with aversion? which aversion of theirs is *now* the occasion of the preachers' turning to the Gentiles. Yet even then the will of God was plainly declared. Thus the Apostle argues strongly both from the place—here in the midst of the Jews—and from the time."

[7] ὥσπερ ἐπ' αὐτῶν: referring to i. 24. as below on καρδιογνώστης. He means, "It was a purpose of the Lord, and a high distinction: therefore he does not say, He would, or was willing that the Gentiles should hear, but He elected me for this work, as He elected us to the Apostleship."

"Chose that the Gentiles by my mouth should hear the word of the Gospel and believe." Whence is this proved? From the Spirit. Then he shows that the testimony given them is not of grace merely, but of their virtue. "And God which knoweth the hearts bare them witness" (v. 8); having afforded to them nothing less (than to us), for, he says," Put no difference between us and them." (v. 9.) Why then, hearts are what one must everywhere look to.[1] And it is very appositely said, "God that knoweth the hearts bare them witness:" as in the former instance, "Thou, Lord, that knowest the hearts of all men." (ch. i. 24.) For to show that this is the meaning, observe what he adds, "Put no difference between us and them." When he has mentioned the testimony borne to them, then he utters that great word, the same which Paul speaks, "Neither circumcision availeth anything, nor uncircumcision." (1 Cor. vii, 19.) "That he may make the twain one in Himself." (Eph. ii. 5.) Of all these the seeds lie in Peter's discourse. And he does not say (between) them of the circumcision, but "Between us," that is the Apostles, "and them." Then, that the expression, "no difference" may not seem an outrage, After faith, he says—"Having purified their hearts by faith" (v. 10)—He thoroughly cleansed them first.[2] Then he shows, not that the Law was evil, but themselves weak.—"But we believe that through the grace of the Lord Jesus we shall be saved even as they." (v. 11.) Mark how he ends with a fearful consideration. He[3] does not discourse to them from the Prophets, but from things present, of which themselves were witnesses. Of course[4] (the Prophets) also themselves anon add their testimony (infra v. 15), and make the reason stronger by what has now come to pass. And observe, he first permits the question to be moved in the Church, and then speaks. "And put no difference between"—he said

not, them of the circumcision, but "us and them," i. e. the Gentiles: for[5] this (gradual advance) little by little is stronger. "Why therefore tempt ye God?" who is become (the) God of the Gentiles: for this was tempting :[6] * * * whether He is able to save even after the Law. See what he does. He shows that they are in danger. For if, what the Law could not do, faith had power to do, "we believe that through the grace of the Lord Jesus we shall be saved even as they" (comp. Gal. ii. 16): but faith falling off, behold, themselves (are) in destruction. And he did not say, Why do ye disbelieve? which was more harsh, but, "Tempt God," and that when the fact is demonstrated.

(c) Great effrontery this, of the Pharisees, that even after faith they set up the Law, and will not obey the Apostles. But see these, how mildly they speak, and not in the tone of authority: such words are amiable, and more apt to fix themselves in the mind. Observe, it is nowhere a display of words, but demonstration by facts, by the Spirit. And yet, though they have such proofs, they still speak gently. And observe they[7] do not come accusing those at Antioch, but "declaring all things that God had done with them :" (v. 4) but thence again these men lay hold upon the occasion (to compass their own objects), "but there rose up," etc. (v. 1.) Such were the pains they took in their love of power: and it was not with the knowledge of the Apostles that they Paul and Barnabas were blamed. But still they brought forward none of these charges: but when they have proved the matter, then (the Apostles) write in stronger terms.

For gentleness[8] is everywhere a great good:

[1] Ἀρα καρδίας δεῖ πανταχοῦ ζητεῖν. i. e. "He implies that God, as knowing the hearts of all men saw the fitness of these Gentiles, therefore chose them, and made no distinction between us and them in point of fitness. Consequently, the heart, not circumcision, is what we must everywhere look to. Nay, he adds, this same expression, καρδιογνώστης was used by the Apostles on the occasion above referred to : so that Peter, by using it here also, declares the Gentiles to be upon a par with the Apostles themselves : no difference between us the Apostles, and them.

[2] Mss. Ἐξεκάθαρε πρότερον τὸν λόγον, καὶ τότε κ. τ. λ. Either τὸν λόγον has come in from another place (perhaps after εἰς φοβερὸν κατέληξε below), or some words are lost, e. g. πίστει τῇ εἰς τὸν λόγον.

[3] The φοβερὸν is in the καθ' ὃν τρόπον κἀκεῖνοι. "Our danger, through the Law, is greater than theirs. Not only are they put upon a par with us, but we may be thankful to be put upon a par with them." To bring out this point, he reviews the tenor and drift of St. Peter's speech.

[4] Εἰκότως καὶ αὐτοὶ λοιπὸν ἐπιμαρτυροῦσι : that αὐτοὶ means the Prophets (cited by St. James), seems to be shown by τοῖς ἤδη γενομένοις, "what they long ago foretold, which is even now come to pass."

[5] τὸ γὰρ καταμικρὸν τοῦτο ἰσχυρότερον γενόμενον τῶν ἐθνῶν· τοῦτο γὰρ πειράζοντος ἦν κ. τ. λ. Mod. text τοῦτο γὰρ κατὰ μικρὸν ἐπαγόμενον ἐγίνετο ἰσχυρότερον· ἐκεῖνο δὲ πειρ. ἦν.—The meaning is : "He does not come at once to the point, but advances to it gradually : first, 'Put no difference'—though, as he afterwards shows, if there be a difference it is in their favor : we are not to think it much that they are to be saved as we, but that we may trust to be saved 'even as they.'"

[6] Above, it was "disbelieving God, as not able to save by faith." Here, "You are tempting God by your unbelief : whereas the question is not so much whether He can save without the Law, as εἰ δύναται καὶ μετὰ νόμον (B. τοῦ νόμου) σῶσαι."

[7] οὐκ ἀπέρχονται διαβάλλοντες τοὺς ἐν Ἀντ. This also shows the ἐπιείκεια of Paul and Barnabas, that when they come to Jerusalem, we do not find them complaining of the Jews who had come to Antioch, but they confine themselves to the recital of "all that God had done with them," v. 4: as he had said above, οὐδὲν λέγουσι περὶ τῶν εἰς τοὺς Ἰουδαίους συμβεβηκότων. The next clause, Ἀλλ' ἐκεῖθεν πάλιν λαμβάνουσιν ἀφορμὴν may be referred to the Apostles, "they again take advantage of this opportunity, viz. of the Judaizing opposition, to establish the freedom of the Gentiles." We have referred it to the Pharisaic brethren, v. 5, for the sake of connection with the following οὕτως ἐμελέτων τὸ φιλαρχεῖν.—In the next clause, καὶ (mod. text οἱ καὶ) οὐκ εἰδότων τῶν ἀποστόλων ἐμέμφθησαν, Sav. marg. has 'πέμφθησαν, "these Judaizers were not sent with knowledge of the Apostles."

[8] Ἐπιείκεια, gentleness, in the sense of moderation and forbearance, keeping one's temper : here distinguished from the temper of the ψυχρὸς, which is unruffled only because he does not feel, and that of the flatterer, who puts up with everything for the sake of pleasing.

gentleness, I say, not stupid indifference; gentleness, not adulation: for between these there is a vast difference. Nothing ruffled Paul, nothing discomposed Peter. When thou hast convincing proofs, why lose thy temper, to render these of none effect? It is impossible for one who is out of temper ever to persuade. Yesterday also we discoursed about anger; but there is no reason why we should not to-day also; perchance a second exhortation coming directly after the first will effect somewhat. For indeed a medicine though of virtue to heal a wound, unless it be constantly renewed, mars all. And think not that our continual discoursing about the same things is a condemning of you: for if we condemned you, we should not discourse; but now, hoping that you will gain much, we speak these things. Would indeed that we did speak constantly of the same things: would that there were no other subject of our discourses, than how we might overcome our passions. For is it not contrary to all reason, that while emperors, living in luxury and so great honor, have no subject of discourse either while sitting at table, or at any other time, save only how to overcome their enemies [1]—and therefore it is that they hold their assemblies each day, and appoint generals and soldiers, and demand taxes and tributes; and that of all state affairs, the moving causes are these two, the overcoming of those who make war upon them, and the establishing of their subjects in peace—we have no mind for such themes as this, nor ever even dream of conversing upon them: but how we may buy land, or purchase slaves, and make our property greater, these are subjects we can talk about every day, and never be tired of them: while concerning things in ourselves and really our own, we neither wish to speak ourselves, nor so much as dream of tolerating advice, nor of enduring to hear others speaking about them? But answer me, what do you talk about? About dinner? Why that is a subject for cooks. Of money? Nay, that is a theme for hucksters and merchants. Of buildings? That belongs to carpenters and builders. Of land? That talk is for husbandmen. But for us, there is no other proper business, save this, how we may make wealth for the soul. Then let not the dis-

course be wearisome to you. Why is it that none finds fault with the physician for always discoursing of the healing art, nor with people of other crafts for talking about their peculiar arts? If indeed the mastery over our passions were really achieved, so that there were no need of putting us in mind, we might reasonably be taxed with ambition and display: or rather, not then either. For even if it were gained, for all that, there would be need of discoursing, that one might not relapse and remain uncorrected: as in fact physicians discourse not only to the sick, but also to the whole, and they have books on this subject, on the one part how to free from disease, on the other how to preserve health. So that even if we are well, still we must not give over, but must do all in order to the preserving of our health. And when we are sick there is a twofold necessity for advice: first, that we may be freed from the disease; secondly, that having been freed, we may not fall into it again. Well then, we are discoursing now by the method of treating the sick, not by the rules for the treatment of the healthy.

How then may one root out this evil passion? how subdue ($\dot{v}\pi o \sigma \kappa \epsilon \lambda i \sigma \epsilon \iota \epsilon$) this violent fever? Let us see whence it had its birth, and let us remove the cause. Whence is it wont to arise? From arrogance and much haughtiness. This cause then let us remove, and the disease is removed together with it. But what is arrogance? whence does it arise? for perhaps we are likely to have to go back to a still higher origin. But whatever course the reason of the thing may point out, that let us take, that we may go to the bottom of the mischief, and pluck it up by the roots. Whence then comes arrogance? From our not looking into our own concerns, but instead of that, busying ourselves about the nature of land, though we are not husbandmen, and the nature of gold, though we are not merchants, and concerning clothing, and everything else: while to ourselves and our own nature we never look at all. And who, you will say, is ignorant of his own nature? Many: perhaps all, save a few: and if ye will, I will show the proof of it. For, tell me, what is man? If one were asked, will he be able to answer outright to the questions, In what he differs from the brutes, in what he is akin to the heavenly inhabitants, what can be made of man? For as in the case of any other material, so also in this case: man is the subject-matter, but of this can be made either an angel or a beast. Does not this seem a strange saying? And yet ye have often heard it in the Scriptures. For of certain human

---

[1] He means, that to βασιλεῖς, when there is an enemy in the field against them, the engrossing theme of discourse, even at table, is how to overcome their enemies. Such was probably the state of things when this Homily was preached: for the note of time in Hom. xliv. implies that it was delivered either at the close of 400 or the beginning of 401 A. D.: now the former of these years was signalized by the revolt and defeat of Gainas. Hence the following passage might be rendered, "they are holding assemblies each day, appointing generals and demanding taxes," etc. The war ended Dec. 400, in the defeat of Gainas.

beings it was said, "he is the angel of the Lord" (Mal. ii. 7): and "from his lips," saith it, "they shall seek judgment" (Mal. iii. 1): and again, "I send My angel before Thy face:" but of some, "Serpents, generation of vipers." (Matt. xii. 34.) So then, it all depends upon the use. Why do I say, an angel? the man can become God, and a child of God. For we read, "I have said, Ye are gods, and all of you are children of the Most High." (Ps. lxxxii. 6.) And what is greater, the power to become both God and angel and child of God is put into his own hands. Yea, so it is, man can be the maker of an angel. Perchance this saying has startled you? Hear however Christ saying: "In the Resurrection they neither marry nor are given in marriage, but are like unto the angels." (Matt. xxii. 30.) And again, "He that is able to receive it, let him receive it." (Matt. xix. 12.) In a word, it is virtue which makes angels: but this is in our power: therefore we are able to make angels, though not in nature, certainly in will. For indeed if virtue be absent, it is no advantage to be an angel by nature; and the Devil is a proof of this, who was an angel once: but if virtue be present, it is no loss to be a man by nature; and John is a proof of this, who was a man, and Elias who went up into heaven, and all those who are about to depart thither. For these indeed, though with bodies, were not prevented from dwelling in heaven: while those others, though without bodies, could not remain in heaven. Let no one then grieve or be vexed with his nature as if it were a hindrance to him, but with his will. He (the Devil) from being incorporeal became a lion: for lo! it saith, "Our adversary, as a roaring lion, walketh about, seeking whom he may devour (1 Pet. v. 8): we from being corporeal, become angels. For just as if a person, having found some precious material, should despise it, as not being an artificer, it will be a great loss to him, whether it be pearls, or a pearl shell, or any other such thing that he has seen; so we likewise, if we are ignorant of our own nature, shall despise it much: but if we know what it is, we shall exhibit much zeal, and reap the greatest profits. For from this nature is wrought a king's robe, from this a king's house, from this nature are fashioned a king's members: all are kingly. Let us not then misuse our own nature to our hurt. He has made us "a little lower than the angels," (Ps. viii. 5), I mean, by reason of death: but even that little we have now recovered. There is nothing therefore to hinder us from becoming nigh to the angels, if we will. Let us then will it, let us will it, and having exercised ourselves thoroughly, let us return honor to the Father, and the Son, and the Holy Spirit, now and ever, world without end, Amen.

HOMILY XXXIII.

ACTS XV. 13, 15.

"And after they had held their peace, James answered, saying, Men and brethren, hearken unto me: Symeon hath declared how God at the first did visit the Gentiles, to take out of them a people for his name. And to this agree the words of the prophets."

THIS (James) was bishop, as they say, and therefore he speaks last, and herein is fulfilled that saying, "In the mouth of two or three witnesses shall every word be established." (Deut. xvii. 6; Matt. xviii. 16.) But observe the discretion shown by him also, in making his argument good from the prophets, both new and old.[1] For he had no acts of his own to declare, as Peter had and Paul. And indeed it is wisely ordered that this (the active) part is assigned to those, as not intended to be locally fixed in Jerusalem, whereas (James) here, who performs the part of teacher, is no way responsible for what has been done, while however he is not divided from them in opinion.[*] (b) "Men and brethren," he says, "hearken unto me." Great is the moderation of the man. His also is a more complete oration, as indeed it puts the completion to the matter under discussion. (a) "Symeon," he says, "declared:" (namely,) in Luke, in that he prophesied, "Which Thou hast prepared before the face of all nations, a light to

[1] All our Mss. and the Cat. ἀπό τε νέων ἀπό τε παλαιῶν βεβαιουμένου τῶν προφητῶν τὸν λόγον, which must be rendered, "Confirming the word of the prophets:" so Ed. Par. Ben. 2, where the other Edd. have παλ. προφ. βεβ. κ. τ. λ., which is in fact what the sense requires: "from the prophets, new (as Symeon) and old."

[*] This was James, the Lord's brother (Gal. i. 19), who, according to the uniform tradition of the early church, was the Bishop of Jerusalem. He evidently was the chief pastor, as he presides at this conference, and when Judaizing teachers

lighten the Gentiles, and the glory of Thy people Israel." [1] (c) " How God at the first did visit the Gentiles, to take out of them a people for His Name." (Luke ii. 25.) Then, since that (witness), though [2] from the time indeed he was manifest, yet had not authority by reason of his not being ancient, therefore he produces ancient prophecy also, saying, " And to this agree the words of the Prophets, as it is written : After this I will return, and will build again the tabernacle of David, which is fallen down ; and I will build again the ruins thereof, and I will set it up." (v. 16.) What ? was Jerusalem raised up ? Was it not rather thrown down ? What [3] sort of raising up does he call that which took place after the return from Babylon ? " That the residue of men," he says, " may seek the Lord, even all the Gentiles upon whom My Name is called." (v. 17.) Then, what makes his word authoritative—" Saith the Lord, which doeth all these things : " and, for that this is no new thing, but all was planned from the beginning, " Known unto God are all His works from everlasting." * (v. 18.) And then again

his authority (καὶ τὸ ἀξίωμα πάλιν) (as Bishop) : " Wherefore my sentence is, that we trouble not them, which from among the Gentiles are turned to God : but that we write unto them, that they abstain from pollution of idols, and from fornication, and from things strangled, and from blood. For Moses of old time hath in every city them that preach him, being read in the synagogues every sabbath day." (v. 19–21.) Since [4] then they had heard of the Law, with good reason he enjoins these things from the Law, that he may not seem to make it of no authority. And (yet) observe how he does not let them be told these things from the Law, but from himself, saying, It is not that I heard these things from the Law, but how ? " We have judged." Then the decree is made in common. " Then pleased it the Apostles and elders, together with the whole Church, to choose men of their own company "—do you observe they do not merely enact these matters, and nothing more ?—" and send them to Antioch with Paul and Barnabas : namely, Judas surnamed Barsabas, and Silas, chief men among the brethren : and they wrote letters by them after this manner." (v. 22.) And observe, the more to authenticate the decree, they send men of their own, that there may be no room for regarding Paul and his company with suspicion. " The Apostles and elders and brethren send greeting unto the brethren which are of the Gentiles in Antioch and Syria and Cilicia." (v. 23.) And mark [5] with what forbearance of all harsh vituperation of those (brethren) they indite their epistle. " Forasmuch as we have heard, that certain which went out from us have troubled you with words, subverting your souls, saying, Ye must be circumcised, and keep the Law : to whom we gave no such commandment." (v. 24.) Sufficient was this charge against the temerity of those men, and worthy of the Apostles' moderation, that they said nothing beyond this. Then to show that they do not act despotically, that all are agreed in this, that with deliberation they write this—" It seemed good to us, being assembled with one accord, to send men of ours whom we have chosen " (v. 25)—then, that it may not look like disparagement of Paul and Barnabas, that those men are sent, observe the encomium passed upon them—" together with our beloved Bar-

---

afterwards went down to Antioch from Jerusalem they are spoken of as coming " from James " (Gal. ii. 12). From this it has been inferred that he was the leader of a Judaistic party, but this view is inconsistent with his address here and also with Paul's testimony who says that the " pillar " apostles " imparted nothing " to him, that is, did not correct or supplement his teaching. He was no doubt of a conservative tendency respecting the questions in dispute and may not have been always self-consistent, as Peter certainly was not, but there can be no doubt of his substantial agreement with Paul. His doctrine of justification by works as well as by faith in his epistle is not against this view, since he uses both the words " faith " and " works " in a different sense from Paul, meaning by the former " belief " and by the latter the deeds which are the fruit of the Christian life, instead of meritorious obedience to the Mosaic law.—G. B. S.

[1] Edd. ἐπιχωριάζειν, Cat. ἐγχρονίζειν, substituted for the less usual ἐγχωριάζειν of A. B. C. Sav.—Below, Συμεών, φησίν, ἐξηγήσατο ἐν τῷ Λουκᾷ προφητεύσας. Cat. " He who in Luke prophesied, Lord, now lettest Thou Thy servant depart."—It is remarkable that it does not occur to Chrys, that Symeon is Simon Peter, though 2 Pet. i. 1 has Συμεών Πέτρος in the Cod. Alexandr., and many other Mss. In the Mod. text Chrys. is made to say : " Some say that this is he who is mentioned by Luke : others, that he is some other person of the same name. (Acts xiii. 1?) But whether it be the one or the other is a point about which there is no need to be particular ; but only to receive as necessary the things which the person declared."

[2] ἀπὸ μὲν τοῦ χρόνου δῆλος ἦν, τὸ δὲ ἀξιόπιστον οὐκ εἶχε : the former clause seems to be corrupt. The sense in general is, He was manifestly (a prophet), but had not the same authority as the old prophets. Probably the form of opposition was this : ἐπειδὴ ἐκεῖνος μὲν * * δῆλος ἦν, ἀπὸ δὲ τοῦ χρόνου τὸ ἀξιόπιστον οὐκ εἶχε διὰ τὸ μὴ παλαιὸς εἶναι. " Since Symeon, though from * * he was manifestly (a prophet), yet from time had not the like authority because he was not ancient."

[3] Mod. text, " But it is not of these things that he speaks. And what raising up, you will say, does he mean ? That after Babylon." We point it, ποίαν λέγει ἔγερσιν τὴν μετὰ Βαβυλῶνα ; " Was it raised up ? was it not rather razed to the ground (by the Romans) ? True it was rebuilt after the return from Babylon, but what sort of raising up does he call that ? " For the answer to these questions, not given here, see the Recapitulation (note 4, p. 207).

* Most modern texts omit πάντα at the end of v. 17 and then join directly to it γνωστὰ ἀπ᾽ αἰῶνος only, dropping out the words of the T. R.: ἐστι τῷ θεῷ πάντα τὰ ἔργα αὐτοῦ. This reading yields the following translation : " the Gentiles upon whom my name is called, saith the Lord, who maketh these things known from the beginning of the world." (So Tischendorf, Alford, Meyer, Westcott and Hort, Gloag, R. V.). This reading encounters the difficulty that the words γνωστὰ ἀπ᾽ αἰῶνος are considered as a part of the quotation which, in reality, they are not. It is probable that this fact may have led to their expansion into an independent sentence.—G. B. S.

---

[4] All our Mss. ἐπειδὴ οὐκ ἦσαν ἀκηκοότες τοῦ νόμου, which contradicts v. 21. We restore ἐπειδὴ οὖν. In B. C. v. 21, with the words ἐπειδὴ οὐκ ἦσαν ἀκ. τοῦ νόμου is repeated after, " We have judged."

[5] Mss. and Edd. Καὶ ὅρα πῶς φορτικῶς ἐκείνους διαβάλλοντες ἐπιστέλλουσιν. The sense absolutely requires πῶς οὐ φορτ. It would be strange if Chrys. made τὸ φορτικὸν and τὸ διαβάλλειν matter of commendation : moreover in his very next remark he says just the contrary, and below, p. 209.

nabas and Paul, men that have hazarded their lives for the name of our Lord Jesus Christ. We have sent therefore Judas and Silas, who shall also tell you the same things by mouth. For it seemed good to the Holy Spirit and to us "—it is not man's doing, it says—" to lay upon you no greater burden "—again it calls the Law a burden : then apologizing even for these injunctions—"save these necessary things" (v. 26-28) : "That ye abstain from meats offered to idols, and from blood, and from things strangled, and from fornication : from which if ye keep yourselves, ye shall do well. (v. 29.) For these things the New Testament did not enjoin : we nowhere find that Christ discoursed about these matters ; but these things they take from the Law. " From things strangled," it says, " and from blood." here it prohibits murder. (Comp. Gen. ix. 5.) " So when they were dismissed, they came to Antioch : and when they had gathered the multitude together, they delivered the epistle : which when they had read, they rejoiced for the consolation." (v. 30-31.) Then those (brethren) also exhorted them : and having established them, for towards Paul they were contentiously disposed, so departed from them in peace. " And Judas and Silas, being prophets also themselves, exhorted the brethren with many words, and confirmed them. And after they had tarried there a space, they were let go in peace from the brethren unto the Apostles." (v. 32-33.) No more factions and fightings, but thenceforth Paul taught.[1]

(Recapitulation.) " Then all the multitude kept silence," etc. (v. 12.) There was no arrogance in the Church. After Peter Paul speaks, and none silences him : James waits patiently, not starts up [2] (for the next word). Great the orderliness (of the proceedings). No word speaks John here, no word the other Apostles, but held their peace, for James was invested with the chief rule, and think it no hardship. So clean was their soul from love of glory. " And after that they had held their peace, James answered," etc. (v. 13.) (b) Peter indeed spoke more strongly, but James here more mildly : for thus it behooves one in high authority, to leave what is unpleasant for others to say, while he himself appears in the milder

part. (a) But what means it, " How God first (πρῶτον) did visit ? " (v. 14.) (It means) from the beginning (ἐξ ἀρχῆς).[3] (c) Moreover he well says, " Symeon expounded " (ἐξηγήσατο) (or, interpreted), implying that he too spake the mind of others. "And to this agree," etc. Observe how he shows that this is a doctrine of old time. " To take out of the Gentiles," he says, " a people for His Name." (v. 15.) Not simply, Chose, but, " for His Name," that is for His glory. His Name is not shamed by the taking (προλήψει) the Gentiles first, but it is even a greater glory.—Here some even great thing is hinted at : that these are chosen before all.[4] " After this I will return, and rebuild the tabernacle of David which is fallen down." (v. 16.) But if one would look into the matter closely, the kingdom of David does in fact now stand, his Offspring reigning everywhere. For what is the good of the buildings and the city, with none obeying there ? And what is the harm arising from the destruction of the city, when all are willing to give their very souls ? There is that come which is more illustrious than David : in all parts of the world is he now sung. This has come to pass : if so, then must this also come to pass, " And I will build again the ruins thereof, and I will set it up : " to what end ? " that the residue of men may seek the Lord, and all the Gentiles, upon whom My Name is called." (v. 17.) If then it was to this end that the city rose again (namely) because of Him (that was to come) of them, it shows that of the building of the city the cause is, the calling of the Gentiles. Who are " the residue ? " those who are then left.[5] " And all the Gentiles, upon whom My Name is called : " but observe, how he keeps the due order, and brings them in second.

---

[1] Παῦλος δὲ λοιπὸν ἐδίδασκεν. Perhaps this may belong to the Recapitulation, v. 12.—In the mod. text the matter is a good deal transposed, without any necessity, and the Recapitulation is made to begin after the sentence ending, " love of glory."—This seems to be the proper place for the first of the sentences following the Recapitulation, p. 210, note [3], viz. " No more faction. On this occasion I suppose it was that they received the right hand, as he says himself, ' They gave to me and Barnabas the right hands of fellowship.' On this (same) occasion he says, ' They added nothing to me.' For they confirmed his view : they praised and admired it."

[2] ἐπιπηδᾷ N. Cat. (ἐπηπιδᾷ sic A. B. C.) mod. text ἀποπηδᾷ, " recoils " from hearing Paul.

[3] The scribes did not perceive that ἐξ ἀρχῆς is the answer to the question, Τί ἐστιν, καθὼς πρῶτον κ. τ. λ. therefore transposed this sentence and gave ἐξ ἀρχῆς to the sentence (a) (Cat. omits them.) Mod. text, the question being thus left unanswered, substitutes " Symeon hath declared "—καθὼς πρ. κ. τ. λ. Ἐξ ἀρχῆς σφοδρότερον μέν. [4] ὅτι πρὸ πάντων οὗτοι. Here also, and in τῇ προλήψει τῶν ἐθνῶν, there seems to be a reference to πρῶτον, as if the meaning were, God " looked upon the Gentiles first to take from them," before the Jews, etc.—After the text, the questions left unanswered above (see note [2], p. 206) might be advantageously introduced. " How could that restoration (after Babylon) be called an ἔγερσις, especially as the city was eventually razed to the ground by the Romans ? True : but the kingdom of David is in fact more gloriously raised up, in the reign of David's offspring throughout the world. As for the buildings and city, what loss is that ? Nay, David himself is more glorious now than he was before, sung as he is in all parts of the world. If then this which the Prophet foretold is come to pass—this is put as St. James's argument—namely that the city was raised from its ruins (and the subsequent overthrow, when the end of that restoration was attained, does not invalidate the fulfilment), then must the διά τι of this restoration also come to pass, namely, that the residue shall seek the Lord, and all the Gentiles upon whom that Name is called. The city, was raised up for the sake of Christ, to come of them, and to reign over all nations. Consequently, the Prophet shows that the αἴτιον (i. e. the διά τι, or final clause) of the building of the city is—the calling of the Gentiles, τὸ τὰ ἔθνη κληθῆναι."

[5] οἱ ὑπολειπόμενοι τότε, the Jews whom that (the Babylonian) judgment leaves.

"Saith the Lord, which doeth these things." Not "saith" (only), but "doeth." Why then, it was God's work.—"But the question is other than this (namely), what Peter spoke more plainly, whether they must be circumcised. Then why dost thou harangue about these matters?" For what the objectors asserted, was not that they must not be received upon believing, but that it must be with the Law. And upon this Peter well pleaded : but then, as this very thing above all others troubled the hearers, therefore he sets this to rights again (θεραπεύει). And observe, that which was needful to be enacted as a rule, that it is not necessary to keep the Law, this Peter introduced : but the milder part,[1] the truth which was received of 'old, this James saith, and dwells upon that concerning which nothing is [2] written, in order that having soothed their minds by that which is acknowledged, he may opportunely introduce this likewise. "Wherefore," saith he, " my sentence is, not to trouble them which from among the Gentiles do turn unto God " (v. 19), that is, not to subvert : for, if God called them, and these observances subvert, we fight against God. And [3] again, "them which from the Gentiles," he saith, " do turn." And he says well, with authority, the "my sentence is. But that we write unto them that they abstain from pollutions of idols, and from fornication "—(b) and yet they often insisted upon these points in discoursing to them [4]—but, that he may seem

also to honor the Law (he mentions), these also, speaking (however) not as from Moses but from the Apostles, and to make the commandments many, he has divided the one into two (saying), " and from things strangled, and from blood." (v. 20.) For these, although relating to the body, were necessary to be observed, because (these things) caused great evils, "For Moses hath of old times in every city," etc. (v. 21.) This above all quieted them. (ἀνέπαυσεν) (a) For this cause I affirm that it is good (so "to write to them.") Then why do we not write the same injunctions to Jews also? Moses discourses unto them. See what condescension (to their weakness)! Where it did no harm, he set him up as teacher, and indulged them with a gratification which hindered nothing, by permitting Jews to hear him in regard of these matters, even while leading away from him them of the Gentiles. See what wisdom! He seems to honor him, and to set him up as the authority for his own people, and by this very thing he leads away the Gentiles from him!* "Being read in the synagogues every sabbath day." Then why do they not learn (what is to be learnt) out of him, for instance * *? [5] Through the perversity of these men. He shows that even these (the Jews) need observe no more (than these necessary things). And

---

[1] Mss. and Edd. τὸ δὲ ἡμέτερον. We must read τὸ δὲ ἡμερώτερον, as above : in the preceding clause something is wanted for antithesis, probably καὶ ὅρα, τὸ μὲν φορτικώτερον, ὅπερ κ. τ. λ.

[2] ὑπὲρ οὗ οὐδὲν γέγραπται. This also requires emendation. The sense demands, "About which there is no dispute." The γέγραπται may have come in from the text referred to : "to wit, Καθὼς γέγραπται," etc.

[3] The report seems to be defective here; and in fact N. (Sav. marg.) inserts after the text, "showing both God's care towards them and mercy, and their ready mind and piety in obeying : and he says well," etc. But this addition is unknown to A. B. C. Cat., and N. frequently adds to or otherwise alters the original text, where the sense or connection is obscure.—Perhaps however these two sentences may be better transposed to follow the part (b), so that the connection would be, " And again, observe he has been speaking concerning the Gentile converts, not openly of the Jewish believers, and yet in fact what he says is no less for them."—Mod. text with partial transposition, "And he well says, To them, etc. declaring both the purpose of God from the beginning with respect to them, and their obedience and readiness for the calling. What means it? I judge? Instead of, With authority I say that this is so. 'But that we write to them,' he says, 'to abstain from' etc. For these, though bodily, etc. (as below.) And that none may object, why then do we not enjoin the same thing to the Jews? He adds, 'For Moses,' etc. : i. e. Moses discourses to them continually : for this is the meaning of, 'Being read every Sabbath day.' See what condescension!"

[4] καίτοι γε πολλάκις αὐτοῖς ὑπὲρ (not περὶ as Ben. renders, de his) διελεχθῆσαν mod. text διελέχθη, referred perhaps to Moses or the Law, as in the trajection this sentence follows the last of (a). The clause seems to refer to "pollutions of idols and fornication." q. d. "Why mention these in the decree? The Apostles, especially Paul, often discoursed to them on behalf of these points of Christian duty, i. e. the abstaining from all approach to idolatry, as in the matter of εἰδωλόθυτα, and from fornication." The answer is : "He mentions them, for the purpose of seeming to maintain the Law, (though at the same

time he does not rest them on the authority of the Law, but on that of the Apostles : still the Jewish believers would be gratified by this apparent acknowledgment of the Law), and (with the same view) to make a greater number of ἐντολαὶ, for which reason also he divides the one legal prohibition of blood into the two, ἀπὸ τῶν πνικτῶν καὶ ἀπὸ τοῦ αἵματος. The latter, he says, though σωματικαὶ, are necessary to be observed because the non-observance of this law on which the Jews laid so much stress led to great evils—especially made it impossible for Jewish and Gentile believers to eat at the same table. For in every city Moses is preached in Jews and proselytes. Therefore I say it is good that we charge them by letter to abstain from these things," Then, giving a different turn to the reason, "for Moses of old times," etc. he adds. "this is for them which from the Gentiles," etc., as for the Jewish believers, they have Moses to teach them. Thus again seeming to uphold Moses, while in fact he shows, what they might learn from Moses himself, that the Law is come to an end for the Jews also.

* The prohibitions imposed by the council upon the Gentiles were chiefly concessions to Jewish prejudice and opinion. Abstinence from meat which had been offered in idols' temples and from things strangled and from blood was forbidden in the Mosaic law (Ex. xxxiv. 15 ; Lev. xvii. 10-14). Failure to abstain from these would expose the Gentile converts needlessly to the suspicions of the Jewish Christians. The prohibition of fornication must rest upon another ground. It is a warning against the custom among Gentiles, which had become so prevalent as to provoke little rebuke or comment. The ground assigned for requiring these abstinences is that Moses is read every Sabbath in the synagogues of the Jews and therefore these very points are kept prominently before the people and therefore unless these indulgences were abandoned, the synagogue preaching would constantly stimulate in the Jews and Judeo-Christians a dislike of the Gentile believers. There is less ground for the view of Chrys. that v. 21. means that the Jewish Christians have no need of instruction on these points because they hear the law read every Sabbath, an explanation. however, which is adopted by such modern scholars as Wordsworth and Neander.—G. B. S.

[5] A. B. ἀπήγ. τὰ ἔθνη ἐξ αὐτοῦ. Διὰ τί οὖν μὴ παρ' αὐτοῦ μανθ; C. ἀπήγ. τὰ ἐξ αὐτοῦ πάντα, οἷον τὰ ἔθνη. Διὰ τί κ. τ. λ. Cat. ἀπήγ. τὰ ἐξ αὐτοῦ μανθ. Hence we read, ἀπήγαγε τὰ ἔθνη. Διὰ τί οὖν μὴ τὰ ἐξ αὐτοῦ μανθάνουσιν, οἷον (τὰ ἔθνη) * * * ;

if we do not write to them, it is not that they are bound to observe anything more, but only that they have one to tell them. And he does not say, Not to offend, nor to turn them back,[1] which is what Paul said to the Galatians, but, "not to trouble them:" he shows that the point (κατόρθωμα) if carried is nothing but a mere troubling. Thus he made an end of the whole matter;[2] and while he seems to preserve the Law by adopting these rules from it, he unbinds it by taking only these. (c) [3] There was a design of Providence in the disputation also, that after the disputation the doctrine might be more firm. "Then pleased it the Apostles to send chosen men of their own company," etc., no ordinary persons, but the "leading men; having written" (letters) "by them after this manner. To those in Antioch," it says, "and Syria and Cilicia," (v. 22, 23) where the disease had its birth. Observe how they say nothing harsher (φορτικώτερον) against those men, but look to one thing only, namely, to undo (the mischief) which has been done. For this would make even the movers of the faction there to confess (that they were wrong). They do not say, The seducers, the pestilent fellows, or suchlike: though where need is, Paul does this, as when he says, "O full of all guile" (ch. xiii. 10): but here, the point being carried, there was no need. And observe, they do not put it, That certain from us ordered you to keep the Law, but, "Troubled you with words, subverting your souls,"—nothing could be more proper (κυριώτερον) than that word: none (of the other speakers) has so spoken of the things done by those men. "The souls," he says, already strongly established, these persons are ἀνασχευάζοντες as in speaking of a building, "taking them down again:" displacing them (μετατιθέντες) from the foundation).[4] "To whom," he says, "we gave no such commandment. It seemed good therefore to us being assembled with one accord, to send chosen men unto you together with our beloved Barnabas and Paul, men that have hazarded their lives for the Name of our Lord Jesus Christ." (v. 25, 26.) If "beloved," they will not despise them, if they "have hazarded their lives," they have themselves a right to be believed. "We have sent," it saith, "Judas

and Silas, who shall also tell you the same things by word of mouth." (v. 27.) For it was necessary that there should be not merely the Epistle there by itself, lest they should say that Paul and Barnabas had suppressed [5] (the real purport), that they said one thing instead of another. The encomium passed upon Paul stopped their mouths. For this is the reason why neither Paul comes alone nor Barnabas (with him), but others also from the Church; that he may not be suspected, seeing it was he that advocated that doctrine: nor yet those from Jerusalem alone. It shows that they have a right to be believed. "For it seemed good," say they, "to the Holy Ghost and to us" (v. 28): not making themselves equal (to Him [6])—they are not so mad. But why does it put this (so)? Why did they add, "And to us," and yet it had sufficed to say, "To the Holy Ghost?" The one, "To the Holy Ghost," that they may not deem it to be of man; the other, "To us," that they may be taught that they also themselves admit (the Gentiles), although themselves being in circumcision. They have to speak to men who are still weak and afraid of them: this is the reason why this also is added. And it shows that it is not by way of condescension that they speak, neither because they spared them, nor as considering them weak, but the contrary; for great was the reverence of the teachers also.[7] "To lay upon you no

[1] καταστρέφειν, Mss. Perhaps, μεταστρέψαι from Gal. i. 7.
[2] ἐξέλυσε τὸ πᾶν, "untied the whole knot," or perhaps "took out of the Law all its strength," as below λύει.
[3] Perhaps the sentence, τοῦτο μάλιστα αὐτοὺς ἀνέπαυσεν, retained above as the end of (b), may belong here, in the sense, "This was conclusive; this made the Judaizers desist, if anything could."
[4] καθάπερ ἐπὶ οἰκοδομῆς τὰ ὑπ' ἐκείνων γεγενημένα μετατιθέντες. Mod. text from E. τιθέντες, "putting, as in respect of a building, the things done by those (Judaizers)." We have transposed τὰ ὑπ' ἐκ γεγ. to its proper place. He interprets ἀνασκ. with reference to Gal. i. 6. μετατίθεσθε.

[5] συνήρπασαν Ben. ipsos extorsisse: but the word is used in the Greek of Chrysostom's time, in the sense "conceal," for which Schneider s. v. refers to Valesius on Harpocrat. p. 145. Gronov. in which sense we have rendered it above. Or perhaps, "had wrested it" to make it speak in their favor. Τὸ ζητούμενον συναρπάζειν is a logical phrase, used of one who commits a petitio principii. St. Chrys. however can hardly be correctly reported here: for the letter itself would show, if it were believed to be genuine, that Paul and Barnabas neither συνήρπασαν nor ἄλλα ἀντ' ἄλλων εἶπαν. He may rather be supposed to have said in substance as follows: "Had Paul and Barnabas returned alone as the bearers of an oral communication, it might be suspected that they gave their own account of the matter: had they come alone, bearing the Epistle, its genuineness might have been called in question: but by sending the Epistle by the hands of men of their own and of high consideration, they left no room for doubt as to the fact of their decision. On the other hand, to have sent these men alone, would have looked like putting a slight upon Barnabas and Paul: but by sending the messengers with them, they showed ὅτι ἀξιόπιστοι εἰσιν, and by the eulogy expressed in the Epistle itself they stopped the mouths of the gainsayers."
[6] The innovator completely mistakes the meaning of this clause: not having the text to guide him, he supposes it to refer to Silas and Judas, and alters thus: "It shows how worthy of credit they are: not making themselves equal, 'it says: they are not so mad. In fact, this is why it adds that expression, Which have hazarded their lives, etc. And why does it say, "It seemed good to the Holy Ghost and to us," and yet it had sufficed," etc.—Below, he has "'To lay upon you no greater burden.' This they say, because they have to speak," etc. But all this belongs to ἔδοξεν ἡμῖν q. d. "You need not fear us, neither is it of condescension that we speak, or to spare you as being weak—quite the contrary—it seems good to the Holy Ghost "and to us."
[7] πολλὴ γὰρ καὶ τῶν διδασκάλων αἰδὼς ἦν. It is not clear whether this means, Great was the reverence shown by the teachers also towards them—as in St. Peter's ὥσπερ κἀκεῖνοι—and therefore they did not treat them as "weak;" or, great was their reverence towards their teachers, so that had they laid upon them a greater burden, they would have borne it.

greater burden "—they[1] are ever calling it a burden—and again, "save these necessary things :" for that was a superfluous burden. See here a brief Epistle, with nothing more in it (than was needed), neither arts of persuasion, (κατασκευὰς) nor reasonings, but simply a command : for it was the Spirit's legislating. "So when they were dismissed they came to Antioch, and having gathered the multitude together, they delivered to them the epistle." (v. 30.) After the epistle, then (Judas and Silas) also themselves exhort them by word (v. 31): for this also was needful, that (Paul and Barnabas) might be quit of all suspicion. "Being prophets also themselves," it says, exhorted the brethren " with many words." It shows here the right that Paul and Barnabas have to be believed. For Paul also might have done this, but it behooved to be done by by these.[2] " And after they had tarried there a space, they were let go in peace. (v. 33.)

No [3] more faction. On this occasion, I suppose, it was that they received the right hand, as he says himself, "They gave to me and Barnabas right hands of fellowship." (Gal. ii. 9.) There he says, "They added nothing to me." * (ib. 6.) For they confirmed his view: they praised and admired it. —It shows that even from human reasonings it is possible to see this, not to say from the Holy Ghost only, that they sinned a sin not easy to be corrected. For such things need not the Spirit.—It shows that the rest are not necessary, but superfluous. seeing these things are necessary. " From which if ye keep yourselves," it saith, "ye shall do well." It shows that nothing is lacking to them, but this is sufficient. For it might have been done also without letters, but that there may be a law in writing (they send this Epistle) : again, that they may obey the law (the Apostles), also told those men (the same things), and they

did this, "and confirmed them, and having tarried a space were let go in peace."

Let us not then be offended on account of the heretics. For look, here at the very outset of the preaching, how many offences there were : I speak not of those which arose from them that were without; for these were nothing : but of the offences which were within. For instance, first Ananias, then the "murmuring," then Simon the sorcerer ; afterwards they that accused Peter on account of Cornelius, next the famine, [4] lastly this very thing, the chief of the evils. For indeed it is impossible when any good thing has taken place, that some evil should not also subsist along with it. Let us not then be disturbed, if certain are offended, but let us thank God even for this, because it makes us more approved. For not tribulations only, but even temptations also render us more illustrious. A man is no such great lover of the truth, only for holding to it when there is none to lead him astray from it : to hold fast to the truth when many are drawing him away, this makes the proved man. What then ? Is this why offences come ? I am not speaking as if God were the author of them : God forbid ! but I mean, that even out of their wickedness He works good to us : it was never His wish that they should arise : "Grant to them," He saith, "that they may be one " (John xvii. 21) : but since offences do come, they are no hurt, to these, but even a benefit: just as the persecutors unwillingly benefit the Martyrs by dragging them to martyrdom, and yet they are not driven to this by God ; just so is it here. Let us not look (only at this), that men are offended : this very thing is itself a proof of the excellence of the doctrine—that many stimulate and counterfeit it : for it would not be so, if it were not good. And this I will now show, and make on all hands plain to you. Of perfumes, the fragrant spices are they which people adulterate and counterfeit ; as, for instance, the amomum leaf. For because these are rare and of necessary use, therefore there come to be spurious imitations likewise. Nobody would care to counterfeit any common article. The pure life gets many a false pretender to it : no man would care to counterfeit the man of vicious life ; no, but the man of monastic life.—What then shall we say to the heathen ? There comes a heathen and says, " I wish to become a Christian, but I know not whom to join : there is much fighting and faction among you, much confusion : which doctrine am I to

---

[1] Mss. and Edd. have this clause, ἄνω κάτω βάρος καλοῦσι after Πνεύματος γάρ ἦν νομοθεσία, and give the καὶ πάλιν to συναγαγόντες. After the clause "For that was a superfluous burden" seems to be the proper place for these sentences from below, see note [3], infra. "It shows that the rest are not necessary but superfluous, seeing these things are necessary. "From which if ye keep yourselves ye shall do well." It shows that nothing is lacking to them, but this is sufficient."

[2] Here insert from below : "For it might have been done also without letters—they did this."

[3] What follows consists of notes which the redactor did not bring to their proper places. "No more faction—admired it," see note [1], p. 207. "It shows—the Spirit," may belong either to the comment on κρίνω ἐγώ, or to that on " It seemed good to the Holy Ghost and to us."—" It shows that the rest—sufficient," see note [1]. These parts being removed, the remainder forms the continuation of the sentence, " it behooved to be done by these," note [2]. The concluding words καὶ μετ'εἰρήνης are the reporter's abridgment of the text " καὶ [ἐπεστήριξαν, ποιήσαντες δὲ χρόνον ἀπελυθησαν] μετ' εἰρήνης.

* The author here assumes the identity of the two visits of Paul to Jerusalem contained in Acts xv. and Gal. i. and ii. This has always been the prevailing view. For a full discussion of this and other views, see Gloag, Com. on the Acts ii. 80-84.—G. B. S.

[4] The famine is mentioned among the offences within, perhaps because it may have led some to question the Providence of God: see above, p. 159.

choose?" How shall we answer him? "Each of you" (says he) "asserts, '*I* speak the truth.'" (*b*) No[1] doubt: this is in our favor. For if we told you to be persuaded by arguments, you might well be perplexed: but if we bid you believe the Scriptures, and these are simple and true, the decision is easy for you. If any agree with the Scriptures, he is the Christian; if any fight against them, he is far from this rule. (*a*) "But which am I to believe, knowing as I do nothing at all of the Scriptures? The others also allege the same thing for themselves. What then (*c*) if the other come, and say that the Scripture has this, and you that it has something different, and ye interpret the Scriptures diversely, dragging their sense (each his own way)?" And you then, I ask, have you no understanding, no judgment? "And how should I be able (to decide)," says he, "I who do not even know how to judge of your doctrines? I wish to become a learner, and you are making me forthwith a teacher." If he say this, what, say you, are we to answer him? How shall we persuade him? Let us ask whether all this be not mere pretence and subterfuge. Let us ask whether he has decided (κατέγνωκε) against the heathen (that they are wrong). The fact[2] he will assuredly affirm, for of course, if he had not so decided, he would not have come to (enquire about) our matters: let us ask the grounds on which he has decided, for to be sure he has not settled the matter out of hand. Clearly he will say, "Because (their gods) are creatures, and are not the uncreated God." Good. If then he find this in the other parties (αἱρέσεις), but among us the contrary, what argument need we? We all confess that Christ is God. But let us see who fight (against this truth), and who not. Now we, affirming Him to be God, speak of Him things worthy of God, that He hath power, that He is not a slave, that He is free, that He doeth of Himself: whereas the other says the reverse. Again I ask: if you would learn (to be) a physician,[3] * * *? And

yet among them are many (different) doctrines. For if you accept without more ado just what you are told, this is not acting like a man: but if you have judgment and sense, you shall assuredly know what is good. We affirm the Son to be God, we verify (ἐπαληθεί-ομεν) what we affirm: but they affirm indeed, but (in fact) confess not.—But[4] to mention (something) even plainer: those have certain persons from whom they are called, openly showing the name of the heresiarch himself, and each heresy in like manner: with us, no man has given us a name, but the faith itself. However, this (talk of yours) is mere pretence and subterfuge. For answer me: how is it that if you would buy a cloak, though ignorant of the art of weaving, you do not speak such words as these—"I do not know how to buy; they cheat me"—but do all you can to learn, and so whatever else it be that you would buy: but here you speak these words? For at this rate, you will accept nothing at all. For let there be one that has no (religious) doctrine whatever: if he should say what you say about the Christians—"There is such a multitude of men, and they have different doctrines; this a heathen, that a Jew, the other a Christian: no need to accept any doctrine whatever, for they are at variance one with another; but I am a learner, and do not wish to be a judge"[5]—but if you have yielded (so far as) to pronounce against (καταγινώσκειν) one doctrine, this pretext no longer has place for you. For just as you were able to reject the spurious, so here also, having come, you shall be able to prove what is profitable. For he that has not pronounced against any doctrine at all, may easily say this: but he that has pronounced against any, though he have chosen none, by going on in the same way, will be able to see what he ought to do. Then let us not make pretexts and excuses, and all will be easy. For, to show you that all this is mere excuse, answer me this: Do you know what you ought to do, and what to leave undone? Then why do you not what you ought? Do that, and by right reason seek of God, and He will assuredly reveal it to thee. "God," it saith, "is no respecter of persons, but in every nation he that feareth Him, and worketh righteousness, is accepted with Him."

---

[1] Mss. and Edd. transpose the parts marked *a* and *b*. The old text, however, by retaining τί οὖν at the end of *a*, as well as at the beginning of *c*, enables us to restore the order, so that then the clause μηδὲν ὅλως εἰδὼς ἐν ταῖς Γραφαῖς, no longer disturbs the sense.

[2] Edd. πάντως τι ἐρεῖ. A. B. C. πάντως ὅτι ἐρεῖ. "In any wise he will affirm the ὅτι, therefore let us ask the αἰτίας δι ἅς."

[3] εἰ ἰατρὸς μέλλοις μανθάνειν. Mod. text adds, "Say, Do you accept out of hand and as it chances, whatever you are told?" The connection is: "Apply your mind to what you hear, whether from us or from them, and see whether of us is consistent. Just as you would if you wished to learn medicine: there also you would find conflicting opinions and you would exercise your judgment upon them, not accept all without examination. Do so here; and in the instance which has been taken, you will see that we, affirming the Son to be God, carry out our affirmation consistently; whereas they (the Arians) say indeed that He is God, but in fact deny Him the essential properties of Deity."—Edd. and all our Mss. Υἱὸν λέγομεν ἡμεῖς ἐπαληθεύομεν κ. τ. λ. We must read either Θεὸν or Υἱὸν Θεόν.

[4] Connection: I have mentioned one simple criterion: here is another palpable and visible mark. Heretics take their names from men, the founders of their sects, τοῦ αἱρεσιάρχου δηλοῦντος A. B. καλοῦντος C., τὸ ὄνομα Sav. marg. δηλοῦντες, which we adopt. But indeed the reasons you allege are mere pretence, etc.

[5] The sentence is left unfinished: "it would be no wonder," "this would be at least consistent," or the like: then εἰ δὲ εἴξω B. C. ἤξω (sic) A., ἤξω D. Mod. text οὐδὲ ἔξω: all corrupt. The sense seems to require, "If you have thought fit," or "gone so far as."

(ch. x. 34, 35.) It cannot be that he who hears without prejudice should not be persuaded. For just as, if there were a rule, by which everything behooved to be put straight, it would not need much consideration, but it would be easy to detect the person who measures falsely (τὸν παραμετροῦντα λαβεῖν), so is it here. "Then how is it they do not see it at a glance?" Many things are the cause of this: both preconceived opinion, and human causes (αἰτίαι). The others, say you, say the same thing about us. How? For are we separated from the Church? have we our heresiarchs? Are we called after men—as one of them has Marcion,[1] another Manichæus, a third Arius, for the author and leader (of his sect)? Whereas if we likewise do receive an appellation from any man, we do not take them that have been the authors of some heresy, but men that presided over us, and governed the Church. We have no "masters upon the earth"—God forbid—we have "One Master

that is in heaven." (Matt. xxiii. 9, 10.) "And those also," says he, "say the same." But there stands the name set over them, accusing them, and stopping their mouths.— How[2] is it, there have been many heathen, and none of them asked these questions: and among the philosophers there were these (differences), and yet none of those holding the right party (αἵρεσιν) was hindered (thereby)?— Why did not (those believers) say, when (the others) raised these questions, "Both these and those are Jews: which must we believe?" But they believed as they ought. Then let us also obey the laws of God, and do all things according to His good pleasure,[3] that having virtuously passed this life present, we may be enabled to attain unto the good things promised to them that love Him, by the grace and mercy of our Lord Jesus Christ, with Whom to the Father and the Holy Ghost together, be glory, dominion, honor, now and ever, world without end. Amen.

HOMILY XXXIV.

ACTS XV. 35.

"Paul also and Barnabas continued in Antioch, teaching and preaching the word of the Lord, with many others also."

OBSERVE again their humility, how they let others also take part in the preaching. "And some days after Paul said unto Barnabas, Let us go again and visit our brethren in every city where we have preached the word of the Lord, and see how they do. And Barnabas determined to take with them John, whose surname was Mark. But Paul thought not good (ἠξίου see note [3], p. 213) to take him with them, who departed from them from Pamphylia, and went not with them to the work. And the contention (or exasperation) was so sharp between them, that they departed asunder one from the other." (v. 36–39.) And already indeed Luke has described to us the

character of the Apostles,[4] that the one was more tender and indulgent, but this one more strict and austere. For the gifts are diverse —(the gifts, I say), for that this is a gift is manifest—but the one befitting one, the other another set of characters, and if they change places, harm results instead of good. (b) In the Prophets[5] too we find this: diverse minds, diverse characters: for instance, Elias austere, Moses meek. So here Paul is more vehement. And observe for all this, how gentle he is. "Thought not good," it says, "to take him with them that had departed from them from Pamphylia." (a) And there seems indeed to be exasperation (παροξυσμός), but in fact the whole matter is a plan of the Divine Providence, that each should receive his proper place: and it behooved that they

---

[1] Sav. marg. adds, "another, Paul of Samosata."
[2] Διὰ τί πολλοὶ γεγόνασιν Ἕλληνες, καὶ οὐδεὶς κ. τ. λ. Mod. text omits διὰ τι. The first clause seems to be corrupt, or misplaced: for to say that "there have been many heathen, and none of them has asked these questions" (about Christian doctrines), would contradict all that precedes: and if it means, There were many Greeks, and diverse schools of philosophy among them, and yet none was deterred from the study of philosophy by those differences, this would not be true. But if this be transposed to the following sentence, which relates to the Ἕλληνες at Antioch, then Chrys. says: "Among philosophers also there were these differences, and yet) etc. How is it that (at Antioch) many Greeks became (Christians) and yet none of them asked these questions? Why did they not say," etc.

[3] Edd. have a longer peroration from F, partly followed by D. "And live according to His will while we are yet in this life present, that with virtue having accomplished the remaining time of our life, we may be able, etc., and together with them which have pleased Him be found worthy of honor, by the grace and loving-kindness of His only-begotten Son, and the All-holy and Life-giving Spirit, the One true Godhead, now and ever, world without end." Amen.
[4] Mss. and Edd. after τῶν ἀποστόλων add τῶν λοιπῶν, which we omit as evidently out of place: for "the Apostles" here are Paul and Barnabas. Possibly it should be διὰ τῶν λοιπῶν, "by the rest of the particulars related on former occasions," but if so, this must be placed after τῶν ἀπ. τὸ ἦθος.
[5] The notes of this Homily have fallen into extreme confusion, and we have but partially succeeded in restoring the true order.

should not be upon a par, but the one should lead, and the other be led. "And so Barnabas took Mark, and sailed unto Cyprus; and Paul chose Silas, and departed, being recommended by the brethren unto the grace of God. And he went through Syria and Cilicia, confirming the Churches." (v. 39–41.) And this also is a work of Providence. For the Cyprians had exhibited nothing of the like sort as they at Antioch and the rest: and those needed the softer character, but these needed such a character as Paul's. "Which[1] then," say you, "did well? he that took, or he that left?" * * * (c) For just as a general would not choose to have a low person always to his baggage-bearer, so neither did the Apostle. This corrected the others, and instructed (Mark) himself. "Then did Barnabas ill?" say you. "And how is it not amiss (ἄτοπον), that upon so small a matter there should arise so great an evil?" In the first place then, no evil did come of it, if, sufficing each for whole nations, they were divided the one from the other, but a great good. And besides, they would not readily have chosen to leave each other. But admire, I pray you, the writer, how he does not conceal this either. "But at any rate," say you, "if they must needs part, let it be without exasperation." Nay, but if nothing more, observe this, that in this too is shown what was of man[2] (in the preaching of the Gospel). For if the like behooved to be shown (even) in what Christ did, much more here. And besides, the contention cannot be said to be evil, when each disputes for such objects (as here) and with just reason. I grant you, if the exasperation were in seeking his own, and contending for his own honor, this might well be (reproved): but if wishing, both the one and the other, to instruct and teach, the one took this way and the other that, what is there to find fault with? For in many things they acted upon their human judgment; for they were not stocks or stones. And observe how Paul impeaches (Mark), and gives the

reason. For of his exceeding humility[3] he reverenced Barnabas, as having been partner with him in so great works, and being with him: but still he did not so reverence him, as to overlook (what was necessary). Now which of them advised best, it is not for us to pronounce: but thus far (we may affirm), that it was a great arrangement of Providence, if these[4] were to be vouchsafed a second visitation, but those were not to be visited even once.*

(a) "Teaching and preaching the word of the Lord." (v. 35.) They[5] did not simply tarry in Antioch, but taught. What did they "teach," and what "preach" (evangelize)? They both (taught) those that were already believers, and (evangelized) those that were not yet such. "And some days after," etc. (v. 36.) For because there were offences without number, their presence was needed. (d) "How they do," he says. And this he did not know: naturally. See him ever alert, solicitous, not bearing to sit idle, though he underwent dangers without end. Do you mark, it was not of cowardice that he came to Antioch? He acts just as a physician does in the case of the sick. And the need of visiting them he showed by saying, "In which we preached the word. And Barnabas determined," etc. (v. 37–40.) (So) Barnabas[6] "departed, and went not with (him)." (b) The point to be considered, is not that they differed in their opinions, but that they accommodated themselves the one to the other (seeing), that thus it was a greater good their being parted:[7] and

[1] Mod. text omits this question: C. for ἀφεὶς has ἀφεθείς, "he that was left, or, dismissed." Part of the answer has dropped out, "Paul did well: for" etc. The interlocutor rejoins: "Then if Paul did well, Barnabas did ill?" Here Edd. and all our Mss. οὐκοῦν, φησί, κακὸς ὁ Βαρνάβας; to which mod. text adds, "By no means: but it is even exceedingly absurd to imagine this. And how is it not absurd to say, that for so small a matter this man became evil?" We restore οὐκοῦν κακῶς ὁ Βαρνάβας;

[2] μάλιστα μὲν οὖν καὶ ἐντεῦθεν (as by other instances of human infirmity, so by this also) δείκνυται τὰ ἀνθρώπινα, i. e. we are shown what in the preaching of the Gospel proceeded from man: that man, as man, did his part, which part is betokened by the ordinary characters of human nature. If even in Christ it behooved that He should not do all as God, but that His Human Nature should also be seen working, much more was it necessary that the Apostles, being but men, should work as men, not do all by the immediate power of the Spirit.

[3] This refers to ἠξίου in the sense "he begged," as he says below, in the beginning of the Recapitulation, καίτοι οὐκ ἔδει ἀξιοῦν αὐτὸν ἔχοντα κατηγορεῖν μετὰ ταῦτα.

[4] If this sentence be in its place, something is wanting for connection: e. g. (It was a great οἰκονομία) for the more extended preaching of the word: since on Barnabas's plan these "at Cyprus" were to have a second visitation, but those "in Asia" not even once. But it may be suspected that this part is altogether misplaced: and that the οὗτοι are the brethren "in the cities where we have preached," and ἐκεῖνοι the people of Macedonia," etc. See end of Recap. where Chrys. says, had it not been for this parting, the word would not have been carried into Macedonia.

* Chrys. has treated the dissension of Paul and Barnabas with discrimination, without, however, placing quite the emphasis upon ἠξίου—"he thought good not to"—"he determined not to"—and upon τὸν ἀποστάντα—"who had fallen away from"—apostated from,"—which those terms seem to require. The conduct of Mark in returning to Jerusalem from Pamphylia (Acts xiii. 13) was clearly regarded as reprehensible by Paul, apparently as an example of fickleness in the service of Christ. It is not strange that Barnabas, Mark's cousin (Col. iv. 10) should have been more lenient in his judgment of his conduct. It is certain that this difference of opinion regarding Mark did not lead to any estrangement of Paul and Mark, for in his imprisonment the apostle speaks of Mark as a trusted fellow-worker (Col. iv. 10; 2 Tim. iv. 11).—G. B. S.

[5] The method of the derangement here is, that there being five portions, these were taken alternately, in the order 1, 3, 5, and then 2, 4.

[6] So Edd. and all our Mss. ἀπέστη ἀπ' αὐτῶν ὁ Βαρνάβας: which may mean, "And so the same may now be said of Barnabas, viz. that he departed (from Paul)," etc. The same word ἀπέστη is applied to Barnabas below, p. 216.

[7] συγκατέβησαν ἀλλήλοις οὕτω μεῖζον ἀγαθὸν εἶναι τὸ χωρισθῆναι. The meaning is as below. that they parted κατὰ σύνεσιν. Mod. text "συγκατ. ἀλλ. ἰδεῖν. The point required

the matter took a pretext from this What then? did they withdraw in enmity? God forbid! In fact you see after this Barnabas receiving many encomiums from Paul in the Epistles. There was "sharp contention," it says, not enmity nor quarrelling. The contention availed so far as to part them. "And Barnabas took Mark," etc. And with reason: for what each supposed to be profitable, he did not forego[1] thereafter, because of the fellowship with the other. Nay, it seems to me that the parting took place advisedly (κατὰ σύνεσιν), and that they said one to another, "As I wish not, and thou wishest, therefore, that we may not fight, let us distribute the places." So that in fact they did this, altogether yielding each to the other: for Barnabas wished Paul's plan to stand, therefore withdrew; on the other hand, Paul wished the other's plan to stand, therefore he withdrew. Would to God we too made such separations, as to go forth for preaching. A wonderful man this is; and exceedingly great! To Mark this contest was exceedingly beneficial. For the awe inspired by Paul converted him, while the kindness of Barnabas caused that he was not left behind: so that they contend indeed, but the gain comes to one and the same end. For indeed, seeing Paul choosing to leave him, he would be exceedingly awed, and would condemn himself, and seeing Barnabas so taking his part, he would love him exceedingly: and so the disciple was corrected by the contention of the teachers: so far was he from being offended thereby. For if indeed they did this with a view to their own honor, he might well be offended: but if for his salvation, and they contend for one and the same object, to show that he who honored him * * * had well determined,[2] what is there amiss (ἄτοπον) in it?

(e) "But Paul," it says, "departed, having chosen Silas, and being commended to the grace of God." What is this? They prayed it says: they besought God. See on all occasions how the prayer of the brethren can do great things. And now he journeyed by land, wishing even by his journeying to benefit

those who saw (τοὺς ὁρῶντας) him. For when indeed they were in haste they sailed, but now not so. (c) "And he went through Syria and Cilicia, confirming the Churches. Then came he to Derbe and Lystra." (v. 41.) Mark the wisdom of Paul: he does not go to other cities before he has visited them which had received the Word. For it is folly to run at random. This let us also do: let us teach the first in the first place, that these may not become an hindrance to them that are to come after.

"And, behold a certain disciple was there, named Timotheus, the son of a certain woman, which was a Jewess, and believed; but his father was a Greek: which was well reported of by the brethren that were at Lystra and Iconium. Him would Paul have to go forth with him; and took and circumcised him because of the Jews which were in those quarters; for they knew all that his father was a Greek." (ch. xvi. 1–3.) It is indeed amazing, the wisdom of Paul! He that has had so many battles about circumcision, he that moved all things to this end, and did not give over until he had carried his point, now that the decree is made sure, circumcises the disciple. He not only does not forbid others, but himself does this thing. (b) "Him," it says, "he would have to go forth with him." And the wonder is this, that he even took him unto him.[3] "Because of the Jews," it says, "which were in those parts: " for they would not endure to hear the word from one uncircumcised. (a) Nothing could be wiser. So that in all things he looked to what was profitable: he did nothing upon his own preference (προλήψει). (c) And what (then)? Mark the success: he circumcised, that he might take away circumcision: for he preached the decrees of the Apostles. "And as they went through the cities, they delivered them the decrees for to keep, that were ordained of the Apostles and elders which were at Jerusalem. And so were the Churches established in the faith, and increased in number daily." (v. 4, 5.) Dost thou mark fighting, and by fighting, edification? Not warred upon by others, but themselves doing contrary things, so they edified the Church! They introduced a decree not to circumcise, and he circumcises! "And so were the Churches," it says, "established in the faith," and in multitude: "increased," it says, "in number daily." Then he does not continue to tarry with these, as having come to visit them: but how? he goes fur-

---

is to see that," etc. Then, Οὕτω μ. ἀ. γέγονε τὸ χωρ. "Thus their being parted became a greater good," etc.—Καὶ πρόφασιν ἐκ τούτου τὸ πρᾶγμα ἔλαβε, i. e. "They saw that it was best to part, viz.: that so the word would be more extensively preached, and this difference gave a pretext for so doing." He means that the contention was οἰκονομία (see the Recap.), the object being, partly this which is here mentioned, partly a lesson to Mark.

[1] Edd. and Mss. οὐ προσήκατο, against the sense of the passage, whence Œcum. omits the negative, not much improving it. The Catena has preserved the true reading, οὐ προήκατο. See instances of confusion the other way in Mr. Field's Index to *Hom. in Matt.* s. v. προσίημι.

[2] ὥστε δεῖξαι τὸν τιμήσαντα αὐτὸν καλῶς βεβουλευμένον. The sense requires τὸν τιμ. αὐτὸν καὶ τὸν μὴ τιμήσαντα καλῶς βεβ. or the like: "that both Barnabas and Paul had taken the course which was for his (Mark's) own good."

[3] ὅτι καὶ ἐπήγετο αὐτόν. The meaning seems to be, (but the confusion into which the text has fallen, leaves it very uncertain), "The wonder is that he took Timothy, being as he was the son of a heathen father, and uncircumcised."

ther. "Now when they had gone throughout Phrygia and the region of Galatia, and were forbidden of the Holy Ghost to preach the word in Asia," (v. 6.) having left Phrygia and Galatia, they hastened into the interior. For, it says, "After they were come to Mysia, they assayed to go into Bithynia: but the Spirit suffered them not." (v. 7.) Wherefore they were forbidden, he does not say, but that they were "forbidden," he does say, teaching us to obey and not ask questions, and showing that they did many things as men. "And the Spirit," it says, "suffered them not: but having passed by Mysia they came down to Troas." (v. 8.) "And a vision appeared to Paul in the night; There stood a man of Macedonia, and prayed him, saying, Come over into Macedonia, and help us." (v. 9.) Why a vision, and not the Holy Ghost? because He forbade the other.[1] He would even in this way draw them over: since to the saints also He appeared in a dream, and in the beginning (Paul) himself saw a vision, " a man coming in and laying his hands upon him." (ch. ix. 12.) In[2] this manner also Christ appears to him, saying, "Thou must stand before Cæsar." Then for this reason also He draws him thither, that the preaching may be extended. This is why he was forbidden to tarry long in the other cities, Christ urging him on. For these were to enjoy the benefit of John for a long time, and perhaps did not extremely need him (Paul), but thither he behooved to go. And now he crosses over and goes forth. "And after he had seen the vision, immediately we endeavored to go into Macedonia, assuredly gathering that the Lord had called us for to preach the Gospel unto them." (v. 10.) Then the writer mentions also the places, as relating a history, and showing where he made a stay (namely), in the greater cities, but passed by the rest. "Therefore loosing from Troas, we came with a straight course to Samothracia, and the next day to Neapolis; and from thence to Philippi, which is the chief city of that part of Macedonia, and a colony." (v. 11, 12.) It is a high distinction for a city, the being a colony. "And in this city we were tarrying certain days." But let us look over again what has been said.

(Recapitulation.) "And after some days,

Paul said," etc. (ch. xv. 36.) He put to Barnabas a necessity for their going abroad, saying "Let us visit the cities in which we preached the word." "But Paul begged," etc. (v. 38.) And yet no need for him to beg, who had to make an accusation presently. This[3] happens even in the case where God and men are the parties: the man requests, God is wroth. For instance, when He saith, "If her father had spit in her face " (Num. xii. 14): and again, "Let me alone, and in Mine anger I will blot out this people." (Ex. xxxii. 32.) And Samuel when he mourns for Saul. (1 Sam. xv. 35.) For by both, great good is done. Thus also here: the one is wroth, the other not so. The same happens also in matters where we are concerned. And the sharp contention with good reason, that Mark may receive a lesson, and the affair may not seem mere stage-playing. For it is not to be thought that he[4] who bids, "Let not the sun go down upon your wrath," (Eph. iv. 26) would have been wroth because of such a matter as this: nor that he who on all occasions gave way would not have given way here, he who so greatly loved Paul that before this he sought him in Tarsus, and brought him to the Apostles, and undertook the alms in common with him, and in common the business relating to the decree. But they take themselves so as to instruct and make perfect by their separation them that need the teaching which was to come from them. And he rebukes others indeed, but bids do good to all men. As in fact he does elsewhere, saying, "But ye, be not weary in well-doing."

---

[1] ὅτι ἐκεῖνο ἐκώλυσεν. Mod. text καὶ μὴ τὸ Πν. τὸ Α. ἐκέλευσεν; But see the Recap. where the question is explained, viz., How is it that when they were to be kept from preaching, the Holy Ghost spoke to them, but here a vision, and that in a dream, is all?

[2] In the Mss. this sentence is placed before "And now he crosses over," etc. v. 10.—'In this manner:' i. e. in a night-vision or dream: the allusion is to xxiii. 11, "the Lord stood by him," confused with xxvii. 23, "the Angel of the Lord."

[3] i. e. just displeasure on the one side; lenity, compassion, intercession, etc. on the other. Thus God is wroth with Miriam, Moses pleads for her, and so in the other cases.

[4] Mod. text omits this clause relating to St. Paul, as in the old text it is incomplete, the remainder of the sentence ("would not have been wroth," etc.) having been transposed to the end of what relates to Barnabas, after "relating to the decree."—Below, ἀλλὰ λαμβάνουσιν ἑαυτοὺς, may perhaps be ἑαυτοῖς, sc. τοὺς δεομένους below, i. e. choose their spheres of action where each was most needed. But the context rather seems to require this sense: "There is no animosity between them, but they take their parts in this dispute for the good of those who, as Mark, need the instruction which was to be derived from the gentleness of Barnabas, and the severity of Paul's character. Paul indeed is stern, but his object is to do good: as 2 Thess. iii. 13, where (comp. the context) rebuking, and enjoining severity to be shown to the disorderly, he says, "And be not weary in well-doing." We have changed the order of the two sentences, "And he rebukes," etc. and, "As he does elsewhere," etc.—Τοῦτο καὶ ἐν τῇ συνηθείᾳ ποιοῦμεν. i. e. this putting on a show of anger, to do good to one whom we would correct: or perhaps, of altercation, as when, for instance, father and mother take opposite parts, the one for punishing, the other for sparing an erring child—συναγανακτῆσαι τῷ Παυλῷ. Ben. indignati esse in Paulum. But whether it means this, or "to have had indignation together with Paul," there is nothing to show: nor is it clear what is the reference of the following sentences; unless it be, But he would not allow these persons who were indignant along with, or at, him, to retain this feeling: he takes them apart, makes them see the thing in its right light, and so departs in peace, "being commended by the brethren to the grace of God," with the prayers of concord and charity. Great is the power of such prayer. (See the former comment on this verse, p. 214.)—Κἂν ὑπὲρ μεγάλου ἀξιοῖς, κἂν ἀνάξιος ἧς. Perhaps it should be ἢ, "Whether it be on behalf of a great man (as Paul), or whether the person be unworthy," etc.

(2 Thess. iii. 13.) This we also do in our common practice. Here it seems to me that others also were alike displeased with Paul. And thereupon taking them also apart, he does all, and exhorts and admonishes. Much can concord do, much can charity. Though it be for a great matter thou askest; though thou be unworthy, thou shalt be heard for thy purpose of heart: fear not.

"He went," it says, "through" the cities "And, behold, there was a disciple, by name Timothy, who had a good report of the brethren which were in Lystra and Iconium." (v. 41; xvi. 1.) Great was the grace of Timothy. When Barnabas departed (ἀπέστη), he finds another, equivalent to him. Of him he saith, "Remembering thy tears and thy unfeigned faith, which dwelt first in thy grandmother Lois, and in thy mother Eunice." (2 Tim. i, 5.) His father continued to be a Gentile,[1] and therefore it was that (Timothy) was not circumcised. (a) Observe the Law already broken. Or if not so, I suppose he was born after the preaching of the Gospel: but this is perhaps not so. (c) He was about to make him a bishop, and it was not meet that he should be uncircumcised. (e) And this was not a small matter, seeing it offended after so long a time:[2] (b) "for from a child," he says, "thou hast known the Holy Scriptures." (ib. iii. 15.) (d) "And as they went through the cities, they delivered them the decrees for to keep." (v. 4.) For until then, there was no need for the Gentiles to keep any such. The beginning of the abrogation was the Gentiles' not keeping these things, and being none the worse for it: nor having any inferiority in respect of faith: anon, of their own will they abandoned the Law. (f) Since therefore he was about to preach, that he might not smite the Jews a

double blow, he circumcised Timothy. And yet he was but half (a Jew by birth),[3] his father being a Greek: but yet, because that was a great point carried in the cause of the Gentiles, he did not care for this: for the Word must needs be disseminated: therefore also he with his own hands circumcised him.[*] "And so were the churches established in the faith." Do you mark here also how from going counter (to his own object) a great good results? "And increased in number daily." (v. 5.) Do you observe, that the circumcising not only did no harm, but was even of the greatest service? "And a vision appeared unto Paul in the night." (v. 9.) Not now by Angels, as to Philip, as to Cornelius, but how? By a vision it is now shown to him: in more human sort, not now as before (i. e., v. 6, 7) in more divine manner. For where the compliance is more easy, it is done in more human sort; but where great force was needed, there in more divine. For since he was but urged to preach, to this end it is shown him in a dream: but to forbear preaching, he could not readily endure: to this end the Holy Ghost reveals it to him. Thus also it was then with Peter, "Arise, go down." (ch. x. 20.) For of course the Holy Spirit did not work what was otherwise easy: but (here) even a dream sufficed him. And to Joseph also, as being readily moved to compliance, the appearance is in a dream, but to the rest in waking vision. (Matt. i. 20; ii. 13, 19.) Thus to Cornelius, and to Paul himself. "And lo, a man of Macedonia," etc. and not simply enjoining, but "beseeching," and from the very persons in need of (spiritual) cure. (ch. x. 3; ix. 3.) "Assuredly gathering," it says, "that the Lord had called us." (v. 10), that is, inferring, both from the circumstance that Paul saw it and none other, and from the having been "forbidden by the Spirit," and from their being on the borders; from all these they gathered. "Therefore loosing from Troas, we came with a straight course," etc. (v. 11.) That is, even the voy-

---

[1] So in Gen. *Serm.* ix. text iv. 695. D. Chrys. infers from this passage with 2 Tim. i. 5, that the father ἔμεινεν ἐν τῇ ἀσεβείᾳ καὶ οὐ μετεβάλλετο. *Hom.* i. *in 2 Tim.* p. 660. E. "Because of his father who was a Gentile, and because of the Jews he took and circumcised him. Do you mark how the Law began to be dissolved, in the taking place of these mixed marriages?" (so here ὅρα ἤδη τὸν νόμον λυόμενον.) In the Mss. all this is extremely confused by transpositions (the method; 1, 4: 2, 5: 3, 6) and misplacing of the portions of sacred text (where these are given). Thus here, "And therefore because of the Jews which were in those parts he circumcised him. Οὐκ ἦν ἐμπερίτομος."—Mod. text "thy mother Eunice. And he took and circumcised him. And wherefore, he himself goes on to say: Because of the Jews, etc. For this reason then he is circumcised. Or also because of his father: for he continued to be a Greek. So then he was not circumcised. Observe the Law already broken. But some think he was born," etc. He is commenting on the fact, that Timothy was uncircumcised: viz., because his father was a heathen. Here then was a devout man, who from a child had known the Holy Scriptures, and yet continued uncircumcised. So that in these mixed marriages we see the Law already broken, independently of the Gospel. It may be indeed that he was born after the conversion of his mother to the faith, and therefore she was not anxious to circumcise him. But this (he adds) is not likely.

[2] For Timothy from a child had been brought up religiously as a Jew, yet now it was an offence that he should continue uncircumcised.

[3] Therefore he might have been exempt by the Apostles' decree. St. Paul, however, having carried his point in securing the immunity of the Gentile converts, did not care to insist upon this in behalf of Timothy.

[*] Our author correctly apprehends the ground on which Paul circumcised Timothy—an act which has often been thought to be inconsistent with his steadfast resistance to the imposition of the Jewish law. It is noticeable that he did not allow Titus to be circumcised (Gal. ii. 3) when the Jewish-Christian faction desired it. The two cases are materially different in the following particulars: (1) Titus was a Gentile; Timothy was born of a Jewish mother. (2) The circumcision of Titus was demanded by the Judaizers; that of Timothy was performed for prudential reasons as a concession to unbelieving Jews in order that Paul might the better win them to Christ. (3) The question of circumcising Titus was a doctrinal question which was not the case in the instance before us. Meyer well says: "Paul acted according to the principle of wise and conciliatory accommodation, not out of concession to the Judaistic dogma of the necessity of circumcision for obtaining the Messianic salvation."—G. B. S.

age made this manifest : for there was no tardiness. It became the very root of Macedonia.[1] It was not always in the way of "sharp contention" that the Holy Spirit wrought : but this so rapid progress (of the Word) was a token that the thing was more than human. And yet it is not said that Barnabas was exasperated, but, "Between them there arose a sharp contention." (v. 39.) If the one was not exasperated neither was the other.

Knowing this, let us not merely pick out (ἐκλέγωμεν) these things, but let us learn and be taught by them : for they were not written without a purpose. It is a great evil to be ignorant of the Scriptures : from the things we ought to get good from, we get evil. Thus also medicines of healing virtue, often, from the ignorance of those who use them, ruin and destroy : and arms which are meant to protect, are themselves the cause of death, unless one know how to put them on. But the reason is, that we seek everything rather than what is good for ourselves. And in the case of a house, we seek what is good for it, and we would not endure to see it decaying with age, or tottering, or hurt by storms : but for our soul we make no account : nay, even should we see its foundations rotting, or the fabric and the roof, we make no account of it. Again, if we possess brute creatures, we seek what is good for them : we call in both horse-feeders and horse-doctors, and all besides :[2] we attend to their housing, and charge those who are entrusted with them, that they may not drive them at random or carelessly, nor take them out by night at unseasonable hours, nor sell away their provender ; and there are many laws laid down by us for the good of the brute creatures : but for that of our soul, there is no account taken. But why speak I of brute creatures which are useful to us ? There are many who keep small birds (or "sparrows") "which are useful for nothing except that they simply amuse, and there are many laws even about them, and nothing is

neglected or without order, and we take care for everything rather than for our own selves. Thus we make our selves more worthless than all. And if indeed a person abusively call us "dog," we are annoyed : but while we are opprobrious to ourselves, not in word, but in deed, and do not even bestow as much care on our soul as on dogs, we think it no great harm. Do you see how all is full of darkness ? How many are careful about their dogs, that they may not be filled with more than the proper food, that so they may be keen and fit for hunting, being set on by famine and hunger : but for themselves they have no care to avoid luxury : and the brute creatures indeed they teach to exercise philosophy, while they let themselves sink down into the savageness of the brutes. The thing is a riddle. "And where are your philosophic brutes ?" There are such ; or, say, do you not take it to be philosophy, when a dog gnawed with hunger, after having hunted and caught his prey, abstains from the food ; and though he sees his meal ready before him, and with hunger urging him on, yet waits for his master ? Be ashamed of yourselves : teach your bellies to be as philosophic. You have no excuse. When you have been able to implant such philosophic self-command in an irrational nature, which neither speaks nor hears reason, shall you not much more be able to implant it in yourself ? For that it is the effect of man's care, not of nature is plain : since otherwise all dogs ought to have this habit. Do you then become as dogs. For it is you that compel me to fetch my examples thence : for indeed they should be drawn from heavenly things ; but since if I speak of those, you say, "Those are (too) great," therefore I speak nothing of heavenly things : again, if I speak of Paul, you say, "He was an Apostle :" therefore neither do I mention Paul : if again I speak of a man, you say, "That person could do it :" therefore I do not mention a man even, but a brute creature ; a creature too, that has not this habit by nature, lest you should say that it effected this by nature, and not (which is the fact) from choice : and what is wonderful, choice not self-acquired, but (the result of) your care. The creature does not give a thought to the fatigue, the wear and tear it has undergone in running down the prey, not a thought to this, that by its own proper toil it has made the capture : but casting away all these regards, it observes the command of its master, and shows itself superior to the cravings of appetite. "True ; because it looks to be praised, it looks to get a greater meal." Say then to yourself, that the dog through hope of

---

[1] A. B. C. Cat. εἰς αὐτὴν τὴν ῥίζαν τῆς Μακεδονίας ἐγένετο (Cat. ἐγένοντο). Οὐκ ἀεὶ (Cat., οὐκ ἂν εἰ) κατὰ παροξυσμὸν ἐνήργησε τὸ Πν. τὸ ᾿Α. The former sentence may possibly mean, that Philippi became the root of the Churches in Macedonia. But it is more probable that the text is mutilated here, and that Chrys. speaks of the parting of Paul and Barnabas, as having become the very root or cause of the extension of the Gospel (into Macedonia and Greece). In the next sentence, the reading of Cat. may perhaps deserve the preference. "Not, if (they had parted) in a state of exasperation, would the Holy Ghost have (thus) wrought."—Mod. text "And besides, even the voyage showed this : for there was no long time ere they arrive at the very root of Macedonia (ὅθεν εἰς . . . παραγίνονται). So that the sharp contention is providentially ordered to be for the best. For (otherwise) the Holy Ghost would not have wrought, Macedonia would not have received the Word. But this so rapid progress," etc.

[2] καὶ πάντα καλοῦμεν. Mod. text substitutes the proverbial expression, καὶ πάντα κάλων κινοῦμεν, "we put every rope in motion," which is hardly suitable here, and not at all necessary. "We call to our aid horse-feeders, and doctors, and every one else who can help us."

future pleasure, despises that which is present: while you do not choose for hope of future good things to despise those which are present; but he indeed knows, that, if he tastes of that food at the wrong time and against his master's will, he will both be deprived of that, and not get even that which was apportioned to him, but receive blows instead of food: whereas you cannot even perceive this, and that which he has learnt by dint of custom, you do not succeed in acquiring even from reason. Let us imitate the dogs. The same thing hawks also and eagles are said to do: what the dogs do with regard to hares[1] and deer, the same do those with regard to birds; and these too act from a philosophy learnt from men. These facts are enough to condemn us, these enough to convict us. To mention another thing:—they that are skilled in breaking horses, shall take them, wild, fierce, kicking, biting, and in a short time so discipline them, that though the teacher be not there, it is a luxury to ride them, their paces are so thoroughly well-ordered: but the paces of the soul may be all disordered, and none cares for it: it bounds, and kicks, and its rider[2] is dragged along the ground like a child, and makes a most disgraceful figure, and yet no one puts curbs on her, and leg-ties, and bits, nor mounts upon her the skilful rider—Christ, I mean. And therefore it is that all is turned upside down. For when you both teach dogs to master the craving of the belly, and tame the fury in a lion, and the unruliness of horses, and teach the birds to speak plainly, how inconsistent must it not be—to implant achievements of reason in natures that are without reason, and to import the passions of creatures without reason into natures endowed with reason? There is no excuse for us, none. All who have succeeded (in mastering their passions) will accuse us, both believers and unbelievers: for even unbelievers have so succeeded; yea, and wild beasts, and dogs, not men only: and we shall accuse our own selves, since we succeed, when we will, but when we are slothful, we are dragged away. For indeed many even of those who live a very wicked life, have oftentimes changed themselves when they wished. But the cause is, as I said, that we go about seeking for what is good for other things, not what is good for ourselves. If you build a splendid house, you know what is good for the house, not what is good for youself: if you

take a beautiful garment, you know what is good for the body, not for yourself: and if you get a good horse, it is so likewise. None makes it his mark how his soul shall be beautiful; and yet, when that is beautiful, there is no need of any of those things: as, if that be not beautiful, there is no good of them. For like as in the case of a bride, though there be chambers hung with tapestry wrought with gold, though there be choirs of the fairest and most beautiful women, though there be roses and garlands, though there be a comely bridegroom, and the maidservants and female friends, and everybody about them be handsome, yet, if the bride herself be full of deformity, there is no good of all those; as on the other hand if she were beautiful, neither would there be any loss arising from (the want of) those, nay just the contrary; for in the case of an ugly bride, those would make her look all the uglier, while in the other case, the beautiful would look all the more beautiful: just so, the soul, when she is beautiful, not only needs none of those adjuncts, but they even cast a shade over her beauty. For we shall see the philosopher shine, not so much when in wealth, as in poverty. For in the former case many will impute it to his riches, that he is not superior to riches:[3] but when he lives with poverty for his mate, and shines through all, and will not let himself be compelled to do anything base, then none claims shares with him in the crown of philosophy. Let us then make our soul beauteous, if at least we would fain be rich. What profit is it, when your mules indeed are white and plump and in good condition, but you who are drawn by them are lean and scurvy and ill-favored? What is the gain, when your carpets indeed are soft and beautiful, full of rich embroidery and art, and your soul goes clad in rags, or even naked and foul? What the gain, when the horse indeed has his paces beautifully ordered, more like dancing than stepping, while the rider, together with his choral[4] train and adorned with more than bridal ornaments, is more crooked than the lame,

---

[1] Our Mss. have ἀλόγων: Savile (from N.?) λαγῶν, which we adopt.

[2] καὶ σύρεται χάμαι καθάπερ παιδίον, καὶ ἀσχημονεῖ μυρία: this cannot be meant for the horse, but for the rider. Perhaps καὶ οὐδεὶς, κἂν σύρεται κ τ. λ.

[3] καὶ τὸ but Sav. Marg. καὶ τῷ μὴ κρείττονα χρημάτων εἶναι: some slight emendation is necessary, but it is not clear whether it should be, καὶ μὴ τῷ . . . . "and not to his being above wealth:" i. e. good in spite of his riches: or καὶ τὸ μὴ . . . with some verb supplied, i. e. "and make it a reproach to him that (though a good man) he is not above riches," seeing he does not abandon his wealth.—Mod. text καὶ τῷ μὴ ἐνδεᾶ χρημάτων εἶναι.

[4] μᾶλλον μετὰ τῆς πορείας καὶ κόσμῳ κεκοσμημένος νυμφικῷ· ὁ δὲ ἐπικαθ. κ. τ. λ. The passage is corrupt: perhaps, as in the Translation, it should be μᾶλλον ἢ νυμφικῷ, but this as a description of the horse is evidently out of place. For πορ., we read χορείας as in mod. text (which has καὶ μετὰ τῆς χορείας κόσμῳ κεκ. ἢ νυμφικῷ.) Then transposing this, we read ὁ δὲ ἐπικαθ., μετὰ τῆς χορ., καὶ.—Below, B. C. ἂν σκολιάζῃ: A. and mod. text ἀσκωλιάζῃ—alluding to the game of leaping on greased bladders or skins, unctos salire per utres; which does not suit τῶν χωλῶν.

and has no more command over hands and feet than drunkards and madmen? Tell me now, if some one were to give you a beautiful horse, and to distort your body, what would be the profit? Now you have your soul distorted, and care you not for it? Let us at length, I beseech you, have a care for our own selves. Do not let us make our own selves more worthless than all beside. If any-one insult us with words, we are annoyed and vexed: but insulting ourselves as we do by our deeds, we do not give a thought to it. Let us, though late, come at last to our senses, that we may be enabled by having much care for our soul, and laying hold upon virtue, to obtain eternal good things, through the grace and mercy of our Lord Jesus Christ, with Whom to the Father, together with the Holy Spirit, be glory, might, honor, now and evermore, world without end. Amen.

HOMILY XXXV.

ACTS XVI. 13, 14.

"And on the sabbath we went out of the city by a river side, where prayer was wont (Chrys. "was thought likely") to be made; and we sat down, and spake unto the women which resorted thither. And a certain woman named Lydia, a seller of purple, of the city of Thyatira, which worshipped God, heard us: whose heart the Lord opened, that she attended unto the things which were spoken of Paul."

SEE again Paul judaizing. "Where[1] it was thought," it says, both from the time and from the place, "that prayer would be.—Out of the city, by a river side:" for it is not to be supposed that they prayed only where there was a synagogue; they also prayed out of synagogue, but then for this purpose they set apart, as it were, a certain place, because as Jews they were more corporeal—and, "on the sabbath-day," when it was likely that a multitude would come together.* "And we sat down, and spake to the women which resorted thither." Mark again the freedom from all pride. "And a certain woman:" a woman and she of low condition, from her trade too: but mark (in her) a woman of elevated mind (φιλόσοφον). In the first place, the fact of God's calling her bears testimony to her: "And when she was baptized," it says, "she and her household"—mark how he persuaded all of them—"she besought us, saying, If ye have judged me to be faithful to the Lord, come into my house, and abide there. And she constrained us[2]" (v. 15): then look at her wisdom, how she importunes (δυσωπεῖ), the Apostles how full of humility her words are, how full of wisdom. "If ye have judged me faithful," she says. Nothing could be more persuasive. Who would not have been softened by these words? She did not request (or, "claim") did not entreat simply: but she left them to decide, and (yet) exceedingly forced them: "And she constrained us," it says, by those words. And again in a different way: for see how she straightway bears fruit, and accounts it a great gain. "If ye have judged me," that is, That ye did judge me is manifest, by your delivering to me such (holy) mysteries (i. e. sacraments, see p. 225, note [3]): and she did not dare to invite them before this. But why was there any unwillingness on the part of Paul and those with them, that they should need to be constrained? It was either by way of calling her to greater earnestness of desire, or because Christ had said, "Enquire who is worthy, and there abide." (Luke x. 8.) (It was not that they were unwilling), but they did it for a purpose.[3]—"And it came to pass," it says, "as we went to prayer, a certain damsel possessed with a spirit of divination met us,†

---

[1] Mss. and Edd. place οὗ ἐν. προσευχὴ εἶναι after ἀπὸ τοῦ τόπου, so that it reads, " See Paul again judaizing both from the time and from the place." Chrys. here explains the ἐνομίζετο (in the sense "was thought"): viz. St. Paul expected to find a congregation assembled for prayer, both because the place was set apart for that purpose, and because it was the sabbath.

* Two variations of text occur in v. 13, which materially affect the meaning. Modern critics read πύλης St. πόλεως—" they went outside the gate" and ἐνομίζομεν instead of ἐνομίζετο—" where we supposed there was a place of prayer." (So B. C. א. R.V., Tischendorf, Westcott and Hort.) If the reading ἐνομίζετο is retained, it more probably means; "where a place of prayer was wont to be" rather than (as Chrys.) "where, it was thought, that prayer would be." The προσευχαι were places of prayer situated often in the open air, and chosen in the neighborhood of streams on account of the custom of washing the hands before prayer. They served the purposes of synagogues in places where they did not exist.—G. B. S.

[2] ἀλλ' αὐτοὺς ἀφῆκε κυρίους εἶναι, καί. Mod. text, οὐκ ἀφῆκε κ. ἐ., ἀλλὰ καί.

[3] Ἀλλὰ δὶ οἰκονομίαν ἐποίουν. B. Cat. "their seeming reluctance was 'economy.'" A. C., Ὅλα δὶ οἰκ. ἐπ. Mod. text, Ὥστε πάντα δὶ οἰκ. ἐπ.

† Most critical editions read in v. 16. πύθωνα st. πύθωνος (following A. B. C. א). In this case the word is in apposition with πνεῦμα and has the force of an adjective, "having a Pythonic spirit," in allusion to the serpent which was said to have guarded Delphi and to have been slain by Apollo. From this feat the God was called Pythius, and in his temple the priestess was called "the Pythian," as being inspired by Apollo. Hence the term became equivalent to a δαιμονίον

which brought her masters much gain by soothsaying: the same followed Paul and us, and cried, saying, These men are the servants of the most high God, which show unto us the way of salvation." (v. 16, 17.) What may be the reason that both the demon spoke these words, and Paul forbade him? Both the one acted maliciously, and the other wisely: the demon wished in fact to make himself credible.[1] For if Paul had admitted his testimony, he would have deceived many of the believers, as being received by him: therefore he endures to speak what made against himself, that he may establish what made for himself: and so the demon himself uses accommodation (συγκαταβάσει) in order to destruction. At first then, Paul would not admit it, but scorned it, not wishing to cast himself all at once upon miracles; but when it continued to do this, and pointed to their work (καὶ τὸ ἔργον ἐδείκνυ) "who preach unto us the way of salvation," then he commanded it to come out. For it says, "Paul being grieved, turned and said to the spirit, I command thee in the name of Jesus Christ to come out of her. And he came out the same hour. (a) [2] And when her masters saw that the hope of their gains was gone, they caught Paul and Silas." (v. 18, 19.) (d) So then Paul did all, both miracles and teaching, but of the dangers Silas also is partaker. And why says it, "But Paul being grieved?" It means, he saw through the malice of the demon, as he saith, "For we are not ignorant of his devices." (2 Cor. ii. 11.) (b) "And when her masters saw that the hope of their gains was gone." Everywhere money the cause of evils. O that heathen cruelty! they wished the girl to be still a demoniac, that they might make money by her. "They caught Paul and Silas," it says, "and dragged them into the marketplace unto the rulers, and brought them unto the magistrates, saying, These men, being Jews, do exceedingly trouble our city!" (v. 20): by doing what? Then why did you not drag them (hither) before this? "Being Jews:" the name was in bad odor. "And teach customs, which are not lawful for

us to receive, neither to observe, being Romans." (v. 21.) They made a charge of treason of it (εἰς καθοσίωσιν ἤγαγον). (e) Why did they not say, Because they cast out the demon, they were guilty of impiety against God? For this was a defeat to them: but instead of that, they have recourse to a charge of treason (ἐπὶ καθοσίωσιν): like the Jews when they said, "We have no king but Cæsar: whoso maketh himself a king speaketh against Cæsar." (John xix. 14, 12.) (c) "And the multitude rose up together against them: and the magistrates rent off their clothes, and commanded to beat them." (v. 22.) O the irrational conduct! They did not examine, did not allow them to speak. And yet, such a miracle having taken place, ye ought to have worshipped them, ought to have held them as saviors and benefactors. For if money was what ye wished, why, having found so great wealth, did ye not run to it? This makes you more famous, the having power to cast out demons than the obeying them. Lo, even miracles, and yet love of money was mightier. (f) "And when they had laid many stripes upon them, they cast them into prison."—great was their wrath—"charging the jailer to keep them safely" (v. 23): "who, having received such a charge, thrust them into the inner prison, and made their feet fast in the stocks." (v. 24.) Observe, he also again thrust them into the "inner" prison: and this too was done providentially, because[3] there was to be a great miracle.*

(Recapitulation.) "Out of the city." (v. 13.) The place was convenient for hearing the word, aloof from troubles and dangers. (b) "On the sabbath." As there was no work going on, they were more attentive to what was spoken. (a) "And a certain woman, named Lydia, a seller of purple" (v. 14): observe how the writer of the history is not ashamed of the occupations (of the converts): (c) moreover neither was this city of the Philippians a great one. Having learnt these things, let us also be ashamed of no man. Peter abides with a tanner (ch. ix. 43): (Paul) with a woman who was a seller of purple, and a foreigner. Where is pride? "Whose heart the Lord opened." Therefore we need God,

---

μαντικόν. In later times the power of the ventriloquist was attributed to such a Pythonic spirit (as by Plutarch) and the LXX. render the word אוב by ἐγγαστρίμυθος in accordance with this view. Meyer maintains that this damsel had the power of ventriloquism which the people attributed to a πνεῦμα πύθωνα. The apostle did not share this opinion but treated the case as one of demoniacal possession.—G. B. S.

[1] B. and Cat. ἐβούλετο λοιπὸν ἀξιόπιστον ἑαυτὸν (B. αὐτὸν) ποιεῖν. The other Mss. ἐβούλετο (ἐβουλεύετο A. C.) γὰρ μὴ ἀξ. αὐτὸν ποιεῖν: wished to make him (Paul) not credible. That the former is the true reading, is shown by what follows: ἵνα στήσῃ τὰ ὑπὲρ ἑαυτοῦ: i. e., to gain credit with the believers in order to deceive them afterwards. In the next clause, we read with Cat. and Sav. τὰ καθ' ἑαυτοῦ, our Mss. ἑαυτοὺς, and so the other Edd.

[2] The scribe has copied the parts in the order 1, 3, 5 : 2, 4, 6. See p. 213, note [5].

---

[3] Edd. have Ἐπειδὴ γὰρ, and join this sentence with the following. The compiler of the Catena perceived that the Recapitulation begins with the next sentence, which he therefore gives to v. 13, though he repeats it wrongly under v. 24.— Mod. text, inserts the Ἀλλ' ἴδωμεν κ. τ. λ. before Γνύη, φ., πορφυρόπωλις.

* This is the first recorded instance of the persecution of Christians by the Roman power. Hitherto the persecutions have proceeded from the Jews and here it is inflicted upon the Christians because they are considered to be Jews who were now under special disfavor, having been shortly before banished from Rome by Claudius.—G. B. S.

to open the heart: but God opens the hearts that are willing: for there are hardened hearts to be seen.[1] "So that she attended to the things which were spoken of Paul." The opening, then, was God's work, the attending was hers: so that it was both God's doing and man's. And she was baptized (v. 15), and receives the Apostles with such earnestness of entreaty; with more than that used by Abraham. And she speaks of no other token than that whereby she was saved (Gen. xviii. 3): she says not, "If ye have judged me" a great, a devout woman; but what? "faithful to the Lord:" if to the Lord, much more to you. "If ye have judged me:" if ye do not doubt it. And she says not, Abide with me, but, "Come into my house and abide:" with great earnestness (she says it). Indeed a faithful woman!—"A certain damsel possessed with a spirit of Python." (v. 16.) Say, what is this demon? The god, as they call him, Python: from the place he is so called. Do you mark that Apollo also is a demon? And (the demon) wished to bring them into temptation: (therefore) to provoke them, "the same followed Paul and us, and cried, saying, These men are the servants of the most high God, which show unto us the way of salvation." (v. 17.) O thou accursed, thou execrable one! if then thou knowest that it is "His way of salvation" that "they show," why dost thou not come out freely? But just what Simon wished, when he said, "Give me, that on whomsoever I lay my hands, he may receive the Holy Ghost" (ch. viii. 19), the same did this demon: since he saw them becoming famous, here also he plays the hypocrite: by this means he thought to be allowed to remain in the body, if he should preach the same things. But if Christ "receive not testimony from man," (John v. 34), meaning John, much less from a demon. "Praise is not comely in the mouth of a sinner" (Ecclus. xv. 9), much less from a demon. For [2] that they preach is not of men, but of the Holy Ghost. Because they did not act in a spirit of boasting. "And Paul being grieved," etc. By their clamor and shouting they thought to alarm them (the magistrates): saying, "These men do exceedingly trouble our city." (v. 18-20.) What sayest thou? Dost thou believe the demon? Why not here also? He saith, They are "servants of the most high God;" thou sayest, "They exceedingly trouble our city:" he saith, "They show us

the way of salvation;" thou sayest, "They teach customs which are not lawful for us to receive." (v. 21.) Observe, how they do not attend even to the demon, but look only to one thing, their covetousness. But observe them (Paul and Silas), how they do not answer, nor plead for themselves; (b) "For when," saith he, "I am weak, then am I strong. My grace is sufficient for thee, for My strength is made perfect in weakness" (2 Cor. xii. 9): so that by reason of their gentleness also they should be admired. (a) "And the magistrates," etc., "charging the jailer to keep them safely" (v. 22): that they may be the means [3] of a greater miracle. (c) The stricter the custody, the greater the miracle. It was probably from the wish to cut short the disturbance, that the magistrates did these things; because they saw the crowd urgent, and wished to stay their passion at the instant, therefore they inflicted the stripes: at the same time it was their wish to hear the matter, and that was why they cast them into prison and gave charge "to keep them safely." And, it says, "he made them fast in the stocks" (v. 24), (τὸ ξύλον) as we should say, the *nervum* (νέρβον).

What tears do not these things call for! (Think) what they suffer, while we (live) in luxury, we in theatres, we perishing and drowning (in dissolute living), seeking always idle amusement, not enduring to suffer pain for Christ, not even as far as words, not even as far as talk. These things I beseech you let us ever call to mind, what things they suffered, what things they endured, how undismayed they were, how unoffended. They were doing God's work, and suffered these things! They did not say, Why do we preach this, and God does not take our part? But even this was a benefit to them, even apart [4] from the truth, in the thing itself; it made them more vigorous, stronger, intrepid. "Tribulation worketh endurance." (Rom. v. 4.) Then let us not seek loose and dissolute living. For as in the one case the good is twofold, that the sufferers are made strong, and that the rewards are great; so in the other the evil is twofold, that such are rendered more enervated, and that it is to no

---

[1] Here mod. text. "But let us look over again what has been said. 'A woman,' it says, 'a seller of purple,'" etc.

[2] Mss. and Edd. τὸ γὰρ κηρύττειν οὐκ ἀνθρώπων ἀλλὰ Πν. Ἐπεὶ οὖν ἀλαζονικῶς ἐποίουν βοῶντες κ. τ. λ. The passage needs emendation. We read οὐκ for οὖν. "They did not catch at praise, least of all from a demon: for they were no braggarts, knowing that the power to preach was not of men," etc.

[3] ἵνα μείζονος θαύματος αἴτιοι γένωνται. B. Cat. Sav. marg. The other Mss. read ἵνα μείζονος ἄξιοι θαύμ. γ., "They forbear to answer, so as to become worthy of more admiration." Hence this clause has been transposed. We refer it to v. 23. "The magistrates give order for their safe custody, thereby becoming the means of a greater miracle."

[4] B. C., καὶ χωρὶς τῆς ἀληθείας, ἐν αὐτῷ τῷ πράγματι. A. and mod. text, καὶ χ. τῆς βοηθείας αὐτῷ. τῷ. πρ., "even without the Divine succour, even though that had been withheld, yet their sufferings were *ipso facto* a benefit." But this alteration is not necessary. "Even apart from the Truth which they preached,—irrespectively of the fact that they were preachers of the Truth—their sufferings were a benefit. Even though they were deceived, and not preachers of the Truth, they gained by suffering: it made them strong," etc.

good, but only evil. For nothing can be more worthless than a man who passes all his time in idleness and luxury. For the man untried, as the saying is, is also unapproved; unapproved not only in the contests, but also in everything else. Idleness is a useless thing, and in luxury itself nothing is so unsuited to the end proposed as the leading a luxurious life: for it palls with satiety, so that neither the enjoyment of the viands is so great, nor the enjoyment of relaxation, but all becomes vapid, and runs to waste.

Then let us not seek after this. For if we will consider which has the pleasanter life, he that is toiled and hardworked, or he that lives in luxury, we shall find it to be the former. For in the first place, [1] the bodily senses are neither clear nor sound, but dull ($\chi\alpha\tilde{v}\nu\alpha\iota$) and languid; and when those are not right, even of health there is plainly no enjoyment. Which is the useful horse, the pampered or the exercised? which the serviceable ship, that which sails, or that which lies idle? which the best water, the running or the stagnant? which the best iron, that which is much used, or that which does no work? does not the one shine bright as silver, while the other becomes all over rusty, useless, and even losing some of its own substance? The like happens also to the soul as the consequence of idleness: a kind of rust spreads over it, and corrodes both its brightness and everything else. How then shall one rub off this rust? With the whetstone of tribulations: so shall one make the soul useful and fit for all things. Else, how, I ask, will she be able to cut off the passions, with her edge turned ($\dot{\alpha}\nu\alpha\kappa\lambda\dot{\omega}\sigma\eta\varsigma$) and bending like lead? How shall she wound the devil?—And then to whom can such an one be other than a disgusting spectacle—a man cultivating obesity, dragging himself along like a seal? I speak not this of those who are naturally of this habit, but of those who by luxurious living have brought their bodies into such a condition, of those who are naturally of a spare habit. The sun has risen, has shot forth his bright beams on all sides, and roused up each person to his work: the husbandman goes forth with his spade, the smith with his hammer, and each artisan with his several instruments, and you will find each handling his proper tools; the woman also takes either her distaff or her webs: while he, like the swine, immediately at the first dawn goes forth to feed his belly, seeking how he may provide sumptuous

fare. And yet it is only for brute beasts to be feeding from morning to night; and for them, because their only use is to be slaughtered. Nay, even of the beasts, those which carry burdens and admit of being worked, go forth to their work while it is yet night. But this man, rising from his bed, when the (noon-tide) sun has filled the market-place, and people are tired of their several works, then this man gets up, stretching himself out just as if he were indeed a hog in fattening, having wasted the fairest part of the day in darkness. Then he sits there for a long time on his bed, often unable even to lift himself up from the last evening's debauch, and having wasted (still) more time in this (listlessness), proceeds to adorn himself, and issues forth, a spectacle of unseemliness, with nothing human about him, but with all the appearance of a beast with a human shape: his eyes rheumy from the effect of wine, [2] * * * while the miserable soul, just like the lame, is unable to rise, bearing about its bulk of flesh, like an elephant. Then he comes and sits in (various) places, and says and does such things, that it were better for him to be still sleeping than to be awake. If it chance that evil tidings be announced, he shows himself weaker than any girl; if good, more silly than any child; on his face there is a perpetual yawn. He is a mark for all that would do harm, if not for all men, at least for all evil passions; and wrath easily excites such a man, and lust, and envy, and all other passions. All flatter him, all pay court to him, rendering his soul weaker than it is already: and each day he goes on and on, adding to his disease. If he chance to fall into any difficulty of business, he becomes dust and ashes, [3] and his silken garments are of no help to him. We have not said all this without a purpose, but to teach you, that none of you should live idly and at random. For idleness and luxury are not conducive to work, to good reputation, to enjoyment. [4] For who will not condemn such a man? Family, friends, kinsfolk (will say), He is indeed a very encumbrance of the ground. Such a man as this has come into the world to no purpose: or rather, not to no purpose, but to ill purpose against his own person, to his own ruin, and to the hurt of others. But that this is more pleasant—let us look to this; for this is the question. Well then, what can be less

---

[1] As no "secondly" follows this "first," the scribes have supplied the seeming deficiency: thus N. (Sav. marg.) πρῶτον μὲν ὅτι τὸ σῶμα ἀνεπιτήδειον πρὸς πάντα καὶ ἐκνενευρισμένον ἐστί· δεύτερον δὲ ὅτι καὶ—. Mod. text Πρ. μὲν γὰρ τοῦ τοιούτου τὸ σῶμα αὐτὸ ἔκλυτον καὶ πεπλαδηκός· ἔπειτα καὶ—.

[2] Mod. text, "his eyes watery, his mouth smelling of wine." It is evident that Chrys. is very imperfectly reported here.

[3] τέφρα καὶ κόνις γίνεται. Unless there be an hiatus here, the meaning is, he has no more solidity in him than so much ashes and dust.

[4] Mod. text, πρὸς δόξαν μόνον, πρὸς ἡδονήν: "but only to vainglory, to pleasure."

pleasant than (the condition of) a man who has nothing to do; what more wretched and miserable? Is it not worse than all the fetters in the world, to be always gaping and yawning, as one sits in the market-place, looking at the passers by? For the soul, as its nature is to be always on the move, cannot endure to be at rest. God has made it a creature of action: to work is of its very nature; to be idle is against its nature. For let us not judge of these things from those who are diseased, but let us put the thing itself to the proof of fact. Nothing is more hurtful than leisure, and having nothing to do: indeed therefore hath God laid on us a necessity of working: for idleness hurts everything. Even to the members of the body, inaction is a mischief. Both eye, if it perform not its work, and mouth, and belly, and every member that one could mention, falls into the worst state of disease: but none so much as the soul. But as inaction is an evil, so is activity in things that ought to be let alone. For just as it is with the teeth, if one eats not, one receives hurt to them, and if one eats things unfitting, it jars them, and sets them on edge:[1] so it is here; both if the soul be inactive, and if inactive in wrong things, it loses its proper force. Then let us eschew both alike; both inaction, and the activity which is worse than inaction. And what may that be? Covetousness,[2] anger, envyings, and the other passions. As regards these, let us make it our object to be inactive, in order that we may obtain the good things promised to us, through the grace and mercy of our Lord Jesus Christ, with Whom to the Father, together with the Holy Spirit, be glory, might, honor, now and ever, world without end. Amen.

HOMILY XXXVI.

ACTS XVI. 25, 26.

" And at midnight Paul and Silas prayed, and sang praises unto God: and the prisoners heard them. And suddenly there was a great earthquake, so that the foundations of the prison were shaken, and immediately all the doors were opened, and every one's bands were loosed."

WHAT could equal these souls? These men had been scourged, had received many stripes, they had been misused, were in peril of their lives, were thrust into the inner prison, and set fast in the stocks: and for all this they did not suffer themselves to sleep, but kept vigil all the night. Do you mark what a blessing tribulation is? But we, in[3] our soft beds, with none to be afraid of, pass the whole night in sleep. But belike this is why they kept vigil, because they were in this condition. Not the tyranny of sleep could overpower them, not the smart of pain could bow them, not the fear of evil cast them into helpless dejection: no, these were the very things that made them wakeful; and they were even filled with exceeding delight. "At midnight," it says, " and the prisoners listened to them:" it was so strange and surprising! "And suddenly there was a great earthquake, so that the foundations of the prison were shaken, and immediately all the doors were opened, and every one's bands were loosed. And the keeper of the prison awaking out of his sleep, and seeing the prison doors open, drew out his sword, and would have killed himself, supposing that the prisoners had been fled." (v. 27.) There was an earthquake, that the keeper should be roused from sleep, and the doors flew open, that he should wonder at what had happened: but these things the prisoners saw not: otherwise they would all have fled: * but the keeper of the prison was about to slay himself, thinking the prisoners were escaped. "But Paul cried with a loud voice, saying, Do thyself no harm: for we are all here." (v. 28.) (b) "Then he called for lights, and sprang in, and came trembling, and fell down before Paul and Silas; and brought them out, and said, Sirs, what must I do

---

[1] ποιεῖ αὐτοὺς βρύχειν καὶ ὠμωδιᾷν (τ. ὠμωδιᾷν). In Jer. xxxi. (Gr. xxxviii.) 29, the phrase is ὀδόντες τῶν τέκνων ᾑμωδίασαν and so Hippocrat. uses the verb. αἱμωδιᾷν. But as Ed. Par. Ben. 2, remarks, the passage of Jer. is sometimes cited with ὠμωδίασαν; Synops. Athanas. t. ii. 167. Isidor. Pelus. iv. Ep. 4.

[2] Here, Edd. before Par. Ben. 2, adopt the amplified peroration of D. F. " Covetings, wrath, envyings, strifes, grudgings, emulations, and all the other passions. In these we ought to aim at being inactive, and with all earnestness to do the work of the virtues, that we may attain," etc.

[3] Mod. text ἡμεῖς δὲ οὐδὲ ἐν ἀπαλοῖς κ. τ. λ. but Sav. justly rejects οὐδὲ, and even Ben. omits it in the Latin.

* The explanation of Chrys. that Paul and Silas could not have known that the doors were open, else they would have escaped, is clearly out of harmony with the narrative. The unwillingness of Paul (v. 37) to go forth from the prison without an explicit vindication from the authorities who had imprisoned him without just cause, shows that he was not bent upon an escape. This would be all the more true in view of the miraculous interposition in their behalf.—G. B. S.

to be saved?" (v. 29–30.) Do you mark how the wonder overpowered him? (*a*) He wondered more at Paul's kindness; he was amazed at his manly boldness, that he had not escaped when he had it in his power, that he hindered him from killing himself.[1] (*c*) "And they said, believe on the Lord Jesus Christ, and thou shalt be saved, and thy house. And they spake unto him the word of the Lord, and to all that were in his house." (v. 31, 32) and (so) immediately gave proof of their kindness towards him. And he took them the same hour of the night and washed their stripes; and was baptized, he and all his, straightway." (v. 33.) He washed them, and was himself baptized, he and his house. "And when he had brought them into his house, he set meat before them, and rejoiced, believing in God with all his house. And when it was day, the magistrates sent the sergeants, saying, Let those men go." (v. 34, 35.) It is likely the magistrates had learnt what had happened, and did not dare of themselves to dismiss them. "And the keeper of the prison told these words to Paul, saying, the magistrates have sent to let you go: now therefore depart, and go in peace. But Paul said unto them, they have beaten us openly uncondemned, being Romans, and have cast us into prison; and now do they thrust as out privily? nay verily; but let them come themselves and fetch us out. And the sergeants told these words unto the magistrates: and they feared, when they heard that they were Romans. And they came and besought them, and brought them out, and desired them to depart out of the city. And they went out of the prison, and entered into the house of Lydia: and when they had seen the brethren, they comforted them, and departed." (v. 36–40.) Even[2] upon the declaration of the magistrates Paul does not go out, but for the sake both of Lydia and the rest he puts them in fear: that they may not be supposed to have come

out upon their own request, that they may set the rest in a posture of boldness. The impeachment was twofold: that "being Romans," and "uncondemned," they had openly cast them into prison. You see that in many things they took their measures as men.

(Recapitulation) "And at midnight," etc. (v. 25.) Let us compare, beloved, with that night these nights of ours, with their revellings, their drunkenness, and wanton excesses, with their sleep which might as well be death, their watchings which are worse than sleep. For while some sleep without sense or feeling, others lie awake to pitiable and wretched purpose, plotting deceits, anxiously thinking about money, studying how they may be revenged upon those who do them wrong, meditating enmity, reckoning up the abusive words spoken during the day: thus do they rake up the smouldering embers of wrath, doing things intolerable.[3] Mark how Peter slept. (ch. xii. 6.) Both there, it was wisely ordered (that he should be asleep); for the Angel came to him, and it behooved that none should see what happened; and on the other hand it was well ordered here (that Paul should be awake), in order that the keeper of the prison might be prevented from killing himself. "And suddenly there was a great earthquake." (v, 26.) And why did no other miracle take place? Because this was, of all others, the thing sufficient for his conversion, seeing he was personally in danger: for it is not so much miracles that overpower us, as the things which issue in our own deliverance. That the earthquake should not seem to have come of itself, there was this concurrent circumstance, bearing witness to it: "the doors were opened, and all their bonds were loosed." And it appears in the night-time; for the Apostles did not work for display, but for men's salvation "And the keeper of the prison," etc. (v. 27.) The keeper was not an evil-disposed man that he "thrust them into the inner prison," (v. 24) was because of his "having received such a command," not of himself. The man[4]

---

[1] i. e. "The miracle amazed him. but he was more astonished at Paul's boldness, was more moved to admiration by his kindness." But besides the transposition marked by the letters, the clauses of (*a*) may perhaps be better re-arranged thus: "He more marvelled at Paul's boldness, in not escaping etc., he was amazed at his kindness in hindering," etc.
[2] The report seems to be defective, but the meaning may be, that in taking this high tone with the magistrates the Apostle was not influenced by personal feelings; but acted thus for the assurance of Lydia and the other believers, by letting it be seen that they were not set at liberty upon their own request. In the recapitulation another consideration is mentioned, viz. in respect of the jailer.—Mod. text "perhaps for the sake of Lydia and the other brethren : or also putting them in fear that they may not, etc., and that they may set the others also in a posture of boldness." Then, Τριπλοῦν, ἀγαπητοί, κ. τ. λ. the third point being καὶ δημοσίᾳ. We reject this καὶ though all our Mss. have it. We have also transferred the ἀγαπητοὶ, which is out of place here to the beginning of the recapitulation.

[3] τὰ ἀφόρητα ἐργαζόμενοι: perhaps, "in imagination wreaking upon their enemies an intolerable revenge."
[4] Mod. text "And why did not Paul shout before this? The man was all in a tumult of perturbation, and would not have received (what was said). Therefore when he saw him about to kill himself, he is beforehand with him, and shouts saying, "We are all here." Therefore also, "Having asked," it says, " for lights, he sprang in, and fell before Paul and Silas." The keeper falls at the feet of the prisoner. And he brings them out, and says, "Sirs," etc. But the question, Διὰ τί μὴ πρὸ τούτου ; evidently cannot be meant for ἐβόησεν ὁ Παῦλος. The meaning is, "Why did he not sooner ask, 'What shall I do to be saved?' Observe his first impulse is to kill himself—such was the tumult of his thoughts. Sud-

was all in a tumult of perturbation. "What shall I do to be saved?" he asks. Why not before this? Paul shouted, until he saw, and is beforehand with him saying, "We are all here. And having called for lights," it says, "he sprang in, and fell down at the feet" of the prisoner; he, the prison-keeper, saying, "Sirs, what must I do to be saved?" (v. 28-30.) Why, what had they said? Observe, he does not, on finding himself safe, think all is well; he is overcome with awe at the miraculous power.

Do you mark[1] what happened in the former case, and what here? There a girl was released from a spirit, and they cast them into prison, because they had liberated her from the spirit. Here, they did but show the doors standing open, and it opened the doors of his heart, it loosed two sorts of chains; that (prisoner)[2] kindled the (true) light; for the light in his heart was shining. "And he sprang in, and fell before them;" and he does not ask, How is this? What is this? but straightway he says, "What must I do to be saved?" What then answers Paul? "Believe on the Lord Jesus Christ, and thou shalt be saved, thou and thine house." (v. 31.) For this above all, wins men: that one's house also should be saved. "And they spake the word to him, and to all that were in his house. And he took them the same hour of the night, and washed their stripes," etc. (v. 32, 33), washed them and was washed: those he washed from their stripes, himself was washed from his sins: he fed and was fed.[3] "And rejoiced," it says: although there was nothing but words only and good hopes: "having believed in God with all his house (v. 34): this was the token of his having believed— that he was released of all. What worse than

a jailer, what more ruthless, more savage? He entertained them with great honor. Not, because he was safe, he made merry, but, having believed God. (a) "Believe on the Lord," said the Apostle: therefore it is that the writer here says, "Having believed.[4]—(d) Now therefore," it says, "depart, and go in peace" (v. 36): that is, in safety, fearing no man. (b) "But Paul said unto them" (v. 37): that he may not seem to be receiving his liberty as one condemned, and as one that has done wrong: therefore it is that he says, "Having openly beaten us uncondemned," etc.—that it may not be matter of grace on their part. (e) And besides, they wish the jailer himself to be out of danger, that he may not be called to account for this afterwards. And they do not say, "Having beaten us," who have wrought miracles: for they (the magistrates) did not even heed these: but, that which was most effectual to shake their minds, "uncondemned, and being Romans." (c) Observe how diversely grace manages things: how Peter went out, how Paul, though both were Apostles. "They feared," (v. 38) it says: because the men were Romans, not because they had unjustly cast them into prison,* "And besought them to depart out of the city" (v. 39): begged them as a favor. And they went to the house of Lydia, and having confirmed her, so departed. For it was not right to leave their hostess in distress and anxiety. But they went out, not in compliance with the request of those rulers, but hasting to the preaching: the city having been sufficiently benefited by the miracle: for it was fit they should not be there any longer. For in the absence of them that wrought it, the miracle appeared greater, itself crying out more loudly: the faith of the jailer was a voice in itself. What equal to this? He is put in bonds, and looses, being bound: looses a twofold bond: him that bound him, he looses by being bound. These are indeed works of (supernatural) grace.

(f) Let us constantly bear in mind this jailer,[5] not the miracle: how, prisoner as he

---

denly awaked, he sees the doors open, and supposes the prisoners were escaped. Therefore Paul shouted to him, to reassure him on that point, until he could satisfy himself with his own eyes: as, it says, 'He called for lights,' for that purpose: and then indeed, relieved of that fears he is overcome with awe: and falls down at the feet of his prisoner saying, 'What shall I do to be saved?' Why, what had they said? Nothing more: but the religious awe now seizes him: for he does not think all is right and no need to trouble himself any further, because he finds himself safe from the temporal danger." For this is the meaning of ὅρα αὐτὸν οὐκ, ἐπειδὴ διεσώθη, ἐπὶ τούτῳ στέργοντα, ἀλλὰ τὴν δύναμιν ἐκπλαγέντα: not as Ben. vide illum non ab hoc diligere quod servatus esset, sed quod de virtute obstupesceret.

[1] This is the sequel to what was said above: "It is not so much miracles that overpower or convince us (αἱρεῖ) as the sense of benefits received." For, they saw the miracle of dispossession wrought upon the girl, and they cast the doers of it into prison: whereas here the jailer sees but the doors open (the prisoners safe, the Apostle's manliness in not escaping, and their kindness to himself), and he is converted. The doors were open, and the door of his heart (like Lydia's) was opened: the prisoner's chains were loosed, and worse chains were loosed from himself: he called for a light, but the true light was lighted in his own heart.

[2] ἦμεν ἐκεῖνος τὸ φῶς. Edd. (from D. F.) ἐκεῖνο.

[3] ἔθρεψε καὶ ἐτράφη: probably meaning the Holy Eucharist immediately after the baptism. So above p. 219, τοσαῦτα μυστήρια, in the case of Lydia.

[4] Edd. "Having believed, that he may not seem to be liberated," etc., as if this (b) were said of the jailer. (Here again the method of the derangement is 1, 3, 5: 2, 4, 6: as in p. 213, note 5, 220, note 2).

* In two respects the treatment of Paul and Silas at Philippi was unjust. It was contrary to natural justice to punish them "uncondemned"—without a fair and impartial trial. Moreover the Lex Valeria (254 U. C.) forbade the punishment of Roman citizens with whips and rods. It was this last violation of law which, upon reflection, the magistrates wished to hush up. Hence their eager desire that Paul and Silas go free forthwith. Every hour of detention was an accusation against themselves.—G. B. S.

[5] All our Mss. δεσμοφύλακος, but Savile δεσμώτου, adopted by Ben. We retain the old reading—Mod. text "What say the heathen? how being a prisoner," etc. Then: "Καὶ τίνα, φησί, πεισθῆναι ἐχρῆν, ἢ μιαρὸν κ. τ. λ. And what man (say they) was (more) to be persuaded than, etc. Moreover,

15

was (the Apostle), persuaded his jailer. What say the heathen? "And of what things," say they, "was such a man as this to be persuaded—a vile, wretched creature, of no understanding, full of all that is bad and nothing else, and easily brought over to anything? For these, say they, are the things, a tanner, a purple-seller, an eunuch, slaves, and women believed." This is what they say. What then will they be able to say, when we produce the men of rank and station, the centurion, the proconsul, those from that time to the present, the rulers themselves, the emperors? But for my part, I speak of something else, greater than this: let us look to these very persons of no consideration. "And where is the wonder?" say you. Why, this, I say, is a wonder. For, if a person be persuaded about any common things, it is no wonder: but if resurrection, a kingdom of heaven, a life of philosophic self-command, be the subjects, and, discoursing of these to persons of mean consideration, one persuades them, it will be more wonderful than if one persuaded wise men. For when there is no danger attending the things of which one persuades people, then (the objector) might with some plausibility allege want of sense on their part: but when (the preacher) says—to the slave, as you will have it—"If thou be persuaded by me, it is at thy peril, thou wilt have all men for thine enemies, thou must die, thou must suffer evils without number," and yet for all this, convinces that man's soul, there can be no more talk here of want of sense. Since, if indeed the doctrines contained what was pleasant, one might fairly enough say this: but if, what the philosohers would never have chosen to learn, this the slave does learn, then is the wonder greater. And, if you will, let us bring before us the tanner himself, and see what were the subjects on which Peter conversed with him: or if you will, this same jailer. What then said Paul to him? "That Christ rose again," say you; "that there is a resurrection of the dead, and a kingdom: and he had no difficulty in persuading him, a man

easily led to anything." How? Said he nothing about the mode of life; that he must be temperate, that he must be superior to money, that he must not be unmerciful, that he must impart of his good things to others? For it cannot be said, that the being persuaded to these things also was from the want of power of mind; no, to be brought to all this required a great soul. For be it so, that as far as the doctrines went, they were rendered more apt to receive these by their want of intelligence: but to accept such a virtuous, self-denying rule of life, how could that be owing to any defect of understanding? So that the less understanding the person may have, if nevertheless he is persuaded to things, to which even philosophers were unable to persuade their fellow-philosophers, the greater the wonder—when women and slaves are persuaded of these truths, and prove it by their actions, of which same truths the Platos and all the rest of them were never able to persuade any man. And why say I, "any man?" Say rather, not themselves even: on the contrary, that money is not to be despised, Plato persuaded (his disciples) by getting, as he did, such an abundance of property, and golden rings, and goblets; and that the honor to be had from the many is not to be despised, this Socrates himself shows, for all that he may philosophize without end on this point: for in everything he did, he had an eye to fame. And if you were conversant with his discourses, I might go at great length into this subject, and show what a deal of insincerity (εἰρωνείαν) there was in them,—if at least we may believe what his disciple says of him,—and how that all his writings have their ground-work in vainglory. But, leaving them, let us direct the discourse to our own selves. For besides the things that have been said, there is this also to be added, that men were persuaded of these things to their own peril. Be not thou therefore shameless, but let us think over that night, the stocks, and the hymns of praise. This let us also do, and we shall open for ourselves—not a prison, but—heaven. If we pray, we shall be able even to open heaven. Elias both shut and opened heaven by prayer. (James v. 17.) There is a prison in heaven also. "Whatsoever," He saith, "ye shall bind on earth, shall be bound in heaven." (Matt. xvi. 19.) Let us pray by night, and we shall loose these bonds. For that prayers loose sins, let that widow convince us, let that friend convince us, who at that untimely hour of the night persists and knocks (Luke xi. 5): let Cornelius convince us, for, "thy prayers," it says, "and thine alms are come up before God." (ch. x. 4.) Let Paul convince

they allege this also: for who but a tanner τίς γὰρ ἢ βυρσεὺς) . . . . believed?"—We take τίνα to be acc. plur. sc. δόγματα. The heathen objection is this, You may see by the character of the first converts, such as this jailer, what is the character of the doctrines: "Since what doctrines behooved (a man like this) to be persuaded of?" St. Chrys. says, "Let us bear in mind this jailer—not to dwell upon the miracle, but to consider how his prisoner persuaded him: how he induced a man like this not only to receive the doctrines, but to submit to the self-denying rule of the Gospel. The heathen raise a prejudice against the Gospel from the very fact, that such men as these were converted. What, say they, must be the teaching to be received by a wretched creature like this jailer? The doctrines were well matched with their first converts, tanner, purple-seller, eunuch," etc. (So in the remarkable argument on this same subject in the Morale of *Hom.* vii. *in* i *Cor.* p. 62, E. "but it is objected: Those who were convinced by them were slaves, women, nurses, eunuchs:" whence it seems, as here, that the case of the eunuch, Acts viii. was made a reproach, as if he must needs be a person of inferior understanding).

us, who says, "Now she that is a widow indeed and desolate, trusteth in God, and continueth in supplications night and day." (1 Tim. v. 5.) If he speaks thus of a widow, a weak woman, much more would he of men. I have both before discoursed to you on this, and now repeat it : let us arouse ourselves during the night: though thou make not many prayers, make one with watchfulness, and it is enough, I ask no more : and if not at midnight, at any rate at the first dawn. Show that the night is not only for the body, but also for the soul : do not suffer it to pass idly, but make this return to thy Master: nay rather (the benefit) itself returns to thee. Say, if we fall into any difficult strait, to whom do we not make request? and if we soon obtain our request, we breathe freely again. What a boon were it for thee, to have a friend to go to with thy request, who shall be ready to take it as a kindness, and to be obliged to thee for thy asking? What a boon, not to have to go about and seek one to ask of, but to find one ready? to have no need of others through whom thou mayest solicit? What could be greater than this? Since here is One who then does most, when we make not our requests of others than Himself : just as a sincere friend then most complains of us for not trusting in his friendship, when we ask of others to make request to him. Thus also let us act.[1] "But what," you will ask, "if I should have offended Him?" Cease to give offence, and weep, and so draw near to Him, and thou wilt quickly render Him propitious as to thy former sins. Say only, I have offended : say it from thy soul and with a sincere mind, and all things are remitted to thee. Thou dost not so much desire thy sins to be forgiven, as He desires to forgive thee thy sins. In proof that thou dost not so desire it, consider that thou hast no mind either to practice vigils, or to give thy money freely: but He, that He might forgive our sins, spared not His Only-begotten and True Son, the partner of His throne. Seest thou how He more desires to forgive thee thy sins (than thou to be forgiven)? Then let us not be slothful, nor put off this any longer. He is merciful and good : only let us give Him an opportunity. And (even) this (He seeks), only that we may not become unprofitable, since even without this He could have freed us from them : but like as we (with the same view) devise and arrange many things for our servants to do, so does He in the matter of our salvation. "Let us anticipate His face

with thanksgiving." (Ps. xcv. 2. "Let us come before His presence." E. V.), since He is good and kind. But if thou call not upon Him, what will *He* do? Thou dost not choose to say, Forgive; thou wilt not say it from thy heart, but with thy mouth only. What is it, to call in truth? (To call) with purpose of heart, with earnestness, with a sincere mind ; just as men say of perfumes, "This is genuine, and has nothing spurious," so here. He who truly calls on Him, he who truly prays to Him, continually attends to it, and desists not, until he obtain (his request): but he who does it in a merely formal manner (ἀφοσιούμενος), and even this only by way of fulfilling a law, does not call in truth. Whosoever thou art, say not only, "I am a sinner," but be earnest also to rid thyself of this character; say not this only, but also grieve. If thou grievest, thou art in earnest : if thou art not in earnest, thou grievest not : if thou grievest not, thou triflest. What sort of man is he who shall say, "I am sick," and not to do all to be freed from his sickness? A mighty weapon is Prayer. "If ye," saith the Lord, "know how to give good gifts to your children, how much more your Father?" (Luke xi. 13.) Then wherefore art thou unwilling to approach Him? He loves thee, He is of more power than all besides. Both willing is He and able, what is there to hinder? Nothing. But then, on our part, let us draw near with faith, draw near, offering the gifts that He desires, forgetfulness of wrongs, kindness, meekness. Though thou be a sinner, with boldness shalt thou ask of Him forgiveness of thy sins, if thou canst show that this has been done by thyself : but though thou be righteous, and possess not this virtue of forgetfulness of injuries, thou art none the better for it. It cannot be that a man who has forgiven his neighbor should not obtain perfect forgiveness : for God is beyond comparison more merciful than we. What sayest thou? If thou sayest, "I have been wronged, I have subdued my anger, I have endured the onset of wrath because of Thy command, and dost Thou not forgive?[2] Full surely He will forgive : and this is plain to all. Therefore let us purge our soul from all resentment. This is sufficient for us, in order that we may be heard ; and let us pray with watching and much perseverance, that having enjoyed His bountiful mercy, we may be found worthy of the good things promised, through the grace and mercy of our Lord Jesus Christ, with Whom to the Father, together with the Holy Spirit, be glory, might, honor, now and ever, world without end. Amen.

---

[1] οὕτω καὶ ἡμεῖς· which mod. text needlessly expands into : "(Thus also we) act in the case of those who ask of us : we then most oblige them. when they approach us by themselves not by others."

[2] καὶ σὺ οὐκ ἀφῇς ; Mod. text, οὐκ ἀφήσει καὶ αὐτός ; "will not He also forgive?"

HOMILY XXXVII.

ACTS XVII. 1, 2, 3.

" Now when they had passed through Amphipolis and Apollonia, they came to Thessalonica, where was a synagogue of the Jews : and Paul, as his manner was, went in unto them, and three sabbath days reasoned with them out of the Scriptures, opening and alleging that Christ must needs have suffered, and risen again from the dead; and that this Jesus, whom I preach unto you, is Christ."

AGAIN they haste past the small cities, and press on to the greater ones, since from those the word was to flow as from a fountain into the neighboring cities. "And Paul, as his manner was, went into the synagogue of the Jews." Although he had said, "We turn to the Gentiles" (ch. xiii. 46), he did not leave these alone : such was the longing affection he had towards them. For hear him saying, "Brethren, my heart's desire and prayer to God for Israel is, that they might be saved" (Rom. x. 1): and, "I wished myself accursed from Christ for my brethren." (ib. ix. 3.) But he did this[1] because of God's promise and the glory : and this, that it might not be a cause of offence to the Gentiles. "Opening," it says, "from the Scriptures, he reasoned with them for three sabbaths, putting before them that the Christ must suffer." Do thou mark how before all other things he preaches the Passion : so little were they ashamed of it, knowing it to be the cause of salvation. "And some of them believed, and consorted with Paul and Silas; and of the devout Greeks a great multitude, and of the chief women not a few." (v. 4.) The writer mentions only the sum and substance of the discoursing : he is not given to redundancy, and does not on every occasion report the sermons. "But the Jews which believed not (the best texts omit "which believed not"), moved with envy, took unto them certain lewd fellows of the baser sort, and gathered a company, and set all the city on an uproar, and assaulted the house of Jason, and sought to bring them out to the people. And when

they found them not, they drew Jason and certain brethren unto the rulers of the city, crying, These that have turned the world upside down are come hither also; whom Jason hath received : and these all do contrary to the decrees of Cæsar, saying that there is another king, one Jesus." (v. 5-7.) Oh! what an accusation ! again they get up a charge of treason against them, " saying, there is another king (one) Jesus. And they troubled the people and the rulers of the city, when they heard these things. And when they had taken security of Jason, and of the other, they let them go." (v. 8, 9.) A man worthy to be admired, that he put himself into danger, and sent them away from it. "And the brethren immediately sent away Paul and Silas by night unto Berea : who coming thither went into the synagogue of the Jews. These were more noble," it says, "than they of Thessalonica : more noble," i. e. more gentle (ἐπιεικέστεροι) (in their behavior) : "in that they received the word with all readiness," and this not inconsiderately, but with a strictness wherein[2] was no passion, "searching the Scriptures whether these things were so." (v. 10, 11.) "Therefore many of them believed ; also of honorable women which were Greeks, and of men, not a few. But when the Jews of Thessalonica had knowledge that the word of God was preached of Paul at Berea, they came thither also, and stirred up the people. And then immediately the brethren sent away Paul to go as it were to the sea : but Silas and Timotheus abode there still." (v. 12-14.) See how he at one time gives way, at another presses on, and in many things takes his measures upon human considerations. "And they that conducted Paul brought him unto Athens : and receiving a commandment unto Silas and Timotheus for to come to him with speed, they departed."

---

[1] This seems meant to refer to the sequel of the passage cited, Rom. ix. 4. " who are Israelites, to whom pertaineth the adoption and *the glory* . . . and *the promises* :" then τοῦτο ἐποίει refers to ἐβουλόμην, indicatively, " I wished :" but καὶ τοῦτο (mod. text omits τοῦτο), " And this solicitude he showed for the sake of the Gentiles also, to whom the unbelief of the Jews might be a stumbling-block :"—unless καὶ τοῦτο refers to v. 3, the discourse of Christ's death and resurrection—that the Cross might not be an offence to the devout Greeks.

[2] μετὰ ἀκριβείας ἔνθα πάθος οὐκ ἦν. It is not easy to see what else this can mean. Below in the Recapitulation οὐ ῥύμη οὐδὲ ζήλῳ.—Mod. text "With exactness they explored the Scriptures—for this is the meaning of ἀνέκρινον—wishing from them to derive assurance rather concerning the Passion: for they had already believed." The last statement, like some other additions in the mod. text, seems to be borrowed from the Catena (Ammonius) whence it is adopted also by Œcumenius : but this was certainly not Chrysostom's meaning.

(v. 15.) But let us look again at what has been said.

(Recapitulation.) "Three sabbath-days," it says, being the time when they had leisure from work, "he reasoned with them, opening out of the Scriptures" (v. 2): for so used Christ also to do: as on many occasions we find Him reasoning from the Scriptures, and not on all occasions (urging men) by miracles. Because to this [1] indeed they stood in a posture of hostility, calling them deceivers and jugglers; but he that persuades men by reasons from the Scriptures, is not liable to this imputation. And on many occasions we find (Paul) to have convinced men simply by force of teaching: and in Antioch "the whole city was gathered together" (ch. xiii. 44): so [2] great a thing is this also, for indeed this itself is no small miracle, nay, it is even a very great one. And that they might not think that they did it all by their own strength, but rather that God permitted it, [3] two things resulted, namely, "Some of them were persuaded," etc. (c) "And of devout Greeks a great multitude, and of the chief women not a few:" * but those others did the contrary: "the Jews moved with envy," etc. (v. 4, 5) (b) and, from the fact that the being called was itself a matter of God's fore-ordering, (a) they neither thought great things of themselves as if the triumph were their own, nor

were terrified as being responsible (for all). But how comes it that he said, "That we should go unto the heathen, and they unto the circumcision" (Gal. ii. 9), and yet discoursed to the Jews? (a) He did this as a thing over and above. (β) For [4] he did other things also more than he was obliged. For instance, Christ ordained that they should "live by the Gospel" (1 Cor. ix. 14; i. 17), but our Apostle did it not: Christ sent him not to baptize, yet he did baptize. Mark how he was equal to all. Peter to the circumcision, he to the Gentiles, to the greater part. (a) Since if it was necessary for him to discourse to Jews, how said he again: "For He that wrought effectually in him toward the circumcision, the same was mighty also in me toward the Gentiles" (Gal. ii. 8)? In the same way as those Apostles also had intercourse with the Gentiles, though they had been set apart for the circumcision, so likewise did our Apostle. The more part of his work indeed was with the Gentiles: still he did not neglect the Jews either, that they might not seem to be severed from them. And how was it, you will ask, that he entered in the first place into the synagogues, as if this were his leading object? True; but he persuaded the Gentiles through the Jews, and from the things which he discoursed of to the Jews. And he knew, that this was most suitable for the Gentiles, and most conducive to belief. Therefore he says: "Inasmuch as I am the "Apostle of the Gentiles." (Rom. xi. 13.) And his Epistles too all fight against the Jews.— That the Christ," he says, "must needs have suffered." (v. 3.) If there was a necessity for His suffering, there was assuredly a necessity for His rising again: for the former [5] was far more wonderful than the latter. For if He gave Him up to death Who had done no wrong, much rather did He raise Him up again. "But the Jews which believed not took unto them certain of the baser sort, and set all the city on an uproar (v. 5): so that the Gentiles were more in number. The Jews thought not themselves enough to raise the disturbance: for because they had no reasonable pretext, they ever effect such purposes by means of uproar, and by taking to themselves base men. "And when they found them not," it says, "they haled Jason and certain brethren."

---

[1] πρὸς τοῦτο, i. e. the working of miracles. Not only it did not win them: they set themselves against it, taxing the doers of the miracles with imposture and magical art, etc.—Mod. text "For because to Him (τοῦτον, Christ) they were opposed, and slandered Him that He was a deceiver and juggler, therefore it is that He also reasons from the Scriptures. For he that attempts to persuade by miracles alone may well be suspected: but he that persuades from the Scriptures," etc.

[2] A. B. οὕτω μέγα τι καὶ τοῦτό ἐστι καὶ τὸ πᾶν. C. omits this: we place it after ἴσχυσαν in the next sentence, where mod. text has it. This thought is brought out more fully below, p. 230. The persuading men by telling them that which even with miracles was hard to believe—a Messiah crucified!—was itself a miracle.

[3] ἀλλ' ὁ Θεὸς συνεχώρησεν, if not corrupt, must mean "but that God permitted all: i. e. that all depended on God's permission, not on their strength.—δύο ἐγένετο, i. e. some believed v. 4., others opposed, v. 5. The sense is confused in the Mss. and Edd. by the transposition of the sentences marked c and a. In c, verse 2 is substituted for v. 4. which we restore. In b, we read τῷ τε (A. B. τό τε) οἰκονομίαν εἶναι καὶ τὸ καλεῖσθαι for καὶ τῷ καλ. The meaning is, And so by reason of the fact that τὸ καλεῖσθαι is itself οἰκονομία—that is of God's ordering, according to His own pleasure, who are called and who not— the preachers are not left either to think too much of themselves when they succeed, ὡς αὐτοὶ καθελόντες, nor to be terrified by failure ὡς, ὑπεύθυνοι, as if they were responsible for men's unbelief.—Mod. text, "And that they may not think that they did it all by their own strength, God suffers them to be driven away (ἐλαύνεσθαι) into unbelief, etc. nor etc. they neither etc. nor etc. So (much) was even the being called a matter of God's ordering. 'And of the devout Greeks,' " etc.

* The "devout Greeks" would include such as were Jewish proselytes and such as were worshippers of the true God and attended the synagogue services, without being connected with Judaism. The "first women" were probably female proselytes to Judaism. These heard the Apostle with interest, but the more ardent and fanatical Jews, reinforced by the baser element—the loungers from the market place, made a tumult of opposition.—G. B. S.

[4] Between the Exposition and the Moral, the original editor or transcriber has thrown together a set of disconnected notes. These are here inserted in what seems to be their proper connection. In the Mss. and Edd. the parts lie in the order as shown by the letters a, β prefixed.

[5] We adopt the reading of B. ἐκεῖνο, "the suffering;" τοῦτον, "the rising again." The others, ἐκείνου, τοῦτο: reversing Chrysostom's meaning.

(v. 6.) O the tyranny! dragged them without any cause out of their houses. "These all," say they, "do contrary to the decrees of Cæsar" (v. 7): for since they spoke nothing contrary to what had been decreed, nor made any commotion in the city, they bring them under a different charge: "saying that there is another king, one Jesus.* And they troubled the people," etc. (v. 8.) And what are ye afraid of, seeing He is dead? (β) "And when they had taken security," etc. (v. 9.) See how by giving security Jason sent Paul away: so that he gave his life (to the hazard) for him.† (a) "And brethren," etc. (v. 10.) See how the persecutions in every case extend the preaching. "Now these," it says, "were more noble than those in Thessalonica" (v. 11): i. e. they were not (men) practising base things, but some [1] were convinced, and the others (who were not), did nothing (of that sort). (β) "Daily," it says, "searching the Scriptures whether these things were so:" not merely upon a sudden impetus or (burst of) zeal. "More noble," it says: i. e. in point of virtue. (a) "Therefore many of them," etc. (v. 12.) And here again are Greeks. (β) "But when the Jews of Thessalonica," etc. (v. 13), because there were lewd persons there. And yet that city was greater. But it is no wonder in the greater city the people were worse: nay, of course to the greater city there go the worse men, where the occasions of disturbances are many. And as in the body, where the disease is more violent for having [2] more matter and fuel, just so is it here. (a) But look, I beg you, how their fleeing was providentially ordered, not from cowardice: otherwise they would have ceased to preach, and would not have exasperated them still more. But from this (flight) two things resulted: both the rage of those (Jews) was quenched, and the preaching spread. But in terms befitting their disorderly conduct, he says, "Agitating the multitude." (β) Just

what was done at Iconium—that they may have the additional condemnation of destroying others besides themselves. (ch. xiv. 2, 19.) This is what Paul says of them: "Forbidding to preach to the Gentiles, to fill up their sins alway, for the wrath is come upon them to the uttermost." (1 Thess. ii. 16.) Why did he not stay? for if (at Lystra, ch. xiv. 19, 21) there, where he was stoned, he nevertheless stayed a long time, much more here. Why? (The Lord) did not wish them to be always doing signs; for this is itself a sign, not less than the working of signs—that being persecuted, they overcame without signs. So that just as now He prevails without signs, so was it on many occasions His will to prevail then. Consequently neither did the Apostles run after signs: as in fact he says himself, "We preach Christ crucified" (1 Cor. i. 23)— to them that crave signs, to them that crave wisdom, we give that which cannot even after signs persuade, and yet we do persuade! So that this was a mighty sign. See then, how when the preaching is extended, they are not in a hurry to run after signs. [3] For it was right that thenceforth the believers should be mighty signs to the rest. Howbeit, by retreating and advancing they did these things. (a) "And immediately," it says, "the brethren sent away Paul." (v. 14.) Here now they send Paul alone: for it was for him they feared, lest he should suffer some harm, the head and front of all being in fact none other than he. (β) "They sent him away," it says, "as it were to the sea:" that it might not be easy for them to seize him. For [4] at present they could not have done much by themselves; and with him they accomplished and achieved many things. For the present, it says, they wished to rescue him. (a) So far is it from being the case, that (supernatural) Grace worked all alike on all occasions: on the contrary, it left them to take their measures upon human judgment, (only) stirring them up and rousing them out of sleep, and making them to take pains. [5] Thus, observe, it brought them safe only as far as Philippi, but no more after that. "And receiving," it says, "a commandment unto Silas and Timotheus for to come to him

---

* The accusation is artfully made. They are accused of the *crimen majestatis*—treason against Cæsar. The Jews knew well that to accuse them of disturbing their worship or opposing their opinions would produce no effect. To arouse the Roman feeling against them it was necessary to prevent their teaching concerning the Kingship of Jesus so as to make it seem to the rulers of this free city as a treasonable doctrine against the Roman state.—G. B. S.

† "When they had taken security"—λαβόντες τὸ ἱκανὸν, a legal term—*satisfactionem accipere*, it is doubtful if, as Chrys. supposes, Jason became surety in person. The surety was more probably a deposit of money and had for its object the guaranty that the peace should be kept, and nothing done contrary to the Emperor and the state.—G. B. S.

[1] Mod. text mistaking the meaning, has: "But they indeed were persuaded, but these do just the contrary, making an uproar among them."

[2] Edd. καθάπερ γὰρ ἐν σώματι, ὅταν ἡ νόσος χαλεπωτέρα ᾖ, πλείονα ἔχει τὴν ὕλην καὶ τὴν τροφήν. Neander, *der heil. Chrysost.* t. i. p. 2. note, corrects the passage thus. καθάπερ γὰρ ἐν σώματι ἡ νόσος χαλεπωτέρα, ὅταν πλ. ἔχοι τὴν ὕλην. But A. C. preserve the true reading ἔχουσα.

[3] Of the Edd. Savile alone has adopted the true reading πῶς οὐ ταχέως ἐπιτρέχουσι τοῖς σημείοις, preserved by B. The other Mss. and Edd. omit οὐ.

[4] Here again Savile (with B.) has the true reading οὔπω γὰρ, the rest οὔτω.

[5] Here (because it seems unsuitable to refer this to χάρις, i. e. supernatural grace, or special miraculous interposition,) B. substitutes, ἀλλ' ἵνα πεῖραν λάβωσι, διανιστῶσαν αὐτοὺς καὶ δυπνίζουσαν καὶ εἰς μέριμναν ἐμβάλλουσαν, ἐποίει αὐτοὺς καὶ ἀνθρώπινα πάσχειν, "but in order that they may get experience, rousing and waking, and making them take pains, (the Lord) made them to suffer (or be affected) after the manner of men."—Below, for "Philippi" the same has "Athens."

with all speed, they departed." (v. 15.) For though he was a Paul, nevertheless he needed them. And with good reason are they urged by God to go into Macedonia, for there lay Greece moreover bright (before them). (ch. xvi. 9.)

See what zeal the rest of the disciples showed with respect to their leaders: not as it is now with us, who are separated and divided into great and small: some of us exalted, while others are envious: for this is the reason why those are envious, because we are puffed up, because we will not endure to be put upon a par with them. The reason why there is harmony in the body, is because there is no puffing up: and there is no puffing up, because the members are of necessity made to stand in need of each other, and the head has need of the feet. And God has made this to be the case with us, and, for all that, we will not endure it: although even without this, there ought to be love among us. Hear ye not how they that are without accuse us when they say, "Needs make friendships?" The laity have need of us; and we again exist for them. Since teacher or ruler would not exist, if there were not persons to be taught, nor would he perform his part, for it would not be possible. As the land has need of the husbandman, and the husbandman of the land, so is it here. What reward is there for the teacher to receive, when he has none to produce that he has taught? and what for the taught, who have not had the benefit of the best teaching? So that we need each other alike in turn, both the governed, them that govern,[1] and leaders, them that obey: for rulers are for the sake of many. Since no one is sufficient to do anything by himself alone, whether need be to ordain (χειροτονῆσαι), or to examine men's counsels and opinions, but they become more honorable by assembly and numbers. For instance, the poor need givers, the givers again need receivers. "Considering one another," he says, "to provoke unto love and to good works." (Heb. x. 24.) On this account the assembly of the whole Church has more power: and what each cannot do by himself singly, he is able to do when joined with the rest. Therefore most necessary are the prayers offered up, here, for the world, for the Church, from the one end of the earth to the other, for peace, for those who are in adversities. And Paul shows this when he says, "That for the gift bestowed upon us by the means of many persons thanks may be given by many on our be-

half " (2 Cor. i. 11); that is, that He might confer the favor on many. And often he asks for their prayers. See also what God says with regard to the Ninevites: "And shall not I spare that city, wherein dwell more than six score thousand persons?" (Jonah iv. 11.) For if, "where two or three," He says, "are gathered together in My Name" (Matt. xviii. 20), they prevail much, how much more, being many? And yet thou mayest prevail, though thou be but one; yet not equally so. For why art thou but one? Why dost thou not make many? Why dost thou not become the maker of love? Why dost thou not create (κατασκευάζεις) friendship? Thou lackest the chief excellence of virtue. For as men's being bad by agreement together more provokes God; so for men to be good by unanimity delights Him more. "Thou shalt not follow a multitude," He says, "to do evil." (Ex. xxiii. 2.) "They are all gone out of the way, they are together become unprofitable" (Rom. iii. 12), and have become as it were men singing in concert in their wickedness. Make for thyself friends in preference to domestics, and all besides. If the peacemaker is a son of God, how much more he who makes friends also? (Matt. v. 9.) If he who reconciles only is called a son of God, of what shall not he be worthy, who makes friends of those who are reconciled? Let us engage ourselves in this trade, let us make those who are enemies to each other friends, and those who are not indeed enemies, but are not friends, them let us bring together, and before all, our own selves. For as he who is at enmity in his house, and has differences with his wife, carries no authority when reconciling others, but will be told, "Physician, heal thyself" (Luke iv. 23), so will a man be told in this case. What then is the enmity that is in us? That of the soul against the body, that of vice against virtue. This enmity let us put an end to, this war let us take away, and then being in peace we shall also address others with much boldness of speech, our conscience not accusing us. Anger fights against gentleness, love of money against contempt of it, envy against goodness of heart. Let us make an end of this war, let us overthrow these enemies, let us set up these trophies, let us establish peace in our own city. We have within us a city and a civil polity, and citizens and aliens many: but let us banish the aliens, that our own people may not be ruined. Let no foreign nor spurious doctrine enter in, no carnal desire. See we not that, if any enemy has been caught in a city, he is judged as a spy? Then let us not only banish aliens, but let us drive out

---

[1] Mss. καὶ ἄρχοντες ἀρχομένων, καὶ ἡγούμενοι (mod. text ἡγούμενος) ὑπήκοων. A change is necessary in one or other clause, and we read ἀρχόντων ἀρχόμενοι.

enemies also. If we see one, let us deliver up to the ruler, (that is), to conscience ($\tau\hat{\varphi}\ \nu\hat{\varphi}$), that imagination which is indeed an alien, a barbarian, albeit tricked out with the garb of a citizen. For there are within us many imaginations of this kind, which are by nature indeed enemies, but are clad in sheep's skins. Just as the Persians, when they have put off the tiara, and the drawers, and the barbarian shoes, and put on the other dress which is usual with us, and have shorn themselves close, and converse in our own tongue, conceal war under their outward garb: but once apply the tortures ($\beta\alpha\sigma\acute{\alpha}\nu\sigma\upsilon\varsigma$ or "tests"), and thou bringest to light what is hidden: so here, examine (or "put to the test,") by torture again and again such an imagination as this, and thou wilt quickly see that its spirit is that of a stranger. But to show you also by way of example the sort of spies which the devil sends into us to spy out what is in us, come let us strip one of them, and examine it strictly at the tribunal: and if you please, let us bring forward some of those which were detected by Paul. "Which things," he says, "have indeed a show of wisdom in will-worship, and humility, and neglecting of the body: not in any honor to the satisfying of the flesh." (Col. ii. 23.) The devil wished to bring in Judaism: now if he had introduced it in its own form, he would not have carried his point. Accordingly, mark how he brought it about. "You must neglect the body," he says: "this is (the true) philosophy, not to admit of meats, but to guard against them: this is humility." And now again in our own times, in the case of the heretics, he wished to bring us down to the creature. See then how he dressed up his deceit. Had he said, "Worship a creature," he would have been detected: but what says he? "God" (viz. the Son and the Holy Ghost), he says, "is a created being." But let us lay bare for the decision of the judges the meaning of the Apostolic writings: there let us bring him: themselves will acknowledge both the preaching and the language. Many make gains "that they may have wherewith to give to the poor," unjust gains: this too is a wicked imagination. But let us undress it, let us convict it, that we may not be taken by it, but that having escaped all the devices of the devil, and holding to the sound doctrines with strictness, we may be able both to pass in safety through this life present, and to obtain the good things promised, through the grace and mercy of our Lord Jesus Christ, with Whom to the Father, together with the Holy Ghost, be glory, might, honor, now and ever, world without end. Amen.

HOMILY XXXVIII.

ACTS XVII. 16, 17.

"Now while Paul waited for them at Athens, his spirit was stirred in him, when he saw the city wholly given to idolatry. Therefore disputed he in the synagogue with the Jews, and with the devout persons, and in the market daily with them that met with him."

OBSERVE how he meets with greater trials among the Jews than among the Gentiles. Thus in Athens he undergoes nothing of this kind; the thing goes as far as ridicule, and there an end: and yet he did make some converts: whereas among the Jews he underwent many perils; so much greater was their hostility against him.—"His spirit," it says, "was roused within him when he saw the city all full of idols." Nowhere else were so many objects [1] of worship to be seen. But again "he disputed with the Jews in the synagogue, and in the market daily with them that met with him. Then certain of the philosophers of the Stoics and Epicureans encountered him." (v. 18.) It is a wonder the philosophers' did not laugh him to scorn, speaking in the way he did. "And some said, What does this babbler mean to say?" insolently, on the instant: [2]—this is far from philosophy. "Other some said, He seemeth to be a setter forth of strange gods," from the preaching, because he had no arrogance. They did not understand, nor comprehend the subjects he was speaking of—how should they? affirming

---

[1] The old text has $\pi\epsilon\iota\rho\alpha\sigma\mu\sigma\acute{\upsilon}\varsigma$, perhaps for $\sigma\epsilon\beta\alpha\sigma\mu\sigma\acute{\upsilon}\varsigma$. Mod. text, $\tau\sigma\sigma\alpha\hat{\upsilon}\tau\alpha\ \epsilon\check{\iota}\delta\omega\lambda\alpha$.

[2] Old text, $\sigma\check{\upsilon}\tau\omega\varsigma\ \alpha\mathring{\upsilon}\tau\sigma\hat{\upsilon}\ \phi\theta\epsilon\gamma\gamma\sigma\mu\acute{\epsilon}\nu\sigma\upsilon\ \mathring{\upsilon}\beta\rho\iota\sigma\tau\iota\kappa\hat{\omega}\varsigma\ \epsilon\mathring{\upsilon}\theta\acute{\epsilon}\omega\varsigma$ (comp. Recapitulation) $\mu\alpha\kappa\rho\grave{\alpha}\nu\ \tau\sigma\hat{\upsilon}\tau\sigma\ \phi\iota\lambda\sigma\sigma\sigma\phi\acute{\iota}\alpha\varsigma\cdot\ \mathring{\alpha}\pi\grave{\sigma}\ \tau\sigma\hat{\upsilon}\ \kappa\eta\rho\acute{\upsilon}\gamma\mu\alpha\tau\sigma\varsigma$. $\mathring{\sigma}\tau\iota\ \sigma\mathring{\upsilon}\delta\acute{\epsilon}\nu\alpha\ \tau\hat{\upsilon}\phi\sigma\nu\ \epsilon\check{\iota}\chi\epsilon\nu$. Hence Mod. text, $\sigma\mathring{\upsilon}\delta\grave{\epsilon}\ \mathring{\alpha}\pi\epsilon\pi\acute{\eta}\delta\eta\sigma\alpha\nu\ \mathring{\alpha}\pi\grave{\sigma}\ \tau\sigma\hat{\upsilon}\ \kappa\eta\rho$., $\epsilon\mathring{\iota}\pi\acute{\sigma}\nu\tau\epsilon\varsigma\cdot\ \mu\alpha\kappa\rho\grave{\sigma}\nu\ \tau\sigma\hat{\upsilon}\tau\sigma\ \phi\iota\lambda$. $\H{\sigma}\tau\iota\ \sigma\mathring{\upsilon}\delta$. τ. $\epsilon\check{\iota}\chi\epsilon\nu\ \check{\alpha}\lambda\lambda\omega\varsigma\ \delta\grave{\epsilon}\ \mathring{\sigma}\tau\iota\ \sigma\mathring{\upsilon}\kappa\ \mathring{\epsilon}\nu\acute{\sigma}\sigma\upsilon\nu\ \kappa.\ \tau.\ \lambda$. The insertion of the texts removes some of the difficulties. Perhaps $\mathring{\alpha}\pi\grave{\sigma}\ \tau\sigma\hat{\upsilon}\ \kappa\eta\rho$. is opposed to $\epsilon\mathring{\upsilon}\theta\acute{\epsilon}\omega\varsigma$: the one sort straightway expressed their disdain, with a supercilious, "What does this $\sigma\pi\epsilon\rho\mu\sigma\lambda\acute{\sigma}\gamma\sigma\varsigma$ mean to say?" the other sort did listen, and condescended to comment on the matter of the preaching, having heard it—$\mathring{\alpha}\pi\grave{\sigma}\ \tau\sigma\hat{\upsilon}\ \kappa\eta\rho$. (as in the phrase $\mathring{\alpha}\pi\grave{\sigma}\ \tau\sigma\hat{\upsilon}\ \delta\epsilon\iota\pi\nu\sigma\hat{\upsilon}$)—saying, "He seemeth," etc. Of these Chrys. may have said, $\mathring{\sigma}\tau\iota\ \sigma\mathring{\upsilon}\delta\acute{\epsilon}\nu\alpha\ \tau\hat{\upsilon}\phi\sigma\nu\ \epsilon\mathring{\iota}\chi\sigma\nu$, opp. to $\mathring{\upsilon}\beta\rho\iota\sigma\tau\iota\kappa\hat{\omega}\varsigma$. But all the Mss. have $\epsilon\check{\iota}\chi\epsilon\nu$, and so we have rendered it.

as they did, some of them, that God is a body; others, that pleasure is the (true) happiness. [1] "Of strange gods, because he preached unto them Jesus and the Resurrection:" for in fact they supposed "Anastasis" (the Resurrection) to be some deity, being accustomed to worship female divinities also.[*] "And having taken him, they brought him to the Areopagus" (v. 19)—not to punish, but in order to learn [2]—"to the Areopagus" where the trials for murder were held. Thus observe, in hope of learning (they ask him), saying, "May we know what is this new doctrine spoken of by thee? For thou bringest certain strange matters to our ears" (v. 20): everywhere novelty is the charge: "we would fain know therefore, what these things may mean." It was a city of talkers, that city of theirs. "For all the Athenians and strangers which were there spent their time in nothing else, but either to tell, or to hear some new thing. Then Paul stood in the midst of Mars hill, and said, Ye men of Athens, I look upon you as being in all things" (v. 21, 22)—he puts it by way of encomium: (the word) does not seem to mean anything offensive—δεισιδαιμονεστέρους, that is, εὐλαβεστέρους, "more religiously disposed. For as I passed by, and beheld your devotions, I found an altar with his inscription, TO AN UNKNOWN GOD. What therefore ye ignorantly worship, this declare I unto you." (v. 23.)—"On which was inscribed, To an Unknown God." The Athenians, namely, as on many occasions they had received gods from foreign parts also—for instance, the temple of Minerva, Pan, and others from different countries—being afraid that there might be some other god not yet known to them, but worshipped elsewhere, for more assurance, forsooth, erected an altar to that god also: and as the god was not known, it was inscribed, "To an Unknown God." This God then, he

tells them, is Christ; or rather, the God of all. [†] "Him declare I unto you." Observe how he shows that they had already received Him, and "it is nothing strange," says he, "nothing new that I introduce to you." All along, this was what they had been saying: "What is this new doctrine spoken of by thee? For thou bringest certain strange matters to our ears." Immediately therefore he removes this surmise of theirs: and then says, "God that made the world and all things therein, He being Lord of heaven and earth" —for, that they may not imagine Him to be one of many, he presently sets them right on this point; adding, "dwelleth not in temples made with hands" (v. 24), "neither is worshipped with men's hands, as though he needed anything"—do you observe how, little by little, he brings in the philosophy? how he ridicules the heathen error? "seeing it is He that giveth to all life, and breath, and all things; and hath made of one blood all nations of men for to dwell on all the face of the earth." This is peculiar to God. Look, then, whether these things may not be predicated of the Son also. "Being Lord," he saith, "of heaven and earth."—which they accounted to be God's. Both the creation he declares to be His work, and mankind also.[3] "Having determined," he says, "the times [4] assigned to them, and the bounds of their habitation," (v. 25, 26), "that they should seek the Lord, if haply they might feel after Him, and find Him, though He be not far from every one of us: for in Him we live, and move, and have our being: as certain also of your own poets have said, For we are also His offspring." (v. 27, 28.) This is said by Aratus the poet. Observe how he draws his arguments from things done by themselves, and from sayings of their own. "Forasmuch then as we are the offspring of God, we ought not to think that the Godhead is like unto gold, or silver,

[1] Here the Mss. have the text v. 18, and v. 19, 20 after "female divinities also."
[*] The view of Chrys. that the Greeks supposed Paul to designate by the Anastasis some goddess, has been shared by many more recent interpreters, but seems very improbable. The apostle could hardly have spoken so abstractly of the resurrection as to give rise to such a misapprehension. Paul doubtless spoke of Jesus' own resurrection and of its relation to that of believers (vid. 1 Cor. xv.), although in the text the absence of αὐτοῦ permits us to find only the idea of the general resurrection expressed.—G. B. S.
[2] Mss. and Edd. οὐχ ὥστε μαθεῖν, ἀλλ' ὥστε κολάσαι. But this cannot be Chrysostom's meaning: for in the opening of the Hom. he remarks, that there was nothing of persecution here (comp. the opening of Hom. xxxix.), and in the Recapitulation, that the Athenians at this time were under Roman Law. Also in the following sentence, he explains that their questions were prompted by the hope of learning, Ὅρα γοῦν (i. e. to show that this was their meaning) καὶ ἐν ἐλπίδι τοῦ μαθεῖν. In the Recapitulation indeed, he says, they brought him ὡς καταπλήξοντες, but this is a different thing from ὥστε κολάσαι. Therefore we have transposed the order of the words. The clause ἔνθα αἱ φονικαὶ δίκαι (and in the Recapitulation ἔνθα τὰς φ. δ. ἐδίκαζον, which we retain from B.), seems to be meant to show that they did not bring him there for trial

[†] The principal points to be noted for the interpretation of v. 23 are as follows: (1) Pausanias (A. D. 174) and Philostratus (A. D. 244) testify to the existence at Athens of altars with the inscription: ἀγνώστῳ θεῷ. (2) "Upon important occasions, when the reference to a god known by name was wanting, as in public calamities of which no definite god could be assigned as the author, in order to honor or propitiate the god concerned by sacrifice, without lighting on a wrong one, altars were erected which were destined and designated ἀγνώστῳ θεῷ." (Meyer.) (3) By these inscriptions the Athenians referred to no particular divinities, but to supposed benefactors or avengers to whom they, in their religious system, could attach no name. (4) No reference is to be found in these inscriptions to the God of the Jews. The true text : ὁ οὖν ἀγνοοῦντες εὐσεβεῖτε, τοῦτο ἐγὼ καταγγέλω ὑμῖν (instead of the masculine ὅν—τοῦτον of the cursives and the T. R.) does not require the supposition of such a reference. They acknowledged an unknown—lying beyond their pantheon. Paul declares what this is : the true God as revealed in Jesus Christ. They would only partially and gradually understand his full meaning.—G. B. S.
[3] προστετ. E. V. "before appointed" (προτετ.)
[4] Edd. καὶ τὴν δημιουργίαν ἐδήλωσε καὶ τοὺς ἀνθρώπους Comp. Recapitulation. whence it appears that he means "Both heaven and earth, and mankind also were created, not generated or emanated."

or stone, graven by art." (v. 29.) And yet
for this reason we ought.[1] By no means: for
surely we are not like (to such), nor are these
souls of ours. "And imagination of man."
How so? * * But some person might say,
"We do not think this." But it was to the
many that he was addressing himself, not now
to Philosophy. How then did they think so
unworthily of Him? Again, putting it upon
their ignorance, he says, "Now the times of
ignorance God overlooked." Having[2] agitated their minds by the fear, he then adds
this: and yet he says, "but now he com-
mandeth all men everywhere to repent."
(v. 30.) "Because He hath appointed a day,
in the which He will judge the world in righteousness by that man whom He hath ordained; whereof He hath given assurance unto
all men, in that He hath raised Him from the
dead." (v. 31.) But let us look over again
what has been said.

(Recapitulation.) (b) "And while Paul waited," etc. (v. 16.) It is providentially ordered
that against his will he stays there, while waiting for those others. (a) "His spirit," it says,
"within him" παρωξίνετο. It does not mean
there anger or exasperation: just as elsewhere
it says, "There was παροξυσμὸς between them."
(ch. xv. 30.) (c) Then what is παρωξίνετο? Was
roused: for the gift is far removed from anger

and exasperation. He could not bear it, but
pined away.[3] "He reasoned therefore in
the synagogue," etc. (v. 17.) Observe him
again reasoning with Jews. By "devout persons" he means the proselytes. For the Jews
were dispersed everywhere before (mod. text
"since") Christ's coming, the Law indeed being henceforth, so to say, in process of dissolution, but at the same time (the dispersed
Jews) teaching men religion.[4] But those prevailed nothing, save only that they got witnesses of their own calamities. (e) "And
certain philosophers," etc. (v. 18.) How
came they to be willing to confer with him?
(They did it) when they saw others reasoning,
and the man having repute (in the encounter).
And observe straightway with overbearing insolence, "some said, What would this babbler
say? For the natural man receiveth not the
things of the Spirit." (1 Cor. ii. 14.) Other
some, He seemeth to be a setter-forth of
strange deities: δαιμονίων, for so they called
their gods. "And having taken him, they
brought him," etc. (v. 19.) (a) The Athenians no longer enjoyed their own laws, but were
become subject to the Romans. (g) (Then) why
did they hale him to the Areopagus? Meaning
to overawe him—(the place) where they held
the trials for bloodshed. "May we know,
what is this new doctrine spoken of by thee?
For thou bringest certain strange things to our
ears; we would fain know therefore what
these things mean. For all the Athenians and
strangers which were there spent their time in
nothing else, but either to tell, or to hear some
new thing." (v. 20, 21.) Here the thing
noted is, that though ever occupied only in this
telling and hearing, yet they thought those
things strange—things which they had never
heard. "Then Paul standing in the midst of
the Areopagus said, Ye men of Athens, I look
upon you as being in all things more religiously disposed" (v. 22): (f) for the cities
were full of gods (δαιμόνων, al. εἰδώλων): (h) this is
why he says δεισιδαιμονεστέρους. "For as I
passed by and viewed the objects of your wor-

---

[1] Καὶ μὴν διὰ τοῦτο ὀφείλομεν. Mod. text inserts a φησὶν, to
make this an interlocution, in the sense, "Nay but for this
reason, viz., being His offspring, we ought to think of Him as
in the likeness of man." But this cannot be Chrysostom's
meaning. Perhaps Chrys. said, οὐδὲ τοῦτο, viz., after the following sentence, so that the sense will be, "We ought not to
think the Godhead like unto gold, etc., the graven work of
man's art. By no means: for certainly we ourselves, our
souls, are not like unto such. Nay, more, we ought not to
think even this, that the Godhead is like unto aught that
man's imagination can conceive, as the Apostle adds, καὶ
ἐνθυμήσεως ἀνθρώπου τὸ Θεῖον εἶκαι ὅμοιον." (See the Recapitulation.) He proceeds: τί δήποτε; i. e. Why having said
χαράγματι τέχνης does he add καὶ ἐνθυμ. ὀνθρ.? The answer,
not expressed here, is, "Because neither is it subject to any
other human conception," (διανοίᾳ, Recapitulation). Then,
the old text has, οὐκ ἔστι ταῦτα τῆς φιλοσοφίαν· πῶς οὖν πάλιν τὸ
ζητούμενον· τοὺς μὲν οὖν χρον. κ. τ. λ. Here we insert from the
Recapitulation a sentence, which, where it stands, is superfluous (p. 236, note [6]): Ἀλλ' εἴποι ἄν τις, Οὐ τοῦτο νομίζομεν.
Ἀλλὰ πρὸς τοὺς πολλοὺς ὁ λόγος ἦν αὐτῷ, and then, οὔκετι (so we
correct οὐκ ἔστι) πρὸς φιλοσοφίαν. i. e. "Philosophers may
say, We do not so think of the Godhead. But he is not dealing with Philosophy, but πρὸς τοὺς πολλούς. Πῶς οὖν οὐχ εὑροῦ;
or the like; Πάλιν τὸ ζητούμενον. Again coming to the question in hand (An 'Unknown' God, Whom ye 'ignorantly
worship, he says). Now the times of ignorance," etc.—Mod.
text. "Why did he not immediately come (ἔστη) to Philosophy, and say, God is incorporeal by nature, invisible and
without form? Because it seemed superfluous at present to
say these things to men who had not yet (μήπω om. E.) learned
that there is but one God. Therefore leaving those matters,
he addresses himself (ἵσταται) to the matter in hand, and says,
Now the times," etc.

[2] Old text inserts here the whole of v. 30, 31, then, καίτοιγέ
φησιν, ὥρισεν ἡμ. ἀναστήσας αὐτὸν ἐκ νεκρῶν. Κατασείσας αὐτῶν
τὴν διανοίαν τῷ φόβῳ, τότε ἐπάγει τοῦτο. It appears from the
Recapitulation that κατ. τῷ φ. refers to the preceding verses,
being explained by δείξας ἀναπολογήτους: and ἐπάγει τοῦτο to
the first clause of v. 30, the overlooking of the times of ignorance. We have arranged the matter accordingly.—Mod. text,
v. 30, 31. "See, having agitated their minds by saying, 'He
hath appointed a day,' and terrified them, then he seasonably
adds this, 'Having raised Him from the dead.'" Which is
clearly not Chrysostom's meaning.

[3] οὐκ ἔφερεν, ἀλλ' ἐτήκετο. The latter word seems incongruous, unless there be a reference to what St. Paul says of
the state of his mind while waiting at Athens, in 1 Thess. ii. 1.
q. d. this is not the state of feeling in which one is apt to give
way to anger and irritation.

[4] ἅμα μὲν τοῦ νόμου λυομένου φησὶν λοιπόν, ἅμα δὲ διδάσκοντες
εὐσέβειαν τοὺς ἀνθρώπους. i. e. "of which dispersion the consequence was indeed a breaking down, it may be said, of the
Law (by intermarriages, etc.), but withal a spreading of the
true religion among men." Mod. text, having mistakenly
changed πρὸ to ἀπὸ, inserts ἐξ ἐκείνου "from that time" before
τοῦ νόμου; and also omits φησὶν λοιπόν, which the innovator
did not understand.—Ἀλλ' οὐδὲν ἴσχυσαν (mod. text, ἐκέρδαναν)
ἐκεῖνοι. But those Jews, for all their success in spreading
their religion, availed nothing, save that they got (more) witnesses (μαρτυρίας perhaps should be μάρτυρας) of their own
proper calamities (when the wrath came upon them to the
uttermost); i. e. they prepared the way for the Gospel, but for
themselves they availed nothing, but only to increase the
number of those who should bear witness to the truth of God's
judgment upon them for their unbelief.

ship—he does not say simply τοὺς δαίμονας (the demons, or deities), but paves the way for his discourse : "I beheld an altar," etc. (v. 23.) This is why he says, "I look upon you as being more religiously disposed," viz. because of the altar. "God," he says, "that made the world." (v. 24.) He uttered one word, by which he has subverted all the (doctrines) of the philosophers. For the Epicureans affirm all to be fortuitously formed and (by concourse) of atoms, the Stoics held it to be body and fire (ἐκπύρωσιν). "The world and all that is therein." Do you mark the conciseness, and in conciseness, clearness? Mark what were the things that were strange to them : that God made the world! Things which now any of the most ordinary persons know, these the Athenians and the wise men of the Athenians knew not. "Seeing He is Lord of heaven and earth :" for if He made them, it is clear that He is Lord. Observe what he affirms to be the note of Deity—creation. Which attribute the Son also hath. For the Prophets everywhere affirm this, that to create is God's prerogative. Not as those affirm [1] that another is Maker but not Lord, assuming that matter is uncreated. Here now he covertly affirms and establishes his own, while he overthrows their doctrine.[2] "Dwelleth not in temples made with hands." For He does indeed dwell in temples, yet not in such, but in man's soul. He overthrows the corporeal worship. What then? Did He not dwell in the temple at Jerusalem? No, indeed : but He wrought therein. "Neither is worshipped by men's hands." (v. 25.) How then was He worshipped by men's hands among the Jews? Not by hands, but by the understanding. "As though He needed anything:" since even those (acts of worship) He did not in this sort seek, "as having need. Shall I eat," saith He, "the flesh of bulls, or drink the blood of goats?" (Ps. l. 13.) Neither is this enough—the having need of naught—which he has affirmed : for though this is Divine, yet a further attribute must be added. "Seeing it is He that giveth unto all, life and breath and all things." Two proofs of Godhead : Himself to have need of naught, and to supply all things to all men. Produce here Plato (and) all that he has philosophized

about God, all that Epicurus has : and all is but trifling to this! "Giveth," he says, "life and breath." Lo, he makes Him the Creator of the soul also, not its begetter. See again how he overthrows the doctrine about matter. "And made," he says, "of one blood every nation of men to dwell upon all the face of the earth." (v. 26.) These things are better than the former : and what an impeachment both of the atoms and of matter, that (creation) is not a partial (work), nor the soul of man either.[3] But this, which those say, is not to be Creator.[4]—But by the mind and understanding He is worshipped.—"It is He that giveth," etc. He not the partial (μερικοὶ δαίμονες) deities. "And all things." It is "He," he saith.—How man also came into being.[5]—First he showed that "He dwelleth not," etc., and then declared[6] that He "is not worshipped as though He had need of aught." If God,[7] He made all : but if He made not, He is not God. Gods that made not heaven and earth, let them perish. He introduces much greater doctrines, though as yet he does not mention the great doctrines ; but he discoursed to them as unto children. And these were much greater than those. Creation, Lordship, the having need of naught, authorship of all good—these he has declared. But[8] how is He worshipped? say. It is not yet the proper time. What equal to this sublimity? Marvellous is this also—of one, to have made so many : but also, having made, Himself sustains them (συγκρατεῖ) in being, "giving life and breath and all things. (b) And hath determined the times appointed, and the bounds of their habitation, that they should seek God, if haply they might feel after Him and find Him." (v. 27.) (a) It means either this, that He did not compel them to go about and seek God, but according to the bounds[9] of their habitation : (c) or this, that He determined

[1] This, as it stands seems to be meant rather for the Manichæans than the heathen philosophers, to whom, he has just before said, the very notion of creation was strange. But the whole exposition is most inadequately given, through the carelessness or incompetency of the reporter. To be referred to the heathen, it should be ἄλλον μὲν εἶναι κύριον (as Jupiter) οὐ ποιητὴν δέ : and this is favored, perhaps, by the unnecessary τὴν δὲ (omitted by A. B.) as remaining from οὐ ποιητὴν δὲ ἀγέννητον ὕλην ὑποτίθεντες.

[2] Ἐνταῦθα λοιπὸν αἰνιγματωδῶς εἶπε τὸ αὐτοῦ ἔστησε—i. e. in speaking of God, he at the same time hints at the coequal Godhead of the Son : for He also is Creator and Lord. See p. 233 in the comments on v. 23, and v. 25, 26.

[3] ὅτι οὐκ ἔστι μερικὴ, οὐδὲ ψυχὴ τοῦ ἀνθρώπου. "This is very obscure, and seems remote from the matter in hand. Hales ap. Sav. thinks it has come into the text from some other place. I should rather think the passage either mutilated or corrupt." BEN. "There is nothing either obscure or corrupt in the passage." ED. PAR. The meaning seems to be, As the whole creation is the work of One God, not μερικῶς but τὸ καθόλου, so are all mankind, universally, HIS work ; the soul too, as well as the body.
[4] This and the following sentences seem to be fragments belonging to the preceding exposition. But the whole is too confused and mangled to admit of any satisfactory restoration.
[5] Πῶς καὶ ἄνθρωπος γέγονε. Or (see note [2].) "How He (the Son) became man"—as belonging to some other place ; e. g. after οὐδέπω τὰ μεγάλα εἶπεν. Or this may be put in the place of πῶς θεραπεύεται, note [8]. Mod. text. "Having before shown, how the heaven was made, then he declared," etc.
[6] ἀπεφήνατο· aoove, τὸ μηδένος δεῖσθαι, ὅπερ ἀπεφήνατο.
[7] This also may be part of the argument against the Arians, which Chrys. seems to have brought into his exposition. See note [2].
[8] This is clearly out of place. Perhaps πῶς καὶ ἄνθρωπος γέγονε (note [5].) belongs here.
[9] Κατὰ τὰς ὁροθεσίας. Perhaps Chrys. may have read κατὰ τὰς ὁρ. in his copy of the Acts : as Cod. Bezæ and S. Irenæus, κατὰ τὴν ὁροθεσίαν.

their seeking God, yet not determined this (to be done) continually, but (determined) certain appointed times (when they should do so) : showing[1] now, that not having sought they had found : for since, having sought, they had not found, he shows that God was now as manifest, as though He were in the midst of them palpably (ψηλαφώμενος). (e) "Though He be not far," he saith, "from every one of us," but is near to all. See again the power (or, "what it is to be God,") of God. What saith he? Not only He gave "life and breath and all things," but, as the sum and substance of all, He brought us to the knowledge of Himself, by giving us these things by which we are able to find and to apprehend Him. But we did not wish to find Him, albeit close at hand. "Though He be not far from every one of us." Why look now, He is near to all, to every one all the world over! What can be greater than this? See how he makes clear riddance of the parcel deities (τοὺς μερικούς)! What say I, "afar off?" He is so near, that without Him we live not : "for in Him we live and move and have our being." (v. 28.) "In him;" to put it by way of corporeal similitude, even as it is impossible to be ignorant of the air which is diffused on every side around us, and is "not far from every one of us," nay rather, which is in us. (d) For it was not so that there was a heaven in one place, in another none, nor yet (a heaven) at one time, at another none. So that both at every "time" and at every "bound" it was possible to find Him. He so ordered things, that neither by place nor by time were men hindered. For of course even this, if nothing else, of itself was a help to them—that the heaven is in every place, that it stands in all time. (f) See how (he declares) His Providence, and His upholding power (συγκράτησιν); the existence of all things from Him, (from Him) their working (τὸ ἐνεργεῖν), (from Him their preservation) that they perish not. And he does not say, "Through Him," but, what was nearer than this, "In him."— That poet said nothing equal to this, "For we are His offspring." He, however, spake it of Jupiter, but Paul takes it of the Creator, not meaning the same being as he, God forbid! but meaning what is properly predicated of God : just as he spoke of the altar with reference to Him, not to the being whom they worshipped. As much as to say, "For certain things are said and done with reference to this (true God), but ye know not that they are with

reference to Him." For say, of whom would it be properly said, "To an Unknown God?" Of the Creator, or of the demon? Manifestly of the Creator : because Him they knew not, but the other they knew. Again, that all things are filled (with the presence)—of God? or of Jupiter—a wretch of a man, a detestable impostor! But Paul said it not in the same sense as he, God forbid! but with quite a different meaning. For he says we are God's offspring, i. e. God's own,[2] His nearest neighbors as it were. For lest, when he says, "Being the offspring of God" (v. 29), they should again say, Thou bringest certain strange things to our ears,[3] he produces the poet. He does not say, "Ye ought not to think the Godhead like to gold or silver," ye accursed and execrable : but in more lowly sort he says, "We ought not." For what (says he)?[4] God is above this? No, he does not say this either : but for the present this— "We ought not to think the Godhead like unto such," for nothing is so opposite to men. "But we do not affirm the Godhead to be like unto this, for who would say that?" Mark[5] how he has introduced the incorporeal (nature of God) when he said, "In Him," etc., for the mind, when it surmises body, at the same time implies the notion of distance. (Speaking) to the many he says, "We ought not to think the Godhead like unto gold, or silver, or stone, the shaping of art,"[6] for if we are not like to those as regards the soul, much more God (is not like to such). So far, he withdraws them from the notion. But neither is the Godhead, he would say, subjected to any other human conception. For[7] if that which art or thought

---

[1] Mod. text spoiling the sense : "And this he says, showing that not even now had they, having sought, found : although He was as plain to be found as anything would be that was (set) in the midst to be handled."

[2] Old text : Τουτέστιν, οἰκείους, ἐγγυτάτους ὥσπερ παροίκους καὶ γείτονας ὅταν λέγῃ : so Cat. The two last words are out of place ; we insert them with the text-words after Ἵνα γὰρ μὴ. The sense is : He does not mean, with the heathen poet, that mankind came from God by generation or emanation : but that we are very near to Him.

[3] Here Mss. and Edd. have οὐδὲν γὰρ οὕτως ἀνθρώποις ἐναντίον, as if it meant, "nothing so goes against men as strangeness." We place it in what seems a more suitable connection : "We ought not to think," etc. for so far from "the Godhead" being "like unto such," nothing is so much the reverse of like unto men, who "are his offspring."

[4] τί γάρ; ὑπὲρ τοῦτο Θεός; οὐδὲ τοῦτο· ἀλλὰ τέως τοῦτο· A. B. C., τί γὰρ τὸ ὑπὲρ τοῦτο Θεός· οὐδὲ κ. τ. λ. Cat. om. τί γὰρ τὸ, and ἀλλὰ τέως τοῦτο. Mod. text, ἀλλ' ὑπὲρ τοῦτο. τί δαὶ τὸ ὑπὲρ τοῦτο; Θεός· ἀλλ' οὐδὲ τοῦτο, ἐνεργείας γάρ ἐστιν ὄνομα· ἀλλὰ τέως τοῦτο.

[5] Possibly the connection may be, "He is not addressing himself to the notions of philosophers, (supra, note[1], p. 234) : for them he insinuated τὸ ἀσώματον by the Ἐν αὐτῷ ζῶμεν, the intimate presence of Deity, the denial of body by the denial of διάστημα which is necessarily implied in the notion of body. But he speaks to the many, and puts it to them in this way, We, being in respect of the soul, akin to God, ought not to think," etc.—Mod. text omits πρὸς τοὺς πολλούς.

[6] Here the Mss. and Edd. have the sentence ἀλλ' εἴποι ἄν τις—ὁ λόγος αὐτῷ, which we have transferred above, p. 234, note[1]. In the next sentence, εἰ γὰρ ἡμεῖς οὐκ ἐσμεν ὅμοιοι ἐκείνοις τὸ κατὰ ψυχήν, A. B. C. omit the negative, which Cat. and mod. text retain.

[7] Εἰ γὰρ ἢ τέχνη ἢ διάνοια εὗρε, A. B. C. but Cat. om. εἰ γάρ, mod. text ἢ γὰρ τέχνη ἢ δ. εὗρε. Διὰ τοῦτο οὕτως εἶπεν· A. also has this last clause, which is unknown to B. C. Cat. In the translation we assume the reading to be, Εἰ γὰρ ὅπερ ἢ τ. ἢ δ. εὗρε—διὰ τοῦτο οὕτως "τέχν. ἢ ἐνθ. ἄ."—ὅπερ οὖν ἢ τ. ἢ δ. ἄ. εὗρε, τοῦτο ὁ Θεός, καὶ ἐν λίθῳ οὐσία θεοῦ.

has found—this is why he says it thus, " of art or imagination of man" —if that, then, which human art or thought has found, is God, then even in the stone (is) God's essence.—How comes it then, if "in Him we live," that we do not find Him? The charge is twofold, both that they did not find Him, and that they found such as these. The (human) understanding in itself is not at all to be relied upon.—But when he has agitated their soul by showing them to be without excuse, see what he says : " The times of ignorance God overlooked, but now commands all men everywhere to repent." (v. 30.) What then? Are none of these men to be punished? None of them that are willing to repent. He says it of these men, not of the departed, but of them whom He commands to repent. He does not call you to account, he would say. He does not say, Took no notice (παρεῖδεν); does not say, Permitted : but, Ye were ignorant. "Overlooked," i. e. does not demand punishment as of men that deserve punishment. Ye were ignorant. And he does not say, Ye wilfully did evil.; but this he showed by what he said above.[1]—" All men everywhere to repent:" again he hints at the whole world. Observe how he takes them off from the parcel deities! " Because He has appointed a day, in the which He will judge the world in righteousness by that Man whom He hath ordained, whereof He hath given assurance to all men, in that He raised Him from the dead." (v. 31.) Observe how he again declares the Passion. Observe the terror again : for, that the judgment is true, is clear from the raising Him up : for it is alleged in proof of that. That all he has been saying is true, is clear from the fact that He rose again. For He did give [2] this "assurance to all men," His rising from the dead : this (i. e. judgment), also is henceforth certain.

These words were spoken indeed to the Athenians : but it were seasonable that one should say to us also, "that all men everywhere must repent, because he hath appointed a day, in the which He will judge the world." See how he brings Him in as Judge also : Him, both provident for the world, and merciful and forgiving and powerful and wise, and, in a word possessing all the attributes of a Creator. " Having given assurance to all men," i. e. He has given proof in the rising (of Jesus) from the dead.[3]

Let us repent then : for we must assuredly be judged. If Christ rose not, we shall not be judged : but if he rose, we shall without doubt be judged. " For to this end," it is said, "did He also die, that he might be Lord both of the dead and living." (Rom. xiv. 9.) " For we shall all stand before the judgment seat of Christ, that every one may receive according to that he hath done." (Rom. xiv. 10, and 2 Cor. v. 10.) Do not imagine that these are but words. Lo! he introduced also the subject of the resurrection of all men ; for in no other way can the world be judged. And that, "In that He hath raised Him from the dead," relates to the body : for that was dead, that had fallen. Among the Greeks, as their notions of Creation, so likewise of the Judgment, are children's fancies, ravings of drunken men. But let us, who know these things accurately, do something that is to the purpose : let us be made friends unto God. How long shall we be at enmity with Him? How long shall we entertain dislike towards Him? "God forbid!" you will say : "Why do you say such things?" I would wish not to say the things I say, if ye did not do the things ye do : but as things are, what is the use now in keeping silence from words, when the plain evidence of deeds so cries aloud? How then, how shall we love Him? I have told you thousands of ways, thousands of times : but I will speak it also now. One way I seem to myself to have discovered, a very great and admirable way. Namely,[4] after acknowledging to Him our general obligations,—what none shall be able to express (I mean), what has been done for each of us in his own person, of these also let us bethink ourselves, because these are of great force : let each one of us reckon them up with himself, and make diligent search, and as it were in a book let him have the benefits of God written down ; for instance, if at any time having fallen into dangers he has escaped the hands of his enemies ; if ever having gone out on a journey at an untimely hour, he has escaped danger ; if ever, having had an encounter with wicked men, he has got the better of them ; or if ever, having fallen into sickness, he has recovered when all had given him over : for this avails much for attaching us to God. For if that Mordecai, when the services done by him were brought to the

---

[1] i. e. in v. 27. " that they should seek the Lord . . . being, as He is, not far from every one of us." But mod. text refers it to the following clause, by adding εἰπών.

[2] Πᾶσι γὰρ ταύτην παρεῖχε πίστιν, i. e. God ; but C. and mod. text παρεῖχον, as if it meant " the Apostles gave assurance of Christ's resurrection," overlooking the πίστιν παρασχὼν of the text.'

[3] Mod. text "The things spoken have given proof of His rising from the dead."

[4] A. B. C. μετὰ γὰρ ταῦτα καθολικὰς εἰδέναι αὑτῷ. The sense would be satisfied by μετὰ τὸ τὰς καθ. εἰδέναι αὑτῷ χάριτας. Mod. text. " Together with the reckoning up of what God has done for us in common (benefits), so many that none is able even to number them, and giving Him thanks for all these, let us all bethink us of what has been done for each one of us, and reckon them up day by day. Since then these," etc.

king's remembrance, found them to be so available, that he in return rose to that height of splendor (Esther vi. 2–11): much more we, if we call to mind, and make diligent enquiry of these two points, what sins we have committed against God, and what good He has done to us, shall thus both be thankful, and give Him freely all that is ours. But no one gives a thought to any of these things : but just as regarding our sins we say that we are sinners, while we do not enquire into them specifically, so with regard to God's benefits (we say), that God has done us good, and do not specifically enquire, where, and in how great number, and at what time. But from this time forth let us be very exact in our reckoning. For if any one can recall even those things which happened long ago, let him reckon up all accurately, as one who will find a great treasure. This is also profitable to us in keeping us from despair. For when we see that he has often protected us, we shall not despair, nor suppose that we are cast off : but we shall take it as a strong pledge of His care for us, when we bethink us how, though we have sinned, we are not punished, but even enjoy protection from Him. Let me now tell you a case, which I heard from a certain person, in which was a child, and it happened on a time that he was in the country with his mother, being not yet fifteen years old. Just then there came a bad air, in consequence of which a fever attacked them both, for in fact it was the autumn season. It happened that the mother succeeded in getting into the town before (they could stop her); but the boy, when the physicians on the spot[1] ordered him, with the fever burning within him, to gargle his throat, resisted, having forsooth his own wise view of the matter, and thinking he should be better able to quench the fire, if he took nothing whatever, therefore, in his unseasonable spirit of opposition, boy-like, he would take nothing. But when he came into the town, his tongue was paralyzed, and he was for a long time speechless, so that he could pronounce nothing articulately; however, he could read indeed, and attended masters for a long time, but[2] that was all, and there was nothing to mark his progress. So all his hopes (in life) were cut off, and his mother was full of grief : and though the physicians suggested many plans, and many others did so too, yet nobody was able to do him any good, until the merciful God loosed the string of his tongue (cf. Mark vii. 35), and then he recovered, and was restored to his former readiness and distinctness of speech. His mother also related, that when a very little child, he had an affection in the nose, which they call a polypus : and then too the physicians had given him over and his father cursed him (for the father was then living), and (even) his mother prayed for him to die ;[3] and all was full of distress. But he on a sudden having coughed, owing to the collection of mucus, by the force of the breath expelled the creature (τὸ θηρίον) from his nostrils, and all the danger was removed. But this evil having been extinguished, an acrid and viscid running from the eyes formed such a thick gathering of the humors (τὰς λήμας), that it was like a skin drawn over the pupil, and what was worse, it threatened blindness, and everybody said this would be the issue. But from this disease also was he quickly freed by the grace of God. So far what I have heard from others : now I will tell you what I myself know. Once on a time a suspicion of tyrants was raised in our city— at that time I was but a youth—and all the soldiers being set to watch without the city as it chanced, they were making strict[4] inquisition after books of sorcery and magic. And the person who had written the book, had flung it unbound (ἀκατασκεύαστον) into the river, and was taken, and when asked for it, was not able to give it up, but was carried all around the city in bonds : when, however, the evidence being brought home to him, he had suffered punishment, just then it chanced that I, wishing to go to the Martyrs' Church, was returning through the gardens by the riverside in company with another person. He, seeing the book floating on the water at first thought it was a linen cloth, but when he got near, perceived it was a book, so he went down, and took it up. I however called shares in the booty, and laughed about it. But let us see, says he, what in

---

[1] τῶν ἰατρῶν τῶν ἐκεῖ. Mod. text omits τῶν, and adds μένειν, καὶ : "the physicians ordering him to stay there." The Mss., except A. which has preserved the true reading εἴρξατο, have ἦρξατο, whence Erasm. Ben. *capit gargarizare*—just what the boy refused to do. He would not take the gargle, nor any other medicine or food.—For σβέννυται we restore with mod. text σβεννύναι.—ὡς δῆθεν φιλοσοφῶν either as above, or "to show his strength of mind forsooth."—ὑπὲρ φιλονεικίας, B. φιλοτιμίας. (Erasmus' translation is altogether wide of the sense.)

[2] ἁπλῶς δὲ (καὶ mod. text.) ἀσημα. Meaning perhaps, "being speechless, he read and heard, but could not give tokens of understanding what he learned."

[3] Mss. καὶ ὁ πατὴρ αὐτῷ κατηρᾶτο, καὶ τελευτῆσαι ηὔχετο καὶ ἡ μητήρ· ἔτι γὰρ ἔτυχε ζῶν ὁ πατὴρ αὐτοῦ. Mod. text, "His mother prayed for him to die, and his father cursed him, for he was yet living."

[4] τυχὸν ἀπλάστως ζητούντων· meaning perhaps, in earnest not for form's sake. The occasion of this strictness was doubtless the affair of Theodorus the Sicilian, see t. i. 343 B. and 470 D. (Πρὸ δέκα τούτων ἐτῶν ἑάλωσαν ἐπὶ τυραννίδι τινὲς κ. τ. λ.) For the history of the treasonable and magical practices against Valens at Antioch, in which Theodorus was implicated, and of the severities exercised in consequence of that attempt, see Ammianus Marcell. xxix. init. Comp. Zosimus iv. 13, 3, Sozomen vi. 35, Socrates iv. 19.

the world it is. So he turns back a part of the page, and finds the contents to be magic. At that very moment it chanced that a soldier came by : * * * then having taken from within,[1] he went off. There were we congealed with fear. For who would have believed our story that we had picked it up from the river, when all were at that time, even the unsuspected, under strict watch ? And we did not dare to cast it away, lest we should be seen, and there was a like danger to us in tearing it to pieces. God gave us means, and we cast it away, and at last we were free for that time from the extreme peril. And I might mention numberless cases, if I had a mind to recount all. And even these I have mentioned for your sakes, so that, if any have other cases, although not such as these, let him bear them in mind constantly : for example, if at any time a stone having been hurled, and being about to strike thee, has not struck thee, do thou bear this ever in thy mind : these things produce in us great affection towards God. For if on remembering any men who have been the means of saving us, we are much mortified if we be not able to requite them, much more (should we feel thus) with regard to God. This too is useful in other respects. When we wish not to be overmuch grieved, let us say : " If we have received good things at the hand of the Lord, shall not we endure evil things ? " (Job ii. 10.) And when Paul told them from whence he had been delivered, (2 Tim. iv. 17) the reason was that he might put them also in mind. See too how Jacob kept all these things in his mind : wherefore also he said : " The Angel which redeemed me from my youth up (Gen. xlviii. 16) ; and not only that he redeemed him, but how and for what purpose. See accordingly how he also calls to mind the benefits he had received in particular. " With my staff," he says, " I passed over Jordan." (Gen. xxxii. 10.) The Jews also always remembered the things which happened to their forefathers, turning over in their minds the things done in Egypt. Then much more let us, bearing in mind the special mercies which have happened to us also, how often we have fallen into dangers and calamities, and unless God had held his hand over us, should long ago have perished : I say, let us all, considering these things and recounting them day by day, return our united thanks all of us to God, and never cease to glorify Him, that so we may receive a large recompense for our thankfulness of heart, through the grace and compassion of His only begotten Son, with Whom to the Father, together with the Holy Ghost, be glory, might, honor, now and ever, world without end. Amen.

HOMILY XXXIX.

ACTS XVII. 32-34. XVIII. 1.

" And when they heard of the resurrection of the dead, some mocked : and others said, We will hear thee again of this matter. So Paul departed from among them. Howbeit certain men clave unto him, and believed : among the which was Dionysius the Areopagite, and a woman named Damaris, and others with them. After these things Paul departed from Athens, and came to Corinth."

WHAT can be the reason that, having persuaded (some so far as to say) that they would hear him again, and there being no dangers, Paul is so in haste to leave Athens ? Probably he knew that he should do them no great good ; moreover he was led by the Spirit to Corinth.[2] (b) For the Athenians, although fond of hearing strange things, nevertheless did not attend (to him) ; for this was not their study, but only to be always having something to say ; which was the cause that made them hold off from him. But if this was their custom, how is it that they accuse him, " he seemeth to be a setter forth of strange gods ? " (ch. xvii. 18.) Yes, but these

---

[1] εἶτα ἔνδοθεν λαβὼν ἀπῄει· ἀπεπάγη τῷ δέει. It is not easy to see what this means, unless the sense intended be, " the soldier paced backward and forward, so that we were intercepted between his walk and the river."—Mod. text, εἶτα ἔ. λ, ἀπῄει καὶ ἀπεπήγει τῷ δέει Erasm *qui hoc animadvertens abiit, et timere nos fecit*. Ben. Hinc. *vero socius. illo occultato abiit et timere tabescebat*. We must certainly read ἀπεπάγην, or ἀπεπάγημεν.

[2] Here in Mss. and Edd. the order is confused by the insertion of the text xvii. 34; xviii. 1-3, and the transposition of the sentence marked (a), in consequence of which the first sentence of (c) has been misunderstood, as if it meant that St. Paul thought it enough merely to sow the seeds at Athens (τέως mod. text Cat. τῶν λόγων), "because the greater part of his life was now passed." So Cat. is further betrayed into a misconception of the following words ἐπὶ μὲν γὰρ Νέρωνος ἐτελειώθη, adding ὁ Παῦλος, as if it referred to St. Paul's martyrdom: and so Ben. mistakes the matter. *major' enim pars vitæ illius jam (ἐνταῦθα) transacta erat. Nam sub Nerone consummatus est*, as Erasm. *occisus est :*' though the opposition to the ἐπὶ μὲν N. in the following clause ἀπὸ δὲ Κλ., might have obviated this misapprehension.

were matters they did not at all know what to make of. Howbeit, he did convert both Dionysius the Areopagite, and some others. For those who were careful of (right) living, quickly received the word; but the others not so. It seemed to Paul sufficient to have cast the seeds of the doctrines. (*a*) To Corinth then, as I said, he was led by the Spirit, in which city he was to abide. (*c*) "And ₁having found a certain Jew named Aquila, of Pontus by birth, lately come from Italy "— for the greater part of his life had been passed there—" and Priscilla his wife, because that Claudius had commanded all the Jews to depart from Rome." (v. 2.) For though it was in the reign of Nero that the war against the Jews was consummated, yet from the time of Claudius and thenceforward it was fanning up, at a distance indeed, [1] so that, were it but so, they might come to their senses, and from Rome they were now driven as common pests. This is why it is so ordered by Providence that Paul was led thither as a prisoner, that he might not as a Jew be driven away, but as acting under military custody might even be guarded there. (Having found these,) "he came to them, and because he was of the same craft, he abode with them and wrought: for by occupation they were tent-makers." (v. 3.) Lo, what a justification he found for dwelling in the same house with them! For because here, of all places, it was necessary that he should not receive, as he himself says, "That wherein they glory, they may be found, even as we" (2 Cor. xi. 12), it is providentially ordered that he there abides. "And he reasoned in the synagogue every sabbath, and persuaded the Jews and the Greeks. And when Silas and Timotheus were come from Macedonia, Paul was straitened in the word, [2] testifying to the Jews that Jesus is the Christ." (v. 4, 5.) "And when the Jews opposed and blasphemed," i. e. they tried to bear him down (ἐπηρέαζον), they set upon him—What then does Paul? He separates from them, and in a very awful manner: and though he does not now say, "It was need that the word should be spoken unto you," yet he darkly intimates it to them :—" and when they opposed themselves, and blasphemed, he shook his raiment, and said unto them, Your blood be upon your own heads; I am clean: from henceforth I will go unto the Gentiles." (v. 6.) "And he departed thence, and entered into a certain man's house, named Justus, one that worshipped God, whose house joined hard to the synagogue." See how having

again said, "Henceforth—" for all that, he does not neglect them ; so that it was to rouse them that he said this, and thereupon came to Justus, whose house was contiguous to the synagogue, so that [3] even from this they might have jealousy, from the very proximity. "And Crispus, the chief ruler of the synagogue, believed on the Lord with all his house." This also was, of all things, enough to bring them over. "And many of the Corinthians hearing believed, and were baptized. Then spake the Lord to Paul in the night by a vision, Be not afraid, but speak, and hold not thy peace : for I am with thee, and no man shall set on thee to hurt thee : for I have much people in this city." (v. 8–10.) See by how many reasons He persuades him, and how He puts last the reason which of all others most prevailed with him, "I have much people in this city." Then how was it, you may ask, that they set upon him? And [4] yet, the writer tells us, they prevailed nothing, but brought him to the proconsul. "And he continued there a year and six months, teaching the word of God among them. And when Gallio was proconsul of Achaia, the Jews made insurrection with one accord against Paul, and brought him to the judgment-seat." (v. 11, 12.) Do you mark why those men were ever contriving to give a public turn to the misdemeanors (they accused them of)? Thus see here : (*b*) "Saying, This fellow seduceth men contrary to the law to worship God. And when Paul was about to open his mouth, Gallio said : If indeed it were any wrong-doing or wicked lewdness, O ye Jews, reason would that I should bear with you. But if it be a question of words and names, and of your law, look ye to it; for I will be no judge of such matters. And he drave them from the judgment-seat." (v. 13–16.) This Gallio seems to me to have been a sensible man. (*a*) Thus observe, when these had said, "Against the law he seduceth men to worship God," he "cared for none of these things :" and observe how he answers them : "If indeed it were" any matter affecting the city, "any wrong-doing or wicked lewdness," etc. (*c*) "Then all the Jews,[5] took Sosthenes the ruler of the synagogue, and beat him before the judgment-seat : and Gallio cared

---

[1] See Recapitulation, p. 239, note [1].
[2] A. B. C. τῷ λόγῳ: so the best Mss. of the Acts, Gr. and Lat. *instabat verbo*.

[3] A. B. C. ὥστε καὶ ἀπὸ (B. om.) τοῦ ζήλου (ζῆλον C.) ἔχειν ἀπὸ τῆς γειτνιάσεως. Cat. has preserved the true reading, ἀπὸ τούτου ζῆλον.
[4] This would be better transposed thus : καὶ μὴν, φησὶν, ἤγαγον αὐτὸν πρὸς τὸν ἀνθ., ἀλλ᾽ ιοὐδὲν σχυσαν. Mod. text, "but they *only* brought him," etc. What follows is confused by the transposition after ὅρα γοὐν ἐνταῦθα of the part (*a*) beginning with the same words.
[5] The Mss. have οἱ Ἕλληνες as in some copies of the Acts and Elz., but the best authorities Gr. and Lat. simply πάντες. We adopt οἱ Ἰουδαῖοι from the Catena, and Chrys. evidently understood it of the Jews.

for none of these things " (v. 17) : but their beating him he did not take as an insult to himself. So petulant were the Jews. But let us look over again what has been said.

(Recapitulation.) " And when they heard," (ch. xvii. 32) what great and lofty doctrines, they did not even attend, but jeered at the Resurrection ! " For the natural man," it saith, " receiveth not the things of the Spirit." (1 Cor. ii. 14.) " And so," it says, " Paul went forth." (v. 33.) How ? Having persuaded some ; derided by others. " But certain men," it says, " clave unto him, and believed, among whom was also Dionysius the Areopagite and some others." [1] (v. 34.) " And after these things," etc. " And having found a certain Jew by name Aquila, of Pontus by birth, lately come from Italy, because that Claudius had ordered all Jews to depart from Rome, he came to them, and because he was of the same craft, he abode with them, and wrought : for by their occupation they were tent-makers." (ch. xviii. 1-3.) Being of Pontus, this Aquila * * * .[2] Observe how, not in Jerusalem, nor near it (the crisis), was hasting to come, but at a greater distance. And with him he abides, and is not ashamed to abide, nay, for this very reason he does abide, as having a suitable lodging-place, for to him it was much more suitable than any king's palace. And smile not thou, beloved, to hear (of his occupation). For (it was good for him) even as to the athlete the palæstra is more useful than delicate carpets ; so to the warrior the iron sword (is useful), not that of gold. " And wrought," though he preached. Let us be ashamed, who though we have no preaching to occupy us, live in idleness. " And he disputed in the synagogue every sabbath day, and persuaded both Jews and Greeks " (v. 4) : but " when they opposed and blasphemed "

he withdrew, by this expecting to draw them more. For wherefore having left that house did he come to live hard by the synagogue ? was it not for this ? For it was not that he saw any danger here. But therefore it is that Paul having testified to them—not teaches now, but testifies—" having shaken his garments," to terrify them not by word only but by action, " said unto them, Your blood be upon your own heads " (v. 6) : he speaks the more vehemently as having already persuaded many. " I," says he, " am clean." Then we also are accountable for the blood of those entrusted to us, if we neglect them. " From this time forth I will go to the Gentiles." So that also when he says, " Henceforth let no man trouble me " (Gal. vi. 17), he says it to terrify. For not so much did the punishment terrify, as this stung them. " And having removed thence he came into the house of one named Justus, that worshipped God, whose house was contiguous to the synagogue " (v. 7), and there abode, by this wishing to persuade them that he was in earnest (πρὸς τὰ ἔθνη ἠπείγετο) to go to the Gentiles. Accordingly, mark immediately the ruler of the synagogue converted, and many others, when he had done this. " Crispus the ruler of the synagogue believed in the Lord, with his whole house : and many of the Corinthians hearing believed, and were baptized."—(v. 8.) " With his whole house : " [3] observe the converts in those times doing this with their entire household. This Crispus he means where he writes, " I baptized none save Crispus and Gaius." (1 Cor. i. 14.) This (same) I take to be called Sosthenes—(evidently) a believer, insomuch that he is beaten, and is always present with Paul.* " And the Lord said in the night," etc. Now even the number (of the " much people ") persuaded him, but Christ's claiming them for His own (moved him) more.[4] Yet He says also, " Fear not : " for the danger

---

[1] Here A. B. C. insert the sentence ὅρα τοὺς πιστοὺς κ. τ. λ. which mod. text rightly removes to the comment on v. 8, and after it, ὅρα πῶς ὁ νόμος καταλύεται λοιπόν : which unless it means, " See here the beginning of the judgment on the Jews, the dissolution of their Law, and overthrow of their nation," of which Chrys. speaks in this sentence, is out of place here, and belongs to the comment on v. 18, i. e. to the beginning of Hom. 40, which in fact opens with these words. So mod. text understands them. " Mark how the Law, begins to be dissolved from henceforth. For this man, being a Jew, having after these things shorn his head in Cenchrea, goes with Paul into Syria. Being a man of Pontus, not in Jerusalem nor near it did he haste to come, but at a greater distance." The innovator's meaning seems to have been, that he shore his head in fulfilment of his vow, not in Jerusalem, nor near Jerusalem, but at a greater distance, viz. in Cenchrea." But St. Chrys. is here commenting on Claudius' edict (see above, p. 240, on v. 2) : " See here the beginning of the judgment on the Jews : it was hasting to come, but it began not in Jerusalem, nor in Palestine, but at a greater distance—at Rome, in this edict of the Emperor : οὐκ ἐν Ἱεροσολύμοις, οὐδὲ πλησίον ἔσπευδεν ἐλθεῖν ἀλλὰ μακροτέρω."

[2] The sentence may be completed with : " had spent the greater part of his life at Rome," etc. ; see above, p. 236, but the copyist make οὗτος nom. to οὐκ ἔσπευδεν ἐλθεῖν.

[3] To this clause, mod. text rightly refers the comment, ὅρα τοὺς πιστοὺς τότε μετὰ τῆς οἰκίας τοῦτο ποιοῦντας ὁλοκλήρου, which the original text has after καὶ ἕτεροι τινές of xvii. 34.

* There is no sufficient ground for the supposition of Chrys. that the Sosthenes here mentioned was a Christian and the same who is saluted in 1 Cor. i. 1. On the contrary, he was the leader of the Jewish party who persecuted the ruler of the synagogue, perhaps the successor of Crispus who had become a Christian. The reading οἱ Ἰουδαῖοι of some inferior Mss. in v. 17 which is followed by Chrys. would easily give rise to this misconception. The true text is most probably πάντες, meaning the officers of the governor. The representatives of the Roman government, then, attacked Sosthenes, the leader of the party which was persecuting Paul. Thus their effort ended in failure. And so indifferent was Gallio that he in no way interfered. Paul's accusers were thus themselves beaten and the whole effort at prosecution miserably failed.— G. B. S.

[4] ἡ δὲ οἰκείωσις τοῦ X. πλέον. Sed familiaritas Christi magis. Ben. Chrys. said above, that the most powerful consideration was this which is put last, " For I have much people in this city." The meaning here is, That there was " much people " to be converted, was a cheering consideration : that Christ should say, λαός μοι πολύς ἐστιν, speaking of them as " His own," was the strongest inducement.

16

was become greater now, both because more believed, and also the ruler of the synagogue. This was enough to rouse him. Not that he was reproved[1] as fearing; but that he should not suffer aught; "I am with thee, and none shall set upon thee to hurt thee." (v. 9, 10.) For He did not always permit them to suffer evil, that they might not become too weak. For nothing so grieved Paul, as men's unbelief and setting themselves (against the Truth): this was worse than the dangers. Therefore it is that (Christ) appears to him now. "And he continued a year and six months," etc. (v. 11.) After the year and six months, they set upon him. "And when Gallio was pro-consul of Achaia," etc. (v. 12, 13), because they had no longer the use of their own laws.[2] (c) And observe how prudent he is: for he does not say straightway, I care not, but, "If," says he, "it were a matter of wrong-doing or wicked lewdness, O ye Jews, reason would that I should bear with you; but if it be a question of doctrine and words and of your law, see ye to it, for I do not choose to be a judge of such matters." (v. 14, 15.) (g) He taught[3] them that not such are the matters which crave a judicial sentence, but they do all things out of order. And he does not say, It is not my duty, but, "I do not choose," that they may not trouble him again. Thus Pilate said in the case of Christ, "Take ye Him, and judge him according to your law." (John xviii. 31.) But they were just like men drunken and mad. (d) "And he drave them from the judgment-seat" (v. 16)—he effectually closed the tribunal against them. "Then all" (the Jews) "having seized Sosthenes the ruler of the synagogue, beat him before the judgment-seat. And Gallio cared for none of these things." (v. 17). (a) This thing, of all others, set them on (to this violence)—their persuasion that the governor would not even let himself down (to notice it). (e) It was a splendid victory. O the shame they were put to! (b) For it is one thing to have come off

victorious from a controversy, and another for those to learn that he cared nothing for the affair. (f) "And Gallio cared for none of these things:" and yet the whole was meant as an insult to him! But, forsooth, as if they had received authority (they did this). Why did he (Sosthenes), though he also had authority, not beat (them)? But they were (otherwise) trained: so that the judge should learn which party was more reasonable. This was no small benefit to those present—both the reasonableness of these, and the audacity of those. (h) [4] He was beaten, and said nothing.

This man let us also imitate: to them that beat us, let us return blow for blow, by meekness, by silence, by long-suffering. More grievous these wounds, greater this blow, and more heavy. For to show that it is not the receiving a blow in the body that is grievous, but the receiving it in the mind, we often smite people, but since it is in the way of friendship, they are even pleased: but if you smite any indifferent person in an insolent manner, you have pained him exceedingly, because you have touched his heart. So let us smite their heart. But that meekness inflicts a greater blow than fierceness, come, let us prove, so far as that is possible, by words. For the sure proof indeed is by acts and by experience: but if you will, let us also make the enquiry by word, though indeed we have often made it already. Now in insults, nothing pains us so much, as the opinion passed by the spectators; for it is not the same thing to be insulted in public and in private, but those same insults we endure even with ease, when we suffer them in a solitary place, and with none by to witness them, or know of them. So true is it that it is not the insult, as it is in itself, that mortifies us, but the having to suffer it in the sight of all men: since if one should do us honor in the sight of all men, and insult us in private, we shall not-withstanding even feel obliged to him. The pain then is not in the nature of the insult, but in the opinion of the beholders; that one may not seem to be contemptible. What then, if this opinion should be in our favor? Is not the man attempting to disgrace us himself more disgraced, when men give their opinion in our favor? Say, whom do the bystanders despise? Him who insults, or him who being insulted keeps silence? Passion indeed suggests, that they despise him who is insulted: but let us look into it now while we are free from that excitement, in order that

---

[1] B. C. ὅτι ἠλέγχθη φοβούμενος ἢ οὐκ ἠλέγχθη ὥστε μὴ (C. μηδὲ) παθεῖν. A., ὅτε ἐλέχθη ὥστε δὲ μὴ παθεῖν, (which is meant for emendation: "This was enough to rouse him when it was spoken: but, that he should not suffer," etc.). Mod. text, ὅτι ἠλ. φοβούμενος, ἢ οὐκ ἠλ. μὲν, ἀλλ' ὥστε μηδὲ τοῦτο παθεῖν. We read Οὐκ ὅτι ἠλέγχθη ὡς φοβούμενος. ὥστε δὲ μὴ παθεῖν, Ἐγὼ εἰμι μετὰ σοῦ. The accidental omission of οὐκ may have been corrected in the margin by the gloss ἢ οὐκ ἠλ. But the sense seems to be otherwise confused by transpositions. "It is true, even the number, and still more Christ's οἰκείωσις of them, prevailed with him. This was enough to rouse him. But Christ begins by saying, "Fear not," etc. And in fact the danger was increased, etc. Not that Paul was reproved as being afraid, etc.

[2] From this point to the end of the Exposition all is confused. To make something like connection, it has been necessary to rearrange the parts, but the restoration is still unsatisfactory.

[3] Καὶ ἐδίδαξεν ὅτι τὰ τοιαῦτα δικαστικῆς ψήφου [οὐ, this we supply,] δεῖται· ἀλλὰ ἀτάκτως πάντα ποιοῦσιν. Mod. text ἐδίδαξε γὰρ (ἢ τε τούτων 'ἐπιείκεια καὶ ἐκείνων θρασύτης, from f) ὅτι τὰ τοι. δικ. ψήφ. δεῖται.

[4] Here, between the parts g and h, the Mss. have two sentences retained by Edd. but clearly out of place, unless they form part of a second recapitulation: "Therefore he departed from Athens." "Because there was much people there."

we may not be carried away when the time comes. Say, whom do we all condemn? Plainly the man who insults: and if he be an inferior, we shall say that he is even mad; if an equal, that he is foolish; if a superior, still we shall not approve of it. For which man, I ask, is worthy of approval, the man who is excited, who is tossed with a tempest of passion, who is infuriated like a wild beast, who demeans himself in this sort against our common nature, or he who lives in a state of calm, in a haven of repose, and in virtuous equanimity? Is not the one like an angel, the other not even like a man? For the one cannot even bear his own evils, while the other bears even those of others also: here, the man cannot even endure himself; there, he endures another too: the one is in danger of shipwreck, the other sails in safety, his ship wafted along the favoring gales: for he has not suffered the squall of passion to catch his sails and overturn the bark of his understanding: but the breath of a soft and sweet air fanning upon it, the breath of forbearance, wafts it with much tranquillity into the haven of wise equanimity. And like as when a ship is in danger of foundering, the sailors know not what they cast away, whether what they lay hands upon be their own or other men's property, but they throw overboard all the contents without discrimination, alike the precious and what is not such: but when the storm has ceased, then reckoning up all that they have thrown out, they shed tears, and are not sensible of the calm for the loss of what they have thrown overboard: so here, when passion blows hard, and the storm is raised, people in flinging out their words know not how to use order or fitness; but when the passion has ceased, then recalling to mind what kind of words they have given utterance to, they consider the loss and feel not the quiet, when they remember the words by which they had disgraced themselves, and sustained most grievous loss, not as to money, but as to character for moderation and gentleness. Anger is a darkness. "The fool," saith Scripture, "hath said in his heart, There is no God." (Ps. xiii. 1.) Perhaps also of the angry man it is suitable to say the same, that the angry man hath said, There is no God. For, saith Scripture, "Through the multitude of his anger he will not seek" (after God).[1] (Ps. x. 4.) For let what pious thought will enter in, (passion) thrusts and drives all out, flings all athwart. (b) When you are told, that he whom you abused uttered not one bitter word, do you not for this feel more pain than you have inflicted?

(a) If you in your own mind do not feel more pain than he whom you have abused, abuse still; (but) though there be none to call you to account, the judgment of your conscience, having taken you privately, shall give you a thousand lashes, (when you think) how you poured out a flood of railings on one so meek, and humble, and forbearing. We are forever saying these things, but we do not see them exhibited in works. You, a human being, insult your fellow-man? You, a servant, your fellow-servant? But why do I wonder at this, when many even insult God? Let this be a consolation to you when suffering insult. Are you insulted? God also is insulted. Are you reviled? God also was reviled. Are you treated with scorn? Why, so was our Master also. In these things He shares with us, but not so in the contrary things. For He never insulted another unjustly: God forbid! He never reviled, never did a wrong. So that we are those who share with Him, not ye. For to endure when insulted is God's part: to be merely abusive, is the part of the devil. See the two sides. "Thou hast a devil" (John vii. 20; ib. xviii. 22), Christ was told: He received a blow on the face from the servant of the high-priest. They who wrongfully insult, are in the same class with these. For if Peter was even called "Satan" (Matt. xvi. 23) for one word; much[2] more shall these men, when they do the works of the Jews, be called, as those were called, "children of the devil" (John viii. 44), because they wrought the works of the devil. You insult; who are you, I ask (that you do so)? Nay, rather the reason why you insult, is this, that you are nothing: no one that is human insults. So that what is said in quarrels, "Who are you?" ought to be put in the contrary way: "Insult: for you are nothing." Instead of that the phrase is, "Who are you, that you insult?" "A better man than you," is the answer. And yet it is just the contrary: but because we put the question amiss, therefore they answer amiss: so that the fault is ours. For as if we thought it was for great men to insult, therefore we ask, "Who are you, that you insult?" And therefore they make this answer. But, on the contrary, we ought to say: "Do you insult? insult still: for you are nobody:" whereas to those who do not insult this should be said: "Who are you that you insult not?—you have surpassed human nature." This is nobility, this is generosity, to speak nothing ungenerous, though a man may deserve to have it spoken to him. Tell me now,

---

[1] Ps. x. 4. "The wicked, through the pride of his countenance, will not," etc. E. V.

[2] Mss. πολλῷ μᾶλλον οὗτοι Ἰουδαῖοι ἀκούσονται, ὅταν τὰ Ἰουδαίων ποιῶσιν ὥσπερ κἀκεῖνοι διαβόλου τέκνα, ἐπειδὴ κ. τ. λ. We omit Ἰουδαῖοι.

how many are there who are not worthy to be put to death? Nevertheless, the judge does not this in his own person, but interrogates them; and not this either, in his own person. But if it is not to be suffered, that the judge, sitting in judgment, should (in his own person) speak with a criminal, but he does all by the intervention of a third person, much more is it our duty not to insult our equals in rank; for[1] all the advantage we shall get of them will be, not so much to have disgraced them, as to be made to learn that we have disgraced ourselves. Well then, in the case of the wicked, this is why we must not insult (even them); in the case of the good there is another reason also because they do not deserve it: and for a third, [2] because it is not right to be abusive. But as things are, see what comes of it; the person abused is a man, and the person abusing is a man, and the spectators men. What then? must the beasts come between them and settle matters? for only this is left. For when both the wrong-doers and those who delight in the wrong-doing are men, the part of reconciler is left for the beasts: for just as when the masters quarrel in a house, there is nothing left but for the servants to reconcile them,—even if this be not the result, for the nature of the thing demands this,—just so is it here.—Are you abusive? Well may you be so, for you are not even human. Insolence seemed to be a high-born thing; it seemed to belong to the great; whereas it belongs rather to slaves; but to give good words belongs to free men. For as to do ill is the part of those, so to suffer ill is

the part of these.—Just as if some slave should steal the master's property, some old hag,—such a thing as that is the abusive man. And like as some detestable thief and runaway, [3] with studied purpose stealing in, looks all around him, wishing to filch something: so does this man, even as he, look narrowly at all on every side, studying how to throw out some (reproach). Or perhaps we may set him forth by a different sort of example. Just as if[4] one should steal filthy vessels out of a house, and bring them out in the presence of all men, the things purloined do not so disgrace the persons robbed, as they disgrace the thief himself: just so this man, by bringing out his words in the presence of all men, casts disgrace not on others but on himself by the words, in giving vent to this language, and befouling both his tongue and his mind. For it is all one, when we quarrel with bad men, as if one for the sake of striking a man who is immersed in putrefying filth should defile himself by plunging his hands into the nastiness. Therefore, reflecting on these things, let us flee the mischief thence accruing, and keep a clean tongue, that being clear from all abusiveness, we may be enabled with strictness to pass through the life present, and to attain unto the good things promised to those that love Him, through the grace and mercy of our Lord Jesus Christ, with Whom to the Father and the Holy Ghost together be glory, might, honor, now and ever, world without end. Amen.

---

[1] οὐ γὰρ οὕτω τὸ ὑβρίσαι πλεονεκτήσομεν αὐτῶν, ὡς τὸ διδαχθῆναι ὅτι ὑβρίσαμεν ἑαυτούς. B. and mod. text τῷ ὑβρ., τῷ διδ. The ὅτι om. by A. B. C. Sav. is supplied by mod. text. A has δειχθῆναι, Sav. διαλεχθῆναι. The construction is πλεονεκτεῖν τί τινός. "We may think we have got something, viz. the pleasure of having disgraced them; whereas all that we get, in advance of them, is the being taught that we have disgraced ourselves."

[2] καὶ τρίτον (om. C.), ὅτι ὑβριστὴν εἶναι οὐ χρή. This cannot be, "for a third reason," or "in the third place," but seems rather to mean "the third party" spoken of in the preceding sentence. Perhaps it may mean, As the judge does not himself arraign nor even interrogate the criminal, but by a third person, because the judge must not seem to be an ὑβριστής, so there is need of a third person, καὶ τρίτον δεῖ εἰς μέσον ἐλθεῖν ὅτι. . . . But the whole scope of the argument is very obscure.

[3] Old text: ὑβριστής, κλέπτης κατάρατος καὶ δραπέτης· καὶ ὡς ἂν εἴποι τις σπουδῇ εἰσιών, καθάπερ ἐκεῖνος πανταχοῦ περιβλέπεται ὠφελέσθαι τι σπουδάζων, οὕτω καὶ οὗτος πάντα περισκοπεῖ ἐκβάλλειν τι θέλων. We read ὑβριστής. Καὶ ὡς ἂν εἴ τις κλέπτης κατάρ. καὶ δραπ. σπουδῇ εἰσιών, παντ. περιβλ. ὑφ. τι θέλων, οὕτω καὶ οὗτος καθάπερ ἐκεῖνος πάνταπερισκ. ἐκβάλλειν τι σπουδάζων. But it can hardly be supposed that Chrys. thus expressed himself. The purport seems to be this: To be abusive is to behave like a slave, like a foul-mouthed hag. (see p. 200.) And the abusive man, when he is eager to catch at something in your life or manners, the exposure of which may disgrace you, is like a thief who should slink into a house, and pry about for something that he can lay hold of—nay, like one who should purposely look about for the filthiest things he can bring out, and who in so doing disgraces himself more than the owner.

[4] Here again ὥσπερ ἂν εἴποι τις, B. for ὥσπερ ἂν εἴ τις, C.—The sentence οὐχὶ τὰ ὑφαιρεθέντα ᾔσχυνε τοσοῦτον is incomplete; viz. "the owner, by the exposure of the noisomeness, as the stealer himself who produces it."

HOMILY XL.

ACTS XVIII. 18.

"And Paul after this tarried there yet a good while, and then took his leave of the brethren, and sailed thence into Syria, and with him Priscilla and Aquila; having shorn his head in Cenchrea: for he had a vow."

SEE how the Law was breaking up; see how they were bound by conscience. This, namely, was a Jewish custom, to shear their heads agreeably with a vow. But then there ought to be also a sacrifice (ch. xxi. 26), which was not the case here.*—"Having yet tarried:" after the beating of Sosthenes.[1] For it was necessary that he should yet tarry, and comfort them concerning these things. "He sailed for Syria." Why does he desire again to come to Syria? It was there that "the disciples were ordered to be called Christians" (ch. xi. 26): there, that he had been "commended to the grace of God" (xiv. 26): there, that he had effected such things concerning the doctrine. "And with him Priscilla"—lo, a woman also[2]—"and Aquila." But these he left at Ephesus. With good reason, namely, that they should teach. For having been with him so long time, they were learning many things: and yet he did not at present withdraw them from their custom as Jews. "And he came to Ephesus, and left them there: but he himself entered into the synagogue, and reasoned with the Jews. When they desired him to tarry longer time with them, he consented not; but bade them farewell, saying, I must by all means keep this feast that cometh in Jerusalem." Therefore[3] it was that he was hindered from coming into Asia, being impelled to what was of pressing moment. Thus observe him here, entreated (by them) to stay, but because he could not comply, being in haste to depart, "he bade them farewell." However, he did not leave them without more ado, but with promise (to return): "But I will return again unto you, if God will. And he sailed from Ephesus." (v. 19–21.) "And when he had landed at Cæsarea, and gone up, and saluted the Church, he went down to Antioch. And after he had spent some time there, he departed, and went over all the country of Galatia and Phrygia in order, strengthening all the disciples." (v. 22–23.) He came again to those places which he had previously visited. "And a certain Jew named Apollos, born at Alexandria, an eloquent man, and mighty in the Scriptures, came to Ephesus." (v. 24.) Lo, even learned men are now urgent, and the disciples henceforth go abroad. Do you mark the spread of the preaching? "This man was instructed in the way of the Lord; and being fervent in the Spirit, he spake and taught diligently the things of the Lord, knowing only the baptism of John. And he began to speak boldly in the synagogue: whom when Aquila and Priscilla had heard, they took him unto them, and expounded unto him the way of God more perfectly." (v. 25–26.)

---

[1] Edd. without stop, ἥτις οὐκ ἐγένετο μετὰ τὸ τυπτηθῆναι τὸν Σωσθένην.—B. N. Cat. ἐγένετο ἔτι, which is the ἔτι of v. 18, and explained by the following words.

* Two points are much disputed in reference to the vow mentioned in v. 18: (1) What kind of a vow it was, whether the Nazarite vow or some other. (2) Whether it had been taken and whether the shaving of the head was done by Paul or by Aquila. The majority of interpreters maintain that this shaving of the head represented the termination of a Nazarite vow which had been taken by Paul. The view encounters two great difficulties: (1) How can we suppose that the champion of liberty from Jewish ceremonies and observances should himself be given to their observance? (2) Luke here places the name of the wife Priscilla first and then Aquila, and κειράμενος stands next to this name. It is most naturally construed with the name to which it stands nearest, especially when this unexpected arrangement of the names of the husband and wife is taken into account. It is true that the same arrangement is found in the salutation of Paul (Rom. xvi. 3; 1 Tim. iv. 19), but this may be due to the predominant Christian activity of the wife; so also in v. 26, which may have been conformed to this passage. The former consideration is the one of chief importance. On the other side it must be acknowledged that there would be less motive for mentioning a vow of Aquila than of Paul. The vow taken was probably akin to that of the Nazarites. It is referred to Paul by the older interpreters by Bengel, Olshausen, Zeller, De Wette, Lange, Hackett, Gloag, Lechler, Bleek, Ewald; to Aquila, by the Vulgate, Grotius, Kuinoel, Wieseler, Meyer, Conybeare and Howson.—G. B. S.

[2] Ἰδοὺ καὶ γυνή: transposed from after the sentence, "For having been—custom as Jews." Mod. text adds, τὸ ἴσον ἀνδράσι ποιοῦσα καὶ διδάσκουσα. But perhaps the comment was, "and mentioned before her husband." See Serm. in illud Salutate Prisc. et Aquil. tom. iii. p. 176. B. where he comments on this position of the names, and adds that "she having taken Apollos, an eloquent man, etc. taught him the way of God and made him a perfect teacher."

[3] Something is wanting here, for in ἐκωλύετο εἰς τὴν Ἀσίαν ἐλθεῖν there seems to be a reference to xvi. 6. κωλυθέντες λαλῆσαι τὸν λόγον ἐν τῇ Ἀσίᾳ, and again in οὐ μὴν αὐτοὺς ἁπλῶς εἴασεν to ibid. 7. οὐκ εἴασεν αὐτοὺς τὸ πνεῦμα. He may have spoken to this effect: This was his first visit to Ephesus, for he was forbidden before to come into Asia. . . . Not however that the Spirit ἁπλῶς οὐκ εἴασεν, but he says, with promise, I will come to you, etc. The prohibition was not absolute, but he was not permitted on the former occasion to preach in Asia (Procons.), because he was impelled to more urgent duties (in Macedonia and Greece); accordingly here also he has other immediate objects in view, and therefore cannot stay. So in Hom. xli. on xix. 10, 11. "For this reason also (the Lord) suffered him not to come into Asia, waiting (or reserving Himself) for this conjuncture."

If this man[1] knew only the baptism of John, how is it that he was "fervent in the Spirit," for the Spirit was not given in that way? And if those after him needed the baptism of Christ, much[2] more would he need it. Then what is to be said? For it is not without a meaning that the writer has strung the two incidents together. It seems to me that this was one of the hundred and twenty who were baptized with the Apostles: or, if not so, then the same that took place in the case of Cornelius, took place also in the case of this man. But neither does he receive baptism. That expression, then, "they expounded more perfectly," seems[3] to me to be this, that he behooved also to be baptized. Because the other twelve knew nothing accurate, not even what related to Jesus. And it is likely[4] that he did in fact receive baptism. But if these (disciples) of John,[5] after that

baptism again received baptism, was this needful for the disciples also? And wherefore the need of water? These are very different from him, men who did not even know whether there were a Holy Ghost.* "He was fervent," then, "in the Spirit, knowing only the baptism of John:" but these "expounded to him more perfectly. And when he was disposed to pass into Achaia, the brethren wrote, exhorting the disciples to receive him; who, when he was come, helped them much which had believed through grace." (v. 27.) He wished then also to depart into Achaia, and these[6] also encouraged (him to do so), having also given him letters. "Who when he was come, helped them much which had believed through grace: for he mightily convinced the Jews, and that publicly, showing by the Scriptures that Jesus was Christ." (v. 28.) "And it came to pass, that, while Apollos was at Corinth, Paul, having passed through the upper coasts"—meaning what we have read as to Cæsarea and the other places—"came to Ephesus, and having found certain disciples (ch. xix. 1), "he said to them, Have ye received the Holy Ghost since ye believed? And they said unto him, We have not so much as heard whether there be any Holy Ghost. And he said unto them, Unto what then were ye baptized? And they said, Unto John's baptism. Then said Paul, John verily baptized with the baptism of repentance, saying unto the people, that they should believe on Him who should come after him, that is, on Christ Jesus." (v. 2-4.) For that they did not even believe in Christ is plain from his saying, "that they should believe on Him that was to come after him." And he did not say, The baptism of John is nothing, but, It is incomplete. Nor does he add this (in so many words), but he taught them, and many received the Holy Ghost. "When they heard this, they were baptized in the name of the Lord Jesus. And when Paul had laid his hands upon them, the Holy Ghost came on them; and they spake with tongues, and prophesied. And all the men were about twelve" (v. 5-7): so that it was likely they had the Spirit, but it did not appear.[7] "And all the men were about twelve."

---

[1] What St. Chrysostom said has been misconceived by the reporter or the copyists. He meant to remark two things concerning Apollos: 1. That having only the baptism of John he nevertheless had the Spirit, nay, was "fervent in the Spirit." How so? He had it, as Cornelius had it; the baptism of the Spirit without the baptism of water. (See Recapitulation *fin.*) 2. That there is no mention of his receiving baptism, as the twelve did in the following narrative. St. Luke, he says, evidently had a meaning in this juxtaposition of the two incidents. Apollos had the baptism of the Spirit "therefore did not need the water." (Hence whether he received it or not, the writer does not think need to mention it.) Those twelve had no accurate knowledge even of the facts relating to Jesus: nor so much as know whether there were a Holy Ghost.—The scribes did not comprehend this view of the case. Hence A. C. omit ἀλλ᾽ οὐ βαπτίζεται, retained by B. mod. text and Cat. Œc. (ἀλλ᾽ οὐδὲ β.)—They take οἱ μετὰ τούτον (i. e. the twelve of the following incident) to mean the Apostles, and therefore make it πολλῷ μᾶλλον καὶ οὗτος ἐδεήθη ἄν, "if Christ's own disciples after John's baptism needed the baptism of Christ, *a fortiori* this man would need it."—They find the baptism in the ἀκριβ. αὐτῷ ἐξέθεντο, "this was one of the points they taught him—that he must be baptized."—St. Chrys. probably spoke of the case of the hundred and twenty who were baptized with the Spirit on the Day of Pentecost: i. e. "Those having" the greater, the baptism of the Spirit, did not need the less, the baptism of water. The scribes absurdly make him suggest that Apollos may have been one of the hundred and twenty.

[2] Perhaps it should be, καὶ εἰ οἱ μετὰ τούτον. . . . τοῦ Χ., πῶς οὐχ οὗτος ἐδεήθη ἄν; Ἀλλ᾽ οὐδὲ βαπτίζεται. Τί οὖν ἐστιν εἰπεῖν; οὐδὲ γὰρ ἁπλῶς ἐφεξῆς ἔθηκεν ἀμφότερα. (By ἀμφ. perhaps the scribes understood. the "knowing only the baptism of John," and, the being "fervent in Spirit") Ἐμοὶ δοκεῖ ὅπερ ἐπὶ τῶν ἑκατὸν εἰκοσι τῶν μετὰ τῶν Ἀπ. βαπτισθέντων, ὅπερ ἐπὶ τοῦ Κορνηλίου γέγονε, γεγένηται καὶ ἐπὶ τούτου..

[3] Here Œcumenius perceived that Chrys. was misrepresented. Accordingly he reads, Τούτου οὖν ἀκριβῶς ἐξετασθέντος (Cat. τὸ οὖν ἀκριβὲν ἐξετασθὲν τὸ, a confusion of the two readings), δοκεῖ τούτο μὴ εἶναι ὅτι. . . "This point being closely examined, it does not seem to mean this. that he also needed to be baptized." But the scribes took it as above, and the innovator (with whom A. partly agrees) enlarges it thus: "But he is not baptized, but when 'they expounded to him more perfectly." But this seems to me to be true, that he did also need to be baptized : since the other twelve," etc. On this the Paris Editor, supposing the twelve Apostles to be meant, strangely remarks, *Itane? duodecim quæ Jesum spectabant nihil noverunt Imo* οἱ κρ′, i. e. οἱ ἑκατὸν εἰκοσι. As if it were likely that those hundred and twenty could be so ignorant.

[4] Εἰκὸς δε αὐτὸν καὶ βαπτισθῆναι. If Chrys. said this (see note [7], p. 247), the meaning may be: "It is likely however that he did receive baptism," viz. though the writer does not mention it. For this is the point—the writer mentions it in the case of those twelve, for it was the means by which they, ignorant hitherto of the existence of a Holy Ghost, received the Spirit : not so in the case of Apollos, for as he had already the baptism of the Spirit, the water was quite a subordinate consideration. See above, Hom. xxiv. p. 157, on the case of Cornelius.

[5] Still overlooking the reference to the following narrative, B. C. read Εἰ δὲ αὐτοὶ οἱ Ἰωάννου—. "But if even John's disciples," etc.: mod. text and A., Πλὴν εἰ καὶ αὐτοὶ—, reading

the next clause affirmatively, Cat. and Œc., εἰ δὲ οὗτοι οἱ Ἰωάννου—, which we adopt. The scribes have further darkened the sense by inserting here v. 27 to the end, and xix. 1-7.

* The utter confusion of the text makes it uncertain what Chrys. said concerning Apollos. The probability is that he still stood upon the plane of John's baptism and teaching, a zealous and able man, but not yet instructed in the Christian doctrine of the Spirit, nor understanding the significance of Christian baptism. It is probable that after receiving instruction he was re-baptized with the twelve at Ephesus (xix. 5-7).—G. B. S.

[6] Προετρέψατο (Sav. marg. αὐτό) καὶ οὗτος (A. οὕτως). We read προετρέψαντο δὲ καὶ οὗτοι.

[7] Viz. the Spirit came upon them in baptism, but it did not appear until Paul had laid his hands upon them : then they spake with tongues, etc.

(Recapitulation.) "And they came to Ephesus, and there he left them" (v. 19): for he did not wish to take them about with him, but left them at Ephesus. But they subsequently dwelt at Corinth, and he bears high testimony to them, and writing to the Romans, salutes them. (Rom. xvi. 3.) Whence it seems to me that they afterwards went back to Rome, in the time of Nero,[1] as having an attachment for those parts whence they had been expelled in the time of Claudius. "But[2] he himself went into the synagogue." It seems to me that the faithful still assembled there, for they did not immediately withdraw them. "And when they besought him to stay, he consented not" (v. 20, 21), for he was hastening to Cæsarea. "And having arrived at Cæsarea," etc., "passing through the region of Galatia and Phrygia, confirming all the disciples." (v. 22, 23.) Through these regions also he merely *passes* again, just enough to establish them by his presence. "And a certain Jew, Apollos by name," etc. (v. 24.) For he was an awakened man, travelling in foreign parts for this very purpose. Writing of him the Apostle said, "Now concerning Apollos our brother."[3] (1 Cor. xvi. 12.) (β) Whom when Aquila and Priscilla had heard," etc. (v. 26.) It was not for nothing that he left them at Ephesus, but for Apollos' sake, the Spirit so ordered it, that he might come with greater force to the attack (ἐπιβῆναι) upon Corinth. What may be the reason that to him they did nothing, but Paul they assault? They knew that he was the leader, and great was the name of the man. "And when he was disposed to pass into Achaia" (v. 27): i. e. in faith, he did all by faith; "the brethren wrote," etc. nowhere envy, nowhere an evil eye. Aquila teaches, or rather this man lets himself be taught. He was minded to depart, and they send letters. (a) "For he mightily convinced the Jews, and that publicly," etc. (v. 28.) Now by this, that he "publicly" convinced them, his boldness was shown: by the clearness of his arguing, his power was declared: by his convicting them out of the Scriptures, his skill (of learning). For neither boldness by itself contributes aught, where there is not power, nor power where there is not boldness. "He mightily con-

vinced," it says. (β) "And it came to pass," etc. (ch. xix. 1.) But whence had those, being in Ephesus, the baptism of John? Probably they had been on a visit at Jerusalem at the time (of John's preaching), and did not even know Jesus. And he does not say to them, Do ye believe in Jesus? but what? "Have ye received the Holy Ghost?" (v. 2.) He knew that they had not, but wishes themselves to say it, that having learnt what they lack, they may ask. "John verily baptized," etc. (v. 4.) From the baptism itself he (John) prophesies:[4] and he leads them (to see) that this is the meaning of John's baptism. (a) "That they should believe on Him that was to come:" on what kind (of Person)? "I indeed baptize you with water, but He that cometh after me, shall baptize you with the Holy Ghost." (Matt. iii. 11.) And when Paul," it says, "had laid his hands upon them, the Holy Ghost came on them; and they spake with tongues, and prophesied." (v. 6.) (β) The gift is twofold: tongues and prophesyings. Hence is shown an important doctrine, that[5] the baptism of John is incomplete. And he does not say, "Baptism" of forgiveness, but, "of repentance." What[6] (is it) then? These had not the Spirit: they were not so fervent, not even instructed. And why did (Apollos) not receive baptism?[7] (The case) seems to me to be this: Great was the boldness of the man. "He taught diligently the things concerning Jesus," but he needed more diligent teaching. Thus, though not knowing all, by his zeal he attracted the Holy Ghost, in the same manner as Cornelius and his company.

Perhaps it is the wish of many, Oh that we had the baptism of John now! But (if we had), many would still be careless of a life of virtue, and it might be thought that each for this, and not for the kingdom of heaven's sake, aimed at virtue. There would be many false prophets: for then "they which are approved" would not be very "manifest." (1 Cor. xi. 19.) As, "blessed are they that have not seen and yet have believed" (John 20, 29), so they that (believe) without signs. "Except," saith (Christ), "ye see signs, ye will not believe." (Ib. iv. 48.) For we lose nothing (by lack of miracles), if we will but

---

[1] ἐπὶ Νέρωνος must be removed from the end of the sentence where the Mss. and Edd. have it.

[2] Instead of this, Edd. have v. 22, 23.

[3] From this point to the end of the Exposition, all is confused, viz. in the old text the order is as here marked by the letters a, a. . β. β. . i. e. it gives two expositions, severally imperfect, but completing each other. In mod. text the parts are rearranged, but so that the first of the portions marked β is placed after the second of those marked a. It also assigns some of the comments to wrong texts, and in many places alters the sense.

[4] Mod. text "From the baptism itself (i. e. immediately after it) they prophesy: but this the baptism of John had not; wherefore it was imperfect. But that they may be made worthy of such gifts, he more prepared them first."

[5] Mod. text "that they who receive baptism are (therein) thoroughly cleansed from their sins: for were it not so, these would not have received the gifts immediately."

[6] Mod. text "And how is it that they who have received the Spirit taught not, but Apollos did, who had not yet received the Spirit?" An entire perversion of Chrysostom's meaning.

[7] In the Mss. it is πῶς δὲ οὐκ ἔλαβον βάπτισμα; which cannot be right. We restore ἔλαβεν.

take heed to ourselves. We have the sum and substance of the good things : through baptism we received remission of sins, sanctification, participation of the Spirit, adoption, eternal life. What would ye more? Signs? But they come to an end (ἀλλὰ καταργεῖται). Thou hast "faith, hope, charity," the abiding things : these seek thou, these are greater than signs. Nothing is equal to charity. For "greater than all," saith he, "is charity." (cf. 1 Cor. xiii. 5.) But now, love is in jeopardy, for only its name is left behind, while the reality is nowhere (seen), but we are divided each from the other. What then shall one do to reunite (ourselves)? For to find fault is easy, but how may one make friendship, this is the point to be studied; how we may bring together the scattered members. For be it so, that we have one Church, or one doctrine—yet this is not the (main) consideration : no, the evil is, that[1] in these we have not fellowship—"living peaceably," as the Apostle says, "with all men" (Rom. xii. 18), on the contrary, we are at variance one with another. For be it that we are not having fights every day, yet look not thou to this, but (to this), that neither have we charity, genuine and unswerving. There is need of bandages and oil. Let us bear it in mind, that charity is the cognizance of the disciples of Christ : that without this, all else avails nothing : that it is an easy task if we will. Yes, say you, we know all this, but how (to go to work) that it may be achieved? What (to do), that it may be effected? in what way, that we may love one another? First, let us put away the things which are subversive of charity, and then we shall establish this. Let none be resentful, none be envious, none rejoicing in (others') misfortunes : these are the things that hinder love; well then, the things that make it are of the other sort. For it is not enough to put away the things that hinder; the things that establish must also be forthcoming. Now Sirach tells us the things that are subversive (of friendship), and does not go on to speak of the things which make union. "Reproaching," he says, "and revealing of a secret, and a treacherous wound." (Ecclus. 22, 27.) But in speaking of the men of those times, these things might well be named, seeing they were carnal : but in our case, God forbid they should be (even) named. Not[2]

from these things do we bring our inducements for you, but from the others. For us, there is nothing good without friendship. Let there be good things without number, but what is the benefit—be it wealth, be it luxury—without friendship? No possession equal to this, even in matters of this life, just as there is nothing worse than men hating (us). "Charity hides a multitude of sins" (1 Pet. iv. 8) : but enmity, even where sins are not, suspects them to be. It is not enough not to be an enemy; no, one must also love. Bethink thee, that Christ has bidden, and this is enough. Even affliction makes friendships, and draws (men) together. "What then," say you, "now, when there is no affliction? say, how (are we to act) to become friends?" Have ye not other friends, I ask? In what way are ye their friends, how do ye continue such? For a beginning, let none have any enemy : this (in itself) is not a small matter : let none envy; it is not possible to accuse the man who envies not. (b) How then shall we be warmly affected? What makes love of persons? Beauty of person. Then let us also make our souls beautiful, and we shall be amiable one to another : for it is necessary, of course, not only to love, but also to be loved. Let us first achieve this point, that we may be loved, and the other will be easy. How to act that we may be loved? Let us become beautiful, and let us do this, that we may always have lovers. Let none make it his study to get money, to get slaves, to get houses, (so much) as to be loved, as to have a good name. Better is a name than much wealth. For the one remains, the other perishes : and the one it is possible to acquire, the other impossible. For he that has got an evil character, will with difficulty lay it aside : but by means of his (good) name the poor man may quickly be rich. Let there be a man having ten thousand talents, and another a hundred friends; the latter is more rich in resources than the former. Then let us not merely do this, but let us work it as a kind of trade. "And how can we?" say you. "A sweet mouth multiplieth its friends, and a gracious tongue." Let us get a well-spoken mouth, and pure manners. It is not possible for a man to be such, and not to be known.

(a) We have one world that we all inhabit, with the same fruits we all are fed. But these are small matters : by the same Sacraments we partake of the same spiritual food. These

---

[1] Mod. text besides other alterations : "that communicating in the other things one with another, in the essentials (ἐν τοῖς ἀναγκαίοις) we do not communicate, and being in peace with all men are at variance one with another."

[2] Οὐκ ἀπὸ τούτων ὑμᾶς ἐνάγομεν, ἀλλ' ἀπὸ τῶν ἄλλων. But the scope seems to require, Οὐκ ἀπὸ τ. ὑ. ἀπάγομεν, i. e. "as these are things not even to be supposed to exist among Chris-

tians, we do not make it our business to lead you away from these ;"—and for the other clause, "But would lead you on to those other things" which Sirach has not mentioned.

surely are justifications of loving! (c) Mark[1] how many (inducements and pleas) for friendship they that are without have excogitated; community of art or trade, neighborhood, relationships: but mightier than all these are the impulses and ties which are among us: this Table is calculated more (than all else) to shame us into friendliness. But many of us who come thereto do not even know one another. The reason, it may be said, is that there are so many of them. By no means; it is only our own sluggish indifference. (Once) there were three thousand (ch. ii. 41)—there were five thousand (iv. 4)—and yet they had all one soul: but now each knows not his brother, and is not ashamed to lay the blame on the number, because it is so great! Yet he that has many friends is invincible against all men: stronger he than any tyrant. Not such the safety the tyrant has with his body-guards, as this man has with his friends. Moreover, this man is more glorious than he: for the tyrant is guarded by his own slaves, but this man by his peers: the tyrant, by men unwilling and afraid of him; this man by willing men and without fear. And here too is a wonderful thing to be seen—many in one, and one in many. (a) Just as in an harp, the sounds are diverse, not the harmony, and they all together give out one harmony and symphony, (c) I could wish to bring you into such a city, were it possible, wherein (all) should be one soul: then shouldest thou see surpassing all harmony of harp and flute, the more harmonious symphony. (b) But the musician is the Might of Love: it is this that strikes out the sweet melody, (d) singing[2]

(withal) a strain in which no note is out of tune. This strain rejoices both Angels, and God the Lord of Angels; this strain rouses (to hear it) the whole audience that is in heaven; this even lulls (evil) passions—it does not even suffer them to be raised, but deep is the stillness. For as in a theatre, when the band of musicians plays, all listen with a hush, and there is no noise there; so among friends, while Love strikes the chords, all the passions are still and laid to sleep, like wild beasts charmed and unnerved: just as, where hate is, there is all the contrary to this. But let us say nothing just now about enmity; let us speak of friendship. Though thou let fall some casual hasty word, there is none to catch thee up, but all forgive thee; though thou do (some hasty thing), none puts upon it the worse construction, but all allowance is made: every one prompt to stretch out the hand to him that is falling, every one wishing him to stand. A wall it is indeed impregnable, this friendship; a wall, which not the devil himself, much less men, can overpower. It is not possible for that man to fall into danger who has gotten many friends. (Where love is) no room is there to get matter of anger, but[3] only for pleasantness of feeling: no room is there to get matter of envying; none, to get occasion of resentment. Mark him, how in all things both spiritual and temporal, he accomplishes all with ease. What then, I pray you, can be equal to this man? Like a city walled on every side is this man, the other as a city unwalled.—Great wisdom, to be able to be a creator of friendship! Take away friendship, and thou hast taken away all, thou hast confounded all. But if the likeness of friendship have so great power, what must the reality itself be? Then let us, I beseech you, make to ourselves friends, and let each make this his art. But, lo! you will say, I do study this, but the other does not. All the greater the reward to thee. True, say you, but the matter is more difficult. How, I ask? Lo! I testify and declare to you, that if but ten of you would knit yourselves together, and make this your work, as the Apostles made the preaching theirs, and the Prophets theirs the teaching, so we the making of friends, great would be the reward. Let us make for ourselves royal portraits. For if this be the common badge of disciples, we do a greater work than if we should put ourselves into the power to raise the dead. The diadem

---

[1] A. substitutes καὶ γὰρ πολλά ἐστι τὰ συνωθοῦντα ἡμᾶς καὶ συνδεσμοῦντα πρὸς φιλίας: "For indeed there are many things which perforce impel us to become and bind us to continue friends," viz. independently of our own choice: which is good in point of sense; but the original reading of the passage implies this meaning: "Even the men of the world acknowledge the necessity of friendship, and look out pleas, inducements, and justifications for friendship: ὅρα πόσα οἱ ἔξωθεν ἐπενόησαν φιλικά"—i. e. which are far-fetched, and therefore need ἐπινοεῖσθαι,, compared with the near and constraining motives which bring and keep us Christians together. For συντεκνίαν which appears in all our Mss. and is retained without suspicion by the Edd. we confidently restore συντεχνίαν, comp. xviii. 2. διὰ τὸ ὁμότεχνον εἶναι. There is a gradation from lower to higher, συντεχνίαν, γειτονίαν (or γειτοσύνην C. A.) συγγενείας.

[2] In the old text both sense and syntax are confused by the transpositions of the parts marked (c) and (b)—occasioned perhaps by the homœoteleuton, viz., συμφωνίαν at the end of (a) and (c): hence (d) οὐδὲν ἀπηχὲς ᾄδουσα μέλος has nothing to agree with, unless it were the μία ψυχὴ of (c); accordingly C. omits ᾄδουσα. Mod. text reforms the whole passage thus: "Just as in an harp, the sounds are diverse, but one the harmony, and one the musician who touches the harp: so here, the harp is Charity itself, and the ringing sounds are the loving words brought forth by Charity, all of them giving out one and the same harmony and symphony: but the musician is the might of Charity: this strikes out the sweet strain. I could wish to lead you into such a city, were it possible, wherein were one soul, and thou shouldest see how than all harp and flute more harmonious is the symphony there, singing no dissonant strain,"—Instead of οὐδὲν ἀπηχὲς ᾄδουσα μέλος. Τοῦτο. . . , we place the full stop after ᾄδουσα, so that the next sentence begins Μέλος τοῦτο καὶ ἀγγέλους κ. τ. λ. and at the end of it, instead of Θεὸν εὐφραίνει τὸ μέλος. Ὅλον . . . ., we read εὐφραίνει. Τοῦτο μέλος ὅλον κ. τ. λ.

[3] The omission in B. C. of this clause and the following which A. and Mod. text retain, may be explained by the like ending ὑπόθεσιν σχεῖν. Mod. text has also after θυμηδίας· the clause ἐν γέλωτι ἀεί ἐστι καὶ τρυφῇ.

and the purple mark the Emperor, and where these are not, though his apparel be all gold, the Emperor is not yet manifest. So now thou art making known thy lineage. Make men friends to thyself, and (friends) to others. There is none who being loved will wish to hate thee. Let us learn the colors, with what ingredients they are mixed, with what (tints) this portrait is composed. Let us be affable: let us not wait for our neighbors to move. Say not, if I see any person hanging back (for me to make the first advances), I become worse than he: but rather when thou seest this, forestall him, and extinguish his bad feeling. Seest thou one diseased, and addest to his malady? This, most of all, let us make sure of—"in honor to prefer one another, to account others better than one's self" (Rom. xii. 10), deem not this to be a lessening of thyself. If thou prefer (another) in honor, thou hast honored thyself more, attracting[1] to thyself a still higher extinction. On all occasions let us yield the precedence to others. Let us bear nothing in mind of the evil done to us, but if any good has been done (let us remember only that). Nothing so makes a man a friend, as a gracious tongue, a mouth speaking good things, a soul free from self-elation, a contempt of vain-glory, a despising of honor. If we secure these things, we shall be able to become invincible to the snares of the Devil, and having with strictness accomplished the pursuit of virtue, to attain unto the good things promised to them that love Him, through the grace and mercy of our Lord Jesus Christ, with Whom to the Father and the Holy Ghost together be glory, dominion, honor, now and ever, world without end. Amen.

HOMILY XLI.

ACTS XIX. 8, 9.

"And he went into the synagogue, and spake boldly for the space of three months, disputing and persuading the things concerning the kingdom of God. But when divers were hardened, and believed not, but spake evil of that way before the multitude, he departed from them, and separated the disciples, disputing daily in the school of one Tyrannus."

(*a*) See him in every place forcing his way into the synagogue, and in this manner departing thence. For in every place, he wished to have the occasion given him by them.[2] (*c*) He wished to separate the disciples thence, and to have the beginning for ceasing to assemble with them, given by (the Jews) themselves. And it was not for nothing that he did this (*b*) which I have said. He was henceforth "provoking them to jealousy." For both the Gentiles readily received him, and the Jews, upon the Gentiles receiving him, repented. (*a*) This is why he continually made a stir among them,[3] "for three months arguing and persuading concerning the kingdom of God:" for you must not suppose because you hear of his "speaking boldly," that there was any harshness: it was of good things that he discoursed, of a kingdom: who would not have heard him? "But when divers were hardened, speaking evil of the way." They might well call it "the way;" this was indeed the way, that led into the kingdom of heaven. "He departed from them, and separated the disciples, disputing daily in the school of one Tyrannus. And this was done for the space of two years, so that all that were in Asia heard the word of the Lord, both Jews and Greeks." (v. 10.) (*a*) Do you mark how much was effected by his persisting?[4] "Both Jews and Greeks

[1] *εἰς τὸ πλέον τιμηθῆναι ἐπισπώμενος.* As *ἐπισπᾶσθαι, ἐπισπάσασθαι* in Chrys. is generally transitive with accusative of the thing, which is here *τὸ πλέον τιμηθῆναι*, we read, *εἰς σαυτὸν τὸ πλ. τ.*.

[2] Mss. and Edd. *Πανταχοῦ γὰρ παρ᾽ αὐτῶν ἐβούλετο λαβεῖν ἀφορμὴν, ὅπερ ἔφην. Τά τε γὰρ ἔθνη παρεζήλου λοιπὸν καὶ ῥαδίως κ. τ. λ.* In *παρεζήλου* there is an allusion to Rom. xi. 14, "if by any means I may provoke them to jealousy:" its subject therefore should be "the Apostle" (*nam et gentes exstimulabat jam*, Erasm.) "he was henceforth provoking to jealousy, being what he said to the Romans, "If by any means I may provoke," etc., not "the Gentiles," as Ben. makes it, *nam gentes jam zelo fervebant.* Besides transposing the parts *b*, *c*, we read, *Παρεζήλου λοιπόν. Τά τε γὰρ ἔθνη ῥαδίως.* . . . But perhaps it should be *Παρεζήλου λοιπὸν, ὅπερ ἔφη "Εἴ πως παραζηλώσω κ. τ. λ."*

[3] *Διὰ τοῦτο ἐνοχλεῖ (ἠνώχλει* Sav.) *αὐτοῖς συνεχῶς μεταπείθων*, old text, retained by Saville. He is explaining why St. Paul still resorted to the synagogues, though an unwelcome visitant. He wished to separate the Church from the Synagogue: but he would not himself take the first step towards this. It must be the act of the Jews. Therefore until they by their outrageous conduct obliged him to depart, he kept on troubling them with his presence (*εἰσωθοῦντα, ἠνώχλει*). Not that his discourse was harsh: that word, *ἐπαρρησ.*, does not mean this, but that he spoke freely and without reserve. (Recapitulation)—The unusual word *μεταπείθων* is probably a corruption of the abbreviation of the text-words, *ἐπὶ μῆνας τρεῖς διαλεγ. καὶ πείθων*, which the reporter may have written thus, *μ. τ. πείθων.*—Mod. text substitutes *Διὰ τοῦτο διελέγετο αὐτοῖς συνεχῶς ὅτι ἔπειθε.*

[4] *πόσον ἤνυσεν ἡ ἐπιστασία.* Cat., *ἀποστασία*, with reference to *ἀποστὰς* in v. 9.—The letters marking the order in which the parts are given in the Mss. will show the extreme confusion into which the notes of this Homily have fallen.

heard: (c) all that dwelt in Asia:" it was for this also that the Lord suffered him not to go into Asia (ch. xvi. 6) (on a former occasion); waiting, as it seems to me, for this same conjuncture. (Hom. xl. p. 245.) (b) "And God wrought special miracles by the hands of Paul: so that from his body were brought unto the sick handkerchiefs or aprons, and the diseases departed from them, and the evil spirits went out of them." (v. 11, 12.) Not touched the wearer only (and so were healed), but also receiving them, they laid them upon the sick (and so healed them).[1] (g) "He that believeth on Me," saith Christ, "doeth greater works than those which I do." (John xiv. 12.) This, and the miracle of the shadows is what He meant (in those words). (d) "Then certain of the vagabond Jews, exorcists, took upon them to call over them which had evil spirits the name of the Lord Jesus, saying, We adjure you by Jesus whom Paul preacheth." (v. 13.) So entirely did they do all by way of trade! Observe: vagabond, or, itinerant, Jewish exorcists. And to believe indeed, they had no mind; but by that Name they wished to cast out the demons. "By Jesus, whom Paul preacheth." Only see what a name Paul had got! "And there were seven sons of one Sceva, a Jew, and chief of the priests, which did so. And the evil spirit answered and said, Jesus I know, and Paul I know; but who are ye? And the man in whom the evil spirit was leaped on them, and overcame them, and prevailed against them, so that they fled out of that house naked and wounded." (v. 14–16.) They did it in secret: then their impotence is publicly exposed. (f) Then not the Name does anything, unless it be spoken with faith. (h) See how they used their weapons against themselves! (j) So far were they from thinking Jesus to be anything great: no, they must needs add Paul, as thinking him to be something great. Here one may marvel how it was that the demon did not coöperate with the imposture of the exorcists, but on the contrary exposed them, and laid open their stage-play. He seems to me (to have done this) in exceeding wrath: just as it might be, if a person being in uttermost peril, should be

exposed by some pitiful creature, and wish to vent all his rage upon him. "Jesus I know, and Paul I know." For, that there may not seem to be any slight put upon the Name of Jesus, (the demon) first confesses (Him), and then has permission given him. For, to show that it was not any weakness of the Name, but all owing to the imposture of those men, why did not the same take place in the case of Paul? "They fled out of that house naked and wounded:" he sorely battered their heads, perhaps rent their garments. (e) "And this became known to all, both Jews and Greeks, that dwelt at Ephesus, and fear fell upon them all, and the name of the Lord Jesus was magnified. And many of them that had believed came confessing and making known their practices." (v. 17, 18.) For since they had got to possess such power as, by means of the demons, to do such things, well might this be the consequence. "And many of them that practised curious arts, brought their books together, and burnt them in the presence of all men;"—having seen that there was no more use of them now that the demons themselves do these things—"and reckoned up the price of them, and found the amount fifty thousand pieces of silver.* So mightily grew the word of God and prevailed." (v. 19, 20.) (i) "And"[2] (so) "he disputed," in the school of one Tyrannus for two years:" where were believers, and believers exceedingly (advanced in the faith). Moreover (Paul) writes (to them) as to great men.

(Recapitulation.) (b) "And having entered in to the synagogue," etc. (v. 8.) But[3] why ἐπαρρησιάζετο? It means, he was ready to confront dangers, and disputed more openly, not veiling the doctrines. (a) "But when some were hardened, and spake evil of the way, having departed from them, he separated the disciples." (v. 9.) He put a stop, it means, to their evil-speaking: he did not wish to kindle their envy, nor to bring them into more contention. (c) Hence let us also learn not to put ourselves in the way of evil-speaking men, but to depart from them: he did not speak evil, when himself evil spoken of. "He disputed daily," and by this gained

---

[1] Οὐχὶ φοροῦντες ἥττοντο μόνον. Edd. i. e., " The process was not only this, that persons bearing these things, by touching the sick healed them, but the things themselves simply laid upon the sick were effectual for their healing." But A. C. Cat. φοροῦντος, which is much better: "It was not only that they touched him (the Apostle) wearing these things " —viz. as the woman was healed by touching the hem of Christ's garment—" but receiving them, they laid them upon the sick," etc.—In the next sentence (g), for τοῦτο καὶ τὸ τῶν σκιῶν ἐστιν ὅπερ ἔλεγεν, (which Sav. gives in marg.), Edd. have τοῦτο τὸ τῶν σκιῶν αἰνιττόμενος, which Ben. renders has umbras insinuans. St. Chrys. elsewhere alleges the miraculous efficacy of St. Paul's garments and of St. Peter's shadow, in illustration of our Lord's saying, t. i. 537. A. t. ii. 53. C.

* Ephesus was famous for its sorcerers and magicians. Plutarch and Eustathius speak of Ephesian letters (Ἐφέσια γράμματα) which, written on slips, were carried about as charms and had power to assure success and avert disaster. The περίεργα were arts connected with this sorcery and the books burned contained, no doubt, mysterious sentences and symbols which gave to them an extravagant worth in the eyes of the superstitious. In this way the large price set upon them may be accounted for.—G. B. S.

[2] The meaning seems to be, Such was the effect of his two years' preaching at Ephesus: and his Epistle shows what high attainments in the faith were made by the Ephesians.

[3] The partial restoration which is here attempted implies this scheme of the derangement: 2, 1.: 1, 3, 2, 4: see note [3], p. 252.

the many, that, being evil intreated and (evil) spoken of, he did not (utterly) break away from them, and keep aloof. (e) The evil-speakers are defeated. They calumniated the doctrine itself; (therefore) so as neither to rouse the disciples to wrath, nor * * them, he withdrew, [1] showing that everywhere alike they repel salvation from them. Here now he does not even apologize, seeing that the Gentiles everywhere have believed. "In the school of one Tyrannus:" it was not that he sought the place, but without more ado where there was a school (there he discoursed).* (d) And look, no sooner is the trial from those without over, than this from the demons begins. Mark the infatuated Jewish hardness. Having seen his garments working miracles, they paid no heed to it. What could be greater than this? But, on the contrary, it resulted in just the opposite effect. If any of the heathens believe not, having seen the (very) dust working these effects, let him believe. [2] (f) Wonderful, how great the power of them that have believed! Both Simon for the sake of merchandise sought the grace of the Spirit, and these for this object did this. What hardness (of heart)! Why does not Paul rebuke them? It would have looked like envy, therefore it is so ordered. This same took place in the case of Christ (Mark ix. 36): but then the person is not hindered, for it was the beginning of the new state of things: since Judas also is not hindered, whereas Ananias and Sapphira were struck dead: and many Jews even for opposing (Christ) suffered nothing, while Elymas was blinded. "For I am not come," saith Christ, "to judge the world, but that the world might be saved." (John iii. 17.) "And seven sons," etc. (v. 14.) See the villany of the men! They still continued to be Jews, while wishing to make a gain of that Name. All that they did was for glory and profit. (g) Look, [3] in every case, how men are converted not so much in consequence of good things as of things fearful. In the case of Sapphira, fear fell upon the Church, and men dared not join themselves to them: here they received handkerchiefs and aprons, and were healed: and after this, then they came confessing their sins. (Hereby) the power of the demons is shown to be a great one, when it is against unbelievers. For why did he not say, "Who is Jesus?" He was afraid, lest he also should suffer punishment; but, that it might be permitted him to take revenge upon those who mocked him, he did this; "Jesus," says he, "I know," etc. He was in dread of Paul. For why did not those wretched men say to him, We believe? How much more splendid an appearance they would have made had they said this, that is, if they had claimed Him as their Master? But instead of that, they spoke even those senseless words, "By Jesus, whom Paul preacheth." Do you mark the forbearance (of the writer), how he writes history and does not call names? This makes the Apostles admirable. "And the evil spirit," etc. (v. 15), for what had happened at Philippi (ch. xvi. 16) had given a lesson to these also. He mentions the name, and the number, thereby giving to the persons then living a credible proof of what he wrote. And why were they itinerant? For the sake of merchandise: not assuredly to bear tidings of the word; how should that be their object? And [4] how ran they anon, preaching by the things they suffered? "Insomuch," it says, "that all that dwelt in Asia heard the word of the Lord." Ought not this to have converted all? And marvel not, for nothing convinces malice. But come now, let us look at the affair of the exorcists, with what an evil disposition (they acted). Why the same was not done in the case of Christ, is an inquiry for another time, and not for the present, save that this also was well and use-

---

[1] ὡς μήτε τοὺς μαθητὰς εἰς θυμὸν ἐγεῖραι, μήτε ἐκείνους ἀναχωρῆσαι. Mod. text. transposes εἰς θ. ἐγεῖραι and ἀναχωρ. We read ἀνεχώρησε. The verb either to ἐκείνους or to τοὺς μαθητάς is probably lost.
* Some have supposed Tyrannus to have been a Jewish teacher, who conducted a school in a private synagogue—a Beth Midrash (so Meyer). In this view, Paul and his companions, on account of the opposition which they encountered, separated themselves from the public synagogue, and betook them to this private Jewish school. But Tyrannus is a Greek name and the more common and preferable opinion is that he was a teacher of philosophy or rhetoric who had become a Christian and in whose apartments both Jews and Gentiles could meet without molestation.—G. B. S.
[2] τὴν κόνιν ταῦτα ἐργαζομένην, πιστευέτω, B. C. Cat. But A. substitutes κόρην, Mod. text σκίαν. He seems to allude here to the miracles effected by the very ashes of the martyrs: see e. g. t. ii. 494, A.: and perhaps with reference to these he says, Βαβαί, πόση τῶν πιστευσάντων ἡ δύναμις: unless this be meant as an exclamation of the persons who "took upon them," etc. i. e. Like Simon, they saw the wonders wrought in the name of Jesus; "Wonderful (said they)! Why, what power is exercised by these men who have believed!" namely, by those who by laying the handkerchiefs, etc., upon the sick restored them to health.—Mod. text adds, "that to others also there comes (the power) of doing the same things: and how great the hardness of those who even after the demonstrations of power yet continue in unbelief."

[3] From this point to the end of the Exposition, having in vain attempted to restore the true order, we take it as it lies in the Mss. and Edd.—Below, "and after this;" i. e. "yet after this," then these itinerant Jewish exorcists took upon them, etc. and not until after their punishment, when "fear fell upon them all," did those of the professed believers (τῶν πεπιστευκότων) who still practiced magic come forward confessing their sins.
[4] Πῶς δὲ ἕτερος λοιπὸν κηρύττοντες δι᾽ ὧν ἔπασχον. The subject to ἔπασχον seems to be "these exorcists" the sons of Sceva: but to ἔτρεχον it seems to be "the Apostles." "This made the Apostles wonderful in men's eyes:" they had wrought miracles, and preached two years, "so that all in Asia heard the word of the Lord," yet still these practices continued: but (see) how they ran (what success they had) now, preaching by the things these men were suffering: "and this became known to all the Jews and Greeks also dwelling in Asia, and the name of the Lord Jesus was magnified."—Mod. text, seemingly referring ἔτρεχον to the exorcists, reads καλῶς δὲ ἔτρ. And in place of v. 10, gives, "Whence, showing this, it saith, 'And this became known to all,'" etc. v. 17.

fully ordered. It seems to me that they did this also in mockery, and that in consequence of this (punishment), none dared even at random to name that Name. Why did this put them upon confession? Because this was a most mighty argument of God's omniscience (therefore), before they should be exposed by the demons, they accused themselves, fearing lest they should suffer the same things. For when the demons their helpers are their accusers, what hope is there thenceforth, save the confession by deeds?

But see, I pray you, after such signs had been wrought, what evils within a short space ensue. Such is human nature: it soon forgets. Or, do ye not remember what has been the case among ourselves? Did not God last year shake our whole city?[1] Did not all run to baptism? Did not whoremongers and effeminate and corrupt persons leave their dwellings, and the places where they spent their time, and change and become religious? But three days passed, and they returned again to their own proper wickedness. And whence is this? From the excessive laziness. And what marvel if, when the things have passed away (this be the case), seeing that, the images lasting perpetually, the result is such? The fate of Sodom—say, does it not still last (in its effects)?[2] Well, did the dwellers beside it become any the better? And what say you to the son of Noah? Was he not such (as he is represented), did he not see with his eyes so vast a desolation, and yet was wicked? Then let us not marvel how, when such things had been done, these Jews (at Ephesus) believe not, when we see that belief itself often comes round for them into its opposite,[3] into malignity; as, for instance, when they say that He hath a devil, He, the Son of God! Do you not see these things even now, and how men are many of them like serpents, both faithless and thankless, men who, viper-like, when they have enjoyed benefits and have been warmed by some, then they sting their benefactors? This we have said, lest any should marvel, how, such signs having been wrought, they were not all converted, For behold, in our own times happened those (miracles) relating to the martyr

Babylas,[4] those relating to Jerusalem, those relating to the destruction of the temples, and not all were converted. Why need I speak of ancient things? I have told you what happened last year; and none gave heed to it, but again little by little they fell off and sunk back. The heaven stands perpetually crying aloud that it has a Master, and that it is the work of an Artificer, all this that we see—I mean the world—and yet some say that it is not so. What happened to that Theodorus last year—whom did it not startle? And yet nothing came of it, but having for a season become religious, they returned to the point from which they had started in their attempt to be religious. So it was with the Jews. This is what the Prophet said of them: "When He slew them, then they sought Him, and turned early unto God." (Ps. lxxviii. 34.) And what need to speak of those things that are common to all? How many have fallen into diseases, how many have promised, if raised up, to work so great a change, and yet they have again become the same as ever! This, if nothing else, shows that we have natural free-will—our changing all at once. Were evil natural, this would not be: things that are natural and necessary, we cannot change from. "And yet," you will say, "we do change from them. For do we not see some, who have the natural faculty to see, but are blinded by fear?" (True—) because this also is natural: * * if a different (necessity of) nature come not also into operation:[5] (thus) it is natural to us, that being terrified we do not see; it is natural to us that when a greater fear supervenes, the other gives way. "What then," you will say, "if right-mindedness[6] be indeed according to nature, but fear having overpowered it cast it out?" What then if I shall show that some even then are not brought to a right mind, but even in these fears are reckless? Is this natural? Shall I speak of ancient things? Well then, of recent? How many in the midst of those fears continued laughing, mocking, and experienced nothing of the sort? Did not Pharaoh change immediately, and (as quickly) run

---

[1] Ben. assigns this to the year 399, and cites the first of the "Eleven Homilies" t. xii. as having been delivered according to St. Chrys. thirty days after that great earthquake, viz., in the year of the fall of Eutropius, therefore A. D. 399. But Ed. Par. justly corrects this mistake : in fact, the σεισμὸς of which St. Chrys. there speaks (t. xii. p. 324. A.) is only a metaphor, meaning the catastrophe of Eutropius.

[2] Perhaps with an allusion to Jude ver. 7, "Sodom and Gomorrah—set forth for an example, suffering the vengeance of eternal fire."

[3] Meaning, perhaps, Even when they believe the miracles to be real, that which should have brought them to faith becomes to them an occasion of greater wickedness.

[4] The miracles at Antioch, when at the instigation of the demon (Apollo) the remains of the martyr Babylas were removed by order of Julian. See the Hom. de S. Babyla, t. ii. p. 567.—The Theodorus mentioned below cannot be the lapsed person of that name to whom St. Chrys. addressed the first of the two Paræneses, t. i. init. But probably πέρυσι is corrupt, and the allusion may be to the troubles at Antioch in connection with Theodorus the Sicilian ; see p. 238, note [4].

[5] ἂν μὴ φύσις ἑτέρα προσέλθῃ. To complete the sense we must supply, "because this also (the being blinded by fear) is a natural affection : but what I have said is true, viz. that τῶν κατὰ φύσιν καὶ ἀνάγκην οὐ δυνάμεθα μεθίστασθαι, ἂν μὴ κ. τ. λ.

[6] τὶ οὖν ἂν καὶ ἡ σωφροσύνη. This is corrupt or mutilated. The sense requires, "What if in some cases 'an evil mind' be a natural necessity—as much as seeing or any other natural property or affection, but when there seems to be a change, it is only that fear casts out the evil mind for a while?"

back to his former wickedness? But here, as if (the demons) knew Him not, they (the exorcists) added, "Whom Paul preacheth," whereas they ought to have said, "the Saviour of the world." "Him that rose again." By this they show that they do know, but they did not choose to confess His glory. Wherefore the demon exposes them, leaping upon them, and saying, "Jesus I know, and Paul I know, but who are ye?" So that not ye are believers, but ye abuse that Name when ye say this. Therefore the Temple is desolate,[1] the implement easy to be overcome. So that ye are not preachers; mine, says he, ye are. Great was the wrath of the demon. The Apostles had power to do this to them, but they did it not as yet. For they that had power over the demons that did these things to them, much more had power over the men themselves. Mark how their forbearance is shown, in that they whom they repulsed do these things, while the demons whom they courted do the contrary. "Jesus," says he, "I know." Be ashamed, ye that are ignorant (of Him). "And Paul I know." Well said, "Think not that it is because I despise them, that I do these things." Great was the fear of the demon. And why without these words did he not rend their garments? For so he would both have sated his wrath, and established the delusion. He feared as I said, the unapproachable force, and would not have had such power had he not said this. But observe how we find the demons everywhere more right minded (than the Jews), not daring to contradict nor accuse the Apostles, or Christ. There they say, "We know Thee who Thou art" (Matt. viii. 29); and, "Why art Thou come hither before the time to torment us" (Mark i. 24): and again, "I know Thee who Thou art, the Son of God." And here, "These men are servants of the most high God" (ch. xvi. 17): and again, "Jesus I know, and Paul I know." For they exceedingly feared and trembled before those holy persons. Perhaps some one of you, hearing of these things, wishes he were possessed of this power, so that the demons should not be able to look him in the face, and accounts those saints happy for this, that they had such power. But let him hear Christ saying, "Rejoice not because the demons are subject unto you" (Luke x. 20), because He knew that all men rejoice most in this, through vainglory. For if thou seekest that which pleaseth God, and that which is for the common good, there is another, a greater way. It is not so great to free from a demon as it

is to rescue from sin. A demon hinders not to attain unto the kingdom of Heaven, nay, even coöperates, unwillingly indeed, but nevertheless coöperates by making him that has the demon more sober-minded; but sin casts a man out.

But it is likely some man will say, "God forbid it should ever befall me to be sobered in this way!" Nor do I wish it for you, but a very different way, that you should do all from love of Christ: if however, which God forbid, it should so befall you, then even on this behalf I would comfort you. If then the demon does not cast out (from the kingdom of heaven), but sin does cast out, to free a man from sin is greater beneficence.

From this let us study to free our neighbors, and before our neighbors, our own selves. Let us see to it, lest we have a demon: let us examine ourselves strictly. More grievous than a demon is sin, for the demon makes men humble. See ye not those possessed with a demon, when they have recovered from the attack, how downcast they are, of how sad a countenance, how fraught with shame their faces are, how they have not even courage to look one in the face? See the strange inconsistency! While those are ashamed on account of the things they suffer, we are not ashamed on account of the things we do; while they are abashed being wronged, we are not abashed when doing wrong: and yet their condition is not a subject for shame, but for pity and tenderness and indulgence: nay, great is the admiration it calls for, and many the praises, when struggling against such a spirit, they bear all thankfully: whereas our condition in very deed is a subject for ridicule, for shame, for accusation, for correction, for punishment, for the worst of evils, for hell-fire; calling for no compassion whatever. Seest thou, that worse than a demon is sin? And those indeed, from the ills they suffer, reap a double profit: first, their being sobered and brought to more self-control; then, that having suffered here the chastisement of their own sins, they depart hence to their Master, purified. For indeed upon this we have often discoursed to you, that those who are punished here, if they bear it thankfully, may naturally be supposed to put away thereby many of their sins. Whereas from sins the mischief resulting is twofold; first, that we offend; secondly, that we become worse. Attend to what I say. Not this is the only injury we get from sin, that we commit a sin: but another and a worse is this, that our soul receives a habit. Just as it is in the case of the body—for it will be more plain when put in the form of an example—as he

---

[1] Meaning perhaps, That which should be the Temple of Christ, the body of the believer.

who has taken a fever has got harm not only in this respect, that he is sick, but also that after the sickness he is become weaker, even though he may return to health after a long disease: just so in the case of sin, though we may regain health, yet we are far from having the strength we need. For [1] take the case of one who has been insolently abusive: does he not suffer his deserts for his abusive conduct? Aye, but there is another and a worse thing to rue (which is), that his soul is become more insensible to shame. For from each several sin that is committed, even after the sin has been done and has ceased, there remains a kind of venom instilled into our souls. Do you not hear people saying, when they are recovered from sickness, "I dare not drink water now?" And yet the man has regained his health: aye, but the disease has done him this harm also. And whereas those (possessed) persons, albeit suffering ill, are thankful, we, when faring well, blaspheme God, and think ourselves very ill used: for you will find more persons behaving thus in health and wealth than in poverty and sickness. For there stands the demon over (the possessed), like a very hangman, fierce, uttering many (menaces), even as a schoolmaster brandishing the lash, and not suffering them to give way to any laxity. And suppose that some are not at all brought to a sober mind, neither are these liable to punishment; [2] no small thing this: even as fools, even as madmen and children, are not called to account, so neither are these: since for things that are done in a state of unconsciousness, none can be so merciless as to call the doers to account. Why then, in a far worse condition than those who are possessed of evil sprits are we that sin. We do not, indeed, foam at the mouth, nor distort our eyes, or throw about our hands convulsively; but as for this, would that we did it in our body and not in our soul! Will you that I show you a soul, foaming, filthy, and a distortion of the mind's eyes? Think of those who are in a passion and drunken with rage; can any form be filthier than the words they discharge? In very deed it is like a sputtering of noisome slaver. And just as the possessed know none of those who are

present, so neither do these. Their understanding darkened, their eyes distorted, they see not who is friend, who foe, who worthy of respect, who contemptible, but they see all alike without a difference. And then, do you not see them, how they tremble, just like those others? But they do not fall to the ground, say you? True, but their soul lies on the ground and falls there in convulsions: since had it stood upright, it would not have come into the condition it is in. Or think you not that it betokens a soul abjectly sprawling and lost to all self-possession, the things men can do and say when drunken with rage? There is also another form of madness worse than this. What may this be? When men cannot so much as suffer themselves to vent their anger, but instead of that nourish within their own bosoms, to their own proper hurt,[3] as it were a very hangman with his lash, the rancorous remembrance of wrongs. For it is a bane to themselves first, the malice that they bear. To say nothing of the things to come, what torture, think you, must that man undergo in the scourging of his soul, as day by day he looks how he may avenge himself on his enemy? He chastises himself first, and suffers punishment, swelling (with suppressed passion), fighting against himself, setting himself on fire. For needs must the fire be always burning within thee: while raising the fever to such a height, and not suffering it to wane, thou thinkest thou art inflicting some evil on the other, whereas thou art wasting thyself, ever bearing about with thee a flame which is always at its height, and not letting thy soul have rest, but evermore being in a state of fury, and having thy thoughts in a turmoil and tempest. What is more grievous than this madness, to be always smarting with pain, and ever swelling and inflamed? For such are the souls of the resentful: when they see him on whom they wish to be revenged, straightway it is as if a blow were struck them: if they hear his voice, they cower and tremble: if they be on their bed, they picture to themselves numberless revenges, hanging, torturing that enemy of theirs: and if, beside all this, they see him also to be in renown, O! the misery they suffer! Forgive him the offence, and free thyself from the torment. Why continue always in a state of punishment, that thou mayest once punish him, and take thy revenge? Why establish for thyself a hectic disease? [4] Why, when thy wrath would fain

---

[1] Mod. text, "For look now at some one who has been abusive, and has not been punished : not for this only is it a subject for weeping, that he does not suffer the punishment for his abusiveness, but also for another reason it is a subject for mourning. What may this be? That his soul is now become more shameless." But Chrys. is speaking of the immediate evil—here the act of ὕβρις for which the man suffers, or will have to give account hereafter—and the permanent effect, the ἕξις which every evil act fixes on 'the soul.—Ἕτερον here and above we render in its pregnant sense, "other and worse," or, "what is quite another and a more serious thing."

[2] Old text. Εἰ δέ τινες μηδ' ὅλως νήφοιεν, οὐδὲ ἐκεῖνοι διδόασι δίκην. Sav. and Ben. οὕτω and δώσουσι. But Par. has resumed the unintelligible reading of mod. text, εἰ δέ τινες μηδ' οὕτω ν., ἀλλ' οὖν ἐκεῖνοι διδόασι δίκην.

[3] ἀλλὰ τρίφωσι παρ ἑαυτοῖς οἰκεῖον κακὸν, καθάπερ τινὰ δήμιον τὴν μνησικακίαν. Mod. text οἰκειακὸν καθ. τ. δ.

[4] For τί κατασκευάζεις ἕκτικον σαυτῷ νόσημα ; B. has, τί κ. ἐκτήκον σαυτὸν 'τῷ νοσήματι, quæ lectio non spernanda, te morbo tabefaciens, Ben. The reading ἐκτήκον is explained by

depart from thee, dost thou keep it back? Let it not remain until the evening, says Paul. (Eph. iv. 26.) For like some eating rot or moth, even so does it gnaw through the very root of our understanding. Why shut up a beast within thy bowels? Better a serpent or an adder to lie within thy heart, than anger and resentment: for those indeed would soon have done with us, but this remains forever fixing in us its fangs, instilling its poison, letting loose upon us an invading host of bitter thoughts. "That he should laugh me to scorn," say you, "that he should despise me!"[1] O wretched, miserable man, wouldest thou not be ridiculed by thy fellow-servant, and wouldest thou be hated by thy Master? Wouldest thou not be despised by thy fellow-servant, and despisest thou thy Master? To be despised by him, is it more than thou canst bear, but thinkest thou not that God is indignant, because thou ridiculest Him, because thou despisest Him, when thou wilt not do as He bids thee? But that thine enemy will not even ridicule thee, is manifest from hence (that), whereas if thou follow up the revenge, great is the ridicule, great the contempt, for this is a mark of a little mind; on the contrary, if thou forgive him, great is the admiration, for this is a mark of greatness of soul. But you will say, he knows not this. Let God know it, that thou mayest have the greater reward. For He says, "Lend to those of whom ye hope not to receive." (Luke vi. 34.) So let us also do good to those who do not even perceive that one is doing them good, that they may not, by returning to us praise or any other thing, lessen our reward. For when we receive nothing from men, then we shall receive greater things from God. But what is more worthy of ridicule, what more paltry, than a soul which is always in anger, and wishing to take revenge? It is womanly, this disposition, it is babyish. For as the babes are angry even with lifeless things, and unless the mother beats the ground, they will not let go their anger:[2] so do these persons wish to revenge themselves on those who have aggrieved them. Why then, it is they who are worthy of ridicule: for to be overcome by passion, is the mark of a childish understanding, but to overcome it, is a sign of manliness. Why then, not we are the objects of ridicule, when we keep our tem-

per, but they. It is not this that makes men contemptible—not to be conquered by passion: what makes them contemptible is this—to be so afraid of ridicule from without, as on this account to choose to subject one's self to one's besetting passion, and to offend God, and take revenge upon one's self. These things are indeed worthy of ridicule. Let us flee them. Let a man say, that having done us numberless ills, he has suffered nothing in return: let him say that he might again frantically assault us, and have nothing to fear. Why, in no other (better) way could he have proclaimed our virtue; no other words would he have sought, if he had wished to praise us, than those which he seems to say in abuse. Would that all men said these things of me: "he is a poor tame creature; all men heap insults on him, but he bears it: all men trample upon him, but he does not avenge himself." Would that they added, "neither, if he should wish to do so, can he:" that so I might have praise from God, and not from men. Let him say, that it is for want of spirit that we do not avenge ourselves. This does us no hurt, when God knows (all): it does but cause our treasure to be in greater safety. If we are to have regard to them, we shall fall away from everything. Let us not look to what they say, but to what becomes us. But, says he, "Let no man ridicule me," and some make a boast of this. O! what folly! "No man," says he, "having injured me, has ridiculed me:" that is, "I had my revenge." And yet for this thou deservest to be ridiculed, that thou didst take revenge. Whence came these words among us—being, as they are, a disgrace to us and a pest, an overthrow of our own proper life and of our discipline? It is in downright opposition to God that thou (so) speakest. The very thing which makes thee equal to God—the not avenging thyself —this thou thinkest a subject for ridicule! Are not we for these things worthy to be laughed at, both by ourselves, and by the heathen, when we thus speak against God? I wish to tell you a story of a thing that happened in the old times (which they tell) not on the subject of anger, but of money. A man had an estate in which there was a hidden treasure, unknown to the owner: this piece of ground he sold. The buyer, when digging it for the purpose of planting and cultivation, found the treasure therein deposited, and came[3] and wanted to oblige the seller to

---

the etacism; the τι in νοσήματι is derived from the following τί βουλόμενον; hence it was necessary to alter σαυτῷ into σαυτὸν τῷ. In the following sentence, B. has τί βουλόμενος, "Why when thou wouldest be quit of it, dost thou keep thine anger?"

[1] Mod. text weakly, "But this I do that he may not laugh me to scorn, that he may not despise me."

[2] Καθάπερ γὰρ ἐκεῖνα (meaning τὰ βρέφη) καὶ πρὸς (om. B. C.) τὰ ἄψυχα ὀργίζεται, κἂν μὴ πλήξῃ τὸ ἔδαφος ἡ μήτηρ, οὐκ ἀφίησι τὴν ὀργήν.—Mod. text and Edd. except Sav. omit ἡ μήτηρ.

[3] Mod. text followed by Edd. perverts the whole story, making the parties contend, not for the relinquishing of the treasure, but for the possession of it, so making the conclusion (the willing cession of it by both to the third party) unintelligible, and the application irrelevant. The innovator was perhaps induced to make this alteration, by an unseasonable

receive the treasure, urging that he had bought a piece of ground, not a treasure. The seller on his part repudiated the gift, saying, "The piece of ground (is not mine), I have sold it, and I have no concern whatever with this (treasure)." So they fell to altercation about it, the one wishing to give it, the other standing out against receiving it. So chancing upon some third person, they argued the matter before him, and said to him, "To whom ought the treasure to be assigned?" The man could not settle that question; he said, however, that he would put an end to their dispute—he would (if they pleased) be master of it himself. So he received the treasure, which they willingly gave up to him; and in the sequel got into troubles without end, and learnt by actual experience that they had done well to have nothing to do with it. So ought it be done likewise with regard to anger; both ourselves ought to be emulous [1] not to take revenge, and those who have aggrieved us, emulous to give satisfaction. But perhaps these things also seem to be matter of ridicule: for when that madness is widely prevalent among men, those who keep their temper are laughed at, and among many madmen he who is not a madman seems to be mad. Wherefore I beseech you that we may recover (from this malady), and come to our senses, that becoming pure from this pernicious passion, we may be enabled to attain unto the kingdom of heaven, through the grace and mercy of His only-begotten Son, with Whom to the Father, together with the Holy Spirit, be glory, might, honor, now and ever, world without end. Amen.

HOMILY XLII.

ACTS XIX. 21, 23.

"After these things were ended, Paul purposed in the Spirit, when he had passed through Macedonia and Achaia, to go to Jerusalem, saying, After I have been there, I must also see Rome. So he sent into Macedonia two of them that ministered unto him, Timotheus and Erastus; but he himself stayed in Asia for a season. And the same time there arose no small stir about the Way."

HE sends Timothy and Erastus into Macedonia, but himself remains at Ephesus. Having made a long enough stay in that city, he wishes to remove elsewhere again. But how is it, that having from the first chosen to depart into Syria, he turns back to Macedonia? "He purposed," it says, "in the Spirit," showing that all (that he did) was done not of his own power. Now he prophesies, saying, "I must also see Rome:" perhaps to comfort them with the consideration of his not remaining at a distance, but coming nearer to them again, and to arouse the minds of the disciples by the prophecy. At this point, [2] I suppose, it was that he wrote his Epistle to the Corinthians from Ephesus, saying, "I would not have you ignorant of the trouble which came to us in Asia." (2 Cor. i. 8.) For since he had promised to go to Corinth, he excuses himself on the score of having loitered, and mentions the trial relating the affair of Demetrius. "There arose no small stir about the Way." * Do you see the renown [3] (acquired)? They contradicted, it says: (then) came miracles, twofold: (then) again, danger: such is the way the threads alternate throughout the whole texture (of the history). "For a certain man named Demetrius, a silversmith, which made silver temples of Diana, brought no small gain unto the craftsmen." (v. 24.). "Which made," it says, "silver temples of Diana." And how is it possible that temples could be made of silver? Perhaps as small boxes

recollection of the Parable of the Treasure hid in a field.— "The seller having learnt this, came and wanted to compel the purchaser ἀπολαβεῖν τὸν θησαυρὸν," (retaining ἀπολ., in the unsuitable sense "that he, the seller, should receive back the treasure.") "On the other hand, the other (the purchaser) repulsed him, saying, that he had bought the piece of ground along with the treasure, and that he made no account of this (καὶ οὐδένα λόγον ποιεῖν ὑπὲρ τούτου.) So they fell to contention, both of them, the one wishing to receive, the other not to give," etc.

[1] καὶ ἡμᾶς φιλονεικεῖν μὴ ἀμύνασθαι, καὶ τοὺς λελυπηκότας φιλονεικεῖν δοῦναι δίκην: as in the story, the parties ἐφιλονείκουν, the one μὴ λαβεῖν ὑπὲρ τοῦ θ., the other δοῦναι.

[2] Ἐντεῦθεν. If St. Chrys. is rightly reported, he means the second Epistle, which he proceeds to quote from. But that

17

Epistle was plainly not written ἀπὸ Ἐφέσου. Perhaps what he said was to this effect: "At this point I suppose it was— viz. after the mission of Timothy and Erastus—that he wrote (his first Epistle) to the Corinthians from Ephesus: and in the second Epistle he alludes to the great trial which ensued in the matter of Demetrius. He had promised to come to Corinth sooner, and excuses himself on the score of the delay." But τὰ κατὰ Δημήτριον διηγούμενος can hardly be meant of St. Paul: it should be αἰνιττόμενος.

* The use of ἡ ὁδός without further definition, to represent the Christian religion, is peculiar to the Acts (ix. 2; xix. 9, 23; xxiv. 22). Κυρίου or σωτηρίας would express the omitted defining idea.—G. B. S.

[3] Ὁρᾳς τὴν εὐδοκίμησιν; This seems to refer to v. 17–20. "But see how successes and trials here, as all along, alternate. Then the Jews contradicted: (v. 9) then miracles, twofold, (11–12 and 13–19): now again (after that εὐδοκίμησις), danger." —Here the Mss. and Edd. give v. 24–27, which we have distributed to their proper places.

(κιβώρια).* Great was the honor paid to this (Diana) in Ephesus; since, when (*Hom. in Eph.* Prol.) their temple was burnt it so grieved them, that they forbade even the name of the incendiary ever to be mentioned. See how, wherever there is idolatry, in every case we find money at the bottom of it. Both in the former instance it was for money, and in the case of this man, for money. (ch. xix. 13.) It was not for their religion, because they thought that in danger; no, it was for their lucrative craft, that it would have nothing to work upon. Observe the maliciousness of the man. He was wealthy himself, and to him indeed it was no such great loss; but to them the loss was great, since they were poor, and subsisted on their daily earnings. Nevertheless, these men say nothing, but only he. And observe : [1] "Whom having collected, and the workmen of like occupation," having themselves common cause with him, "he said, Sirs, ye know that by this craft we have our wealth" (v. 25); then he brought the danger home to them, that we are in danger of falling from this our craft into starvation. "Moreover ye see and hear, that not alone at Ephesus, but almost throughout all Asia, this Paul hath persuaded and turned away much people, saying that they be no gods, which are made with hands : so that not only this our craft is in danger to be set at naught; but also, that the temple of the great goddess Diana should be despised, and her magnificence should be destroyed, whom all Asia and the world worshippeth. And when they heard these sayings, they were full of wrath, and cried out, saying, Great is Diana of the Ephesians." (v. 26–28.) And yet the very things he spoke were enough to bring them to true religion : but being poor senseless creatures, this is the part they act. For if this (Paul being) man is strong enough to turn away all, and the worship of the gods is in jeopardy, one ought to reflect, how great must this man's God be, and that he will much more give you those things, for which ye are afraid. Already (at the outset) he has secured a hold upon their minds by saying, "This Paul hath turned away much people, saying, that they be no gods, which are made with men's hands." See what it is that the heathen are so indignant at; because he said

that "they which be made of men are no gods." Throughout, he drives his speech at their craft. Then that which most grieved them he brings in afterwards. But, with the other gods, he would say, we have no concern, but that "the temple also of the great goddess Diana is in danger to be destroyed." Then, lest he should seem to say this for the sake of lucre, see what he adds : "Whom the whole world worshippeth." Observe how he showed Paul's power to be the greater, proving all (their gods) to be wretched and miserable creatures, since a mere man, who was driven about, a mere tentmaker, had so much power. Observe the testimonies borne to the Apostles by their enemies, that they overthrew their worship.[2] There (at Lystra) they brought "garlands and oxen." (ch. xiv. 13.) Here he says, "This our craft is in danger to be set at naught.—Ye have filled (all) everywhere with your doctrine." (ch. v. 28.) So said the Jews also with regard to Christ : "Ye see how the world is going after Him" (John xii. 19); and, "The Romans shall come and take away our city." (ch. xi. 48). And again on another occasion, "These that have turned the world upside down are come hither also." (ch. xvii. 6).—"And when they heard these sayings, they were full of wrath." Upon what was that wrath called forth ? On hearing about Diana, and about their source of gain. "And cried out, saying, Great is Diana of the Ephesians. And the whole city was filled with confusion : and rushed with one accord into the theatre." (v. 29). Such is the way with vulgar minds, any trivial occasion shall hurry them away and inflame their passions. Therefore[3] it behooves to do (things) with (strict) examination. But see how contemptible they were, to be so exposed to all (excitements) ! "Having caught Gaius and Aristarchus, men of Macedonia, Paul's companions in travel, they dragged them :" (here) again recklessly, just as did the Jews in the case of Jason ; and everywhere they set upon them.[4] "And when Paul would

---

* These silver "temple" (ναοὺς) were shrines, small models of the temple containing images of the goddess, which pilgrims to the temple purchased and carried away and probably used in their homes as objects of domestic worship.—G. B. S.
[1] Καὶ ὅρα κοινωνοὺς ὄντας αὐτούς· εἶτα τὸν κίνδυνον ἐπέστησεν (so Cat. C. -σαν, A. B. ἐπέτησεν). Mod. text, "But being themselves partners of the craft, he takes them as partners also of the riot. Then also he exaggerated (ηὔξησεν) the danger, adding, This our craft is in danger of coming into contempt. For this is pretty nearly what he declares by this, that from this art," etc.
[2] ὅτι καθαιρῶν (Cat. ὅτε ἐκαθήρουν) αὐτῶν τὰ σεβάσματα, ἐκεῖ στέμματα καὶ ταύρους προσέφερον· ἐνταῦθα φησιν ὅτι κινδυνεύει κ. τ. λ. These seem to be only rough notes or hints of what Chrys. said. The first words καθ. αὐτ. τὰ σεβ. look like a reference to Acts xvii. 23, ἀναθεωρῶν τὰ σεβάσματα ὑμῶν: "thus at Athens, surveying the objects of their worship, and finding an Altar, etc. he thence takes occasion to preach the Unknown God. At Lystra, they brought garlands and oxen, and the Apostles thereupon, etc. Therefore these men here might well say, Our craft is in danger. For it was true, as was said on another occasion (at Jerusalem), Ye have filled, etc.: and, They that have turned the world, etc. Nay, of Christ also the Jews said the same, The world is going after Him."
[3] Διὰ ταῦτα μετ᾽ ἐξετάσεως δεῖ ποιεῖν, Mod. text adds πάντα. This sentence, om. by A., seems to be out of place, and to belong rather to v. 36. We have transposed the text v. 28, 29, which in Mss. and Edd. is given after ὡς πᾶσι προκεῖσθαι.
[4] καὶ πανταχοῦ αὐτοῖς προκεῖνται. To make some sense of the passage, we adopt προσκεῖνται from B. We also transpose v. 30 which is given with 31 after the following sentence.

have entered in unto the people, the disciples suffered him not," (v. 30) so far were they from all display and love of glory. "And certain of the Asiarchs, which were his friends, sent unto him, desiring him that he would not adventure himself into the theatre" (v. 31) to a disorderly populace and tumult. And Paul complies, for he was not vainglorious, nor ambitious. "Some therefore cried one thing, and some another : for the assembly was confused." Such is the nature of the multitude : it recklessly follows, like fire when it has fallen upon fuel ; and the more part knew not wherefore they were come together." (v. 32.) "And they drew Alexander out of the multitude, the Jews putting him forward." It was the Jews that thrust him forward ;[1] but as providence ordered it, this man did not speak. "And Alexander beckoned with the hand, and would have made his defence unto the people." (v. 33.) "But when they knew that he was a Jew, all with one voice about the space of two hours cried out, Great is Diana of the Ephesians." (v. 34.) A childish understanding indeed! as if they were afraid, lest their worship should be extinguished, they shouted without intermission. For two years had Paul abode there, and see how many heathen there were still! "And when the town clerk had appeased the people, he said, Ye men of Ephesus, what man is there that knoweth not how that the city of the Ephesians is temple-keeper of the great goddess Diana, and of the image which fell down from Jupiter?" (v. 35.) As if the thing were not palpable. With this saying first he extinguished their wrath. "And of the Diopetes." There was another sacred object (ἱερὸν) that was so called. Either he means the piece of burnt earth or her image.[2]* This (is) a lie. "Seeing then that

these things cannot be spoken against, ye ought to be quiet, and to do nothing rashly. For ye have brought hither these men, which are neither robbers of churches, nor yet blasphemers of your goddess." (v. 36, 37.) All this however he says to the people ; but in order that those (workmen) also might become more reasonable, he says : "Wherefore if Demetrius, and the craftsman which are with him, have a matter against any man, the law is open, and there are deputies : let them implead one another. But if ye enquire anything concerning other matters, it shall be determined in a lawful assembly. For we are in danger to be called in question for this day's uproar, there being no cause, for which (matter) we shall not be able to give an account for this concourse." v. 38-40.) "A lawful assembly," he says, for there were three assemblies according to law in each month ; but this one was contrary to law. Then he terrified them also by saying, "We are in danger to be called to account" for sedition. But let us look again at the things said.

(Recapitulation.) "After these things were ended," it says, "Paul purposed in the Spirit, when he had passed through Macedonia and Achaia, to go to Jerusalem," saying, "After I have been there, I must also see Rome." (v. 21.) He no longer speaks here after the manner of a man,[3] or, He purposed to pass through those regions, without tarrying longer. Wherefore does he send away Timothy and Erastus? Of this I suppose he says, "Wherefore when we could no longer forbear, we thought it good to be left at Athens alone. He sent away," it says, "two of those who ministered to him" (1 Thess. iii. 1), both to announce his coming, and to make them more

---

[1] Προεβάλοντο Ἰουδαῖοι οἰκονομικῶς δὲ (supplied by Cat.) οὗτος οὐκ ἐφθέγξατο. Mod. text "The Jews thrust him forward, as Providence ordered it, that they might not have (it in their power) to gainsay afterwards. This man is thrust forward, and speaks: and hear what (he says)."

[2] Old text: Ἱερὸν ἕτερον οὕτως ἐκαλεῖτο—meaning, as we take it, the Palladium of Troy, which was also called "the Diopetes," τὸ Παλλάδιον τὸ Διοπετὲς καλούμενον, Clem. Alex. Protrept. iv. 47."—ἤτοι τὸ ὄστρακον αὐτῆς φησιν. Something more is needed, therefore we supply ἢ τὸ ἄγαλμα αὐτῆς φησιν. But ἱερὸν in this sense is not usual. Ὅστρακον, whatever it mean, cannot be the image of Diana, which was known to be of wood. The passage seems to be corrupt, and one might conjecture that ἱερὸν ἕτερον relates to "another Temple" of Diana built after the first which was burned by Herostratos, and that the name of this man is latent in the unintelligible ηποιτοοστρακον, and that Chrysostom's remark is this, that together with that former Temple perished the original Diopetes: so that to speak of that image as still in being was a lie (τοῦτο ψεῦδος)—Mod. text "But a different ἱερὸν was thus called διοπετές: either then the idol of Diana they called Diopetes, ὡς ἐκ τοῦ Διὸς τὸ ὄστρακον ἐκεῖ νοπεπτωκὸς, and not made by man: or a different ἄγαλμα was thus called among them."—Isidore of Pelus. in the Catena: "Some say that it is spoken of the image of Diana, i. e. '(a worshipper) of the great Diana and of her διοπετὲς ἄγαλμα:' some that the Palladium also (is here named as διοπ.), i. e. the image of Minerva, which they worshipped along with Diana." Ammonius ibid., "the ναὸς τοῦ Διός: or the στρογγυλοειδὲς"—meaning the ὄστρακον?—

"or rather, which is the true explanation, this image of Diana: or the Palladium, which they thought came from Jupiter, and was not the work of men." Œcum. gives the same variety of explanations, from the Catena. The words τοῦτο ψεῦδος, which in the Mss. follow the text v. 36, 37, are better referred to the Diopetes, as in our translation.—Mod. text ἄρα τὸ πᾶν ψεῦδος: and then, "these things however he says to the people, in order that those also," etc. omitting δὲ preserved by the old text.

* This Diopetes, the image which was supposed to have fallen down from Jupiter or heaven (Διός—πίπτω), was the image of Diana which was in the great temple at Ephesus. This was the superstitious belief of the people as is clear from the many instances in classic mythology in which statues are famed to have fallen from heaven. This image was of wood and was probably found there by the Greeks when they colonized Ionia.—G. B. S.

[3] i. e. In this, he prophesies (see above on this verse): but in his purpose of going to Jerusalem from Achaia, he was disappointed, for he had to return through Macedonia: ἢ προείλετο, i. e. this is the meaning of ἔθετο ἐν πνεύματι. Mod. text om. οὐκέτι ἐγχρονίσας, and adds: "for this is the meaning of ἔθετο, and such is the force of the expression." Then: "But why he sends away T. and E., the writer does not say: but it seems to me that of this also he says, Ἐν πνεύματι. Wherefore when," etc.—The meaning is: "He sends them away on this occasion, as he did at Athens: viz. because he could no longer forbear, therefore he thought it good to be left alone."

eager. "But he himself tarried awhile in Asia." (v. 22.) Most of all does he pass his time in Asia; and with reason : there, namely, was the tyranny, of the philosophers.[1] (Afterwards) also he came and discoursed to them again. "And the same time" etc. (v. 23), for indeed the superstition was excessive. (a) "Ye both see and hear," so palpable was the result that was taking place—"that not alone at Ephesus, but almost throughout all Asia, this Paul by persuading hath turned away," not by violence : this is the way to persuade a city. Then, what touched them closely, "that they be no gods which are made with hands." (v. 26.) He overturns, says he, our craft : (e) "From this work we have our wealth. Hath persuaded." How[2] did he persuade—he, a man of mean consideration ? How prevail over so great a force of habit? by doing what—by saying what ? It is not for a Paul (to effect this), it is not for a man. Even this is enough, that he said, "They are no gods." Now if the impiety (of the heathen religions) was so easy to detect, it ought to have been condemned long ago : if it was strong, it ought not to have been overthrown so quickly. (b) For, lest they should consider within themselves (how strange), that a human being should have such power as this, and if a human being has power to effect such things, why then one ought to be persuaded by that man, he adds : (f) "not only is this our craft in danger to be set at naught, but also," as if forsooth alleging a greater consideration, "the temple of the great goddess Diana," etc. (c) "whom all Asia and the world worshippeth." (v. 27.) (g) "And when they heard, they were filled with wrath, and shouted, Great is Diana of the Ephesians!" (v. 28.) For each city had its proper gods. (d) They thought to make their voice a barrier against the Divine Spirit. Children indeed, these Greeks ! (h) And their feeling was as if by their voice they could reinstate the worship of her, and undo what had taken place ! "And the whole city," etc. (v. 29.) See a disorderly multitude ! "And when Paul," etc. (v. 30.) Paul then wished to enter in that he might harangue them : for he took his persecutions as occasions for teaching : "but the disciples suffered him not." Mark, how great forethought we always find them taking for him. At the very first they brought him out that they might not (in his person) receive a mortal blow; and yet they had heard him

say, "I must also see Rome." But it was providential that he so predicts beforehand, that they might not be confounded at the event. But they would not that he should even suffer any evil. "And certain of the Asiarchs besought him that he would not enter into the theatre." Knowing his eagerness, they "besought him :" so much did all the believers love him.—"And they drew Alexander," etc. (v. 33.) This Alexander, why did he wish to plead ? Was he accused ? No, but it was to find an opportunity, and overturn the whole matter, and inflame[3] the anger of the people. "But when they knew that he was a Jew, all with one voice about the space of two hours cried out, Great is Diana of the Ephesians." (v. 34.) Do you mark the inordinate rage? Well, and with rebuke does the town clerk say, "What man is there that knoweth not how that the city of the Ephesians—"(v. 35) (coming to the point) which they were frightenened about. Is it this,[4] says he, that ye do not worship her ? And he does not say, "That knoweth not" Diana, but, "our city," that it always worshipped her.[5] "Seeing then that these things cannot be spoken against." (v. 36.) Why then do ye make a question about them, as if these things were not plain ? (b) Then he quietly chides them, showing that they had come together without reason. "And to do nothing rashly," he says. Showing that they had acted rashly. (a) "For ye have brought hither," etc. (v. 37.) They wanted to make religion the pretext for what concerned their own money-making : (c) and it was not right on account of private charges to hold a public assembly. For he put them to a nonplus, and left them not a word to say for themselves.[6] "There being no cause," he says, "for this concourse, for which" (matter) "we shall not[7] be able to give the account." (v. 40.) See how prudently, how cleverly, the unbelievers (act). Thus he extinguished their wrath. For as it is easily

---

[3] ἐκκαῦσαι. Erasm. ut et confutaret totum et furorem populi extingueret. Ben. subverteret . . . . extingueret. But ἐκκαῦσαι will not bear this sense, nor does the context suggest it. Alexander's object, it is represented, was to overthrow the preaching, and kindle the rage of the people yet more.—Cat. and Sav. marg. ἐλκύσαι.
[4] Mod. text "As if he had said, Do ye not worship her ?"
[5] Mod. text "But, Our city, paying court to them: θεραπεύων αὐτοὺς:" for which the old text has. But, Your city. Ἐθεράπευσεν αὐτήν. Which may mean, Thus he, the town clerk, paid homage to the city, by speaking of its honors. But θεραπεύετε αὐτὴν in the preceding sentence requires the sense given in the translation.
[6] Σφόδρα γὰρ αὐτοὺς ἠλόγησεν καὶ διηπόρησεν. Mod. text Τούτῳ σφ. αὐτοὺς διηπ., omitting, ἠλόγησεν, which, if not corrupt is here put in an unusual sense.
[7] οὐ δυνησόμεθα old text, here and above, as in the Alexandrine Ms. of the N. T. (received by Griesbach) but here with τῆς συστρ. τ. transposed. (If the negative be retained, it is better to read περὶ τῆς σ. τ. as in the leading authorities of the text: so that this clause is epexegetical to περὶ οὗ· for which, namely, for this concourse.)

kindled, so also is it easily extinguished. "And when he had thus spoken," it says, "he dismissed the assembly." (v. 41.)

Seest thou how God permits trials, and by them stirs up and awakens the disciples, and makes them more energetic? Then let us not sink down under trials: for He Himself will "also make the way of escape, that we may be able to bear them." (1 Cor. x. 13.) Nothing so makes friends, and rivets them so firmly, as affliction: nothing so fastens and compacts the souls of believers: nothing is so seasonable for us teachers in order that the things said by us may be heard. For the hearer when he is in ease is listless and indolent, and seems to suffer annoyance from the speaker: but when he is in affliction and distress, he falls into a great longing for the hearing. For when distressed in his soul, he seeks on all sides to find comfort for his affliction: and the preaching brings no small comfort. "What then," you will say, "of the Jews? How was it that in consequence of their weakheartedness, they did not hear?" Why, they were Jews, those ever weak and miserable creatures: and besides, the affliction in their case was great, but we speak of affliction in moderation. For observe: they expected to be freed from the evils that encompassed them, and they fell into number-less greater evils: now this is no common distress to the soul. Afflictions cut us off from the sympathy we have for the present world, as appears in this, that we wish for death immediately, and cease to be loving of the body: which very thing is the greatest part of wisdom, to have no hankering, no ties to the present life. The soul which is afflict-ed does not wish to be concerned about many things: repose and stillness are all it desired, content for its part to have done with the things present, even though there be nothing else to follow. As the body when wearied and distressed does not wish to indulge in amours, or gormandizing, but only to repose and lie down in quiet; so the soul, harassed[1] by numberless evils, is urgent to be at rest and quiet. The soul which is at ease is (apt to be) fluttered, alarmed, unsettled: whereas in this there is no vacuity, no run-ning to waste: and the one is more manly, the other more childish; the one has more gravity, in the other more levity. And as some light substance, when it falls upon deep water, is tossed to and fro, just so is the soul when it falls into great rejoicing. Moreover, that our greatest faults arise out of overmuch pleasure, any one may see. Come, if you

will, let us represent to ourselves two houses, the one where people are marrying, the other where they are mourning: let us enter in imagination into each: let us see which is better than the other. Why, that of the mourner will be found full of seriousness (φιλοσοφίας); that of the marrying person, full of indecency. For look, (here are) shameful words, unrestrained laughter, more unre-strained motions, both dress and gait full of indecency, words fraught with mere nonsense and foolery: in short, all is ridicule there, all ridiculous.[2] I do not say the marriage is this; God forbid; but the accompaniments of the marriage. Then nature is beside itself in excess of riot. Instead of human beings, those present become brute creatures, some neighing like horses, others kicking like asses: such utter license, such dissolute unre-straint: nothing serious, nothing noble: (it is) the devil's pomp, cymbals, and pipes, and songs teeming with fornication and adultery. But not so in that house where there is mourning; all is well-ordered there: such silence, such repose, such composure; nothing disorderly, nothing extravagant: and if any one does speak, every word he utters is fraught with true philosophy: and then the wonderful circumstance is, that at such times not men only, but even servants and women speak like philosophers—for such is the nature of sorrow—and while they seem to be consoling the mourner, they in fact utter numberless truths full of sound philosophy. Prayers are there to begin with, that the afflic-tion may stop there, and go no further: many a one comforting the sufferer, and recitals without number of the many who have the like cause for mourning. "For what is man?" (they ask) (and thereupon) a serious examination of our nature—"aye, then, what is man!" (and upon this) an impeachment of the life (present) and its worthlessness, a reminding (one another) of things to come, of the Judgment. (So from both these scenes) each returns home: from the wed-ding, grieved, because he himself is not in the enjoyment of the like good fortune; from the mourning, light-hearted, because he has not himself undergone the like affliction, and having all his inward fever quenched. But what will you? Shall we take for another contrast the prisons and the theatres? For the one is a place of suffering, the other of pleasure. Let us again examine. In the former there is seriousness of mind; for where there is sadness, there must needs be seriousness. He who aforetime was rich, and

---

[1] ταραχθεῖσα B. The other Mss. ταριχευθεῖσα, which is unsuitable here.

[2] ὅλως οὐδὲν ἕτερον ἢ πάντα γέλως καὶ κατάγελως τὰ ἐκεῖ.

inflated with his own importance, now will even suffer any common person to converse with him, fear and sorrow, like some mightier fire, having fallen on his soul, and softening down his harshness : then he becomes humble, then of a sad countenance, then he feels the changes of life, then he bears up manfully against everything. But in a theatre all is the reverse of this—laughter, ribaldry, devil's pomp, dissoluteness, waste of time, useless spending of days, planning for extravagant lust, adultery made a study of, practical training to fornication, schooling in intemperance, encouragement to filthiness, matter for laughter, patterns for the practice of indecency. Not so the prison : there you will find humbleness of mind, exhortation, incentive to seriousness, contempt of worldly things ; (these) are all trodden under foot and spurned and, fear stands over (the man there), as a schoolmaster over a child, controlling him to all his duties. But if you will, let us examine in a different way.[1] I should like you to meet a man on his return from a theatre, and another coming out of prison ; and while you would see the soul of the one fluttered, perturbed, actually tied and bound, that of the other you would see enlarged, set free, buoyant as on wings. For the one returns from the theatre, enfettered by the sight of the women there, bearing about chains harder than any iron, the scenes, the words, the gestures, that he saw there. But the other on his return from the prison, released from all (bounds), will no longer think that he suffers any evil as comparing his own case with that of (those) others. (To think) that he is not in bonds will make him thankful ever after ; he will despise human affairs, as seeing so many rich men there in calamity, men (once) having power to do many and great things, and now lying bound there : and if he should suffer anything unjustly, he will bear up against this also ; for of this too there were many examples there : he will be led to reflect upon the Judgment to come and will shudder, seeing here[2] (in the earthly prison) how it will be there. For as it is with one here shut up in prison, so in that world also before the Judgment, before the Day that is to come. Towards wife, children, and servants, he will be more gentle.

Not so he that comes from the theatre : he will look upon his wife with more dislike, he will be peevish with his servants, bitter towards his children, and savage towards all. Great are the evils theatres cause to cities, great indeed, and we do not even know that they are great. Shall we examine other scenes of laughter also, I mean the feasts, with their parasites, their flatterers, and abundance of luxury, and (compare with them) places where are the halt and blind? As before, in the former is drunkenness, luxury, and dissoluteness, in the latter the reverse.— See also with regard to the body, when it is hot-blooded, when it is in good case, it undergoes the quickest change to sickness : not so, when it has been kept low. Then let me make my meaning clearer to you :—let there be a body having plenty of blood, plenty of flesh, plump with good living : this body will be apt even from any chance food to engender a fever, if it be simply idle. But let there be another, struggling rather with hunger and hardship : this is not easily overcome, not easily wrestled down by disease. Blood, though it may be healthy in us, does often by its very quantity engender disease : but if it be small in quantity, even though it be not healthy, it can be easily worked off. So too in the case of the soul, that which leads an easy, luxurious life, has its impulses quickly swayed to sin : for such a soul is next neighbor to folly, to pleasure, to vainglory also, and envy, and plottings, and slanderings. Behold this great city of ours, what a size it is ! Whence arise the evils? is it not from those who are rich? is it not from those who are in enjoyment? Who are they that "drag" men "before the tribunals?" Who, that dissipate properties? Those who are wretched and outcasts, or those who are inflated with consequence, and in enjoyment? It is not possible that any evil can happen from a soul that is afflicted. (James ii. 6.) Paul knew the gain of this : therefore he says, "Tribulation worketh patience, and patience experince, and experience hope, and hope maketh not ashamed." (Rom. v. 3.) Then let us not sink in our afflictions, but in all things give thanks, that so we may get great gain, that we may be well-pleasing to God, who permits afflictions. A great good is affliction : and we learn this from our own children : for without affliction (a boy) would learn nothing useful. But we, more than they, need affliction. For if there, when the passions (as yet) are quiet, (chastisement) benefits them, how much more us, especially possessed as we are by so many ! Nay, we behoove rather to have schoolmasters than

---

[1] C., Ἀλλ' εἰ βούλει πάλιν πολλοὺς ἐξετάσωμεν τόπους· B.; Ἀλλὰ πάλιν εἰ βούλει ἑτέρους ἐξετ. τόπους. Mod. text Ἀλλ' εἰ β., πάλιν ἑτέρως ἐξετ. τοὺς αὐτοὺς τόπους. In the Translation we adopt ἑτέρως and omit τόπους.

[2] The text is corrupt: καὶ φρίξει τοὺς τόπους—perhaps it should be τοὺς ἐκεῖ τόπους—ἐνταῦθα ὁρῶν· καθάπερ γὰρ ἐνταῦθα ἐν δεσμωτηρίῳ τυγχάνων οὕτω κἀκεῖ πρὸ τῆς κρίσεως, πρὸ τῆς μελλούσης ἡμέρας, sc. φρίξει. i. e. "just as here, being shut up in prison he looks forward with dread to the coming trial, so will he in that world," etc. Mod. text quite misrepresenting the sense: "For, as he that is here shut up in prison is gentle towards all, so those also before the Judgment, before the coming Day, will be more gentle," etc.

they : since the faults of children cannot be great, but ours are exceeding great. Our schoolmaster is affliction. Let us then not draw it down willingly upon ourselves, but when it is come let us bear it bravely, being, as it is, always the cause of numberless good things ; that so we may both obtain grace from God, and the good things which are laid up for them that love Him, in Christ Jesus our Lord, with Whom to the Father, together with the Holy Spirit, be glory, might, honor, now and evermore, world without end. Amen.

HOMILY XLIII.

ACTS XX. I.

"And after the uproar was ceased, Paul called unto him the disciples, and embraced them, and departed for to go into Macedonia."

There was need of much comforting after that uproar. Accordingly, having done this, he goes into Macedonia, and then into Greece. For, it says, "when he had gone over those parts, and had given them much exhortation, he came into Greece, and there abode three months. And when the Jews laid wait for him, as he was about to sail into Syria, he purposed to return through Macedonia." (v. 2, 3.) Again he is persecuted by the Jews, and goes into Macedonia. "And there accompanied him into Asia Sopater of Berea ; and of the Thessalonians, Aristarchus and Secundus ; and Gaius of Derbe, and Timotheus ; and of Asia, Tychicus and Trophimus. These going before tarried for us at Troas." (v. 4. 5.) But how does he call Timothy a man "of Thessalonica ?"* This is not his meaning, but, "Of Thessalonians, Aristarchus and Secundus and Gaius : of Derbe, Timothy,"[1] etc., these, he says, went before him to Troas, preparing the way for him. "And we sailed away from Philippi after the days of unleavened bread, and came unto them to Troas in five days ; where we abode seven days." (v. 6.) For it seems to me that he made a point of keeping the feasts in the large cities. "From Philippi," where the affair of the prison had taken place. This was his third coming into Macedonia, and it is a high testimony that he bears to the Philippians, which is the reason why he makes some stay there. "And upon the first day of the week, when the disciples came together to break bread, Paul preached unto them, ready to depart on the morrow ; and continued his speech until midnight." (v. 7.) It was then the (season between Easter and) Pentecost.[2] See how everything was subordinate to the preaching. It was also, it says, the Lord's day.† Not even during night-time was he silent, nay he discoursed the rather then, because of stillness. Mark how he both made a long discourse, and beyond the time of supper itself. But the Devil disturbed the feast—not that he prevailed, however— by plunging the hearer in sleep, and causing him to fall down. "And," it says, "there were many lights in the upper chamber, where they were gathered together. And there sat in a window a certain young man named Eutychus, being fallen into a deep sleep : and as Paul was long preaching, he sunk down with sleep, and fell down from the third loft, and was taken up dead. And Paul went down, and fell on him, and embracing him, said, Trouble not yourselves ; for his life is in him. When he therefore was come up

---

* The phrase ἄχρι τῆς Ἀσίας are omitted by ℵ and B. and are now discarded in the leading critical editions. The residence of Timothy is not given, as being well known. It was probably Lystra (Acts xvi.).—G. B. S.

[1] St. Chrysostom's reading of v. 4 is peculiar, but does not appear in the vv. ll. of N. T. perhaps because the Edd. of Chrys. conform it to the usual text, which is Θεσσαλ. δὲ, Ἀρ. καὶ Σεκ. καὶ Γάιος Δερβαῖος καὶ Τιμόθεος, i. e. two Thessalonians, and beside them Gaius of Derbe, and Timothy, etc. But in the preceding chapter, v. 29, a Gaius was mentioned along with Aristarchus, and both as Macedonians. Hence it seems St. Chrys. read it with a stop after Γάιος, of Thessalonians, Aristarchus and Secundus and Gaius. In his remark, he seems to be giving a reason for striking out καὶ before Τιμόθεος : viz. "How does he call Timothy a Thessalonian. (as a negligent reader might suppose to be the case, viz., Of Thess. Ar. and Sec. and Gaius Derbæus and Timothy ?) He does not say this, but, of Thessalonians he mentions three, and then, of Derbe, Timothy, cf. xvi. 1., whereas Gaius was not of Derbe, but of Macedonia, xix. 29." The note of Œcumen. on the passage shows that Δερβαῖος was supposed by some to be a proper name : "Of the rest, he tells us what countries they were of : for Timothy he is content with the name, his personal character was distinction enough, and besides he has already told us where T. came from : viz. xvi. 1. But if Δερβαῖος here is a noun of nation and not a proper name, perhaps he has here also mentioned his country."

[2] Πεντηκοστὴ, meaning the whole of the seven weeks. The scope of the remark is, Being met for celebration of the Holy Eucharist, which followed the Sermon, and the discourse being lengthened out until midnight, they were fasting all the time (for the Eucharist was taken fasting, see Hom. xxvii. in 1 Cor.): so that, though it was during the weeks after Easter, when there was no fast, and not only so, but the Lord's Day moreover, here was a fast protracted till midnight.

† That the religious observance of Sunday is here alluded to has been generally assumed. Taken in connection with 1 Cor. xvi. 2 and Rev. i. 10, the passage renders it highly probable that at this time (about A.D. 57) the first day of the week was regularly observed by the Christians in memory of the Lord's resurrection, although it is certain that the Jewish Christians still observed the Jewish Sabbath.—G. B. S.

again, and had broken bread, and eaten, and talked a long while, even till break of day, so he departed. And they brought the young man alive, and were not a little comforted." (v. 8–12.) But observe, I pray you, the theatre, how crowded it was: and the miracle, what it was. "He was sitting in a window," at dead of night. Such was their eagerness to hear him! Let us take shame to ourselves! "Aye, but a Paul," say you, "was discoursing then." Yes, and Paul discourses now, or rather not Paul, either then or now, but Christ, and yet none cares to hear. No window in the case now, no importunity of hunger, or sleep, and yet we do not care to hear: no crowding in a narrow space here, nor any other such comfort. And the wonderful circumstance is, that though he was a youth, he was not listless and indifferent; and though (he felt himself) weighed down by sleep, he did not go away,[1] nor yet fear the danger of falling down. It was not from listlessness that he slumbered, but from necessity of nature. But observe, I beseech you, so fervent was their zeal, that they even assembled in a third loft: for they had not a Church yet. "Trouble not yourselves," he says. He said not, "He shall come to life again, for I will raise him up:" but mark the unassuming way in which he comforts them: "for his life," says he, "is in him. When he was come up again, and had broken bread, and eaten." This thing cut short the discourse; it did no harm, however. "When he had eaten," it says, "and discoursed a long while, even till break of day, so he departed." Do you mark the frugality of the supper? Do you observe how they passed the whole night? Such were their meals, that the hearers came away sober, and fit for hearing. But we, in what do we differ from dogs? Do you mark what a difference (between us and those men)? "And they brought the young man alive, and," it says, "were not a little comforted," both because they received him back alive, and because a miracle had been wrought.* "And we went before to ship, and sailed unto Thasos,[2] there intending to

take in Paul: for so had he appointed, minding himself to go afoot." (v. 13.) We often find Paul parting from the disciples. For behold again, he himself goes afoot: giving them the easier way, and himself choosing the more painful. He went afoot, both that he might arrange many matters, and by way of training them to bear a parting from him.[3] "And when he had joined us at Thasos, having taken him on board, we came to Mytilene; and having sailed thence on the morrow, we come over against Chios"—then they pass the island—"and on the next day we touched at Samos, and having stopped at Trogylium, on the following day we came to Miletus. For Paul had determined to sail by Ephesus, because he would not spend the time in Asia: for he hasted, if it were possible for him, to be at Jerusalem the day of Pentecost." (v. 14–16.) Why this haste? Not for the sake of the feast, but of the multitude. At the same time, by this he conciliated the Jews, as being one that did honor the feasts, wishing to gain even his adversaries: at the same time also he delivers the word.[4] Accordingly, see what great gain accrued, from all being present. But that the interests of the people of Ephesus might not be neglected on that account, he managed for this in a different way. But let us look over again what has been said.

(Recapitulation.) "And having embraced them," it says, "he departed for to go into Macedonia." (v. 1.) By this again he refreshed them (ἀνεκτήσατο), giving them much consolation. "And having exhorted" the Macedonians, "with much discourse, he came into Greece." (v. 2.) Observe how we everywhere find him accomplishing all by means of preaching, not by miracles. "And we sailed," etc. The writer constantly shows him to us as hasting to get to Syria; and the reason of it was the Church, and Jerusalem, but still he restrained his desire, so as to set all right in those parts also[5] And yet Troas

[1] οὐκ ἀπέστη, so as to lose the opportunity of hearing, and forego the "breaking of bread," which was to follow the discourse. Comp. Hom. x. in Gen. init.
* The narrative requires the interpretation of Chrys. that this was a case of restoration to life, not merely of revival from suspended animation (as Olshausen, Ewald, DeWette). This is established by the fact that Eutychus is said to have seen taken up νεκρός, not ὡς νεκρός. Moreover to ἤρθη νεκρός (v. 9) is opposed ἤγαγον ζῶντα (v. 12). He was dead; they brought him alive. It is true that the apostle says: "His life (soul) is in him," but this is said after he had fallen upon and embraced him, or this may have been said from the standpoint of his confidence of a miraculous restoration, as Jesus said of Jairus' daughter: "The damsel is not dead, but sleepeth," meaning that from his standpoint and in view of his power she still lived, although she was in reality dead.—G. B. S.
[2] Old text instead of Ἄσσον has Θάσον, a misreading which appears in some Mss. and Versions of the Acts: Cat., Νάσον.

[3] παιδεύων τε αὐτοὺς χωρίζεσθαι αὐτοῦ: but mod. text ἅμα καὶ παιδεύων αὐτοὺς μηδὲ χωρίζεσθαι αὐτοῦ. After this, old text has ἀνήχθημεν, φησιν, εἰς τὴν Θάσον evidently confusing this clause of v. 13, with the first of v. 14, then, εἶτα παρέχονται (for παρέρχ.) τὴν νῆσον, followed by v. 15, 16. Mod. text, v. 15 followed by "See, how Paul being urgent, they put to sea, and lose no time, but παρέρχονται τὰς νήσους," and v. 16.
[4] καὶ τοὺς ἐχθροὺς ἑλεῖν (F. ἐλεεῖν βουλόμενος, wishing by this means to overcome (for their good) even those who hated him. Then, ἅμα καὶ τὸν λόγον καθίει. Mod. text ἅμα ἔσπευδε τὸν λόγον καθεῖναι. Mr. Field remarks on Hom. in 2 Cor. p. 553 B. where we have παραίνεσιν καθῆσι, that the much more usual expression is, εἴς τι καθεῖναι, and adds: "semel tantum ap. Nostrum reperimus λόγον καθεῖναι, viz. t. ix. p. 236. E."—our passage.
[5] ἀλλ᾽ ὅμως κατεῖχε τὸν πόθον καὶ τὰ ἐκεῖ κατορθοῦν. The infinitive requires βουλόμενος or the like: i. e. "though desirous to get to Jerusalem, he restrained his desire, and made a stay at Troas of seven days, wishing, etc.:" but B. gives the same sense by reading κατορθῶν, Cat. κατώρθου. Mod. text οὕτως εἶχε τὸν πόθον καὶ τὰ ἐκεῖ κατορθοῦν.

is not a large place : why then do they pass seven days in it ? Perhaps it was large as regarded the number of believers. And after he had passed seven days there, on the following day he spent the night in teaching : so hard did he find it to tear himself away from them, and they from him. "And when we came together," it says, "to break bread." (v. 7-12.) At the very time (of breaking bread) the discourse having taken its commencement, * extended :[1] as representing that they were hungry, and it was not unseasonable : for the principal object (which brought them together) was' not teaching, but they came together "to break bread;" discourse however having come up, he prolonged the teaching. See how all partook also at Paul's table. It seems to me, that he discoursed while even sitting at table, teaching us to consider all other things as subordinate to this. Picture to yourselves, I beseech you, that house with its lights, with its crowd, with Paul in the midst, discoursing, with even the windows occupied by many : what a thing it was to see, and to hear that trumpet, and behold that gracious countenance ![2] But why did he discourse during night time ? Since "he was about to depart," it says, and was to see them no more : though this indeed he does not tell them, they being too weak (to bear it), but he did tell it to the others. At the same time too the miracle which took place would make them evermore to remember that evening ; so that the fall turned out to the advantage of the teacher. Great was the delight of the hearers, and even when interrupted it was the more increased. That (young man) was to rebuke all that are careless (of the word), he whose death was caused by nothing else than this, that he wished to hear Paul. "And we went before to ship,", etc. (v. 13.) Wherefore does the writer say where they came, and where they went to ? To show in the first place that he was making the voyage more leisurely—and this upon human grounds—and sailing past (some) : also (for the same reason he tells) where he made a stay, and what parts he sailed past ; (namely,) "that he might not have to spend the time in Asia." (v. 16.) Since had he come there, he could not have sailed by ; he

did not like to pain those who would have begged him to remain. "For he hasted," it says, "if it were possible for him to keep the day of Pentecost in Jerusalem :" and (this) was not possible (if he stayed). Observe, how he is also moved like other men. For therefore it is that all this is done, that we may not fancy that he was above human nature : (therefore) you see him desiring (something), and hasting, and in many instances not obtaining (his object) : for those great and holy men were partakers of the same nature with us; it was in the will and purpose that they differed, and so it was that also they attracted upon themselves the great grace they did. See, for instance, how many things they order by an economy of their own. "That we give not offence" (2 Cor. vi. 3) to those who wish (to take offence), and, "That our ministry be not blamed." Behold, both an irreproachable life and on the other hand condescension. This is (indeed to be) called. economy, to the (very) summit and height (of it).[3] For he that went beyond the commandments of Christ, was on the other hand more humble than all. "I am made all things to all men," he says, "that I might gain all." (1 Cor. ix. 22.) He cast himself also upon dangers, as he says in another place ; "In much patience, in afflictions, in necessities, in distresses, in stripes, in imprisonments." (2 Cor. vi. 4, 5.) And great was his love for Christ. For if there be not this, all else is superfluous, both the economy (of condescending accommodation), and the irreproachable life, and the exposing himself to dangers. "Who is weak," he says, "and I am not weak ? Who is offended, and I burn not ?" (2 Cor. xi. 29.) These words let us imitate, and let us cast ourselves upon dangers for our brethren's sake. Whether it be fire, or the sword, cast thyself on it, beloved, that thou mayest rescue (him that is) thy member : cast thyself, be not afraid. Thou art a disciple of Christ, Who laid down His life for His brethren : a fellow-disciple with Paul, who chose to suffer numberless ills for his enemies, for men that were

---

[1] Πρὸς αὐτὸν τὸν καιρὸν, ἀρχὴν ὁ λόγος λαβὼν παρέτεινεν ὡς ἐνδεικνύμενος πεινῆν· καὶ οὐκ ἦν ἄκαιρον· οὐ γὰρ προηγουμένως εἰς διδασκαλίαν καθῆκεν. This is evidently mutilated ; the verb to ὁ λόγος is wanting : ὡς ἐνδεικ. πεινῆν, either "making a display of," or, "pleading as excuse the being hungry," is unintelligible ; so is οὐκ ἦν ἄκ. Mod. text attempts to make sense by reading : "At the very time ᾧ ἐνεδείκνυτο πεινῆν, καὶ οὐκ ἦν ἄκαιρον, ἀρχὴν ὁ λόγος λαβὼν παρετάθη, ὥστε οὐ προηγ."

[2] Mod. text "many occupying even the windows, to hear that trumpet, and see that gracious countenance. What must the persons taught have been, and how great the pleasure they must have enjoyed !"

[3] Τοῦτο οἰκονομία λέγεται εἰς ἀκρότητα καὶ εἰς ὕψος. "This" —the blameless life and therewith συγκατάβασις described in 2 Cor. vi. 3 ff—"is what one may indeed call Οἰκονομία—managing or dispensing things for the good of others, so that they shall have what is best for them in the best manner, without shocking their prejudices. Οἰκον., in the moral sense of the word, implies συγκατάβασις, letting one's self down to the level of others for their good. (Hence below, καὶ τὰ τῆς οἰκονομίας, καὶ (τὰ) τοῦ ἀλήπτου βίου.) "Talk of 'economy'— here you have it at its very top and summit, in a degree not to be surpassed." Instead of ὕψος the context seems to require "the lowest depth." Hence mod. text τὸ εἰς ἀκρότητα εἶναι καὶ ὕψους ἀρετῆς, καὶ ταπεινοφροσύνης συγκαταβάσεως. Καὶ ἄκουε πῶς ὁ ὑπερβαίνων. . . "the being at the summit both of loftiness of virtue and of lowliness of condescension." In the next sentence St. Paul is described as ὁ ὑπερβαίνων τὰ παραγγέλματα τοῦ Χριστοῦ, namely, the precept "that they which preach the Gospel should live by the Gospel," 1 Cor. ix. 14.

warring against him; be thou filled with zeal, imitate Moses. He saw one suffering wrong, and avenged him; he despised royal luxury, and for the sake of those who were afflicted he became a fugitive, a wanderer, lonely and deserted; he passed his days in a foreign land; and yet he blamed not himself, nor said, "What is this? I despised royalty, with all that honor and glory: I chose to avenge those who were wronged, and God hath overlooked me: and not. only hath He not brought me back to my former honor, but even forty years am I passing in a foreign land. Truly, handsomely[1] have I received my wages, have I not!" But nothing of the kind did he say or think. So also do thou: be it that thou suffer any evil for doing good, be it that (thou have to wait) a long time, be not thou offended, be not discomposed: God will of a surety give thee thy reward. The more the recompense is delayed, the more is the interest of it increased. Let us have a soul apt to sympathize, let us have a heart that knows how to feel with others in their sorrows: no unmerciful temper (ὠμόν), no inhumanity. Though thou be able to confer no relief, yet weep thou, groan, grieve over what has happened: even this is not to no purpose. If it behooves us to feel for those who are justly punished by God, much more for those who suffer unjustly at the hands of men. (They of) "Ænan,"[2] it saith, "came not forth to mourn for the house which was near her" (Micah i. 11): they shall receive pain, "in return for that they built for derision." And again, Ezekiel makes this an accusation against them, that they did not grieve for (the afflicted). (Ezek. xvi. 2.) What sayest thou, O Prophet? God punisheth, and shall I grieve for those that He is punishing? Yea verily: for God Himself that punisheth wisheth this: since neither does He Himself wish to punish, nay, even Himself grieves when punishing. Then be not thou glad at it. You will say, "If they are justly punished, we ought not to grieve." Why, the thing we ought to grieve for is this —that they were found worthy of punishment. Say, when thou seest thy son undergoing cautery or the knife, dost thou not grieve? and sayest thou not to thyself,

"What is this? It is for health this cutting, to quicken his recovery; it is for his deliverance, this burning?" but for all that, when thou hearest him crying out, and not able to bear the pain, thou grievest, and the hope of health being restored is not enough to carry off the shock to nature. So also in the case of these, though it be in order to their health that they are punished, nevertheless let us show a brotherly feeling, a fatherly disposition. They are cuttings and cauteries, the punishments sent by God: but it is for this we ought to weep, that they are sick, that they needed such a mode of cure. If it be for crowns that any suffer these things, then grieve not; for instance, as Paul, as Peter suffered: but when it is for punishment that one suffers justice, then weep, then groan. Such was the part the prophets acted; thus one of them said, "Ah! Lord, dost thou destroy the residue of Israel?" (Ezek. ix. 8.) We see men-slayers, wicked men, suffering punishment, and we are distressed, and grieve for them. Let us not be philosophical beyond measure: let us show ourselves pitiful, that we may be pitied; there is nothing equal to this beautiful trait: nothing so marks to us the stamp of human nature as the showing pity, as the being kind to our fellow-men. In fact, therefore do the laws consign to public executioners the whole business of punishment: having compelled the judge to punish so far as to pronounce the sentence, thereafter they call forth those to perform the act itself. So true is it, that though it be justly done, it is not the part of a generous (φιλοσόφου) soul to inflict punishment, but it requires another sort of person for this: since even God punishes not by His own hand, but by means of the angels. Are they then executioners, the angels? God forbid: I say not this, but they are avenging powers. When Sodom was destroyed, the whole was done by them as the instruments: when the judgments in Egypt were inflicted, it was through them. For, "He sent," it says, "evil angels among them." (Psalm lxxviii. 50.) But when there is need of saving, God does this by Himself: thus, He sent the Son:—(b) but,[3] "He that receiveth you, receiveth Me, and he that receiveth Me, receiveth Him that sent Me." (Matt. x. 40.) (a) And again He saith, "Then will I say unto the angels, Gather together them that do iniquity, and cast them into the furnace." (Matt. xiii. 30, 41, 42.) But concerning the just, not so. (c) And again, "Bind him hand and foot, and

---

[1] Edd. καλῶς γε· οὐ γὰρ τοὺς μισθοὺς ἀπέλαβον: as if it meant, "And well that it is so: for I have not received my wages— therefore the reward is yet to come: not as it is with those who ἀπέχουσι τὸν μισθὸν αὐτῶν in this life, Matt. vi. 2 ff." If this were the meaning, the sentence would be out of place; it should be, "He said nothing of the kind, but would rather have repressed such thoughts with the consideration, It is well: for I have not received my wages—they are yet to come." But in fact here as elsewhere the Edd. overlook the ironical interrogation οὐ γάρ. Read καλῶς γε (οὐ γάρ;) τοὺς μισθοὺς ἀπ᾽ ἐλαβον (or καλούς γε.).

[2] Αἰνάν. Sav. marg., Σαινάν LXX. Edd., Σενναάρ. Hebr., Zaanan.

[3] This clause is evidently misplaced, and moreover requires to be completed. The meaning may be: "So in the highest of all God's saving acts, the mission of the Son: for he that receiveth Him receiveth the Father."

cast him into outer darkness." (Matt. xxii. 13.) Observe how in that case His servants minister: but when the point is to do good, see Himself doing the good, Himself calling: "Come, ye blessed of My Father, inherit the Kingdom prepared for you." (Matt. xxv. 34.) When the matter is, to converse with Abraham, then Himself comes to him: when it is, to depart to Sodom, He sends His servants, like a judge raising up those who are to punish. "Thou hast been faithful over a few things, I will make thee ruler over many things" (Matt. xxv. 21); *I* (will make thee): but that other, not Himself, but His servants bind. Knowing these things, let us not rejoice over those who are suffering punishment, but even grieve: for these let us mourn, for these let us weep, that for this also we may receive a reward. But now, many rejoice even over those who suffer evil unjustly. But not so, we: let us show all sympathy: that we also may have God vouchsafed us, through the grace and mercy of His only-begotten Son, with Whom to the Father and the Holy Ghost together be glory, might, honor, now and ever, world without end. Amen.

HOMILY XLIV.

ACTS XX. 17-21.

" And from Miletus he sent to Ephesus, and called the elders of the Church. And when they were come to him, he said unto them, Ye know, from the first day that I came into Asia, after what manner I have been with you at all seasons, serving the Lord with all humility of mind, and with many tears, and temptations, which befell me by the lying in wait of the Jews: and how I kept back nothing that was profitable unto you, but have showed you, and have taught you publicly, and from house to house, testifying both to the Jews, and also to the Greeks, repentance toward God, and faith toward our Lord Jesus Christ."

SEE him, hasting to sail by, and yet not overlooking them, but taking order for all. Having sent for the rulers, through those he discourses to them (the Ephesians): but it is worthy of admiration, how finding himself under a necessity of saying certain great things about himself, he tries to make the least he can of it ($\pi\epsilon\iota\rho\hat{\alpha}\tau\alpha$ $\mu\epsilon\tau\rho\iota\acute{\alpha}\zeta\epsilon\iota\nu$). "Ye know." For just as Samuel, when about to deliver up the government to Saul says in their presence, "Have I taken aught of your hands? Ye are witnesses, and God also" (1 Sam. xii. 3, 5); (so Paul here). David also, when disbelieved, says, "I was with the flock keeping my father's sheep: and when the bear came, I scared her away with my hands" (1 Sam. xvii. 34, 35): and Paul himself too says to the Corinthians, "I am become a fool; ye have compelled me." (2 Cor. xii. 11.) Nay, God Himself also does the same, not speaking of himself upon any and every occasion, but only when He is disbelieved, then He brings up His benefits. Accordingly, see what Paul does here: first he adduces their own testimony; that you may not imagine his words to be mere boast-ing, he calls the hearers themselves as witnesses of the things he says, since he was not likely to speak lies in their presence. This is the excellence of a teacher, to have for witnesses of his merits those who are his disciples. And what is wonderful, Not for one day nor for two, says he, have I continued doing this. He wishes to cheer them for the future, that they may bravely bear all things, both the parting from him, and the trials about to take place—just as it was in the case of Moses and Joshua. And see how he begins: "How I have been with you the whole time, serving the Lord with all humility of mind." Observe, what most becomes rulers: "hating pride" (Exod. xviii. 21, LXX.), says (Moses): which (qualification) is especially in point for rulers, because to them there is (almost) a necessity of becoming arrogant. This (humility) is the groundwork of all that is good, as in fact Christ saith,[1] "Blessed are the poor in spirit." (Matt. v. 3.) And (here) not simply, "with humility of mind," but, "with all humility." For there are many kinds of humility, in word and in action, towards rulers, and toward the ruled. Will you that I mention to you some kinds of humility? There are some who are lowly towards those who are lowly, and high towards the high: this is not the character of humility.[2] Some then are such. Then, that he

---

[1] i. e. putting this foremost of the Beatitudes.
[2] Something more ought to follow, but the report is imperfect. Mod. text " Others again there are who are not such as these, but who in the case of both characters preserve according to the occasion both the lowly and the high bearing: which thing indeed above all is characteristic of humility. Since then he is about to teach them such things, lest he should seem to be arrogant," etc.

may not seem to be arrogant, he lays a foundation beforehand, removing that suspicion: For, "if, says he, I have acted 'with all humility of mind,' it is not from arrogance that I say the things I say." Then for his gentleness, ever with much condescension making them his fellows, "With you," he says, "have I been serving the Lord;" he makes the good works common to them with himself: none of it his own peculiar. "What?" (you will say) "why, against God could he possibly bear himself arrogantly?" And yet there are many who do bear themselves arrogantly against God: but this man not even against his own disciples. This is the merit of a teacher, by his own achievements of virtue to form the character of his disciples. Then for his fortitude, upon which also he is very concise. "With many tears," he says, "and temptations which befell me by the lying in wait of the Jews." Do you see that he grieves at their doings? But here too he seems to show how sympathizing he was: for he suffered for those who were going to perdition, for the doers themselves: what was done to himself, he even rejoiced at it; for he belonged to that band which "rejoiced that they were counted worthy to suffer shame for that Name (Acts v. 41): and again he says, "Now I rejoice in my sufferings for you" (Col. i. 24): and again, "For our light affliction, which is but for the moment, worketh for us a far more exceeding and eternal weight of glory." (2 Cor. iv. 17). These things, however, he says, by way of making the least of his merits ($\mu\epsilon\tau\rho\iota\acute{\alpha}\zeta\omega\nu$). But here he shows his fortitude, not so much of daring, as of enduring: "I," says he, "have been evil entreated, but it was with you: and what is indeed the grievous part of the business, at the hands of Jews." Observe, he puts here both love and fortitude. Mark, here, I pray you, a character of teaching: "I kept back nothing," he says, ungrudging fulness, unshrinking promptness—"of what was profitable unto you:" because there were things which they did not need to learn. For as the hiding some things would have been like grudging, so the saying all things would be folly. This is why he adds, "that was profitable unto you. But have showed you, and have taught you:" have not only said, but also taught: not doing this either as a mere matter of form. For that this is what he means, observe what he says: "publicly, and from house to house:" thereby representing the exceeding toil, the great earnestness and endurance. "Both Jews, and Greeks." Not (addressing myself) to you alone. "Testifying:" here, the boldness of speech: and that, even though we do

no good, yet we must speak: for [1] this is the meaning of "testifying," when we speak to those who do not pay attention: and so the word $\delta\iota\alpha\mu\alpha\rho\tau\acute{\upsilon}\rho\alpha\sigma\theta\alpha\iota$ is for the most part used. "I call heaven and earth to witness" (Deut. iv. 26), $\delta\iota\alpha\mu\alpha\rho\tau\acute{\upsilon}\rho\text{o}\mu\alpha\iota$, Moses says: and now Paul himself, $\Delta\iota\alpha\mu\alpha\rho\tau\upsilon\rho\acute{\text{o}}\mu\epsilon\nu\text{o}\varsigma$ "both to Jews and Greeks repentance toward God." What testifiest thou? That they should be careful about their manner of life: that they should repent, and draw near to God. "Both to Jews and Greeks"—for neither did the Jews know Him—both [2] by reason of their works, he says, "repentance towards God," and, by reason that they knew not the Son, he adds, "and faith in the Lord Jesus." To what end, then, sayest thou these things? to what end dost thou put them in mind of them? What has come of it? hast thou anything to lay to their charge? Having first alarmed their feelings, then he adds, "And now, behold, I go bound in the Spirit unto Jerusalem, not knowing the things that shall befall me there: save that the Holy Ghost witnesseth in every city, saying that bonds and afflictions abide me. But none of these things move me, neither count I my life dear unto myself, so that I might finish my course with joy, and the ministry, which I have received of the Lord Jesus, to testify the Gospel of the grace of God." (v. 22–24). Wherefore says he this? By way of preparing them to be always ready to meet dangers, whether seen or unseen, and in all things to obey the Spirit.* He shows that it is for great objects that he is led away from them. "Save that the Holy Ghost," he says, "in every city witnesseth to me, saying"—to show that he departs willingly; that (see Hom. xlv. p. 273) you may not imagine it any bond or necessity, when he says, "bound in the Spirit—that in every city bonds and afflictions await me." Then also he adds this, "I count not my life dear, until I shall have fulfilled my course and the ministry, which I received of the Lord Jesus." Until I shall have finished my course,

---

[1] Τὸ γὰρ διαμαρτύρασθαι τοῦτό ἐστιν, ὅταν. . . . . Τὸ γὰρ διαμαρτύρασθαι ὡς ἐπὶ τὸ πολὺ τοῦτό ἐστιν.

[2] Old text διά τε τὰ ἔργα, διά τε τὸν Υἱὸν ἀγνοεῖν· καὶ πίστιν τὴν εἰς τὸν Κ. Ἰ. as if all this were said in explanation of the preceding Οὐδὲ γὰρ Ἰουδαῖοι ᾔδεσαν αὐτόν. But δία τε τὰ ἔργα explains the clause τὴν εἰς τὸν Θεὸν μετάνοιαν, which requires to be inserted as in the Translation. Mod. text "both because they were ignorant of the Son, and because of their works, and their not having faith in the Lord Jesus."

* Chrys. understands "bound in the spirit" to mean constrained by the Holy Spirit (so Theophylact, Beza, Calvin, Wordsworth et al.). The fact that the Holy Spirit is mentioned in the next verse (23) in such a way as to be distinguished apparently from "the spirit" here mentioned, has led most critics to believe that "the spirit" was Paul's own spirit (so Meyer, Lechler, Lange, DeWette, Ewald, Alford, Hackett, Gloag). Δεδεμένος should not be taken as meaning bound with chains in prospect, i. e., as seen in his spirit in advance (as Bengel, Conybeare and Howson), but rather constrained, inwardly constrained.—G. B. S.

says he, with joy. Do you mark how (clearly) these were the words not of one lamenting, but of one who forbore to make the most (of his troubles) (μετριάζοντος), of one who would instruct those (whom he addressed), and sympathize with them in the things which were befalling He says not, "I grieve indeed,[1] but one must needs bear it:" "but," says he, "of none of these things do I make account, neither do I have," i. e. account "my life dear to me." Why this again? not to extol himself, but to teach them, as by the former words, humility, so by these, fortitude and boldness: "I have it not precious," i. e. "I love it not before this: I account it more precious to finish my course, to testify." And he says not, "to preach," "to teach"—but what says he? "to testify (διαμαρτύρασθαι)—the Gospel of the grace of God." He is about to say something more uncomfortable (φορτικώτερον), namely, "I am pure from the blood of all men (because on my part) there is nothing lacking:" he is about to lay upon them the whole weight and burden: so he first mollifies their feelings by saying, "And now behold I know that ye shall see my face no more." The consolation[2] is twofold: both that "my face ye shall see no more," for in heart I am with you: and that it was not they alone (who should see him no more): for, "ye shall see my face no more, ye all, among whom I have gone about preaching the Kingdom." * So that he may well (say), "Wherefore I take you to record (read διὸ μαρτ. for διαμαρτ.),—seeing I shall be with you no more—"that I am pure from the blood of all men." (v. 26.) Do you mark how he terrifies them, and troubled and afflicted as their souls are, how hard he rubs them (ἐπιτρίβει)? But it was necessary. "For I have not shunned," he says, "to declare unto you all the counsel of God." (v. 27.) Why then, he who does not *speak*, has blood to answer for: that is, mur-

der! Nothing could be more terrifying than this. He shows that they also, if they *do* it not, have blood to answer for. So, whereas he seems to be justifying himself, in fact he is terrifying them. "Take heed therefore unto yourselves, and to all the flock, over the which the Holy Ghost hath made you overseers (or, bishops) to feed the Church of God (see note [3]), which He hath purchased with His own blood." (v. 28.) Do you mark? he enjoins them two things. Neither success in bringing others right of itself is any gain—for, I fear, he says, "lest by any means, when I have preached to others, I myself should be a castaway" (1 Cor. ix. 27); nor the being diligent for one's self alone. For such an one is selfish, and seeks his own good only, and is like to him who buried his talent. "Take heed to yourselves:" this he says, not because our own salvation is more precious than that of the flock, but because, when we take heed to ourselves, then the flock also is a gainer. "In which the Holy Ghost hath made you overseers, to feed the Church of God." See, it is from the Spirit ye have your ordination. This is one constraint: then he says, "To feed the Church of the Lord."[3] Lo! another obligation: the Church is the Lord's.† And a third: "which He hath purchased with His own blood." It shows[4] how precious the concern is; that the peril is about no small matters, seeing that even His own blood He spared not. He indeed, that he might reconcile those who were enemies, poured out even His blood: but thou, even when they are become thy friends, art not able to retain them. "For I know this, that after my departing shall grievous wolves enter in among you, not sparing the flock." (v. 29.) Again he engages (ἐπιστρέφει) them from another quarter, from the things which should come after: as when he says, "We wrestle not against flesh and blood. After my departing," he says, "grievous wolves shall enter in among you" (Eph. vi. 12); twofold the evil, both that he himself would not be present, and that others would assail them. "Then why depart, if thou knowest this beforehand?" The Spirit

---

[1] Mss. Cat. and Edd. ἀλγῶμεν "let us grieve:" but Savile, ἀλγῶ μέν. The next clause ἀλλ' οὐδὲ ἡγοῦμαι, or, ἀλλ' οὐδὲ, Ἡγοῦμαι, requires something to make sense of it, as in the Translation.

[2] Διπλῆ ἡ παραμυθία. The meaning is, "It was his face that they would see no more: he chooses that expression by way of softening matters, implying that in spirit he would be present: and again, all ye, not they only, so that the grief was not peculiar to them:" but this being rather obscure, A. substitutes ἀθυμία, and mod. text Διπλῆ ἡ λύπη, i. e. "the dejection (or, the sorrow) was twofold, both the being to see his face no more, and the, All of them."

* Neither of the two ideas which Chrys. draws from v. 25—(a) that though absent in body, he would be present with them in spirit; (b) that the "all" addressed refers to the whole company—comes naturally from the text. The apostle states his firm conviction that he shall not again visit Ephesus. Whether he ever did so or not, we do not know. The probabilities in the case would depend upon the question of a release from his Roman imprisonment. He hoped for such a release and intended to visit Colossæ (Philem. 22). On the supposition of such a release and on the consequent supposition of the Pauline authorship of the Pastoral Epistles, a visit after this time to Ephesus becomes very probable, especially since we find the apostle (2 Tim. iv. 13, 20) at Troas and Miletus.—G.B.S.

[3] Hence it appears that St. Chrys. reads Κυρίου not Θεοῦ in this text, though in the citation the Scribes give it according to the other reading, Θεοῦ.

† It is an interesting fact that in this passage where the reading vacillates between Κυρίου and Θεοῦ, while the report of the Homily has given us θεοῦ, the citation of the N. T. text favors the reading Κυρίου. The great majority of Mss. read τοῦ Κυρίου: א and B. have τοῦ θεοῦ (the usual Pauline formula). Many critics hold that Κυρ. was changed to θ. in accordance with Pauline usage in the Epistles. The idea of the "blood of God" is against the reading θεοῦ. Modern critics are nearly equally divided. Alford, Westcott and Hort, read θεοῦ; Meyer, Tischendorf, Κυρίου; to us the latter seems decidedly preferable.—G. B. S.

[4] δείκνυσι τίμιον τὸ πρᾶγμα, ὅτι. Mod. text. πολὺ δείκν. δι ὧν εἶπε τίμιον τὸ πρ. So Edd. *Multum ostendit dum dicit pretiosam rem.* Ben.

draws me, he says. Both "wolves," and "grievous, not sparing the flock;" and what is worse, even "from among your own selves :" the grievous thing (this), when the war is moreover an intestine war. The matter is exceeding serious, for it is "the Church of the Lord :" great the peril, for with blood He redeemed it : mighty the war, and twofold. "Also of your own selves shall men arise, speaking perverse things, to draw away disciples after them." (v. 30.) "How then? what comfort shall there be?" "Therefore watch, and remember, that by the space of three years I ceased not to warn every one night and day with tears." (v. 31.) See how many strong expressions are here : "with tears," and "night and day," and "every one." For it was not that if he saw many,[1] then he came in (to the work), but even were it for a single soul, he was capable of doing everything (for that one soul). So it was, in fact, that he compacted them together (συνεκρότησεν) (so firmly as he did). "Enough done on my part : three years have I remained :" they had establishing enough, he says ; enough of rooting. "With tears," he says. Seest thou that the tears were on this account? The bad man grieves not : grieve thou : perhaps he will grieve also. As, when the sick man sees his physician partaking of food, he also is incited to do the same : so likewise here, when he sees thee weeping, he is softened : he will be a good and great man.[2]

(Recapitulation.) "Not knowing," he says, "the things that shall befall me." (v. 22, 23.) Then is this why thou departest? By no means ; on the contrary (I know that), "bonds and afflictions await me." That (there are) trials, I know, but of what kind I know not : which was more grievous. "But none of these things move me" (v. 24): for do not suppose that I say these things as lamenting them : for "I hold not my own life dear." It is to raise up their minds that he says all this, and to persuade them not only not to flee, but also to bear nobly. Therefore it is that he calls it a "course" and a "ministry," on the one hand, showing it to be glorious from its being a race, on the other, showing what was due from it, as being a ministry. I am a minister : nothing more. Having comforted them, that they might not grieve that he was so evil entreated, and having

told them that he endured those things "with joy," and having shown the fruits of them, then (and not before) he brings in that which would give them pain, that he may not overwhelm their minds. "And[3] now behold," etc. "Wherefore I take you to record, that I am pure from the blood of all men, because I have not shrunk from declaring unto you the whole counsel of God" (v. 25-27): * * * that (counsel) which concerns the present matter. "For I know this," etc. (v. 29.) "What then," someone might say, "thinkest thou thyself so great? if thou shouldest depart, are we to die?" I say not this, he replies, that my absence causeth this : but what? That there should rise up against you certain of another sort : he says not, "because of my departing," but "after my departing:" that is, after his going on his journey.—And yet this thing has happened already : much more (then will it happen) hereafter. Then we have the cause, "to draw away disciples after them." (v. 30.) That there are heresies, this is the cause, and no other than this. Then comes also consolation. But if He "purchased" it "with His own blood," He will assuredly stand forward in its defence. "Night and day," he says, "I cease not to warn with tears." (v. 31.) This might well be said in our case also : and though the speech seems to refer peculiarly to the teachers, it is common also to the disciples. For what, though I speak and exhort and weep night and day, while the disciple obeys not? Therefore[4] it is that he says, "I take you to record :" since also himself says, "I am pure from the blood of all men : for I have not shunned to declare unto you." (v. 26, 27.) Why then, this only is to be a teacher, to declare, to preach, to instruct, shrink from nothing, to exhort night and day : but if, while one is doing all this, nothing comes of it, ye know what remains. Then

---

[1] Οὐ γὰρ εἰ πολλοὺς εἶδε τότε ἐφείσατο (mod. ἐφείδετο). Non enim si multos vidisset, eis pepercisset, Ben. But Cat. has preserved the true reading, ἐφίστατο.

[2] Ἔσται χρηστὸς καὶ μέγας ἀνήρ. The second epithet being evidently unsuitable, mod. text gives, χρηστὸς ἀνὴρ καὶ πρᾶος γενήσεται. But perhaps χ. ἀ. καὶ μ. belongs to the next sentence, as an exclamation on v. 22. "A good and great man!" and for μαλάσσεται· ἔσται we may read μαλαχθήσεται.

[3] Old text: ἵνα μὴ καταχώσῃ αὐτῶν τὴν διάνοιαν, followed by the latter part of v. 27. Τοῦ ἀναγγεῖλαι ὑμῖν κ. τ. λ. But the connection may also be, "I have not shrunk—of course in due order and proportion" (or something of that kind) "that he may not overwhelm their minds, from declaring," etc. It might seem, however, from the comment which follows, viz τὴν περὶ τοῦ παρόντος πράγματος, that Chrys. is here proposing an interpretation of v. 27 different from what was implied in the first exposition, p. 269, and from that of v. 20: i. e. "painful as it is, I have not shrunk from announcing to you all the counsel of God, to wit, as touching the present matter, my separation from you, so that ye shall see my face no more." But this being very unsatisfactory, it is better to take the connection thus : Nor does he now shrink from declaring to them the whole counsel of God concerning the coming events, and their duty and responsibility therein. (We have therefore placed the mark of an hiatus before this clause.)—Mod. text substitutes, "But what is this (that he adds), 'Also of your own selves shall men arise, speaking perverse things.' What then," etc.

[4] The text is evidently confused or defective here. Mod. text "For that none may fancy it plea enough for his justification, that he is a disciple while yet he does not yield, therefore having said, I take you to record, he adds, for I have not shunned," etc.

ye have another justification: "I am pure from the blood of all men." Think not that these words are spoken to us only: for indeed this speech is addressed to you also, that ye should attend to the things spoken, that ye should not start away from the hearing. What can I do? Lo! each day I rend myself with crying out, "Depart from the theatres:" and many laugh at us: "Desist from swearing, from covetousness:" numberless are our exhortations, and there is none to hear us. But I do not discourse during night? Fain would I do this also in the night time, and at your tables, if it were possible that one could be divided into ten thousand pieces, so as to be present with you and discourse. But if once in the week we call to you, and ye shrink back, and some of you do not even come here, and you that do come, depart having received no profit,—what shall we do? Many I know even sneer at us, that we are forever discoursing about the same things: so wearisome are we become to you by very satiety. But for this not we are to blame, but the hearers may thank themselves. For he indeed who is making good progress, rejoices to hear the same things always; it seems to be his praises that he hears spoken: but he who does not wish to get on, seems even to be annoyed, and though he hear the same thing but twice, it seems to him that he is hearing it often.

"I am pure," he says, "from the blood of all men." (v. 26.) This was fit and proper for Paul to say, but we dare not say it, conscious as we are of numberless faults. Wherefore for him the ever vigilant, ever at hand, the man enduring all things for the sake of the salvation of his disciples, it was fit and proper to say this: but we must say that of Moses, "The Lord was wroth with me for your sakes" (Deut. iii. 26), because ye lead us also into many sins. For when we are dispirited at seeing you make no progress, is not the greater part of our strength struck down? For what, I ask you has been done? Lo! by the grace of God we also have now passed the space of three years,[1] not indeed night and day exhorting you, but doing this, often every third day, or every seventh. What more has come of it? We accuse, we rebuke, we weep, we are in anguish, although not openly, yet in heart. But those (inward) tears are far more bitter than these (outward ones): for these indeed bring a kind of relief

to the feelings of the sorrowful, whereas those aggravate it, and bind it fast. Since when there is any cause of grief, and one cannot give vent to the sorrow, lest he should seem to be vainglorious, think what he suffers! Were it not that people would tax me with excessive love of display, you would see me each day shedding fountains of tears: but to those my chamber is witness, and my hours of solitude. For believe me I have (at times) despaired of my own salvation, but from my mourning on your account, I have not even leisure to bemoan my own evils: so entirely are ye all in all to me. And whether I perceive you to be advancing, then, for very delight, I am not sensible of my own evils: or whether I see you not advancing, such is my grief, I again dismiss my own cares from my thoughts: brightening up on account of your good things, though I myself have evils without number, and saddened on account of your painful things, though my own successes are without number. For what hope is there for the teacher, when his flock is destroyed? What kind of life, what kind of expectation is there for him? With what sort of confidence will he stand up before God? what will he say? For grant that he has nothing laid to his charge, has no punishment to suffer, but is "pure from the blood of all men:" yet even so will he suffer a grief incurable: since fathers also though they be not liable to be called to account for their children's sins, nevertheless have grief and vexation. And this profits them nothing,[2] nor shields them ($\pi\rho o i \sigma \tau a \tau a\iota$). "For it is they that watch for our souls, as those that must give account." (Heb. xiii. 17.) This seems to be a fearful thing: to me this gives no concern after your destruction. For whether I give account, or not, it is no profit to me. Might it be, that ye were saved, and I to give account because of you: ye saved, and I charged with not having fulfiled my part! For my anxiety is not that you should be saved through me as the means, but only that you should be saved, no matter by what person as the instrument. Ye know not the pangs of spiritual childbirth, how overpowering they

---

[1] St. Chrysostom succeeded Nectarius in the Archbishopric of Constantinople, 26th Feb. Coss. Honorius iv. and Eutychianus A.D. 398. Socrat. vi. 2.—From the following passage it appears that these Homm. though begun after Easter, perhaps of A.D. 400, extended over a considerable period of time, not being preached every day.—Below, mod. text spoils the sense by altering πικρότερα into κουφότερα.

[2] Mod. text inserts a φησίν, and makes the sentence interrogative. "And does this, you will say, profit them nothing nor shield them, that they watch for our souls? But then they watch as they that must give an account: and to some indeed this seems to be terrible." The meaning in general seems to be: "If they perish, yet surely you can comfort yourself with the thought, that you at least are pure from their blood. No, this thought avails nothing to ward off (that sorrow). "Because they watch," etc.—this seems a fearful thing. But if you be lost, it is not the thought of my accountability that gives me most concern—it is the thought of your perishing. Oh! that I might in the last day find you saved though not through me, yea, though I myself thereafter were called to account as not having done my part by you!"

are; how he who is in travail with this birth, would rather be cut into ten thousand pieces, than see one of those to whom he has given birth perishing and undone. Whence shall we persuade you? By no other argument indeed, but by what has been done, in all that regards you we shall clear ourselves.[1] We too shall be able to say, that in nothing have we "shrunk from declaring" to you the whole truth: nevertheless we grieve: and that we do grieve, is manifest from the numberless plans we lay and contrivances we devise. And yet we might say to ourselves, What matters it to me? I have done my part, "I am pure from" (their) "blood:" but this is not enough for comfort. If we could tear open our heart, and show it to you, ye would see with what largeness it holds (you) within it, both women and children and men; for such is the power of love, that it makes the soul more spacious than the heaven. "Receive us," says (Paul): "we have wronged no man, ye are not straitened in us." (2 Cor. vii. 2; vi. 12.) He had all Corinth in his heart, and says, "Ye are not straitened: be ye also enlarged (2 Cor. vi. 13); but I myself could not say this, for I well know, that ye both love me and receive me. But what is the profit either from my love or from yours, when the things pertaining to God thrive not in us? It is a ground for greater sorrow, an occasion of worse mischief (λύμης, al. λύπης). I have nothing to lay to your charge: "for I bear you record, that, if it had been possible, ye would have plucked out your own eyes, and have given them to me." (Gal. iv. 15.) "We yearn not only to give you the Gospel, but also our own souls." (1 Thess. ii. 8.) We are loved and we love (you): but this is not the question. But let us love Christ, "for the first commandment is, Thou shalt love the Lord thy God: and the second is like unto it, And thy neighbor as thyself." (Matt. xxii. 37-39.) We have the second, we need the first: need the first, exceedingly, both I and you. We have it, but not as we ought. Let us love Him: ye know how great a reward is laid up for them that love Christ: let us love Him with fervor of soul, that, enjoying his goodwill, we may escape the stormy waves of this present life, and be found worthy to obtain the good things promised to them that love Him, through the grace and mercy of His only-begotten Son, with whom to the Father, together with the Holy Ghost, be glory, might, honor, now and ever, world without end. Amen.

HOMILY XLV.

ACTS XX. 32.

"And now, brethren, I commend you to God, and to the word of His grace, which is able to build you up, and to give you an inheritance among all them that are sanctified."

WHAT he does when writing in an Epistle, this he does also when speaking in council: from exhorting, he ends with prayer: for since he had much alarmed them by saying, "Grievous wolves shall enter in among you" (v. 29), therefore, not to overpower them, and make them lose all self-possession, observe the consolation (he gives). "And now," he says, as always, "I commend you, brethren, to God, and to the word of His grace: that is, to His grace: it is grace that saveth. He constantly puts them in mind of grace, to make them more earnest as being debtors, and to persuade them to have confidence. "Which is able to build you up."[*] He does not say, to build, but, "to build up," showing that they had (already) been built. Then he puts them in mind of the hope to come; "to give you an inheritance," he says, "among all them which are sanctified." Then exhortation again: "I have coveted no man's silver, or gold, or apparel." (v. 33.) He takes away that which is the root of evils, the love of money. "Silver, or gold," he says. He says not, I have not taken, but, not even "coveted." No great thing this, but what follows after is great. "Yea, ye yourselves know, that these hands have ministered unto

---

[1] Ἑτέρωθεν μὲν οὐδαμόθεν, ἀπὸ δὲ τῶν γενομένων) meaning perhaps, "From what has been done by us in our ministry: we will endeavor to persuade you by reminding you of all our care and pains for our salvation:") τὰ καθ᾽ ὑμᾶς πάντα ἀπολυσόμεθα. Ἀπολύεσθαι (ἐγκλήματα), is frequent in Chrys., often confused with ἀπολούεσθαι and ἀποδύεσθαι. See Mr. Field's *Index and Annotat. in Hom. Matth.*

[*] The phrase "which is able" (τῷ δυναμένῳ) may be connected with the word "God," or with "the word of His grace." As standing nearer the latter, this would be the natural construction. So our author has taken it, understanding by "the word of His grace" rather the grace itself than the doctrine concerning it. Most critics have preferred to connect the phrase with τῷ θεῷ on the ground that it is more appropriate to ascribe the giving of an inheritance among the sanctified directly to God than to His word. (So DeWette, Meyer, Alford, Gloag). —G. B. S.

my necessities, and to them that were with me. I have showed you all things, how that so laboring, ye ought to support the weak." (v. 34, 35.) Observe him employed in work, and not simply that, but toiling. "These hands have ministered unto my necessities, and to them that were with me :" so as to put them to shame. And see how worthily of them. For he says not, Ye ought to show yourselves superior to money, but what ? "to support the weak"—not all indiscriminately —"and to hear the word of the Lord which He spake, It is more blessed to give than to receive."* For lest any one should think that it was spoken with reference to them, and that he gave himself for an ensample, as he elsewhere says, "giving an ensample to you" (Phil. iii. 17), he added the declaration of Christ, Who said, " It is more blessed to give than to receive." He prayed over them while exhorting them : he shows it both by action,— "And when he had thus spoken, he kneeled down, and prayed with them all," (v. 36)—he did not simply pray, but with much feeling : (κατανύξεως): great was the consolation—and by his saying, " I commend you to the Lord. And they all wept sore, and fell on Paul's neck, and kissed him, sorrowing most of all for the words which he spake, that they should see his face no more." (v. 37, 38.) He had said, that "grievous wolves should enter in ;" had said, " I am pure from the blood of all men :" and yet the thing that grieved them most of all was this, "that they should see him no more :" since indeed it was this that made the war grievous. "And they accompanied them," it says, "unto the ship. And it came to pass, that after we had torn ourselves from them "—so much did they love him, such was their affection towards him— " and had launched, we came with a straight course unto Coos, and the day following unto Rhodes, and from thence unto Patara : and finding a ship sailing over unto Phenicia, we went aboard, and set forth. Now when we had discovered Cyprus, we left it on the left hand, and sailed into Syria, and landed at Tyre" (Acts xxi. 1-3): he came to Lycia, and having left Cyprus, he sailed down to Tyre—"for there the ship was to unlade her burden. And finding disciples, we tarried there seven days : who said to Paul through the Spirit, that he should not go up to Jerusalem." (v. 4.) They too prophesy of the afflictions. It is so ordered that they should

be spoken by them also, that none might imagine that Paul said those things without cause, and only by way of boasting. And there again they part from each other with prayer. "And when we had accomplished those days, we departed, and went our way ; and they all brought us on our way, with wives and children, till we were out of the city : and we kneeled down on the shore, and prayed. And when we had taken our leave one of another, we took ship ; and they returned home again. And when we had finished our course from Tyre, we came to Ptolemais, and saluted the brethren, and abode with them one day. And the next day we that were of Paul's company departed, and came unto Cæsarea : and we entered into the house of Philip the evangelist, which was one of the seven ; and abode with him." (v. 5-8.) Having come to Cæsarea, it says, we abode with Philip, which was one of the seven. "And the same man had four· daughters, virgins, which did prophesy." (v. 9.) But it is not these that foretell to Paul, though they were prophetesses ; it is Agabus. "And as we tarried there many days, there came down from Judea a certain prophet, named Agabus. And when he was come unto us, he took Paul's girdle, and bound his own hands and feet, and said, Thus saith the Holy Ghost, So shall the Jews at Jerusalem bind the man that owneth this girdle, and shall deliver him into the hands of the Gentiles." (v. 10, 11.) He who formerly had declared about the famine, the same says, This "man, who owneth this girdle, thus shall they bind." (ch. xi. 28.) The same that the prophets used to do, representing events to the sight, when they spoke about the captivity—as did Ezekiel—the same did this (Agabus). " And," what is the grievous part of the business, "deliver him into the hands of the Gentiles. And when we heard these things, both we, and they of that place, besought him not to go up to Jerusalem." (v. 12.) Many even besought him not to depart, and still he would not comply. " Then Paul answered, What mean ye to weep and to break mine heart ? " [1]   (v. 13.)   Do you mark ?   Lest, having heard that saying, "I go bound in the Spirit" (ch. xx. 22), you should imagine it a matter of necessity, or that he fell into it ignorantly, therefore these things are foretold. But they wept, and he comforted them, grieving at their tears. For, " what mean ye," he says, " to weep and to break my heart ?"   Nothing could be more affectionate : because he saw them weeping, he grieved, he that felt no pain

* By " the weak " Chrys. evidently understands the physically weak, the sick and poor (see the Recapitulation) and we think correctly as opposed to the " weak in faith." The apostle counsels labor in order to liberality toward the needy. So Olshausen, DeWette, Hackett, Gloag, Alford, vs. Neander, Tholuck, Lechler, Meyer.—G. B. S.

[1] The remainder of v. 13 and 14 we have removed from this to its proper place.

at his own trials. "For I am ready not to be bound only, but also to die at Jerusalem for the name of the Lord Jesus. And when he would not be persuaded, we ceased, saying, The will of the Lord be done." (v. 13, 14.) Ye do me wrong in doing this: for do I grieve? Then they ceased, when he said, "to break my heart." I weep, he says, for you, not on account of my own sufferings: as for those (men), I am willing even to die for them. But let us look over again what has been said.

(Recapitulation.) "Silver, or gold, or apparel," etc. (ch. xx. 33, 34; 1 Cor. ix.; 2 Cor. xi.) So then, it was not in Corinth only that they did this [1]—they that corrupted the disciples, but in Asia as well. But he nowhere casts this up as a reproach to the Ephesians, when writing to them. And why? Because he did not fall upon any subject that obliged him to speak of this. But to the Corinthians he says, "My boasting has not been stopped in the regions of Achaia." (2 Cor. xi. 10.) And he does not say, Ye did not give to me; but, "Silver, or gold, or apparel, I coveted not," that it might not seem to be their doing, that they had not given. And he does not say, From no man have I coveted the necessaries of life, that again it might not look like accusing them: but he covertly hints as much, seeing that he provided subsistence for others as well as himself. See how he worked with earnestness, "night and day" discoursing (to others), "with tears, warning each one of them." (v. 31.) (Here) again he puts them in fear: "I have showed you all things," he says: ye cannot take refuge in the plea of ignorance: "have shown you" by works "how that so laboring ye ought to work." And he does not say, that to receive is bad, but that not to receive is better. For, "remember," he says, "the words of the Lord which he spake: It is more blessed to give than to receive." (v. 35.) And where said He this? Perhaps the Apostles delivered it by unwritten tradition; or else it is plain from (recorded sayings, from) which one could infer it.[2] For in fact here he has shown both boldness in meeting dangers, sympathy with those over whom he ruled, teaching with (unshrinking) boldness, humility, (voluntary) poverty: but, what we have here is even more than that poverty. For if

He says there (in the Gospel), "If thou wilt be perfect, sell what thou hast and give to the poor" (Matt. xix. 21), when, besides receiving nothing himself, he provides sustenance for others also, what could equal this? It is one degree to fling away one's possessions; a second, to be sufficient for the supply of one's own necessities: a third, to provide for others also; a fourth, for one (to do all this)· who preaches and has a right to receive. So that here is a man far better than those who merely forego possessions. "Thus it is right to support the weak:" this is (indeed) sympathy with the weak; for to give from the labors of others, is easy. "And they fell on his neck," it says, "and wept." (v. 37.) He shows their affection also by saying, "Upon his neck," as taking a last and yet a last embrace, such was the love they conceived from his discourse, such the spell of love that bound them. For if we groan when simply parting from each other, although we know that we shall receive one another back again, what a tearing away of themselves it must have been to them! Methinks Paul also wept. "Having torn ourselves away," he says: he shows the violence of it by saying, "having torn ourselves away from them." And with reason: otherwise they could never have got to sea. What means, "We came with a straight course unto Coos?" Instead of saying, "we did not go round nor make stay in other places." Then "unto Rhodes." (ch. xxi. 1.) See how he hastes on. "And finding a ship sailing over unto Phenicia. (v. 2.) Possibly that ship (in which they had come) was making a stay there: wherefore they shifted to another, and not having found one going to Cæsarea, but (finding this) for Phenice, they embarked in it (and pursued their voyage), having left Cyprus also and Syria: but the expression, "having left it on the left hand," is not said simply (in that meaning), but that they made speed not to get to Syria either.[3] "We landed at Tyre." (v. 3.) Then they tarry with the brethren seven days. Now that they were come near to Jerusalem, they no longer run. (*b*) "Who said to Paul through the Spirit, that he should not go up to Jerusalem." (v. 4.) Observe how, when the Spirit does not forbid, he complies. They said, "Adventure not thyself into the theatre, and he did not adventure" (ch. xix. 31): often they bore him off (from dangers), and he complied: again he es-

---

[1] Οὐκ ἄρα ἐν Κορίνθῳ τοῦτο εἰργάσαντο μόνον οἱ διαφθείροντες τοὺς μαθητὰς κ. τ. λ. One would have expected εἰργάσατο μόνον, καὶ οὐχ ὡς οἱ δ. But the connection, not fully expressed, may be this : " So different from those "grievous wolves not sparing the flock," the false teachers who would make a gain of them ! So then" etc.
[2] Some text or texts of the Gospels should be supplied here : beginning perhaps like the next sentence with a Καὶ γάρ.

[3] By Syria he seems here to mean the northern parts, about Antioch. "They left Cyprus on the left, but nearer to it than the opposite coast of Syria, because he did not wish to come near that either." Mod. text "This is not said idly, but to show that he did not think fit even to come near it (Cyprus), they sailing straight for Syria." What follows required transposition : the derangement, 2, 1 : 3, 5, 7 : 4, 6, 8.

caped by a window: and now, though number-less persons, so to say, beseech him, both those at Tyre and those at Cæsarea, weeping also and predicting numberless dangers, he refuses to comply. And yet it is not (merely), they predicted the dangers, but "said by the Spirit." If then the Spirit bade, why did he gainsay? "By the Spirit," that is, they knowing "by the Spirit" (what would be the consequences, said to him): for of course it does not mean that the exhortation they made was by the Spirit. For they did not simply foretell to him the dangers (through the Spirit), but (added of themselves) that it be-hooved him not to go up—sparing him. But "after we had accomplished the days," i. e. had fulfilled the appointed days, "we sep-arated, and went on our way: they all bring-ing us on our way with wives and children." (v. 5.)—See how great was the entreaty. And again they part with prayer. Also in Ptole-mais they stay one day, but in Cæsarea many. (v. 6-8.) (a) Now that they are near to Jeru-salem, they no longer hurry. For observe, I pray you, all the days. "After the day of un-leavened bread" they came "to Troas in five days" (ch. xx. 6); then they there spent "seven;" in all, twelve: then to "Thasos," to "Mytilene," to "Trogylium" and "over against Chios," and to "Samos" and "Mile-tus" (ib. 13-17); eighteen in all. Then to "Cos," to "Rhodes," to "Patara," twenty-one: then say[1] five to "Tyre;" twenty-six: there "seven;" thirty-three; "Ptolemais," thirty-four; then to "Cæsarea, many days" (ch. xxi. 1-10); and then, thereafter, the prophet puts them up thence. (c) When Paul has heard that he has to suffer numberless perils, then he is in haste, not flinging himself upon the dangers but accounting it to be the command of the Spirit. (e) And Agabus does not say, "They shall bind" Paul, that he may not seem to speak upon agreement (with Paul), but "the man that owneth this girdle" (v. 11)—so then he had a girdle also.[2] But when they could not persuade him—this was why they wept—then they "held their peace." Do you mark the resignation? do you mark the affection? "They held their peace," it says, "saying, The will of the Lord be done." (v. 12-14.) (g) The Lord, say they, Himself will do that which is pleasing in his sight. For they perceived that it was the will of God.

Else Paul would not be so bent (upon going) —he that on all (other occasions delivers him-self out of dangers. (d) "And after these days," it says, "having taken up our bag-gage"—i. e. having received the (supplies) necessary for the journey—"we went up to Jerusalem." (v. 15.) "And there went with us also certain of the disciples from Cæsarea, bringing us to one with whom we should lodge, one Mnason, an ancient disciple of Cy-prus."* (v. 16.) "And when we were come to Jerusalem, the brethren received us gladly." (v. 17.) (f) "Bringing us," it says, "(to him) with whom we should lodge"—not to the church: for on the former occasion (ch. xv. 4), when they went up concerning the decrees, they lodged with the Church, but now with a certain "ancient disciple." (The expression) shows that the preaching had been going on a long time: whence it seems to me that this writer in the Acts epitomizes the events of many years, relating (only) the matters of chief importance. (h) So unwilling were they to burthen the Church, when there was another to lodge them; and so little did they stand upon their dignity. "The brethren," it says, "received us gladly." Affairs among the Jews were now full of peace: there was not much warfare (among them). "Bringing us," it says, "to one with whom we should lodge." Paul was the guest he entertained. Per-chance some one of you says: Aye, if it were given me to entertain Paul as a guest, I read-ily and with much eagerness would do this. Lo! it is in thy power to entertain Paul's Mas-ter for thy guest, and thou wilt not: for "he that receiveth one of these least," he saith, "receiveth Me." (Matt. xviii. 5; Luke ix. 48.) By how much the brother may be least, so much the more does Christ come to thee through him. For he that receives the great, often does it from vainglory also; but he that receives the small, does it purely for Christ's sake. It is in thy power to entertain even the Father of Christ as thy guest, and thou will not: for,[3] "I was a stranger," He says, "and ye took me in" (Matt. xxv. 35): and again, "Unto one of the least of these the breth-ren that believe on Me, ye have done it unto Me."(ib. 40.) Though it be not Paul, yet if it be a believer and a brother, although the least,

---

[1] A. C. Cat. (in B. the original characters are written over by a later hand), Εἶτα βουληθῆναι πέντε εἰς Τύρον. Perhaps βούλει θεῖναι. Mod. text εἶτα ἐκεῖθεν δι ἡμερῶν πέντε.

[2] *Hom. x. in Matt.* E. "But why, you may ask, did he (the Baptist) use a girdle also with his garment? This was a custom with the ancients, before this present soft and dissolute fashion of ours came in. Thus Peter appears girdled, and Paul likewise: as it says, 'The man that owneth this girdle."

* The meaning of the latter part of v. 16 (ἄγοντες παρ᾽ ᾧ ξενισθῶμεν Μνασωνί τινι Κυπρίῳ κ. τ. λ.), according to Chrys., is that the disciples from Cæsarea conducted Paul to the house of Mnason at Jerusalem where he was to lodge, not (as our Eng. vss.), that they brought with them Mnason on their journey from Cæsarea to Jerusalem. The former seems the preferable view as there is nothing in the context to intimate that Mnason was at this time in Cæsarea and his residence was evidently Jerusalem. The construction of attraction is also equally well resolved in this way.—G. B. S.

[3] Here supply, "He that receiveth Me, receiveth Him that sent Me."

Christ cometh to thee through him. Open thine house, take Him in. "He that receiveth a prophet," He saith, "shall receive a prophet's reward." (Matt. x. 41.) Therefore too he that receives Christ, shall receive the reward of him who has Christ for his guest.[1] Do not thou disbelieve His words, but be believing. Himself hath said, Through them I come to thee: and that thou mayest not disbelieve, He lays down both punishments for those who do not receive, and honors for those who do receive; since He would not have done this, unless both the person honored and the person insulted were Himself. "Thou receivedst Me," He saith, "into thy lodging, I will receive thee into the Kingdom of My Father; thou tookest away My hunger, I take away thy sins; thou sawest Me bound, I see thee loosed; thou sawest Me a stranger, I make thee a citizen of heaven; thou gavest Me bread, I give thee an entire Kingdom, that thou mayest inherit and possess it." He saith not, "Receive," but, "Inherit," the word which is spoken of those who have possession by right of ownership; as when we say, "This have I inherited." Thou didst it to Me in secret, I will proclaim it openly: and of thine acts indeed I say, that they were of free gift, but Mine are of debt. "For since thou," He saith, "didst begin, I follow and come after: I am not ashamed to confess the benefits conferred on Me, nor from what things thou didst free Me, hunger and nakedness and wandering. Thou sawest Me bound, thou shalt not behold the fire of hell; thou sawest Me sick, thou shalt not behold the torments nor the punishments." O hands, truly blessed, which minister in such services as these, which are accounted worthy to serve Christ! Feet which go into prisons for Christ's sake, with ease defy the fire: no trial of bonds have they, (the hands)[2] which saw Him bound! Thou clothedst Him with a garment, and thou puttest on a garment of salvation: thou wast in prison with Him, and with Him thou findest thyself in the Kingdom, not ashamed, knowing that thou visitedst Him. The Patriarch knew not that he was entertaining Angels, and he did entertain them. (Gen. xviii. 3.) Let us take shame to ourselves, I beseech you: he was sitting in mid-day, being in a foreign land, where he had none inheritance, "not so much as to set his foot on" (ch. vii. 5): he was a stranger, and the stranger entertained strangers: for he was a citizen of heaven. Therefore, not even while he was on earth was he a stranger (to Him). We are rather strangers than that stranger, if we receive not strangers. He had no home, and his tent was his place of reception. And mark his liberality—he killed a calf, and kneaded fine meal: mark his ready mind—by himself and his wife: mark the unassuming manner—he worships and beseeches them. For all these qualities ought to be in that man who entertains strangers—readiness, cheerfulness, liberality. For the soul of the stranger is abashed, and feels ashamed; and unless (his host) show excessive joy, he is as (if) slighted, and goes away, and it becomes worse than not to have received him, his being received in this way. Therefore he worships them, therefore he welcomes them with speech, therefore with a seat. For who would have hesitated, knowing that this work was done unto Him? "But we are not in a foreign land." If we will, we shall be able to imitate him. How many of the brethren are strangers? There is a common apartment, the Church, which we call the "Xenon." Be inquisitive (περιεργάζεσθε), sit before the doors, receive those who come yourselves; though you may not wish to take them into your houses, at any rate in some other way (receive them), by supplying them with necessaries. "Why, has not the Church means" you will say? She has: but what is that to you? that they should be fed from the common funds of the Church, can that benefit you? If another man prays, does it follow that you are not bound to pray? Wherefore do you not say, "Do not the priests pray? then why should I pray?" "But I," you will say, "give to him who cannot be received there." Give, though it be to that one: for what we are anxious for is this, that you should give at any rate. Hear what Paul says: "That it may relieve them that are widows indeed; and that the Church be not burdened." (1 Tim. v. 16.) Be it how you will, only do it. But I put it, not, "that the Church be not burdened," but, "that thou be not burdened;" for at this rate thou wilt do nothing, leaving all to the Church. This is why there is a common room set apart by the Church, that you may not say these things. "The Church," say you, "has lands,[3] has money, and revenues." And has she not charges? I ask; and has she not a daily expenditure? "No doubt," you will say. Why then do you not lend aid to her moderate means? I am ashamed indeed to say these things: however, I compel no man, if any one imagines what I am saying to

---

[1] οὐκοῦν καὶ ὁ Χριστὸν (should it be Χριστιανὸν?) δεχόμενος, λήψεται μισθὸν τοῦ Χριστὸν ξενίζοντος.—Ben. renders the latter clause, *recipiet mercedem Christi peregrinantis.*

[2] All our Mss. omit χεῖρες, but the text αἱ δεδεμένον αὐτὸν ἰδοῦσαι requires more than this for its emendation. Below, before "not ashamed." mod. text inserts, "These things He (Christ) confesseth."

[3] Ἀλλ᾽ ἔχει ἰούγα ἡ ἐκκλησία. On ἰούγα, *juga*, see p. 74. Here also B. ἰυγγα., mod. text substitutes δαπανήματα.

be for gain. Make for yourself a guest-chamber in your own house : set up a bed there, set up a table there and a candlestick. (comp. 2 Kings iv. 10.) For is it not absurd, that whereas, if soldiers should come, you have rooms set apart for them, and show much care for them, and furnish them with everything, because they keep off from you the visible war of this world, yet strangers have no place where they might abide? Gain a victory over the Church. Would you put us to shame? This do : surpass us in liberality : have a room, to which Christ may come ; say, " This is Christ's cell ; this building is set apart for Him." Be it but an underground[1] chamber, and mean, He disdains it not. " Naked and a stranger," Christ goes about, it is but a shelter He wants : afford it, though but this. Be not uncompassionate, nor inhuman ; be not so earnest in worldly matters, so cold in spiritual. Let also the most faithful of thy servants be the one entrusted with this office, and let him bring in the maimed, the beggars, and the homeless. These things I say to shame you. For ye ought indeed to receive them in the upper part of your house ; but if ye will not do this, then though it be below, though but where thy mules are housed, and thy servants, there receive Christ. Perchance ye shudder at hearing this. What then, when ye do not even this? Behold, I exhort, behold, I bid you ; let this be a matter to be taken up in earnest. But ye do not wish it thus, perhaps? Do it some other way. There are many poor men and poor women : set apart some one (of these) constantly to remain there : let the poor man be (thine inmate) though but as a guard to thy house : let him be to thee wall and fence, shield and spear. Where alms are, the devil dares not approach, nor any other evil thing. Let us not overlook so great a gain. But now a place is set apart for a chariot, and for litters (βαστερνίοις) another ; but for Christ Who is wandering, not even one ! Abraham received the strangers in the place where he abode himself ; his wife stood in the place of a servant, the guests in the place of masters. He knew not that he was receiving Christ ; knew not that he was receiving Angels ; so that had he known it, he would have lavished his whole substance. But we, who know that we receive Christ, show not even so much zeal as he did who thought that he was receiving men. " But they are impostors," you will say, " many of them, and unthankful." And for this the greater thy reward, when thou receivest for the sake of Christ's name. For if thou knowest indeed that they are impostors, receive them not into thy house : but if thou dost not know this, why dost thou accuse them lightly? " Therefore I tell them to go to the receiving house." But what kind of excuse is there for us, when we do not even receive those whom we know, but shut our doors against all? Let our house be Christ's general receptacle : let us demand of them as a reward, not money, but that they make our house the receptacle for Christ ; let us run about everywhere, let us drag them in, let us seize our booty : greater are the benefits we receive than what we confer. He does not bid thee kill a calf : give thou bread to the hungry, raiment to the naked, shelter to the stranger. But that thou mayest not make this thy pretext, there is a common apartment, that of the Church ; throw thy money into that, and then thou hast received them : since (Abraham) there had the reward of those things also which were done by his servants. " He gave the calf to a young man, and he hasted to dress it." (Gen. xviii. 7.) So well trained were his servants also ! They ran, and murmured not as ours do : for he had made them pious. He drew them out to war, and they murmured not : so well disciplined were they. (Gen. xiv. 14.) For he had equal care for all as for himself : he all but said as Job did, " We were alike formed in the same womb." (Job xxxiii. 6.) Therefore let us also take thought for their salvation, and let us make it our duty to care for our servants, that they may be good ; and let our servants also be instructed in the things pertaining to God. Then will virtue not be difficult to us, if we train them orderly. Just as in war, when the soldiers are well-disciplined, the general carries on war easily, but the contrary happens, when this is not so ; and when the sailors too are of one mind, the pilot easily handles the rudder-strings ; so here likewise. For say now, if thy servants have been so schooled, thou wilt not have to find fault, wilt not be made angry, wilt not need to abuse them. It may be, thou wilt even stand in awe of thy servants, if they are worthy of admiration, and they will be helpers with thee, and will give thee good counsel. But from all these shall all things proceed that are pleasing to God, and thus shall the whole house be filled with blessing, and we, performing things pleasing to God, shall enjoy abundant succor from above, unto which may we all attain, through the grace and mercy of our Lord Jesus Christ, with Whom to the Father and the Holy Ghost, together be glory, might, honor, now and ever, world without end. Amen.

---

[1] A. B. C. κᾰν καταγώγιον ᾖ so Morel. Ben. But E. has here preserved the true reading κατώγεον, so Savil. with marg. κατάγαιον.

HOMILY XLVI.

ACTS XXI. 18, 19.

"And the day following Paul went in with us unto James: and all the elders were present. And when he had saluted them, he declared particularly what things God had wrought among the Gentiles by his ministry."

THIS was the Bishop of Jerusalem; and to him (Paul) is sent on an earlier occasion. This (James) was brother of the Lord; a great and admirable man. (To him, it says,) "Paul entered in with us." Mark the (Bishop's) unassuming behavior: "and the elders" (were present). Again Paul relates to them the things relating to the Gentiles, not indulging in vainglory, God forbid, but wishing to show forth the mercy of God, and to fill them with great joy. (ch. xv.) See accordingly: "when they heard it," it says, "they glorified God,"—not praised nor admired Paul: for in such wise had he narrated, as referring all to Him—"and said unto him, Thou seest, brother, how many thousands of Jews there are which believed." Observe with what modest deference they too speak: "they said to him:" not (James) as Bishop discourses authoritatively, but they take Paul as partner with them in their view; "Thou seest, brother:" as though immediately and at the outset apologizing for themselves, and saying, "We did not wish this. Seest thou the necessity of the thing? 'how many thousands,' say they, 'of Jews there are which' have come together." And they say not, "how many thousands we have made catechumens," but, "there are. And these," say they, "are all zealous for the law." (v. 20.) Two reasons—the number of them, and their views. For neither had they been few, would it have been right to despise them: nor, if they were many and did not all cling to the law, would there have been need to make much account of them. Then also a third cause is given: "And they all," it says, "have been informed of thee"—they say not, "have heard," but κατηχήθησαν, that is, so they have believed, and have been taught, "that thou teachest apostasy from Moses to all the Jews which are among the Gentiles, by telling them not to circumcise their children, neither to walk after the customs." (v. 21.) "What is it therefore? the multitude must needs come together: for they will hear that thou art come. Do therefore this that we say to thee" (v. 22, 23): they say these things as advising, not as commanding. "We have four men which have a vow on them; them take, and purify thyself with them, and be at charges with them." Make thy defence in act, not in word—"that they may shave themselves," it says, "and all may know that those things, whereof they were informed concerning thee, are nothing; but that thou thyself also walkest orderly, and keepest the law" (v. 23, 24): they say not, "teachest," but, of superabundance, "that thou thyself also keepest the law." For of course not this was the matter of chief interest, whether he did not teach others, but, that he did himself observe the law. "What then" (he might say), "if the Gentiles should learn it? I shall injure them." How so? say they, seeing that even we, the teachers of the Jews, have sent unto them. "As touching the Gentiles which believe, we have written and concluded that they observe no such thing, save only that they keep themselves from things offered to idols, and from blood, and from strangled, and from fornication." (v. 25.) Here with a kind of remonstrance (ἐντρεπτικῶς), As "we," say they, commanded them, although we are preachers to the Jews, so do thou, although a preacher to the Gentiles, coöperate with us. Observe Paul: he does not say, "Well, but I can bring forward Timothy, whom I circumcised: well, but I can satisfy them by what I have to say (of myself):" but he complied, and did all: for in fact thus was it expedient (to do).* For it was one thing to take (effec-

---

* It has been much disputed whether the charge: "Thou teachest apostacy from Moses," etc., was true or not. There certainly was truth in the charge. Paul maintained that the Mosaic law, as such, was not binding upon Christians. But it was against those who made it a yoke of bondage upon believers, that he waged a polemic. Where there was no imposition of the law as necessary to salvation, Paul in no way antagonized it, but rather trusted to the free working of the principles of the gospel to gradually accomplish the abolition of its rites and forms. The truth seems to be that Paul was tolerant of Judaism where it did not impose burdens upon believers or threaten the completeness and sufficiency of the gospel; he even accommodated himself to Jewish requirements, as in shaving his head at Cenchrea and circumcising Timothy. He never unnecessarily opposed the law of Moses, but taught that it had been fulfilled in Christ. So far as he accommodated himself to its ceremonies, it was only that he might remove prejudice and so win the Jews to Christ.—G. B. S.

tual) measures for clearing himself, and another to have done these things without the knowledge of any (of the parties). It was a step open to no suspicion, the fact of his even bearing the expenses. "Then Paul took the men, and the next day purifying himself with them entered into the temple, signifying the accomplishment of the days of purification, until that an offering should be offered for every one of them." (v. 26.) "Signifying," διαγγέλλων, i. e. καταγγέλλων, publicly notifying : so that it was he who made himself conspicuous. "And when the seven days were about to be completed, the Jews from Asia"—for (his arrival) most keeps times with theirs [1]—"when they saw him in the temple, stirred up all the people, and laid hands on him, crying out, Men of Israel, help : This is the man, that teacheth all men everywhere against the people, and the law, and this place : and further brought Greeks also into the temple, and hath polluted this holy place." (v. 27, 28.) Mark their habitual conduct, how turbulent we everywhere find it, how men who with or without reason make a clamor in the midst.[2] "For they had seen before with him in the city Trophimus an Ephesian, whom they supposed that Paul had brought into the temple. And all the city was moved, and the people ran together : and they took Paul, and drew him out of the temple and forthwith the doors were shut." (v. 29, 30.) "Men of Israel," it says, "help : this is the man that (teaches) against the people, and the law, and this place,"—the things which most trouble them, the Temple and the Law. And Paul does not tax the Apostles with being the cause of these things to him. "And they drew him," it says, "out of the Temple : and the doors were shut." For they wished to kill him ; and therefore were dragging him out, to do this with greater security. "And as they went about to kill him, tidings came unto the tribune of the cohort, that all Jerusalem was in an uproar. Who immediately took soldiers and centurions, and ran down unto them : and when they saw the tribune and the soldiers, they left beating of Paul. Then the tribune came near, and took him, and commanded him to be bound with two chains ; and demanded

who he was, and what he had done. And some cried one thing, some another, among the multitude." (v. 31-34.) But the tribune having come down delivered him, and "commanded him to be bound with two chains : " (hereby) appeasing the anger of the people. "And when he could not know the certainty for the tumult, he commanded him to be carried into the castle. And when he came upon the stairs, so it was, that he was borne of the soldiers for the violence of the people. For the multitude of the people followed after, crying, Away with him ! " (v. 34-36.) What means, "Away with him ? " that is, what they say with us according to the Roman custom, To the standards with him![3] "And as Paul was to be led into the castle, he said unto the tribune, May I speak unto thee ? " (v. 37.) In the act of being borne along up the stairs, he requests to say something to the tribune : and observe how quietly he does it. "May I speak unto thee ? " he says. "Who said, Canst thou speak Greek ? Art thou not then that Egyptian, which before these days madest an uproar, and leddest out into the wilderness four thousand men that were murderers ? " (v. 38.) For (this Egyptian) was a revolutionary and seditious person. With regard to this then Paul clears himself, and * * *[4]

(Recapitulation.) "Do therefore this that we say unto thee," etc. (v. 23, 24.) He shows that it was not necessary to do this upon principle (προηγουμένως)—whence also they obtain his compliance—but that it was economy and condescension.* "As touching the Gentiles," etc. (v. 25.) Why, then, this was no hindrance to the preaching, seeing they themselves

---

[1] Old text : μάλιστα γὰρ ἐκείνοις συγχρονίζει, as the comment on οἱ ἀπὸ τῆς Ἀσίας Ἰουδαῖοι, meaning apparently that his arrival at Jerusalem would naturally fall at the same time with that of the Jews who, like himself, came from the same parts. Mod. text transfers the comment to the first clause of the verse, "And as the days were about to be fulfilled: ὅρα πῶς μάλιστα δὴ αὐτοῖς ἐγχρονίζει," it is not easy to see with what meaning.

[2] ὅρα τὸ ἦθος αὐτῶν πανταχοῦ ταραχῶδες, καὶ ἁπλῶς βοώντων ἐν τῷ μέσῳ. Meaning perhaps that the conduct of these Ephesian Jews was of a piece with that of their heathen countrymen, ch. xix. 28.

[3] ἐν τοῖς σίγνοις αὐτὸν ἔμβαλε. Ammonius in the Catena, "It was a custom of the Jews to utter this cry against the just, as they did against the Lord, Αἶρε αὐτόν ! i. e. away with Him from among the living." Hence Œcumen. combining this with the explanation in the text, "It was the custom of the Jews, etc. But some say, That is, what they say with us," etc. And so mod. text, "It was a custom of the Jews to say this against those whom they would condemn, as also in the case of Christ they appear doing this, and saying, Ἀρον αὐτόν ! that is, Make him to disappear from among the living. "But some," what among us they say according to the Roman custom, Ἐν τοῖς σίγνοις αὐτὸν ἔμβαλε, the same is the Αἶρε αὐτόν.
[4] Mod. text supplies the evident lacuna with, "And by what he says, takes him off from his suspicion. "But let us look again at what has been read. "There are," they say, "with us seven men," etc.
* This vow appears to have been the Nazarite vow described in Num. vi. 1-21, taken by the apostle as an accommodation to Jewish prejudices and to allay the suspicions of the legal party in Jerusalem. This was done upon the recommendation of James, the "Bishop" of the church, and his associates. The significance of Paul's paying the expenses is, perhaps, that the period during which the others' vow had run was on this condition reckoned to his account also. It is noticeable that the party of James distinctly admits that adherence to the legal ceremonies is not required of the Gentile Christians; it is equally important to notice that Paul yielded to the advice to take this view, as a concession in a matter of indifference, since he was living for the time as a Jew among Jews, that he might give no needless offence and might win the more. It was not a compromise, but an expedient concession to convictions and prejudices which it was not wise or necessary to oppose or increase.—G. B. S.

legislated for them to this effect. Why, then,[1] in his taking Peter to task he does not absolutely (ἀπλῶς) charge him with doing wrong: for precisely what he does on this occasion himself, the same does Peter on that occasion, (merely) holding his peace, and establishing his doctrine. (Gal. ii. 11.) And he says not, For why? it is not right to teach those among the Gentiles. "It is not enough to have not (so) preached there, but there was need also to do something more, that those may be persuaded that thou observest the law. The affair is one of condescension, be not alarmed." They do not advise him (to this course) sooner, until they have first spoken of the economy and the gain. "And besides, the doing this in Jerusalem, is a thing to be borne. 'Do thou this thing therefore' here, that it may be in thy power abroad to do the other." (b) "The next day," it says, "he took them" (v. 26): he deferred it not; for when there is economy in the case, this is the way of it. (a) "Jews from Asia having seen him," for it was natural that they were spending some days there, "in the Temple." (v. 27.) (c) Mark the economy (of Providence) that appeared (in this). (p. 279, note [1].) After the (believing) Jews had been persuaded (concerning him), then it is that those (Jews of Asia) set upon him in order that those (believing Jews) may not also set upon him. Help, say they, "ye men of Israel!" as though it were some (monster) difficult to be caught, and hard to be overcome, that has fallen into their hands. "All men," they say, "everywhere, he ceaseth not to teach;" not here only. And then the accusation (is) more aggravated by the present circumstances. "And yet more," say they, "he has polluted the temple, having brought into it men who are Greeks." (v. 28.) And yet in Christ's time there "came up (Greeks) to worship" (John xii. 20): true, but here it speaks of Greeks who had no mind to worship. "And they seized Paul," etc. (v. 30-35.) They no longer wanted laws nor courts of justice: they also beat him. But he forbore to make his defence then; he made it afterward: with reason; for they would not even have heard him then. Pray, why did they cry, "Away with him?" (v. 36.) They feared he might escape them. Observe how submissively Paul speaks to the tribune. "May I speak unto thee? Then art not thou that Egyptian?" (v. 37, 38.) This Egyptian, namely, was a cheat and impostor, and the

devil expected to cast a cloud over (the Gospel) through him, and implicate both Christ and His Apostles in the charges pertaining to those (imposters): but he prevailed nothing, nay the truth became even more brilliant, being nothing defeated by the machinations of the devil, nay rather shining forth all the more. Since if there had not been impostors, and then these (Christ and His Apostles) had prevailed, perhaps some one might have laid hold upon this: but when those impostors did actually appear, this is the wonder. "In order," says (the Apostle), "that they which are approved may be made manifest." (1 Cor. xi. 19.) And Gamaliel says, "Before these days stood up Theudas."[2] Then let us not grieve that heresies exist, seeing that false Christs wished to attack even Christ both before this and after; with a view to throw Him into the shade, but on every occasion we find the truth shining out transparent. So it was with the Prophets: there were false prophets, and by contrast with these they shone the more: just as disease enhances health, and darkness light, and tempest calm. There is no room left for the Greeks to say that (our teachers) were impostors and mountebanks: for those (that were such) were exposed. It was the same in the case of Moses: God suffered the magicians, on purpose that Moses might not be suspected to be a magician: He let them teach all men to what length magic can go in making a fantastic show: beyond this point they deceived not, but themselves confessed their defeat. Impostors do us no harm, rather do us good, if we will apply our mind to the matter. What then, you will say, if we are partners with them in common estimation? The estimation is not among us, but with those who have no judgment. Let not us greatly care for the estimation of the many, nor mind it more than needs. To God we live, not to men: in heaven we have our conversation, not on earth: *there* lie the awards and the prizes of our labors, thence

---

[1] Mod. text, "Using this economy then, he himself at a later time (?) accuses Peter, and he does not do this ἀπλῶς." St. Chrysostom's view of St. Peter's dissimulation at Antioch as an "economy," is most fully given in his exposition of the passage, *Comment. in Gal.* cap. ii. §. 4, 5.

[2] Mod. text adds, "But as for the *sicarii*, some say they were a kind of robbers, so called from the swords they bore, which by the Romans are called *sicæ*: others, that they were of the first sect among the Hebrews. For there are among them three sects, generally considered (αἱρέσεις αἱ γενικαί): Pharisees, Sadducees, and Essenes who are also called ὅσιοι, for that is the meaning of the name 'Essenes,' on account of their reverend manner of life: but the same (?) are also called *sicarii*, because of their being zealots." For a further illustration of the way in which the modern text was formed, especially in respect of its use of the *Catena* (see p. 279, note [3]), compare the latter with Œcumenius on this passage. The Catena, namely, cites from Origen: "Among the Jews are τρεῖς αἱρέσεις γενικαί· Pharisees, Sadducees, Essenes: these (last) exercise a more reverend manner of life, being lovers one of another and temperate: whence also they are called Essenes, i. e. ὅσιοι: but others called them (?) *sicarii*, i. e. zealots." (Œcumen. using the Catena, makes a continuous exposition from Chrys., Origen, and Josephus. Mod. text from the same materials, interpolates the text of Chrys. as above.

we look for our praises, thence for our crowns. Thus far let us trouble ourselves about men— that we do not give and afford them a handle against us. But if, though we afford none, those choose to accuse us thoughtlessly and without discrimination, let us laugh, not [1] weep. "Provide" thou "things honest before the Lord and before men" (2. Cor. viii. 21): if, though thou provide things honest, that man derides, give thyself no more concern (for that). Thou hast thy patterns in the Scriptures. For, saith he, "do I now persuade men or God?" (Gal. i. 10) and again, "We persuade men, but we are made manifest unto God." (2 Cor. v. 11.) And Christ (spoke) thus of them that take offence: "Let them alone, they be blind guides of the blind (Matt. xv. 14); and again, "Woe unto you, when all men speak well of you" (Luke vi. 26): and again, "Let your works shine, that men may see, and glorify your Father which is in heaven." (Matt. v. 16.) And, "Whoso shall offend one of these little ones, it were better for him that a millstone were hanged about his neck, and he were drowned in the depths of the sea." (Matt. xviii. 6.) These sayings are not contrary, nay, they are exceedingly in accord. For when the offence is with us, then woe unto us, but when not with us, not so. And again, Woe to (that man) through whom "the name of God is blasphemed." (Rom. ii. 24.) How then if I do what is right in anything, but another blasphemes? That is nothing to me, but only to him: for through him (God) was blasphemed. "And how is it possible to do what is right in anything, and yet give a handle to the rest?" Whence will ye that I bring examples—from present, or from old times? Not to be easily scared (ψοφοδεεῖς), shall we speak to the very point now in hand? Paul judaized in Jerusalem, but in Antioch not so: he judaized, and they were offended (p. 282, note [8]), but those had no right to be offended. He is said to have saluted both Nero's cupbearer and his concubine:[2] what, think ye, must they have said against him because of this? But they had no right to do so. Since, if he drew them to him for [3] loose living or any wicked acts, one might well be offended: but if in order to right living, what is there to be offended at? Let me mention something

that happened to one of my acquaintance. The wrath of God once fell upon (a city), and he being very young (was) in the order of deacon. The bishop was absent at the time, and of the presbyters none took thought for the matter, but indiscriminately they caused in one night immense numbers [4] of people to be baptized all at once, and they did indiscriminately receive baptism, all of them ignorant of everything: these he took apart by a hundred or two hundred together, and discoursed to them, not upon any other subject, but only on the sacraments, so that the unbaptized also were not allowed to be present. Many thought he did this because he coveted rule. But he cared not for that: neither however did he continue the thing for a (longer) time, but immediately desisted. When then? Was he the cause of the scandal? I think not. For if indeed he had done this without cause, they might with reason have ascribed it to him: and so again, if he had continued to do so. For when aught of what is pleasing to God is hindered by another's taking offence, it is right to take no notice: but then is the time to mind it, when we are not forced because of him to offend God. For, say, if, while we are discoursing and putting drunkards to shame (σκωπτόντων), any one take offence—am I to give over speaking? Hear Christ say, "Will ye also go away?" (John vi. 67.) So then, the right thing is, neither to take no notice, nor to take too much, of the weakness of the many. Do we not see the physicians acting thus: how, when it may be done, they humor the whims of their patients, but when the gratification does harm, then they will not spare? Always it is good to know the right mean. Many reviled, because a certain beautiful virgin stayed, and they railed upon those who catechised (her). What then? Was it their duty to desist for that? By no means. For let us not look to this only, whether some be offended, but whether they are justly offended, and [5] so that it is no hurt to ourselves (to give way). "If meat," saith (Paul), "offend my brother, I will eat no meat as long as the world lasts." (1 Cor. viii. 13.) With reason: for the not eating did (him) no harm. If however it offend him, that I wish to renounce (ἀποτάξασθαι) (the world), it is not right to mind him. And whom, you will ask,

---

[1] B. alone of our Mss. gives the negative which the sense requires; restored to the text by Ed. Par. Ben. 2.

[2] The cupbearer may be Narcissus (Rom. xvi. 11): the name of the concubine is not mentioned. In one of his earliest works, *Adv. Oppugn. Vitæ Monast.* i. § 3. t. i. p. 59. D. St. Chrys. relates that Nero cast St. Paul into prison, and in the end beheaded him, in his rage at the loss of a favorite concubine, converted by him to the faith.

[3] Ben. ἠσπάσατο, which is the reading of D. only: all the rest ἐπεσπάσατο.

[4] In the original, μυριάδας πολλάς. The deacon is probably Chrys. himself; the bishop, Flavian.

[5] καὶ μὴ μετὰ τῆς ἡμετέρας βλαβῆς. Mod. text and Edd. καὶ εἰ μὴ, which is ambiguous. "The thing to be considered is, whether they are offended δικαίως καὶ μὴ μετὰ τ. ἡ. β. justly, and not with concomitant hurt to ourselves should we give way." As in the case afterwards mentioned, the sitting at meat in an idol's temple; the "weak brothers" were offended δικαίως, and to abstain from such conduct was not attended with any moral hurt or loss to the men of "knowledge."

does this offend ? Many, to my knowledge. When therefore the hindrance is a thing indifferent, let (the thing) be done [1]. Else, if we were to look only to this, many are the things we have to desist from : just as, on the other hand, if we should despise (all objections), we have to destroy many (brethren). As in fact Paul also took thought beforehand concerning offence : "Lest," he says, "in this liberality which is administered by us : " for it was attended with no loss (to him) to obviate an ill surmise. But when we fall into such a necessity as that great evils should ensue through the other's taking offence,[2] let us pay no heed to that person. He has to thank himself for it, and we are not now accountable, for it was not possible to spare

him without hurt (to ourselves). Some were offended, because certain believers sat down to meat in (heathen) temples. It was not right to sit down : for no harm came of this (their not doing it). They were offended, because Peter ate with the Gentiles. But he indeed spared them, but (Paul) [3] not so. On all occasions it behooves us in following the laws of God to take great pains that we give no matter of offence; that both ourselves may not have to answer for it, and may have mercy vouchsafed us from God, by the grace and loving-kindness of His only-begotten Son, with Whom to the Father and Holy Ghost together be glory, dominion, honor, now and ever, world without end. Amen.

HOMILY XLVII.

ACTS XXI. 39, 40.

"But Paul said, I am a man which am a Jew of Tarsus, a city in Cilicia, a citizen of no mean city : and I beseech thee, suffer me to speak unto the people. And when he had given him license, Paul stood on the stairs, and beckoned with the hand unto the people. And when there was made a great silence, he spake unto them in the Hebrew tongue, saying."

OBSERVE how, when he discourses to those that are without, he does not decline availing himself of the aids afforded by the laws. Here he awes the tribune by the name of his city. And again, elsewhere he said, " Openly, uncondemned, Romans as we are, they have cast us into prison." (ch. xix. 37.) For since the tribune said, " Art thou that Egyptian ? " he immediately drew him off from that surmise : then, that he may not be thought to deny his nation, he says at once, " I am a Jew : " he means his religion.[4] (b) What

then ? he did not deny (that he was a Christian) : God forbid : for he was both a Jew and a Christian, observing what things he ought : since indeed he, most of all men, did obey the law : (a) as in fact he elsewhere calls himself, "Under the law to Christ." (1 Cor. ix. 21.) What is this, I pray ? (c) The man [5] that believes in Christ. And when discoursing with Peter, he says : "We, Jews by nature.—But I beseech thee, suffer me to speak unto the people." (Gal. ii. 15.) And this is a proof, that he does not speak lies, seeing he takes all as his witnesses. Observe again how mildly he speaks. This again is a very strong argument that he is chargeable with no crime, his being so ready to make his defence, and his wishing to come to discourse with the people of the Jews. See a man well-prepared (τεταγμένον ἄνδρα) !—Mark the providential ordering of the thing : unless the

---

[1] ὅταν τοίνυν ἀδιάφορον ᾖ τὸ κώλυμα, γινέσθω. Ben. *quando igitur indifferens est, abstineatur.* But the κώλυμα (which is overlooked in this rendering) seems to mean, the hindrance to the ἀποτάξασθαι, which latter will be the subject to γίνεσθω. For instance, if the impediment urged by others against a person's taking the monastic vows be a thing indifferent, let him take them. Else, if we were to look to this only—viz. that this or that man is offended—πολλῶν ἔχομεν ἀποστῆναι—many are the right undertakings we should have to forego or desist from: as on the other hand were we to make it a rule to despise all considerations of offence, we should have to be the ruin of many a brother.

[2] Namely, in a matter where the duty of persisting in our course is plain—viz. where the other is offended οὐ δικαίως, and to give way would be μετὰ τῆς ἡμετέρας βλάβης—then, even though great evils to him or others result from our not giving way, we must take no notice of the offence, must allow it no weight.

[3] αὐτὸς δὲ οὐκ ἔτι. Here, as above, p. 118, it seems to be assumed that St. Paul's judaizing at Jerusalem gave offence to the Gentile brethren in his company.

[4] Εἶτα ἵνα μὴ νομισθῇ τὸ ἔθνος Ἰουδαῖος, λέγει τὴν θρησκείαν· καὶ γὰρ καὶ ἀλλαχοῦ ἔννομον ἑαυτὸν Χριστοῦ καλεῖ. Τί (A. B. C.

add οὖν, Cat. δὴ) τοῦτό ἐστιν ; (Mod. text adds, Παῦλος ψεύδεται ; Ἄπαγε) Τί οὖν ; οὐκ ἠρνήσατο ; κ. τ. λ. The sense is confused by omission and transposition. It seems to be this: He gives the tribune to understand that he is a Roman : but because he would not have the Jews to suppose that he was not a Jew, therefore he declares his religion, that he is a Jew. And herein was no denial of his Christianity, etc. See below on v. 3. ἵνα μὴ πάλιν νομίσωσι τὸ ἔθνος ἄλλο, τὴν θρησκείαν ἐπήγαγεν. Hence we restore the sense as in the text.—Œcumen. gives it, " He immediately drew him off from this surmise, καὶ τὸ ἔθνος καὶ τὴν θρησκείαν εἰπών, as in fact he elsewhere calls himself, Under the law to Christ."

[5] Mod. text omits the article. Ὁ τῷ Χριστῷ πιστεύων, as we take it, is the answer to the question, τί δὴ τοῦτό ἐστιν ; In the next sentence (which Edd. separate from this only by a comma) he says: in the same sense he calls himself and Peter, φύσει Ἰουδαῖοι, " born Jews (not proselytes,) and Jews still." But Ammonius in the Catena: " I am a man which am a Jew: for we Christians are φύσει Ἰουδαῖοι, as confessing the true faith: which is what the name Judah signifies."

tribune had come, unless he had bound him, he would not have desired to speak for his defence, he would not have obtained the silence he did. "Standing on the stairs." Then there was the additional facility afforded by the locality, that he should have a high place to harangue them from—in chains too! What spectacle could be equal to this, to see Paul, bound with two chains, and haranguing the people! (To see him,) how he was not a whit perturbed, not a whit confused; how, seeing as he did so great a multitude all hostility against him, the ruler standing by, he first of all made them desist from their anger: then, how prudently (he does this). Just what he does in his Epistle to the Hebrews, the same he does here: first he attracts them by the sound of their common mother tongue: then by his mildness itself. "He spake unto them," it says, "in the Hebrew tongue, saying, Men, brethren, and fathers, hear ye my defence which I make now unto you." (ch. xxii. 1.) Mark his address, at once so free from all flattery, and so expressive of meekness. For he says not, "Masters," nor "Lords," but, "Brethren," just the word they most liked: "I am no alien from you," he says, nor "against you." "Men," he says, "brethren, and fathers:" this, a term of honor, that of kindred. "Hear ye," says he, "my"—he says not, "teaching," nor "harangue," but, "my defence which I now make unto you." He puts himself in the posture of a suppliant. "And when they heard that he spake in the Hebrew tongue to them, they kept the more silence." (v. 2.) Do you observe how the using the same tongue subdued them? In fact, they had a sort of awe for that language. Observe also how he prepares the way for his discourse, beginning thus: "I am verily a man which am a Jew, born in Tarsus, a city in Cilicia, yet brought up in this city at the feet of Gamaliel, and taught according to the perfect manner of the law of the fathers, and was zealous toward God, as ye all are this day." (v. 3.) "I am a man," he says, "which am a Jew:" which thing they liked most of all to hear; "born in Tarsus, a city of Cilicia." That they may not again think him to be of another nation, he adds his religion: "but brought up in this city." (p. 282, note *.) He shows how great was his zeal for the worship, inasmuch as having left his native city, which was so great and so remote too, he chose to be brought up here for the Law's sake. See how from the beginning he attached himself to the law.*

But this he says, not only to defend himself to them, but to show that not by human intent was he led to the preaching of the Gospel, but by a Divine power: else, having been so educated, he would not have suddenly changed. For if indeed he had been one of the common order of men, it might have been reasonable to suspect this: but if he was of the number of those who were most of all bound by the law, it was not likely that he should change lightly, and without strong necessity. But perhaps some one may say: "To have been brought up here proves nothing: for what if thou camest here for the purpose of trading, or for some other cause?" Therefore he says, "at the feet of Gamaliel:" and not simply, "by Gamaliel," but "at his feet," showing his perseverance, his assiduity, his zeal for the hearing, and his great reverence for the man. "Taught according to the perfect manner of the law of the fathers." Not simply, "the law," but "the law of the fathers;" showing that he was such from the beginning, and not merely one that knew the Law. All this seems indeed to be spoken on their side, but in fact it told against them, since he, knowing the law, forsook it. "Yes, but what if thou didst indeed know the law accurately, but dost not vindicate it, no, nor love it?" "Being a zealot," he adds: not simply (one that knew it). Then, since it was a high encomium he had passed upon himself, he makes it theirs as well as his, adding, "As ye all are this day." For he shows that they act not from any human object, but from zeal for God; gratifying them, and preoccupying their minds, and getting a hold upon them in a way that did no harm. Then he brings forward proofs also, saying, "and I persecuted this way unto the death, binding and delivering into prisons both men and women. As also the high priest doth bear me witness, and all the estate of the elders" (v. 4, 5): "How does this appear." As witnesses he brings forward the high-priest himself and the elders. He says indeed, "Being a zealot, as ye" (Hom. xix. p. 123): but he shows by his actions, that he went beyond them. "For I did not wait for an opportunity of seizing them: I both stirred up the priests, and undertook

---

* The whole purpose of Paul's defence here is to appease the prejudice against him as an apostate from Moses. He addresses the people of Jerusalem in their own tongue and as "brethren." He shows them that although born in a Greek city, he had received his education in Jerusalem, under one of their most famous Rabbis. He sketches his history as a zealous adherent of Judaism. After his conversion he did not desert the religion of his fathers. It was while praying in the temple that the call of God came to him which summoned him to go as an apostle to the Gentiles. From this apology, it would be seen how far Paul was from despising the Mosaic law and also, how manifestly providential had been the call by which he had been set apart to a distinct work among the Gentiles. It is a guarded defence which neither antagonizes the law, nor admits its binding force over the apostle or his converts.

journeys : I did not confine my attacks, as ye
did, to men, I extended them to women also :
" both binding, and casting into prisons both
men and women." This testimony is incontrovertible ; the (unbelief) of the Jews (is left)
without excuse. See how many witnesses he
brings forward, the elders, the high-priest,
and those in the city. Observe his defence,
how it is not of cowardly fear (for himself,
that he pleads), no, but for teaching and
indoctrination. For had not the hearers been
stones, they would have felt the force of what
he was saying. For up to this point he had
themselves as witnesses : the rest, however,
was without witnesses : " From whom also I
received letters unto the brethren, and went
to Damascus, to bring them which were there
bound unto Jerusalem, for to be punished.
And it came to pass, that, as I made my journey, and was come nigh unto Damascus
about noon, suddenly there shone from
heaven a great light round about me. And I
fell unto the ground, and heard a voice saying
unto me, Saul, Saul, why persecutest thou
Me ? And I answered, Who art Thou, Lord ?
And he said unto me, I am Jesus of Nazareth,
Whom thou persecutest." (v. 6, 7, 8.) Why
then, these very things ought to have been
held worthy of credit, from those that went
before : otherwise he would not have undergone such a revolution. How if he is only
making a fine story of it, say you? Answer
me, Why did he suddenly fling away all this
zeal? Because he looked for honor? And
yet he got just the contrary. But an easy
life, perhaps? No, nor that either. Well,
but something else? Why it is not in the
power of thought to invent any other object.
So then, leaving it to themselves to draw the
inference, he narrates the facts. " As I came
nigh," he says, " unto Damascus, about noon-
day." See how great was the excess of the
light. What if he is only making a fine story,
say you? Those who were with him are
witnesses, who led him by the hand, who saw
the light. " And they that were with me saw
indeed the light, and were afraid ; but they
heard not the voice of Him that spake to
me." (v. 9.) But in another place he says,
" Hearing the voice, but seeing no man."
(Acts ix. 7.) It is not at variance : no, there
were two voices, that of Paul and the Lord's
voice : in that place, the writer means Paul's
voice (Hom. xix. p. 124, note [2]) ; as in
fact (Paul) here adds, " The voice of Him
that spake unto me. Seeing no man : " he
does not say, that they did not see the light :
but, " no man," that is, " none speaking."
And good reason that it should be so, since
it behooved him alone to have that voice

vouchsafed unto him. For if indeed they
also had heard it, (the miracle) would not
have been so great. Since persons of grosser
minds are persuaded more by sight, those
saw the light, and were afraid. In fact,
neither did the light take so much effect on
them, as it did on him : for it even blinded
his eyes : by that which befel him, (God)
gave them also an opportunity of recovering
their sight, if they had the mind. It seems
to me at least, that their not believing was
providentially ordered, that they might be
unexceptionable witnesses. " And he said
unto me," it says, " I am Jesus of Nazareth,
Whom thou persecutest." (comp. ch. ix. 5.)
Well is the name of the city (Nazareth) also
added, that they might recognize (the Person) : moreover, the Apostles also spoke thus.
(ch. ii. 22 ; iv. 10 ; x. 38.) And Himself bore
witness, that they were persecuting Him.
" And they that were with me saw indeed the
light, and were afraid, but they heard not the
voice of Him that spake to me. And I said,
What shall I do, Lord? And the Lord said
unto me, Arise, and go into Damascus ; and
there it shall be told thee of all things which
are appointed for thee to do. And when I
could not see for the glory of that light, being
led by the hand of them that were with me, I
came into Damascus. And one Ananias, a
devout man according to the law, having a
good report of all the Jews which dwelt there,
came unto me, and stood, and said unto me,
Brother Saul, receive thy sight. And the
same hour I looked up upon him. Enter into
the city," it says, " and there it shall be
spoken to thee of all that is appointed for
thee to do." (v. 10-13.) Lo! again another
witness. And see how unexceptionable he
makes him also. " And one Ananias," he
says, " a devout man according to the law,"
—so far is it from being anything alien !—
" having a good report of all the Jews that
dwelt " (there). " And I in the same hour
received sight." Then follows the testimony
borne by the facts. Observe how it is interwoven, of persons and facts ; and the persons,
both of their own and of aliens : the priests,
the elders, and his fellow-travellers : the facts,
what he did and what was done to him : and
facts bear witness to facts, not persons only.
Then Ananias, an alien ; [1] then the fact itself,
the recovery of sight ; then a great prophecy.
" And he said, The God of our fathers hath
chosen thee, that thou shouldest know His
will, and see That Just One." (v. 14.) It is
well said, " Of the fathers," to show that they

---

[1] Perhaps it should be, " And he too, not an alien : " viz.
being a " devout man according to the Law : " as above, he says
of Ananias, οὕτως οὐδὲν ἀλλότριόν ἐστι.

were not Jews, but aliens from the law, and that it was not from zeal (for the law) that they were acting. "That thou shouldest know His will." Why then His will is this. See how in the form of narrative it is teaching. "And see That Just One, and hear the voice of His mouth. For thou shalt be His witness unto all men of what thou hast seen and heard. And see," he says, "that Just One." (v. 15.) For the present he says no more than this : if He is Just, they are guilty. "And hear the voice of His mouth." See how high he raises the fact ! "For thou shalt be His witness—for this, because thou wilt not betray the sight and hearing (i. e. "prove false to ")—"both of what thou hast seen, and of what thou hast heard :" by means of both the senses he claims his faithfulness—"to all men. And now why tarriest thou ? arise, and be baptized, and wash away thy sins, calling on His name." (v. 16.) Here it is a great thing he has uttered. For he said not, "Be baptized in His name :" but, "calling on the name of Christ." It shows that He is God : since it is not lawful to "call upon" any other, save God. Then he shows also, that he himself was not compelled : for, "I said," says he, "What must I do ?" Nothing is (left) without witness : no ; he brings forward the witness of a whole city, seeing they had beheld him led by the hand. But see the prophecy fulfilled. "To all men," it is said. For he did become a witness to Him, and a witness as it ought to be ; by what he suffered, by what he did, and by what he said. Such witnesses ought we also to be, and not to betray the things we have been entrusted withal : I speak not only of doctrines, but also of the manner of life. For observe : because he had seen, because he had heard, he bears witness to all men, and nothing hindered him. We too bear witness (Mod. text "have heard") that there is a Resurrection and numberless good things : we are bound to bear witness of this to all men. "Yes, and we do bear witness," you will say, "and do believe." How, when ye act the contrary ? Say now : if any one should call himself a Christian, and then having apostatized should hold with the Jews, would this testimony suffice ? By no means : for men would desire the testimony which is borne by the actions. Just so, if we say that there is a Resurrection and numberless good things, and then despise those things and prefer the things here, who will believe us ? Not what we say, but what we do, is what all men look to. "Thou shalt be a witness," it says, "unto all men :" not only to the friendly, but also to the unbelievers : for this

is what witnesses are for ; not to persuade those who know, but those who know not. Let us be trustworthy witnesses. But how shall we be trustworthy ? By the life we lead. The Jews assaulted him : our passions assault us, bidding us abjure our testimony. But let us not obey them : we are witnesses from God. (Christ) is judged that He is not God :[1] He has sent us to bear witness to Him. Let us bear witness and persuade those who have to decide the point : if we do not bear witness, we have to answer for their error also. But if in a court of justice, where worldly matters come in question, nobody would receive a witness full of numberless vices, much less here, where such (and so great) are the matters to be considered. *We* say, that we have heard Christ, and that we believe the things which He has promised : Show it, say they, by your works : for your life bears witness of the contrary—that ye do not believe. Say, shall we look at the money-getting people, the rapacious, the covetous ? the people that mourn and wail, that build and busy themselves in all sorts of things, as though they were never to die ? "Ye do not believe that ye shall die, a thing so plain and evident : and how shall we believe you when ye bear witness ?" For there are, there are many men, whose state of mind is just as if they were not to die. For when in a lengthened old age they set about building and planting, when will they take death into their calculations ? It will be no small punishment to us that we were called to bear witness, but were not able to bear witness of the things that we have seen. We have seen Angels with our eyes, yea, more clearly than those who have (visibly) beheld them. We shall be (Mod. text "Then let us be") witnesses to Christ : for not those only are "martyrs," (or witnesses, whom we so call), but ourselves also. This is why they are called martyrs, because when bidden to abjure (the faith), they endure all things, that they may speak the truth : and we, when we are bidden by our passions to abjure, let us not be overcome. Gold saith : Say that Christ is not Christ. Then listen not to it as to God, but despise its biddings. The evil lusts[2] "profess that they know God, but in works they deny Him." (Tit. i. 16.) For this is not to witness, but the contrary. And indeed that others should deny (Him) is nothing wonderful : but that we who have been called to bear witness should deny Him, is a grievous

[1] Κρίνεται παρ ἀνθρώποις (τισὶν ὁ Θεὸς add. mod. text) ὅτι οὐκ ἐστι Θεός. The subject, not expressed, is Christ. He is brought before the bar of men's judgment for trial whether He be God : so below τοὺς δικάζοντας.
[2] Mod. text adds: " say the same : but be not thou seduced, but stand nobly that it may not be said of us also, They profess," etc.

and a heinous thing: this of all things does the greatest hurt to our cause. "It shall be to (your)selves for a testimony." (Luke xxi. 13), He saith: but (this is) when we ourselves stand to it firmly. If we would all bear witness to Christ, we should quickly persuade the greater number of the heathen. It is a great thing, my beloved, the life (one leads). Let a man be savage as a beast, let him openly condemn thee on account of thy doctrine,[1] yet he secretly approves, yet he will praise, yet he will admire. For say, whence can an excellent life proceed? From no source, except from a Divine Power working in us. "What if there be heathen also of such a character?" If anywhere any of them be such, it is partly from nature, partly from vainglory. Wilt thou learn what a brilliancy there is in a good life, what a force of persuasion it has? Many of the heretics have thus prevailed, and while their doctrines are corrupt, yet the greater part of men out of reverence for their (virtuous) life did not go on to examine their doctrine: and many even condemning them on account of their doctrine, reverence them on account of their life: not rightly indeed, but still so it is, that they do thus feel (towards them). This has brought slanders on the awful articles of our creed, this has turned everything upside down, that no one takes any account of good living: this is a mischief to the faith. We say that Christ is God; numberless other arguments we bring forward, and this one among the rest, that He has persuaded all men to live rightly: but this is the case with few. The badness of the life is a mischief to the doctrine of the Resurrection, to that of the immortality of the soul, to that of the Judgment: many other (false doctrines) too it draws on with itself, fate, necessity, denial of a Providence. For the soul being immersed in numberless vices, by way of consolations to itself tries to devise these, that it may not be pained in having to reflect that there is a Judgment, and that virtue and vice lie in our own power. (Such a) life works numberless evils, it makes men beasts, and more irrational than beasts: for what things are in each several nature of the beasts, these it has often collected together in one man, and turned everything upside down. This is why the devil has brought in the doctrine of Fate: this is why he has said that the world is without a Providence (Hom. ii. p. 15): this is

why he advances his hypothesis of good natures, and evil natures, and his hypothesis of evil (uncreated and) without beginning, and material (in its essence): and, in short, all the rest of it, that he may ruin our life. For it is not possible for a man who is of such a life either to recover himself from corrupt doctrines, or to remain in a sound faith: but of inevitable necessity he must receive all this. For I do not think, for my part, that of those who do not live aright, there could be easily found any who do not hold numberless satanical devices—as, that there is a nativity (or birth-fate) (γένεσις), that things happen at random, that all is hap-hazard and chance-medley. Wherefore I beseech you let us have a care for good living, that we may not receive evil doctrines. Cain received for punishment that he should be (ever) groaning and trembling. (Gen. iv. 14.) Such are the wicked, and being conscious within themselves of numberless bad things, often they start out of their sleep, their thoughts are full of tumult, their eyes full of perturbation; everything is fraught for them with misgivings, everything alarms them, their soul is replete with grievous expectation and cowardly apprehension, contracted with impotent fear and trembling. Nothing can be more effeminate than such a soul, nothing more inane.[2] Like madmen, it has no self-possession. For it were well for it that in the enjoyment of calm and quiet it were enabled to take knowledge of its proper nobility. But when all things terrify and throw it into perturbation, dreams, and words, and gestures, and forebodings, indiscriminately, when will it be able to look into itself, being thus troubled and amazed? Let us therefore do away with its fear, let us break asunder its bonds. For were there no other punishment, what punishment could exceed this—to be living always in fear, never to have confidence, never to be at ease? Therefore knowing these things assuredly, let us keep ourselves in a state of calm and be careful to practise virtue, that maintaining both sound doctrines and an upright life, we may without offence pass through this life present, and be enabled to attain unto the good things which God hath promised to them that love Him, through the grace and mercy of His only-begotten Son, with Whom to the Father and the Holy Ghost together be glory, might, honor, now and ever, world without end. Amen.

---

[1] Κἂν φανερῶς οὐ καταγινώσκῃ (B. C. -ει) διὰ το δόγμα, αλλ᾽ ἀποδέχεται κ. τ. λ. Ben. retains this, in the sense, *saltem aperte non damnabit propter dogma:* taking κἂν in different senses in this and the former clause. Ed. Par. Ben. 2, *Legendum videtur* φανερῶς οὖν καταγ. *Licet sit quispiam valde efferus, licet aperte ob dogma condemnet, at clam* etc. Erasm. *Etiam si per dogma non condemnetur.* The emendation is sure and easy: κἂν φανερῶς ΣΟΥ καταγινώσκῃ. So below. Πολλοὶ δὲ καὶ καταγινώσκοντες αὐτῶν διὰ τὸ δόγμα, αἰδοῦνται διὰ τον βίον.

[2] Old text ἐξηχότερον: a word unknown to the Lexicons, and of doubtful meaning. If we could suppose a comparative of the perfect participle in κως (analogous to the comparison of ἐρρωμένος and ἄσμενος), ἐξεστηκότερον would suit the sense very well: but such a form seems to be quite unexampled.—Mod. text ἀνοηπότερον. Then: "Even as madmen have no self-possession, so this has no self-possession. When therefore is this to come to consciousness of itself, having such a dizziness: which it were well," etc.

HOMILY XLVIII.

ACTS XXII. 17-20.

"And it came to pass, that, when I was come again to Jerusalem, even while I prayed in the temple, I was in a trance; and saw him saying unto me, Make haste, and get thee quickly out of Jerusalem: for they will not receive thy testimony concerning me. And I said, Lord, they know that I imprisoned and beat in every synagogue them that believed on thee: and when the blood of thy martyr Stephen was shed, I also was standing by, and consenting unto his death, and kept the raiment of them that slew him."

SEE how he thrusts himself (into danger). I came, he says, after that vision, "to Jerusalem. I was in a trance," etc. Again, this is without witness: but observe, the witness follows from the result. He said, "They will not receive thy testimony:" they did not receive it. And yet from calculations of reason the surmise should have been this, that they would assuredly receive him. For I was the man that made war upon the Christians: so that they ought to have received him. Here he establishes two things: both that they are without excuse, since they persecuted him contrary to all likelihood or calculation of reason; and, that Christ was God, as prophesying things contrary to expectation, and as not looking to past things, but foreknowing the things to come. How then does He say, "He shall bear My name before the Gentiles and kings and children of Israel?" (Acts ix. 15.) Not, certainly persuade. Besides which, on other occasions we find the Jews were persuaded, but here they were not. Where most of all they ought to have been persuaded, as knowing his former zeal (in their cause), here they were not persuaded. "And when the blood of Thy martyr Stephen," etc. See where again his discourse terminates, namely, in the forcible main point (εἰς τὸ ἰσχυρὸν κεφάλαιον): that it was he that persecuted, and not only persecuted but killed, nay, had he ten thousand hands (μυρίαις χερσὶν ἀναιρῶν) would have used them all to kill Stephen. He reminded them of the murderous spirit heinously indulged (by him and them). Then of course above all they would not endure him, since this convicted them; and truly the prophecy was having its fulfilment: great the zeal, vehement the accusation, and the Jews themselves witnesses of the truth of Christ!

"And he said unto me, Depart: for I will send thee far hence unto the Gentiles. And they gave him audience unto this word, and then lifted up their voices, and said, Away with such a fellow from the earth: for it is not fit that he should live." (v. 21, 22.) The Jews [1] would not endure to hear out all his harangue,[*] but excessively fired by their wrath, they shouted, it says, "Away with him; for it is not fit that he should live. And as they cried out, and cast off their clothes, and threw dust into the air, the tribune commanded him to be brought into the castle, and bade that he should be examined by scourging; that he might know wherefore they cried so against him." (v. 23, 24.) Whereas both the tribune ought to have examined whether these things were so—yes, and the Jews themselves too —or, if they were not so, to have ordered him to be scourged, he "bade examine him by scourging, that he might know for what cause they so clamored against him." And yet he ought to have learnt from those clamorers, and to have asked whether they laid hold upon aught of the things spoken: instead of that, without more ado he indulges his arbitrary will and pleasure, and acts with a view to gratify them: for he did not look to this, how he should do a righteous thing, but only how he might stop their rage unrighteous as it was. "And as they bound him with thongs,[†] Paul said unto the centurion that stood by, Is it

[1] The sense is confused in old text by misplacing the portions of sacred text. Mod. text "witnesses of the truth of Christ speaking boldly. But the Jews," etc. v. 21-24, which verses are followed in old text by φησιν· αἶρε αὐτὸν οὐ γὰρ καθῆκει αὐτὸν ζῆν. Below, mod. text "or the Jews themselves also," and omits "or if it were not so, to have ordered him to be scourged."

[*] The words, "I will send thee to the *Gentiles*," were those at which the Jews took offence. That a word should come from heaven to Paul in the Temple, commanding him to leave the chosen people and the Holy City and go to the uncircumcised heathen, was a statement verging upon blasphemy. This admission they would regard as proof of Paul's apostasy from Moses. It implied that he regarded the heathen as standing upon the same plane as themselves. The thought roused all their native bigotry. Beyond "this word" they would not hear him, nor did they think that one who should so estimate the privileges and character of the Jews as compared with the Gentiles was fit to live.—G. B. S.

[†] Προέτειναν αὐτὸν τοῖς ἱμᾶσιν is commonly rendered, as here, "When they stretched him out, or bound him with thongs." But this rendering seems to overlook the force of πρό in the verb and the force of the article τοῖς. The preferable interpretation seems to be, (Thayer's Lex.): "When they had stretched him out for the thongs, i. e. to receive the blows of the thongs, by tying him up to a beam or pillar." (So Meyer, DeWette, Lechler, Gloag).—G. B. S.

lawful for you to scourge a man that is a Roman, and uncondemned?" (v. 25.) Paul lied not, God forbid: for he was a Roman:[1] if there was nothing else, he would have been afraid (to pretend this), lest he should be found out, and suffer a worse punishment. (See Sueton. Vit. Claud. § 25.) And observe, he does not say it peremptorily (ἁπλῶς), but, "Is it lawful for you?" The charges brought are two, both its being without examination, and his being a Roman. They held this as a great privilege at that time: for they say that (it was only) from the time of Hadrian that all[2] were named Romans, but of old it was not so. He would have been contemptible had he been scourged: but as it is, he puts *them* into greater fear (than they him). Had they scourged him, they would also have dismissed[3] the whole matter, or even have killed him; but as it is, the result is not so. See how God permits many (good results) to be brought about quite in a human way, both in the case of the Apostles and of the rest (of mankind). Mark how they suspected the thing to be a pretext,[4] and that in calling himself a Roman, Paul lied: perhaps surmising this from his poverty. "When the centurion heard that, he went and told the tribune, saying, Take heed what thou doest: for this man is a Roman. Then the tribune came, and said unto him, Tell me, art thou a Roman? He said, Yea. And the tribune answered, With a great sum obtained I this freedom. And Paul said, But I was free born. Then straightway they departed from him which should have examined him: and the tribune also was afraid, after he knew that he was a Roman, and because he had bound him." (v. 26-29.)—"But I," he says, "was free

born." So then his father also was a Roman. What then comes of this? He bound him, and brought him down to the Jews.[5] "On the morrow, because he would have known the certainty whereof he was accused of the Jews, he loosed him from his bands, and commanded the chief priests and all their council to appear, and brought Paul down, and set him before them." (v. 30.) He discourses not now to the multitude, nor to the people. "And Paul, earnestly beholding the council, said, Men and brethren, I have lived in all good conscience before God until this day." (ch. xxiii. 1.) What he means is this: I am not conscious to myself of having wronged you at all, or of having done anything worthy of these bonds. What then said the high priest?[6] Right justly, and ruler-like, and mildly: "And the high priest Ananias commanded them that stood by him to smite him on the mouth. Then said Paul unto him, God shall smite thee, thou whited wall: for sittest thou to judge me after the law, and commandest me to be smitten contrary to the law? And they that stood by said, Revilest thou God's high priest? Then said Paul, I wist not, brethren, that he was the high priest: for it is written, Thou shalt not speak evil of the ruler of thy people."[7] (v. 3-5.) Because "I knew not that he was high priest." Some say, Why then does he defend himself as if it was matter of accusation, and adds, "Thou shalt not speak evil of the ruler of thy people?" For if he were not the ruler, was it right for no better reason than that to abuse (him or any) other? He says himself, "Being reviled, we bless; being persecuted, we suffer it" (1 Cor. iv. 12); but here he does the contrary, and not only reviles, but curses.[8] They are the words of boldness, rather than of anger; he did not choose to appear in a contemptible light to the tribune. For suppose the tribune himself had spared to scourge him, only as he was about to be delivered up to the Jews, his being beaten by their servants would have more emboldened him: this is why Paul does not attack the servant, but the person who gave the order. But that saying, "Thou

---

[1] Mod. text entirely mistaking the sense, interpolates, "On which account also the tribune fears on hearing it. And why, you will say, did he fear?" as if it meant, The tribune would have been afraid to be condemned for this, etc.

[2] Meaning that all provincial subjects of the Roman Empire came to be called Romans, only in the time of this Emperor: therefore in St. Paul's time it was a great thing to be able to call one's self a Roman. If it means, "All the citizens of Tarsus," the remark is not apposite. Certain it is that Tarsus, an *urbs libera* by favor of M. Anthony, enjoyed neither *jus colon-iarum* nor *jus civitatis* until long afterwards, and the Apostle was not a Roman because a citizen of Tarsus. This however is not the point of St. Chrysostom's remark. In the Catena and Œcumen. it will be seen, that in later times the extended use of the name "Roman" as applied to all subjects of the Roman Empire made a difficulty in the understanding of this passage. Thus Ammonius takes it that St. Paul was a "Roman," because a native of Tarsus which was subject to the Romans (so Œc.): and that the Jews themselves for the like reason were Romans; but these scorned the appellation as a badge of servitude; Paul on the contrary avouched it, setting an example of submission to the powers that be.—After this sentence mod. text interpolates, "Or also he called himself a Roman to escape punishment: for," etc.

[3] παρέπεμψαν ἄν: mod. text (after Cat.) needlessly alters to παρέτρεψαν.

[4] πρόφασιν εἶναι τὸ πρᾶγμα καὶ τὸ εἰπεῖν αὐτὸν ʹΡωμαῖον τὸν Παῦλον· καὶ ἴσως. . . . We read τῷ εἰπεῖν and καὶ ψεύδεσθαι τὸν Π. ἴσως. "But the tribune by answering, 'with a great sum,' etc., shows that he suspected it to be a pretext, Paul's saying that he was a Roman: and perhaps he surmised this from Paul's apparent insignificance."

[5] Mod. text interpolates: "So far was it from being a false-hood, his saying, etc., that he also gained by it, being loosed from his chains. And in what way, hear." And below, altering the sense: "He no longer speaks to the tribune, but to the multitude and the whole people."

[6] Mod. text "When he ought to have been pricked to the heart, because (Paul) had been unjustly bound to gratify them, he even adds a further wrong, and commands him to be beaten: which is plain from the words subjoined."

[7] Mod. text "Now some say, that he knowing it speaks ironically (or feigns ignorance, εἰρωνεύεται); but it seems to me, that he did not at all know that it was the high priest: otherwise he would even have honored him: wherefore," etc. In old text τινές φασι, placed before ὅτι οὐκ ᾔδειν, κ. τ. λ. requires to be transposed.

[8] Mod. text "Away with the thought: he appears to have done neither the one nor the other: but to one accurately considering it, the words," etc.

whited wall, and dost thou sit to judge me after the law?" (is) instead of, Being (thyself) a culprit: as if he had said, And (thyself) worthy of stripes without number. See accordingly how greatly they were struck with his boldness; for whereas the point was to have overthrown the whole matter, they rather commend him.[1] (*infra*, v. 9.) "For it is written," etc. He wishes to show that he thus speaks, not from fear, nor because (Ananias) did not deserve to be called this, but from obedience to the law in this point also. And indeed I am fully persuaded that he did not know that it was the high priest,[2] since he had returned now after a long interval, and was not in the habit of constant intercourse with the Jews; seeing him too in the midst among many others: for the high priest was no longer easy to be seen at a glance, there being many of them and diverse.* So, it seems to me, in this also he spoke with a view to his plea against them: by way of showing that he does obey the law; therefore he (thus) exculpates himself.

(Recapitulation.) (*b*) But let us review what has been said. (*a*) "And when I was came again to Jerusalem," etc. (v. 17.) How was it,[3] that being a Jew, and there brought up and taught, he did not stay there? Nor did he abide there, unless he had a mind to furnish numberless occasions against him:

everywhere just like an exile, fleeing about from place to place. (*c*) "While I prayed in the temple," he says, "it came to pass that I was in a trance." (To show) that it was not simply a phantom of the imagination, therefore "while he prayed" (the Lord) stood by him. And he shows that it was not from fear of their dangers that he fled, but because they would "not receive" his "testimony." (v. 18.) But why said he "They know I imprisoned?" (v. 19.) Not to gainsay Christ, but because he wished to learn this which was so contrary to all reasonable expectation. Christ, however, did not teach him (this),[4] but only bade him depart, and he obeys: so obedient is he. "And they lifted up their voices," it says, "and said, Away with him: it is not fit that this fellow should live." (v. 22.) Nay, ye are the persons not fit to live; not he, who in everything obeys God. O villains and murderers! "And shaking out their clothes," it says, "they threw dust into the air" (v. 23), to make insurrection more fierce, because they wished to frighten the governor.† And observe; they do not say what the charge was, as in fact they had nothing to allege, but only think to strike terror by their shouting. "The tribune commanded," etc. and yet he ought to have learnt from the accusers, "wherefore they cried so against him. And as they bound him, etc. And the chief captain was afraid, after he learnt that he was a Roman." Why then it was no falsehood. "On the morrow, because he would know the certainty wherefore he was accused of the Jews, etc., he brought him down before the council." (v. 24–30.) This he should have done at the outset. He brought him in, loosed. This above all the Jews would not know what to make of.[5] "And Paul," it says, "earnestly beholding them." It shows his boldness, and how it awed them (τὸ ἐντρεπτικόν). "Then the high priest Ananias," etc. (ch. xxiii. 1, 2.) Why, what has he said that

---

[1] Παραινοῦσι, all our Mss. But Erasm. *debacchantur*, and all the Edd. παροινοῦσιν, contrary to the sense.

[2] Other interpretations are given in the Catena and Œcum. "Anonym.: The high priest being a hypocrite deserved to be called a 'whited wall.' Whence also Paul says he did not even know him as high priest, since it is the work of a high priest to save the flock put under his charge: but this man made havoc upon it, etc. Severus: Paul justly reproached him, but then, as if repenting, said: 'I knew not,' etc. Not know that he was high priest? Then how saidst thou, 'And sittest thou to judge me?'—But he pretends ignorance: an ignorance which does no harm, but is an 'economy' (οἰκονομοῦσαν): for reserve (μεταχειρισμὸς) may be more forcible than speaking out (παρρησία): an unseasonable παρρησία often hinders the truth: a seasonable μεταχ. as often advances it."

* Other methods of dealing with Paul's much debated statement: "I did not know that he was the high priest," besides the view given in the text (with which agree Beza, Wolff, Lechler, *et al.*) are: (1) Paul did not perceive who it was that addressed him and thus did not know that it was the high priest whom he rebuked (Alford). (2) Paul did not acknowledge Ananias to be high priest; he would not recognize so unjust a man as a real high priest (Calvin, Meyer, Stier). (3) Ananias was not high priest at this time (Lightfoot, Whiston, Lewin). (4) Paul did not recollect or consider that it was the high priest whom he was addressing (Bengel, Olshausen, Neander, Schaff, Hackett, Conybeare and Howson, Gloag). In this view Paul apologizes for his rash words, spoken inadvertently and without reflection, by adding: "for it is written, Thou shalt not speak evil of the ruler of thy people." Baur and Zeller suppose that the apostle never said what he is reported as saying. The choice appears to lie between views (2) and (4).—G. B. S.

[3] Mod. text omits the whole of the portion marked (*a*). The sense is: St. Paul is concerned to explain how it was that having been bred and taught in Jerusalem, he did not remain there. It was by command of Christ in a vision that he departed. In fact he could not stay there unless, etc. Accordingly we find him everywhere fleeing about from place to place, like one exiled from his own land. The words which are corrupt, are: οὐκ ἐκεῖ ἔμενεν; οὐδὲ ἐκεῖ διέτριβεν (οὐδὲ γὰρ ἐξῆν ἐκεῖ διατρίβειν?) εἰ μὴ μυρία κατ' αὐτῶν (αὑτοῦ A) κατασκενάσαι (sic) ἤθελε πανταχοῦ· καθάπερ τις φυγὰς περιφυγών.

[4] τὸ οὕτω παράδοξον, viz. that the Jews would not receive the testimony of one, who from his known history had, of all men, the greatest claim to be heard by them: "'Lord, they know,' etc., therefore surely they will listen to me." (So St. Chrysostom constantly interprets these words: see *Cat. in loco*.) But Christ did not gratify his wish for information on this point: He only bade him depart.—The innovator, who has greatly disfigured this Homily by numerous interpolations, has here: "did not teach him what he must do."

† Better: "they cast off their clothes" as a signal of their anger and readiness to stone Paul. Others understand it to mean: waving their garments as a signal of their assent to the exclamations against Paul of those who were near.—G. B. S.

[5] τοῦτο μάλιστα ἠπόρησαν ἂν οἱ Ἰουδαῖοι: i. e. perhaps "they would be at a loss to know the reason of his being brought before them ere they loosed, not knowing what had passed between him and the tribune." Mod. text amplifies: "This he ought to have done at the outset, and neither to have bound him, nor have wished to scourge him, but to have left him, as having done nothing such as that he should be put in bonds. 'And he loosed him,' it says, etc. This above all the Jews knew not what to make of."

was affronting? What is he beaten for? Why what hardihood, what shamelessness! Therefore (Paul) set him down (with a rebuke): "God shall smite thee thou whited wall." (v. 3.) Accordingly (Ananias) himself is put to a stand, and dares not say a word: only those about him could not bear Paul's boldness. They saw a man ready to die [1] * * * for if this was the case, (Paul) had but to hold his peace, and the tribune would have taken him, and gone his way; he would have sacrificed him to them. He both shows that he suffers willingly what he suffers, and thus excuses himself before them, not that he wished to excuse himself to them—since as for those, he even strongly condemns them— but for the sake of the people. [2] "Violating the law, commandest thou me to be beaten?" Well may he say so: for to kill a man who had done (them) no injury, and that an innocent person, was a violating of the law. For neither was it abuse that was spoken by him, unless one would call Christ's words abusive, when He says, "Woe unto you, Scribes and Pharisees, for ye are like unto whited walls." (Matt. xxiii. 27.) True, you will say: but if he had said it before he had been beaten, it would have betokened not anger, but boldness. But I have mentioned the reason of this. [3] And (at this rate) we often find Christ Himself "speaking abusively" to the Jews when abused by them; as when He says, "Do not think that I will accuse you." (John v. 45.) But this is not abuse, God forbid. See, with what gentleness he addresses these men: "I wist not," he says, "that he was God's high priest" (v. 4, 5): and, (to show) that he was not dissembling (εἰρωνεύεται), he adds, "Thou shalt not speak evil of the ruler of thy people." He even confesses him to be still ruler. Let us also learn the gentleness also, [4] that in both the one and the other we may be perfect. For one must look narrowly into them, to learn what the one is and what the other: narrowly, because these virtues have their corresponding vices hard by them: mere forwardness passing itself off for boldness, mere cowardice for gentleness: [5] and need being to scan them, lest any person possessing the vice should seem to have the virtue: which would be just as if a person should fancy that he was cohabiting with the mistress, and not know that it was the servant-maid. What then is gentleness, and what mere cowardice? When others are wronged, and we do not take their part, but hold our peace, this is cowardice: when we are the persons ill-treated, and we bear it, this is gentleness. What is boldness? Again the same, when others are the persons for whom we contend. What forwardness? When it is in our own cause that we are willing to fight. So that magnanimity and boldness go together, as also (mere) forwardness and (mere) cowardice. For he that (does not) resent on his own behalf, [6] will hardly but resent on behalf of others: and he that does not stand up for his own cause, will hardly fail to stand up for others. For when our habitual disposition is pure from passion, it admits virtue also. Just as a body when free from fever admits strength, so the soul, unless it be corrupted by the passions, admits strength. It betokens great strength, this gentleness; it needs a generous and a gallant soul, and one of exceeding loftiness, this gentleness. Or, think you, is it a small thing to suffer ill, and not be exasperated? Indeed one would not err if in speaking of the disposition to stand up for our neighbors, one should call it the spirit of manly courage. For he that has had the strength to be able to overcome so strong a passion (as this of selfishness), will have the strength to dare the attack on another. For instance, these are two passions, cowardice and anger: if thou have overcome anger, it is very plain that thou overcomest cowardice also: but thou gettest the mastery over anger, by being gentle: therefore (do so) with cowardice also, and thou wilt be manly. Again, if thou hast not got the better of anger, thou art become

---

[1] εἶδον ἄνθρωπον θανατῶντα· εἰ γὰρ τοῦτο ἦν, κἂν ἐσίγησεν· καὶ λαβὼν αὐτὸν ἀπῆλθεν· κἂν ἐξέδωκεν αὐτὸν αὐτοῖς ὁ χιλίαρχος. The meaning (see above p. 289.) may be: "The wrong was not to be put up with, for to hold his peace under such treatment would have been to embolden the tribune to sacrifice him to his enemies, as a person who might be insulted with impunity." But the passage is corrupt: perhaps it should be οὐκ (mod. text has οὕτως) εἶδον ἄνθρ. θαν. "They did not see before them one who was willing to die, i. e. to let them take away his life. For if this were the case, he had but to hold his peace, and the tribune would," etc. Mod. text "In such wise saw they a man ready to die; and they would not endure it. 'I knew not that he was the high priest.' Why then: the rebuke was of ignorance. For if this were not the case, κἂν λαβὼν αὐτὸν ἀπῆλθε καὶ οὐκ ἐσίγησε, κἂν ἐξέδωκεν, κ. τ. λ."

[2] Mod. text quite perverting the sense: "Obeying the law, not from a wish to show (ἐνδείξασθαι) to them: for those he had even strongly condemned. For the law's sake, therefore, he defends himself, not for the sake of the people, with reason," etc.

[3] Viz. it was because he did not choose to let the tribune despise him, p. 289. And so mod. text adds, ὅτι οὐκ ἐβούλετο καταφρονηθῆναι.

[4] Μάθωμεν καὶ τὴν ἐπιείκειαν, i. e. Paul's, as well as his παρρησία. Mod. text "Let us then also learn gentleness."

[5] ὅτι παρυφεστᾶσιν αὐταῖς αἱ κακίαι, τῇ μὲν παρρησίᾳ θρασύτης τῇ δὲ ἐπιεικείᾳ ἀνανδρία. It is seldom possible to match the ethical terms of one language with exact equivalents in another. Here θρασύτης, as opposed to παρρησία "courage in speaking one's mind," is not merely "audacity," or "hardihood," or "pugnacity," or "the spirit of the bully," though it may be applied to all these. On the whole, "forwardness" seems to be most suitable for the antithesis: the one character comes forward boldly and speaks up in the cause of truth and justice: the other thrusts itself forward, in its own cause, for resentment of wrongs done to one's self. Below, in connection with ἀνανδρία it means what we call "bullying."

[6] All our Mss. ὁ γὰρ ὑπὲρ ἑαυτοῦ μὴ ἀλγῶν, δυσκόλως ὑπὲρ ἑτέρων ἀλγήσει, but Sav. marg. οὐκ ἀλγήσει: which we adopt as indispensable to the sense. In the next sentence, C. omits the μὴ before ἀμύνων, and A. the οὐκ before ἀμυνεῖται.

forward (and pugnacious); but not having got the better of this, neither canst thou get the better of fear; consequently, thou wilt be a coward too: and the case is the same as with the body; if it be weak, it is quickly overcome both by cold and heat: for such is the ill temperament, but the good temperament is able to stand all (changes). Again, greatness of soul is a virtue, and hard by it stands prodigality: economy is a virtue, the being a good manager; hard by it stands parsimony and meanness. Come, let us again collate and compare the virtues (with their vices). Well, then, the prodigal person is not to be called great-minded. How should he? The man who is overcome by numberless passions, how should he be great of soul? For this is not despising money; it is only the being ordered about by other passions: for just as a man, if he were at the beck and bidding of robbers to obey their orders, could not be free (so it is here). His large spending does not come of his contempt of money, but simply from his not knowing how to dispose of it properly: else, were it possible both to keep it and to lay it out on his pleasure, this is what he would like. But he that spends his money on fit objects, this is the man of high soul: for it is truly a high soul, that which is not in slavery to passion, which accounts money to be nothing. Again, economy is a good thing: for thus that will be the best manager, who spends in a proper manner, and not at random without management. But parsimony is not the same thing with this. For the former[1] indeed, not even when an urgent necessity demands, touches the principal of his money: but the latter will be brother to the former. Well, then, we will put together the man of great soul, and the prudent economist, as also the prodigal and the mean man: for both of these are thus affected from littleness of soul, as those others are (from the opposite). Let us not then call him high-souled, who simply spends, but him who spends aright: nor let us call the economical manager mean and parsimonious, but him who is unseasonably sparing of his money. What a quantity of wealth that rich man spent, "who was clothed in purple and fine linen?" (Luke xvi. 19.) But he was not high-souled: for his soul was possessed by an unmerciful disposition and by numberless lusts: how then should it be great? Abraham had a great soul, spending as he did for the reception of his guests, killing the calf, and, where need was, not only not sparing his property, but not even his life. If then we see a person having his sumptuous table, having his harlots and his parasites, let us not call him a man of a great mind, but a man of an exceedingly little mind. For see how many passions he is enslaved and subject to—gluttony, inordinate pleasure, flattery: but him who is possessed by so many, and cannot even escape one of them, how can any one call magnanimous? Nay, then most of all let us call him little-minded, when he spends the most: for the more he spends, the more does he show the tyranny of those passions: for had they not excessively got the mastery over him, he would not have spent to excess. Again, if we see a person, giving nothing to such people as these, but feeding the poor, and succoring those in need, himself keeping a mean table—him let us call an exceedingly high-souled man: for it is truly a mark of a great soul, to despise one's own comfort, but to care for that of others. For tell me, if you should see a person despising all tyrants, and holding their commands of no account, but rescuing from their tyranny those who are oppressed and evil entreated; would you not think this a great man? So let us account of the man in this case also. The passions are the tyrant: if then we despise them, we shall be great: but if we rescue others also from them, we shall be far greater, as being sufficient not only for ourselves, but for others also. But if any one, at a tyrant's bidding, beat some other of his subjects, is this greatness of soul? No, indeed: but the extreme of slavery, in proportion as he is great. And now also there is set before us (πρόκειται) a soul that is a noble one and a free: but this the prodigal has ordered to be beaten by his passions: the man then that beats himself, shall we call high-souled? By no means. Well then * *, but let us see what is greatness of soul, and what prodigality; what is economy, and what meanness; what is gentleness, and (what) dulness and cowardice; what boldness, and what forwardness: that having distinguished these things from each other, we may be enabled to pass (this life) well-pleasing to the Lord, and to attain unto the good things promised, through the grace and mercy of our Lord Jesus Christ, to Whom be the glory for ever and ever. Amen.

---

[1] Ἐκεῖνος μὲν γὰρ οὐδὲ ἀναγκαίας ἀπαιτούσης χρείας, τῆς οὐσίας ἅπτεται τῶν χρημάτων, οὗτος δὲ ἐκείνου γένοιτο ἂν ἀδελφός. We leave this as it stands, evidently corrupt. Something is wanting after οὗτος δὲ. "The former, the οἰκονομικὸς, is careful not to touch his principal or capital, but will confine his outlay within his income: the latter," etc. But οὐδὲ ἀναγκ. ἀπ. χρείας is hardly suitable in the former case, and should rather come after οὗτος δέ "the latter, the niggard, though the need be ever so urgent, has not the heart to touch either principal or income"—or something to that effect. Then perhaps, πῶς οὖν οὗτος ἐκείνου γένοιτο ἂν ἀδελφός; Mod. text "For the former spends all upon proper objects; the latter, not even when urgent need requires, touches the principal of his money. The οἰκον. therefore will to brother to the μεγαλόψ."

HOMILY XLIX.[1]

ACTS. XXIII. 6–8.

"But when Paul perceived that the one part were Sadducees, and the other Pharisees, he cried out in the council, Men and brethren, I am a Pharisee, the son of a Pharisee: of the hope and resurrection of the dead I am called in question. And when he had so said, there arose a dissension between the Pharisees and the Sadducees: and the multitude was divided. For the Sadducees say that there is no resurrection, neither angel, nor spirit: but the Pharisees confess both."

AGAIN he discourses simply as man, and he does not on all occasions alike enjoy the benefit of supernatural aid. "I am a Pharisee, the son of a Pharisee:"[2] both in this, and in what comes after it, he wished to divide the multitude, which had an evil unanimity against him. And he does not speak a falsehood here either: for he was a Pharisee by descent from his ancestors. "Of the hope and resurrection of the dead I am called in question." For since they would not say for what reason they arraigned him, he is compelled therefore to declare it himself. "But the Pharisees," it says, "confess both." And yet there are three things: how then does he say both? "Spirit and Angel" is put as one.[3] When he is on their side, then they plead for him. "And there arose a great cry: and the scribes that were of the Pharisees' part arose, and strove, saying, We find no evil in this man: but" (what) "if a spirit has spoken to him, or an angel?"[4] * (v. 9.) Why did they

not plead for him before this? Do you observe, how, when the passions give way, the truth is discovered? Where is the crime, say they, if an angel has spoken to him, or a spirit? Paul gives them no handle against him. "And when there arose a great dissension, the tribune, fearing lest Paul should have been pulled in pieces of them, commanded the soldiers to go down, and to take him by force from among them, and to bring him into the castle." (v. 10.) The tribune is afraid of his being pulled in pieces, now that he has said that he is a Roman: and the matter was not without danger. Do you observe that Paul had a right to profess himself a Roman? Else, neither would (the tribune) have been afraid now. So it remains that the soldiers must bear him off by force. But when the wretches saw all to be without avail, they take the whole matter into their own hands, as they would fain have done before, but were prevented: and their wickedness stops nowhere, though it received so many checks: and yet how many things were providentially ordered, on purpose that they might settle down from their rage, and learn those things through which they might possibly recover themselves! But none the less do they set upon him. Sufficient for proof of his innocence was even this, that the man was saved when at the point to be pulled in pieces, and that with these so great dangers about him, he escaped them all. "And the night following the Lord stood by him, and said, Be of good cheer, Paul: for as thou hast testified of Me in Jerusalem, so must thou bear witness also at Rome. And when it was day, certain of the Jews banded together, and bound themselves under a curse, saying that they would neither eat nor drink till they had killed Paul.

---

[1] This Homily is wanting in C. The mod. text swarms with interpolations.

[2] καὶ ἐν τούτῳ, viz. in saying "I am a Pharisee," καὶ ἐν τῷ μετὰ ταῦτα, i. e. "Of the hope of resurrection," etc. Mod. text "but is also permitted to contribute somewhat of himself, which also he does and καὶ ἐν τ., καὶ ἐν τῷ μ. τ. both on this occasion and on that which followed (?) he pleads for himself, wishing," etc.

[3] Mod. text "Either because spirit and angel is one, or because the term ἀμφότερα is taken not only of two but of three." (This is taken from Ammonius in the Catena. The innovator adds): "the writer therefore uses it καταχρηστικῶς, and not according to strict propriety."

[4] The last clause in the Vulgate text, μὴ θεομαχῶμεν, is unknown to St. Chrys., being in fact quite a modern addition. Chrys. interprets it as an aposiopesis—viz. ποῖον ἔγκλημα; St. Isidore of Pelusium in the Cat. τὸ γὰρ εἰ ἤ ἐστι· τοῦτ' ἐστιν, ἤ πν. ἐλάλησεν αὐτῷ ἤ ἄγγελος. Ammonius ibid. "Either the sentence is left incomplete, viz. but whether a spirit or an angel has spoken to him. . . is not certain: or, it is to be spoken as on the part of the Pharisees, Εἴδε (?) πν. κ. τ. λ. that is, Behold, he is manifestly asserting the resurrection, taught (κατηχηθείς) either by the Holy Ghost or by an angel the doctrine of the resurrection." Mod. text using the latter: "Where is the crime, if an angel has spoken to him, if a spirit, and taught (κατηχηθείς) by him, he thus teaches the doctrine of the resurrection?" (and then, adopting the modern addition μὴ θεομ.), "then let us not stand off from him, lest warring with him, we be found also fighting against God."

* The Pharisees were uniformly more favorably inclined to

Christianity than the rival sect of the Sadducees. The latter, as disbelieving in the resurrection and the spirit-world, would be especially prejudiced against a system which made these tenets so central. The Pharisees, on the other hand, agreed on these points with Christianity. It is evident that in his defence here before the Sanhedrin Paul wishes to conciliate the Pharisaic party so far as can be done by emphasizing his own agreement with them respecting the resurrection. They, as believers in this doctrine, would have less prejudice against Paul's teaching concerning Christ's resurrection. In asserting his Pharisaic ancestry, Paul wishes to establish a point of connection with them and thus gain a foothold for the defence of his central truth of Christ's resurrection, which justifies him in being His disciple and servant.—G. B. S.

And they were more than forty which had made this conspiracy." (v. 11-13.) "They bound themselves under a curse," it says. See how vehement and revengeful they are in their malice! What means, "bound under a curse?"[1] Why then those men are accused forever, seeing they did not kill Paul. And forty together. For such is the nature of that nation: when there needs concerting together for a good object, not even two concur with each other: but when it is for an evil object, the entire people does it. And they admit the rulers also as accomplices. "And they came to the chief priests and elders, and said, We have bound ourselves under a great curse, that we will eat nothing until we have slain Paul. Now therefore ye with the council signify to the tribune that he bring him down unto you to-morrow, as though ye would enquire something more perfectly concerning him: and we, or ever he come near, are ready to kill him. And when Paul's sister's son heard of their lying in wait, he went and entered into the castle, and told Paul. Then Paul called one of the centurions unto him, and said, Bring this young man unto the tribune: For he hath a certain thing to tell him. So he took him, and brought him to the tribune, and said, Paul the prisoner called me unto him, and prayed me to bring this young man unto thee, who hath something to say unto thee. Then the tribune took him by the hand, and went with him aside privately, and asked him, What is that thou hast to tell me? And he said, the Jews have agreed to desire thee that thou wouldest bring down Paul to-morrow into the council, as though they would enquire somewhat of him more perfectly. But do not thou yield unto them: for there lie in wait for him of them more than forty men, which have bound themselves with an oath, that they will neither eat nor drink till they have killed him: and now are they ready, looking for a promise from thee. So the tribune then let the young man depart, and charged him, See thou tell no man that thou hast showed these things to me." (v. 14-22). Again he is saved by man's forethought. And observe: Paul lets no man learn this, not even the centurion, that the matter might not become known. And the centurion having come, reported to the tribune. And it is well done of the tribune also, that he bids him keep it secret, that it might not become known: moreover he gives his orders to the centurions only at the time when the thing was to be done: and so Paul

is sent into Cæsarea, that there too he might discourse in a greater theatre and before a more splendid audience: that so the Jews may not be able to say, "If we had seen Paul, we would have believed—if we had heard him teaching." Therefore this excuse too is cut off from them. "And the Lord," it said, "stood by him, and said, Be of good cheer: for as thou hast testified of Me in Jerusalem, so must thou bear witness also at Rome." (Yet) even after He has appeared to him, He again suffers him to be saved by man's means. And one may well be astonished at Paul;[2] he was not taken aback, neither said, "Why, what is this? Have I then been deceived by Christ?" but he believed: yet, because he believed, he did not therefore sleep: no; what was in his own power by means of human wisdom, he did not abandon. "Bound themselves by a curse:" it was a kind of necessity that those men fastened on themselves by the curse. "That they would neither eat nor drink." Behold fasting the mother of murder! Just as Herod imposed on himself that necessity by his oath, so also do these. For such are the devil's (ways): under the pretext forsooth of piety he sets his traps. "And they came to the chief priests," etc. And yet they ought to have come (to the tribune), ought to have laid a charge, and assembled a court of justice: for these are not the doings for priests, but for captains of banditti, these are not the doings for rulers, but for ruffians. They endeavor also to corrupt the ruler: but it was providentially ordered, to the intent that he also should learn of their plot. For not (only) by their having nothing to say, but also by their secret attempt, they convicted themselves that they were naught. It is likely too that after (Paul was gone) the chief priests came to (the tribune) making their request, and were put to shame. For[3] of course he would not have liked either to deny or to grant their request. How came he to believe (the young man's tale)? He did so in consequence of what had already taken place; because it was likely they would do this also. And observe their wickedness: they as good as laid a necessity on the chief priests also: for if they undertook so great a thing themselves, and engaged themselves in the whole risk, much more ought those to do thus much. Do you observe, how Paul is

---

[1] To this question mod. text interpolates for answer from Ammonius in the Catena, "that is, they declared themselves to be out of the pale of the faith to Godward, if they should not do that which was determined against Paul."

[2] Καὶ ἄξιον ἐκπλαγῆναι τὸν Παῦλον· (A. and Cat. omit this) τί δὴ τοῦτο; οὐκ ἐθορυβήθη, οὐδὲ εἶπε. Here mod. text rightly transposes τί δὴ τοῦτο.

[3] Mod. text "And with reason the tribune does this (i. e. sends Paul away): for of course he did not wish either to gratify (χαρίσασθαι) or to assent." But the meaning is : "If he had not been informed of their plot, he would have been embarrassed by the request, not liking to refuse, nor yet to grant it."

held innocent by those that are without, as was also Christ by Pilate? See their malice brought to naught: they delivered him up, to kill and condemn him: but the result is just the contrary; he is both saved, and held innocent. For had it not been so,[1] he would have been pulled in pieces: had it not been so, he would have perished, he would have been condemned. And not only does (the tribune) rescue him from the rush (made upon him), but also from much other [2] (violence): see how he becomes a minister to him, insomuch that without risk he is carried off safe with so large a force. "And he called unto him two centurions, saying, Make ready two hundred soldiers to go to Cæsarea, and horsemen threescore and ten, and spearmen two hundred, at the third hour of the night; and provide them beasts, that they may set Paul on, and bring him safe unto Felix the governor. And he wrote a letter after this manner: Claudius Lysias unto the most excellent governor Felix sendeth greeting. This man was taken of the Jews, and should have been killed of them: then came I with an army, and rescued him, having understood that he was a Roman. And when I would have known the cause wherefore they accused him, I brought him forth into their council: whom I perceived to be accused of questions of their law, but to have nothing laid to his charge worthy of death or of bonds. And when it was told me how that the Jews laid wait for the man, I sent straightway to thee, and gave commandment to his accusers also to say before thee what they had against him. Fare ye well." (v. 23–30). See how the letter speaks for him as a defence—for it says, "I found nothing worthy of death," but as accusation against them (rather) than against him. "About to have been killed of them:" so set upon his death were they. First, "I came with the army, and rescued him:" then also "I brought him down unto them:" and not even so did they find anything to lay to his charge: and when they ought to have been stricken with fear and shame for the former act, they again attempt to kill him, insomuch that again his cause became all the more clear. "And his accusers," he says, "I have sent unto thee:" that at the tribunal where these things are more strictly examined, he may be proved guiltless.

(Recapitulation.) Let us look then to what has been said above. "I," he says, "am a Pharisee:" then, that he may not seem to pay court, he adds, "Of the hope and resurrection of the dead it is, that I am called in question." (v. 6.) From this charge and calumny he commends himself. "For the Sadducees indeed," etc. The Sadducees have no knowledge of anything incorporeal, perhaps not even God; so gross (παχεῖς) are they: whence neither do they choose to believe that there is a Resurrection. "And the scribes," etc. Look; the tribune also hears that the Pharisees have acquitted him of the charges, and have given sentence (Mss. and Edd. ἐψηφίσατο, "he gave sentence") in his favor, and with greater confidence carries him off by force. Moreover all that was spoken (by Paul) was full of right-mindedness (φιλοσοφίας). "And the night following the Lord stood by him," etc. See what strong consolation! First he praises him, "As thou hast testified to My cause in Jerusalem;" then He does not leave him to be afraid for the uncertain issue of his journey to Rome: for thither also, He saith, thou shalt not depart alone (μόνος, Cat. and Edd. μόνον), but thou shalt also have all this boldness of speech. Hereby it was made manifest, not (only) that he should be saved, but that (he should be so) in order to great crowns in the great city. But why did He not appear to him before he fell into the danger? Because it is evermore in the afflictions that God comforts us; for He appears more wished-for, while even in the dangers He exercises and trains us. Besides, he was then at ease, when free from bonds; but now great perils were awaiting him. "We have bound ourselves," they say, "under a curse, that we will not eat nor drink." (v. 14.) What is all this zeal? "That he may bring him down," it says, "unto you, as though ye would enquire into his case more perfectly." (v. 15.) Has he not twice made a speech unto you? has he not said that he is a Pharisee? What (would ye have) over and above this? So reckless were they and afraid of nothing, not tribunals, not laws: such their hardihood which shrunk from nothing. They both declare their purpose, and announce the way of carrying it into effect. "Paul's sister's son heard of it." (v. 16.) This was of God's providence, their not perceiving that it would be heard. What then did Paul? he was not alarmed, but perceived that this was God's doing: and casting all upon Him, so he acquits himself (from further concern about it:) "having called one of the centurions," etc. (v. 17.) He told of the plot, he was believed; he is saved. If he was acquitted of the charge, why did (the tribune) send the accusers? That the enquiry might be more strict: that the man might be the more entirely cleared.

---

[1] εἰ γὰρ μὴ οὕτω. Cat. οὗτος· "but for this man (the tribune.)"
[2] Mod. text omits ἀλλὰ καὶ ἄλλης πολλῆς· ὅρα πῶς.

Such are God's ways of ordering: the very things by which we are hurt, by these same are we benefited. Thus it was with Joseph: his mistress sought to ruin him: and she seemed indeed to be contriving his ruin, but by her contriving she placed him in a state of safety: for the house where that wild beast (of a woman) was kept was a den in comparison with which the prison was gentle. (Gen. xxxix. 1–20.) For while he was there, although he was looked up to and courted, he was in constant fear, lest his mistress should set upon him, and worse than any prison was the fear that lay upon him: but after the accusation he was in security and peace, well rid of that beast, of her lewdness and her machinations for his destruction: for it was better for him to keep company with human creatures in miserable plight, than with a maddened mistress. Here he comforted himself, that for chastity's sake he had fallen into it: there he had been in dread, lest he should receive a death-blow to his soul: for nothing in the world is more annoying than a woman in love can be to a young man who will not (meet her advances): nothing more detestable (than a woman in such case), nothing more fell: all the bonds in the world are light to this. So that the fact was not that he got into prison, but that he got out of prison. She made his master his foe, but she made God his friend; brought him into closer relation to Him Who is indeed the true Master; she cast him out of his stewardship in the family, but made him a familiar friend to that Master. Again, his brethren sold him (Gen. xxxvii. 18); but they freed him from having enemies dwelling in the same house with him, from envy and much ill will, and from daily machinations for his ruin: they placed him far aloof from them that hated him. For what can be worse than this, to be compelled to dwell in the same house with brethren that envy one; to be an object of suspicion, to be a mark for evil designs? So that while they and she were severally seeking to compass their own ends, far other were the mighty consequences working out by the Providence of God for that just man. When he was in honor, then was he in danger; when he was in dishonor, then was he in safety. The eunuchs did not remember him, and right well it was that they did not, that the occasion of his deliverance might be more glorious: that the whole might be ascribed, not to man's favor, but to God's Providence (Gen. xl. 23): that at the right moment, Pharaoh, reduced to need, might bring him out; that not as conferring but as receiving a benefit, the king might release him from the prison. (ib. xli. 40.) It behooved to be no servile gift, but

that the king should be reduced to a necessity of doing this: it behooved that it should be made manifest what wisdom was in him. Therefore it is that the eunuch forgets him, that Egypt might not forget him, that the king might not be ignorant of him. Had he been delivered at that time, it is likely he would have desired to depart to his own country: therefore he is kept back by numberless constraints, first by subjection to a master, secondly by being in prison, thirdly by being over the kingdom, to the end that all this might be brought about by the Providence of God. Like a spirited steed that is eager to bound off to his fellows, did God keep him back there, for causes full of glory. For that he longed to see his father, and free him from his distress, is evident from his calling him thither. (Gen. xlv. 9.)

Shall we look at other instances of evil designing, how they turn out to our good, not only by having their reward, but also by their working at the very time precisely what is for our good? This (Joseph's) uncle (Esau) had ill designs against his father (Jacob), and drove him out of his native land: what then? (Gen. xxvii. 41.) He too set him (thereby) aloof from the danger; for he too got (thereby) to be in safety. He made him a wiser and a better man ($\phi\iota\lambda o\sigma o\phi\acute{\omega}\tau\epsilon\rho o\nu$); he was the means of his having that dream (Gen. xxviii. 12.) But, you will say, he was a slave in a foreign land? Yes, but he arrives among his own kindred, and receives a bride, and appears worthy to his father-in-law. (ib. xxix. 23.) But he too cheated him? Yes, but this also turned out to his good, that he might be the father of many children. But it was in his mind to design evil against him? True, but even this was for his good, that he might thereupon return to his own country; for if he had been in good circumstances, he would not have so longed for home. But he defrauded him of his hire? Aye, but he got more by the means. (ib. xxxi. 7.) Thus, in every point of these men's history, the more people designed their hurt, the more their affairs flourished. If (Jacob) had not received the elder daughter, he would not soon have been the father of so many children; he would have dragged out a long period in childlessness, he would have mourned as his wife did. For she indeed had reason to mourn, as not having become a mother (ib. xxx. 1, 2.); but he had his consolation: whence also he gives her a repulse. Again, had not (Laban) defrauded him of his hire, he would not have longed to see his own country; the higher points ($\phi\iota\lambda o\sigma o\phi\acute{\iota}\alpha$) of the man's character would not have come to light, (his wives) would not have become more closely attached to him. For see what they say: "With devouring hath he devoured us and our money." (Gen. xxxi. 15.) So that this became the means of riveting their love to him. After this he had in them not merely wives, but (devoted) slaves; he was beloved by them: a thing that no possession can equal: for nothing, nothing whatever, is more precious than to be thus loved by a wife and to love her. "And a wife," Scripture says, "that agrees with her husband." (Ecclus. xxv. 1. "A man and a wife that agree together." E. V.) One thing this, as the Wise Man puts it, of the things for which a man is to be counted happy; for where this is, there all wealth, all prosperity abounds: as also, where it is not, there all besides profits nothing, but all goes wrong, all is mere unpleasantness and confusion. Then let us seek this before all things. He that seeks money, seeks not this. Let us seek those things which can remain fixed. Let us not seek a wife from among the rich, lest the excess of wealth on her side produce arrogance, lest that arrogance be the means of marring all. See you not what God did? how He put the woman in subjection? (Gen. iii. 16.) Why art thou ungrateful, why without perception? The very benefit God has given thee by nature, do not thou mar the help it was meant to be. So that it is not for her wealth that we ought to seek a wife: it is that we may receive a partner of our life, for the appointed order of the procreation of children. It was not that she should bring money, that God gave the woman; it was that she might be an helpmate. But she that brings money, becomes, instead of a wife, a setter up of her own will (ἐπίβουλος), a mistress—it may be a wild beast instead of a wife—while she thinks she has a right to give herself airs upon her wealth. Nothing more shameful than a man who lays himself out to get riches in this way. If wealth itself is full of temptations, what shall we say to wealth so gotten? For you must not look to this, that one or another as a rare and unusual case, and contrary to the reason of the thing, has succeeded: as neither ought we in other matters to fix our regards upon the good which people may enjoy, or their chance successes, out of the common course: but let us look to the reason of the thing as it is in itself, and see whether this thing be not fraught with endless annoyance. Not only you bring yourself into a disreputable position; you also disgrace your children by leaving them poor, if it chance that you depart this life before the wife: and you give her incomparably more occasions for connecting herself with a second bridegroom. Or do you not see that many women make this the excuse for a second marriage—that they may not be despised; that they want to have some man to take the management of their property? Then let us not bring about so great evils for the sake of money; but let us dismiss all (such aims), and seek a beautiful soul, that we may also succeed in obtaining love. This is the exceeding wealth, this the great treasure, this the endless good things: whereunto may we all attain by the grace and loving kindness of our Lord Jesus Christ, with Whom to the Father and the Holy Ghost together be glory, dominion, honor, now and ever, world without end. Amen.

HOMILY L.

ACTS XXIII. 31, 32, 33.

"Then the soldiers, as it was commanded them, took Paul, and brought him by night to Antipatris. On the morrow they left the horsemen to go with him, and returned to the castle: who, when they came to Cæsarea, and delivered the epistle to the governor, presented Paul also before him."

LIKE some king whom his body-guards escort, so did these convey Paul; in such numbers too, and by night, for fear of the wrath of the people.[1] Now then you will say that they have got him out of the city, they desist from their violence? No indeed. But (the tribune) would not have sent him off with such care for his safety, but that while he himself had found nothing amiss in him, he knew the murderous disposition of his adversaries. "And when the governor had

---

[1] τοῦ δήμου τὴν ὀργὴν τῆς ὁρμῆς. Ἐπεὶ οὖν τῆς πόλεως αὐτὸν ἐξέβαλον, τότε ἀφίστανται. So Edd. and our Mss. but Cat. simply τὴν ὀργήν. The next sentence, if referred affirmatively to the Jews, would be untrue, for in fact the Jews οὐκ ἀπέστησαν.

Possibly the scribes took it to refer to the soldiers: but this is very unsatisfactory. To make sense, it must be read interrogatively: "Well then, at any rate that now, they have got him out of the city, they desist from further attempts? By no means; and in fact the precautions taken for his safety show what was the tribune's view of the matter, both that Paul was innocent and that they were set on murdering him." We read ἀφίστανται τῆς ὁρμῆς.

read the letter, he asked of what province he was. And when he understood that he was of Cilicia ; I will hear thee, said he, when thine accusers are also come." Already Lysias has spoken for his exculpation ; (but the Jews seek to) gain the hearer beforehand. "And he ordered him to be kept in custody in Herod's prætorium" (v. 34, 35) : again Paul is put in bonds. "And after five days came down the high priest Ananias with the elders." See how for all this they do not desist ; hindered as they were by obstacles without number, nevertheless they come, only to be put to shame here also. "And with an orator, one Tertullus." [1] And what need was there of " an orator ? Which (persons) also informed the governor against Paul." (c. xxiv. 1.) See how this man also from the very outset (b) with his praises seeks to gain the judge beforehand. "And when he was called forth, Tertullus began to accuse him, saying, Seeing that by thee we enjoy great quietness, and that very worthy deeds are done unto this nation by thy providence, we accept it always, and in all places, most noble Felix, with all thankfulness." (v. 2, 3.) Then as having much to say, he passes by the rest : " Notwithstanding, that I be not further tedious unto thee, I pray thee that thou wouldest hear us of thy clemency a few words. For we have found this man a pestilent fellow, and a mover of sedition among all the Jews throughout the world." (a) As a revolutionary and seditious person he wishes to deliver him up. And yet, it might be answered, it is ye that have done this. (c) And see how he would put up the judge to a desire of punishing, seeing he had here an opportunity to coerce the man that turned the world upside down ! As if they had achieved a meritorious action, they make much of it : " Having found this fellow," etc., " a mover of sedition," say they, " among all the Jews throughout the world." (Had he been such), they would have proclaimed him as a benefactor and saviour of the nation ! [2] "And a ringleader of the sect of the Nazarenes." (v. 4, 5.) They thought this likely to tell as a reproach—" of the Nazarenes : " and by this also they seek to dam-

age him—for Nazareth was a mean place. And, " we have found him," say they : see how maliciously they calumniate him : (found him), as if he had been always giving them the slip, and with difficulty they had succeeded in getting him : though he had been seven days in the Temple ! " Who also hath gone about to profane the temple ; whom we took, [and would have judged according to our law."] (v. 6.) See how they insult even the Law ; it was so like the Law, forsooth, to beat, to kill, to lie in wait ! And then the accusation against Lysias : though he had no right, say they, to interfere, in the excess of his confidence he snatched him from us : [" But the tribune Lysias came upon us, and with great violence took him away out of our hands, commanding his accusers to come unto thee] : * by examining of whom thyself mayest take knowledge of all these things, whereof we accuse him. And the Jews also assented, saying that these things were so." (v. 7–9.) What then says Paul ? " Then Paul ; after that the governor had beckoned unto him to speak, answered, Forasmuch as I know that thou hast been of many years a just judge unto this nation, I do the more cheerfully answer for myself." (v. 10.) This is not the language of flattery, his testifying to the judge's justice : [3] no, the adulation was rather in that speech of the orator, " By thee we enjoy great quietness." If so, then why are ye seditious ? What Paul sought was justice. " Knowing thee to be a just judge, I cheerfully," says he, " answer for myself." Then also he enforces this by the length of time : that (he had been judge) "of many years. Because that thou mayest understand, that there are yet but twelve days since I went up to Jerusalem for to worship." (v. 11.) And what is this ? [4] (It means), "that I could not immediately have raised a commotion." Because the accuser had nothing to show (as done) in Jerusalem, observe what he said : " among all the Jews throughout the world." Therefore it is that Paul here forcibly attracts him—" to worship," he says, " I came up," so

[1] It has been necessary to rearrange the texts, and also to transpose the parts mark a, b.—Καὶ μὴν ὑμεῖς, φησὶ τοῦτο πεποιήκατε. The φησί here is hypothetical : " Tertullus wishes to arraign Paul as a seditious person. And yet, Felix might say, it is ye Jews that have been the movers of sedition : in these words ye describe yourselves."—Mod. text " v. 2, 3, 4. And yet ye have done this : then what need of an orator ? See how this man, also from the very outset wishes to deliver him up as a revolutionary and seditious person, and with his praises preoccupies the judge. Then as having much to say, he passes it by, and only says this, But that I be not further tedious unto thee."

[2] So much was sedition to their taste, they would have been the last to arraign him for that ; on the contrary etc.—But Mod. text ὡς λυμεῶνα λοιπὸν καὶ κοινὸν ἐχθρὸν τοῦ ἔθνους διαβάλλουσι.

[3] Hence it appears that Chrys. read ὄντα σε κριτὴν δίκαιον in v. 10, though the old text in the citation omits the epithet. Cat. retains it.—See p. 299, note [2].

[4] As Felix had been many years a judge, he was conversant enough with the habits of the Jews to be aware that the Pentecost which brought Paul to Jerusalem was but twelve days past : so that there had not been time to raise a commotion. Mod. text. "And what did this contribute to the proof ? A great point : for he shows that Felix himself knew that Paul had done nothing of all that he was accused of. But if he had ever raised an insurrection, Felix would have known it, being judge, and such an affair would not have scaped his notice."—Below, διὰ τοῦτο ἐνταῦθα αὐτὸν ἕλκει, we suppose αὐτὸν to be Felix : Mod. text substitutes ἐντεῦθεν ἀφέλκων, referring it to the accuser. The meaning is obscure, but it seems to be, " draws the attention of his judge to this point," viz., of his having come up to worship, and therefore ἐνδιατρίβει τούτῳ τῷ δικαίῳ lays the stress upon this point, of Felix being a just judge. Perhaps, however, the true reading here is τῷ δεκαδύο, " of its being not more than twelve days."

* The bracketed passage in vv. 6–8 om. in A. B. G. H. א. and R. V.—G. B. S.

far am I from raising sedition—and lays a stress upon this point of justice, being the strong point. "And they neither found me in the Temple disputing with any man, neither raising up the people, neither in the synagogues, nor in the city" (v. 12); which in fact was the truth. And the accusers indeed use the term "ringleader," as if it were a case of fighting and insurrection; but see how mildly Paul here answers. "But this I confess unto thee, that after the way which they call heresy,* so worship I the God of my fathers, believing all things which are written in the Law and the Prophets: and have hope toward God, which they themselves also allow, that there shall be a resurrection of the dead, both of the just and unjust." (v. 14, 15.) The accusers were separating him (as an alien), but he indentifies himself with the Law, as one of themselves. "And in this," says he, "do I exercise myself, to have always a conscience void of offence toward God and toward men. Now after many years I came to bring alms to my nation, and offerings. In which they found me purified in the temple, not with multitude, neither with tumult." (v. 16, 17, 18.) Why then camest thou up? What brought thee hither? To worship, says he; to do alms. This was not the act of a factious person. Then also he casts out their person:[1] "but," says he, (they that found me, were) "certain Jews from Asia, who ought to have been here before thee, and object, if they had ought against me. Or else let these same here say, if they have found any evil doing in me while I stood before the council, except it be for this one voice, that I cried, standing among them, Touching the resurrection of the dead I am called in question by you this day." (v. 19, 20, 21.) For this is justification in superabundance, not to flee from his accusers, but to be ready to give account to all.† "Of the

resurrection of the dead," says he, "am I this day called in question." And not a word said he of what he had to say, how they had conspired against him, had violently kept him, had laid wait for him—for these matters are course spoken of by the tribune[2]—but by Paul, though there was danger, not so: no, he is silent, and only defends himself, though he had very much to say. (b) "In which"[3] (alms), says he, "they found me in course of purifying in the Temple." Then how did he profane it? For it was not the part of the same man both to purify himself and worship and come for this purpose, and then to profane it. This has with it a surmise of the justice of his cause, that he does not fall into a long discourse. And he gratifies the judge, I suppose, by that also (namely, by), making his defence compendious: (d) seeing that Tertullus before him did make a long harangue. (f) And this too is a proof of mildness, that when one has much to say, in order not to be troublesome one says but few words. (c) But let us look again at what has been said.

(Recapitulation.) "Then the soldiers," etc. (v. 31-33.) (a) This also made Paul famous in Cæsarea, his coming with so large a force. —"But," says Tertullus, 'that I be not further tedious," (e) showing that (Felix) does find him tedious (ἐγκόπτεται): "I beseech thee," he does not say, Hear the matter, but, "hear us of thy clemency." (ch. xxiv. 4.) Probably it is to pay court, that he thus lays out his speech. (g) "For having found this man, a pestilent fellow, and a mover of sedition among all the Jews throughout the world" (v. 5): how then, it might be said, if he did this elsewhere (and not here)? No, says he; among us also he has profaned the Temple; "attempted," says he, "to profane it:" but the how, he leaves untold. "Whom

* Ἅιρεσις in v. 14 has the same meaning as in v. 5. The meaning is therefore obscured by rendering it (as A. V.) in the former verse by "sect" and in the latter by "heresy." It is *party* or *sect* in both cases, used as a term of reproach. Paul's accusers considered him a member of a sect which they contemptuously called the Nazarenes. In his defence he takes up their own word.—G. B. S.

1 Εἶτα καὶ ἐκβάλλει αὐτῶν τὸ πρόσωπον, rejects their person, repudiates their pretension. They had said, "We found him:" he answers, "There found me, in a condition as far as possible from that of a mover of sedition—not they, 'but certain of the Jews from Asia.' In the Recapitulation, he says, καλῶς δὲ οὐδὲ τοῦτο ἐκβάλλει referring to v. 21. Hence one might conjecture here, εἶτα οὐκ ἐκβ., to be placed after v. 20; but see p. 299, note 3.—Mod. text ἐκβ. ἀ. τ. πρ. λέγων ἀδιορίστως, Ἐν οἷς εὑρόν μέ τινες τῶν κ. τ. λ. "Saying indefinitely, 'In which there found me,' (and then adding), 'certain of the Jews from Asia.'"

† Vv. 5 and 6 had contained the three charges preferred by Tertullus, viz.: sedition, sectarianism and profanation of the temple. Paul was charged with creating disturbances among the Jews (5). To this he replies (11, 12), that the charge is not sustained by facts; he worshipped in the temple, but neither there, nor in the synagogues, nor in the city, did he create a disturbance or gather a crowd. To the second charge that he is a ringleader of the sect of the Nazarenes (5), Paul replies by conceding that he worships the God of his fathers after a way

which they call a sect, but he denies that this fact involves rejection or contempt of the law or the prophets (14). To the third charge that he had attempted to profane the Temple (6), he replies by alleging that he had, on the contrary, brought offerings to the Temple service and that he had there peaceably taken part in the religious rites of the Nazarites (17, 18). He concludes by insisting that his whole offence consists in having stoutly maintained the doctrine of the resurrection of the dead.—G. B. S.

2 Old text ταῦτα γὰρ εἰκότως περὶ ἐκείνου λέγεται, παρὰ δὲ τούτου. . . We read παρὰ ἐκείνου. in the sense, "All that is to be said on those points comes from Lysias: from Paul, not a word." Mod. text ταῦτα γὰρ παρ' ἐκείνων λέγεται γενέσθαι. "these things are said to have been done by those."

3 Here old text has the reading ἐν αἷς, above it was ἐν οἷς.— Here the first Redactor has confused the matter, in consequence of his supposing that at the mention of Tertullus (d) Chrys. must have gone into the Recapitulation. Hence he places (c) the formula ἀλλ' ἴδωμεν κ. τ. λ. immediately before this. Accordingly to (d) as being comment on v. 4, he joins (e), and then supposing the ἐπιεικείας of (f) to refer to ἐπιεικείᾳ v. 4, he places this next. The part (b) he keeps in its place, viz. before the Recapitulation: there remained (a), and this he prefixes to b, though its contents clearly show that it belongs to the Recapitulation of v. 31.

also we took," etc. "But the tribune," etc. And while he thus exaggerates what relates to the tribune,[1] see how he extenuates the part of the accusers themselves. "We took him," he says, "and would have judged him according to our Law." (v. 6.) He shows that it is a hardship to them that they have to come to foreign tribunals, and that they would not have troubled him had not the tribune compelled them, and that he, having no concern in the matter, had seized the man by force: for in fact the wrongs done were against us, and with us the tribunal ought to have been. For that this is the meaning, see what follows: "with great violence" (v. 7), he says. For this conduct is violence. "From whom thou mayest know." He neither dares to accuse him (the tribune)—for the man was indulgent (forsooth)—nor does he wholly pass it by. Then again, lest he should seem to be lying, he adduces Paul himself as his own accuser. "From whom, by examining him, thou mayest take knowledge of all these things." (v. 8.) Next, as witnesses also of the things spoken, the accusers, the same persons themselves both witnesses and accusers: "And the Jews also assented," etc. (v. 9.) But Paul, "Forasmuch as I know that thou hast been of many years a just judge." (v. 10.) Why then, he is no stranger or alien or revolutionary person, seeing he had known the judge for many years. And he does well to add the epithet "just,"[2] that he (Felix) might not look to the chief priest, nor to the people, nor the accuser. See, how he did not let himself be carried away into abuse, although there was strong provocation. "Believing," he says, "that there will be a resurrection:" now a man who believed a resurrection, would never have done such things—"which" (resurrection) "they themselves also allow. (v. 15.) He does not say it of them, that they believe "all things written in the Prophets:" it was he that believed them all, not they: but how "all," it would require a long discourse to show. And he nowhere makes mention of Christ. Here by saying, "Believing," he does (virtually) introduce what relates to Christ; for the present he dwells on the subject of the resurrection, which doctrine was common to them also, and removed the suspicion of any sedition. And for the cause of his going up, "I came," he says, "to bring alms to my nation and offerings." (v. 17.) How then should I have troubled those, for the bringing offerings to whom I had come so long a journey? "Neither with multitude, nor with tumult." (v. 18.) Everywhere he does away the charge of sedition. And he also does well to challenge his accusers who were from Asia, "Who ought to accuse before thee," etc., but he does well also not to reject this either;[3] "or else," says he, "let these same here say. Touching the resurrection of the dead," etc. (v. 19, 20, 21): for in fact it was on this account they were sore troubled from the first, because he preached the Resurrection. This being proved, the things relating to Christ also were easily introduced, that He was risen. "What evil doing," he says, "they found in me. In the council (ch. iv. 2) he says: the examination not having taken place in private. That these things which I say are true, those witness who bring this charge against me. "Having," he says, "a conscience void of offence both toward God, and toward men." (v. 16.) This is the perfection of virtue, when even to men we give no handle against us, and are careful to be void of offence with God. "That I cried," he says, "in the council." He also shows their violence.[4] They have it not to say, Thou didst these things under the pretext of alms: for (it was) "not with multitude, nor with tumult:" especially as upon enquiry made concerning this thing, nothing further was found. Do you observe his moderation, though there were dangers? do you observe how he keeps his tongue from evil-speaking, how he seeks only one thing, to free himself from the charges against himself, not that he may criminate them, except so far as he might be obliged to do so while defending himself? Just as Christ also said: "I have not a devil, but I honor My Father: but ye do dishonor Me." (John viii. 49.)

Let us imitate him, since he also was an imitator of Christ. If he, with enemies, who went even to the length of murder and slaughter, said nothing offensive to them, what pardon shall we deserve, who in reviling

---

[1] τὰ μὲν ἐκείνου, evidently the tribune, but Ben. quæ Paulum quidem spectabant.—They made the most of what the tribune had done, of their own violence they make as little as possible.

[2] See above, p. 197, note [3]. The principal authorities for the δίκαιον are Laud's Cod. Gr. and Cat. of Acts.

[3] καλῶς δὲ (B.) οὐδὲ τοῦτο ἐκβάλλει. i. e. but while he does well to challenge the parties who found him viz. the Jews from Asia, he does well also that he does not cast out or repudiate this particular which he goes on to mention—viz. his exclamation before the Sanhedrim. This may consist with what was said above, ἐκβάλλει αὐτῶν τὸ πρόσωπον: (see p. 297, note [1]) viz. though he does this, and deprives them of the credit they took to themselves, for it was not that they found him ; and as to his behavior in the temple, he will not admit their testimony, for they were not present: yet even these he challenges to testify to that of which they were cognizant.—Mod. text " from Asia, saying, Who ought to accuse me before thee, if they had aught against me. So confident was he to be clear as to the matters of which he was accused, that he even challenges them. But not only those from Asia, nay, those also from Jerusalem."

[4] Mod. text adds, " by saying, Ἐκέκραξα: as much as to say, They have it not," etc. But their violence was shown not by his crying out, but by the fact that they had nothing more against him than this exclamation.

and abuse become infuriated, calling our enemies villains, detestable wretches? what pardon shall we deserve, for having enemies at all? Hear you not, that to honor (another) is to honor one's self? So it is: but we disgrace ourselves. You accuse (some one) that he has abused you: then why do you bring yourself under the same accusation? Why inflict a blow on yourself? Keep free from passion, keep unwounded: do not, by wishing to smite another, bring the hurt upon yourself. What, is the other tumult of our soul not enough for us, the tumult that is stirred up, though there be none to stir it up—for example, its outrageous lusts, its griefs and sorrows, and such like—but we must needs heap up a pile of others also? And how, you will say, is it possible, when one is insulted and abused, to bear this? And how is it not possible, I ask? Is a wound got from words; or do words inflict bruises on our bodies? Then where is the hurt to us? So that, if we will, we can bear it. Let us lay down for ourselves a law not to grieve, and we shall bear it: let us say to ourselves, "It is not from enmity; it is from infirmity"—for it is indeed owing to an infirmity, since, for proof that it comes not from enmity nor from malignity of disposition, but from infirmity, the other also would fain have restrained (his anger), although he had suffered numberless wrongs. If we only have this thought in our minds, that it is from infirmity, we shall bear it, and while we forgive the offending person, we shall try not to fall into it ourselves. For I ask all you who are present: would ye have wished to be able to exercise such a philosophic temper, as to bear with those who insult you?[1] I think so. Well, then, he insulted unwillingly; he would rather not have done so, but he did it, forced by his passion: refrain thyself. Do you not see (how it is with) the demoniacs (in their fits)? Just then as it is with them, so with him: it is not so much from enmity, as from infirmity (that he behaves as he does): endure it. And as for us—it is not so much from the insults as they are in themselves that we are moved, as from our own selves: else how is it that when madmen offer us the same insults, we bear it? Again, if those who insult us be

our friends, in that case too we bear it: or also our superiors, in that case also we bear it: how then is it not absurd, that in the case of these three, friends, madmen, and superiors, we bear it, but where they are of the same rank or our inferiors, we do not bear it? I have oftentimes said: It is but an impulse of the moment, something that hurries us away on the sudden: let us endure it for a little, and we shall bear the whole thing. The greater the insults, the more weak the offender. Do you know when it behooves us to grieve? When we have insulted another, and he keeps silence: for then he is strong, and we weak: but if the contrary be the case, you must even rejoice: you are crowned, you are proclaimed conqueror, without having even entered into the contest, without having borne the annoyance of sun, and heat, and dust, without having grappled with an antagonist and let him close with you; nothing but a mere wish on your part, sitting or standing, and you have got a mighty crown: a crown far greater than those (combatants earn): for to throw an enemy standing to the encounter, is nothing like so great as to overcome the darts of anger. You have conquered, without having even let him close with you, you have thrown down the passion that was in you, have slain the beast that was roused, have quelled the anger that was raging, like some excellent herdsman. The fight was like to have been an intestine one, the war a civil war. For, as those who sit down to besiege from without (endeavor to), embroil (the besieged) in civil discords, and then overcome them; so he that insults, unless he rouse the passion within us, will not be able to overcome us: unless we kindle the flame in ourselves, he has no power. Let the spark of anger be within us, so as to be ready for lighting at the right moment, not against ourselves, nor so as to involve us in numberless evils. See ye not how the fire in houses is kept apart, and not thrown about at random everywhere, neither among straw, nor among the linen, nor just where it may chance, that so there may not be danger, if a wind blow on it, of its kindling a flame: but whether a maid-servant have a lamp, or the cook light a fire, there is many an injunction given, not to do this in the draught of the wind, nor near a wooden panel, nor in the night-time: but when the night has come on, we extinguish the fire, fearing lest perchance while we are asleep and there is none to help, it set fire, and burn us all. Let this also be done with regard to anger; let it not be scattered everywhere up and down in our thoughts, but let it be in some deep recess of the mind, that the wind

---

[1] Old text ἆρα ἂν ἠθελήσατε οὕτω φιλοσοφεῖν δύνασθαι—; Mod. text ἆρα ἂν οὕτω φιλοσοφεῖν δύνησθε—; and so Ben. against grammar and the sense. Savile and Ed. Par. Ben. 2, ἆρα ἂν ἐθελήσητε, ... δύνασθε; But our Mss. give it as above: and Savile's reading does not suit the sense: which is, "Would not you have wished—? Well, then, so would he."— Below, ὥσπερ οὖν ἐκεῖνος οὐκ (B., ἐκείνοις and om. οὐκ) ἀπὸ ἔχθρας τοσοῦτον, ὅσον ἀπὸ ἀσθενείας, τοῦτο ὑπομένει· οὕτω καὶ ἡμεῖς οὐκ ἀπὸ τῆς φύσεως τῶν ὑβρέων κινούμεθα, ὅσον ἀφ' ἡμῶν αὐτῶν. The scribes have made nonsense of the passage, and the Edd. retain it. If for ὑπομένει we read ὑπόμενε, this will answer to ἐπίσχες in the preceding sentence: to τοῦτο we supply πάσχει: so we read, ὥσπερ οὖν ἐκεῖνοι. οὕτω καὶ οὗτος οὐκ ἀπὸ ἔ. ὅσον ἀπὸ ἀσθ. τοῦτο πάσχει· ὑπόμενε. Καὶ ἡμεῖς etc.

arising from the words of him who is opposing us may not easily reach to it, but that it receive the wind (which is to rouse it) from ourselves, who know how to rouse it in due measure and with safety. If it receive the wind from without, it knows no moderation; it will set everything on fire: oftentimes when we are asleep this wind will come upon it, and will burn up all. Let it therefore be with us (in safe keeping) in such sort as only to kindle a light: for anger does kindle a light when it is managed as it ought to be: and let us have torches against those who wrong others, against the devil. Let not the spark lie anywhere as it may chance, nor be thrown about; let us keep it safe under ashes: in lowly thoughts let us keep it slumbering. We do not want it at all times, but when there is need to subdue and to make tender, to mollify obduracy, and convict the soul. What evils have angry and wrathful passions wrought! And what makes it grievous indeed is, that when we have parted asunder, we have no longer the power to come together again, but we wait for others (to do this): each is ashamed, and blushes to come back himself and reconcile the other. See, he is not ashamed to part asunder and to be separated; no, he takes the lead as author of the evil: but to come forward and patch that which is rent, this he is ashamed to do: and the case is just the same, as if a man should not shrink from cutting off a limb, but should be ashamed to join it together again. What sayest thou, O man? Hast thou committed great injuries, and thyself been the cause of the quarrel? Why, then, thou wouldest justly be the first to go and be reconciled, as having thyself furnished the cause. But he did the wrong, he is the cause of the enmity? Why then, for this reason also thou must do it, that men may the more admire thee, that in addition to the former, thou mayest get the first prize in the latter also: as thou wast not the cause of the enmity, so neither of its being extended further. Perhaps also the other, as conscious within himself of numberless evils, is ashamed and blushes. But he is haughty? On this account above all, do not thou hesitate to run and meet him: for if the ailment in him be twofold, both haughtiness and anger, in this thou hast mentioned the very reason why thou oughtest to be the first to go to him, thou that art the one in sound health, the one who is able to see: as for him, he is in darkness: for such is anger and false pride. But do thou, who art free from these and in sound health, go to him—thou the physician, go to the sick. Does any of the physicians say, Because such an one is sick, I do not go to

him? No, this is the very reason above all why they do go, when they see that he is not able to come to them. For of those who are able (to come) they think less, as of persons not extremely ill, but not so of those who lie at home sick. Or are not pride and anger, think you, worse than any illness? is not the one like a sharp fever, the other like a body swollen with inflammation? Think what a thing it is to have a fever and inflammation: go to him, extinguish the fire, for by the grace of God thou canst: go, assuage the heat as it were with water. "But," you will say, "how if he is only the more set up by my doing this very thing?" This is nothing to thee: thou hast done thy part, let him take account for himself: let not our conscience condemn us, that this thing happens in consequence of any omission of what ought to have been done on our part. "In so doing," says the Scripture, "thou shalt heap coals of fire on his head." (Rom. xii. 20, cf. *Hom. in l.* xxii. § 3.) And yet, for all that this is the consequence, it bids us go and be reconciled and do good offices—not that we may heap coals of fire, but that (our enemy) knowing that future consequence,[1] may be assuaged by the present kindness, that he may tremble, that he may fear our good offices rather than our hostilities, and our friendships rather than our ill designs. For one does not so hurt his hater by showing his resentment as an enemy, as by doing him good and showing kindness. For by his resentment, he has hurt both himself and perhaps the other also in some little degree: but by doing good offices, he has heaped coals of fire on his head. "Why then," you will say, "for fear of thus heaping coals one ought not to do this (*b*) but to carry on the enmity to greater lengths." By no means: it is not you that cause this, but he with his brutish disposition. For if, when you are doing him good, and honoring him, and offering to be reconciled, he persists in keeping up the enmity, it is he has kindled the fire for himself, he has set his own head on fire; you are guiltless. Do not want to be more merciful than God (*b*), or rather, if you wish it, you will not be able, not even in the least degree. How should you? "As far as the heaven is from the earth," Scripture says, "so far are My counsels from your counsels" (Isa. xlv. 8): and again, "If ye," He says, "being evil, know how to give good gifts unto your children, how much more your heavenly Father" (Matt.

---

[1] B. C. ἵνα εἰδὼς ἐκεῖνο (mod. text ἐκεῖνος) τοῦτο (we read τούτῳ) καταστέλληται. Here, as often, ἐκεῖνο refers to the other world, τοῦτο to this life: "knowing what will come of it there, (i. e. the coals of fire) he may," etc.

vii. 11)? But in fact this talk is mere pretext and subterfuge. Let us not prevaricate with God's commandments. "And how do we prevaricate," you will say? He has said, "In so doing, thou wilt heap coals of fire on his head:" and you say, I do not like to do this. (a) But are you willing to heap coals after another fashion, that is upon your own head? For in fact this is what resentment does: (c) since you shall suffer evils without number. (e) You say, "I am afraid for my enemy, because he has done me great injuries:" in reality is it this you say? But how came you to have an enemy? But how came you to hate your enemy? You fear for him that has injured you, but do you not fear yourself? Would that you had a care for yourself! Do not act (the kindness) with such an aim as this: or rather do it, though it be but with such an aim. But you do it not at all. I say not to you, "thou wilt heap coals of fire:" no, I say another and a greater thing: only do it. For Paul says this only by way of summoning thee (if only), in hope of the vengeance, to put an end to the enmity. Because we are savage as wild beasts in disposition, and would not otherwise endure to love our enemy, unless we expected some revenge, he offers this as a cake, so to say, to a wild beast. For to the Apostles (the Lord) says not this, but what says He? "That ye may be like to your Father which is in heaven." (Matt. v. 45.)

And besides, it is not possible that the benefactor and the benefited should remain in enmity. This is why Paul has put it in this way. Why, affecting a high and generous principle in thy words, why in thy deeds dost thou not even observe (common) moderation? (It sounds) well; thou dost not feed him, for fear of thereby heaping upon him coals of fire: well then, thou sparest him? well then, thou lovest him, thou actest with this object in view? God knows, whether thou hast this ojbect in so speaking, and are not [1] palming this talk upon us as a mere pretence and subterfuge. Thou hast a care for thine enemy, thou fearest lest he be punished, then wouldest thou not have extinguished thine anger? For he that loves to that degree that he overlooks his own interest for the sake of the other's advantage, that man has no enemy. (Then indeed) thou mightest say this. How long shall we trifle in matters that are not to be trifled with, and that admit of no excuse? Wherefore I beseech you, let us cut off these pretexts; let us not despise God's laws: that we may be enabled with well-pleasing to the Lord to pass this life present, and attain unto the good things promised, through the grace and mercy of our Lord Jesus Christ, with Whom to the Father and the Holy Ghost together be glory, might, honor, now and ever, world without end. Amen.

HOMILY LI.

ACTS XXIV. 22, 23.

"And when Felix heard these things, having more perfect knowledge of that way, he deferred them, and said, When Lysias the tribune shall come down, I will know the uttermost of your matter. And he commanded a centurion to keep Paul, and to let him have liberty, and that he should forbid none of his acquaintance to minister or come unto him."

SEE how much close investigation is made by the many in a long course of time, that it should not be said that the trial was hurried over. For, as the orator had made mention of Lysias, that he took "him away with violence, Felix," he says, "deferred them. Having knowledge of that way:" that is, he put them off on purpose: not because he wanted to learn, but as wishing to get rid of the Jews. On their account, he did not like to let him

go: to punish him was not possible; that would have been (too) barefaced. "And to let him have liberty,* and to forbid none of his acquaintance to minister to him." So entirely did he too acquit him of the charges. Howbeit, to gratify them, he detained him, and besides, expecting to receive money, he called for Paul. "And after certain days, when Felix came with his wife Drusilla, which was a Jewess, he sent for Paul, and heard him

---

[1] καὶ μὴ . . . Mod text καὶ μὴν . . . "And yet thou art," etc.

* Ἄνεσις is better rendered "relaxation" or "indulgence" (R. V.) than "liberty" (A. V.). Meyer understands by this that he was to be allowed *rest*, "to be spared all annoyance." Others (DeWette, Lange) suppose ἄνεσις to refer to release from *chains*, the so-called *custodia libera* of the Romans in which the prisoner went free on bail or upon the responsibility of some magistrate. This view is, however, inconsistent with the fact that Felix committed Paul to the keeping of a centurion (23) as well as with his leaving Paul bound (27). The custody was doubtless the *custodia militaris* and ἄνεσις denotes the relaxation of the rigors of his imprisonment.—G.B.S.

concerning the faith in Christ. And as he reasoned of righteousness, temperance (i. e. self-control or chastity), and judgment to come, Felix trembled, and answered, Go thy way for this time; when I have a convenient season, I will call for thee. He hoped also that money should have been given him of Paul, that he might loose him; wherefore he sent for him the oftener, and communed with him. But after two years Porcius Festus came into Felix's room : and Felix, willing to show the Jews a pleasure, left Paul bound." (v. 24-27.) See how close to the truth are the things written. But he sent for him- frequently, not that he admired him, nor that he praised the things spoken, nor that he wished to believe, but why? " Expecting," it says, "that money should have been given him." Observe how he does not hide here the mind of the judge. "Wherefore he sent for him," etc. And yet if he had condemned him, he would not have done this, nor have wished to hear a man, condemned and of evil character. And observe Paul, how, though reasoning with a ruler, he says nothing of the sort that was likely to amuse and entertain, but (" he reasoned," it says,) "of righteousness, and of the coming judgment," and of the resurrection. And such was the force of his words, that they even terrified the governor.* This man is succeeded in his office by another, and he leaves Paul a prisoner : and yet he ought not to have done this; he ought to have put an end to the business : but he leaves him, by way of gratifying them. They however were so urgent, that they again besought the judge. Yet against none of the Apostles had they set themselves thus pertinaciously; there, when they had attacked, anon they desisted. So providentially is he removed from Jerusalem, having to do with such wild beasts. And they nevertheless request that he might be brought again there to be tried. " Now when Festus was come into the province, after three days he ascended from Cæsarea to Jerusalem. Then the high priest and the chief of the Jews informed him against Paul, and besought him, and desired favor against him, that he would send for him to Jerusalem, laying wait in the way to kill him." (ch. xxv. 1-3.) Here now God's providence interposed, not permitting the governor to do this : for it was natural that he having just come to

the government would wish to gratify them : but God suffered him not. " But Festus answered, that Paul should be kept at Cæsarea, and that he himself would depart shortly thither. Let them therefore, said he, which among you are able, go down with me, and accuse this man, if there be any wickedness in him. And when he had tarried among them more than ten days, he went down unto Cæsarea; and the next day sitting on the judgment seat commanded Paul to be brought." (v. 4-6.) But after they came down, they forthwith made their accusations shamelessly and with more vehemence : and not having been able to convict him on grounds relating to the Law, they again according to their custom stirred the question about Cæsar, being just what they did in Christ's case. For that they had recourse to this is manifest by the fact, that Paul defends himself on the score of offences against Cæsar. "And when he was come, the Jews which came down from Jerusalem stood round about, and laid many and grievous complaints against Paul, which they could not prove. While he answered for himself, Neither against the law of the Jews, neither against the temple, nor yet against Cæsar, have I offended anything at all. But Festus, willing to do the Jews a pleasure, answered Paul, and said, Wilt thou go up to Jerusalem, and there be judged of these things before me"? (v. 7-9.) Wherefore he too gratifies the Jews, the whole people, and the city. Such being the case, Paul terrifies him also, using a human weapon for his defence. "Then said Paul, I stand at Cæsar's judgment seat, where I ought to be judged; to the Jews have I done no wrong, as thou very well knowest. For if I be an offender, or have committed anything worthy of death, I refuse not to die : but if there be none of these things whereof these accuse me, no man may deliver me unto them. I appeal unto Cæsar." (v. 10-11.) Some one might say, How is it, that having been told, "Thou must also bear witness of Me in Rome," (ch. xxiii. 11), he, as if unbelieving, did this? God forbid : nay, he did it, because he so strongly believed. For it would have been a tempting of God to be bold on account of that declaration, and to cast himself into numberless dangers, and to say : "Let us see if God is able even thus to deliver me." But not so does Paul; no, he does his part, all that in him lies, committing the whole to God. Quietly also he reproves the governor : for, "If, says he, I am an offender, thou doest well : but if not, why dost thou give me up ?" "No man," he says, "may sacrifice me." He put him in fear, so that even if he wished, he

---

* Paul's reasoning " concerning righteousness " was directed against the well-known injustice of a prince of whom Tacitus says that he acted as if there were no penalty for villainy. His reasoning "concerning self-control" (ἐκράτεια) was in opposition to his sensuality. He had unlawfully married Drusilla who was the wife of Azizus, the king of Emesa (Jos. Ant. xx. 7, 2). His references to the judgment to come might well have been directed against the governor's murder of Jonathan, the high priest.—G. B. S.

could not sacrifice him to them; while also as
an excuse to them he had Paul's appeal to
allege. "Then Festus, when he had conferred with the council, answered, Hast thou
appealed unto Cæsar? unto Cæsar shalt thou
go. And after certain days king Agrippa and
Bernice came unto Cæsarea to salute Festus."
(v. 12, 13.) Observe, he communicates the
matter to Agrippa, so that there should be
other hearers once more, both the king, and
the army, and Bernice. Thereupon a speech
in his exculpation. "And when they had
been there many days, Festus declared Paul's
cause unto the king, saying, There is a certain
man left in bonds by Felix: about whom,
when I was at Jerusalem, the chief priests and
the elders of the Jews informed me, desiring
to have judgment against him. To whom I
answered, It is not the manner of the Romans
to deliver any man to die, before that he
which is accused have the accusers face to
face, and have license to answer for himself
concerning the crime laid against him.
Therefore, when they were come hither, without any delay on the morrow I sat on the
judgment seat, and commanded the man to
be brought forth. Against whom when the
accusers stood up, they brought none accusation of such things as I supposed: but had
certain questions against him of their own
superstition, and of one Jesus, which was
dead, whom Paul affirmed to be alive. And
because I doubted of such manner of questions, I asked him whether be would go to
Jerusalem, and there be judged of these
matters. But when Paul had appealed to be
reserved unto the hearing of Augustus, I
commanded him to be kept till I might send
him to Cæsar. Then Agrippa said unto Festus, I would also hear the man myself. To-
morrow, said he, thou shalt hear him." (v.
14–22.) And observe a crimination of the
Jews, not from Paul, but also from the govern-
or. "Desiring," he says, "to have judgment
against him." To whom I said, to their
shame, that "it is not the manner of the
Romans," before giving an opportunity to
speak for himself, "to sacrifice a man." But
I did give him (such opportunity), and I
found no fault in him. "Because I doubted,"
says he, of "such manner of questions: he
casts a veil also over his own wrong. Then
the other desires to see him. (*b*) But let us
look again at what has been said.[1]

(Recapitulation.) "And when Felix," etc.

(v. 22.) Observe on all occasions how the
governors try to keep off from themselves the
annoyance of the Jews, and are often compelled to act contrary to justice, and seek
pretexts for deferring: for of course it was
not from ignorance that he deferred the cause,
but knowing it. And his wife also hears,
together with the governor. (v. 24.) This
seems to me to show great honor. For he
would not have brought his wife to be present
with him at the hearing, but that he thought
great things of him. It seems to me that she
also longed for this. And observe how Paul
immediately discourses not only about faith, nor
about remission of sins, but also about practical points of duty. "Go thy way," he says,
"for this time: when I have a convenient
season, I will call for thee." (v. 25.) Observe
his hardness of heart: hearing such things,
"he hoped that he should receive money from
him!" (v. 26.) And not only so, but even
after conversing with him—for it was towards
the end of his government—he left him
bound, "willing to show the Jews a pleasure"
(v. 27): so that he not only coveted money,
but also glory. How, O wretch, canst thou
look for money from a man who preaches the
contrary? But that he did not get it, is evident from his leaving him bound; he would
have loosed him, had he received it. "Of temperance," it says, he reasoned; but the other
was hankering to receive money from him who
discoursed these things! And to ask indeed
he did not dare: for such is wickedness: but
he hoped it. "And when two years were
completed," etc., so that it was but natural
that he showed them a pleasure, as he had
been so long governor there. "Now when
Festus was come into the province," etc.
(ch. xxv. 1, 2.) At the very beginning, the
priests came to him, who would not have hesitated to go even to Cæsarea, unless he had
been seen immediately coming up, since immediately on his arrival they come to him.
And he spends ten days,[2] in order, I suppose,
to be open to those who wished to corrupt
him with bribes. But Paul was in the prison.
"They besought him," it says, "that he would
send for him:" why did they desire it as a
favor, if he was deserving of death? But thus
their plotting became evident even to him, so
that discoursing of it (to Agrippa), he says,
"desiring to have judgment against him."
They wanted to induce him to pass sentence
now immediately, being afraid of Paul's tongue.
What are ye afraid of? What are ye in

such a hurry? In fact, that expression, "that he should be kept"[1] (v. 4), shows this. Does he want to escape? "Let them therefore," he says, "which among you are able, accuse him." (v. 5.) Again accusers, again at Cæsarea, again Paul is brought forth. And having come, immediately "he sat on the judgment-seat" (v. 6); with all his haste: they so drove, so hurried him. While as yet he had not got acquainted with the Jews, nor experienced the honor paid to him by them, he answered rightly: but now that he had been in Jerusalem ten days, he too wants to pleasure them (by sacrificing Paul to them): then, also to deceive Paul, "Wilt thou," says he, "be judged there of these things by me?" (v. 9.) I am not giving thee up to them—but this was the fact—and he leaves the point to his own choice, that by this mark of respect he might get him to yield: since his was the sentence,[2] and it would have been too barefaced, when he had been convicted of nothing here, to take him back thither. "But Paul said, At Cæsar's tribunal am I standing," etc. (v. 10): he did not say, I will not, lest he should make the judge more vehement, but (here) again is his great boldness: They cast me out once for all, themselves, and by this they think to condemn me, by their showing that I have offended against Cæsar: at his bar I choose to be judged, at the bar of the injured person himself. "To the Jews have I done no wrong, as thou also very well knowest." Here now he reproved him, that he too wished to sacrifice him to the Jews: then, on the other hand, he relaxes (the sternness of) his speech: "if then I be an offender, or have committed anything worthy of death, I refuse not to die." I utter sentence against myself. For along with boldness of speech there must be also justness of cause, so as to abash (the hearer). "But if there be nothing in the things whereof these accuse me, no man"—however he may wish it—"no man may sacrifice me to please them." He said, not, I am not worthy of death, nor, I am worthy to be acquitted, but, I am ready to take my trial before Cæsar. At the same time too, remembering the dream, he was the more confident to appeal. (ch. xxiii. 11.) And he

said not, Thou (mayest not), but, neither any other man may sacrifice me, that it might be no affront to him. "Then Festus, when he had conferred with the council"—do you observe how he seeks to gratify them? for this is favor —"having conferred," it says, "with the council, he said, Hast thou appealed unto Cæsar? unto Cæsar shalt thou go." (v. 12.) See how his trial is again lengthened out, and how the plot against him becomes an occasion for the preaching: so that with ease and in safe custody he should be taken away to Rome,[3] with none to plot evil against him: for it was not the same thing his simply coming there, and his coming on such a cause. For, in fact this was what made the Jews come together there. (ch. xxviii. 17.) Then again, some time passes while he tarries at Jerusalem, that you may learn, that, though some time passed, the evil design against him prevails nothing, God not permitting it. But this king Agrippa, who was also a Herod, was a different Agrippa, after him of James' time, so that this is the fourth (Herod). See how his enemies coöperate with him against their will. To make the audience large, Agrippa falls into a desire of hearing: and he does not simply hear, but with much parade. And see what a vindication (ἀπολογίαν)! So writes Festus,[4] and the ruthlessness of the Jews is openly made a show of: for when it is the governor that says these things, he is a witness above all suspicion: so that the Jews are condemned by him also. For, when all had pronounced sentence against them, then, and not sooner, God brings upon them the punishment. But observe: Lysias gave it against them, Felix against them, Festus against them—although he wished to gratify them[5]—Agrippa against them. What further? The Pharisees—even they gave it against themselves. No evil, says Festus, "of such things as I supposed: no accusation did they bring against him." (v. 18.) And yet they did bring it: true, but they did not prove it: for their evil design and daring plot against him gave cause to surmise this, but the examination brought out nothing of the kind. "And of one Jesus," he says, "which was dead." (v. 19.) He says naturally enough, "of one" (Jesus), as being a man in office, and not caring for these things.

---

[1] τὸ, "φυλάττεσθαι;" this seems to refer to xxiii. 35: in v. 4, the expression is τηρεῖσθαι. Perhaps Chrys. said, "He was safe in custody, for Felix had ordered him φυλάττεσθαι, and there he was still. Then what needs this fresh order that he should τηρεῖσθαι? He is not attempting to escape, is he? It shows the spirit of the governor: 'we have him safe; come down and accuse him.'"

[2] ἐπειδὴ ἦν καὶ ἡ ἀπόφασις. Mod. text and Sav. omit the καὶ. Ben. ἐπειδὴ εἰ ἦν ἀπόφασις, with no authority of Mss. We have marked the clause as corrupt. Possibly, καλὴ πρόφασις is latent in the words, with the sense "since some handsome pretext was necessary" (or the like): or, perhaps, ἐπειδὴ Καὶ [σαρος] ἦν ἡ ἀπόφασις, as comment upon the clause, Ἐπὶ τοῦ βήματος Καίσαρος ἐστώς εἰμι.

[3] εἰς τὰ Ἱεροσόλυμα all our Mss., and so Edd. without remark. Yet the sense plainly requires εἰς Ῥώμην, and in fact the Catena has preserved the true reading. In the next sentence, he seems to be commenting upon the πλείους ἡμέρας of v. 14 to this effect: "See how his cause is lengthened out by all these delays: the time (ten days) of Festus' stay at Jerusalem; then the second hearing; now again, πλείους ἡμέρας: but for all this, his enemies are not able to effect their design.

[4] Alluding to v. 26, 27 (which mod. text inserts here): i. e. "to this same effect Festus also writes, in his report to the Emperor."

[5] For καὶ οἱ χαριζόμενοι αὐτοῖς, Mss. and Edd. we restore from the Catena καίτοι χαριζόμενος αὐτοῖς.

20

" And not knowing, for my part, what to make of the enquiry concerning these things " (v. 20)—of course, it went beyond a judge's hearing, the examining into these matters. If thou art at a loss, why dost thou drag him to Jerusalem ? But the other would not deign this : no, " To Cæsar " (says he) ; as in fact it was touching Cæsar that they accused him. Do you hear the appeal ? hear the plotting of the Jews ? hear their factious spirit ? All these things provoked him to a desire (of hearing him) : and he gives them the gratification, and Paul becomes more renowned. For such, as I said, are the ill designs (of enemies). Had not these things been so, none of these rulers would have deigned to hear him, none would have heard with such quietness and silence. And he seems indeed to be teaching, he seems to be making a defence ; but he rather makes a public harangue with much orderliness. Then let us not think that ill designs against us are a grievous thing. So long as we do not make ill designs against ourselves, no one will be able to have ill designs against us : or rather, people may do this, but they do us no hurt ; nay, even benefit us in the highest degree : for it rests with ourselves, whether we shall suffer evil, or not suffer evil. Lo ! I testify, and proclaim with a loud voice, more piercing even than the sound of a trumpet—and were it possible to ascend on high and cry aloud, I would not shrink from doing it—him that is a Christian, none of all the human beings that inhabit the earth will have power to hurt. And why do I say, human beings ? Not even the Evil Spirit himself, the tyrant, the Devil, can do this, unless the man injure himself ; be what it may that any one works, in vain he works it. For even as no human being could hurt an angel, if he were on earth, so neither can one human being hurt another human being. But neither again will he himself be able to hurt another, so long as he is good. What then can be equal to this, when neither to be hurt is possible, nor to hurt another ? For this thing is not less than the former, the not wishing to hurt another. Why, that man is a kind of angel, yea, like God. For such is God ; only, He indeed (is such) by nature, but this man, by moral choice : neither to be hurt is possible (for either), nor to hurt another. But this thing, this " not possible,' think not that it is for any want of power—for the contrary to this is want of power—no, I speak of the morally incompatible (τὸ ἀνενδεκτόν). For the (Divine) Nature is neither Itself susceptible of hurt, nor capable of hurting another : since this very thing in itself is a hurt. For in no other way do we hurt ourselves, than by

hurting another, and our greatest sins become such from our doing injury to ourselves. So that for this reason also the Christian cannot be hurt, namely, because neither can he hurt. But how in hurting others we hurt ourselves, come, let us take this saying in hand for examination in detail. Let a man wrong another, insult, overreach ; whom then has he hurt ? is it not himself first ? This is plain to every one. For to the one, the damage is in money, to himself, it is in the soul ; to destruction, and to punishment. Again, let another be envious : is it not himself he has injured ? For such is the nature of injustice : to its own author first it does incalculable hurt. " Yes,[1] but to another also ? " True, but nothing worth considering : or rather, not even a little—nay, it even benefits him. For let there be,—as the whole matter lies most in these examples,—let there be some poor man, having but little property and (barely) provided with necessary food,[2] and another rich and wealthy, and having much power, and then let him take the poor man's property, and strip him naked, and give him up to starvation, while he shall luxuriate in what he has unjustly taken from the other : not only has he not hurt that man at all—he has even benefited him, while himself he has not only not benefited, but even hurt. For how should it be otherwise ? In the first place, harassed by an evil conscience, and day by day condemning himself and being condemned by all men : and then, secondly, in the judgment to come. But the other, how is he benefited ? Because to suffer ill and bear it nobly, is great gain : for it is a doing away of sins, this suffering of ill, it is a training to philosophy, it is a discipline of virtue. Let us see which of the two is in evil case, this man or that. For the one, if he be a man of well-ordered mind, will bear it nobly : the other will be every day in a constant tremor and misgiving : which then is hurt, this man or that ? " You talk idly," say you : " for when a man has nothing to eat, and is forced to bewail himself and to feel himself very wretched, or comes and begs, and gets nothing, is not that a ruining of both soul and body ? " No, it is you that talk idly : for I show facts in proof. For say, does none of the rich feel himself wretched ? What then ? Is poverty the cause of his wretchedness ? " But he does not starve." And what of that ? The greater is the punishment, when having riches he does

---

[1] 'Αλλὰ καὶ ἕτερον· ἀλλ' οὐδὲν ἀξιόπιστον· μᾶλλον δὲ οὐδὲ μικρόν, ἀλλὰ καὶ ὠφελεῖ. So B. C.; in A. all this is omitted, Mod. text—"incalculable mischief, but little to another, or rather not even a little does it hurt, nay even benefits. But I have said nothing worthy of belief ἀλλ' οὐδὲν ἀξιόπιστον εἴρηκα. Well then, let there be," etc.

[2] χρήματα ἔχων ὀλίγα καὶ τῆς ἀναγκαίας εὐπορῶν τροφῆς, ἕτερος δὲ πλούσιος καὶ εὔπορος. So the Mss. and Edd. without comment. We assume it to be ἀπορῶν.

this. For neither does wealth make a man strong-minded, nor poverty make him weak: otherwise none of those living in wealth would pass a wretched life, nor would any of those in poverty (not) curse his fate. But that yours is indeed the idle talk, I will make manifest to you from hence. Was Paul in poverty or in wealth? did he suffer hunger, or did he not? You may hear himself saying, "In hunger and thirst." (2 Cor. xi. 27.) Did the prophets suffer hunger, or did they not? They too had a hard time of it. "Again, you fetch up Paul to me, again the prophets, some ten or twenty men." But whence shall I bring examples? "Show me from the many some who bear ills nobly." But[1] the rare is ever such: however, if you will, let us examine the matter as it is in itself. Let us see whose is the greater and sharper care, whose the more easy to be borne. The one is solicitous about his necessary food, the other about numberless matters, freed from that care. The rich man is not afraid on the score of hunger, but he is afraid about other things: oftentimes for his very life. The poor man is not free from anxiety about food, but he is free from other anxieties, he has safety, has quietness, has security.

If to injure another is not an evil, but a good, wherefore are we ashamed? wherefore do we cover our faces? Wherefore, being reproached, are we vexed and disconcerted? If the being injured is not a good thing, wherefore do we pride ourselves, and glory in the thing, and justify ourselves on its account? Would you learn how this is better than that? Observe those who are in the one condition, and those who are in the other. Wherefore are laws? Wherefore are courts of justice? Wherefore punishments? Is it not, on account of those men, as being diseased and unsound? But the pleasure lies great, you will say. Let us not speak of the future: let us look into the present. What is worse than a man who is under such a suspicion as this? what more precarious? what more unsound? is he not always in a state of shipwreck? Even if he do any just thing, he is not credited, condemned as he is by all on account of his power (of injuring): for in all who dwell with him he has accusers: he cannot enjoy friendship: for none would readily choose to become the friend of a man who has such a character, for fear of becoming implicated with him in the opinion held of him. As if he were a wild beast, all men turn away from him; as from a pest, a foe, a man-slayer, and an enemy of nature, so they shrink from the unjust man. If he who has wronged another happen to be brought into a

court of justice, he does not even need an accuser, his character condemns him in place of any accuser. Not so he who is injured; he has all men to take his part, to condole with him, to stretch out the hand of help: he stands on safe ground. If to injure another be a good and a safe thing, let any one confess that he is unjust: but if he dares not do this, why then does he pursue it as a good thing? But let us see in our own persons, if this same be done there, what evils come of it: (I mean,) if any of the parts or functions within us having overstepped its proper bounds, grasp at the office of some other. For let the spleen, if it will, have left its proper place, and seize on the part belonging to some other organ along with its own, is not this disease? The moisture within us, let it fill every place, is it not dropsy and gout?[2] is not this to ruin itself, along with the other? Again, let the bile seek for a wide room, and let the blood be diffused throughout every part. But how is it in the soul with anger, lust, and all the rest, if the food exceed its proper measure? Again in the body, if the eye wish to take in more, or to see more than is allotted to it, or admit a greater light than is proper. But if, when the light is good, yet the eye is ruined, if it choose to see more than is right: consider what it must be in the case of an evil thing. If the ear take in a (too) loud voice, the sense is stunned: the mind, if it reason about things above itself, is overpowered: and whatever is in excess, mars all. For this is πλεονεξία, the wanting to have more than what is marked off and allotted. So too in respect of money; when we will needs put upon (us) more burdens (than is meet), although we do not perceive it, to our sore hurt we are nourishing within ourselves a wild beast; much having, yet much wanting, numberless the cares we entangle ourselves withal, many the handles we furnish the devil against ourselves. In the case of the rich, however, the devil has not even need of labor, so surely do their very concerns of business of themselves ruin them. Wherefore I beseech you to abstain from the lust of these things, that we may be enabled to escape the snares of the evil one, and having taken hold of virtue, to attain unto the good things eternal, through the grace and mercy of our Lord Jesus Christ, with Whom to the Father and the Holy Ghost together be glory forever. Amen.

---

[1] Ἀλλὰ τὸ σπάνιον ἀεὶ τοιοῦτον. One would expect Ἀλλὰ σπάνιον ἀεὶ τὸ τοιοῦτον.—Mod. text adds, καὶ ὀλίγοι οἱ καλοί.

[2] καὶ ποδαλγία; οὐχὶ ἑαυτὸν συνδιέφθειρε μετ' ἐκείνου; ἡ χολὴ πάλιν εὐρυχωρίαν ζητείτω. Mod. text "is not this dropsy? μετ' ἐκείνου ἡ χολὴ κ. τ. λ. and below ἐὰν ὑπερβῇ τὸ μέτρον, οὐχὶ ἑαυτὸν συνδιέφθειρε; οὕτω καὶ ἡ τροφή. adding, "if it be taken beyond what can be digested, it involves the body in diseases. For whence comes the gout? whence the paralyzing and commotion of the body? Is it not from the immediate quantity of aliments? Again in the body," etc.

HOMILY LII.

ACTS XXV. 23.

"And on the morrow, when Agrippa was come, and Bernice with great pomp, and was entered into the place of hearing, with the chief captains, and principal men of the city, at Festus' commandment Paul was brought forth.

SEE what an audience is gathered together for Paul. Having collected all his guards, the governor is come, and the king, and the tribunes, "with the principal men," it says, "of the city." Then Paul being brought forth, see how he is proclaimed as conqueror. Festus himself acquits him from the charges, for what says Festus? "And Festus said, King Agrippa, and all men which are here present with us, ye see this man, about whom all the multitude of the Jews have dealt with me, both at Jerusalem, and also here, crying that he ought not to live any longer. But when I found that he had committed nothing worthy of death, and that he himself hath appealed to Augustus, I have determined to send him. Of whom I have no certain thing to write unto my lord. Wherefore I have brought him forth before you, and especially before thee, O king Agrippa, that, after examination had, I might have somewhat to write. For it seemeth to me unreasonable to send a prisoner, and not withal to signify the crimes laid against him." (v. 24-27.) Mark how he accuses them, while he acquits him. O what an abundance of justifications! After all these repeated examinations, the governor finds not how he may condemn him. They said he was worthy of death. On this account he said also: "When I found," says he "that he had committed nothing worthy of death.— Of whom I have no certain thing to write to my lord." This too is a proof of Paul's spotlessness, that the judge found nothing to say concerning him. "Therefore I have brought him forth," he says, "before you. For it seemeth to me unreasonable to send a prisoner, and not withal to signify the crime laid against him." Such were the great straits into which the Jews brought themselves and their rulers! What then? "Agrippa said to Paul, Thou art permitted to speak for thyself." (ch. xxvi. 1.) From his great desire to hear, the king permits him to speak. But Paul speaks out forthwith with boldness, not flattering, but for this reason saying that he is happy, namely, because (Agrippa) knew all. "Then Paul stretched forth the hand, and answered for himself. I think myself happy, king Agrippa, because I shall answer for myself this day before thee touching all the things whereof I am accused of the Jews. Especially because I know thee to be expert in all questions which are among the Jews: wherefore I beseech thee to hear me patiently." (v. 2, 3.) And yet, had he been conscious of guilt, he should have feared at being tried in the presence of one who knew all the facts: but this is a mark of a clear conscience, not to shrink from a judge who has an accurate knowledge of the circumstances, but even to rejoice, and to call himself happy. "I beseech thee," he says, "to hear me patiently." Since he is about to lengthen out his speech, and to say something about himself, on this account, he premises an entreaty, and (then) says: "My manner of life from my youth, which was at the first among mine own nation at Jerusalem, know all the Jews: which knew me from the beginning, if they would testify, that after the most straitest sect of our religion I lived a Pharisee." (v. 4, 5.) Then how should I have become a seditious person, who when young was (thus) testified of by all? Then too from his sect: "after the most straitest sect," says he, "of our religion I lived." "What then, if though the sect indeed be worthy of admiration, thou art evil?" Touching this also I call all to witness—touching my life and conversation. "And now I stand and am judged for the hope of the promise made of God unto our fathers: unto which promise our twelve tribes, instantly serving God day and night, hope to come. For which hope's sake, king Agrippa, I am accused of the Jews. Why should it be thought a thing incredible with you, that God should raise the dead?" (v. 6-8.) Two arguments he lays down for the Resurrection: one, the argument from the prophets: and he does not bring forward any prophet (in particular,) but the doctrine itself as held by the Jews: the other and stronger one, the argument from the facts—(especially from this,) that Christ Himself held discourse with him. And he lays the ground for this by (other) arguments, relating accurately his former madness. Then too, with high commendation of the Jews, he says, "Night and day," says he, "serving (God) look to attain unto." So that even if I had not been of unblemished life, it is not for this (doctrine) that I ought to be brought to trial :—"for which hope, king Agrippa, I am accused of the Jews." And then another argument: "Why should it be thought a thing incredible with you, that God should raise the dead?" Since, if such an opinion had not existed, if they had not been brought up in these dogmas, but they were now for the first time brought in, perhaps[1] some one might not have received the saying. Then he tells, how he persecuted : this also helps the proof: and he brings forward the chief priests as witnesses, and the "strange cities," and that he heard Him saying to him, "It is hard for thee to kick against the pricks," and shows the mercifulness of God, that, though being persecuted He appeared (to men), and did that benefit not to me only, but also sent me as teacher to others : and shows also the prophecy, now come to pass, which he then heard, "Delivering thee from the people, and from the Gentiles, unto whom I send thee." Showing all this, he says : "I verily thought with myself, that I ought to do many things contrary to the name of Jesus of Nazareth. Which thing I also did in Jerusalem : and many of the saints did I shut up in prison, having received authority from the chief priests ; and when they were put to death, I gave my voice against them. And I punished them oft in every synagogue, and compelled them to blaspheme ; and being exceedingly mad against them, I persecuted them even unto strange cities. Whereupon as I went to Damascus with authority and commission from the chief priests, at midday, O king, I saw in the way a light from heaven, above the brightness of the sun, shining round about me and them which journeyed with me. And when we were all fallen to the earth, I heard a voice speaking unto me, and saying in the Hebrew tongue, Saul, Saul, why persecutest thou Me? it is hard for thee to kick against the pricks. And I said, Who art Thou, Lord? And he said, I am Jesus whom thou persecutest ; but rise, and stand upon thy feet: for I have appeared unto thee for this purpose, to make thee a minister and a witness both of these things which thou hast seen, and of those things in the which I will appear unto thee : delivering thee from the

people, and from the Gentiles, unto whom now I send thee, to open their eyes, and to turn them from darkness to light, and from the power of Satan unto God, that they may receive forgiveness of sins (v. 9–18):—observe[2] how mildly he discourses—God, he says, said (this) to me, "that they may receive forgiveness of sins, and inheritance among them which are sanctified by faith that is in Me." By these things, says he, I was persuaded, by this vision He drew me to Himself, and so persuaded me, that I made no delay. "Whereupon, O king Agrippa, I was not disobedient unto the heavenly vision : but showed first unto them of Damascus, and at Jerusalem, and throughout all the coasts of Judea, and then to the Gentiles, that they should repent and turn to God, and do works meet for repentance." (v. 19, 20.) I therefore, who instructed others also concerning the most excellent way of living, how should I myself have become the author of sedition and contention ? "For these causes the Jews caught me in the temple, and went about to kill me. Having therefore obtained help of God, I continue unto this day, witnessing both to small and great, saying none other things than those which the prophets and Moses did say should come." (v. 21, 22.) See how free from flattery his speech is, and how he ascribes the whole to God. Then his boldness—but neither do I now desist : and the sure grounds—for it is from the prophets that I urge the question, "Whether the Christ was to suffer: " then[3] the Resurrection and the promise, "Whether He, as the first to rise from the dead, should show light unto the people and to the Gentiles." (v. 23.) Festus saw the boldness, and what says he? For Paul was all along addressing himself to the king—he was in a manner annoyed,[4] and says to him, "Thou art beside thyself, Paul : " for, "while he thus discoursed, Festus said with a loud voice, Paul, thou art beside thyself: much learning doth make thee mad." (v. 24.) What then says Paul? With gentleness, "I am not mad," says he, "most noble Festus ; but speak forth the words of truth

---

[1] Old text omits ἴσως, and puts it as a question, "Who would not have received the saying?"

[2] This is the comment on "forgiveness of sins:" the ἐπιεικὲς consisting in the not enlarging upon the greatness and aggravation of their sins. In the Mss. and Edd. this is placed at the end of v. 18, and then, "God said to me, I have appeared to thee," and the rest repeated to "forgiveness of sins."

[3] Mod. text "Whether He (as) first to rise from the dead should declare light: as if he had said, Christ as the first that rose dieth no more." It is manifest from the declaring this to all, that they also (have to) expect it for themselves. Then Festus seeing the boldness, since he all along addressed himself to the king, not once ceasing to look full towards him, was as annoyed (ὥσπερ ἔπαθέ τι), and says, " Thou art mad, Paul." And that he says this in annoyance (or passion), hear from what follows. " And as he thus discoursed," etc.

[4] ὥσπερ ἔπαθέ τι. This is explained in the Recapitulation: " with a loud voice—οὕτω θυμοῦ ἦν καὶ ὀργῆς."

and soberness." (v. 25.) Then too he gives him to understand why, turning from him, he addressed his speech to the king: "For the king knoweth of these things, before whom also I speak freely: for I am persuaded that none of these things are hidden from him: for this thing was not done in a corner." (v. 26.) He shows, that (the king) knows all perfectly; at the same time, all but saying to the Jews, And ye indeed ought to have known these things—for this is the meaning of that which he adds, "For this thing was not done in a corner. And Agrippa, said to Paul, Ἐν ὀλίγῳ thou persuadest me to be a Christian." What is ἐν ὀλίγῳ?[1] "Within a little, παρὰ μικρόν. "And Paul said, I could pray to God," καὶ ἐν ὀλίγῳ καὶ ἐν πολλῷ, (that is) "I could pray to God," for my part, not "in little" (but "in much"): he does not simply pray, he prays (not briefly, but) with largeness— "that not only thou, but also all that hear me this day, were such as I am."* Then he

adds, "except these bonds;" and yet it was matter of glory; true, but looking to their notion of it, therefore says he, "except these bonds." (v. 27–29.)

(Recapitulation.) "And on the morrow," etc. (v. 23.) The Jews desisted ever since Paul exercised his right of appeal.[2] Then also for him the theatre becomes a splendid one: "with great pomp" they were present. "And Festus said," etc. "The whole multitude of the Jews—" not some of them only, and others not so—"both at Jerusalem, and also here," they said "that he ought not to live any longer." (v. 24.) "And I having found," etc. It shows that he did right in appealing to Cæsar. For if[3] though they had no great matter to allege against him, yet those (at Jerusalem) were mad against him, with good reason may he go to Cæsar. "That after examination had by you," he says, "I may get somewhat to write." Observe how the matter is repeatedly put to the test. The Jews therefore may thank themselves for this vindication[4] (of Paul), which would come to the ears of those also who were at Rome. See how they become the unwilling heralds both of their own wickedness and of Paul's virtue, even to the emperor himself: so that Paul was carried away (to Rome) with more renown than if he had gone thither without bonds: for not as an impostor and a deceiver, after so many judges had acquitted him, was he now carried thither. Quit therefore of all charges,[5] among those with whom he was bred and born, and not only so, (but) thus free from all suspicion, he makes his appearance at Rome. "Then Paul," etc. (ch.

---

[1] Old text: ".v. 27-29. Εὐξαιμην ἄν, φησίν, ἔγωγε οὐκ ἐν ὀλίγῳ, τί ἐστι; παρὰ μικρόν. Καὶ οὐχ ἅπλως εὔχεται ἀλλὰ καὶ ἐπιτεταμένως. From the Recapitulation it appears that Chrys. supposes that Paul, as an ἰδιώτης, i. e. not conversant with the elegancies of Greek style, οὐκ ἐνόησεν τί ἐστιν Ἐν ὀλίγῳ ἀλλ' ἐνόμισεν ὅτι ἐξ ὀλίγου: did not perceive what Agrippa's phrase meant (viz. as here explained. παρὰ μικρόν), but supposed it to be the same as ἐξ ὀλίγου." "With little ado"—i. e. thou makest short work to persuade me, as if this were an easy thing, to be done in brief: therefore Paul answers, Be it in little, or be it in much, I could pray to God, with no brief and hasty prayer, but ἐπιτεταμένως, much and earnestly.—For καὶ οὐχ ἅπλως, we read καὶ ἐν πολλῷ· οὐχ ἅ. and transpose τί ἐστιν ἐν ὀλίγῳ; παρὰ μικρόν, to its fitting place. Mod. text οὐκ ἐν ὀλίγῳ· τουτέστι, μικρόν, omitting παρὰ, meaning this as the explanation of St. Paul's εὔξ. ἐν ὀλίγῳ. Of the Edd., Commel. Sav. Ben. give παρὰ, and so Par. Ben. 2, who however rejects the οὐκ.

* The correct interpretation of v. 28, 29 depends upon the ff. points: (1) Whether the remark of Agrippa is sincere or ironical. (2) Whether the true text in v. 29 is ἐν πολλῷ or ἐν μεγάλῳ. (3) What noun, if any, is to be supplied with the adjectives ὀλίγῳ and μεγάλῳ (or πολλῷ). Regarding the first question, the considerations in favor of the view that Agrippa's remark is ironical are (a) the frivolous character of the man, (b) the current use of Christian among Jews and Romans as a term of reproach and contempt. Touching the second point, we find that μεγάλῳ is favored by א A. B. Syr. Copt. Aram. Vulg., as against G. H. for πολλῷ. The former reading is adopted by Tischendorf, Lachmann, Meyer, Westcott and Hort, and most modern critics, and the evidence in its favor may be considered decisive. Whether any noun is to be supplied to ὀλίγῳ and μεγάλῳ (as most) or not (as Meyer) is not important. In any case the sense must be completed. What do "in little" and "in great" mean? The sense may be completed by supplying (a) the idea of time—"in a little time," i. e. almost. In this case, ἐν μεγάλῳ would have to be rendered "wholly" or "altogether," a meaning which ἐν μεγάλῳ cannot well convey. Another rendering which might be derived from supplying the idea of time—differing but slightly from the foregoing—would be: "in a little time thou art persuading me!" i. e. dost thou think so soon to persuade me? and Paul replies: "Whether in a little time or in a long time—whether soon or late—I could wish," etc. The first interpretation lays emphasis upon the state of Agrippa's mind—persuaded almost—persuaded altogether; the second upon the element of time required to accomplish the persuasion (ironically spoken of). (b) The idea of labor, trouble or argument may be supplied thus: "Easily—with few words—or with little trouble thou persuaded me!" and Paul's answer is: Whether with little (labor) or with much, I would to God that," etc. This view we prefer, because, (a) it harmonizes best with the natural meaning of ἐν μεγάλῳ which (if the true reading) requires taking both phrases in a quantitative sense. (b) It is favored by the evidently ironical character of Agrippa's remark. There is no ground for the opinion of Chrys. (followed by Calvin) tnat ἐν ὀλίγῳ is used in different senses in the language of Agrippa and Paul, much less for the idea that Paul did not understand what ἐν ὀλίγῳ meant!—G. B. S.

[2] Ἀπέστησαν λοιπὸν οἱ Ἰ. τῇ ἀφέσει χρησαμένου ἐκείνου A. B. (C. has lost a leaf here). Mod. text ἐφέσει. Cat. Ἐπέστησαν λοιπὸν οἱ Ἰ τῇ ἐφέσει χρησάμενοι ἐκείνου. If this be the true reading, it should seem to belong to πᾶν τὸ πλ. τῶν Ἰουδ., viz. "'concerning whom all the multitude of the Jews besought me:' the Jews thereupon had set upon him, using his, Festus' permission." But ἀπεστ. and ἐφέσει give a better sense as comment on v. 23, i. e. "No mention now of the Jews—they had left him, when he had made his appeal."—Then, μετὰ πολλῆς φαντ. (mod. text adds ὁ βασιλεὺς καὶ) πᾶν τὸ πλῆθος τῶν Ἰ. παρῆσαν οὐχ οἱ μὲν οἱ δὲ οὔ. Which is not true, for it could not be said that all the Jews were present at this hearing before Agrippa. We read μετὰ π. φ. παρῆσαν. Then from v. 24, "πᾶν τὸ πλῆθος sc. ἐνέτυχόν μοι.

[3] Εἰ γὰρ οὐδὲν μὲν εἶχον δεινὸν εἰπεῖν. i. e. "As far as the matter of accusation was concerned, he knew that he had nothing to fear: ἐκεῖνοι δὲ ἐμεμήνεσαν, but the people yonder (at Jerusalem) were mad against him: therefore εἰκότως ἐπ' ἐκεῖνον ἔρχεται, no wonder he is for going to Cæsar."

[4] The ἀπολογία is Festus' written report of the hearings before him, which would be sent to Rome, and would at once testify to Paul's innocence, and to the malignity of the Jews.

[5] Πάντα τοίνυν ἀποδυσάμενος, not as Ben. "omnibus ergo relictis, apud quos natus, etc." but in the sense of the phrase ἀποδύεσθαι (ἐγκλήματα) which is frequent in Chrys. That is, "the consequence is that Paul makes his first appearance at Rome, not merely as one who has cleared himself of all charges brought against him at home, but, after these repeated examinations, clear from all suspicion."—Below οἵστε κυρίων οὐκ ὄντων τῶν καταδικαζόντων αὐτόν: the sense intended may be, "seeing they were not his judges, even if they wished to condemn him."

xxvi. 1-3.) And he said not, Why is this? once for all I have appealed to Cæsar: I have been tried many times: when will there be an end of this? but what did he? Again he is ready to render an account, and that, before the man who was the best informed on the subject; and with much boldness, seeing they were not his judges to condemn him: but still, though they were not his judges, since that declaration was in force, " Unto Cæsar shalt thou go, he renders an account and gives full answers, " touching all the things," and not merely on one and another here and there. They accuse me of sedition, accuse me of heresy, accuse me that I have profaned the temple: " touching all these things I answer for myself:" now that these are not things in accordance with my ways, my accusers themselves are witnesses: " my manner of life from my youth," etc. (v. 4.) which is what he says on a former occasion " Being a zealot." (ch. xxii. 3.) And when the whole people was present, then he challenges their testimony: not [1] before the tribunal, but before Lysias, and again here, when more were present: whereas in that hearing there needed not much vindication of himself, since Lysias' letter exculpated him. " Know all the Jews," he says, " which knew me from the beginning." And he does not say what kind of life his was, but leaves it to their own conscience, and lays the whole stress on his *sect*, as he would not have chosen that sect, if he had been a man of evil disposition and bad character (πονηρὸς καὶ μοχθηρός). " But, for this hope " (Mss. and Edd. αἱρέσεως) he says, " I stand and am judged." (v. 6, 7.) This hope is honored among themselves also, because of this they pray, because of this they worship, that unto this they may attain: this same do I show forth. Why then, it is acting like madmen, to be doing all things for the sake of attaining to this, and yet to persecute him who believes in the same. " I indeed thought with myself," that is, I determined, " to do many things contrary to the name of Jesus of Nazareth." (v. 9.) I was not one of Christ's disciples: among those who fought against Him, was I. Whence also he is a witness who has a right to be believed, because he, a man who was doing numberless things, makes war on the believers, persuading them to blaspheme, stirring up all against them, cities, rulers, and by himself doing all

this of his own accord, was thus suddenly changed. Then again the witnesses, those who were with him: next he shows what just cause he had to be persuaded, both from the light, and from the prophets, and from the results, and from the things which have now taken place. See accordingly, how both from the prophets, and from these particulars, he confirms the proof to them. For that he may not seem to be broaching some novelty, although he had great things to say, yet he again takes refuge with the prophets, and puts this as a question for discussion.[2] Now this had a stronger claim upon belief, as having actually come to pass: but since he alone saw (Christ), he again fetches proof of it from the prophets. And see how he does not discourse alike in the court of justice, and in the assembly (of his own people); there indeed he says, " ye slew Him: " but here no such thing, that he might not kindle their anger more: but he shows the same thing, by saying, " Whether the Christ was to suffer." He so frees them from accusations: for the prophets, he says, say this. Therefore receive ye also the rest. Since he has mentioned the vison, he then without fear goes on to speak also of the good wrought by it. " To turn them from darkness to light, and from the power of Satan unto God. For to this end have I appeared unto thee" (v. 16-18), not to punish, but to make thee an Apostle. He shows the evils which possess unbelievers, " Satan, darkness; " the good things belonging to believers, light, God, " the inheritance of the saints. Whereupon, O king Agrippa," etc. (v. 19, 20.) He not only exhorts them to repent, but also to show forth a life worthy of admiration. And see how everywhere the Gentiles are admitted into connection with the people (Israel): for those who were present were of the Gentiles. " Testifying," he says, " both to great and small," (v. 22) that is, both to distinguished and undistinguished. This is also for the soldiers. Observe: having left the post of defendant, he took up that of teacher—and therefore also it is that Festus says to him, " Thou art beside thyself "—but then, that he may not seem to be himself the teacher, he brings in the prophets, and Moses: " Whether the Christ was to suffer, whether He as the first to rise from the dead should show light both to the people, and to the Gentiles."

---

[1] Mod. text " But not before the tribunal of Lysias alone does he this, but also before Festus, and again here." Ben. cites the old text only to condemn it. Inconsiderately: for it *was* in the hearing ἐπὶ Λυσίου xxii. 3-5. (Lysias had no " tribunal ") and here, that St. Paul thus challenged the testimony of the Jews: not before Felix, which is what is meant by ἐκεῖ, still less before Festus.

[2] καὶ τοῦτο μέσον τίθησι. The innovator not understanding the phrase, and its reference to Εἰ παθητὸς ὁ Χριστὸς etc., substitutes, " And puts their (words) in the midst."—The meaning is: " He had greater things to say than what the prophets had said:" he could say, " The Christ whom ye slew is risen, for I have seen Him: but instead of this, he put it as a subject for discussion, Did the prophets teach that the Christ was to suffer and to rise again ? "

(v. 23.) "And Festus said with a loud voice" —in such anger and displeasure (did he speak)—"Paul, thou art beside thyself." What then said Paul? "I am not mad," etc. "For this thing," he says, "was not done in a corner." (v. 25, 26.) Here he speaks of the Cross, of the Resurrection: that the doctrine was come to every part of the world. "King Agrippa," he says, "believest thou"—he does not say, the Resurrection, but—"the prophets?" (v. 27.) Then he forestalls him, and says: "I know that thou believest." Ἐν ὀλίγῳ (i. e. within a little,) "almost thou persuadeth me to be a Christian." (v. 28.) Paul did not understand what the phrase ἐν ὀλίγῳ meant: he thought it meant ἐξ ὀλίγου (i. e. with little cost or trouble), wherefore also he answers (as) to this: so unlearned was he.[1] And he said not, I do not wish (that), but, "I pray that not only thou, but also all that hear." Mark how free from flattery his speech is.—"I pray that this day they may be all such as I am, except these bonds." (v. 29.) He, the man that glories in his bonds, that puts them forth as a golden chain, deprecates them for these men: for they were as yet too weak in their minds, and it was rather in condescension that he so spake. For what could be better than those bonds which always in his Epistles he prefers (to all things else), saying, "Paul, a prisoner of Jesus Christ:" (Eph. iii. 1) and again, "On this account I am bound with this chain" (Acts xxviii. 20), "but the word of God is not bound;" and, "Even unto bonds, as an evil-doer." (2 Tim. ii. 9.) The punishment was twofold. For if indeed he had been so bound, as with a view to his good, the thing would have carried with it some consolation: but now (he is bound) both "as an evil-doer," and as with a view to very ill consequences; yet for none of these things cared he.[2]

Such is a soul winged with heavenly love. For if those who cherish the foul (earthly passion which men call) love, think nothing either glorious or precious, but those things alone which tend to gratify their lust, they think both glorious and honorable, and their mistress is everything to them; much more do those, who have been taken captive by this heavenly love, think nothing of the cost (τὰ ἐπιτίμια). But if we do not understand what I am saying, it is no marvel, while we are unskilled in this Divine Wisdom. For if any one be caught with the fire of Christ's love, he becomes such as a man would become who dwelt alone upon the earth, so utterly careless is he for glory or disgrace: but just as if he dwelt alone, he would care for nothing, no more does he in this case. As for trials, he so despises them, both scourges and imprisonments, as though the body in which he suffers these things were another's and not his own, or as though he had got a body made of adamant: while as for the sweet things of this life, he so laughs them to scorn, is so insensible to them, as we are insensible of dead bodies, being ourselves dead. He is as far from being taken captive by any passion, as the gold refined in the fire and purified is free from alloy. For even as flies would not dart into the midst of a flame, but fly from it, so the passions dare not even to come near this man. Would that I could bring forward examples of all this from among ourselves: but since we are at a loss for such, we must needs betake ourselves to this same Paul. Observe him then, how he felt towards the whole world. "The world is crucified unto me," he says, "and I unto the world" (Gal. vi. 14): I am dead to the world, and the world is dead to me. And again: "It is no longer I that live, but Christ liveth in me."[3] (ib. ii. 20.) And, to show you that he was as it were in solitude, and so looked upon the things present, hear himself saying, "While we look not at the things which are seen, but at the things which are not seen." (2 Cor. iv. 18.) What sayest thou? Answer me. And yet what thou sayest is the contrary; thou seest the things invisible, and the visible thou seest not. Such eyes as thou hadst gotten, such are the eyes which are given by Christ: for as these bodily eyes see indeed the things that are seen, but things unseen they see not: so those (heavenly eyes) do the contrary: none that beholds the invisible things, beholds the visible: no one beholding the things seen, beholds the invisible. Or is not this the case with us also? For when having turned our mind inwards we think of any of the unseen things, our views become raised above the

---

[1] See above, p. 310, note [1], and.* Yet some modern commentators assert that ἐν ὀλίγῳ cannot mean, as Chrys. says, παρὰ μικρόν: that this sense requires ὀλίγου, or ὀλίγου δεῖν, or παρ᾽ ὀλίγον: so that, in their view, Chrysostom's remark οὕτως ἰδιώτης ἦν would be quite out of place.—In the next sentence οὐ βούλομαι, all our Mss. and Edd. But Ben. renders it without the negative, Et non dixit, Vellem.

[2] He is commenting upon 2 Tim. ii. 9. "I suffer trouble as an evil-doer even unto bonds." To others, this might seem a twofold aggravation: both that he was treated as a malefactor, and that his destruction was intended. For if indeed he was put in bonds ὡς ἐπ᾽ ἀγάθῳ, the thing bore its comfort with it, and such was the case to him, but not in their intention; which was, that he should be in chains καὶ ὡς κακούργος καὶ ὡς ἐπὶ τοῖς δεινοῖς. Of the Mss. A. C. have ὡς ἐπὶ τοῖς δεινοῖς ἄλλοὺς· ἀλλ᾽ οὐδενὸς τούτων ἐφρόντιζεν. B. ἀλλοὺς· and so mod. text. But ἀλλοὺς seems to be only the abbreviation of the following ἀλλ᾽ οὐδενὸς. —

[3] Mod. text adds, "To say this, belongs to Paul only: ours it is, who are so far removed from him as the heaven is from the earth, to hide our faces, so that we dare not even to open our mouth."

things on earth.[1] Let us despise glory : let us be willing to be laughed at rather than to be praised. For he indeed who is laughed at is nothing hurt: but he who is praised is much hurt. Let us not think much of those things which terrify men, but as we do in the case of children, this let us do here : namely, if we see any one terrifying children, we do not hold that man in admiration : since in fact whoever does frighten, only frightens children ; for were it a man, he could not frighten him. Just as those who frighten (children in sport), do this either by drawing up their eyelids, or by otherwise distorting their face, but with the eye looking naturally and mild they would not be able to do this : so these others do this, by distorting their mental vision (τὸ διορατικὸν τῆς διανοίας). So that of a mild man and beautiful in soul nobody would be afraid ; on the contrary, we all respect him, honor and venerate him. See ye not, how the man who causes terror is also an object of hatred and abhorrence to us all ? For of those things which are only able to terrify what do we not turn away from ? Is it not so with wild beasts, with sounds, with sights, with places, with the air, such as darkness ? Let us not therefore think it a great thing, if men fear us. For, in the first place, no man indeed is frightened at us : and, secondly, it is no great thing (if they were). Virtue is a great good : and see how great. However wretched we may deem the things by means of which it consists, yet we admire virtue itself, and count them blessed (that have it). For who would not count the patient sufferer blessed, although poverty and such like things seem to be wretched ? When therefore it shines forth through those things which seem to be wretched, see how surpassingly great this is ! Thinkest thou much, O man, because thou art in power ? And what sort of power ? say, was it conferred by appointment ? (If so,) of men thou hast received power : appoint thyself to it from within. For the ruler is not he who is so called, but he who is really so. For as a king could not make a physician or an orator, so neither can he make a ruler : since it is not the (imperial) letters nor the name that makes a ruler. For, if you will, let any man build a medicine-shop, let him also have pupils, let him have instruments too and drugs, and let him visit those who are sick : are these things sufficient to make a physician ? By no means : but there is need of art, and without that, not only do these things

profit nothing, but they even hurt : since it were better that he who is not a physician should not even possess medicines. He that possesses them not, neither saves nor destroys : but he that possesses them, destroys, if he knows not how to use them : since the healing power is not only in the nature of the medicines, but also in the art of the person applying them : where this is not, all is marred. Such also is the ruler : he has for instruments, his voice, anger, executioners, banishments, honors, gifts, and praises ; he has also for medicines, the law ; has also for his patients, men ; for a place to practise in, the court of justice ; for pupils, he has the soldiers : if then he know not the science of healing, all these profit him nothing. The judge is a physician of souls, not of bodies : but if this art of healing the bodies needs so much care, much more that of healing the soul, since the soul is of more importance than the body. Then not the mere having the name of ruler is to be a ruler : since others also are called by great names : as Paul, Peter, James, and John : but the names do not make them that which they are called, as neither does my name make me (to be that which John was) ; I bear indeed the same name with that blessed man, but I am not the same thing (ὁμώνυμος, οὐ μὴν συνώνυμος), I am not John, but am called so. In the same way they are not rulers, but are called so. But those others are rulers even without these adjuncts, just as also a physician, though he may not actually practise his science, yet if he have it in his soul, he is a physician. Those are rulers, who bear rule over themselves. For there are these four things,[2] soul, family ; city, world : and the things form a regular progression (ὁδῷ προβαίνει). He therefore that is to superintend a family, and order it well, must first bring his own soul into order ; for it is his family : but if he cannot order his own family, where there is but one soul, where he himself is master, where he is always along with himself, how shall he order others ? He that is able to regulate his own soul, and makes the one part to rule, the other to be subject, this man will be able to regulate a family also : but he that can do this by a family, can do it by a city also : and if by a city, then also by the world. But if he cannot do this for his own soul, how then shall he be able to do it for the world ? These things have been spoken by me, that we may not be excited about offices of rule ; that we may know what ruling is : for this (which is

---

[1] μετέωροι τῶν ἐνεργειῶν ἡμῖν γίνονται αἱ ὄψεις. Unable to discover any meaning in this, (Ben. *sublimes nobis sunt : operationum oculi*), we conjecture τῶν ἐπιγειῶν.

[2] Mss. and Edd., τρία γὰρ ταῦτά ἐστι ψυχῇ (only F. has ψυχή): "there are for the soul these three subjects."—Below, Mss. and Edd. οἰκοδομεῖν for οἰκονομεῖν.

so called) is not ruling, but a mere object of derision, mere slavery, and many other names one might call it by. Tell me, what is proper to a ruler? is it not to help one's subjects, and to do them good? What then, if this be not the case? how shall he help others, who has not helped himself? he who has numberless tyrannies of the passions in his own soul, how shall he root out those of others? Again, with respect to "luxury" or delightful living: the true luxury or delight is not this (which is so called), but quite another thing. For as we have shown that the ruler is not he who is so called, but another (who has something more than the name), so the person who lives indeed in delight is another sort of person (than he whom we so describe). For "luxury" or delightful living seems indeed to be, the enjoying pleasure and the gratifying the belly: yet it is not this thing, but the contrary: it is, to have a soul worthy of admiration, and to be in a state of pleasure. For let there be a man eating, drinking, and wantoning; then let him suffer cares and loss of spirits: can this man be said to be in a state of delight? Therefore, it is not eating and drinking, it is the being in pleasure, that makes true luxury or delightful living. Let there be a man who gets only dry bread, and let him be filled with gladness: is not this pleasure? Well then, it is the true luxury. Let us see then, to whom this befalls— whether to the rich, or to those who are not rich? Neither to the one part altogether, nor to the other, but to those who so order their own souls, that they may not have many grounds for sorrows. And where is such a life as this to be found? for I see you all eager and wishing to hear what this life is which has no sorrows. Well then, let this be acknowledged first by you, that this is pleasure, this the true luxury, to have no sorrow to cause annoyance; and ask not of me meats, and wine, and sauces, and silken robes, and a sumptuous table. But if I shall show that apart from all these such a life as that is present (within our reach), then welcome thou this pleasure, and this life: for the most part of painful things happen to us from our not calculating things as we ought. Who then will have the most sorrows—he that cares for none of these things, or he that cares for them? He that fears changes, or he that does not fear? He that is in dread of jealousy, of envy, of false accusations, of plottings, of destruction, or he that stands aloof from these fears? He that wants many things, or he that wants nothing? He that is a slave to masters without number, or he that is a slave to none? He that has need of many things, or he that is free? He that has one lord to fear, or he that fears despots innumerable? Well then, greater is the pleasure here. This then let us pursue, and not be excited about the things present: but let us laugh to scorn all the pomp of life, and everywhere practise moderation, that we may be enabled so to pass through this life, that it may be without pain, and to attain unto the good things promised, through the grace and mercy of our Lord Jesus Christ, with Whom to the Father and the Holy Ghost together be glory, might, honor, now and ever, world without end. Amen.

HOMILY LIII.

ACTS XXVI. 30-32.

"And when he had thus spoken, the king rose up, and the governor, and Bernice, and they that sat with them: and when they were gone aside, they talked between themselves, saying, This man doeth nothing worthy of death or of bonds. Then said Agrippa unto Festus, This man might have been set at liberty, if he had not appealed unto Cæsar."

SEE how again also they pass sentence in his favor, and after having said, "Thou art beside thyself," (v. 24) they acquit him, as undeserving not only of death, but also of bonds, and indeed would have released him entirely, if he had not appealed to Cæsar. But this was done providentially, that he should also depart with bonds. "Unto bonds," he says, "as an evil doer." (1 Tim. ii. 9.) For if his Lord "was reckoned among the transgressors" (Mark xv. 28), much more he: but as the Lord did not share with them in their character, so neither did Paul. For in this is seen the marvellous thing, the being mixed up with such, and yet receiving no harm from them. "And when it was determined that we should sail into Italy, they delivered Paul and certain other prisoners unto one named Julius, a centurion of Augustus' band. And entering into a ship of Adramyttium, we launched, meaning to sail by the coasts of Asia; one Aristarchus, a Macedonian of Thessalonica, being with us. And the next day we touched at Sidon." (ch. xxvii. 1–3.) See how far Aristarchus also accompanies Paul. To good and useful purpose is Aristarchus present, as he would take back the report of all to Macedonia. "And Julius courteously entreated Paul, and gave him liberty to go unto his friends to refresh himself. Julius gave Paul liberty," it says, acting "courteously, that he might refresh himself;" as it was but natural that he should be much the worse from his bonds, and the fear, and the being dragged hither and thither. See how the writer does not hide this either, that Paul wished " to refresh himself. And when we had launched from thence, we sailed under Cyprus, because the winds were contrary." (v. 4.) Again trials, again contrary winds. See how the life of the saints is thus interwoven throughout: escaped from the court of justice, they fall in with shipwreck and storm. "And when we had sailed over the sea of Cilicia and Pamphylia, we came to Myra, a city of Lycia. And there the centurion found a ship of Alexandria sailing into Italy; and he put us therein." (v. 5, 6.) "A ship of Alexandria," it says. It is likely that both those (in the former ship) would bear to Asia the report of what had befallen Paul, and that these[1] would do the same in Lycia. See how God does not innovate or change the order of nature, but suffers them to sail into the unfavorable winds. But even so the miracle is wrought. That they may sail safely, He did not let them go out in the (open) sea, but they always sailed near the land. "And when we had sailed slowly many days, and scarce were come over against Cnidus, the wind not suffering us, we sailed under Crete, over against Salmone; and, hardly passing it, came unto a place which is called The fair havens; nigh whereunto was the city of Lasea. Now when much time was spent, and when sailing was now dangerous, because the fast was now already past, Paul admonished them." (v. 7–9.) By "the fast" here, I suppose he means that of the Jews.[*] For they departed thence a long time after the Pentecost, so that it was much about midwinter that they arrived at the coasts of Crete. And this too was no slight miracle, that they also should be saved on his account.

"Paul admonished them, and said unto them, Sirs, I perceive that this voyage will be with hurt and much damage, not only of the lading and ship, but also of our lives. Nevertheless the centurion believed the master and the owner of the ship, more than those things which were spoken by Paul. And because the haven was not commodious to winter in, the more part advised to depart thence also, if by any means they might attain to Phenice, and there to winter; which is an haven of Crete, and lieth toward the southwest and northwest. And when the south wind blew softly, supposing that they had obtained their purpose, loosing thence, they sailed close to Crete. But not long after there arose against it a tempestuous wind, called Euroclydon.† And when the ship was caught, and could not bear up into the wind, we let her drive" (R. V. "were driven.") (v. 10–15.) Paul therefore advised them to remain, and he foretells what would come of it: but they, being in a hurry, and being prevented by the place, wished to winter at Phenice. Mark then the providential ordering of the events: first indeed, "when the south wind blew softly, supposing they had obtained their purpose," they loosed the vessel, and came forth; then when the wind bore down upon them, they gave way to it driving them, and were with difficulty saved. "And running under a certain island which is called Clauda, we had much work to come by the boat: which when they had taken up, they used helps, undergirding the ship; and, fearing lest they should fall into the quicksands, ‡ strake sail,§ and so were driven. And we being exceedingly tossed with a tempest, the next day they lightened the ship; and the third day we cast out with our own hands the tackling of the ship. And when neither sun nor stars in many days appeared, and no small tempest lay on us, all hope that we

---

[1] Καὶ τούτους, meaning perhaps those who remained at Myra.

[*] The fast referred to was that which occurred on the great day of atonement (Lev. xxiii. 27) i. e. on the tenth of the seventh month (Tisri). This would be about the end of September, after the autumnal equinox, when navigation was considered dangerous.—G. B. S.

† Preponderant authority favors the reading εὐρακύλων from εὖρος, the S. E. wind and the Latin *Aquilo*, a N. wind (so א, B* A. Vulgate Erasmus Mill, Bengel, Olshausen, Hackett, Tischendorf, Lachmann, Tregelles, Westcott and Hort, R.V.) If εὐροκλύδων is read, it is disputed whether the first part of the word is εὖρος (Alford, Gloag, Howson,) or εὐρύς, broad. Meyer defends the latter reading, on the ground that the phrase ὁ καλούμενος requires that the word εὐρ. denote a *name* and not merely the direction of the wind and that it is easier to suppose that this reading should be modified into the former than the reverse. Alford supposes that εὐρακύλων was the name of the wind, which the Greek sailors did not understand and pronounced εὐροκλύδων. Meyer's argument is inadequate, and the probabilities favor the reading εὐρακύλων with the meaning, N. E. wind, a signification, moreover, which answers all the conditions of the narrative. (See Bib. Dict. *sub voce*.)—G.B.S.

‡ Rather, "on the Syrtis" (εἰς τὴν Σύρτιν.) There were two shoals on the coast of Africa, called by this name, the Syrtis Major and the Syrtis Minor. The former to the S. W. of Crete is the one here referred to.—G. B. S.

§ R. V. "they lowered the gear" (σκεῦος). The word σκεῦος—utensil, implement—is in itself indefinite and must be understood from the context. It has here been taken to mean "anchor;" "mast" (Olshausen); "sail" (Meyer, Lechler, Hackett, A. V.); "gear," meaning the ropes and topsails in order to set the ship in a direction off shore.—G. B. S.

should be saved was then taken away. But after long abstinence Paul stood forth in the midst of them, and said, Sirs, ye should have hearkened unto me, and not have loosed from Crete, and to have gained this harm and loss." (v. 16–21.) Then after so great a storm he does not speak as insultingly over them, but as wishing that at any rate he might be believed for the future. Wherefore also he alleges what had taken place for a testimony of the truth of what was about to be said by him. "And now I exhort you to be of good cheer : for there shall be no loss or any man's life among you, but of the ship. For there stood by me this night the angel of God, whose I am, and whom I serve, saying, Fear not, Paul ; thou must be brought before Cæsar : and, lo God hath given thee all them that sail with thee. Wherefore, sirs, be of good cheer, for I believe God, that it shall be even as it was told me. Howbeit we must be cast upon a certain island." (v. 22–26.) And he foretells two things ; both that they must be cast upon an island, and that though the ship would be lost, those who were in it should be saved—which thing he spoke not of conjecture, but of prophecy—and that he "must be brought before Cæsar." But this that he says, "God hath given thee all," is not spoken boastfully, but in the wish to win those who were sailing in the ship : for (he spoke thus), not that they might feel themselves bound to him, but that they might believe what he was saying. "God hath given thee ; " as much (as to say), They are worthy indeed of death, since they would not listen to thee : however, this is done out of favor to thee. "But when the fourteenth night was come, as we were driven up and down in Adria, about midnight the shipmen deemed that they drew near to some country ; and sounded, and found it twenty fathoms ; and when they had gone a little further, they sounded again, and found it fifteen fathoms. Then fearing lest they should have fallen upon rocks, they cast four anchors out of the stern, and wished for the day. And as the shipmen were about to flee out of the ship, when they had let down the boat into the sea, under color as though they would have cast anchors out of the foreship, Paul said to the centurion and to the soldiers, Except these abide in the ship, ye cannot be saved. Then the soldiers cut off the ropes of the boat, and let her fall off." (v. 27–32.) The sailors however, were about to escape, having no faith in what was said : but the centurion does believe Paul, For he says, If these flee, "ye cannot be saved : " so saying, not on this account, but that he might restrain them, and the prophecy

might not fall to the ground. See how as in a church they are instructed by the calmness of Paul's behavior, how he saved them out of the very midst of the dangers. And it is of providential ordering that Paul is disbelieved, that after proof of the facts, he might be believed : which accordingly was the case. And he exhorts them again to take some meat, and they do as he bids them, and he takes some first, to persuade them not by word, but also by act, that the storm did them no harm, but rather was a benefit to their souls. "And while the day was coming on, Paul besought them all to take meat, saying, This day is the fourteenth day that ye have tarried and continued fasting having taken nothing." (v. 33.) (b) And how, say you, did they go without food, having taken nothing ? how did they bear it ? Their fear possessed them, and did not let them fall into a desire of food, being, as they were, at the point of extreme jeopardy ; (f) but they had no care for food. "Wherefore I pray you to take some meat : for this is for your health : for there shall not an hair fall from the head of any of you. And when he had thus spoken, he took bread, and gave thanks to God in presence of them all : and when he had broken it, he began to eat. Then were they all of good cheer, and they also took some meat," (v. 34–36) seeing that there was no question about their lives being saved. (d) "And we were in all in the ship two hundred threescore and sixteen souls. And when they had eaten enough, they lightened the ship, and cast out the wheat into the sea. And when it was day, they knew not the land : but they discovered a certain creek with a shore, into the which they were minded, if it were possible, to thrust in the ship. And when they had taken up the anchors, they committed themselves unto the sea, and loosed the rudder bands, and hoisted up the mainsail to the wind, and made toward

---

[1] The confusion here has arisen from the scribe's taking the four last portions a, c, e, g, i. e. 4, 5, 6, 7, and inserting between them the first three b, f, d, but in the order b, d, f, i. e. 1, 3, 2 : so that the confused order becomes 4, (1), 5, (3), 6, (2), 7. The texts also needed to be redistributed. Of our Mss. A, C, omit all the latter part d, e, f, g : so that B and Cat. are the authorities here followed for the old text. (of N. we have no collation).—In (f), for ἅτε οὐ περὶ τῶν ψυχῶν αὐτῶν ὄντος τοῦ λόγου which we have referred to, " Then were they of good cheer," viz. because they believed Paul's assurance that their lives were safe. mod. text substitutes " (they had no care for food,) ἅτε οὐ περὶ τῶν τυχόντων ὄντος τοῦ κινδύνου." In (d), " κατεῖχον," τοὺς οἴακας τῇ πνεούσῃ δόντες, the meaning seems to be, they bore right down (upon the shore), letting the rudder-handles go, so that the wind was right astern : πόλλακις γὰρ οὐχ οὕτῳ ποιοῦσιν, for oftentimes they steer not so, but more or less transverse to the line of the wind. Κατέφερον τὸ σκεῦος, τ. ε. τὰ ἱστία : what this can mean, we do not understand : but above in v. 17, old text has χαλάσαντες τὸ σκεῦος for χαλ. τὰ ἱστία : hence we read here κατεφέροντο (χαλάσαντες, or some such word) τὸ σκεῦος, τ. ε. τὰ ἱ.—For ἐγκοπτομένης τῆς ῥύμης we read with the Catena ἐγκ. τῆς πρύμνης. Mod. text substitutes ἐγκόπτοντες (Sav. τος) τοῦ πνεύματος τὴν ῥύμην.

shore." (v. 37–41.) "They made towards shore," having given the rudder-handles to the wind : for oftentimes they do it not in this way. They were borne along, having loosed the rigging, i. e. the sails. "And falling into a place where two seas met, they ran the ship aground ; and the forepart stuck fast, and remained unmovable, but 'the hinder part was broken with the violence of the waves ;" for when there is a strong wind, this is the consequence, the stern bearing the brunt (of the storm). (a) "And the soldiers' counsel was to kill the prisoners, lest any of them should swim out, and escape." (v. 42.) Again the devil tries to hinder the prophecy, and they had a mind to kill some, but the centurion suffered them not, that he might save Paul, so much was the centurion attached to him. "But the centurion, willing to save Paul, kept them from their purpose ; and commanded that they which could swim should cast themselves first into the sea, and get to land : and the rest, some on boards, and some on broken pieces of the ship. And so it came to pass, that they escaped all safe to land." (v. 43, 44.) "And when they were escaped, then they knew that the island was called Melita." (ch. xxviii. 1.) Do you mark what good came of the storm ? Why then it was no mark of their being forsaken, that the storm came upon them. (c) Now this that happened was in consequence of the season of the year ; but the wonder is greater, that at such a season they were saved from the midst of the dangers, both he, and for his sake the rest, (e) and this too in the Hadriatic. There were two hundred and seventy-six souls in all : no small matter this also, if indeed they believed. The voyage was at an unseasonable time. (g) It is natural to suppose they would ask the reason why they were sailing, and would learn all. Nor was it for nothing that the voyage was so protracted ; it afforded Paul an opportunity for teaching.

(Recapitulation.) And Paul says, "I perceive that (this voyage will be) with hurt and loss." (v. 10.) And observe how unassuming the expression is. That he may not seem to prophesy, but to speak as of conjecture, "I perceive," says he. For they would not have received it, had he said this at the outset. In fact he does prophesy on this former occasion, as he does afterward, and says (there), "The God whom I serve," leading them on. Then how comes it that it was not "with loss" (of any) "of their lives ?" It would have been so, but that God brought them safe through it. For as far as depended on the nature of the thing, they had perished, but

God prevented it. Then, to show that it was not from conjecture that he so spake, the master of the ship said the contrary (v. 11), and he a man of experience in the matter : so far was it from being the case that Paul's advice was given from conjecture. Moreover, the place suggested this same (which the master said), "being not commodious ;" and it was evident that from conjecture "the more part advised" (v. 12) as they did, rather than Paul. Then, severe the storm (that ensued), deep the darkness : and that they may not forget, the vessel also goes to pieces, and the corn is flung out and all beside, that they may not have it in their power after this to be shameless. For this is why the vessel goes to pieces, and [1] their souls are tightly braced. Moreover, both the storm and the darkness contributed not a little to his obtaining the hearing he did. Accordingly observe how the centurion does as he bids him, insomuch that he even let the boat go, and destroyed it. And if the sailors did not as yet comply with his bidding, yet afterwards they do so : for in fact this is a reckless sort of people. (v. 13–20.) "Sirs, ye should have hearkened to me," etc. (v. 21.) One is not likely to have a good reception, when he chides in the midst of calamity ; but [1] when he tells them what more there is (to come) of the calamity, and then predicts the good, then he is acceptable. Therefore he attacks them then first, when "all hope that they should be saved was taken away :" that none may say, Nothing has come of it. And their fear also bears witness. Moreover, the place is a trying one, for it was in the Adriatic, and then their long abstinence. They were in the midst of death. It was now the fourteenth day that they were going without food, having taken nothing. "Wherefore," said he, "I pray you to take some meat : for this is for your health" (v. 34), that ye should eat, lest ye perish of hunger. Observe, his giving thanks after all that had happened strengthened them. For this showed an assured mind that they would be saved. (b) "Then were they all of good cheer, and they also took some meat." (v. 36.) And not only so, but henceforth they so cast all their care upon Paul, that they even cast

---

[1] Καὶ ἐπισφίγγονται αὐτῶν αἱ ψυχαί. Hom. in Matt. p. 60, A. ἐπισφ. is applied to the action of salt in stopping corruption ; and ib. 167 B. Christians are the salt of the earth, ἵνα ἐπισφίγγωμεν τοὺς διαρρέοντας. Here in a somewhat similar sense, "the vessel goes to pieces and their (dissolute) souls (which were in danger of going to pieces) are powerfully constricted, held in a close strain, braced to the uttermost." Mod. text omits this, and for ἵνα μὴ λάθωνται—ἀναισχυντεῖν, substitutes, "That they may not perish, the corn is thrown out and all the rest."—Below, ἀλλ' ὅταν καὶ τὰ πλείονα λέγῃ τῆς συμφορᾶς : mod. text absurdly substitutes παρατρέχῃ : we insert after this the clause τότε τὰ χρηστὰ προλέγει which our Mss. have below after καὶ ὁ φόβος μαρτυρεῖ.

out the corn (v. 37), being so many. (a) Two hundred and seventy-six souls (v. 38): whence had they victuals?[1] (c) See how they do their part as men, and how Paul does not forbid them. "And when it was day," etc., "they loosed the rudder-bands." (v. 39, 40.) And the vessel goes to pieces in the daytime, that they may not be clean dissolved with the terror: that you may see the prophecy brought out as fact. "And the soldiers' counsel," etc. (v. 42.) Do you mark that in this respect also they were given to Paul? since for his sake the centurion suffered them not to be slain. So confessedly wicked do those men seem to me to have been: insomuch that they would have chosen even to slay them: but some swam on shore, others were borne on boards, and they all were thus saved, and the prophecy received accomplishment; (a prophecy,) although not solemn from length of time, since he did not deliver it a number of years before, but keeping close to the nature of the things themselves: (still a prophecy it was,) for all was beyond the reach of hope. And (so) it was through themselves being saved that they learnt who Paul was. But some one may say: why did he not save the ship? That they might perceive how great a danger they had escaped: and that the whole matter depended, not on the help of man, but on God's hand saving them independently of a ship. So that righteous men, though they may be in a tempest, or on the sea, or in the deep, suffer nothing dreadful, but even save others together with themselves. If (here was) a ship in danger and suffering wreck, and prisoners were saved for Paul's sake, consider what a thing it is to have a holy man in a house: for many are the tempests which assail us also, tempests far more grievous than these (natural ones), but He can also give[2] us to be delivered, if only we obey holy men as those (in the ship) did, if we do what they enjoin. For they are not simply saved, but themselves also contributed to other men's believing (πίστιν εἰσήνεγκαν). Though the holy man be in bonds, he does greater works than those who are free. And look how this was the case here. The free centurion stood in need of his bound prisoner: the skilful pilot was in want of him who was no pilot—nay rather, of him who was the true pilot. For he steered as pilot not a vessel of this (earthly) kind, but the Church of the whole world, having

learnt of Him Who is Lord also of the sea; (steered it,) not by the art of man, but by the wisdom of the Spirit. In this vessel are many shipwrecks, many waves, spirits of wickedness, "from within are fightings, from without are fears" (2 Cor. vii. 5): so that he was the true pilot. Look at our whole life: it is just such (as was this voyage). For at one time we meet with kindliness, at another with a tempest; sometimes from our own want of counsel, sometimes from our idleness, we fall into numberless evils; from our not hearkening to Paul, when we are eager to go somewhither, where he bids us not. For Paul is sailing even now with us, only not bound as he was then: he admonishes us even now, and says to those who are (sailing) on this sea, "take heed unto yourselves: for after my departing grievous wolves shall enter in among you" (Acts xx. 29): and again, "In the last times perilous times shall come: and men shall be lovers of their own selves, lovers of money, boasters." (2 Tim. iii. 2.) This is more grievous than all storms. Let us therefore abide where he bids us—in faith, in the safe haven: let us hearken unto him rather than to the pilot that is within us, that is, our own reason. Let us not straightway do just what this may suggest; not what the owner of the ship: no, but what Paul suggests: he has passed through many such tempests. Let us not learn (to our cost) by experience, but before the experience let us "avoid both harm and loss." Hear what he says: "They that will be rich fall into temptation." (1 Tim. vi. 9.) Let us therefore obey him; else, see what they suffered, because they did not take his counsel. And again he tells in another place what causes shipwrecks: "Who," he says, "have made shipwreck concerning the faith. But do thou continue in the things which thou hast learned and wast assured of." (1 Tim. i. 19.) Let us obey Paul: though we be in the midst of a tempest, we shall surely be freed from the dangers: though we remain without food fourteen days, though hope of safety may have left us, though we be in darkness and mist, by doing his bidding, we shall be freed from the dangers. Let us think that the whole world is a ship, and in this the evildoers and those who have numberless vices, some rulers, others guards, others just men, as Paul was, others prisoners, those bound by their sins: if then we do as Paul bids us, we perish not in our bonds, but are released from them: God will give us also to him. Or think you not that sins and passions are grievous bonds? for it is not the hands only that are bound, but the whole man. For tell

---

[1] πόθεν τὰ σιτηρέσια εἶχον; i. e. what were they to subsist upon, having thrown out the rest of the corn? But they trusted Paul's assurance for all.

[2] χαρίσασθαι i. e. to the holy man, to be saved for his sake, in like manner as "He gave (κεχάρισται) to Paul them that sailed with him," v. 24.

me, when any one possessed of much money uses it not, nor spends it, but keeps it close, is he not bound more grievously than any prisoner by his miserliness, a bond that cannot be broken? What again, when a man gives himself up to (the belief in) Fate, is not he too bound with other fetters? What, when he gives himself up to observations (of times)? What, when to omens? are not these more grievous than all bonds? What again, when he gives himself up to an unreasonable lust and to love? Who shall break in pieces these bonds for you? There is need of God's help that they may be loosed. But when there are both bonds and tempest, think how great is the amount of dangers. For which of them is not enough to destroy? The hunger, the tempest, the wickedness of those on board, the unfitness of the season? But against all these, Paul's glory stood its ground. So is it now: let us keep the saints near us, and there will be no tempest: or rather, though there be a tempest, there will be great calm and tranquillity, and freedom from dangers: since that widow had the saint for her friend, and the death of her child was loosed, and she received back her son alive again. (1 Kings xvii. 17.) Where the feet of saints step, there will be nothing painful; and if such should happen, it is for proving us and for the greater glory of God. Accustom the floor of thy house to be trodden by such feet, and an evil spirit will not tread there. For as where a sweet odor is, there a bad odor will not find place: so where the holy unguent is, there the evil spirit is choked, and it gladdens those who are near it, it delights, it refreshes the soul. Where thorns are, there are wild beasts: where hospitality is, there are no thorns: for almsgiving having entered in, more keenly than any sickle it destroys the thorns, more violently than any fire. Be not thou afraid: (the wicked one) fears the tracks of saints, as foxes do lions. For "the righteous," it says, "is as bold as a lion." (Prov. xxviii. 1.) Let us bring these lions into our house, and all the wild beasts are put to flight, the lions not needing to roar, but simply to utter their voice. For not so much does the roaring of a lion put the wild beasts to flight, as the prayer of a righteous man puts to flight evil spirits: let him but speak, they cower. And where are such men now to be found, you will say? Everywhere, if we believe, if we seek, if we take pains. Where hast thou sought, tell me? When didst thou take this work in hand? When didst thou make this thy business? But if thou seekest not, marvel not that thou dost not find. For "he that seeketh findeth" (Matt. vii. 7), not he that seeketh not. Listen to those who live in deserts: away with thy gold and silver: (such holy men) are to be found in every part of the world. Though thou receive not such an one in thy house, yet go thou to him, live with the man, be at his dwelling-place, that thou mayest be able to obtain and enjoy his blessing. For a great thing it is to receive a blessing from the saints: which let us be careful to obtain, that being helped by their prayers we may enjoy mercy from God, through the grace and loving-kindness of His only-begotten Son, with Whom to the Father and the Holy Ghost together be glory, might, honor, now and ever, world without end. Amen.

HOMILY LIV.

ACTS XX. 1.

" And the barbarous people showed us no little kindness: for they kindled a fire, and received us every one, because of the present rain, and because of the cold. And when Paul had gathered a bundle of sticks, and laid them on the fire, there came a viper out of the heat, and fastened on his hand."

" SHOWED," he says, " no little kindness to us—barbarians " (as they were *)—" having kindled a fire: " else it were of no use that their lives be saved, if the wintry weather must destroy them. Then Paul having taken brushwood, laid it on the fire. See how active he is; observe how we nowhere find him doing miracles for the sake of doing them, but only upon emergency. Both during the storm when there was a cause he prophesied, not for the sake of prophesying, and here again in the first instance he lays on brushwood:— nothing for vain display, but (with a simple view) to their being preserved, and enjoying some warmth. Then a viper " fastened on his hand. And when the barbarians saw the

---

* The Maltese, though undoubtedly civilized, were βάρβαροι in the Greek and Roman sense of speaking an unintelligible language (cf. 1 Cor. xiv. 11). The word might be appropriately rendered "foreigners." The Maltese were of Phœnician descent and spoke a mixed dialect.—G. B. S.

venomous beast hang on his hand, they said among themselves, No doubt this man is a murderer, whom, though he hath escaped the sea, yet vengeance suffereth not to live." (v. 4.) Well also was this permitted, that they should both see the thing and utter the thought, in order that, when the result ensued, there might be no disbelieving the miracle. Observe their good feeling (towards the distressed), in saying this (not aloud, but) among themselves—observe (also) the natural judgment clearly expressed even among barbarians, and how they do not condemn without assigning a reason. And these also behold, that they may wonder the more. "And he shook off the beast into the fire, and felt no harm. Howbeit they looked when he should have swollen, or fallen down dead suddenly: but after they had looked a great while, and saw no harm come to him, they changed their minds, and said that he was a god." (v. 5, 6.) They expected him, it says, to fall down dead: and again, having seen that nothing of the kind happened to him, they said, He is a god. Again (viz. as in ch. xiv. 11), another excess on the part of these men. "In the same quarters were possessions of the chief man of the island, whose name was Publius; who received us, and lodged us three days courteously. And it came to pass, that the father of Publius lay sick of a fever and of a bloody flux: to whom Paul entered in, and prayed, and laid his hands on him, and healed him." (v. 7, 8.) Behold again another hospitable man, Publius, who was both rich and of great possessions: he had seen nothing, but purely out of compassion for their misfortune, he received them, and took care of them. So that he was worthy to receive kindness: wherefore Paul as a requital for his receiving them, "healed him. So when this was done, others also, which had diseases in the island, came, and were healed: who also honored us with many honors; and when we departed, they laded us with such things as were necessary" (v. 9, 10), both us and the rest. See how when they were quit of the storm, they did not become[1] more negligent, but what a liberal entertainment was given to them for Paul's sake: and three months were they there, all of them provided with sustenance. See how all this is done for the sake of Paul, to the end that the prisoners should believe, and the soldiers, and the centurion. For if they were very stone, yet from

the counsel they heard him giving, and from the prediction they had heard him making, and from the miracles they knew him to have wrought, and from the sustenance they by his means enjoyed, they must have got a very high notion of him. See, when the judgment is right, and not preoccupied by some passion, how immediately it gets right judgings, and gives sound verdicts. "And after three months we departed in a ship of Alexandria, which had wintered in the isle, whose sign was Castor and Pollux.* And landing at Syracuse, we tarried there three days. And from thence we fetched a compass, and came to Rhegium: and after one day the south wind blew, and we came the next day to Puteoli: where we found brethren, and were desired to tarry with them seven days: and so we went toward Rome. And from thence, when the brethren heard of us, they came to meet us as far as Appii forum, and the Three Taverns: whom when Paul saw, he thanked God, and took courage." (v. 11–15.) Already the preaching has reached to Sicily: see how it has run through (even to those lands): at Puteoli also they found some: others also came to meet them. Such was the eagerness of the brethren, it nothing disconcerted them, that Paul was in bonds. But observe also how Paul himself also was affected after the manner of men. For it says, "he took courage, when he saw the brethren." Although he had worked so many miracles, nevertheless even from sight he received an accession (of confidence). From this we learn, that he was both comforted after the manner of men, and the contrary. "And when we came to Rome, Paul was suffered to dwell by himself with a soldier that kept him." (v. 16.) Leave was given him to dwell by himself. No slight proof this also of his being held in much admiration: it is clear they did not number him among the rest. "And it came to pass, that after three days he called together them that were the chief of the Jews." After three days he called the chief of the Jews, that their ears might not be preoccupied. And what had he in common with them? for they would not (else) have been like to accuse him. Nevertheless, it was not for this that he cared; it was for the teaching that he was concerned, and that what he had to say might not offend them.

(Recapitulation.) "And the barbarians," etc. (v. 2.) The Jews then, beholding all the many miracles they did, persecuted and har-

1 ἀμελεστέρους γενομένους, i. e. the impression left on their minds by the storm was not suffered to wear out, when the danger was over. What happened on shore, Paul's miracles, the kindness and honors shown them by the barbarians for Paul's sake, all helped to keep them from relapsing into indifference.

* Or with the sign of the Dioscuri. The reference is to the ships *insigne*, an image or picture of the divinities Castor and Pollux on the prow of the ship. In the current mythology they were the sons of Jupiter and Leda, and were regarded as the tutelary divinities of sailors.—G. B. S.

assed (Paul); but the barbarians, who had seen none, merely on the ground of his misfortune, were kind to him.—"No doubt," say they, "this man is a murderer." (v. 4). They do not simply pronounce their judgment, but say, "No doubt," (i. e.) as any one may see, "and vengeance," say they, "suffereth him not to live." Why then, they held also the doctrine of a Providence, and these barbarians were far more philosophic than the philosophers, who allow not the benefit of a Providence to extend to things "below the moon:" whereas (these barbarians) suppose God to be present everywhere, and that although a (guilty) man may escape many (a danger), he will not escape in the end. And they do not assail him forthwith, but for a time respect him on account of his misfortune: nor do they openly proclaim their surmise, but speak it "among themselves: a murderer;" for the bonds led them to suspect this. "They showed no small kindness," and yet (some of them) were prisoners. Let those be ashamed that say, Do not do good to those in prison: let these barbarians shame us; for they knew not who these men were, but simply because they were in misfortune (they were kind): thus much they perceived, that they were human beings, and therefore they considered them to have a claim upon their humanity. "And for a great while," it says, "they expected that he would die." (v. 6.) But when he shook his hand, and flung off the beast, then they saw and were astonished. And the miracle did not take place suddenly, but the men went by the length of time, "after they had looked a great while," so plainly was there no deceit, no haste here (συναρπαγή). "Publius," it says, "lodged them courteously" (v. 7): two hundred and seventy-six persons. Consider how great the gain of his hospitality: not as of necessity, not as unwilling, but as reckoning it a gain he lodged them for three days: thereafter having met with his requital, he naturally honored Paul much more, when the others also received healing. "Who also," it says, "honored us with many honors" (v. 10): not that he received wages, God forbid; but as it is written, "The workman is worthy of his meat. And when we departed, they laded us with such things as were necessary." (Matt. x. 10.) It is plain that having thus received them, they also received the word of the preaching: for it is not to be supposed, that during an entire three months they would have had all this kindness shown them,[1] had these persons not believed strongly,

and herein exhibited the fruits (of their conversion): so that from this we may see a strong proof of the great number there was of those that believed. Even this was enough to establish (Paul's) credit with those (his fellow-voyagers). Observe how in all this voyage they nowhere touched at a city, but (were cast) on an island, and passed the entire winter (there, or) sailing—those being herein under training for faith, his fellow-voyagers, I mean. (a) "And after three months we departed in a ship of Alexandria, which had wintered in the isle, whose sign was Castor and Pollux." (v. 11.) Probably this was painted on it: so addicted were they to their idols. (d) "And when the south wind blew, we came the next day to Puteoli: where we found brethren, and were desired to tarry with them seven days: and so we went toward Rome." (v. 13, 14.) (b) Observe them tarrying a while, and again hasting onwards. (e) "And from thence, when the brethren heard of us, they came to meet us as far as Appii forum, and the Three Taverns" (v. 15): not fearing the danger. (c) Paul therefore was now so much respected, that he was even permitted to be by himself: for if even before this they used him kindly, much more would they now. (g) "He was suffered," it says, "to dwell by himself, with a soldier that kept him." (v. 16.) That it might not be possible for any plot to be laid against him there either—for there could be no raising of sedition now. So that in fact they were not keeping Paul in custody, but guarding him, so that nothing unpleasant should happen: for it was not possible now, in so great a city, and with the Emperor there, and with Paul's appeal, for anything to be done contrary to order. So surely is it the case, that always through the things which seem to be against us, all things turn out for us. "With the soldier"— for he was Paul's guard. "And having called together the chief of the Jews" (v. 17), he discourses to them, who both depart gainsaying, and are taunted by him, yet they dare not say anything: for it was not permitted them to deal with his matter at their own will. For this is a marvellous thing, that not by the things which seem to be for our security, but by their very opposites, all comes to be for us. And that you may learn this—Pharaoh commanded the infants to be cast into the river.

---

lation), "would not have been so hospitably and liberally entertained, such a number as there were of them, two hundred and seventy-six souls and this for a period of three months:" but in διελέχθ. perhaps διηλέγχθησαν is latent: "they would not have been so honored etc., but rather would have been convicted," etc.—In what follows, the parts had fallen out of their places thus, 2, 4. 6: 3, 5: 1, 7. Mod. text in e, ὅτι φοβηθέντες τὸν κίνδυνον ἐξῆλθον, connecting this with the first clause of f, καὶ ταῦτα ἱκανὰ ἐκείνους πιστώσασθαι.

---

[1] οὐ γὰρ ἂν ἐν τριμήνῳ τοσούτῳ διελέχθησαν μὴ σφόδρα αὐτῶν πιστευσάντων. (Mod. text τοσαῦτα διελέχθη.) This is evidently corrupt. The context requires (as we have given in the trans-

(Exod. i. 22.) Unless the infants had been cast forth, Moses would not have been saved, he would not have been brought up in the palace. When he was safe, he was not in honor; when he was exposed, then he was in honor. But God did this, to show His riches of resource and contrivance. The Jew threatened him, saying, "Wouldest thou kill me?" (ib. ii. 14) and this too was of profit to him. It was of God's providence, in order that he should see that vision in the desert, in order that the proper time should be completed, that he should learn philosophy in the desert, and there live in security. And in all the plottings of the Jews against him the same thing happens: then he becomes more illustrious. As also in the case of Aaron; they rose up against him, and thereby made him more illustrious (Num. xvi. xvii.): that so his ordination should be unquestionable, that he might be held in admiration for the future also from the plates of brass (τῶν πετάλων τοῦ χαλκοῦ). Of course you know the history: wherefore I pass over the narration. And if ye will, let us go over the same examples from the beginning. Cain slew his brother, but in this he rather benefited him: for hear what Scripture says, "The voice of thy brother's blood crieth unto Me" (Gen. iv. 10): and again in another place, "To the blood that speaketh better things than that of Abel." (Heb. xii. 24.) He freed him from the uncertainty of the future, he increased his reward: we have all learnt hereby what love God had for him. For what was he injured? Not a whit, in that he received his end sooner. For say, what do they gain, who die more slowly? Nothing: for the having good days does not depend on the living many years or few years, but in the using life properly. The Three Children were thrown into the furnace, and through this they became more illustrious: Daniel was cast into the pit, and thence was he made more renowned. (Dan. iii. and vi.) You see that trials in every case bring forth great good even in this life, much more in the life to come: but as to malice, the case is the same, as if a man having a reed should set himself to fight with the fire: it seems indeed to beat the fire, but it makes it brighter, and only consumes itself. For the malice of the wicked becomes food and an occasion of splendor to virtue: for by God's turning the unrighteousness to good account, our character shines forth all the more. Again, when the devil works anything of this kind, he makes those more illustrious that endure. How then, you will say, was this not the case with Adam, but, on the contrary, he became more disgraced? Nay, in this case of all others God turned (the malice of) that (wicked one)

to good account: but if (Adam) was the worse for it, it was he that injured himself: for it is the wrongs that are done to us by others that become the means of great good to us, not so the wrongs which are done by ourselves. As indeed, because the fact is that when hurt by others, we grieve, but not so when hurt by ourselves, therefore it is that God shows, that he who suffers unjustly at the hands of another, gets renown, but he who injures himself, receives hurt: that so we may bear the former courageously, but not the latter. And besides, the whole thing there was Adam's own doing. Wherefore didst thou the woman's bidding? (Gen. iii. 6.) Wherefore when she counselled thee contrary (to God), didst thou not repel her? Thou wast assuredly thyself the cause. Else, if the devil was the cause, at this rate all that are tempted ought to perish: but if all do not perish, the cause (of our destruction) rests with ourselves.[1] "But," you will say, "all that are tempted ought (at that rate) to succeed." No: for the cause is in ourselves. "At that rate it ought to follow that (some) perish without the devil's having anything to do with it." Yes: and in fact many do perish without the devil's being concerned in it: for surely the devil does not bring about all (our evil doings); no, much comes also from our own sluggishness by itself alone: and if he too is anywhere concerned as a cause, it is from our offering the occasion. For say, why did the devil prevail in Judas' case? When "Satan entered into him" (John xiii. 27), you will say. Yes, but hear the cause: it was because "he was a thief, and bare what was put in the bag." (ib. xii. 6.) It was he that himself gave the devil a wide room for entering into him: so that it is not the devil who puts into us the beginning, it is we that receive and invite him. "But," you will say, "if there were no devil, the evils would not have become great." True, but then our punishment would admit of no plea for mitigation: but as it is, beloved, our punishment is more mild, whereas if we had wrought the evils of ourselves, the chastisements would be intolerable. For say, if Adam, without any counsel,

---

[1] The dialogue seems to proceed thus. "If the devil was the cause of Adam's fall, at this rate it ought to follow that all whom the devil tempts should perish (ἔδει κατὰ τοῦτο πάντας τοὺς πειραζομένους ἀπόλλυσθαι): if this be not the case, as certainly it is not, then, the cause (of our perishing) is with ourselves (εἰ δὲ μὴ ἀπόλλυνται, παρ᾽ ἡμᾶς ἡ αἰτία)." Then: 'Αλλ᾽ ἔδει, φησί, πάντας τοὺς πειραζομένους κατορθοῦν· οὐ παρ᾽ ἡμᾶς γὰρ ἡ αἰτία· ἔδει, φησί, καὶ χωρὶς τοῦ διαβόλου ἀπόλλυσθαι. "But," say you, "(at this rate) all that are tempted ought to succeed (against the Tempter, to come off victorious from the encounter)." No: for the cause (of our being tempted) is with ourselves. "Then people ought to perish even without the devil:" i. e. 'It should follow that those who perish, perish independently of the tempter.' Yes: in fact many do," etc. In the printed text ἀλλ᾽ ἔδει—κατορθοῦν, ... ἔδει ἀπόλλυσθαι are put interrogatively, and in place of the οὐ παρ ἡμᾶς γὰρ ἡ αἰτία of the Mss. (which we point Οὐ. παρ᾽ ἡμᾶς γ. η. ἁ.) it has ἡ, εἰ παρ ἡ. η. ἁ.

had committed the sin he did, who would
have snatched him out of the dangers? "But
he would not have sinned," you will say?
What right hast thou to say this? For he
who had so little solidity, that was so inert
and so ready for folly as to receive such
advice as this, much more would he without
any counsel have become this (that he did
become). What devil incited the brethren of
Joseph to envy? If then we be watchful,
brethren, the devil becomes to us the cause
even of renown. Thus, what was Job the
worse for his falling into such helplessness of
distress? "Speak not of this instance," you
will say: "(Job was not the worse,) but the
weak person is the worse." Yes, and the
weak person is the worse, even if there be no
devil. "But in a greater degree," you will
say, "when there is the devil's power working
along with him." True, but he is the less
punished, when he has sinned through the
devil's working with him; for the punishments are not the same for all sins. Let us
not deceive ourselves: the devil is not the
cause of our taking harm, if we be watchful:[1]
rather what he does, is to awake us out of our
sleep; what he does, is to keep us on the
alert. Let us for a while examine these
things: suppose there were no wild beasts,
no irregular states of the atmosphere; no
sicknesses, no pains, no sorrows, nor anything
else of the kind: what would not man have
become? A hog rather than a man, revelling
in gluttony and drunkenness, and troubled by
none of those things. But as it is, cares and
anxieties are an exercise and discipline of
philosophy, a method for the best of training.
For say, let a man be brought up in a palace,
having no pain, nor care, nor anxiety, and
having neither cause for anger nor failure,
but whatever he sets his mind upon, that let
him do, in that let him succeed, and have all
men obeying him: (see whether) such a man
would not become more irrational than any
wild beast. But as it is, our reverses and our
afflictions are as it were a whetstone to
sharpen us. For this reason the poor are for
the most part wiser than the rich, as being
driven about and tost by many waves. Thus
a body also, being idle and without motion, is
sickly and unsightly: but that which is exercised, and suffers labor and hardships, is
more comely and healthy: and this we should
find to hold also in the case of the soul.

Iron also, lying unused, is spoilt, but if
worked it shines brightly; and in like manner
a soul which is kept in motion. Now these
reverses are precisely what keeps the soul in
motion. Arts again perish, when the soul is
not active: but it is active when it has not
everything plain before it: it is made active
by adverse things. If there were no adverse
things, there would be nothing to stir it: thus,
if everything existed ready-made in beautiful
sort, art would not have found wherein to exercise itself. So, if all things were level to
our understanding, the soul would not find
wherein to exert itself: if it had to be carried
about everywhere, it would be an unsightly
object. See you not, that we exhort nurses
not to make a practice of carrying children
always, that they may not bring them into a
habit (of wanting to be carried) and so make
them helpless? This is why those children
which are brought up under the eyes of their
parents are weak, in consequence of the indulgence, which by sparing them too much
injures their health. It is a good thing, even
pain in moderation; a good thing, care; a
good thing, want; for[2] they make us strong:
good also are their opposites: but each of
these when in excess destroys us; and the
one relaxes, but the other (by overmuch
tension) breaks us. Seest thou not, that
Christ also thus trains His own disciples?
If they needed these things, much more do
we. But if we need them, let us not grieve,
but even rejoice in our afflictions. For these
are remedies, answering to our wounds, some
of them bitter, others mild; but either of
them by itself would be useless. Let us
therefore return thanks to God for all these
things: for He does not suffer them to happen
at random, but for the benefit of our souls.
Therefore, showing forth our gratitude, let us
return Him thanks, let us glorify Him, let us
bear up courageously, considering that it is
but for a time, and stretching forward our
minds to the things future, that we may both
lightly bear the things present, and be counted
worthy to attain unto the good things to come,
through the grace and mercy of His only begotten Son, with Whom to the Father and the
Holy Ghost together be glory, might, honor,
now and ever, world without end. Amen.

[1] *Hom.* xxiii. *in Gen.* § 6, p. 215, A. "I exhort you never to
lay the blame upon Satan, but upon your own remissness. I
say not this to exculpate him, for he 'goeth about,' etc. 1 Pet.
v. 8, but to put ourselves in more security, that we may not
exculpate ourselves when we so easily go over to the evil one,
that we may not speak those heartless, senseless words, 'Why
has God left the evil one so much freedom to seduce men.'
These words betoken the greatest ingratitude. Consider this:
God has left him that freedom, to this very end, that by fear
of the enemy he may keep us ever watchful and sober."

[2] The printed text, ἰσχυροὺς γὰρ ἡμᾶς ποιεῖ καλὰ καὶ τὰ
ἐναντία. Ben., *fortes enim nos reddunt quæ bona et contraria
sunt.* But καλὰ καὶ τὰ ἐναντία clearly answers to καλὸν καὶ
λυπὴ σύμμετρος, καλὸν καὶ φροντίς, καλὸν καὶ ἐνδεια. Only it may
be doubted whether τὰ ἐναντία is to be taken here as above,
"Good also are adverse things, or, "their opposites," i. e.
"freedom from sorrow, and care, and want, if in moderation."
But the context speaks for the latter: viz. "(In moderation),
for each of them (both these things and of their opposites) being out of measure destroys: and as the one leaves no solidity
or stability (καὶ τὸ μὲν χαυνοῖ, i. e. immoderate joy, ease, comfort), so the other by excessive tension breaks."—So below by
ταῦτα we understand "these things and their opposites,"
which are described as τὰ μὲν πικρὰ, τὰ δὲ ἥμερα (mod. text
ἥδέα).

HOMILY LV.

ACTS XXVIII. 17-20.

" And it came to pass, that after three days Paul called the chief of the Jews together: and when they were come together, he said unto them, Men and brethren, thought I have committed nothing against the people, or customs of our fathers, yet was I delivered prisoner from Jerusalem into the hands of the Romans. Who, when they had examined me, would have let me go, because there was no cause of death in me. But when the Jews spake against it, I was constrained to appeal unto Cæsar; not that I had aught to accuse my nation of. For this cause therefore have I called for you, to see you, and to speak with you: because that for the hope of Israel I am bound with this chain."

HE wished to exculpate both himself and others; himself, that they might not accuse him, and by so doing hurt themselves; and those (others), that it might not seem that the whole thing was of their doing. For it was likely that a report was prevalent, that he had been delivered up by the Jews; and this was enough to alarm them. He therefore addresses himself to this, and defends himself as to his own conduct.* "How then is it reasonable," it might be said, "that they should deliver thee up without a cause?" The Roman governors, he says, bear me witness, who wished to let me go. "How was it then that they did not let (thee) go?" "When the Jews spake against it," he says. Observe how he extenuates (in speaking of) their charges against him.[1] Since if he had wished to aggravate matters, he might have used them so as to bear harder upon them.

* Paul's prompt summoning of the unbelieving Jews was due as Chrys. reminds us, to his desire to conciliate them and thus to prevent the rise of new obstacles to the progress of the gospel. The apostle might naturally suppose that the Jews of Jerusalem, who were bent upon destroying him, had lodged information against him with their brethren at Rome and that his appearance as a prisoner might still further excite their prejudice and opposition. This view of Paul's action removes the objection that he could not have given attention to the Jews before making the acquaintance of the Christian church (Zeller). He had, however, made their acquaintance; the brethren had gone out to meet him on his approach to the city and he had probably spent the most of the three days referred to in their company. Zeller has objected still more zealously to Paul's statement. "I have done nothing against this people or the customs of the fathers." Paul's meaning, however, is, that he had never sought the destruction or subversion of the Jewish law and customs, but had ever labored in the line of the Messianic fulfilment of them. Meyer fitly says : " His antagonism to the law was directed against *justification* by the Law."

[1] viz. by saying only ἀντιλεγόντων τῶν Ἰουδ., whereas they had shown the utmost malignity against him, accusing him of crimes which they could not prove, and "saying that he was not fit to live:" but he is so forbearing, that though he might have turned all this against them, he sinks the mention of it, etc.

Wherefore, he says, "I was constrained to appeal unto Cæsar:" so that his whole speech is of a forgiving nature. What then? didst thou this, that thou mightest accuse them? No, he says: "Not that I had aught to accuse my nation of:" but that I might escape the danger. For it is for your sakes "that I am bound with this chain." So far am I, he says, from any hostile feeling towards you. Then they also were so subdued by his speech, that they too apologized for those of their own nation: "And they said unto him, We neither received letters out of Judea concerning thee, neither any of the brethren that came showed or spake any harm of thee." (v. 21.) Neither through letters, nor through men, have they made known any harm of thee. Nevertheless, we wish to hear from thyself: "But we desire to hear of thee what thou thinkest" (v. 22): and then forestalled him by showing their own sentiments. "For as concerning this sect, it is known to us, that everywhere it is spoken against. And when they had appointed him a day, there came many to him into his lodging; to whom he expounded and testified the kingdom of God, persuading them concerning Jesus, both out of the Law of Moses and out of the Prophets, from morning till evening. And some believed the things which were spoken, and some believed not." (v. 23, 24.) They said not, we speak against it, but "it is spoken against." Then he did not immediately answer, but gave them a day, and they came to him, and he discoursed, it says, "both out of the Law of Moses, and out of the Prophets. And some believed, and some believed not. And when they agreed not among themselves, they departed, after that Paul had spoken one word, Well spake the Holy Ghost by Esaias the prophet unto our fathers, saying, Go unto this people, and say, Hearing ye shall hear, and shall not understand; and seeing ye shall see, and not perceive: for the heart of this people is waxed gross, and their ears are dull of hearing, and their eyes have they closed; lest they should see with their eyes, and hear with their ears, and understand with their heart, and should be converted, and I should heal them." (v. 25-27.) But when they departed, as they were opposed to each other, then he reproaches them, not because he wished to reproach those (that believed not), but to confirm these (that believed). "Well said Esaias," says he to them. So that to the Gentiles it is given to know this mystery. No wonder then, if they did gainsay: this was foretold from the first. Then again he moves their jealousy (on the score) of them of the Gentiles. "Be it known therefore unto you, that the salvation of God is sent unto the Gentiles, and that they will hear it. And when he had said these words, the Jews departed, and had great reasoning among themselves. And Paul dwelt two whole years in his own hired house, and received all that came in unto him, preaching the kingdom of God, and teaching those things which concern the Lord Jesus Christ, with all confidence, no man forbidding him. Amen." (v. 28-31.) It shows the freedom he had now: without hindrance in Rome, he who had been hindered in Judea; and he remained teaching there for two years. What of the (years) after these?[1]

(Recapitulation.) (d) "Who having examined me," says he, "found nothing in me" (v. 18). When those ought to have rescued, they "delivered (him) into the hands of the Romans." And such the superabundance,[2] * * because those had not power to condemn, but delivered him prisoner. "Not as having aught to accuse my nation of," (v. 19) am I come. See what friendliness of expression! "my nation:" he does not hold them as aliens. He does not say, I do not accuse, but, "I have not (whereof) to accuse:" although he had suffered so many evils at their hands. But nothing of all this does he say, nor make his speech offensive: neither does he seem to be sparing them as matter of favor. For this was the main point, to show that they delivered him prisoner to the Romans,[3] when those ought to have con-

demned him. (a) "For this cause," he says, "I wished to see you" (v. 20): that it might not be in any man's power to accuse me, and to say what (naturally) might suggest itself (τὰ παριστάμενα), that having escaped their hands I have come for this: not to bring evils upon others, but myself fleeing from evils. "I was compelled to appeal unto Cæsar." Observe them also speaking more mildly to him. "We beg," say they: and wish to speak in exculpation of those (at Jerusalem). (e) Whereas they ought to accuse them, they plead for them: by the very fact of their exonerating them, they do in fact accuse them.[4] (b) For this very thing was a proof that they knew themselves exceedingly in the wrong. Had they been confident, they would at any rate have done this, so that he should not have it in his power to make out his story in his own way, and besides they shrank from coming. And by their many times attempting they showed * * (f) "As for this sect, it is known to us," say they, "that it is everywhere spoken against." (v. 21, 21.) * True, but (peo-

---

[1] Τί δὴ τὰ μετὰ ταῦτα; For the answer to this question, see the Recapitulation.—The remainder of the Exposition had fallen into extreme confusion, in consequence of the original redactor's having read the notes in the order 2, 4, 6 : 1, 3, 5: 7: and this is followed by another series of trajections. The restoration of the true order here, and in the numerous cases of the like kind in the former homilies, was no easy matter; but being effected, it speaks for itself. Later scribes (of the old text) have altered a few words here and there: but the framer of the mod. text has endeavored to make it read smoothly, in point of grammar, little regarding the sense and coherence of the whole.

[2] Καὶ τοσαύτη ἡ περιουσία, i. e. not only the Jews could prove nothing against him, but the Romans also, to whom they delivered him, after strict and repeated examinations, found nothing in him worthy of death. So ex abundanti, enough and more than enough, was his innocence established. Mod. text adds τῆς ἐλευθερίας.

[3] This clause τὸ δεῖξαι ὅτι Ῥωμαίοις παρέδωκαν δέσμιον is wanting in A. C. In the next clause. δέον ἐκείνους καταδικάσαι, "whereas, had I been guilty, those, the Jews at Jerusalem, ought to have condemned me, instead of that, ' they delivered me prisoner to the Romans,' and the consequence was, that 'I was compelled to appeal unto Cæsar.'" But this clause being fol-

lowed by e, mod. text connects thus: τοὺς δὲ καταδικάσαι δέον ἐκείνους, δέον κατηγορῆσαι: but whereas these (the Jews at Rome) ought to have condemned those (the Jews at Jerusalem), ought to have accused them, they rather apologize for them, etc.

[4] δέον ἐκείνων κατηγορῆσαι· ἀπολογοῦνται δι' ὧν κατηγοροῦσιν αὐτῶν. We restore it thus, ἀπολογοῦνται· δι' ὧν ἀπολογοῦνται, κατηγοροῦσιν αὐτῶν. And in (b), Τοῦτο μὲν γὰρ αὐτὸ for—αὐτοῦ. "This very thing," i. e. their neither sending letters concerning him to Rome, nor coming themselves; "if they had been confident of their cause (ἐθάρρουν), κἂν τοῦτο ἐποίησαν, they would at any rate have sent letters concerning him, if they did not come themselves. ὥστε μὴ δυνηθῆναι συναρπάσαι με, Erasmus, who here makes his version from the old text, ita ne possent me simul rapere. The mod. text "for if they had been confident, they would at least have done this and come together, ὥστε αὐτὸν συναρπάσαι, ut ipsum secum attraherent." (Ben.) It does not appear what με has to do here, unless the words, defectively reported, are put in St. Paul's mouth : "if," he might say, "they were confident, they would have done this, so that I should not be able συναρπάσαι." The expression συναρπάσαι (sc. τὸ ζητούμενον) is a term of logic, "to seize to one's self as proved some point which is yet in debate and not granted by the opponent:" therefore a petitio principii. Above, p. 321, we had συναρπαγή in the sense of "jumping hastily to a conclusion." Later authors also use it in the sense, "to suppress." See above, p. 209, note[5]. Here, "they would at any rate have written letters concerning him (or, me), that so he (or, I) might not be able to have it all his (or, my) own way:" to beg the point in dispute, and run off with his own justification.—ἄλλως τε καὶ ἐλθεῖν ᾤκνησαν," especially as they shrunk from coming: καὶ τὸ πολλάκις ἐπιχειρίσαι ἔδειξαν, A., ἐπιχῆραι ἔδειξαν." Read καὶ τῷ π. ἐπιχειρῆσαι "by their repeated attempts (to slay him ?)" ἔδειξαν ὅτι οὐκ ἐθάρρουν, or ὅτι ἔδεισαν. Mod. text. "But now, not being confident they shrunk from coming; especially as by their frequent attempting, they showed that they were not confident."

* Needless difficulties have been found in v. 22. It is said that the Jews speak as if they had heard of the Christian Church at Rome, which some years before is represented by Paul's Epistle to the Romans as large and flourishing (Rom. i. 8), only from hearsay, and that Luke must have represented them as so speaking in order to represent Paul as the founder of the Roman Church. For the reserve of the Jews, however, plausible and sufficient reasons can be given, if the fact that they say no more than they do requires explanation. To us it does not seem to require any. The Jews do not state that they know nothing concerning the Roman Christians. They speak of the "sect" in general, but do not say that they know of it only by hearsay. They simply state one thing which they know, not how they know it, nor that it is all that they know. This statement served their purpose to commit themselves in no way against Paul concerning whom they had received no official information from Jerusalem (v. 21) as also the purpose to encourage Paul to explain himself and defend his cause fully and frankly to them.—G. B. S.

ple) are also everywhere persuaded (as, in fact, here), "some were persuaded, and some believed not. And when they had appointed him a day," etc. (v. 23–25.) See again how not by miracles but by Law and Prophets he puts them to silence, and how we always find him doing this. And yet he might also have wrought signs; but then it would no longer have been matter of faith. In fact, this (itself) was a great sign, his discoursing from the Law and the Prophets. Then that you may not deem it strange (that they believed not), he introduces the prophecy which saith, "Hearing ye shall hear and not understand," more now than then: "and ye shall see and not perceive" (v. 26) more now than then. This is not spoken for the former sort, but for the unbelievers. How then? Was it contrary to the prophecy, that those believed? ("Go,") it says, "unto this people" (that is), to the unbelieving people. He did not say this to insult them, but to remove the offence. "Be it known then," he says, "unto you, that unto the Gentiles is sent the salvation of God. They," says he, "will hear it too." (v. 28.) Then why dost thou discourse to us? Didst thou not know this? Yes, but that ye might be persuaded, and that I might exculpate myself, and give none a handle (against me). (c) The unbelieving were they that withdrew. But see how they do not now form plots against him. For in Judea they had a sort of tyranny. Then wherefore did the Providence of God order that he should go thither, and yet the Lord had said, "Get thee out quickly from Jerusalem?" (ch. xxii. 18.) That both their wickedness might be shown, and Christ's prophecy made good, that they would not endure to hear him: and so that all might learn that he was ready to suffer all things, and that the event might be for the consolation of those in Judea: for there also (the brethren) were suffering many grievous evils. But if while preaching the Jewish doctrines, he suffered this, had he preached the doctrines of the glory of Christ, how would they have endured him? While "purifying himself" (ch. xxi. 26) he was intolerable, and how should he have been tolerable while preaching? What [1] lay ye to his charge? What have ye heard? He spoke nothing of the kind. He was simply seen, and he exasperated all against him. Well might he then be set apart for the Gentiles: well might he be sent afar off: there also destined to discourse to the Gentiles. First he calls the

Jews, then having shown them the facts he comes to the Gentiles. (ch. xxiv. 18.) "Well spake the Holy Ghost," etc. But this saying, "The Spirit said," is nothing wonderful: for an angel also is said to say what the Lord saith: but [2] He (the Spirit) not so. When one is speaking of the things said by the angel, one does not say, Well said the angel, but, Well said the Lord. "Well said the Spirit:" as much as to say, It is not me that ye disbelieve. But God foreknew this from the first. "He discoursed," it says, "with boldness, unhindered" (v. 31): for it is possible to speak with boldness, yet hindered. His boldness nothing checked: but in fact he also spoke unhindered. (c) "Discoursed,[3]" it says, "the things concerning the kingdom of God:" mark, nothing of the things of sense, nothing of the things present. (f) But of his affairs after the two years, what say we? (b) (The writer) leaves the hearer athirst for more: the heathen authors do the same (in their writings), for to know everything makes the reader dull and jaded. Or else he does this, (e) not having it in his power to exhibit it from his own personal knowledge. (a) Mark the order of God's Providence,[4] "I have been much hindered from coming unto you . . . having a great desire these many years to

---

[1] i. e. "You say, He is accused of preaching everywhere against the Law—but of what do ye accuse him? what have you heard him say? Not a word of the kind did he speak. They did but see him in the Temple, xxi. 27, and straightway stirred up all the people against him."

[2] ἀλλ' ἐκεῖνος οὐκέτι. A., ἐκείνων. Cat., ἐκεῖνο. Mod. text ἀλλ' ἐνταῦθα μὲν οὕτως, κεῖ δὲ οὐκέτι. Ἄλλως δὲ καὶ—. He makes this an argument against those who affirmed the Holy Ghost to be a created Angel. There are many places where an Angel speaks in the name of the Lord, and what the Angel says, is the Lord's saying. But in speaking of such a communication, one would not say, Well spake the Angel, but, Well spake the Lord. So here, if the Spirit were but an Angel, St. Paul would not have said, "Well spake the Holy Spirit: he would have said, Well spake the Lord. Hence the clause ἀλλ' ἐκεῖνος or ἐκεῖνο (sc. τὸ Πν.) οὐκέτι means, "But not so the Spirit," i. e. What has been said of the case of an Angel speaking in the name of the Lord, does not apply here: the Holy Spirit speaks in His own name. The sense is obscured by the insertion of the clause καλῶς εἶπε, φ., τὸ Πν. τὸ Ἅ. (which we omit) before ἀλλ' ἐκεῖνος οὐκέτι.

[3] Here follows another series of trajections: the parts, as it seems, having been transcribed from the notes in this order, 5, 3, 1: 6, 4, 2: 7, 9: 8, 10. Mod. text inserts here: "But Paul," it says, "dwelt two whole years in his own hired house." So without superfluity was he, rather so did he imitate his Master in all things, since he had even his dwelling furnished him, not from the labors of others, but from his own working: for the words, "in his own hired house," signify this. But that the Lord also did not possess a house, hear Him saying to the man who had not rightly said, "I will follow Thee whithersoever Thou goest: The foxes" said He "have holes, and the birds of the air have nests: but the Son of Man hath not where to lay His head." Thus did He from His own self teach that we should possess nothing, nor be exceedingly attached to things of this life. "And he received," it says, "all that came in unto him, preaching the kingdom of God." See him speaking nothing of the things of sense; nothing concerning the present things, but all concerning the kingdom of God." And below after b, in place of c—g, the same has: "But he does this, and tells not what things came afterwards, deeming it would be superfluous for those who would take in hand the things he had written, and who would learn from these how to add on to the narration: for what the things were which went before, such doubtless he found these which came after. Hear too what he says, writing after these things (?) to the Romans, "Whensoever I take my journey into Spain, I will come to you."

[4] The report is very defective, but the meaning in general is this: See how his desire of coming to Rome is accomplished, but not in the way which he proposed. Hence in (h) we do not hesitate to supply the negative which is omitted in the Mss. and the printed text. Ὁρᾷς πῶς ΟΥ πάντα προεώρα.

come unto you." (Rom. xv. 22, 23.) (*d*) But he fed them with hopes. (*g*) I am in haste to go to Spain, and "I hope," says he, "to see you in my journey, and to be brought thitherward on my journey by you, if first I be filled with your company in some measure." (ib. 24.) (*i*) Of this he says, I will come and rest together with you "in the fulness of the blessing of the Gospel" (ib. 29): and again "I am going to Jerusalem to minister to the saints" (ib. 25): this is the same that he has said here, "To do alms to my nation I came." (Acts xxiv. 17.) (*h*) Do you mark how he did not foresee everything—that sacred and divine head, the man higher than the heavens, that had a soul able to grasp all at once, the holder of the first place—Paul? The man whose very name, to them that know him, suffices for rousing of the soul, for vigilance, for shaking off all sleep! Rome received him bound, coming up from the sea, saved from a shipwreck—and was saved from the shipwreck of error. Like an emperor that has fought a naval battle and overcome, he entered into that most imperial city. (*k*) He was nearer now to his crown. Rome received him bound, and saw him crowned and proclaimed conqueror. There he had said, I will rest together with you: but this was the beginning of a course once more, and he added trophies to trophies, a man not to be overcome. Corinth kept him two years, and Asia three, and this city two for this time; a second time he again entered it, when also he was consummated. Thus he escaped then, and having filled the whole world, he so brought his life to a close. Why didst thou wish to learn what happened after these two years? Those too are such as these: bonds, tortures, fightings, imprisonments, lyings in wait, false accusations, deaths, day by day. Thou hast seen but a small part of it? How much soever thou hast seen, such is he for all the rest. As in the case of the sky, if thou see one part of it, go where thou wilt thou shalt see it such as this: as it is with the sun, though thou see its rays but in part, thou mayest conjecture the rest: so is it with Paul. His Acts thou hast seen in part; such are they all throughout, teeming with dangers. He was a heaven having in it the Sun of Righteousness, not such a sun (as we see): so that that man was better than the very heaven. Think you that this is a small thing—when you say "The Apostle," immediately every one thinks of him (as), when you say "The Baptist," immediately they think of John? To what shall one compare his words? To the sea, or even to the ocean? But nothing is equal to them. More copious than this (sea) are (his) streams;

purer and deeper; so that one would not err in calling Paul's heart both a sea and a heaven, the one for purity, the other for depth. He is a sea, having for its voyagers not those who sail from city to city, but those from earth to heaven: if any man sail in this sea, he will have a prosperous voyage. On this sea, not winds, but instead of winds the Holy and Divine Spirit wafts the souls which sail thereon: no waves are here, no rock, no monsters: all is calm. It is a sea which is more calm and secure than a haven, having no bitter brine, but a pure fountain both sweeter than * *, and brighter and more transparent than the sun: a sea it is, not having precious stones, nor purple dye as ours, but treasures far better than those. He who wishes to descend into this sea, needs not divers, needs not oil, but much loving-kindness (φιλανθρωπίας): he will find in it all the good things that are in the kingdom of Heaven. He will even be able to become a king, and to take the whole world into his possession, and to be in the greatest honor; he who sails on this sea will never undergo shipwreck, but will know all things well. But as those who are inexpert in this (our visible sea) are suffocated (in attempting to dive therein), so is it in that other sea: which is just the case with the heretics, when they attempt things above their strength. It behooves therefore to know the depth, or else not to venture. If we are to sail on this sea, let us come well-girded. "I could not," he says, "speak unto you as unto spiritual, but as unto carnal." (1 Cor. iii. 1.) Let no one who is without endurance sail on this sea. Let us provide for ourselves ships, that is, zeal, earnestness, prayers, that we may pass over the sea in quiet. For indeed this is the living water. Like as if one should get a mouth of fire, such a mouth does that man get who knows Paul well: like as if one should have a sharp sword, so again does such an one become invincible. And for the understanding of Paul's words there is needed also a pure life. For therefore also he said: "Ye are become such as have need of milk, seeing ye are dull of hearing." (Heb. v. 11, 12.) For there is, there is an infirmity of hearing. For as a stomach which is infirm could not take in wholesome food (which it finds) hard of digestion, so a soul which is become tumid and heated, unstrung and relaxed, could not receive the word of the Spirit. Hear the disciples saying, "This is a hard saying: who can hear it" (John vi. 60)? But if the soul be strong and healthy, all is most easy, all is light: it becomes more lofty and buoyant: it is more able to soar and lift itself on high.

Knowing then these things, let us bring our soul into a healthy state: let us emulate Paul, and imitate that noble, that adamantine soul: that, advancing in the steps of his life, we may be enabled to sail through the sea of this present life, and to come unto the haven wherein are no waves, and attain unto the good things promised to them that love Him, through the grace and mercy of our Lord Jesus Christ, with Whom to the Father and Holy Ghost together be glory, might, honor, now and ever, world without end.   Amen.

THE HOMILIES OF ST. JOHN CHRYSOSTOM,

ARCHBISHOP OF CONSTANTINOPLE,

ON THE

EPISTLE OF ST. PAUL THE APOSTLE

TO THE

ROMANS

TRANSLATED BY

REV. J. B. MORRIS, M. A.,

OF EXETER COLLEGE, OXFORD, AND

REV. W. H. SIMCOX,

FELLOW OF QUEEN'S COLLEGE, OXFORD.

REVISED, WITH NOTES, BY

GEORGE B. STEVENS, PH.D. D.D.,

PROFESSOR IN YALE UNIVERSITY.

PREFACE TO HOMILIES ON ROMANS.

ST. CHRYSOSTOM'S Commentary on the Epistle to the Romans is one of the closest and most argumentative of those he has left us. The style of the Epistle itself called for this, being such as almost constantly to remind an attentive reader of the necessity of forming some notion of the views and feelings of the persons to whom it was originally addressed. To this point St. Chrysostom has paid much attention, and has consequently obtained a far clearer view of the doctrinal bearing of the Epistle than most other commentators. His early rhetorical education would probably have given him even too strong a bias toward that kind of exposition, but for his subsequent course of severe discipline and ascetic devotion. As it is, the rhetorical element in his commentary is of very great value. His ready apprehension of the effect intended to be produced by the style and wording of a sentence, is often the means of clearing up what might otherwise seem obscure or even inconsistent. An example of this occurs in the beginning of the seventh chapter, which he expounds in the 12th Homily. The illustration of our release from the Law of Moses by partaking in the Death of Christ, by the dissolution of marriage at death, is so stated in the Epistle as to contain an apparent inconsistency, as though the death of the Law, and the death of the person, were confounded. And the various readings only shift the difficulty, without removing it. This, however, he has very ably shown to be, in fact, an argument *a fortiori*. Other cases will strike other persons as they happen to have found difficulty in the Text.

A far higher qualification for interpreting St. Paul, in whom, as much as in any of the sacred writers, the Man appears as well as the guiding Spirit, was that peculiar affection with which he regarded him, and which he expresses particularly in the beginning of the Introduction, and at the close of the last Homily. The effect of this is perhaps best traced in the commentary on Rom. ix. 3, Hom. xvi.

The elaborate composition of these Homilies, and the close attention which it must have required, has been thought an indication that they must have been delivered before the Author was engaged in the cares of the Bishopric of Constantinople. But Tillemont has detected even surer indications, which place the point clearly beyond all question. In his exhortation to Charity, Hom. viii. he speaks of himself and his hearers as under one Bishop. It has been objected that he speaks of himself as Pastor, in Hom. xxix. but he does the same in other Homilies, certainly delivered by him when he was only a preacher at Antioch, and the terms are less definite than in the other case, v. ad. P. Ant. Hom. xx. on the Statues. Besides, he seems to address persons who have ready access to the place in which St. Paul taught and was bound, which cannot be shown to tally with Constantinople, but evidently agrees with Antioch. The binding of St. Paul there mentioned is not, however, on record, and it is just possible he may mean in that expression to refer to another place.

Some account of the life of the Author has been given in the Preface to the Homilies on the First Epistle to the Corinthians, already translated.[1] It may be worth while, however, to notice particularly, in connection with this work, the manner in which St. Chrysostom was quoted in the Pelagian controversy, as some of the passages are taken from it.

St. Augustin, *adv. Julianum*, l. 1, c. vi. discusses a passage in a Homily to the newly baptized, which was alleged against the doctrine of Original Sin. He had spoken of infants as not having sins, meaning of course actual sins, as the plural number implies. The words were, however, easily turned in translation so as to bear another sense. St. Augustin quotes on the other side his Letter to Olympias, that "Adam by his sin condemned the whole race of men." And Hom. ix. in Gen. c. 1. v. 28, where he speaks of the loss of command over the creation, as a penalty of the Fall. And finally, a passage from the Homily before quoted (as

---

[1] [For this a more complete sketch of the Life and Work of St. Chrysostom has been given by the Editor in the Prolegomena to the first volume.]

ad Neophytos), in which he speaks of our Lord finding us " bound by a hereditary debt ; " and one in Hom. x. of this Commentary, viz. that on Rom. v. 14. These are sufficient to make it clear, that St. Chrysostom did not hold any Pelagian doctrine on this point.

With respect to Free-will, he has one or two passages, as in Hom. on the words of St. Paul, 2 Cor. iv. 13. Ben. t. iii. p. 264. " That first believing, and obeying when called, is of our good will; but when the foundation of faith is laid, we need the assistance of the Spirit." And on St. John i. 38. Ben. 8. p. 107, p. 154, O. T. " that God does not precede our wills with His gifts ; but when we have begun, when we have sent our will before, then He gives us abundant opportunities of salvation." However, in Hom. lviii. in Gen. he says, " though he received help from above, yet he first did his own part. So let us persuade ourselves, that though we strive ever so much, we can do no good thing at all, except we are aided by help from above. For as we can never do anything aright without that help, so unless we contribute our own share, we shall not be able to obtain help from above." This illustrates his meaning about doing our own part *first*, and shows that he does not mean to exclude Divine aid in the very beginning of good actions, only not *superseding* the motion of our will. The word *gifts* is also to be observed. He probably did not think of its being applicable to the first motions of prevenient grace, intending himself the Evangelical gifts. This view of his meaning seems to solve the difficulties of his expressions, so far as is necessary in a writer more rhetorical than logical. Some passages in this Commentary bear on the point, as on Rom. ii. 16, and viii. 26.

In a Letter to Olympias, shortly before his death, he laments the errors of a " Monk Pelagius," and it is supposed that he means the well-known heretic.

The present Translation is from the text of Savile, except where otherwise noted. For the first sixteen Homilies, several Mss. have been collated in Paris, with a view to an Edition of the original, the rest of the collation is not yet come to hand. Four contain nearly the whole of the Commentary, and three more several parts of it: two of these were partially used by the Benedictine Editors, and supply some valuable readings in the latter Homilies. There is also one Ms. in the Bodleian Library, which has many mistakes, but agrees in general with the best readings in those which have been collated. It contains nearly the whole text as far as Hom. xxx. and has been entirely collated after Hom. xvi. and for a great part of the earlier Homilies.

The Editors are indebted for the Translation, and much of the matter contained in the Notes, to the Reverend J. B. MORRIS, M. A., of Exeter College, as well as for the Index.

C. MARRIOTT.

The Benedictine text having been revised by Mr. Field with singular acumen by aid of collations of all European Mss. of any account, it was not thought right to republish this important volume without revising the translation by that text. This was kindly undertaken by the Rev. W. H. Simcox, late Fellow of Queen's College, and has been executed with the care and exactness to be expected from that accomplished scholar. In other respects, he has with a remarkable modesty left the previous translation untouched.

1876   E. B. PUSEY.

CONTENTS OF THE HOMILIES

333

HOMILIES

OF

ST. JOHN CHRYSOSTOM,

ARCHBISHOP OF CONSTANTINOPLE,

ON THE

EPISTLE OF ST. PAUL THE APOSTLE

TO THE

ROMANS

THE ARGUMENT.[1]

As I keep hearing the Epistles of the blessed Paul read, and that twice every week, and often three or four times, whenever we are celebrating the memorials of the holy martyrs, gladly do I enjoy the spiritual trumpet, and get roused and warmed with desire at recognizing the voice so dear to me, and seem to fancy him all but present to my sight, and behold him conversing with me. But I grieve and am pained, that all people do not know this man, as much as they ought to know him; but some are so far ignorant of him, as not even to know for certainty the number of his Epistles. And this comes not of incapacity, but of their not having the wish to be continually conversing with this blessed man. For it is not through any natural readiness and sharpness of wit that even I am acquainted with as much as I do know, if I do know anything, but owing to a continual cleaving to the man, and an earnest affection towards him. For, what belongs to men beloved, they who love them know above all others; because they are interested in them. And this also this blessed Apostle shows in what he said to the Philippians; "Even as it is meet for me to think this of you all, because I have you in my heart, both in my bonds, and in the defence and confirmation of the Gospel." (Phil. i. 7.) And so ye also, if ye be willing to apply to the reading of him with a ready mind, will need no other aid. For the word of Christ is true which saith, "Seek, and ye shall find; knock, and it shall be opened unto you." (Matt. vii. 7.) But since the greater part of those who here gather themselves to us, have taken upon themselves the bringing up of children, and the care of a wife, and the charge of a family, and for this cause cannot afford to give themselves wholly to this labor, be ye at all events aroused to receive those things which have been brought together by others, and bestow as much attention upon the hearing of what is said as ye give to the gathering together of goods. For although it is unseemly to demand only so much of you, yet still one must be content if ye give as much. For from this it is that our countless evils have arisen—from ignorance of the Scriptures; from this it is that the plague of heresies has broken out; from this that there are negligent lives; from this labors without advantage. For as men deprived of this daylight would not walk aright, so they that look not to the gleaming of the Holy Scriptures must needs be frequently and constantly sinning, in that they are walking in the worst darkness. And that this fall not out, let us hold our eyes open to the bright shining of the Apostle's words; for this man's tongue shone forth above the sun, and he abounded more than all the rest in the word of doctrine; for since he labored more abundantly than they, he also drew upon himself a large measure of the Spirit's grace.

---

[1] Field counts this as the first Homily: but it seemed needless to disturb the usual numeration.

(1 Cor. xv. 10.) And this I constantly affirm, not only from his Epistles, but also from the Acts. For if there were anywhere a season for oratory, to him men everywhere gave place. Wherefore also he was thought by the unbelievers to be Mercurius, because he took the lead in speech. (Acts xiv. 12.) And as we are going to enter fully into this Epistle, it is necessary to give the date also at which it was written. For it is not, as most think, before all the others, but before all that were written from Rome, yet subsequent to the rest, though not to all of them. For both those to the Corinthians were sent before this: and this is plain from what he wrote at the end of this, saying as follows: "But now I go unto Jerusalem to minister unto the saints: for it hath pleased them of Macedonia and Achaia to make a certain contribution for the poor saints which are at Jerusalem." (Rom. xv. 25, 26.) For in writing to the Corinthians he says: "If it be meet that I go also, they shall go with me" (1 Cor. xvi. 4); meaning this about those who were to carry the money from thence. Whence it is plain, that when he wrote to the Corinthians, the matter of this journey of his was in doubt, but when to the Romans, it stood now a decided thing. And this being allowed, the other point is plain, that this Epistle was after those. But that to the Thessalonians also seems to me to be before the Epistle to the Corinthians: for having written to them before, and having moved the question of alms to them, when he said, "But as touching brotherly love, ye need not that I write unto you: for ye yourselves are taught of God to love one another. And indeed ye do it toward all the brethren" (1 Thess. iv. 9, 10): then he wrote to the Corinthians. And this very point he makes plain in the words, "For I know the forwardness of your mind, for which I boast of you to them of Macedonia, that Achaia was ready a year ago, and your zeal hath provoked very many" (2 Cor. ix. 2): whence he shows that they were the first he had spoken to about this. This Epistle then is later than those, but prior ($\pi\rho\acute{\omega}\tau\eta$) to those from Rome; for he had not as yet set foot in the city of the Romans when he wrote this Epistle, and this he shows by saying, "For I long to see you, that I may impart unto you some spiritual gift." (Rom. i. 11.) But it was from Rome he wrote to the Philippians; wherefore he says, "All the saints salute you, chiefly they that are of Cæsar's household" (Phil. iv. 22): and to the Hebrews from thence likewise, wherefore also he says, "all they of Italy salute them." (Heb. xiii. 24.) And the Epistle to Timothy he sent also

from Rome, when in prison; which also seems to me to be the last of all the Epistles; and this is plain from the end: "For I am now ready to be offered," he says, "and the time of my departure is at hand." (2 Tim. iv. 6.) But that he ended his life there, is clear, I may say, to every one. And that to Philemon is also very late, (for he wrote it in extreme old age, wherefore also he said, "as Paul the aged, and now also a prisoner in Christ Jesus,") (Philem. 9), yet previous to that to the Colossians. And this again is plain from the end. For in writing to the Colossians, he says, "All my state shall Tychicus declare unto you, whom I have sent with Onesimus, a faithful and beloved brother." (Col. iv. 7.) For this was that Onesimus in whose behalf he composed the Epistle to Philemon. And that this was no other of the same name with him, is plain from the mention of Archippus. For it is he whom he had taken as worker together with himself in the Epistle to Philemon, when he besought him for Onesimus, whom when writing to the Colossians he stirreth up, saying, "Say to Archippus, Take heed to the ministry which thou hast received, that thou fulfil it." (Col. iv. 17.) And that to the Galatians seems to me to be before that to the Romans.[*] But if they have a different order in the Bibles, that is nothing wonderful, since the twelve Prophets, though not exceeding one another in order of time, but standing at great intervals from one another, are in the arrangement of the Bible placed in succession. Thus Haggai and Zachariah and the Messenger[1] prophesied after Ezekiel and Daniel, and long after Jonah and Zephaniah and all the rest. Yet they are nevertheless joined with all those from whom they stand so far off in time.

But let no one consider this an undertaking beside the purpose, nor a search of this kind a piece of superfluous curiosity; for the date of the Epistles contributes no little to what we are looking after.[†] For when I see him writing to

---

[1] "Or 'Angel,' i. e. Malachi; who was so called from the expression Mal. i. 1 (LXX. διὰ χειρὸς ἀγγέλου αὐτοῦ. cf. E. V. in margin 'by the hand of Malachi'), cf. 2 Esdr. i. 40."

[*] It is remarkable that the conclusions of Chrys. should harmonize so well with the results of modern scholarship in regard to the order of the Pauline epistles. Except in assigning the Epistle to the Hebrews to Paul and in apparently interposing a considerable period between Philemon and Colossians, his statements may be taken as giving the best conclusions of criticism.—G. B. S.

[†] Our author rightly attaches much importance to the time and occasion of writing as bearing upon the meaning of the epistles. The earliest epistles—those to the Thessalonians—relate to Paul's missionary labors and are but a continuation of the apostle's preaching. They might almost be called samples of his sermons. The group which falls next in order (Gal., 1 and 2 Cor., and Rom.) comprehends the great doctrinal discussions of the problems of law and grace, and reflects the conflict of the Apostle to the Gentiles with the Judaizing tendency in all its phases. This group is most important for the study of the Pauline theology. The third group—the epistles of the (first) imprisonment—Col., Philem., Eph. and Phil.—besides containing a wonderful fulness and richness

the Romans and to the Colossians about the same subjects, and yet not in a like way about the same subjects; but to the former with much condescension, as when he says, "Him that is weak in the faith receive ye, but not to doubtful disputations; for one believeth that he may eat all things, another, who is weak, eateth herbs" (Rom. xiv. 1, 2): but to the Colossians he does not write in this way, though about the same things, but with greater boldness of speech : " Wherefore if ye be dead with Christ," he says, "why, as though living in the world, are ye subject to ordinances (touch not, taste not, handle not), which all are to perish with the using, not in any honor to the satisfying of the flesh" (Col. ii. 20-23);—I find no other reason for this difference than the time of the transaction. For at the first it was needful to be condescending, but afterwards it became no more so. And in many other places one may find him doing this. Thus both the physician and the teacher are used to do. For neither does the physician treat alike his patients in the first stage of their disorder, and when they have come to the point of having health thenceforth, nor the teacher those children who are beginning to learn and those who want more advanced subjects of instruction. Now to the rest he was moved to write by some particular cause and subject, and this he shows, as when he says to the Corinthians, "Touching those things whereof ye wrote unto me" (1 Cor. vii. 1): and to the Galatians too from the very commencement of the whole Epistle writes so as to indicate the same thing; but to these for what purpose and wherefore does he write? For one finds him bearing testimony to them that they are "full of goodness, being filled with all knowledge, and able also to admonish others." (Rom. xv. 14.) Why then does he write to them? "Because of the grace of God," he says, "which is given unto me, that I should be the minister of Jesus Christ" (ib. 15, 16): wherefore also he says in the beginning: "I am a debtor ; as much as in me is, I am ready to preach the Gospel to you that are at Rome also ; " for what is said—as that they are "able to exhort others also" (Rom. i. 14, 15),—and the like, rather belongs to encomium and encouragement : and the correction afforded by means

of a letter, was needful even for these ; for since he had not yet been present, he bringeth the men to good order in two ways, both by the profitableness of his letter and by the expectation of his presence. For such was that holy soul, it comprised the whole world and carried about all men in itself thinking the nearest relationship to be that in God. And he loved them so, as if he had begotten them all, or rather showed (so 4 Mss.) a greater instinctive affection than any father (so Field: all Mss. give "a father's toward all"); for such is the grace of the Spirit, it exceedeth the pangs of the flesh, and displays a more ardent longing than theirs. And this one may see specially in the soul of Paul, who having as it were become winged through love, went continually round to all, abiding nowhere nor standing still. For since he had heard Christ saying, "Peter, lovest thou Me? feed My sheep" (John xxi. 15); and setting forth this as the greatest test of love, he displayed it in a very high degree. Let us too then, in imitation of him, each one bring into order, if not the world, or not entire cities and nations, yet at all events his own house, his wife, his children, his friends, his neighbors. And let no one say to me, "I am unskilled and unlearned : " nothing were less instructed than Peter, nothing more rude than Paul, and this himself confessed, and was not ashamed to say, "though I be rude in speech, yet not in knowledge." (2 Cor. xi. 6.) Yet nevertheless this rude one, and that unlearned man,* overcame countless philosophers, stopped the mouths of countless orators, and did all by their own ready mind and the grace of God. What excuse then shall we have, if we are not equal to twenty names, and are not even of service to them that live with us? This is but a pretence and an excuse—for it is not want

* The "learning" of the Apostle Paul has been greatly exaggerated on both sides. It has been customary to overestimate it. He has been described as learned in Greek literature. The quotation of a few words from Aratus (Acts xvii. 28) and the use of two (probably) proverbial sayings which have been traced to Menander and Epimenides (1 Cor. xv. 33; Titus i. 12) furnish too slender support for this opinion. (vid. Meyer *in locis*). It is said that Paul had abundant opportunity to become acquainted with the Greek literature in Tarsus. But he left Tarsus at an early age and all the prejudices of his family would disincline him to the study of Heathen literature. His connection with Gamaliel and the style of his epistles alike show that his education was predominantly Jewish and Rabbinic. He was learned after the manner of the strictest Pharisees and from his residence in Tarsus and extended travel had acquired a good writing and speaking knowledge of the Greek language. Chrys. is uniformly inclined, however, to depreciate the culture of Paul. This springs from a desire to emphasize the greatness of his influence and power as compared with his attainments. The apostle's confession that he is an ἰδιώτης τῷ λόγῳ (2 Cor. xi. 6), means only that he was unskilled in eloquence and is to be taken as his own modest estimate of himself in that particular. Moreover it is immediately qualified by ἀλλ' οὐ τῇ γνώσει which is entirely inconsistent with the idea that he was rude or illiterate in general, or that he considered himself to be so.—G. B. S.

of Christian thought, exhibits to us the rise and spread of Gnostic heresies,—the introduction of heathen philosophical ideas which were destined to exert a mighty influence upon the theology, religion and life of the church for centuries. The last group—the Pastoral epistles—has a peculiar private and personal character from being addressed to individuals. They have a special value, for all who hold their genuineness, from being the latest Christian counsels of "Paul the aged." —G. B. S.

of learning or of instruction which hindereth our teaching, but drowsiness and sleep. (Acts i. 15; ii. 41.) Let us then having shaken off this sleep with all diligence cleave to our own members, that we may even here enjoy much calm, by ordering in the fear of God them that are akin to us, and hereafter may partake of countless blessings through the grace and love of our Lord Jesus Christ towards man, through Whom, and with Whom, be glory to the Father, with the Holy Ghost, now, and evermore, and to all ages. Amen.

HOMILY I.

ROM. I. 1, 2.

"Paul, a servant of Jesus Christ, called to be an Apostle, separated unto the Gospel of God, (which He promised afore by His prophets in the Holy Scriptures.)"

MOSES having written five books, has nowhere put his own name to them, neither have they who after him put together the history of events after him, no nor yet has Matthew, nor John, nor Mark, nor Luke; but the blessed Paul everywhere in his Epistles sets [1] his own name. Now why was this? Because they were writing to people, who were present, and it had been superfluous to show themselves when they were present. But this man sent his writings from afar and in the form of a letter, for which cause also the addition of the name was necessary. But if in the Epistle to the Hebrews he does not do the same, this too is after his own wise judgment.[*] For since they felt prejudiced against him, lest on hearing the name at the outstart, they should stop up all admission to his discourse, he subtly won their attention by concealing the name. But if some Prophets and Solomon have put their names, this I leave as a subject for you to look further into hereafter, why some of them wished to put it so, and some not. For you are not to learn everything from me, but to take pains yourselves also and enquire further, lest ye become more dull-witted.

"Paul, a servant of Jesus Christ." Why did God change his name, and call him Paul, who was Saul? It was, that he might not even in this respect come short of the Apostles, but that that preëminence which the chief of the Disciples had, he might also acquire (Mark iii. 16); and have whereon to ground a closer union with them. And he calls himself, the servant of Christ, yet not merely this;[2] for there be many sorts of servitude. One owing to the Creation, according to which it says, "for all are Thy servants" (Ps. cxix. 91); and according to which it says, "Nebuchadnezzar, My servant" (Jer. xxv. 9), for the work is the servant of Him which made it. Another kind is that from the faith, of which it saith, "But God be thanked that ye were the servants of sin, but ye have obeyed from a pure heart that form of doctrine which was delivered unto you: being then made free from sin, ye became the servants of righteousness." (Rom. vi. 17, 18.) Another is that from civil subjection (πολιτείας), after which it saith, "Moses my servant is dead" (Jos. i. 2); and indeed all the Jews were servants, but Moses in a special way as shining most brightly in the community. Since then, in all the forms of the marvellous servitude, Paul was a servant; this he puts in the room of the greatest title of dignity, saying, "a servant of Jesus Christ." And the Names appertaining to the dispensation [3] he sets forth, going on upwards from the lowest. For with the Name Jesus, did the Angel come from Heaven when He was conceived of the Virgin, and Christ He is called from being anointed, which also itself belonged to the flesh. And with what oil, it may be asked, was He anointed? It was not with oil that He was anointed, but with the Spirit. And Scripture has instances of calling such "Christs": inasmuch as the Spirit is the chief point in the unction, and that for which the oil is used. And where does it call those "Christs" who are not anointed with oil? "Touch not," it says, "Mine anointed, and do My prophets no harm" (Ps. cv. 15), but at that time the institution of anointing with oil did not yet even exist.

"Called an Apostle." He styles himself

---

[1] In every one of his Epistles prefixes (Savile).
[*] This expression is significant as showing the confidence of Chrys. in the Pauline authorship of the Epistle to the Hebrews. It need hardly be said that the reason for the omission of the Apostle's name is purely fanciful and that the non-Pauline character of the Epistle is almost demonstrable.—G. B. S.

[2] Or, "not in one way only."
[3] οἰκονομίας, viz. the concealment of His glory in the Incarnation.

"called" in all his Epistles, so showing his own candor (εὐγνωμοσύνην), and that it was not of his own seeking that he found, but that when called he came near and obeyed. And the faithful, he styles, " called to be saints," * but while they had been called so far as to be believers, he had besides a different thing committed to his hands, namely, the Apostleship, a thing full of countless blessings, and at once greater than and comprehensive of, all the gifts.

And what more need one say of it, than that whatsoever Christ was doing when present, this he committed to their hands when He departed. Which also Paul cries aloud, speaking thereof and magnifying the dignity of the Apostles' office; "We are ambassadors for Christ, as though God did beseech by us;" i. e. in Christ's stead. "Separated to the Gospel of God." (2 Cor. v. 20.) For as in a house, each one is set apart for divers works; thus also in the Church, there be divers distributions of ministrations. And herein he seems to me to hint, that he was not appointed by lot only, but that of old and from the first he was ordained to this office; which also Jeremy saith, that God spake concerning himself, "Before thou camest forth out of the womb, I sanctified thee, I ordained thee a prophet unto the nations." (Jer. i. 5.) For in that he was writing to a vainglorious city, and one every way puffed up, he therefore uses every mode of showing that his election was of God. For He Himself called him, and Himself separated him. And he does this, that he may make the Epistle deserve credit, and meet an easy reception. "To the Gospel of God." Not Matthew then alone is an Evangelist, nor Mark, as neither was this man alone an Apostle, but they also; even if he be said preëminently to be this, and they that. And he calleth it the Gospel, not for those good things only which have been brought to pass, but also for those which are to come. And how comes he to say, that the Gospel "of God" is preached by himself? for he says, "separated to the Gospel of God"—for the Father was manifest, even before the Gospels. Yet even if He were manifest, it was to the Jews only, and not even to all of these as were fitting. For neither did they know Him to be a Father, and many things did they conceive unworthily of Him. Where-

fore also Christ saith, "The true worshippers" shall come, and that "the Father seeketh such to worship Him." (John iv. 23.) But it was afterwards that He Himself with the Son was unveiled to the whole world, which Christ also spake of beforehand, and said, "that they might know Thee the only true God, and Jesus Christ Whom Thou has sent." (John xvii. 3.) But he calls it the "Gospel" of God, to cheer the hearer at the outstart. For he came not with tidings to make the countenance sad, as did the prophets with their accusations, and charges, and reproofs, but with glad tidings, even the "Gospel of God;" countless treasures of abiding and unchangeable blessings.

Ver. 2. "Which He promised afore by His Prophets in the Holy Scriptures."

For the Lord, saith he, "shall give the word to them that proclaim glad tidings with great power" (Ps. lxviii. 12, Sept.); and again, "How beautiful are the feet of them that preach the Gospel of peace." (Is. lii. 7; Rom. x. 15.) See here both the name of the Gospel expressly and the temper of it, laid down in the Old Testament. For, we do not proclaim it by words only, he means, but also by acts done; since neither was it human, but both divine and unspeakable, and transcending all nature. Now since they have laid against it the charge of novelty also, He shows it to be older than the Greeks, and described aforetime in the Prophets. And if He gave it not from the beginning because of those that were unwilling to receive it, still, they that were willing did hear it. "Your father Abraham," He says, "rejoiced to see My day, and he saw it, and was glad." (John viii. 56.) How then comes He to say, Many prophets desired to see the things which ye see, and have not seen them?" (Matt. xiii. 17.) He means not so, as ye see and hear, the Flesh itself, and the very miracles before your eyes. But let me beg you to look and see what a very long time ago these things were foretold. For when God is about to do openly some great things, He announces them of a long time before, to practise men's hearing for the reception of them when they come.

"In the Holy Scriptures." Because the Prophets not only spake, but also writ what they spake; nor did they write only, but also shadowed them forth by actions, as Abraham when he led up Isaac, and Moses when he lifted up the Serpent, and when he spread out his hands[1] against Amalek, and when he offered the Paschal Lamb.

---

* It is noticeable that in the New Testament the apostles call the body of believers "saints," but never apply this term to themselves or to one another. In later times the body of believers returned the compliment and fixed the term as a title upon the Apostles, New Testament writers, Church Fathers, and a large number of Christians more or less distinguished for learning or piety. Most Christians find the title more appropriate to the two first classes than to the two last.—G. B. S.

---

[1] Which the Fathers teach to be a type of Christ upon the Cross. See on *Tert. Apol.* c. 30, p. 70. Oxf. Tr.

Ver. 3. "Concerning His Son which was made of the seed of David, according to the flesh."

What dost, thou, O Paul, that after lifting up our souls so, and elevating them, and causing great and unutterable things to pass in show before them, and speaking of the Gospel, and that too the Gospel of God, and bringing in the chorus of the Prophets, and showing the whole of them heralding forth many years before those things which were to come: why dost thou again bring us down to David? Art thou conversing, oh tell me, of some man, and giving him Jesse's son for a father? And wherein are these things worthy of what thou hast just spoken of? Yea, they are fully worthy. For our discourse is not, saith he, of any bare man. Such was my reason for adding, "according to the flesh;" as hinting that there is also a Generation of the Same after the Spirit. And why did he begin from that and not from this the higher? It is because that was what Matthew, and Luke, and Mark, began from. For he who would lead men by the hand to Heaven, must needs lead them upwards from below. So too was the actual dispensation ordered. First, that is, they saw Him a man upon earth, and then they understood Him to be God. In the same direction then, as He Himself had framed His teaching, did His disciple also shape out the way which leadeth thither. Therefore the generation according to the flesh is in his language placed first in order, not because it was first, but because he was for leading the hearer from this up to that.

Ver. 4. "And declared to be the Son of God with power, according to the Spirit of Holiness, by the resurrection from the dead, even Jesus Christ."

What is said has been made obscure by the close-folding of the words, and so it is necessary to divide it. What then is it, which he says? We preach, says he, Him Who was made of David. But this is plain. Whence then is it plain, that this incarnate "Person" was also the Son of God? First, it is so from the prophets; wherefore he says, "Which He had promised afore by the Prophets in the Holy Scriptures." (v. 2.) And this way of demonstration is no weak one. And next also from the very way of His Generation: which also he sets forth by saying, "of the seed of David according to the flesh:" for He broke the rule of nature. Thirdly, from the miracles which He did, yielding a demonstration of much power, for "in power" means this. Fourthly, from the Spirit which He gave to them that believe upon Him, and through which He made

them all holy, wherefore he saith, "according to the Spirit of holiness." For it was of God only to grant such gifts. Fifthly, from the Resurrection; for He first and He alone raised Himself: and this Himself too said to be above all a miracle sufficient to stop the mouths even of them that behaved shamelessly. For, "Destroy this Temple," He says, "and in three days I will raise it up" (John xix.); and, "When ye have lifted" Me "up from the earth, then shall ye know that I am He" (ib. viii. 28); and again, This "generation seeketh after a sign; and there shall no sign be given unto it, but the sign of Jonas." (Matt. xii. 39.) What then is the being "declared?" being shown, being manifested, being judged, being confessed, by the feeling and suffrage of all; by Prophets, by the marvellous Birth after the Flesh, by the power which was in the miracles, by the Spirit, through which He gave sanctification, by the Resurrection, whereby He put an end to the tyranny of death.

Ver. 5. "By Whom we have received grace and Apostleship for obedience to the faith."

See the candor of the servant. He wishes nothing to be his own, but all his Master's. And indeed it was the Spirit that gave this. Wherefore He saith, "I have many things to say unto you, but ye cannot bear them now. Howbeit when He, the Spirit of Truth, is come, He will guide you into all truth" (John xvi. 12): and again, "Separate Me Paul and Barnabas." (Acts xiii. 2.) And in the Epistle to the Corinthians, he says, that "to one is given by the Spirit the word of wisdom, to another the word of knowledge" (1 Cor. xii. 8, 11); and that It divideth all as It willeth. And in addressing the Milesians, he says, "Over which the Holy Ghost hath made you shepherds and overseers." (Acts xx. 28.) You see, he calls the things of the Spirit, the Son's, and the things of the Son, the Spirit's. "Grace and Apostleship;" that is, it is not we that have achieved for ourselves, that we should become Apostles. For it was not by having toiled much and labored that we had this dignity allotted to us, but we received grace, and the successful result is a part of the heavenly gift. "For obedience to the faith." So it was not the Apostles that achieved it, but grace that paved the way before them. For it was their part to go about and preach, but to persuade was of God, Who wrought in them. As also Luke saith, that "He opened their heart" (Acts xvi. 14); and again, To whom it was given to hear the word of God.[1] "To obedience;" he

---

[1] Supposed to be a vague recollection of St. Luke viii. 10, or of Acts xix. 10.

says not, to questioning and parade (κατασκευὴν) of argument but "to obedience." For we were not sent, he means, to argue, but to give those things which we had trusted to our hands. For when the Master declareth aught, they that hear should not be nice and curious handlers of what is told them, but receivers only; for this is why the Apostles were sent, to speak what they had heard, not to add aught from their own stock, and that we for our part should believe—that we should believe what?—"concerning His Name." Not that we should be curious about the essence, but that we should believe on the Name; for this it was which also wrought the miracles. For it says, "in the Name of Jesus Christ rise up and walk." (Acts iii. 6.) And this too requireth faith, neither can one grasp aught of these things by reasoning (λογισμῷ καταλαβεῖν). "Among all nations, among whom are ye also the called of Jesus Christ." What? did Paul preach then to all the nations? Now that he ran through the whole space from Jerusalem to Illyricum, and from thence again went forth to the very ends of the earth, is plain from what he writes to the Romans; but even if he did not come to all, yet still what he says is not false, for he speaks not of himself alone, but of the twelve Apostles, and all who declared the word after them. And in another sense, one should not see any fault to find with the phrase, if about himself, when one considers his ready mind, and how that after death he ceaseth not to preach in all parts of the world. And consider how he extols the gift, and shows that it is great and much more lofty than the former, since the old things were with one nation, but this gift drew sea and land to itself. And attend to this too, how free the mind of Paul is from all flattery; for when conversing with the Romans, who were seated as it were upon a sort of summit of the whole world, he attaches no more to them than to the other nations, nor does he on the score of their being then in power and ruling, say, that they have in spiritual things also any advantage. But as (he means) we preach to all the nations, so do we to you, numbering them with Scythians and Thracians: for if he did not wish to show this, it were superfluous to say "Among whom are ye also." * And this he does to take down their high spirit (κενῶν

τὸ φύσημα) and to prostrate the swelling vanity of their minds, and to teach them to honor others alike to themselves: and so he proceeds to speak upon this very point.

Ver. 6. "Among whom are ye also the called of Jesus Christ."

That is, along with whom ye also are: and he does not say, that he called the others with you, but you with the others. For if in Christ Jesus there is neither bond nor free, much less is there king and private man. For even ye were called and did not come over of yourselves.

Ver. 7. "To all that be in Rome, beloved of God, called to be saints: grace to you and peace from God our Father, and the Lord Jesus Christ."

See how continually he puts the word "called," saying, "called to be an Apostle; among whom ye also are called; to all that be in Rome, called:" and this he does not out of superfluity of words, but out of a wish to remind them of the benefit. For since among them which believed, it was likely that there would be some of the consuls (ὑπάτων; Ben. *consulares*) and rulers as well as poor and common men, casting aside the inequality of ranks, he writes to them all under one appellation. But if in things which are more needful and which are spiritual, all things are set forth as common both to slaves and to free, for instance, the love from God, the calling, the Gospel, the adoption, the grace, the peace, the sanctification, all things else, how could it be other than the uttermost folly, whom God had joined together, and made to be of equal honor in the greater things, those to divide on account of things on earth? on this ground, I presume, from the very outstart, this blessed Apostle, after casting out this mischievous disease, conducts them to the mother of blessings, humble-mindedness. This made servants better, since they learnt that they should take no harm from their servitude, while they had the true freedom; this would incline masters to be gentle, as being instructed that they have no advantage in being free, unless the goods of faith have the first place given them. And that you may learn that he was not doing this to work confusion, by dashing all things, but still knew the best distinction, he wrote not simply to all that were in Rome, but with a definition added, "beloved of God." For this is the best discrimination, and shows whence the sanctification was. Whence then was the sanctification? from Love. For after saying, "beloved," then he proceeds, "called to be saints," showing that it is from this that the

---

* The expression has also another important bearing upon a question much debated by modern scholars, viz.: was the Roman Church predominantly Jewish or Gentile? The Pauline usage is strongly in favor of understanding by the words τὰ ἔθνη Gentiles as opposed to Jews. If this is correct the expression together with ἐν οἷς ἐστὲ would seem decisive as showing the predominantly Gentile character of the Roman Christian community.—G. B. S.

fount of all blessings is. But saints he calls all the faithful. "Grace unto you and peace."

Oh address, that bringeth countless blessings to us! This also Christ bade the Apostles to use as their first word when entering into houses. (Luke x. 5.) Wherefore it is from this that Paul also in all places takes his beginning, from grace and peace; for it was no small war which Christ put an end to, but indeed one varying and of every kind and of a long season (ποικίλον καὶ παντοδαπὸν); and this not from our labors, but through His grace. Since then love presented us with grace, and grace with peace, having set them down in the due order of an address, he prays over them that they may abide perpetual and unmoved, so that no other war may again be blown into flame, and beseeches Him that gave, to keep these things firmly settled, saying as follows, "Grace be unto you and peace from God our Father, and the Lord Jesus Christ." See in this passage, the " from " is common to the Son and the Father, and this is equivalent to " of whom." [1] For he did not say, Grace be unto you and peace from God the Father, "through" our Lord Jesus Christ; but, "from God the Father, and the Lord Jesus Christ." Strange! how mighty is the love of God! we which were enemies and disgraced, have all at once become saints and sons. For when he calls Him Father, he shows them to be sons; and when he says sons, he has unveiled the whole treasure of blessings.

Let us then keep showing a conversation worthy of the gift, and hold on in peace and holiness. For other dignities are but for a time, and are brought to an end along with this life present, and may be bought with money (whence one might say they are not dignities at all but names of dignities only, having their strength in the investiture of fine array and the servility of attendants), but this as having been given of God, the gift of sanc-

tification and adoption, is not broken through even by death, but even here maketh men conspicuous, and also departs with us upon our journey to the life to come. For he that holdeth on in the adoption, and keeps an exact watch upon his holiness, is much brighter and more happy even than he that is arrayed with the diadem itself, and has the purple; and has the delight of abundant peace in the present life and is nurtured up with goodly hopes, and hath no ground for worry and disturbance, but enjoys constant pleasure; for as for good spirits and joy, it is not greatness of power, not abundance of wealth, not pomp of authority, not strength of body, not sumptuousness of the table, not the adorning of dresses, nor any other of the things in man's reach that ordinarily produces them, but spiritual success, and a good conscience alone. And he that hath this cleansed, even though he be clad in rags and struggling with famine, is of better spirits than they that live so softly. So too he that is conscious of wicked deeds, even though he may gather to himself all men's goods, is the most wretched of all men. For this cause Paul, living in continual hunger and nakedness, and being scourged every day was joyful, and went more softly than they that were then emperors. But Ahab though a king, and indulging in a sumptuous luxury, when he had done that one sin, groaned and was out of spirits, and his countenance was fallen both before the sin and after the sin. If then we wish to enjoy pleasure, above all things else let us shun wickedness, and follow after virtue; since it is not in the nature of things for one to have a share thereof on any other terms, even if we were mounted upon the king's throne itself. Wherefore also Paul saith, " But the fruit of the Spirit is love, joy, peace." (Gal. v. 22.) This fruit then let us keep growing by us, that we may be in the fruition of joy here, and may obtain the kingdom to come, by the grace and love towards man of our Lord Jesus Christ, through Whom and with Whom, be glory to the Father, and to the Holy Spirit, now and always, even unto all ages. Amen.

[1] See St. Basil *de Spiritu Sancto*, c. 2, 4. and 5. St. Chrysostom is arguing against the Arian abuse of 1 Cor. viii. 6, as he does on the passage itself.

HOMILY II.

ROM. I. 8.

" First, I thank my God through Jesus Christ for you all, that your faith is spoken of throughout the whole world."

An exordium worthy of this blessed spirit, and able to teach all men to offer unto God the firstlings of their good deeds and words, and to render thanks not only for their own, but also for others' well-doings : which also maketh the soul pure from envy and grudging, and draweth God in a greater measure towards the loving spirit of them that so render thanks. Wherefore also elsewhere he says, " Blessed be God and the Father of our Lord Jesus Christ, Who hath blessed us with all spiritual blessing." (Eph. i. 3.) And it is fitting that we render thanks not only when rich, but also when poor, not when in health only, but also when sick, not when we thrive only, but also when we have to bear the reverse. For when our affairs are borne onward with a fair wind, to be thankful is not matter of wonder. But when no small tempests be upon us, and the vessel veers about and is in jeopardy, then is the great time for displaying patience and goodness of heart. For this cause Job also gained a crown from hence, and the shameless mouth of the devil did he stop, and show clearly that not even when he saw good days was it through his wealth that he was thankful, but through his much love toward God. And see too what things he is thankful for : not for things earthly and perishing, as power and authority and glory (for these things are of no account), but for real blessings, faith and boldness of speech. And with how much feeling [1] he gives thanks : for he saith not " to God," but " to my God," which also the Prophets do, so making that which is common to all their own. And what is there wonderful in the Prophets doing so ? For God himself plainly does it continually to His servants, calling Himself the God of Abraham and Isaac and Jacob, as peculiarly theirs. " That your faith is spoken of throughout the whole world." What then, had the whole world heard of the faith of the Romans ? Yes, the whole, according to him.

(Or, since that time, πᾶσα ἐξ ἐκείνου). And it is not a thing unlikely. For the city was not one of no note, but as being upon a sort of eminence it was on every account conspicuous. But consider, I pray, the power of the preaching, how in a short time by means of publicans and fishermen it took hold upon the very head of all cities, and Syrians became the teachers and guides of Romans. He attests then two excellencies in them, both that they believed, and that they believed with boldness, and that so great as that the fame of them reached into all the world. " For your faith," he says " is spoken of throughout the whole world. Your faith," not your verbal disputations, nor your questionings, nor your syllogisms. And yet there were there many hindrances to the teaching. For having recently acquired the empire of the world they were elated, and lived in riches and luxury, and fishermen brought the preaching there, and they Jews and of the Jews, a nation hated and had in abomination among all men ; and they were bidden to worship the Crucified, Who was brought up in Judea. And with the doctrine the teachers proclaimed also an austere life to men who were practised in softness, and were agitated about things present. And they that proclaimed it were poor and common men, of no family, and born of men of no family. But none of these things hindered the course of the word. So great was the power of the Crucified as to carry the word round everywhere. " For it is spoken of," he says, " in all the world." He says not, it is manifested, but, is spoken of, as if all men had them in their mouths. And indeed when he bears witness of this in the Thessalonians, he adds another thing also. For after saying, " from you sounded out the word of God," he adds, " so that we need not to speak anything." (1 Thess. i. 8.) For the disciples had come into the place of teachers, by their boldness of speech instructing all, and drawing them to themselves. For the preaching came not anywhere to a stand, but went over the whole world more rapidly than fire. But here there is only thus much —" it is spoken of." He well says that " it

---

[1] διαθέσεως, see *Ernesti Lex. Technol.* in v.

is spoken of," showing that there was no need to add aught to what was said, or to take away. For a messenger's business is this, to convey from one to another only what is told him. For which cause also the priest is called a "messenger" (Mal. ii. 7), because he speaks not his own words, but those of Him that sent him. And yet Peter had preached there. But he reckons what was his, to be his own as well. In such degree, as I said before, was he beyond measure clear of all grudging!

Ver. 9. "For God is my witness, whom I serve with my spirit in the Gospel of His Son."

Words these of an Apostle's bowels of affection, the showing forth this of fatherly concernment![1] And what is it which he says, and why does he call God to witness? He had to declare his feeling toward them. Since then he had not as yet ever seen them, he therefore called no man to witness, but Him Who entereth in the hearts. For since he was saying, "I love you," and as a token thereof alleged his praying continually for them, and wishing to come to them, and neither was this self-evident, he betakes himself to the trustworthy testimony. Will then any one of you be able to boast that he remembers, when praying at his house (ἐπὶ τῆς οἰκίας) the entire body of the Church? I think not. But Paul drew near to God in behalf not of one city only, but of the whole world, and this not once, or twice, or thrice, but continually. But if the continually bearing any one about in one's memory would not happen without much love; to have any in one's prayers, and to have them there continually, think what great affection and friendship that implies. But when he says, "Whom I serve with my spirit in the Gospel of His Son," he shows us at once the grace of God, and also his own humble-mindedness; the grace of God because He entrusted to him so great a matter; but his own humility, because he imputes it all not to his own zeal, but to the assistance of the Spirit. But the addition of "the Gospel," shows the kind of ministry. For there are many and diverse modes of service. And as under kings all are ranged under one that beareth kingly power, and all have not to minister (διακονοῦνται) about the same thing, but to one belongeth the ministry of ruling armies and to another that of ordering cities and to another again that of keeping treasures in the storehouses, thus also in spiritual things, one serveth God and laboreth (λατρεύει καὶ δουλεύει) in believing and

ordering his own life well, and another in undertaking the care of strangers, and another in taking in hand the patronship of them that be in need. As even during the Apostle's own time, they of Stephen's company served God in the guardianship of the widows, others (ἄλλοι 2 Mss., all ὧν) in the teaching of the word, of whom also Paul was, serving in the preaching of the Gospel. And this was the fashion of his service : for it was to this that he was appointed. On this account, he not only calls God to witness, but also says what he was entrusted with, to show that having so great things put into his hands, he would not have called Him Who trusted them to him to witness what was false. And therewith he wished to make another point out also, viz. that he could not but have this love and care for them. For that they might not say "who art thou? and, from whence? that thou sayest that thou art anxious over a city so great, and most imperial," he shows that he must needs have this care,[2] if at least the sort of service that was committed to him, was to declare the Gospel : for he that hath this put into his hands, must needs have continually upon his mind them that are to receive the word. And he shows another thing besides this by saying, "in my spirit;" that this service is much higher than either the Gentile or the Jewish. For the Gentile is both fleshly and in error, and the Jewish is true indeed, yet even this is fleshly. But that of the Church is the opposite of the Gentile, but more lofty than the Jewish by a great deal. For the mode of our service is not with sheep and oxen and smoke and fat, but by a spiritual soul, which Christ also shows in saying that "God is a Spirit, and they that worship Him must worship Him in spirit and in truth." (John iv. 24.)

"In the Gospel of His Son." Having said above that it was the Father's Gospel, here he says it is the Son's. So indifferent is it to say the Father's or the Son's! For he had learnt from that blessed voice that the things of the Father are the Son's, and the things of the Son are the Father's. For "all Mine are Thine, and Thine are Mine." (John xvii. 10.)

"That without ceasing I make mention of you always in my prayers." This is the part of genuine love, and he seems indeed to be saying some one thing, yet states four things even here. Both that he remembers, and that he does so continually, and that it is in his prayers, and that it is to ask great things for them.

---

[1] Four Mss. διδασκαλίας, a father's mode of Teaching. S. κηδεμονίας.

[2] One Ms. adds, if Christ hath given him this care, and

Ver. 10, 11. "Making request, if by any means now at length I might have a prosperous journey by the will of God to come unto you."

You see him painfully desiring to see them, and yet not enduring to see them contrary to what seemed good unto God, but having his longing mingled with the fear of God. For he loved them, and was eager to come to them. Yet he did not, because he loved them, desire to see them, contrary to what seemed good unto God. This is true love, not as we love who err on both sides from the laws of love : for either we love no one, or if we ever do love, we love contrary to what seemeth good unto God, acting in both against the Divine law. And if these things be grievous (φορτικὰ) when spoken of, they are more grievous when done. And how do we love contrary to what seems good to God? (you will say.) When we neglect Christ pining with hunger, and provide our children and friends and relations above their needs. Or rather what need to carry the subject further. For if any one will examine his own conscience, he will find that this takes place in many things. But such was not that blessed person, but he knew both how to love and to love as he ought (3 Mss. omit "as he ought"), and as was fitting, and though exceeding all men in loving, he transgressed not the measures of love. See then two things thrive extremely in him, fear of God, and also longing towards the Romans. For to be praying continually, and not to desist when he obtained not, shows exceeding love. But while loving, thus to continue yielding to the will of God, shows intense reverence. In another place, however, having "thrice besought the Lord " (2 Cor. xii. 8), he not only did not receive, but on the contrary, when he did not receive, he was very thankful for not having been heard. So, in all things did he look to God. But here he received, though not when he asked, but after delay, and neither hereat was he discontented. And these things I mention that we may not repine at not being heard, or at being heard slowly. For we are not better than Paul, who confesses his thankfulness for both, and with good ground. For when he had once given himself up to the all-governing Hand, and put himself with as much subjection under it, as clay under the potter, he followed wheresoever God led. Having then said that he desired to see them, he mentioned also the cause of his desire ; and what is it ?

Ver. 11. "That I may impart unto you some spiritual gift, to the end ye may be established."

For it was not merely as many now go travelling in a needless and profitless way that he also went, but for necessary and very urgent ends. And he does not tell them his meaning openly, but by way of hints, for he does not say that I may teach you, that I may instruct you, that I may fill up that which is wanting ; but, " that I may impart ; " showing, that it is not his own things which he is giving them, but that he was imparting to them what he had received. And here again he is unassuming, in saying " some," he means, a small one, and suited to my powers. And what may this small one be which thou art now going to impart ? This it is, he says, " to the end that ye may be established." This then also cometh of grace, namely, the being unwavering and standing fast. But when you hear of grace, think not that the reward of resolve on our part is thereby cast aside ; for he speaks of grace, not to disparage the labor of resolve on our part, but to undermine (ὑποτεμνόμενος, as piercing a thing inflated) the haughtiness of an insolent spirit (ἀπονοίας). Do not thou then, because that Paul hath called this a gift of grace, grow supine. For he knows how, in his great candor, to call even well doings, graces ; because even in these we need much influence from above. But in saying, " to the end that ye may be established," he covertly shows that they needed much correction : for what he would say is this : Of a " long time I have both desired " and prayed to see you, for no other reason than that I may "stablish, strengthen, fix" you thoroughly in the word of God, so that ye be not continually wavering. But he does not express himself so (for he would have shocked them), but in another way he hints to them the same thing, though in a subdued tone. For when he says, "to the end that ye may be established," he makes this plain. Then since this also was very irksome, see how he softens it by the sequel. For that they may not say, are we wavering, and carried about ? and need we speech of yours in order to stand fast ? he anticipates and does away any gainsaying of the kind, by saying as follows.

Ver. 12. "That is, that I may be comforted together with you by the mutual faith both of you and me."

As if he said, Do not suspect that I spoke to accuse you. It was not with this feeling that I said what I did. But what may it be that I wished to say ? Ye are undergoing many tribulations, being drenched on every side (by those who persecute you περιαντλούμενοι. 3 Mss. παρενοχλούμενοι, harassed). I desired then to see you, that

I might comfort you, or rather, not that I might comfort you only, but that I might myself receive comfort. See the wisdom of the teacher. He said, to the end that "ye may be strengthened ; he knew that what he had said would be heavy and irksome to the disciples. He says, "to the end that ye may be comforted." But this again is heavy, not indeed to such a degree as the former, still it is heavy. He then pares down what is galling in this also, smoothing his speech on every side, and rendering it easy of acceptance. For he does not say barely, "to be comforted," but, "to be comforted together with you;" nor was he content with this but he puts in a further lenitive, when he says, "by the mutual faith both of you and me." * Oh how great was his humble-mindedness ! He showed himself also to be in need of them, and not them only of him. And he puts the disciples in the position of teachers, not letting any superiority remain upon his own side, but pointing out their full equality. For the gain is mutual, he means, and I need the comfort from you, and you that from me. And how comes this to pass? "Through the mutual faith both of you and me." For as in the case of fire, if any one gather together many lights, it is a bright flame that he kindles, thus also does it naturally happen with the faithful. For when we be by ourselves, torn away from others, we are somehow in worse spirits. But when we see one another, and are entwined [1] with the members of our own selves, great is the comfort we receive. You must not look to the present time, during which, by God's grace, both in city and in the desert itself, there be many hosts of believers, and all impiety hath been driven out ; but consider, in that time, how great a good it was both for disciples to see their master, and for brethren who had come from another city to be seen of brethren. But that I may make what I am saying plainer, let me bring the matter to an example. For if it should even happen and come to pass (may it never do so!) that we had been carried away to the land of the Persians or Scythians or other barbarians, and had been scattered (7 Mss. "torn asunder") by twos and threes in their cities, and were then suddenly to see any one of those here coming to us, reflect what a

harvest of comfort we should reap of it ! See ye not those too who are in the prisons, if they see any of their acquaintance, how they revive, and are quite fluttering with the pleasure? But if I compare those days with captivity and imprisonment, count it no wonder. For these suffered far harder things than those, scattered as they were, and driven about, and dwelling in the midst of famine and of wars, and tremblingly expecting daily death, and suspecting friends and kindred and relatives, and dwelling in the world as in a strange land, aye, and in far harder plight than they who live in another's country. This is why he says, "to the end that ye may be established and comforted with us by our mutual faith." And this he says, not as though himself needed any assistance from them (far from it ; for how should the pillar of the Church, who was stronger than iron and the rock, the spiritual adamant, who was equal to the charge of countless cities), but that he should not make his language impetuous and his reproof vehement, he says, that he himself also needs their consolation. But if any one here should say, that the comfort was his gladness at the increase of their faith, and that Paul needed this, he would not be mistaking his meaning in this way either. If then thou desire, one might say, and pray, and wilt gain comfort and give comfort by it, what is there to hinder thy coming? By way of dissipating this suspicion then, he proceeds.

Ver. 13. "Now I would not have you ignorant, brethren, that oftentimes I desired to come unto you (but was let hitherto)."

Here is a compliance great as that of slaves, and a plain exhibition of his excellent temper (εὐγνωμοσύνης) ! For, that he was let, he says, but why, he does not go on to say. For he does not pry into the command of his Master, but only obeys. And yet one might expect a person to start questions, as to why God hindered a city so conspicuous and great, and towards which the whole world was looking, from enjoying such a teacher, and that for so long a time. For he that had overcome the governing city, could easily go on to the subjects of it. But he that let alone the more royal one, and lay in wait about the dependents, had the main point left neglected. But none of these things does he busy himself with, but yields to the incomprehensibleness of Providence, thereby both showing the right tone of his soul, and instructing us all never to call God to account for what happens, even though what is done seem to trouble the minds of many. For the Master's part it is alone to enjoin, the servants' to obey. And

---

* Verse 12 is best understood as a quasi-correction, or modification of v. 11, to show that he does not mean that his coming to them would be a blessing to them alone, but also to himself ; thus : I mean to say that I want to visit you not only that I may impart (μεταδῶ, v. 11) something unto you, but that I may be encouraged in you (or among you) through the action and reaction of our common (ἐν ἀλλήλοις) faith. Thus τοῦτο δὲ ἐστιν is taken not as simply explanatory, but as mildly adversative.—G. B. S.

[1] περιπλακῶμεν seems here to have a double sense from the context.

this is why he says, that he was let, but not for what cause; for he means, even I do not know; ask not then of me the counsel or mind of God. For neither "shall the thing formed say to him that formed it, Why hast thou made me thus?" For why, tell me, do you even seek to learn it? do you not know that all things are under His care, that He is wise, that He doeth nothing at a mere hazard, that He loveth thee more than they who begat thee, and goes exceeding far beyond a father's yearnings of affection to thee, and a mother's anxiousness. Seek then no more, and go not a step further; for this is sufficient consolation for thee: since even then it was well ordered for the Romans. And if thou knowest not the manner, take it not to heart: for this is a main feature of faith, even when in ignorance fo the manner of the dispensation, to receive what is told us of His Providence.

Paul then having succeeded in what he was earnest about (and what was this? to show that it was not as slighting them that he did not come to them, but because, though greatly desiring it, he was hindered), and having divested himself of the accusation of remissness, and having persuaded them that he was not less desirous to see them than themselves, further shows his love to them by other things. For even when I was hindered, he means, I did not stand aloof from the attempt, but I kept attempting always yet was always hindered, yet never did I stand aloof, thus, without falling out with the will of God, still keeping my love. For by his purposing it to himself and not standing aloof from it, he showed his affection; but through his being hindered and yet not struggling against it, all his love to God. "That I might have some fruit among you also." Yet he had told them the cause of his longing before, and shown that it was becoming him; but still here also, he states it, clearing away all their suspicion. For since the city was conspicuous, and in the whole extent of sea and land had no equal to many even the mere desire of becoming acquainted with it became a reason (πρόφασις) for a journey to it; that they might not think anything of the sort about Paul, or suspect that, merely with a view to glory in claiming them to himself he desired to be present there, he repeatedly lays down the ground of his desire, and before he says, it was that "I may impart to you some spiritual gift," that I desired to see you; but here more clearly, "that I might have some fruit among you also even as among other Gentiles." The rulers he puts with the subjects, and after the countless triumphs and victories and the glory of the consuls, he puts them

with the barbarians, and with good reason too. For where the nobility of faith is, there is none barbarian, none Grecian, none stranger, none citizen, but all mount up to one height of dignity. And see him here also unassuming, for he does not say, that I may teach and instruct, but what? "that I might have some fruit." And not fruit, simply, but "some fruit." Again, depreciating his own share therein just as he had said above, "that I may impart some gift." And then to repress them too, as I said also before, he says, "even as among other Gentiles." * For, I do not, because you are rich, and have the advantage of others, show less concern about the others. For it is not the rich that we are seeking, but the faithful. Where now are the wise of the Greeks, they that wear long beards and that are clad in open dress,[1] and puff forth great words (τὰ μεγάλα φυσῶντες)? All Greece and all barbarian lands has the tentmaker converted. But Plato, who is so cried up and carried about[2] among them, coming a third time to Sicily with the bombast of those words of his, with his brilliant reputation (ὑπολήψεως), did not even get the better of a single king, but came off so wretchedly, as even to have lost his liberty. But this tentmaker ran over not Sicily alone or Italy, but the whole world; and while preaching too he desisted not from his art, but even then sewed skins, and superintended the workshop. And even this did not give offence to those who were born of consuls, and with very good reason, for it is not their trades and occupations, but falsehood and forged doctrines, which usually render teachers easy subjects of contempt. And for this reason, even Athenians still laugh at the former. But this man even barbarians attend to, and even foolish and ignorant men. For his preaching is set forth to all alike, it knows no distinction of rank, no preëminence of nation, no other thing of the sort; for faith alone does

---

* Verse 13 adds a new reason for his wish to visit Rome—ἵνα τινὰ καρπὸν σχῶ. It seems to me that more is here meant than the establishing and encouragement of v. 11, 12; that the Apostle is not here merely repeating the idea of τι μεταδῶ χάρισμα (Meyer, Alford), but is thinking of the conversion of those outside of the Roman Christian community. This is confirmed by the generalization of v. 14: "And to Greeks and Barbarians, I am debtor." It was not merely a joy that he might experience, but a conquest which he might win for Christ. His purpose to go to Rome is grounded upon his fixed purpose to carry the gospel to all Gentile nations without distinction of race or culture (so Godet, Hofmann). Chrysostom's exposition proceeds upon the supposition of the simple identity of these statements.—G. B. S.

[1] ἐξωμίδας, a short tunic leaving the arms and shoulders bare, which had with it a kind of mantle. It was used by slaves, and adopted perhaps by these philosophers as a badge of austerity. See Ælian. *Var. Hist.* I. IX. c. 34. Ed. Varior. note of Perizonius.

[2] Field reads ἀδόμενος καὶ περιφερόμενος, Vulg. ἀγόμενος which may mean "alleged."

it require, and not reasonings. Wherefore it is most worthy of admiration, not only because it is profitable and saving, but that it is readily admissible and easy (Sav. " lovable)," and comprehensible to all : which is a main object in the Providence of God, who setteth forth His blessings to all in common.

For what He did in respect of the sun and the moon and the earth and the sea and other things, not giving the rich and the wise a greater share of the benefits of these, and a less to the poor, but setting forth the enjoyment of them to all alike, this also did He with regard to the preaching, and even in a much greater degree, by how much this is more indispensable than they. Wherefore Paul repeatedly says, " among all the Gentiles," to show that he in no respect favors them, but is fulfilling his Master's command, and sending them away to thanksgiving to the God of all, he says ;

Ver. 14. " I am a debtor to the Greeks and to the Barbarians, both to the wise and to the unwise."

Which also he said when writing to the Corinthians. And he says it, to ascribe the whole to God. (1 Cor. ix. 16.)

Ver. 15. "So, as much as in me is, I am ready to preach the Gospel to you that are at Rome also."

Oh, noble soul! having taken on him a task laden of so great dangers, a voyage across the sea, temptations, plottings, risings—for it was likely, that one who was going to address so great a city which was under the tyrannic sway of impiety, should undergo temptations thick as snowflakes ; and it was in this way that he lost his life in this city, being cut off by the tyrant of it—yet still expecting to undergo so great troubles, for none of these did he become less energetic, but was in haste and was in travail and was ready-minded. Wherefore he says, " So, as much as in me is, I am ready to preach the Gospel to you that are at Rome also."

Ver. 16. " For I am not ashamed of the Gospel."

" What sayest thou, O, Paul ? When it were fitting to say, that I boast, and am proud, and luxuriate in it ; thou sayest not this, but what is less than this, that thou art " not ashamed," which is not what we usually say of things very glorious. What then is this which he says, and why does he thus speak ? while yet he exults over it more than over heaven. At least, in writing to the Galatians, he said, " God forbid that I should glory, save in the Cross of our Lord Jesus Christ." (Gal. vi. 14.) How then comes he here to say, not that I even glory, but that " I

am not ashamed ? " The Romans were most anxiously eager about the things of the world, owing to their riches, their empire, their victories ; and their kings they reckoned to be equal to the gods, and so they even called them. And for this cause too, they worshipped them with temples and with altars and with sacrifices. Since then they were thus puffed up, but Paul was going to preach Jesus, who was thought to be the carpenter's son, who was brought up in Judea, and that in the house of a mean woman, who had no body guards, who was not encircled in wealth, but even died as a culprit with robbers, and endured many other inglorious things ; and it was likely that they were concealing themselves as not as yet knowing any of the unspeakable and great things : for this reason he says, " I am not ashamed," having still to teach them not to be ashamed. For he knew that if they succeeded in this, they would speedily go on and come to glorying also : and do you then, if you hear any one saying, Dost thou worship the Crucified ? be not ashamed, and do not look down, but luxuriate in it, be bright-faced at it, and with the eyes of a free man, and with uplifted look, take up your confession ; and if he say again, Dost thou worship the Crucified ? say in reply to him, Yes ! and not the adulterer, not the insulter of his father, not the murderer of his children (for such be all the gods they have[1]), but Him who by the Cross stopped the mouths of devils, and did away with their countless juggleries. For the Cross is for our sakes, being the work of unspeakable Love towards man, the sign of His great concern for us. And in addition to what has been said, since they were puffed up with great pomposity of speech and with their cloak of external wisdom, I, he means to say, bidding an entire farewell to these reasonings, come to preach the Cross, and am not ashamed because of it : " for it is the power of God to salvation." For since there is a power of God to chastisement also (for when He chastised the Egyptians, He said, " This is My great power,[2] ") (Joel ii. 25) and a power to destruction, (for, "fear Him," He says, " that is able to destroy both body and soul in hell "), (Matt. x. 28) for this cause he says, it is not these that I come to bring, the powers of chastisement and punishment, but those of salvation. What then ? Did not the Gospel tell of these things also, namely, the account of hell, and that of the outer

---

[1] And this the wiser heathen urge, as Plato, Rep. xi. and Euthyph. and Aristoph. Nub.
[2] Joel ii. 25. S. Ephrem considers that passage to allude to the plagues of Egypt ; and so others.

darkness, and of the venomous worm? And yet we know of these from no other source than the Gospel. In what sense then does he say, "the power of God unto salvation?" Attend only to what follows. "To every one that believeth; to the Jew first, and also to the Greek."

For it is not to all absolutely, but to them that receive it. For though thou be a Grecian (i. e. Heathen), and even one that has run into every kind of vice, though a Scythian, though a barbarian, though a very brute, and full of all irrationality, and burdened with the weights of endless sins, no sooner hast thou received the word concerning the Cross, and been baptized, than thou hast blotted out all these; and why says he here, "to the Jew first, and also to the Greek?" What meaneth this difference? and yet he has often said, "Neither circumcision is anything, nor uncircumcision" (1 Cor. vii. 19. see Gal. v. 6 and vi. 15); how then doth he here discriminate, setting the Jew before the Greek? Now why is this? seeing that by being first he does not therefore receive any more of the grace (for the same gift is bestowed both on this person and that,) but the "first" is an honor in order of time only. For he has no such advantage as that of receiving greater righteousness, but is only honored in respect of his receiving it first. Since in the case of those that are enlightened (you that are initiated know what is meant,) all run [1] to the baptism, yet not all at the same hour, but one first and another second. Yet the first doth not receive more than the second, nor he than the person after him, but all enjoy the same gifts. The "first" then here is an honor in word, not a superiority in grace. Then after saying, "unto salvation," he enhances the gift further, by showing that it stayeth not at the present point, but proceedeth farther. [*] For this is what he sets forth, when he says,

Ver. 17. "For therein is the righteousness of God revealed."

But he who hath become just shall live, not for the present life only, but for that which is to come. And he hints not only this, but also another thing along with this, namely, the brightness and gloriousness of such a life.

For since it is possible to be saved, yet not without shame (as many are saved of those, who by the royal humanity are released from punishment), that no one may suspect this upon hearing of safety, he adds also righteousness; and righteousness, not thine own, but that of God; hinting also the abundance of it and the facility. [†] For you do not achieve it by toilings and labors, but you receive it by a gift from above, contributing one thing only from your own store, "believing." Then since his statement did not seem credible, if the adulterer and effeminate person, and robber of graves, and magician, is not only to be suddenly freed from punishment but to become just, and just too with the highest righteousness; he confirms his assertion from the Old Testament. And first with a short sentence, he lays open a vast sea of histories to one who has a capacity for seeing them. For after having said, "from faith to faith," he sends the hearer back to the dispensations of God, which took place thus in the Old Testament, which, when writing to the Hebrews, he explains with his usual great wisdom, showing that both the just and the sinners were justified in that way even then, wherefore also he made mention both of the harlot and of Abraham. But then here, after having just hinted at it (for he was running on to another and a pressing subject), he again confirms what he had said from the Prophets, bringing in Habakkuk before them, crying, and saying, that it is not in the nature of things for him who is to live, to live otherwise save by faith; for " the just," he says, "shall live by faith " (Hab. ii. 4), speaking about the life to come. For since what God giveth transcends reasoning entirely, it is but reason that we need faith. But the man that thinks meanly of it, and is contemptuous and vainglorious, will not effect anything at all. Let heretics hearken to the voice of the Spirit, for such is the nature of reasonings. They are like some labyrinth or puzzles which have no end to them anywhere, and do not let the reason stand upon the rock, and have their very origin in vanity. For being ashamed to allow of faith, and to seem ignorant of heavenly things, they involve themselves in the dust-cloud of

---

[1] See the Ceremonies of Baptism, St. Cyril Lect. xx. (ii. on Myst.) c. 4. He says they "were led to the holy pool." p. 264. ⊖. T.

[*] Verse 16 might almost be considered as a summary of the apostle's doctrine. It could be expressed thus: subject: The gospel, what is it? God's power. For what? Salvation. For whom? Every one that believeth. On what historic conditions? To the Jew first and also to the Greek. Πρῶτον is best taken, not as simply chronological (Chrys. Godet, Hodge), but as denoting a providential, economic precedence (Meyer, De Wette, Tholuck, Philippi, Alford).—G. B. S.

[†] Δικαιοσύνη θεοῦ (17) means a righteousness which is from God (gen. orig.) and of which God's character is the norm. The δίκαιος stands in an ethical relation which, on its divine side, is designated as δικ. θεοῦ. God is the author of this right condition, but man is placed in it on condition and in consequence of faith. The δικ. is ἐκ πίστεως as its conditioning cause and its aims at faith and terminates in faith—εἰς πίστιν. How closely and vitally are faith and righteousness connected! And yet they are to be distinguished. Faith is a subjective exercise; righteousness is a status. The former is that which man does; the latter is the relation and condition in which God places the believer. They represent respectively the human and the divine sides of salvation and are so vitally related that Paul can say: λογίζεται ἡ πίστις εἰς δικαιοσύνην (Rom. iv. 5 sq).—G. B. S.

countless reasonings. Then oh miserable and painful man, fit object for endless tears, should any one ask thee, how the heaven was made, and how the earth,—and why do I say the heaven and the earth? how thou wert thyself born,[1] how nourished, and how thou grewest, art thou then not ashamed of thine ignorance? But if anything be said about the Only-begotten, dost thou thrust thyself through shame into a pit of destruction, thinking that it is unworthy of thee not to know everything? And yet disputatiousness is an unworthy thing, and so is ill-timed curiosity. And why do I speak of doctrines? for even from the corruption in our present life we have escaped by no other means than through the faith. Thus shone also all those aforetime, thus Abraham, thus Isaac, thus Jacob, thus too the harlot was saved, the one in the Old Testament, and likewise the one in the New. For, "by faith," he says, "the harlot Rahab perished not with them that believed not when she had received the spies." (Heb. xi. 31.) For if she had said to herself, " and how can they that are captives and exiles, and refugees, and live the life of vagabond tribes, get the better of us who have a city, and walls, and towers?" she would have destroyed both herself and them. Which also the forefathers of those who were then saved did suffer. For when, upon the sight of men great and tall, they questioned the manner of victory, they perished, without battle or array, all of them. Seest thou what a pit is that of unbelief! what a wall that of faith! For the one carried down endless thousands, the other not only saved a harlot, but made her the patroness of so numerous a people!

Now since we know of these and more than these, never let us call God to account for what is done, but whatsoever He may lay on us, that let us take up with, and let us not run into niceties and curious questions, though to human reasoning the thing commanded appears even amiss. For what, let me ask, looks more amiss than for a father to slay with his own hands his only and legitimate son? (Gen. xxii. 3.) But still when the righteous man was bid do it, he raised no nice scruples about it, but owing to the dignity of the bidder, he merely accepted the injunction. And another too that was bidden of God to strike a prophet, when he raised nice scruples about the seeming unreasonableness of the injunction, and did not simply obey, he was punished to the extreme. (1 Kings xx. 35, 36.) But he that struck, gained a good report. And Saul too, when he saved men contrary to the decree of God, fell from the kingdom, and was irretrievably punished. And one might find other instances beside these: by all which we learn, never to require a reason for God's injunctions,[2] but to yield and obey only. But if it be dangerous to raise nice scruples about aught that He may enjoin, and extreme punishment is appointed for those who are curious questioners, what possible excuse shall they have who curiously question things far more secret and awful than these, as for instance, how He begat the Son, and in what fashion, and what His Essence is? Now as we know this, let us with all kindliness receive the mother of all blessings, faith; that sailing as it were in a still harbor, we may at once keep our doctrines orthodox, and by steering our life safely in a straight course, may attain those eternal blessings by the grace and love toward man of our Lord Jesus Christ, through Whom and with Whom be glory unto the Father, with the Holy Ghost, for ever and ever. Amen.

HOMILY III.

ROM. I. 18.

" For the wrath of God is revealed from Heaven against all ungodliness and unrighteousness of men, who hold down the truth in unrighteousness."

OBSERVE the discretion of Paul, how after encouraging by the gentler things, he turns his discourse to the more fearful. For after saying that the Gospel is the cause of salvation and of life, that it is the power of God, that it gendereth salvation and righteousness, he mentions what might well make them fear that were heedless of it. For since in general most men are not drawn so much by the promise of what is good as by the fear of what is painful, he draws them on both sides. For this cause too did God not only promise a kingdom, but also threaten hell. And the Prophets spake thus with the Jews, ever inter-

---

[1] See Eccles. xi. 5. and Homer, *Odys.* i. 216, also Menander as quoted by Eustathius on that passage.
[2] 2 Mss. " to call God to account for His injunctions."

mingling the evil with the good. For this cause too Paul thus varies his discourse, yet not any how, but he sets first the good things, and after the evil, to show that the former came of the guiding purpose of God, but the latter of the wickedness of the backsliding. And in this way the prophet puts the good first, saying, "If ye be willing and will obey me, ye shall eat the good of the land: but if ye be not willing and will not obey me, the sword shall devour you." (Is. i. 19, 20.) So here too does Paul conduct his discourse. But observe him; Christ, he means, came to bring forgiveness, righteousness, life, yet not in any way, but by the Cross, which is greatest too and wonderful, that He not only gave such things, but that He also suffered such things. If then ye insolently scorn the gifts, then will the penalties await you. And see how he raises his language, "For the wrath of God," he says, "is revealed from heaven." Whence does this appear? If it be a believer who says this, we will tell him of the declarations of Christ, but if the unbeliever and the Grecian, him Paul silences, by what he says presently of the judgment of God, bringing an uncontrovertible demonstration from the things which were done by them. And this too is by far the most striking point in him, how he exhibits those who speak against the truth, as themselves bearing witness by the things which they do daily, and say, to the doctrines of the truth. But of this in the sequel: but for the present, let us keep to what is set before us. "For the wrath of God is revealed from heaven." And indeed even here this often takes place in famines and pestilences and wars: for each individually and all in common are punished. What will be the new thing then? That the chastisement will be greater, and common to all, and not by the same rules. For now what takes place is for correction; but then for vengeance.* And this also St. Paul showed, when he said, "We are chastened now, that we should not be condemned with the world." (1 Cor. xi. 32.) And now indeed to many such things usually seem to come not of the wrath from above, but of the malice of man. But then the punishment from God shall be manifest, when the Judge, sitting upon the

fearful tribunal, shall command some to be dragged to the furnaces, and some to the outer darkness,[1] and some to other inexorable and intolerable punishments. And why is it that he does not speak as plainly as this, the Son of God is coming with ten thousand angels, and will call each man to account, but says, that "the wrath of God is revealed?" His hearers were as yet novices, and therefore he draws them first by things quite allowed by them. And besides what is here mentioned, he also seems to me to be aiming against the Greeks. And this is why he makes his beginning from this, but afterwards he introduces the subject of Christ's judgment.

"Against all ungodliness and unrighteousness of men who hold the truth in unrighteousness." Here he showeth that the ways of ungodliness are many, and that of truth, one. For error is a thing various and multiform and compound, but the truth is one. And after speaking of doctrines he speaks of life, mentioning the unrighteousness of men. For there be various kinds of unrighteousness also. One is in money affairs, as when any one deals unrighteously by his neighbor in these; and another in regard to women, when a man leaves his own wife, and breaks in upon the marriage of another. For St. Paul calls this also defrauding, saying thus, "That no man go beyond or defraud his brother in the matter." (1 Thess. iv. 6.) Others again injure not the wife or property, but the reputation of their neighbor, and this too is unrighteousness. For "a good name is better than great riches." (Prov. xxii. 1.) But some say that this also is said of Paul about doctrines. Still there is nothing to prevent its having been said of both. But what it is "to hold the truth in unrighteousness," learn from the sequel.

Ver. 19. "Because that which may be known of God is manifest in them, for God hath showed it unto them."

But this glory they invested stocks and stones with. As then he which is entrusted with the goods of the king, and is ordered to spend them upon the king's glory, if he waste these upon robbers, and harlots, and witches, and make these splendid out of the king's stores, he is punished as having done the

---

* The author does not make it plain in what he understands the revelation of God's wrath here spoken of to consist. He mentions famines and pestilences as things in which it "often takes place." Paul evidently means that God's wrath is manifest in the judicial hardening of the people for their sins (vid. vv. 21, 28). Their shameful deeds and lives are the penalty of their sin. "God punishes their sin by sin" (Weiss), that is, He made them reap the bitter fruit in sinful lives of their sinful choices and acts. The view of Ritschl that ὀργὴ θεοῦ is here eschatological in meaning seems very inadequately supported (vid. Godet on Romans—Am. ed. p. 102). —G. B. S.

[1] St. Basil speaks similarly of various punishments, *Regulæ. Br. Tr. int.* 267, ed. Ben. text ii. p. 507. Theophylact on Matt. viii. 12, seems to allude to this passage. Both say that "outer darkness" implies an "inner," but seemingly in opposite senses, Theoph. taking ἔσω to be towards Heaven. Origen on Matt. xxii. 13 makes it a temporary punishment. St. Chrys. on Matt. xxii. 13. St. Aug. on Ps. vi. 6. St. Jerome on Matt. viii. 12, take it otherwise. See also St. Bas. on Ps. 33 (4), 11, text i. 151 e. See Maldonatus on Matt. viii. 12, and St. Chrys. on Rom. xvi. 16, *infra* on the difference of punishments.

kingdom the greatest wrong. Thus they also who after having received the knowledge of God and of His glory, invested idols therewith, "held the truth in unrighteousness," and, at least as far as was in their power, dealt unrighteously by the knowledge, by not using it upon fitting objects. Now, has what was said become clear to you, or must one make it still clearer? Perhaps it were needful to say somewhat more. What then is it which is here said? The knowledge of Himself God placed in men from the beginning. But this knowledge they invested stocks and stones with, and so dealt unrighteously to the truth, as far at least as they might. For it abideth unchanged, having its own glory immutable. "And whence is it plain that He placed in them this knowledge, O Paul?" "Because," saith he, "that which may be known of Him is manifest in them." This, however, is an assertion, not a proof. But do thou make it good, and show me that the knowledge of God was plain to them, and that they willingly turned aside. Whence was it plain then? did He send them a voice from above? By no means. But what was able to draw them to Him more than a voice, that He did, by putting before them the Creation, so that both wise, and unlearned, and Scythian, and barbarian, having through sight learned the beauty of the things which were seen, might mount up to God.[1] Wherefore he says,

Ver. 20. "For the invisible things of Him from the Creation of the world are clearly seen, being understood by the things which are made."

Which also the prophet said, "The heavens declare the glory of God." (Ps. xix. 1.) For what will the Greeks (i. e. Heathen) say in that day? That "we were ignorant of Thee?" Did ye then not hear the heaven sending forth a voice by the sight, while the well-ordered harmony of all things spake out more clearly than a trumpet? Did ye not see the hours of night and day abiding unmoved continually, the goodly order of winter, spring, and the other seasons remaining both sure and unmoved, the tractableness (εὐγνωμοσύνην) of the sea amid all its turbulence and waves? All things abiding in order and by their beauty and their grandeur, preaching aloud of the Creator? For all these things and more than these doth Paul sum up in saying, "The invisible things of Him from the creation of the world are clearly seen, being understood by the things which are made, even His eternal Power and Godhead; so that they are without excuse." And yet it is not for this God hath

made these things, even if this came of it. For it was not to bereave them of all excuse, that He set before them so great a system of teaching, but that they might come to know Him. But by not having recognized[2] Him they deprived themselves of every excuse, and then to show how they are bereaved of excuse, he says,

Ver. 21. "Because that, when they knew God, they glorified Him not as God."

This is the one greatest charge; and the second after it is their also worshipping idols, as Jeremy too in accusing them said, "This people hath committed two evils: they have forsaken me the fountain of living water, and have dug for themselves broken cisterns." (Jer. ii. 13.) And then as a sign of their having known God, and not used their knowledge upon a fit object, he adduces this very thing, that they knew gods. Wherefore he adds, "because that, when they knew God, they glorified Him not as God." And he names the cause through which they fell into such senselessness. What then is it? They trusted everything to their reasonings. Still he does not word it so, but in a much sharper language, "but became vain in their reasonings, and their foolish heart was darkened." For as in a night without a moon, if any one attempt to go by a strange road, or to sail over a strange sea, so far will he be from soon reaching his destination, that he will speedily be lost. Thus they, attempting to go the way leading to Heaven, and having destroyed the light from their own selves, and, in lieu of it, trusted themselves to the darkness of their own reasoning, and seeking in bodies for Him who is incorporeal, and in shapes for Him who hath no shape, underwent a most rueful shipwreck. But beside what has been said, he names also another cause of their error, when he says,

Ver. 22. "Professing themselves to be wise, they became fools."

For having some great conceit of themselves, and not enduring to go the way which God had commanded them, they were plunged into the reasonings of senselessness (1 Ms. διανοίας). And then to show and give in outline, what a rueful surge it was, and how destitute of excuse, he goes on to say,

Ver. 23. "And changed the glory of the uncorruptible God into an image made like to corruptible man, and to birds, and to four-footed beasts, and creeping things."

The first charge is, that they did not find God; the second was, that it was while they had great and clear (Sav. marg. "wise") means

---

[1] Pascal. Pen. c. 20, thinks an inward illumination implied here.

[2] ἀγνοήσαντες 4 Mss. and Sav. marg.; in text ἀγνωμονήσαντες, having been obstinate.

to do it ; the third, that withal they said they were wise ; the fourth, that they not only did not find that Reverend Being, but even lowered Him to devils and to stones and stocks. Now he takes down their haughtiness also in the Epistle to the Corinthians, but not in the same way there as here. For there it is from the Cross he gives them the blow, saying, "The foolishness of God is wiser than men." (1 Cor. i. 25.) But here, without any comparison, he holds their wisdom by itself up to ridicule, showing it to be folly and a mere display of vain boasting. Then, that you may learn that when they had the knowledge of God they gave it up thus treacherously, "they changed," he says. Now he that changeth, hath something to change. For they wished to find out more, and not bear with the limits given them, and so they were banished from these also. For they were lusters after new devices, for such is all that is Grecian. And this is why they stood against one another, and Aristotle rose up against Plato, and the Stoics blustered (ἐφρυάξαντο 6 Mss. "fenced themselves," ἐφράξαντο: which Field inclines to prefer) against him, and one has become hostile to one, another to another. So that one should not so much marvel at them for their wisdom, as turn away from them indignant and hate them, because through this very thing they have become fools. For had they not trusted what they have to reasonings, and syllogisms, and sophistries, they would not have suffered what they did suffer. Then, to strengthen the accusation against them, he holds the whole of their idolatry up to ridicule. For in the first place the changing even were a very fit subject of scorn. But to change to such things too, is beyond all excuse. For what then did they change it, and what was it which they invested with His Glory? Some conceptions they ought to have had about Him, as, for instance, that He is God, that He is Lord of all, that He made them, which were not, that He exerciseth a Providence, that He careth for them. For these things are the "Glory of God." To whom then did they ascribe it ? Not even to men, but "to an image made like to corruptible man." Neither did they stop here, but even dropped down to the brutes, or rather to the images of these. But consider, I pray, the wisdom of Paul, how he has taken the two extremes, God the Highest, and creeping things the lowest : or rather, not the creeping things, but the images of these ; that he might clearly show their evident madness. For what knowledge they ought to have had concerning Him Who is incomparably more excellent than all, with that they invested what

was incomparably more worthless than all. But what has this to do with the philosophers? a man may say. To these belongs most of all what I have said to do with them. For they have the Egyptians who were the inventors of these things to their masters. And Plato, who is thought more reverend than the rest of them, glories in these masters. (Plat. Tim. 21. B. etc.) And his master is in a stupid awe of these idols, for he it is that bids them sacrifice the cock to Æsculapius[1] (his last words, Phædo), where (i. e. in his temple. So Field from Mss.) are the images of these beasts, and creeping things. And one may see Apollo and Bacchus worshipped along with these creeping things. And some of the philosophers even lifted up to Heaven bulls, and scorpions, and dragons, and all the rest of that vanity. For in all parts did the devil zealously strive to bring men down before the images of creeping things, and to range beneath the most senseless of all things, him whom God hath willed to lift up above the heavens. And it is not from this only, but also from other grounds, that you will see their chief man to come under the remarks now made. For having made a collection of the poets, and having said that we should believe them upon matters relating to God, as having accurate knowledge, he has nothing else to bring forward but the "linked sweetness" of these absurdities, and then says, that this utterly ludicrous trifling is to be held for true.[2] *

---

[1] Thus Tert. Ap. 46. Lact. iii. 20. Origen cont. Cels. vi. c. 4, quotes this as showing the Philosophers guilty of St. Paul's charge, at the same time speaking of Socrates' previous discourse as "what God had shown them ;" the note of Spencer, Ed. Ben. i. 631, quotes an allegorical explanation. Theodoret, Græc. Aff. Cur. Dis. vii. de Sacr. says it was done to disprove the charge of Atheism.
[Probably Socrates' real judgment on the popular mythology was, that it was an imperfect and economical revelation of a higher truth than it expressed : and its ceremonies the legitimate though conventional expression of true devotion. Thus "the cock to Æsculapius" was the sick man's thank-offering for recovery from "life's fitful fever."]

[2] See Plat. Io 533 E. and perhaps Euthyph. 6 A. B : passages certainly not fairly representative of Plato's deliberate opinions. But Greek Philosophy is here treated as attempting to rival the Gospel. The Fathers who most value what is true in it, as Clement of Alexandria and Justin Martyr, speak of it as from partial Divine Light, and use it against the false ; as Cl. A. *Str.* 1. recommends the study of it for subordinate knowledge, and Cohort. *ad Gr.* quotes Heathens against the mythology, whose authors he considers led by demons to deceive men. So too Justin, Ap. i. 46, allows Heathens a partaking of the Λόγος, and 20, 55, 58, 62, etc., refers idol rites to the demons. St. Augustin *de Civ. Dei*, viii. 10, and elsewhere, gives a fair estimate of Gentile Philosophy. The Apostolical Constitutions, i. i. c. 6, forbid studying heathen books. Coterius in his note quotes on the same side, i. ii. c. 61, recog. x. 15, 42. Isid. Sent. iii. 13, etc., and the blame cast on Origen by many. On the other side, Tert. *de Idol.* c. 10, who however only defends learning in heathen schools, rather than Christians should conform to heathen customs as teachers. Origen Philocal. c. 13. Greg. Naz. Or. 20. Hieron. ep. 84. 70 Vall. *ad Magnum Oratorem* Greg. Papa. ad 1 Reg. xiii. 19, 20. Theod. H. E. iv. 26, as checking excess in such studies, Greg. ad Desiderium, l. ix. Ep. 48. Hier. adv. Luciferianos, c. 5. Ep. 61, c. 1. Cassian. Coll. xiv. c. 12, etc.
* The steps of this degeneracy of the Gentile world as indicated in v. 21-23 may be indicated thus : (1) ceasing to give glory to God and to recognize his power and divineness.

Ver. 24. "Wherefore also God gave them up to uncleanness, through the lusts of their own hearts, to dishonor their own bodies between themselves."

Hence he shows, that even of the perversion of the laws it was ungodliness which was the cause, but He "gave them up," here is, let them alone.* For as he that hath the command in an army, if upon the battle lying heavy upon him he retreat and go away, gives up his soldiers to the enemies, not by thrusting them himself, but by stripping them of his own assistance; thus too did God leave those that were not minded to receive what cometh from Him, but were the first to bound off from Him, though Himself having wholly fulfilled His own part. But consider; He set before them, for a form of doctrine, the world; He gave them reason, and an understanding capable of perceiving what was needful. None of these things did the men of that day use unto salvation, but they perverted to the opposite what they had received. What was to be done then? to drag them by compulsion and force? But this were not to make them virtuous. It remained then, after that, for Him to leave them alone, and this He did too, that in this way, if by no other, having by trial come to know the things they lusted after, they might flee from what was so shameful (3 Mss. add εἰκότως, and with reason). For if any that was a king's son, dishonoring his father, should choose to be with robbers and murderers, and them that break up tombs, and prefer their doings to his father's house; the father leaves him, say, so that by actual trial, he may learn the extravagance of his own madness. But how comes he to mention no other sin, as murder, for instance, or covetousness, or other such besides, but only unchasteness? He seems to me to hint at his audience at the time, and those who were to receive the Epistle. "To uncleanness, to dishonor their own bodies between themselves."

Note the emphasis here, as it is most severe.

(2) Thanklessness. They lost the sense of their relation to him as recipients of his bounty. (3) They entered into vain and foolish speculations—διαλογισμοί. (4) These ended only in blindness of mind and heart to the truth which they once possessed. (5) Mistaking all this folly for wisdom, they were ripe for complete self-deception. They perverted their religious feeling by ceasing to make the glorious perfection of God the object of their worship and by substituting images of men and animals.—G. B. S.

* The expression: "God gave them up," etc. is not to be so softened down into the idea of mere permission. With this v. (24) begins the description of God's revelation of his wrath against them. This is introduced by διὸ; because they had pursued the course outlined in the preceding verses (19-23) God set in operation against them those moral and providential forces which reduced them to the lowest depth of misery and shame. Vv. 25-32 show what this exhibition of his wrath was and what were its consequences. For historic illustration of the condition of the Heathen world at this time, see Fisher, *Beginnings of Christianity*, chap. vi. —G. B. S.

For they stood not in need of any others, it means, to do insolent violence to them, but the very treatment the enemies would have shown them, this they did to themselves. And then, taking up the charge again, he says,

Ver. 25. "Who changed the truth of God into a lie, and worshipped and served the creature more than the Creator."

Things which were matter for utter scorn, he puts down specially, but what seemed of a graver cast than the rest, in general terms; and by all he shows, that serving the creature is Grecian. And see how strong he makes his assertion, for he does not say, barely, "they served the creature," but "more than the Creator:" thus everywhere giving fresh force to the charge, and, by the comparison, taking from them all ground of mitigation. "Who is blessed forever. Amen." But by this, he means, He was not any whit injured. For Himself abideth "blessed for ever." Here he shows, that it was not in self-defence that He left them alone, inasmuch as He suffered nothing Himself. For even if these treated Him insolently, yet He was not insolently treated, neither was any scathe done to the bearings of His glory, but He abideth continually blessed. For if it often happen, that man through philosophy would not feel the insults men offered him, much less would God, the imperishable and unalterable Nature, the unchangeable and immovable Glory.

For men are in this respect made like unto God,[1] when they do not feel what is inflicted by them who would do them despite, and are neither insulted of others who insult them, nor beaten of them when beating them, nor made scorn of when they make scorn of them. And how in the nature of things can this be? it may be said. It is so, yea most certainly it is possible, when thou art not vexed at what is done. And how, it may be said, is it possible not to be vexed? Nay rather, how is it possible to be vexed? Tell me now, if your little child were to insult you, would you then reckon the insult an insult? What, but would you be vexed? Surely not. But and if you were to be vexed, would you not then be ridiculous? Thus too let us then get to feel disposed towards our neighbors, and then we shall have no sense of displeasure. For they that insult us are more senseless than children. Neither let us even seek to be free from insults, but when we are insulted to bear them. For this is the only secure honor. But why so? Because this you are master of, but that, another person. Do you not see the adamant rever-

[1] Greg. Nyss. i. p. 720. ἐπεὶ ἀπαθὲς τὸ Θεῖον, ὁ ἐν πάθει ὢν τῆς πρὸς τὸ Θεῖον συναφείας ἀποσχοινίζεται.

berating the blows it receives? But nature, you will say, gives it this property. Yet you too have it in your power to become by free choice such, as that happens to be by nature. How? do you not know that the children in the furnace were not burned? and that Daniel in the den suffered no harm? This may even now come to pass. There stand by us too lions, anger and lust, with fearful teeth tearing asunder him that falleth among them. (Plato *Rep.* viii.) Become then like that (ἐκεῖνον 3 Mss.) Daniel, and let not these affections fasten their fangs into thy soul. But that, you will say, was wholly of grace. Yes; because the acts[1] of free-will led the way thereto. So that if we be willing to train ourselves to a like character, even now the grace is at hand. And even though the brutes be an hungered, yet will they not touch thy sides. For if at the sight of a servant's body they were abashed, when they have seen the members of Christ, (and this is what we believers are,) how shall they do else than be still? Yet if they be not still, it is owing to the fault of those cast among them. For indeed many spend largely upon these lions, by keeping harlots, breaking through marriages, taking vengeance upon enemies. And so before ever they come to the bottom of the den they get torn in pieces. (Dan. vi. 24.) But with Daniel this did not so happen, neither yet would it with us, if we were so minded, but even a greater thing would take place than what then happened. For the lions hurt not him; and if we be sober-minded, then will they that hurt us even profit us. Thus then did Paul grow bright out of those that thwarted him and plotted against him, thus Job out of the many scourges, thus Jeremy out of the miry pit, thus Noah out of the flood, thus Abel out of the treachery, thus Moses out of the bloodthirsty Jews, thus, Elisha, thus each of the worthies of old, not out of relaxedness and softness, but out of tribulations and trials, came to be attired with their bright crowns. Wherefore also Christ, inasmuch as He knew this to be the groundwork of a good report, said to His disciples, " In the world ye shall have tribulation, but be of good cheer, I have overcome the world." (John xvi. 33.) What then, they will say, Have not many been turned to flight by these terrors? Yes, but that was not of the nature of temptation, but of their own remissness. But He that " with the temptation maketh also an escape, so that ye may be able to bear it " (1 Cor. x. 13), may He stand by all of us, and reach forth His hand, that being gloriously proclaimed victorious we may attain to the everlasting crowns, through the grace and love towards man (5 Mss. add the rest and so Field *passim*) of our Lord Jesus Christ, through Whom, and with Whom, to the Father be glory, with the Holy Ghost, for ever and ever. Amen.

HOMILY IV.

ROM. I. 26, 27.

" For this cause God gave them up unto vile affections: for even their women did change the natural use into that which is against nature : and likewise also the men, leaving the natural use of the woman, burned in their lust one towards another."

ALL these affections then were vile, but chiefly the mad lust after males; for the soul is more the sufferer in sins, and more dishonored, than the body in diseases. But behold how here too, as in the case of the doctrines, he deprives them of excuse, by saying of the women, that "they changed the natural use." For no one, he means, can say that it was by being hindered of legitimate intercourse that they came to this pass, or that it was from having no means to fulfil their desire that they were driven into this monstrous insaneness. For the changing implies possession. Which also when discoursing upon the doctrines he said, "They changed the truth of God for a lie." And with regard to the men again, he shows the same thing by saying, " Leaving the natural use of the woman." And in a like way with those, these he also puts out of all means of defending themselves by charging them not only that they had the means of gratification, and left that which they had, and went after another, but that having dishonored that which was natural, they ran after that which was contrary to nature. But that which is contrary to nature hath in it an irksomeness and displeasingness, so that they could not fairly allege even

---

[1] τὰ τῆς πρ. i. e. his fastings. etc. S. Ephrem notes that it was not the miracles which were supernatural, but the grace of the doers thereof, in *Nat. Dom.* ix. text 2. p. 427. f.

pleasure. For genuine pleasure is that which is according to nature. But when God hath left one, then all things are turned upside down. And thus not only was their doctrine Satanical, but their life too was diabolical. Now when he was discoursing of their doctrines, he put before them the world and man's understanding, telling them that, by the judgment afforded them by God, they might through the things which are seen, have been led as by the hand to the Creator, and then, by not willing to do so, they remained inexcusable. Here in the place of the world he sets the pleasure according to nature, which they would have enjoyed with more sense of security and greater glad-heartedness, and so have been far removed from shameful deeds. But they would not; whence they are quite out of the pale of pardon, and have done an insult to nature itself. And a yet more disgraceful thing than these is it, when even the women seek after these intercourses, who ought to have more sense of shame than men. And here too the judgment of Paul is worthy of admiration, how having fallen upon two opposite matters he accomplishes them both with all exactness. For he wished both to speak chastely and to sting the hearer. Now both these things were not in his power to do,[1] but one hindered the other. For if you speak chastely you shall not be able to bear hard upon the hearer. But if you are minded to touch him to the quick, you are forced to lay the naked facts before him in plain terms. But his discreet and holy soul was able to do both with exactness, and by naming nature has at once given additional force to his accusation, and also used this as a sort of veil, to keep the chasteness of his description. And next, having reproached the women first, he goes on to the men also, and says, " And likewise also the men leaving the natural use of the woman." Which is an evident proof of the last degree of corruptness, when both sexes are abandoned, and both he that was ordained to be the instructor of the woman, and she who was bid to become an helpmate to the man, work the deeds of enemies against one another. And reflect too how significantly he uses his words. For he does not say that they were enamoured of, and lusted after one another, but, " they burned in their lust one toward another." You see that the whole of desire comes of an exorbitancy which endureth not to abide within its proper limits. For everything which transgresseth the laws by God appointed, lusteth after monstrous things and not those which be customary. For as many oftentimes having left the desire of food get to feed upon earth and small [2] stones, and others being possessed by excessive thirst often long even for mire, thus these also ran into this ebullition of lawless love. But if you say, and whence came this intensity of lust? It was from the desertion of God :[3] and whence is the desertion of God? from the lawlessness of them that left Him; " men with men working that which is unseemly." Do not, he means, because you have heard that they burned, suppose that the evil was only in desire. For the greater part of it came of their luxuriousness, which also kindled into flame their lust. And this is why he did not say being swept along or being overtaken,[4] an expression he uses elsewhere; but what? working. They made a business of the sin, and not only a business, but even one zealously followed up. And he called it not lust, but that which is unseemly, and that properly.[5] For they both dishonored nature, and trampled on the laws. And see the great confusion which fell out on both sides. For not only was the head turned downwards but the feet too were upwards, and they became enemies to themselves and to one another, bringing in a pernicious kind of strife, and one even more lawless than any civil war, and one rife in divisions, and of varied form. For they divided this into four new, and lawless kinds. Since (3 Mss. whence) this war was not twofold or threefold, but even fourfold. Consider then. It was meet, that the twain should be one, I mean the woman and the man. For " the twain," it says, " shall be one flesh." (Gen. ii. 24.) But this the desire of intercourse effected, and united the sexes to one another. This desire the devil having taken away, and having turned the course thereof into another fashion, he thus sundered the sexes from one another, and made the one to become two parts in opposition to the law of God. For it says, " the two shall be one flesh ; " but he divided the one flesh into two : here then is one war. Again, these same two parts he provoked to war both against themselves and against one another. For even women again abused women, and not men only. And the men stood against one another, and against the female sex, as happens in a battle by night. You see a second

---

[1] 3 Mss. ταῦτα δὲ (βουλομένῳ) ἀμφότερα οὐκ ἐνὸν (κατορθοῦν). (Sav. ἐνῆν) but in these one cannot succeed merely by wishing it.

[2] μικρὰς, Mss. the fem. is used of jewels. The Translator once had some earth which the natives of Mozambique eat in this way ; it becomes a dram to them, its taste is like magnesia with iron, which last would give it a stimulant property. There are some other instances, but cases of madness are perhaps intended.

[3] 3 Mss. I should say, ... and if you ask whence is the desertion of God, I shall answer you again.

[4] Gal. 6, 1. προληφθέντες, but 5 Mss. παραλ.

[5] κυρίως, perhaps " as by name."

and third war, and a fourth and fifth ; there is also another, for beside what have been mentioned they also behaved lawlessly against nature itself. For when the Devil saw that this desire it is, principally, which draws the sexes together, he was bent on cutting through the tie, so as to destroy the race, not only by their not copulating lawfully, but also by their being stirred up to war, and in sedition against one another.

"And receiving in themselves that recompense of their error which was meet." See how he goes again to the fountain head of the evil, namely, the impiety that comes of their doctrines, and this he says is a reward of that lawlessness. For since in speaking of hell and punishment, it seemed he would not at present be credible to the ungodly and deliberate choosers of such a life, but even scorned, he shows that the punishment was in this pleasure itself. (So Plato *Theæt.* p. 176, 7.) But if they perceive it not, but are still pleased, be not amazed. For even they that are mad, and are afflicted with phrenzy (cf. Soph. *Aj.* 265-277) while doing themselves much injury and making themselves such objects of compassion, that others weep over them, themselves smile and revel over what has happened. Yet we do not only for this not say that they are quit of punishment, but for this very reason are under a more grievous vengeance, in that they are unconscious of the plight they are in. For it is not the disordered but those who are sound whose votes one has to gain. Yet of old the matter seemed even to be a law,[1] and a certain lawgiver among them bade the domestic slaves neither to use unguents when dry (i. e. except in bathing) nor to keep youths, giving the free this place of honor, or rather of shamefulness. Yet they, however, did not think the thing shameful, but as being a grand privilege, and one too great for slaves, the Athenian people, the wisest of people, and Solon who is so great amongst them, permitted it to the free alone. And sundry other books of the philosophers may one see full of this disease. But we do not therefore say that the thing was made lawful, but that they who received this law were pitiable, and objects for many tears. For these are treated in the same way as women that play the whore. Or rather their

plight is more miserable. For in the case of the one the intercourse, even if lawless, is yet according to nature : but this is contrary both to law and nature. For even if there were no hell, and no punishment had been threatened, this were worse than any punishment. Yet if you say "they found pleasure in it," you tell me what adds to the vengeance. For suppose I were to see a person running naked, with his body all besmeared with mire, and yet not covering himself, but exulting in it, I should not rejoice with him, but should rather bewail that he did not even perceive that he was doing shamefully. But that I may show the atrocity in a yet clearer light, bear with me in one more example. Now if any one condemned a virgin to live in close dens (θαλαμευομένην), and to have intercourse with unreasoning brutes, and then she was pleased with such intercourse, would she not for this be especially a worthy object of tears, as being unable to be freed from this misery owing to her not even perceiving the misery? It is plain surely to every one. But if that were a grievous thing, neither is this less so than that. For to be insulted by one's own kinsmen is more piteous than to be so by strangers : these I say (5 Mss. "I consider ") are even worse than murderers : since to die even is better than to live under such insolency. For the murderer dissevers the soul from the body, but this man ruins the soul with the body. And name what sin you will, none will you mention equal to this lawlessness. And if they that suffer such things perceived them, they would accept ten thousand deaths so they might not suffer this evil. For there is not, there surely is not, a more grievous evil than this insolent dealing. For if when discoursing about fornication Paul said, that "Every sin which a man doeth is without the body, but he that committeth fornication sinneth against his own body" (1 Cor. vi. 18); what shall we say of this madness, which is so much worse than fornication as cannot even be expressed? For I should not only say that thou hast become a woman, but that thou hast lost thy manhood, and hast neither changed into that nature nor kept that which thou haddest, but thou hast been a traitor to both of them at once, and deserving both of men and women to be driven out and stoned, as having wronged either sex. And that thou mayest learn what the real force of this is, if any one were to come and assure you that he would make you a dog instead of being a man, would you not flee from him as a plague? But, lo! thou hast not made thyself a dog out of a man, but an animal more disgraceful than this. For this is useful unto

---

[1] See Müller's *Dorians,* l. iv. c. 4, § 6, where it is shown that this charge is more than exaggerated from confounding earlier times with later. Aristotle, *Pol.* ii. and Plato, *Leg.* i. 636, accuse the Lacedæmonians in like manner, but see Xen. *de Rep. Lac.* ii. 13. Ælian. v. H. iii. I. 12, and other writers quoted by Müller. At Athens opinion was, according to Plato, rather lax than positively immoral : it may be doubted if Solon's law (Aesch. *in Tim.* 19, 25,) was meant to bear the worst sense, though censured by Plutarch in almost the same terms as here. That there was however a fearful prevalence of this vice among the heathen cannot be disputed.

service, but he that hath thus given himself up is serviceable for nothing. Or again, if any one threatened to make men travail and be brought to bed, should we not be filled with indignation? But lo! now they that have run into this fury have done more grievously by themselves. For it is not the same thing to change into the nature of women, as to continue a man and yet to have become a woman; or rather neither this nor that. But if you would know the enormity of the evil from other grounds, ask on what account the lawgivers punish them that make men eunuchs, and you will see that it is absolutely for no other reason than because they mutilate nature. And yet the injustice they do is nothing to this. For there have been those that were mutilated and were in many cases useful after their mutilation. But nothing can there be more worthless than a man who has pandered himself. For not the soul only, but the body also of one who hath been so treated, is disgraced, and deserves to be driven out everywhere. How many hells shall be enough for such? But if thou scoffest at hearing of hell and believest not that fire, remember Sodom. For we have seen, surely we have seen, even in this present life, a semblance of hell. For since many would utterly disbelieve the things to come after the resurrection, hearing now of an unquenchable fire, God brings them to a right mind by things present. For such is the burning of Sodom, and that conflagration! And they know it well that have been at the place, and have seen with their eyes that scourge divinely sent, and the effect of the lightnings from above. (Jude 7.) Consider how great is that sin, to have forced hell to appear even before its time! For whereas many thought scorn of His words, by His deeds did God show them the image thereof in a certain novel way. For that rain was unwonted, for that the intercourse was contrary to nature, and it deluged the land, since lust had done so with their souls. Wherefore also the rain was the opposite of the customary rain. Now not only did it fail to stir up the womb of the earth to the production of fruits, but made it even useless for the reception of seed. For such was also the intercourse of the men, making a body of this sort more worthless than the very land of Sodom. And what is there more detestable than a man who hath pandered himself, or what more execrable? Oh, what madness! Oh, what distraction! Whence came this lust lewdly revelling and making man's nature all that enemies could? or even worse than that, by as much as the soul is better than the

body. Oh, ye that were more senseless than irrational creatures, and more shameless than dogs! for in no case does such intercourse take place with them, but nature acknowledgeth her own limits. But ye have even made our race dishonored below things irrational, by such indignities inflicted upon and by each other. Whence then were these evils born? Of luxury; of not knowing God. For so soon as any have cast out the fear of Him, all that is good straightway goes to ruin.*

Now, that this may not happen, let us keep clear before our eyes the fear of God. For nothing, surely nothing, so ruins a man as to slip from this anchor, as nothing saves so much as continually looking thereto. For if by having a man before our eyes we feel more backward at doing sins, and often even through feeling abashed at servants of a better stamp we keep from doing anything amiss, consider what safety we shall enjoy by having God before our eyes! For in no case will the Devil attack us when so conditioned, in that he would be laboring without profit. But should he see us wandering abroad, and going about without a bridle, by getting a beginning in ourselves he will be able to drive us off afterwards any whither. And as it happens with thoughtless servants at market, who leave the needful services which their masters have entrusted to them, and rivet themselves at a mere haphazard to those who fall in their way, and waste out their leisure there; this also we undergo when we depart from the commandments of God. For we presently get standing on, admiring riches, and beauty of person, and the other things which we have no business with, just as those servants attend to the beggars that do jugglers' feats, and then, arriving too late, have to be grievously beaten at home. And many pass the road set before them through following others, who are behaving in the same unseemly way. But let not us so do. For we have been sent to dispatch many affairs that are urgent. And if we leave those, and stand gaping at these useless things, all our time will be wasted in vain and to no profit, and we shall suffer the extreme of punishment. For if you

* There is no more forcible exhibition of the meaning of the apostle in the volume, then that found in this Homily. The depravity of the heathen world of which Paul has drawn but an outline picture is here painted in full in dark and awful colors. The force of διὰ τοῦτο (26) is rightly brought out as showing the relation of this depravity to the divine penalty for unbelief and irreligion. This deplorable moral condition is the judicial consequence of not following the light which God had given. It follows from the recoil of the moral law upon those who violate it. It is an example of the Saviour's warning: "If the light that is in thee be darkness, how great is the darkness?" (Matt. vi. 23). The inevitable result of continued sin is a constantly increased and inveterate sinfulness which, as Chrys. says, is itself a most bitter punishment. —G. B. S.

wish yourself to be busy, you have whereat you ought to wonder, and to gape all your days, things which are no subject for laughter, but for wondering and manifold praises. As he that admires things ridiculous, will himself often be such, and even worse than he that occasioneth the laughter. And that you may not fall into this, spring away from it forthwith. For why is it, pray, that you stand gaping and fluttering at sight of riches? What do you see so wonderful, and able to fix your eyes upon them? these gold-harnessed horses, these lackeys, partly savages, and partly eunuchs, and costly raiment, and the soul that is getting utterly soft in all this, and the haughty brow, and the bustlings, and the noise? And wherein do these things deserve wonder? what are they better than the beggars that dance and pipe in the market-place? For these too being taken with a sore famine of virtue, dance a dance more ridiculous than theirs, led and carried round at one time to costly tables, at another to the lodging of prostitute women, and at another to a swarm of flatterers and a host of hangers-on. But if they do wear gold, this is why they are the most pitiable, because the things which are nothing to them, are most the subject of their eager desire. Do not now, I pray, look at their raiment, but open their soul, and consider if it is not full of countless wounds, and clad with rags, and destitute, and defenceless! What then is the use of this madness of shows? for it were much better to be poor and living in virtue, than to be a king with wickedness; since the poor man in himself enjoys all the delights of the soul, and doth not even perceive his outward poverty for his inward riches. But the king, luxurious in those things which do not at all belong to him, is punished in those things which are his most real concern, even the soul, the thoughts, and the conscience, which are to go away with him to the other world. Since then we know these things, let us lay aside the gilded raiment, let us take up virtue and the pleasure which comes thereof. For so, both here and hereafter, shall we come to enjoy great delights, through the grace and love towards man of our Lord Jesus Christ, through Whom, and with Whom, be glory to the Father, with the Holy Spirit, for ever and ever. Amen.

HOMILY V.

ROM. I. 28.

"Even as they did not like to retain God in their knowledge, God gave them over to a reprobate mind, to do those things which are not convenient."

LEST he should seem to be hinting at them by delaying in his discourse so long over the unnatural sin, he next passes on to other kinds of sins also, and for this cause he carries on the whole of his discourse as of other persons. And as he always does when discoursing with believers about sins, and wishing to show that they are to be avoided, he brings the Gentiles in, and says, "Not in the lust of concupiscence, even as the other Gentiles which know not God." (1 Thess. iv. 5.) And again: "sorrow not, even as others which have no hope." (ib. 13.) And so here too he shows that it was to them the sins belonged, and deprives them of all excuse. For he says, that their daring deeds came not of ignorance, but of practice. And this is why he did not say, "and as they knew not God;" but, "as they did not like to retain God in their knowledge;" as much as to say, that the sin was one of a perverted determination of obstinacy, more than of a sudden ravishment, and shows that it was not the flesh (as some heretics say) but the mind,[1] to the wicked lust whereof the sins belonged, and that it was thence the fount of the evils flowed.[*] For since the mind is become undistinguishing,[2] all else is then dragged out of course and overturned, when he is corrupted that held the reins! (Plat. *Phaedr.* 246 A. B.)

Ver. 29. "Being filled with all unrighteous-

---

[1] Mss. the evil mind and negligence (or self-will, ῥαθυμίας) to which the sins belonged. See St. Aug. *Conf.* b. 3, c. 16, b. 5, c. 18, b. 7, c. 4, Oxf. Tr. pp. 40, 78, 110, etc.

[*] Chrys. is correct in denying that Paul refers sin to the flesh (in the sense of the *body*), as its cause and seat. With the apostle σάρξ is not the same as σῶμα in its relation to sin. Σάρξ comprehends the whole unregenerate man and not merely his body or the impulses and passions connected with his physical life. It is true that Paul regards the body as the sphere in which sin makes many of its worst manifestations. It may be due to this that he chose the word σάρξ to denote unrenewed human nature. With Paul the cause and seat of sin are in the will. He nowhere identifies evil with the body and therefore lays no basis for asceticism or for the contempt or ill-treatment of the body. Of the "works of the flesh" which he enumerates in Gal. v. 19-21 more than half are sins having no special relation to the body and not manifesting themselves through physical appetites or passions, as, e. g. "idolatry, enmities, jealousies, divisions, heresies."—G. B. S.

[2] ἀδόκιμος, usually rendered "reprobate" as in the text, here seems to be used with a consciousness of its etymology, as St. Paul plays on the word in οὐκ ἐδοκίμασαν.

ness, wickedness, covetousness, maliciousness."

See how everything here is intensitive. For he says, "being filled," and "with all," and having named maliciousness in general, he also further pursues the particulars, and these too in excess, saying, "Full of envy, murder," for the latter of these comes from the former, as was shown in Abel's case and Joseph's, and then after saying, "debate, deceit, malignity ; "

Ver. 30. "Whisperers, backbiters, haters of God, despiteful," and classing things which to many seem indifferent among his charges, he further strengthens his accusation, going up to the stronghold of their wickednesses, and styles them " boasters." For even worse than sinning is it, even though sinning to be haughty-minded. Wherefore also he charges the Corinthians with it, saying, " Ye are puffed up." (1 Cor. v. 2.) For if in a good action he that puffs himself up loseth all, if any one do so among his sins, what vengeance is there of which he is not worthy, since such an one cannot repent any more ? Next, he says, " inventors of evil things ; " showing that they were not content with those already existing, but even invented others. And this again is like men that are full purposed and in earnest, not those that are hurried away and forced out of their course ; and after mentioning the several kinds of maliciousness, and showing that here too they stood against nature itself (for he says, " disobedient to parents "), he then goes on to the root of the great pestilence, calling them,

Ver. 31. "Without natural affection, implacable."

For this Christ Himself also pronounces to be the cause of wickedness, saying, " When iniquity shall abound, the love of many shall wax cold." (Matt. xxiv. 12). This too St. Paul here says, calling them " covenant-breakers, without natural affection, implacable, unmerciful," and showing that they were traitors even to the gift of nature. For we have a sort of family feeling even by nature towards one another, which even beasts have got towards each other. " For every beast," it says, " loveth his like, and every man his neighbor." (Ecclus. xiii. 15.) But these became more ferocious even than they. The disorder then which resulted to the world by evil doctrines, he proves to us by these witnesses, and clearly shows that the malady in either case came of the negligence of them that were disordered. He shows besides, what he did in the case of the doctrines, that they were here also deprived of all excuse ; and so he says,

Ver. 32. "Who knowing the judgment of God, that they which commit such things are worthy of death, not only do the same, but have pleasure in them that do them."

Having assumed here two objections, he in the first place removes them. For what reason have you to say, he means, that you know not the things which ought to be done ? At best, even if you did not know, you are to blame in having left God who instructs you. But as it is by many arguments we have shown that you do know, and transgress willingly. But are you drawn by passion ? Why then do you both coöperate therewith and praise it ? For they " not only do such things," he says, " but have pleasure in them that do them." Having then put the more grievous and the unpardonable sin first, that he might have done with it (Or " convict you of it," ἵνα ἐλῃ) ; (for he that praiseth the sin is far worse than even he that trespasseth ;) having then put this the first, he by this method grapples more powerfully with him in the sequel, speaking on this wise,

Chap. ii. ver. 1. " Therefore thou art inexcusable, O man ; whosoever thou art that judgest ; for wherein thou judgest another, thou condemnest thyself."

These things he says, with an aim at the rulers, inasmuch as that city then had the rule of the world put into its hands.[*] He anticipated them therefore by saying, Thou art depriving thyself of defence, whoever thou mayest be ; for when thou condemnest an adulterer, and thyself committest adultery, although no man condemneth thee, in thy judgment upon the guilty person thou hast also passed sentence against thyself.

Ver. 2. " For we are sure that the judgment of God is according to truth against them who commit such things."

For lest any should say, until now I have escaped, to make him afraid, he says, that it is not so with God as it is here. For here (Plato in _Theæt. et Phædon._) one is punished, and another escapes while doing the same thing. But hereafter it is not so. That he that judgeth then knoweth the right, he has

---

[*] The author seems here to overlook the fact that Paul at the beginning of ch. ii. turns to the Jews. Chrys. speaks as if he were now addressing specifically " rulers." But as the argument goes on, the language shows more and more clearly that he is here thinking of the Jewish world (see v. 12 sq and esp. 17). The " therefore " grounds the fact of universal condemnation upon the description of sin as universal, contained in i. 18–32. The only peculiarity is that the statement that this picture of Gentile depravity is a picture of universal application, is made afterwards, " For wherein," etc. The argument proceeds as if after i. 32 the apostle had been interrupted with the objection, " But your description does not apply to us." The apostle answers: " It does, for you do the same things." The " therefore " is proleptic so far as it assumes as shown what he now asserts: τὰ γὰρ αὐτὰ πράσσεις ὁ κρίνων. The conclusion is thus stated before the major premiss.—G. B. S.

said : but whence he knoweth it, he hath not added ; for it was superfluous. For in the case of ungodliness, he shows both that the ungodly was so even with a knowledge of God, and also whence he got that knowledge, namely, from the Creation. For inasmuch as it was not plain to all, he gave the cause also ; but here he passes it over as a thing admitted. But when he says, "whosoever thou art that judgest," he is not addressing himself to the rulers only, but to all private individuals and subjects also. For all men, even if they have no chair of state, nor executioners, nor stocks at command, yet even they judge those that offend, in conversations and public meetings (Gr. κοινοῖς συλλόγοις) and by the vote of their conscience. And no one would venture to say, that the adulterer does not deserve punishment. But it is others, he says, they condemn, and not themselves. And for this cause he stands forth vehemently against them, and says,

Ver. 3. "And thinkest thou this" (4 Mss. om. this), "O man, that judgest those which do such things, and doest the same, that thou shalt escape the judgment of God ? "

For since he had shown the sin of the world to be great, from its doctrines, from its doings, and that they did yet sin though wise, and though they had the creation to lead them by the hand, and not by leaving God only, but also by choosing the images of creeping things, and by their dishonoring virtue, and deserting, in spite of nature's drawings back, to the service of vice even contrary to nature : he goes on next to show, that they who do such things are punished too. He did indeed at once point out a punishment by mentioning their very practice. For "they received," he says, "in themselves that recompense of their error which was meet." But as they do not perceive that, he mentions another also, which they stood most in fear of. And indeed already he chiefly pointed at this. For when he says, "That the judgment of God is according to truth," he is speaking of no other than this. But he establishes the same again upon other further grounds, saying thus, "And thinkest thou this, O man, that judgest them which do such things, and doest the same, that thou shalt escape the judgment of God ? " Thou hast not been acquitted of thine own judgment, and wilt thou escape through God's ? Who indeed would say this ? And yet thou hast judged thyself (3 Mss. "and not been acquitted "). But since the rigorousness of the judgment-court was such, and thou wert not able to spare even thyself, how should not God, that cannot do amiss, and who is in the highest sense just, be much surer to do the

same ? But hast thou condemned thyself, and is God to approve of thee and praise thee ? And how can this be reasonable ? And all the while thou art deserving of a greater punishment, than he who is of thee condemned. For sinning merely, is not the same thing with falling again into the same sins you have chastised another for committing. See, how he has strengthened the charge ! For if you, he means, punish a person who has committed less sins, though by it you will put yourself to shame, how shall not God cast you in your suit, and condemn you more severely, who have committed greater transgressions, and this too when He will never make Himself ashamed, and you are already condemned by your own reckoning. But if thou say, I know that I deserve punishment ; yet through His long-suffering thinkest slightingly of it, and art confident because thou dost not suffer punishment forthwith ; this surely is a reason why thou oughtest to be afraid and tremble. For the fact that thou hast not yet suffered punishment, will not result in thy not suffering any punishment, but in thy suffering a more severe one if thou abidest unamended.[1] And so he goes on to say :

Ver. 4. "Or despiseth thou the riches of His goodness and forbearance and long-suffering ; not knowing that the goodness of God leadeth thee to repentance ? "

For after praising God's long-suffering, showing the gain thereof to be very great to them that heeded it (and this was the drawing sinners to repentance); he adds to the terror. For as to them, who avail themselves of it aright, it is a ground of safety ; so to them that slight it, it is conducive to a greater vengeance. For whenever you utter this common notion, that God doth not exact justice, because He is good and long-suffering, he says, You do but mention what will make the vengeance intenser. For God showeth His goodness that you may get free from your sins, not that you may add to them. If then thou make not this use thereof, the judgment will be more fearful. Wherefore it is a chief ground for abstaining from sin, that God is long-suffering, and not for making the benefit a plea for obstinacy. For if He be long-suffering, He most certainly punisheth. Whence does this appear ? from what is next said. For if the wickedness be great and the wicked have not been requited, it is absolutely necessary that they should be requited. For if men do not overlook these things, how

---

[1] So Field, from Mss: the old reading would have to mean "For it is not that thou shouldst not suffer any punishment, but that thou mayest suffer a worse if thou abide unamended, that He delayeth—and may that never befall thee."

should God make an oversight ? And so from this point he introduces the subject of the judgment. For the fact of showing many who, if they repent not, are liable, yet still are not punished here, introduces with it necessarily the judgment, and that with increase. Wherefore he says,

Ver. 5. " But after thy hardness and impenitent heart treasurest up unto thyself wrath."

For when a man is neither to be softened by goodness nor to be turned back by fear, what can be harder than such an one ? For after that he had showed the goodness of God towards men, he then shows His vengeance that it is unbearable for him who[1] does not even so return to repentance. And observe with what propriety he uses the words! " Thou treasurest up unto thyself wrath," he says, so making it plain what is certainly laid up, and showing that it is not He that judgeth, but he that is condemned, who is the author of this. For he says, " thou treasurest up for thyself," not God for thee. For He did all, whatsoever things were fitting, and created thee with a power to discern between good and what was not so, and showed long-suffering over thee, and called thee to repentance, and threatened a fearful day, so by every means drawing thee to repentance. But if thou shouldst continue unyielding, " thou treasurest up unto thyself wrath against the day of wrath and revelation and (so all Mss. but two) the righteous judgment of God." For lest on hearing of wrath thou shouldest think of any passion, he adds, " the righteous judgment of God." And he said " revelation " with good reason, for then is this revealed when each man receives his desert. For here many men often annoy and practise harm to one without justice. But hereafter it is not so.

Ver. 6, 7. " Who will render to every man according to his deeds, to them who by patient continuance in well doing," etc.

Since he had become awestriking and harsh by discoursing of the judgment and of the punishment that shall be, he does not forthwith, as one might expect, enter upon the vengeance, but turns his discourse to what was sweeter, to the recompense of good actions, saying as follows,

Ver. 7. " To them who by patient continuance in well doing seek for glory and honor and immortality, eternal life."

Here also he awakens those who had drawn back during the trials, and shows that it is not right to trust in faith only. For it is deeds also into which that tribunal will enquire.

But observe, how when he is discoursing about the things to come, he is unable to tell clearly the blessings, but speaketh of glory and honor. For in that they transcend all that man hath, he hath no image of them taken from this to show, but by those things which have a semblance of brightness among us, even by them he sets them before us as far as may be, by glory, by honor, by life. For these be what men earnestly strive after, yet are those things not these, but much better than these, inasmuch as they are incorruptible and immortal. See how he has opened to us the doors toward the resurrection of the body by speaking of incorruptibility. For incorruptibility belongs to the corruptible body. Then, since this sufficed not, he added glory and honor. For all of us are to rise incorruptible, but not all to glory, but some to punishment, and some to life.

Ver. 8. " But unto them that are contentious,"* he says. Again, he deprives of excuse those that live in wickedness, and shows that it is from a kind of disputatiousness and carelessness that they fall into unrighteousness.

" And do not obey the truth, but obey unrighteousness." See, here is another accusation again. For what defence can he set up, who flees from the light and chooses the dark ? And he does not say, who are " compelled by," " lorded over by," but who " obey unrighteousness," that one may learn that the fall is one of free choice, the crime not of necessity.

Ver. 9. " Indignation and wrath, tribulation and anguish, upon every soul of man that doeth evil."

That is, if a man be rich, if a consul, if a very sovereign (so Field: several Mss. and Edd. " the emperor himself "), by none of them is the account of the judgment out-faced. Since in this dignities have no place. Having then shown the exceeding greatness of the disease, and having added the cause, that it was from the carelessness of the disordered, and finally, that destruction awaits them and that amendment is easy, in the punishment also he again gives the Jew the heavier lot. For he that had enjoyed a larger share of instruction would also deserve to undergo a larger share of vengeance if doing lawlessly. And so the wiser or mightier men we are, the more are we punished if we sin. For if thou art rich, thou wilt have more money demanded of thee than of the poor ; and if wiser than others, a stricter obedience ; and if thou hast been

---

[1] Or, "he" (St. Paul, according to Field) "is terribly severe upon him who:" for most Mss. omit "he shows that."

* Ἐριθεία is probably derived from ἔριθος, *a hired laborer* and not from ἔρις (strife) as commonly. Hence the meaning is : labor for hire—*Lohnarbeit*, party spirit. Better translate "factious" (R. V.) than "contentious" (A. V.). So Weiss, Thayer's *Lex.*—G. B. S.

invested with authority, more shining acts of goodness; and so in the case of all the other things, thou wilt have to bring in measures proportioned to your power.

Ver. 10. "But glory, honor, and peace to every man that worketh good, to the Jew first, and also to the Gentile."

What Jew does he here mean? or about what Gentiles is he discoursing? It is of those before Christ's coming. For his discourse had not hitherto come to the times of grace, but he was still dwelling upon the earlier times, so breaking down first from afar off and clearing away the separation between the Greek and the Jew, that when he should do this in the matter of grace, he might no more seem to be devising some new and degrading view. For if in the earlier times when this Grace had not shone forth in such greatness, when the estate of the. Jews was solemn and renowned and glorious before all men, there was no difference, what could they say for themselves (τίνα ἂν ἔχοιεν λόγον εἰπεῖν;) now after so great a display of grace? And this is why he establishes it with so great earnestness. For when the hearer has been informed that this held in the earlier times, much more will he receive it after the faith. But by Greeks he here means not them that worshipped idols, but them that adored God, that obeyed the law of nature, that strictly kept all things, save the Jewish observances, which contribute to piety, such as were Melchizedek and his (οἱ περὶ), such as was Job, such as were the Ninevites, such as was Cornelius. Here then he is first breaking through the partition between the circumcision and the uncircumcision: and at a distance dissipates this distinction beforehand, so as to do it without being suspected, and to strike into it as compelled by another occasion, which is ever a characteristic of his Apostolic wisdom. For if he had showed it in the times of grace, what he said would have had a very suspicious look. But on describing the vice which possessed the world, and where end the ways of wickedness, to pass from that consecutively into the treatment of these points renders his teaching unsuspected. And that he means this, and for this purpose so put this together, is plain from hence: for if he were not intent upon effecting this, it were enough for him to have said, "According to thy hardness and impenitent heart thou treasurest up unto thyself wrath against the day of wrath;" and then to have dropped this subject, since it would have been complete. But in that what he had in view was not to speak of the judgment to come only, but to show also that the Jew had no advantage of

such a Greek, and so was not to be haughty-spirited, he advances farther, and speaks[1] of them in order. But consider! He had put the hearer in fear, had advanced[2] against him the fearful day, had told him what an evil it is to be living in wickedness, had showed him that no man sinneth of ignorance, nor with impunity, but that even though he suffer no punishment now, yet he certainly will suffer it: then he wishes to make good next that the teaching of the Law was not a thing of great importance. For it is upon works that both punishment and reward depend, not upon circumcision and uncircumcision. Since then he had said, that the Gentile shall by no means go unpunished and had taken this for granted, and upon it had made good that he shall also be rewarded, he next showed the Law and circumcision to be superfluous. For it is the Jews that he is here chiefly opposing. For inasmuch as they were somewhat captiously disposed, first, of their haughtiness, not deigning to be reckoned along with the Gentiles, and secondly thinking it ridiculous if the faith is to do away all sins; for this cause he accused the Gentiles first, in whose behalf he is speaking, that without suspicion and with boldness of speech, he may attack the Jews. And then having come to the enquiry concerning the punishment, he shows that the Jew is so far from being at all profited by the Law, that he is even weighed down by it. And this was his drift some way back. For if the Gentile be on this score inexcusable, because, when the creation led him on and his own reasonings, he yet did not amend, much more were the Jew so, who besides these had the teaching of the Law also. Having then persuaded him to a ready admission of these reasonings, in the case of other men's sins, he now compels him even against his will to do so in the case of his own. And in order that what he says may be more readily allowed, he leads him forward with the better things also in view, speaking on this wise: "But glory and honor and peace to every man that worketh good, to the Jew first, and also to the Gentile." For here whatever good things a man hath, he hath with fightings, even if he be rich, if a prince, if a king. Even if he be not at variance with others, yet is he often so with himself, and has abundant war in his own thoughts. But there it is no such thing, but all is still and void of trouble, and in possession of true peace. Having then made good from what was said above, that they too which have not the Law are to enjoy the same blessings, he adds his reason in the following words :

Ver. 11. "For there is no respect of persons with God."

For when he says that as well the Jew as the Gentile is punished if he sin, he needs no reasonings : but when he wants to prove that the Gentile is honored also, he then needs a foundation for it also ; as it seemed wonderful and extravagant if he who had heard neither Law nor Prophets, were to be honored upon his working good. And this is why (as I also said before) he exercises their hearing in the times before grace, that he might afterwards more treatably bring in, along with the faith, the acquiescence in these things also. For here he is not at all suspected, as seeming not to be making his own point good. Having then said, "Glory and honor and peace to every man that worketh good, to the Jew first, and also to the Gentile," he adds, " For there is no respect of persons with God." Wonderful ! What more than victory has he gained ! For he shows, by reducing it to an absurdity, that it was not meet with God that it should be otherwise. For it would then be a case of respecting of persons. But of such character God is not. And he does not say, " for if this were not so, God would be a respecter of persons," but with more of dignity, " For there is no respect of persons with God." That it is not quality of persons, but difference of actions. Which He maketh inquisition for. By so saying he shows that it was not in actions but in persons only that the Jew differed from the Gentile. The consequence of this would be thus expressed ; For it is not because one is a Jew and the other a Gentile, that one is honored and the other disgraced, but it is from the works that either treatment comes. But he does not say so, since it would have roused the anger of the Jew, but he sets down something more, so bringing their haughty spirit yet lower, and quelling it for the admission of the other. But what is this ? The next position.

Ver. 12. "For as many," he says, " as have sinned without law shall also perish without law : and as many as have sinned in the law shall be judged by the law."

For here, as I said before, he shows not only the equality of the Jew and the Gentile, but that the Jew was even much burdened by the gift of the Law. For the Gentile is judged without law. But this " without law " (Gr. lawlessly) here expresses not the worse plight but the easier, that is, he has not the Law to accuse him. For " without law " (that is, without the condemnation arising from it), is he condemned solely from the reasonings of

nature, but the Jew, " in the Law," that is, with nature and the Law too to accuse him. For the greater the attention he enjoyed, the greater the punishment he will suffer. See how much greater is the necessity which he lays upon the Jews of a speedy recourse to grace ! For in that they said, they needed not grace, being justified by the Law, he shows that they need it more than the Gentiles, considering they are liable to be punished more. Then he adds another reason again, and so farther contends for what has been said.*

Ver 13. " For not the hearers of the law are just before God."

Well doth he add "before God ; " for haply before men they may be able to appear dignified and to vaunt great things, but before God it is quite otherwise—the doers of the Law alone are justified. You see with what advantage he combats, by turning what they said to an opposite bearing. For if it is by the Law you claim to be saved, in this respect, saith he, the Gentile will stand before you,[1] when seen to be a doer of what is written in the Law. And how is it possible (one may say) for one who hath not heard to be a doer ? Not this only, he says, is possible, but what is much more even than this. For not only is it possible without hearing to be a doer, but even with hearing not to be so. Which last thing he makes plainer, and that with a greater advantage over them, when he says, "Thou that teachest another, teachest thou not thyself ? " (Rom. ii. 21.) But here he is still making the former point good.

Ver. 14. " For when the Gentiles," he says, " which have not the law, do by nature the things contained in the law, these, having not the law, are a law unto themselves."

I am not, he means, rejecting the Law, but even on this score I justify the Gentiles. You see how when undermining the conceit of Judaism, he giveth no handle against himself as villifying the Law, but on the contrary by extolling it and showing its greatness he so makes good his whole position. But whenever he saith " by nature," he means by the

---

* Verse 12 assigns the ground of v. 11. " Sin brings penalty and death whether committed under the Mosaic law or under the ethical law of conscience." The first member of the sentence (v. 12) applies to the Gentiles. They have sinned without the standard and guidance of positive law ; they are, therefore, not brought to the test of that law's demands, but to the tests of natural, moral law (which the apostle will directly describe), and by that test their sins meet their penalty. Death, as sin's penalty, is coextensive with sin, not with the Mosaic law. Sin existed before the Mosaic law and apart from it ; it is imputed to the Gentiles—not, indeed, in the same way and degree (Rom. v. 13)—because they have a law of conscience. Each class is judged by the standard which has been given to them. All the terms relating to law here signify the Mosaic law, which was to Paul the specific statutory expression of the divine will and the embodiment of moral principles and duties.—G. B. S.

[1] πρῶτός σοῦ. cf. St. John i. 30.

reasonings of nature. And he shows that others are better than they, and, what is more, better for this, that they have not received the Law, and have not that wherein the Jews seem to have an advantage over them. For on this ground he means they are to be admired, because they required not a law, and yet exhibited all the doings of the Law, having the works, not the letters, graven upon their minds. For this is what he says,

Ver. 15. "Which show the work of the Law written in their hearts, their conscience also bearing witness, and their thoughts the meanwhile accusing or else excusing one another."

Ver. 16. "In the day when God shall judge the secrets of men by Jesus Christ, according to my Gospel."

See how he again puts that day before them, and brings it close to them, battering down their conceit, and showing, that those were to be the rather honored who without the Law strove earnestly to fulfil the things of the Law. But what is most to be marvelled at in the discretion of the Apostle, it is worth while to mention now. For having shown, from the grounds given, that the Gentile is greater than the Jew; in the inference, and the conclusion of his reasoning, he does not state it, in order not to exasperate the Jew. But to make what I have said clearer, I will give the very words of the Apostle. For after saying, that it is not the hearers of the Law, but the doers of the Law, that shall be justified, it followed to say, " For when the Gentiles, which have not the Law, do by nature the things contained in the Law," they are much better than those who are instructed by the Law. But this he does not say, but he stays at the encomium of the Gentiles, and does not yet awhile carry on his discourse by way of comparison, that so at least the Jew may receive what is said. And so he does not word it as I was doing, but how? " For when the Gentiles, which have not the Law, do by nature the things contained in the Law, these, not having the Law, are a law unto themselves; which show the work of the Law, written in their hearts, their conscience also bearing witness." For the conscience and reason doth suffice in the Law's stead. By this he showed, first, that God made man independent,[1] so as to be able to choose virtue

and to avoid vice. And be not surprised that he proves this point, not once or twice, but several times. For this topic was very needful for him to prove owing to those who say, Why ever is it, that Christ came but now? And where in times before was the (most Mss. this mighty) scheme of Providence? Now it is these that he is at present beating off by the way, when he shows that even in former times, and before the Law was given, the human race (Gr. nature) fully enjoyed the care of Providence. For " that which may be known of God was manifest in them," and they knew what was good, and what bad; by means whereof they judged others, which he reproaches them with, when he says, " wherein thou judgest another, thou condemnest thyself." But in the case of the Jews, besides what has been mentioned, there was the Law, and not reason or conscience only. And why does he put the words " accusing or else excusing ?"—for, if they have a Law written, and show the work of it in them, how comes reason to be able to accuse them still? But he is not any longer speaking of those only who do well, but also of mankind (Gr. the nature) universally. For then our reasonings stand up, some accusing and some excusing. And at that tribunal a man needeth no other accuser. Then to add to their fear, he does not say the sins of men, but the secrets of men. For since he said, " Thinkest thou, that judgest them that do such things, and doest the same, that thou shalt escape the judgment of God ; " that thou mayest not expect such a sentence as thou passest thyself, but mayest know, that that of God is far more exact than thine own, he brings in, " the secrets of men," and adds, " through Jesus Christ according to my Gospel." For men sit in judgment upon overt acts alone. And above too he spake of the Father alone, but as soon as he had crushed them with fear, he brought in the mention of Christ also. But he does not do barely this, but even here, after having made mention of the Father, he so introduceth Him. And by the same things he raises the dignity of his preaching. For this preaching, he means, openly speaks out what nature taught by anticipation. Do you see with what wisdom he has bound them both to the Gospel and to Christ, and demonstrated that our affairs come not here to a stand, but travel further. And this he made good before also, when he said, " thou treasurest up to thy-

---

[1] αὐτάρκης, writing before the Pelagian controversy, he does not notice the distinction between a sufficiency of knowledge, etc., and a supply of grace which must be presupposed. See Aug. *ad Dardanum, Ep.* 188, al. 143, c. 11, 12. See also De C. D. x. c. 29 and 32. Conc. Araus. A. D. 529, cap. 19. Labbe IV. 1670, B. declares grace needed even before the fall, much more after. See Bp. Bull on the state of man before the fall, Works, II. also Vinc. Lir. c. 24. The question is here whether men had means to attain salvation. It is taken for granted they had power given them to choose the right, but whether in the way of nature or of grace is not defined. The grace given

to Christians was always regarded as so distinct from and superior to everything granted to Jews or Heathens, that it was difficult to speak of the manner in which they received Divine assistance. But the gift spoken of by Justin Martyr, Ap. i. 13, is clearly supernatural. See also. St. Basil, *Const. Mon.* 16, t. 2, p. 559, B. and Macarius, Hom. 56.

self wrath against the day of wrath : " and here again, " God shall judge the secrets of men."

Now let each man enter into his own conscience, and reckoning up his transgressions, let him call himself to a strict account, that we be not then condemned with the world. (1 Cor. xi. 32.) For fearful is that court, awful the tribunal, full of trembling the accounts, a river of fire rolls along (ἕλκεται). " A brother doth not redeem : shall man redeem ? " (Ps. xlix. 8. LXX.) Call then to mind what is said in the Gospel, the Angels running to and fro, of the bridechamber being shut, of the lamps going out, of the powers which drag to the furnaces. And consider this, that if a secret deed of any one of us were brought forth into the midst, to-day, before the Church only, what could he do but pray to perish, and to have the earth to gape for him, rather than have so many witnesses of his wickedness ? How then shall we feel, when, before the whole world, all things are brought into the midst, in a theatre so bright and open, with both those known and those unknown to us seeing into everything ? But alas ! wherewith am I forced to affright you ! with men's estimation ! when I ought to use the fear of God, and His condemnation. For what, pray, is to become of us then when bound, and gnashing our teeth, we are led away to the outer darkness ? Or, rather, what shall we do (and this is the most fearful thought of all) when we offend (προσκρούσωμεν) God ? For if any one have sense and reason, he has already endured a hell when he is out of sight of God. But since this doth not pain, fire is therefore threatened. For we ought to smart not when we are punished, but when we sin. Thus listen to Paul wailing and lamenting over sins, for which he was not to be punished. For " I am not meet," he says, " to be called an Apostle, because I persecuted the Church." (1 Cor. xv. 9.) Hear also David, when he is set free from the punishment, yet, as thinking that he had offended God, calling vengeance down upon himself, and saying, " Let thy hand be upon me and upon my father's house." (2 Sam. xxiv. 17.) For to have offended God is more distressing than to be punished. But now we are so wretchedly disposed, that, were there no fear of hell, we should not even choose readily to do any good thing. Wherefore were it for nothing else, yet for this at least, we should deserve hell, because we fear hell more than Christ (several Mss. God). But not so the blessed Paul, but contrariwise. But since we feel otherwise, for this reason are we condemned to hell : since, did we but love Christ as we

should love Him, we should have known that to offend Him we love were more painful than hell. But since we love Him not, we know not the greatness of His punishment. And this is what I bewail and grieve over the most ! And yet what has God not done, to be beloved of us ? What hath He not devised ? What hath He omitted ? We insulted Him, when He had not wronged us in aught, but had even benefited us with blessings countless and unspeakable. We have turned aside from Him when calling and drawing us to Him by all ways, yet hath He not even upon this punished us, but hath run Himself unto us, and held us back, when fleeing, and we have shaken Him off and leaped away to the Devil. And not even on this hath He stood aloof, but hath sent numberless messengers to call us to Him again, Prophets, Angels,[1] Patriarchs : and we have not only not received the embassy, but have even insulted those that came. But not even for this did He spew us out of His mouth, but like those slighted lovers that be very earnest, He went round beseeching all, the heaven, the earth, Jeremiah, Micah, and that not that He might weigh us down, but that He might speak in behalf of His own ways (Is. i. 2 ; Jer. ii. 12 ; iii. 12 ; etc.; Mic. vi. 1) : and along with the prophets He went also Himself to those that turned aside from Him, being ready to submit to examination, and deigning to condescend to a conference, and drawing them that were deaf to every appeal into a disputation with Himself. For He saith, " O my people, what have I done unto thee, and wherein have I wearied thee ? Answer me." (Mic. vi. 3.) After all this we killed the Prophets, we stoned them, we did them other cruel wrongs without number. What then ? In their place He sent no longer Prophets, no longer Angels, no longer Patriarchs, but the Son Himself. He too was killed when He had come, and yet not even then did He quench His love, but kindled it even more, and keepeth on beseeching us, after even His own Son was killed, and entreating us, and doing all things to turn us unto Himself. And Paul crieth aloud, saying, " Now then we are ambassadors for Christ, as though God did beseech you by us : be ye reconciled to God." (2 Cor. v. 20.) None of these things however reconciled us. Yet not even then did He leave us, but keeps on both threatening hell, and promising a kingdom, that even so He may draw us unto Himself. But we be still in an insensible mood. What can be worse than this brutishness ? For had a man

[1] Perhaps human " messengers," inspired teachers other than those strictly called Prophets.

done these things, should we not many times over have let ourselves become slaves to him? But God when doing so we turn us away from! O what listlessness! O what unfeelingness! We that live continually in sins and wickednesses, if we happen to do any little good, like unfeeling domestics, with what a niggardly spirit do we exact it, and how particular are we about the recompense made, if what we have done has any recompense to come of it. And yet the recompense is the greater if you do it without any hope of reward. Why saying all this, and making exact reckoning, is language fitter for an hireling than a domestic of willing mind. For we ought to do everything for Christ's sake, not for the reward, but for Him. For this also was why He threatened hell and promised the kingdom, that He might be loved of us. Let us then so love Him as we ought to love Him. For this is the great reward, this is royalty and pleasure, this is enjoyment, and glory, and honor, this is light, this is the great happiness,[1] which language (or reasoning) cannot set before us, nor mind conceive. Yet indeed I do not know how I was led so far in this way of speaking, and came to be exhorting men who do not even think slightly of power and glory here for Christ's sake, to think slightly of the kingdom. Yet still those great and noble men even attained to this measure of love. Hear, for instance, how Peter burns with love towards Him, setting Him before soul, and life, and all things. And when he had denied Him, it was not the punishment he was grieved for, but that he had denied Him Whom he longed for, which was more bitter to him than any punishment. And all this did he show before the grace of the Spirit was given.[2] And he perseveringly pressed the question, "Whither goest thou?" (John xiii. 36) and before this; "To whom shall we go?" (vi. 67); and again; "I will follow Thee whithersoever Thou goest." (Luke xxii. 33?) Thus He was all things to them, and neither heaven nor the kingdom of heaven did they count of, in comparison of Him they longed for. For Thou art all these things unto me, he means. And why doest thou marvel that Peter was so minded? Hear now what the Prophet says: "What have I in heaven, and what is there upon earth, that I should desire in comparison of Thee?" (Ps. lxxiii. 25.) Now what he means is nearly this. Neither of things above nor of things below desire I any, save Thee only.

This is passion;[3] this is love. Can we so love, it will not be things present only, but even things to come, which we shall reckon as nothing compared with that love-charm, and even here shall we enjoy the Kingdom, delighting ourselves in the love of Him. And how is this to be? one may say. Let us reflect how oft we insult Him after numberless goodnesses, yet He standeth and calleth us to Him, and how often we run by Him, but He still doth not overlook us, but runneth to us, and draweth us to Him, and catcheth us in unto Himself. For if we consider these things, and such as these, we shall be enabled to kindle this longing. For if it were a common man that so loved, but a king who was thus beloved, would he not feel a respect for the greatness of the love? Most assuredly he would. But when the case is reversed, and His Beauty (S. "that beauty") is unspeakable, and the glory and the riches too of Him that loveth us, and our vileness so great, surely we deserve the utmost punishment, vile as we are and outcasts, who are treated with so exceeding great love by One so great and wonderful, and yet wax wanton against His love? He needeth not anything of ours, and yet He doth not even now cease loving us. We need much what is His, and for all that we cleave not unto His love, but money we value above Him, and man's friendship, and ease of body, and power, and fame, before Him who valueth nothing more than us. For He had One Son, Very (Lit. "true-born") and Only-Begotten, and He spared not even Him for us. But we value many things above Him. Were there not then good reason for a hell and torment, even were it twofold or threefold or manifold what it is? For what can we have to say for ourselves, if even Satan's injunctions we value more than the Laws of Christ, and are reckless of our own salvation that we may choose the works of wickedness, before Him who suffered all things for us? And what pardon do these things deserve? what excuse have they? Not one even. (5 Mss. οὐδὲ μιᾶς.) Let us stop then after this in our headlong course, and let us grow again sober; and reckoning up all these things, let us send up glory unto Him by our works (for words alone suffice not thereto), that we may also enjoy the glory that cometh of Him, which ·may we all attain unto by the grace and love toward man of our Lord Jesus Christ, through Whom, and with Whom, to the Father be glory, with the Holy Spirit, for ever and ever. Amen.

---

[1] The Ms. reading means no more: but the Edd. have μυριομακαριότης "countless blessedness," which is more like St. Chrysostom than a copyist.

[2] Origen on Matt. xxvi. 69, notices the same. Ed. Ben. p. 913, D.

[3] ἔρως . . . φιλία: the whole of this glorious passage suffers grievously in translation, owing to the impossibility of expressing the climax from ἀγαπᾶν, the common ecclesiastical word, to φιλεῖν and even ἐρᾶν.

HOMILY VI.

ROM. II. 17, 18.

"Behold,[1] thou art called a Jew, and restest in the Law, and makest thy boast of God, and knowest His will, and approvest the things that are more excellent, being instructed out of the Law."

AFTER saying that the Gentile wanteth nothing appertaining to salvation if he be a doer of the Law, and after making that wonderful comparison, he goes on to set down the glories of the Jews, owing to which they thought scorn of the Gentiles: and first the very name itself, which was of great majesty, as the name Christian is now. For even then the distinction which the appellation made was great. And so he begins from this, and see how he takes it down. For he does not say, Behold, thou art a Jew, but "art called" so, "and makest thy boast in God;" that is, as being loved by Him, and honored above all other men. And here he seems to me to be gently mocking their unreasonableness, and great madness after glory, because they misused this gift not to their own salvation, but to set themselves up against the rest of mankind, and to despise them. "And knowest His will, and approvest the things that are more excellent." Indeed this is a disadvantage, if without working: yet still it seemed to be an advantage, and so he states it with accuracy. For he does not say, thou doest, but knowest; and approvest, not followest and doest.*

Ver. 19. "And art confident that thou thyself."

Here again he does not say that thou art "a guide of the blind," but "thou art confident," so thou boastest, he says. So great was the unreasonableness of the Jews. Wherefore he also repeats nearly the very words, which they used in their boastings. See for instance what they say in the Gospels.

"Thou wast altogether (ὅλος 4 Mss. ὅλως) born in sin, and dost thou teach us?" (John ix. 34.) And all men they utterly looked down upon, to convince them of which, Paul keeps extolling them and lowering the others, that so he may get more hold on them, and make his accusation the weightier. Wherefore he goes on adding the like things, and making more of them by different ways of relating them. For "Thou art confident," he saith, "that thou thyself art a leader of the blind,"

Ver. 20. "An instructor of the foolish, a teacher of babes, which hast the form of knowledge and truth, which is in the Law."

Here again he says not, in the conscience and in actions and in well-doings, but "in the Law;" and after saying so, he does here also what he did with regard to the Gentiles. For as there he says, "for wherein thou judgest another, thou condemnest thyself," so saith he here also.

Ver. 21. "Thou therefore which teachest another, teachest thou not thyself?"

But there he frames his speech with more of sharpness, here with more of gentleness. For he does not say, However on this score thou deservest greater punishment, because though entrusted with so great things thou hast not made a good use of any of them, but he carries his discourse on by way of question, turning them on themselves (ἐντρέπων), and saying, "Thou that teachest another, teachest thou not thyself?" And here I would have you look at the discretion of Paul in another case. For he sets down such advantages of the Jews, as came not of their own earnestness, but by a gift from above, and he shows not only that they are worthless to them if neglectful, but that they even bring with them increase of punishment. For neither is the being called a Jew any well doing of theirs, nor yet is the receiving of the Law, nor the other things he has just enumerated, but of the grace from above. And towards the beginning he had said, that the hearing of the Law is valueless unless the doing be thereto added ("for not the hearers of the Law," he says, "are just before God,") but now he

---

[1] One Ms. appears to have εἰ δὲ "but if," with most Mss. of the N. T., instead of ἴδε, "behold," which St. Chrysostom appears to have read with the present T. R.

* From the 17th verse on the apostle speaks of the Jew by name and clearly shows that he had him in mind from the beginning of the chapter. The correct text reads εἰ δὲ instead of ἴδε to which the question of v. 21 corresponds as apodosis. Chrys.' interpretation of δοκιμάζεις τὰ διαφέροντα is that which is followed by the Vulgate ("probas utiliora"), most anct. vss., Wordsworth, Meyer, and our Eng. vss. The majority of modern commentators, however, adopt the interpretation: "testest things that differ." So Weiss, Godet, Wilke (Clavis N. T.), Lange, Tholuck. Alford, Philippi. This interpretation has the advantage of following the original meaning of both verbs.—G. B. S.

shows further still, that not only the hearing, but, what is more than the hearing, the teaching of the Law itself will not be able to screen the teacher, unless he do what he says; and not only will it not screen him, but will even punish him the more. And he has used his expressions well too, since he does not say, Thou hast received the Law, but "Thou restest in the Law." For the Jew was not wearied with going about to seek what was to be done, but had on easy terms the Law pointing the way leading to virtue. For if even the Gentiles have natural reason (and it is on this ground that these are better than they, in that they do the Law without hearing), yet still the others had greater facility. But if you say, I am not only a hearer, but even a teacher, this very thing is an aggravation of your punishment. For because they prided themselves upon this,[1] from this above all he shows them to be ridiculous. But when he says, "a guide of the blind, an instructor of the foolish, a teacher of babes," he is speaking their own pompous language. For they treated proselytes extremely ill, and these were the names they called them by. And this is why he dwells at large upon what were supposed to be their praises, well knowing that what was said gave ground for greater accusation; "Which hast the form of knowledge and of the truth in the Law." As if any one who had a picture of the king, were to draw nothing after it, and they that were not entrusted with it were to imitate it exactly even without the original. And then after mentioning the advantages they had from God, he tells them of their failings, bringing forward what the prophets accused them of. "Thou therefore which teachest another, teachest thou not thyself? Thou that preachest a man should not steal, dost thou steal? Thou that sayest a man should not commit adultery, dost thou commit adultery? Thou that abhorrest idols, dost thou commit sacrilege?"* For it was strictly forbidden them to touch any of the treasures upon the idols (so Field from the Mss: Vulg. "in the idol temples") by reason of the defilement. But the tyranny of avarice, he says, has persuaded you (4 Mss. and

mar. "us") to trample this Law also under foot. Then he brings the far more grievous charge afterwards, saying,

Ver. 23. "Thou that makest a boast in the Law through breaking the Law dishonorest thou God?"

There are two accusations which he makes, or rather three. Both that they dishonor, and dishonor that whereby they were honored; and that they dishonor Him that honored them, which was the utmost extreme of unfeelingness. And then, not to seem to be accusing them of his own mind, he brings in the Prophet as their accuser, here briefly and concisely as it were in a summary, but afterwards more in detail, and here Isaiah, and after that David, when he had shown the grounds of reproof to be more than one. For to show, he means, that it is not I who speak these things to your reproach, hear what Isaiah saith.

Ver. 24. "For the name of God is blasphemed among the Gentiles through you." (Is. lii. 5; Ez. xxxvi. 20, 23.)

See again another double accusation. For they not only commit insolence themselves, but even induce others to do so. What then is the use of your teaching when ye teach not your own selves? Above, however, he merely said this, but here he has even turned it round to the contrary. For not only yourselves, but even others, do ye not teach what should be done. And what is far worse—ye not only teach not the things of the Law, but ye even teach the opposite, viz. to blaspheme God, which is opposite to the Law. But the circumcision, one will say, is a great thing. Yea, I also confess it, but when? when (So all Mss. S. "then, when") it hath the inward circumcision. And observe his judgment, in bringing in what he says about it so opportunely. For he did not begin straightway with it, since the conceit men had of it was great. But after he had shown them to have offended in that which was greater[2] and to be responsible for the blasphemy against God, then having henceforth possession of the reader's judgment against them, and having stripped them of their pre-eminence, he introduces the discussion about circumcision, feeling sure that no one will any more advocate it, and says,

Ver. 25. "For circumcision verily profiteth, if thou keep the Law."

And yet, were this not so, a man might have rejected it and said, What is circumcision? for is it any good deed on his part that hath it? is it any manifestation of a right

---

[1] The younger Buxtorf, in his preface to his father's *Synagoga Judaica*, gives specimens of their language, as from Cad Hakkemach, "Such is the power of Circumcision, that none who is circumcised goeth down into Hell," and R. Abraham, than the Israelites were "all wise, all understanding, all skilled in the Law." See also Smith's *Select Discourses*, No. 7.

* There are three interpretations of ἱεροσυλεῖς (22) (1) "rob (heathen) temples." So Wilke, Meyer, Godet, Philippi, Alford, Conybeare and Howson, R. V. (2) "Rob the temple" (at Jerusalem, by embezzling or withholding the temple-tribute). So Hofmann, Ewald, Lange, Weiss. (3) "commit sacrilege," Calvin, Bengel. Luther, A. V. marg. of R.V. The contrast with ὁ βδελ, τὰ εἴδωλα strongly favors (1) which is adopted by Chrys. That such robbery had taken place among the Jews seems implied in Acts xix. 37, and is clearly referred to in Josephus' *Ant.* iv. 8, 10.—G. B. S.

[2] ἀπὸ τοῦ μείζονος. Perhaps "the more guilty," as having offended with greater advantages.

24

choice? For it takes place at an unripe age, and those in the wilderness too remained uncircumcised for a long time. And from many other points of view also, one might look at it as not necessary. And yet it is not on this foot that he rejects it, but upon the most proper ground, from the case of Abraham. For this is the most exceeding victory,—to take the very reason for showing it to be of small regard, whence it was held by them in reverence. Now he might have said that even the prophets call the Jews uncircumcised. But this is no disparagement of circumcision, but of those that hold ill to it. For what he aims at is to show that even in the very best life, it has not the least force. This is what he next proves. And here he does not bring forward the Patriarch, but having previously overturned it upon other grounds, he keeps him till afterwards, when he brings in what he has to say of faith, on the words—"How then was it reckoned" to Abraham? "when he was in circumcision, or in uncircumcision?" For so long as it is struggling against the Gentile and the uncircumcised, he is unwilling to say aught of this, lest he should be over irksome to them. But when it comes in opposition to the faith, then he disengages himself more completely for a combat with it. Up to the present point then it is uncircumcision that the contest is against, and this is why he advances in his discourse in a subdued tone, and says,

"For circumcision verily profiteth if thou keep the Law; but if thou be a breaker of the Law, thy circumcision is made uncircumcision." For here he speaks of two uncircumcisions, and two circumcisions, as also two laws. For there is a natural law and there is a written law. But there is one also between these, that by works. And see how he points these three out, and brings them before you. "For when the Gentiles," he says, "which have not the Law." What Law, say? The written one. "Do by nature the things of the Law." Of what Law? Of that by works. "These having not the Law." What Law? The written one. "Are a law unto themselves." How so? By using the natural law. "Who show the work of the Law." Of what law? Of that by actions. For that which is by writing lieth outside; but this is within, the natural one, and the other is in actions. And one the writing proclaims; and another, nature; and another, actions. Of this third there is need,[1] for the sake of which also those two exist, both the natural and the written. And if this be not present they are

of no good, but even very great harm. And to show this in the case of the natural he said, "For wherein thou judgest another, thou condemnest thyself." But of the written Law, thus—"Thou that preachest a man should not steal, dost thou steal? Thus also there are two uncircumcisions, one that of nature, and the second from conduct: and one circumcision in the flesh, and the other from the will. I mean for instance, a man has been circumcised upon the eighth day; this is circumcision of the flesh: a man has done all the Law bids him; this is circumcision of the mind which St. Paul requires above all, yea rather the Law also. See now how having granted it in words, he in deed does away with it. For he does not say the circumcision is superfluous, the circumcision is of no profit, of no use. But what saith he? "Circumcision verily profiteth if thou keepest the Law." (Deut. x. 16; xxx. 6.) He approves it so far, saying, I confess and deny not that the circumcision is honorable. But when? When it has the Law kept along with it.

"But if thou be a breaker of the Law, thy circumcision is made uncircumcision." He does not say, it is no more profitable, lest he should seem to insult it. But having stripped the Jew of it, he goes on to smite him. And this is no longer any insult to circumcision, but to him who through listlessness has lost the good of it. As then in the case of those who are in dignified stations and are after convicted of the greatest misdemeanors, the judges deprive them of the honors of their stations and then punish them; so has Paul also done. For after saying, if thou art a breaker of the Law, thy "circumcision is made uncircumcision," and having shown him to be uncircumcised, he condemns him after that without scruple.

Ver. 26. "Therefore if the uncircumcision keep the righteousness of the Law, shall not his uncircumcision be turned [2] into circumcision?"

See how he acts. He does not say that the uncircumcision overcomes circumcision (for this was highly grating to those who then heard him), but that the uncircumcision hath become circumcision. And he next enquires what circumcision is, and what uncircumcision and he says that circumcision is well doing and uncircumcision is evil doing. And having first transferred into the circumcision the uncircumcised, who has good deeds, and

---

[1] See Butler, *Anal. II.* i. v. fin.

[2] Four Mss. have μετατραπήσεται, both here and a little below: the others read λογισθήσεται here, and then contradict themselves, by putting τραπήσεται there. The old Edd. have περιτραπήσεται. Nearly all Mss. of the N. T. have λογισθήσεται: so we must either think with Heyse that St. Chrysostom expresses his definite opinion in favor of μετατρ. or with Matthiae that he made a slip of memory.

having thrust out the circumcised man that lived a corrupt life into the uncircumcision, he so gives the preference to the uncircumcised. And he does not say, To the uncircumcised, but goes on to the thing itself, speaking as follows: "Shall not his uncircumcision be turned into circumcision?" And he does not say "reckoned," but "turned to," which was more expressive. As also above he does not say thy circumcision is reckoned uncircumcision, but has been made so.

Ver. 27. "And shall not the uncircumcision which is by nature judge?"

You see, he recognizes two uncircumcisions, one from nature, and the other from the will. Here, however, he speaks of that from nature, but does not pause here, but goes on, "if it fulfil the Law, judge thee, who by the letter and circumcision dost transgress the Law?" See his exquisite judgment. He does not say, that the uncircumcision which is from nature shall judge the circumcision, but while where the victory had been, he brings in the uncircumcision, yet where the defeat is, he does not expose the circumcision as defeated; but the Jew himself who had it, and so by the wording spares offending his hearer. And he does not say, "thee that hast the Law and the circumcision," but yet more mildly, "thee who by the letter and circumcision dost transgress the Law." That is, such uncircumcision even stands up for the circumcision, for it has been wronged and comes to the Law's assistance, for it has been insulted, and obtains a notable triumph. For then is the victory decided, when it is not by Jew that Jew is judged, but by the uncircumcised; as when he says, "The men of Nineveh shall rise in judgment against this generation, and shall condemn it." (Matt. xii. 41.) It is not then the Law that he dishonors (for he reverences it greatly), but him that does disgrace to the Law. Next, having settled these grounds clearly, he goes on confidently to define what the Jew really is; and he shows that it is not the Jew, nor the circumcision, but he that is no Jew, and uncircumcised, whom he is rejecting. And he seemeth indeed to stand up in its behalf, but yet does away with the opinion regarding it, securing men's concurrence by the conclusion he comes to. For he shows not only that there is no difference between the Jew and the uncircumcised, but that the uncircumcised has even the advantage, if he take heed to himself, and that it is he that is really the Jew; and so he says:

Ver. 28. "For he is not a Jew which is one outwardly."

Here he attacks them as doing all things for show.

Ver. 29. "But he is a Jew which is one inwardly; and circumcision is that of the heart, in the spirit, and not in the letter."

By saying this he sets aside all things bodily. For the circumcision is outwardly, and the sabbaths and the sacrifices and purifications: all of which he hints in a single word, when he says, "For he is not a Jew which is one outwardly." But since much was made of the circumcision, inasmuch[1] as even the sabbath gave way to it (John vii. 22), he has good reason for aiming more especially against it. But when he has said "in the spirit" he thereafter paves the way for the conversation[2] of the Church, and introduces the faith. For it too is in the heart and spirit and hath its praise of God. And how cometh he not to show that the Gentile which doeth aright is not inferior to the Jew which doeth aright, but that the Gentile which doeth aright is better than the Jew which breaketh the Law? It was that he might make the victory an undoubted one. For when this is agreed upon, of necessity the circumcision of the flesh is set aside, and the need of a good life is everywhere demonstrated. For when the Greek is saved without these, but the Jew with these is yet punished, Judaism stands by doing nothing. And by Greek he again means not the idolatrous Greek, but the religious and virtuous, and free from all legal observances.

Chap. iii. ver. 1. "What advantage then hath the Jew?"*

Since he has set all aside, the hearing, the teaching, the name of the Jew, the circumcision, and all the other particulars by his saying that "he is not a Jew which is one outwardly, but he which is one inwardly;" he

---

[1] It might be observed, that all St. Paul's reasoning here and to the Galatians holds against circumcision and the Sabbath alike.

[2] πολιτεία. We want a word to express at once the spiritual citizenship and the corresponding life.

* The passage iii. 1-8 considers four possible objections. (1) "This placing of Jews and Gentiles in the same condition, takes away all the theocratic prerogatives." (v. 1.) No, answers Paul, they have a great advantage as to light and privilege, though none as to righteousness. (v. 2.) (2) "They have the O. T. scriptures, you say; but what if those scriptures have not attained their end in bringing the Jews to believe in Jesus as the Messiah? If some have not believed, does not that render void God's promises to his people in the O. T., so that he is no longer bound by them?" (v. 3.) The answer is: "No, God is faithful to his promises in all conditions (v. 4). (3) "Then the unbelief of the Jews seems to be the occasion of eliciting God's faithfulness. The conclusion would be that falseness contributes to God's glory." To this Paul gives no specific reply but develops the argument so as to show that it leads to a (5) position: "Let us do evil that good may come." (v. 8.) He thinks it enough to exhibit the logical conclusion of such an objection. It is enough to know that it obliterates all moral distinctions and impugns the justice of God. Paul might have shown that from God's overruling of sin to his praise the approval of sin does not follow. But he is content to make it clear that the objection is inconsistent with a righteous judgment of the world.—G. B. S.

next sees an objection which starts up, and against this makes his stand. Now what is this objection? If, he means, these things are no use, what reason was there for that nation being called, and the circumcision too being given? What does he then and how does he solve it? By the same means as he did before : for as there, he told, not of their praises, but the benefits of God ; nor their well doings (for to be called a Jew and to know His Will and to approve the things which are more excellent, was no well doing of their own, but came of the grace of God : and this the Prophet also says, upbraiding them ; " He hath not done so to any nation, neither hath he showed His judgments unto them ; " (Ps. cxlvii. 20.) and Moses again ; " Ask now whether there hath been any such thing as this ? " he says, " did ever people hear the voice of God speaking out of the midst of the fire, and live ? ") (Deut. iv. 32, 33), this then he does here also. For as, when speaking of circumcision, he did not say, Circumcision is valueless without a good life, but, Circumcision is of value with a good life, pointing out the same thing but in a more subdued tone. And again he does not say, If thou be a breaker of the Law, thou who art circumcised art no whit profited, but " thy circumcision is made uncircumcision : " and after this again, " the uncircumcision," saith he, shall " judge," not the circumcision, but " thee that dost transgress the Law," so sparing the things of the Law, and smiting the persons. So he doth here also. For after setting before himself this objection, and saying, " what advantage then hath the Jew?" he says not, None, but he concurs with the statement, and confutes it again by the sequel, and shows that they were even punished owing to this preëminence. And how he does so, I will tell you when I have stated the objection. "What advantage then," he says, " hath the Jew," or " what profit is there of circumcision ? "

Ver. 2. "Much every way : chiefly, because that they were entrusted with the oracles of God."

Do you see that, as I said above, it is not their well doings, but the benefits of God, that he everywhere counts up? And what is the word ἐπιστεύθησαν? (they were trusted.) It means, that they had the Law put into their hands because He held them[1] to be of so much account that He entrusted to them oracles which came down from above. I know indeed that some take the " entrusted " not of the Jews, but of the oracles, as much as to

say, the Law was believed in. But the context does not admit of this being held good. For in the first place he is saying this with a view to accuse them, and to show that, though in the enjoyment of many a blessing from above, they yet showed great ingratitude. Then, the context also makes this clear. For he goes on to say, " For what if some did not believe ? " If they did not believe, how do some say, the oracles were believed in ? [2] What does he mean then ? Why that God entrusted the same to them, and not that they trusted to the oracles : [3] how else will the context make sense ? For he farther goes on to say,

Ver. 3. " For what if some did not believe ? " [4]

And what comes next makes the same point clear. For he again adds and follows ; " Shall their unbelief make the faith of God without effect ? "

Ver. 4. " God forbid." The word ἐπιστεύθησαν, then, proclaims God's gift.

And I would have you here also note his judgment. For again he does not bring in his accusation of them on his own part, but as it were by way of objection, as if he said, But perhaps you will say, ' What then is the use of this circumcision since they used it not as was fitting, since they were trusted with the Law and were unfaithful to the trust ? ' And hitherto he is not a severe accuser, but as if to clear God of complaints against Him, he by this means turns the whole of the accusation round upon themselves. For why, he would say, do you complain that they did not believe ? and how doth this affect God ? For as for His benefit, doth the ingratitude of those benefited overturn it ? Or doth it make the honor to be no honor ? For this is what the words, " Shall their unfaithfulness make the faith of God without effect," amount to. " God forbid." As if one should say, I have honored such an one. And if he did not receive the honor, this gives no ground for accusing me, nor impairs my kindness, but shows his want of feeling. But Paul does not say this merely, but what is much more. That not only does their unbelief not leave the soil of complaint upon God, but even shows His honor and love of man to be the greater, in that He is seen to have bestowed honor upon one who would dishonor Him. See how he has brought them

---

[1] See Gen. xviii. 19 ; Deut. iv. 37, and x. 15.

[2] For this use of the word, see 1 Tim. iii. 16.
[3] Field reads λόγοις " His words: " probably by a misprint.
[4] A practical, not a theoretical unbelief. It might be clearer to use the word " unfaithful " throughout, but that ἀπιστεῖν is treated as the exact negative of πιστεύειν: in fact we cannot translate idiomatically all that either St. Paul or St. Chrysostom has to say of πίστις, without using the three words " faith " " trust " and " belief " for it and its correlatives.

out guilty of misdemeanors by means of what they gloried in ; forasmuch as the honor with which God treated them was so great, that even when He saw what would come thereof, He withheld not His good-will toward them! Yet they made the honors bestowed on them a means of insulting Him that Honor them! Next, since he said, "For what if some did not believe?" (while clearly it was all of them that did not believe,) lest by speaking here too as the history allowed him, he should seem to be a severe accuser of them like an enemy, he puts that, which really took place, in the method of reasoning and syllogism, saying as follows: "Yea, let God be true, but every man a liar." What he says is something of this sort. I do not mean, he says, that some did not believe, but if you will, suppose that all were unbelieving, so waiving what really happened, to fall in with the objector, that he might seem overbearing or to be suspected. Well, he says, in this way God is the more justified. What does the word justified mean? That, if there could be a trial and an examination of the things He had done for the Jews, and of what had been done on their part towards Him, the victory would be with God, and all the right on His side. And after showing this clearly from what was said before, he next introduces the Prophet also as giving his approval to these things, and saying, "that Thou mightest be justified in Thy sayings, and clear when Thou art judged." (Ps. li. 4.) He then for His part did everything, but they were nothing the better even for this. Then he brings forward after this another objection that arises, and says,

Ver. 5. "But if our unrighteousness commend the righteousness of God, what shall we say? is God unrighteous Who taketh vengeance? I speak as a man."

Ver. 6. "God forbid."

He solves one perplexity by another again. Yet as this is not clear, we must needs declare it more clearly. What is it then he means? God honored the Jews: they did despite to Him. This gives Him the victory, and shows the greatness of His love towards man, in that He honored them even such as they were. Since then, he means, we did despite to Him and wronged Him, God by this very thing became victorious, and His righteousness was shown to be clear.[1] Why then (a man may say) am I to be punished, who have been the cause of His victory by the despite I did Him? Now how does he meet this? It is, as I was

saying, by another absurdity again. For if it were you, he says, that were the cause of the victory, and after this are punished, the thing is an act of injustice. But if He is not unjust, and yet you are punished, then you are no more the cause of the victory. And note his apostolic reverence; (or caution : εὐλάβεια); for after saying, "Is God unrighteous Who taketh vengeance?" he adds, "I speak as a man." As if, he means, any body were to argue in the way men reason. For what things seem with us to be justice, these the just judgment of God far exceedeth, and has certain other unspeakable grounds for it. Next, since it was indistinct, he says the same thing over again :

Ver. 7. "For if the truth of God hath more abounded through my lie unto His glory : why yet am I also judged as a sinner?"

For if God, he means is shown to be a Lover of man, and righteous, and good, by your acts of disobedience, you ought not only to be exempt from punishment but even to have good done unto you. But if so, that absurdity will be found to result, which is in circulation with so many, that good comes of evil, and that evil is the cause of good; and one of the two is necessary, either that He be clearly unjust in punishing, or that if He punish not, it is from our vices that He hath the victory. And both of these are absurd to a degree. And himself meaning to show this too, he introduces the Greeks (i. e. heathens) as the fathers of these opinions, thinking it enough to allege against what he has mentioned the character of the persons who say these things. For then they used to say in ridicule of us, "let us do evil that good may come." And this is why he has stated it clearly in the following language.

Ver. 8. "If [2] not (as some affirm that we say,) Let us do evil that good may come? Whose damnation is just."

For whereas Paul said,[3] "where sin abounded grace did much more abound" (Rom. v. 20), in ridicule of him and perverting what he said to another meaning, they said, We must cling to vice that we may get what is good. But Paul said not so; however[4] to correct this notion it is that he says, "What then? shall we continue in sin that grace may abound? God forbid!" (ib. vi. 1, 2.) For I said it, he means, of the times which are past, not that we should make this a practice. To lead them away then from this suspicion, he

---

[1] Field thinks that St. Chrysostom wrote "Therefore if, because we did despite to Him . . . . . . was shown to be clear, why am I to be punished," etc.? Heyse would have "Then, since through our despite and wrong God became victorious. . . . why," etc.?

[2] So Field with most Mss. and Interp.
[3] ἔλεγεν. St. Chrysostom treats it as his habitual teaching, so that it had been already misrepresented, though not yet embodied in this Epistle.
[4] γοῦν. He is evidently aiming at some who still used such reasonings.

said, that henceforth this was even impossible. For "how shall we," he says, "that are dead unto sin, live any longer therein?" Against the Greeks then he inveighs (κατέδραμεν) without difficulty. For their life was exceeding abandoned. But of the Jews, even if their life seemed to have been careless, still they had great means of cloaking these things in the Law and circumcision, and the fact of God having conversed with them, and their being the teachers of all. And this is why he strips them even of these, and shows that for these they were the more punished, and this is the conclusion to which he has here drawn his discussion. For if they be not punished, he would say, for so doing, that blasphemous language—let us do evil that good may come—must necessarily gain currency. But if this be impious, and they who hold this language shall be punished (for this he declared by saying, "whose damnation is just"), it is plain that they are punished. For if they who speak it be deserving of vengeance, much more are they who act it, but if deserving thereof, it is as having done sin. For it is not man that punishes them, that any one should suspect the sentence, but God, that doeth all things righteously. But if they are righteously punished, it is unrighteously that they, who make ridicule of us, said what they did. For God did and doth everything, that our conversation might shine forth and be upright on every side.

Let us then not be listless; for so we shall be able to recover the Greeks also from their error. But when we are in words lovers of wisdom, but in deeds behave unseemly, with what looks shall we face them? with what lips shall we discourse concerning doctrines? For he[1] will say to each of us, How can you that have failed in what is less, claim to teach me about what is greater? you who as yet have not learnt that covetousness is a vice, how can you be wise upon the things in heaven? But do you know that it is a vice? Then, the charge is the greater, because you transgress knowingly. And why speak I of the Greek, for even our laws allow us not to speak thus boldly when our life has become abandoned. For to "the sinner," it says, "saith God, what hast thou to do to declare my statutes?" (Ps. l. 16.) There was a time when the Jews were carried away captive, and when the Persians were urgent with them, and called upon them to sing those divine songs unto them, they said, "How shall we sing the Lord's song in a strange land?" (Ps. cxxxvii. 4.) Now if it were un-

lawful to sing the oracles of God in a strange land, much less might the estranged soul do it. For estranged[2] the merciless soul is. If the Law made those who were captives and had become slaves to men in a strange land, to sit in silence; much more is it right for those who are slaves to sin and are in an alien community (πολιτεία) to have a curb upon their mouths. And however they had their instruments then. For it says, "Upon the willows in the midst thereof did we hang our instruments," but still they might not sing. And so we also, though we have a mouth and tongue, which are instruments of speech, have no right to speak boldly, so long as we be slaves to what is more tyrannical than any barbarian, sin. For tell me what have you to say to the Greek, if you plunder, and be covetous? will you say, Forsake idolatry, acknowledge God, and draw not near to gold and silver? Will he not then make a jest of you, and say, Talk to thyself first in this way? For it is not the same thing for a Gentile to practise idolatry, and a Christian to commit this same (4 Mss. om. "same") sin. For how are we to draw others away from that idolatry if we draw not ourselves away from this? For we are nearer related to ourselves[3] than our neighbor is, and so when we persuade not ourselves, how are we to persuade others? For if he that doth not rule well over his own house, will not take care of the Church either (1 Tim. iii. 5), how shall he that doth not rule even over his own soul be able to set others right? Now do not tell me, that you do not worship an image of gold, but make this clear to me, that you do not do those things which gold bids you. For there be different kinds of idolatry, and one holds mammon lord, and another his belly his god, and a third some other most baneful lust. But, "you do not sacrifice oxen to them as the Gentiles do." Nay, but what is far worse, you butcher your own soul. But "you do not bow the knee and worship." Nay, but with greater obedience you do all that they command you, whether it be your belly, or money, or the tyranny of lust. For this is just what makes Gentiles disgusting, that they made gods of our passions; calling lust Venus, and anger Mars, and drunkenness Bacchus. If then you do not grave images as did they, yet do you with great eagerness bow under the very same passions, when you make the members

---

[1] i. e. The Greek, see a few lines below. Savile's punctuation was first corrected by the Benedictines.

[2] Βάρβαρος, Though this word is not equivalent to Barbarian, it has force enough to give a fitness to the term "merciless." St. Chrysostom excels in these side-strokes, which he so much admires too in the Apostle.

[3] κάκιστος ὁ πρὸς ἑαυτὸν χρώμενος τῇ μοχθηρίᾳ, etc. Arist. Eth. v. 1.

of Christ members of an harlot, and plunge yourself into the other deeds of iniquity. (1 Cor. vi. 15.) I therefore exhort you to lay to heart the exceeding unseemliness hereof, and to flee from idolatry :—for so doth Paul name covetousness—and to flee not only covetousness in money, but that in evil desire, and that in clothing, and that in food, and that in everything else : since the punishment we shall have to suffer if we obey not God's laws is much severer. For, He says, "the servant that knew his Lord's will," and did it not, "shall be beaten with many stripes." (Luke xii. 47.) With a view then to escaping from this punishment, and being useful both to others and to ourselves, let us drive out all iniquity from our soul and choose virtue. For so shall we attain to the blessings which are to come, whereto may it be granted us all to attain by the grace and love toward man, etc.

HOMILY VII.

ROM. III. 9–18.

"What then have we more [1] than they? [*] For we have proved both Jews and Gentiles, that they are all under sin. As it is written, There is none righteous, no, not one : there is none that understandeth, there is none that seeketh after God. They are all gone out of the way, they are together become unprofitable; there is none that doeth good, no not one. Their throat is an open sepulchre; with their tongues have they used deceit; the poison of asps is under their lips : whose mouth is full of cursing and bitterness : their feet are swift to shed blood : destruction and misery are in their ways : and the way of peace have they not known : there is no fear of God before their eyes."

HE had accused the Gentiles, he had accused the Jews; it came next in order to mention the righteousness which is by faith. For if the law of nature availed not, and the written Law was of no advantage, but both weighed down those that used them not aright, and made it plain that they were worthy of greater punishment, then after this the salvation which is by grace was necessary. Speak then of it, O Paul, and display it. But as yet he does not venture, as having an eye to the violence of the Jews, and so turns

afresh to his accusation of them ; and first he brings in as accuser, David speaking of the same things at length, which Isaiah mentioned all in short compass, so furnishing a strong curb for them, so that they might not bound off, nor any of his hearers, while the matters of faith were laid open to them, might after this start away; being beforehand safely held down by the accusations of the prophets. For there are three excesses which the prophet lays down ; he says that all of them together did evil, and that they did not do good indifferently with evil, but that they followed after wickedness alone, and followed it also with all earnestness. And next that they should not say, "What then, if these things were said to others ? " he goes on :

Ver. 19. "Now we know that what things soever the Law saith, it saith to them who are under the Law."

This then is why, next to Isaiah, who confessedly aimed at them, he brought in David ; that he might show that these things also belonged to the same subject. For what need was there, he means, that a prophet who was sent for your correction should accuse other people. For neither was the Law given to any else than you. And for what reason did he not say, we know that what things soever the prophet saith, but what things soever the Law saith ? It is because Paul uses to call the whole Old Testament the Law. And in another place he says, "Do ye not hear the Law, that Abraham had two sons?" (Gal. iv. 21, 22.) And here he calls the Psalm the Law [2] when he says, "We know that what things soever the Law saith, it saith to them who are under the Law. Next he shows that

---

[1] So St. Chrysostom here and in the next homily, but in both places some Mss. (and Vulg. ante Field) had inserted the common reading of the text of the N. T. "what then? are we better than they? No, in no wise."

[*] The meaning of προεχόμεθα here is much disputed. What is its subject? Most agree (vs. Olshausen, Reiche) that it is Ἰουδαῖοι. Is προεχ. middle or passive? If middle. it may mean (1) Do we hold (a place) before them? Are we superior to them (the Gentiles) as respects the condition of sinfulness? So Vulgate ("præcellimus") Luther, Calvin, Bengel, Tholuck, Baur, De Wette, Alford, Weiss ; or (2) Do we hold before us (any protection)? Have we any excuse or pretext? So Meyer, Godet, Schaff, on the ground that (1) is against the admitted advantage of the few (vv. 1, 2). If passive, it can mean (a) Are we held superior to them ? This is substantially the same as (1) or (b) Are we surpassed by them? This is the sense given in the trans. of the R. V. : " Are we in worse case than they ? " It connects v. 9 immediately with the special points of v. 1-8. It seems to me that it is better to suppose that he here breaks away from these special objections and recurs to the larger subject. In this view the προ in compos. points back to such passages as i. 18-32 ; ii. 15 and 17-29. The argument is: "We have established the sinfulness of all ; therefore we Jews have no advantage in relation to sin, repentance and justification."—G. B. S.

[2] The term Law was commonly applied to all the Pentateuch by Jewish writers: but to the Psalms not so. They, however, viewed the whole Old Testament as an evolved form of the Law.

neither are these things he said merely for accusation's sake, but that he[1] may again be paving the way for faith. So close is the relationship of the Old Testament with the New, since even the accusations and reproofs were entirely with a view to this, that the door of faith might open brightly upon them that hear it. For since it was the principal bane of the Jews that they were so conceited with themselves (which thing he mentioned as he went on, " how that being ignorant of the righteousness of God, and going about to establish their own righteousness, they submitted not themselves to the righteousness of God ") (Rom. x. 3), the Law and the Prophet by being beforehand with them cast down their high thoughts, and laid low their conceit, that being brought to a consideration of their own sins, and having emptied out the whole of their unreasonableness, and seen themselves in danger of the last extremity, they might with much earnestness run unto Him Who offered them the remission of their sins, and accept grace through faith. And this it is then which St. Paul hints even here, when he says,

" Now we know that what things soever the Law saith, it saith to them who are under the Law, that every mouth may be stopped, and all the world may become guilty before God."

Here then he exhibits them as destitute of the boldness of speech which comes of works, and only using a parade of words and behaving in a barefaced way. And this is why he uses so literal an expression, saying, " that every mouth may be stopped," so pointing out the barefaced and almost uncontrollable pomposity of their language, and that their tongue was now curbed in the strictest sense. For as an unsupportable torrent, so had it been borne along. But the prophet stopped it. And when Paul saith, " that every mouth may be stopped," what he means is, not that the reason of their sinning was that their mouth might be stopped, but that the reason of their being reproved was that they might not commit this very sin in ignorance. " And all the world may become guilty before God." He does not say the Jew, but the whole of mankind.[2] For the phrase, " that every mouth may be stopped," is the language of a person hinting at them, although he has not stated it clearly, so as to prevent the language being too harsh. But the words " that all the

world may become guilty before God," are spoken at once both of Jews and of Greeks. Now this is no slight thing with a view to take down their unreasonableness. Since even here they have no advantage over the Gentiles, but are alike given up as far as salvation is concerned. For he would be in strict propriety called a guilty person, who cannot help himself to any excuse, but needeth the assistance of another : and such was the plight of all of us, in that we had lost the things pertaining to salvation.

Ver. 20. " For by the Law is the knowledge of sin."

He springs upon the Law again, with forbearance however (for what he says is not an accusation of it, but of the listlessness of the Jews). Yet nevertheless he has been earnest here with a view (as he was going to introduce his discourse about faith) to show its utter feebleness. For if thou boastest in the Law, he means, it puts thee to the greater shame : it solemnly parades forth your sins before you. Only he does not word it in this harsh way, but again in a subdued tone ; " For by the Law is the knowledge of sin." And so the punishment is greater, but[3] that because of the Jew. For the Law accomplished the disclosure of sin to you, but it was your duty then to flee it. Since then you have not fled it, you have pulled the punishment more sorely on yourself, and the good deed of the Law has been made to you a supply of greater vengeance. Now then having added to their fear, he next brings in the things of grace, as having brought them to a strong desire of the remission of their sins, and says,

Ver. 21. " But now the righteousness of God without the Law is manifested." *

Here he utters a great thing, and such as needed much proof. For if they that lived in the Law not only did not escape punishment, but were even the more weighed down thereby, how without the Law is it possible not only to escape vengeance, but even to be

---

[1] So Field with 2 Mss: others " that the Word," one Mss. and Vulg. " that the Law."

[2] ἡ φύσις, here used probably for the particular nature or kind in question, viz. the human. Somewhat in the same manner it is used of individual beings. For the several uses of the term, see Arist. *Metaph.* 4, where he calls this use metaphorical.

[3] Mss. " yet not owing to the feebleness of the Law, but to the listlessness of the Jews."

* With iii. 21 begins the great central argument of the epistle : the positive development of the doctrine of justification by faith. He had prepared the way for this negatively by showing that all men were sinners and could not hope for justification on the condition of obedience to the law of God. This he proved in regard to the Gentiles in i. 18-32, and in regard to the Jews in ii. 1–iii. 20. Having now showed that justification cannot be by law he proceeds to prove that it is by faith. This central argument extends to the end of chap. viii. It may be analyzed as follows ; (1) General introductory statement, iii. 21-31. (2) O. T. proof, iv. (3) Consequences of justification, v. 1-11. (4) Universality of the principles of sin and grace, showed by the parallel between Adam and Christ, v. 12-21. (5) Objections answered and false inferences refuted, vi. vii. (6) Triumphant conclusion ; the blessedness of justification, viii. This argument concludes the doctrinal portion of the Epistle so far as the question of justification is concerned. chaps. ix.-xi. treat of the rejection of the Jews and may be considered a kind of doctrinal appendix to the main argument. The remaining chaps. (xii.-xvi.) are chiefly practical. —G. B. S.

justified? For he has here set down two high points,[1] the being justified, and the obtaining these blessings, without the Law. And this is why he does not say righteousness simply, but the righteousness of God, so by the worthiness of the Person displaying the greater degree of the grace, and the possibility of the promise. For to Him all things are possible. And he does not say, "was given," but "is manifested," so cutting away the accusation of novelty. For that which is manifested, is so as being old, but concealed. And it is not this only, but the sequel that shows that this is no recent thing. For after saying, "is manifested," he proceeds :

"Being witnessed by the Law and the Prophets."

Do not be troubled, he means, because it has but now been given, nor be affrighted as though at a thing new and strange. For of old both the Law and the Prophets foretold it. And some passages he has pointed out in the course of this argument, and some he will shortly, having in what came before brought in Habakkuk as saying, "the just shall live by faith" (i. 17), but in what comes after, Abraham and David, as themselves also conversing with us about these things. Now the regard they had for these persons was great, for one was a patriach and a prophet, and the other a king and a prophet: and further the promises about these things had come to both of them. And this is why Matthew in the first beginning of his Gospel mentions both of these first, and then brings forward in order the forefathers. For after saying, "the Book of the Generation of Jesus Christ" (Matt. i. 1), he does not wait after Abraham to name Isaac also and Jacob, but mentions David along with (5 Mss. "after ") Abraham. And what is wonderful indeed is, that he has even set David before Abraham speaking on this wise, "the Son of David, the Son of Abraham," and then begins the catalogue of Isaac and Jacob, and all the rest in order. And this is why the Apostle here keeps presenting them in turns, and speaks of the righteousness of God being witnessed by the Law and the Prophets. Then that no one should say, How are we to be saved without contributing anything at all to the object in view? he shows that we also offer no small matter toward this, I mean our faith. Therefore after saying, "the righteousness of God," he adds straightway, "by faith unto all and upon all that believe."

Here again the Jew is alarmed by his not having anything better than the rest, and being numbered with the whole world. Now that he may not feel this, he again lowers him with fear by adding, " For there is no difference, for all have sinned." For tell me not that it is such and such a Greek,[2] such and such a Scythian, such and such a Thracian, for all are in the same plight. For even if you have received the Law, one thing alone is there which you have learnt from the Law— to know sin, not to flee from it. Next, that they may say, "even if we have sinned, still it is not in the same way that they did," he added, "and have come short of the glory of God." So that even if you have not done the same sins as others, still you are alike bereft of the glory, since you belong to those who have offended, and he that hath offended belongeth not to such as are glorified, but to such as are put to shame. Yet, be not afraid : for the reason of my saying this was not that I might thrust you into despair, but that I might show the love of the Lord (Δεσπότου) toward man : and so he goes on ;

Ver. 24, 25. "Being justified freely by His grace through the redemption that is in Christ Jesus : Whom God hath set forth to be a propitiation through faith[3] in His blood, to declare His righteousness."[4]

See by how many proofs he makes good what was said. First, from the worthiness of the person, for it is not a man who doeth these things, that He should be too weak for it, but God all-powerful. For it is to God, he says, that the righteousness belongs. Again, from the Law and the Prophets. For you need not be afraid at hearing the "without the Law," inasmuch as the Law itself approves this. Thirdly, from the sacrifices under the old dispensation. For it was on this ground that he said, " In His blood," to call to their minds those sheep and calves. For if the sacrifices of things without reason, he means, cleared from sin, much more would this blood. And he does not say barely λυτρώσεως, but ἀπολυτρώσεως, entire redemption, to show[5] that we should come no more into such slavery. And for this same reason he calls it a propitiation, to show that if the type had such force, much more would the reality display the same. But to show again that it was no novel thing or recent, he says, "fore-ordained" (Auth. Version marg.) ; and by saying God "fore-or-

---

[1] ἄκρα high or excellent things ; thus Longinus. Or perhaps "terms." See Arist. *Anal. Pr.* l. i. where this use of the word is explained.

[2] 4 Mss. read ὁ δεῖνα Ἕλλην, etc. for ὁ δεῖνα ὁ Ἕλλην, making the sense, do not say (in contempt) "such an one is a Greek! such an one a Scythian ! " etc.

[3] So Sav. Mor. Ben., against the Mss. and the Ed. of Verona, which omits these words.

[4] v. 26, 3 P. Mss. ἐν τῷ νῦν καιρῷ.

[5] 4 Mss. add, "to show that this was so brought about."

dained," and showing that the good deed is the Father's, he showeth it to be the Son's also. For the Father "fore-ordained," but Christ in His own blood wrought the whole aright.

"To declare His righteousness." What is declaring of righteousness? Like the declaring of His riches, not only for Him to be rich Himself, but also to make others rich, or of life, not only that He is Himself living, but also that He makes the dead to live; and of His power, not only that He is Himself powerful, but also that He makes the feeble powerful. So also is the declaring of His righteousness not only that He is Himself righteous, but that He doth also make them that are filled with the putrefying sores (κατασαπέντας) of sin suddenly righteous. And it is to explain this, viz. what is "declaring," that he has added, "That He might be just, and the justifier of him which believeth in Jesus." Doubt not then: for it is not of works, but of faith: and shun not the righteousness of God, for it is a blessing in two ways; because it is easy, and also open to all men. And be not abashed and shamefaced. For if He Himself openly declareth (ἐνδείκνυται) Himself to do so, and He, so to say, findeth a delight and a pride therein, how comest thou to be dejected and to hide thy face at what thy Master glorieth in? Now then after raising his hearers' expectations by saying that what had taken place was a declaring of the righteousness of God, he next by fear urges him on that is tardy and remissful about coming; by speaking as follows:

"On account of the relaxing[1] of sins that were before." Do you see how often he keeps reminding them of their transgressions? Before, he did it by saying, "through the Law is the knowledge of sin;" and after by saying, "that all have sinned," but here in yet stronger language. For he does not say for the sins, but, "for the relaxing," that is, the deadness. For there was no longer any hope of recovering health, but as the paralyzed body needed the hand from above, so doth the soul which hath been deadened. And what is indeed worse, a thing which he sets down as a charge, and points out that it is a greater accusation. Now what is this? That the last state was incurred in the forbearance of God. For you cannot plead, he means, that you have not enjoyed much forbearance and goodness. But the words "at this time" are those of one who is pointing out the greatness of the power (Sav. forbearance) and love toward man. For after we had given all over, (he would say,) and it were time to sentence us, and the evils were waxed great and the sins were in their full, then He displayed His own power, that thou mightest learn how great is the abundancy of righteousness with Him. For this, had it taken place at the beginning, would not have had so wonderful and unusual an appearance as now, when every sort of cure was found unavailing.

Ver. 27. "Where is boasting then? it is excluded," he says. "By what law? of works? Nay, but by the law of faith."

Paul is at great pains to show that faith is mighty to a degree which was never even fancied of the Law. For after he had said that God justifieth man by faith, he grapples with the Law again. And he does not say, where then are the well doings of the Jews? where their righteous dealing? but, "where is then the boasting?" so taking every opportunity of showing, that they do but use great words, as though they had somewhat more than others, and have no work to show. And after saying, "Where then is the boasting?" he does not say, it is put out of sight and hath come to an end, but "it is excluded," which word rather expresses unseasonableness; since the reason for it is no more. For as when the judgment is come they that would repent have not any longer the season for it, thus now the sentence being henceforth passed, and all being upon the point of perishing, and He being at hand Who by grace would break these terrors, they had no longer the season for making a plea of amelioration wrought by the Law. For if it were right to strengthen themselves upon these things, it should have been before His coming. But now that He who should save by faith was come, the season for those efforts[2] was taken from them. For since all were convicted, He therefore saveth by grace. And this is why He is come but now, that they may not say, as they would had He come at the first, that it was possible to be saved by the Law and by our own labors and well-doings. To curb therefore this their effrontery, He waited a long time: so that after they were by every argument clearly convicted of inability to help themselves, He then saved them by His grace. And for this reason too when he had said above, "To declare His righteousness," he added, "at this time." If any then were to gainsay, they do the same as if a person who after committing great sins was unable to defend himself in court, but was condemned

---

[1] πάρεσιν. Our translation cannot be kept without losing St. Chrysostom's meaning. He takes this word in a medical sense, for the cessation of vital energy. It was sometimes used thus, or for paralysis. It does not occur elsewhere in the New Testament; the usual word for remission is ἄφεσις.

[2] Or "pleading the same."

and going to be punished, and then being by the royal pardon forgiven, should have the effrontery after his forgiveness to boast and say that he had done no sin. For before the pardon came, was the time to prove it: but after it came he would no longer have the season for boasting. And this happened in the Jews' case. For since they had been traitors to themselves, this was why He came, by His very coming doing away their boasting. For he who saith that he is a "teacher of babes, and maketh his boast in the Law," and styles himself "an instructor of the foolish," if alike with them he needed a teacher and a Saviour, can no longer have any pretext for boasting. For if even before this, the circumcision was made uncircumcision, much rather was it now, since it is cast out from both periods. But after saying that "it was excluded," he shows also, how. How then does he say it was excluded? "By what law? of works? Nay, but by the law of faith." See he calls the faith also a law, delighting to keep to the names, and so allay the seeming novelty. But what is the "law of faith?" It is, being saved by grace. Here he shows God's power, in that He has not only saved, but has even justified, and led them to boasting,[1] and this too without needing works, but looking for faith only. And in saying this he attempts to bring the Jew who has believed to act with moderation, and to calm him that hath not believed, in such way as to draw him on to his own view. For he that has been saved, if he be high-minded in that he abides by the Law, will be told that he himself has stopped his own mouth, himself has accused himself, himself has renounced claims to his own salvation, and has excluded boasting. But he that hath not believed again, being humbled by these same means, will be capable of being brought over to the faith. Do you see how great faith's preëminence is? How it hath removed us from the former things, not even allowing us to boast of them?

Ver. 28. "Therefore we conclude that a man is justified by faith without the deeds of the Law."

When he had shown that by faith they were superior to the Jews, then he goes on with great confidence to discourse upon it also, and what seemed therein to annoy he again heals up. For these two things were what confused the Jews; one, if it were possible for men, who with works were not saved, to be saved without them, and another, if it were just for the uncircumcised to enjoy the same blessings with those, who had during so long a period been nurtured in the Law; which last confused them more by far than the former. And on this ground having proved the former, he goes on to the other next, which perplexed the Jews so far, that they even complained on account of this position against Peter after they believed. What does he say then? "Therefore we conclude, that by faith a man is justified." He does not say, a Jew, or one under the Law, but after leading forth his discourse into a large room, and opening the doors of faith to the world, he says "a man," the name common to our race. And then having taken occasion from this, he meets an objection not set down. For since it was likely that the Jews, upon hearing that faith justifieth every man, would take it ill and feel offended, he goes on,

Ver. 29. "Is He the God of the Jews only?"

As if he said, On what foot does it then seem to you amiss that every man should be saved? Is God partial? So showing from this, that in wishing to flout the Gentiles, they are rather offering an insult to God's glory, if, that is, they would not allow Him to be the God of all. But if He is of all, then He taketh care of all; and if He care for all, then He saveth all alike by faith. And this is why he says, "Is He the God of the Jews only? is He not also of the Gentiles? Yes, of the Gentiles also." For He is not partial as the fables of the Gentiles (cf. Ov. Tr. I. ii. 5. sqq) are, but common to all, and One. And this is why he goes on,

Ver. 30. "Seeing it is one God."

That is, the same is the Master of both these and those. But if you tell me of the ancient state of things, then too the dealings of Providence were shared by both, although in diverse ways. For as to thee was given the written law, so to them was the natural; and they came short in nothing, if, that is, only they were willing, but were even able to surpass thee. And so he proceeds, with an allusion to this very thing, "Who shall justify the circumcision by faith, and the uncircumcision through faith," so reminding them of what he said before about uncircumcision and circumcision, whereby he showed that there was no difference.[2] But if then there was no difference, much less is there any now, And this accordingly he now establishes upon still clearer grounds, and so demonstrates,

---

[1] The term καυχᾶσθαι, here rendered boasting, is used in a good sense also, and sometimes rendered glorying in our Version. See Rom. v. 2, 3, 11 ; xv. 17; 1 Cor. i. 31; 2 Cor. x. 17; xii. 9; Gal. vi. 4 and 14 ; Phil. iii. 5 ; 1 Thess. ii. 19; James i. 9, etc.

[2] Field omits "there was no difference;" but most Mss. have the words; and at any rate they must be supplied.

that either of them stand alike in need of faith.

Ver. 31. "Do we then," he says, "make void the Law through faith? God forbid: yea, we establish the Law."

Do you see his varied and unspeakable judgment? For the bare use of the word "establish" shows that it was not then standing, but was worn out (καταλελυμένον). And note also Paul's exceeding power, and how superabundantly he maintains what he wishes. For here he shows that the faith, so far from doing any disparagement to the "Law," even assists it, as it on the other hand paved the way for the faith. For as the Law itself before bore witness to it (for he saith, "being witnessed by the Law and the Prophets"), so here this establisheth that, now that it is unnerved. And how did it establish? he would say. What was the object of the Law, and what the scope of all its enactments? Why, to make man righteous. But this it had no power to do. "For all," it says, "have sinned:" but faith when it came accomplished it. For when a man is once a believer, he is straightway justified. The intention then of the Law it did establish, and what all its enactments aim after, this hath it brought to a consummation. Consequently it has not disannulled, but perfected it. Here then three points he has demonstrated; first, that without the Law it is possible to be justified; next, that this the Law could not effect; and, that faith is not opposed to the Law. For since the chief cause of perplexity to the Jews was this, that the faith seemed to be in opposition to it, he shows more than the Jew wishes, that so far from being contrary, it is even in close alliance and coöperation with it, which was what they especially longed to hear proved.

But since after this grace, whereby we were justified, there is need also of a life suited to it, let us show an earnestness worthy the gift. And show it we shall, if we keep with earnestness charity, the mother of good deeds. Now charity is not bare words, or mere ways of speaking (προσρήσεις) to men, but a taking care (προστασία) of them, and a putting forth of itself by works, as, for instance, by relieving poverty, lending one's aid to the sick, rescuing from dangers, to stand by them that be in difficulties, to weep with them that weep, and to rejoice with them that rejoice. (Rom. xii. 15.) For even this last is a part of charity. And yet this seems a little thing, to be rejoicing with them that rejoice: nevertheless it is exceedingly great, and requireth for it the spirit of true wisdom. And we may find many that perform the more irksome part

(πεικρότερον), and yet want vigor for this. For many weep with them that weep, but still do not rejoice with them that rejoice, but are in tears when others rejoice; now this comes of grudging and envy. The good deed then of rejoicing when our brother rejoices is no small one, but even greater than the other: and haply not only greater than weeping with them that weep, but even than standing by them that are in danger. There are many, at all events, that have shared danger with men in danger, but were cut to the heart when they came into honor. So great is the tyranny of a grudging spirit! And yet the one is a thing of toils and labors, and this of choice and temper only. Yet at the same time many that have endured the harder task have not accomplished the one easier than it, but pine and consume away when they see others in honor, when a whole Church is benefited, by doctrine, or in any other fashion. And what can be worse than this? For such an one doth not any more fight with his brother, but with the will of God. Now consider this, and be rid of the disease: and even if you be unwilling to set your neighbor free, at least set yourself free from these countless evils. Why do you carry war into your own thoughts? Why fill your soul with trouble? why work up a storm? why turn things upside down? How will you be able, in this state of mind, to ask forgiveness of sins? For if those that allow not the things done against themselves to pass, neither doth He forgive, what forgiveness shall He grant to those who go about to injure those that have done them no injury? For this is a proof of the utmost wickedness. Men of this kind are fighting with the Devil, against the Church, and haply even worse than he. For him one can be on one's guard against. But these cloaking themselves under the mask of friendliness, secretly kindle the pile, throwing themselves the first into the furnace, and laboring under a disease not only unfit for pity, but even such as to meet with much ridicule. For why is it, tell me, that thou art pale and trembling and standing in fear? What evil has happened? Is it that thy brother is in honor, and looked up to, and in esteem? Why, thou oughtest to make chaplets, and rejoice, and glorify God, that thine own member is in honor and looked up to! But art thou pained that God is glorified?[1] Seest thou to what issue the war tends? But, some will say, it is not because God is glorified, but because my brother is. Yet through him the glory ascendeth up to God: and so will the war from thee do also.

---

[1] 4 Mss. add what madness doth not this exceed?

But it is not this, he will say, that grieves me, for I should wish God to be glorified by me. Well then! rejoice at thy brother's being in honor, and then glorified is God again through thee also; and[1] all will say, Blessed be God that hath His household so minded, wholly freed from envy, and rejoicing together at one another's goods! And why do I speak of thy brother? for if he were thy foe and enemy, and God were glorified through him, a friend shouldest thou make of him for this reason. But thou makest thy friend an enemy because God is glorified by his being in honor. And were any one to heal thy body when in evil plight, though he were an enemy, thou wouldest count him thenceforward among the first of thy friends: and dost thou reckon him that gladdens the countenance of Christ's Body, that is, the Church, and is thy friend, to be yet an enemy? How else then couldest thou show war against Christ? For this cause, even if a man do miracles, have celibacy to show, and fasting, and lying on the bare ground, and doth by this virtue advance even to the angels, yet shall he be most accursed of all, while he has this defect, and shall be a greater breaker of the Law than the adulterer, and the fornicator, and the robber, and the violator of supulchres. And, that no one may condemn this language of hyperbole, I should be glad to put this question to you. If any one were come with fire and mattock, and were destroying and burning this House, and digging down this Altar, would not each one of those here stone him with stones as accursed and a law-breaker? What then, if one were to bring a flame yet more consuming than that fire, I mean envy, that doth not ruin the buildings of stone nor dig down an Altar of gold, but subverteth and scornfully marreth what is far more precious than either walls or Altar, the Teachers' building, what sufferance would he deserve? For let no one tell me, that he has often endeavored and been unable: for it is from the spirit that the actions are judged. For Saul did kill David, even though he did not hit him. (1 Sam. xix. 10.) Tell me, dost thou not perceive that thou art plotting against the sheep of Christ when thou warrest with His Shepherd? those sheep for whom also Christ shed His Blood, and bade us both to do and to suffer all things? Dost thou not remind thyself that thy Master sought thy glory and not His own, but thou art seeking not that of thy Master but thine own? And yet if thou didst see His then thou wouldst have obtained thine own also. But by seeking thine

own before His, thou wilt not ever gain even this.

What then will be the remedy? Let us all join in prayer, and let us lift up our voice with one accord in their behalf as for those possessed, for indeed these are more wretched than they, inasmuch as their madness is of choice. For this affliction needeth prayer and much entreaty. For if he that loveth not his brother, even though he empty out his money, yea, and have the glory of martyrdom, is no whit advantaged; consider what punishment the man deserves who even wars with him that hath not wronged him in anything; he is even worse than the Gentiles: for if to love them that love us does not let us have any advantage over them, in what grade shall he be placed, tell me, that envieth them that love him? For envying is even worse than warring; since he that warreth, when the cause of the war is at an end, puts an end to his hatred also: but the grudger would never become a friend. And the one shows an open kind of battle, the other a covert: and the one often has a reasonable cause to assign for the war, the other, nothing else but madness, and a Satanic spirit. To what then is one to compare a soul of this kind? to what viper? to what asp? to what canker-worm? to what scorpion? since there is nothing so accursed or so pernicious as a soul of this sort. For it is this, it is this, that hath subverted the Churches, that hath gendered the heresies, this it was that armed a brother's hand, and made his right hand to be dipped in the blood of the righteous, and plucked away the laws of nature, and set open the gates for death, and brought that curse into action, and suffered not that wretch to call to mind either the birth-pangs, or his parents, or anything else, but made him so furious, and led him to such a pitch of phrenzy, that even when God exhorted him and said, "Unto thee shall be his recourse,[2] and thou shalt rule over him" (Gen. iv. 7, LXX.); he did not even then give in. Yet did He both forgive him the fault, and make his brother subject to him: but his complaint is so incurable, that even if thousands of medicines are applied, it keeps sloughing with its own corruption. For wherefore art thou so vexed, thou most miserable of men? Is it because God hath had honor shown Him? Nay, this would show a Satanical spirit. Is it then because thy brother outstrips thee in good name? As for

---

[1] 4 Mss. for "and" have "for when thou art so disposed toward thy brother."

[2] ἀποστροφὴ, "turning away," some read ἐπιστροφὴ, as Cyr. Al. Glaph. ad. loc. who speaks of the ἀποστροφὴ or turning away of God's face from Cain; but to render it thus here is inconsistent with Gen. iii. 16, and with St. Chrysostom's interpretation in Gen. iv. Hom. xix. which illustrates several expressions here.

that, it is open to thee in turn to outstrip him. And so, if thou wouldest be a conqueror, kill not, destroy not, but let him abide still, that the material for the struggle may be preserved, and conquer him living. For in this way thy crown had been a glorious one; but by thus destroying thou passest a harder sentence of defeat upon thyself. But a grudging spirit hath no sense of all this. And what ground hast thou to covet glory in such solitude? for those were at that time the only inhabitants of the earth. Still even then this restrained him not, but he cast away all from his mind, and stationed himself in the ranks of the devil; for he it was who then led the war upon Cain's side. For inasmuch as it was not enough for him that man had become liable to death, by the manner of the death he tried to make the tragedy still greater, and persuaded him to become a fratricide. For he was urgent and in travail to see the sentence carried into effect, as never satisfied with our ills. As if any one who had got an enemy in prison, and saw him under sentence, were to press, before he was out of the city, to see him butchered within it, and would not wait even the fitting time, so did the devil then, though he had heard that man must return to earth, travail with desire to see something worse, even a son dying before his father, and a brother destroying a brother, and a premature and violent slaughter. See you what great service envy hath done him? how it hath filled the insatiate spirit of the devil, and hath prepared for him a table great as he desired to see?

Let us then escape from the disease; for it is not possible, indeed it is not, to escape from the fire prepared for the devil, unless we get free from this sickness. But free we shall get to be if we lay to mind how Christ loved us, and also how He bade us love one another. Now what love did He show for us? His precious Blood did He shed for us when we were enemies, and had done the greatest wrong to Him. This do thou also do in thy brother's case (for this is the end of His saying "A new commandment I give unto you, That ye so[1] love one another as I have loved you") (John xiii. 34); or rather even so the measure does not come to a stand. For it was in behalf of His enemies that He did this. And are you unwilling to shed your blood for your brother? Why then dost thou even shed his blood, disobeying the commandment even to reversing it? Yet what He did was not as a due: but you, if you do it, are but fulfilling a debt. Since he too, who, after receiving the

ten thousand talents, demanded the hundred pence, was punished not merely for the fact that he demanded them, but because even by the kindness done him he had not become any better, and did not even follow where his Lord had begun, or remit the debt. For on the part of the servant the thing done was but a debt after all, if it had been done. For all things that we do, we do towards the payment of a debt. And this is why Himself said, "When ye have done all, say, We are unprofitable servants, we have done that which was our duty to do." (Luke xvii. 10.) If then we display charity, if we give our goods to them that need, we are fulfilling a debt; and that not only in that it was He who first began the acts of goodness, but because it is His goods that we are distributing if we ever[2] do give. Why then deprive thyself of what He willeth thee to have the right of? For the reason why He bade thee give them to another was that thou mightest have them thyself. For so long as thou hast them to thyself even thou thyself hast them not. But when thou hast given to another, then hast thou received them thyself. What charm then will do as much as this? Himself poured forth His Blood for His enemies: but we not even money for our benefactor. He did so with His Blood that was His own: we will not even with money that is not ours. He did it before us, we not even after His example. He did it for our salvation, we will not do it even for our own advantage. For He is not to have any advantage from our love toward man, but the whole gain accrueth unto us. For this is the very reason why we are bidden to give away our goods, that we may not be thrown out of them. For as a person who gives a little child money and bids him hold it fast, or give it the servant to keep, that it may not be for whoever will to snatch it away, so also doth God. For He says, Give to him that needeth, lest some one should snatch it away from thee, as an informer, for instance, or a calumniator, or a thief, or, after all these are avoided, death. For so long as thou holdest it thyself, thou hast no safe hold of it. But if thou givest it Me through the poor, I keep it all for thee exactly, and in fit season will return it with great increase. For it is not to take it away that I receive it, but to make it a larger amount and to keep it more exactly, that I may have it preserved for you against that time, in which there is no one to lend or to pity. What then can be more hard-hearted, than if we, after such promises, cannot make

---

[1] οὕτως and ἐγὼ are not in the text in St. John. 1 Ms. (Bodl.) here omits οὕτως.

[2] 5 Mss. "if we give all."

up our minds to lend to him? Yes, it is for this that we go before Him destitute and naked and poor, not having the things committed to our charge, because we do not deposit them with Him who keepeth them more exactly than any. And for this we shall be most severely punished. For when we are charged with it, what shall we be able to say about the loss of them?[1] what pretext to put forward? what defence? For what reason is there why you did not give? Do you disbelieve that you will receive it again? And how can this be reasonable? For He that hath given to one that hath not given, how shall He not much rather give after He has received? Does the sight of them please you? Well then, give much the more for this reason, that you may there be the more delighted, when no one can take them from you. Since now if you keep them, you will even suffer countless evils. For as a dog, so doth the devil leap upon them that are rich, wishing to snatch from them, as from a child that holdeth a sippet or a cake. Let us then give them to our Father, and if the devil see this done, he will certainly withdraw: and when he has withdrawn, then will the Father safely give them all to thee, when he cannot trouble, in that world to come. For now surely they that be rich differ not from little children that are troubled by dogs, while all are barking round them, tearing and pulling; not men only, but ignoble affections; as gluttony, drunkenness, flattery, uncleanness of every kind. And when we have to lend, we are very anxious about those that give much, and look particularly for those that are frank dealers. But here we do the opposite. For God, Who dealeth frankly, and giveth not one in the hundred, but a hundred-fold, we desert, and those who will not return us even the capital, these we seek after. For what return will our belly make us, that consumeth the larger share of our goods? Dung and corruption. Or what will vainglory? Envy and grudging. Or what nearness? Care and anxiety. Or what uncleanness? Hell and the venomous worm! For these are the debtors of them that be rich, who pay this interest upon the capital, evils at present, and dreadful things in expectation. Shall we then lead to these, pray, with such punishment for interest, and shall we not trust the same to Christ (4 Mss. om. τῷ) Who holdeth forth unto us heaven, immortal life, blessings unutterable? And what excuse shall we have? For how comest thou not to give to Him, who will assuredly return, and return in greater abundance?

Perhaps it is because it is so long before He repays. Yet surely He repays even here. For He is true which saith, "Seek the kingdom of heaven, and all these things shall be added to you." (Matt. vi. 33.) Seest thou this extreme munificence? Those goods, He says, have been stored up for thee, and are not diminishing: but these here I give by way of increase and surplus. But, besides all this, the very fact of its being so long before thou wilt receive it, does but make thy riches the greater: since the interest is more. For in the case of those who have money lent them, we see that this is what the lenders do, lending, that is, with greater readiness to those who refund a long time after. For he that straightway repays the whole, cuts off the progression of the interest, but he that keeps possession of it for a longer time, makes also the gain from it greater. Shall we then, while in man's case we are not offended at the delay, but even use artifices to make it greater, in the case of God be so little-minded, as on this very ground to be backward and to retract? And yet, as I said, He both giveth here, and along with the reason mentioned, as planning also some other greater advantage to us, He there keepeth the whole in store. For the abundance of what is given, and the excellency of that gift, transcends this present worthless life. Since in this perishable and doomed body there is not even the possibility of receiving those unfading crowns; nor in our present state, perturbed and full of trouble, and liable to many changes as it is, of attaining to that unchangeable unperturbed lot.[2] Now you, if any one were to owe you gold, and while you were staying in a foreign country, and had neither servants, nor any means to convey it across to the place of your abode, were to promise to pay you the loan, would beseech him in countless ways to have it paid down not in the foreign land, but at home rather. But do you think right to receive those spiritual and unutterable things in this world? Now what madness this would show! For if you receive them here, you must have them corruptible to a certainty; but if you wait for that time, He will repay you them incorruptible and unalloyed. If you receive here, you have gotten lead; but if there, tried gold. Still He does not even deprive thee of the goods of this life. For along with that promise He has placed another also, to the following effect, That every one that loveth the things of the world to come, shall receive "an hundred-fold in this life present, and shall inherit eternal life." (Matt. xix. 29.) If then

[1] Savile, "about our own self-destruction," περὶ τῆς ἀπωλείας ἑαυτῶν. but the Mss. αὐτῶν, which makes better sense.

[2] λῆξιν, which may mean "rest."

we do not receive the hundred-fold, it is ourselves that are to blame for not lending to
Him Who can give so much, for all who have
given have received much, even though they
gave but little. For what great thing, tell me,
did Peter give? was it not a net that was
broken (Luke v. 6, 11), and a rod and a hook
only? Yet still God opened to him the
houses of the world, and spread before him
land and sea, and all men invited him to their
possessions. Or rather they sold what was
their own, and brought it to their[1] feet, not
so much as putting it into their hands, for
they dared not, so great was the honor they
paid him, as well as their profuseness. But
he was Peter, you will say! And what of
this? O man! For it was not Peter only to
whom He made this promise, neither said He,
Thou, O Peter, only art to receive an hundred-fold, but "every one whosoever hath left
houses or brethren shall receive an hundred-
fold." For it is not distinction of persons
that He recognizes, but actions that are
rightly done. But a circle of little ones is
round about me, one will say, and I am desirous of leaving them with a good fortune.[2]
Why then do we make them paupers? For if
you leave them everything, you are still committing your goods to a trust that may deceive
you. But if you leave God their joint-heir
and guardian, you have left them countless
treasures. For as when we avenge ourselves
God assisteth us not, but when we leave it to
Him, more than we expect comes about; so
in the case of goods, if we take thought about
them ourselves, He will withdraw from any
providence over them, but if we cast all upon
Him, He will place both them and our children in all safety. And why art thou amazed
that this should be so with God? for even
with men one may see this happening. For
if you do not when dying invite any of your
relatives to the care of your children, it often
happens, that one who is abundantly willing
feels reluctancy, and is too modest to spring
to the task of his own accord. But if you
cast the care upon him, as having had a very
great honor shown him, he will in requital
make very great returns. If then thou wouldest leave thy children much wealth, leave them
God's care. For He Who, without thy having
done anything, gave thee a soul, and formed
thee a body, and granted thee life, when He
seeth thee displaying such munificence and
distributing their goods to Himself along with
them, must surely open to them every kind of
riches. For if Elijah after having been

nourished with a little meal, since he saw that
that woman honored him above her children,
made threshing-floors and oil-presses appear
in the little hut of the widow, consider what
loving caring the Lord of Elijah will display!
Let us then not consider how to leave our
children rich, but how to leave them virtuous.
For if they have the confidence of riches, they
will not mind aught besides, in that they have
the means screening the wickedness of their
ways in their abundant riches. But if they
find themselves devoid of the comfort to be
got from that source, they will do all so as by
virtue to find themselves abundant consolation
for their poverty. Leave them then no
riches that you may leave them virtue. For
it is unreasonable in the extreme, not to make
them, whilst we are alive, lords of all our
goods, yet after we are dead to give the easy
nature of youth full exemption from fear.
And yet while we are alive we shall have
power to call them to good account, and to
sober and bridle them, if they make an ill use
of their goods: but if after we are dead we
afford them, at the time of the loss of ourselves, and their own youthfulness, that power
which wealth gives, endless are the precipices
into which we shall thrust those unfortunate
and miserable creatures, so heaping fuel upon
flame, and letting oil drop into a fierce furnace. And so, if you would leave them rich
and safe withal, leave God a debtor to them,
and deliver the bequest to them into His
hands. For if they receive the money themselves, they will not know even who to give it
to, but will meet with many designing and
unfeeling people. But if thou beforehand
puttest it out to interest with God, the treasure henceforward remains unassailable, and
great is the facility wherewith that repayment
will be made. For God is well pleased at
repaying us what He oweth, and both looks
with a more favorable eye upon those who
have lent to Him, than on those who have
not; and loveth those the most to whom He
oweth the most. And so, if thou wouldest
have Him for thy Friend continually, make
Him thy Debtor to a large amount. For
there is no lender so pleased at having those
that owe to him, as Christ (6 Mss. God) is
rejoiced at having those that lend to Him.
And such as He oweth nothing to, He fleeth
from; but such as He oweth to, He even
runneth unto. Let us then use all means to
get Him for our Debtor; for this is the season
for loans, and He is now in want. If then
thou givest not unto Him now, He will not
ask of thee after thy departing hence. For it
is here that he thirsteth, here that He is an hungered. He thirsteth, since He thirsteth after

---

[1] So the Mss. ; i. e. the Apostles'.
[2] See St. Cypr. *Of works and alms,* c. 15 : *Treatises,* pp. 243
244, O. T.

thy salvation; and it is for this that He even begs; for this that He even goeth about naked, negotiating immortal life for thee. Do not then neglect Him; since it is not to be nourished that He wishes, but to nourish; it is not to be clothed, but to clothe and to accoutre thee with the golden garment, the royal robe. Do you not see even the more attached sort of physicians, when they are washing the sick, wash themselves also, though they need it not? In the same way He also doth all for the sake of thee who art sick. For this reason also He uses no force in demanding, that He may make thee great returns: that thou mayest learn that it is not because He is in need that He asketh of thee, but that He may set right that thou needest. For this reason too He comes to thee in a lowly guise, and with His right hand held forth. And if thou givest Him a farthing, He turneth not away: and even if thou rejectest Him, He departeth not but cometh again to thee. For He desireth,[1] yea desireth exceedingly, our salvation: let us then think scorn of money, that we may not be thought scorn of by Christ. Let us think scorn of money, even with a view to obtain the money itself. For if we keep it here, we shall lose it altogether both here and hereafter. But if we distribute it with abundant expenditure, we shall enjoy in each life abundant wealthiness. He then that would become rich, let him become poor, that he may be rich. Let him spend that he may collect, let him scatter that he may gather. But if this is novel and paradoxical, look to the sower, and consider, that he cannot in any other way gather more together, save by scattering what he hath and, letting go of what is at hand. Let us now sow and till the Heaven, that we may reap with great abundance, and obtain everlasting goods, through the grace and love toward man, etc.

HOMILY VIII.

ROM. IV. 1, 2.

" What shall we then say that Abraham, our father as pertaining to the flesh, hath found? For if Abraham were justified by works, he hath whereof to glory; but not before God."

HE had said (5 Mss. εἶπεν), that the world had become guilty before God, and that all had sinned, and that boasting was excluded, and that it was impossible to be saved otherwise than by faith. He is now intent upon showing that this salvation, so far from being matter of shame, was even the cause of a bright glory, and a greater than that through works. For since the being saved, yet with shame, had somewhat of dejection in it, he next takes away this suspicion too. And indeed he has hinted at the same already, by calling it not barely salvation, but "righteousness. Therein" (he says) "is the righteousness of God revealed." (Rom. i. 17.) For he that is saved as a righteous man has a confidence accompanying his salvation. And he calls it not "righteousness" only, but also the setting forth of the righteousness of God. But God is set forth in things which are glorious and shining, and great. However, he nevertheless draws support for this from what he is at present upon, and carries his discourse forward by the method of question. And this he is always in the habit of doing both for clearness sake, and for the sake of confidence in what is said. Above, for instance, he did it, where he says, "What advantage then hath the Jew?" (ib. iii. 1.) and, "What then have we more than they?"[2] (ib. 9) and again, "where then is boasting? it is excluded" (Rom. iii. 27): and here, "what then shall we say that Abraham our father?" etc. Now since the Jews kept turning over and over the fact, that the Patriarch, and friend of God, was the first to receive circumcision, he wishes to show, that it was by faith that he too was justified. And this was quite a vantage ground to insist upon (περιουσία νίκης πολλῆς). For for a person who had no works, to be justified by faith, was nothing unlikely. But for a person richly adorned with good deeds, not to be made just from hence, but from faith, this is the thing to cause wonder, and to set the power of faith in a strong light. And this is why he passes by all the others, and leads his discourse back to this man. And he calls him "father, as pertaining to the flesh," to throw them out of the

---

[1] ἐρᾷ; cf. p. 367, note ³.

[2] Rom. iii. 9, τί οὖν προκατέχομεν περισσόν; as 2 Mss. of Matt. read at the beginning of the last Homily. So too some Mss. of the text, and the Syriac version.

genuine relationship (συγγενείας γνησίας) to him;
and to pave the Gentiles' way to kinsmanship[1]
with him. And then he says, "For if Abraham were justified by works, he hath whereof
to glory: but not before God." After saying
that God "justified the circumcision by faith
and the uncircumcision through faith," and
making the same sufficiently sure in what he
said before, he now proves it by Abraham
more clearly than he promised, and pitches
the battle for faith against works, and makes
this righteous man the subject of the whole
struggle; and that not without special meaning. Wherefore also he sets him up very high
by calling him "forefather," and putting a
constraint upon them to comply with him in
all points. For, Tell me not, he would say,
about the Jews, nor bring this man or that
before me. For I will go up to the very head
of all, and the source whence circumcision
took its rise. For "if Abraham," he says,
"was justified by works, he hath whereof to
glory: but not before God."[2] What is here
said is not plain, and so one must make it
plainer. For there are two "gloryings," one
of works, and one of faith. After saying then,
"if he was justified by works, he hath whereof
to glory; but not before God;" he points out
that he might have whereof to glory from faith
also,[3] yea and much greater reason for it.
For the great power of Paul is especially displayed in this, that he turns what is objected
to the other side, and shows that what seemed
rather to be on the side of salvation by works,
viz. glorying or boldness of claim (παρρησιάζεσ-
θαι) belonged much more truly to that by
faith. For he that glorieth in his works has
his own labors to put forward: but he that
finds his honor in having faith in God, has a
much greater ground for glorying to show, in
that it is God that he glorifieth and magnifieth.
For those things which the nature of the visible
world tells him not of, in receiving these by
faith in Him, he at once displays sincere love
towards Him, and heralds His power clearly
forth. Now this is the character of the noblest
soul, and the philosophic[4] spirit, and lofty
mind. For to abstain from stealing and mur-

dering is trifling sort of acquirement, but to
believe that it is possible for God to do things
impossible requires a soul of no mean stature,
and earnestly affected towards Him; for this
is a sign of sincere love. For he indeed
honors God, who fulfils the commandments,
but he doth so in a much greater degree who
thus followeth wisdom (φιλοσοφῶν) by his faith.
The former obeys Him, but the latter receives
that opinion of Him which is fitting, and glorifies Him, and feels wonder at Him more than
that evinced by works. For that glorying
pertains to him that does aright, but this
glorifieth God, and lieth wholly in Him.
For he glorieth at conceiving great things
concerning Him, which redound to His
glory. And this is why he speaks of
having whereof to glory before God.
And not for this only, but also for another
reason: for he who is a believer glorieth again,
not only because he loveth God in sincerity,
but also because he hath enjoyed great honor
and love from him. For as he shows his love
to Him by having great thoughts about Him,
(for this is a proof of love), so doth God also
love him, though deserving to suffer for
countless sins, not in freeing him from punishment only, but even by making him righteous.
He then hath whereof to glory, as having been
counted worthy of mighty love.

Ver. 4. "For[5] to him that worketh is the
reward not reckoned of grace, but of debt."

Then is not this last the greatest? he means.
By no means: for it is to the believer that it
is reckoned. But it would not have been
reckoned, unless there were something that he
contributed himself. And so he too hath God
for his debtor, and debtor too for no common
things, but great and high ones. For to show
his high-mindedness and spiritual understanding, he does not say "to him that believeth"
merely, but

Ver. 5. "To him that believeth on Him
that justifieth the ungodly."

For reflect how great a thing it is to be
persuaded and have full confidence that God
is able on a sudden not to free a man
who has lived in impiety from punishment
only, but even to make him just, and to count
him worthy of those immortal honors. Do
not then suppose that this one is lowered in
that it is not reckoned unto the former of
grace. For this is the very thing that makes
the believer glorious; the fact of his enjoying
so great grace, of his displaying so great faith.
And note too that the recompense is greater.
For to the former a reward is given, to the
latter righteousness. Now righteousness is

---

[1] ἀγχιστείαν, which the orators use for right of inheritance as next of kin. See verses 13, 14; c. viii. 17; ix. 8; Gal. iii. 7, 15, 16, 18; Heb. ix. 16, 26; which renders it probable that there is reference to the death of Christ, (see Rev. xiii. 8.) and so to the idea of "Testament," in the Ep. to the Galatians.

[2] St. Chrysostom understands πρὸς τὸν θεὸν not "as claiming credit with God," but "glorying in reference to God," in which He has a share. He takes the argument to be, "If Abraham was justified by works, he hath not whereof to glory before God" (in this sense), "but can only glory in himself: as it is, he hath whereof to glory before God, and therefore was not justified by works."

[3] 4 Mss. that he that is of faith might also have whereof to glory.

[4] φιλοσόφου γνώμης, the word is used (as frequently by Christian writers) in the sense of choosing wisdom for the guide of life.

[5] So the Mss., omitting v. 3.

much greater than a reward. For righteousness is a recompense which most fully comprehends several rewards. Therefore after proving this from Abraham, he introduces David also as giving his suffrage in favor of the statement made. What then doth David say? and whom doth he pronounce blessed? is it him that triumphs[1] in works, or him that hath enjoyed grace? him that hath obtained pardon and a gift? And when I speak of blessedness, I mean the chiefest of all good things; for as righteousness is greater than a reward, so is blessedness greater than righteousness. Having then shown that the righteousness is better, not owing to Abraham's having received it only but also from reasonings (for he[2] hath whereof to boast, he says, before God[3]); he again uses another mode of showing that it is more dignified, by bringing David in to give his suffrage this way. For he also, he says, pronounces him blessed who is so made righteous, saying,

Ver. 7. "Blessed are they whose iniquities are forgiven."

And he seems to be bringing a testimony beside his purpose. For it does not say, Blessed are they whose faith is reckoned for righteousness. But he does so on purpose, not through inadvertency, to show the greater superiority. For if he be blessed that by grace received forgiveness, much more is he that is made just, and that exhibits faith. For where blessedness is, there all shame is removed, and there is much glory, since blessedness is a greater degree both of reward and of glory. And for this cause what is the advantage of the other he states as unwritten, "Now to him that worketh is the reward reckoned not of grace;" but what the advantage of the faithful is, he brings Scriptural testimony to prove, saying, As David saith, "Blessed are they whose iniquities are forgiven, and whose sins are covered."[4] What, he means, is it that you say? Is it that "it is not of debt but of grace that he[5] receives forgiveness?" But see it is this person who is pronounced blessed. For he would not have pronounced him so, unless he saw him in the enjoyment of great glory. And he does not say this "forgiveness" then comes upon the circumcision; but what saith he?

Ver. 9. "Cometh this blessedness then"

(which is the greater thing) "upon the circumcision or upon the uncircumcision?"

For now the subject of enquiry is, With whom is this good and great thing to be found; is it with the circumcision or with the uncircumcision? And notice its superiority! For he shows that it is so far from shunning the uncircumcision, that it even dwelt gladly with it before the circumcision. For since he that pronounced it blessed was David, who was himself also in a state of circumcision, and he was speaking to those in that state, see how eagerly Paul contends for applying what he said to the uncircumcised. For after joining the ascription of blessedness to righteousness, and showing that they are one and the same thing, he enquires how Abraham came to be righteous. For if the ascription of blessedness belong to the righteous, and Abraham was made righteous, let us see how he was made righteous, as uncircumcised or circumcised? Uncircumcised, he says.

"For we say that faith was reckoned to Abraham for righteousness."*

After mentioning the Scripture above (for he said, "What saith the Scripture? Abraham believed in God, and it was counted unto him for righteousness,") here he goes on to secure also the judgment of the speakers, and shows that justification took place in the uncircumcision. Then from these grounds he solves another objection which is starting up. For if when in uncircumcision, one might say he was justified, to what purpose was the circumcision brought in?

Ver. 11. "He received it," he says, "a sign and[6] seal of the righteousness that was by the faith, which he had being yet uncircumcised."

See you how he shows the Jews to be as it were of the class of parasites (i. e. guests), rather than those in uncircumcision, and that these were added to the others?[7] For if he

---

[1] So Vulg. and Field: most Mss. have καμόντα "that hath toiled."
[2] Or "it"; i. e. the righteousness of faith.
[3] So several Mss. Vulg. "but not before God." But the text suits St. Chrysostom's view of the argument: see p. 112, note c.
[4] 6 Mss. om. and whose, etc.
[5] So 5 Mss. Sav. "thou receivest," which scarcely makes sense.

* Chrys. is free from the polemical treatment of the subject of justification which has been so prominent in modern expositions. The following points may be suggested: (1) It is the imputation of faith which here receives chief emphasis—λογίζεται ἡ πίστις αὐτοῦ εἰς δικαιοσύνην (vv. 3, 5, 6, 8, 9). (2) Although λογίζεσθαι is an actus forensis, it has an ethical counterpart involved in the very conception of faith and righteousness. (3) While faith is not to be identified with righteousness, it can be reckoned as such because it involves the soul's commitment to a life of fellowship with Christ, in which a perfect righteousness is guaranteed and increasingly secured. This righteousness is real as well as putative. (4) The power and value of faith are in its object, not in its own inherent moral excellence. It brings the believer into real and vital union with God and Christ. The δικαιοσύνη θεοῦ is the righteousness of which God is the author but in faith we appropriate it and God makes it ours. Man does not attain it by any act of goodness; he receives it from God as a gift of grace. It is God's righteousness as coming from God; it is man's as being imparted to him on condition of faith.—G. B. S.
[6] Text, "the sign of circumcision, a seal," etc. All our copies, however, and those of Matth. agree. The whole verse, in fact, is paraphrased rather than quoted.
[7] The meaning seems to be that the faithful Jews were brought in as it were to the house of Abraham, and added to

was justified and crowned while in uncircumcision, the Jews came in afterwards, Abraham is then the father first of the uncircumcised, which through faith appertain to him, and then of those in the circumcision. For he is a forefather of two lines. See you faith lightening up? for till it came the patriarch was not justified. See you the uncircumcision offering no hindrance? for he was uncircumcised, yet was not hindered from being justified. The circumcision therefore is behind the faith. And why wonder that it is behind the faith, when it is even behind the uncircumcision. Nor is it behind faith only, but very far inferior to it, even so far as the sign is to the reality of which it is the sign; for instance, as the seal is to the soldier. (See Hom. iii. on 2 Cor. at the end.) And why, he says, did he want a seal then? He did not want it himself. For what purpose then did he receive it? With a view to his being the father alike of them that believe in uncircumcision and in circumcision. But not of those in circumcision absolutely: wherefore he goes on to say, "To them who are not of the circumcision only." For if to the uncircumcised, it is not in that he is uncircumcised that he is their father, although justified in uncircumcision; but in that they imitated his faith; much less is it owing to circumcision that he is the forefather of those in the state of circumcision, unless faith also be added. For he says that the reason of his receiving circumcision was that either of us two parties might have him for a forefather, and that those in the uncircumcision might not thrust aside those in the circumcision.[1] See how the former had him for their forefather first. Now if the circumcision be of dignity owing to its preaching righteousness, the uncircumcision even hath no small preëminence in having received it before the circumcision. Then wilt thou be able to have him as a forefather when thou walkest in the steps of that faith, and art not contentious, nor a causer of division in bringing in the Law. What faith? tell me.

Ver. 12. "Which he had being yet uncircumcised."

Here again he lays low the lofty spirit of the Jews by reminding them of the time of the justification. And he well says, "the steps," that you as well as Abraham may believe in the resurrection of bodies that are dead. For he also displayed his faith upon this point. And so if you reject the uncircumcision, be informed for certain that the circumcision is of no more use unto you. For if you follow not in the steps of his faith, though you were ten thousand times in a state of circumcision, you will not be Abraham's offspring. For even he received the circumcision for this end, that the man in a state of uncircumcision might not cast thee off. Do not then demand this of him too.[2] For it was you whom the thing was to be an assistance to, not he. But he calls it a sign of the righteousness. And this also was for thy sake, since now it is not even this: for thou then wert in need of bodily signs, but now there is no need of them. "And was it not possible," one might say, "from his faith to learn the goodness of his soul?" Yes, it was possible but thou stoodest in need of this addition also. For since thou didst not imitate the goodness of his soul, and wert not able to see it, a sensible circumcision was given thee, that, after having become accustomed to this of the body, thou mightest by little and little be led on to the true love of wisdom in the soul also, and that having with much seriousness received it as a very great privilege, thou mightest be instructed to imitate and revere thine ancestor. This object then had God not only in the circumcision, but in all the other rites, the sacrifices, I mean, and the sabbath, and feasts. Now that it was for thy sake that he received the circumcision, learn from the sequel. For after saying that he received a sign and a seal, he gives the reason also as follows. That he might be the father of the circumcision—to those who received the spiritual circumcision also, since if you have only this (i. e. the carnal), no farther good will come to you. For this is then a sign, when the reality of which it is the sign is found with thee, that is, faith; since if thou have not this, the sign to thee has no longer the power of a sign, for what is it to be the sign of? or what the seal of, when there is nothing to be sealed? much as if you were to show one a purse with a seal to it, when there was nothing laid up within. And so the circumcision is ridiculous if there be no faith within. For if it be a sign of righteousness, but you have not righteousness, then you have no sign either. For the reason of your receiving a sign was that you might seek diligently for that reality whereof you have the sign: so that if you had been sure of diligently seeking thereafter without it, then you had not

---

the number of the faithful already existing as uncircumcised, and children of Abraham by their faith. The reading of Savile's text, ῇ καὶ τούτους τοὺς ἐν ἀκροβυστίᾳ ἐκείνοις προσερριμμένους, means, "in that these too, that were in uncircumcision, were added to them," which is inconsistent with the context, and is not noticed in the Ben. Edition. Possibly the passage is still corrupt.

[1] 4 Mss. "and that neither those in circumcision might thrust away the uncircumcised, nor the uncircumcised those in circumcision."

[2] i. e. "do not require him to be circumcised." See Rom. xiv. 3; Gal. vi. 12, 15, etc.

needed it. But this is not the only thing that circumcision proclaims, namely righteousness, but righteousness in even an uncircumcised man. Circumcision then does but proclaim, that there is no need of circumcision.

Ver. 14. " For if they which are of the Law be heirs, faith is made void, and the promise made of none effect." *

He had shown that faith is necessary, that it is older than circumcision, that it is more mighty than the Law, that it establisheth the Law. For if all sinned, it was necessary: if one being uncircumcised was justified, it is older: if the knowledge of sin is by the Law and yet it was without the Law made evident,[1] it is more mighty: if it has testimony borne to it by the Law, and establisheth the Law, it is not opposed to it, but friendly and allied to it. Again, he shows upon other grounds too that it was not even possible by the Law to attain to the inheritance, and after having matched it with the circumcision, and gained it the victory, he brings it besides into contrast with the Law in these words, " For if they which are of the Law be heirs, faith is made void." To prevent them any-one from saying that one may have faith and also keep up the Law, he shows this to be impracticable. For he that clings to the Law, as if of saving force, does disparagement to faith's power; and so he says, " faith is made void," that is, there is no need of salvation by grace. For then it cannot show forth its own proper power; " and the promise is made of none effect." This is because the Jew might say, What need have I of faith? If then this held, the things that were promised, would be taken away along with faith. See how in all points he combats with them from the early times and from the Patriarch. For having shown from thence that righteousness and faith went together in the inheritance, he now shows that the promise did likewise. For to prevent the Jew from saying, What matters it to me if Abraham was justified by faith? Paul says, neither can what you are interested with, the promise of the inheritance, come into effect apart from it: which was what scared them most. But what promise is he speaking of? That of his being " the heir of

the world," and that in him all should be blessed. And how does he say that this promise is made of none effect?

Ver. 15. " Because the Law worketh wrath: for where no Law is, there is no transgression."

Now if it worketh wrath, and renders them liable for transgression, it is plain that it makes them so to a curse also. But they that are liable under a curse, and punishments, and transgression, are not worthy of inheriting, but of being punished and rejected. What then happens? faith comes, drawing on it the grace, so that the promise comes into effect. For where grace is, there is a remitting, and where remitting is, there is no punishment. Punishment then being removed, and righteousness succeeding from faith, there is no obstacle to our becoming heirs of the promise.

Ver. 16. " Therefore it is of faith," he says, " that it might be by grace; to the end the promise might be sure to all the seed."

You see that it is not the Law only that faith establisheth, but the promise of God also that it will not allow to fall to the ground. But the Law, on the other hand, by being kept[2] to unseasonably, makes even the faith of none effect, and hindereth the promise. By this he shows that faith, so far from being superfluous, is even necessary to that degree, that without it there is no being saved. For the Law worketh wrath, as all have transgressed it. But this doth not even suffer wrath to arise at all: for " where no Law is," he says, " there is no transgression." Do you see how he not only does away with sin after it has existed, but does not even allow it to be produced? And this is why he says " by grace." For what end? Not with a view to their being put to shame, but to the end that the promise might be sure to all the seed. Here he lays down two blessings, both that the things given are sure, and also that they are to all the seed, so gathering in those of the Gentiles, and showing that the Jews are without, if they contend against the faith. For this is a surer thing than that. For faith doeth thee no hurt (be not contentious), but even now thou art in danger from the Law, it preserves thee. Next having said, " to all the seed," he defines what seed he meaneth. That which is of faith, he says, so blending with it[3] their relationship to the Gentiles, and showing that they must not be proud of Abraham who do not believe as he

---

* According to vv. 14–17, the promise cannot be through the law because that would annul faith and destroy the promise entirely (14). The principle of law is *quid pro quo* and on that basis alone there is no room for faith and promise. Claim, debt and reward, are the ideas which stand on the plane of law. Justification by law would imply no act of trust, obedience or gracious promise, but would be matter of reward simply. But since man is a sinner, it is inconceivable that he be justified on this basis, and the gospel of a gracious salvation is the only hope. To reject the latter is to exclude the possibility of any salvation whatever. Only by clinging to the Gospel can the Jew find any ground of hope in the ancient promises and covenants.—G. B. S.

[1] i. e. as justifying. Rom. iii. 21.

[2] These words are very important, as they show that the Law was not held empty in itself, but at this time, i. e. since Christianity.

[3] Or perhaps " fixing the relationship," i. e. of Abraham to the Gentiles, συνάπτων.

did. And see a third thing which faith effected besides. It makes the relationship to that righteous man more definite (ἀκρι βεστέ-ραν), and holds him up as the ancestor of a more numerous issue. And this is why he does not say merely Abraham, but "our father," ours who believe. Then he also seals what he has said by the testimony—

Ver. 17. "As it is written," he says, "I have made thee a father of many nations."

Do you observe that this was ordered by Providence from of old? What then, he means, does He say this on account of the Ishmaelites, or of the Amalekites, or of the Hagarenes? This however, as he goes on he proves more distinctly not to be said of these. But as yet he presses forward to another point, by which means he proves this very thing by defining the mode of the relationship, and establishing it with a vast reach of mind. What then does he say?

"Before (or, answering to, κατέναντ.) Him Whom he believed, even God."

But his meaning is something of this sort, as God is not the God of a part, but the Father of all, so is he also. And again, as God is a father not by way of the relationship of nature, but by way of the affiance of faith, so is he also, inasmuch as it is obedience that makes him father of us all. For since they thought nothing of this relationship, as clinging to that grosser one, he shows that this is the truer relationship by lifting his discourse up to God. And along with this he makes it plain that this was the reward of faith that he received. Consequently, if it were not so, and he were the father of all the dwellers upon earth, the expression before (or answering to) would be out of place, while the gift of God would be curtailed. For the "before," is equivalent to "alike with." Since where is the marvel, pray, in a man's being the father of those sprung from himself? This is what is every man's lot. But the extraordinary thing is, that those whom by nature he had not, them he received by the gift of God. And so if thou wouldest believe that the patriarch was honored, believe that he is the father of all. But after saying, "before Him Whom he believed, even God," he does not pause here, but goes on thus; "Who quickeneth the dead, and calleth those things which be not as though they were," so laying beforehand his foundations for discoursing upon the resurrection. And it was serviceable also to his present purpose. For if He could "quicken the dead" and bring in "those things that were not as though they were," then could He also make those who were not born of him to be his children. And

this is why he does not say, bringing in the things which are not, but calling them, so showing the greater ease of it. For as it is easy to us to call the things which are by name, so to Him it is easy, yea, and much easier to give a subsistence to things that are not. But after saying, that the gift of God was great and unspeakable, and having discoursed concerning His power, he shows farther that Abraham's faith was deserving of the gift, that you may not suppose him to have been honored without reason. And after raising the attention of his hearers to prevent the Jew from clamoring and making doubts, and saying, "And how is it possible for those who are not children to become children?" he passes on to speak of the patriarch, and says,

Ver. 18. "Who against hope believed in hope, that he might become the father of many nations, according to that which was spoken, So shall thy seed be."

How was it that he "believed in hope against hope?" It was against man's hope, in hope which is of God. (For he is showing the loftiness of the action, and leaving no room for disbelieving what is said.) Things which are contrary to one another, yet faith blends them together. But if he were speaking about such as were from Ishmael, this language would be superfluous : for it was not by faith but by nature that they were begotten. But he bringeth Isaac also before us. For it was not concerning those nations that he believed, but concerning him who was to be from his barren wife. If then it be a reward to be father of many nations, it would be so of those nations clearly of whom he so believed. For that you may know that he is speaking of them, listen to what follows.

Ver. 19. "And being not weak in faith, he considered [1] his own body now dead."

Do you see how he gives the obstacles, as well as the high spirit of the righteous man which surmounts all? "Against hope," he says, was that which was promised : this is the first obstacle. For Abraham had no other person who had received a son in this way to look to. They that were after him looked to him, but he to no one, save to God only. And this is why he said, "against hope." Then, "his body now dead." This is a second. And, "the deadness of Sarah's womb." This is a third, aye and a fourth [2] obstacle.

Ver. 20. "But he staggered not at the promise of God through unbelief."

For God neither gave any proof nor made

---

[1] Nearly all Mss. omit "not": as do the oldest of the N. T.
[2] i. e. Sarah's personal barrenness, and her present age.

any sign, but there were only bare words promising such things as nature did not hold out any hopes of. Yet still he says, " he staggered not." He does not say, " He did not disbelieve," but, " He staggered not," that is, he neither doubted nor hesitated, though the hindrances were so great. From this we learn, that if God promise even countless impossibilities, and he that heareth doth not receive them, it is not the nature of things that is to blame, but the unreasonableness of him who receiveth them not. " But was strong in faith." See the pertinacity of Paul.[1] For since this discourse was about them that work and them that believe, he shows that the believer works more than the other, and requires more power, and great strength, and sustains no common degree of labor. For they counted faith worthless, as having no labor in it. Insisting then upon this, he shows that it is not only he that succeeds in temperance, or any other virtue of this sort, but he that displays faith also who requires even greater power. For as the one needs strength to beat off the reasonings[2] of intemperance, so hath the faithful also need of a soul endued with power, that he may thrust aside the suggestions of unbelief. How then did he become " strong?" By trusting the matter, he replies, to faith and not to reasonings : else he had fallen. But how came he to thrive in faith itself? By giving glory to God, he says.

Ver. 21. " And being fully persuaded that what He had promised, He was able also to perform."

Abstaining then from curious questionings is glorifying God, as indulging in them is transgressing. But if by entering into curious questions, and searching out things below, we fail to glorify Him, much more if we be over curious in the matter of the Lord's generation, shall we suffer to the utmost for our insolence. For if the type of the resurrection is not to be searched into, much less those unutterable and awestriking subjects.[3] And he does not use the word " believed " merely, but, " being fully persuaded." For such a thing is faith, it is clearer than the demonstration by reasons, and persuades more fully. For it is not possible for another reasoning succeeding to it to shake[4] it afterwards. He indeed that is persuaded with words may have his persuasion

altered too by them. But he that stays himself upon faith, hath henceforward fortified his hearing against words that may do hurt to it. Having said then, that he was justified by faith, he shows that he glorified God by that faith ; which is a thing specially belonging to a good life. For, " Let your light so shine before men, that they may see your good works, and glorify your Father Which is in heaven." (Matt. v. 16.) But lo! this is shown also to belong to faith! Again, as works need power, so doth faith. For in their case the body often shareth the toil, but in the faith the well-doing belongeth to the soul alone. And so the labor is greater, since it has no one to share the struggles with it. Do you observe how he shows that all that belonged to works attached to faith in a far greater degree, as having whereof to glory before God,—requiring power and labor,— and again, glorifying God? And after saying, that " what He had promised, He is able also to perform," he seems to me to speak beforehand of things to come. For it is not things present merely that He promises, but also things to come. For the present are a type of the other. It is then a sign of a weak, little, and pitiful mind not to believe. And so when any make faith a charge against us, let us make want of faith a charge against them in return, as pitiful, and little-minded, and foolish, and weak, and no better in disposition than asses. For as believing belongs to a lofty and high-born soul, so disbelieving doth to a most unreasonable and worthless one, and such as is sunken drowsily (κατενηνεγμένης) into the senselessness of brutes. Therefore having left these, let us imitate the Patriarch, and glorify God as he gave Him glory. And what does it mean, gave Him glory? He held in mind His majesty, His boundless power. And having formed a just conception of Him, he was also " fully persuaded " about His promises.

Let us then also glorify Him by faith as well as by works, that we may also attain to the reward of being glorified by Him. " For them that glorify Me, I will glorify" (1 Sam. ii. 30), He says : and indeed, if there were no reward, the very privilege of glorifying God were itself a glory. For if men take a pride in the mere fact of speaking eulogies of kings, even if there be no other fruit of it ; consider how glorious it must be, that our Lord is glorified by us : as again, how great a punishment to cause Him to be by our means blasphemed. And yet this very being glorified, He wisheth to be brought about for our sakes, since He doth not need it Himself. For what distance dost thou suppose to be between God and

---

[1] 6 Mss. φιλονεικίαν, Sav. φιλοσοφίαν, 1 Ms. σοφίαν, which makes better sense than the reading of Savile.
[2] λογισμούς. It may be used for imaginations, as by Macarius : but perhaps St. Chrysostom is thinking of Arist. *Eth.* vii. iii. 9, 10.
[3] *Tertull. de Res.* Carn. cap. xii. *Totus hic ordo revolubilis rerum,* etc.
[4] Or, " destroy "—διαλῦσαι, for διασαλεῦσαι. Savile's reading seems the most forcible, but the other makes good sense.

man? as great as that between men and worms? or as great as between Angels and worms? But when I have mentioned a distance even thus great, I have not at all expressed it: since to express its greatness is impossible. Would you, now, wish to have a great and marked reputation among worms? Surely not. If then thou that lovest glory, wouldest not wish for this, how should He Who is far removed from this passion, and so much farther above us, stand in need of glory from thee? Nevertheless, free from the want of it as He is, still He saith that He desireth it for thy sake. For if He endured for thy sake to become a slave, why wonder that He upon the same ground layeth claim to the other particulars also? For He counts nothing unworthy of Himself which may be conducive to our salvation. Since then we are aware of this, let us shun sin altogether, because by reason of it He is blasphemed. For it says, "flee from sin, as from the face of a serpent: if thou comest too near unto it, it will bite thee" (Ecclus. xxi. 2): for it is not it that comes to us, but we that desert to it. God has so ordered things that the Devil should not prevail over us by compulsion (Gr. tyranny): since else none would have stood against his might. And on this account He set him a distant abode, as a kind of robber and tyrant.[1] And unless he find a person unarmed and solitary for his assaults, he doth not venture to attack him. Except he see us travelling by the desert,[2] he has not the courage to come near us. But the desert and place of the Devil is nothing else than sin. We then have need of the shield of faith, the helmet of salvation, the sword of the Spirit, not only that we may not get evil intreated, but that ever should he be minded to leap[3] upon us, we may cut off his head. Need we have of continual prayer that he may be bruised under our feet, for he is shameless and full of hardihood, and this though he fights from beneath. But yet even so he gets the victory: and the reason is, that we are not earnestly set upon being above his blows. For he has not even the power to lift himself very high, but he trails along upon the ground. And of this the serpent is a type. But if God set him in that rank from the beginning, much more will He now. But if thou dost not know what fighting

from beneath may be, I also will try to explain to thee the manner of this war. What then may this fighting "from beneath" (John viii. 23) be? It is standing upon the lower things of the world to buffet us, such as pleasure and riches and all the goods of this life. And for this reason, whoever he seeth flying toward heaven, first, he will not even be able to leap so far. Secondly, even if he should attempt he will speedily fall. For he hath no feet; be not afraid: he hath no wings; fear not. He trails upon the earth, and the things of the earth. Do thou then have naught in common with the earth, and thou wilt not need labor even. For he hath not any knowledge of open fight: but as a serpent he hideth him in the thorns, nestling evermore in the "deceitfulness of riches." (Matt. xiii. 22.) And if thou wert to cut away the thorns, he will easily be put to flight, being detected:[4] and if thou knowest how to charm him with the inspired charms he will straightway be struck. For we have, we surely have, spiritual charms, even the Name of our Lord Jesus Christ and the might of the Cross. This charm will not only bring the serpent out of his lurking places, and cast him into the fire (Acts xxviii. 5), but even wounds it healeth. But if some that have said this Name have not been healed, it came of their own little faith, and was not owing to any weakness in what they said. For some did throng Jesus and press Him (Luke viii. 44, 45), and got no good therefrom. But the woman with an issue, without even touching His Body, but merely the hem of His garment, stanched a flux of blood of so long standing. (So St. Aug. Serm. LXII. iii. 4, p. 124 O. T.) This Name is fearful alike to devils, and to passions, and to diseases. In this then let us find a pleasure, herewith let us fortify ourselves. It was thus Paul waxed great, and yet he was of the like nature with ourselves, so the whole choir of the Disciples. But faith had made him a perfectly different person, and so much did it abound in them, that even their garments had great force. (Acts xix. 12.) What excuse then shall we deserve, if even the shadows and the garments of those men drave off death (Acts v. 15), but our very prayers do not so much as bring the passions down? What is the reason[5] of it? Our temper is widely different. For what nature gives, is as much ours as theirs. For he was born and brought up just as we are, and dwelt upon the earth and breathed the air, as we do. But in other points he was far greater and better

---

[1] Tyrant was the name given to any rebel who set himself up for Emperor.
[2] See St. Chrys. on Matt. iv. 1; Hom. 13 in St. Matt. p. 174 O. T., and the Catena Aurea on the same place, Oxf. Trans. p. 117, etc. Being alone is represented as always exposing us to temptation, though it is sometimes done for holy purposes, and for greater victory.
[3] Alluding perhaps to the sons of Sceva, and then to Goliath.

[4] Sav. mar. and 5 Mss. δῆλος: Vulg. δειλὸς a coward.
[5] Compare Bp. Taylor, Worthy Communicant, Sect. iv. 10 t. xv. p. 480.

than we are, in zeal, in faith, and love. Let us then imitate him. Let us allow Christ to speak through us. He desireth it more than we do : and by reason of this, He prepared this instrument, and would not have it remain useless and idle, but wisheth to keep it ever in hand. Why then dost thou not make it serviceable for the Maker's hand, but lettest it become unstrung, and makest it relaxed through luxury, and unfittest the whole harp for His use, when thou oughtest to keep the members [1] of it in full stretch, and well strung, and braced with spiritual salt. [2] For if Christ see our soul thus attuned, He will send forth His sounds even by it. And when this taketh place, then shalt thou see Angels leaping for joy, (σκιρτῶντας) and Archangels too, and the Cherubim. Let us then become worthy of His spotless hands. Let us invite Him to strike even upon our heart. For He rather needeth not any inviting. Only make it worthy of that touch, and He will be foremost in running unto thee. For if in consideration of their attainments not yet reached, He runneth to them (for when Paul was not yet so advanced He yet framed that praise for him) when He seeth one fully furnished, what is there that He will not do? But if Christ shall sound forth and the Spirit shall indeed light upon us, and we shall be better than the heaven, having not the sun and the moon fixed in our body, but the Lord of both sun and moon and angels dwelling in us and walking in us. And this I say, not that we may raise the dead, or cleanse the lepers, but that we may show forth what is a greater miracle than all these—charity. For wheresoever this glorious thing shall be there the Son taketh up His abode along with the Father, and the grace of the Spirit frequenteth. For "where two or three are gathered together in My Name," it says, "there am I in the midst of them." (Matt. xviii. 20.) Now this is for great affection, and for those that are very intimate friends, to have those whom they love on either side of them. Who then, he means, is so wretched as not to wish to have Christ in the midst? We that are at variance with one another! And haply some one may ridicule me and ask, What is it that you mean? Do you not see that we are all within the same walls, and under the same enclosure of the Church, standing under the same fold with unanimity; that no one fighteth, that we be under the same shepherd, crying aloud in common, listening in common to what is being said, sending up our prayers in common,

—and yet mention fighting and variance? Fighting I do mention, and I am not mad nor out of my sober mind. For I see what I see, and know that we are under the same fold, and the same shepherd. Yet for this cause I make the greater lamentation, because, though there are so many circumstances to draw us together, we are at variance. And what sedition, it will be said, see you here? Here truly I see none. But when we have broken up, such an one accuses such another, another is openly insulting, another grudges, another is fraudulent, and rapacious, and violent, another indulges in unlawful love, another frames countless schemes of deceit. And if it were possible to open your souls, then ye would see all things distinctly, and know that I am not mad. Do you not see in a camp, that when it is peace, men lay down their arms and cross over unarmed and undefended into the camp of the enemy, but when they are protected with arms, and with guards and outposts, the nights are spent in watching, and the fires are kept continually burning, this state of things is no longer peace but war? Now this is what may be seen among us. For we are on our guard against one another, and fear one another and talk each of us into his neighbor's ear. And if we see any one else present, we hold our peace, and draw in all we were going to say. And this is not like men that feel confidence, but like those that are strictly on their guard. "But these things we do (some one may say,) not to do wrong, but to escape having it done us." Yea, for this I grieve, that living as we do among brethren, we need be on our guard against having wrong done us ; and we light up so many fires, and set guards and out-posts! The reason is the prevalence of falsehood, the prevalence of craft, the prevailing secession of charity, and war without truce. By this means one may find men that feel more confidence in Gentiles (Greeks) than in Christians. And yet, how ashamed we ought to be of this; how we ought to weep and bewail at it! "What then, some may say, is to become of me? such and such an one is of ungainly temper, and vexatious." Where then is your religion (Gr. philosophy)? where are the laws of the Apostles, which bid us bear one another's burdens? (Gal. vi. 2.) For if you have no notion of dealing well by your brother, when are you to be able to do so by a stranger? If you have not learnt how to treat a member of your own self, when are you likely to draw to you any from without, and to knit him to yourself? But how am I to feel? I am vexed exceedingly almost to tears, for I could have

---

[1] Or tunes, the word is ambiguous in the original.
[2] The substance used was probably not salt, but something possessing astringent properties.

sent forth large fountains from mine eyes
(Jer. ix. 1), as that Prophet says, seeing as I
do countless enemies upon the plain more
galling than those he saw. For he said, upon
seeing the aliens coming against them, "My
bowels! I am pained at my bowels." (ib.
iv. 19.) But when I see men arrayed under one
leader, yet standing against one another, and
biting and tearing their own members, some for
money's sake, and some for glory's, and others
quite at random ridiculing and mocking and
wounding one another in countless ways, and
corpses too worse treated than those in war,
and that it is but the bare name of the
brethren that is now left, myself feel my inability to devise any lament fitting such a
catastrophe as this! Reverence now, oh
reverence, this Table whereof we all are
partakers! (1 Cor. x. 16–18.) Christ, Who
was slain for us, the Victim that is placed
thereon! (Heb. xiii. 10.) Robbers when
they once partake of salt, cease to be robbers
in regard to those with whom they have par-
taken thereof; that table changes their dispositions, and men fiercer than wild beasts it
makes gentler than lambs. But we though
partakers of such a Table, and sharers of such
food as that, arm ourselves against one
another, when we ought to arm against him
who is carrying on a war against all of us, the
devil. Yet this is why we grow weaker and
he stronger every day. For we do not join to
form in defence against him, but along with
him we stand against each other, and use him
as a commander for such hostile arrays, when
it is he alone that we ought to be fighting
with. But now letting him pass, we bend the
bow against our brethren only. What bows,
you will say? Those of the tongue and the
mouth. For it is not javelins and darts only,
but words too, keener far than darts, that
inflict wounds. And how shall we be able to
bring this war to an issue? one will ask. If
thou perceivest that when thou speakest ill
of thy brother, thou art casting up mire out
of thy mouth, if thou preceivest that it is a
member of Christ that thou art slandering,
that thou art eating up thine own flesh (Ps.
xxvii. 2), that thou art making the judgment set for thee more bitter (fearful and
uncorrupt as it is), that the shaft is killing
not him that is smitten, but thyself that
shot it forth. But he did you some wrong,
may be, and injured you? Groan at it, and
do not rail. Weep, not for the wrong done
thee, but for his perdition, as thy Master
also wept at Judas, not because Himself
was to be crucified, but because he was a
traitor. Has he insulted thee and abused
thee? Beseech God for him, that He may

speedily become appeased toward him. He
is thy brother, he is a member of thee, the
the fruit of the same pangs as thyself, he
has been invited to the same Table. But
he only makes fresh assaults upon me, it
may be said. Then is thy reward all the
greater for this. On this ground then there
is the best reason for abating one's anger,
since it is a mortal wound that he has received, since the devil hath wounded him.
Do not thou then give a further blow, nor
cast thyself down together with him. For
so long as thou standest thou hast the means
of saving him also. But if thou dash thyself
down by insulting deeds in return, who is then
to lift you both up? Will he that is wounded?
Nay, for he cannot, now that he is down.
But wilt thou that art fallen along with him?
And how shalt thou, that couldest not support thine own self, be able to lend a hand
to another? Stand therefore now nobly, and
setting thy shield before thee, and draw him,
now he is dead, away from the battle by thy
long-suffering. Rage hath wounded him, do
not thou also wound him, but cast out even
that first shaft. For if we associate with each
other on such terms, we shall soon all of us
become healthful. But if we arm ourselves
against one another, there will be no farther
need even of the devil to our ruin. For all
war is an evil, and civil war especially. But
this is a sorer evil than even a civil one, as
our mutual rights are greater than those of
citizenship, yea, than of kindred itself. Of
old, Abel's brother slew him and shed the
blood of his kinsman. But this murder is
more lawless than that, in that the rights of
kinsmanship are greater, and the death a sorer
evil. For he wounded the body, but thou
hast whetted thy sword against the soul.
"But thou didst first suffer ill." Yes, but it
is not suffering ill, but doing it, that is really
suffering ill. Now consider; Cain was the
slayer, Abel was the slain. Who then was the
dead? He that after death crieth, (for He
saith, "The voice of thy brother's blood
crieth to Me,") (Gen. iv. 10), or he who
while he lived was yet trembling and in fear?
He was, assuredly he was, more an object of
pity than any dead man. Seest thou how to
be wronged is better, though a man come even
to be murdered? learn that to wrong is worse,
though a man should be strong enough even
to kill. He smote and cast down his brother,
yet the latter was crowned, the former was
punished. Abel was made away with and
slain wrongfully, but he even when dead
accused (comp. John v. 45), and convicted
and overcame: the other, though alive, was
speechless, and was ashamed, and was con-

victed, and effected the opposite of what he intended. For he made away with him because he saw him beloved, expecting to cast him out of the love also. Yet he did but make the love more intense, and God sought him more when dead, saying, " Where is thy brother Abel ? " (Gen. iv. 9.) For thou hast not extinguished the desire towards him by thine envy, but hast kindled it up the more. Thou hast not lessened his honor by slaying him, but hast made it the more ample. Yet before this God had even made him subject to thee, whereas since thou hast slain him, even when dead, he will take vengeance upon thee. So great was my love towards him. Who then was the condemned person, the punisher or the punished ? He that enjoyed so great honor from God, or he that was given up to a

certain novel and unexpected punishment ? Thou didst not fear him (he would say) while alive, thou shalt fear him therefore when dead. Thou didst not tremble when on the point of thrusting with the sword. Thou shalt be seized, now the blood is shed, with a continual trembling. While alive he was thy servant, and thou showedst no forbearance to him. For this reason, now he is dead, he hath become a master thou shalt be afraid of. Thinking then upon these things, beloved, let us flee from envy, let us extinguish malice, let us recompense one another with charity, that we may reap the blessings rising from it, both in the present life and the life which is to come, by the grace and love toward man, etc. Amen.

HOMILY IX.

ROM. IV. 23.

"Now it was not written for his sake alone, that it was imputed to him for righteousness; but for us also, to whom it shall be imputed, if we believe on Him that raised up Jesus our Lord from the dead."

AFTER saying many great things of Abraham, and his faith, and righteousness, and honor before God, lest the hearer should say, What is this to us, for it is he that was justified ? he places us close to the Patriarch again. So great is the power of spiritual words. For of one of the Gentiles, one who was recently come near, one who had done no work, he not only says that he is in nothing inferior to the Jew who believes (i. e. as a Jew), but not even to the Patriarch, but rather, if one must give utterance to the wondrous truth, even much greater. For so noble is our birth, that his faith is but the .type of ours. And he does not say, If it was reckoned unto him, it is probable it will be also to us, that he might not make it matter of syllogism. But he speaks in authentic words of the divine law, and makes the whole a declaration of the Scripture. For why was it written, he says, save to make us see that we also were justified in this way ? For it is the same God Whom we have believed, and upon the same matters, if it be not in the case of the same persons. And after speaking of our faith, he also mentions God's unspeakable love towards man, which he ever presents on all sides, bringing the Cross before us. And this he now makes plain by saying,

Ver. 25. "Who was delivered for our offences, and was raised again for our justification."

See how after mentioning the cause of His death, he makes the same cause likewise a demonstration of the resurrection. For why, he means, was He crucified ? Not for any sin of His own. And this is plain from the Resurrection. For if He were a sinner, how should He have risen ? But if He rose, it is quite plain that He was not a sinner. But [1] if He was not a sinner, how came He to be crucified ?—For others,—and if for others, then surely he rose again. Now to prevent your saying, How, when liable for so great sins, came we to be justified ? he points out One that blotteth out all sins, that both from Abraham's faith, whereby he was justified, and from the Saviour's Passion, whereby we were freed from our sins, he might confirm what he had said. And after mentioning His Death, he speaks also of His Resurrection. For the purpose of His dying was not that He might hold us liable to punishment and in condemnation, but that He might do good unto us. For for this cause He both died and rose again, that He might make us righteous.

Chap. v. ver. 1. " Therefore being justi-

---

[1] If a fresh argument commences here, there is no vicious circle. For there was independent proof of each proposition, and so, when shown to involve one another, they were mutually confirmed.

fied by faith, let us [1]* have peace with God through our Lord Jesus Christ."

What does "Let us have peace" mean? Some say, "Let us not be at variance, through a peevish obstinacy for bringing in the Law." But to me he seems to be speaking now of our conversation. For after having said much on the subject of faith, he had set it before righteousness which is by works, to prevent any one from supposing what he said was a ground for listlessness, he says, "let us have peace," that is, let us sin no more, nor go back to our former estate. For this is making war with God. And "how is it possible," saith one, "to sin no more?" How [2] was the former thing possible? For if when liable for so many sins we were freed from all by Christ, much more shall we be able through Him to abide in the estate wherein we are. For it is not the same thing to receive peace when there had been none, and to keep it when it has been given, since to acquire surely is harder than to keep. Yet nevertheless the more difficult hath been made easy, and carried out into effect. That which is the easier thing then will be what we shall easily succeed in, if we cling to Him who hath wrought even the other for us. But here it is not the easiness only which he seems to me to hint at, but the reasonableness. For if He reconciled us when we were in open war with Him, it is reasonable that we should abide in a state of reconciliation,[3] and give unto Him this reward for that He may not seem to have reconciled untoward and unfeeling creatures to the Father.

Ver. 2. "By Whom also we have access," he says, "by faith unto this grace. (7 Mss. add, unto, etc.)

If then He hath brought us near to Himself, when we were far off, much more will He keep us now that we are near. And let me beg you to consider how he everywhere sets down these two points; His part, and our part. On His part, however, there be things varied and numerous and diverse. For He died for us, and farther reconciled us, and brought us to Himself, and gave us grace unspeakable. But we brought faith only as our contribution. And so he says," "by faith, unto this grace." What grace is this? tell me. It is the being counted worthy of the knowledge of God, the being forced from error, the coming to a knowledge of the Truth, the obtaining of all the blessings that come through Baptism. For the end of His bringing us near was that we might receive these gifts. For it was not only that we might have simple remission of sins, that we were reconciled; but that we might receive also countless benefits. Nor did He even pause at these, but promised others, namely, those unutterable blessings that pass understanding alike and language. And this is why he has set them both down also. For by mentioning grace he clearly points at what we have at present received, but by saying, "And we rejoice in hope of the glory of God," he unveils the whole of things to come. And he had well said, "wherein also we stand." For this is the nature of God's grace. It hath no end, it knows no bound, but evermore is on the advance to greater things, which in human things is not the case. Take an instance of what I mean. A person has acquired rule and glory and authority, yet he does not stand therein continuously, but is speedily cast out of it. Or if man take it not from him, death comes, and is sure to take it from him. But God's gifts are not of this kind; for neither man, nor occasion, nor crisis of affairs, nor even the Devil, nor death, can come and cast us out of them. But when we are dead we then more strictly speaking have possession of them, and keep going on enjoying more and more. And so if thou feel in doubt about those to come; from those now present, and what thou hast already received, believe in the other also. For this is why he says, "And we rejoice (καυχώμεθα) in hope of the glory of God," that you may learn, what kind of soul the faithful ought to have. For it is not only for what hath been given, but for what is to be given, that we ought to be filled with confidingness, as though it were already given. For one "rejoices" in what is already given. Since then the hope of things to come is even as sure and clear as that of what is given, he says that in that too we in like manner "rejoice." For this cause also he called them glory. For if it contributeth unto God's glory, come to pass it certainly will, though it do not for our sakes, yet for Him it will. And why am I saying (he means) that the

---

[1] So nearly all Mss. here; and there is good authority for the reading in the text of the N. T. both from Mss., versions, and Fathers. It is accepted by Tregelles: Tischendorf retains the received text "we have."

* The text of Chrys. adds confirmation to the strongly attested ἔχωμεν (so א A. B. C. D.) as against the reading (ἔχομεν) of the T. R. Strong and clear as is the external evidence here, it is to me very doubtful whether it is not overborne by the internal evidence. There seems to be no appropriateness in an exhortation here. The thought has been developed in a didactic form thus far and we should now expect a didactic conclusion (οὖν). Nor should we expect an exhortation to have peace with God which would be the natural consequence of justification and scarcely the proper object of an exhortation. De Wette, Meyer, Godet and Weiss reject the better authenticated reading ἔχωμεν on these grounds. It is difficult to see how Chrys. can think that the Apostle is here treating of our "Conversation"—when he proceeds at once to enumerate the new comfort, patience and hope which follow from justification.—G. B. S.

[2] 3 Mss. If thou wilt consider how, etc.

[3] Or perhaps "by the terms of reconciliation," for so the text may be understood. The reading in Savile's margin, τοῖς καταλλαγεῖσι, seems also to bear the same sense.

blessings to come are worthy of being gloried in (καυχήσεως)? Why even the very evils of this time present are able to brighten up our countenances, and make us find in them even our repose. Wherefore also he added,

Ver. 3. "And not only so, but we glory in tribulations also."

Now, consider how great the things to come are, when even at things that seem to be distressful we can be elated; so great is God's gift, and such a nothing any distastefulness in them! For in the case of external goods, the struggle for them brings trouble and pain and irksomeness along with it; and it is the crowns and rewards that carry the pleasure with them. But in this case it is not so, for the wrestlings have to us no less relish than the rewards. For since there were sundry temptations in those days, and the kingdom existed in hopes, the terrors were at hand, but the good things in expectation, and this unnerved the feebler sort, even before the crowns he gives them the prize now, by saying that we should "glory even in tribulations." And what he says is not "you should glory," but we glory, giving them encouragement in his own person. Next since what he had said had an appearance of being strange and paradoxical, if a person who is struggling in famine, and is in chains and torments, and insulted, and abused, ought to glory, he next goes on to confirm it. And (what is more), he says they are worthy of being gloried in, not only for the sake of those things to come, but for the things present in themselves. For tribulations are in their own selves a goodly thing. How so? It is because they anoint us unto patient abiding. Wherefore after saying we glory in tribulations, he has added the reason, in these words, "Knowing that tribulation worketh patience." Notice again the argumentative spirit of Paul, how he gives their argument an opposite turn. For since it was tribulations above all that made them give up the hopes of things to come, and which cast them into despondency, he says that these are the very reasons for confidingness, and for not desponding about the things to come, for "tribulation," he says, "worketh patience."

Ver. 4, 5. "And patience experience, and experience hope; and hope maketh not ashamed." *

Tribulations, that is, are so far from confuting these hopes, that they even prove them. For before the things to come are realized, there is a very great fruit which tribulation hath—patience; [1] and the making of the man that is tried, experienced. And it contributes in some degree too to the things to come,[2] for it gives hope a vigor within us, since there is nothing that so inclines a man to hope for blessings as a good conscience. Now no man that has lived an upright life is unconfiding about things to come, as of those who have been negligent there are many that, feeling the burden of a bad conscience, wish there were neither judgment nor retribution. What then? do our goods lie in hopes? Yes, in hopes—but not mere human hopes, which often slip away, and put him that hoped to shame; when some one, who was expected to patronize him, dies, or is altered though he lives. No such lot is ours; our hope is sure and unmoveable. For He Who hath made the promise ever liveth, and we that are to be the enjoyers of it, even should we die, shall rise again, and there is absolutely nothing which can put us to shame, as having been elated at random, and to no purpose, upon unsound hopes. Having then sufficiently cleared them of all doubtfulness by these words of his, he does not let his discourse pause at the time present, but urges again the time to come, knowing that there were men of weaker character, who looked too for present advantages, and were not satisfied with these mentioned. And so he offers a proof for them in blessings already given. For lest any should say, But what if God be unwilling to give them to us? For that He can, and that He abideth and liveth, we all

---

begets hope; it takes away fear for what the future may bring. —G. B. S.

[1] We do not see what use patience will be of in a future state. cf. Butler's *Anal.* part i. c. v. § 4.

[2] That such is the power of conscience even in a heathen is plain from Plato, *Rep.* 1. § 5. Steph. p., 350. e. "For you must know, Socrates," said he, "that when a man is near the time when he must expect to die, there comes into his mind a fear and anxiety about things that were never so thought of before. For the stories that are told of things in Hades, how a man that has done wrong here must satisfy justice for it there, which have hitherto been laughed at, come then to perplex his soul with alarms that they may be true. And even of himself, whether from the infirmity of age, or in that he is in a manner already nearer to that state, he sees somewhat more of it. However it be, he becomes full of suspicion and alarm; and takes account and considers whether he has at all wronged any one. And then a man who finds a number of guilty actions in his life is often roused by alarm from his sleep, like children, and lives ever in expectation of misery. But one who is conscious in himself of no wrong has a pleasing hope ever with him, as the kind nurse of his old age, as Pindar too says. For beautifully indeed, Socrates, has he expressed this, that whoever has passed his life in justice and holiness,

Sweet Hope, best helpmate of the heart,
　　With cheerful tenderness,
Soothes his declining years.
　　She whom we mortals trust
　　In many an anxious doubt
To sway life's wavering helm.

Well said indeed! one wonders to think how well," etc.

---

* The word rendered "patience," (ὑπομονή) means rather patient endurance, constancy. It is active rather than passive in meaning. Then the endurance which is developed under tribulation helps to form a tried, tested character, Δοκιμή means a tested state—approved character. The R. V. renders "probation," which is more nearly correct than "experience" (A. V.). We have no word which makes a felicitous translation. The meaning is that steadfastness under trials develops a tested moral manhood, and this kind of character

know : but how do we know, that He is willing, also, to do it ? From the things which have been done already. "What things done?" The Love which He hath shown for us. In doing what ? some may say. In giving the Holy Ghost. Wherefore after saying "hope maketh not ashamed," he goes on to the proof of this, as follows :

"Because the love of God is," he does not say "given," but "shed abroad in our hearts," so showing the profusion of it. That gift then, which is the greatest possible, He hath given ; not heaven and earth and sea, but what is more precious than any of these, and hath rendered us Angels from being men, yea sons of God, and brethren of Christ. But what is this gift ? The Holy Spirit. Now had He not been willing to present us after our labors with great crowns, He would never have given us such mighty gifts before our labors. But now the warmth of His Love is hence made apparent, that it is not gradually and little by little that He honors us ; but He hath shed abroad the full fountain of His blessings, and this too before our struggles. And so, if thou art not exceedingly worthy, despond not, since thou hast that Love of thy Judge as a mighty pleader for thee. For this is why he himself by saying, "hope maketh not ashamed," has ascribed everything not to our well-doings, but to God's love. But after mentioning the gift of the Spirit, he again passes to the Cross, speaking as follows :

Ver. 6–8. "For while we were yet without strength, Christ in due time died for the ungodly. For scarcely for a righteous man will one die : yet pervadenture for a good man some would even dare to die.* But God commendeth His love towards us."

Now what he is saying is somewhat of this kind. For if for a virtuous man, no one would hastily choose to die, consider thy Master's love, when it is not for virtuous men, but for sinners and enemies that He is seen to have been crucified—which he says too after this, "In that, if when we were sinners Christ died for us,"

Ver. 9, 10. "Much more then, being now justified by His Blood, we shall be saved from wrath through Him. For if, when we were

enemies, we were reconciled to God by the death of His Son, much more, being reconciled, we shall be saved by His life."

And what he has said looks indeed like tautology, but it is not to any one who accurately attends to it. Consider then. He wishes to give them reasons for confidence respecting things to come. And first he gives them a sense of shame from the righteous man's decision, when he says, that he also "was fully persuaded that what God had promised He was able also to perform ; " and next from the grace that was given ; then from the tribulation, as sufficing to lead us into hopes ; and again from the Spirit, whom we have received. Next from death, and from our former viciousness, he maketh this good. And it seems indeed, as I said, that what he had mentioned was one thing, but it is discovered to be two, three, and even many more. First, that "He died : " second, that it was "for the ungodly ; " third, that He "reconciled, saved, justified " us, made us immortal, made us sons and heirs. It is not from His Death then only, he says, that we draw strong assertions, but from the gift which was given unto us through His Death. And indeed if He had died only for such creatures as we be, a proof of the greatest love would what He had done be ! but when He is seen at once dying, and yielding us a gift, and that such a gift, and to such creatures, what was done casts into shade our highest conceptions, and leads the very dullest on to faith. For there is no one else that will save us, except He Who so loved us when we were sinners, as even to give Himself up for us. Do you see what a ground this topic affords for hope ? For before this there were two difficulties in the way of our being saved ; our being sinners, and our salvation requiring the Lord's Death, a thing which was quite incredible before it took place, and required exceeding love for it to take place. But now since this hath come about, the other requisites are easier. For we have become friends, and there is no further need of Death. Shall then He who hath so spared his enemies as not to spare His Son, fail to defend them now they are become friends, when He hath no longer any need to give up his Son ? For it is either because a person does not wish it, or because though he may wish it perhaps,[1] yet he is unable to do it, that he does not save. Now none of these things can be said of God. For that He is willing is plain from His having given up His Son.[2] But that He is able also is the very thing He proved

---

* Meyer and Weiss make no distinction between δικαίου and ἀγαθοῦ here. Most have held (I think, rightly) that the latter expresses more than the former. It comprehends those qualities of benevolence, kindness, etc., which may be considered as the peculiar bonds of friendship and would lead to the greatest sacrifices. Hofman, Godet and Weiss (following Jerome) take τοῦ ἀγαθοῦ as neuter. J. Müller supposes it to refer to God. The force of the argument is : For an upright man one would hardly be moved to die, but in the case of a benefactor to whom one owed much, the motives of love and pity might move one strongly enough to lead him to summon up the resolution (τολμᾷ) to die, but this would be the highest and a very improbable reach of human love. But Christ died for his *enemies*, etc.—G. B. S.

[1] πολλάκις, Heind. ad Plat. *Phæd.* p. 140, § 12.
[2] So Field, from one Ms. and Brixius' version : the old reading could only mean " Now none of these things can be said of God, considering He hath given up."

likewise, from the very fact of His having justified men who were sinners. What is there then to prevent us any more from obtaining the things to come? Nothing! Then again, lest upon hearing of sinners, and enemies, and strengthless ones, and ungodly, thou shouldest be inclined to feel abashed and blush; hear what he says.

Ver. 11. "And not only so, but we also joy in God through our Lord Jesus Christ, by Whom we have now received the atonement."

What meaneth the "not only so?" Not only were we saved, he means, but we even glory[1] for this very reason, for which some suppose we ought to hide our faces. For, for us who lived in so great wickedness to be saved, was a very great mark of our being exceedingly beloved by Him that saved us. For it was not by angels or archangels, but by His Only-begotten Son Himself, that He saved us. And so the fact of His saving us, and saving us too when we were in such plight, and doing it by means of His Only-begotten, and not merely by His Only-begotten, but by His Blood, weaves for us endless crowns to glory in. For there is not anything that counts so much in the way of glory and confidence, as the being treated as friends (φιλεῖσθαι) by God, and finding a Friend (φιλεῖν) in Him that loveth (ἀγαπῶντα) us. This it is that maketh the angels glorious, and the principalities and powers. This is greater than the Kingdom, and so Paul placed it above the Kingdom. For this also I count the incorporeal powers blessed, because they love Him, and in all things obey Him. And on this score the Prophet also expressed his admiration at them. "Ye that excel in strength, that fulfil His Word." (Ps. ciii. 20.) And hence too Isaiah extolleth the Seraphim, setting forth their great excellency from their standing near that glory, which is a sign of the greatest love.

Let us then emulate the powers above, and be desirous not only of standing near the throne, but of having Him dwelling in us who sitteth upon the Throne. He loved us when we hated Him, and also continueth to love us. "For He maketh His sun to rise on the evil and on the good and sendeth rain on the just and on the unjust." (Matt. v. 45.) As then He loveth us, do thou love Him. For He is our Friend (φιλεῖ γὰρ). And how cometh it, some will say, that one who is our Friend threateneth hell, and punishment, and vengeance? It is owing to His loving us alone. For all He doeth and is busied with, is with

a view to strike out thy wickedness, and to refrain with fear, as with a kind of bridle, thy inclinableness to the worse side, and by blessings and by pains recovering thee from thy downward course, and leading thee up to Him, and keeping thee from all vice, which is worse than hell. But if thou mockest what is said, and wouldest rather live continually in misery, than be punished for a single day, it is no marvel. For this is but a sign of thy unformed judgment (ἀτελοῦς γνώμης), drunkenness, and incurable disorder. Since little children even when they see the physician going to apply burning or the knife, flee and leap away screaming and convulsed, and choose to have a continual sore eating into their body, rather than to endure a temporary pain, and so enjoy health afterwards. But those who have come to discretion, know that to be diseased is worse than submitting to the knife, as also to be wicked is worse than to be punished. For the one is to be cured and to be healthy, the other to ruin one's constitution and to be in continual feebleness. Now that health is better than feebleness, surely is plain to every one. Thieves then ought to weep not when they have their sides pierced through, but when they pierce through walls and murder. For if the soul be better than the body (as it is), when the former is ruined there is more reason to groan and lament; but if a man does not feel it, so much the more reason to bewail it. For those that love with an unchastened love ought to be more pitied than those who have a violent fever, and those that are drunken, than those that are undergoing torture. But if these are more painful (some may say), how come we to give them the preference? Because there are many of mankind, who, as the proverb saith, like the worse, and they choose these, and pass by the better. And this one may see happening as well in victuals as in forms of government, in emulous aims of life too, and in the enjoyment of pleasure, and in wives, and in houses, and in slaves, and in lands, and in the case of all other things. For which is more pleasurable pray, cohabiting with women or with males? with women or with mules? Yet still we shall find many that pass over women, and cohabit with creatures void of reason, and abuse the bodies of males. Yet natural pleasures are greater than unnatural ones. But still many there are that follow after things ridiculous and joyless, and accompanied with a penalty, as if pleasurable. Well but to them, a man may say, these things appear so. Now this alone is ground enough to make them miserable, that they think those things to be pleasurable which are not so. Thus

---

[1] Same word as joy. See v. 2, etc.

they assume punishment to be worse than sin, which it is not, but just the contrary. Yet, if it were an evil to the sinner, God would not have added evils to the evil; for He that doeth everything to extinguish evil, would not have increased it. Being punished then is no evil to the man who has done wrong, but not being punished, when in that plight, is evil, just as for the infirm not to be cured. (Plat. *Gorg.* p. 478, sqq.) For there is nothing so evil as extravagant desire. And when I say, extravagant, I mean that of luxury, and that of ill-placed glory, and that of power, and in general that of all things which go beyond what is necessary. For such is he who lives a soft and dissolute life, who seems to be the happiest of men, but is the most wretched, as superinducing upon his soul harsh and tyrannical sovereigns. For this cause hath God made the present a life of labor to us, that He may rid us of that slavery, and bring us into genuine freedom. For this cause He threatened punishment, and made labors a part of our portion in life, so muzzling our vaunting spirit. In this way the Jews also, when they were fettered to the clay and brick making, were at once self-governed, and called continually upon God. But when they were in the enjoyment of freedom, then they murmured, and provoked the Lord, and pierced themselves through with countless evils. What then, it may be said, will you say to those frequent instances of men being altered for the worse by tribulations? Why, that this is no effect of tribulation, but of their own imbecility. For neither if a man had a weak stomach and could not take a bitter medicine which would act as a purgative, but was made even worse by it, would it be the drug we should find fault with, but the weakness of the part, as we should therefore here too with the yieldingness of temper. For he who is altered so by tribulation, is much more likely to be affected in this way by laxity. If he falls even when splinted, (or tied) (this is what affliction is), much more will he when the bandage is removed. If when braced up he is altered, much more when in a state of tumor (χαυνούμενος). And how am I, one may ask, to keep from being so altered by tribulation? Why, if thou reflectest that, wish it or not, thou wilt have to bear the thing inflicted: but if thou dost it with a thankful spirit, thou wilt gain very greatly thereby; but if thou art indignant at it, and ragest[1] and blasphemest, thou wilt not make the calamity lighter, but thou wilt render its wave more troublous. By feeling then in this way, let us

turn what is necessary into a matter of our own choice. What I mean is this—suppose one has lost his own son, another all his property: if you reflect that it is not in the nature of things for what has taken place to be undone, while it is to gain fruit from the misfortune, though irremediable, even that of bearing the circumstance nobly; and if instead of using blasphemous words, thou wert to offer up words of thanksgiving to the Lord, so would evils brought upon thee against thy will become to thee the good deeds of a free choice. Hast thou seen a son taken prematurely away? Say, "the Lord hath given, the Lord hath taken away." Do you see your fortune exhausted? Say, "naked came I out of my mother's womb, and naked shall I return thither." (Job. i. 21.) Do you see evil men faring well, and just men faring ill and undergoing ills without number, and dost thou not know where to find the cause? Say, "I became even as it were a beast before Thee. Yet I am ever with Thee." (Ps. lxxiii. 22.) But if thou wilt search out the cause, reflect that He has fixed a day in which He will judge the world, and so you will throw off perplexity, for then every man will meet his deserts, even as Lazarus and the rich man. Call to mind the Apostles, for they too rejoiced at being scourged, at being driven about and undergoing numberless sufferings, because they were "counted worthy to suffer shame for His Name's sake." (Acts v. 41.) And do thou, then, if thou art sick, bear it nobly, and own thyself indebted to God for it, and thou shalt receive the same reward with them. But how, when in feebleness and pain, art thou to be able to feel grateful to the Lord? Thou wilt if thou lovest Him sincerely. For if the Three Children who were thrown into the furnace, and others who were in prisons, and in countless other evils, ceased not to give thanks, much more will they who are in a state of disease, be able to do this. For there is not, assuredly there is not, anything which vehement desire doth not get the better of. But when the desire is even that of God, it is higher than anything, and neither fire, nor the sword, nor poverty, nor infirmity, nor death, nor aught else of the kind appeareth dreadful to one who hath gotten this love, but scorning them all, he will fly to heaven, and will have affections no way inferior to those of its inhabitants, seeing nothing else, neither heaven, nor earth, nor sea, but gazing only at the one Beauty of that glory. And neither the vexations of this life present will depress him, nor the things which are goodly and attended with pleasure elate him or puff him up. Let us then love with this love (for there

---

[1] Several Mss. "art in pain."

is not anything equal unto it) both for the sake of things present and for the sake of things to come. Or rather, more than for these, for the nature of the love itself. For we shall be set free both from the punishments of this life and of that which is to come, and shall enjoy the kingdom. Yet neither is the escape from hell, nor the fruition of the kingdom, anything great in comparison of what is yet to be said. For greater than all these things is it to have Christ our beloved at once and our lover. For if when this happens with men it is above all pleasure; when both happen from God, what language or what thought is able to set before one the blessedness of this soul? There is none that can, save the experience of it only. That then we may by experience come to know what is this spiritual joy, and life of blessedness, and untold treasure of good things, let us leave everything to cling to that love, with a view as well to our own joy as to the glory of God. For unto Him is the glory and power, with His Only-begotten, and the Holy Ghost, now, and ever, and unto all ages evermore. Amen.

HOMILY X.

ROM. V. 12.

" Wherefore as by one man sin entered into the world, and death by sin, and so death passed upon (διῆλθεν 6 Mss. εἰσ. . .) all men, for that all have sinned."

As the best physicians always take great pains to discover the source of diseases, and go to the very fountain of the mischief, so doth the blessed Paul also. Hence after having said that we were justified, and having shown it from the Patriarch, and from the Spirit, and from the dying of Christ (for He would not have died unless He intended to justify), he next confirms from other sources also what he had at such length demonstrated. And he confirms his proposition from things opposite, that is, from death and sin. How, and in what way? He enquires whence death came in, and how it prevailed. How then did death come in and prevail? " Through the sin of one." But what means, "for that all have sinned?" This; he having once fallen, even they that had not eaten of the tree did from him, all of them, become mortal.*

Ver. 13. " For until the Law sin was in the world, but sin is not imputed where there is no law."

The phrase " till the Law " some think he used of the time before the giving of the Law —that of Abel, for instance, or of Noah, or of Abraham—till Moses was born. What was the sin in those days, at this rate? some say he means that in Paradise. For hitherto it was not done away, (he would say,) but the fruit of it was yet in vigor. For it had borne that death whereof all partake, which prevailed and lorded over us. Why then does he proceed, " But sin is not imputed when there is no law?" It was by way of objection from the Jews, say they who have spoken on our side,[1] that he laid this position down and said, if there be no sin without the Law, how came death to consume all those before the Law? But to me it seems that the sense presently to be given has more to be said for it, and suits better with the Apostle's meaning. And what sense is this? In saying, that " till the Law sin was in the world," what he seems to me to mean is this, that after the Law was given the sin resulting from the transgression of it prevailed, and prevailed too so long as the Law existed. For sin, he says, can have no existence if there be no law.† If then it was this sin, he means, from

---

* This whole passage is introduced to show the glory and power of Christ's salvation as able to conquer the power of sin and death. The case of Adam's sin is not introduced for its own sake but as a background on which to exhibit the greatness of God's grace. Two erroneous assumptions are often made in respect to this passage (1) that Adam's sin and not God's grace in Christ is the chief theme, and (2) that the Apostle intends here to set forth a theory of original sin. This verse contains four points (1) Sin came into the world by the agency of one man—Adam. (2) In consequence of sin came death. (3) In virtue of the causal relation between sin and death, the latter extended itself to all men, for the reason (4) that all sinned. The ὥσπερ shows that this is used as an illustrative parallel to magnify the greatness of grace which is mightier than sin (cf. πολλῷ μᾶλλον vv. 15-17).—G. B. S.

[1] οἱ τὰ ἡμέτερα εἰρηκότες. The passage is corrupt in Savile: most Mss. read φασὶν and λέγοντα.

† The apostle does not say that there can be no sin if there is no law. He says the exact contrary. He elsewhere says (iv. 15) that where there is no law there is no transgression. By " law " here he means positive, statutory commands and prohibitions. His meaning here is : God does not reckon ἁμαρτία as παράβασις where there is no explicit commandment. But sin was in the world during all this period previous to the Mosaic law, as proved by the reign of death. It extended its sway and penalty even to those who had not sinned, as Adam did, against positive enactment. We know well on what principle the apostle justifies his position that there is sin even where no written commandment is transgressed. The principle has been already developed viz.: there is a moral law implanted in the human heart (i. 19, 21; ii. 15). To offend against this is sin (though not transgression, which implies positive law) and induces death as its consequence.—G. B. S.

26

the transgression of the Law that brought forth death, how was it that all before the Law died? For if it is in sin that death hath its origin, but when there is no law, sin is not imputed, how came death to prevail? From whence it is clear, that it was not this sin, the transgression, that is, of the Law, but that of Adam's disobedience, which marred all things. Now what is the proof of this? The fact that even before the Law all died: for "death reigned," he says, "from Adam to Moses, even over them that had not sinned."

How did it reign? "After the similitude of Adam's transgression, who is the figure of Him that was to come." Now this is why Adam is a type of Christ. How a type? it will be said. Why in that, as the former became to those who were sprung from him, although they had not eaten of the tree, the cause of that death which by his eating was introduced; thus also did Christ become to those sprung from Him, even though they had not wrought righteousness, the Provider[1] of that righteousness which through His Cross[2] He graciously bestowed on us all. For this reason, at every turn he keeps to the "one," and is continually bringing it before us, when he says, "As by one man sin entered into the world"—and, "If through the offence of one many be dead:" and, "Not as it was by one that sinned, so is the gift;" and, "The judgment was by one to condemnation:" and again, "If by one (or, the one) man's offence death reigned by one;" and "Therefore as by the offence of one." And again, "As by one man's disobedience many (or, the many) were made sinners." And so he letteth not go of the one, that when the Jew says to thee, How came it, that by the well-doing of this one Person, Christ, the world was saved? thou mightest be able to say to him, How by the disobedience of this one person, Adam, came it to be condemned? And yet sin and grace are not equivalents, death and life are not equivalents, the Devil and God are not equivalents, but there is a boundless space between them. When then as well from the nature of the thing as from the power of Him that transacteth it, and from the very suitableness thereof (for it suiteth much better with God to save than to punish), the preëminence and victory is upon this side, what one word have you to say for unbelief, tell me? However, that what had been done was reasonable, he shows in the following words.

Ver. 15. "But not as the offence, so is also the free gift. For if through the offence of one many be dead, much more the grace of God, and the gift by grace, which is by one man, Jesus Christ, hath abounded unto the many."

For what he says is somewhat of this kind. If sin had so extensive effects, and the sin of one man too; how can grace, and that the grace of God, not the Father only, but also the Son, do otherwise than be the more abundant of the two? For the latter is far the more reasonable supposition. For that one man should be punished on account of another does not seem to be much in accordance with reason. But for one to be saved on account of another is at once more suitable and more reasonable. If then the former took place, much more may the latter. Hence he has shown from these grounds the likelihood and reasonableness of it. For when the former had been made good, this would then be readily admitted. But that it is even necessarily so, he makes good from what follows. How then does he make it good?

Ver. 16. "And not as it was by one that sinned, so is the gift. For the judgment was by one to condemnation, but the free gift is of many offences unto justification."

And what is this that he is speaking of? It is that sin had power to bring in death and condemnation; but grace did not do away that one sin only, but also those that followed after in its train. Lest then the words "as" and "so" might seem to make the measure of the blessings and the evils equal, and that you might not think, upon hearing of Adam, that it was only that sin which he had brought in which was done away with, he says that it was from many offences that an indemnity was brought about. How is this plain? Because after the numberless sins committed after that in paradise, the matter issued in justification. But where righteousness is, there of necessity follows by all means life, and the countless blessings, as does death where sin was. For righteousness is more than life, since it is even the root of life. That there were several goods then brought in, and that it was not that sin only that was taken away, but all the rest along with it, he points out when he says, that "the gift was of many offences unto justification." In which a proof is necessarily included, that death was also torn up by the roots. But since he had said, that the second was greater than the first, he is obliged to give further grounds again for this same thing. For, before, he had said that if one man's sin slew all, much more will the grace of One have the power to save. After that he shows that it was not that sin only that was done away by the grace, but all the rest too, and that it was not that the sins were done away only, but that righteousness was given. And Christ did not merely do the same amount of good that Adam did of harm, but far more and greater good. Since then he had made such declarations as these, he wants again here also further confirmation of these. And how does he give this confirmation? He says,

Ver. 17. "For if by one man's offence death reigned by one, much more they which receive abundance of grace and of the gift and (so Field with most Mss.) of righteousness shall reign in life by one, Jesus Christ."

What he says, amounts to this nearly. What armed death against the world? The one man's eating from the tree only. If then death attained so great power from one offence, when it is found that certain received a grace and righteousness out of all proportion to that sin, how shall they still be liable to death? And for this cause, he does not here say " grace," but " superabundance of grace." For it was not as much as we must have to do away the sin only, that we received of His grace, but even far more. For we were at once freed from punishment, and put off all iniquity, and were also born again from above (John iii. 3) and rose again with the old man buried, and were redeemed, justified, led up to adoption, sanctified, made brothers of the Only-begotten, and joint heirs and of one Body with Him, and counted for His Flesh, and even as a Body with the Head, so were we united unto Him! All these things then Paul calls a "superabundance" of grace, showing that what we received was not a medicine only to countervail the wound, but even health, and comeliness, and honor, and glory and dignities far transcending our natural state. And of these each in itself was enough to do away with death, but when all manifestly run together in one, there is not the least vestige of it left, nor can a shadow of it be seen, so entirely is it done away. As then if any one were to cast a person who owed ten mites (ὀβόλους) into prison, and not the man himself only, but wife and children and servants for his sake ; and another were to come and not to pay down the ten mites only, but to give also ten thousand talents of gold, and to lead the prisoner into the king's courts, and to the throne of the highest power, and were to make him partaker of the highest honor and every kind of magnificence, the creditor would not be able to remember the ten mites ; so hath our case been. For Christ hath paid down far more than we owe, yea as much more as the illimitable ocean is than a little drop. Do not then, O man, hesitate as thou seest so great a store of blessings, nor enquire how that mere spark of death and sin was done away, when such a sea of gifts was brought in upon it. For this is what Paul intimated by saying that "they who have received the abundance of the grace and righteousness shall reign in life." And as he had now clearly demonstrated this, he again makes use of his former argument, clenching it by taking up the same word afresh, and saying that if for that offence all were punished, then they may be justified too by these means.* And so he says,

Ver. 18. "Therefore as by the offence of one judgment came upon all men to condemnation ; even so by the righteousness of One the free gift came upon all men unto justification of life."

And he insists again upon it, saying,

Ver. 19. "For as by one man's disobedience many were made sinners, so by the obedience of One shall many be made righteous.

What he says seems indeed to involve no small question : but if any one attends to it diligently, this too will admit of an easy solution. What then is the question? It is the saying that through the offence of one many were made sinners. For the fact that when he had sinned and become mortal, those who were of him should be so also, is nothing unlikely. But how would it follow that from his disobedience another would become a sinner? For at this rate a man of this sort will not even deserve punishment, if, that is, it was not from his own self that he became a sinner. What then does the word "sinners" mean here? To me it seems to mean liable to punishment and condemned to death. Now that by Adam's death we all became mortals, he had shown clearly and at large. But the question now is, for what purpose was this done? But this he does not go on to add : for it contributed nothing to his present object. For it is against a Jew that the contest is, who doubted and made scorn of the righteousness by One. And for this reason after showing that the punishment too was brought in by one upon all, the reason why this was so he has not added. For he is not for superfluities, but keeps merely to what is necessary. For this is what the principles

---

* Chrys. has well apprehended v. 15-17 as an argument *a fortiori*. Here are three contrasts between the principles of sin and grace to show the superior power of the latter : (1) It is a much more reasonable and supposable case that many should find life in one man's act than that many should suffer death in consequence of one man's sin, v. 15. (2) The condemnation has in it (so to speak) only the power of one sin ; the gracious gift overcomes many trespasses, v. 16. (3) Life in Christ must be greater than death in Adam.—G. B. S.

of disputation did not oblige him to say any more than the Jew; and therefore he leaves it unsolved. But if any of you were to enquire with a view to learn, we should give this answer: That we are so far from taking any harm from this death and condemnation[1], if we be sober-minded, that we are the gainers even by having become mortal, first, because it is not an immortal body in which we sin; secondly, because we get numberless grounds for being religious (φιλοσοφίας). For to be moderate, and to be temperate, and to be subdued, and to keep ourselves clear of all wickedness, is what death by its presence and by its being expected persuades us to. But following with these, or rather even before these, it hath introduced other greater blessings besides. For it is from hence that the crowns of the martyrs come, and the rewards of the Apostles. Thus was Abel justified, thus was Abraham, in having slain his son, thus was John, who for Christ's sake was taken off, thus were the Three Children, thus was Daniel. For if we be so minded, not death only, but even the devil himself will be unable to hurt us. And besides there is this also to be said, that immortality awaits us, and after having been chastened a little while, we shall enjoy the blessings to come without fear, being as if in a sort of school in the present life, under instruction by means of disease, tribulation, temptations, and poverty, and the other apparent evils, with a view to our becoming fit for the reception of the blessings of the world to come.

Ver. 20. "Moreover the Law entered: that the offence might abound."

Since then he had shown that the world was condemned from Adam, but from Christ was saved and freed from condemnation, he now seasonably enters upon the discussion of the Law, here again undermining the high notions of it. For it was so far from doing any good, he means, or from being any way helpful, but the disorder was only increased by its having come in. But the particle "that" again does not assign the cause, but the result. For the purpose of its being given was not "in order that" it might abound, for it was given to diminish and destroy the offence. But it resulted the opposite way, not owing to the nature of the Law, but owing to the listlessness of those who received it.*

But why did he not say the Law was given, but "the Law entered by the way?" It was to show that the need of it was temporary, and not absolute or imperative. And this he says also to the Galatians, showing the very same thing another way. "For before faith came," he says, "we were kept under the Law, shut up unto the faith which should afterwards be revealed." And so it was not for itself, but for another, that it kept the flock. For since the Jews were somewhat gross-minded, and enervated, and indifferent to the gifts themselves, this was why the Law was given, that it might convict them the more, and clearly teach them their own condition, and by increasing the accusation might the more repress them. But be not thou afraid, for it was not that the punishment might be greater that this was done, but that the grace might be seen to be greater. And this is why he proceeds,

"But where sin abounded, grace did much more abound."

He does not say did abound, but "did much more abound." For it was not remission from punishment only that He gave us, but that from sins, and life also. As if any were not merely to free a man with a fever from his disease, but to give him also beauty, and strength, and rank; or again, were not to give one an hungered nourishment only, but were to put him in possession of great riches, and were to set him in the highest authority. And how did sin abound? some will say. The Law gave countless commands. Now since they transgressed them all, trangression became more abundant. Do you see what a great difference there is between grace and the Law? For the one became an addition to the condemnation, but the other, a further abundance of gifts. Having then mentioned the unspeakable munificence, he again discusses the beginning and the root both of death and of life. What then is the root of death? It is sin. Wherefore also he saith,

Ver. 21. "That as sin reigned unto death, even so might grace reign through righteousness unto eternal life, through our Lord Jesus Christ."

This he says to show that the latter ranks as a king, the former, death, as a soldier, being marshalled under the latter, and armed by it. If then the latter (i. e. sin) armed death, it is plain enough that the righteousness destructive hereof, which by grace was introduced, not only disarms death, but even destroys it, and undoes entirely the dominion thereof, in that it is the greatest of the two,

---

[1] i. e. since we have been redeemed. See on Rom. ix. 11.

* The Author's view of ἵνα πλεονάσῃ cannot be exegetically justified. Paul teaches that it was the purpose of the dispensation of law which came in between Adam and Christ to make transgression abound (cf. Gal. iii. 9). The meaning is not that its purpose in coming in alongside (παρεισῆλθεν) of this reign of sin was to increase sin; but to make sin appear as such, to exhibit it as transgression and to reveal it in its true character to the consciousness of men. Only through the law could sin appear as transgression and thus be apprehended by men in the clearest manner as contrary to God's will (cf. iv. 15 and v. 13).—G. B. S.

as being brought in not by man and the devil, but by God and grace, and leading our life unto a goodlier estate, and to blessings unlimited. For of it there will never be any end (to give you a view of its superiority from this also). For the other cast us out of our present life, but grace, when it came, gave us not the present life, but the immortal and eternal one. But for all these things Christ is our voucher. Doubt not then for thy life if thou hast righteousness, for righteousness is greater than life as being mother of it.

Chap. vi. ver. 1. "What then? shall we continue in sin, that grace may abound? God forbid."

He is again turning off to exhortation, yet introducing it not directly, lest he should seem to many to be irksome and vexing, but as if it rose out of the doctrines. For if, even so diversifying his address, he was afraid of their being offended at what he said, and therefore said, "I have written the more boldly unto you in some sort," (Rom. xv. 15) much more would he have seemed to them, had he not done so, to be too harsh. Since then he showed the greatness of the grace by the greatness of the sins it healed, and owing to this it seemed in the eyes of the unthinking to be an encouragement to sin (for if the reason, they would say, why greater grace was shown, was because we had done great sins, let us not give over sinning, that grace may be more displayed still), now that they might not say this or suspect it, see how he turns the objection back again. First he does it by his deprecation. "God forbid." And this he is in the habit of doing at things confessed on all hands to be absurd. And then he lays down an irrefragable argument. And what is it?

Ver. 2. "How shall we," he says, "that are dead to sin, live any longer therein?"

What does "we are dead" mean? Does it mean that as for that, and as far as it goes, we have all received the sentence[1] of death? or, that we became dead to it by believing any being[2] enlightened. This is what one should rather say, since the sequel makes this clearly right. But what is becoming dead to it? The not obeying it in anything any more. For this baptism effected once for all, it made us dead to it. But this must of our own earnestness thenceforth continually be maintained, so that, although sin issue countless commands to us, we may never again obey it, but abide unmovable as a dead man doth. And indeed he elsewhere saith that sin itself is dead. But there he sets that

down as wishing to show that virtue is easy. (Rom. vii. 8?) But here, as he earnestly desires to rouse the hearer, he puts the death on his side. Next, since what was said was obscure, he again explains, using what he had said also in the way of reproof.

Ver. 3, 4. "Know ye not," he says, "my brethren, that so many of us as were baptized into Christ were baptized into His death? therefore we are buried with Him by baptism into death."

What does being "baptized into His Death" mean? That it is with a view to our dying as He did. For Baptism is the Cross. What the Cross then, and Burial, is to Christ, that Baptism hath been to us, even if not in the same respects. For He died Himself and was buried in the Flesh, but we have done both to sin. Wherefore he does not say, planted together in His Death, but in the likeness of His Death. For both the one and the other is a death, but not of the same subject; since the one is of the Flesh, that of Christ; the other of sin, which is our own. As then that is real, so is this. But if it be real, then[3] what is of our part again must be contributed. And so he proceeds,

"That as Christ was raised up from the dead by the Glory of the Father, even so we also should walk in newness of life."

Here he hints, along with the duty of a careful walk, at the subject of the resurrection. In what way? Do you believe, he means, that Christ died, and that He was raised again? Believe then the same of thyself. For this is like to the other, since both Cross and Burial is thine. For if thou hast shared in Death and Burial, much more wilt thou in Resurrection and Life. For now the greater is done away with, the sin I mean, it is not right to doubt any longer about the lesser, the doing away of death.

But this he leaves for the present to the conscience of his hearers to reason out, but himself, after the resurrection to come had been set before us, demands of us another, even the new conversation, which is brought about in the present life by a change of habits.[4] When then the fornicator becomes chaste, the covetous man merciful, the harsh subdued, even here a resurrection has taken place, the prelude to the other. And how is it a resurrection? Why, because sin is mortified, and righteousness hath risen again, and the old life hath been made to vanish, and

---

[1] ἀπόφασιν ἐδεξάμεθα, see the same phrase, Hom. vii. p. 382.
[2] i. e. baptized, St. Cyr. Cat. Intr. § 1. p. 1, O. T.

[3] Or "still," εἰ καὶ ἀληθής.
[4] St. Gr. Naz. Iamb. xx. 271, p. 228 (in Ed. Ben. xxiv. 277, p. 508). B. What? have I not the cleansing laver yet? A. You have, but mind! B. Mind what? A. Not for your habits, but for past transgressions. B. Nay, but for habits! What? A. Only if thou be first at work to cleanse them. See Tert. de Pœn. § 6, 7, and the beginning of the next Homily.

this new and angelic one is being lived in. But when you hear of a new life, look for a great alteration, a wide change. But tears come into my eyes, and I groan deeply to think how great religiousness (φιλοσοφίαν) Paul requires of us, and what listlessness we have yielded ourselves up to, going back after our baptism to the oldness we before had, and returning to Egypt, and remembering the garlic after the manna. (Num. xi. 5.) For ten or twenty days at the very time of our Illumination, we undergo a change, but then take up our former doings again. But it is not for a set number of days, but for our whole life, that Paul requires of us such a conversation. But we go back to our former vomit, thus after the youth of grace building up the old age of sins. For either the love of money, or the slavery to desires not convenient, or any other sin whatsoever, useth to make the worker thereof old. "Now that which decayeth and waxeth old is ready to vanish away." (Heb. viii. 13.) For there is no body, there surely is none, to be seen as palsied by length of time, as a soul is decayed and tottering with many sins. Such an one gets carried on to the last degree of doting, yielding indistinct sounds, like men that are very old and crazed, being surcharged with rheum, and great distortion of mind, and forgetfulness, and with scales upon its eyes, and[1] disgustful to men, and an easy prey to the devil. Such then are the souls of sinners; not so those of the righteous, for they are youthful and well-favored, and are in the very prime of life throughout, ever ready for any fight or struggle. But those of sinners, if they receive even a small shock, straightway fall and are undone. And it was this the Prophet made appear, when he said, that like as the chaff which the wind scattereth from the face of the earth (Ps. i. 4), thus are they that live in sin whirled to and fro, and exposed to every sort of harm. For they neither see like a healthy person, nor hear with simplicity, they speak not articulately, but are oppressed with great shortness of breath. They have their mouth overflowing with spittle. And would it were but spittle, and nothing offensive! But now they send forth words more fetid than any mire, and what is worst, they have not power even to spit this saliva of words away from them, but taking it in their hand with much lewdness, they smear it on again, so as to be coagulating, and hard to perspire through.[2] Perhaps ye are sickened with this description.

Ought ye not then to be more so at the reality? For if these things when happening in the body are disgustful, much more when in the soul. Such was that son who wasted out all his share, and was reduced to the greatest wretchedness, and was in a feebler state than any imbecile or disordered person. But when he was willing, he became suddenly young by his decision alone and his change. For as soon as he had said, "I will return to my Father," this one word conveyed to him all blessings; or rather not the bare word, but the deed which he added to the word. For he did not say, "Let me go back," and then stay there; but said, Let me go back, and went back, and returned the whole of that way. Thus let us also do; and even if we have gotten carried beyond the boundary, let us go up to our Father's house, and not stay lingering over the length of the journey. For if we be willing, the way back again is easy and very speedy. Only let us leave the strange and foreign land; for this is what sin is, drawing us far away from our Father's house; let us leave her then, that we may speedily return to the house of our Father. For our Father hath a natural yearning towards us, and will honor us if we be changed, no less than those that are unattainted, if we change, but even more, just as the father showed that son the greater honor. For he had greater pleasure himself at receiving back his son. And how am I to go back again? one may say. Do but put a beginning upon the business, and the whole is done. Stay from vice, and go no farther into it, and thou hast laid hold of the whole already. For as in the case of the sick, being no worse may be a beginning of getting better, so is the case with vice also. Go no further, and then your deeds of wickedness will have an end. And if you do so for two days, you will keep off on the third day more easily; and after three days you will add ten, then twenty, then an hundred, then your whole life. (Cf. Hom. xvii. on St. Matt. p. 267, O. T.) For the further thou goest on, the easier wilt thou see the way to be, and thou wilt stand on the summit itself, and wilt at once enjoy many goods. For so it was when the prodigal came back, there were flutes, and harps, and dancings, and feasts, and assemblings: and he who might have called his son to account for his ill-timed extravagance, and flight to such a distance, did nothing of the sort, but looked upon him as unattainted, and could not find it in him even to use the language of reproach, or rather, even to mention barely to him the former things, but threw himself upon him, and kissed him, and killed the calf, and put a robe upon him, and placed on him abundant honors. Let us then, as we have such examples before us, be of good cheer and keep from despair. For He is not so well pleased with being called Master, as Father, nor with having a slave as with having a son. And this is what He liketh rather than that. This then is why He did all that He has done; and "spared not even His Only-begotten Son" (Rom. viii. 32), that we might receive the adoption of sons, that we might love Him, not as a Master only, but as a Father. And if He obtained this of us, He taketh delight therein as one that has glory given him, and proclaimeth it to all, though He needeth nothing of ours. This is what, in Abraham's case for instance, He everywhere does, using these words, "I am the God of Abraham, Isaac, and Jacob." And yet it was they of His household who should have found an honor in this; but now it is the Lord evidently who does this; for this is why He says to Peter, "Lovest thou Me more than these?" (John xxi. 17) to show that He seeketh nothing so much as this from us. For this too He bade Abraham offer his son to Him, that He might make it known to all that He was greatly beloved[1] by the patriarch. Now this desire to be loved exceedingly comes from loving exceedingly. For this cause too He said to the Apostles, "He that loveth father or mother more than Me, is not worthy of Me." (Matt. x. 37.) For this cause He bids us esteem that even which is in the most close connection with us, our soul (or, life, v. 39, and John xii. 25), as second to the love of him, since He wisheth to be beloved by us with exceeding entireness. For we too, if we have no strong feelings about a person, have no strong desire for his friendship either, though he be great and noble; whereas when we love any one warmly and really, though the person loved be of low rank and humble, yet we esteem love from him as a very great honor. And for this reason He Himself also called it glory not to be loved by us only, but even to suffer those shameful things in our behalf. (ib. 23.) However, those things were a glory owing to love only. But whatever we suffer for Him, it is not for love alone; but even for the sake of the greatness and dignity of Him we long for, that it would with good reason both be called glory, and be so indeed. Let us then incur dangers for Him as if running for the greatest crowns, and let us esteem neither poverty, nor disease, nor affront, nor calumny, nor death itself, to be heavy and burdensome,

when it is for Him that we suffer these things. For if we be right-minded, we are the greatest possible gainers by these things, as neither from the contrary to these shall we if not right-minded gain any advantage. But consider; does any one affront thee and war against thee? Doth he not thereby set thee upon thy guard, and give thee an opportunity of growing like unto God? For if thou lovest him that plots against thee, thou wilt be like Him that "maketh His Sun to rise upon the evil and good." (Matt. v. 45.) Does another take thy money away? If thou bearest it nobly, thou shalt receive the same reward as they who have spent all they have upon the poor. For it says, "Ye took joyfully the spoiling of your goods, knowing that ye have in heaven a better and an enduring substance." (Heb. x. 34.) Has any one reviled thee and abused thee, whether truly or falsely, he weaves for thee a very great crown if thou bearest meekly his contumely; since he too, who calumniates, provides for us an abundant reward. For "rejoice," it says, "and be exceeding glad, when men say all manner of evil against you falsely, because great is your reward in Heaven." (Matt. v. 12, 11.) And he too that speaketh truth against us is of the greatest service, if we do but bear meekly what is said. For the Pharisee spake evil of the Publican, and with truth, still instead of a Publican he made him a righteous man. (Luke xviii. 11.) And what need to go into particular instances. For any one that will go to the conflicts of Job may learn all these points accurately. And this is why Paul said, "God for us, who against us?" (Rom. viii. 31.) As then by being earnest, we gain even from things that vex us, so by being listless, we do not even improve from things that favor us. For what did Judas profit, tell me, by being with Christ? or what profit was the Law to the Jew? or Paradise to Adam? or what did Moses profit those in the wilderness? And so we should leave all, and look to one point only, how we may husband aright our own resources. And if we do this, not even the devil himself will ever get the better of us, but will make our profiting the greater, by putting us upon being watchful. Now in this way it is that Paul rouses the Ephesians, by describing his fierceness. Yet we sleep and snore, though we have to do with so crafty an enemy. And if we were aware of a serpent[2] nestling by our bed, we should make much ado to kill him. But when the devil nestleth in our souls, we fancy that we take no harm, but lie at our ease; and the reason is, that

---

[1] This passage is one among many which show how the *fides formata* was that which the Fathers contemplated.

[2] See Macarius on the *Keeping of the Heart*, c. 1. translated in Penn's *Institutes of Christian Perfection*, p. 2.

we see him not with the eyes of our body. And yet this is why we should rouse us the more and be sober. For against an enemy whom one can perceive, one may easily be on guard; but one that cannot be seen, if we be not continually in arms, we shall not easily escape. And the more so, because he hath no notion of open combat (for he would surely be soon defeated), but often under the appearance of friendship he insinuates the venom of his cruel malice. In this way it was that he suborned Job's wife, by putting on the mask of natural affectionateness, to give that wretchless advice. And so when conversing with Adam, he puts on the air of one concerned and watching over his interests, and saith, that "your eyes shall be opened in the day that ye eat of the tree." (Gen. iii. 5.) Thus Jephtha too he persuaded, under the pretext of religion, to slay his daughter, and to offer the sacrifice the Law forbade. Do you see what his wiles are, what his varying warfare? Be then on thy guard, and arm thyself at all points with the weapons of the Spirit, get exactly acquainted with his plans, that thou mayest both keep from being caught, and easily catch him. For it was thus that Paul got the better of him, by getting exactly acquainted with these. And so he says, "for we are not ignorant of his devices." (2 Cor. ii. 11.) Let us then also be earnest in learning and avoiding his stratagems, that after obtaining a victory over him, we may, whether in this present life or in that which is to come, be proclaimed conquerors, and obtain those unalloyed blessings, by the grace and love toward man, etc.

HOMILY XI.

ROM. VI. 5.

"For if we have been planted together * in the likeness of His death, we shall be also in the likeness of His resurrection."

WHAT I had before occasion to remark, that I mention here too, that he continually digresseth into exhortation, without making any twofold division as he does in the other Epistles, and setting apart the former portion for doctrines, and the latter for the care of moral instruction. Here then he does not do so, but blends the latter with the subject throughout, so as to gain it an easy admission. Here then he says there are two mortifyings, and two deaths, and that one is done by Christ in Baptism, and the other it is our duty to effect by earnestness afterwards. For that our former sins were buried, came of His gift. But the remaining dead to sin after baptism must be the work of our own earnestness, however much we find God here also giving us large help. For this is not the only thing Baptism has the power to do, to obliterate our former transgressions; for it also secures against subsequent ones. As then in the case of the former, thy contribution was faith that they might be obliterated, so also in those subsequent to this, show thou forth the change in thine aims, that thou mayest not defile thyself again. For it is this and the like that he is counselling thee when he says, "for if we have been planted together in the likeness of His Death, we shall be also in the likeness of His Resurrection." Do you observe, how he rouses the hearer by leading him straightway up to his Master, and taking great pains to show the strong likeness? This is why he does not say "in death," lest you should gainsay it, but, "in the likeness of His Death." For our essence itself hath not died, but the man of sins, that is, wickedness. And he does not say, "for if we have been" partakers of "the likeness of His Death;" but what? "If we have been planted together," so, by the mention of planting, giving a hint of the fruit resulting to us from it. For as His Body, by being buried in the earth, brought forth as the fruit of it the salvation of the world; thus ours also, being buried in baptism, bore as fruit righteousness, sanctification, adoption, countless blessings. And it will bear also hereafter the gift of the resurrection. Since then we were buried in water, He in earth, and we in regard to sin, He in regard to His Body, this is why he did not say, "we were planted together in His Death," but "in the likeness of His Death." For both the one and the other is death, but not that of the same subject. If then he says, "we have been planted together in His Death, [1] we shall be in that

---

* Better: "United with him by the likeness" or "united with the likeness." See, note *, p. 409.—G. B. S.

[1] The construction here is harsh, and seems to require "in the likeness of."

of His Resurrection," speaking here of the Resurrection which (Gr. be of His Resurrection) is to come. For since when he was upon the subject of the Death before, and said, "Know ye not, brethren, that so many of us as were baptized into Christ were baptized into His Death?" he had not made any clear statement about the Resurrection, but only about the way of life after baptism, bidding men walk in newness of life; therefore he here resumes the same subject, and proceeds to foretell to us clearly that Resurrection. And that you may know that he is not speaking of that resulting from baptism, but about the other, after saying, "for if we were planted together in the likeness of His Death," he does not say that we shall be in the likeness of His Resurrection,[1] but we shall belong to the Resurrection.* For to prevent thy saying, and how, if we did not die as He died, are we to rise as He rose? when he mentioned the Death, he did not say, "planted together in the Death," but, "in the likeness of His Death." But when he mentioned the Resurrection, he did not say, "in the likeness of the Resurrection," but we shall be "of the Resurrection" itself. And he does not say, We have been made, but we shall be, by this word again plainly meaning that Resurrection which has not yet taken place, but will hereafter. Then with a view to give credibility to what he says, he points out another Resurrection which is brought about here before that one, that from that which is present thou mayest believe also that which is to come. For after saying, "we shall be planted together in the Resurrection," he adds,

Ver. 6. "Knowing this, that our old man is crucified with Him, that the body of sin might be destroyed."

So putting together both the cause and the demonstration of the Resurrection which is to come. And he does not say is crucified, but is crucified with Him, so bringing baptism near to the Cross. And on this score also it was that he said above, "We have been planted together in the likeness of His Death that the body of sin might be destroyed," not giving that name to this body of ours, but to all iniquity. For as he calls the whole sum of wickedness the old man, thus again the wickedness which is made up of the different parts of iniquity he calls the body of that man. And that what I am saying is not mere guesswork, hearken to Paul's own interpretation of this very thing in what comes next. For after saying, "that the body of sin might be destroyed," he adds, "that henceforth we should not serve sin."† For the way in which I would have it dead is not so that ye should be destroyed and die, but so that ye sin not. And as he goes on he makes this still clearer.

Ver. 7. "For he that is dead," he says, "is freed (Gr. justified) from sin."

This he says of every man, that as he that is dead is henceforth freed from sinning, lying as a dead body, so must[2] he that has come up from baptism, since he has died there once for all, remain ever dead to sin. If then thou hast died in baptism, remain dead, for any one that dies can sin no more; but if thou sinnest, thou marrest God's gift. After requiring of us then heroism (Gr. philosophy) of this degree, he presently brings in the crown also, in these words.

Ver. 8. "Now if we be dead with Christ."

And indeed even before the crown, this is in itself the greater crown, the partaking with our Master. But he says, I give even another reward. Of what kind is it? It is life eternal. For "we believe," he says, "that we shall also live with Him." And whence is this clear?

Ver. 9. "That Christ being raised from the dead, dieth no more."

And notice again his undauntedness,[3] and how he makes the thing good from opposite grounds. Since then it was likely that some would feel perplexed at the Cross and the

---

[1] The word likeness in our version is in italics as an addition, and unless it is understood, the construction is scarcely grammatical; but this interpretation favors the reading questioned in the last note. Perhaps also St. Chrysostom may have taken the words thus, "If we have been in likeness planted together with His Death," which would be a parallel construction.

* The word σύμφευτοι should be rendered "united with" (as in R V.)—literally "grown together," from συν—φύω, not "planted together" (A. V.) as if from συν—φευτεύω. The Dat. τῷ ὁμοιώματι may be taken as instrumental after σύμ. γεγόν. (R. V., Weiss), or (I think better), after σύν in composition (Thayer's *Lex.*, Meyer), because there is no indirect object expressed and on the former view one must be supplied (as αὐτῷ, or χριστῷ). We must supply in the apodosis, σύμφευτοι τῷ ὁμοιώματι. The ὁμοίωμα here means that which corresponds to the death and resurrection of Christ, i. e. our moral death to sin and resurrection to a holy life (vid. vv. 2, 4), or (dropping the figure) the cessation of the old life and the beginning of the new. If the former occurs, the latter also must take place and thus the objection that if sin makes grace abound we should continue in sin, contradicts the very idea of the Christian life which is that of freedom from sin and continuance in holiness. The interp. of Chrys. is somewhat confused, apparently by not clearly apprehending the fact that Paul is dealing with an *analogy* to the death and resurrection of Christ.—G. B. S.

† Verse 6 urges the same thought under the specific figure of the crucifixion of the body. The use of this figure almost necessitates the use of the word *body* to carry it out. As the one is figurative, so is the other. By σῶμα τῆς ἁμαρτίας is not meant "the body which is sin—or sinful," but the body which is under the sway of sin. In the moral process of the new life the body so far 'as ruled by sin—as being the seat of evil passions and desires—is destroyed *in this character*. Paul could hardly have employed this figure had he not regarded the body as the special manifestation-point of sin.—G. B. S.

[2] The necessity spoken of is clearly, from the context, that of obligation.

[3] φιλονεικίαν, his determination to take the highest ground, and give up no single point.

Death, he shows that this very thing is a ground for feeling confident henceforward.

For suppose not, he says, because He once died, that He is mortal, for this is the very reason of His being immortal. For His death hath been the death of death, and because He did die, He therefore doth not die. For even that death

Ver. 10. "He died unto sin."

"What does "unto sin"[1] mean? It means that He was not subject even to that one, but for our sin, that He might destroy it, and cut away its sinews and all its power, therefore He died. Do you see how he affrighteth them? For if He does not die again, then there is no second laver, then do thou keep from all inclinableness to sin. For all this he says to make a stand against the "let us do evil that good may come. Let us remain in sin that grace may abound." To take away this conception then, root and branch, it is, that he sets down all this. But in that "He liveth, He liveth unto God," he says,— that is, unchangeably, so that death hath no more any dominion over Him. For if it was not through any liability to it that He died the former death, save only for the sin of others, much less will He die again now that He hath done that sin away. And this he says in the Epistle to the Hebrews also, "But now once," he says, "in the end of the world hath He appeared to put away sin by the Sacrifice of Himself. And as it is appointed unto men once to die, and after that the judgment; so Christ was once offered to bear the sins of many, and unto them that look for Him shall He appear the second time without sin unto salvation." (Heb. ix. 26–28.) And he both points out the power of the life that is according to God, and also the strength of sin. For with regard to the life according to God, he showeth that Christ shall die no more. With regard to sin, that if it brought about the death even of the Sinless, how can it do otherwise than be the ruin of those that are subject to it? And then as he had discoursed about His life; that none might say, What hath that which you have been saying to do with us? he adds,

Ver. 11. "Likewise reckon ye also yourselves to be dead indeed unto sin, but alive unto God."

He well says, "reckon," because there is no setting that, which he is speaking of, before the eyes as yet. And what are we to reckon? one may ask. That we "are dead unto sin, but alive unto God. In Jesus Christ our Lord." For he that so liveth will lay hold of every virtue, as having Jesus Himself for his ally. For that is what, " in Christ," means, for if He raised them when dead, much more when alive will He be able to keep them so.

Ver. 12. "Let not sin therefore reign in your mortal body, that ye should obey it in the lusts thereof."

He does not say, let not the flesh live or act, but, "let not sin reign,"[2] for He came not to destroy our nature, but to set our free choice aright. Then to show that it is not through any force or necessity that we are held down by iniquity, but willingly, he does not say, let it not tyrannize, a word that would imply a necessity, but let it not reign. For it is absurd for those who are being conducted to the kingdom of heaven to have sin empress over them, and for those who are called to reign with Christ to choose to be the captives of sin, as though one should hurl the diadem from off his head, and choose to be the slave of a frantic woman, who came begging, and was clothed in rags. Next since it was a heavy task to get the upper hand of sin, see how he shows it to be even easy, and how he allays the labor by saying, "in your mortal body." For this shows that the struggles were but for a time, and would soon bring themselves to a close. At the same time he reminds us of our former evil plight, and of the root of death, as it was from this that, contrary even to its beginning, it became mortal. Yet it is possible even for one with a mortal body not to sin. Do you see the abundancy of Christ's grace? For Adam, though as yet he had not a mortal body, fell. But thou, who hast received one even subject to death, canst be crowned. How then, is it that "sin reigns?" he says. It is not from any power of its own, but from thy listlessness. Wherefore after saying, "let it not reign," he also points out the mode of this reigning, by going on to say "that ye should obey it in the lusts thereof." For it is not honor to concede to it (i. e. to the body) all things at will, nay, it is slavery in the extreme, and the height of dishonor; for when it doth what it listeth, then is it bereft of all liberties; but when it is put under restraints, then it best keeps its own proper rank.

Ver. 13. "Neither yield ye your members as instruments of unrighteousness unto sin . . . . but as instruments of righteousness."

The body then is indifferent between vice

---

[1] Or "by sin."

[2] In all this there is a design to obviate Manichæan notions concerning matter, and the opinion resulting from them, that we must be content to live in sin as unavoidable.

and virtue, as also instruments (or arms) are. But either effect is wrought by him that useth it. As if a soldier fighting in his country's behalf, and a robber who was arming against the inhabitants, had the same weapons for defence. For the fault is not laid to the suit of armor, but to those that use it to an ill end. And this one may say of the flesh too, which becomes this or that owing to the mind's decision, not owing to its own nature. For if it be curious after the beauty of another, the eye becomes an instrument of iniquity, not through any agency of its own (for what is of the eye, is but seeing, not seeing amiss), but through the fault of the thought which commands it. But if you bridle it, it becomes an instrument of righteousness. Thus with the tongue, thus with the hands, thus with all the other members. And he well calls sin unrighteousness. For by sinning a man deals unrighteously either by himself or by his neighbor, or rather by himself more than by his neighbor. Having then led us away from wickedness, he leads us to virtue, in these words :

"But yield yourselves unto God, as those that are alive from the dead."

See how by his bare words he exhorts them, on that side naming " sin " and on this "God." For by showing what a difference there is between the rulers, he casts out of all excuse the soldier that leaveth God, and desireth to serve under the dominion of sin. But it is not only in this way, but also by the sequel, that he establishes this; by saying, " as alive from the dead." For by these he shows the wretchedness of the other, and the greatness of God's gift. For consider, he says, what you were, and what you have been made. What then were ye? Dead, and ruined by a destruction which could not from any quarter be repaired. For neither was there any one who had the power to assist you. And what have ye been made out of those dead ones? Alive with immortal life. And by whom? By the all-powerful God. Ye ought therefore to marshal yourselves under Him with as much cheerful readiness, as men would who had been made alive from being dead.

"And your members as instruments of righteousness."

Hence, the body is not evil, since it may be made an arm[1] of righteousness. But by calling it an arm, he makes it clear that there is a hard warfare at hand for us. And for this reason we need strong armor, and also a noble spirit, and one acquainted too with the ways of this warfare ; and above all we need a commander. The Commander however is standing by, ever ready to help us, and abiding unconquerable, and has furnished us with strong arms likewise. Farther, we have need of a purpose of mind to handle them as should be, so that we may both obey our Commander, and take the field for our country. Having then given us this vigorous exhortation, and reminded us of arms, and battle, and wars, see how he encourages his soldier again and cherishes[2] his ready spirit.

Ver. 14. " For sin shall no more have dominion over you ; for ye are not under the Law, but under grace."

If then sin hath no more dominion over us, why does he lay so great a charge upon them as he does in the words, " Let not sin reign in your mortal body," and, " yield not ye your members as instruments of unrighteousness unto sin ? " What does that here said mean then ? He is sowing a kind of seed in this statement, which he means to develop afterwards, and to cultivate in a powerful argument. What then is this statement ? It is this ; that our body, before Christ's coming, was an easy prey to the assaults of sin. For after death a great swarm of passions entered also. And for this cause it was not lightsome for running the race of virtue. For there was no Spirit present to assist, nor any baptism of power to mortify. (John vii. 39.) But as some horse (Plato *Phædr.* § 74) that answereth not the rein, it ran indeed, but made frequent slips, the Law meanwhile announcing what was to be done and what not, yet not conveying into those in the race anything over and above exhortation by means of words. But when Christ had come, the effort became afterwards more easy, and therefore we had a more distant goal (μείζονα τὰ σκάμματα) set us, in that the assistance we had given us was greater. Wherefore also Christ saith, " Except your righteousness shall exceed the righteousness of the Scribes and Pharisees, ye shall in no case enter into the Kingdom of Heaven. (Matt. v. 20.) But this he says more clearly in the sequel. But at present he alludes here briefly to it, to show that unless we stoop down very low to it, sin will not get the better of us. For it is not the Law only that exhorteth us, but grace too which also remitted our former sins, and secures us against future ones. For it promised them crowns after toils, but this (i. e. grace) crowned them first, and than led them to the contest. Now it seems to me that he is not signifying here the

---

[1] ὅπλα is most usually arms, secondarily any instruments.

[2] ἀλείφει. anoints. Hannibal, before his victory on the Trebia, sent oil round to his battalions to refresh their limbs. *Ignibus ante tentoria factis, oleoque per manipulos, ut mollirent artus, misso, et cibo per otium capto,* etc. Liv. xxi. 55.

whole life of a believer, but instituting a comparison between the Baptism and the Law. And this he says in another passage also; "The letter killeth, but the Spirit giveth life." (2 Cor. iii. 6.) For the Law convinceth of transgression, but grace undoes transgression. As then the former by convincing establisheth sin so the latter by forgiving suffereth us not to be under sin. And so thou art in two ways set free from this thraldom; both in thy not being under the Law, and in thy enjoying grace. After then he had by these words given the hearer a breathing time, he again furnishes him a safeguard, by introducing an exhortation in reply to an objection, and by saying as follows.

Ver. 15. "What then? shall we sin, because we are not under the Law, but under grace? God forbid."

So he first adopted a form of adjuration, because it was an absurb thing he had named. And then he makes his discourse pass on to exhortation, and shows the great facility of the struggle, in the following words. *

Ver. 16. "Know ye not, that to whom ye yield yourselves servants to obey, his servants ye are to whom ye obey; whether of sin unto death, or of obedience unto righteousness?

I do not, he would say, mention hell as yet, nor that great (Ms. Bodl. long) punishment, but the shame it is in this world, when ye become slaves, and slaves of your own accord too, and sin's slaves, and when the wages are such as a second death. For if before baptism, it wrought death of the body, and the wound required so great attendance, that the Lord of all came down to die, and so put a stop to the evil; if after so great a gift, and so great liberty, it seize thee again, while thou bendest down under it willingly, what is there that it may not do? Do not then run into such a pit, or willingly give thyself up. For in the case of wars, soldiers are often given up even against their will. But in this case, unless thou desertest of thyself, there is no one who will get the better of thee. Having then tried to shame them by a sense of duty, he alarms them also by the rewards, and lays before them the wages of both; righteousness, and death, and that a death not like the former, but far worse. For if Christ is to die no more, who is to do away with death? No one! We must then be punished, and have

vengeance taken upon us forever. For a death preceptible to the senses is not still to come in this case, as in the former, which gives the body rest, and separates it from the soul. "For the last enemy, death, is destroyed" (1 Cor. xv. 26), whence the punisment will be deathless. But not to them that obey, for righteousness, and the blessings springing from it, will be their rewards.

Ver. 17. "But God be thanked, that ye were the servants of sin, but ye have obeyed from the heart that form of doctrine which was delivered unto you." (Lit. "into which ye were delivered.")

After shaming them by the slavery, after alarming them by the rewards, and so exhorting them, he again rights them by calling the benefits to mind. For by these he shows that they were great evils from which they were freed, and that not by any labors of their own, and that things henceforth would be more manageable. Just as any one who has rescued a captive from a cruel tyrant, and advises him not to run away back to him, reminds him of his grievous thraldom; so does Paul set the evils passed away most emphatically before us, by giving thanks to God. For it was no human power that could set us free from all those evils, but, "thanks be to God," who was willing and able to do such great things. And he well says, "Ye have obeyed from the heart." Ye were neither forced nor pressed, but ye came over of your own accord, with willing mind. Now this is like one that praises and rebukes at once. For after having willingly come, and not having had any necessity to undergo, what allowance can you claim, or what excuse can you make, if you run away back to your former estate? Next that you may learn that it came not of your own willing temper only, but the whole of it of God's grace also, after saying, "Ye have obeyed from the heart," he adds, "that form of doctrine which was delivered you." For the obedience from the heart shows the free will. But the being delivered, hints the assistance from God. But what is the form of doctrine?[1] It is living aright, and in conformity with the best conversation.

Ver. 18. "Being then made free from sin, ye became the servants of righteousness."

There are two gifts of God which he here points out. The "freeing from sin," and also the "making them servants to righteousness," which is better than any freedom. For God hath done the same as if a person were to

---

* The Argument of the vv. 15-23 is briefly this: Does the principle that we are not under the (Mosaic) law lead to lawlessness and sin? No! for, although we are freed from the Mosaic law as such, we are still under the law of righteousness (cf. 1 Cor. ix. 21 "Not being without law to God, but under law to Christ). We are free from the law and free from sin, but are bondsmen to righteousness. See esp. 18. "And being made free from sin, ye became servants of righteousness."—G. B. S.

[1] Tit. ii. 12; 1 Tim. i. 10; are instances of a similar use of the term "doctrine." Compare Eph. iv. 19-24, from which context the phrase, "Even as Truth is in Jesus," appears to be used nearly in the same sense.

take an orphan, who had been carried away by savages into their own country, and were not only to free him from captivity, but were to set a kind father ever him, and bring him to very great dignity. And this has been done in our case. For it was not our old evils alone that He freed us from, since He even led us to the life of angels, and paved the way for us to the best conversation, handing us over to the safe keeping of righteousness, and killing our former evils, and deadening the old man, and leading us to an immortal life.

Let us then continue living this life; for many of those who seem to breathe and to walk about are in a more wretched plight than the dead. For there are different kinds of deadness; and one there is of the body, according to which Abraham was dead, and still was not dead. For "God," He says, "is not a God of the dead, but of the living." (Matt. xxii. 32.) Another is of the soul, which Christ alludes to when He says, "Let the dead bury their dead." (ib. viii. 22.) Another, which is even the subject of praise, which is brought about by religion (φιλοσοφίας), of which Paul saith, "Mortify your members which are upon the earth." (Col. iii. 5.) Another, which is the cause even of this, the one which takes place in baptism. "For our old man," he says, "has been crucified" (ver. 6), that is, has been deadened. Since then we know this, let us flee from the deadness by which, even though alive, we die. And let us not be afraid of that with which common death comes on. But the other two, whereof one is blissful, having been given by God, the other praiseworthy (cf. Ar. Eth. i. 12), which is accomplished by ourselves together with God, let us both choose and be emulous of. And of those two, one doth David pronounce blessed, when he says, "Blessed are they whose iniquities are forgiven" (Ps. xxxii. 1); and the other, Paul holds in admiration, saying, and writing to the Galatians, "They that be Christ's have crucified the flesh." (Gal. v. 24.) But of the other couple, one Christ declares to be easy to hold in contempt, when He says, "Fear not them which kill the body, but are not able to kill the soul:" and the other fearful, for, "Fear" (He says) "Him that is able to destroy both body and soul in hell." (Matt. x. 28.) And therefore let us flee from this, and choose [1] that deadness which is held blessed and admirable; that of the other two, we may escape the one and not [2] fear the other: for it is not the least good to us to see

the sun, and to eat and drink, unless the life of good words be with us. For what would be the advantage, pray, of a king dressed in a purple robe and possessed of arms, but without a single subject, and exposed to all that had a mind to attack and insult him? In like manner it will be no advantage to a Christian to have faith, and the gift of baptism, and yet be open to all the passions. In that way the disgrace will be greater, and the shame more. For as such an one having the diadem and purple is so far from gaining by this dress any honor to himself, that he even does disgrace to that by his own shame: so the believer also, who leadeth a corrupt life, is so far from becoming, as such, an object of respect, that he is only the more one of scorn. "For as many," it says, "as sinned without law, shall also perish without law; and as many as have sinned in the law, shall be judged by the law." (Rom. ii. 12). And in the Epistle to the Hebrews, he says, "He that despised Moses' law died without mercy under two or three witnesses: of how much sorer punishment, suppose ye, shall he be thought worthy, who had trodden under foot the Son of God?" (Heb. x. 28, 29.) And with reason. For I placed (He might say) all the passions in subjection to thee by baptism. How then comes it that thou hast disgraced so great a gift, and hast become one thing instead of another? I have killed and buried thy former transgressions, like worms—how is it that thou hast bred others?—for sins are worse than worms, since these do harm to the body, those to the soul; and those make the more offensive stench. Yet we perceive it not, and so we are at no pains to purge them out. Thus the drunkard knows not how disgustful the stale wine is, but he that is not drunken has a distinct perception of it. So with sins also, he that lives soberly knows thoroughly that other mire, and the stain. But he that gives himself up to wickedness, like a man made drowsy with drunkenness, does not even know the very fact that he is ill. And this is the most grievous part of vice, that it does not allow those who fall into it even to see the greatness of their own bane, but as they lie in the mire, they think they are enjoying perfumes. And so they have not even the power of getting free, but when full of worms, like men that pride themselves in precious stones, so do they exult in these. And for this reason they have not so much as the will to kill them, but they even nourish these up, and multiply them in themselves, until they send them on to the worms of the world to come. For these are providers for those, and are not only providers, but even the fathers of

---

[1] So 4 Mss. Sav. and 3 Mss. omit "not," but the sense requires it.

those that never die ; as it says, "their worm shall not die." (Mark ix. 44.) These kindle the hell which never extinguishes. To prevent this from happening then, let us do away with this fountain of evil, and extinguish the furnace, and let us draw up the root of wickedness from beneath, since you will do no good by cutting the tree off from above, if the root remains below, and sends up fresh shoots of the same kind again. What then is the root of the evils? Learn from the good husbandman (i. e. St. Paul 1 Cor. iii. 6–9), who has an accurate knowledge of such things, and tends the spiritual vine and cultivates the whole world. Now what does he say is the cause of all the evils? The love of money. For the "love of money is the root of all evils." (1 Tim. vi. 10). Hence come fightings, and enmities and wars; hence emulations, and railings, and suspicions, and insults; hence murders, and thefts, and violations of sepulchres. Through this, not cities and countries only, but roads and habitable and inhabitable parts, and mountains, and groves, and hills, and, in a word, all places are filled with blood and murder. And not even from the sea has this evil withdrawn, but even there also with great fury hath it revelled, since pirates beset it on all sides, thus devising a new mode of robbery. Through this have the laws of nature been subverted, and the claims of relationship set aside, and the laws of piety itself[1] broken through. For the thraldom of money hath armed, not against the living only, but even against the departed too, the right hands of such men. And at death even, they make no truce with them, but bursting open the sepulchres, they put forth their impious hands even against dead bodies, and not even him that hath let go of life will they suffer to be let go from their plotting. And all the evils that you may find, whether in the house or in the market-place, or in the courts of law, or in the senate, or in the king's palace, or in any other place whatsoever, it is from this that you will find they all spring. For this evil it is, this assuredly, which fills all places with blood and murder, this lights up the flame of hell, this makes cities as wretchedly off as a wilderness, yea, even much worse. For those that beset the high roads, one can easily be on one's guard against, as not being always upon attack. But they who in the midst of cities imitate them are so much the worse than them, in that these are harder to guard against, and dare to do openly what the others do with

secrecy. For those laws, which have been made with a view to stopping their iniquity, they draw even into alliance and fill the cities with this kind of murders and pollutions. Is it not murder, pray, and worse than murder, to hand the poor man over to famine, and to cast him into prison, and to expose him not to famine only, but to tortures too, and to countless acts of insolence? For even if you do not do these things yourself to him, yet you are the occasion of their being done, you do them more than the ministers who execute them. The murderer plunges his sword into a man at once, and after giving him pain for a short time, he does not carry the torture any farther. But do you who by your calumnies, by your harassings, by your plottings, make light darkness to him, and set him upon desiring death ten thousand times over, consider how many deaths you perpetrate instead of one only? And what is worse than all, you plunder and are grasping, not impelled to it by poverty, without any hunger to necessitate you, but that your horse's bridle may be spattered over with gold enough, or the ceiling of your house, or the capitals of your pillars. And what hell is there that this conduct would not deserve, when it is a brother, and one that has shared with yourself in blessings unutterable, and has been so highly honored by the Lord, whom you, in order that you may deck out stones, and floors, and the bodies of animals with neither reason, nor perception of these ornaments, are casting into countless calamities? And your dog[2] is well attended too, while man, or rather Christ, for the sake of the hound, and all these things I have named, is straitened with extreme hunger. What can be worse than such confusion? What more grievous than such lawlessness as this? What streams of fire will be enough for such a soul? He that was made in the Image of God stands in unseemly plight, through thy inhumanity; but the faces of the mules that draw thy wife glisten with gold in abundance, as do the skins and woods which compose that canopy. And if it is a seat that is to be made, or a footstool, they are all made of gold and silver. But the member of Christ, for whom also He came hither from Heaven, and shed His precious Blood, does not even enjoy the food that is necessary for him, owing to thy rapaciousness. But the couches are mantled with silver on every side, while the bodies of the saints are deprived even of necessary clothing. And to thee Christ is less precious than anything else, servants, or mules, or couch, or chair, or footstool; for I

---

[1] So Field from one Ms. Vulg. "of our very being,"—οὐσίας for ὁσίας.

[2] Or "the pillar" and so in the next line κιών and κιόνα for κύων and κύνα.

pass over furniture of still meaner use than these, leaving it to you to know of it. But if thou art shocked at hearing this, stand aloof from doing it, and then the words spoken will not harm thee. Stand aloof, and cease from this madness. For plain madness it is, such eagerness about these things. Wherefore letting go of these things, let us look up, late as it is, towards Heaven, and let us call to mind the Day which is coming, let us bethink ourselves of that awful tribunal, and the exact accounts, and the sentence incorruptible. Let us consider that God, who sees all these things, sends no lightnings from Heaven; and yet what is done deserves not thunderbolts merely. Yet Hé neither doth this, nor doth He let the sea loose upon us, nor doth He burst the earth in twain, He quencheth not the sun, nor doth He hurl the heaven with its stars upon us. He doth not move aught from its place, but suffereth them to hold their course, and the whole creation to minister to us. Pondering all this then, let us be awestruck with the greatness of His love toward man, and let us return to that noble origin which belongs to us, since at present certainly we are in no better plight than the creatures without reason, but even in a much worse one. For they do love their kin, and need but the community of nature to cause affection towards each other. But thou who besides nature hast countless causes to draw thee together and attach thee to the members of thyself; the being honored with the Word, the partaking in one religion, the sharing in countless blessings; art become of wilder nature than they, by displaying so much carefulness about profitless things, and leaving the Temples of God to perish in hunger and nakedness, and often surrounding them also with a thousand evils. For if it is from love of glory that you do these things, it is much more binding on you to show your brother attention, than your horse. For the better the creature that enjoys the act of kindness, the brighter the crown that is woven for such carefulness. Since now while thou fallest into the contrary of all this, thou pullest upon thyself accusers without number, yet perceivest it not. For who is there that will not speak ill of thee? who that will not indite thee as guilty of the greatest atrocity and misanthrophy, when he sees that thou disregardest the human race, and settest that of senseless creatures above men, and besides senseless creatures, even the furniture of thy house? Hast thou not heard the Apostles say, that they who first received the word sold both "houses and lands" (Acts iv. 34), that they might support the brethren? but you

plunder both houses and lands, that you may adorn a horse, or wood-work, or skins, or walls, or a pavement. And what is worse is, that it is not men only, but women too are afflicted with this madness, and urge their husbands to this empty sort of pains, by forcing them to lay out their money upon anything rather than the necessary things. And if any one accuse them for this, they are practised with a defence, itself loaded with much to be accused. For both the one and the other are done at once, says one. What say you? are you not afraid to utter such a thing, and to set the same store by horses and mules and couches and footstools, as by Christ an hungered? Or rather not even comparing them at all, but giving the larger share to these, and to Him meting out with difficulty a scant share? Dost thou not know that all belongs to Him, both thou and thine? Dost thou not know that He fashioned thy body, as well as gave thee a soul, and apportioned thee the whole world? but thou art not for giving a little recompense to Him. But if thou lettest a little hut, thou requirest the rent with the utmost rigor, and though reaping the whole of His creation, and dwelling in so wide a world, thou hast not courage to lay down even a little rent, but has given up to vainglory thyself and all thou hast. For this is that whereof all these things come. The horse is none the better above his natural excellence for having this ornament, neither yet is the person mounted upon him, for sometimes he is only in the less esteem for it; since many neglect the rider and turn their eyes to the horse's ornaments, and to the attendants behind and before, and to the fan-bearers. But the man, who is lackeyed by these, they hate and turn their heads from, as a common enemy. But this does not happen when thou adornest thy soul, for then men, and angels, and the Lord of angels, all weave thee a crown. And so, if thou art in love with glory, stand aloof from the things which thou art now doing, and show thy taste not in thy house, but in thy soul, that thou mayest become brilliant and conspicuous. For now nothing can be more cheap than thou art, with thy soul unfurnished, and but the handsomeness of thy house for a screen. But if thou art impatient of hearing me speak in this way, listén to what one of those that are without did, and at all events be shamed by their philosophy. For it is said that a certain one of them, who went into a palace that shone with gold in abundance, and glistened with the great beauty of the marbles and the columns, when he saw the floor strewed with carpets in all directions, spat in the face of the master of the house, and when found fault with for it said, that since there was no other part of the house 'where he could do this, he was obliged to do this affront to his face. See how ridiculous a man is, who displays his taste in exteriors, and how little he is in the eyes of all reasonable men. And with good reason. For if a person were to leave thy wife to be clad in rags, and to be neglected, and clothed thy maid-servants with brilliant dresses, thou wouldest not bear it meekly, but wouldest be exasperated, and say that it was insulting in the extreme. Reason then in this way about your soul. When you display your taste in walls then, and pavement, and furniture, and other things of the kind, and do not give liberally in alms, or practise the other parts of a religious life (φιλοσοφίαν); you do nothing less than this, or rather what is worse than this by far. For the difference between servant and mistress is nothing, but between soul and flesh, there is a great disparity. But if it be so with the flesh, much more is it with a house or a couch or a footstool. What kind of excuse then dost thou deserve, who puttest silver on all these, but for it hast no regard, though it be covered with filthy rags, squalid, hungry, and full of wounds, torn by hounds unnumbered (Luke xvi. 20, 21); and after all this fanciest that thou shalt get thee glory by displaying thy taste in externals wound about thee? And this is the very height of phrenzy, while ridiculed, reproached, disgraced, dishonored, and falling into the severest punishment, still to be vain of these things! Wherefore, I beseech you, laying all this to heart, let us become sober-minded, late as it is, and become our own masters, and transfer this adorning from outward things to our souls. For so it will abide safe from spoiling, and will make us equal to the angels, and will entertain us with unaltering good, which may we all attain by the grace and love toward man, etc.

HOMILY XII.

ROM. VI. 19.

"I speak after the manner of men because of the infirmity of your flesh: for as ye have yielded your members (so 4 Mss. Sav. the members of your flesh) servants to uncleanness and to iniquity unto iniquity; even so now yield your members servants to righteousness unto holiness."

SINCE he had required great strictness of life, charging us to be dead to the world, and to have died unto wickedness, and to abide with no notion towards the workings of sin, and seemed to be saying something great and burdensome, and too much for human nature; through a desire to show that he is not making any exorbitant demand, nor even as much as might be expected of one who enjoyed so great a gift, but one quite moderate and light, he proves it from contraries, and says, "I speak after the manner of men," as much as to say, Going by human reasonings; by such as one usually meets with. For he signifies either this, or the moderateness of it, by the term applied, "after the manner of men." For elsewhere he uses the same word. "There hath no temptation taken you but such as is common to man" (1 Cor. x. 13), that is, moderate and small. "For as ye have yielded your members servants to uncleanness and to iniquity unto iniquity; even so now yield your members servants to righteousness unto holiness." And truly the masters are very different ones, but still it is an equal amount of servitude that I ask. For men ought to give a much larger one, and so much the larger as this is a greater and better mastership than the other. Nevertheless I make no greater demand "because of the infirmity," and that, he does not say of your free will or readiness of spirit, but "of your flesh," so making what he says the less severe. And yet on one side there is uncleanness, on the other holiness: on the one iniquity, and on the other righteousness. And who is so wretched, he says, and in such straits as not to spend as much earnestness upon the service of Christ, as upon that of sin and the devil? Hear then what follows, and you will see clearly that we do not even spend this little. For when (stated in this naked way) it does not seem credible or easy to admit, and nobody would endure to hear that he does not serve Christ so much as he did serve the devil, he proves it by what follows, and renders it credible by bringing that slavery before us, and saying how they did serve him.*

---

* The ground for Paul's speaking "after the manner of men because of the infirmity of their flesh" can hardly be, as Chrys. suggests, because he would only demand for the ser-

Ver. 20. " For when ye were the servants of sin, ye were free from righteousness."

Now what he says is somewhat of this kind, When ye lived in wickedness, and impiety, and the worst of evils, the state of compliance ye lived in was such that ye did absolutely no good thing at all. For this is, " ye were free from righteousness." That is ye were not subject to it, but estranged from it wholly. For ye did not even so much as divide the manner of servitude between righteousness and sin, but gave yourselves wholly up to wickedness. Now, therefore, since ye have come over to righteousness, give yourselves wholly up to virtue, doing nothing at all of vice, that the measure you give may be at least equal. And yet it is not the mastership only that is so different, but in the servitude itself there is a vast difference. And this too he unfolds with great perspicuity, and shows what conditions they served upon then, and what now. And as yet he says nothing of the harm accruing from the thing, but hitherto speaks of the shame.

Ver. 21. " What fruit had ye then in those things whereof ye are now ashamed ? "

So great was the slavery, that even the recollection of it now makes you ashamed ; but if the recollection makes one ashamed, the reality would much more. And so you gained now in two ways, in having been freed from the shame, and also in having come to know the condition you were in ; just as then ye were injured in two ways, in doing things deserving shame, and in not even knowing to be ashamed. And this is worse than the former. Yet still ye kept in a state of servitude. Having then proved most abundantly the harm of what took place then from the shame of it, he comes to the thing in question. Now what is this thing ?

" For the end of those things is death."

Since then shame seems to be no such serious evil, he comes to what is very fearful, I mean death ; though in good truth what he had before mentioned were enough. For consider how exceeding great the mischief must be, inasmuch as, even when freed from the vengeance due to it, they could not get free of the shame. What wages then, he says, do you expect from the reality, when from the

bare recollection, and that too when you are freed from the vengeance, you hide your face and blush, though under such grace as you are ! But God's side is far otherwise.

Ver. 22. " For now being made free from sin, and become servants to God, ye have your fruit unto holiness, and the end everlasting life."

Of the former, the fruit was shame, even after the being set free. Of these the fruit is holiness, and where holiness is, there is all confidence. But of those things the end is death, and of these everlasting life. Do you see how he points out some things as already given, and some as existing in hope, and from what are given he draws proof of the others also, that is from the holiness of the life. For to prevent your saying (i. e. as an objection) everything lies in hope, he points out that you have already reaped fruits, first the being freed from wickedness, and such evils as the very recollection of puts one to shame ; second, the being made a servant unto righteousness ; a third, the enjoying of holiness ; a fourth, the obtaining of life, and life too not for a season, but everlasting. Yet with all these, he says, do but serve as ye served it. For though the master is far preferable, and the service also has many advantages, and the rewards too for which ye are serving, still I make no further demand. Next, since he had mentioned arms and a king, he keeps on with the metaphor in these words:

Ver. 23. " For the wages of sin is death, but the gift of God is eternal life, through Jesus Christ our Lord."

After speaking of the wages of sin, in the case of the blessings, he has not kept to the same order (τάξιν, rank or relation): for he does not say, the wages of good deeds, " but the gift of God ; " to show, that it was not of themselves that they were freed, nor was it a due they received, neither yet a return, nor a recompense of labors, but by grace all these things came about.* And so there was a superiority for this cause also, in that He did not free them only, or change their condition for a better, but that He did it without any labor or trouble upon their part : and that He not only freed them, but also gave them much more than before, and that through His Son. And the whole of this he has interposed as having discussed the subject of grace, and

---

vice of the gospel an earnestness equal to that which they had formerly displayed in sin. The reference to the infirmity of their flesh gives the reason for his manner of speech in illustrating the character of the Christian life, rather than a ground for the moderateness of his demand. His meaning might be thus expressed : " I am carrying the figure of bondage to its utmost length in applying it to righteousness because I wish to make it clear to you that we are not in a lawless condition, but are still *under authority ;* hence I use the strongest language and press it almost beyond its proper limits in calling our relation to God and righteousness a *servitude.*" —G. B. S.

* Verse 23 is a confirmation of what he had said in 21, 22 about death and life. They are the results of the two courses spoken of. The servant of sin receives death as his wages. It follows on the principle of desert. Not so, however, on the other side. Respecting eternal life there can be no thought of wages or deserts. There all is grace. And thus Paul closes this refutation of objections by triumphantly maintaining the praise of God's grace in Christ, as he had closed the argument constructed upon the parallel between Adam and Christ (v. 21).—G. B. S.

being on the point of overthrowing the Law next. That these things then might not both make them rather listless, he inserted the part about strictness of life, using every opportunity of rousing the hearer to the practice of virtue. For when he calls death the wages of sin, he alarms them again, and secures them against dangers to come. For the words he uses to remind them of their former estate, he also employs so as to make them thankful, and more secure against any inroads of temptations. Here then he brings the hortatory part to a stop, and proceeds with the doctrines again, speaking on this wise.

Chap. vii. ver. 1. "Know ye not, brethren, for I speak to them that know the Law."

Since then he had said, we are "dead to sin," he here shows that not sin only, but also the Law, hath no dominion over them. But if the Law hath none, much less hath sin: and to render his language palatable, he uses a human example to make this plain by. And he seems to be stating one point, but he sets down at once two arguments for his proposition. One, that when a husband is dead, the woman is no longer subject to her husband, and there is nothing to prevent her becoming the wife of another man: and the other, that in the present case it is not the husband only that is dead but the wife also. So that one may enjoy liberty in two ways. Now if when the husband is dead, she is freed from his power, when the woman is shown to be dead also, she is much more at liberty. For if the one event frees her from his power, much more does the concurrence of both. As he is about to proceed then to a proof of these points, he starts with an encomium of the hearers, in these words, "Know ye not, brethren, for I speak to them that know the Law, that is, I am saying a thing that is quite agreed upon, and clear, and to men too that know all these things accurately,

"How that the Law hath dominion over a man as long as he liveth?"

He does not say, husband or wife, but "man," which name is common to either creature; "For he that is dead," he says, "is freed (Gr. justified) from sin." The Law then is given for the living, but to the dead it ceaseth to be ordained (or to give commands). Do you observe how he sets forth a twofold freedom? Next, after hinting this at the commencement, he carries on what he has to say by way of proof, in the woman's case, in the following way.

Ver. 2, 3. "For the woman which hath an husband is bound by the Law to her husband, so long as he liveth: but if the husband be dead, she is loosed from the Law of her

husband. So then, if while her husband liveth, she be married to another man, she is called an adulteress: but if her husband be dead, she is free from that law; so that she is no adulteress, though she be married to another man."

He keeps continually upon this point, and that with great exactness, since he feels quite sure of the proof grounded on it: and in the husband's place he puts the Law, but in the woman's, all believers. Then he adds the conclusion in such way, that it does not tally with the premiss; for what the context would require would be, "and so, my brethren, the Law doth not rule over you, for it is dead."* But he does not say so, but only in the premiss hinted it, and in the inference, afterwards, to prevent what he says being distasteful, he brings the woman in as dead by saying,

"Wherefore, my brethren, ye also are become dead to the Law."

As then the one or the other event gives rise to the same freedom, what is there to prevent his showing favor to the Law without any harm being done to the cause? "For the woman which hath an husband is bound by the Law to her husband as long as he liveth." What is become now (3 Mss. then)

* Chrys. rightly apprehends the incongruous logical form of the argument in vii. 1-6. The Apostle starts out with a general principle: "The law rules a man as long as he lives." It is a question of the *man's* living or dying not of the *law's*. Now (v. 2.) he introduces in confirmation of this a specific example. He takes the case of a woman who is "under the law of her husband." Here the "law of the husband must correspond to ὁ νόμος of the general principle; the γυνή to ὁ ἄνθρωπος (v. 1). That is, the "husband" of the illustration corresponds to the "law" of the general principle and the "woman" of the illustration to the "man" of the principle. But in v. 1, it is a question of the man's (not of the law's) living or dying, while in the illustration this order is reversed. Here it is a question of the husband's living or dying (who corresponds to the "law") and not of the wife's, (who corresponds to the "man" of v. 1). How can this incongruity be explained? We answer that if Paul will use the illustration from the dissolution of the marriage relation at all, he can use it only as he has done. In order to make the illustration harmonize *in form* with the principle (v. 1) and with the application (v. 4.) it would be necessary to suppose the wife as dying and then marrying again after death—which is impossible;—so that in order in any way to carry out the idea of the wife's marrying another (as illustrating the Christian's becoming free, as it were, from one husband—the law—and joining himself to another—Christ), he must suppose the husband as dying and not the wife. Nor can the thought which the apostle wishes to bring out (the freedom to espouse another master) be brought out by adhering to the form of verse 1. There it is the man who dies and so gets free from the law, but with this figure it is impossible to take the next step (which is necessary to the argument) and say : He being dead to his former master, is free to take up allegiance to another. In order to carry out the idea the thought of verse 1 must change form and represent as dying, not the person under authority, but the person exercising it. The essential point of the argument is, that the relation of the Christian to the Mosaic law is as fully terminated as the marriage bond is by the death of one of the parties. There is in each case a termination *by death*, this term being used of the relation of the Christian to the law as a strong figure. (Cf. Rom. vi. 6, where the "death" is predicated of the man, and Gal. vi. 14 where it is applied to both terms in the relation of the Christian to the world: "By whom the *world* is crucified unto me and *I* unto the world.") The key to the whole passage is the idea of *death* figuratively applied to the termination of the Christian's relation to the law, and its central thought is, that having died to the law, we must live unto Christ.—G. B. S.

of those that speak evil of the Law?[1] Let them hear, how even when forced upon it, he does not bereave it of its dignity, but speaks great things of its power; if while it is alive the Jew is bound, and they are to be called adulterers who transgress it, and leave it whiles it is alive. But if they let go of it after it has died, this is not to be wondered at. For in human affairs no one is found fault with for doing this: "but if the husband be dead, she is loosed from the law of her husband." You see how in the example he points out the Law as dead, but in the inference he does not do so. So then if it be while her husband liveth, the woman is called an adulteress. See how he dwells upon the accusations of those who transgress the Law, while it is yet living. But since he had put an end to it, he afterwards favors it with perfect security, without doing any harm hereby to the faith. "For if while her husband liveth, she be married to another man, she is called an adulteress." Thus it would have been natural to say next, ye also, my brethren, now the Law is dead, will not be judged guilty of adultery, if ye become married to another husband. Yet he does not use these words, but what? "Ye are become dead to the Law;" if ye have been made dead, ye are no longer under the Law. For if, when the husband is dead, the woman is no longer liable to it, much more when herself is dead also she is freed from the former. Do you note the wisdom of Paul, how he points out that the Law itself designs that we should be divorced from it, and married to another? For there is nothing, he means, against your living with another husband, now the former is dead; for how should there be, since when the husband was alive it allowed this to her who had a writing of divorcement?[2] But this he does not set down, as it was rather a charge against the woman; for although this had been granted, still it was not cleared of blame. (Matt. xix. 7, 8.) For in cases where he has gained the victory by requisite and accredited proofs, he does not go into questions beyond the purpose; not being captious. The marvel then is this, that it is the Law itself that acquits us who are divorced from it of any charge, and so the mind of it was that we should become Christ's. For it is dead itself, and we are dead; and the grounds of its power over us are removed in a twofold way. But he is not content with this alone, but also adds the reason of it. For he has not set down death without special purpose, but brings the cross in again, which had wrought these things, and in this way too he puts us under an engagement. For ye have not been freed merely, he means, but it was through the Lord's death. For he says,

"Ye are become dead to the Law by the Body of Christ."

Now it is not on this only he grounds his exhortation, but also on the superiority of this second husband. And so he proceeds: "that ye should be married to another, even to Him Who is raised from the dead."

Then to prevent their saying, If we do not choose to live with another husband, what then? For the Law does not indeed make an adulteress of the widow who lives in a second marriage, but for all that it does not force her to live in it. Now that they may not say this, he shows that from benefits already conferred, it is binding on us to choose it: and this he lays down more clearly in other passages, where he says, "Ye are not your own;" and, "Ye are bought with a price;" and, "Be not ye the servants of men" (1 Cor. vi. 19, 20; vii. 23); and again, "One died for all, that they which live should not henceforth live unto themselves, but unto Him which died for them." (2 Cor. v. 15.) This is then what he here alludes to in the words, "By the Body." And next he exhorts to better hopes, saying, "That we should bring forth fruit unto God." For then, he means, ye brought forth fruit unto death, but now unto God.

Ver. 5. "For when we were in the flesh, the motions of sins, which were by the Law, did work in our members to bring forth fruit unto death."

You see then the gain to be got from the former husband! And he does not say when we were in the Law, so in every passage shrinking from giving a handle to heretics;[3] but "when we were in the flesh," that is, in evil deeds, in a carnal life. What he says then is, not that they were in the flesh before, but now they went about without any bodies;[4] but by saying what he does, he neither says that the Law is the cause of sins, nor yet frees it from odium. For it held the rank of a bitter accuser, by making their sins bare: since that, which enjoins more to him who is not minded to obey at all, makes the offence greater. And this is why he does not say, the "motions of sins" which were produced by the Law, but which "were through the Law" (Rom. ii. 27), without adding any

---

[1] The Manichees, who said the Law was given by an evil being.

[2] Deut. xxiv. and xxv. It is applied by Is. l. 1; and Jer. iii. 8, to the then existing Church.

[3] Cf. Origen in Rom. v. 8, p. 537.

[4] Perhaps alluding to Menander (J. Mart. *Ap.* i. 26; Iren. i. 21; Eus. iii. 26), who pretended that those who received his baptism became immortal.

"produced," but simply "through the Law," that is to say, which through the Law were made apparent, were made known. Next that he might not accuse the flesh either; he does not say which the members wrought, but "which did work (or were wrought) in our members," to show that the origin of the mischief was elsewhere, from the thoughts which wrought in us, not from the members which had them working in them. For the soul ranks as a performer, and the fabric of the flesh as a lyre, sounding as the performer obliges it. So the discordant tune is to be ascribed not to the latter, but to the former sooner than to the latter.

Ver. 6. "But now," he says, "we are delivered from the Law." (κατηργήθημεν, "made of no effect.")

See how he again in this place spares the flesh and the Law. For he does not say that the Law was made of no effect, or that the flesh was made of no effect, but that we were made of no effect (i. e., were delivered). And how were we delivered? Why by the old man, who was held down by sin, being dead and buried. For this is what he sets forth in the words, "being dead to that, wherein we were held." As if he had said, the chain by which we were held down was deadened and broken through, so that that which held down, namely sin, held down no more. But do not fall back or grow listless. For you have been freed with a view to being servants again, though not in the same way, but "in newness of spirit, and not in the oldness of the letter." Now what does he mean here? for it is necessary to disclose it here, that when we come upon the passage, we may not be perplexed with it. When then Adam sinned (he means), and his body became liable to death and sufferings, it received also many physical losses, and the horse[1] became less active and less obedient. But Christ, when He came, made it more nimble for us through baptism, rousing it with the wing of the Spirit. And for this reason the marks for the race, which they of old time had to run, are not the same as ours.[2] Since then the race was not so easy as it is now. For this reason, He desires them to be clear not from murder only, as He did them of old time, but from anger also; nor is it adultery only that He bids them keep clear of, but even the unchaste look; and to be exempt not from false swearing only, but even from true. (Matt. v. 21, 27, 33.) And with their friends He orders them to love

their enemies also. And in all other duties, He gives us a longer ground to run over, and if we do but obey, threatens us with hell, so showing that the things in question are not matters of free-will offering for the combatants, as celibacy and poverty are, but are binding upon us absolutely to fulfil. For they belong to necessary and urgent requisites, and the man who does not do them is to be punished to the utmost. This is why He said, "Except your righteousness exceed the righteousness of the Scribes and Pharisees, ye shall in no case enter into the kingdom of heaven." (Matt. v. 20.) But he that does not see the kingdom, shall certainly fall into hell. For this cause Paul too says, "Sin shall not have dominion over you, because ye are not under the Law, but under grace." And here again, "that ye should serve in newness of spirit, and not in the oldness of the letter." For it is not the letter that condemneth, that is the old Law, but the Spirit that helpeth. And for this reason among the ancients, if any were found practising virginity, it was quite astonishing. But now the thing is scattered over every part of the world. And death in those times some few men did with difficulty despise, but now in villages and cities there are hosts of martyrs without number, consisting not of men only, but even of women.[3] And next having done with this, he again meets an objection which is rising, and as he meets it, gives confirmation to his own object. And so he does not introduce the solution of it as main argument, but by way of opposing this; that by the exigency of meeting it, he may get a plea for saying what he wishes, and make his accusation not so unpalatable. Having then said, "in the newness of the Spirit, and not in the oldness of the letter," he proceeds.

Ver. 7. "What then? is the Law sin? God forbid."

Even before this he had been saying, that "the motions of sins, which were by the Law did work in our members" (ver. 5): and, "sin shall have no dominion over you, for ye are not under the Law." (vi. 14.) And that "where no law is, there is no transgression." (iv. 15.) And, "but the Law came in, that the offence might abound" (v. 20); and, "the Law worketh wrath." (iv. 15.) Now as all these things seem to bring the Law into disrepute, in order to correct the suspicion arising from them, he supposes also an objection, and says, "What then, is the Law sin? God forbid." Before the proof he uses this adjuration to conciliate the hearer, and by

---

[1] Alluding to Plato's *Phædrus* again as in the word wing too.
[2] So St. Aug. interprets "shall be least in the kingdom." See *Cat. Aur. ad loc.*

[3] See St. Athan. *de. Incarn.* c. 27, t. i. p. 70.

way of soothing any who was troubled at it. For so, when he had heard this, and felt assured of the speaker's disposition, he would join with him in investigating the seeming perplexity, and feel no suspicions of him. Wherefore he·has put the objection, associating the other with him. Hence, he does not say, What am I to say? but "What shall we say then?" As though a deliberation and a judgment were before them, and a general meeting called together, and the objection came forward not of himself, but in the course of discussion, and from real circumstances of the case. For that the letter killeth, he means, no one will deny, or that the Spirit giveth life (2 Cor. iii. 6); this is plain too, and nobody will dispute it. If then these are confessedly truths, what are we to say about the Law? that "it is sin? God forbid." Explain the difficulty then. Do you see how he supposes the opponent to be present, and having assumed the dignity of the teacher, he comes to the explaining of it. Now what is this? Sin, he says, the Law is not. "Nay, I had not known sin, but by the Law." Notice the reach of his wisdom! What the Law is not, he has set down by way of objection, so that by removing this, and thereby doing the Jew a pleasure, he may persuade him to accept the less alternative. And what is this? Why that "I had not known sin, but by the Law. For I had not known lust, except the Law had said, Thou shalt not covet."

Do you observe, how by degrees he shows it to be not an accuser of sin only, but in a measure its producer? Yet not from any fault of its own, but from that of the froward Jews, he proves it was, that this happened. For he has taken good heed to stop the mouths of the Manichees, that accuse the Law; and so after saying, "Nay, I had not known sin, but by the Law;" and, "I had not known lust, except the Law had said, Thou shall not covet;" he adds,

Ver. 8. "But sin, taking occasion by the commandment, wrought in me all manner of concupiscence."

Do you see how he has cleared it of all blame? For "sin," he says, "taking occasion by the commandment," it was, and not the Law, that increased the concupiscence, and the reverse of the Law's intent was brought about. This came of weakness, and not of any badness. For when we desire a thing, and then are hindered of it, the flame of the desire is but increased. Now this came not of the Law; for it hindered us (3 Mss. endeavored) of itself to keep us off from it; but sin, that is, thy own listlessness and bad disposition, used what was good for the reverse.

But this is no fault in the physician, but in the patient who applies the medicine wrongly. For the reason of the Law being given was, not to inflame concupiscence, but to extinguish it, though the reverse came of it. Yet the blame attaches not to it, but to us. Since if a person had a fever, and wanted to take cold drink when it was not good for him, and one were not to let him take his fill of it, and so increase his lust after this ruinous pleasure, one could not deservedly be found fault with. For the physician's business is simply prohibiting it, but the restraining himself is the patient's. And what if sin did take occasion from it? Surely there are many bad men who by good precepts grow in their own wickedness. For this was the way in which the devil ruined Judas, by plunging him into avarice, and making him steal what belonged to the poor. However it was not the being entrusted with the bag that brought this to pass, but the wickedness of his own spirit. And Eve, by bringing Adam to eat from the tree, threw him out of Paradise. But neither in that case was the tree the cause, even if it was through it that the [1] occasion took place. But if he treats the discussion about the Law with somewhat of vehemence, do not feel surprise. For Paul is making a stand against the present exigency, and suffers not his language to give a handle even to those that suspected otherwise, but takes great pains to make the present statement correct. Do not then sift what he is now going on to say (4 Mss. "here saying") by itself, but put beside it the purpose by which he is led on to speak of these things, and reckon for the madness of the Jews, and their vigorous spirit of contention, which as he desires earnestly to do away with, he seems to bear violently (πολὺς πνεῖν) against the Law, not to find fault with it, but to unnerve their vigor. For if it is any reproach to the Law that sin taketh occasion by it, this will be found to be the case in the New Testament also. For in the New Testament there are thousands of laws, and about many more ("far more," Field) important matters. And one may see the same come to pass there also, not with regard to covetousness (lust, as v. 7) only, but to all wickedness generally. For He says, "if I had not come and spoken unto them, they had not had sin," (John xv. 22.) Here then sin finds a footing in this fact, and so the greater punishment. And again when Paul discourseth about grace, he says, "Of how much sorer punishment, suppose ye, shall he be counted worthy, who hath trodden under foot the Son of God."

---

[1] See the *Analogy*, l. v. § 4, p. 132.

(Heb. x. 29.) Has not then the worse punishment its origin from hence, from the greater benefit? And the reason why he says the Greeks were without excuse was, because being honored with the gift of reason, and having gotten a knowledge of the beauty of the creation, and having been placed in a fair way for being led by it to the Creator, they did not so use the wisdom of God, as it was their duty. Seest thou that to the wicked in all cases occasions of greater punishment result from good things? But we shall not in this accuse the benefits of God, but rather upon this even admire them the more : but we shall throw the blame on the spirit of those who abuse the blessings to contrary purpose. Let this then be our line with regard to the Law also. But this is easy and feasible—the other is what is a difficulty. How is it that he says "I had not known lust except the Law had said, Thou shalt not covet?" Now if man had not known lust, before he received the Law, what was the reason for the flood, or the burning of Sodom? What does he mean then? He means vehement lust : and this is why he did not say, lust, but "all manner of concupiscence," intimating, in that, its vehemency. And what, it will be said, is the good of the Law, if it adds to the disorder? None ; but much mischief even. Yet the charge is not against the Law, but the listlessness of those who received it. For sin wrought it, though by the Law. But this was not the purpose of the Law, nay, the very opposite, Sin then became stronger, he says, and violent. But this again is no charge against the Law but against their obstinacy. "For without the Law sin is dead." That is, was not so ascertainable. For even those before the Law knew that they had sinned, but they came to a more exact knowledge of it after the giving of the Law. And for this reason they were liable to a greater accusation : since it was not the same thing to have nature to accuse them, and besides nature the Law, which told them distinctly every charge.

Ver. 9. "For I was alive without the Law once."

When, pray, was that? Before Moses. See how he sets himself to show that it, both by the things it did, and the things it did not do, weighed down human nature. For when "I was alive without the Law," he means, I was not so much condemned.

"But when the commandment came, sin revived, and I died."

This seems indeed to be an accusing of the Law. But if any one will look closely at it, it will be seen to be even an encomium of it. For it did not give existence to sin that be-

fore was not, but only pointed out what had escaped notice. And this is even a praise of the Law, if at least before it they had been sinning without perceiving it. But when this came, if they gained nothing besides from it, at all events this they were distinctly made acquainted with, the fact that they had been sinning. And this is no small point, with a view to getting free from wickedness. Now if they did not get free, this has nothing to do with the Law ; which framed everything with a view to this end, but the accusation lies wholly against their spirit, which was perverse beyond all supposition. [1] For what took place was not the natural thing,—their being injured by things profitable. And this is why he says "And the commandment, which was ordained to life, I found to be unto death." He does not say, "it was made," or "it brought forth" death, but "was found," so explaining the novel and unusual kind of discrepancy, and making the whole fall upon their own pate. For if, he says, you would know the aim of it, it led to life, and was given with this view. But if death was the issue of this, the fault is with them that received the commandment, and not of this, which was leading them to life.   And this is a point on which he has thrown fresh light by what follows.

Ver. 11. "For sin taking occasion by the commandment deceived me, and by it slew me."

You observe how he everywhere keeps to sin, and entirely clears the Law of accusation. And so he proceeds as follows.

Ver. 12. "Wherefore the law is holy, and the commandment holy, and just, and good."

But, if ye be so minded, we will bring before you the language of those who wrest these declarations. For this will make our own statements clearer. For there are some that say, that he is not here saying what he does of the Law of Moses, but some take it of the law of nature ; some, of the commandment given in Paradise. Yet surely Paul's object everywhere is to annul this Law, but he has not any question with those. And with much reason ; for it was through a fear and a horror of this that the Jews obstinately opposed grace. But it does not appear that he has ever called the commandment in Paradise "Law" at all ; no, nor yet any other writer. Now to make this plainer from what he has really said, let us follow out his words, retracing the argument a little. Having then spoken to them about strictness of conversa-

---

[1] This expression seems strange with respect to the acts of God, but it may be referred to what man could have imagined beforehand ; as indeed one use of the Law was to make men sensible of their real state. It may also be taken in the sense suggested by Is. v. 4 ; Matt. xxi. 19 ; Luke xiii. 6.

tion, he goes on to say, "Know ye not, brethren, how that the Law hath dominion over a man as long as he liveth? Wherefore ye are become dead to the Law." Therefore if these things are said about the natural law, we are found to be without the natural law. And if this be true, we are more senseless than the creatures which are without reason. Yet this is not so, certainly. For with regard to the law in Paradise, there is no need to be contentious, lest we should be taking up a superfluous trouble, by entering the lists against things men have made up their minds upon. In what sense then does he say, "I should not have known sin but by the Law?" He is speaking, not of absolute want of knowledge, but of the more accurate knowledge. For if this were said of the law of nature, how would what follows suit? "For I was alive," he says, "without the Law once." Now neither Adam, nor any body else, can be shown ever to have lived without the law of nature. For as soon as God formed him, He put into him that law of nature, making it to dwell by him as a security to the whole kind (Gr. Nature, see p. 365). And besides this, it does not appear that he has anywhere called the law of nature a commandment. But this he calls as well a commandment, and that "just and holy," as a "spiritual law." But the law of nature was not given to us by the [1] Spirit. For barbarians, as well as Greeks and other men, have this law. Hence it is plain, that it is the Mosaic Law that he is speaking of above, as well as afterwards, and in all the passages. For this cause also he calls it holy, saying, "Wherefore the Law is holy, and the commandment holy, and just, and good." For even though the Jews have been unclean since the Law, and unjust and covetous, this does not destroy the virtue of the Law, even as their unbelief doth not make the faith of God of none effect. So from all these things it is plain, that it is of the Law of Moses that he here speaks.

Ver. 13. "Was then that which is good made death unto me? God forbid. But sin, that it might appear sin." (4 Mss. om. *ἡ*.)

That is, that it might be shown what a great evil sin is, namely, a listless will, an inclinableness to the worse side, the actual doing (3 Mss. om. this clause), and the perverted judgment. For this is the cause of all the evils; but he amplifies it by pointing out the exceeding grace of Christ, and teaching them what an evil He freed the human race from, which, by the medicines used to cure it, had become worse, and was increased by the preventives. Wherefore he goes on to say: "That sin, by the commandment, might become exceeding sinful." Do you see how these things are woven together everywhere? By the very means he uses to accuse sin, he again shows the excellency of the Law. Neither is it a small point which he has gained by showing what an evil sin is, and unfolding the whole of its poison, and bringing it to view. For this is what he shows, by saying, "that sin by the commandment might become exceeding sinful." That is, that it may be made clear what an evil sin is, what a ruinous thing. And this is what was shown by the commandment. Hereby he also shows the preëminence of grace above the Law, the preëminence above, not the conflict with, the Law. For do not look to this fact, that those who received it were the worse for it; but consider the other, that the Law had not only no design of drawing wickedness out to greater lengths, but even seriously aimed at hewing down what already existed. But if it had no strength, give to it indeed a crown for its intention, but adore more highly the power of Christ, which abolished, cut away: and plucked up the very roots an evil so manifold and so hard to be overthrown. But when you hear me speak of sin, do not think of it as a substantial [2] power, but evil doing, as it comes upon men and goes from them continually, and which, before it takes place, has no being, and when it has taken place, vanishes again. This then was why the Law was given. Now no law is ever given to put an end to things natural, but in order to correct a way of acting purposely wicked. And this the lawgivers that are without too are aware of, and all mankind in general. For it is the evils from viciousness alone that they are for setting right, and they do not undertake to extirpate those allotted us along with our nature; since this they cannot do. For things natural remain unalterable (Arist. *Eth.* b. 2, c. 1), as we have told you frequently in other discourses also.

And so let us leave these contests, and again practise ourselves in exhortation. Or rather, this last part belongs to those contests. For if we cast out wickedness, we should bring virtue in also: and by these means we shall clearly teach that wickedness is no natural evil, and shall be able easily to stop the mouths of them that enquire for the origin of evil, not by means of words only, but of actions also, since we share the same nature

---

[1] Gen. vi. 3; and Psalm xciv. 10. do not contradict this, since St. C. is using the word in its limited sense, as in St. John vii. 39.

[2] See Herbert's *Poems*, 2d. on Sin. "Oh that I could a sin once see!" etc. Also Möhler *Symb.* l. i. c. 8. also St. Aug. *Conf.* vii. § 12 (18) p. 122, O. T. and *De Civ. Dei.* xi. § 9, xii. § 2.

with them, but are freed from their wickedness. For let us not be looking at the laboriousness of virtue, but at the possibility of succeeding in it. But if we be in earnest, it will be at once light and palatable to us. But if you tell me of the pleasure of vice, tell out its end too. For it issueth in death, even as virtue leadeth us to life. Or if you think fit, let us rather scrutinize them both even before their end; for we shall see that vice has a great deal of pain attached to it, and virtue great pleasure. For what pray is so painful as a bad conscience? or what more pleasing than a good hope? For there is nothing, assuredly there is nothing, which is used to cut us so deep, and press so hard on us, as the expectation of evil: nothing that so keeps us up, and all but gives us wings, as a good conscience. And this we may get a knowledge of even by what takes place before our eyes. For they that dwell in a prison, and are in expectation of sentence against them, let them have the enjoyment of luxury repeated beyond count, live a more afflicting life than those that go a begging by the by-roads, yet with nothing upon their consciences to trouble them. For the expectation of a dreadful end will not let them perceive those pleasures which they have in their hands. And why do I speak of prisoners? Why, as for those that are living out of prison, and have a good fortune, yet have a bad conscience about them, handicraftsmen that work for their bread, and spend the whole day amid their labor, are in a far better plight than they. And for this reason too we say, How miserable the gladiators are (though seeing them as we do in taverns, drunken, luxurious, gormandizing), and call them the most miserable of men, because the calamity of the end which they must expect is too great to admit of comparison with that pleasure. Now if to them a life of this sort seems to be pleasing, remember what I am continually telling you, that it is no such marvel that a man who lives in vice should not flee from the misery and pain of vice. For see how a thing so detestable as that, yet seems to be delectable to those who practice it. Yet we do not on this account say, how happy they are, for this is just the very reason why we think them pitiable, because they have no notion of the evils they are amongst. And what would you say of adulterers, who for a little pleasure undergo at once a disgraceful slavery, and a loss of money, and a perpetual fear (Hor. Sat. II. vii. 58–67), and in fact the very life of a Cain, or rather one that is even much worse than his, filled with fears for the present, and trembling for the future, and suspecting alike friend and foe, and those that know about it, and those that know nothing? Neither when they go to sleep are they quit of this struggle, their bad conscience shaping out for them dreams that abound with sundry terrors, and in this way horrifying them. Far otherwise is the chaste man, seeing he passes the present life unshackled and at full liberty. Weigh then against the little pleasure, the sundry fluctuations of these terrors, and with the short labor of continency, the calm of an entire life; and you will find the latter hath more of pleasantness than the former. But as for the man that is set upon plundering and laying hands upon other men's goods, tell me if he has not to undergo countless pains in the way of running about, fawning upon slaves, freemen, doorkeepers; alarming and threatening, acting shamelessly, watching, trembling, in agony, suspecting everything. Far otherwise is the man that holds riches in contempt, for he too enjoys pleasure in abundance, and lives with no fear, and in perfect security. And if any one were to go through the other instances of vice, he would find much trouble, and many rocks. But what is of greater importance is, that in the case of virtue the difficulties come first, and the pleasant part afterwards, so the trouble is even thus alleviated. But in the case of vice, the reverse. After the pleasure, the pains and the punishments, so that by these besides the pleasure is done away. For as he who waits for the crown, perceives nothing of present annoyance, so he that has to expect the punishments after the pleasures has no power of gathering in a gladness that is unalloyed, since the fear puts everything in confusion. Or rather if any one were to scrutinize the thing with care, even before the punishment which follows upon these things, he would find that even at the very moment when vice is boldly entered upon, a great deal of pain is felt. And, if you think fit, let us just examine this in the case of those who plunder other men's goods. Or those who in any way get together money, and setting aside the fears, and dangers, and trembling, and agony, and care, and all these things, let us suppose the case of a man, who has got rich without any annoyance, and feels sure about maintaining his present fortune (which he has no means of doing, still for all that let it be assumed for argument's sake). What sort of pleasure then is he to gather in from having so much about him? On the contrary, it is just this very thing that will not let him be glad-hearted. For as long as ever he desires other things besides, he is still upon the rack.

Because desire gives pleasure at the time it has come to a stand. If thirsty, for instance, we feel refreshed, when we have drunk as much as we wish; but so long as we keep thirsty, even if we were to have exhausted all the fountains in the world, our torment were but growing greater; even if we were to drink up ten thousand rivers, our state of punishment were more distressing. And thou also, if thou wert to receive the goods of the whole world, and still to covet, wouldest make thy punishment the greater, the more things thou hadst tasted of. Fancy not then, that from having gathered a great sum together thou shalt have aught of pleasure, but rather by declining to be rich. But if thou covetest to be rich thou wilt be always under the scourge. For this is a kind of love that does not reach its aim; and the longer journey thou hast gone, the further off thou keepest from the end. Is not this a paradox then, a derangement, a madness in the extreme? Let us then forsake this first of evils, or rather let us not even touch this covetousness at all. Yet, if we have touched it, let us spring away from its first motions (προοιμίων). For this is the advice the writer of the Proverbs gives us, when he speaks about the harlot: "Spring away," he says, "tarry not, neither go thou near to the door of her house" (Prov. v. 8): this same thing I would say to you about the love of money. For if by entering gradually you fall into this ocean of madness, you will not be able to get up out of it with ease, and as if you were in whirlpools,[1] struggle as often as ever you may, it will not be easy for you to get clear; so after falling into this far worse abyss of covetousness, you will destroy your own self, with all that belongs to you. (Acts viii. 20.) And so my advice is that we be on our watch against the beginning, and avoid little evils, for the great ones are gendered by these. For he who gets into a way of saying at every sin, This matters nothing! will by little and little ruin himself entirely. At all events it is this which has introduced vice, which has opened the doors to the robber (5 Mss. devil), which has thrown down the walls of cities, this saying at each sin, "This matters nothing!" Thus in the case of the body too, the greatest of diseases grow up, when trifling ones are made light of. If Esau had not first been a traitor to his birthright, he would not have become unworthy of the blessings. If he had not rendered himself unworthy of the blessings, he would not have had the desire of going on to fratricide. If Cain had not fallen

in love with the first place, but had left that to God, he would not have had the second place. Again, when he had the second place, if he had listened to the advice, he would not have travailed with the murder. Again, if after doing the murder he had come to repentance, when God called him, and had not answered in an irreverent way, he would not have had to suffer the subsequent evils. But if those before the Law did owing to this listlessness come to the very bottom of misery, only consider what is to become of us, who are called to a greater contest, unless we take strict heed unto ourselves, and make speed to quench the sparks of evil deeds before the whole pile is kindled. Take an instance of my meaning. Are you in the habit of false swearing? do not stop at this only, but away with all swearing, and you will have no further need of trouble. For it is far harder for a man that swears to keep from false swearing, than to abstain from swearing altogether.[2] Are you an insulting and abusive person? a striker too? Lay down as a law for yourself not to be angry or brawl in the least, and with the root the fruit also will be gotten rid of. Are you lustful and dissipated? Make it your rule again not even to look at a woman (Job xxxi. 1), or to go up into the theatre, or to trouble yourself with the beauty of other people whom you see about. For it is far easier not even to look at a woman of good figure, than after looking and taking in the lust, to thrust out the perturbation that comes thereof, the struggle being easier in the preliminaries (προοιμίοις). Or rather we have no need of a struggle at all if we do not throw the gates open to the enemy, or take in the seeds of mischief (κακίας). And this is why Christ chastised the man who looks unchastely upon a woman (Matt. v. 28), that He might free us from greater labor, before the adversary became strong, bidding us cast him out of the house while he may be cast out even with ease. For what need to have superfluous trouble, and to get entangled with the enemies, when without entanglement we may erect the trophy, and before the wrestling seize upon the prize? For it is not so great a trouble not to look upon beautiful women, as it is while looking to restrain one's

---

[1] Such is apparently the sense, though Field with most Mss. reads ἰλίγγοις not ἰλιγξι.

[2] See St. Chrys. on Eph. i. 14, *Hom. ii. Mor.* (p. 119 O. T.) also *Hom. x. on the Statutes*, p. 186 O. T. and index and St. Gr. Naz. *Iamb. xx.* (Ben. xxiv.) The practice of swearing seems to have prevailed to such an extent, as to call for the utmost exertions to put it down. St. Jerome on Jer. iv. 2; Ez. xvii. 19, seems however to allow oaths. St. Athanasius speaks strongly against swearing generally, *de Pass. et Cruc.* § 4, 5, 6, t. 2, p. 82–4, and seems to allow it on Ps. lxii. 12 (Eng. lxiii. 11.) t. 1, 1107, b. In *Apol. ad Imp. Const.* Hist. Tracts, p. 161 O. T. he wishes some one present, "that he might question him by the very Truth" (ἐπ᾽ αὐτῆς τῆς ἀληθείας) "for what we say as in the presence of God, we Christians hold for an oath."

self. Or rather the first would be no trouble at all, but immense toil and labor comes on after looking. Since then this trouble is less (most Mss. add, " to the incontinent"), or rather there is no labor at all, nor trouble, but the greater gain, why do we take pains to plunge into an ocean of countless evils? And farther, he who does not look upon a woman, will overcome such lust not only with greater ease, but with a higher purity, as he on the other hand who does look, getteth free with more trouble, and not without a kind of stain,[1] that is, if he does get free at all. For he that does not take a view of the beautiful figure, is pure also from the lust that might result. But he who lusteth to look, after first laying his reason low, and polluting it in countless ways, has then to cast out the stain that came of the lust, that is, if he do cast it out. This then is why Christ, to prevent our suffering in this way, did not prohibit murder only, but wrath; not adultery only, but an unchaste look even: not perjury only, but all swearing whatsoever. Nor does he make the measure of virtue stop here, but after having given these laws, He proceeds to a still greater degree. For after keeping us far away from murder, and bidding us to be clear of wrath, He bids us be ready even to suffer ill, and not to be prepared to suffer no more than what he who attacks us pleases, but even to go further, and to get the better of his utmost madness by the overflowingness of our own Christian spirit (τῆς οἰκείας φιγοσοφίας). For what He says is not, " If a man smite thee on thy right cheek, bear it nobly and hold thy peace ;" but He adds to this the yielding to him the other too. For He says, " Turn to him the other also." (Matt. v. 39.) This then is the brilliant victory, to yield him even more than what he wishes, and to go beyond the bounds of his evil desire by the profuseness of one's own patient endurance. For in this way you will put a stop to his madness, and also receive from the second act again the reward of the first, besides putting a stop to wrath against him. See you, how in all cases it is we that have it in our power not to suffer ill, and not they that inflict it? Or rather it is not the not suffering ill alone, but even the having benefits (Sav. conj. παθεῖν εὖ, so 2 Mss.) done us that we have in our own power. And this is the truest wonder, that we are so far from being injured, if we be right-minded, that we are even benefited, and that too by the very things that we suffer unjustly at the hands of others. Reflect then ; has such an one done you an affront ?

You have the power of making this affront redound to your honor. For if you do an affront in return, you only increase the disgrace. But if you bless him that did you the affront, you will see that all men give you victory, and proclaim your praise. Do you see how by the things wherein we are wronged, we get good done unto us if we be so minded? This one may see happening in the case of money matters, of blows, and the same in everything else. For if we requite them with the opposite, we are but twining a double crown about us, one for the ills we have suffered, as well as one for the good we are doing. Whenever then a person comes and tells you that "such an one has done you an affront, and keeps continually speaking ill of you to everybody," praise the man to those who tell you of him. For thus even if you wish to avenge yourself, you will have the power of inflicting punishment. For those who hear you, be they ever so foolish, will praise you, and hate him as fiercer than any brute beast, because he, without being at all wronged, caused you pain, but you, even when suffering wrong, requited him with the opposite. And so you will have it in your power to prove that all that he said was to no purpose. For he who feels the tooth of slander, gives by his vexation a proof that he is conscious of the truth of what is said. But he who smiles at it, by this very thing acquits himself of all suspicion with those who are present. Consider then how many good things you cull together from the affair. First, you rid yourself of all vexation and trouble. Secondly (rather this should come first), even if you have sins, you put them off,[2] as the Publican did by bearing the Pharisee's accusation meekly. Besides, you will by this practice make your soul heroic (Gr. philosophic), and will enjoy endless praises from all men, and will divest yourself of any suspicion arising from what is said. But even if you are desirous of taking revenge upon the man, this too will follow in full measure, both by God's punishing him for what he has said, and before that punishment by thy heroic conduct standing to him in the place of a mortal blow.[3] For there is nothing that cuts those who affront us so much to the heart, as for us who are affronted to smile at the affront. As then from behaving with Christian heroism so many honors will accrue to us, so from being little-minded just the

---

[1] " There is some little sensuality in being tempted." Bp. Taylor on *Repentance*, c. 5. sect. 6. § 4. t. 8, p. 494.

[2] An instance of the rhetorical arrangement he admires in the Apostle. His object is of course to make men patient under reproaches even when partly deserved, and he thus takes them by surprise.

[3] See on Rom. xii. 20, Hom 22, which illustrates the subsidiary use of inferior motives.

opposite will befall us in everything. For we disgrace ourselves, and also seem to those present to be guilty of the things mentioned, and fill our soul with perturbation, and give our enemy pleasure, and provoke God, and add to our former sins. Taking then all this into consideration, let us flee from the abyss of a little mind (μικροψυχίας), and take refuge in the port of patient endurance (μακροθυμίας), that here we may at once "find rest unto our souls" (Matt. xi. 29), as Christ also set forth, and may attain to the good things to come, by the grace and love toward man, etc.

HOMILY XIII.

ROM. VII. 14.

"For we know that the Law is spiritual: but I am carnal, sold under sin."

AFTER having said that great evils had taken place, and that· sin, taking occasion by the commandment, had grown stronger, and the opposite of what the Law mainly aimed at had been the result, and after having thrown the hearer into a great deal of perplexity, he goes on next to give the rationale of these events, after first clearing the Law of any ill suspicion. For lest—upon hearing that it was through the commandment that sin took that occasion, and that it was when it came that sin revived, and through it deceived and killed—any one should suppose the Law to be the source of these evils, he first sets forth its defence with considerable advantage, not clearing it from accusation only, but encircling it also with the utmost praise. And this he lays down, not as granting it for his own part, but as declaring a universal judgment. "For we know," he says, "that the Law is spiritual." As if he had said, This is an allowed thing, and self-evident, that it "is spiritual," so far is it from being the cause of sin, or to blame for the evils that happened. And observe, that he not only clears it of accusation, but bestows exceeding great praise upon it. For by calling it spiritual, he shows it to be a teacher of virtue and hostile to vice; for this is what being spiritual means, leading off from sin of every kind· And this the Law did do, by frightening, admonishing, chastening, correcting, recommending every kind of virtue. Whence then, was sin produced, if the teacher was so admirable? It was from the listlessness of its disciples. Wherefore he went on to say, "but I am carnal;" giving us a sketch now of man, as comporting himself in the Law, and before the Law.* "Sold under sin." Because with death (he means) the throng of passions also came in. For when the body had become mortal, it was henceforth a necessary thing for it to receive concupiscence, and anger, and pain, and all the other passions, which required a great deal of wisdom (φιλοσοφίας) to prevent their flooding us, and sinking reason in the depth of sin. For in themselves they were not sin,[1] but, when their extravagancy was unbridled, it wrought this effect. Thus (that I may take one of them and examine it as a specimen) desire is not sin: but when it has run into extravagance, being not minded to keep within the laws of marriage,[2] but springing even upon other men's wives; then the thing henceforward becomes adultery, yet

---

* Chrys. gives no hint of any controversy as to the interpretation of the passage vii. 14–25. In modern times the question has been greatly disputed: Whom does the apostle represent by the "I" who is waging such an unsuccessful combat with sin? Passing by the views that he refers to himself personally (Hofmann) and that he refers to the Jewish people under the old dispensation (Grotius, Reiche), two opinions have prevailed among interpreters (1) that he is representing the *regenerate* man. (For the arguments by which this view is supported see Hodge on Romans *in loco*). (2) That he is here personating the *unregenerate* man who, however, has become awakened under the law to a sense of his sinful condition. This view is preferred on the following grounds. (1) The connection of 14–25 with the argument of 7–13 which shows the power of the law to awaken the consciousness of sin and can therefore apply only to the Jew aroused by the law. (2) The relation of the passage to chap. viii. In vii. 25 the apostle mounts to the Christian plane and in ch. viii. exults in the liberation from the conflict just described which Christ brings to the soul. (3) Much of the language of vii. 14–25 is inconsistent with the consciousness of a regenerate man and especially with Paul's joyous and triumphant view of the Christian life. (4) The language throughout is appropriate, not, indeed, to the morally indifferent man, but to the unconverted Jew whom the law has awakened to a knowledge of his sin and need, and this is precisely the subject under consideration in the earlier verses of the Chap. So Tholuck, De Wette, Alford, Olshausen, Lange, Meyer, Weiss, Godet). Chrys. rather takes for granted, than states the same view, in saying that it is "a sketch of *man* as comporting himself in the law and before the law."—G. B. S.

[1] The words of the Fathers on this subject become more definite after the Pelagian Controversy. St. Aug. *contr. Julianum*, i. 2, § 32. (Ben. t. 10), speak thus of concupiscence, (not in act, but as an inherited habit). "It is not however called sin in the sense of making one guilty, but in that it is caused by the guilt of the first man, and in that it rebels, and strives to draw us into guilt except grace aid us."

[2] So Field from most Mss. Sav. lawful marriage.

not by reason of the desire, but by reason of its exorbitancy. And observe the wisdom of Paul. For after praising the Law, he hastens immediately to the earlier period, that he may show the state of our race, both then and at the time it received the Law, and make it plain how necessary the presence of grace was, a thing he labored on every occasion to prove. For when he says, "sold under sin," he means it not of those who were under the Law only, but of those who had lived before the Law also, and of men from the very first. Next he mentions the way in which they were sold and made over.

Ver. 15. "For that which I do, I know not."

What does the "I know not" mean?— I am ignorant. And when could this ever happen? For nobody ever sinned in ignorance. Seest thou, that if we do not receive his words with the proper caution, and keep looking to the object of the Apostle, countless incongruities will follow? For if they sinned through ignorance, then they did not deserve to be punished. As then he said above, "for without the Law sin is dead," not meaning that they did not know they were sinning, but that they knew indeed, but not so distinctly; wherefore they were punished, but not so severely: and again; "I should not have known lust;" not meaning an entire ignorance of it, but referring to the most distinct knowledge of it; and said, that it also "wrought in me all manner of concupiscence, not meaning to say that the commandment made the concupiscence, but that sin through the commandment introduces an intense degree of concupiscence; so here it is not absolute ignorance that he means by saying, "For what I do, I know not;" since how then would he have pleasure in the law of God in his inner man? What then is this, "I know not?" I get dizzy, he means, I feel carried away,[1] I find a violence done to me, I get tripped up without knowing how. Just as we often say, Such an one came and carried me away with him, without my knowing how; when it is not ignorance we mean as an excuse, but to show a sort of deceit, and circumvention, and plot. "For what I would, that I do not: but what I hate, that I do." How then canst thou be said not to know what thou art doing? For if thou willest the good, and hatest the evil, this requires a perfect knowledge. Whence it appears that

he says, "that I would not," not as denying free will, or as adducing any constrained necessity. For if it was not willingly, but by compulsion, that we sinned, then the punishments that took place before would not be justifiable. But as in saying "I know not," it was not ignorance he set before us, but what we have said; so in adding the "that I would not," it is no necessity he signifies, but the disapproval he felt of what was done.[2] Since if this was not his meaning in saying, "That which I would not, that I do:" he would else have gone on, "But I do what I am compelled and enforced to." For this is what is opposed to willing and power (ἐξουσία). But now he does not say this, but in the place of it he has put the word, "that I hate," that you might learn how when he says, "that I would not," he does not deny the power. Now, what does the "that I would not" mean? It means, what I praise not, what I do not approve, what I love not. And in contradistinction to this, he adds what follows; "But what I hate, that I do."

Ver. 16. "If then I do that which I would not, I consent unto the Law, that it is good."

You see here, that the understanding is not yet perverted, but keeps up its own noble character even during the action. For even if it does pursue vice, still it hates it the while, which would be great commendation, whether of the natural or the written Law. For that the Law is good, is (he says) plain, from the fact of my accusing myself, when I disobey the Law, and hate what has been done. And yet if the Law was to blame for the sin, how comes it that he felt a delight in it, yet hated what it orders to be done? For, "I consent," he says, "unto the Law, that it is good."

Ver 17, 18. "Now then it is no more I that do it, but sin that dwelleth in me. For I know that in me, that is, in my flesh, dwelleth no good thing."

On this text, those who find fault with the flesh, and contend it was no part of God's creation, attack us. What are we to say then? Just what we did before, when discussing the Law: that as there he makes sin answerable for everything so here also. For he does not say, that the flesh worketh it, but just the contrary, "it is not I that do it, but sin that dwelleth in me." But if he does say that "there dwelleth no good thing in it," still this is no charge against the

---

[1] ἐμποδισμὸς ταῖς βουλήσεσι. Arist. Rhet. ii.

[2] This seems to have been Plato's view of free-will. See Tenneman, Plat. Philos. iv. p. 34, οὐδεὶς ἑκὼν πονηρὸς, etc.

flesh. For the fact that "no good thing dwelleth in it," does not show that it is evil itself. Now we admit, that the flesh is not so great as the soul, and is inferior to it, yet not contrary, or opposed to it, or evil; but that it is beneath the soul, as a harp beneath a harper, and as a ship under the pilot. And these are not contrary to those who guide and use them, but go with them entirely, yet are not of the same honor with the artist. As then a person who says, that the art resides not in the harp or the ship, but in the pilot or harper, is not finding fault with the instruments, but pointing out the great difference between them [1] and the artist; so Paul in saying, that "in my flesh dwelleth no good thing," is not finding fault with the body, but pointing out the soul's superiority. For this it is that has the whole duty or pilotage put into its hands, and that of playing. And this Paul here points out, giving the governing power to the soul, and after dividing man into these two things, the soul and the body, he says, that the flesh has less of reason, and is destitute of discretion, and ranks among things to be led, not among things that lead. But the soul has more wisdom, and can see what is to be done and what not, yet is not equal to pulling in the horse as it wishes. And this would be a charge not against the flesh only, but against the soul also, which knows indeed what it ought to do, but still does not carry out in practice what seems best to it. "For to will," he says, "is present with me; but how to perform that which is good, I find not." Here again in the words, "I find not," he does not speak of any ignorance or perplexity, but a kind of thwarting and crafty assault made by sin, which he therefore points more clearly out in the next words.

Ver. 19, 20. "For the good that I would I do not: but the evil which I would not that I do. Now if I do that I would not, it is no more I that do it but sin that dwelleth in me."

Do you see, how he acquits the essence of the soul, as well as the essence of the flesh, from accusation, and removes it entirely to sinful actions? For if the soul willeth not the evil, it is cleared : and if he does not work it himself, the body too is set free, and the whole may be charged upon the evil moral choice. Now the essence of the soul and body and of that choice are not the same, for the two first are God's works,

and the other is a motion from ourselves towards whatever we please to direct it. For willing is indeed natural (ἔμφυτον), and is from God : but willing on this wise is our own, and from our own mind.

Ver. 21. "I find then a law, that when I would do good, evil is present with me."

What he says is not very clear. What then is it that is said ? I praise the law, he says, in my conscience, and I find it pleads on my side so far as I am desirous of doing what is right, and that it invigorates this wish. For as I feel a pleasure in it, so does it yield praise to my decision. Do you see how he shows, that the knowledge of what is good and what is not such is an original and fundamental part of our nature, and that the Law of Moses praises it, and getteth praise from it ? For above he did not say so much as I get taught by the Law, but "I consent to the Law ; " nor further on that I get instructed by it, but "I delight in " it. Now what is "I delight ? " It is, I agree with it as right, as it does with me when wishing to do what is good. And so the willing what is good and the not willing what is evil was made a fundamental part of us from the first. But the Law, when it came, was made at once a stronger accuser in what was bad, and a greater praiser in what was good. Do you observe that in every place he bears witness to its having a kind of intensitiveness and additional advantage, yet nothing further ? For though it praises and I delight in it, and wish what is good the "evil is" still "present with me," and the agency of it has not been abolished. And thus the Law, with a man who determines upon doing anything good, only acts so far as auxiliary to him, as that it has the same wish as himself. Then since he had stated it indistinctly, as he goes on he gives a yet more distinct interpretation, by showing how the evil is present, how too the Law is a law to such a person only who has a mind to do what is good.

Ver. 22. "For I delight," he says, "in the law of God after the inward man."

He means, for I knew even before this what was good, but when I find it set down in writing, I praise it.

Ver. 23. "But I see another law warring against the law of my mind."

Here again he calls sin a law warring against the other, not in respect of good order, but from the strict obedience yielded to it by those who comply with it. As then it gives the name of master (κύριον Matt. vi. 24; Luke xvi. 13) to Mammon, and of god

---

[1] So the Mss. Sav. has τῆς τέχνης, which seems to have been put in to show that it was not the maker, but the user of the instrument, that was meant.

(Phil. iii. 19) to the belly, not because of their intrinsically deserving it, but because of the extreme obsequiousness of their subjects ; so here he calls sin a law, owing to those who are so obsequious to it, and are afraid to leave it, just as those who have received the Law dread leaving the Law. This then, he means, is opposed to the law of nature ; for this is what is meant by " the law of my mind." And he next represents an array and battle, and refers[1] the whole struggle to the law of nature. For that of Moses was subsequently added over and above : yet still both the one and the other, the one as teaching, the other as praising what was right, wrought no great effects in this battle ; so great was the thraldom of sin, overcoming and getting the upper hand as it did. And this Paul setting forth, and showing the decided ($\kappa\alpha\tau\grave{\alpha}$ $\kappa\rho\acute{\alpha}\tauο\varsigma$) victory it had, says, " I see another law warring against the law of my mind, and bringing me into captivity." He does not use the word conquering only, but "bringing me into captivity to the law of sin." He does not say the bent of the flesh, or the nature of the flesh, but " the law of sin." That is, the thrall, the power. In what sense then does he say, "Which is in my members ?" Now what is this ? Surely it does not make the members to be sin, but makes them as distinct from sin as possible. For that which is in a thing is diverse from that wherein it is. As then the commandment also is not evil, because by it sin took occasion, so neither is the nature of the flesh, even if sin subdues us by means of it. For in this way the soul will be evil, and much more so too, since it has authority in matters of action. But these things are not so, certainly they are not. Since neither if a tyrant and a robber were to take possession of a splendid mansion and a king's court, would the circumstance be any discredit to the house, inasmuch as the entire blame would come on those who contrived such an act. But the enemies of the truth, along with their impiety, fall unawares also into great unreasonableness. For they do not accuse the flesh only, but they also disparage the Law. And yet if the flesh were evil, the Law would be good. For it wars against the Law, and opposes it. If, however, the Law be not good, then the flesh is good.* For it wars

and fights against it even by their own account. How come they then to assert that both belong to the devil, putting things opposed to each other before us ? Do you see, along with their impiety, how great is their unreasonableness also ? But such doctrines as these are not the Church's, for it is the sin only that she condemns ; and both the Laws which God has given, both that of nature and that of Moses, she says are hostile to this, and not to the flesh ; for the flesh she denies to be sin, for it is a work of God's, and one very useful too in order to virtue, if we live soberly.

Ver. 24. " O wretched man that I am ! who shall deliver me from the body of this death ? "

Do you notice what a great thraldom that of vice is, in that it overcomes even a mind that delighted in the Law ? For no one can rejoin, he means, that I hate the Law and abhor it, and so sin overcomes me. For " I delight in it, and consent to it," and flee for refuge to it, yet still it had not the power of saving one who had fled to it. But Christ saved even one that fled from Him. See what a vast advantage grace has ! Yet the Apostle has not stated it thus ; but with a sigh only, and a great lamentation, as if devoid of any to help him, he points out by his perplexity the might of Christ, and says, " O wretched man that I am ! who shall deliver me from the body of this death ? " The Law has not been able : conscience has proved unequal to it, though it praised what was good, and did not praise it only, but even fought against the contrary of it. For by the very words " warreth against " he shows that he was marshalled against it for his part. From what quarter then is one to hope for salvation ?

Ver. 25. " I thank God through Jesus Christ our Lord."

Observe how he shows the necessity of having grace present with us, and that the well-doings herein belong alike to the Father and the Son. For if it is the Father Whom he thanketh, still the Son is the cause of this thanksgiving. But when you hear him say, "Who shall deliver me from the body of this death ? " do not suppose him to be accusing the flesh. For he does not say "body of sin," but "body of death :" that is, the mortal body—that which hath been overcome by death, not that which gendered death. And this is no proof of the evil of the flesh, but of the marring ($\grave{\epsilon}\pi\eta\rho\epsilon\acute{\iota}\alpha\varsigma$, thwarting) it has under-gone. As if any one who was take captive by the savages were to be said to belong to the savages, not as being a savage, but as being detained by them : so the body is said to be

---

[1] Ver. and Sav. Marg. $\grave{\epsilon}\nu\tau\acute{\iota}\theta\eta\sigma\iota$, which makes much the same sense ; his conj. and 2 Mss. $\grave{\alpha}\nu\tau\iota\tau\acute{\iota}\theta\eta\sigma\iota$, " sets in opposition."

* It is peculiarly interesting to see how vigorously Chrys. combats the idea that the flesh is essentially evil, as if it were a current notion of his time. This view—derived from heathen sources—exerted a powerful influence in the Church from early times and became the fruitful source of ascetic rigors.— G. B. S.

of death, as being held down thereby, not as producing it. Wherefore also it is not the body that he himself wishes to be delivered from, but the mortal body, hinting, as I have often said, that from its becoming subject to suffering,[1] it also became an easy prey to sin. Why then, it may be said, the thraldom of sin being so great before the times of grace, were men punished for sinning? Because they had such commands given them as might even under sin's dominion be accomplished. For he did not draw them to the highest kind of conversation, but allowed them to enjoy wealth, and did not forbid having several wives, and to gratify anger in a just cause, and to make use of luxury within bounds.[2] (Matt. v. 38.) And so great was this condescension, that the written Law even required less than the law of nature. For the law of nature ordered one man to associate with one woman throughout. And this Christ shows in the words, " He which made them at the beginning, made them male and female." (ib. xix. 4.) But the Law of Moses neither forbade the putting away of one and the taking in of another, nor prohibited the having of two[3] at once! (ib. v. 31.) And besides this there are also many other ordinances of the Law, that one might see those who were before its day fully performing, being instructed by the law of nature. They therefore who lived under the old dispensation had no hardship done them by so moderate a system of laws being imposed upon them. But if they were not, on these terms, able to get the upper hand, the charge is against their own listlessness. Wherefore Paul gives thanks, because Christ, without any rigorousness about these things, not only demanded no account of this moderate amount,[4] but even made us able to have a greater race set before us. And therefore he says, " I thank my God through Jesus Christ." And letting the salvation which all agreed about pass, he goes from the points he had already made good, to another further point, in which he states that it was not our former sins only that we were freed from, but we were also made invincible for the future. For " there is," he says, " now no condemnation to them which are in Christ Jesus, who walk not after the flesh." Yet he did not say it before he had first recalled to mind our former condition again in the words, " So then

with the mind I myself serve the law of God, but with the flesh the law of sin."

Chap. viii. ver. 1. " There is therefore no condemnation to them which are in Christ Jesus."

Then as the fact that many fall into sin even after baptism presented a difficulty (ἀντέπιπτεν), he consequently hastened to meet it, and says not merely "to them that are in Christ Jesus," but adds, "who walk not after the flesh;" so showing that all afterward comes of our listlessness. For now we have the power of walking not after the flesh, but then it was a difficult task. Then he gives another proof of it by the sequel, in the words,

Ver. 2. " For the law of the Spirit of life hath made me free."

It is the Spirit he is here calling the law of the Spirit. For as he calls sin the law of sin, so he here calls the Spirit the law of the Spirit. And yet he named that of Moses as such, where he says, " For we know that the Law is spiritual." What then is the difference? A great and unbounded one. For that was spiritual, but this is a law of the Spirit. Now what is the distinction between this and that? The other was merely given by the Spirit, but this even furnisheth those that receive it with the Spirit in large measure. Wherefore also he called it the law of life[5] in contradistinction to that of sin, not that of Moses. For when he says, It freed me[6] from the law of sin and death, it is not the law of Moses that he is here speaking of, since in no case does he style it the law of sin : for how could he one that he had called "just and holy " so often, and destructive of sin too? but it is that which warreth against the law of the mind. For this grievous war did the grace of the Spirit put a stop to, by slaying sin, and making the contest light to us and crowning us at the outstart, and then drawing us to the struggle with abundant help. Next as it is ever his wont to turn from the Spirit to the Son and the Father, and to reckon all our estate to lean upon the Trinity,[7] so doth he here also. For after saying, "Who shall deliver me from the body of this death," he pointed at the Father as doing this by the Son, then again at the Holy Spirit along with the Son. " For the law of the Spirit of Life in Christ Jesus hath made me free, he says. Then again, at the Father and the Son;

Ver. 3. " For what the Law could not do,"

---

[1] παθητὸν, which may also mean liable to passions.
[2] He is speaking of the actual precepts. Men under the Law were encouraged to higher aims, but it was in looking beyond the letter.
[3] The typical fitness of this permission is illustrated by the case of Sarah and Hagar; the coincidence of typical with moral fitness is in many cases above our understanding.
[4] So Field from 1 Ms.: others " past sins:" Vulg. " our doings."

[5] It may be right to consider τῆς ζωῆς as forming part of the attribute of νόμος in conformity with the Hebr. idiom; see Lee's Gram. Art. 224, 8.
[6] " Thee " most Mss., and Edd. before Field.
[7] τῇ τριάδι πάντα τὰ παρ ἡμῶν λογιζόμενος, or "imputing all things (done) by us to the Trinity."

he saith, "in that it was weak through the flesh, God sending His own Son in the likeness of sinful flesh, and for sin, condemned sin in the flesh."

Again, he seems indeed to be disparaging the Law. But if any one attends strictly, he even highly praises it, by showing that it harmonizes with Christ, and gives preference to the same things. For he does not speak of the badness of the Law, but of " what it could not do ; " and so again, " in that it was weak," not, " in that it was mischievous, or designing." And even weakness he does not ascribe to it, but to the flesh, as he says, " in that it was weak through the flesh," using the word " flesh " here again not for the essence and subsistency itself, but giving its name to the more carnal sort of mind. In which way he acquits both the body and the Law of any accusation. Yet not in this way only, but by what comes next also. For supposing the Law to be of the contrary part, how was it Christ came to its assistance, and fulfilled its requisitions, and lent it a helping hand by condemning sin in the flesh? For this was what was lacking, since in the soul the Lord had condemned it long ago. What then ? is it the greater thing that the Law accomplished, but the less that the Only-Begotten did ? Surely not. For it was God that was the principal doer of that also, in that He gave us the law of nature, and added the written one to it. Again, there were no use of the greater, if the lesser had not been supplied. For what good is it to know what things ought to be done, if a man does not follow it out ? None, for it were but a greater condemnation. And so He that hath saved the soul it is, Who hath made the flesh also easy to bridle. For to teach is easy, but to show besides a way in which these things were easily done, this is the marvel. Now it was for this that the Only-Begotten came, and did not depart before He had set us free from this difficulty. But what is greater, is the method of the victory; for He took none other flesh, but this very one which was beset with troubles. So it is as if any one were to see in the street a vile woman of the baser sort being beaten, and were to say he was her son, when he was the king's, and so to get her free from those who ill treated her. And this He really did, in that He confessed that He was the Son of Man, and stood by it (i. e. the flesh), and condemned the sin. However, He did not endure to smite it besides ; or rather, He smote it with the blow of His death, but in this very act it was not the smitten flesh which was condemned and perished, but the sin which had been smiting.

And this is the greatest possible marvel. For if it were not in the flesh that the victory took place, it would not be so astonishing, since this the Law also wrought. But the wonder is, that it was with the flesh ($\mu\epsilon\tau\grave{\alpha}\ \sigma\alpha\rho\kappa\grave{o}\varsigma$) that His trophy was raised, and that what had been overthrown numberless times by sin, did itself get a glorious victory over it. For behold what strange things there were that took place ! One was, that sin did not conquer the flesh ; another, that sin was conquered, and conquered by it too. For it is not the same thing not to get conquered, and to conquer that which was continually overthrowing us. A third is, that it not only conquered it, but even chastised it. For by not sinning it kept from being conquered, but by dying also, He overcame and condemned it, having made the flesh, that before was so readily made a mock of by it, a plain object of fear to it. In this way then, He at once unnerved its power, and abolished the death by it introduced. For so long as it took hold of sinners, it with justice kept pressing to its end. But after finding a sinless body, when it had given it up to death, it was condemned as having acted unjustly. Do you observe, how many proofs of victory there are ? The flesh not being conquered by sin, Its even conquering and condemning it, Its not condemning it barely, but condemning it as having sinned. For after having convicted it of injustice, he proceeds to condemn it, and that not by power and might barely, but even by the rules of justice. For this is what he means by saying, "for sin condemned sin in the flesh." As if he had said that he had convicted it of great sin, and then condemned it. So you see it is sin that getteth condemned everywhere, and not the flesh, for this is even crowned with honor, and has to give sentence against the other. But if he does say that it was "in the likeness " of flesh that he sent the Son, do not therefore suppose that His flesh was of a different kind. For as he called it "sinful," this was why he put the word "likeness."[1] For sinful flesh it was not that Christ had, but like indeed to our sinful flesh,

---

[1] The Fathers lay great stress upon this phrase of the Apostles. August. *contr. Faust.* xiv. 5, argues, that this likeness consisted in our Lord's flesh being mortal; death being the penalty of sin: vid. also *de Nuptiis et Concupisc.* 1. 12. vid. also Basil, *Ep.* 261, where writing against the Apollinarians, he interprets this text to mean, that whereas Christ had all affections of human nature, which implied the reality of His assumption of it, He had not those which infringe our nature, i. e. which arise from sin. Athanasius, writing against the same heretics, observes, that Christ's sinlessness was like Adam's before the fall (In Apoll. ii. 6): nor as St. Cyril observes, greater than before the fall, because He has a physical inability to sin, arising from His personality being Divine. vid. Cyr. Alex. *in Esai. l. i. Orat.* 4, *fin.* At the same time He took the flesh, not of Adam unfallen, but fallen, such as ours. *Vid. Leont. contra Nest. et Eutych. lib.* 2 *apud Canis.* vol. i. p. 568. Gall. xii. 681. Fulgent. *Ep. ad. Regin.* Tertull. *de Carn. Christi.* xvi.

yet sinless, and in nature the same with us. And so even from this it is plain that by nature the flesh was not evil. For it was not by taking a different one instead of the former, nor by changing this same one in substance, that Christ caused it to regain the victory: but He let it abide in its own nature, and yet made it bind on the crown of victory over sin, and then after the victory raised it up, and made it immortal. What then, it may be said, is this to me, whether it was this flesh that these things happened in? Nay, it concerns thee very much. Wherefore also he proceeds:

Ver. 4. "That the righteousness[1] of the Law might be fulfilled in us, who walk not after the flesh."

What meaneth this word, righteousness? Why, the end, the scope, the well-doing. For what was its design, and what did it enjoin? To be without sin. This then is made good to us (κατώρθωται ἡμῖν) now through Christ. And the making a stand against it, and the getting the better of it, came from Him. But it is for us to enjoy the victory. Then shall we never sin henceforth? We never shall unless we have become exceedingly relaxed and supine. And this is why he added, "to them that walk not after the flesh. For lest, after hearing that Christ hath delivered thee from the war of sin, and that the requisition (δικαίωμα) of the Law is fulfilled in thee, by sin having been "condemned in the flesh," thou shouldest break up all thy defences; therefore, in that place also, after saying, "there is therefore no condemnation," he added, "to them that walk not after the flesh;" and here also, "that the requisition of the Law might be fulfilled in us," he proceeds with the very same thing; or rather, not with it only, but even with a much stronger thing.[2] For after saying, "that the righteousness of the Law might be fulfilled in us that walk not after the flesh," he proceeds, "but after the Spirit."

So showing, that it is not only binding upon us to keep ourselves from evil deeds, but also to be adorned (κομᾷν) with good. For to give thee the crown is His; but it is thine to hold it fast when given. For the righteousness of the Law, that one should not become liable to its curse, Christ has accomplished for thee. Be not a traitor then to so great a gift, but keep guarding this goodly treasure. For in

this passage he shows that the Font will not suffice to save us, unless, after coming from it, we display a life worthy of the Gift. And so he again advocates the Law in saying what he does. For when we have once become obedient to Christ, we must use all ways and plans so that its righteousness, which Christ fulfilled, may abide in us, and not come to naught.

Ver. 5. "For they that are after the flesh do mind the things of the flesh."

Yet even this is no disparaging of the flesh. For so long as it keeps its own place, nothing amiss cometh to pass. But when we let it have its own will in everything, and it passes over its proper bounds, and rises up against the soul, then it destroys and corrupts everything, yet not owing to its own nature, but to its being out of proportion, and the disorder thereupon ensuing. "But they that are after the Spirit do mind the things of the Spirit."

Ver. 6. "For to be carnally minded is death." He does not speak of the nature of the flesh, or the essence of the body, but of being carnally "minded," which may be set right again, and abolished. And in saying thus, he does not ascribe to the flesh any reasoning power of its own. Far from it. But to set forth the grosser motion of the mind, and giving this a name from the inferior part, and in the same way as he often is in the habit of calling man in his entireness, and viewed as possessed of a soul, flesh. "But to be spiritually minded." Here again he speaks of the spiritual mind, in the same way as he says further on, "But He that searcheth the hearts knoweth what is the mind of the spirit" (ver. 27); and he points out many blessings resulting from this, both in the present life, and in that which is to come. For as the evils which being carnally minded introduces, are far outnumbered by those blessings which a spiritual mind affords. And this he points out in the words "life and peace." The one is in contraposition to the first—for death is what he says to be carnally minded is. And the other in contraposition to the following. For after mentioning peace, he goes on,

Ver. 7. "Because the carnal mind is enmity against God:" and this is worse than death. Then to show how it is at once death and enmity; "for it is not subject to the Law of God," he says, "neither indeed can be." But be not troubled at hearing the "neither indeed can be." For this difficulty admits of an easy solution. For what he here names "carnal mindedness" is the reasoning (or "way of thinking," λογισμὸν) that is

---

[1] Aristotle defines δικαίωμα to be τὸ δίκαιον ὅταν πραχθῇ· but rather in the sense of correcting wrong than in the more general meaning: *Eth.* b. v. c. 7, § 7. It may mean here what the Law claims of right.

[2] St. Chr. evidently used a text which read in v. 1 μὴ κατὰ σάρκα περιπ., but omitted ἀλλὰ κατὰ Πνεῦμα. Most Mss. of the N. T. and all recent critical editions, omit both clauses there: here there is no doubt of either.

earthly, gross, and eager-hearted after the things of this life and its wicked doings. It is of this he says "neither yet can" it "be subject" to God. And what hope of salvation is there left, if it be impossible for one who is bad to become good? This is not what he says. Else how would Paul have become such as he was? how would the (penitent) thief, or Manasses, or the Ninevites, or how would David after falling have recovered himself? How would Peter after the denial have raised himself up? (1 Cor. v. 5.) How could he that had lived in fornication have been enlisted among Christ's fold? (2 Cor. ii. 6–11.) How could the Galatians who had "fallen from grace" (Gal. v. 4), have attained their former dignity again? What he says then is not that it is impossible for a man that is wicked to become good, but that it is impossible for one who continues wicked to be subject to God. Yet for a man to be changed, and so become good, and subject to Him, is easy. For he does not say that man cannot be subject to God, but, wicked doing cannot be good. As if he had said, fornication cannot be chastity, nor vice virtue. And this it says in the Gospel also, "A corrupt tree cannot bring forth good fruit" (Matt. vii. 18), not to bar the change from virtue to vice, but to say how incapable continuance in vice is of bringing forth good fruits. For He does not say that an evil tree cannot become a good one, but that bring forth good fruit it cannot, while it continues evil. For that it can be changed, He shows from this passage, and from another parable, when He introduces the tares as becoming wheat, on which score also He forbids their being rooted up; "Lest," He says, "ye root up also the wheat with them (ib. xiii. 29); that is, that which will spring (γίνεσθαι, 4 Mss.. τίκτεσθαι) from them. It is vice then he means by carnal mindedness, and by spiritual mindedness the grace given, and the working of it discernible in the right determination of mind, not discussing in any part of this passage, a substance and an entity, but virtue and vice. For that which thou hadst no power to do under the Law, now, he means, thou wilt be able to do, to go on uprightly, and with no intervening fall, if thou layest hold of the Spirit's aid. For it is not enough not to walk after the flesh, but we must also go after the Spirit, since turning away from what is evil will not secure our salvation, but we must also do what is good. And this will come about, if we give our souls up to the Spirit, and persuade our flesh to get acquainted with its proper position, for in this way we shall make it also spiritual; as also if we be listless we shall make our soul

carnal. For since it was no natural necessity which put the gift into us, but the freedom[1] of choice placed it in our hands, it rests with thee henceforward whether this shall be or the other. For He, on His part, has performed everything. For sin no longer warreth against the law of our mind, neither doth it lead us away captive as heretofore, for all that state has been ended and broken up, and the affections cower in fear and trembling at the grace of the Spirit. But if thou wilt quench the light, and cast out the holder of the reins, and chase the helmsman away, then charge the tossing thenceforth upon thyself. For since virtue hath been now made an easier thing (for which cause also we are under far stricter obligations of religious living), consider how men's condition lay when the Law prevailed, and how at present, since grace hath shone forth. The things which aforetime seemed not possible to any one, virginity, and contempt of death, and of other stronger sufferings, are now in full vigor through every part of the world, and it is not with us alone, but with the Scythians, and Thracians, and Indians, and Persians, and several other barbarous nations, that there are companies of virgins, and clans of martyrs, and congregations of monks, and these now grown even more numerous than the married, and strictness of fasting, and the utmost renunciation of property. Now these are things which, with one or two exceptions, persons who lived under the Law never conceived even in a dream. Since thou seest then the real state of things voiced with a shriller note than any trumpet, let not thyself grow soft and treacherous to so great a grace. Since not even after the faith is it possible for a listless man to be saved! For the wrestlings are made easy that thou mayest strive and conquer, not that thou shouldest sleep, or abuse the greatness of the grace by making it a reason for listlessness, so wallowing again in the former mire. And so he goes on to say,

Ver. 8. "So then they that are in the flesh cannot please God."

What then? Are we, it will be said, to cut our bodies in pieces to please God, and to make our escape from the flesh? and would you have us be homicides, and so lead us to virtue? You see what inconsistencies are gendered by taking the words literally. For by "the flesh" in this passage, he does not mean the body, or the essence of the body,

---

[1] i. e. as exercised in coming to the font. Field proposes to soften the strong expression by reading, "it was by no natural necessity that He put, etc., but by freedom of choice He placed it."

but that life which is fleshly and worldly, and uses self-indulgence and extravagance to the full, so making the entire man flesh. For as they that have the wings of the Spirit, make the body also spiritual, so do they who bound off from this, and are the slaves of the belly, and of pleasure, make the soul also flesh, not that they change the essence of it, but that they mar its noble birth. And this mode of speaking is to be met with in many parts of the Old Testament also, to signify by flesh the gross and earthly life, which is entangled in pleasures that are not convenient. For to Noah He says, "My Spirit shall not always make its abode in these men, because they are flesh." (Gen. vi. 3 as the LXX. give it.) And yet Noah was himself also compassed about with flesh. But this is not the complaint, the being compassed about with the flesh, for this is so by nature, but the having chosen a carnal life. Wherefore also Paul saith, "But they that are in the flesh cannot please God." Then he proceeds:

Ver. 9. "But ye are not in the flesh, but in the Spirit."

Here again, he does not mean flesh absolutely, but such sort of flesh, that which was in a whirl and thraldom of passions. Why then, it may be said, does he not say so, nor state any difference? It is to rouse the hearer, and to show that he that liveth aright is not even in the body. For inasmuch as it was in a manner clear to every one that the spiritual man was not in sin, he states the greater truth that it was not in sin alone, that the spiritual man was not, but not even in the flesh was he henceforward, having become from that very moment an Angel, and ascended into heaven, and henceforward barely carrying the body about. Now if this be thy reason for disparaging the flesh, because it is by its name that he calls the fleshly life, at this rate you are also for disparaging the world, because wickedness is often called after it, as Christ also said to His disciples, "Ye are not of this world;" and again to His brethren, He says, "The world cannot hate you, but me it hateth." (John xv. 19. ib. vii. 7.) And the soul too Paul must afterwards be calling estranged from God, since to those that live in error, he gives the name of men of the soul (1 Cor. ii. 14, ψυχικὸς A. V. natural). But this is not so, indeed it is not so. For we are not to look to the bare words, but always to the sentiment of the speaker, and so come to a perfectly distinct knowledge of what is said. For some things are good, some bad, and some indifferent. Thus the soul and the flesh belong to things indifferent, since each

may become either the one or the other. But the spirit belongs to things good, and at no time becometh any other thing. Again, the mind of the flesh, that is, ill-doing, belongs to things always bad. "For it is not subject to the law of God." If then thou yieldest thy soul and body to the better, thou wilt have become of its part. If on the other hand thou yield to the worse, then art thou made a partaker of the ruin therein, not owing to the nature of the soul and the flesh, but owing to that judgment which has the power of choosing either. And to show that these things are so, and that the words do not disparage the flesh, let us take up the phrase itself again, and sift it more thoroughly. "But ye are not in the flesh but in the Spirit," he says. What then? were they not in the flesh, and did they go about without any bodies? What sense would this be? You see that it is the carnal life that he intimates. And why did he not say, But ye are not in sin? It is that you may come to know that Christ hath not extinguished the tyranny of sin only, but hath even made the flesh to weigh us down less, and to be more spiritual, not by changing its nature, but rather by giving it wings. For as when fire cometh in company with iron, the iron also becomes fire, though abiding in its own nature still; thus with them that believe, and have the Spirit, the flesh henceforth goeth over into that manner of working, and becometh wholly spiritual, crucified in all parts, and flying with the same wings as the soul, such as was the body of him who here speaks. Wherefore all self-indulgence and pleasure he made scorn of, and found his self-indulgence in hunger, and stripes, and prisons, and did not even feel pain in undergoing them. (2 Cor. xi.) And it was to show this that he said, "For our light affliction, which is but for a moment," etc. (ib. iv. 17.) So well had he tutored even the flesh to be in harmony with the spirit. "If so be that the Spirit of God dwell in you" (εἴπερ.) He often uses this "if so be," not to express any doubt, but even when he is quite persuaded of the thing, and instead of "since," as when he says, "If it is a righteous thing," for "seeing it is a righteous thing with God to recompense tribulation to them that trouble you." (2 Thess. i. 6.) Again, "Have ye suffered so many things in vain, if it be yet in vain?" (Gal. iii. 4.)

"Now if any man have not the Spirit of Christ." He does not say, if ye have not, but he brings forward the distressing word, as applied to other persons. "He is none of His." he says.

Ver. 10. "And if Christ be in you."

Again, what is good he applies to them,[1] and the distressing part was short and parenthetic. And that which is an object of desire, is on either side of it, and put at length too, so as to throw the other into shade. Now this he says, not as affirming that the Spirit is Christ, far from it, but to show that he who hath the Spirit not only is called Christ's, but even hath Christ Himself. For it cannot but be that where the Spirit is, there Christ is also. For wheresoever one Person of the Trinity is, there the whole Trinity is present. For It is undivided in Itself, and hath a most entire Oneness. What then, it may be said, will happen, if Christ be in us? "The body is dead because of sin; but the Spirit is life because of righteousness." You see the great evils that come of not having the Holy Spirit; death, enmity against God, inability to satisfy His laws, not being Christ's as we should be, the want of His indwelling. Consider now also what great blessings come of having the Spirit. Being Christ's, having Christ himself, vying with the Angels (for this is what mortifying the flesh is), and living an immortal life, holding henceforward the earnests of the Resurrection, running with ease the race of virtue. For he does not say so little as that the body is henceforward inactive for sin, but that it is even dead, so magnifying the ease of the race. For such an one without troubles and labors gains the crown. Then afterward for this reason he adds also, "to sin," that you may see that it is the viciousness, not the essence of the body, that He hath abolished at once. For if the latter had been done, many things even of a kind to be beneficial to the soul would have been abolished also. This however is not what he says, but while it is yet alive and abiding, he contends, it is dead. For this is the sign of our having the Son, of the Spirit being in us, that our bodies should be in no respect different from those that lie on the bier with respect to the working of sin (so the Mss. Sav. "of the body." The preceding words are slightly corrupt.) But be not affrighted at hearing of mortifying. For in it you have what is really life, with no death to succeed it: and such is that of the Spirit. It yieldeth not to death any more, but weareth out death and consumeth it, and that which it receiveth, it keepeth it immortal. And this is why after saying "the body is dead," he does not say, "but the Spirit 'liveth,'" but, "is life," to point out that He (the Spirit) had the power of giving this to others also. Then again to brace up his hearer, he tells him the cause of the Life,

and the proof of it. Now this is righteousness; for where there is no sin, death is not to be seen either; but where death is not to be seen, life is indissoluble.

Ver. 11. "But if the Spirit of Him that raised up Jesus from the dead dwell in you, He that raised up our Lord shall also quicken your mortal bodies by His Spirit that dwelleth in you."

Again, he touches the point of the Resurrection, since this was the most encouraging[2] hope to the hearer, and gave him a security from what had happened unto Christ. Now be not thou afraid because thou art compassed about with a dead body. Let it have the Spirit, and it shall assuredly rise again. What then, shall the bodies which have not the Spirit not rise? How then must "all stand before the judgment-seat of Christ?" (Rom. xiv. 10) or how will the account of hell be trustworthy? For if they that have not the Spirit rise not, there will not be a hell at all. What then is it which is said? All shall rise, yet not all to life, but some to punishment and some to life. (John v. 29.) This is why he did not say, shall raise up, but shall quicken. (Dan. xii. 2.) And this is a greater thing than resurrection, and is given to the just only. And the cause of this honor he adds in the words, "By His Spirit that dwelleth in you." And so if while here thou drive away the grace of the Spirit, and do not depart with it still safe, thou wilt assuredly perish, though thou dost rise again. For as He will not endure then, if he see His Spirit shining in thee, to give thee up to punishment, so neither will He allow them, if He see It quenched, to bring thee into the Bride-chamber, even as He admitted not those virgins. (Matt. xxv. 12.)

Suffer not thy body then to live in this world, that it may live then! Make it die, that it die not. For if it keep living, it will not live: but if it die, then shall it live. And this is the case with resurrection in general. For it must die first and be buried, and then become immortal. But this has been done in the Font. It has therefore had first its crucifixion and burial, and then been raised. This has also happened with the Lord's Body. For that also was crucified and buried (7 Mss. died) and rose again. This then let us too be doing: let us keep continually mortifying it in its works. I do not mean in its substance—far be it from me—but in its inclinations towards evil doings. For this is a life too, or rather this only is life, undergoing nothing that is common to man, nor being

---

[1] τὸ χρηστὸν for τὸν Χριστὸν Field, with the Catena and the Version of Musculus.

[2] ἤλειφεν, v. p. 170, n. Sav. εἴληφεν.

a slave to pleasures. For he who has set himself under the rule of these, has no power even to live through the low spirits, the fears, and the dangers, and the countless throng of ills, that rise from them. For if death must be expected, he hath died, before death, of fear. And if it be disease he dreads, or affront, or poverty, or any of the other ills one cannot anticipate, he is ruined and hath perished. What then can be more miserable than a life of this sort? But far otherwise is he that liveth to the Spirit, for he stands at once above fears and grief and dangers and every kind of change: and that not by undergoing no such thing, but, what is much greater, by thinking scorn of them when they assail him. And how·is this to be? It will be if the Spirit dwell in us continually. For he does not speak of any short stay made thereby, but of a continual indwelling. Hence he does not say "the Spirit which" dwelt, but "which dwelleth in us," so pointing to a continual abiding. He then is most truly alive, who is dead to this life. Hence he says, "The Spirit is life because of righteousness." And to make the thing clearer, let me bring[1] before you two men, one who is given up to extravagances and pleasures, and the deceitfulness of this life; and the other made dead to all these; and let us see which is more really the living one. For let one of these two be very rich and much looked up to, keeping parasites and flatterers,[2] and let us suppose him to spend the whole day upon this, in revelling and drunkenness: and let the other live in poverty, and fasting, and hard fare, and strict rules (φιλοσοφία), and at evening partake of necessary food only; or if you will let him even pass two or three days without food.[3] Which then of these two think we (3 Mss. you) is most really alive? Men in general will, I know, reckon the former so, the man that takes his pleasure (Sav. σκιρτῶντα, Mss. τρυφῶντα) and squanders his goods. But we reckon the man that enjoys the moderate fare. Now then since it is still a subject of contest and opposition let us go into the houses of them both, and just at the very time too when in your judgment the rich man is living in truest sense, in the very season of self-indulgence, and when we have got in, let us look and see the real condition of each of these men. For it is from the actions that it appears which is alive and which dead. Shall we not find the one among his books, or in prayer and fasting, or some other necessary duty, awake and sober, and conversing with God? but the

other we shall see stupid in drunkenness, and in no better condition than a dead man. And if we wait till the evening, we shall see this death coming upon him more and more, and then sleep again succeeding to that: but the other we shall see even in the night keeping from wine and sleep. Which then shall we pronounce to be most alive, the man that lies in a state of insensibility, and is an open laughing-stock to everybody? or the man that is active, and conversing with God? For if you go up to the one, and tell him something he ought to know, you will not hear him say a word, any more than a dead man. But the latter, whether you choose to be in his company at night or by day, you will see to be an angel rather than a man, and will hear him speak wisdom about things in Heaven. Do you see how one of them is alive above all men living, and the other in a more pitiable plight even than the dead? And even if he have a mind to stir he sees one thing instead of another, and is like people that are mad, or rather is in a worse plight even than they. For if any one were to do them any harm, we should at once feel pity for the sufferer, and rebuke the doer of the wrong. But this man, if we were to see a person trample on him, we should not only be disinclined to pity, but should even give judgment against him, now that he was fallen. And will you tell me this is life, and not a harder lot than deaths unnumbered? So you see the self-indulgent man is not only dead, but worse than dead, and more miserable than a man possessed. For the one is the object of pity, the other of hatred. And the one has allowance made him, the other suffers punishment for his madness. But if externally he is so ridiculous, as having his saliva tainted, and his breath stinking of wine, just consider what case his wretched soul, inhumed as it were in a grave, in such a body as this, is probably in. For one may look upon this as much the same as if one were to permit a damsel, comely, chaste, free-born, of good family, and handsome, to be trampled on, and every way insulted by a serving woman, that was savage, and disgustful, and impure; drunkenness being something of this sort. And who, being in his senses, would not choose to die a thousand deaths, rather than live a single day in this way? For even if at daylight he were to get up, and seem to be sober from that revelling (or absurd show, κωμῳδίας, 1 Ms. κώμου) of his, still even then it is not the clear brightness of temperance which he enjoys, since the cloud from the storm of drunkenness still is hanging before his eyes. And even if we were to grant him the clearness of sobriety,

---

[1] See Ernesti in v. παραγωγή.
[2] The Plutus evidently in his mind.
[3] This was not uncommon in warmer climates, Euseb. ii. 17.

what were he the better? For this soberness would be of no service to him, except to let him see his accusers. For when he is in the midst of his unseemly deeds, he is so far a gainer in not perceiving those that laugh at him. But when it is day he loses this comfort even, and while his servants are murmuring, and his wife is ashamed, and his friends accuse him, and his enemies make sport of him, he knows it too. What can be more miserable than a life like this, to be laughed at all day by everybody, and when it is evening to do the same unseemly things afresh. But what if you would let me put the covetous before you? For this is another, and even a worse intoxication. But if it be an intoxication, then it must be a worse death by far than the former, since the intoxication is more grievous. And indeed it is not so sad to be drunk with wine as with covetousness. For in the former case, the penalty ends with the sufferings (several Ms. "sufferer,") and results in insensibility, and the drunkard's own ruin. But in this case the mischief passes on to thousands of souls, and kindles wars of sundry kinds upon all sides. Come then and let us put this beside the other, and let us see what are the points they have in common, and in what again this is worse than it, and let us make a comparison of drunkards to-day. For with that blissful man, who liveth to the Spirit, let them not be put at all in comparison, but only tried by one another. And again, let us bring the money-table before you, laden as it is with blood. What then have they in common, and in what are they like each other? It is in the very nature of the disease. For the species of drunkenness is different, as one comes of wine, the other of money, but its way of affecting them is similar, both being alike possessed with an exorbitant desire. For he who is drunken with wine, the more glasses he has drunk off, the more he longs for; and he that is in love with money, the more he compasses, the more he kindles the flame of desire, and the more importunate he renders his thirst. In this point then they resemble each other. But in another the covetous man has the advantage (in a bad sense). Now what is this? Why that the other's affection is a natural one. For the wine is hot, and adds to one's natural drought, and so makes drunkards thirsty. But what is there to make the other man always keep desiring more? how comes it that when he is increased in riches, then he is in the veriest poverty? This complaint then is a perplexing one, and has more of paradox about it. But if you please, we will take a view of them after the drunkenness also. Or

rather, there is no such thing as ever seeing the covetous man after his drunkenness, so continual a state of intoxication is he in! Let us then view them both in the state of drunkenness, and let us get a distinct notion which is the most ridiculous, and let us again figure to ourselves a correct sketch of them. We shall see then the man who dotes with his wine at eventide with his eyes open, seeing no one, but moving about at mere hap-hazard, and stumbling against such as fall in his way, and spewing, and convulsed, and exposing his nakedness in an unseemly manner. (See Habak. ii. 16.) And if his wife be there, or his daughter, or his maid-servant, or anybody else, they[1] will laugh at him heartily. And now let us bring before you the covetous man. Here what happens is not deserving of laughter only, but even of a curse, and exceeding wrath, and thunderbolts without number. At present however let us look at the ridiculous part, for this man as well as the other has an ignorance of all, whether friend or foe. And like him too, though his eyes are open, he is blinded. And as the former takes all he sees for wine, so does this man take all for money. And his spewing is even more disgusting. For it is not food that he vomits, but words of abuse, of insolence, of war, of death, that draws upon his own head lightnings without number from above. And as the body of the drunkard is livid and dissolving, so also is the other's soul. Or rather, even his body is not free from this disorder, but it is taken even worse, care eating it away worse than wine does (as do anger too and want of sleep), and by degrees exhausting it entirely. And he that is seized with illness from wine, after the night is over may get sober. But this person is always drunken day and night, watching or sleeping, so paying a severer penalty for it than any prisoner, or person at work in the mines, or suffering any punishment more grievous than this, if such there be. Is it then life pray, and not death? or rather, is it not a fate more wretched than any death? For death gives the body rest, and sets it free from ridicule, as well as disgrace and sins: but these drunken fits plunge it into all these, stopping up the ears, dulling the eyesight, keeping down the understanding in great darkness. For it will not bear the mention of anything but interest, and interest upon interest, and shameful gains, and odious traffickings, and ungentlemanly and slavelike trans-

---

[1] ἐγγελάσεται Mss., "he will be laughed at" or rather "she (the supposed spectator) will laugh at him." Field reads ἐγελάσατε with one or two Mss., and alters the punctuation; so that the passage will run "exposing, etc., even if his wife be there . . . . or anybody else. Do you laugh heartily? Then let us bring before you," etc.

actions, barking like a dog at everybody, and hating everybody, averse to everybody, at war with everybody, without any reason for it, rising up against the poor, grudging at the rich, and civil to nobody. And if he have a wife, or children, or friends, if he may not use them all towards getting gain, these are to him more his enemies than natural enemies. What then can be worse than madness of this sort, and what more wretched? when a man is preparing rocks for his own self on every side, and shoals, and precipices, and gulfs, and pits without number, while he has but one body, and is the slave of one belly. And if any thrust thee into a state office, thou wilt be a runaway, through fear of expense. Yet to thyself thou art laying up countless charges far more distressing than those, enlisting thyself for services not only more expensive, but also more dangerous, to be done for mammon, and not paying this tyrant a money contribution only, nor of bodily labor, torture to the soul, and grief, but even of thy blood itself, that thou mayest have some addition to thy property (miserable and sorrow-stricken man!) out of this barbarous slavery. Do you not see those who are taken day by day to the grave, how they are carried to tombs . naked and destitute of all things, unable to take with them aught that is in the house, but bearing what clothes they have about them to the worm? Consider these day by day, and perchance the malady will abate, unless you mean even by such an occasion to be still more mad at the expensiveness of the funeral rites—for the malady is importunate, the disease terrible! This then is why we address you upon this subject at every meeting, and constantly foment your hearing, that at all events by your growing accustomed to such thoughts, some good many come. But be not conten-

tious, for it is not only at the Day to come, but even before it, that this manifold malady brings with it sundry punishments. For if I were to tell you of those who pass their days in chains, or of one nailed to a lingering disease, or of one struggling with famine, or of any other thing whatsoever, I could point out no one who suffers so much as they do who love money. For what severer evil can befall one, than being hated by all men, than hating all men, than not having kindly feeling towards any, than being never satisfied, than being in a continual thirst, than struggling with a perpetual hunger, and that a more distressing one than what all men esteem such? than having pains day by day, than being never sober, than being continually in worries and harasses? For all these things, and more than these, are what the covetous set their shoulder to; in the midst of their gaining having no perception of pleasure, though scraping to themselves from all men, because of their desiring more. But in the case of their incurring a loss, if it be but of a farthing, they think they have suffered most grievously, and have been cast out of life itself. What language then can put these evils before you? And if their fate here be such, consider also what comes after this life, the being cast out of the kingdom, the pain that comes from hell, the perpetual chains, the outer darkness, the venomous worm, the gnashing of teeth, the affliction, the sore straitening, the rivers of fire, the furnaces that never get quenched. And gathering all these together, and weighing them against the pleasure of money, tear up now this disease root and branch, that so receiving the true riches, and being set free from this grievous poverty, thou mayest obtain the present blessings, and those to come, by the grace and love toward man, etc.

HOMILY XIV.

ROM. VIII. 12, 13.

"Therefore, brethren, we are debtors, not to the flesh, to live after the flesh. For if ye live after the flesh, ye shall die; but if ye through the Spirit do mortify the deeds of the body, ye shall live."

AFTER showing how great the reward of a spiritual life is, and that it maketh Christ to dwell in us, and that it quickeneth our mortal bodies, and wingeth them to heaven, and rendereth the way of virtue easier, he next fitly introduces an exhortation to this pur-

pose. "Therefore" we ought "not to live after the flesh." But this is not what he says, for he words it in a much more striking and powerful way, thus, "we are debtors to the Spirit." For saying, "we are debtors not to the flesh," indicates this. And this is a point he is everywhere giving proof of, that what God hath done for us is not matter of debt, but of mere grace. But after this, what we do is no longer matter of free-will offering, but of debt. For when he saith, " Ye are bought with a price, be not ye the servants of men " (1 Cor. vii. 23) ; and when he writes, " Ye are not your own " (ib. vi. 19) ; and again in another passage he calls these selfsame things to their mind, in these words, " If (most Mss. om. " if") One died for all, then all died [1] that they should not henceforth live unto themselves." (2 Cor. v. 15.) And it is to establish this that he says here also, " We are debtors ; " then since he said we are " not " debtors " to the flesh," lest you should again take him to be speaking against the nature of the flesh, he does not leave speaking, but proceeds, " to live after the flesh." For there are many things which we do owe it, as giving it food, warmth, and rest, medicine when out of health, clothing, and a thousand other attentions. To prevent your supposing then that it is this ministration he is for abrogating when he says, " We are not debtors to the flesh," he explains it by saying, " to live after the flesh." For the care that I am for abrogating is, he means, that which leadeth to sin, as I should be for its having what is healing to it. And this he shows further on. For when he says, " Make not provision for the flesh," he does not pause at this, but adds, " to fulfil the lusts thereof." (Rom. xiii. 14.) And this instruction he gives us here also, meaning, Let it have attention shown it indeed, for we do owe it this, yet let us not live according to the flesh, that is, let us not make it the mistress of our life. For it must be the follower, not the leader, and it is not it that must regulate our life, but the laws of the Spirit must it receive. Having then defined this point, and having proved that we are debtors to the Spirit, to show next for what benefits it is that we are debtors, he does not speak of those past (a thing which serves as a most striking proof of his judgment), but those which were to come ; although even the former were enough for the purpose. Yet still he does not set them down in the present case, or mention even those unspeakable blessings, but the things to come. For a benefit once for all conferred does not, for the most part, draw men on so much as one which is expected, and is to come. After adding this then, he first uses the pains and ills that come of living after the flesh, to put them in fear, in the following words ; " For if ye live after the flesh ye shall die," so intimating to us that deathless death, punishment, and vengeance in hell. Or rather if one were to look accurately into this, such an one is, even in this present life, dead. And this we have

made clear to you in the last discourse. " But if ye through the Spirit, do mortify the deeds of the body, ye shall live." You see that it is not the essence of the body whereof we are discoursing, but the deeds of the flesh. For he does not say, " if ye through the Spirit do mortify " the essence " of the body," but " the deeds of " it, and these not all deeds, but such as are evil. And this is plain in what follows : for if ye do this, " ye shall live," he says. And how is it in the nature of things for this to be, if it was all deeds that his language applied to? for seeing and hearing and speaking and walking are deeds of the body ; and if we mortify these, we shall be so far from living, that we shall have to suffer the punishment of a manslayer. What sort of deeds then does he mean us to mortify? Those which tend toward wickedness, those which go after vice, which there is no other way of mortifying save through the Spirit. For by killing yourself you may put an end to the others.[2] And this you have no right to do. But to these (you can put an end) by the Spirit only. For if This be present, all the billows are laid low, and the passions cower under It, and nothing can exalt itself against us.[3] So you see how it is on things to come, as I said before, that he grounds his exhortations to us, and shows that we are debtors not owing to what has been already done only. For the advantage of the Spirit is not this only, that He hath set us free from our former sins, but that He rendereth us impregnable against future ones, and counts us worthy of the immortal life. Then, to state another reward also, he proceeds :

Ver. 14. " For as many as are led by the Spirit of God, they are the sons of God."

Now this is again a much greater honor than the first. And this is why he does not say merely, As many as live [4] by the Spirit of God, but, " as many as are led by the Spirit of God," to show that he would have Him use such power over our life as a pilot doth over a ship, or a charioteer over a pair of horses. And it is not the body only, but the soul itself too, that he is for setting under reins of this sort. For he would not have even that independent, but place its authority [5] also under the power of the Spirit. For lest through a confidence in the Gift of the Font they should turn negligent of their conversation after it, he would say, that even supposing you receive

---

[1] So St. Chrysostom reads, as appears from his Commentary on this passage.

[2] Sav. τὰς μὲν γὰρ ἄλλας ἀποκτείναντα, σεαυτὸν ἀνελεῖν ἐστιν; to give this sense we should punctuate τὰς μὲν γὰρ ἄλλας, ἀποκτ. ἑαυτὸν, ἀνελεῖν ἐστιν.
[3] κατεξανίσταται. The word used in the last Homily for the conduct of the covetous towards the poor. See p. 439.
[4] See Gal. v. 25, where " live " means " have life," and is distinguished from " walk."
[5] Or the command of it, ἐξουσίαν.

baptism, yet if you are not minded to be "led by the Spirit" afterwards, you lose the dignity bestowed upon you, and the pre-eminence of your adoption. This is why he does not say, As many as have received the Spirit, but, "as many as are led by the Spirit," that is, as many as live up to this all their life long, "they are the sons of God." Then since this dignity was given to the Jews also, for it says, "I said ye are Gods, and all of you children of the Most High" (Ps. lxxxii. 6); and again, "I have nourished and brought up children" (Is. i. 2); and so, "Israel is My first-born" (Ex. iv. 22); and Paul too says, "Whose is the adoption" (Rom. ix. 4)—he next asserts the great difference between the latter and the former honor. For though the names are the same, he means, still, the things are not the same. And of these points he gives a clear demonstration, by introducing a comparison drawn both from the persons so advanced (κατορθούντων) and from what was given them, and from what was to come. And first he shows what they of old had given them. What then was this? "A spirit of bondage:" and so he thus proceeds,

Ver. 15. "For ye have not received the spirit of bondage again to fear."

Then not staying to mention that which stands in contradistinction to bondage, that is, the spirit of freedom, he has named what is far greater, that of adoption, through which he at the same time brings in the other, saying, "But ye have received the Spirit of adoption."

But this is plain. But what the spirit of bondage may be, is not so plain, and there is need of making it clearer. Now what he says is so far from being clear, that it is in fact very perplexing. For the people of the Jews did not receive the Spirit. What then is his meaning here? It is the letter he giveth this name to, for spiritual it was, and so he called the Law spiritual also, and the water from the Rock, and the Manna. "For they did eat," he says, "of the same spiritual meat, and all drank of the same spiritual drink." (1 Cor. x. 3, 4.) And to the Rock he gives this name, when he says, "For they drank of that spiritual Rock which followed them." Now it is because all the rites then wrought were above nature that he calls them spiritual, and not because those who then partook of them received the Spirit. And in what sense were those letters, letters of bondage? Set before yourself the whole dispensation, and then you will have a clear view of this also. For recompenses were with them close at hand, and the reward followed forthwith, being at once proportionate, and like a kind of daily ration

given to domestic servants, and terrors in abundance came to their height before their eyes, and their purifications concerned their bodies, and their continency extended but to their actions. But with us it is not so, since the imagination even and the conscience getteth purged out. For He does not say, "Thou shalt do no murder," only, but even thou shalt not be angry: so too, it is not, "Thou shalt not commit adultery," but thou shalt not look unchastely. So that it is not to be from fear of present punishment, but out of desire towards Himself, that both our being habitually virtuous, and all our single good deeds are to come. Neither doth he promise a land flowing with milk and honey, but maketh us joint-heir with the Only-Begotten, so making us by every means stand aloof from things present, and promising to give such things especially as are worth the acceptance of men made sons of God, nothing, that is, of a sensible kind or corporeal, but spiritual all of them. And so they, even if they had the name of sons, were but as slaves; but we as having been made free, have received the adoption, and are waiting for Heaven. And with them He discoursed through the intervention of others, with us by Himself. And all that they did was through the impulse of fear, but the spiritual act through a coveting and a vehement desire. And this they show by the fact of their [1] overstepping the commandments. They, as hirelings and obstinate persons, so never left murmuring: but these do all for the pleasing of the Father. So too they blasphemed when they had benefits done them: but we are thankful at being jeoparded. And if there be need of punishing both of us upon our sinning, even in this case the difference is great. For it is not on being stoned and branded and maimed by the priests, as they were, that we are brought round. But it is enough for us to be cast out from our Father's table, and to be out of sight for certain days. And with the Jews the honor of adoption was one of name only, but here the reality followed also, the cleansing of Baptism, the giving of the Spirit, the furnishing of the other blessings. And there are several other points besides, which go to show our high birth and their low condition. After intimating all these then by speaking of the Spirit, and fear, and the adoption, he gives a fresh proof again of having the Spirit of adoption. Now what is this? That "we cry, Abba, Father." And how

---

[1] ὑπερβαίνειν means to go beyond as well as to go against. He refers to such things as St. Paul's refusing sustenance from the Achæans. 1 Cor. ix. 4, etc. The tenses prove this to be St. Chrysostom's meaning.

great this is, the initiated know (St. Cyr. Jer. Cat. 23, § 11, p. 276, O. T.), being with good reason bidden to use this word first in the Prayer of the initiated. What then, it may be said, did not they also call God Father? Dost thou not hear Moses, when he says, "Thou desertedst the God that begot thee?" (Deut. xxxii. 15. LXX.) Dost thou not hear Malachi reproaching them, and saying, that "one God formed you," and there is "one Father of you all?" (Mal. ii. 10. LXX.) Still, if these words and others besides are used, we do not find them anywhere calling God by the name, or praying in this language. But we all, priests and laymen, rulers and ruled, are ordered to pray herein. And this is the first language we give utterance to, after those marvellous throes, and that strange and unusual mode of labor. If in any other instances they so called Him, that was only of their own mind. But those in the state of grace do it through being moved by the in-working of the Spirit. For as there is a Spirit of Wisdom, after which they that were unwise became wise, and this discloses itself in their teaching: and a Spirit of Power there is, whereby the feeble raised up the dead, and drove out devils; a Spirit also of the gift of healing, and a Spirit of prophecy, and a Spirit of tongues, so also a Spirit of adoption. And as we know the Spirit of prophecy, in that he who hath it foretelleth things to come, not speaking of his own mind, but moved by the Grace; so too is the Spirit of adoption, whereby he that is gifted with it calleth God, Father, as moved by the Spirit. Wishing to express this as a most true descent, he used also the Hebrew[1] tongue, for he does not say only, "Father," but "Abba, Father," which name is a special sign of true-born children to their fathers. After mentioning then the diversity resulting from their conversation, that resulting from the grace which had been given, and that from their freedom, he brings forward another demonstration of the superiority which goes with this adoption. Now of what kind is this?

Ver. 16. "The Spirit Itself beareth witness with our spirit, that we are the children of God."

For it is not from the language merely, he says, that I make my assertion, but from the cause out of which the language has its birth; since it is from the Spirit suggesting it that we so speak. And this in another passage he has put into plainer words, thus: "God hath sent forth the Spirit of his Son into our

hearts, crying, Abba Father." (Gal. iv. 6.) And what is that, "Spirit beareth witness with spirit?" The Comforter, he means, with that Gift, which is given unto us. For it is not of the Gift alone that it is the voice, but of the Comforter also who gave the Gift, He Himself having taught us through the Gift so to speak. But when the "Spirit beareth witness," what farther place for doubtfulness? For if it were a man, or angel, or archangel, or any other such power that promised this, then there might be reason in some doubting. But when it is the Highest Essence that bestoweth this Gift, and "beareth witness" by the very words He bade us use in prayer, who would doubt any more of our dignity? For not even when the Emperor elects any one, and proclaims in all men's hearing the honor done him, does anybody venture to gainsay.

Ver. 17. "And if children, then heirs."

Observe how he enhances the Gift by little and little. For since it is a possible case to be children, and yet not become heirs (for it is not by any means all children that are heirs), he adds this besides—that we are heirs. But the Jews, besides their not having the same adoption as we, were also cast out from the inheritance. For "He will miserably destroy those wicked men, and will let out the vineyard to other husbandmen" (Matt. xxi. 41): and before this, He said that "many shall come from the East and from the West, and shall sit down with Abraham, but the children of the Kingdom shall be cast out." (ib. viii. 11, 12.) But even here he does not pause, but sets down something even greater than this. What may this be then? That we are heirs of God; and so he adds, "heirs of God." And what is more still, that we are not simply heirs, but also "joints heirs with Christ." Observe how ambitious he is of bringing us near to the Master. For since it is not all children that are heirs, he shows that we are both children and heirs; next, as it is not all heirs that are heirs to any great amount, he shows that we have this point with us too, as we are heirs of God. Again, since it were possible to be God's heir, but in no sense "joint heir with" the Only-Begotten, he shows that we have this also. And consider his wisdom. For after throwing the distasteful part into a short compass, when he was saying what was to become of such as "live after the flesh," for instance, that they "shall die," when he comes to the more soothing part, he leadeth forth his discourse into a large room, and so expands it on the recompense of rewards, and in pointing out

---

[1] i. e. the Syriac, which the Hebrew means in the N. T. probably in all cases—it being then the language of the Hebrews.

that the gifts too are manifold and great. For if even the being a child were a grace unspeakable, just think how great a thing it is to be heir! But if this be great, much more is it to be "joint heir." Then to show that the Gift is not of grace only, and to give at the same time a credibility to what he says, he proceeds, "If so be that we suffer with Him, that we may be also glorified together." If, he would say, we be sharers with Him in what is painful, much more shall it be so in what is good. For He who bestowed such blessings upon those who had wrought no good, how, when He seeth them laboring and suffering so much, shall he do else than give them greater requital? Having then shown that the thing was a matter of return, to make men give credit to what was said, and prevent any from doubting, he shows further that it has the virtue of a gift. The one he showed, that what was said might gain credit even with those that doubted, and that the receivers of it might not feel ashamed as being ever-more receiving salvation for nought; and the other, that you might see that God outdoeth the toils by His recompenses. And the one he has shown in the words, "If so be that we suffer with Him, that we may be also glorified together." But the other in proceeding to add;

Ver. 18. "The sufferings of the present time are not worthy to be compared with the glory which shall be revealed in (Gr. εἰς) us."

In what went before, he requires of the spiritual man the correcting of his habits (Mar. and 6 Mss. passions), where he says, "Ye are not debtors to live after the flesh," that such an one, for instance, should be above lust, anger, money, vainglory, grudging. But here having reminded them of the whole gift, both as given and as to come, and raised him up aloft with hopes, and placed him near to Christ, and showed him to be a joint-heir of the Only-Begotten; he now leads him forth with confidence even to dangers. For to get the better of the evil affections in us, is not the same thing with bearing up under those trials, scourges, famine, plunderings, bonds, chains, executions. For these last required much more of a noble and vigorous spirit. And observe how he at once allays and rouses the spirit of the combatants. For after he had shown that the rewards were greater than the labors, he both exhorts to greater efforts, and yet will not let them be elated, as being still outdone by the crowns given in requital. And in another passage he says, "For our light affliction, which is but for a moment, worketh a far more exceed-ing and eternal weight of glory" (2 Cor. iv. 17): it being the deeper sort of persons he was then speaking to. Here, however, he does not allow that the afflictions were light; but still he mingles comfort with them by the compensation which good things to come afford, in the words, "For I reckon that the sufferings of this present time are not worthy to be compared," and he does not say, with the rest (ἄνεσιν) that is to come, but what is much greater, "with the glory which is to come." For it does not follow, that where rest is there is glory; but that where glory is there is rest, does follow: then as he had said that it is to come, he shows that it already is. For he does not say, that which is to be, but "which shall be revealed in us," as if already existing but unrevealed. As also in another place he said in clearer words, "Our life is hid with Christ in God."[1] Be then of a good heart about it. For already hath it been prepared, and awaiteth thy labors. But if it vexes you that it is yet to come, rather let this very thing rejoice you. For it is owing to its being great and unutterable, and transcending our present condition, that it is stored up there. And so he has not put barely "the sufferings of this present time," but he speaks so as to show that it is not in quality only, but in quantity also, that the other life has the advantage. For these sufferings, whatever they are, are attached to our present life; but the blessings to come reach themselves out over ages without end. And since he had no way of giving a particular description of these, or of putting them before us in language, he gives them a name from what seems to be specially an object of desire with us, "glory." For the summit of blessings and the sum of them, this seems to be. And to urge the hearer on in another way also, he gives a loftiness to his discourse by the mention of the creation, gaining two points by what he is next saying, the contempt of things present, and the desire of things to come, and a third beside these, or rather the first, is the showing how the human race is cared for on God's part and in what honor He holds our nature. And besides this, all the doctrines of the philosophers, which they had framed for themselves about this world, as a sort of cobweb or child's mound,[2] he throws down with this one doctrine. But that these things may stand in a clearer light, let us hear the Apostle's own language.

Ver. 19, 20. "For the earnest expectation of the creation waiteth," he says, "for the

---

[1] Col. iii. 3. Ver. 4. confirms his application of it.
[2] Perhaps alluding to Il. xv. 362.

revelation of the sons of God. For the creation was made subject to vanity, not willingly, but by reason of him who hath subjected the same in hope."

And the meaning is something of this kind. The creation itself is in the midst of its pangs, waiting for and expecting these good things whereof we have just now spoken. For "earnest expectation" (ἀποκαραδοκία, looking out) implies expecting intensely. And so his discourse becomes more emphatic, and he personifies this whole world as the prophets also do, when they introduce the floods clapping their hands, and little hills leaping, and mountains skipping, not that we are to fancy them alive, or ascribe any reasoning power to them, but that we may learn the greatness of the blessings, so great as to reach even to things without sense also.* The very same thing they do many times also in the case of afflicting things, since they bring in the vine lamenting, and the wine too, and the mountains, and the boardings[1] of the Temple howling, and in this case too it is that we may understand the extremity of the evils. It is then in imitation of these that the Apostle makes a living person of the creature here, and says that it groaneth and travaileth: not that he heard any groan conveyed from the earth and heaven to him, but that he might show the exceeding greatness of the good things to come; and the desire of freedom from the ills which now pervaded them. "For the creature was made subject to vanity, not willingly, but by reason of him who hath subjected the same." What is the meaning of, "the creation was made subject to vanity?" Why that it became corruptible. For what cause, and on what account? On account of thee, O man. For since thou hast taken a body mortal and liable to suffering, the earth too hath received a curse, and brought forth thorns and thistles. But that the heaven, when it is waxen old along with the earth, is to change afterwards

to a better portion (λῆξιν v. p. 384) hear from the Prophet in his words; "Thou, O Lord, from the beginning hast founded the earth, and the heavens are the work of Thy hands. They shall perish, but thou shalt endure; and they all shall wax old as doth a garment, and as a cloak shalt Thou fold them up, and they shall be changed." (Ps. cii. 25, 26.) Isaiah too declares the same, when he says, "Look to the heaven above, and upon the earth beneath, for the heavens are as a firmament of smoke,[2] and the earth shall wax old like a garment, and they that dwell therein shall perish in like manner. (Is. li. 6.) Now you see in what sense the creation is "in bondage to vanity," and how it is to be freed from the ruined state. For the one says, "Thou shalt fold them up as a garment, and they shall be changed;" and Isaiah says, "and they that dwell therein shall perish in like manner," not of course meaning an utter perishing. For neither do they that dwell therein, mankind, that is, undergo such an one, but a temporary one, and through it they are changed into an incorruptible (1 Cor. xv. 53) state, and so therefore will the creature be. And all this he showed by the way, by his saying "in like manner" (2 Pet. iii. 13), which Paul also says farther on. At present, however, he speaks about the bondage itself, and shows for what reason it became such, and gives ourselves as the cause of it. What then? Was it harshly treated on another's account? By no means, for it was on my account that it was made. What wrong then is done it, which was made for my sake, when it suffereth these things for my correction? Or, indeed, one has no need to moot the question of right and wrong at all in the case of things void of soul and feeling. But Paul, since he had made it a living person, makes use of none of these topics I have mentioned, but another kind of language, as desiring to comfort the hearer with the utmost advantage. And of what kind is this? What have you to say? he means. It was evil intreated for thy sake, and became corruptible; yet it has had no wrong done it. For incorruptible will it be for thy sake again. This then is the meaning of "in hope." But when he says, it was "not willingly" that it was made subject, it is not to show that it is possessed of judgment that he says so, but that you may learn that the whole is brought about by Christ's care, and this is no achievement of its own. And now say in what hope?

---

* Chrysostom's interpretation of ἡ κτίσις is undoubtedly correct in principle, although he probably gives to it too general an idea in calling it "this whole world"—reaching "even to things without sense also." It is more likely that the apostle has in mind distinctively the *irrational creation*. (So Meyer, Godet, Thayer, Dwight). Nature is subject to "vanity"—i. e. the law of decay and death, and is poetically spoken of as awaiting the revelation of the sons of God in the hope of sharing in it. The apostle explains that the κτίσις was placed in this condition not of its own accord but on account of the will of God, who, however, subjected it to the forces of decay and death on the ground of hope. Hope was the attendant condition of this subjection which took place in consequence of the fall. Hence this condition is not final and the creation desires and groans to be delivered and to share in the "manifestation of the sons of God"—the revelation of them in their true character in the presence of the universe at the coming of Christ.—G. B. S.

[1] φατνώματα, Heb. שירות. Amos viii. 3. LXX. Hesych. σανιδώματα. See Schleusner, *Lex. Gr. Vet. Test.* for conjectures to account for the translation.

[2] Eng. "shall vanish away like smoke." LXX. render נמלחו ἐστερεώθη, they give the same for גמה. Is. xlv. 12.

Ver. 21. " That the creature itself also shall be delivered from the bondage of corruption."

Now what is this creation? Not thyself alone, but that also which is thy inferior, and partaketh not of reason or sense, this too shall be a sharer in thy blessings. For " it shall be freed," he says, " from the bondage of corruption," that is, it shall no longer be corruptible, but shall go along with the beauty given to thy body; just as when this became corruptible, that became corruptible also; so now it is made incorruptible, that also shall follow it too. And to show this he proceeds. (εἰς) " Into the glorious liberty of the children of God." That is, because of[1] their liberty. For as a nurse who is bringing up a king's child, when he has come to his father's power, does herself enjoy the good things along with him, thus also is the creation, he means. You see how in all respects man takes the lead, and that it is for his sake that all things are made. See how he solaces the struggler, and shows the unspeakable love of God toward man. For why, he would say, dost thou fret at thy temptations? thou art suffering for thyself, the creation for thee. Nor does he solace only, but also shows what he says to be trustworthy. For if the creation which was made entirely for thee is "in hope," much more oughtest thou to be, through whom the creation is to come to the enjoyment of those good things. Thus men (3 Mss. fathers) also when a son is to appear at his coming to a dignity, clothe even the servants with a brighter garment, to the glory of the son; so will God also clothe the creature with incorruption for the glorious liberty of the children.

Ver. 22. " For we know that the whole creation groaneth and travaileth in pain together until now."

Observe, how he shames the hearer, saying almost, Be not thou worse than the creation, neither find a pleasure in resting in things present. Not only ought we not to cling to them, but even to groan over the delay of our departure hence. For if the creation doth this, much more oughtest thou to do so, honored with reason as thou art. But as this was not yet enough to force their attention, he proceeds.

Ver. 23. " And not only they, but ourselves also, which have the first-fruits of the Spirit, even we ourselves groan within ourselves."

That is, having had a taste of the things to come. For even if any should be quite stone hard, he means what has been given already is enough to raise him up, and draw him off from things present, and to wing him after things to come in two ways, both by the greatness of the things that are given, and by the fact that, great and numerous as they are, they are but first-fruits. For if the first-fruits be so great that we are thereby freed even from our sins, and attain to righteousness and sanctification, and that those of that time both drave out devils, and raised the dead by their shadow (Acts v. 15), or garments (ib. xix. 12), consider how great the whole must be. And if the creation, devoid as it is of mind and reason, and though in ignorance of these things, yet groaneth, much more should we. Next, that he may give the heretics no handle, or seem to be disparaging our present world, we groan, he says, not as finding fault with the present system, but through a desire of those greater things. And this he shows in the words, "Waiting for the adoption." What dost thou say, let me hear? Thou didst insist on it at every turn, and didst cry aloud, that we were already made sons, and now dost thou place this good thing among hopes, writing that we must needs wait for it? Now it is to set this right by the sequel that he says, "to wit, the redemption[2] of our body." That is, the perfect glory. Our lot indeed is at present uncertainty to our last breath, since many of us that were sons have become dogs and prisoners. But if we decease with a good hope, then is the gift unmovable, and clearer, and greater, having no longer any change to fear from death and sin. Then therefore will the grace be secure, when our body shall be freed from death and its countless ailments (or passions). For this is full redemption (ἀπολύτρωσις), not a redemption[3] only, but such, that we shall never again return to our former captivity. For that thou mayest not be perplexed at hearing so much of glory without getting any distinct knowledge of it, he partially exposes to thy view the things to come, setting before thee the change of thy body (Gr. changing thy body), and along with it the change of the whole creation. And this he has put in a clearer light in another passage, where he says, "Who shall change our vile body, that it may be fashioned like unto His glorious Body." (Phil. iii. 21.) And in another place again he writes and says, "But when this mortal shall have put on

---

[1] διὰ τὴν. St. Chrysostom does not mean to say that one preposition is used for another, as his illustration shows. For the liberty of the sons of God is both the thing of which the creation partakes, and the cause of its partaking ; so that the one is put in a sense which implies the other too.

[2] ἀπολύτρωσιν. In the meaning of this word sometimes the manner, and sometimes the completeness of redemption predominates; see Rom. iii. 24, p. 377.

[3] λύτρωσις, showing that the completeness is implied in the preposition, which should be observed in the doctrinal use of the term.

immortality, then shall be brought to pass the saying that is written, Death is swallowed up in victory." (1 Cor. xv. 54.) But to show, that with the corruption of the body the constitution of the things of this life will also come to an end, he wrote again elsewhere, "For the fashion of this world passeth away." (1 Cor. vii. 31.)

Ver. 24. "For we are saved by hope," he says.

Now since he had dwelt upon the promise of the things to come, and this seemed to pain the weaker hearer, if the blessings are all matter of hope; after proving before that they are surer than things present and visible, and discoursing at large on the gifts already given, and showing that we have received the first fruits of those good things, lest we should seek our all in this world, and be traitors to the nobility that faith gives us, he says, "For we are (Gr. were) saved by hope." And this is about what he means. We are not to seek our all in this life, but to have hope also. For this is the only gift that we brought in to God, believing Him in what He promised shall come, and it was by this way alone we were saved. If then we lose this hope, we have lost all that was of our own contributing. For I put you this question, he would say, Wert thou not liable for countless sins? wert thou not in despair? wert thou not under sentence? were not all out of heart about thy salvation? What then saved thee? It was thy hoping[1] in God alone, and trusting to Him about His promises and gifts, and nothing besides hadst thou to bring in. If it was this then that saved thee, hold it fast now also. For that which afforded thee so great blessings, to a certainty will not deceive thee in regard to things to come. For in that it found thee dead, and ruined, and a prisoner, and an enemy, and yet made thee a friend, and a son, and a freeman, and righteous, and a joint-heir, and yielded such great things as no one ever expected even, how, after such munificence and attachment, will it betray[2] thee in what is to follow? Say not to me, hopes again! expectations again! faith again! For it is in this way thou wert saved from the beginning, and this dowry was the only one that thou didst bring in to the Bridegroom. Hold it then fast and keep it: for if thou demandest to have everything in this world, thou hast lost that well-doing of thine, through which thou didst become bright, and this is why he

proceeds to say, "But hope that is seen is not hope; for what a man seeth, why doth he yet hope for?"

Ver. 25.—"But if we hope for that we see not, then do we with patience wait for it."

That is, if thou art to be looking for everything in this world, what need is there for hope? What is hope then? It is feeling confidence in things to come. What great demand then doth God make upon thee, since He Himself giveth thee blessings quite entire from His own stores? One thing only, hope, He asks of thee, that thou too mayest have somewhat of thine own to contribute toward thy salvation. And this he intimates in what he proceeds with: "For if we hope for that we see not, then do we with patience wait for it." As then God crowneth him that undergoes labors, and hardnesses, and countless toils, so doth He him that hopeth. For the name of patience belongs to hard work and much endurance. Yet even this He hath granted to the man that hopeth, that He might solace the wearied soul. And then to show that for this light task we enjoy abundant aid, he proceeds:

Ver. 26. "Likewise the Spirit also helpeth our infirmities."*

For the one point is thy own, that of patience, but the other comes of the Spirit's furnishings, Who also cherisheth (Gr. anointeth) thee unto this hope, and through it again lighteneth thy labors. Then that thou mightest know that it is not in thy labors only and dangers that this grace standeth by thee, but even in things the most easy seemingly,[3] it worketh with thee, and on all occasions bears its part in the alliance, he proceeds to say,

"For we know not what we should pray for as we ought."

And this he said to show the Spirit's great concern about us, and also to instruct them not to think for certainty that those things are desirable which to man's reasonings appear so. For since it was likely that they, when they were scourged, and driven out, and suffering grievances without number, should be seeking a respite, and ask this favor of God, and think it was advantageous to them, by no means (he says) suppose that what seem blessings to you really are so. For we

---

[1] This blending of faith and hope illustrates the connection of faith and love, the Object of love being now known by faith, and appropriated by hope. The personification which follows is a powerful way of representing that in us which apprehends God as itself His gift.

[2] So the Mss. and Catena: the old reading was οὐ προσήσεται, "will it not satisfy."

* *Magna est vis Græci verbi συναντιλαμβάνεσθαι*, said Calvin. The word means: "takes hold together with us, as if on the other side or as if instead of us" (Godet). The notion of lifting the other end of a burden, or perhaps, of taking hold of it in our place, seems to lie at the basis of this expressive word. Cf. Luke x. 40.—G. B. S.

[3] These words show that St. Chrysostom does not mean that we do any good unaided, however much he insists on the freedom of our will.

need the Spirit's aid even to do this. So feeble is man, and such a nothing by himself. For this is why he says, " For we know not what we should pray for as we ought." In order that the learner might not feel any shame at his ignorance, he does not say, ye know not, but, "we know not." And that he did not say this merely to seem moderate, he plainly shows from other passages. For he desired in his prayers unceasingly to see Rome. Yet the time when he obtained it was not at once when he desired it. And for "the thorn" that was given him " in the flesh " (2 Cor. xii. 8), that is the dangers, he often besought God, and was entirely unsuccessful.[1] And so was Moses, who in the Old Testament prays to see Palestine (Deut. iii. 26), and Jeremiah when he made supplication for the Jews (Jer. xv. 1), and Abraham when he interceded for the people of Sodom. "But the Spirit Itself maketh intercession for us with groanings which cannot be uttered." This statement is not clear, owing to the cessation of many of the wonders which then used to take place. Wherefore I must needs inform you of the state of things at that time, and in this way the rest of the subject will be cleared. What therefore was the state of things then? God did in those days give to all that were baptized certain excellent gifts, and the name that these had was spirits. For "the spirits of the Prophets," it says, " are subject to the prophets." (1 Cor. xiv. 32.) And one had the gift of prophecy and foretold things to come; and another of wisdom, and taught the many; and another of healings, and cured the sick; and another of miracles, and raised the dead; another of tongues, and spake different languages. And with all these there was also a gift of prayer, which also was called a spirit, and he that had this prayed for all the people. For since we are ignorant of much that is profitable for us and ask things that are not profitable, the gift of prayer came into some particular person of that day, and what was profitable for all the whole Church alike, he was the appointed person to ask for in behalf of all, and the instructor of the rest. Spirit then is the name that he gives here to the grace of this character, and the soul that receiveth the grace, and intercedeth to God, and groaneth. For he that was counted worthy of such grace as this, standing with much compunction, and with many mental groanings falling before God, asked the things that were profitable for all. And of this the Deacon of the present day is a symbol when he offers up the prayers for the people. This then is what Paul means when he says,[2] " the Spirit itself maketh intercession for us with groanings that cannot be uttered."

Ver. 27. " But He that searcheth the hearts."

You see that it is not about the Comforter that he is speaking, but about the spiritual heart. Since if this were not so, he ought to have said, " He that searcheth " the Spirit. But that thou mayest learn that the language is meant of a spiritual man, who has the gift of prayer, he proceeds, " And he that searcheth the hearts knoweth what is the mind of the Spirit," that is, of the spiritual man.

" Because he maketh intercession for the saints according to the will of God."

Not (he means) that he informs God as if ignorant, but this is done that we may learn to pray for proper things, and to ask of God what is pleasing to Him. For this is what the " according to God " is. And so this was with a view to solace those that came to Him, and to yield them excellent instruction. For He that furnished the gifts, and gave besides blessings without number, was the Comforter. Hence it says, " all these things worketh one and the self-same Spirit." (1 Cor. xii. 11.) And it is for our instruction that this takes place, and to show the love of the Spirit, it condescendeth even to this. And it is from this that the person praying getteth heard, because the prayer is made " according to the will of God."

You see from how many points he instructs them in the love that was shown them and the honor that was done them. And what is there that God hath not done for us? The world He hath made corruptible for us, and again for us incorruptible. He suffered His Prophets to be ill-treated for our sake, sent them into captivity for us, let them fall into the furnace, and undergo ills without number. Nay, He made them prophets for us, and the Apostles also He made for us. He gave up for us His Only-Begotten, He punisheth the devil for us, He hath seated us on the Right Hand, He was reproached for us. " For the reproaches of them that reproached thee," it says, " fell upon me." (Ps. lxix. 9.) Yet still, when we are drawing back after so great favor, He leaveth us not, but again entreats, and on our account inciteth others to entreat for us, that He may show us favor. And so it was with Moses. For to him He says, " Let Me alone, that I may blot them out " (Ex. xxxii. 10), that He might drive him upon supplicating on their behalf. And now

---

[1] See Bishop Bull, *Serm. V.* who discusses what this was.

[2] St. Ambrose. *Epist.* 36, gives the same interpretation.

He doth the same thing. Hence He gave the gift of prayer. But this He doth, not as Himself standing in need of entreaty, but that we might [1] not, from being saved without effort (ἀπλῶς), grow indifferent. For this cause it is on account of David, and of this person and that, He often says, that He is reconciled with them, to establish again this very thing, that the reconciliation may be with all due formality.[2] Still He would have looked more loving toward man, if it had not been through this and the other prophet, but of Himself, that He told them that He ceased to be wroth. But the reason of His not holding to that point was, that this ground of reconciliation might not become an occasion for listlessness. Wherefore to Jeremiah also He said, " Pray not for this people, for I will not hear thee " (Jer. xi. 14), not as wishing to stop his praying (for He earnestly longeth for our salvation), but to terrify them : and this the prophet also seeing did not cease praying. And that you may see that it was not through a wish to turn him from it, but to shame [3] them that He said this, hear what it says. " Seest thou not what these are doing ? " (Ez. viii. 6, not verbally from LXX.) And when He says to the city " Though thou wash thee with nitre, and take thee much soap (Gr. herb), yet thou art stained before Me " (Jer. ii. 22), it is not that He may cast them into despair that He so speaks, but that He may rouse them to repentance. For as in the case of the Ninevites, by giving the sentence without limitation, and holding out no good hope, He scared them the more, and led them to repentance, so He doth here also, both to rouse them, and to render the prophet more venerated, that in this way at least they may hear him. Then, since they kept on in a state of incurable madness, and were not to be sobered even by the rest being carried away, he first exhorts them to remain there. But when they kept not up to this, but deserted to Egypt, this indeed He allowed them, but requires of them not to desert to irreligion as well as to Egypt. (Jer. xliv. 8.) But when they did not comply in this either, He sendeth the prophet along with them, so that they might not after all suffer total wreck. (Ver. 28.) For since they did not follow Him when He called, He next followeth them to discipline them, and hinder their being hurried further into vice, and as a father full of affection does a child who takes all treatment

in the same peevish way, conducting him about everywhere with himself, and following him about. This was the reason why He sent not Jeremiah only into Egypt, but also Ezekiel into Babylon, and they did not refuse to go. For when they found their Master love the people exceedingly, they continued themselves to do so likewise. Much as if a right-minded servant were to take compassion upon an intractable son when he saw his father grieving and lamenting about him. And what was there that they did not suffer for them ? They were sawn asunder, they were driven out, they were reproached, they were stoned, they underwent numberless grievances. And after all this they would run back to them. Samuel, for instance, ceased not to mourn for Saul, miserably insulted as he was by him, and injured irreparably. (1 Sam. xv. 35.) Still he held none of these things in remembrance. And for the people of the Jews, Jeremiah has composed Lamentations in writing. And when the general of the Persians had given him liberty to dwell securely, and with perfect freedom, wherever he pleased, he preferred above dwelling at home the affliction of the people, and their hard durance in a strange land. (Jer. xi. 5.) So Moses left the palace and the sort of living herein, and hasted to be among their calamities.   And Daniel abode for twenty days following without food, pinching himself with the most severe fast, that he might reconcile God to them. (Dan. x. 2.) And the three Children too, when in the furnace, and so fierce a fire, put up a supplication for them. For it was not on their account that they were grieved, as they were saved ; but since they considered that then was the time for the greatest boldness of speech, they consequently prayed in their behalf ; hence too they said, " In a contrite heart and an humble spirit let us be accepted." (Song. ver. 16.) For them Joshua also rent his garments. (Josh. vii. 6.) For them Ezekiel too wailed and lamented when he saw them cut down. (Ez. ix. 8.) And Jeremy [4] said, " Let me alone, I will weep bitterly." (Is. xxii. 4.) And before this, when he did not venture openly to pray for a remittance of their sad estate, he sought for some limited period, when he says, " How long, O, Lord ? " (ib. vi. 11.) For full of affectionateness is the whole race of the saints. Wherefore also St. Paul saith, " Put on therefore, as the elect saints of God, bowels of mercy, kindness, humbleness of mind." (Col. iii. 12.) You see the strict. propriety of the word, and how he would have

---

[1] The peculiar position of the negative resembles that in Eur. *Hec.* 1131 (al. 1149), ἵν' ἄλλος μή τις εἰδείη τάδε.
[2] 6 Mss. with glorying, i. e. with something good done on man's part.
[3] ἐντρέψαι perhaps " to urge him to compassion ; " (there is no pronoun with this verb).

[4] So all Mss. but one, and that is obviously an emendation : both the passages cited are from Isaiah.

us continually merciful. For he does not say, "show mercy" only, but put it on, that like as our garment is always with us, so may mercy be. And he does not say merely mercy, but "bowels of mercy," that we may imitate the natural affection of relations. But we do just the contrary, and if any one comes to ask a single penny of us, we insult them, abuse them, call them impostors. Dost thou not shudder, man, and blush to call him an impostor for bread? Why even supposing such an one is practising imposture, he deserves to be pitied for it, because he is so pressed with famine as to put on such a character. This then is a reproach to our cruelty. For since we had not the heart to bestow with readiness, they are compelled to practise a great many arts, so as to put a cheat off upon our inhumanity, and to soften down our harshness. Now if it was gold and silver that he asked of thee, then there would be some reason in thy suspicions. But if it is necessary food that he comes to thee for, why be showing thyself wise so unseasonably, and take so over exact an account of him, accusing him of idleness and sloth? For if we must talk in this way, it is not others but ourselves that we ought to address. When therefore thou art going to God to ask forgiveness for thy sins, then call these words to mind, and thou wilt know thou deservest to have these things said to thee by God, much more than the poor man by thee. And yet God hath never said such words to thee as " Stand off, since thou art an impostor, always coming to church and hearing My laws, but when abroad, setting gold, and pleasure (ἐπιθυμίαν), and friendship, and in fact anything above My commandments. And now thou makest thyself humble, but when thy prayers are over thou art bold, and cruel, and inhuman. Get thee hence, therefore, and never come to Me any more." Yet this, and more than this, we deserve to have said to us; but still He never did reproach us in any such way, but is long-suffering and fulfils everything on His own part, and gives us more than we ask for. Calling this to mind then, let us relieve the poverty of those that beg of us, and if they do impose upon us, let us not be over exact about it. For such a salvation is it that we ourselves require, one with pardon, with kindness (φιλανθρωπίας), with much mercy along with it. For it is not possible, it certainly is not, if our estate were searched into strictly, that we should ever be saved, but we must needs be punished and brought to ruin altogether. Let us not then be bitter judges of others lest we also get a strict account demanded of us. For we have sins that are too great to

plead any excuse. And therefore let us show more mercy towards those who have committed inexcusable sins, that we also may lay up for ourselves the like mercy beforehand. And yet be as large-hearted as we may, we shall never be able to contribute such love toward man as we stand in need of at the hand of a God that loveth man. How then is it other than monstrous, when we are in need of so many things ourselves, to be over exact with our fellow servants, and do all we can against ourselves? For thou dost not in this way so much prove him unworthy of thy liberality, as thyself of God's love toward man. For he that deals over exactly with his fellow servant, will be the more sure to find the like treatment at God's hand. Let us not speak against ourselves, but even if they come out of idleness or wilfulness,[1] let us bestow. For we also do many sins through wilfulness, or rather we do them all through wilfulness, and yet God doth not presently call us to punishment, but gives us a set time for penance, nurturing us day by day, disciplining us, teaching us, supplying us with all other things, that we too may emulate this mercy of His. Let us then quell this cruelty, let us cast out this brutal spirit, as benefiting thereby ourselves rather than others. For to these we give money, and bread, and clothing, but for ourselves we are laying up beforehand very great glory, and such as there is no putting into words. For we receive again our bodies incorruptible, and are[2] glorified together and reign together with Christ. And how great this is we shall see from hence— or rather there is no means of making us see it clearly now. But to start from our present blessings, and to get from them at least some kind of scanty notice of it, I will endeavor so far as I may be able to put before you what I have been speaking of. Tell me then, if when you were grown old, and were living in poverty, and any one were to promise suddenly to make you young, and to bring you to the very prime of life, and to render you very strong, and preëminently beautiful, and were to give you the kingdom of the whole earth for a thousand years, a kingdom in the state of the deepest peace, what is there that you would not choose to do, and to suffer to gain this promise? (4 Mss. and Sav. Mar. object.) See then, Christ promises not this, but much more than this. For the distance between old age and youth is not to be compared with

[1] All Mss. read κἂν δι' ἀργίαν κἂν διὰ ῥᾳθυμίαν, which order agrees with the stronger sense here given to ῥᾳθυμία: "listlessness" is generally too little expressive of that readiness to yield to temptations which this word implies. But 1 Ms. reads "rather all through vice," κακίαν, which tends to give the other word a lighter sense.
[2] 6 Mss. pres., and so all just above.

the difference of corruption and incorruption, nor that of a kingdom and poverty to that of the present glory and the future, but the difference is that of dreams and a reality. Or rather I have yet said nothing to the purpose, since there is no language capable of setting before you the greatness of the difference between things to come and things present. And as for time, there is no place for the idea of difference. For what mode is there for a man to compare with our present state a life that hath no limit? And as for the peace it is as far removed from any present peace, as peace is different from war; and for the incorruption, it is as much better as a clear pearl is than a clod of clay. Or rather, say as great a thing as one may, nothing can put it before you. For were I even to compare the beauty of our bodies then to the light of the sunbeam, or the brightest lightning, I shall not yet be saying aught that is worthy of that brilliancy. Now for such things as these what money so much that it were not worth the while to give up? what bodies, or rather what souls[1] is it not worth one's while to give up? At present if any one were to lead thee into the palace, and in presence of all were to give thee an opportunity of conversing with the king, and make thee sit at his table, and join in his fare, thou wouldest call thyself the happiest of men. But when you are to go up to Heaven, and stand by the King of the universe Himself, and to vie with angels in brightness, and to enjoy even that unutterable glory, do you hesitate whether you ought to give up money? whereas if you had to put off life itself, you ought to leap and exult, and mount on wings of pleasure. But you, that you may get an office (ἀρχὴν), as a place to pillage from (for call a thing of this sort gain, I cannot), put all you have to hazard, and after borrowing of others, will, if need be, pawn your wife and children too without hesitation. But when the kingdom of Heaven is set before you, that office (ἀρχῆς) which hath none to supersede you in it, and God bids you take not a part of a corner of the earth, but the whole of Heaven entirely, are you hesitating, and reluctant, and gaping after money, and forgetful that if the parts of that Heaven which we see are so fair and delightful, how greatly so must the upper Heaven be, and the Heaven[2] of Heaven? But since we have as yet no means of seeing this with our bodily eyes, ascend in thy thought, and standing above this Heaven, look up unto that

Heaven beyond this, into that height without a bound, into that Light surcharged with awe, into the crowds of the Angels, into the endless ranks of Archangels, into the rest of the incorporeal Powers. And then lay hold again of the image (cf. Plat. *Rep.* vii. p. 516) thereof we have, after coming down from above, and make a sketch of the estate of a king with us, as his men in gold armor, and his pairs of white mules proudly decked with gold, and his chariots set with jewels[3] and his snow-like cushions (στρωμνὴν Poll. x. 41), and the spangles that flutter about the chariot, and the dragons shaped out in the silken hangings, and the shields with their gold bosses, and the straps that reach up from these to the rim of them through so many gems, and the horses with the gilded trappings and the gold bits. But when we see the king we immediately lose sight of all these. For he alone turns our eyes to him, and to the purple robe, and the diadem, and the throne, and the clasp, and the shoes, all that splendor of his appearance. After gathering all these things together then with accuracy, then again remove your thoughts from these things to things above, and to that awful day in which Christ is coming. For then you will not see any pairs of mules, nor golden chariots, nor dragons and shields, but things that are big with a mighty awe, and strike such amazement that the very incorporeal Powers are astonished. For the "powers of the Heavens," He says, "shall be shaken." (Matt. xxiv. 29.) Then is the whole Heaven thrown open, and the gates of those concaves unfold themselves, and the Only-begotten Son of God cometh down, not with twenty, not with a hundred men for His body-guard, but with thousands, ten thousands of Angels and Archangels, Cherubim and Seraphim, and other Powers, and with fear and trembling shall everything be filled, whiles the earth is bursting itself up, and the men that ever were born, from Adam's birth up to that day, are rising from the earth, and all are caught up; (1 Thess. iv. 17) when Himself appears with such great glory as that the sun, and the moon, and all light whatever, is cast into the shade, being outshone by that radiance. What language is to set before us that blessedness, brightness, glory? Alas! my soul. For weeping comes upon me and great groaning, as I reflect what good things we have fallen from, what blessedness we are estranged from. For estranged we are (I am now speaking of my own case still), unless we do some great and astonishing work; speak

---

[1] Or lives, but see above, p. 433, where the spirit seems to be considered apart from the soul.

[2] See St. Augustin's *Confessions*, p. 250, Oxf. Tr. Clem. *Recog.* iii. 75; Aristot. *Metaph.* p. 997; 15, p. 1071, 23, Bekker.

[3] λιθοκόλλητα, v. Jungerm. *ad Polluc.* x. 145, V. l. χρυσοκόλλητα.

not then of hell to me now, for more grievous than any hell is the fall from this glory, and worse than punishments unnumbered the estrangement from that lot. But still we are gaping after this present world, and we take not thought of the devil's cunning, who by little things bereaves us of those great ones, and gives us clay that he may snatch from us gold, or rather that he may snatch Heaven from us, and showeth us a shadow that he may dispossess us of the reality, and puts phantoms before us in dreams (for such is the wealth of this world), that at daybreak[1] he may prove us the poorest of men. Laying these things to heart, late though it be, let us fly from this craft, and pass to the side of things to come. For we cannot say that we were ignorant how exposed to accidents the present life is, since things every day din in our ears more loudly than a trumpet, the worthlessness, the ridiculousness, the shamefulness, the dangers, the pitfalls, of the present scene. What defence then shall we have to set up for pursuing things so subject to hazards, and laden with shame, with so much eagerness, and leaving things unfailing, which will make us glorious and bright, and giving our whole selves up to the thraldom of money? For the slavery to these things is worse than any bondage. And this they know who have been counted worthy to obtain their freedom from it. That ye then may also feel this goodly liberty, burst the bonds asunder, spring out of the snare. And let there be no gold lying by in your houses, but that which is more precious than millions of money, alms and love to man, for your treasure. For this gives us boldness toward God, but the other covers us with deep shame, and causes the devil to bear hard (σφοδρὸν πνεῖν) upon us. Why then arm thy enemy, and make him stronger? Arm thy right hand against him, and transfer all the splendor of thy house into thy soul, and stow away all thy fortune in thy mind, and instead of a chest and a house, let heaven keep thy gold. And let us put all our property about our own selves; for we are much better than the walls, and more dignified than the pavement. Why then do we, to the neglect of our own selves, waste all our attention upon those things, which when we are gone we can no longer reach, and often even while we stay here we cannot keep hold of, when we might have such riches as to be found not in this life only, but also in that, in the easiest circumstances? For he who carries about his farms and house and gold upon his soul, wherever he appears, appears

with all this wealth. And how is this possible to be effected? one may ask. It is possible, and that with the utmost ease. For if you transfer them to Heaven by the poor man's hand, you will transfer them entire into your own soul. And if death should afterwards come upon thee, no one will take them from thee, but thou wilt depart to be rich in the next world too. This was the kind of treasure Tabitha had. Hence it was not her house that proclaimed her wealth, nor the walls, nor the stones, nor the pillars, but the bodies of widows furnished with dress, and their tears that were shed, and death that played the runaway, and life that came back again. Let us also make unto ourselves such-like treasures, let us build up for ourselves such-like houses. In this way we shall have God for our Fellow-worker, and we ourselves shall be workers together with Him. For Himself brought the poor from not being into being, and you will prevent them, after they have been brought into life and being, from perishing with hunger and other distress, by tending them and setting them upright, staying up the Temple of God in every quarter. What can be equal to this in respect both of utility and of glory? Or if as yet you have not gained any clear notion of the great adornment He bestowed upon thee when He bade thee relieve poverty, consider this point with thyself. If He had given thee so great power, that thou wert able to set up again even the Heaven if it were falling, wouldest thou not think the thing an honor far too great for thee? See now He hath held thee worthy of a greater honor. For that which in His esteem is more precious than the Heavens,[2] He hath trusted thee to repair. For of all things visible there is nothing in God's esteem equal to man. For Heaven and earth and sea did He make for him, and finds more pleasure in dwelling with him than in the Heaven. And yet we, though with a knowledge of this, bestow no attention nor forethought upon the temples of God; but leaving them in a neglected state, we provide houses splendid and large for ourselves. This is why we are devoid of all good things, and greater beggars than the poorest poor, because we pride ourselves in these houses which we cannot take away with us when we go hence, and leave those alone which we might move away along with our own selves. For the bodies of the poor after dissolution must needs rise again; and God, Who hath given this charge, will bring them forth, and praise those who have taken care of them,

---

[1] Night being put for the time of our sojourn here. Cf. Rom. xiii. 12.

[2] Several Mss. "which is more precious than the Heavens themselves."

and treat such with regard (θαυμάσεται), because when they were on the point of falling to ruin at one time by starvation, at another by nakedness and cold, these repaired them by all means in their power. But still, even with all these praises set before us, we loiter yet, and decline undertaking this honorable charge. And Christ indeed hath not where to lodge, but goeth about a stranger, and naked, and hungry, and you set up houses out of town, and baths, and terraces, and chambers without number, in thoughtless vanity; and to Christ you give not even a share of a little hut, while for daws and vultures you deck out upper chambers. What can be worse than such insanity as this? What more grievous than such madness? for madness it is in the last stage of it, or rather one

has no name to suit it, use whatever one may. Yet still if we be so minded, it is possible to beat off the disorder, tenacious as it is; and not possible only, but even easy; and not easy merely, but even easier is it to get rid of this pest than of the sufferings of the body, since the Physician is so much greater. Let us then draw Him to ourselves, and invite Him to aid us in the attempt, and let us contribute our share, good-will, I mean, and energy. For He will not require anything further, but if He can meet with this only, He will confer all that is His part. Let us then contribute our share, that in this world we may enjoy a genuine health, and may attain to the good things to come, by the grace and love towards man, etc.

HOMILY XV.

ROM. VIII. 28.

"And we know that all things work together for good to them that love God."

HERE he seems to me to have mooted this whole topic with a view to those who were in danger; or, rather, not this only, but also what was said a little before this. For the words, "the sufferings of this present time are not worthy to be compared with the glory which shall be revealed in us;" and those, that "the whole creation groaneth;" and the saying, that "we are saved by hope;" and the phrase, "we with patience wait for;" and that, "we know not what we should pray for as we ought;" are all of them said to these. For he instructs them not to choose just what they may think, themselves, to be useful, but what the Spirit may suggest; for many things that seem to one's self profitable, do sometimes even cause much harm. Quiet, for instance, and freedom from dangers, and living out of fear, seemed to be advantageous for them. And what wonder if they did to them, since the blessed Paul himself this seemed to be so? still he came afterwards to know that the opposite to all these are the things advantageous, and when he came to know it, he was content. So he that besought the Lord thrice to be freed from hazards,[1] when once he heard Him say, "My grace is sufficient for thee, for My Power is perfected in weakness" (2 Cor. xii. 8, 9), was after-

wards delighted at being persecuted, and insulted, and having irreparable ills done him. For, "I glory," he says, "in persecutions, in insults" (Eng. V. reproaches), "in necessities." (2 Cor. xii. 10.) And this was his reason for saying, "For we know not what we should pray for as we ought." And he exhorted all men to give up these matters to the Spirit. For the Holy Spirit is very mindful of us, and this is the will of God. Having then cheered them by all methods, he proceeds to what we have heard to-day, putting forward a reason strong enough to reclaim them. For he says, "we know that all things work together for good to them that love God." Now when he speaks of "all things," he mentions even the things that seem painful. For should even tribulation, or poverty, or imprisonment, or famines, or deaths, or anything else whatsoever come upon us, God is able to change all these things into the opposite. For this is quite an instance of His unspeakable power, His making things seemingly painful to be lightsome to us, and turning them into that which is helpful to us. And so he does not say, that "them that love God," no grievance approacheth, but, that it "works together for good," that is to say, that He useth the grievous things themselves to make the persons so plotted against approved. And this is a much greater thing than hindering the approach of such grievances, or stopping them when they have come.

[1] See p. 447, and on 2 Cor. xii. 7, Hom. 26, p. 294 O. T.

And this is what He did even with the furnace at Babylon. For He did not either prevent their falling into it, or extinguish the flame after those saints were cast into it, but let it burn on, and made them by this very flame greater objects of wonder, and with the Apostles too He wrought other like wonders continually. (St. Mark xvi. 18.) For if men who have learnt to be philosophic can use the things of nature to the opposite of their intention, and appear even when living in poverty in easier circumstances than the rich, and shine [1] through disgrace: much more will God work for those that love Him both these and also greater things by far. For one needs only one thing, a genuine love of Him, and all things follow that. As then things seemingly harmful do good to these, so do even things profitable harm those who love Him not. For instance, the exhibition of miracles and wisdom in His teaching only injured the Jews, as did the rightness of doctrine; and for the former they called Him a possessed person (John viii. 48), for the other one that would be equal to God (ib. v. 18): and because of the miracles (ib. xi. 47, 53), they even went about to kill Him. But the thief when crucified, when nailed to the Cross, and reviled, and suffering ills unnumbered, not only was not hurt, but even gained the greatest good therefrom. See how for those who love God all things work together for good. After mentioning then this great blessing, one which far exceeds man's nature, since to many this seemed even past belief, he draws a proof of it from past blessings, in these words, " to them who are called according to His [2] purpose." Now consider, he means, from the calling, for instance, what I have just said. Why then did He not from the first call all? or why not Paul himself as soon as the rest? Does it not seem that the deferring was harmful? But it was still by the event shown to be for the best. The purpose he here mentions, however, that he might not ascribe everything to the calling; since in this way both Greeks and Jews would be sure to cavil. For if the calling alone were sufficient, how came it that all were not saved? Hence he says, that it is not the calling alone, but the purpose of those called too, that works the salvation. For the calling was not forced upon them, nor compulsory. All then were called, but all did not obey the call.

Ver. 29. " For whom· He did foreknow, He also did predestinate to be conformed to the Image of His Son."

See what superb honor! for what the Only-begotten was by Nature, this they also have become by grace. And still he was not satisfied with this calling of them conformed thereto, but even adds another point, " that He might be the first-born." And even here he does not come to a pause, but again after this he proceeds to mention another point, " Among many brethren." So wishing to use all means of setting the relationship [3] in a clear light. Now all these things you are to take as said of the Incarnation.[4] For according to the Godhead He is Only-begotten. See, what great things He hath given unto us! Doubt not then about the future. For he showeth even upon other grounds His concern for us by saying, that things were foreordered [5] in this way from the beginning. For men have to derive from things their conceptions about them, but to God these things have been long determined upon,[6] and from of old He bare good-will toward us (πρὸς ἡμᾶς διέκειτο), he says.

Ver. 30. " Moreover whom He did predestinate, them He also called; and whom He called, them He also justified."

Now He justified them by the regeneration of the laver. " And whom He justified, them He also glorified " by the gift, by the adoption.

Ver. 31. " What shall we then say to these things? "

As if he should say, Let me then hear no more about the dangers and the malicious devices from every quarter. For even if some disbelieve the things to come, still they have not a word to say against the good things that have already taken place; as, for instance, the friendship of God towards thee from the first, the justifying, the glory. And yet these things He gave thee by means seemingly distressing. And those things which you thought to be disgracing, the Cross, scourges, bonds, these are what have set the whole world aright. As then by what Himself suffered, though of aspect forbidding in man's eye, even by these He effected the liberty and salvation of the whole race; so also is He wont to do in regard to those things which thou endurest, turning thy sufferings unto glory and renown for thee. " If God be for us, who can be against us? "

---

[1] καὶ ἐν τούτοις διαλάμπει τὸ καλὸν, *Eth.* i. 2. "even in these (misfortunes) the noble character shines forth."

[2] The word His perhaps rightly inserted in our version, is not in the Greek, and Theodoret seems not to have taken it so; he says, "for he calleth not any as it may be (ἁπλῶς), but those who have a purpose " (a predisposition), πρόθεσιν, and so does St. Chrysostom below, and Œcumenius. See on Eph. i. 11, Hom. ii. p. 112 O. T. and note. St. Augustin rejects this exposition and adopts that of our version, Ad Bonif. l. ii. § 22, De Corr. *et. Gr.* § 23.

[3] συγγένειαν, but Mar. and 6 Mss. εὐγ. nobility.

[4] Gr. *Economy*, see p. 338, note [3].

[5] Or "marked out." προτετυπῶσθαι.

[6] See Sir Thomas Brown, *Rel. Med.* pt. i. p. 22.

Why, it may be said, who is there that is not against us? Why the world is against us, both kings and peoples, both relations and countrymen. Yet these that be against us, so far are they from thwarting us at all, that even without their will they become to us the causes of crowns, and procurers of countless blessings, in that God's wisdom turneth their plots unto our salvation and glory. See how really no one is against us! For it was this which gave new lustre to Job, the fact that the devil was in arms against him. For the devil moved at once friends against him, his wife against him, and wounds, and servants, and a thousand other machinations. And it turned out that none of them was against him on the whole. And yet this was no great thing to him, though it was great in itself, but what is a far greater thing is, that it turned out that they were all for him. For since God was for him, even things seemingly against him all became for him. And this happened with the Apostles also, inasmuch as both the Jews, and they of the Gentiles, and false brethren, and rulers, and peoples, and famines, and poverty, and ten thousand things were against them; and yet nothing was against them. For the things which made them the most bright and conspicuous, and great in the sight both of God and of men, were these. Just reflect then what a word Paul hath uttered about the faithful, and those who are truly (ἀκριβῶς) crucified, such as not even the Emperor with his diadem can achieve. For against him there are abundance of barbarians that arm themselves, and of enemies that invade, and of body-guards that plot, and of subjects many that oftentimes are ever and anon rebelling, and thousands of other things. But against the faithful who taketh good heed unto God's laws, neither man, nor devil, nor aught besides, can stand! For if you take away his money, you have become the procurer of a reward to him. If you speak ill of him, by the evil report he gains fresh lustre in God's sight. If you cast him into starvation, the more will his glory and his reward be. If (what seems the most severe stroke of all) you give him over to death, you are twining a crown of martyrdom about him.* What

then is equivalent to this way of life, being that against which nothing can be done, but even they that seem to devise mischief are no less of service to him than benefactors? This is why he says, "If God be for us, who can be against us? Next, not being satisfied with what he had already said, the greatest sign of His love for us, and that which he always is dwelling over, that he sets down here also; I mean, the slaying of His Son. For He did not only justify us, he means, and glorify us, and make us conformed to that Image, but not even His Son did He spare for thee. And therefore he proceeds to say,

Ver. 32. "He that spared not His own Son, but delivered Him up for us all, how shall He not with Him also freely give us all things?"

And here the words he uses are high-wrought (μεθ᾽ ὑπερβολῆς) and exceedingly warm, to show his love. How then is He to neglect us, in whose behalf "He spared not His own Son, but delivered Him up for us all? For reflect what goodness it is not to spare even His own Son, but to give Him up, and to give Him up for all, and those worthless, and unfeeling, and enemies, and blasphemers. "How then shall He not with Him also freely give us all things? What he means then is much as follows; If He gave His own Son, and not merely gave Him, but gave Him to death, why doubt any more about the rest, since thou hast the Master? why be dubious about the chattels, when thou hast the Lord? For He that gave the greater thing to His enemies, how shall He do else than give the lesser things to His friends?

Ver. 33. "Who shall lay anything to the charge of God's elect?"

Here he is against those who say, that faith is no profit, and will not believe the complete change. (i. e. in baptism see p. 349.) And see how swiftly he stops their mouths, by the worthiness of Him that elected. He does not say, "Who shall lay anything to the charge of God's " servants? or of God's faithful ones? but " of God's elect?" And election is a sign of virtue. For if when a horse-breaker has selected colts fit for the race, no one can find fault with them, but he would get laughed at who should find fault; much more when God selecteth souls are they that "lay any charge against" them deserving of laughter.

"It is God that justifieth."

Ver. 34. "Who is He that condemneth?

---

* Chrys. apprehends well the practical purpose for which the apostle introduced verses 28-30. Notwithstanding all the imperfections of the Christian's spiritual life (26, 27) and the trials which have been so fully described (1-24) we have the assurance that all these things are working in accordance with God's gracious plan for his ultimate good. In passing over from the idea of believers as those who love God to its counterpart that they are those called according to His purpose (not to be taken of the *believer's* purpose, as Chrys.) the apostle develops from this idea of *purpose* a series of conceptions designed to emphasize the believer's security. "You who love God can be sure of the outcome of all suffering in good for you are included in God's purpose which he purposed in

Christ Jesus our Lord." (Eph. iii. 11.) You have all the strength and solidity of God's eternal plan on your side. When the divine purpose of redemption was before the mind of God in eternity, you were the prospective participants in it, as truly as you now are the real participants. What you are God from eternity intended you to be. The stability of his immutable counsel is pledged to you."—G. B. S.

He does not say, it is God that forgave our sins, but what is much greater, "It is God that justifieth." For when the Judge's sentence declares us just, and a Judge such as that too, what signifieth the accuser? Hence neither is it right to fear temptations, for God is for us, and hath shown it by what He hath done; nor again Jewish triflings, for He has both elected and justified us, and the wondrous thing is that it was also by the death of His Son that He did so. Who then is to condemn us, since God crowns us, and Christ was put to death for us, and not only was put to death, but also after this intercedeth for us? *

For, "It is Christ," he says, "that died, yea rather, that is risen from the dead, Who is at the right hand of God, Who also maketh intercession for us."

For though seen now in His own dignity, He hath not left caring for us, but even "maketh intercession for us," and still keepeth up the same love. For He was not contented with being put to death alone. And this is a sign for the most part of very great love, to be doing not only what falls to His lot, but also to address Another on this behalf. For this is all he meant to signify by the interceding, using a way of speaking better suited to man, and more condescending, that he might point out love. Since unless we take the words, "He spared not," also with the same understanding, many inconsistencies will come of it. And that you may see that such is the point he is aiming at, after first saying, that He "is at the Right Hand, he next proceeds to say, that He "maketh intercession for us," when he had shown an equality of honor and rank, so that hence it may appear that the Intercession is not a sign of inferiority,[1] but of love only. For being Life itself ($\alpha\dot{\upsilon}\tau o\zeta\omega\dot{\eta}$) (Ps. xxxvi. 9.), and a Well of good things of every kind, and with the same power as the Father, both to raise up the dead and to quicken them, and do all besides that He doth, how could He need to be a suppliant in order to help us? (John v. 19, 21, 36.) He that of His own power set free those who were given over and condemned, even from that condemnation; and made them righteous, and sons, and led them to the very highest honors, and brought

to pass things which had never been hoped for: how should He, after having achieved all this, and having shown our nature on the King's throne, require to be a suppliant to do the easier things? (Acts vii. 55; Heb. x. 12; Rev. vii. 17.) You see how it is shown by every argument, that there is no other reason for his having mentioned intercession, save to show the warmth and vigorousness of His love for us; for the Father also is represented to us as beseeching men to be reconciled to Him. "For we are ambassadors of Christ, as though God did beseech you by us." (2 Cor. v. 20.) Still, though God beseecheth, and men are "ambassadors in Christ's stead" to men, we do not understand on that account anything done unworthy of that dignity; but one thing only do we gather from all that is told us, namely, the intenseness of the love. This then let us do here also. If then the Spirit even "maketh intercession for us with groanings that cannot be uttered," and Christ died and intercedeth for us, and the Father "spared not His own Son" for thee, and elected thee, and justified thee, why be afraid any more? Or why tremble when enjoying such great love, and having such great interest taken in thee? In this way then, after showing His great providence over us from the first, he afterwards brings out what comes next in a bold style, and does not say, ye ought also to love Him, but, as if grown enthusiastic at this unspeakable Providence over us, he says,

Ver. 35. "Who shall separate us from the love of Christ?"

And he does not say of God, so indifferent is it to him whether he mentions the Name of Christ or of God. "Shall tribulation, or distress, or persecution, or famine, or nakedness, or peril, or sword?" Observe the blessed Paul's judgment. For he does not mention the things that we are daily getting taken by, love of money and desire of glory and the thraldom of anger, but things that are far more enthralling than these, and of power to put a force[2] upon nature itself, and to wrench open the sternness of the resolution many times even against our will, are what he puts down here, tribulations and distresses. For even if the things mentioned are easy to tell up, still each single word has in it thousands of lines of temptation. For when he says, tribulation, he mentions prisons and bonds, and calumnies, and banishments, and all the other hardships, so in one word running through an ocean of dangers without

---

* The argument of vv. 33, 34 which is so condensed in form, may be paraphrased thus: "Who shall lay anything to the charge of God's elect? No one shall. Why? Because their justifier is God himself. No one may accuse whom He acquits. Who, then, can appear against them and condemn them? No one can, for it is no less a person than Christ who died and rose on their behalf."—G. B. S.

[1] Theodoret notices the same thing, *ad loc.* St. Basil, *De Sp. S.* c. xx. answers a similar argument against the equal Divinity of the Holy Spirit, by showing that it would apply to the Son if at all.

[2] Shakespeare, *Lear*, act ii. sc. iv. "We are not ourselves when nature being oppressed commands the mind to suffer with the body," etc.

stint, and exhibiting to us, in fact by a single word, all the evils that men meet with. Yet still he dares them all! Wherefore he brings them forward in the shape of questions, as if it was incontrovertible that nothing could move a person so beloved, and who had enjoyed so much providence over him. Then that this might not seem as if he had forgotten himself, he brings in the Prophet also, who declared this before, a long while ago and saith,

Ver. 36. "For Thy sake we are killed all the day long, we are accounted as sheep for the slaughter." (Ps. xliv. 22.)

That is, we are exposed to all to be evil entreated of them. But yet against so many and so great dangers and these recent horrors, the object of our conflicts is given as a sufficient consolation, or rather not sufficient only, but even much more. For it is not for men, nor for any other of the things of this life that we suffer, but for the King (he says) of the universe. But this is not the only crown, for he encircles them with another besides, and that varied and manifold. Since then, as they were men they could not have deaths without number to undergo, he shows that in this way the prize is none the less. For even if by nature it were fated to die once, by choice God hath granted us to suffer this every day, if we be so minded. Whence it is plain that we shall depart with as many crowns as we have lived days, or rather with many more. For it is possible in a day to die not once alone or twice, but many times. For he who is always ready unto this, keeps continually receiving a full reward. This then is what the Psalmist (Προφήτης) hints at, when he says, "all the day." And for this reason the Apostle also brought him before them to rouse them up the more. For if, he means, those in the old dispensation, who had the land as their reward, and the other things which come to a close along with this life, did so look down upon the present life and the temptations and dangers of it, what pardon should we find if we deal so languidly after the promise of Heaven, and the Kingdom above, and its unutterable blessings, so as not to come even up to the same measure as they? And this he does not say indeed, but leaves it to his hearers' consciences, and is satisfied with the quotation alone. He shows too that their bodies become a sacrifice, and that we must not be disturbed or troubled at God having so ordered it. And he exhorts them in other ways besides. For to prevent any from saying that he is merely philosophizing here before having any experience of realities, he adds, "we are ac-

counted as sheep for the slaughter," meaning the daily deaths of the Apostles. You see his courage and his goodness. For as they, he means, when slaughtered make no resistance, so neither do we. But since the feebleness of the mind of man, even after so great things, was afraid of the multitude of temptations, see how he again rouses the hearer, and gives him a lofty and exulting spirit, by saying,

Ver. 37. "Nay, in all these things we are more than conquerors through Him that loved us."

For what is indeed wonderful is this, not that we are conquerors only, but that we are so by the very things meant as plots against us. And we are not merely conquerors, but we are "more than conquerors," that is, are so with ease, without toil and labor. For without undergoing the real things, by only setting our mind aright, we raise our trophies against our enemies. And with good reason. For it is God that striveth together with us. Do not then be doubtful, if though beaten we get the better of our beaters, if driven out we overcome our persecutors, if dying we put the living to fight. For when you take the power and also the love of God into account, there is nothing to prevent these wondrous and strange things from coming to pass, and that victory the most advantageous should shine upon us. For they did not merely conquer, but in a wondrous way, and so that one might learn that those who plotted against them had a war not against men, but against that invincible Might. See the Jews then with these among them, and at a loss quite, and saying, "What are we to do to these men?" (Acts iv. 16.) For it is marvellous indeed, that though they had hold of them and had got them liable to their courts, and imprisoned them and beat them, they were yet at a loss and in perplexity, as they got overcome by the very things whereby they expected to conquer. And neither kings nor people, nor ranks of demons, nor the devil himself, had power to get the better of them, but were all overcome at a very great disadvantage, finding that all they planned against them became for them. And therefore he says, "we are more than conquerors." For this was a new rule of victory for men to prevail by their adversaries, and in no instance to be overcome, but to go forth to these struggles as if they themselves had the issue in their own hands.

Ver. 38, 39. "For I am persuaded, that neither death nor life, nor angels, nor principalities, nor powers, nor things present, nor things to come, nor height, nor depth, nor any other creature, shall be able to separate us from the love of God, which is in Christ Jesus our Lord."

These are great things here mentioned. But the reason we do not enter into them is, because we have not so great love. Yet still though they are great, as he wished to show that they were nothing beside the love wherewith he was loved of God; after it he then places his own, lest he should seem to be saying great things about himself. And what he says is somewhat of this kind. Why speak, he means, of things present, and evils inherited in this life? For even if a person were to tell me of things to come, and of powers; of things, such as death and life; of powers, such as angels and archangels, and all the superior orders of beings; even these would be little to me compared with the love of Christ. For even if a person were to threaten me with that future death to which there is no death, to separate me from Christ, nor if he promised the life without end, would I agree to it. Why mention kings here below and consuls? and this one or that? for if you tell me of angels, or all the powers above, or all existing things, or all that are to come, they are all small to me, both those in the earth, and those in heaven, and those under the earth, and those above heaven, compared to this charm. Then as though these were not enough to set before them the strong desire which he had, he gives a being to others again of like magnitude, and says, "nor any other creation." And what he means is nearly this, even if there were any other creation as great as the visible, and as great as the intelligible,[1] none of them could part me from that love. This he says not as if the Angels attempted it, or the other Powers, far from it, but as wishing to show quite to the utmost the charm he had toward Christ. For Christ he loved not for the things of Christ, but for His sake the things that were His, and to Him alone he looked, and one thing he feared, and that was falling from his love for Him. For this thing was in itself more dreadful than hell, as to abide in it was more desirable than the Kingdom.

What then should we now deserve, when he is found not to esteem even the things in Heaven as compared with the desire for Christ, and we set more store by things of mire and clay than by Christ? And he out of desire of Him would take up with falling into hell, and being banished from the Kingdom, if the choice between the two were put

to him: but we are not even above the present life. Are we worthy then to touch his very shoes, when we have come to be so far short of his largeness of mind? For he for Christ's sake does not think anything even of a kingdom; but we think slightingly of Himself, but things of His we make great account of. And would it were of things of His. But now it is not even this; but with a Kingdom held out to us, we let that alone, and keep pursuing shadows and dreams all our days. And yet God in His love toward man and exceeding gentleness, hath done the same as if an affectionate father should, on his son's becoming disinclined to a continual stay with him, manage to bring this about in another way. For since we have not the right feeling of desire after Him, He keeps putting divers other things before us, so as to hold us to Himself. Yet not even for this do we abide with Him, but we keep springing off to childish playthings. Not so Paul, but like a noble spirited child, who is open and attached to his father, he seeks only after the Father's presence, and other things he sets not so much store by; or rather, it is much more than a child. For he does not value the Father and things that are His at the same rate, but when he looks to the Father, he counts them nothing, but would choose rather to be chastised and beaten, so he was with Him, than to be apart from Him and indulge his ease. Let us then shudder, all of us that do not even feel above money for the sake of Christ, or rather such of us as do not feel above it for our own sakes. For it was Paul alone who suffered in good earnest all things for Christ's sake, not for the sake of the kingdom, or his own honor, but owing to his affection to Him. But as for us, neither Christ nor the things of Christ draw us from the things of this life; but as serpents, or snakes, or swine, or even as all of them at once, so do we keep dragging on in the mire. For wherein are we better than those brutes, when with so many and such great examples before us we still keep bowing down, and have not the heart to look up to Heaven for ever so little a time? Yet did God give up even His Son. But thou wilt not so much as share thy bread with Him, Who was given up for thee, Who was slain for thee. The Father for thy sake spared not Him, and this too when He was indeed His Son, but thou doest not look upon Him even when pining with starvation, and this too when thou shouldest but spend of His own, and spend it too for thy own good! What can be worse than such a breach of law as this? He was given up for thee, He was slain for thee, He goeth about in

---

[1] Intelligible is used in old Platonist writers for invisible, as in German.

hunger for thee, it is of His own thou should-est give, that thou mayest thyself get the gain, and still thou dost not give! What sort of stone is there than which these are not more senseless, who in despite of such great induce-ments, continue in this diabolical cruel-heartedness? For He was not satisfied even with death and the Cross only, but He took up with becoming poor also, and a stranger, and a beggar, and naked, and being thrown into prison, and undergoing sickness, that so at least He might call thee off. If thou wilt not requite Me, He says, as having suffered for thee, show mercy on Me for My poverty. And if thou are not minded to pity Me for My poverty, do for My disease be moved, for My imprisonment be softened. And if even these things make thee not charitable, for the easiness of the request comply with Me. For it is no costly gift I ask, but bread and lodg-ing, and words of comfort; but if even after this thou still continuest unsubdued, still for the Kingdom's sake be improved for the rewards which I have promised. Hast thou then no regard even for these? yet still for very nature's sake be softened at seeing Me naked, and remember that nakedness where-with I was naked on the Cross for thee; or, if not this, yet that wherewith I am now naked through the poor. I was then bound for thee, nay, still am so for thee, that whether moved by the former ground or the latter, thou mightest be minded to show some pity. I fasted for thee, again I am hungry for thee. I was athirst when hanging on the Cross, I am athirst also through the poor, that by the former as also by the latter I may draw thee to Myself, and make thee chari-table to thine own salvation. Hence also of thee that owest Me the requital of benefits without number, I make not demand as of one that oweth, but crown thee as one that favoreth Me, and a kingdom do I give thee for these small things. For I do not say so much as put an end to My poverty, or give Me riches, and yet I did become poor for thee; yet still I ask for bread and clothing, and a small solace for My hunger. And if I

be thrown into prison, I do not insist upon thy loosing My bonds and setting Me free, but one thing only do I seek after, that thou wouldest visit Me, Who was (or am) bound for thee, and I shall have received favor enough, and for this only will I give thee Heaven. And yet I delivered thee from most galling bonds, but for Me it is quite enough, if thou wilt but visit Me when in prison. For I am able indeed to crown thee even without all this; yet I would fain be a debtor to thee, that the crown may give thee some feeling of confidence. This is why, though I am able to support Myself, I come about begging, and stand beside thy door, and stretch out Mine hand, since My wish is to be supported by thee. For I love thee exceedingly, and so desire to eat at thy table, which is the way with those that love a person. And I glory (John xv. 8) in this. And when the whole world are spectators, then am I to herald thee forth, and in the hearing of all men to display thee as My supporter. Yet we, when we are supported by any one, feel ashamed, and cover our faces; but He, as loving us exceed-ingly, even if we hold our peace, will then tell out what we did with much praise, and is not ashamed to say, that when Himself was naked we clothed Him, and fed Him when hungry. Let us then lay all these things to heart, and not be contented with passing mere praises upon them, but let us even accomplish what I have been speaking of. For what is the good of these applauses and clamors? I demand one thing only of you, and that is the display of them in real action, the obedience of deeds. This is my praise, this your gain, this gives me more lustre than a diadem. When you have left the Church then, this is the crown that you should make for me and for you, through the hand of the poor; that both in the present life we may be nourished with a goodly hope, and after we have departed to the life to come, we may attain to those good things without number, to which may all of us attain by the grace and love toward man, etc.

HOMILY XVI.

ROM. IX. 1.

'I say the truth in Christ, I lie not, my conscience also bearing me witness in the Holy Ghost."

DID I not seem yesterday to you to have spoken some great and exorbitant things of Paul's love toward Christ? And great indeed they were, too great for any words to express. Yet what you have heard to-day are as far above those things, as those things were above ours. And yet I did not think they could be exceeded, still when I came to what has been read to-day [1] it did appear far more glorious than the whole of the former. And that he was aware of this himself he shows by his exordium. For as on the point of entering upon greater things than those, and therefore liable to be disbelieved by the generality, he first uses a strong asseveration about the matter he is going to speak of; which many are in the habit of doing when they are going to say somewhat which is not believed by the generality, and about which they feel the utmost certainty in their own minds. Hence he says, "I say the truth in Christ, I lie not, and my conscience beareth witness,"

Ver. 2, 3. "That I have a great heaviness and continual sorrow in my heart. For I could wish that myself were accursed from Christ." *

What sayest thou, O Paul? from Christ, thy beloved One, from Whom neither kingdom nor hell, nor things visible nor intelligible, nor another world as great, would separate thee, is it from Him that thou wouldst now be accursed? What has happened? Hast thou changed, hast thou given over that love? No, he replies, fear not. Rather I have even made it more intense. How then is it that thou wouldest fain be accursed, and seekest a separation, and a removal to such a distance, that after it there is no possibility of finding a more distant one? Because I love Him ex-

ceedingly, he may reply. How, pray, and in what manner? For the things seem a riddle. Or rather, if you will, let us learn what the curse is, and then we will question him upon these points, and shall understand this unspeakable and extraordinary love. What then is the curse? Hear his own words, " If any man love not our Lord Jesus Christ, let him be accursed." (anathema, 1 Cor. xvi. 22.) That is, let him be set apart from all, removed from all. For as in the case of a thing dedicated (ἀνάθημα), which is set apart for God, no one would venture so much as to touch it with his hand or even to come near it ; so too with a man who is put apart from the Church, in cutting him off from all, and removing him as far off as possible, he calls him by this name (ἀνάθεμα) in a contrary sense,[2] thus with much fear denouncing to all men to keep apart from him, and to spring away from him. For the thing set apart, no one, from respect of it, ventures to come near to. But from him who is cut off, all men separate themselves from a very opposite feeling. And so the separation is the same, and both the one and the other are equally removed from the generality. Still, the mode of separation is not the same, but in this case it is the opposite to what it is in that. For from the one they keep back as being dedicated to God ; from the other as being estranged from God, and broken off from the Church. This then is what Paul means when he says, " I could wish that myself were accursed from Christ." And he does not say merely that I could be willing, but using a stronger term, he says even, " I could wish" (or pray ηὐχόμην). But if what he says trouble you in your (ἀσθενέστερον) feebleness, consider the real state of the case, not only that he wished to be separated, but also the cause for which he wished it, and then you will see the greatness of his love.† For he even

---

[1] So Field from one Ms. Vulg. "what has been read to-day, as it reached my ears."

* Chaps. ix. x. and xi. may be viewed as a kind of appendix to the doctrinal part of the epistle, in which the apostle considers the problems to which the unbelief and rejection of the Jews gave rise. It is Paul's purpose in these chapters to show that his doctrine does not contradict God's promises to the Jews. Chap. ix. contains strong assertions that the providential dealing of God with the Jews is not to be called in question. It is evident from the gradual approach of the apostle to this theme, how painful it was to him to be compelled to contemplate it.—G. B. S.

[2] Thus *sacer* is used in both senses, and devoted in our own language somewhat similarly.

† The force of ηὐχόμην here is : "I would wish, if it were a thing which could possibly be realized for the advantage of my brethren." The word ἀνάθεμα means anything devoted to God and then (as in the N. T.) something devoted to his wrath, i. e. accursed. The expression is to be understood as the language of intense passion and can scarcely mean anything less than a readiness to perish if by so doing he could save his people Israel.—G. B. S.

circumcised (Timothy, Acts xvi. 3), and we pay no attention to what was done, but to the intention of it, and the cause of it, and hence we wonder at him the more. And he not only circumcised a person, but he even shaved himself and sacrificed (Acts xviii. 18; xxi. 24), and yet surely we do not therefore assert him to be a Jew, but upon this very score to be perfectly free from Judaizing, and clear of it, and a genuine worshipper of Christ. As then when you see him circumcising and sacrificing, you do not therefore condemn him as Judaizing, but upon this very score have the best reason for crowning him as quite an alien to Judaism; thus when thou seest him to have become desirous of being accursed, do not therefore be troubled, but upon this very ground give him the loudest praise, when thou knowest the cause why he wishes this. For if we do not look narrowly into the causes, we shall call Elijah a manslayer, and Abraham not a manslayer only, but a murderer of his son.[1] And Phinees and Peter we shall implead for murder likewise. Nor is it in the case of the saints alone, but also of the God of the universe, that he who does not keep to this rule, will be suspecting sundry unbecoming things. Now to prevent this happening in all cases of the kind, let us bring together both the cause, and the intention, and the time, and all that makes in behalf of what is so done, and in this way let us investigate the actions. And this we must do now also in the case of this blessed soul. Now what is the cause? It is Jesus Himself Who is so beloved. And yet he does not say *for* Him; for what he says is, I would wish that I were accursed *from* Him for my brethren. And this comes of his humbleness of mind. For he has no wish to make himself conspicuous, as if he were saying something great, and doing Christ a favor in this. Wherefore also he said "my kinsmen," that he may conceal his high aim (πλεονέκτημα). Since to see that he wished it all for Christ's sake, just hear what comes next. After speaking of kinsmen then, he proceeds,

Ver. 4, 5. "To whom pertaineth the adoption, and the glory, and the covenants, and the giving of the Law, and the service of God, and the promises; whose are the father's, and of whom as concerning the flesh Christ came, Who is over all, God blessed for ever. Amen."

And what is this? one asks. For if with a view to the belief of others he was willing to become accursed, he ought to have also wished for this in the Gentiles' behalf. But if he wishes it in the Jews' behalf only, it is a proof that he did not wish it for Christ's sake, but for his own relationship to them. But in fact if he had prayed for the Gentiles only, this would not have been equally clear. But since it is for the Jews only, it is a clear proof that it is only for Christ's glory that he is thus earnest. And I am aware that what I am saying will seem a paradox to you. Still if ye do not make a disturbance,[2] I will presently endeavor to make it clear. For what he has said he has not said nakedly; but since all were talking and accusing God, that after being counted worthy of the name of sons, and receiving the Law, and knowing Him beyond all men, and enjoying such great glory, and serving him beyond the whole world, and receiving the promises, and being from fathers who were His friends, and what was the greatest thing of all, having been forefathers of Christ Himself (for this is the meaning of the words, " of whom, as concerning the flesh, Christ came "), they are now cast out and disgraced; and in their place are introduced men who had never known Him, of the Gentiles. Now since they said all this, and blasphemed God, Paul hearing it, and being cut to the heart, and vexed for God's glory's sake, wished that he were accursed, had it been possible, so that they might be saved, and this blasphemy be put a stop to, and God might not seem to have deceived the offspring of those to whom He promised the gifts. And that you may see that it was in sorrow for this, that the promise of God might not seem to fall to the ground, which said to Abraham, " I will give this land to thee and to thy seed," that he uttered this wish, he proceeds,

Ver. 6. " Not as though the word of God had taken none effect."

To show that he had courage (Mar. and 4 Mss. wished) to bear all these things for the word of God, that is, the promise made to Abraham. For as Moses seemed to be pleading for the Jews, yet was doing everything for God's glory (for he says, " Lest they say, Because He was not able to save them, He led them forth to destroy them in the wilderness " (Deut. ix. 28); stay Thy wrath), so also does Paul, That they may not say (he means) that the promise of God has fallen to the ground, and He has disappointed us of that. He vouched to us, and this word has not issued in deed, I could wish to be accursed. This then was why he did not speak of the

---

[1] Aug. *de Civ. Dei*, i. 21. Butler, *Anal.* p. 262, ii. 3, v. fin.

[2] This was sometimes done; but the Mss. vary unusually in this word, and three different readings mean, " if ye are not disturbed." See Twining on Arist. *Poet.* note 22, and Gaisf. on *Rhet.* p. 46.

Gentiles (for to them no promises had been made by Him, nor had they worshipped Him, wherefore neither did any blaspheme Him on their account), but it was for the Jews who had both received the promise, and had also been brought into closer connection with Him than others, that he expressed this wish. Do you see, that if he had expressed it for the Gentiles, he would not have been shown to be doing this so purely for Christ's glory? But since he was willing to become accursed in the Jews' behalf, then it was most evidenced that it was for Christ's sake only that he desired this.[1] And for this cause he says,

"To whom pertaineth the adoption, and the glory, and the service of God, and the promises."

For the Law, he means, which speaks of Christ, comes from thence, and all the covenants made with them, and Himself came from them, and the Fathers who received the promises were all from them. Yet still the opposite has resulted, and they have fallen from all their good things. Hence, he means, I am vexed, and if it were possible to be separated from the company about Christ, and to be made an alien, not from the love of Him (that be far from him; for even all this he was doing through love), but from all that enjoyment and glory, I would accept that lot, provided my Master were not to be blasphemed, that He might not have to hear some saying, that it has been all for stage-effect; He promises to one, and gives to another. He was sprung from one race, He saved another. It was to the forefathers of the Jews that He made the promises, and yet He has deserted their descendants, and put men, who never at any time knew Him, into their good things. They labored in the practice of the Law, and reading the Prophets, while men who have come but yesterday from heathen altars and images have been set up above them. What foresight is there in all this? Now that these things may not be said of my •Master, he means, even if they are said unjustly, I would willingly lose even the kingdom and that glory unutterable, and any sufferings would I undergo, as considering it the greatest consolation possible no longer to hear Him Whom I so long for, so blasphemed. But if you be still against allowing this explanation, just reflect that many fathers have at many times taken up with thus much for their children, and have chosen to be separated from them, and rather to see them in honor, considering their honor dearer to them than their company. But since we are so short of love like this

[1] As galled at the blasphemies against Him for breaking His promise.

(Bacon, N. O. Aph. lib. 2, § 7), we cannot even form an idea of what is here meant. For there be some that are so wholly unworthy even to hear the name of Paul, and that stand at such an interval and distance from that vehemency of his, as to fancy that he says this of temporal death. Who I should say were as ignorant of Paul, as the blind of the sun's rays, or even much more so. For he that died daily, and set before him dangers thick as a snow-storm, and then said, "Who shall separate us from the love of Christ? shall tribulation, or distress, or persecution, or famine?" and still unsatisfied with what he had said, and after going above the heaven and the heaven of heavens, and running through the Angels and Archangels, and all the higher orders of beings, and taking in at once things present, things to come, things visible, things intelligible, things grievous, and things good, that were on either part, and leaving nothing out at all, yet not even thus satiated, but even bodying forth another non-existing creation, how should he, by way of saying some great thing after all those things, make mention of a temporal death? It is not so, surely it is not! But such a notion is that of worms nestling in their dunghill. For had he said this, in what sense would he be wishing himself accursed from Christ? For death (Phil. i. 23) of that sort would have joined him more closely with the band of Christ, and made him enjoy that glory the more. Yet some there are who venture to say things different from these, even more ridiculous. It was not then, they say, death that he wished to have, but to be a treasure, a thing set apart, of Christ's. And who even of the most worthless and indolent that would not wish for this? And in what way was this likely to be in his kinsmen's behalf? Let us then leave these fables and trifles (for it is no more worth while making a reply to these things than to children babbling at play), and let us go back again to the words themselves, luxuriating in this very ocean of love, and fearlessly swimming there in every direction, and reflecting upon the unspeakable flame of love—or rather say what one may, one shall say nothing worthy the subject. For there is no ocean so wide, no flame so intense, as this. And no language can set it forth as it deserves, but he alone knew it who in good earnest gained it. And now let me bring the words themselves before you again.

"For I could wish that I myself were accursed." What does the "I myself" mean? It means I that have been a teacher (1 Cor. ix. 27) of all, that have gathered together countless good deeds, that am waiting for countless crowns, that desired Him so much, as to value His love above all things, who all my days am burning for Him, and hold all things (Phil. iii. 8) of second importance to the love of Him. For even being loved by Christ was not the only thing he cared for, but loving Him exceedingly also. And this last he cared most for (τούτου μάλιστα ἦν). So it was that he looked to this only, and took all things light-heartedly. For he kept one aim in view in all circumstances, the fulfilling of this excellent love. And this he wishes for. But since things were not to take this course, nor he to become accursed,[1] he next attempts to go into a defence against the charges, and so to bring what was bruited abroad by all before them as to overthrow it. And before he openly enters into his defence against these, he first lays down some seeds of it beforehand. For when he says, " to whom pertaineth the adoption, and the glory, and the giving of the Law, and the service of God, and the promises," he does but say that God willed them indeed to be saved, and this he showed by His former dealings, and by Christ's having sprung from them, and by what He promised to the Fathers. But they out of their own untreatable temper thrust the benefit away from them. And this is also the reason of his setting down such things as set forth God's gift, not such as were encomiums upon them. For the adoption came of His grace, and so too the glory, and the promises, and the Law. After taking all these things then into consideration, and reflecting how earnest God along with His Son, had been for their salvation, he lifts up his voice aloud, and says," Who is[2] blessed forever. Amen."

So himself offering up thanksgiving for all men unto the Only-Begotten of God. What, he says, if others do blaspheme? Still we who know His mysteries, and His unspeakable Wisdom, and great Providence over us, know well that it is not to be blasphemed, but to be glorified, that He is worthy. Still not satisfied with being himself conscious of it, he endeavors next to use arguments, and to use a sharper way of speech against them. And he does not direct his aim at them, without first divesting them of a suspicion they had. Lest then he should seem to be addressing them as enemies, further on he says " Brethren, my heart's desire and prayer to God for Israel is,

that they might be saved." (Rom. x. 1.) And here, along with other remarks, he so ordered things, as not to seem to be saying what he was going to say out of enmity against them. Hence he does not decline calling them even kinsmen and brothers. For even if it was for Christ's sake that he said what he did, still he is for drawing (ἐπισπᾶται) their mind to him also,[3] and paves his way to what he has to say, and quits himself of all suspicion owing to what had to be said against them, and then he at last goes into the subject most of them were looking for. For many, as I have already stated, wanted to know what was the reason why they who had received the promise fell short of it, while those who had even never heard of it were saved before them. Therefore, to clear up this difficulty, he brings forward the answer before the objection. For to prevent any from saying, What? Art thou more thoughtful for God's glory than God is for His own? And does He need thy aid that His word may not fall to the ground? In reply to these things he says, I spoke this not as if God's Word had fallen to the ground, but to show my love for Christ. For as things have had this issue, we are in no want of words in God's behalf, or of showing that stand His promise did. God said to Abraham, "To thee and to thy seed will I give the land." And, "In thy seed shall all the nations of the earth be blessed." (Gen. xii. 7, 3.) Let us see then, he says, of what sort this seed is. For it is not all that are from him that are his seed. Whence he says, "For they are not all Israel that are of (or from) Israel."

Ver. 7. "Neither, because they are the seed of Abraham, are they all children."

Now when you come to know of what kind the seed of Abraham is, you will see that the promise is given to his seed, and know that the word hath not fallen to the ground. * Of what kind, pray, is the seed then? It is no saying of mine, he means, but the Old Testament itself explains itself by saying as

---

[1] This passage makes, perhaps, a comment on the words, Luke ix. 24, Whosoever will lose his life (τὴν ψυχὴν), the same shall save it.

[2] So all copies of St. Chrys. The following words, however, imply that this was not his reading of the text, (which had before been read at length, as the first words of this Homily show, see p. 459), he quotes it as in our text, in Hom. xx. on I Cor. viii. 5, p. 266 O. T. and elsewhere. See note in Mill's G. T. All Mss. agree with the rec. text.

[3] I Ms. he is aware of their way of thinking, ἐπίσταται, this gives a more common sense to διάνοιαν.

* At v. 6 begins Paul's theodicy in view of the lapse of the Israelites. The argument of vv. 6-13 is : God's promise cannot fail because it applies to the *true Israel*. This point he illustrates from Old Testament examples. The argument throughout this chapter is conducted from the point of view of God's sovereign election. In the two subsequent chapters, other considerations drawn from the freedom and disobedience of the people are introduced. It is as if the apostle had said: God has done according to His sovereign good pleasure. We might leave the matter there. To one who should say : why then does he blame me? (v. 19), or : why has he made me thus? (23), we might reply : who art thou to reply against God? The apostle does not rest the consideration of the case with the presentation of this view. In the closing verses of the chap. he shifts the point of view and asks: *why* did Israel fail? why was she cut off and the Gentiles chosen? (31). He answers, because they did not seek righteousness by faith ; they were not trustful and obedient, and hence they found the Messiah a stone of stumbling and failed to realize the ideal of their prophetic history.—G. B. S.

follows, "In Isaac shall thy seed be called."
(Gen. xxi. 12.) What is, "In Isaac?"
Explain.

Ver. 8. "That is, they which are the
children of the flesh, these are not the children of God: but the children of the promise, these are counted for the seed."

And observe the judgment and depth of
Paul's mind. For in interpreting, he does
not say, "they which are the children of the
flesh, these are not" the children of Abraham, but, "the children of God:" so blending the former things with the present, and
showing that even Isaac was not merely
Abraham's son. And what he means is
something of this sort: as many as have been
born as Isaac was, they are sons of God, and
of the seed of Abraham. And this is why he
said, "in Isaac shall thy seed be called."
That one may learn that they who are born
after the fashion of Isaac, these are in the
truest sense Abraham's children. In what
way was Isaac born then? Not according to
the law of nature, not according to the power
of the flesh, but according to the power of the
promise. What is meant then by the power
of "the promise?"

Ver. 9. "At this time will I come, and
Sarah shall have a son."

This promise then and word of God it was
that fashioned Isaac, and begat him. For
what if a womb was its instrument and the
belly of a woman? Since it was not the
power of the belly, but the might of the
promise that begat the child. Thus are we
also gendered by the words of God. Since in
the pool of water it is the words of God
which generate and fashion us. For it is by
being baptized into the Name of the Father
and of the Son and of the Holy Ghost that
we are gendered. And this birth is not of
nature, but of the promise of God. (John iii.
3; Eph. v. 26; James i. 18; 1 Pet. iii. 21.)
For as after first foretelling the birth of
Isaac, He then accomplished it; so ours also
He had announced before, many ages ago by
all the Prophets, and afterwards brought it
to pass. You know how great He has set it
forth as being, and how, as He promised a
great thing, He furnished it with abundant
ease! (Hos. ii. 1, etc.) But if the Jews
were to say, that the words, "In Isaac shall
thy seed be called," mean this, that those born
of Isaac should be reckoned to him for a
seed, then the Edomites too, and all those
people, ought to be denominated his sons,
since their forefather Esau was a son of his.
But now so far are they from being called
sons, that they are the greatest possible
aliens. You see then that it is not the chil-

dren of the flesh that are the children of God,
but that even in nature itself the generation
by means of baptism from above was sketched
out beforehand. And if you tell me of the
womb, I in return have to tell you of the
water. But as in this case all is of the Spirit,
so in the other all was of promise. For the
womb was more chilled than any water owing
to barrenness and to old age. Let us then
gain accurate knowledge of our own nobility,
and display a life worthy of it. For in it is
nothing fleshly or earthy: hence neither let
there be in us. For it was neither sleep, nor
the will of the flesh (John i. 13), nor em-
braces, nor the madness of desire, but "God's
love toward man," which wrought the whole.
(Tit. iii. 5.) And as in that case it was when
the age was past hope, so in this also it was
when the old age of sins had come over us,
that Isaac[1] suddenly sprang up in youth, and
we all became the children of God, and the
seed of Abraham. (Is. xl. 31.)

Ver. 10. "And not only this; but when
Rebecca also had conceived by one, even by
our father Isaac."

The subject in question was an important
one. Hence he turns to several arguments,
and endeavors by all means to solve the
difficulty. For if it was at once strange and
new for them to be cast out after so great
promises, it is much more strange that we
even should come into their good things, who
did not expect anything of the kind. And
the case was the same as if a king's son, who
had promises made him that he should succeed to the power he had, were to be cast
into the level of disreputable men, and in
his place a condemned man, and one laden
with evils unnumbered, after being taken out
of prison, were to come into the power, which
properly was the other's. For he means,
what have you to say? that the son is unworthy? Well, but so is this man unworthy, and
much more so. Hence he ought either to
have been punished along with the former,
or to have been honored along with him.
Now it was something of this sort which befel
the Jews and the Gentiles, or something far
more strange than this. Now that all were
unworthy, he has shown above, where he
says, "For all have sinned, and come short
of the glory of God." (Rom. iii. 23.) But the
new thing is, that when all were unworthy,
the Gentiles were saved alone. And beside
this there is another difficulty that some one
may start, he says. If God had no intention
of fulfilling the promises to them, why make
them at all? For men who know not the

---

[1] i. e. the true Seed of promise.

future, and are many times deceived, do promise even the undeserving that they shall have their largesses. But He Who knoweth beforehand things to come as well as things present, and hath a clear knowledge that they will make themselves undeserving of the promises, and therefore will not receive any of the things specified,—why should He promise at all? Now what is Paul's way of meeting all this? It is by showing what the Israel is to whom He made the promise. For when this has been shown, there is at the same time demonstrated the fact that the promises were all fulfilled. And to point this out he said, "For they are not all Israel that are of Israel." And this is why he does not use the name of Jacob,[1] but that of Israel, which was a sign of the virtue of that just man, and of a gift from above, and of having seen God. (Gen. xxxii. 28.) Yet, "all," he says, "have sinned, and come short of the glory of God." (Rom. iii. 23.) Now if all have sinned, how come some to be saved, and some to perish? It is because all were not minded to come to Him, since for His part all were saved, for all were called. However, he does not set this down yet awhile, but meets it from an advantageous position, and from other examples, by bringing before them another question, and as in the former case meets a difficulty very great, by another difficulty. For when he was discussing how by Christ being justified all the rest enjoyed that righteousness, he brought in Adam's case, saying, "For if by one man's offence death reigned, much more they which receive abundance of grace shall reign in life." (Rom. v. 17. And the case of Adam, indeed, he does not clear up, but from it he clears up His (or his own), and shows that it was more reasonable that He Who died in their behalf should have power over them at His will. For that when one had sinned all should be punished, does not seem to be so very reasonable to most men. But that when One had done aright all should be justified, is at once more reasonable and more suited to God. Yet still he has not solved the difficulty he raised. For the more obscure that point remained, the more the Jew was put to silence. And the difficulty of his position passed over to the other, and this become clearer from it (Mar. and 4 Mss. "than that"). So in this passage also, it is by raising other difficulties that he meets the questions raised, inasmuch as it was against Jews that he was contending. Hence he takes no pains to solve the exam-

ples which he has brought before us. For he was not answerable for[2] them as in the fight against the Jews. But from them he makes his own subject throughout clearer. Why do you feel surprised, he means, that some of the Jews were saved, and some not saved at this time? Why of old, in the patriarch's times, one may see this happening. For why was Isaac only called the seed, and yet he was the father of Ishmael also, and of several others. "But he was of a mother that was a slave." And what has this to do with his father? Still I will not be captious. Let this son be set aside on his mother's account. What are we to say of those sprung from Keturah? were they not free, and from a mother that was free? How came they not to be honored with the same preference as Isaac? And why do I speak of these? for Rebecca was even Isaac's only wife, and bearing two children she bore them both to Isaac; still those so born, though of the same father, and the same mother, and the fruit of the same labor, being both of one father and one mother, and twins besides, yet did not enjoy the same lot. And yet here you have no mother's slavery to account for it, as in Ishmael's case, nor can you say that one was begotten of this womb and the other of a different one, as in the case of Keturah and Sarah, since in this case they had the same hour in common to them for their birth. This was why Paul then, in order to give a clearer example, says that this happened not in Isaac's case only, "but when Rebecca also had conceived by one, even by our father Isaac."

Ver. 11-13. "For the children being not yet born, neither having done any good or evil, that the purpose of God according to election might stand, not of works, but of him that calleth, it was said unto her, the elder shall serve the younger. As it is written, Jacob have I loved, but Esau have I hated."

What was the cause then why one was loved and the other hated? why was it that one served, the other was served? It was because one was wicked, and the other good.[3] And yet the children being not yet born, one was honored and the other condemned. For when they were not as yet born, God said, "the elder shall serve the younger." With what intent then did God say this? Because He doth not wait, as man doth, to see from the issue of their acts the good and him who

---

[1] Didymus in Psalm xcvii. 3, and Hesych. ps. lii. 7, ap. Corderium, t. 2.

[2] Gr. to them, i. e. to them considered as objections. Compare Matt. xxi. 27. "Neither tell I you by what authority I do these things.
[3] If this is to be read interrogatively, so as to imply the negative, it must be understood of that time exclusively, as the context shows.

is not so, but even before these He knoweth which is the wicked and which not such. And this took place in the Israelites' case also, in a still more wonderful way. Why, he says, do I speak of Esau and of Jacob, of whom one was wicked and the other good? For in the Israelites' case, the sin belonged to all, since they all worshipped the calf. Yet notwithstanding some had mercy shown them, and others had not.[1]

Ver. 15. "For I will have mercy, He says, on whom I will have mercy, and I will show compassion on whom I will show compassion." (Ex. xxxiii. 19.)

This one may see also in the case of those who are punished, for what would you say of Pharaoh who was punished, and had to pay so heavy a penalty? You say he was hardened and disobedient. Was he then alone such, and not even one person else? How came he then to be so severely punished? Why even in the case of the Jews did he call that a people which was no people, or again, why not count all worthy of equal honor? "For if they be" (it says) "as the sand of the sea, yet shall a remnant be saved." (Is. x. 22.) And why is it to be only a remnant? You see what difficulty he has filled the subject with. And with great propriety. For when you have power to throw your adversary into perplexity, do not at once bring forward the answer, because if he be found himself responsible for the same ignorance, why take unnecessary dangers upon yourself? Why make him more bold, by drawing it all upon yourself? Now tell me, O thou Jew, that hast so many perplexing questions, and art unable to answer any of them, how thou comest to annoy us on account of the call of the Gentiles? I, however, have a good reason to give you why the Gentiles were justified and ye were cast out. And what is the reason? It is that they are of faith, ye of the works of the Law. And it is owing to this obstinacy of yours that ye have in every way (Mar. and several Mss. all) been given up. For, "they being ignorant of God's righteousness, and going about to establish their own righteousness, have not submitted themselves unto the righteousness of God." (Rom. x. 3.) The clearing up then of the whole passage, to give the whole sense summarily, is here brought out by that blessed person. But that this may be clearer, let us investigate the things he says also one by one; this knowing, that what the blessed Paul aimed at was, to show by all that he said that God only knoweth who are worthy, and no man whatever knoweth, even if he

seem to know ever so well, but that in this sentence of his there are sundry aberrations. For He that knoweth the secrets of the hearts, He only knoweth for a certainty who deserve a crown, and who punishment and vengeance. Hence it is that many of those, by men esteemed good, He convicts and punishes, and those suspected to be bad He crowns, after showing it not to be so; thus forming his sentence not after the judgment of us slaves, but after his own keen and uncorrupt decision, and not waiting for the issue of actions to look at the wicked and him who is not so therefrom. But that we may not make the subject more obscure, again let us go to the very words of the Apostle.

Ver. 10. "And not only this, but when Rebecca also had conceived by one."

I might, he implies, have mentioned the children by Keturah besides, but I do not. But to gain the victory from a vantage ground it is those born of one and the same father, and mother too, that I bring forward. For they were both sprung from Rebecca, and from Isaac the true-born, the elect, the son honored above all, of whom He said, "In Isaac shall thy seed be called," who became "the father of us all;" but if he was our father, then should his sons have been our fathers; yet it was not so. You see how this happens not in Abraham's case only, but also in that of his son himself, and how it is faith and virtue in all cases that is conspicuous, and gives the real relationship its character. For hence we learn that it is not only from the manner of birth, but owing to their being worthy of the father's virtue, that the children are called children of him. For if it were only owing to the manner of the birth, then ought Esau to have enjoyed the same as Jacob did. For he also was from a womb as good as dead, and his mother was barren. Yet this was not the only thing required, but the character too, which fact contributes no common amount of practical instruction for us. And he does not say that one is good and another bad, and so the former was honored; lest this kind of argument should be wielded against him, "What, are those of the Gentiles good men rather than those of the circumcision?" For even supposing the truth of the matter was so, still he does not state it yet, as that would have seemed to be vexatious. But it is upon God's knowledge that he has cast the whole, and this no one would venture to gainsay, though he were ever so frantic. "For the children being not yet born," he says, "it was said unto her, The elder shall serve the younger." And he shows that noble birth after the flesh is of no avail, but

---

[1] He refers to the occasion on which the words next quoted were spoken, viz. when Moses interceded for them after that sin.

we must seek for virtue of soul, which even before the works of it God knoweth of. For "the children," he says, "being not yet born, nor having done any good or evil, that the purpose¹ of God according to election might stand, it was said unto her that the elder shall serve the younger:" for this was a sign of foreknowledge, that they were chosen from the very birth. That the election made according to foreknowledge, might be manifestly of God, from the first day He at once saw and proclaimed which was good and which not. Do not then tell me that thou hast read the Law (he means) and the Prophets, and hast been a servant for such a long time. For He that knoweth how to assay the soul, knoweth which is worthy of being saved. Yield then to the incomprehensibleness of the election. For it is He alone Who knoweth how to crown aright. How many, for instance, seemed better than St. Matthew; to go by the exhibition of works more visible. But He that knoweth things undeclared, and is able to assay the mind's aptitude, knew the pearl though lying in the mire, and after passing by others, and being well pleased with the beauty of this, He elected it, and by adding to the noble born free-will grace from Himself, He made it approved. For if in the case of these arts which are perishable, and indeed in other matters, those that are good judges do not use the grounds on which the uninstructed form their decision, in selecting out of what is put before them; but from points which they are themselves well aware of, they many times disparage that which the uninstructed approve, and decide upon what they disparage: and horse-breakers often do this with horses, and so the judges of precious stones, and workmen in other arts: much more will the God that loveth man, the infinite Wisdom, Who alone hath a clear knowledge of all things, not allow of man's guesses, but will out of His own exact and unfailing Wisdom pass his sentence upon all men. Hence it was that He chose the publican, the thief, and the harlot; but dishonored priests, and elders, and rulers, and cast them out. And this one may see happening in the martyrs' case also. Many accordingly of those who were utterly cast aside, have in the time of trial been crowned. And, on the other hand, some that have been held great ones by many have stumbled² and fallen. Do not then call the Creator to account, nor say, Why is it that one was crowned and another punished? For He knoweth how to do these things with exact-

ness. Whence also he says, "Jacob have I loved, and Esau have I hated." That it was with justice, you indeed know from the result: but Himself even before the result knew it clearly. For it is not a mere exhibition of works that God searcheth after, but a nobleness of choice and an obedient temper (γνώμην εὐγνώμονα) besides. For a man of this kind, if he should ever sin through some surprise,³ will speedily recover himself. And if he should even stay long haply in a state of vice, he will not be overlooked, but God Who knoweth all things will speedily draw him out. And so he that is herein corrupted, even if he seem to do some good things, will perish, in that he doth this with an ill intention. Hence even David, after committing murder and adultery, since he did this as being carried away by surprise, and not from habitual practice of wickedness, speedily washed it out. The Pharisee, however, who had not perpetrated any such crime (Luke xviii. 11), but even had good deeds besides to boast of, lost all by the bad spirit he had chosen.

Ver. 14. "What shall we say then? Is there unrighteousness with God? God forbid."

Hence there is no such thing in the case of us and the Jews. And then he goes on with another thing, a more clear than this. And of what sort is it?

Ver. 15. "For he saith to Moses, I will have mercy on whom I will have mercy, and I will have compassion on whom I will have compassion."

Here again he adds force to the objection by dividing it in two and meeting it, and starting another fresh difficulty. But to make what I have said clearer, one must needs explain it. God, he means, said that "the elder shall serve the younger," before the travail. What then? "Is God unrighteous?" By no means. Now listen to what follows also. For in that case the virtue or the vice, might be the decisive thing. But here there was one sin on which all the Jews joined, that of the molten calf, and still some were punished, and some were not punished. And this is why He says, "I will have mercy on whom I will have mercy, and I will have compassion on whom I will have compassion." (Ex. xxxiii. 19: observe context.) For it is not thine to know, O Moses, he means, which are deserving of My love toward man, but leave this to Me. But if Moses had no right to know, much less have we. And this is why he did not barely quote the passage, but also called to our

¹ This expression supports St. Augustin's interpretation of Rom. viii. 28.
² Perhaps alluding to the supplanting of Esau.
³ Literally under some circumstance, but περιστάσις implies surrounding and assault.

minds to whom it was said. For it is Moses, he means, that he is speaking to, that at least by the dignity of the person he might make the objector modest. Having then given a solution of the difficulties raised, he divides it in two, by bringing forward another objection besides, as follows :

Ver. 16, 17. "So then it is not of him that willeth, nor of him that runneth, but of God that showeth mercy.¹ For the Scripture saith unto Pharaoh, Even for this same purpose have I raised thee up, that I might show my power in thee, and that my name might be declared throughout all the earth."

As then in the one case, he means, some were saved and some were punished, so here also. This man was reserved for this very purpose. And then he again urges the objection.

Ver. 18, 19. "Therefore He hath mercy on whom He will have mercy, and whom He will He hardeneth. Thou wilt say then unto me, Why doth he then find fault? For who hath resisted His will?"

See what pains he takes to embarrass the subject in every way. And the answer he does not produce forthwith, it being a useful thing not to do so, but he first stops the disputant's mouth, saying as follows,

Ver. 20. "Nay but, O man, who art thou that repliest against God?"

This he does to take down the objector's unseasonable inquisitiveness, and excessive curiosity, and to put a check upon it, and teach him to know what God is, and what man, and how incomprehensible His fore-knowledge is, and how far above our reason, and how obedience to Him in all points is binding. So when he has made this preparatory step in his hearer, and has hushed and softened down his spirit, then with great felicity he introduces the answer, having made what he says easy of admittance with him. And he does not say, it is impossible to answer questions of this kind, but that (5 Mss. No, but what? that) it is presumptuous to raise them. For our business is to obey what God does, not to be curious even if we do not know the reason of them. Wherefore he said, "Who art thou that repliest against God?" You see how very light he makes of him, how he bears down his swelling spirit! "Who art thou?" art thou a sharer of His power? (compare

Job xxxviii.) nay, art thou sitting in judgment upon God? Why in comparison with Him thou canst not have a being even! nor this or that sort of being, but absolutely none! For the expression, "who art thou?" doth much more set him at naught than "thou art nothing." And he takes other ways of showing further his indignation in the question, and does not say, "Who art thou that" answerest "God?" but, "that repliest against," that is, that gainsayest, and that opposest. For the saying things ought to be so, and ought not to be so, is what a man does that "replieth against." See how he scares them, how he terrifies them, how he makes them tremble rather than be questioning and curious. This is what an excellent teacher does ; he does not follow his disciples' fancy everywhere, but leads them to his own mind, and pulls up the thorns, and then puts the seed in, and does not answer at once in all cases to the questions put to him.

Ver. 20, 21. "Shall the thing formed say to Him that formed it, Why hast Thou made me thus? Hath not the potter (Read Jer. xviii. 1–10) power, of the same lump to make one vessel unto honor, and another unto dishonor?"

Here it is not to do away with free-will that he says this, but to show, up to what point we ought to obey God. For in respect of calling God to account, we ought to be as little disposed to it as the clay is. For we ought to abstain not from gainsaying or questioning only, but even from speaking or thinking of it at all, and to become like that lifeless matter, which followeth the potter's hands, and lets itself be drawn about anywhere he may please. And this is the only point he applied the illustration to, not, that is, to any enunciation of the rule of life, but to the complete obedience and silence enforced upon us. And this we ought to observe in all cases, that we are not to take the illustrations quite entire, but after selecting the good of them, and that for which they were introduced, to let the rest alone. As, for instance, when he says, "He couched, he lay down as a lion;" (Numb. xxiv. 9) let us take out the indomitable and fearful part, not the brutality, nor any other of the things belonging to a lion. And again, when He says, "I will meet them as a bereaved bear" (Hos. xiii. 8), let us take the vindictiveness. And when he says, "our God is a consuming fire" (Deut. iv. 24; and Heb. xii. 29), the wasting power exerted in punishing. So also here must we single out the clay, the potter, and the vessels. And when he does go on to say, "Hath not the

---

¹ One Ms. adds, "Isaac, for his part, wished to bless Esau, he ran to the field (παιδίον, by a common mistake for πεδίον) to do his father's bidding, desirous of the blessing. But God brought in Jacob who was worthy, and by a just judgment declared him deserving of the blessing."

potter power over the clay, of the same lump to make one vessel unto honor, and another unto dishonor?" do not suppose that this is said by Paul as an account of the creation, nor as implying a necessity over the will, but to illustrate the sovereignty and difference of dispensations; for if we do not take it in this way, divers incongruities will follow, for if here he were speaking about the will, and those who are good and those not so, He will be Himself the Maker of these, and man will be free from all responsibility. And at this rate, Paul will also be shown to be at variance with himself, as he always bestows chief honor upon free choice. There is nothing else then which he here wishes to do, save to persuade the hearer to yield entirely to God, and at no time to call Him to account for anything whatever. For as the potter (he says) of the same lump makes what he pleaseth, and no one forbids it; thus also when God, of the same race of men, punisheth some, and honoreth others, be not thou curious nor meddlesome herein, but worship only, and imitate the clay. And as it followeth the hands of the potter, so do thou also the mind of Him that so ordereth things. For He worketh nothing at random, or mere hazard, though thou be ignorant of the secret of His Wisdom. Yet thou allowest the other of the same lump to make divers things, and findest no fault: but of Him you demand an account of His punishments and honors, and will not allow Him to know who is worthy and who is not so; but since the same [1] lump is of the same substance, you assert that there are the same dispositions. And how monstrous this is! And yet not even is it on the potter that the honor and the dishonor of the things made of the lump depends, but upon the use made by those that handle them, so here also it depends on the free choice. Still, as I said before, one must take this illustration to have one bearing only, which is that one should not contravene God, but yield to His incomprehensible Wisdom. For the examples ought to be greater than the subject, and than the things on account of which they are brought forward, so as to draw on the hearer better. Since if they were not greater and did not mount far above it, he could not attack as he ought, and shame the objectors. However, their ill-timed obstinacy he silenced in this way with becoming superiority. And then he introduces his answer. Now what is the answer?

Ver. 22, 23, 24. "What if God, willing to show His wrath, and to make His power known, endured with much long-suffering the vessels of wrath fitted to destruction: and that He might make known the riches of His glory on the vessels of mercy, which He had afore prepared unto glory, even us, whom He hath chosen, not of the Jews only, but also of the Gentiles."

What he means is somewhat as follows. Pharaoh was a vessel of wrath, that is, a man who by his own hard-heartedness had kindled the wrath of God. For after enjoying much long-suffering, he became no better, but remained unimproved. Wherefore he calleth him not only "a vessel of wrath," but also one "fitted for destruction." That is, fully fitted indeed, but by his own proper self.[2] For neither had God left out aught of the things likely to recover him, nor did he leave out aught of those that would ruin him, and put him beyond any forgiveness. Yet still, though God knew this, "He endured him with much long-suffering," being willing to bring him to repentance. For had He not willed this, then He would not have been thus long-suffering. But as he would not use the long-suffering in order to repentance, but fully fitted himself for wrath, He used him for the correction of others, through the punishment inflicted upon him making them better, and in this way setting forth His power. For that it is not God's wish that His power be so made known, but in another way, by His benefits, namely, and kindnesses, he had shown above in all possible ways. For if Paul does not wish to appear powerful in this way ("not that we should appear approved," he says, "but that ye should do that which is honest,") (2 Cor. xiii. 7), much less doth God. But after that he had shown long-suffering, that He might lead to repentance, but he did not repent, He suffered him a long time, that He might display at once His goodness and His power, even if that man were not minded to gain anything from this great long-suffering. As then by punishing this man, who continued incorrigible, He showed His power, so by having pitied those who had done many sins but repented, He manifested His love toward man. But it does not say, love towards man, but glory, to show that this is especially God's glory, and for this He was above all things earnest. But in saying, "which He had afore prepared unto glory," he does not mean that all is God's doing. Since if this were so, there were nothing to hinder all men from being saved. But he is setting forth again

[1] Such is plainly the sense, but most Mss. have τὸ αὐτὸ φύραμα τῆς οὐσίας ἐστὶ, it is the same lump in regard of the substance.

[2] The Greek word, κατηρτισμένον, makes this more obvious.

His foreknowledge, and doing away with the difference between the Jews and the Gentiles. And on this topic again he grounds a defence of his statement, which is no small one. For it was not in the case of the Jews only that some men perished, and some were saved, but with the Gentiles also this was the case. Wherefore he does not say, all the Gentiles, but, "of the Gentiles," nor, all the Jews, but, "of the Jews." As then Pharaoh became a vessel of wrath by his own lawlessness, so did these become vessels of mercy by their own readiness to obey. For though the more part is of God, still they also have contributed themselves some little. Whence he does not say either, vessels of well-doing, or vessels of boldness (παρρησίας), but "vessels of mercy," to show that the whole is of God. For the phrase, "it is not of him that willeth, nor of him that runneth," even if it comes in the course of the objection, still, were it said by Paul, would create no difficulty. Because when he says, "it is not of him that willeth, nor of him that runneth," he does not deprive us of free-will, but shows that all is not one's own, for that it requires grace from above. For it is binding on us to will, and also to run : but to confide not in our own labors, but in the love of God toward man. And this he has expressed elsewhere. "Yet not I, but the grace which was with me." (1 Cor. xv. 10.) And he well says, "Which He had afore prepared unto glory." For since they reproached them with this, that they were saved by grace, and thought to make them ashamed, he far more than sets aside this insinuation. For if the thing brought glory even to God, much more to them through whom God was glorified. But observe his forbearance, and unspeakable wisdom. For when he had it in his power to adduce, as an instance of those punished, not Pharaoh, but such of the Jews as had sinned, and so make his discourse much clearer, and show that where there were the same fathers, and the same sins, some perished, and some had mercy shown them, and persuade them not to be doubtful-minded, even if some of the Gentiles were saved, while the Jews were perishing; that he might not make his discourse irksome, the showing forth of the punishment he draws from the foreigner, so that he may not be forced to call them "vessels of wrath." But those that obtained mercy he draws from the people of the Jews. And besides, he also has spoken in a sufficient way in God's behalf, because though He knew very well that the nation was fitting itself as a vessel of destruction, still He contributed all on His part, His patience, His long-suffering, and that not merely long-suffering, but "much

long-suffering;" yet still he was not minded to state it barely against the Jews. Whence then are some vessels of wrath, and some of mercy? Of their own free choice. God, however, being very good, shows the same kindness to both. For it was not those in a state of salvation only to whom He showed mercy, but also Pharaoh, as far as His part went. For of the same long-suffering, both they and he had the advantage. And if he was not saved, it was quite owing to his own will : since, as for what concerneth God, he had as much done for him as they who were saved. Having then given to the question that answer which was furnished by facts, in order to give his discourse the advantage of other testimony in its favor, he introduces the prophets also making the same declarations aforetime. For Hosea, he says, of old put this in writing, as follows :

Ver. 25. "I will call them My people, which were not My people ; and her beloved, which was not beloved."

Here to prevent their saying, that you are deceiving us here with specious reasoning, he calls Hosea to witness, who crieth and saith, "I will call them My people, who were not My people." (Hos. ii. 23.) Who then are the not-people ? Plainly, the Gentiles. And who the not-beloved ? The same again. However, he says, that they shall become at once people, and beloved, and sons of God.

Ver. 26. "For even they shall be called," he says, "the children of the living God."

But if they should assert that this was said of those of the Jews who believed, even then the argument stands. For if with those who after so many benefits were hard-hearted and estranged, and had lost their being as a people, so great a change was wrought, what is there to prevent even those who were not estranged after being taken to Him, but were originally aliens, from being called, and, provided they obey, from being counted worthy of the same blessings? Having then done with Hosea, he does not content himself with him only, but also brings Isaiah in after him, sounding in harmony with him.

Ver. 27. "For Esaias," he says, "crieth concerning Israel."

That is, speaks out boldly, and uses no dissimulation. Why then lay a charge against us, when they afore declared the same thing with more than trumpet's loudness? And what does Isaiah cry? "Though the number of the children of Israel be as the sand of the sea, a remnant shall be saved. (Is. x. 22.)

Do you see that he too does not say that all are to be saved, but that those that are worthy shall? For I regard not the multitude, he means, nor does a race diffused so far distress me, but those only do I save that yield themselves worthy of it. And he does not mention the "sand of the sea" without a reason, but to remind them of the ancient promise whereof they had made themselves unworthy. Why then are you troubled, as though the promise had failed, when all the Prophets show that it is not all that are to be saved? Then he mentions the mode of the salvation also. Observe the accuracy of the Prophet, and the judgment of the Apostle, what a testimony he has cited, how exceedingly apposite! For it not only shows us that those to be saved are some and not all, but also adds the way they are to be saved. How then are they to be saved, and how will God count them worthy of the benefit?

Ver. 28. "He will finish the work, and cut it short in righteousness," he says, "because a short work will the Lord make upon the earth." (Ib. 23, LXX.)

What he means then is somewhat of this sort. There is no need of fetching a circuit, and of trouble, and the vexation of the works of the Law, for the salvation is by a very short way. For such is faith, it holds salvation in a few short words. "For if thou shalt confess with thy mouth the Lord Jesus, and believe in thine heart that God hath raised Him from the dead, thou shalt be saved." (Rom. x. 9.) Now you see what this, "the Lord shall make a short word (LXX. lit.) upon earth," is. And what is indeed wonderful is, that this short word carries with it not salvation only, but also righteousness.

Ver 29. "And as Esaias said before, Except the Lord of Sabaoth had left us a seed, we had been as Sodoma, and had been made like unto Gomorrha." (Is. i. 9.)

Here again he shows another thing, that not even those few were saved from their own resources. For they too would have perished, and met with Sodom's fate, that is, they would have had to undergo utter destruction (for they (of Sodom) were also destroyed root and branch, and left not even the slightest remnant of themselves,) and they too, he means, would have been like these, unless God had used much kindness to them, and had saved them by faith. And this happened also in the case of the visible captivity, the majority having been taken away captive and perished, and some few only being saved.

Ver. 30, 31. "What shall we say then? That the Gentiles, which followed not after righteousness, have attained to righteousness, even the righteousness which is by faith. But Israel, which followed after the law of right-

eousness, hath not attained to the law of righteousness."

Here at last is the clearest answer. For since he had used a proof as well from facts ("for they are not all Israel that are of Israel") as from the case of the forefathers Jacob and Esau, and from the prophets Hosea and Isaiah, he further gives the most decisive answer, after first adding to the perplexity. The points discussed, then, are two; one that the Gentiles attained, and the other that they attained it without following after it, that is, without taking pains about it. And again in the Jews' case also there are two difficulties of the same kind; one that Israel attained not, the other that, though they took pains, they attained not. Whence also his use of words is more emphatical. For he does not say that they had, but that they "attained to righteousness." For what is especially new and unusual is, that they who followed after it attained not, but they which followed not after it attained. And he seems to be indulging them by saying, "followed after." But afterwards he strikes the blow home. For since he had a strong answer to give them, he had no fear of making the objection a little harsher. Hence he doth not speak of faith either, and the righteousness ensuing thereon, but shows that before the faith even, on their own ground they were worsted and condemned. For thou, O Jew, he says, hast not found even the righteousness which was by the Law. For thou hast transgressed it, and become liable to the curse. But these that came not through the Law, but by another road, have found a greater righteousness than this, that, namely, which is of faith. And this he had also said before. "For if Abraham was justified by works, he hath whereof to glory, but not before God" (Rom. iv.): so showing that the other righteousness was greater than this. Before, then, I said that there were two difficulties, but now they have even become three questions: that the Gentiles found righteousness, and found it without following after it, and found a greater than that of the Law. These same difficulties are again felt in the Jews' case with an opposite view. That Israel did not find, and though he took pains he did not find, and did not find even the less. Having then thrust his hearer into perplexity, he proceeds to give a concise answer, and tells him the cause of all that is said. When then is the cause?

Ver. 32. "Because they sought it not by faith, but as it were by the works of the Law."

This is the clearest answer in the passage, which if he had said immediately upon starting, he would not have gained so easy a hearing. But since it is after many perplexities, and preparations, and demonstrations that he sets it down, and after using countless preparatory steps, he has at last made it more intelligible, and also more easily admitted. For this he says is the cause of their destruction : " Because it was not by faith, but as it were by the works of the Law," that they wished to be justified. And he does not say, " by works," but, " as it were by the works of the Law," to show that they had not even this righteousness.

" For they stumbled at that stumblingstone ; "

Ver. 33. " As it is written, Behold I lay in Sion a stumbling-stone, and rock of offence : and whosoever believeth on Him shall not be ashamed."

You see again how it is from faith that the boldness comes, and the gift is universal; since it is not of the Jews only that this is said, but also of the whole human race. For every one, he would say, whether Jew, or Grecian, or Scythian, or Thracian, or whatsoever else he may be, will, if he believes, enjoy the privilege of great boldness. But the wonder in the Prophet is that he foretells not only that they should believe, but also that they should not believe. For to stumble is to disbelieve. As in the former passage he points out them that perish and them that are saved, where he says, " If the number of the children of Israel be as the sand of the sea, the remnant shall be saved. And, If the Lord of Sabaoth had not left us a seed, we should have been as Sodoma." And, " He hath called not of the Jews only, but also of the Gentiles ; " so here too he implies that some will believe, and some will stumble. But stumbling comes of not taking heed, of gaping after other things. Since then they did give heed to the Law, they stumbled on the stone, " And a stone of stumbling and rock of offence " he calls it from the character and end of those that believe not.

Is then the language used made plain to you? or does it still want much in clearness? I think indeed that, to those who have been attending, it is easy to get a clear view of it. But if it has slipped anybody's memory, you can meet in private, and learn what it was. And this is why I have continued longer upon this explanatory part of the discourse, that I might not be compelled to break off the continuity of the context, and so spoil the clearness of the statements. And for this cause too I will bring my discourse to a conclusion here, without saying anything to you on the more immediately practical points, as I generally do, lest I should make a fresh indistinctness in your memories by saying so much. It is time now to come to the proper conclusion, by shutting up the discourse with the doxology to the God of all. Let us then both pause, me that am speaking and you that are hearing, and offer up glory to Him. For His is the kingdom, and the power, and the glory, for ever and ever. Amen.

HOMILY XVII.

ROM. X. 1.

" Brethren, my heart's desire and prayer to God for them is, that they might be saved."

HE is now going again to rebuke them more vehemently than before.* Wherefore he again does away with every suspicion of hatred, and makes a great effort beforehand to correct misapprehension. Do not then, he says, mind words or accusations, but observe

---

* In ix. 30-33 Paul had stated that the reason of Israel's rejection was, that they sought after righteousness not by faith but by works, while the Gentiles sought it by faith and attained it. Chap. x. is an illustration and confirmation of this position. Its leading idea is, that the Jews could not be justified by works of the law, because a new system, that of faith, had come in with Christ and had displaced the old. The argument may be summarized thus: (1) Vv. 1, 2. Conciliatory introduction in which the apostle avows his love for his people. (2) Vv. 3, 4. Their method, however, of seeking righteousness by works is an effort to obtain a righteousness of their own, which is impossible. Christ has put an end to the system of works and He is himself the only means of attaining God's righteousness. At v. 5 begins the Scriptural argument concerning the two systems of works and faith. (3) Vv. 5-10. The principle of the system of works as stated by Moses is, keep the law and you will be saved by it. The principle of faith, on the other hand, is, not that of striving to reach something afar off, but of accepting the present truth. It is not struggle but acceptance; not attaining by merit, but receiving by grace. (4) Vv. 11-13. The Scriptures emphasize this principle of faith as the true principle of salvation, speaking of the assurance which it brings and that to all, regardless of nationality or outward condition. (5) Vv. 14, 15. But in order that men may accept this message, preachers must be sent to proclaim the glad tidings. (6) Vv. 16-21. This has been done in the case of the Jews. They cannot shelter themselves behind the excuse that they have not known God's message. The scriptures of the Old Testament reveal God and require faith in Him and also intimate the larger destination of the gospel for Gentiles as well as Jews.—G. B. S.

that it is not in any hostile spirit that I say
this. For it is not likely that the same person
should desire their salvation, and not desire it
only, but even pray for it, and yet should also
hate them, and feel aversion to them. For
here he calls his exceeding desire, and the
prayer which he makes (εὐδοκίαν), "heart's
desire." For it is not the being freed from
punishment only, but that they may also be
saved, that he makes so great a point of,
and prays for. Nor is it from this only, but
also from the sequel that he shows the good-
will that he hath towards them. For from
what is open to him, as far as he can, he
forces his way, and is contentious to find out
some shadow at least of an excuse for them.
And he hath not the power, being overcome
by the nature of the facts.

Ver. 2. "For I bear them record," says he,
"that they have a zeal of God, but not according to knowledge."

Ought not this then to be a ground for
pardoning and not for accusing them? For
if it is not of man[1] that they are separated, but
through zeal, they deserved to be pitied
rather than punished. But observe how
adroitly he favors them in the word, and yet
shows their unseasonable obstinacy.

Ver. 3. "For they being ignorant," he
says, "of God's righteousness."

Again the word would lead to pardon. But
the sequel to stronger accusation, and such as
does away with defence of any kind.

"And going about," he says, "to establish
their own righteousness, have not submitted
themselves unto the righteousness of God.

And these things he says to show, that it
was from a petulancy and love of power that
they erred, rather than from ignorance, and
that not even this righteousness from the deeds
of the Law did they establish. (Matt. xxi.
38; John. xii. 19, 42.) For saying "going
about to establish" is what one would do to
show this. And in plain words indeed he has
not stated this (for he has not said, that they
fell short of both righteousnesses), but he has
given a hint of it in a very judicious manner,
and with the wisdom so befitting him. For
if they are still "going about" to establish
that, it is very plain that they have not yet
established it. If they have not submitted
themselves to this, they have fallen short of
this also. But he calls it their "own righteousness," either because the Law was no
longer of force, or because it was one of
trouble and toil. But this he calls God's
righteousness, that from faith, because it
comes entirely from the grace from above, and

because men are justified in this case, not by
labors, but by the gift of God. But they that
evermore resisted the Holy Ghost, and vexa-
tiously tried to be justified by the Law, came
not over to the faith. But as they did not
come over to the faith, nor receive the righteousness thereupon ensuing, and were not
able to be justified by the Law either, they
were thrown out of all resources.

Ver. 4. "For Christ is the end of the
Law for righteousness to every one that
believeth.

See the judgment of Paul. For as he had
spoken of a righteousness, and a righteousness, lest they of the Jews which believed
should seem to have the one but be excluded
from the other, and to be accused of lawlessness (for even these there was no less cause
to fear about as being still newly come in),
and lest Jews should again expect to achieve
it, and should say, Though we have not at
present fulfilled it, yet we certainly will fulfil
it, see what ground he takes. He shows that
there is but one righteousness, and that has its
full issue[2] in this, and that he that hath taken
to himself this, the one by faith, hath fulfilled
that also. But he that rejects this, falls short
as well of that also. For if Christ be "the
end of the Law," he that hath not Christ,
even if he seem to have that righteousness,
hath it not. But he that hath Christ, even
though he have not fulfilled the Law aright,
hath received the whole. For the end of the
physician's art is health. As then he that can
make whole, even though he hath not the
physician's art, hath everything; but he that
knows not how to heal, though he seem to be
a follower of the art, comes short of everything: so is it in the case of the Law and of
faith. He that hath this hath the end of that
likewise, but he that is without this is an alien
from both. For what was the object of the
Law? To make man righteous. But it had
not the power, for no one fulfilled it. This
then was the end of the Law and to this it
looked throughout, and for this all its parts
were made, its feasts, and commandments, and
sacrifices, and all besides, that man might be
justified. But this end Christ gave a fuller
accomplishment of through faith.* Be not

---

[1] Referring to the expression, "a zeal of God," see 1 Cor.
iii. 3, Gr.

[2] Gr. "is summed up," ἀνακεφαλαιοῦται. See Irenæus,
31, 32; iii. 21, 9, 10; xxii. 1 Massuet pp. 293, 294 O. T. where he
says the creation is "recapitulated" in Christ. Also iv. 74,
78, v. 1; iv. 38, 1; 40. 3: v. 1, 2. Mass. pp. 436, 444, 451 O. T.
much to the same purpose, and v. 29, p. 518 O. T. of the recapitulation or consummation of iniquity in Antichrist; the word
is the same.
* By the "end of the law," the author seems to understand
the ability to secure righteousness to men which was the ideal
aim of the law but which it could not do. While this view is
correct enough in itself, it seems not to present the full force
of τέλος νόμου which is best taken, with most recent interpreters, (as Meyer, Godet, De Wette, Olshausen, Dwight) to
signify literally the end or termination of the law. Christ
puts an end to the law system by fulfilling it. The meaning

then afraid, he says, as if transgressing the Law in having come over to the faith. For then dost thou transgress it, when for it thou dost not believe Christ. If thou believest in Him, then thou hast fulfilled it also, and much more then it commanded. For thou hast received a much greater righteousness. Next, since this was an assertion, he again brings proof of it from the Scriptures.

Ver. 5. "For Moses," he says, " describeth the righteousness which is of the Law."

What he means is this. Moses showeth us the righteousness ensuing from the Law, what sort it is of, and whence. What sort is it then of, and what does it consist in? In fulfilling the commandments. "He (R. T. the man), that doeth these things," He says, "shall live by (or in), them." (Lev. xviii. 5.) And there is no other way of becoming righteous in the Law save by fulfilling the whole of it. But this has not been possible for any one, and therefore this righteousness has failed them. (διαπέπτωκεν). But tell us, Paul, of the other righteousness also, that which is of grace. What is that then, and of what does it consist? Hear the words in which he gives a clear sketch of it. For after he had refuted [1] the other, he next goes on to this, and says,

Ver. 6, 7, 8, 9. "But the righteousness which is of faith speaketh on this wise, Say not in thine heart, Who shall ascend into heaven (that is, to bring Christ down from above): or, Who shall descend into the deep? (that is, to bring up Christ again from the dead.) But what saith it? The word is nigh thee, even in thy mouth, and in thy heart, that is, the word of faith which we preach. That if thou shalt confess with thy mouth the Lord Jesus, and shalt believe in thine heart that God hath raised Him from the dead, thou shalt be saved.

To prevent the Jews then from saying, How came they who had not found the lesser righteousness to find the greater? he gives a reason there was no answering, that this way was easier than that. For that requires the fulfilment of all things (for when thou doest all, then thou shalt live); but the righteousness which is of faith doth not say this, but what? "If thou confess with thy mouth the Lord Jesus, and believe in thy heart that God hath raised Him from the dead, thou shalt be saved." Then again that we may not seem to be making it contemptible by showing it to be

easy and cheap,[2] observe how he expands his account of it. For he does not come immediately to the words just given, but what does he say? " But the righteousness which is of faith saith on this wise; Say not in thine heart, Who shall go up into heaven? (that is, to bring Christ down); or, Who shall descend into the deep? (that is, to bring up Christ again from the dead.") For as to the virtue manifested in works there is opposed a listlessness, which relaxeth our labors,[3] and it requireth a very wakeful soul not to yield to it: thus, when one is required to believe, there are reasonings which confuse and make havoc of the minds of most men, and it wants a soul of some vigor to shake them thoroughly off. And this is just why he brings the same before one. And as he did in Abraham's case, so he does here also. For having there shown that he was justified by faith, lest he should seem to have gotten so great a crown by a mere chance, as if it were a thing of no account, to extol the nature of faith, he says, "Who against hope believed in hope, that he might become the father of many nations. And being not weak in faith, he considered his own body now dead, and the deadness of Sarah's womb. He staggered not at the promise of God through unbelief; but was strong in faith, giving glory to God; and being fully persuaded that what He had promised He was able also to perform " (Rom. iv. 18–21): so he showed that there is need of vigor, and a lofty soul, that takes in things beyond expectation, and stumbles not at appearances. This then he does here also, and shows that it requires a wise mind, and a spirit heavenly (Gr. heaven-reaching) and great. And he does not say merely, " Say not," but, " Say not in thine heart," that is, do not so much as think of doubting and saying with thyself, And how can this be? You see that this is a chief characteristic of faith, to leave all the consequences [4] of this lower world, and so to seek for that which is above nature, and to cast out the feebleness of calculation, and so to accept everything from the Power of God. The Jews, however, did not merely assert this, but that it was not possible to be justified by faith. But himself turns even what had taken place to another account, that having shown the thing to be so great, that even after it had taken place it required faith, he might seem with good reason to bestow a crown on these: and he uses the words which

---

is well given in Meyer's paraphrase: " For the validity of the law has come to an end in Christ, in order that every believer may be a partaker of righteousness."—G. B. S.

[1] He seems to consider the words quoted from Lev. xviii. a sufficient refutation, as the Jews thought to be justified by the Law without fulfilling it. See Rom. ii.

[2] This term is admissible with respect to the method of attainment; but there are two other readings of the passage; one is " that the easiness may not seem to make it contemptible and cheap."

[3] "sinews" Field, from Catena.

[4] πᾶσαν ἀκολουθίαν, i. e. the common order of cause and effect.

are found in the Old Testament, being always at pains to keep quite clear of the charges of love of novelties, and of opposition to it. For this, which he here says of faith, Moses says to them of the commandment,[1] so showing that they had enjoyed at God's hand a great benefit. For there is no need to say, he means, that one must go up to heaven, or cross a great sea, and then receive the commandments, but things so great and grand hath God made of easy access to us. And what meaneth the phrase, " The Word is nigh thee ? " That is, It is easy. For in thy mind and in thy tongue is thy salvation. There is no long journey to go, no seas to sail over, no mountains to pass, to get saved. But if you be not minded to cross so much as the threshold, you may even while you sit at home be saved. For " in thy mouth and in thy heart" is the source of salvation. And then on another score also he makes the word of faith easy, and says, that " God raised Him from the dead." For just reflect upon the worthiness of the Worker, and you will no longer see any difficulty in the thing. That He is Lord then, is plain from the resurrection. And this he said at the beginning even of the Epistle. " Which was declared to be the Son of God with power . . . by the resurrection from the dead." (Rom. i. 4.) But that the resurrection is easy too, has been shown even to those who are very unbelieving, from the might of the Worker of it. Since then the righteousness is greater, and light and easy to receive, is it not a sign of the utmost contentiousness to leave what is light and easy, and set about impossibilities ? For they could not say that it was a thing they declined as burdensome. See then how he deprives them of all excuse. For what do they deserve to have said in their defence, who choose what is burdensome and impracticable, and pass by what is light, and able to save them, and to give them those things which the Law could not give ? All this can come only from a contentious spirit, which is in a state of rebellion against God. For the Law is galling (ἐπαχθὴς), but grace is easy. The Law, though they dispute never so much, does not save ; Grace yieldeth the righteousness resulting from itself, and that from the Law likewise. What plea then is to rescue them, since they are disposed to be contentious against this, but cling to that to no purpose whatever? Then, since he had made a strong assertion, he again confirms it from the Scripture. *

Ver. 11–13. " For the Scripture saith, " he proceeds, " Whosoever believeth on Him, shall not be ashamed. For there is no difference between the Jew and the Greek ; for the same Lord over all is rich unto all that call upon Him. For whosoever shall call upon the Name of the Lord shall be saved."

You see how he produces witnesses, whether to the faith, or to the confession of it. For the words, " Every one that believeth," point out the faith. But the words, " Whosoever shall call upon," set forth confession. Then again to proclaim the universality of the grace, and to lay their boasting low, what he had before demonstrated at length, he here briefly recalls to their memory, showing again that there is no difference between the Jew and the uncircumcised. " For there is," he says, "no difference between the Jew and the Greek." And what he had said about the Father, when he was arguing this point, that he says here about the Son. For as before he said in asserting this, " Is He the God of the Jews only ? Is He not of the Gentiles also ? Yes, of the Gentiles also : seeing it is one God " (Rom. iii. 29, 30) :—so he says here also, " For the same Lord over all is rich unto all (and upon all)." (Rom. iii. 22.) You see how he sets Him forth as exceedingly desiring our salvation, since He even reckons this to be riches to Himself ; so that they are not even now to despair, or fancy that, provided they would repent, they were unpardonable. For He who considereth it as riches[2] to Himself to save us, will not cease to be rich. Since even this is riches, the fact of the gift being shed forth unto all. For since what distresseth him the most was, that they, who were in the enjoyment of a prerogative over the whole world, should now by the faith be degraded from these thrones, and be no wit better off than others, he brings the Prophets in constantly as foretelling, that they would have equal honor with them. " For whosoever," he says, " believeth on Him shall not be ashamed" (Is. xxviii. 16) ; and, " Whosoever shall call upon the Name of the

---

[1] St. Augustin Quæst. in Deut. lib. v. q. 54, discusses this passage and its application, and considers it to refer to the spiritual meaning of the Law.

* The following analysis of Paul's meaning in vv. 6–10 may be useful in connection with the exposition of Chrys. The

apostle quotes Deut. xxx. 11–14 in which God assures the people that his commandments are not beyond their power to obey. He brings truth and duty near to them. These expressions are typical of the principles of the Christian faith. No striving, journeying or climbing are needful to reach Christ and his truth and law. Christian truth and duty are brought near in the apostolic message. After this presentation of the faith-idea in Old Testament language, which all might not grasp, he presents the message of the gospel in vv. 9, 10 in unmistakable terms. It includes two points, (1) confession, (2) faith, and the object of both is stated. It is Christ. Confess Christ ; believe heartily in his resurrection (which would carry belief in all the essential facts of his life and person with itself). And then, reversing the order, and throwing καρδία and στόματι into special prominence, he repeats the assurance that faith and confession conduct to the true goal—εἰς δικαιοσύνην—εἰς σωτηρίαν (10).—G. B. S.

[2] Hooker, v. 23, " The higher any cause is, the more it coveteth to impart virtue unto things beneath it."

Lord shall be saved." (Joel ii. 32.) And the "whosoever" is put in all cases, that they might not say aught in reply. But there is nothing worse than vainglory. For it was this, this most especially, which proved their ruin. Whence Christ also said to them, "How can ye believe, which receive glory one of another, and seek not the glory which cometh of God only?" (John v. 44.) This, with ruin, exposes men also to much ridicule; and before the punishment in the other world, involves them in ills unnumbered in this. And if it seem good, that you may learn this clearly, leaving for the present the heavens which that puts us out of, and the hell which it thrusts us into, let us investigate the whole matter as here before us. What then can be more wasteful than this? what more disgraceful, or more offensive? For that this disorder is a wasteful one is plain from the people who spend to no purpose whatsoever on theatres, horse-races, and other such irrelevant expenditures: from those that build the fine and expensive houses, and fit up everything in a useless style of extravagance, on which I must not enter in this discourse. But that a person diseased in this way must needs be extravagant, and expensive, and rapacious, and covetous, anybody can see. For that he may have food to give the brute, he thrusteth his hand into the substance of others. And why do I talk of substance? It is not money only but souls also that this fire devoureth, and it worketh not death here only, but also hereafter. For vanity is the mother of hell, and greatly kindleth that fire, and the venomous worm. One may see that it hath power even over the dead. And what can be worse than this? For the other passions are put an end to by death, but this even after death shows its force, and strives to display its nature even in the dead corpse. For when men give orders on their death-bed to raise to them fine monuments, which will waste all their substance, and take pains to lay out beforehand a vast extravagance in their funeral, and in their lifetime insult the poor that come to them for a penny and a single loaf, but when they are dead give a rich banquet to the worm, why seek any more exorbitant thraldom to the disease? From this mischief also irregular loves are conceived. For there are many whom it is not the beauty of the appearance, nor the desire of lying with her, but the wish to boast that "I have made conquest of such an one," hath even drawn into adultery. And why need I mention the other mischiefs that spring of this? For I had rather be long (3 Mss. διηνεκῶς) the slave of ten thousand savages, than of vanity once. For even they

do not put such commands upon their captives, as this vice lays upon its votaries. Because it says, Be thou every one's slave, be he nobler or be he lower than thyself. Despise thy soul, neglect virtue, laugh at freedom, immolate thy salvation, and if thou doest any good thing, do it not to please God, but to display it to the many, that for these things thou mayest even lose thy crown. And if thou give alms, or if thou fast, undergo the pains, but take care to lose the gain. What can be more cruel than these commands? Hence grudging beareth sway, hence haughtiness, hence covetousness, the mother of evils. For the swarm of domestics, and the black servants liveried in gold, and the hangers on, and the flatterers, and the silver-tinselled chariots, and the other absurdities greater than these, are not had for any pleasure's sake or necessity, but for mere vanity. Yes, one will say, but that this affliction is an evil, anybody can see; but how we are to keep quite clear of it, this is what you should tell us. Well then, in the first place, if you persuade yourself that this disorder is a baneful one, you will have made a very good beginning towards correcting it. For when a man is sick, he speedily sends for the physician, if he be first made acquainted with the fact that he is sick. But if thou seekest for another way besides to escape from hence, look to God continually, and be content with glory from Him; and if thou find the passion tickling thee, and stirring thee to tell thy well-doings to thy fellow-servants, bethink thyself next, that after telling them thou gainest nothing. Quench the absurd desire, and say to thy soul, Lo, thou hast been so long big with thy own well-doings to tell them, and thou hast not had the courage to keep them to thyself, but hast blabbed them out to all. What good then hast thou gotten from this? None at all, but loss to the utmost, and avoidance of all that had been gathered together with much labor. And besides this, consider another thing also, which is, that most men's opinion is perverted, and not perverted only, but that it withers away so soon. For supposing they do admire you for the time, when the occasion has gone by they will have forgotten it all, and have taken away from thee the crown God had given, and have been unable to secure to thee that from themselves. And yet if this were abiding, it were a most miserable thing to exchange that for this. But when even this hath gone, what defence shall we be able to make for betraying the abiding one for the sake of the unabiding one, for losing such blessings for the sake of credit with a few? And indeed even if they who praise were numerous, even for this they were to be pitied, and the more so the more numerous those who do it. But if thou art surprised at what I have said, hear Christ giving His sentence in this way, "Woe unto you, when all men speak well of you." (Luke vi. 26.) And so indeed it should seem. For if in every art you look to the workmen (δημιουργους) in it to be judges of it, how come you to trust the proving of virtue to the many, and not most of all to Him Who knoweth it more surely then any, and is best able to applaud[1] and to crown it? This saying then, let us inscribe both on our walls and our doors and our mind, and let us keep constantly saying to ourselves, "Woe unto us, when all men speak well of us." For even they that so speak slander one afterward as a vain person, and fond of honor, and covetous of their good word. But God doeth not so. But when He seeth thee coveting the glory that cometh of Him, then He will praise thee most, and respect (θαυμάσεται om. in most Mss.) thee, and proclaim thee conqueror. Not so man; but, when he finds thee slavish instead of free, by gratifying thee often by bare words with false praise, he snatches from thee thy true meed, and makes thee more of a menial than a purchased slave. For those last men get to obey them after their orders, but thou even without orders makest thyself a slave. For thou dost not even wait to hear something from them, but if thou merely knowest wherein thou mayest gratify them, even without their command thou doest all. What hell then should we not deserve, for giving the wicked pleasure, and courting their service before they give orders, while we will not hearken to God, even when He every day commands and exhorts us? And yet if thou art covetous of glory and praise, avoid the praise that cometh of men, and then thou wilt attain to glory. Turn aside from fair speeches, and then thou wilt obtain praises without number both from God and from men. For there is no one we are used to give so much glory to, as the man who looks down upon glory, or to praise and respect so much as the man who thinks scorn of getting respected and praised. And if we do so, much more will the God of the universe. And when He glorifieth thee and praiseth thee, what man can be more justly pronounced blessed? For there is not a greater difference between glory and disgrace, than between the glory from above and that of men. Or rather, there is a much greater, aye an infinite difference. For if this, even when it does not get put beside any other, is

but a base and uncomely one, when we come to scrutinize it by the other's side, just consider how great its baseness will be found to be! For as a prostitute stands at her place[2] and lets herself out to any one, so are they that be slaves of vanity. Or rather, these be more base than she. For that sort of women do in many instances treat those enamoured of them with scorn. But you prostitute yourself to everybody, whether runaway slaves, or thieves, or cut-purses (for it is of these and such as these that the play-houses that applaud you consist), and those whom as individuals you hold to be nothing worth, when in a body, you honor more than your own salvation and show yourself less worthy of honor than any of them. For how can you be else than less worthy, when you stand in need of the good word of others, and fancy that you have not enough by yourself, unless you receive the glory that cometh of others? Do you not perceive, pray, beside what I have said, that as you are an object of notice, and known to every body, if you should commit a fault, you will have accusers unnumbered; but if unknown, you will remain in security? Yes, a man may say, but then if I do well I shall have admirers unnumbered. Now the fearful thing is, that it is not only when you sin, but even when you do aright, that the disorder of vanity does you mischief, in the former case subverting thousands, in the present bereaving thee entirely of thy reward. It is then a sad thing, and replete with disgrace of every kind, to be in love with glory even in civil matters. But when even in spiritual you are in the same plight what excuse is there left remaining for you, when you are not minded to yield God even as much honor as you have yourself from your servants? For even the slave "looketh to the eyes of his master" (Ps. cxxiii. 2), and the hireling to his employer, who is to pay him wages, and the disciple to his master. But you do just the contrary. Having left the God that hired thee, even thy Master, thou lookest to thy fellow-servants; and this knowing that God remembers thy well-doings even after this life, but man only for the present. And when thou hast spectators assembled in Heaven, thou art gathering together spectators upon earth. And where the wrestler struggles, there he would be honored; but thou, while thy wrestling is above, art anxious to gain thee a crown below. And what can be worse than madness like this? But let us look, if it seem proper, at the crowns also. For one is formed by haughtiness, and a second by grudging against another, and a third by dissimulation and flattery, another again by wealth, and another by servile obsequiousness. And like as children at their childish play put crowns of grass upon one another, and many a time laugh at him that is crowned behind his back; thus now also they that pass their praises upon thee, many a time joke by themselves at their putting the grass upon us. And would it were grass only! But now the crown is laden with much mischief, and ruins all our well-doings. Taking then the vileness of it into consideration, flee from the damage entailed. For how many would you have to praise you? A hundred? or twice, or thrice, or four times as many? Or rather, if you please, put them at ten times or twenty times as many, and let there be two or four thousand, or if you will, even ten thousand to applaud you. Still these be no better than so many daws cawing from above. Or rather taking the assemblage of the angels into consideration, these will seem more vile than even worms, and their good word of not so much solidity as a cobweb, or a smoke, or a dream. Hear then how Paul, who saw through these things thoroughly, is so far from seeking after them, that he even deprecates them, in the words, "But God forbid that I should glory, save in the cross of Christ." (Gal. vi. 14.) This glory then be thou also emulous of, that thou mayest not provoke the Master, because in so doing thou art insulting God, and not thyself alone. For if thou even wert a painter, and hadst some pupil, and he were to omit showing thee his practice of the art, but set forth his painting publicly just to any body that chanced to observe it, thou wouldest not take it quietly. But if this even with thy fellow-servants were an insult, how much more with the Master! But if you have a mind to learn on other grounds to feel scorn for the thing, be of a lofty mind, laugh at appearances, increase thy love of real glory, be filled with a spiritual temper, say to thy soul as Paul did, "Knowest thou not that we shall judge angels?" (1 Cor. vi. 3) and having by this roused it up, go on to rebuke it, and say, Thou that judgest the angels, wilt thou let thyself be judged of off-scourings, and be praised with dancers, and mimics, and gladiators, and horse-drivers? For these men do follow after applause of this sort. But do thou poise thy wing high above the din of these, and emulate that citizen of the wilderness, John, and learn how he was above regarding the multitude, and did not turn him to look at flatterers, but when he saw all the dwellers in Palestine poured forth about him, and wondering, and astonished at him, he was not puffed up with such honor as this, but rose up against them, and discoursing to his great concourse as if to one youth, he thus rebuked them and said, "Ye serpents, ye generation of vipers!" (Matt. iii. 7.) Yet it was for him that they had run together, and left the cities, in order to see that holy personage, and still none of these things unnerved him. For he was far above glory, and free from all vanity. So also Stephen, when he saw the same people again, not honoring him, but mad upon him, and gnashing their teeth, being lifted above their wrath, said, "Ye stiff-necked and uncircumcised in heart." (Acts vii. 51.) Thus also Elias, when those armies were present, and the king, and all the people, said, "How long halt ye upon both your hips?" (1 Kings xviii. 21, LXX. true sense of "halt.") But we flatter all, court all, with this servile obsequiousness buying their honor. Wherefore all things are turned upside down, and for this favor [1] the business of Christianity is betrayed, and everything neglected for the opinion of the generality. Let us then banish this passion, and then we shall have a right notion of liberty, and of the haven, and the calm. For the vain man is ever like persons in a storm, trembling, and fearing, and serving a thousand masters. But he that is clear of this thraldom, is like men in havens, enjoying a liberty untainted. Not so that person, but as many acquaintances as he has, so many masters has he, and he is forced to be a slave to all of them. How then are we to get free from this hard bondage? It is by growing enamoured of another glory, which is really glory. For as with those that are enamoured of persons, the sight of some handsomer one doth by its being seen take them off from the first: so with those that court the glory which cometh from us men, the glory from heaven, if it gleameth on them, has power to lead them off from this. Let us then look to this, and become thoroughly acquainted with it, that by feeling admiration of its beauty, we may shun the hideousness of the other, and have the benefit of much pleasure by enjoying this continually. Which may we all attain to by the grace and love toward man, etc.

---

[1] ἐξεπέσομεν καὶ added after χάριτος in 2 Mss. and in Ben from Mss. "we have fallen from this grace, and the business of Christianity is treacherously given up."

HOMILY XVIII.

ROM. X. 14, 15.

"How then shall they call on Him in Whom they have not believed? and how shall they believe in Him of Whom they have not heard? and how shall they hear without a preacher? and how shall they preach except they be sent? as it is written."

HERE again·he takes from them all excuse. For since he had said, "I bear them record that they have a zeal of God, but not according to knowledge," and that "being ignorant of God's righteousness, they submitted not themselves" to it: he next shows, that for this ignorance itself they were punishable before God. This he does not say indeed so, but he makes it good by carrying on his discourse in the way of question, and so convicting them more clearly, by framing the whole passage out of objections and answers. But look further back. The Prophet, saith he, said, "Whosoever shall call upon the Name of the Lord shall be saved." Now somebody might say perhaps, "But how could they call upon Him Whom they had not believed? Then there is a question from him after the objection; And why did they not believe? Then an objection again. A person certainly may say, And how could they believe, since they had not heard? Yet hear they did, he implies. Then another objection again. "And how could they hear without a preacher?" Then an answer again. Yet preach they did, and there were many sent forth for this very purpose. And whence does it appear that these are those persons sent? Then he brings the prophet in next, who says, "How beautiful are the feet of them that preach the Gospel of peace, and bring glad tidings of good things!" (Is. iii. 7.) You see how by the kind of preaching he points out the preachers. For there was nothing else that these men went about telling everywhere, but those unspeakable good things, and the peace made by God with men. And so by disbelieving, it is not we, he implies, whom you disbelieve, but Isaiah the prophet, who spake many years ago, that we were to be sent, and to preach, and to say what we do say. If the being saved, then, came of calling upon Him, and calling upon Him from believing, and believing from hearing, and hearing from preaching, and preaching from being sent, and if they were sent, and did preach, and the prophet went round with them to point them out, and proclaim them, and say that these were they whom they showed of so many ages ago, whose feet even they praised because of the matter of their preaching; then it is quite clear that the not believing was their own fault only. And that because God's part had been fulfilled completely.*

Ver. 16, 17. "But they have not all obeyed the Gospel. For Esaias saith, Lord, who hath believed our report? So then faith cometh by hearing, and hearing by the word of God." (ib. liii. 1.)

Since they pressed him with another objection again to this effect, that if these were the persons sent upon the mission by God, all ought to have hearkened to them: observe Paul's judgment, and see how he shows that this very thing which made the confusion, did in fact do away with confusion and embarrassment. What offends you, O Jew, he would say, after so great and abundant evidence, and demonstration of the points? that all did not submit to the Gospel? Why this very thing, when taken along with the others, is of force to certify thee of the truth

---

* Vv. 14, 15 state a threefold objection to Paul's doctrine of the Jews' responsibility. Vv. 16-21 are the reply to this objection. Paul takes up three points which are summarized in the objections. (1) Shall the fact that they have not believed constitute any excuse? (16, 17). The apostle answers that the real fact is that the message of faith and of the Messianic salvation has been proclaimed to the Jews and a large part of them have rejected and disobeyed it. They must therefore have heard, for disobedience, on the one hand, and faith, on the other, depends upon hearing the message and hearing it depends upon God having spoken it. (2) Then comes the prior question concerning the hearing on which disobedience or hearing is dependent (18). Certainly they have heard, answers Paul, for we might apply to God's message the words of the Psalm (xix. 5) which describe the movements of the heavenly bodies, so plain and wide-spread have been God's messages concerning Christ and the principles on which his Gospel is based. (3) Since Israel has heard, does it not follow that they knew and are therefore inexcusable? (19). Yes. The Jews complain that God's promise has failed; that He has not preserved to them their promised prerogatives. Hence it is excusable for them to fall away from confidence in Him, etc. The apostle answers that this is an entire misunderstanding of their own providential history. The coming of the Gentiles into the kingdom of God was already foreshadowed in the Old Testament, e. g. Moses (Deut. xxxii. 21) speaks of Israel being made jealous and angry by a "no-people"—"a foolish nation" (heathen). And again, Isaiah (lxv. 1, 2) uses very bold words which the apostle applies to the relation of Jews and Gentiles. The three points placed in close relation are : (1) Israel has heard and (2) hence knows, and (3) is blameworthy for the rejection of the Messiah.—G. B. S.

of my statements, even in that some do not believe. For this too the prophet foretold. Notice his unspeakable wisdom too; how he shows more than they were looking for, or expected him to have to say in reply. For what is it that you say? he means. Is it that all have not believed the Gospel? Well! Isaiah foretold this too from of old. Or rather, not this only, but even much more than this. For the complaint you make is, Why did not all believe? But Isaiah goes further than this. For what is it he says? "Lord, who hath believed our report? Then since he had rid himself of this embarrassment by making the Prophet a bulwark against them, he again keeps to the line he was before upon. For as he had said that they must call upon Him, but that they who call must believe, and they who believe must hear first, but they who are to hear must have preachers, and the preachers be sent, and as he had shown that they were sent, and had preached; as he is going to bring in another objection again, taking occasion first of another quotation from the Prophet, by which he had met the objection a little back, he thus interweaves it, and connects it with what went before. For since he had produced the Prophet as saying, "Lord, who hath believed our report" (ἀκοῇ)? he happily seizes on the quotation, as proving what he says, "So then faith cometh by hearing" (ἀκοῆς). And this he makes not a mere naked statement. But as the Jews were forever seeking a sign, and the sight of the Resurrection, and were gaping after the thing much; he says, Yet the Prophet promised no such thing, but that it was by hearing that we were to believe. Hence he makes this good first, and says, "so then faith cometh by hearing." And then since this seemed a mean thing to say, see how he elevates it. For he says, I was not speaking of mere hearing, nor of the need of hearing men's words and believing them, but I mean a great sort of hearing. For the hearing is "by the word of God." They were not speaking their own, but they were telling what they learnt from God. And this is a higher thing than miracles. For we are equally bound to believe and to obey God, whether speaking or working miracles.[1] Since both works and miracles come of His words. For both the heaven and everything else was established in this way. (Ps. xxxiii. 6–8.) After showing then that we ought to believe the prophets, who always speak God's words, and not to look after anything more,

he proceeds next to the objection I mentioned, and says,

Ver. 18. "But I say, Have they not heard?"

What, he means, if the preachers were sent, and did preach what they were bid, and these did not hear? Then comes a most perfect reply to the objection.

"Yes, verily, their sound went into all the earth, and their words unto the ends of the world."[2]

What do you say? he means. They have not heard? Why the whole world, and the ends of the earth, have heard. And have you, amongst whom the heralds abode such a long time, and of whose land they were, not heard? Now can this ever be? Sure if the ends of the world heard, much more must you. Then again another objection.

Ver. 19. "But I say, Did not Israel know?"

For what if they heard, he means, but did not know what was said, nor understand that these were the persons sent? Are they not to be forgiven for their ignorance? By no means. For Isaiah had described their character in the words, "How beautiful are the feet of them that preach the Gospel of peace." (Is. lii. 7.) And before him the Lawgiver himself. Hence he proceeds.

"First Moses saith, I will provoke you to jealousy by them that are no people, and by a foolish nation I will anger you. (Deut. xxxii. 21.)

And so they ought even from him to have been able to distinguish the preachers, not from the fact of these disbelieving only, not from the fact of their preaching peace, not from the fact of their bringing the glad tidings of those good things, not from the word being sown in every part of the world, but from the very fact of their seeing their inferiors, those of the Gentiles, in greater honor. For what they had never heard, nor their forefathers, that wisdom did these[3] on a sudden embrace (ἐφιλοσόφουν). And this was a mark of such intense honor, as should gall them, and lead them to jealousy, and to recollection of the prophecy of Moses, which said,

[1] Four Mss. The believing and obeying God equally when He speaks and when He works wonders.

[2] Ps. xix. 4 (V. and LXX. xviii). The mystical interpretation of this Psalm here indicated, is acknowledged by the Church in using it on Christmas day. An ancient Latin hymn has this paraphrase on a part of it:

From Chastity, His Palace bright,
Forth came the Bridegroom decked with light,
Giant! God and Man in one!
Glad His glorious race to run.
From the Eternal Father sent
Back to Him His circuit bent,
Down to hell His path descends,
At the throne of God it ends.

Origen on this passage (t. iv. p. 627), and St. Augustin on the Psalm. enlarge upon its Christian interpretation.
[3] "They" "their" i. e. the Jews: "these" i. e. the Gentiles.

"I will provoke you to jealousy by them that are no people." For it was not the greatness of the honor alone that was enough to throw them upon jealousy, but the fact too that a nation had come to enjoy these things which was of so little account that it could hardly be considered a nation at all. "For I will provoke you to jealousy, by them which are no nation, and by a foolish nation will I anger you." For what more foolish than the Greeks (Heathen, see pp. 373, 377)? or what of less account? See how by every means God had given from of old indications and clear signs of these times, in order to remove their blindness. For it was not any little corner in which the thing was done, but in land, and in sea, and in every quarter of the globe. And they saw those in the enjoyment of countless blessings now, who had formerly been objects of their contempt. One should consider then that this is that people of which Moses said, "I will provoke you to jealousy by them that are no people, and by a foolish nation will I anger you." Was it Moses only then that said this? No, for Isaiah also after Him saith so. And this is why Paul said, "First Moses," to show that a second will come who says the same things in a clearer and plainer way. As then he says above, that Esaias crieth, so too here.

Ver. 20. "But Esaias is very bold, and saith."

Now what he means is something of this kind. He put a violence on himself, and was ambitious to speak, not some thing veiled over, but to set things even naked before your eyes, and choosing rather to run (Origen *in loc.*) into dangers from being plain spoken, than by looking to his own safety, to leave you any shelter for your impenetrableness; although it was not the manner of prophecy to say this so clearly; but still to stop your mouths most completely, he tells the whole beforehand clearly and distinctly. The whole! what whole? Why your being cast out, and also their being brought in; speaking as follows, "I was found of them that sought Me not, I was made manifest of them that asked not after Me." (Is. lxv. 1.) Who then are they that sought not? who they that asked not after Him? Clearly not the Jews, but they of the Gentiles, who hitherto had not known Him. As then Moses gave their characteristic mark in the words, "no people" and "a foolish nation," so here also he takes the same ground to point them out from, viz. their extreme ignorance. And this was a very great blame to attach to the Jews, that they who sought Him not found Him, and they who sought Him lost Him.

Ver. 21. "But unto Israel He saith, All the day long have I stretched forth My hands unto a disobedient and gainsaying people." (Is. lxv. 2.)

Observe now that difficulty, which so many make a subject of question, is discovered laid up from of old in the words of the Prophet, and with a clear solution to it too. And what is this? You heard Paul say before. "What shall we say then? That the Gentiles which followed not after righteousness have attained unto righteousness. But Israel which followed after the law of righteousness hath not attained to the law of righteousness." (Rom. ix. 30, 31.) This Esaias also says here. For to say, "I was found of them that sought me not, I was made manifest unto them which asked not after me," is the same with saying, "that the Gentiles which followed not after righteousness have attained unto righteousness." Then to show that what was happening was not of God's grace only, but also of the temper of those who came to Him, as also the casting off of the others came of the disputatiousness of those who disobeyed, hear what he proceeds with. "But to Israel He saith, All the day long have I stretched forth My hands to a disobedient and gainsaying people;" here meaning by the day the whole period of the former dispensation. But the stretching out of the hands, means calling and drawing[1] them to Him, and inviting them. Then to show that the fault was all their own, he says "to a disobedient and gainsaying people." You see what a great charge this is against them! For they did not obey Him even when He invited them, but they gainsaid Him, and that when they saw Him doing so, not once or twice or thrice, but the whole period. But others who had never known Him, had the power to draw Him to them. Not that he says they themselves had the power to do it, but to take away lofty imaginings even from those of the Gentiles, and to show that it was His grace that wrought the whole, He says, *I* was made manifest, and *I* was found. It may be said, Were they then void of everything? By no means, for the taking of the things found, and the getting a knowledge of what was manifested to them, was what they contributed themselves.[2] Then to prevent these saying, But why wast Thou not made manifest to us also? he sets down what is more than this, that I not only

---

[1] This of course does not exclude the other interpretation of J. Martyr. *Apol.* i. 35. p. 27 O. T. *Tryph.* 97, p. 193 O. T. and others. See, on the contrary, St. John xii. 32, also St. Cyr. Hier. Cat. xiii. 27, and note, p. 157 O. T. add St. Cyprian, Test. ii. 20, p. 56, O. T. and note.

[2] As in Cornelius' case. See p. 379, and context.

was made manifest, but I even continue with My hands stretched out, inviting them, and displaying all the concern of an affectionate father, and a mother that is set on her child. See how he has brought us a most lucid answer to all the difficulties before raised, by showing that it was from their own temper that ruin had befallen them, and that they are wholly undeserving of pardon. For though they had both heard and understood what was said, still not even then were they minded to come to Him. And what is far more, He did not cause them to hear these things and to understand them only, but a thing which hath more force to rouse them up and draw them to Him, when they were disobedient and gainsaying, He added to the others. Now what is this? It is His exasperating them, and making them jealous. For ye know the domineering might of the passion, and how great the power is which jealousy is naturally possessed of for bringing all disputatiousness to an end, and rousing those who have grown remiss. And why need one say this of man, when in brutes without reason, and children before they are of full age, the power it shows is so great? For a child often will not submit to its father when it is called, but continues obstinate. But when another child has notice taken of it, then it even though not called comes to its father's bosom, and what calling could not do, provoking to jealousy will. This then God also did. For He not only called and stretched out His hands, but stirred up in them the feeling of jealousy also, by bringing those far inferior to them (a thing which makes men excessively jealous) not into their good things, but (what was a much stronger step, and makes the feeling even more domineering,) into much greater good things, and of greater necessity than theirs, and such as they had never even fancied in a dream. But still they did not submit. What pardon then do they deserve who exhibit such excessive obstinacy? None. Yet this he does not say himself, but leaves it to the consciences of his hearers, to gather it from the conclusion of what he had stated, and again also confirms it by what he goes on to in his usual wisdom. And this he did also above, by introducing objections both in the case of the Law (see on Rom. vii. 7, pp. 420, 1) and of the people, which presented an accusation beyond the true one; and then in the answer, which was to overthrow this, yielding as much as he pleased, and as the case allowed, so as to make what he was saying not unwelcome. And this he doth here, writing as follows:

Chap. xi. ver. 1 "I say then, Hath God

cast away His people whom He foreknew? God forbid."*

And he introduces the form a person would use in doubt, as though taking occasion from what had been said, and after making this alarming statement, by the denial of it he causes the sequel to be allowed with readiness; and what by all the former arguments he had been laboring to show that he makes good here also. What then is this? That even if there be but a few saved, the promise yet stands good. This is why he does not merely say "people," but "people which He foreknew." Then proceeding with the proof that the "people" were not cast off, "For I also am an Israelite, of the seed of Abraham, of the tribe of Benjamin."

I, he says, the instructor, the preacher. Now since this seemed contrary to what was said before in the words, "Who hath believed our report?" and, "All the day long have I stretched forth My hands to a disobedient and gainsaying people;" and, "I will provoke you to jealousy by them which are no people;" he was not satisfied with the deprecation, nor with having said, "God forbid," but makes it good by taking it up again and saying, "God hath not cast away His people." But this is not a confirmation, men may say, but an assertion. Observe then the confirmation, both the first, and that which follows it. For the first is that he was himself of that race. But He would not, if on the point of casting them off, have chosen from them to whom He entrusted all the preaching, and the affairs of the world, and all mysteries, and the whole economy. This then is one proof, but the next, after it, is his saying, that "people whom He foreknew," that is, who He knew clearly were suited to it, and would receive the faith. (Pococke on Hos. p. 23. See Acts ii. 41; iv. 4; xxi. 20.) For three, five, even ten thousand were believers from among them. And so to prevent any from saying, Art thou the people, then? And because thou hast been called, hath the nation been called? he proceeds.

Ver. 2. "He hath not cast off His people, whom He foreknew."

As though he said, I have with me three, five, or ten thousand. What then? has the

* The central thought of chap. xi. is that Israel's rejection is not forever; the nation is to be restored. The order of thought is as follows: (1) The rejection is *partial*. The Scriptures furnish analogous examples of partial falls and rejections of the nation, 1-10. (2) The fall of Israel is *temporary*. Some branches were cut off because of unbelief and Gentile branches inserted in their place, but the natural branches shall yet be restored, 11-24. (3) Reflections upon the wise and gracious purposes of God in all these dispensations, 25-36.—G. B. S.

people come to be[1] three, five, or ten thousand? that seed that compared with the stars of heaven for multitude, or the sand of the sea? Is this the way you deceive us and put a cheat upon us, by making the whole people thyself and the few that are with thee; and didst thou inflate us with idle hopes, and say that the promise has been fulfilled, when all are lost, and the salvation comes down to a few? This is all bombast and vanity! we cannot away with such sophistry as this! Now, that they may not say this, see how in the sequel he proceeds to the answer, not giving the objection indeed, but before it grounding the answer to it upon ancient history. What then is the answer?

Ver. 2–5. "Wot ye not," he says, "what the Scripture saith of Elias? how he (so most; Mss. Sav. who) maketh intercession to God against Israel, saying, Lord, they have killed Thy prophets, and digged down Thine altars; and I am left alone, and they seek my life. But what saith the answer of God unto him? I have reserved to Myself seven thousand men, who have not bowed the knee to the image of Baal. Even so then at this present time also, there is a remnant according to the election of grace."

What he means is nearly this. "God hath not cast off His people." For had He done so, He would have admitted none of them. But if He did admit some, He hath not cast them off. Still it is said, if He had not cast off, He would have admitted all. This does not follow; since in Elijah's time the part to be saved had come down to "seven thousand:" and now also there are probably many that believe. But if you do not know who they are, this is no wonder, for that prophet, who was so great and good a man, did not know. But God ordered things for Himself when even the prophet knew them not. But consider his judgment. Now in proving what was before him, he covertly augments the charge against them. For this is why he gave the whole passage, that he might parade before them their untowardness, and show that they had been so from of old. For if he had not wished this, but had directed his whole attention to prove that the people lay in the few, he would have said that even in Elijah's time, seven thousand were left. But now he reads to them the passage further back, as having been throughout at pains to show that it was no strange thing that they did with Christ, and the Apostles,

but their habitual practice. For to prevent their saying that it was as a deceiver we put Christ to death, and as impostors that we persecute the Apostles, he brings forward the text which says, "Lord, they have killed Thy prophets, and digged down thine altars." (1 Kings xix. 14.) Then in order not to make his discourse galling to them, he attaches another reason to the bringing forward of the text. For he quotes it not as if it was on purpose to accuse them, but as if intent upon showing some other things. And he leaves them without any excuse even by what had before been done. For observe how strong the accusation is even from the person speaking. For it is neither Paul, nor Peter, nor James, nor John, but one whom they held in the greatest estimation, the chief of the Prophets, the friend of God, a man who had been so very zealous[2] in their behalf as even to be given up to hunger for them, who even to this day hath never died. What then doth this man say? "Lord, they have killed Thy prophets, and digged down Thine altars; and I am left alone, and they seek my life." What could be more brutal cruelty than this? For when they should have besought pardon for the offences they had already committed, they were minded even to kill him. And all these things put them quite beyond pardon. For it was not during the prevalence of the famine, but when the season was favorable, and their shame was done away, and the devils (i. e. false gods) had been put to shame, and the power of God had been shown, and the king had bowed beneath it, that they committed these audacities, passing from murder to murder, and making away with their teachers, and such as would bring them to a better mind. What then could they have to say to this? Were they too deceivers? Were they too impostors? Did they not know whence they were either? But they distressed you. Yes, but they also told you goodly things. But what of the altars? the altars too did not surely distress you? Did they too exasperate you? See of what obstinacy, of what insolence they were ever yielding proofs! This is why in another passage too Paul says, when writing to the Thessalonians, "Ye also have suffered like things of your own countrymen, even as they have of the Jews, who both killed the Lord, and their own prophets, and have persecuted us, and please not God, and are contrary to all men (1 Thess. ii. 14, 15); which is what he says here too, that they both digged down the altars, and killed the prophets. But what

---

[1] Field with one Ms. reads "What then? Is this the people? is that seed . . . . come to be 3, 5, or 10,000?" and mentions with approval the reading of the Catena "What then? are the people come down to thee and 3, 5, or 10,000?"

[2] Referring to his words, 1 Kings xix. 14, and to his sharing in the famine, xvii. 13.

saith the answer of God unto him? "I have reserved to Myself seven thousand men who have not bowed the knee to the image of Baal." (1 Kings xix. 18.) And what has this to do with the present subject? some may say. It hath a great deal to do with the present subject. For he shows here that it is the worthy that God useth to save, even if the promise be made to the whole nation. And this he pointed out above when he said, " Though the number of the children of Israel be as the sand of the sea, a remnant shall be saved." And, " Except the Lord of Sabaoth had left us a seed, we should have become as Sodoma." (Rom. ix. 27, 29.) And he points it out from this passage also. Wherefore he proceeds to say, " Even so then at this present time also, there is a remnant according to the election of grace." Observe that each word maintains its own rank, showing at once God's grace, and the obedient temper of them that receive salvation. For by saying election, he showed the approval of them, but by saying grace, he showed the gift of God.

Ver. 6. " And if by grace, then it is no more of works, otherwise grace is no more grace : but if it be of works, then is it no more grace,[1] otherwise work is no more work."

He again springs upon the disputatiousness of the Jews, in what has just been quoted; and on this ground bereaves them of excuse. For you cannot, he means, so much as say, that the Prophets called indeed, and God invited, and the state of things cried aloud, and the provoking to jealousy was enough to draw us to Him, but what was enjoined was grievous, and this is why we could not draw nigh, since we had a display of works demanded of us, and laborious well-doings. For you cannot even say this. For how should God have demanded this of you, when this would just throw His grace into the shade? And this he said out of a wish to show that He was most desirous that they might be saved. (Deut. v. 29.) For not only would their salvation be easily brought about, but it was also God's greatest glory to display His love toward man. Why then are you afraid of drawing nigh, since you have no works demanded of you? Why are you bickering and quarrelsome, when grace is before you, and why keep putting me the Law forward to no purpose whatsoever? For you will not be saved by that, and will mar this gift also; since if you pertinaciously insist on being saved by it, you do away with this grace of God. Then that they might not think this

strange, having first taken those seven thousand ; he said that they were saved by grace. For when he says, " Even so then at this present time also there is a remnant according to the election of grace ; " he shows that they also were saved by grace. And not hereby only, but likewise by saying, " I have reserved unto Myself." For this is the language of One Who showeth that He Himself was the chief Contributor. And if by grace, it will be said, how came we all not to be saved? Because ye would not. For grace, though it be grace, saves the willing, not those who will not have it, and turn away from it, who persist in fighting against it, and opposing themselves to it. Observe how throughout the point he is proving is, " Not as though the Word of God had taken none effect," by showing that the worthy were those to whom the promise came, and that these, few though they be, may yet be the people of God ; and indeed he had stated it in the beginning of the Epistle with much force, where he says, " For what if some did not believe " (Rom. iii. 3), and did not even stop at this, but proceeded, " Yea, let God be true, and every man a liar." (ib. 4.) And here again he confirms it another way, and shows the force of grace, and that always the one were being saved, the other perished. Let us then give thanks, that we belong to them that are being saved, and not having been able to save ourselves by works, were saved by the gift of God. But in giving thanks, let us not do this in words only, but in works and actions. For this is the genuine thanksgiving, when we do those things whereby God is sure to be glorified, and flee from those from which we have been set free. For if we, after insulting the King, instead of being punished have been honored, and then go and insult Him afresh, since we are detected in the utmost ingratitude, we should with justice have to suffer the utmost punishment, one greater far than the former. For the former insolence did not show us so ungrateful as that committed after honor and much attention shown us. Let us then flee those things from which we have been set free, and not give thanks with our mouths only, lest it be said of us also, " This people honoreth Me with their lips, but with their heart is far from Me." (Is. xxix. 13.) For how is it else than unseemly, when the " heavens declare the glory of God " (Ps. xix. 1), and thou, for whom the heavens were made that glorify Him, doest such things that through thee the God that made thee is blasphemed? It is for this that not only he that blasphemeth, but thyself also, wilt be

---

[1] 4 Mss. omit these words: most early Mss. and versions of the N. T. omit the whole second half of the verse.

liable to punishment. For the heavens also do not glorify God by sending forth a voice, but by putting others upon doing it at the sight of them, and yet they are said "to declare the glory of God." Thus too they that furnish a life to be wondered at, even though they hold their peace, yet glorify God, when others through them glorify Him. For He is not so much reverenced because of the heaven, as of a spotless life. When then we are discoursing with the Gentiles, we cite (4 Mss. read or point to the reading, "let us not cite") not the heavens before them, but the men, whom though they were in worse plight than brutes, He hath persuaded to be the Angels' competitors. And we (1 Ms. "let us") stop their mouths by speaking of this change. For far better than the heaven is man, and a soul brighter than their beauty may he possess. For it, though visible for so long a time, did not persuade much. But Paul, after preaching a short time, drew the whole world unto him. (St. Aug. on Ps. xix. 4.) For he possessed a soul no less than the heaven, which was able to draw all men unto him. Our soul is not a match even for the earth: but his is equal to the heavens. That stands indeed keeping to its own boundary and rule; but the loftiness of his soul transcended all the heavens, and conversed with Christ Himself. (2 Cor. x. 15; Rom. xv. 19, etc.) And the beauty of it was so great, that even God heraldeth it forth. For the stars did the angels marvel at when they were made. (Job xxxviii. 7.) But this He marvelled at when He saith, "He is a chosen vessel unto Me." (Acts ix. 15.) And this Heaven doth a cloud many times overshadow. But Paul's soul no temptation overshadowed, but even in storms he was clearer to the sight than the hard sky (σταθερᾶς μεσημβρίας) at noon, and shone constantly as it had done before the clouds came on. For the Sun who shone in him sent not forth such rays as to be overclouded by the concourse of temptations, but even then shone forth the more. Wherefore he says, "My grace is sufficient for thee, for My Strength is made perfect in weakness." (2 Cor. xii. 9.) Let us then strive to be like him, and then even to what we are this heaven will be as nothing, if we wish it, nor yet the sun, nor the whole world. For these are for us, and not we for them. Let us show that we are worthy of having had these made for us. For if we be found unworthy of these, how shall we be worthy a kingdom? For indeed all that live so as to blaspheme God are unworthy to see the sun. They who blaspheme Him are unworthy to enjoy the creatures who glorify Him: since even a son

who insulteth his father is unworthy to be waited upon by the approved servants. Hence these will enjoy glory, and that great glory; but we shall have to undergo punishment and vengeance. How miserable then will it be for the creation which was made for thee to be fashioned "according to the glorious liberty of the children of God," (Rom. viii. 21) but for us who were made children of God, through our much listlessness, to be sent away to destruction and hell, for whose sake the creation shall enjoy that great festal time? Now to keep this from coming to pass, let such of us as have a pure soul keep it still such, or rather let us make its brightness more intense. And let those of us that have a soiled one, not despair. For "if" (he says) "your sins be as purple, I will make them white as snow. And if they be as scarlet, I will make them white as wool." (Is. i. 18.) But when it is God that promiseth, doubt not, but do those things whereby thou mayest draw to thee these promises. Are they unnumbered, the fearful and outrageous acts done by thee? And what of this? For hitherto thou art not gone away into the grave where no man shall confess. (ib. xxxviii. 18; Ps. vi. 5.) Hitherto the arena (θέατρον) is not broken up for thee, but thou art standing within the line, and thou art able even by a struggle at the last to recover all thy defeats. Thou art not yet come to where the rich man was, for thee to hear it said, "there is a gulf betwixt you and us." (Luke xvi. 26.) The Bridegroom is not yet at hand, that one should fear to give you of his oil. Still canst thou buy and store up. And there is not one yet to say, "Not so; lest there be not enough for us and and you" (Matt. xxv. 9); but there are many that sell, the naked, the hungry, the sick, the imprisoned. Give food to these, clothing to those, visit the sick, and the oil will come more than from fountains. The day of account is not here. Use the time as need be, and make deductions from the debts, and to him that oweth "an hundred measures of oil, say, Take thy bill and write fifty." (Luke xvi. 6.) And with money, and with words,[1] and with every other thing do in like manner, imitating that steward. And advise this to thyself, and also to thy relatives, for thou hast still the power of saying so. Thou art not yet come to the necessity of calling in another in their behalf, but thou hast power to give advice at once to thyself and to others. (ib. 28.) But when thou art gone away thither, neither of these things wilt thou have

---

[1] All Field's Mss. om. "words," which however may mean offence given by words.

it in thy power to do at need. And with good reason. For thou who hast had so long a period fixed thee, and neither done thyself good, nor any else, how when thou art under the Judge's hands shalt thou be able to obtain this grace? Putting all these things together then, let us cling fast to our own salvation, and not lose the opportunity of this life present. For it is possible, it is, even at our last breath to please God. It is possible to gain approval by thy last will, not indeed in such way as in our lifetime, still it is possible. How, and in what way? If thou leavest Him among thine heirs, and givest Him also (καὶ αὐτῷ) a portion of thine whole estate. Hast thou not fed Him in thy lifetime? At all events when departed, when thou art no longer owner, give Him a share of thy goods. He is loving unto man, He doth not deal niggardly by thee. It is a mark to be sure of a greater desire, and so it will be more rewarded, to feed Him in thy lifetime. But if thou hast not done this, at all events do the next best thing. Leave Him joint-heir (see p. 384) with thy children, and if thou art dilatory over this, bethink thyself that His Father made thee joint-heir with Him, and break down thy inhuman spirit. For what excuse wilt thou have if thou dost not even make Him a sharer with thy children, who made thee share the Heaven, and was slain for thee? And yet all that ever He did, He did not in repayment of a debt, but as bestowing a favor. But you after so great benefits, have been made a debtor as well. And yet, though things are so, it is as if receiving a favor, not as demanding payment of a debt, that He crowneth thee; and this too when what He is to receive is His own. Give then thy money, which is now no longer of any use to thee, and of which thou art no longer owner; and He will give thee a Kingdom which shall be of service to thee perpetually, and with it will bestow also the things of this life. For if He be made the joint-heir of thy children, He doth lighten their orphanage for them, do away with plots against them, beat off insults, stop the mouths of pettifoggers. And if they themselves be unable to stand up for their bequeathments, He will Himself stand up, and not let them be broken through. But if He do even allow this, then He makes up of Himself all that was ordered in the will with still greater liberality, because He has been but mentioned in it. Leave Him then thine heir. For it is to Him that thou art upon the point of going. He will be thy Judge Himself in the trial for all that hath been done here. But there are some so miserable and pinched, that though they have no children,

still they have not the courage to do this, but approve of giving that they have to hangers on, and to flatterers, and to this person and to that, sooner than to Christ, Who hath done them so great benefits. And what can be more unreasonable than this conduct? For if one were to compare men of this cast to asses, aye, or to stones, one shall not still be saying anything tantamount to their unreasonableness and senselessness. Nor could one find a similitude to put before you their madness and dementedness. For what pardon shall they obtain for not having fed Him in their lifetime, who, even when they are on the point of departing to Him, have not the inclination to give Him but a trifle out of those goods, of which they are no longer the owners, but are of such an inimical and hostile disposition, as not even to give Him a share in what is useless to themselves? Do you not know how many of mankind have not even been counted worthy to obtain an end of this kind, but have been snatched off suddenly? But thee doth God empower to give orders to thy kindred, and to speak with them about thy property, and set all that is in thy house in order. What defence then wilt thou have to set up, when even after receiving this favor from Him, thou hast treacherously given up the benefit, and art standing as it were in diametrical opposition to thy forefathers in the faith? For they even in their lifetime sold all, and brought it to the Apostle's feet. But thou, even at thy death, dost not give any share to them that need. What is the better part, and gives one much boldness, is to remedy poverty in one's lifetime. But if thou hast not been minded to do this, at all events do upon thy death-bed some noble act. For this is not what a strong love for Christ would do, yet still it is an act of love. For if thou wilt not have the high place with the Lambs, still even to be after them at all is no light thing, and so not to be placed with the goats nor on the left hand. But if thou wilt not do even this, what plea is to rescue thee, when neither the fear of death nor thy money having become henceforth of no use to thee, nor the leaving of safety behind thee to thy children, nor the laying up of much pardon there against the time to come, will make thee merciful to man? Wherefore I advise, as the best thing, that in your lifetime you give the larger half of your goods to the poor. But if there be any of so narrow a soul as not to have the heart to do so, at all events let them by necessity become merciful. For when you were living as if there were no death, then you clung close to your goods. But now since you have learnt that you are to die, at least now give over your opinion, and deliberate about your affairs as one that must die. Or rather as one that ought to enjoy immortal life for evermore. For if what I am going to say be distasteful, and big with horror, still it must be said. Reckon with thy slaves the Lord. Art thou giving thy slaves liberty? Give Christ liberty from famine, from distress, from imprisonment, from nakedness. Art thou horrified at the words? Is it not then more horrible when thou dost not even thus much? And here the word makes thy blood curdle. But when thou art gone to that world, and hast to hear things far more grievous than these, and seest the tortures which are incurable, what wilt thou say? To whom wilt thou flee for refuge? Whom wilt thou call to thy alliance and assistance? Will it be Abraham? He will not hearken to thee. Or those virgins? They will not give thee of their oil. Thy father then or thy grandfather? But none even of these, if he be ever so holy, will have it in his power to reverse that sentence. Weighing then all these things, to Him Who alone is Lord to blot out the bill against thee and to quench that flame, to Him make prayer and supplication, and propitiate Him, by now feeding Him and clothing Him continually: that in this world thou mayest depart with a good hope, and when thou art there thou mayest enjoy eternal blessings, which may we all attain to by the grace and love toward man, etc.

HOMILY XIX.

ROM. XI. 7.

"What then?[1] Israel hath not obtained that, which he seeketh for; but the election hath obtained it, and the rest were blinded."

HE had said that God did not cast off His people; and to show in what sense He had not cast them off, he takes refuge in the Prophets again.* And having shown by them that the more part of the Jews were lost, that he might not seem to be again bringing forward an accusation of his own, and to make his discourse offensive, and to be attacking them as enemies, he takes refuge in David and Isaiah, and says,

Ver. 8. "According as it is written, God hath given them the spirit of slumber." (Is. xxix. 10.)

Or rather we should go back to the beginning of his argument. Having then mentioned the state of things in Elijah's time, and shown what grace is, he proceeds, "What then? Israel hath not obtained that which he seeketh for." Now this is as much what an accuser would say, as what one who was putting a question. For the Jew, he means, is inconsistent with himself when he seeketh for righteousness, which he will not accept. Then to leave them with no excuse, he shows, from those who have accepted it, their unfeeling spirit, as he says, "But the election hath obtained it," and they are the condemnation of the others. And this is what Christ says, "But if I by Beelzebub cast out devils, by whom do your children cast them out? Wherefore they shall be your judges." (Luke xi. 19.) For to prevent any one from accusing the nature of the thing, and not their own temper, he points out those who had obtained it. Hence he uses the word[2] with great propriety, to show at once the grace from above and the zeal of these. For it is not to deny free-will that he speaks of their having "obtained" (as by chance, Gr. ἐπέτυχε) it, but to show the greatness of the good things, and that the greater part was of grace, though not the whole.[3] For we too are in the habit of saying, "so and so chanced to get" (same word), "so and so met with," when the gain has been a great one. Because it is not by man's labors, but by God's gift, that the greater part was brought about.

"And the rest was blinded."

See how he has been bold enough to tell with his own voice the casting off of the rest. For he had indeed spoken of it already, but it

---

[1] Field punctuates so as to give the sense "Why then hath not Israel attained to that which he seeketh after? Nay, but the election hath obtained it;" which seems to be (at all events) St. Chrysostom's view of the passage.

* The course of thought here may be thus exhibited: God in his gracious promise made simple faith the condition of salvation, but Israel sought it in the line of works and has not attained it. But the election obtained it because the avowed principle of the election was grace, to which corresponds faith. In other words: those who complied with the express principle of the election and who sought salvation by faith, receiving it as a gift of divine grace, were accepted. Those who thought to establish their own righteousness have failed, and this failure corresponds to that judicial hardening with which God through Moses and Isaiah threatens the disobedient Israelites in the Old Testament.—G. B. S.

[2] Or "language." He has before remarked on the term election as implying an approved character; see on v. 5, p. 483.
[3] So on x. 21. But see on viii. 26, and xi. 22.

was by bringing the prophets in as accusers. But from this point he declares it in his own person. Still even here he is not content with his own declaration, but brings Isaiah the prophet in again. For after saying, "were blinded," he proceeds; "according as it is written, God hath given them the spirit of slumber." Now whence came this blinding? He had indeed mentioned the causes of it before, and turned it all upon their own heads, to show that it was from their unseasonable obstinacy that they had to bear this. And now he speaks of it too. For when he says, "Eyes that they should not see, and ears that they should not hear," he is but finding fault with their contentious spirit. For when they had "eyes to see" the miracles, and were possessed of "ears to hear" that marvellous Teaching, they never used these as were fitting. And the "He gave," do not imagine to mean here an agency, but a permission only. But "slumber" (κατάνυξις lit. piercing) is a name he here gives to the habit of soul inclinable to the worse, when incurably and unchangeably so. For in another passage David says, "that my glory may sing unto Thee, and I may not be put to slumber" (Ps. xxx. 12, LXX.): that is, I may not alter, may not be changed. For as a man who is hushed to slumber in a state of pious fear would not easily be made to change his side; so too he that is slumbering in wickedness would not change with facility. For to be hushed[1] to slumber here is nothing else but to be fixed and riveted to a thing. In pointing then to the incurable and unchangeable character of their spirit, he calls it "a spirit of slumber." Then to show that for this unbelief they will be most severely punished, he brings the Prophet forward again, threatening the very things which in the event came to pass.

Ver. 9. "Let their table be made a snare, and a trap, and a stumbling-block." (Ps. lxix. 22, 23.)

That is, let their comforts and all their good things change and perish, and let them be open to attack from any one. And to show that this is in punishment for sins that they suffer this, he adds, "and a recompense unto them."

Ver. 10. "Let their eyes be darkened that they may not see, and bow Thou down their back alway."

Do these things then still require any inter-

preting? Are they not plain even to those ever so senseless? And before our words, the very issue of facts has anticipated us in bearing witness to what was said. For at what time have they ever been so open to attacks? at what time such an easy prey? at what time hath He so "bowed down their backs?" At what time have they been set under such bondage? And what is more, there is not to be any unloosing from these terrors. And this the prophet hath also hinted. For he does not say only, "bow Thou down their back," but, "forever bow Thou down." But if thou art disposed to dispute, O Jew, about the issue, from what hath gone before learn also the present case. Thou didst go down to Egypt; and two hundred years passed, and God freed thee speedily from that bondage, and that though thou wert irreligious, and wentest a whoring with the most baneful whoredom. Thou wast freed from Egypt, and thou didst worship the calf, thou didst sacrifice thy sons to Baalpeor, thou didst defile the temple, thou didst go after every sort of vice, thou didst grow not to know nature itself. The mountains, the groves, the hills, the springs, the rivers, the gardens didst thou fill with accursed sacrifices, thou didst slay the prophets, didst overthrow the altars, didst exhibit every excess of wickedness and irreligion. Still, after giving thee up for seventy years to the Babylonians, He brought thee back again to thy former freedom, and gave thee back the temple, and thy country, and thy old form of polity,[2] and there were prophets again, and the gift of the Spirit. Or rather, even in the season of thy captivity thou wast not deserted, but even there were Daniel, and Ezekiel, and in Egypt Jeremiah, and in the desert Moses. After this thou didst revert to thy former vice again, and wast a reveller (ἐξεβακχεύθης 2 Macc. xiv. 33), therein, and didst change thy manner of life (πολιτείαν to the Grecian in the time of Antiochus the impious Dan. viii. 14; 1 Macc. iv. 54). But even then for a three years and a little over only were ye given up to Antiochus, and then by the Maccabees ye raised those bright trophies again. But now there is nothing of the sort, for the reverse hath happened throughout. And this is ground for the greatest surprise, as the vices have ceased, and the punishment hath been increased, and is without any hope of a change. For it is not seventy years only that have passed away, nor a hundred, nor yet twice as many, but three hundred, and a good deal over, and there is no finding even a shadow of a hope of the

---

[1] Accommodated to the A. V. Gr. "to feel compunction": the word is used thus on Rom. viii. 26, p. 447. In Is. xxix. 10, it is for הרדמה a deep (often supernatural) sleep, as Gen. ii. 21, xv. 12; 1 Sam. xxvi. 12; Ps. lxxvi. 7. In Ps. xxx. (al. 29), 13, the verb is דמם which signifies stillness (from horror or amazement). We speak of being penetrated with horror; here the notion of piercing is taken, and applied to fixing. See Schleusner on κατανύσσομαι.

[2] Most Mss. "prophecy," which if right must be interpreted "theocracy."

kind. And this though ye neither are idol-aters, nor do the other audacious acts ye did before. What then is the cause? The reality hath succeeded to the type, and grace hath shut out the Law. And this the prophet fore-telling from of old said, "And ever bow Thou down their back." See the minuteness of prophecy, how it foretells their unbelief, and also points out their disputatiousness, and shows the judgment which should follow, and sets forth the endlessness of the punishment. For as many of the duller sort, through unbe-lief in what was to come to pass, wished to see things to come by the light of things present, from this point of time God gave proof of His power on either part, by lifting those of the Gentiles who believed, above the heaven, but bringing down such of the Jews as believed not to the lowest estate of desola-tion, and giving them up to evils not to be ended. Having then urged them severely both about their not believing, and about what they had suffered and were yet to suffer, he again allays what he had said by writing as follows:

Ver. 11. "I say then, Have they stumbled, that they should fall? God forbid."

When he has shown that they were liable to evils without number, then he devises an allayment. And consider the judgment of Paul. The accusation he had introduced from the prophets, but the allayment he makes come from himself. For that they had sinned greatly, he would say, none will gainsay. But let us see if the fall is of such kind as to be incurable, and quite preclude their being set up again. But of such kind it is not.* You see how he is attacking them again, and

under the expectation of some allayment he proves them guilty of confessed sins. But let us see what even by way of allayment he does devise for them. Now what is the allayment? "When the fulness of the Gentiles," he says, "shall have come in, then shall all Israel be saved," at the time of his second coming, and the end of the world. Yet this he does not say at once. But since he had made a hard onset upon them, and linked accusations to accusations, bringing prophets in after prophets crying aloud against them, Isaiah, Elijah, David, Moses, Hosea, not once or twice, but several times; lest in this way he should both by driving these into despair, make a wall to bar their access to the faith, and should further make such of the Gentiles as believed unreasonably elated, and they also by being puffed up should take harm in matter of their faith, he further solaces them by say-ing, "But rather through their fall salvation is come unto the Gentiles." But we must not take what is here said literally, but get ac-quainted with the spirit and object of the speaker, and what he aimed to compass. Which thing I ever entreat of your love. For if with this in our minds we take up what is here said, we shall not find a difficulty in any part of it. For his present anxiety is to remove from those of the Gentiles the haughtiness which might spring in them from what he had said. For in this way they too were more likely to continue unshaken in the faith, when they had learnt to be reasonable, as also those of the Jews were, when quit of despair, more likely to come with readiness to grace. Having regard then to this object of his, let us so listen to all that is said on this

<hr/>

* The following paraphrase of the apostle's argument in vv. 16-24 by which he would show that the Jews' rejection is but temporary may be serviceable in connection with the exposition of Chrysostom : granting then that the Jews have sadly stumbled, have they done so in order that (ἵνα, accord-ing to a providential intention) they may fall (completely away from God and be lost to all hope)? No. There is a providential purpose in this sad lapse. God has overruled it for the salvation of the Gentiles. When the Jews rejected Christianity, then the gospel turned from them and went to the Gentiles, so that the rejection of the Jews facilitated the conversion of the heathen. And the acceptance of the Gen-tiles reacted again in favor of the Jews because it provoked them to jealousy and so stimulated them to accept the bless-ings which the Gentiles were receiving. Thus their fall has a twofold beneficial effect, (a) on the Gentiles, (b) through them on themselves. (vv. 11-12) Now, if so much good can come out of their fall, how much more out of their restoration! If their fault, by which they come so far short of their ideal mission, could be such an (indirect) blessing to the Gentiles, how much greater a blessing will the repairing of that defect prove? (vv. 13-16.) I say the return of the Jews will be a great blessing to you, my Gentile Christian brethren, and I urge this point with you. It is all to be to your advantage. In hoping and laboring for the conversion of my own people, I am still laboring in the line of my mission as apostle to the Gentiles. If I can save any of the Jews and stimulate their jealousy so that they will be desirous of availing themselves of the blessings of the gospel, I shall be doing the greatest possible good to the Gentile world. Why? (15) Because if their rejection is the "reconciliation of the world"—the means of securing salvation to the Gentiles, their reception back again shall be a veritable "resurrection from the dead."—from it shall flow streams of spiritual life, compared with

which that indirect blessing which sprang from their rejec-tion is as nothing (16). And such is the divine, final destina-tion of the Jewish people. They are still holy unto the Lord, a peculiar possession, and cannot be finally and utterly cast away. (vv. 17-24) Hence you Gentiles have no ground of glorying over the Jews, either in the fact that some of them have been cut off or that you have been grafted in. Israel is still the stock. At most you are but branches and that wild-olive branches! If now you seize upon what was said (in vv. 11-12) and maintain that the Jews were rejected to make place for you (19), I reply that there is another to the matter (20). From the point of view of the divine providence this is true, but from the point of view of the Jews' own action, unbelief explains their rejection. You have nothing to do with God's providential purposes in the case. What you have to do is to be obedient and faithful. If you draw an assurance from the one view, I shall draw a warning from the other and that too from the side with which you have to do and for which you are responsible. "Be not high-minded but fear." God will deal with you on the same principles upon which he has dealt with the Jews (21). These dispensations reveal the two sides of God's nature—his severity toward disobedience and his goodness to all who continue in relation to his goodness (22). Those portions of the nation which have been cut off shall be grafted in again unless they persist in unbelief (23). And if the branches from a wild-olive tree were grafted into the genuine olive tree, contrary to their nature, how much more natural to suppose that the branches which originally belonged to the true olive stock shall be returned and grafted again into that stock to which they naturally belong (24). There is no good ground for the opinion of Chrys. (11) that the salvation of Israel is to occur at the second coming and the end of the world.—G. B. S.

passage. What does he say then? And whence does he show that their fall was not irremediable, nor their rejection final? He argues from the Gentiles, saying as follows:

"Through their fall salvation is come unto the Gentiles, for to provoke them to jealousy."

This language is not his own only, but in the Gospels too the parables mean this. For He who made a marriage feast for His Son, when the guests would not come, called those in the highways. (Matt. xxii. 9.) And He who planted the Vineyard, when the husband-men slew the Heir, let out His Vineyard to others. (ib. xxi. 38, etc.) And without any parable, He Himself said, "I am not sent but unto the lost sheep of the House of Israel." (ib. xv. 24.) And to the Syrophœnician woman, when she persevered, He said some-what further besides. "It is not meet," He says, "to take the children's bread, and cast it to the dogs." (ib. xv. 26.) And Paul to those of the Jews that raised a sedition, "It was necessary that the word of God should first have been spoken unto you : but seeing ye judge yourselves unworthy, lo, we turn unto the Gentiles." (Acts xiii. 46.) And through-out it is clear that the natural course of things was this, that they should be the first to come in, and then those of the Gentiles ; but since they disbelieved, the order was reversed ; and their unbelief and fall caused these to be brought in first. Hence it is that he says, "through their fall salvation is come to the Gentiles, for to provoke them to jealousy." But if he mentions what the course of things issued in, as if the chief design of Providence, do not feel surprised. For he wishes to sol-ace their down-stricken souls, and his mean-ing is about this. Jesus came to them; they did not receive Him, though He did countless miracles, but crucified Him. Hence He drew the Gentiles to Him, that the honor they had, by cutting them to the heart for their insensi-bility might at least out of a moroseness against others persuade them to come over. For they ought to have been first admitted, and then we. And this was why he said, "For it is the power of God unto salvation unto every one that believeth ; to the Jew first, and also to the Gentile." (Rom. i. 16.) But as they had started off, we the last became first. See then how great honors he gathers for them even from this. One that he says, we were then called, when they were not will-ing ; a second that he says, the reason of our being called was not that we only might be saved, but that they also, growing jealous at our salvation, might become better. What does he say then? that if it were not for the Jews' sake, we should not have been called and saved at all? We should not before them, but in the regular order. Wherefore also when He was speaking to the disciples, He did not say barely, "Go to the lost sheep of the House of Israel" (Matt. x. 6), but, "Go rather to the sheep," to show that to those parts also they must come after these. And Paul again saith not, "It was necessary that the word of God should have been spoken unto you," but "should first have been spoken unto you" (Acts xiii. 46), to show that in the second place it must be to us also. And this was both done and said, that they might not be able, shameless though they were, to pre-tend that they were overlooked, and that was why they did not believe. This then was why Christ, though he knew all things before, yet came to them first.

Ver. 12. "Now if the fall of them be the riches of the world, and the diminishing of them the riches of the Gentiles, how much more their fulness?"

Here he is speaking to gratify them. For even if these had fallen a thousand times, the Gentiles would not have been saved unless they had shown faith. As the Jews likewise would not have perished unless they had been unbelieving and disputatious. But as I said, he is solacing them now they are laid low, giv-ing them so much the more ground to be con-fident of their salvation if they altered. For if when they stumbled, he says, so many en-joyed salvation, and when they were cast out so many were called, just consider what will be the case when they return. But he does not put it thus, When they return. Now he does not say "how much more their" return, or their altering, or their well-doing, but "how much more their fulness," that is, when they are all about coming in. And this he said to show that then also grace and God's gift will do the larger part, or almost the whole.

Ver. 13, 14. "For I speak to you Gentiles ; inasmuch as I am the Apostle of the Gentiles, I magnify mine office ; if by any means I may provoke to emulation them which are my flesh, and might save some of them."

Again he endeavors much to get himself clear of untoward suspicion. And he seems to be blaming the Gentiles, and to be hum-bling their conceits, yet he gives a gentle prov-ocation to the Jew also. And indeed he goes round about seeking to veil and allay this great ruin of theirs. But he finds no means of doing it, owing to the nature of the facts. For from what he had said, they deserved but the greater condemnation, when those who were far short of them had taken the good things prepared for them. This is why then he passes from the Jews to those of the Gentiles, and puts in between his discourse the part about them, as wishing to show that he is saying all these things in order to instruct them to be reasonable. For I praise you, he means, for these two reasons; one, because I am necessitated to do so as being your commissioned minister; the other, that through you I may save others. And he does not say, my brethren, my kinsmen; but, "my flesh." And next, when pointing out their disputatious spirit, he does not say, "if by any means I may" persuade, but, "provoke to jealousy and save;" and here again not all, but, "some of them." So hard were they! And even amid his rebuke he shows again the Gentiles honored, for they are causes of their salvation, and not in the same way. For they became purveyors of blessings to them through unbelief, but these to the Jews by faith. Hence the estate of the Gentiles seems to be at once equal and superior. For what wilt thou say, O Jew? that if we had not been cast out, he would not have been called so soon? This the man of the Gentiles may say too, If I had not been saved, thou wouldest not have been moved to jealousy. But if thou wouldest know wherein we have the advantage, I save thee by believing, but it is by stumbling that thou hast afforded us an access before thyself. Then perceiving again that he had touched them to the quick, resuming his former argument, he says,

Ver. 15. "For if the casting away of them be the reconciling of the world, what shall the receiving of them be but life from the dead?"

Yet this again condemns them, since, while others gained by their sins, they did not profit by other men's well doings. But if he asserts that to be their doing which necessarily happened, be not surprised: since (as I have said several times) it is to humble these, and to exhort the other, that he throws his address into this form. For as I said before, if the Jews had been cast away a thousand times over, and the Gentiles had not shown faith, they would never have been saved. But he stands by the feeble party, and gives assistance to the distressed one. But see also even in his favors to them, how he solaces them in words only. "For if the casting away of them be the reconciling of the world," (and what is this to the Jews?) "what shall the receiving of them be but life from the dead?" Yet even this was no boon to them, unless they had been received. But what he means is to this effect. If in anger with them He gave other men so great gifts, when He is reconciled to them what will He not give? But as the resurrection of the

dead was not by the receiving of them, so neither now is our salvation through them. But they were cast out owing to their own folly, but it is by faith that we are saved, and by grace from above. But of all this nothing can be of service to them, unless they show the requisite faith. Yet doing as he is wont, he goes on to another encomium, which is not really one, but which only seems to be, so imitating the wisest physicians, who give their patients as much consolation as the nature of the sickness allows them. And what is it that he says?

Ver. 16. "For if the first-fruits be holy, the lump also is holy; and if the root be holy, so are the branches;"

So calling in this passage by the names of the first-fruit and root Abraham, and Isaac, and Jacob, the prophets, the patriarchs, all who were of note in the Old Testament; and the branches, those from them who believed. Then since the fact met him that many had disbelieved, observe how he undermines (ὑποτέμνεται, see p. 345) it again, and says,

Ver. 17. "And if some of the branches be broken off."

And yet above thou didst say that the more part perished, and a few were saved only. How came it then that speaking of those that perished, thou hast used a "some," which is indicative of fewness? It is not, he replies, in opposition to myself, but out of a desire to court and recover those that are distressed. Observe how in the whole of the passage one finds him working at this object, the wish to solace them. And if you deny it, many contradictions will follow. But let me beg you to notice his wisdom, how while he seems to be speaking for them, and devising a solace for them, he aims a secret blow at them, and shows that they are devoid of all excuse, even from the "root," from the "first-fruit." For consider the badness of the branches, which, when they have a sweet root, still do not imitate it; and the faultiness of the lump, when it is not altered even by the first-fruit. "And if some of the branches were broken off." However, the greater part were broken off. Yet, as I said, he wishes to comfort them. And this is why it is not in his own person, but in theirs, that he brings in the words used, and even in this gives a secret stroke at them, and shows them to have fallen from being Abraham's kinsmen. (Matt. iii. 9.) For what he was desirous of saying was, that they had nothing in common with them. (John viii. 39.) For if the root be holy, and these be not holy, then these are far away from the root. Then under the appearance of solacing the Jews, he again by his accusation smiteth them of the Gentiles. For after saying, "And if some of the branches were broken off," he proceeds.

"And thou being a wild olive wert grafted in."

For the less esteem the man of the Gentiles is of, the more the Jew is vexed at seeing him enjoy his goods. And to the other, the disgrace of the little esteem he was of, is nothing to the honor of the change. And consider his skilfulness. He does not say, "thou wert" planted "in," but "thou wert grafted in," by this again cutting the Jew to the heart, as showing that the Gentile man was standing in his own tree, and himself lying on the ground. Wherefore he does not stop even here, nor after he had spoken of grafting in does he leave off (and yet in this he declared the whole matter), but still he dwells over the prosperous state of the Gentile, and enlarges upon his fair fame in the words, " And with them partakest of the root and fatness of the olive tree." And he seems indeed to have viewed him in the light of an addition. But he shows that he was no whit the worse on that account, but in possession of everything, that the branch which had come up out of the root had. Lest then on hearing the words, " and thou wert grafted in," thou shouldest suppose him to be lacking when compared with the natural branch, see how he makes him equal to it by saying, that "with them thou partakest of the root and fatness of the olive : " that is, hast been put into the same noble rank, the same nature. Then in rebuking him, and saying,

Ver. 18. " Boast not against the branches."

He seems indeed to be comforting the Jew, but points out his vileness and extreme dishonor. And this is why he says not, "boast not," but, "boast not against," do not boast against them so as to sunder them. For it is into their place that ye have been set, and their goods that ye enjoy. Do you observe how he seems to be rebuking the one, while he is sharp upon the other?

"But if thou boast," he says, " thou bearest not the root, but the root thee."

Now what is this to the branches that are cut off? Nothing. For, as I said before, while seeming to devise a sort of weak shadow of consolation, and in the very midst of his aiming at the Gentile, he gives them a mortal blow; for by saying, "boast not against them," and, "if thou boast, thou bearest not the root," he has shown the Jew that the things done deserved boasting of, even if it was not right to boast, thus at once rousing him and provoking him to faith, and smiting at him, in the attitude of an advocate, and

pointing out to him the punishment he was undergoing, and that other men had possession of what were their goods.

Ver. 19. "Thou wilt say then," he goes on, "The branches were broken off that I might be grafted in."

Again he establishes, by way of objection, the opposite to the former position, to show that what he said before, he had not said as directly belonging to the subject, but to draw them to him. For it was no longer by their fall that salvation came to the Gentiles, nor was it their fall that was the riches of the world. Nor was it by this that we were saved, because they had fallen, but the reverse. And he shows that the providence in regard to the Gentiles was a main object, even though he seems to put what he says into another form. And the whole passage is a tissue of objections, in which he clears himself of the suspicion of hatred, and makes his language such as will be acceptable.

Ver. 20. "Well," he praises what they said, then he alarms them again by saying, "Because of unbelief they were broken off, and thou art grafted in [1] by faith."

So here another encomium, and for the other party an accusation. But he again lays their pride low by proceeding to say, "be not high-minded, but fear." For the thing is not matter of nature, but of belief and unbelief. And he seems to be again bridling the Gentile, but he is teaching the Jew that it is not right to cling to a natural kinsmanship. Hence he goes on with, "Be not high-minded," and he does not say, but be humble, but, fear. For haughtiness genders a contempt and listlessness. Then as he is going into all the sorrows of their calamity, in order to make the statement less offensive, he states it in the way of a rebuke given to the other as follows :

Ver. 21. " For if God spared not the natural branches," and then he does not say, neither will He spare thee," but "take heed, lest He also spare not thee." So paring (ὑποτεμνόμενος) away the distasteful from his statement, representing the believer as in the struggle, he at once draws the others to him, and humbles these also.

Ver. 22. " Behold therefore the goodness and severity of God: on them which fell, severity ; but toward thee, goodness, if thou continue in His goodness : otherwise thou also shalt be cut off."

And he does not say, Behold thy well doing, behold thy labors, but, " Behold the goodness

1 So all Mss. but one, but we need not suppose a various reading in the text, as there is no authority for it: rec. t. standest.

of God" toward man, to show that the whole comes of grace from above, and to make us tremble. For this reason for boasting should make thee to fear: since the Lord ($\delta\epsilon\sigma\pi\acute{o}\tau\eta\varsigma$) hath been good unto thee, do thou therefore fear. For the blessings do not abide by thee unmovable if thou turnest listless, as neither do the evils with them, if they alter; "For thou also," he says, "unless thou continue in the faith, wilt be cut off."

Ver. 23. "And they also, if they abide not in unbelief, shall be grafted in."

For it was not God that cut them off, but they have broken themselves off and fallen, and he did well to say have[1] broken themselves off. For He hath never yet so (Sav. conj. Ms. corr. $o\hat{v}\tau o\varsigma$) cast them off, though they have sinned so much and so often. You see what a great thing a man's free choice is, how great the efficacy of the mind is. For none of these things is immutable, neither thy good nor his evil. You see too how he raises up even him in his despondency, and humbles the other in his confidence; and do not thou be faint at hearing of severity, nor thou be confident at hearing of goodness. The reason why He cut thee[2] off in severity was, that thou mightest long to come back. The reason why He showed goodness to thee was, that thou mightest continue in (he does not say the faith, but) His goodness, that is, if thou do things worthy of God's love toward man. For there is need of something more than faith. You see how he suffers, neither these to lie low, nor those to be elated, but he also provokes them to jealousy, by giving through them a power to the Jew to be set again in this one's place, as he also had first taken the other's ground. And the Gentile he put in fear by the Jews, and what had happened to them, lest they should feel elated over it. But the Jew he tries to encourage by what had been afforded to the Greek. For thou also, he says, wilt be cut off if thou growest listless, (for the Jew was cut off), and he will be grafted in if he be earnest, for thou also wast grafted in. But it is very judicious in him to direct all he says to the Gentile, as he is always in the habit of doing, correcting the feeble by rebuking the stronger. This he does in the end of this Epistle too, when he is speaking of the observance of meats. Then, he grounds this on what had already happened, not upon what was to come only. And this was more likely to persuade his hearer. And as he means to

enter on consecutiveness of reasonings, such as could not be spoken against, he first uses a demonstration drawn from the power of God. For if they were cut off, and cast aside, and others took precedence of them in what was theirs, still even now despair not.

"For God is able," he says, "to graft them in again," since He doeth things beyond expectation. But if thou wishest for things to be in order, and reasons to be consecutive, you have from yourselves a demonstration which more than meets your wants.

Ver. 24. "For if thou wert cut out of the olive tree, which is wild by nature, and were grafted contrary to nature into a good olive tree, how much more shall these, which be the natural branches, be grafted[3] into their own olive tree."

If then faith was able to do what was contrary to nature, much more will it that which is according to nature. For if this person, who was cut off from those by nature his fathers,[4] came contrary to nature unto Abraham, much more wilt thou be able to recover thine own. For the Gentile's evil lot is according to nature (he being by nature a wild olive), and the good contrary to nature (it being contrary to nature for him to be grafted into Abraham), but thy lot on the contrary is the good by nature. For it is not upon another root, as the Gentile, but on thine own that thou art to be fixed if thou art minded to come back. What then dost thou deserve, when after the Gentile had been able to do what was contrary to nature, thou art not able to do that which is according to nature, but hast given up even this? Then as he had said "contrary to nature," and, "wert grafted in," that you may not suppose the Jew to have the advantage, he again corrects this by saying that he also is grafted in. "How much more shall these," says he, "which be the natural branches be grafted into their own olive-tree?" And again, "God is able to graft them in." And before this he says, that if they "abide not still in unbelief, they shall be also grafted in." And when you hear that he keeps speaking of "according to nature," and "contrary to nature," do not suppose that he means the nature that is unchangeable, but he tells us in these words of the probable and the consecutive, and on the other hand of the improbable. For the good things and the bad are not such as[5] are by nature, but by

---

[1] $\dot{\epsilon}\xi\epsilon\kappa\lambda\acute{a}\sigma\theta\eta\sigma\alpha\nu$. In earlier Greek this use of the passive belongs to the second aorist, but in later times it extends to the first.

[2] Most Mss. "cut thee not off," which is perhaps the better reading. See on the last verse.

[3] There is no authority for the reading of the old edd., " these, if according to nature they be grafted."

[4] Ms. " from these that were his by nature by others."

[5] Ben. and several Mss. $\phi\upsilon\sigma\iota\kappa\grave{a}$ for $\phi\acute{v}\sigma\epsilon\iota$. Savile's reading would be a general position which is not so much to the purpose, such as that of St. Augustin, *nullam esse naturam mali*. This reading however will also bear that meaning.

temper and determination alone. And consider also how inoffensive he is. For after saying that thou also wilt be cut off, if thou dost not abide in the faith, and these will be grafted in, if they "abide not still in unbelief," he leaves that of harsh aspect, and insists on that of kindlier sound, and in it he ends, putting great hopes before the Jews if they were minded not to abide so. Wherefore he goes on to say,

Ver. 25. "For I would not, brethren, that ye should be ignorant of this mystery, lest ye should be wise in your own conceits."

Meaning by mystery here, that which is unknown and unutterable, and hath much of wonder and much of what one should not expect about it. As in another passage too he says, "Behold, I tell you a mystery. We shall not all sleep, but we shall all be changed." (1 Cor. xv. 51.) What then is the mystery?

"That blindness in part hath happened unto Israel." Here again he levels a blow at the Jew, while seeming to take down the Gentile. But his meaning is nearly this, and he had said it before, that the unbelief is not universal, but only "in part." As when he says, "But if any hath caused grief, he hath not grieved me, but in part" (2 Cor. ii. 5) : And, so here too he says what he had said above, "God hath not cast off His people whom He foreknew" (Rom. xi. 2): and again, "What then? Have they stumbled that they should fall? God forbid" (ib. 11): This then he says here also; that it is not the whole people that is pulled up, but many have already believed, and more are likely to believe. Then as he had promised a great thing, he adduces the prophet in evidence, speaking ·as follows. Now it is not for the fact of a blindness having happened that he quotes the passage (for every one could see that), but that they shall believe and be saved, he brings Isaiah to witness, who crieth aloud and saith,

Ver. 26. "There shall come out of Sion the Deliverer, and shall turn away ungodliness from Jacob." (Is. lix. 20.)

Then to give the mark that fixes its sense to salvation, to prevent any one from drawing it aside and attaching it to times gone by, he says,

Ver. 27. "For this is my covenant unto them,[1] when I shall take away their sins."

Not when they are circumcised, not when they sacrifice, not when they do the other deeds of the Law, but when they attain to the forgiveness of sins. If then this hath been

promised, but has never yet happened in their case, nor have they ever enjoyed the remission of sins by baptism, certainly it will come to pass. Hence he proceeds,

Ver. 29. "For the gifts and calling of God are without repentance."

And even this is not all he says to solace them, for he uses what had already come about. And what came in of consequence, that he states as chiefly intended, putting it in these words,

Ver. 28. "As concerning the Gospel, they are enemies for your sakes : but as touching the election, they are beloved for the fathers' sakes."

That the Gentile then might not be puffed up, and say, "I am standing, do not tell me of what would have been, but what has been," he uses this consideration to bring him down, and says, "As concerning the Gospel, they are enemies for your sakes." For when you were called they became more captious. Nevertheless God hath not even now cut short the calling of you, but He waiteth for all the Gentiles that are to believe to come in, and then they also shall come. Then he does them another kind favor, by saying, "As touching election, they are beloved for the fathers sakes." And what is this? for wherein they are enemies, punishment is theirs : but wherein they are beloved, the virtue of their ancestors has no influence on them, if they do not believe. Nevertheless, as I said, he ceaseth not to solace them with words, that he may bring them over. Wherefore by way of fresh proof for his former assertion, he says,

Ver. 30–32. "For as ye in times past have not believed God, yet have now obtained mercy through their unbelief; even so have these also now not believed, that through your mercy they may also obtain mercy. For God hath concluded them all in unbelief, that He might have mercy upon all."

He shows here that those of the Gentiles were called first. Then, as they would not come, the Jews were elected, and the same result occurred again. For when the Jews would not believe, again the Gentiles were brought over. And he does not stop here, nor does he draw the whole to a conclusion at their rejection, but at their having mercy shown them again. See how much he gives to those of the Gentiles, as much as he did to the Jews before. For when ye, he would say, "in times past did not obey," being of the Gentiles, then the Jews came in. Again, when these did not obey, ye have come. However, they will not perish forever. "For God hath concluded them all in unbelief," that is, hath convinced

---

[1] So LXX. except in *when*, etc., which the sequel implies. See Jer. xxxi. 31, 34.

them, hath shown them disobedient; not that they may remain in disobedience, but that He may save the one by the captiousness of the other, these by those and those by these. Now consider; ye were disobedient, and they were saved. Again, they have been disobedient, and ye have been saved. Yet ye have not been so saved as to be put away again, as the Jews were, but so as to draw them over through jealousy while ye abide.

Ver. 33. "Oh, the depth of the riches, both of the wisdom and knowledge of God! How unsearchable are His judgments!"

Here after going back to former times, and looking back to God's original dispensation of things whereby the world hath existed up to the present time, and having considered what special provision He had made for all occurrences, he is stricken with awe, and cries aloud, so making his hearers feel confident that certainly that will come to pass which he saith. For he would not have cried aloud and been awe-struck, unless this was quite sure to come to pass. That it is a depth then, he knows: but how great, he knows not. For the language is that of a person wondering, not of one that knew the whole. But admiring and being awe-struck at the goodliness, so far forth as in him lay, he heralds it forth by two intensive words, riches and depth, and then is awestruck at His having had both the will and the power to do all this, and by opposites effecting opposites. "How unsearchable are His judgments." For they are not only impossible to be comprehended, but even to be searched. "And His ways past finding out;" that is, His dispensations for these also are not only impossible to be known, but even to be sought into. For even I, he means, have not found out the whole, but a little part, not all. For He alone knoweth His own clearly. Wherefore he proceeds:

Ver. 34, 35. "For who hath known the mind of the Lord? or who hath been His counsellor? Or who hath first given to Him, and it shall be recompensed unto him again?"

What he means is nearly this: that though He is so wise, yet He has not His Wisdom from any other, but is Himself the Fountain of good things. And though He hath done so great things, and made us so great presents, yet it was not by borrowing from any other that He gave them, but by making them spring forth from Himself; nor as owing any a return for having received from him, but as always being Himself the first to do the benefits; for this is a chief mark of riches, to overflow abundantly, and yet need no aid. Wherefore he proceeds to say, "For

of Him, and through Him, and to Him, are all things." Himself devised, Himself created, Himself worketh together (Vulg. συγκρατεῖ, Mss. συγκροτεῖ). For He is rich, and needeth not to receive from another. And wise, and needeth no counsellor. Why speak I of a counsellor? To know the things of Him is no one able, save Himself alone, the Rich and Wise One. For it is proof of much riches that He should make them of the Gentiles thus well supplied; and of much wisdom that He should constitute the inferiors of the Jews their teachers. Then as he was awe-struck he offers up thanksgiving also in the word, "To Whom be glory forever. Amen.

For when he tells of any great and unutterable thing of this kind, he ends in wonder with a doxology. And this he does in regard to the Son also. For in that passage also he went on to the very same thing that he does here. "Of whom is Christ according to the flesh, Who is over all God blessed forever. Amen. (Rom. ix. 5.)

Him then let us also imitate, and let us glorify God in all things, by a heedful way of life, and let us not feel confidence in the virtues of our ancestry, knowing the example that has been made of the Jews. For this is not, certainly it is not, the relationship of Christians, for theirs is the kinsmanship of the Spirit. So the Scythian becometh Abraham's son: and his son on the other hand more of an alien to him than the Scythian. Let us not then feel confidence in the well-doings of our fathers (most Mss. "of others"), but if you have a parent who is a marvel even, fancy not that this will be enough to save you, or to get you honor and glory, unless you have the relationship of character to him. So too if you have a bad one, do not think that you will be condemned on this account, or be put to shame if at least you order your own doings aright. For what can be less honorable than the Gentiles? still in faith they soon became related to the Saints. Or what more nearly connected than the Jews? Yet still by unbelief they were made aliens. For that relationship is of nature and necessity, after which we are all relations. For of Adam we all sprung, and none can be more a relation than another, both as regards Adam and as regards Noah, and as regards the earth, the common mother of all. But the relationship worthy of honors, is that which does distinguish us from the wicked. For it is not possible for all to be relations in this way, but those of the same character only. Nor do we call them brothers who come of the same labor with ourselves, but those who display the same zeal. In this way Christ giveth men the name of children of God, and so on the other hand children of the devil, and so too children of disobedience, of hell, and of perdition likewise. So Timothy was Paul's son from goodness and was called "mine own son"[1] (1 Tim. i. 2): but of his sister's son we do not know even the name. And yet the one was by nature related to him, and still that availed him not. But the other being both by nature and country far removed from him (as being a native of Lystra), still became most nearly related. Let us then also become the sons of the Saints, or rather let us become even God's sons. For that it is possible to become sons of God, hear what he says, "Be ye therefore perfect, as your father which is in Heaven." (Matt. v. 48.) This is why we call Him Father in prayer, and that not only to remind ourselves of the grace, but also of virtue, that we may not do aught unworthy of such a relationship. And how it may be said is it possible to be a son of God? by being free from all passions, and showing gentleness to them that affront and wrong us. For thy Father is so to them that blaspheme Him. Wherefore, though He says various things at various times, yet in no case does He say that ye may be like your Father, but when He says, "Pray for them that despitefully use you, do good to them that hate you" (ib. v. 44), then He brings in this as the reward. For there is nothing that brings us so near to God, and makes us so like Him, as this well-doing. Therefore Paul also, when he says, "Be ye followers of God" (Eph. v. 1), means them to be so in this respect. For we have need of all good deeds, chiefly however of love to man and gentleness, since we need so much of His love to man ourselves. For we commit many transgressions every day. Wherefore also we have need to show much mercy. But much and little is not measured by the quantity of things given, but by the amount of the givers' means. Let not then the rich be high-minded, nor the poor dejected as giving so little, for the latter often gives more than the former. We must not then make ourselves miserable because we are poor, since it makes almsgiving the easier for us. For he that has got much together is seized with haughtiness, as well as a greater affection to that (or "lust beyond that") he has. But he that hath but a little is quit of either of these domineering passions: hence he finds more occasions for doing well. For this man will go cheerfully into a prison-house, and will visit the sick, and will give a cup of cold water. But the other will not take upon him any office of this sort, as pampered up ($\phi\lambda\epsilon\gamma\mu\alpha\acute{\iota}\nu\omega\nu$, by his riches. Be not then out of heart at thy poverty. For thy poverty makes thy traffic for heaven the easier to thee. And if thou have nothing, but have a compassionating soul, even this will be laid up as a reward for thee. Hence too Paul bade us "weep with them that weep" (Rom. xii. 15), and exhorted us to be to prisoners as though bound with them. (Heb. xiii. 3.) For it is not to them that weep only that it yieldeth some solace that there be many that compassionate them, but to them who are in other afflicting circumstances. For there are cases where conversation has as much power to recover him that is cast down as money. For this then God exhorts us to give money to them that ask, not merely with a view to relieve their poverty, but that He may teach us to compassionate the misfortunes of our neighbors. For this also the covetous man is odious, in that he not only disregards men in a beggared state, but because he gets himself trained ($\dot{\alpha}\lambda\epsilon\acute{\iota}\phi\epsilon\tau\alpha\iota$) for cruelty and great inhumanity. And so he that, for their sakes, thinks little of money, is even on this account an object of love, that he is merciful and kind to man. And Christ, when He blesseth the merciful, blesseth and praiseth not those only that give the alms of money, but those also who have the will to do so. Let us then be so inclinable to mercy, and all other blessings will follow, for he that hath a spirit of love and mercy, if he have money, will give it away, or if he see any in distress, will weep and bewail it; if he fall in with a person wronged, will stand up for him; if he sees one spitefully entreated, will reach out his hand to him. For as he has that treasure-house of blessings, a loving and merciful soul, he will make it a fountain for all his brethren's needs, and will enjoy all the rewards that are laid up with God (Field with 4 Mss. $\tau\hat{\omega}$ $\Theta\epsilon\hat{\omega}$). That we then may attain to these, let us of all things frame our souls accordingly. For so, while in this world, we shall do good deeds without number, and shall enjoy the crowns to come. To which may we all attain by the grace and love toward man, etc.

---

[1] Field reads, So also Timothy was called Paul's son from goodness.

HOMILY XX.

ROM. XII. 1.

"I beseech you therefore, brethren, by the mercies of God, that ye present your bodies a living sacrifice, holy, acceptable unto God, which is your reasonable service."

AFTER discoursing at large upon the love of God toward man, and pointing out His unspeakable concern for us, and unutterable goodness, which cannot even be searched into, he next puts it forward with a view of persuading those who have received the benefit to exhibit a conversation worthy of the gift. And though he is so great and good a person, yet he does not decline beseeching them, and that not for any enjoyment he was likely to get himself, but for that they would have to gain. And why wonder that he does not decline beseeching, where he is even putting God's mercies before them? For since, he means, it is from this you have those numberless blessings, from the mercies of God, reverence them, be moved to compassion by them. For they themselves take the attitude of suppliants, that you would show no conduct unworthy of them. I entreat you then, he means, by the very things through which ye were saved. As if any one who wished to make a person, who had had great kindnesses done him, show regard, was to bring him the benefactor himself as a suppliant. And what dost thou beseech? let me hear. "That ye would present your bodies a living sacrifice, holy, acceptable unto God, which is your reasonable service." For when he had said sacrifice, to prevent any from thinking he bade them kill themselves, he forthwith added (Greek order) "living." Then to distinguish it from the Jewish, he calls it "holy, acceptable to God, your reasonable[1] service." For theirs was a material one, and not very acceptable either.[*] Since He saith, "Who hath required this at your hands?" (Isa. i. 12.) And in sundry other passages He clearly

throws them aside. For it was not this, but this with the other, that He looked to have presented. Wherefore he saith, "The sacrifice of praise shall glorify Me." And again, "I will praise the name of my God with a song, and this shall please him better than a bullock that putteth forth horns and hoofs." (Ps. l. 23; lxix. 30, 31.) And so in another place He rejects it, and says, "Shall I eat the flesh of bulls, or drink goat's blood?" (ib. l. 13) and proceeds with, "Offer unto God a sacrifice of praise, and pay thy vows unto the Most High." (ib. 14.) So Paul also here bids us "present our bodies a living sacrifice." And how is the body, it may be said, to become a sacrifice? Let the eye look upon no evil thing, and it hath become a sacrifice; let thy tongue speak nothing filthy, and it hath become an offering; let thine hand do no lawless deed, and it hath become a whole burnt offering. Or rather this is not enough, but we must have good works also: let the hand do alms, the mouth bless them that cross one, and the hearing find leisure evermore for lections of Scripture.[2] For sacrifice allows of no unclean thing: sacrifice is a first-fruit of the other actions. Let us then from our hands, and feet, and mouth, and all other members, yield a first-fruit unto God. Such a sacrifice is well pleasing, as that of the Jews was even unclean, for, "their sacrifices," it says, "are unto them as the bread of mourning." (Hos. ix. 4.) Not so ours. That presented the thing sacrificed dead: this maketh the thing sacrificed to be living. For when we have mortified our members, then we shall be able to live. For the law of this sacrifice is new, and so the sort of fire is a marvellous one. For it needeth no wood or matter under it; but our fire liveth[3] of itself, and doth not burn up the victim, but rather quickeneth it. This was the sacrifice that God sought of old. Wherefore the Prophet saith, "The sacrifice of God is a broken spirit." (Ps. li. 17.) And the three Children offer this when they say,

---

[1] Reasonable is here used for what has been termed supersensuous, as in the Syriac, and later Latin, see p. 498.

[*] Evidently Chrys. understands by λογικήν here rational as opposed to material service such as the Jews offered in animal sacrifices. Others have understood of it of spiritual service as opposed to the superstitious service of the heathen (Calvin). Others find in it a contrast with the irrational animals (ζῶα ἄλογα) offered in sacrifice (Theodoret, Grotius). The first view is preferable. *Christianus omnia recte reputat, et ex beneficio Dei miserentis colligit officium suum,* says Bengel.—G. B. S.

[2] θείαις ἀκροάσεσιν. See Suicer in ἀκροάομαι. lit. "divine hearings." The place where those stood who were not yet admitted to Communion, but heard the Scriptures read, was called the ἀκρόασις or hearing; here the act of hearing is meant.

[3] 2 or 3 Mss. "boileth" which Heyse prefers.

"At this time there is neither prince, or prophet, or leader, or burnt offering, or place to sacrifice before Thee, and to find mercy. Nevertheless, in a contrite heart and an humble spirit let us be accepted." (Song of 3 Ch. 15, 16.) And observe how great the exactness wherewith he useth each word. For he does not say, offer (ποιήσατε Ex. xxix. 39. LXX.) your bodies as a sacrifice, but "present" (παραστήσατε see below) them, as if he had said, never more have any interest in them. Ye have given them up to another. For even they that furnish (same word) the war-horses have no further interest in them. And thou too hast presented thy members for the war against the devil, and for that dread battle-array. Do not let them down to selfish appliances. And he shows another thing also from this, that one must make them approved, if one means to present them. For it is not to any mortal being that we present them, but to God, the King of the universe; not to war only, but to have seated thereon the King Himself. For He doth not refuse even to be seated upon our members, but even greatly desireth it. And what no king who is but our fellow-servant would choose to do, that the Lord of Angels chooseth. Since then it is both to be presented (i. e. as for a King's use) and is a sacrifice, rid it of every spot, since if it have a spot, it will no longer be a sacrifice. For neither can the eye that looks lecherously be sacrificed, nor the hand be presented that is grasping and rapacious, nor the feet that go lame and go to play-houses, nor the belly that is the slave of self-indulgence, and kindleth lusts after pleasures, nor the heart that hath rage in it, and harlots' love, nor the tongue that uttereth filthy things. Hence we must spy out the spots on our body upon every side. For if they that offered the sacrifices of old were bid to look on every side, and were not permitted to offer an animal "that hath anything superfluous or lacking, or is scurvy, or scabbed" (Lev. xxii. 22, 23), much more must we, who offer not senseless animals, but ourselves, exhibit more strictness, and be pure in all respects, that we also may be able to say as did Paul, "I am now ready to be offered, and the time of my departure is at hand." (2 Tim. iv. 6.) For he was purer than any sacrifice, and so he speaks of himself as "ready to be offered." But this will be brought about if we kill the old man, if we mortify our members that are upon the earth, if we crucify the world unto ourselves. In this way we shall not need the knife any more, nor altar, nor fire, or rather we shall want all these, but not made with the hands, but all of them will come to us from above, fire from above, and knife also, and our altar will the breadth of Heaven be. For if when Elijah offered the visible sacrifice, a flame, that came down from above consumed the whole water, wood, and stones, much more will this be done upon thee. And if thou hast aught in thee relaxed and secular, and yet offerest the sacrifice with a good intention, the fire of the Spirit will come down, and both wear away that worldliness, and perfect (so Field: Mss. "carry up") the whole sacrifice. But what is "reasonable (λογικῇ) service?" It means spiritual ministry, conversation according to Christ. As then he that ministereth in the house of God, and officiateth, of whatever sort he may be, then collects himself (συστέλλεται Ezech. xliv. 19), and becomes more dignified;[1] so we ought to be minded all our whole life as serving and ministering. And this will be so, if every day you bring Him sacrifices (3 Mss. "thyself as a sacrifice"), and become the priest of thine own body, and of the virtue of thy soul; as, for example, when you offer soberness, when almsgiving, when goodness and forbearance. For in doing this thou offerest "a reasonable service" (or worship, λατρείαν), that is, one without aught that is bodily, gross, visible. Having then raised the hearer by the names bestowed, and having shown that each man is a priest of his own flesh by his conversation, he mentions also the way whereby we may compass all this. What then is the way?

Ver. 2. "And be not fashioned[2] after this world; but be ye transformed by the renewing of your mind."

For the fashion of this world is grovelling and worthless, and but for a time, neither hath ought of loftiness, or lastingness, or straightforwardness, but is wholly perverted. If then thou wouldest walk upright (or aright ὀρθὰ), figure not thyself after the fashion of this life present. For in it there is nought abiding or stable. And this is why he calls it a *fashion* (σχῆμα); and so in another passage, "the fashion of this world passeth away." (1 Cor. vii. 31.) For it hath no durability or fixedness, but all in it is but for a season; and so he calls it this age (or world, Gr. αἰών), hereby to indicate its liableness to misfortune, and by the word fashion its unsubstantialness. For speak of riches, or of glory, or beauty of person, or of luxury, or of whatever other of its seemingly great things you will, it is a fashion only, not reality, a show and a mask, not any

---

[1] σεμνότερος, which implies reverence as well as dignity. The word before probably refers also to dress. See Ex. xxviii. 43, but in this case the outward act so truly represents the inward, that it is difficult to separate them.

[2] A. V. conformed to. The translation is altered to express the distinction noticed in the comment.

abiding substance (ὑπόστασις). But "be not thou fashioned after this, but be transformed," he says, "by the renewing of your mind." He says not change the fashion, but "be transformed" (μεταμορφοῦ), to show that the world's ways are a fashion, but virtue's not a fashion, but a kind of real form,[1] with a natural beauty of its own, lacking not the trickeries and fashions of outward things, which no sooner appear than they go to nought. For all these things, even before they come to light, are dissolving. If then thou throwest the fashion aside, thou wilt speedily come to the form.[*] For nothing is more strengthless than vice, nothing so easily wears old. Then since it is likely that being men they would sin every day, he consoles his hearer by saying, "renew thyself" from day to day. This is what we do with houses, we keep constantly repairing them as they wear old, and so do thou unto thyself. Hast thou sinned to-day? hast thou made thy soul old? despair not, despond not, but renew it by repentance, and tears (Hilary on Ps. cxix.), and confession, and by doing of good things. And never fail of doing this. And how are we to do this?

"That ye may prove (things more expedient (διαφέροντα), and know[2]) what is that good, and acceptable, and perfect will of God."

Either he means by this, be renewed, that ye may learn what is more expedient for you, and what the will of God. Or rather, that ye can get so renewed if ye learn the things expedient, and what God may will. For if thou see this, and know how to distinguish the nature of things, thou art in possession of the whole way of virtue. And who, it may be said, is ignorant of what is expedient, and what is the will of God? They that are flurried with the things of this world, they that deem riches an enviable thing, they that make light of poverty, they that follow after power, they that are gaping after outward glory, they that think themselves great men when they raise fine houses, and buy costly sepulchres, and keep herds of slaves, and carry a great swarm of eunuchs about with them; these know not what is expedient for them, or what the will of God is. For both of these are but one thing. For God willeth what things are expedient for

us, and what God willeth, that is also expedient for us. What then are the things which God willeth? to live in poverty, in lowliness of mind, in contempt of glory; in continency, not in self-indulgence; in tribulation, not in ease; in sorrow, not in dissipation and laughter; in all the other points whereon He hath given us laws. But the generality do even think these things of ill omen;[3] so far are they from thinking them expedient, and the will of God. This then is why they never can come near even to the labors for virtue's sake. For they that do not know so much even as what virtue may be, but reverence vice in its place, and take unto their bed the harlot instead of the modest wife, how are they to be able to stand aloof from the present world? Wherefore we ought above all to have a correct estimate of things, and even if we do not follow after virtue, to praise virtue, and even if we do not avoid vice, to stigmatize vice, that so far we may have our judgments uncorrupted. For so as we advance on our road, we shall be able to lay hold on the realities. This then is why he also bids you be renewed, "that ye may prove what is the will of God." But here he seems to me to be attacking the Jews too, who cling to the Law. For the old dispensation was a will of God, yet not the ultimate purpose, but allowed owing to their feebleness. But that which is a perfect one, and well-pleasing, is the new conversation. So too when he called it "a reasonable service," it was to set it in contrast with that other (v. note p. 496) that he gave it such a name.

Ver. 3. "For I say, through the grace given unto me, to every man that is among you, not to think of himself more highly than he ought to think, but to think soberly, according as God hath dealt to every man the measure of faith."

After saying above, "I beseech you by the mercies," here he says again, "by the grace." Observe the teacher's lowliness of mind, observe a spirit quite subdued! He means to say that he is in no respect worthy to be trusted in such an exhortation and counsel. But at one time he takes the mercies of God along with him, at another His grace. It is not my word, he would say, that I am speaking, but one from God. And he does not say, For I say unto you by the wisdom of God, or, for I say unto you by the Law given of God, but, "by the grace," so reminding them continually of the benefits done them, so as

---

[1] μορφή. See Phil. ii. 6, 7, 8, and St. Chrysostom on the passage, Hom. vi. pp. 363, sqq. O. T.

[*] The two words here rendered: "be fashioned" and "be transformed" differ as the terms (σχῆμα and μορφή) which underlie them differ. "The term μορφή, form, strictly denotes, not an external pose suitable for imitation, like σχῆμα, attitude, but an organic form, the natural product of a principle of life which manifests itself thus." Godet. "Be not conformed, but be transformed" (A. V.) marks well the distinction.—G. B. S.

[2] See the note of Matthiæ on the place. Nearly all Mss. have and know; it seems a slip of memory; see Rom. ii. 18.

[3] οἰωνίζονται, v. Jung. ad J. Poll. v. 163. Dem. adv. Aristog. 1. (794, 5), it means to make a sign of detestation on meeting anything counted unlucky.

to make them more submissive, and to show that even on this account, they were under an obligation to obey what is here said. "To every man that is among you." Not to this person and to that merely, but to the governor and to the governed, to the slave and to the free, to the unlearned and to the wise, to the woman and to the man, to the young and to the old. For the Law is common to all as being the Lord's. And by this he likewise makes his language inoffensive, setting the lessons he gives to all, even to such as do not come under them, that those who do come under them may with more willingness accept such a reproof and correction. And what dost thou say? Let me hear. "Not to think more highly than he ought to think." Here he is bringing before us the mother of good deeds, which is lowliness of mind, in imitation of his own Master. For as He, when He went up into the mountain, and was going to give a tissue of moral precepts, took this for his first beginning, and made this the foundation, in the words, "Blessed are the poor in spirit" (Matt. v. 3); so Paul too, as he has now passed from the doctrinal parts to those of a more practical kind, has taught us virtue in general terms, by requiring of us the admirable sacrifice; and being on the point of giving a more particular portrait of it, he begins from lowliness of mind as from the head, and tells us, "not to think more highly of one's self than one ought to think," (for this is His will), (many Mss. om. for etc.), "but to think soberly." But what he means is about this. We have received wisdom not that we should use it to make us haughty, but to make us sober-minded. And he does not say in order to be lowly in mind, but in order to sobriety, meaning by sobriety (σωφροσύνη) here not that virtue which contrasts with lewdness, nor the being free from intemperance, but being sober and healthful in mind. And the Greek name of it means keeping the mind safe.[1] To show then that he who is not thus modest (μετριάζοντα), cannot be sober either, that is, cannot be staid and healthful minded (because such an one is bewildered, and out of his wits, and is more crazed than any madman), he calls lowliness of mind, soberness of mind.

"According as God hath dealt to every man the measure of faith." For since having gifts given them had made many unreasonably elated, both with these and with the Corinthians, see how he lays open the cause of the disease, and gradually removes it. For after saying that we should think soberly, he pro-

ceeds, "according as God hath dealt to every man the measure of faith," meaning here the gift by faith: and by using the word "dealt," he solaces him who had the less, and humbles him who had the greater share. For if God dealt it, and it is no achievement of thine, why think highly of thyself? But if any one says that faith here does not mean the gift, this would only the more show that he was humbling the vain boasters. For if that which is the cause of the gift (so Field with most Mss.: Vulg. "If the faith by which miracles are wrought is the cause of the gift"), that faith by which miracles are wrought, be itself from God, on what ground dost thou think highly of thyself? If He had not come, or been incarnate, then the things of faith would not have fared well either. And it is from hence that all the good things take their rise. But if it is He that giveth it, He knoweth how He dealeth it. For He made all, and taketh like care of all. And as His giving came of His love towards man, so doth the quantity which He giveth. For was He Who had shown His goodness in regard to the main point, which is the giving of the gift, likely to neglect thee in regard to the measure? For had He wished to do thee dishonor, then He had not given them at all. But if to save thee and to honor thee was what He had in view (and for this He came and distributed such great blessings), why art thou confounded and disturbed, and abusest thy wisdom to foolishness, making thyself more disgraceful than one who is by nature so? For being foolish by nature is no ground of complaint. But being foolish through wisdom, is at once bereaving one's self of excuse, and running into greater punishment.

Such then are those, who pride themselves upon their wisdom, and fall into the excess of recklessness.[2] For recklessness of all things makes a person a fool. Wherefore the Prophet calls the barbarian by this name. But "the fool," he says, "shall speak folly." (Is. xxxii. 6.) But that you may see the folly of him from his own words, hear what he says. "Above the stars of heaven will I place my throne, and I will be like the Most High." (ib. xiv. 14.) "I will take hold of the world as a nest, and as eggs that are left will I take them away." (ib. x. 14.) Now what can be more foolish than these words? And every instance of haughty language immediately draws on itself this reproach. And if I were to set before you every expression of them that are reckless, you would not

---

[1] σώζουσαν τὴν φρόνησιν, Aristot. Eth. vi.

[2] This word has been sometimes translated haughtiness, but means something more; usually the recklessness of despair, but sometimes that of pride.

be able to distinguish whether the words are those of a reckless man or a fool. So entirely the same is this failing and that. And another of a strange nation says again, "I am God and not man" (Ezech. xxviii. 2); and another again, Can God save you, or deliver you out of my hand?" (Dan. iii. 15.) And the Egyptian too, "I know not the Lord, neither will I let Israel go." (Ex. v. 2.) And the foolish body in the Psalmist is of this character, who hath "said in his heart, There is no God." (Ps. xiv. 1.) And Cain, "Am I my brother's keeper?" (Gen. iv. 9.) Can you now distinguish whether the words are those of the reckless or those of the fool? For recklessness going out of due bounds, and being a departure from reason (whence its name recklessness, ἀπόνοια), maketh men both fools and vainglorious. For likewise, "the beginning of wisdom is the fear of the Lord" (Prov. ix. 10), so then the beginning of folly is surely not knowing the Lord. If then knowing be wisdom, and not knowing Him folly, and this ignorance come of haughtiness (ὑπερηφανία), (for the beginning of haughtiness is the not knowing of the Lord), then is haughtiness the extreme of folly. Such was Nabal, if not to Godward, at least toward man, having become senseless from his recklessness. But he afterwards died of fear. For when any falleth from the measure of wisdom, he becomes at once a coward and bold (θρασύδειλοί Ar. Eth. iii.), his soul having been made feeble. For as the body when it loseth its proper tone having become out of condition, is a prey to any disease, thus too the soul when it hath lost its greatness of nature and lowly-mindedness, having gotten any feeble habit (ἕξιν), becomes fearful, as well as bold and unreasonable, and loses its powers of self-consciousness. And he that has lost these, how is he to know things above himself? For as he that is seized with a frenzy, when he has so lost them, knoweth not even what is right before him; and the eye, when it is dimmed, darkeneth all the other members; so doth it happen with this recklessness. Wherefore these are more miserable than the mad, or than those silly by nature. For like them they stir laughter, and like them they are ill-tempered. And they are out of their wits as the others are, but they are not pitied as they are. And they are beside themselves, as are these, but they are not excused, as are these, but are hated only. And while they have the failings of either, they are bereaved of the excuse of either, being ridiculous not owing to their words only, but to their whole appearance also. For why, pray, dost thou stiffen up thy neck? or why walk on tiptoe? why knit up thy brows? why stick thy breast out? Thou canst not make one hair white or black, (Matt. v. 36) and thou goest with as lofty gait as if thou couldest command everything. No doubt thou wouldest like to have wings, and not go upon the earth at all! No doubt thou wouldest wish to be a prodigy! For hast thou not made thyself prodigious now, when thou art a man and triest to fly? or rather flying from within, and bloated in every limb? What shall I call thee to quit thee of thy recklessness? Shall I call thee ashes, and dust, and smoke, and pother? I have described thy worthlessness to be sure, but still I have not laid hold of the exact image I wanted. For I want to put their bloatedness before me, and all its emptiness. What image am I to find then which will suit with all this? To me it seems to be like tow in a blaze. For it seems to swell when lighted, and to lift itself up; but when it is submitted to a slight touch of the hand, it all tumbles down, and turns out to be more worthless than the veriest ashes. Of this sort are the souls of these men; that empty inflatedness of theirs even the commonest attack may humble and bring down. For he that behaves recklessly must of necessity be a throughly feeble person, since the height he has is not a sound one, but even as bubbles are easily burst, so are these men easily undone. But if thou dost not believe, give me a bold reckless fellow, and you will find him more cowardly than a hare even at the most trivial circumstance. For as the flame that rises from dry sticks is no sooner lighted than it becomes dust, but stiff logs do not by their nature easily kindle up, and then keep up their flame a long time burning; so souls that be stern and firm are not easily kindled or extinguished; but these men undergo both of these in a single moment. Since then we know this, let us practise humble-mindedness. For there is nothing so powerful as it, since it is stronger even than a rock and harder than adamant, and places us in a safety greater than that of towers and cities and walls, being too high for any of the artillery of the devil. As then recklessness makes men an easy prey even to ordinary occurrences, being, as I was saying, easier broken than a bubble, and rent more speedily than a spider's web, and more quickly dissolved than a smoke; that we then may be walking upon the strong rock, let us leave that and take to this. For thus in this life present we shall find rest, and shall in the world to come have every blessing, by the grace and love toward man, etc.

HOMILY XXI.

ROM. XII. 4, 5.

"For as we have many members in one body, and all members have not the same office; so we, being many, are one body in Christ, and every one members one of another."

AGAIN he uses the same ensample as he does to the Corinthians, and that to allay the same passion. For great is the power of the medicine, and the force of this illustration for the correcting of this disease of haughtiness. Why (he means) dost thou think highly of thyself? Or why again does another utterly despise himself? Are we not all one body, both great and small? When then we are in the total number but one, and members one of another, why dost thou by thy haughtiness separate thyself? Why dost thou put thy brother to shame? For as he is a member of thee, so art thou also of him. And it is on this score that your claims to honor are so equal. For he has stated two things that might take down their haughty spirit: one that we are members one of another, not the small of the great only, but also the great of the small; and another, that we are all one body. Or rather there are three points, since he shows that the gift was one of grace. "Therefore be not high-minded." For it was given thee of God; thou didst not take it, nor find it even. Hence too, when he touches upon the gifts, he does not say that one received more, and another less, but what? *different*. For his words are, "having then gifts," not less and greater, but, "differing." And what if thou art not appointed to the same office, still the body is the same. And beginning with gifts, he ends with a good deed (4 Mss. pl.); and so after mentioning prophecy, and ministry, and the like, he concludes with mercy, diligence, and succor. Since then it was likely that some would be virtuous, yet not have prophecy, he shows how that this too is a gift, and a much greater one than the other (as he shows in the Epistle to the Corinthians), and so much the greater, as that one has a reward, the other is devoid of a recompense. For the whole is matter of gift and grace. Wherefore he saith,

Ver. 6. "Having then gifts differing according to the grace of God that is given unto us, whether prophecy, let us prophesy according to the proportion of faith."

Since then he had sufficiently comforted them, he wishes also to make them vie with each other,[1] and labor more in earnest, by showing that it is themselves that give the grounds for their receiving more or less. For he says indeed that it is given by God (as when he says, "according as God hath dealt to every man the measure of faith;" and again, "according to the grace given unto us") (Rom. xii. 3), that he may subdue the haughty. But he says also that the beginnings lie with themselves, to rouse the listless. And this he does in the Epistle to the Corinthians also, to produce both these emotions. For when he saith, "covet earnestly the gifts," (1 Cor. xii. 31), he shows that they were themselves the cause of the differences in what was given. But when he says, "Now all these things worketh one and the selfsame Spirit, dividing to every man severally as he will" (ib. 11), he is proving that those who have received it ought not to be elated, so using every way open to him to allay their disorder. And this he does here also. And again, to rouse those who have fallen drowsy, he says, "Whether prophecy, let us prophesy according to the proportion of faith." For though it is a grace, yet it is not poured forth at random, but framing its measure according to the recipients, it letteth as much flow as it may find the vessel of faith that is brought to be capable of.*

Ver. 7. "Or ministry, let us wait on our ministering."

Here he names a comprehensive thing. For the Apostleship even is called a ministry, and every spiritual work is a ministry. This is indeed a name of a peculiar office (viz. the

---

[1] Or feel they need an effort ἐναγωνίους. See on Rom. xi. 21 p. 349.

* Prophecy is to be κατὰ τὴν ἀναλογίαν τῆς πίστεως (6). In the view of some (as Meyer) the man's own faith is meant. He should not exceed in his speaking the limits of his faith. Others (as Philippi) take "faith" in the objective sense as a body of doctrine and find the idea here which was later associated with the expression *analogia fidei*: the word πίστις will not bear this meaning and the individual's own faith seems too narrow a criterion of prophecy. It seems better to understand the expression as meaning that the prophet is to regulate his utterance by the character and contents of the faith of the church; that he should in his prophetic utterances keep to the line of the Church's trust and hope and not feel at liberty to add new or heterogeneous elements. The terms διακονία (7) and διδάσκων seem to refer to the two offices of the church deacons and presbyters, although others hold the view (of Chrys.) that the words are merely general.—G. B. S.

diaconate); however, it is used in a general sense. "Or he that teacheth, on teaching." See with what indifference he places them, the little first and the great afterwards, again giving us the same lesson, not to be puffed up or elated.

Ver. 8. "Or he that exhorteth, on exhortation."

And this is a species of teaching too. For "if ye have any word of exhortation," it says, "speak unto the people." (Acts xiii. 15.) Then to show that it is no great good to follow after virtue unless this is done with the proper rule, he proceeds,

"He that giveth " (μεταδιδοὺς, imparteth), "let him do it with simplicity." For it is not enough to give, but we must do it with munificence also, for this constantly answereth to the name of simplicity. Since even the virgins had oil, still, since they had not enough, they were cast out from everything. "He that defendeth" (A. V. ruleth, προϊστάμενος,) "with diligence;" for it is not enough to do undertake the defence.[1] "He that showeth mercy, with cheerfulness." For it is not enough to show mercy, but it behooves us to do it with a largeness and an ungrudging spirit, or rather not with an ungrudging, but even with a cheerful and rejoicing one, for not grudging does not amount to rejoicing. And this same point, when he is writing to the Corinthians also, he insisted very strongly upon. For to rouse them to such largeness he said, "He that soweth sparingly shall reap also sparingly, and he which soweth bountifully shall reap also bountifully. (2 Cor. ix. 6.) But to correct their temper he added, "Not grudgingly or of necessity." (ib. 7.) For both the shower of mercy ought to have, both ungrudgingness and pleasure. And why dost thou bemoan thyself of giving alms? (Aristot. Eth. N. ii. 3 and iv. l.) Why dost thou grieve at showing mercy, and lose the advantage of the good deed? For if thou grievest thou dost not do mercy, but art cruel and inhuman. For if thou grievest, how shalt thou be able to raise up him that is in sorrow? For it is much if he suspects no ill, even, when thou art giving with joyfulness. For since nothing seems to men such a disgrace as to be receiving from others, unless by an exceedingly cheerful look thou removest the suspicion, and showest that thou art receiving rather than giving, thou wilt even cast down the receiver rather than raise him up. This is why he says, "He that

showeth mercy, with cheerfulness." For who that is receiving a kingdom, is of sad countenance? Who that is receiving pardon for his sins continueth of dejected look? Mind not then the expenditure of the money; but the increase that comes of that expenditure. For if he that soweth rejoiceth though sowing with uncertainty of return, much more should he do so that farms the Heaven. For in this way, even though thou give but little, thou wilt be giving much; even as how much soever thou givest with a sad countenance, thou wilt have made thy much a little. Thus the widow outweighed many talents by the two mites, for her spirit was large. And how is it possible, it may be said, for one that dwells with poverty in the extreme, and empties forth his all, to do this with a ready mind? Ask the widow, and thou wilt hear the way, and wilt know that it is not poverty[2] that makes narrow circumstances, but the temper of a man that effects both this and its opposite. For it is possible even in poverty to be munificent (μεγαλόψυχον), and in riches to be niggardly. Hence in giving he looks for simplicity, and in showing mercy for cheerfulness, and in patronizing for diligence. For it is not with money only that he wishes us to render every assistance to those in want, but both with words, and deeds, and in person, and in every other way. And after mentioning the chief kind of aiding (προστασίαν), that which lies in teaching, namely, and that of exhorting (for this is a more necessary kind, in that it nurtures the soul), he proceeds to that by way of money, and all other means; then to show how these may be practised aright, he bringeth in the mother of them, love.

Ver. 9. For, "Let love be without dissimulation," he says,

If thou hast this, thou wilt not perceive the loss of thy money, the labor of thy person, the toil of thy words, thy trouble, and thy ministering, but thou wilt bear all courageously, whether it be with person, or money, or word, or any other thing whatsover, that thou art to assist thy neighbor. As then he doth not ask for giving only, but that with simplicity, nor aiding, but that with diligence, nor alms, but that with cheerfulness; so even love too he requires not alone, but that without dissimulation. Since this is what love is. And if a man have this, everything else follows. For he that showeth mercy does so with cheerfulness (for he is giving to himself): and he that aideth, aideth with diligence; for it is for himself he is aiding: and he that imparteth doth this with largeness; for he is bestowing it on

[1] Near the end of Hom. 19, we have κἂν ἀδικουμένῳ περιτύχῃ προστήσεται, which proves that he takes the word in the sense here given. "Unless," added by Ben. and 2 Mss. "he do it with diligence and zeal."

[2] πενία here seems distinguished from πτωχεία, as in the Plutus.

himself. Then since there is a love even for ill things, such as is that of the intemperate, that of those who are of one mind for money, and for plunder's sake, and for revels and drinking clubs, he clears it of all these, by saying, "Abhor (ἀποστυγοῦντες) that which is evil." And he does not speak of refraining from it, but of hating it, and not merely hating it, but hating it exceedingly. For this word [1] ἀπὸ is often of intensive force with him, as where he speaks of "earnest expectation,"[2] looking out for,"[3] (complete) "redemption."[4] For since many who do not evil things still have a desire after them, therefore he says, "Abhor." For what he wants is to purify the thought, and that we should have a mighty enmity, hatred and war against vice. For do not fancy, he means, because I said, "Love one another," that I mean you to go so far as to coöperate even in bad actions with one another; for the law that I am laying down is just the reverse. Since it would have you an alien not from the action only, but even from the inclination towards vice; and not merely an alien from this same inclination, but to have an excessive aversion and hatred of it too. And he is not content with only this, but he also brings in the practice of virtue. "Cleave to that which is good."

He does not speak of doing only, but of being disposed too. For this the command to "cleave to" it indicates. So God, when He knit the man to the woman, said, "For he shall cleave to his wife." (Gen. ii. 24.) Then he mentions reasons why we ought to love one another.

Ver. 10. "Be kindly affectioned one to another with brotherly love."

Ye are brethren, he means, and have come of the same pangs. Hence even on this head you ought to love one another. And this Moses said to those who were quarrelling in Egypt, "Ye are brethren, why do ye wrong one to another?" (Exod. ii. 13.) When then he is speaking of those without, he says, "If it be possible, as much as in you lieth, live peaceably with all men." (Rom. xii. 18.) But when he is speaking of his own, he says, "Be kindly affectioned one to another with brotherly love." For in the other case he requires abstinence from quarrelling, and hatred, and aversion: but here loving too, and not merely loving, but the loving of relatives. For not only must one's "love be without dissimulation," but intense also, and warm, and glowing. Because, to what purpose would

you love without fraud, and not love with warmth? Whence he says, "kindly affectioned one towards another, that is, be friends, and warm ones too. Do not wait to be loved by another, but leap at it thyself, and be the first to begin it. For so wilt thou reap the wages of his love also. Having mentioned the reason then why we ought to love one another, he tells us also the way in which the affection may grow unchangeable. Whence he proceeds, "In honor preferring one another." For this is the way that affection is produced, and also when produced abideth. And there is nothing which makes friends so much, as the earnest endeavor to overcome one's neighbor in honoring him.* For what he had mentioned before comes of love, and love of honor, as honor does too of love. Then that we may not honor only, he looks for something besides, when he says,

Ver. 11. "Not backward in zeal."[5]

For this also gendereth love when with honor we also show a readiness to protect: as there is nothing that makes men beloved so much as honor and forethought. For to love is not enough, but there must be this also: or rather this also comes of loving, as also loving has its warmth from this, and they are confirmative one of another. For there are many that love in mind, yet reach not forth the hand. And this is why he uses every means to build up love. And how are we to become "not backward in zeal?"

"Fervent in spirit." See how in every instance he aims after higher degrees; for he does not say "give" only, but "with largeness;" nor "rule," but do it "with diligence;" nor "show mercy," but do it "with cheerfulness;" nor "honor," but "prefer one another;" nor "love," but do it "without dissimulation;" nor refrain from "evil" things, but "hate" them; nor hold to "what is good," but "cleave" to it; nor "love," but to do it "with brotherly affection;" nor be zealous, but be so without backwardness; nor have the "Spirit," but have it "fervent," that is, that ye may be warm and awakened. For if thou hast those things aforesaid, thou wilt draw the Spirit to thee. And if This abide with thee, It will likewise make thee good for those purposes, and all things will be easy from the Spirit and the love, while thou art made to glow from both sides. Dost thou not see the bulls (Hannibal. ap. Liv. xxii. 16)

---

[1] Viz. in composition.

[2] ἀποκαραδοκία, Rom. viii. 19.

[3] ἀπεκδεχόμενοι, Rom. viii. 23.

[4] ἀπολύτρωσις, Rom. viii. 23, see *ad loc.* Hom. xiv. p. 445.

* Chrys. evidently takes προηγούμενοι (10) in the sense of *excelling;* others understand the word temporally and render *anticipating.* The word (*hapax.*) is better taken as in our vss. *preferring,* i. e. "going before, as guides, namely, with the conduct which incites others to follow," (Meyer). — G. B. S.

[5] A. V. not slothful in business; R. V. In diligence not slothful.

that carry a flame upon their back, how nobody is able to withstand them? So thou also wilt be more than the devil can sustain, if thou takest both these flames. "Serving the Lord."* For it is possible to serve God in all these ways; in that whatever thou doest to thy brother passes on to thy Master, and as having been Himself benefited, He will reckon thy reward accordingly. See to what height he has raised the spirit of the man that worketh these things! Then to show how the flame of the Spirit might be kindled, he says,

Ver. 12. "Rejoicing in hope, patient in tribulation, continuing instant in prayer."

For all these things are fuel for that fire. For when he had required the expenditure of money and the labor of the person, and ruling, and zeal, and teaching, and other laborious occupations, he again supplies the wrestler with love, with the Spirit, through hope. For there is nothing which makes the soul so courageous and venturesome for anything as a good hope. Then even before the good things hoped for, he gives another reward again. For since hope is of things to come, he says, "patient in tribulation." And before the things to come, in this life present thou wilt gain a great good (see on Rom. v. 4, p. 397) from tribulation, that of becoming hardy and tried. And after this he affords them another help, when he says, "continuing instant in prayer." When therefore love maketh things easy, and the Spirit assisteth, and hope lighteneth, and tribulation maketh thee tried and apt for bearing everything nobly, and thou hast along with these another very great weapon, to wit, "prayer" and the aidances that come of prayer, what further grievousness can there be in what he is enjoining? Surely none. You see how in every way he gives the wrestler firm footing and shows that the injunctions are perfectly easy. Consider again how he vindicates almsgiving, or rather not almsgiving absolutely, but that to the saints. For above when he says, "he that showeth mercy with cheerfulness," he makes us open-handed to everybody. Here, however, it is in behalf of the faithful that he is speaking. And so he proceeds to say,"

Ver. 13. "Sharing with the necessity (χρείαις, al. μνείαις, memories) of the saints."

He does not say, Bestow upon, but "share

with the necessity[1] of the saints," to show that they receive more than they give, that it is a matter of merchandise, because it is a community. Do you bring in money? They bring you in boldness toward God. "Given to (Gr. pursuing) hospitality." He does not say doing it, but "given" to it, so to instruct us not to wait for those that shall ask it, and see when they will come to us, but to run to them, and be given to finding[2] them.

Thus did Lot, thus Abraham. For he spent the whole day upon it, waiting for this goodly prey, and when he saw it, leaped upon it, and ran to meet them, and worshipped upon the ground, and said, "My Lord, if now I have found favor in Thy sight, pass not away from Thy servant." (Gen. xviii. 3.) Not as we do, if we happen to see a stranger or a poor man, knitting our brows, and not deigning even to speak to them. And if after thousands of entreaties we are softened, and bid the servant give them a trifle, we think we have quite done our duty. But he did not so, but assumed the fashion of a suppliant and a servant, though he did not know who he was going to take under his roof. But we, who have clear information that it is Christ Whom we take in, do not grow gentle even for this. But he both beseeches, and entreats, and falls on his knees to them, yet we insult those that come to us. And he indeed did all by himself and his wife, whereas we do it not even by our attendants. But if you have a mind to see the table that he set before them, there too you will see great bounteousness, but the bounteousness came not from excess of wealth, but of the riches of a ready will. Yet how many rich persons were there not then? Still none did anything of the kind. How many widows were there in Israel? Yet none showed hospitality to Elijah. How many wealthy persons again were there not in Elisha's day? But the Shunamite alone gathered in the fruits of hospitality; as did Abraham also,[3] whom beside his largeness and ready mind it is just especially to admire, on this ground, that when he had no knowledge who they were that had come, yet he so acted. Do not thou then be curious either: since for Christ thou dost receive him. And if thou art always so scrupulous, many a time wilt thou pass by a man of esteem, and lose thy reward from him. And yet he that receiveth one that is not of esteem, hath no fault found with him,

---

* Here the Mss. and vss. vary between τῷ κυρίῳ and τῷ καιρῷ (v. 11). The latter text gives the idea of serving the time or adapting one's self to the opportunity and is adopted by many (as Meyer, Godet) on the ground that the precept: *serving the Lord* is too general to be in point here among these specific exhortations. The Mss. evidence for τῷ κυρίῳ, however, is too strong to be overthrown by a consideration so subjective (א, B, A, E, L, P, It. Syr. vs. D. F. G.).—G. B. S.

[1] St. Chrysostom (on 2 Tim. i. 16, p. 189 O. T.) adopts and argues on the reading, μνείαις, for which there is some authority. See *Brit. Crit.* No. LI. pp. 80, 81.
[2] καταδιώκειν. lit. hunt them down.
[3] So Field: the passage is corrupt in the MSS. Vulg. "As did Abraham also then with largeness and ready mind. And on this ground he deserves one's admiration most, that when," etc.

but is even rewarded. For " he that receiveth a prophet in the name of a prophet, shall receive a prophet's reward." (Matt. x. 41.) But he who out of this ill-timed scrupulousness passeth one that should be admired, shall even suffer punishment. Do not then busy thyself with men's lives and doings. For this is the very extreme of niggardliness, for one loaf to be exact about a man's entire life. For if this person be a murderer, if a robber, or what not, does he therefore seem to thee not to deserve a loaf and a few pence? And yet thy Master causeth even the sun to rise upon him! And dost thou judge him unworthy of food even for a day? I will put another case to you besides. Now even if you were positively certain that he were laden with countless iniquities, not even then wouldest thou have an excuse for depriving him of this day's sustenance. For thou art the servant of Him Who said, " Ye know not what spirit ye are of." (Luke ix. 55.) Thou art servant to Him Who healed those that stoned Him, or rather Who was crucified for them. And do not tell me that he killed another, for even if he were going to kill thee thyself, even then thou shouldest not neglect him when starving. For thou art a disciple of Him Who desired the salvation even of them that crucified Him, Who said upon the Cross itself, " Father, forgive them, for they know not what they do." (Luke xxiii. 34.) Thou art the servant of Him Who healed him that smote Him, Who upon the Cross itself crowned the man who had scorned Him. And what can equal this? For both the robbers at first scorned Him. Still to one of these He opened Paradise.[1] And He bewails those who were upon the point of killing Him, and is troubled and confounded at seeing the traitor, not because He was going to be crucified, but because he was lost. He was troubled then as having foreknowledge of the hanging, and the punishment after the hanging. And though He knew his wickedness, He bore with him[2] to the last hour, and thrust not away the traitor, but even kissed him. Thy Master kisseth, and with His lips receiveth him who was on the very point of shedding His precious Blood. And dost thou count the poor not worthy even of a loaf, and reverencest not the Law which Christ laid down? Now by this He shows that we ought not to turn aside, not only from the poor, but not even from those that would lead us away to death. Do not tell me then, that so and so hath done me grievous mischief, but just consider what Christ did near the Cross itself, wishing to amend by His kiss the traitor by whom He was on the point of being betrayed. And see with how much power to shame him. For He says, " Judas, betrayest thou the Son of Man with a kiss?" (ib. xxii. 48.) Who is there He would not have softened? who is there that this address would not have made yielding? What beast? what adamant? yet not that wretched man. Do not then say, that such an one murdered such an one, and that is why I turn aside from him. For even if he were upon the point of thrusting a sword down into thee, and to plunge his hand into thy neck itself, kiss this very right hand! since even Christ kissed that mouth which wrought His death! And therefore do not thou either hate, but bewail and pity him that plotteth against thee. For such an one deserveth pity at our hands, and tears. For we are the servants of Him Who kissed even the traitor (I will not leave off dwelling over that continually), and spoke words unto him more gentle than the kiss. For He did not even say, O thou foul and villanous traitor, is this the sort of recompense thou returnest us for so great a benefit? But in what words? " Judas;" using his own name, which is more like a person bemoaning, and recalling him, than one wroth at him. And he does not say, thy Teacher, thy Master, and Benefactor, but, " the Son of Man." For though He were neither Teacher nor Master, yet is it with One Who is so gently, so unfeignedly affected towards thee, as even to kiss thee at the time of betrayal, and that when a kiss too was the signal for the betrayal; is it with Him that thou playest the traitor's part? Blessed art Thou, O Lord! What lowliness of mind, what forbearance hast Thou given us ensamples of! And to him He so behaved. But to those who came with staves and swords to Him, was it not so too? What can be more gentle than the words spoken to them? For when He had power to demolish them all in an instant, He did nothing of the kind, but as expostulating (ἐντρεπτικῶς), addressed them in the words, " Why are ye come out as against a thief with swords and staves?" (Matt. xxvi. 55.) And having cast them down backwards (John xviii. 6), as they continued insensible, He of His own accord gave Himself up next, and forbore while He saw them putting manacles upon His holy hands, while He had the power at once to confound all things, and overthrow them. But dost thou even after this deal fiercely with the poor? And even were he guilty of ten thousand sins, want and famine were enough to soften down a soul ever so blunted. But thou standest brutalized, and imitating the rage of lions. Yet they never

---

[1] Some MSS. add, " first of all men."
[2] Or " dealt kindly with him."

taste of dead bodies. But thou, while thou seest him a very corpse (τεταριχευμένον lit. salter, or, a mummy) for distresses, yet leapest upon him now that he is down, and tearest his body by thine insults, and gatherest storm after storm, and makest him as he is fleeing to the haven for refuge to split upon a rock, and bringest a shipwreck about more distressing than those in the sea. And how wilt thou say to God, Have mercy upon me, and ask of Him remission of sins, when thou art insolent to one who hath done no sin, and callest him to account for this hunger and great necessity, and throwest all the brute beasts into the shade by thy cruelty. For they indeed by the compulsion of their belly lay hold of the food needful for them. But thou, when nothing either thrusts thee on or compels thee, devourest thy brother, bitest, and tearest him, if not with thy teeth, yet with words that bite more cuttingly. How then wilt thou receive the sacred Host (προσφορὰν), when thou hast empurpled thy tongue in human gore? how give the kiss of peace, with mouth gorged with war? Nay, how enjoy every common nourishment, when thou art gathering so much venom? Thou dost not relieve the poverty, why make it even more grinding? thou dost not lift up him that is fallen, why throw him down also? thou dost not remove despondency, why even increase it? thou givest no money, why use insulting words besides? Hast thou not heard what punishment they suffer that feed not the poor? to what vengeance they are condemned? For He says, "Depart to the fire prepared for the devil and his angels." (Matt. xxv. 41.) If then they that feed not are so condemned, what punishment are they to suffer, who besides not feeding, even insult? What punishment shall they undergo? what hell? That we kindle not so great evils against ourselves, whiles we have it in our power, let us correct this evil complaint also, and put a bridle on the tongue. And let us be so far from insulting, as even to invite them, both by words and actions, that by laying up much mercy for ourselves, we may obtain the blessings promised us. Which God grant that we may all attain unto by the grace and love towards man, etc.

HOMILY XXII.

ROM. XII. 14,

"Bless them which persecute you ; bless, and curse not."

AFTER teaching them how they ought to be minded towards one another, and after joining the members closely into one, he next proceeds to lead them forth to the battle without, which he makes easier as from this point. For as he who hath not managed things well with those of his own side, will find more difficulty in arranging affairs with strangers, so he, that has practised himself duly among these, will with the more ease have the advantage of those without also. Hence then Paul also as he goes on in his journey, after the one places the other, and says, "Bless them that persecute you." He did not say, be not spiteful or revengeful, but required something far better. For that a man that was wise might do, but this is quite an angel's part. And after saying "bless," he proceeds, "and curse not," lest we should do both the one and the other, and not the former only. For they that persecute us are purveyors of a reward to us. But if thou art sober-minded, there will be another reward after that one, which thou wilt gain thyself. For he will yield thee that for persecution, but thou wilt yield thyself the one from the blessing of another, in that thou bringest forth a very great sign of love to Christ. For as he that curseth his persecutor, showeth that he is not much pleased at suffering this for Christ, thus he that blesseth showeth the greatness of his love. Do not then abuse him, that thou thyself mayest gain the greater reward, and mayest teach him that the thing is matter of inclination, not of necessity, of holiday and feast, not of calamity or dejection. For this cause Christ Himself said, "Rejoice when men speak all manner of evil against you falsely." (Matt. v. 11.) Hence too it was that the Apostles returned with joy not from having been evil spoken of only, but also at having been scourged. (Acts v. 40, 41.) For besides what I have mentioned, there will be another gain, and that no small one, that you will make, both the abashing of your adversaries hereby, and instructing of them by your actions that you are travelling to another life; for if he see thee joyous, and elevated, (πτερούμενον) from suffering ill, he will see clearly from the actions that thou hast other hopes greater than those of this life. So that if thou dost not so, but weepest and lamentest, how is he to be able to learn from that that thou art tarrying for any other life? And besides this, thou wilt compass yet another thing. For provided he see thee not vexed at the affronts done thee, but even blessing him, he will leave harassing thee. See then how much that is good comes from this, both a greater reward for thyself and a less temptation, and he will forbear persècuting thee, and God too will be glorified : and to him that is in error thy endurance will be instruction in godliness. For this reason it was not those that insult us only, but even those that persecute us and deal despitefully with us, that he bade us requite with the contrary. And now he orders them to bless, but as he goes on, he exhorts them to do them good in deeds also.

Ver. 15. " Rejoice with them that do rejoice, and weep with them that weep."

Since it is possible to bless and not to curse, and yet not to do this out of love, he wishes us to be penetrated with the warmth of friendship throughout. And this is why he goes on in these words, that we are not only to bless, but even feel compassion for their pains and sufferings, whenever we happen to see them fallen into trouble. Yes, it will be said, but to join in the sorrows of mourners one can see why he ordered them, but why ever did he command them the other thing, when it is no such great matter? Aye, but that requires more of a high Christian temper, to rejoice with them that do rejoice, than to weep with them that weep. For this nature itself fulfils perfectly : and there is none so hard-hearted as not to weep over him that is in calamity : but the other requires a very noble soul, so as not only to keep from envying, but even to feel pleasure with the person who is in esteem. And this is why he placed it first. For there is nothing that ties love so firmly as sharing both joy and pain one with another. Do not then, because thou art far from difficulties thyself, remain aloof from sympathizing too. For when thy neighbor is ill-treated, thou oughtest to make the calamity thine own. Take share then in his tears, that thou mayest lighten his low spirits. Take share in his joy, that thou mayest make the joy strike deep root, and fix the love firmly, and be of service to thyself rather than to him in so doing, by thy weeping rendering thyself merciful, and by thy feeling his pleasure, purging thyself of envy and grudging. And let me draw your attention to Paul's considerateness. For he does not say, Put an end to the calamity, lest thou shouldest say in many cases (or perchance πολλάκις) that

it is impossible : but he has enjoined the easier task, and that which thou hast in thy power. For even if thou art not able to remove the evil, yet contribute tears, and thou wilt take the worst half away. And if thou be not able to increase a man's prosperity, contribute joy, and thou wilt have made a great addition to it. Therefore it is not abstaining from envy only, but what is a much greater thing that he exhorts us to, namely, joining in the pleasure. For this is a much greater thing than not envying.

Ver. 16. " Be of the same mind one towards another. Mind not high things, but condescend to men of low estate."

Here again he insists much upon lowliness of mind, the subject he had started this exhortation with. For there was a probability of their being full of high-mindedness, both on account of their city (see p. 343), and from sundry other causes ; he therefore keeps drawing off (ὑποσύρει, 2 Mss. ὑπορύττει) the morbid matter, and lowers the inflammation. For there is nothing that makes such schisms in the Churches as vanity does. And what does he mean by, " Be of the same mind one towards another?" Has a poor man come into thy house? Be like him in thy bearing, do not put on any unusual pompous air on account of thy riches. There is no rich and poor in Christ. Be not then ashamed of him because of his external dress, but receive him because of his inward faith. And if thou seest him in sorrow, do not disdain to comfort him, nor if thou see him in prosperity, feel abashed at sharing his pleasure, and being gladdened with him, but be of the same mind in his case, that thou wouldest be of in thine own. For it says, " Be of the same mind one towards another." For instance, if thou thinkest thyself a great man, therefore think him so likewise. Dost thou suspect that he is mean and little? Well then, pass this same sentence upon thyself, and cast aside all unevenness. And how is this to be? By thy casting aside that reckless temper. Wherefore he proceeds : " Mind not high things, but condescend to men of low estate." That is, bring thyself down to their humble condition, associate with them, walk with them, do not be humbled in mind only, but help them also, and reach forth thy hand to them, not by means of others, but in thine own person, as a father taking care of a child, as the head taking care of the body. As he says in another place, "being bound with them that are in bonds." (Heb. xiii. 3. But here he means by those of low estate not merely the lowly-minded, but those of a low rank, and which one is apt to think scorn of.*

"Be not wise in your own conceits." This is, do not think that you can do for your-selves. Because the Scripture saith in another place besides, "Woe to them that are wise in their own eyes, and prudent in their own sight." (Is. v. 22.) And by this again, he secretly draws off recklessness, and reduces conceit and turgidity. For there is nothing that so elates men and makes them feel differ-ent from other people, as the notion that they can do by themselves. Whence also God hath placed us in need one of another, and though thou be wise thou wilt be in need of another: but if thou think that thou art not in need of him, thou wilt be the most foolish and feeble of men. For a man of this sort bares himself of all succor, and in whatever error he may run into, will not have the advantage either of correction or of pardon, and will provoke God by his recklessness, and will run into many errors. For it is the case, aye, and often too, that a wise man does not perceive what is needful, and a man of less shrewdness hits upon somewhat that is applicable. And this happened with Moses and his father-in-law, and with Saul and his servant, and with Isaac and Rebecca. Do not then suppose that you are lowered by needing another man. For this exalts you the more, this makes you the stronger, and the brighter too, and the more secure.

Ver. 17. "Recompense to no man evil for evil."

For if thou findest fault with another who plots against thee, why dost thou make thyself liable to this accusation? If he did amiss, how comest thou not to shun imitating him? And observe how he puts no difference here, but lays down one law for all. For he does not say, "recompense not evil" to the believer, but to "no man," be he heathen, be he contaminated, or what not. "Provide things honest in the sight of all men."

Ver. 18. "If it be possible, as much as lieth in you, live peaceably with all men."

This is that: "let your light shine before men" (Matt. v. 16), not that we are to live for vanity, but that we are not to give those

who have a mind for it a handle against us. Whence he says also in another place, "Give none offence, neither to the Jews, nor to the Gentiles, nor to the Church of God." (1 Cor. x. 32.) And in what follows he limits his meaning well, by saying, "If it be possible." For there are cases in which it is not possible, as, for instance, when we have to argue about religion, or to contend for those who are wronged. And why be surprised if this be not universally possible in the case of other persons, when even in the case of man and wife he broke through the rule? "But if the unbelieving depart, let him depart." (1 Cor. vii. 15.) And his meaning is nearly as follows: Do thine own part, and to none give occasion of war or fighting, neither to Jew nor Gentile. But if you see the cause of religion suffering anywhere, do not prize concord above truth, but make a noble stand even to death. And even then be not at war in soul, be not averse in temper, but fight with the things only. For this is the import of "as much as in you lieth, be at peace with all men." But if the other will not be at peace, do not thou fill thy soul with tempest, but in mind be friendly (φίλος, several Mss. φιλόσοφος) as I said before, without giving up the truth on any occasion.

Ver. 19. "Dearly beloved, avenge not your-selves, but rather give place unto wrath. For it is written, Vengeance is mine; I will repay, saith the Lord."

Unto what wrath? To the wrath of God. Now since what the injured man desires most to see is, himself having the pleasure of revenge, this very thing he gives him in full measure, that if thou dost not avenge thyself, he means, God will be thy avenger. Leave it then to Him to follow up thy wrongs. For this is the force of "give place unto wrath." Then to give further comfort, he brings the quotation forward also, and after winning him more throughly to himself in this way, he demands more Christian heroism (φιλοσοφίαν) of him, and says:

Ver. 20, 21. "If thine enemy hunger, feed him; if he thirst, give him to drink; for in so doing thou shalt heap coals of fire upon his head. Be not overcome of evil, but overcome evil with good."

Why, he means, am I telling you that you must keep peace? for I even insist upon your doing kindness. For he says, "give him to eat, and give him to drink." Then as the command he gave was a very difficult and a great one, he proceeds: "for in so doing thou shalt heap coals of fire upon his head." And this he said both to humble the one by fear, and to make the other more ready-minded

---

* τοῖς ταπεινοῖς is best taken here as *neuter* (Meyer, De Wette, R. V.) corresponding in this respect to τὰ ὑψηλὰ. Meyer renders and interprets thus: "*being drawn onward by the lowly;* i. e. instead of following the impulse to high things, rather yielding to that which is humble, to the claims and tasks which are presented to you by the humbler rela-tions of life, entering into this impulse towards the lower strata and spheres of life which lays claim to you, and follow-ing it. The ταπεινά ought to have for the Christian a force of attraction in virtue of which he yields himself to fellowship with them and allows himself to be guided by them in the determination of his conduct." Those who understand ταπεινοῖς as masculine are divided between the meanings: *of low rank* and *of humble disposition.* Chrys.' interpretation combines both ideas.—G. B. S.

through hope of a recompense.[1] For he that is wronged, when he is feeble, is not so much taken with any goods of his own as with the vengeance upon the person who has pained him. For there nothing so sweet as to see an enemy chastised. What he is longing for, then, that he gives him first, and when he has let the venom go, then he again gives advice of a higher tone, saying, "Be not overcome of evil." For he knew that if the enemy were a very brute, he would not continue an enemy when he had been fed.[2] And if the man injured be of ever so little[3] a soul, still when feeding him and giving him to drink, he will not himself even have any farther craving for his punishment. Hence, out of confidence in the result of the action, he does not simply threaten, but even dwells largely upon the vengeance. For he did not say, "thou shalt take vengeance," but, "thou shalt heap coals of fire upon his head."[*] Then he further declares him victor, by saying, "be not overcome of evil, but overcome evil with good." And he gives a kind of gentle hint, that one is not to do it with that intention, since cherishing a grudge still would be "being overcome of evil." But he did not say it at once, as he did not find it advisable yet.[4] But when he had disburdened the man of his anger, then he proceeded to say, "overcome evil with good." Since this would be a victory. For the combatant is rather then the conqueror, not when he brings himself under to take the blows, but when he withdraws himself, and makes his antagonist waste his strength upon the air. And in this way he will not be struck himself, and will also exhaust the whole of the other's strength. And this takes place in regard to affronts also. For when you do affronts in return,

you have the worse, not as overcome (so 1 Ms. νικηθεὶς, Sav. κινηθεὶς) by a man, but what is far more disgraceful, by the slavish passion of anger. But if you are silent, then you will conquer, and erect a trophy without a fight, and will have thousands to crown you, and to condemn the slander of falsehood. For he that replies, seems to be speaking in return as if stung. And he that is stung, gives reason to suspect that he is conscious of being guilty of what is said of him. But if you laugh at it, by your laughing you do away with the sentence against you. And if you would have a clear proof of what has been said, ask the enemy himself, when he is most vexed? when you are heated, and insult him in return? or when you laugh at him as he insults you? and you will be told the last rather. For he too is not so much pleased with not being insulted in return, as he is vexed because his abuse was not able to gain any hold upon you. Did you never see men in a passion, how they make no great account of their own wounds, but rush on with much violence, and are worse than very wild boars for seeking the hurt of their neighbor, and look to this alone, and are more given to this than to being on their guard against getting harmed? When therefore thou deprivest him of that he desires most, thou bereavest him of everything, by holding him thus cheap, and showing him to be easy to be despised, and a child rather than a man; and thou indeed hast gained the reputation of a wise man, and him dost thou invest with the character of a noisome beast. This too let us do when we are struck, and when we wish to strike, let us abstain from striking again. But, would you give a mortal blow? "Turn to him the other cheek also" (Matt. v. 39), and thou wilt smite him with countless wounds. For they that applaud, and wonder at thee, are more annoying to him than men to stone him would be; and before them, his conscience will condemn him, and will exact the greatest punishment of him, and so he will go off with a confused look as if he had been treated with the utmost rigor. And if it is the estimation of the multitude that you look for, this too you will have in larger share. And in a general way we have a kind of sympathy with those who are the sufferers; but when we also see that they do not strike (several Mss. resist, ἀντιπίπτοντας) in return, but even give themselves up to it, we not only pity them, but even feel admiration for them.

Here then I find reason to lament, that we who might have things present, if we listened to Christ's Law as we should, and also attain to things to come, are cast out of both by not

---

[1] ἀντιδόσεως. It means a recompense upon the other.

[2] Most Mss. omit "he would not . . . . . fed."

[3] μικρόψυχος, Ed. Ben. quotes St. Bas. *Ep.* 74 and St. Ath. t. i. p. 142 a and 152 f. Hist. tracts pp. 41 and marg., 55, to show that this word may be used in the sense of "malicious." It sometimes means "niggardly," both being characteristics of a little mind. v. p. 106 and 373.

[*] The meaning which is here attached to the expression: *thou shalt heap coals of fire upon his head,* viz.: thou shalt bring the divine vengeance upon him, is very improbable. Such a consideration could not be urged as a motive of Christian love. Augustin well says: "How does any one love the man to whom he gives food and drink for the very purpose of heaping coals of fire upon his head, if 'coals of fire' in this place signify some heavy punishment?" The meaning is: thou shalt by returning good for evil, bring the evil-doer to shame and remorse. This course will be the dictate of Christian love because it will tend to reveal the man's wrong-doing to himself, induce repentance for it and lead him to forsake it. The repentance of Saul is an example (1 Sam. xxiv. 17), "And Saul lifted up his voice and wept. And he said: thou art more righteous than I: for thou hast rendered unto me good, whereas I have rendered unto thee evil."—G. B. S.

[4] It may be objected that St. Paul was not speaking to a person in a rage, but generally to all. However, it is plain that the admonition is meant for those who want it. And there are many people who justify themselves in bearing malice, so as to require such management even in a general admonition.

paying attention to what has been told us, but giving ourselves to unwarranted philosophising about them. For He has given us laws upon all these points for our good, and has shown us what makes us have a good name, what brings us to disgrace. And if it was likely to have proved His disciples ridiculous, He would not have enjoined this. But since this makes them the most notable of men, namely, the not speaking ill, when we have ill spoken of us; the not doing ill when we have ill done us; this was His reason for enjoining it. But if this be so, much more the speaking of good when we have ill spoken of us, and the praising of those that insult us, and the doing good to those that plot against us, will make us so. This then was why He gave these laws. For He is careful for His own disciples, and knowing well what it is that maketh little or great. If then He both careth and knoweth, why dost thou quarrel with Him, and wish to go another road? For conquering by doing ill is one of the devil's laws. Hence in the Olympic games which were celebrated to him [1] it is so that all the competitors conquer. But in Christ's race this is not the rule about the prize, for, on the contrary, the law is for the person smitten, and not for the person smiting, to be crowned. For such is the character of His race, it has all its regulations the other way; so that it is not in the victory only, but also in the way of the victory, that the marvel is the greater. Now when things which on the other side are signs of a victory, on this side he showeth to be productive of defeat, this is the power of God, this the race of Heaven, this the theatre of Angels. I know that ye are warmed thoroughly now, and are become as soft as any wax, but when ye have gone hence ye will spew it all out. This is why I sorrow, that what we are speaking of, we do not show in our actions, and this too though we should be greatest gainers thereby. For if we let our moderation be seen, we shall be invincible to any man; and there is nobody either great or small, who will have the power of doing us

any hurt. For if any one abuseth thee, he has not hurt thee at all, but himself severely. And if again he wrong thee, the harm will be with the person who does the wrong. Did you never notice that even in the courts of law those who have had wrong done them are honored, and stand and speak out with entire freedom, but those who have done the wrong, are bowed down with shame and fear? And why do I talk of evil-speaking (Sav. conj. and 5 Mss. κακηγορίαν) and of wrong? For were he even to whet his sword against thee, and to stain his right hand in thy life-blood (εἰς τὸν λαιμὸν, as p. 505), it is not thee that he hath done any harm to, but himself that he hath butchered. And he will witness what I say who was first taken off thus by a brother's hand. For he went away to the haven without a billow, having gained a glory that dieth not away; but the other lived a life worse than any death, groaning, and trembling, and in his body bearing about the accusation of what he had done. Let us not follow after this then, but that. For he that hath ill done him, has not an evil that taketh up its constant abode with him, since he is not the parent of it; but as he received it from others, he makes it good by his patient endurance. But he that doeth ill, hath the well of the mischief in himself. Was not Joseph in prison, but the harlot that plotted against him in a fine and splendid house? Which then wouldest thou wish to have been? And let me not hear yet of the requital, but examine the things that had taken place by themselves. For in this way thou wilt rate Joseph's prison infinitely above the house with the harlot in it. For if you were to see the souls of them both, you would find the one full of enlargement and boldness, but that of the Egyptian woman in straitness, shame, dejection, confusion, and great despondency. And yet she seemed to conquer; but this was no real victory. Knowing all this then, let us fit ourselves for bearing ills, even that we may be freed from bearing ills, and may attain to the blessings to come. Which that we may all attain to, God grant, by the grace and love toward man, etc.

[1] The Fathers generally believed the devils were connected with idol-worship. See Tertullian *de Spectac.* p. 202 O. T. St. Augustin *de Civ. Dei*, i. 32, etc. Clem. *Al. Protr.* c. 3.

HOMILY XXIII.

ROM. XIII. 1.

"Let every soul be subject unto the higher powers."

OF this subject he makes much account in other epistles also, setting subjects under their rulers as household servants are under their masters. And this he does to show that it was not for the subversion of the commonwealth that Christ introduced His laws, but for the better ordering of it, and to teach men not to be taking up unnecessary and unprofitable wars. For the plots that are formed against us for the truth's sake are sufficient, and we have no need to be adding temptations superfluous and unprofitable. And observe too how well-timed his entering upon this subject is. For when he had demanded that great spirit of heroism, and made men fit to deal either with friends or foes, and rendered them serviceable alike to the prosperous and those in adversity and need, and in fact to all, and had planted a conversation worthy of angels, and had discharged anger, and taken down recklessness, and had in every way made their mind even, he then introduces his exhortation upon these matters also. For if it be right to requite those that injure us with the opposite, much more is it our duty to obey those that are benefactors to us. But this he states toward the end of his exhortation, and hitherto does not enter on these reasonings which I mention, but those only that enjoin one to do this as a matter of debt. And to show that these regulations are for all, even for priests, and monks, and not for men of secular occupations only, he hath made this plan at the outset, by saying as follows: "let every soul be subject unto the higher powers," if thou be an Apostle even, or an Evangelist, or a Prophet, or anything whatsoever, inasmuch as this subjection is not subversive of religion. And he does not say merely "obey," but "be subject." And the first claim such an enactment has upon us, and the reasoning that suiteth the faithful, is, that all this is of God's appointment.

"For there is no power," he says, "but of God."

What say you? it may be said; is every ruler then elected by God? This I do not say, he answers. Nor am I now speaking about individual rulers, but about the thing in itself. For that there should be rulers, and some rule and others be ruled, and that all things should not just be carried on in one confusion, the people swaying like waves in this direction and that; this, I say, is the work of God's wisdom. Hence he does not say, "for there is no ruler but of God;" but it is the thing he speaks of, and says, "there is no power but of God.* And the powers that be, are ordained of God." Thus when a certain wise man saith, "It is by the Lord that a man is matched with a woman" (Prov. xix. 14, LXX.), he means this, God made marriage, and not that it is He that joineth together every man that cometh to be with a woman. For we see many that come to be with one another for evil, even by the law of marriage, and this we should not ascribe to God. But as He said Himself, "He which made them at the beginning, made them male and female, and said, For this cause shall a man leave father and mother, and shall cleave to his wife, and they twain shall be one flesh." (Matt. xix. 4, 5; Gen. ii. 24.) And this is what that wise man meant to explain. For since equality of honor does many times lead to fightings, He hath made many governments and forms of subjection; as that, for instance, of man and wife, that of son and father, that of old men and young, that of bond and free,[1] that of ruler and ruled, that of master and disciple. And why are you surprised in the case of mankind, when even in the body He hath done the same thing? For even here He hath not made all parts of equal honor,

---

* The distinction which Chrys. carries through his interpretation of this passage on human government, between authority *in abstracto* and *in concreto* belongs rather to a philosophical treatment of the subject than to an exposition of the apostle's language. The use of general terms like ἐξουσία and οὐσία cannot have been designed to leave room for concrete exceptions since the apostle blends general and specific terms throughout the passage [ἄρχοντες (3) θεοῦ διάκονος (4)]. The question of obeying unjust rulers and supporting the "powers" in unjust measures, the apostle does not raise. He is stating a general principle and he says nothing of exceptions. His language does not exclude the possibility of exceptions when the reign of rulers becomes clearly subversive of moral order and opposed to the principles of the divine government.—G. B. S.

[1] See 1 Cor. vii. 21; Col. iii. 22; 1 Tim. vi. 2. Slavery is clearly recognized as a lawful state of life, appointed by Providence, and in Col. iv. 1, is shown to have a typical meaning; this does not necessarily imply the common opinion of the Greeks (*Ar. Pol.* i. 1), that there is a natural distinction of men into the free and the slavish.

but He hath made one less and another greater, and some of the limbs hath He made to rule and some to be ruled. And among the unreasoning creatures one may notice this same principle, as amongst bees, amongst cranes, amongst herds of wild cattle. And even the sea itself is not without this goodly subordination; for there too many of the clans are ranged under one among the fishes, and are led thus as an army, and make long expeditions from home. For anarchy, be where it may, is an evil, and a cause of confusion. After having said then whence governments come, he proceeds, "Whosoever therefore resisteth the power, resisteth the ordinance of God." See what he has led the subject on to, and how fearful he makes it, and how he shows this to be a matter of debt. For lest the believers should say, You are making us very cheap and despicable, when you put us, who are to enjoy the Kingdom of Heaven, under subjection to rulers, he shows that it is not to rulers, but to God again that he makes them subject in doing this. For it is to Him, that he who subjects himself to authorities is obedient. Yet he does not say this—for instance that it is God to Whom a man who listens to authorities is obedient—but he uses the opposite case to awe them, and gives it a more precise form by saying, that he who listeneth not thereto is fighting with God, Who framed these laws. And this he is in all cases at pains to show, that it is not by way of favor that we obey them, but by way of debt. For in this way he was more likely to draw the governors who were unbelievers to religion, and the believers to obedience. For there was quite a common report in those days (Tert. *Ap.* 1, 31, 32), which maligned the Apostles, as guilty of a sedition and revolutionary scheme, and as aiming in all they did and said at the subversion of the received institutions. When then you show our common Master giving this in charge to all His, you will at once stop the mouths of those that malign us as revolutionists, and with great boldness will speak for the doctrines of truth. Be not then ashamed, he says, at such subjection. For God hath laid down this law, and is a strong Avenger of them if they be despised. For it is no common punishment that He will exact of thee, if thou disobey, but the very greatest; and nothing will exempt thee, that thou canst say to the contrary, but both of men thou shalt undergo the most severe vengeance, and there shall be no one to defend thee, and thou wilt also provoke God the more. And all this he intimates when he says,

"And they that resist shall receive to them-selves damnation." Then to show the gain of the thing after the fear, he uses reasons too to persuade them as follows :

Ver. 3. "For rulers are not a terror to good works, but to the evil."

For when he has given a deep wound, and stricken them down, he again uses gentler treatment, like a wise physician, who applies soothing medicines, and he comforts them, and says, why be afraid? why shudder? For does he punish a person that is doing well? Or is he terrible to a person who lives in the practice of virtue? Wherefore also he proceeds, "Wilt thou then not be afraid of the power? Do that which is good, and thou shalt have praise of the same." You see how he has made him friends (ᾠκείωσεν) with the ruler, by showing that he even praises him from his throne. You see how he has made wrath unmeaning.

Ver. 4. "For he is the minister of God to thee for good."

So far is he from terrifying thee, he says, that he even praises thee : so far from being a hindrance to thee, that he even works with thee. When then thou hast his praise and his succor, how is it that thou art not in subjection to him? For he maketh virtue easier for thee in other ways also, by chastising the wicked, by benefiting and honoring[1] the good, and by working together with the will of God. Whence too he has even given him the name of "Minister."[2] And consider : I give you counsel to be sober-minded, and he, by the laws, speaks the same language. I exhort you not to be rapacious and grasping. And he sits in judgment in such cases, and so is a worker together with us, and an assistant to us, and has been commissioned by God for this end.[3] Hence there are both reasons for reverencing him, both because he was commissioned by God, and because it was for such an object. "But if thou do that which is evil, be afraid." It is not then the ruler that maketh the fear, but our own wickedness.

"For he beareth not the sword in vain." You see how he hath furnished him with arms, and set him on guard like a soldier, for a terror to those that commit sin. "For he is the minister of God to execute wrath, a re-

---

[1] Most Mss. omit "and honoring."
[2] Or Deacon ; the Coronation Service illustrates the sacred view of the kingly office ; as by the use of the Dalmatic (sect. x.), which belongs also to Deacons ; see Palmer, *Or. Lit.* append. sect. iv.
[3] Compare Butler, *Analogy* 1, 2, and Arist. *Eth.* v. 1. "The law commands to do the acts of a brave man, such as not quitting one's post, not flying, not throwing away one's arms. And those of a sober man, as not to commit adultery, or to insult any one. And those of a meek person, as not to strike, not to defame ; and so with other virtues and vices, . . ." Where he means that the law cannot enforce the character but can demand the acts, and is so far drawing man towards what is suitable to his nature. Butler shows that this is a part of God's moral government.

venger upon him that doeth evil." Now lest you should start off at hearing again of punishment, and vengeance, and a sword, he says again that it is God's law he is carrying out. For what if he does not know it himself? yet it is God that hath so shaped things (οὕτως ἐτύπωσεν). If then, whether in punishing, or in honoring, he be a Minister, in avenging virtue's cause, in driving vice away, as God willeth, why be captious against him, when he is the cause of so many good doings, and paves the way for thine too? since there are many who first practised virtue through the fear of God. For there are a duller sort, whom things to come have not such a hold upon as things present. He then who by fear and rewards gives the soul of the majority a preparatory turn towards its becoming more suited for the word of doctrine, is with good reason called "the Minister of God."

Ver. 5. "Wherefore ye must needs be subject, not only for wrath but also for conscience sake."

What is the meaning of, "not only for wrath?" It means not only because thou dost resist God by not being subject, nor only because thou art procuring great evils for thyself, both from God and the rulers, but also because he is a benefactor to thee in things of the greatest importance, as he procures peace to thee, and the blessings of civil institutions. For there are countless blessings to states through these authorities; and if you were to remove them, all things would go to ruin, and neither city nor country, nor private nor public buildings, nor anything else would stand, but all the world will be turned upside down, while the more powerful devour the weaker. And so even if some wrath were not to follow man's disobedience, even on this ground thou oughtest to be subject, that thou mayest not seem devoid of conscience and feeling towards the benefactor.

Ver. 6. "For, for this cause pay ye tribute also; for they are God's ministers, attending continually on this very thing."

Without going one by one into the benefits done to states by the rulers, as that of good order and peace, the other services, as regarding the soldiery, and those over the public business, he shows the whole of this by a single case. For that thou art benefited by him, he means, thou bearest witness thyself, by paying him a salary. Observe the wisdom and judgment of the blessed Paul. For that which seemed to be burdensome and annoying —the system of imposts—this he turns into a proof of their care for men. What is the reason, he means, that we pay tribute to a king? It is not as providing for us? And yet we

33

should not have paid it unless we had known in the first instance that we were gainers from this superintendence. Yet it was for this that from of old all men came to an agreement that governors should be maintained by us, because to the neglect of their own affairs, they take charge of the public,[1] and on this they spend their whole leisure, whereby our goods also are kept safe. After saying then what the external goods are, he again averts to the former line of argument (for in this way he was more likely to attract the believer to him), and he shows again that this is God's decree, and on it he makes his advice rest finally, in these words, "they are God's ministers." Then to show the pains they take, and their hard life, he proceeds,

"Waiting continually upon this very thing."

For this is their life, this their business, that thou mayest enjoy peace. Wherefore in another Epistle, he bids them not only be subject, but also "pray" in their behalf. And as showing there too that the advantage was common to all, he adds, "that we may lead a quiet and peaceable life in all things."[2] (1 Tim. ii. 1, 2.) For it is in no small degree that they contribute to the settled state of the present life, by keeping guard, beating off enemies, hindering those who are for sedition in the cities, putting an end to differences among any. For do not tell me of some one who makes an ill use of the thing, but look to the good order that is in the institution itself, and you will see the great wisdom of Him who enacted this law from the first.

Ver. 7, 8. "Render therefore to all their dues; tribute to whom tribute, custom to whom custom, fear to whom fear, honor to whom honor. Owe (or ye owe) no man anything, but to love one another."

He still keeps upon the same line, bidding them pay them not money only, but honor and fear. And how is it when he said above, "Wilt thou not be afraid of the power? do that which is good;" that he here says "render fear?" He does it meaning exceeding honor, and not the fear which comes from a bad conscience, which he alluded to before And it is not "give," that he says, but "render" (or "give back," ἀπόδοτε), and then adds to it, the "dues." For it is not a favor that you confer by so doing, since the thing is

---

[1] Arist. *Eth.* viii. 8, "The political union of men seems to have been first formed for advantage, and for this it is upheld." See *Pol.* i. 2, where he says of it, that "it is formed that men may live, but is (in the nature of things) that they may live well."

[2] St. Augustin *de Civ. Dei,* xix. 17, writes, "But the heavenly city, or rather that part of it which sojourneth in this mortal state, and liveth by faith, must likewise make use of this kind of peace, till that mortality, for which such peace is needful, pass away." And xix. 26, he quotes 1 Tim. ii. 2, and Jer. xxix. 7, to the same purpose.

matter of due. And if you do it not, you will be punished as obstinate. Do not suppose that you are lowering yourself, and detracting from the dignity of your own philosophy, if you rise up at the presence of a ruler, or if you uncover your head. For if he laid these laws down at that time, when the rulers were Gentiles, much more ought this to be done with them now they are believers. But if you mean to say, that you are entrusted with greater privileges, be informed that this is not thy time. For thou art a stranger and a sojourner. A time will be when thou shalt appear brighter than all. Now thy "life is hid with Christ in God. When Christ shall appear, then shall ye also appear with Him in glory." (Col. iii. 3, 4.) Seek not then in this life of accidents thy change, but even if thou hast to be with fear in a ruler's presence, do not think that this is unworthy thy noble birth. For so God willeth, that the ruler who has his place marked[1] by Him, should have his own power. And when he who is conscious of no evil in himself, stands with fear in the judge's presence, much more will he who doth evil things be affrighted, and thou in this way wilt be the more respected. For it is not from honoring that the lowering of self comes but from dishonoring him. And the ruler will treat thee with greater respect, and he will glorify thy Master owing to this, even if he be an unbeliever. "Owe[2] no man anything, but to love one another." Again he has recourse to the mother of good deeds, and the instructress of the things spoken of, who is also productive of every virtue, and says that this is a debt also, not however such as the tribute or the custom, but a continuous one. For he does not wish it ever to be paid off, or rather he would have it always rendered, yet never fully so, but to be always owing. For this is the character of the debt, that one keeps giving and owing always. Having said then how he ought to love, he also shows the gain of it, saying,

"For he that loveth another hath fulfilled the Law."

And do not, pray, consider even this a favor; for this too is a debt. For thou owest love to thy brother, through thy spiritual relationship. And not for this only, but also because "we are members one of another." And if love leave us, the whole body is rent in pieces. Love therefore thy brother. For if from his friendship thou gainest so much as

to fulfil the whole Law, thou owest him love as being benefited by him.

Ver. 9. "For this, Thou shalt not commit adultery, Thou shalt not kill, Thou shalt not steal, Thou shalt not bear false witness,[3] and any other commandment, is briefly comprehended in this saying, Thou shalt love thy neighbor as thyself."

He does not say merely it is fulfilled, but "it is briefly comprehended,[4] that is, the whole work of the commandments is concisely and in a few words completed. For the beginning and the end of virtue is love. This it has for its root, this for its groundwork, this for its summit. If then it be both beginning and fulfilment, what is there equal to it? But he does not seek love merely, but intense love. For he does not say merely "love thy neighbor," but, "as thyself." Hence also Christ said[5] that "the Law and the Prophets hang upon" it. And in making two kinds of love, see how He has raised this! For after saying that the first commandment is, "Thou shalt love the Lord thy God," He added a second;[6] and He did not stay, but added, "like unto it; Thou shalt love thy neighbor as thyself." What can be equal to this love to man, or this gentleness? That when we were at infinite distance from Him, He brings the love to us into comparison with that toward Himself, and says that that "is like unto this." Hence then, to put the measures of either as nearly the same, of the one He says, "with all thy heart, and with all thy soul," but of this towards one's neighbor, He says, "as thyself." But Paul said, that when this did not exist even the other was of no great profit to us. As then we, when we are fond of any one, say, if you love him, then you love me; so He also to show this saith, "is like unto it;" and to Peter, "If thou lovest Me, feed My sheep." (John xxi. 16.)

Ver. 10. "Love worketh no ill to his neighbor, therefore love is the fulfilling of the Law."

Observe how it has both virtues, abstinence from evils (for it "worketh no ill," he says), and the working of good deeds. "For it is," he says, "the fulfilling (or filling up) of the Law;" not bringing before us instruction only on moral duties in a concise form, but making the accomplishment of them easy also. For that we should become acquainted with

[1] τυπωθείς, see p. 513, οὕτως ἐτύπωσεν. The sense appears to be, "whose precise character in every form of government Himself determines."
[2] Or "ye owe," it may seem that this is his sense, from "thou owest," but he would have it look the other way.
[3] St. Chrysostom omits "Thou shalt not covet." Many Mss. of the New Testament omit "Thou shalt not bear false witness," but all known Mss. of St. Chrysostom have it, as well as the printed copies.
[4] ἀνακεφαλαιοῦται, see p. 472, note [3].
[5] Matt. xxii. 39. St. Hilary on the place notices that the second could not be called like unto it, were it not that our Neighbor means Christ, i. e. as present in His members.
[6] So most Mss. while the old edd. read "added, and the second—"

things profitable to us was not all that he was careful for (which is the Law's care), but also with a view to the doing of them it brought us great assistance; accomplishing not some part of the commandments, but the whole sum of virtue in us. Let us then love one another, since in this way we shall also love God,[1] Who loveth us. For in the case of men, if you love a man's beloved, he that loveth him is contentious at it. But here He deemeth thee worthy to share His love, and hateth thee when thou sharest not. For man's love is laden with envy and grudging;[2] but God's is free from all passion, whence also He seeketh for those to share His love. For He says, love thou with Me, and then thyself also will I love the more. You see the words of a vehement lover! If thou love My beloved, then will I also reckon Myself to be greatly beloved of thee. For He vehemently desireth our salvation, and this He showed from of old. Now hear what He saith when He was forming the man, "Let Us make man in Our Image:" and again, "Let Us[3] make an help meet for him. It is not good for him to be alone." (Gen. i. 26.) And when he had transgressed, He rebuked him, observe how gently;[4] and He does not say, Wretch! thou very wretch! after receiving so great benefits, hast thou after all trusted to the devil? and left thy Benefactor, to take up with the evil spirit? But what saith He? "Who told thee that thou art naked, unless thou hast eaten of the Tree, from which alone I commanded thee not to eat?" (ib. iii. 11.) As if a father were to say to a child, who was ordered not to touch a sword, and then disobeyed and got wounded, " How camest thou wounded? Thou camest so by not listening to me." You see they are the words of a friend rather than a master, of a friend despised, and not even then forsaking. Let us then imitate Him, and when we rebuke, let us preserve this moderation. For even the woman He also rebuketh again with the same gentleness. Or rather what He said was not so much rebuke as admonition and correction, and security against the future. This is why He saith nothing[5] to the serpent. For he was the designer of the mischiefs, and had it not in his power to put off the accusation on any one else, wherefore He punished him severely: and even here He did not come to

a pause, but made the earth also to share in the curse. But if He cast them out of paradise, and condemned them to labor, even for this we ought to adore and reverence Him the most. For since self-indulgence issues in listlessness, He trenches upon the pleasure by building a fort of pain against listlessness, that we may return to the love of Him. And what of Cain's case? Doth he not meet with the same gentleness? For being by him also insulted, He doth not reproach (same word as insult) in return, but entreats (or comforts) him, and says, "Why is thy countenance fallen?" (Gen. iv. 6.) And yet what he had done allowed of no excuse whatever. And this the younger brother shows. But still even then He doth not rebuke him: but what saith He? "Hast thou sinned: keep peace;" "do so no more." "To thee shall his turning be, and thou shalt rule over him"[6] (ib. 7, LXX.), meaning his brother. "For if thou art afraid, lest for this sacrifice," He means, "I should deprive thee of the preëminence of the firstborn, be of good cheer, for the entire command over him do I put into thy hands. Only be thou better, and love him that hath done thee no wrong; for I have an interest in you both. And what maketh Me most glad is, that ye be not at variance one with another." For as a devoted mother, so doth God do and plan everything to keep one from being torn from another; but that you may get a clearer view, by an example, of my meaning, call to your mind, pray, Rebecca in her trouble, and running about everywhere, when the elder son was at enmity with the younger. For if she loved Jacob, still she did not feel averse to Esau. And therefore she said, Lest by any means "I be deprived of both of you, my children, in one day." (ib. xxvii. 45.) Therefore also God upon that occasion said, "Thou hast sinned: be at peace: unto thee shall his turning be" (ib. iv. 7), so repressing the murder beforehand, and aiming at the peace of them both. But when he had murdered him, He did not even then bring His care for him to a close, but again answers the fratricide in gentle terms, saying, "Where is thy brother Abel?" that even now, if he would, he might make a full confession. But he struggled in defence of his former misdeeds, with a greater and sadder shamelessness. But even then God doth not leave him, but again speaks the language of an injured and despised lover, and says, "The voice of thy brother's blood crieth unto Me." (Gen. iv. 10.) And again He rebukes the earth with the murderer, turning His wrath off to it, and saying, " Cursed

---

[1] Ms. "be beloved of God," which makes a fair sense with the context.

[2] Plato, *Phædr.* p. 217, B. ὁ φθόνος ἔξω Θείου χοροῦ ἵσταται, Envy standeth without the Divine circle.

[3] Gen. ii. 18. This plural is in the LXX., not in the Hebrew. See in Gen. c. ii. Hom. xiv.

[4] On the Fall, see Hom. xvii. in Gen.

[5] Nothing before or beside his sentence. Nothing of admonition. See Ben.

[6] See *Hom.* xix. *in Gen.* St. Cyr. *Al. Glaph.* lib. i. § 2, p. 20 B. takes this as said to Abel.

be the earth, which opened her mouth to receive thy brother's blood" (ib. ii.); and doing like those who lament (ἀνακαλοῦντας), as David also did when Saul was fallen. For he made an address to the mountains which received him as he died, in the words, "Ye mountains of Gilboa, let there fall on you neither rain nor dew, because there were the shields of the mighty cast away." (2 Sam i. 21.) And thus God also, as though singing some solitary dirge (μονῳδίαν), saith, "The voice of thy brother's blood crieth unto Me; and now art thou cursed from the earth, which hath opened her mouth to receive thy brother's blood from thy hand." And this He said to humble his fiery passion, and to persuade him to love him at least now he was gone. Hast thou extinguished his life? He would say; why dost thou not now extinguish the hatred also? But what doth He do? He loveth both the one and the other, since He made them both. What then?[1] doth (4 Mss. will) He let the murderer go unpunished? Nay, he would but have grown worse. Will He punish him then? Nay, He hath more tenderness than a father. See then how He at once punisheth and also displays, even in this, His love. Or rather, He doth not so much as punish, but only corrects. For He doth not kill him, but only fetters him with trembling, that he may divest himself of the crime, that so at least he may come back to a natural tenderness for the other, and that so at last he may make a truce with him now he hath gone; for He were fain he should not go away to the other world in enmity with him that was deceased. This is the way wherein they that love, when in doing acts of kindness they meet with no love in return, are led on to be vehement and to threaten, not with their will indeed, but led by their love to do this: that at least in this way they may win over those that scorn them. Yet affection of this sort is one of compulsion, and still this even solaces them, through the vehemency of their love. And so punishment itself comes from affection, since unless pained at being hated, they would not choose to punish either. Now observe, how this is what Paul says to the Corinthians. For "who is he" (says he) "that maketh me glad, but the same which is made sorry by me?" (2 Cor. ii. 2.) And so when he is going to the full extent of punishment, then he shows his love. Thus the Egyptian woman too, from her vehement love, as vehemently punished Joseph: and she

indeed did so for mischief, the love being unchaste; but God for good, since the love was worthy of Him who loved. This is why He does not refuse even to condescend to grosser words, and to speak the names of human passions, and to call Himself jealous. For "I am a jealous God" (Ex. xx. 5), He saith, that you may learn the intenseness of the love. Let us then love Him as He would have us: for He sets great store thereby. And if we turn away, He keepeth inviting us, and if we will not be converted, He chasteneth us through His affection, not through a wish to exact punishment of us. And see what He saith in Ezekiel to the city that was beloved, yet had despised Him. "I will bring thy lovers against thee, and will deliver thee into their hands, and they shall stone thee, and shall slay thee, and My jealousy shall be taken away from thee, and I will rest, and I will not trouble Myself any more." (From Ezek. xvi. 37–42.) What more than this could a vehement lover have said, when despised by his beloved, and after all again ardently loving her? For God doeth everything that He may be loved by us, and owing to this He spared not even His Son. But we are unbending, and savage. Yet let us become gentle at last, and love God as we ought to love Him, that we may with pleasure enjoy virtue. For if any that hath a beloved wife does not perceive any of the vexations that come day by day, He that loveth with this divine and pure love, only consider what great pleasure he will have to enjoy! For this is, indeed it is, the kingdom of Heaven; this is fruition of good things, and pleasure, and cheerfulness, and joy, and blessedness. Or rather, say as many things as I may, I shall still be unable to give you any such representation of it as should be, but the trial of it alone can give a knowledge of this goodly thing. Wherefore also the Prophet saith, "Delight thyself in the Lord" (Ps. xxxvii. 4), and, "Taste and see that the Lord is gracious." (Ib. xxxiv. 8.) Let us then be persuaded, and indulge ourselves in His love. For in this way we shall both see His Kingdom even from out of this life, and shall be living the life of Angels, and while we abide on earth, we shall be in as goodly a condition as they that dwell in heaven; and after our departing hence, shall stand the brightest of beings by the judgment-seat of Christ, and shall enjoy that glory unutterable, which may we all attain unto, by the grace and love toward man of our Lord Jesus Christ. For to Him is the glory forever, Amen.

---

[1] Alluding to the στένων καὶ τρέμων of the LXX., v. 12.

HOMILY XXIV.

ROM. XIII. 11.

" And that, knowing the time, that now it is high time to awake out of sleep."

SINCE he had given them what commands were fitting, he again thrusts them on to the performance of good works, in consideration of what was pressing upon them. For the time of judgment, he means, is at the doors. So too he wrote to the Corinthians also, " The remaining time is short.¹ " (1 Cor. vii. 29.) And to the Hebrews again, " For yet a little while, and He that shall come will come, and will not tarry." (Heb. x. 37.) But in those cases it was to cheer those in trouble, and to solace the toils of their closely successive temptations, that he said those things : but in the passage before us he does it to rouse those that are asleep, this language being useful to us for both the purposes : and what is that which he says, " Now it is high time to awake out of sleep ? " It is, that near is the Resurrection, near the awful Judgment, and the day that burneth as a furnace, near. Henceforward then we must be free from our listlessness ; " for now is our salvation nearer than when we believed."* You see how he puts the Resurrection now close by them. For as the time advances, he means, the season of our present life is wasting away, and that of the life to come waxes nearer. If then thou be prepared, and hast done all whatsoever He hath commanded, the day is salvation to thee (3 Mss. and Cat. σωτηρία σοι) ; but if the contrary, not so. For the present however, it is not upon alarming grounds that he exhorts them, but upon kindly ones, thus also to untie them from their fellow-feeling for the things of this present world. Then since it was not unlikely, that in the beginning of their early endeavors they would be most earnest, in that their desire was then at its full vigor, but that as the time went on,

the whole of their earnestness would wither down to nothing ; he says that they ought however to be doing the reverse, not to get relaxed as time went on, but to be the more full of vigor. For the nearer the King may be at hand, the more ought they to get themselves in readiness ; the nearer the prize is, the more wide awake ought they to be for the contest, since even the racers do this, when they are upon the end of the course, and towards the receiving of the prize, then they rouse themselves up the more. This is why he said, " Now is our salvation nearer than when we believed."

Ver. 12. " The night is far spent, the day is at hand."

If then this is upon ending, and the latter is drawing near, let us henceforth do what belongs to the latter, not to the former. For this is what is done in the things of this life. And when we see the night pressing on towards the morning, and hear the swallow twittering, we each of us awake our neighbor, although it be night still. But so soon as it is actually departing, we hasten one another, and say, It is day now ! and we all set about the works of the day, dressing, and leaving our dreams, and shaking our sleep thoroughly off, that the day may find us ready, and we may not have to begin getting up, and stretching ourselves, when the sunlight is up. What then we do in that case, that let us do here also. Let us put off imaginings, let us get clear of the dreams of this life present, let us lay aside its deep slumber, and be clad in virtue for garments. For it is to point out all this that he says,

" Let us therefore cast off the works of darkness, and let us put on the armor of light."

Yes, for the day is calling us to battle-array, and to the fight. Yet fear not at hearing of array and arms. For in the case of the visible suit of armor, to put it on is a heavy and abhorred task. But here it is desirable, and worth being prayed for. For it is of Light the arms are ! Hence they will set thee forth brighter than the sunbeam, and giving out a great glistening, and they place thee in security : for they are arms, and glit-

---

¹ 1 Cor. vii. 29. The stopping only is altered, as in Hom. xix. on the Hebrews (Matthiæ) p. 225 ed. Field.

* Ἡμῶν is better taken with ἐγγύτερον : " For now is salvation nearer *to us* than when we believed." (So R. V.) Both the position of the words and the requirements of emphasis favor this construction. Chrys. is essentially correct in referring ἡ σωτηρία here to the last things. The reference is to the Messianic salvation which is to be ushered in by the *Parousia* of the Lord from heaven. The period which shall intervene between the time of writing and the advent of Christ is designated as " night " (12), but the " day " which the Messianic σωτηρία shall usher in is near(ἤγγικεν).—G. B. S.

tering do they make thee : for arms of light are they! What then, is there no necessity for thee to fight ? yea, needful is it to fight, yet not to be distressed and toil. For it is not in fact war, but a solemn dance and feast-day, such is the nature of the arms, such the power of the Commander. And as the bride-groom goes forth with joyous looks from his chamber, so doth he too who is defended with these arms. For he is at once soldier and bridegroom. But when he says, "the day is at hand," he does not even allow it to be but near, but puts it even now beside us. For he says,

"Let us walk becomingly," (A. V. honestly, in this sense) "as in the day." For day it already is. And what most people insist upon very much in their exhortations, that he also uses to draw them on, the sense of the becoming. For they had a great regard to the esteem of the multitude.[1] And he does not say, walk ye, but let us walk, so making the exhortation free from anything grating, and the reproof gentle.

"Not in rioting and drunkenness." Not that he would forbid drinking, but the doing it immoderately; not the enjoying of wine, but doing it to excess ($\mu\epsilon\tau\grave{\alpha}$ $\pi\alpha\rho o\iota\nu\acute{\iota}\alpha\varsigma$). As also the next thing he states likewise with the same measure, in the words,

"Not in chambering and wantonness;" for here also he does not prohibit the inter-course of the sexes, but committing forni-cation. "Not in strife and envying." It is the deadly kind of passions then that he is for extinguishing, lust, namely, and anger. Wherefore it is not themselves only, but even the sources of them that he removes. For there is nothing that so kindles lust, and in-flames wrath, as drunkenness, and sitting long at the wine. Wherefore after first saying, "not in rioting and drunkenness," then he proceeded with, "not in chambering and wantonness, not in strife and envying." And even here he does not pause, but after strip-ping us of these evil garments, hear how he proceeds to ornament us, when he says,

Ver. 14. "But put ye on the Lord Jesus Christ."

He no longer speaks of works, but he rouses them to greater things. For when he was speaking of vice, he mentioned the works of it : but when of virtue, he speaks not of works, but of arms, to show that virtue put-teth him that is possessed of it into complete safety, and complete brightness. And even here he does not pause, but leading his dis-

course on to what was greater, a thing far more awestriking ; he gives us the Lord Him-self for a garment, the King Himself : for he that is clad with Him, hath absolutely all virtue.* But in saying, "Put ye on," he bids us be girt about with Him upon every side. As in another place he says, "But if Christ be in you." (Rom. viii. 10.) And again, "That Christ may dwell in the inner man." (Eph. iii. 16. 17, *al. punct.*) For He would have our soul to be a dwelling for Himself, and Himself to be laid round about us as a garment, that He may be unto us all things both from within and from without. For He is our fulness ; for He is "the fulness of Him that filleth all in all" (ib. i. 23): and the Way, and the Husband, and the Bridegroom ;—for "I have espoused you as a chaste virgin to one husband," (2 Cor. xi. 2): and a root, and drink, and meat, and life ;—for he says, "I live, yet not I, but Christ liveth in me ; " (Gal. ii. 20) and Apostle, and High-Priest, and Teacher, and Father, and Brother, and Joint-heir, and sharer of the tomb and Cross ;—for it says, "We were buried together with Him," and "planted together in the likeness of His Death" (Rom. vi. 4, 5): and a Suppliant ;—" For we are ambassadors in Christ's stead " (2 Cor. v. 20): and an "Advocate to the Father ; "—for " He also maketh," it says, " intercession for us: " (Rom. viii. 34) and house and inhabitant ;—for He says, " He that abideth in Me and I in Him " (John xv. 5): and a Friend ; for, " Ye are My friends " (ib. 14): and a Foundation, and Corner-stone. And we are His members and His heritage, and building, and branches, and fellow-workers. For what is there that He is not minded to be to us, when He makes us cleave and fit on to Him in every way ? And this is a sign of one loving exceedingly. Be persuaded then, and rousing thee from sleep, put Him on, and when thou hast done so, give thy flesh up to His bridle. For this is what he intimates in saying,

"And make not provision for the flesh, to fulfil the lusts thereof." For as he does not forbid drinking, but drinking to excess, not marrying, but doing wantonness ; so too he does not forbid making provision for the flesh either, but doing so with a view " to fulfil the lusts thereof," as, for instance, by going be-yond necessaries. For that he does bid make provision for it, hear from what he says to Timothy, " Use a little wine for thy stom-

---

[1] St. Augustin *de Civ. Dei*, v. 13-15, discusses this motive, and the temporal good that comes of it, as to the Roman state ; quoting Matt. vi. 2.

* In one of the apostle's favorite figures, that of putting off, or on, as clothing, he states again the essential qualities of the Christian life. The Christian is even now to belong to that sphere of light into whose full glory he shall shortly be raised. The culminating thought is : "put on Christ." Chrys.' application of the apostle's exhortation is one of his most eloquent passages.—G. B. S.

ach's sake, and thine often infirmities."
(1 Tim. v. 23.) So here too he is for taking
care of it, but for health, and not wantonness.
For this would cease to be making provision
for it, when you were lighting up the flame,
when you were making the furnace powerful.
But that you may form a clearer notion what
" making provision " for it " to fulfil the lusts
thereof " is, and may shun such a provision,
just call to mind the drunken, the gluttonous,
those that pride themselves in dress, those
that are effeminate, them that live a soft and
relaxed life, and you will see what is meant.
For they do everything not that they may be
healthy, but that they may be wanton and
kindle desire. But do thou, who hast put on
Christ, prune away all those things, and seek
for one thing only, to have thy flesh in health.
And to this degree do make provision for it,
and not any further, but spend all thy industry
on the care of spiritual things. For then you
will be able to rouse yourself out of this sleep,
without being weighed down with these manifold desires. For the present life is a sleep,
and the things in it are no way different from
dreams. And as they that are asleep often
speak and see things other than healthful, so
do we also, or rather we see much worse
even. For he that doeth anything disgraceful
or says the like in a dream,[1] when he is rid
of his sleep, is rid of his disgrace, also, and
is not to be punished. But in this case it is
not so, but the shame, and also the punishment, are immortal. Again, they that grow
rich in a dream, when it is day are convicted
of having been rich to no purpose. But in
this case even before the day the conviction
often comes upon them, and before they
depart to the other life, those dreams have
flown away.

Let us then shake off this evil sleep, for if
the day find us sleeping, a deathless death
will succeed, and before that day we shall be
open to the attacks of all the enemies that are
of this world, both men and devils: and if
they be minded to undo us, there is nobody
to hinder them. For if there were many
watching, then the danger would not be so
great; since however, one perhaps there is, or
two, who have lighted a candle, and would be
as it were watching in the depth of night,
while men were sleeping; therefore now we
have need of much sleeplessness, much
guardedness, to prevent our falling into the
most irremediable evils. Doth it not now
seem to be broad daylight? do we not think
that all men are awake and sober? yet still

(and perhaps you will smile at what I say,
still say it I will) we seem all of us like men
sleeping and snoring in the depth of night.
And if indeed an incorporeal being could be
seen, I would show you how most men are
snoring, and the devil breaking through walls,
and butchering us as we lie, and stealing
away the goods within, doing everything fearlessly, as if in profound darkness. Or rather,
even if it be impossible to see this with our
eyes, let us sketch it out in words, and consider how many have been weighed down by
evil desires, how many held down by the sore
evil of wantonness, and have quenched the
light of the Spirit. Hence it comes that they
see one thing instead of another, hear one
thing instead of another, and take no notice
of any of the things here told them. Or if I
am mistaken in saying so, and thou art awake,
tell me what has been doing here this day, if
thou hast not been hearing this as a dream.
I am indeed aware that some can tell me
(and I do not mean this of all); but do thou
who comest under what has been said, who
hast come here to no purpose, tell me what
Prophet, what Apostle hath been discoursing
to us to-day? and on what subjects? And
thou wouldest not have it in thy power to tell
me. For thou hast been talking a great deal
here, just as in a dream, without hearing the
realities. And this I would have said to the
women too, as there is a great deal of sleeping amongst them. And would it were sleep!
For he that is asleep says nothing either good
or bad. But he that is awake as ye are puts
forth many a word even for mischief on his
own head, telling his interest, casting up his
creditor accounts, calling to memory some
barefaced bargaining, planting the thorns
thick in his own soul, and not letting the seed
make even ever so little advance. But rouse
thyself, and pull these thorns up by the roots,
and shake the drunkenness off: for this is the
cause of the sleep. But by drunkenness I
mean, not that from wine only, but from
worldly thoughts, and with them that from
wine also. (See p. 443.) And this advice[2] I
am giving not to the rich only, but the poor
too, and chiefly those that club together for
social parties. For this is not really indulgence or relaxation, but punishment and vengeance. For indulgence lies not in speaking
filthy things, but in talking solemnly, in being
filled, not being ready to burst. But if thou
thinkest this is pleasure, show me the pleasure
by the evening! Thou canst not! And
hitherto I say nothing of the mischiefs it leads

---

[1] On this see St. Augustin, Conf. x. 30, p. 205 O. T. de Gen. ad
lit. x. 12, xii. 15. St. Greg. Mor. viii. § 42 sq. pp. 449, 450 O. T.
Cassian. Collat.

[2] This is a good illustration of Aristotle's remark, that
" general discourses on moral matters are pretty well useless,
while particular ones are more like the truth." Eth. ii. 7.

to, but at present have only been speaking to you of the pleasure that withers away so quickly. For the party is no sooner broken up, than all that went for mirth is flown away. But when I come to mention the spewing, and the headaches, and the numberless disorders, and the soul's captivity, what have you to say to all this? Have we any business, because we are poor, to behave ourselves unseemly too? And in saying this I do not forbid your meeting together, or taking your suppers at a common table, but to prevent your behaving unseemly, and as wishing indulgence to be really indulgence, and not a punishment, nor a vengeance, or drunkenness and revelling. Let the Gentiles (ἕλληνες) see that Christians know best how to indulge, and to indulge in an orderly way. For it says, "Rejoice in the Lord with trembling." (Ps. ii. 11.) But how then can one rejoice? Why, by saying hymns, making prayers, introducing psalms in the place of those low songs. Thus will Christ also be at our table, and will fill the whole feast with blessing, when thou prayest, when thou singest spiritual songs, when thou invitest the poor to partake of what is set before thee, when thou settest much orderliness and temperance over the feast. So thou wilt make the party a Church,[1] by hymning, in the room of ill-timed shouts and cheers, the Master of all things. And tell me not, that another custom has come to prevail, but correct what is thus amiss. "For whether ye eat," it says, "or whether ye drink, or whatsoever ye do, do all to the glory of God." (1 Cor. x. 31.) For from banquets of that sort you have evil desires, and impurities, and wives come to be in disrepute, and harlots in honor among you. Hence come the upsetting of families and evils unnumbered, and all things are turned upside down, and ye have left the pure fountain, and run to the conduit of mire. For that an harlot's body is mire, I do not enquire of any one else but of thine own self that wallowest in the mire, if thou dost not feel ashamed of thyself, if thou dost not think thyself unclean after the sin is over. Wherefore I beseech you flee fornication, and the mother of it, drunkenness. Why sow where reaping is impossible, or rather even if thou dost reap, the fruit brings thee great shame? For even if a child be born, it at once disgraces thyself, and has itself had injustice done it in being born through thee illegitimate and base. And if thou leave it never so much money, both the son of an harlot, and that of a servant-maid, is disreputable at home, disreputable in the city, disreputable in a court of law: dis-

reputable too wilt thou be also, both in thy lifetime, and when dead. For if thou have departed even, the memorials of thy unseemliness abide. Why then bring disgrace upon all these? Why sow where the ground makes it its care to destroy the fruit? where there are many efforts at abortion? where there is murder before the birth? for even the harlot thou dost not let continue a mere harlot, but makest her a murderess also. You see how drunkenness leads to whoredom, whoredom to adultery, adultery to murder; or rather to a something even worse than murder. For I have no name to give it, since it does not take off the thing born,[2] but prevent its being born.[2] Why then dost thou abuse the gift of God, and fight with His laws, and follow after what is a curse as if a blessing, and make the chamber of procreation a chamber for murder, and arm the woman that was given for childbearing unto slaughter? For with a view to drawing more money by being agreeable and an object of longing to her lovers, even this she is not backward to do, so heaping upon thy head a great pile of fire. For even if the daring deed be hers, yet the causing of it is thine. Hence too come idolatries, since many, with a view to become acceptable, devise incantations, and libations, and love-potions, and countless other plans. Yet still after such great unseemliness, after slaughters, after idolatries, the thing seems to many to belong to things indifferent, aye, and to many that have wives too. Whence the mingle (φορυτὸς) of mischief is the greater. For sorceries[3] are applied not to the womb that is prostituted, but to the injured wife, and there are plottings without number, and invocations of devils, and necromancies, and daily wars, and truceless fightings, and home-cherished jealousies. Wherefore also Paul, after saying, "not in chamberings and wantonness," proceeds, "not in strife and envying," as knowing the wars that result therefrom; the upsetting of families, the wrongs done to legitimate children, the other ills unnumbered. That we may then escape from all these, let us put on Christ, and be with Him continually. For this is what putting Him on is; never being without Him, having Him evermore visible in us, through our sanctification, through our moderation. So we say of friends, such an one is wrapped up (ἐνεδύσατο) in such another, meaning their great love, and keeping together incessantly. For he that is wrapped up in anything, seems to be that which he is wrapped in. Let then Christ be seen in every

---

[1] *Ora et ibi templum est*, D. Bernard.

[2] See Arist. *Polit.* vii. Tertull. *Apol.* i. 9, p. 22 O. T. and note r.

[3] Or poisonings.

part of us. And how is He to be seen? If thou doest His deeds. And what did He do? "The Son of Man," He says, "hath not where to lay His head." (Luke ix. 58.) This do thou also aim after.[1] He needed the use of food, and He fared upon barley loaves. He had occasion to travel, and there were no horses or beast of burden anywhere, but He walked so far as even to be weary. He had need of sleep, and He lay "asleep upon the pillow in the fore (πρύμνῃ, here πρώρας) part of the ship." (Mark iv. 38.) There was occasion for sitting down to meat, and He bade them lie down upon the grass. And His garments were cheap; and often He stayed alone, with no train after Him. And what He did on the Cross, and what amidst the insults, and all, in a word, that He did, do thou learn by heart (καταμαθὼν) and imitate. And so wilt thou have put on Christ, if thou "make no provision for the flesh to fulfil the lusts thereof." For the thing has no real pleasure, since these lusts gender again others more keen, and thou wilt never find satisfaction, but wilt only make thee one great torment. For as one who is in a continual thirst, even if he have ten thousand fountains hard by him, gets no good from this, as he is not able to extinguish the disorder, so is he that liveth continually in lusts. But if thou keep to what is necessary, thou wilt never come to have this fear, but all those things will go away, as well drunkenness as wantonness. Eat then only so much as to break thy hunger, have only so much upon thee as to be sheltered, and do not curiously deck thy flesh with clothing, lest thou ruin it. For thou wilt make it more delicate, and wilt do injury to its healthfulness, by unnerving it with so much softness. That thou mayest have it then a meet vehicle for the soul, that the helmsman may be securely seated over the rudder, and the soldier handle his arms with ease, thou must make all parts to be fitly framed together. For it is not the having much, but requiring little, that keeps us from being injured. For the one man is afraid even if he is not wronged: this other, even if he be wronged, is in better case than those that have not been wronged, and even for this very thing is in the better spirits. Let the object of our search be then, not how we can keep any one from using us spitefully, but how even if he wish to do it, he may be without the power. And this there is no other source whence to obtain, save by keeping to necessaries, and not coveting anything more. For in this way we shall be able to enjoy ourselves here, and shall attain to the good things to come, by the grace and love toward man, etc.

HOMILY XXV.

ROM. XIV. 1, 2.

"Him that is weak in the faith receive ye, but not to doubtful disputations. For one believeth that he may eat all things; another, who is weak, eateth herbs."

I AM aware that to most what is here said is a difficulty. And therefore I must first give the subject of the whole of this passage, and what he wishes to correct in writing this. What does he wish to correct then? There were many of the Jews which believed, who adhered of conscience to the Law, and after their believing, still kept to the observance of meats, as not having courage yet to quit the service of the Law entirely. Then that they might not be observed if they kept from swine's flesh only, they abstained in consequence from all flesh, and ate herbs only, that what they were doing might have more the appearance of a fast than of observance of the Law.* Others again were farther advanced, (τελειότεροι) and kept up no one thing of the kind, who became to those, who did keep them, distressing and offensive, by re-

---

[1] Lying on the bare ground was a common part of asceticism.

* Chrys. adopts the view which was common in antiquity as to who the "weak" here mentioned were. He regards them as judaizing Christians who were over-zealous for the Mosaic law and even went beyond its explicit requirements to abstain from swine's flesh and abstained from meat altogether. Another class of interpreters have supposed that the scruples of the "weak" concerning meat had the same ground as in 1 Cor. viii. and x., viz., the fear of eating flesh and drinking wine that had been used in the heathen sacrificial worship (So Rückert, Philippi, Neander). The chief objection to the former view is that they could not have derived their doctrine of entire abstinence from meat and wine from the Mosaic law, which prohibits only the flesh of certain unclean animals, and does not prohibit wine at all except in particular cases. The difficulty with the second view is that the whole passage has no allusion to heathen sacrifices, which could hardly have been the case if they had been the ground of the scruple. On the contrary in v. 14 Paul in correcting these ascetic notions declares his conviction that nothing is "unclean *of itself*," showing that their view was that flesh and wine possessed *in themselves* some power of pollution. The difficulties connected with these explanations have led many recent scholars to different explanations. Baur regarded the "weak" as Ebionitic Christians, but the Ebionites abstained from flesh as inherently sinful and it would seem that if this had been the opinion of the "weak" that Paul could hardly

proaching them, accusing them, driving them to despondency. Therefore the blessed Paul, out of fear lest, from a wish to be right about a trifle, they should overthrow the whole, and from a wish to bring them to indifferency about what they ate, should put them in a fair way for deserting the faith, and out of a zeal to put everything right at once, before the fit opportunity was come, should do mischief on vital points, so by this continual rebuking setting them adrift from their agreement in (ὁμολογίας εἰς) Christ, and so they should remain not righted in either respect: observe what great judgment he uses and how he concerns himself with both interests with his customary wisdom. For neither does he venture to say to those who rebuke, Ye are doing amiss, that he may not seem to be confirming the other in their observances; nor again, Ye are doing right, lest he should make them the more vehement accusers: but he makes his rebuke to square with each. And in appearance he is rebuking the stronger, but he pours forth all he has to say [1] against the other in his address to these. For the kind of correction most likely to be less grating is, when a person addresses some one else, while he is striking a blow at a different person, since this does not permit the person rebuked to fly into a passion, and introduces the medicine of correction unperceived. See now with what judgment he does this, and how well-timed he is with it. For after saying, "make not provision for the flesh to fulfil the lusts thereof," then he proceeds to the discussion of these points, that he might not seem to be speaking in defence of those who were the rebukers, and were for eating of anything. For the weaker part ever requires more forethought. Wherefore he aims his blow against the strong, immediately saying as follows, "Him that is weak in the faith." You see one blow immediately given to him. For by calling him weak (ἀσθενοῦντα), he points out that he is

not healthy (ἄρρωστον). Then he adds next, "receive," and point out again that he requires much attention. And this is a sign of extreme debility. "Not to doubtful disputations." [*] See, he has laid on a third stripe. For here he makes it appear that his error is of such a nature, that even those who do not transgress in the same manner, and who nevertheless admit him to their affection, and are earnestly bent upon curing him, are at doubt.[2] You see how in appearance he is conversing with these, but is rebuking others secretly and without giving offence. Then by placing them beside each other, one he gives encomiums, the other accusations. For he goes on to say, "One believeth that he may eat all things," commending him on the score of his faith. "Another who is weak, eateth herbs," disparaging this one again, on the score of his weakness. Then since the blow he had given was deadly (καιρίαν, used hyperbolically), he comforts him again in these words,

Ver. 3. "Let not him that eateth, despise him that eateth not."

He does not say, let him alone, nor does he say, do not blame him, nor yet, do not set him right; but do not reproach him, do not "despise" him, to show they were doing a thing perfectly ridiculous. But of this he speaks in other words. "Let not him which eateth not, judge him that eateth." For as the more advanced made light of these, as of little faith, and falsely healed, and spurious, and still Judaizers, so they too judged these as law-breakers, or as given to

---

have treated it so mildly. Since the Ebionites date from about 70 A. D., these ascetics at Rome could have been Ebionitic only in the sense of having the germs of subsequent Ebionism. An opinion similar to this has been advocated by Ritschl, Meyer and Mangold. In their view the root of this asceticism was Essenic. There was certainly a Judeo-Christian minority in the Roman church. The ideas of the Essenes were widely disseminated among the Jews at the time. It is natural to suppose that among the Roman Jews there were Essenes or those of Essenic tendencies who upon their conversion would associate their rigorous asceticism with the Christian doctrine of the subjugation of the flesh. This view best meets the requirements of the passage. The Essenes abstained wholly from wine and practised a supra-legal regimen in regard to food. They would have no occasion to array themselves against the apostle's doctrine and he therefore treats their scruples not in a polemic but in a cautious and conciliatory spirit.—G. B. S.

[1] κενοί, i. e. so as not to have to say anything against them directly. St. Chrysostom turns the passage in that way more than Theodoret. See on v. 4, which Theod. applies directly against the Judaizers. His general remarks on the rhetoric of the passage are independent of this question.

[*] Verse 2 counsels receiving to Christian fellowship those affected by these ascetic scruples but μὴ εἰς διακρίσεις διαλογισμῶν. These words have been variously rendered: (1) "not to doubtful disputations" (A. V., R. V.); (2) "for decisions of doubts" (marg. R. V.); (3) not to judgings of thoughts" (Meyer); "not to discussions of opinions" (Godet). It is clear that the apostle exhorts the church against allowing the scruples in question to be matter of debate and division but whether he means to place a limitation upon the church's duty to receive the weak brethren or whether he exhorts them to refrain from making the opinions of the weak a matter of discussion and judgment, is a question still unsettled. The following consideration deserve attention in the decision of the question (1) Paul treats the "weak" throughout with great forbearance and tenderness. (2) The church is the party exhorted. (3) It is probably that the διακρίσεις διαλογισμῶν refer to actions or judgments which the church would be in danger of exercising toward the weak. (4) It is likely that the question of eating meats or herbs only (v. 2) is a specimen of the διαλογισμοί referred to. (5) Διακρίσις means an act of distinguishing things that differ, i. e. a logical or moral judgment. (6) The question remains whether διαλογισμός means a doubt, or a thought, an opinion. The latter is the primary meaning and seems preferable here. Then the meaning would be: receive these persons to fellowship and abstain from criticisms and judgments upon their conscientious opinions. The translation of our Eng. vs. "not to doubtful disputations" is as ambiguous as the original phrase is in Greek. and is, therefore, a faithful rendering in respect of ambiguity. These translators seem to take διακρίσεις as meaning "doubts"—a meaning which that word cannot be shown to bear.—G. B. S.

[2] He seems to mean, "are at doubt whether they may acknowledge such." So Œcumenius seems to take it, who paraphrases this comment, and adds καὶ χωρίζεσθαι, " and separate themselves."

gluttony. And of these it is likely that many were of the Gentiles too. Wherefore he proceeds, "for God hath received him. But in the other's case he does not say this. And yet to be despised was the eater's share, as a glutton, but to be judged, his that did not eat, as of little faith. But he has made them change places, to show that he not only does not deserve to be despised, but that he can even despise. But do I condemn him? he means. By no means. For this is why he proceeds, "for God hath received him." Why then speakest thou to him of the law, as to a transgressor? "For God hath received him:" that is, has shown His unspeakable grace about him, and hath freed him from all charges against him; then again he turns to the strong.

Ver. 4. "Who art thou that judgest another man's servant?"

Whence it appears that they too judged, and did not despise only. "To his own Master he standeth or falleth." See here is another stroke. And the indignation seems to be against the strong man, and he attacks him. When he says, "Yea, he shall be holden up," he shows that he is still wavering, and requireth so much attention as to call in God as a physician for this, "for God," he says, "is able to make him stand." And this we say of things we are quite in despair about. Then, that he may not despair he both gives him the name of a servant when he says, "Who art thou that judgest another man's servant?" And here again he secretly attacks him. For it is not because he does things worthy to exempt him from being judged, that I bid you not judge him, but because he is Another's servant, that is, not thine, but God's. Then to solace him again he does not say, "falleth," but what? "standeth or falleth." But whether it be the latter or the former, either of these is the Master's concernment, since the loss also goes to Him, if he does fall, as the riches too, if he stand. And this again if we do not attend to Paul's aim in not wishing them to be rebuked before a fitting opportunity, is very unworthy of the mutual care becoming for Christians. But (as I am always saying) we must examine the mind with which it is spoken, and the subject on which it is said, and the object he would compass when he says it. But he makes them respectful by no slight motive, when he says this: for what he means is, if God, Who undergoeth the loss, hitherto doth nothing, how can you be else than ill-timed and out of all measure exact, when you seize on (ἀγκων, throttle) him and annoy him?

Ver. 5. "One man esteemeth one day above another, another esteemeth every day alike."

Here he seems to me to be giving a gentle hint about fasting. For it is not unlikely that some who fasted were always judging those who did not, or among the observances it is likely that there were some that on fixed days abstained, and on fixed days did not.[1] Whence also he says, "Let every man be fully persuaded in his own mind." And in this way he released those who kept the observances from fear, by saying that the thing was indifferent, and he removed also the quarrelsomeness of those who attacked them, by showing that it was no very desirable (or urgent, περισπούδαστον) task to be always making a trouble about these things. Yet it was not a very desirable task, not in its own nature, but on account of the time chosen, and because they were novices in the faith. For when he is writing to the Colossians, it is with great earnestness that he forbids it, saying, "Beware lest any man spoil you through philosophy and vain deceit, after the traditions of men, after the elements of the world, and not after Christ." (Col. ii. 8, see p. 4.) And again, "Let no man judge you in meat or in drink" (ib. 16), and, "let no man beguile you of your reward." (ib. 18.) And when writing to the Galatians with great precision, he exacts of them Christian spirit and perfectness in this matter. But here he does not use this vehemency, because the faith was lately planted in them. Let us therefore not apply the phrase, "Let every man be persuaded in his own mind," to all subjects. For when he is speaking of doctrines, hear what he says, "If any one preacheth unto you any gospel other than that ye have received, let him be accursed" (Gal. i. 9), "even" if it be "an angel." And again, "I fear lest by any means, as the serpent beguiled Eve through his subtilty, so your minds should be corrupted." (2 Cor. xi. 3.) And in writing to the Philippians, he says, "Beware of dogs, beware of evil workers, beware of the concision." (Phil. iii. 2.) But with the Romans, since it was not yet the proper time for setting things of this sort right, "Let every man," he says, "be fully persuaded in his own mind." For he had been speaking of fasting. It was to clear away the vanity of the others and to release these from fear then, that he said as follows:

Ver. 6. "He that regardeth the day, regardeth it unto the Lord; and he that

---

[1] ἐχομένους, here opposed to ἀπεχομένους.

regardeth not the day, to the Lord he doth not regard it." And, "He that eateth, eateth to the Lord, for he giveth God thanks; and he that eateth not, to the Lord he eateth not, and giveth God thanks."

He still keeps to the same subject. And what he means is about this. The thing is not concerned with fundamentals. For the thing requisite is, if this person and the other are acting for God's sake, the thing requisite is (these words are repeated 3 Mss.), if both terminate in thanksgiving. For indeed both this man and that give thanks to God. If then both do give thanks to God, the difference is no great one. But let me draw your notice to the way in which here also he aims unawares a blow at the Judaizers. For if the thing required be this, the "giving of thanks," it is plain enough that he which eateth it is that "giveth thanks," and not "he which eateth not." For how should he, while he still holds to the Law? As then he told the Galatians, "As many of you as are justified by the Law are fallen from grace" (Gal. v. 4); so here he hints it only, but does not unfold it so much. For as yet it was not time to do so. But for the present he bears with it (see p. 337): but by what follows he gives it a further opening. For where he says,

Ver. 7, 8. "For none of us liveth unto himself, and no man dieth unto himself. For whether we live, we live unto the Lord; and whether we die, we die unto the Lord," by this too he makes the same clearer. For how can he that liveth unto the Law, be living unto Christ? But this is not the only thing that he effects by this, he also holds back the person who was in so much haste for their being set right, and persuades him to be patient, by showing that it is impossible for God to despise them, but that in due time He will set them right. What is the force then of "none of us liveth to himself?" It means, We are not free, we have a Master who also would have us live, and willeth not that we die, and to whom both of these are of more interest than to us. For by what is here said he shows that he hath a greater concern for us than we have ourselves, and considereth more than we do, as well our life to be wealth, as our death to be a loss. For we do not die to ourselves alone, but to our Master also, if we do die. But by death here he means that from the faith. However, this were enough to convince us that He taketh care for us, in that it is to Him we live, and to Him we die. Still he is not satisfied with saying this, but proceeds further. For after saying, "Whether we live, therefore, or die, we are the Lord's,"

and passing from that death to the physical one, that he may not give an appearance of harshness to his language, he gives another very great indication of His care for us. Now of what kind is this?

Ver. 9. "For to this end Christ both died, and rose, and revived, that He might be Lord both of the dead and living."

And so let us at least convince thee, that He is thoughtful for our salvation. For had He not had this great care for us, where were the need of the Dispensation (or Incarnation, οἰκονομίας)? He then that hath shown so much anxiety about our becoming His, as to take the form of a servant, and to die, will He despise us after we have become so? This cannot be so, assuredly it cannot! Nor would He choose to waste so much pains. "For to this end (he says) he also died," as if any one were to say, Such an one will not have the heart to despise his servant. For he minded his own purse. (Cf. Ex. xxi. 21.) For indeed we are not so much in love with money, as is He with our salvation. Wherefore it was not money, but His own Blood that He gave as bail for us. And for this cause He would not have the heart to give them up, for whom He had laid down so great a price. See too how he shows that His power also is unspeakable. For he says, "to this end He both died and revived, that He might be Lord both of the dead and the living." And above he said, "for whether we live or die, we are His." See what a wide extended Mastery! see what unconquerable might! see what exact providence over us! For tell me not, he means, of the living. Even for the departed He taketh care. But if He doth of the departed, it is quite plain that He doth of the living also. For He hath not omitted any point for this Mastery, making out for Himself more claims than men do, and especially beside[1] all other things in order to take care of us. For a man puts down money, and for this clings strongly to his own slave. But He Himself paid down His death; and the salvation of one who was purchased at so great a price, and the Mastery over whom He had gained with so much anxiety and trouble, He is not likely to count of no value. But this he says to make the Judaizer abashed, and to persuade him to call to mind the greatness of the benefit, and how that when dead he had come to be alive, and that there was nothing that he gained from the Law, and how that it would be the

---

[1] χωρὶς: The construction seems imperfect: the Translator suggests χωρισθείς, "separating Himself from all others." If the passage be not corrupt, χωρὶς τῶν ἄλλων ἁπάντων is merely = in primis; and so Field.

last degree of unfeelingness, to leave Him Who had shown so much care toward him, and run away back to the Law. After attacking him then sufficiently, he relaxes again, and says,

Ver. 10. " But why dost thou judge thy brother? or why dost thou set at nought thy brother?"

And so he seems to be setting them upon a level, but from that he has said, he shows that the difference between them is great. First then by the appellation of "brother" he does away with disputatiousness, and then also by calling that awful day to their mind. For after saying, "Why dost thou set at nought thy brother?" he proceeds, "For we shall all stand before the judgment-seat of Christ."

And he seems indeed to be again rebuking the more advanced in saying this, but he is putting the mind of the Judaizer to confusion by not only calling for his reverence to the benefit that had been done him, but also making him afraid of the punishment to come. "For we shall all," he says, "stand before the judgment-seat of Christ."

Ver. 11, 12. " For it is written, As I live, saith the Lord, every knee shall bow to Me, and every tongue shall confess to God. So then every one of us shall give account of himself to God."

See how he again puts his mind into confusion, while he seems to be rebuking the other. For he intimates some such thing, as if he had said, How does it affect you? Are you to be punished for him? But this he does not say, but hints at it by putting it in a milder form, and saying, " For we shall all stand before the judgment-seat of Christ:" and, " So then every one of us shall give account of himself to God." And he introduces the prophet [1] in witness of the subjection of all to Him, yea a subjection extended even to those in the Old Testament, and of all absolutely. For he does not barely say every one shall worship, but "shall confess," that is, shall give an account of what he has done. Be in anxiety then as seeing the Master of all sitting on His judgment-seat, and do not make schisms and divisions in the Church, by breaking away from grace, and running over to the Law. For the Law also is His. And why say I so of the Law? Even those in the Law and those before the Law are His. And it is not the Law that will demand an account of thee, but Christ, of thee and of all the human race. See how he has re-

leased us from the fear of the Law. Then that he may not seem to be saying this to frighten them for the occasion, but to have come to it in the course he had proposed himself, he again keeps to the same subject, and says,

Ver. 13. " Let us not therefore judge one another any more : but judge this rather, that no man put a stumbling-block or an occasion to fall in his brother's way."

This does not apply to one less than the other : wherefore it may well fit with both, both the advanced man that was offended at the observance of meats, and the unadvanced that stumbled at the vehement rebuke given him. But consider, I pray you, the great punishment we shall suffer, if we give offence at all. For if in a case where the thing was against law, yet, as they rebuked unseasonably, he forbade their doing it, in order that a brother might not be made to offend and stumble ; when we give an offence without having anything to set right even, what treatment shall we deserve? For if not saving others be a crime (and that it is so, he who buried the talent proves), what will be the effect of giving him offence also? But what if he gives himself the offence, you may say, by being weak? Why this is just why thou oughtest to be patient. For if he were strong, then he would not require so much attention. But now, since he is of the feebler sort, he does on this ground need considerable care. Let us then yield him this, and in all respects bear his burdens, as it is not of our own sins only that we shall have to give an account, but for those also wherein we cause others to offend. For if that account, were even by itself hard to pass, when these be added too, how are we to be saved? And let us not suppose, that if we can find accomplices in our sins, that will be an excuse ; as this will prove an addition to our punishment. Since the serpent too was punished more than the woman, as was the woman likewise more than the man (1 Tim. ii. 14); and Jezebel also was punished more severely than Ahab, who had seized the vineyard ; for it was she that devised the whole matter, and caused the king to offend. (1 Kings xxi. 23, 25, 29.) And therefore thou, when thou art the author of destruction to others, wilt suffer more severely [2] than those who have been subverted by thee. For sinning is not so ruinous as leading others also into the same. Wherefore he speaks of those who " not only do the same, but have pleasure in them that do them." (Rom. i. 32.) And

---

[1] Some Mss. and edd. " with all attesting the subjection to Him." The passage is found Is. xlv. 23, probably the reading of the LXX., till it was corrected to suit the Hebrew. See Parsons *ad loc.*

[2] Sav. Mar. and one Ms. end the sentence, " having punishment exacted of the for those who have been made by thee to offend."

so when we see any sinning, let us, so far from thrusting them on, even pull them back from the pit of iniquity, that we may not have to be punished for the ruin of others besides ourselves. And let us be continually in mind of the awful judgment-seat, of the stream of fire, of the chains never to be loosed, of the darkness with no light, the gnashing of teeth, and the venomous worm. "Ah, but God is merciful!" Are these then mere words? and was not that rich man punished for despising Lazarus? Are not the foolish [1] virgins cast out of the Bride-chamber? Do not they who did not feed Him go away into "the fire prepared for the devil?" (Matt. xxv. 41.) Will not he that hath soiled garments be "bound hand and foot" (ib. xxii. 13), and go to ruin? Will not he that demanded the hundred pence to be paid, be given over to the tormentors? Is not that said of the adulterers [2] true, that "their worm shall not die, nor their fire be quenched?" [3] (Mark ix. 43.) Are these but mere threats then? Yea, it is answered. And from what source pray dost thou venture to make such an assertion, and that too when thou passest judgment of thine own opinion? Why, I shall be able to prove the contrary, both from what He said, and from what He did. (See John v. 22.) For if you will not believe by the punishments that are to come, at least believe by those that have happened already. For what have happened, and have come forth into reality, surely are not threats and words. Who then was it that flooded the whole world, and affected that baleful wreck, and the utter destruction of our whole race! Who was it that after this hurled those thunders and lightnings upon the land of Sodom? Who that drowned all Egypt in the sea? Who that consumed the six hundred thousand men in the wilderness? Who that burnt up the synagogue of Abiram? Who that bade the earth open her mouth for the company of Core and Dathan, and swallow them up? Who that carried off the threescore and ten thousand at one sweep in David's time? Shall I mention also those that were punished individually! Cain, who was given up to a

continual vengeance? (the son of) Charmi,[4] who was stoned with his whole family? Or him, that suffered the same thing for gathering sticks on the sabbath? The forty children who were consumed by those beasts, and obtained no pardon even on the score of their age? And if you would see these same things even after the times of grace, just consider what great suffering the Jews had, how the women ate their children, some roasting them, and some consuming them in other ways:[5] how after being given up to irremediable famine, and wars varied and severe, they threw all previous catastrophes into the shade by the exceeding greatness of their own calamities. For that it was Christ Who did these things unto them, hear Him declaring as much, both by parables, and clearly and explicitly. By parables, as when He says, "But those that would not that I should reign over them, bring hither and slay them" (Luke xix. 27); and by that of the vineyard, and that of the marriage. But clearly and explicitly, as when He threatens that they shall fall by the edge of the sword, and shall be led away captive into the nations, and there shall be upon the earth "distress of nations with perplexity, at the roaring of the sea and waves;[6] men's hearts failing them for fear." (ib. xxi. 24, 25, 26.) "And there shall be tribulation, such as there never was, no, nor ever shall be." (Matt. xxiv. 21.) And what a punishment Ananias too and Sapphira suffered, for the theft of a few pieces of money, ye all know. Seest thou not the daily calamities also? Or have these too not taken place? Seest thou not now men that are pining with famine? those that suffer elephantiasis, or are maimed in body? those that live in constant poverty, those that suffer countless irreparable evils? Now then will it be reasonable for some to be punished, and some not? For if God be not unjust (and unjust He is not), thou also wilt assuredly suffer punishment, if thou sinnest. But if because He is merciful He doth not punish, then ought not these either to have been punished. But now because of these words of yours, God even here punisheth many, that when ye believe not the words of the threatening, the deeds of vengeance ye may at least believe. And since things of old do not affright you so much, by things which happen in every generation, He correcteth those that in every generation are growing listless. And what is the reason, it may be said, why

---

[1] The oil representing especially deeds of mercy. Hil. ad. l. See St. Chrys. on Rom. xi. 6. p. 485.

[2] See Matt. v. 28, and 2 Pet. ii. 14. And with respect to giving cause of offence to others, Mark. ix. 44.

[3] Field's punctuation will give the sense, "These then are mere words—the rich man is not punished, nor the foolish virgins cast out, etc., but these are only threats!" which is perhaps more vigorous. Compare Hom. xxxi. p. 496: also Browning's *Heretic's Tragedy.*

"Who maketh God's menace an idle word?
    Saith, it no more means what it proclaims
Than a damsel's threat to her wanton bird?
    —For she too prattles of ugly names.
Saith, he knoweth but one thing—what he knows?
    That God is good and the rest is breath."

[4] Most Mss. have "Charmi" or "Charmin;" one "Achar," one "Achar the son of Charmi."

[5] Josephus, B. J. vi., vii. c. 8., Euseb. H. E. iii. 6.

[6] So most Mss. of St. Chrysostom, and the best of the N. T..

He doth not punish all here? That He may give the others an interval[1] for repentance. Why then does He not take vengeance upon all in the next world?[2] It is lest many should disbelieve in His providence. How many robbers are there who have been taken, and how many that have left this life unpunished? Where is the mercy of God then? it is my turn now to ask of thee. For supposing no one at all had vengeance taken upon him, then you might have taken refuge in this. But now that some are punished, and some are not, though they be the worse sinners, how can it be reasonable that there be not the same punishments for the same sins? How can those punished appear to be else than wronged? What reason is there then why all are not punished here? Hear His own defence for these things. For when some had died by the falling of a tower on them; He said to those who raised a question upon this, " Suppose ye that they were sinners above all men? I tell you nay, but except ye repent, ye shall all likewise perish " (Luke xiii. 4, 5); so exhorting us not to feel confident when others suffer punishment, and we ourselves, though we have committed many transgressions, do not. For except we change our conduct, we assuredly shall suffer. And how, it may be said, is it that we are to be punished without end for sinning a short time here? how, I ask, is it that in this world,[3] those who in a short moment of time have done one murder, are condemned to constant punishment in the mines? " But it is not God that does this," it may be said. How then came He to keep the man with a palsy for thirty and eight years in so great punishments? For that it was for sins that He punished him, hear what He says, " Behold, thou art made whole, sin no more." (John v. 14.) Still it is said, he found a release. But the case is not so with the other life. For that there, there will never be any release,[4] hear from His own mouth, " Their worm will not die, nor their fire be quenched." (Mark ix. 44.) And " these shall go into everlasting life, but these into everlasting punishment." (Matt. xxv. 46.) Now if the life be eternal, the punishment is eternal. Seest thou not how severely He threatened the Jews? Then have the things threatened come to pass, or were those that were told them a mere talk? " One stone shall not remain upon another." (Luke xxi. 6.) And has it remained? But what, when He says, " There shall be tribula-

tion such as hath not been? " (Matt. xxiv. 21.) Has it not come then? Read the history of Josephus, and thou wilt not be able to draw thy breath even, at only hearing what they suffered for their doings. This I say, not that I may pain you, but that I may make you secure, and lest by having humored you overmuch, I should but make a way for the endurance of sorer punishments. For why, pray, dost thou not deem it right thou shouldest be punished for sinning? Hath He not told thee all beforehand? Hath He not threatened thee? not come to thy aid?[5] not done things even without number for thy salvation's sake? Gave He thee not the laver of Regeneration, and forgave He not all thy former sins? Hath He not after this forgiveness, and the laver, also given thee the succor of repentance if thou sin? Hath He not made the way to forgiveness of sins, even after all this, easy[6] to thee? Hear then what He hath enjoined: " If thou forgive thy neighbor, I also will forgive thee " (ib. vi. 14), He says. What hardship is there in this? " If ye judge the cause of the fatherless, and see that the widow have right, come and let us converse together," He saith, " and if your sins be as purple, I will make them white as snow." (Is. i. 17, 18.) What labor is there here? " Tell thy sins, that thou mayest be justified." (Is. xliii. 26. LXX.) What hardship is there in this? " Redeem thy sins with alms." (Dan. iv. 24.) What toilsomeness is there in this? The Publican said, " Be merciful to me a sinner," and " went down home justified." (Luke xviii. 13, 14.) What labor is it to imitate the Publican? And wilt thou not be persuaded even after this that there is punishment and vengeance? At that rate thou wilt deny that even the devil is punished. For, " Depart," He says, " into the fire prepared for the devil and his angels." (Matt. xxv. 41.) Now if there be no hell, then neither is he punished. But if he is punished, it is plain that we shall also. For we also

---

[1] προθεσμίαν, lit. a set time. He has used the term before with especial view to the length of the time.
[2] i. e. so as to spare all in this.
[3] See Butler's *Anal.* i. 2. " But all this," and i. 3. iii.
[4] So Mss. λύσιν. Sav. λῆξιν, cessation: see 383, note [9].

[5] So Field: Vulg. " made thee afraid."
[6] St. Chrysostom must not be understood here as making light of the labor of an effectual repentance, nor as excluding the office of the Church in accepting the Penitent. His object is to show that there is no such difficulty in repentance, as need be an objection to our belief in eternal punishment. He is speaking of repentance in the lowest degree, and he certainly held that different degrees of it would obtain different degrees of benefit. As of almsgiving on Rom. xi. 6, p. 485. etc. " It is possible to gain approval by thy last will, not indeed in such way as in thy lifetime," and more generally *ad Theodorum Lapsum*, t. i. p. 11, 12. Ben. where he represents it as difficult, though not so much so as it might seem to those who did not try it, and know its consolations: and Hom i. *de S. Pentec. fin.* he says, " It is possible by diligence, prayer, and exceeding watchfulness, to wipe out all our sins that are written down. This then let us make our business all our days, that when we depart thither, we may obtain some forgiveness, and all escape irrevocable punishments." Of confession he speaks strongly, *de Cruce et Latrone*, Hom. i. t. 2, 407: B. *ad Pop. Ant.* Hom. 3, p. 42 E. on the Statues, p. 66 O. T. and of the power of the Priesthood to absolve, *de Sac.*, c. 3, § 5, t. i. p. 384 E. quoting Ja. v. 14, 15.

have disobeyed, even if it be not in the same way. And how comest thou not to be afraid to speak such daring things? For when thou sayest that God is merciful, and doth not punish, if He should punish he will be found in thy case to be no longer merciful. See then unto what language the devil leadeth you? And what? are the monks that have taken up with the mountains, and yield examples of such manifold self-denial,[1] to go away without their crown? For if the wicked are not to be punished, and there is no recompense made to any one, some one else will say, perhaps, that neither are the good crowned. Nay, it will be said, For this is suitable with God, that there should be a kingdom only, and not a hell. Well then, shall the whoremonger, and the adulterer, and the man who hath done evils unnumbered, enjoy the same advantages with the man who has exhibited soberness and holiness, and Paul is to stand with Nero, or rather even the devil with Paul? For if there be no hell and yet there will be a Resurrection of all, then the wicked will attain to the same good things! And who would say this? Who even of men that were quite crazed? or rather, which of the devils even would say this? For even they confess that there is a hell. Wherefore also they cried out and said, "Art Thou come hither to torment us before the time?" (ib. viii. 29.) How then comest thou not to fear and tremble, when even the devils confess what thyself art denying? Or how is it that thou dost not see who is the teacher of these evil doctrines? For he who deceived the first man, and under the pretext of greater hopes, threw them out even of the blessings they had in possession, he it is who now suggests the saying and fancying of these things. And for this reason he persuades some to suspect there is no hell, that he may thrust them into hell. As God on the other hand threateneth hell, and made hell ready, that by coming to know of it thou mightest so live as not to fall into hell. And yet if, when there is a hell, the devil persuades thee to these things, how came the devils to confess it, if it did not exist,[2] whose aim and desire it is that we should not suspect anything of the kind, that through fearlessness we might become the more listless, and so fall with them into that fire? How then (it

will be said) came they to confess it? It was through their not bearing the compulsion laid upon them. Taking all these things into consideration then, let those who talk in this way leave off deceiving both themselves and others since even for these words of theirs they will be punished for detracting (διασύροντες) from those awful things, and relaxing the vigor [3] of many who are minded to be in earnest, and do not even do as much as those barbarians, for they, though they were ignorant of everything, when they heard that the city was to be destroyed, were so far from disbelieving, that they even groaned, and girded themselves with sackcloth, and were confounded, and did not cease to use every means until they had allayed the wrath. (Jonah iii. 5.) But dost thou, who hast had so great experience of facts and of teaching, make light of what is told thee? The contrary then will be thy fate. For as they through fear of the words had not to undergo the vengeance in act, so thou who despisest the threatening by words, wilt have to undergo the punishment in very deed. And if now what thou art told seems a fable to thee, it will not, however, seem so when the very things convince thee, in that Day. Have you never noticed what He did even in this world? How when He met with two thieves, He counted them not worthy of the same estate, but one He led into the Kingdom, and the other He sent away into Hell? And why speak I of a robber and murderer? For even the Apostle He did not spare, when he had become a traitor, but even when He saw him rushing to the halter, and hanging, and bursting asunder in the midst (for he did "burst asunder, and all his bowels gushed out") (Acts i. 18), still when He foresaw all these things, He let him suffer all the same, giving thee from the present a proof of all that is in the other world also. Do not then cheat yourselves, through being persuaded of the devil. These devices are his. For if both judges, and masters, and teachers, and savages, respect the good, and punish the evil, with what reason is the contrary to be the case with God, while the good man and he who is not so are deemed worthy of the same estate? And when will they leave off their wickedness? For they who now are expecting punishment, and are amongst so many terrors, those from the judges and from the laws, and yet do not for this depart from iniquity; when on their departing this life they are to lay aside even this fear, and are not only not to be cast into hell, but are even to obtain a kingdom; when will they leave doing

---

[1] μυρίαν ἄσκησιν: the term asceticism is an insufficient translation of ascesis, since its termination takes off the reality. The word "crown" hints at a play on its secular sense, of gymnastic training.

[2] This sentence may be read so as to avoid the fault in reasoning; he breaks off the supposition as too absurd, and after a pause gives the true account of the case, which he in fact assumes in the first clause. The whole passage is rhetorical, and the first mention of the devils is introduced with tremendous power, as almost any one must have felt in reading it.

[3] Or "undoing the awe," as edd. before Field, and some Mss.

wickedly? Is this then mercy, pray? to add to wickedness, to set up rewards for iniquity, to count the sober and the unchastened, the faithful and the irreligious, Paul and the devil, to have the same deserts? But how long am I to be trifling? Wherefore I exhort you to get you free from this madness, and having grown to be your own masters, persuade your souls to fear and to tremble, that they may at once be saved from the hell to come, and may, after passing the life in this world soberly, attain unto the good things to come by the grace and love towards man, etc.

HOMILY XXVI.

ROM. XIV. 14.

"I know, and am persuaded by (Gr. in) the Lord Jesus, that there is nothing unclean of itself, but to him that esteemeth anything to be unclean, to him it is unclean."

AFTER first rebuking the person who judgeth his brother, and moving him to leave off this reproaching, he then explains himself further upon the doctrinal part, and instructs in a dispassionate tone the weaker sort, displaying in this case too a great deal of gentleness. For he does not say he shall be punished, nor anything of the sort, but merely disburdens him of his fears in the matter, and that with a view to his being more easily persuaded with what he tells him; and he says, "I know, and am persuaded." And then to prevent any of those who did not trust him (or "believe," τῶν οὐ πιστῶν) saying, And what is it to us if thou art persuaded? for thou art no trustworthy evidence to be set in competition with so great a law, and with oracles brought down from above, he proceeds, "in the Lord." That is, as having learned from Him, as having my confidence from Him. The judgment then is not one of the mind of man. What is it that thou art persuaded of and knowest? Tell us. "That there is nothing unclean of itself." By nature, he says, nothing is unclean but it becomes so by the spirit in which a man uses it. Therefore it becomes so to himself only, and not to all. "For to him that esteemeth anything to be unclean, to him it is unclean." What then? Why not correct thy brother, that he may think it not unclean? Why not with full authority call him away from this habit of mind and conception of things, that he may never make it common? My reason is, he says, I am afraid to grieve him. Wherefore he proceeds,

Ver. 15. "But if thy brother be grieved with thy meat, now walkest thou not charitably."

You see how far, for the present, he goes in affection for him, showing that he makes so great account of him, that with a view not to grieve him he does not venture even to enjoin things of great urgency, but by yieldingness would rather draw him to himself, and by charity. For even when he has freed him of his fears, he does not drag him and force him, but leaves him his own master. For keeping a person from meats is no such matter as overwhelming with grief.[1] You see how much he insists upon charity. And this is because he is aware that it can do everything. And on this ground he makes somewhat larger demand upon them. For so far he says from its being proper for them to distress you at all, they ought even, if need be, not to hesitate at condescending to you. Whence he proceeds to say, "Destroy not him with thy meat, for whom Christ died." Or dost thou not value thy brother enough even to purchase his salvation at the price of abstinence from meats? And yet Christ refused not to become a slave, nor yet to die for him; but thou dost not despise even food, that thou mayest save him. And yet with it all Christ was not to gain all, yet still He died for all; so fulfilling His own part. But art thou aware that by meat thou art overthrowing him in the more important matters, and yet makest a disputing? And him who is the object of such care unto Christ, dost thou consider so contemptible, and dishonor one whom He loveth? Yet He died not for the weak only, but even for an enemy. And wilt not thou refrain from meats even, for him that is weak? Yet Christ did what was greatest even, but thou not even the less. And He was Master, thou a brother. These words then were enough to tongue-tie him. For they show him to be of a little spirit, and after having the

---

[1] i. e. "better deprive the strong of his meats, than deeply grieve the weak."

34

benefit of great things from God, not to give in return even little ones.

Ver. 16, 17. "Let not then your good be evil spoken of. For the kingdom of God is not meat and drink."

By their "good," he means here either their faith, or the hope of rewards hereafter, or the perfectness of their religious state.* For it is not only that you fail to profit your brother, he means, but the doctrine itself, and the grace of God, and His gift, you cause to be evil spoken of. Now when thou fightest, when thou quarrellest, when thou art vexatious, when thou makest schism in the Church, and reproachest thy brother, and art distant with him, those that are without will speak evil of you. And so good is so far from coming of this, that just the opposite is the case. For your good is charity, love of the brotherhood, being united, being bound together, living at peace, living in gentleness (ἐπιεικείας). He again, to put an end to his fears and the other's disputatiousness, says, "For the kingdom of God is not meat and drink." Is it by these, he means, that we are to be approved? As he says in another passage too, ¹ "Neither if we eat are we the better, neither if we eat not are we the worse." And he does not need any proof, but is content with stating it. And what he says is this, If thou eatest, does this lead thee to the Kingdom? And this was why, by way of satirizing them as mightily pleased with themselves herein, he said, not "meat" only, but "drink." What then are the things that do bring us here? "Righteousness, and peace, and joy," and a virtuous life, and peace with our brethren (whereto this quarrelsomeness is opposed), the joy from unanimity, which this rebuking puts an end to. But this he said not to one party only, but to both of them, it being a fit season for saying it to both. Then as he had mentioned peace and joy, but there is a peace and joy over bad actions also, he adds, "in the Holy Ghost." Since he that ruins his brother, hath at once subverted peace, and wronged joy, more grievously than he that plunders money. And what is worse is, that Another saved him, and thou wrongest and ruinest him. Since then eating, and the supposed perfect state, does not bring in these virtues, but the things subversive of them it does bring in, how can it be

else than right to make light of little things, in order to give firmness to great ones? Then since this rebuking took place in some degree out of vanity, he proceeds to say,

Ver. 18. "For he that in these things serveth Christ, is acceptable to God, and approved of men."

For they will not admire thee so much for thy perfect state, as all will for peace and amity. For this is a goodly thing, that all will have the benefit of, but of that not one even will.

Ver. 19. "Let us therefore follow after the things which make for peace, and things wherewith one may edify one another."

This applies to the other, that he may grow peaceable. But the other to the latter too, that he may not destroy his brother. Still he has made both apply to either again, by saying, "one another," and showing that without peace it is not easy to edify.

Ver. 20. "For meat destroy not the work of God."

Giving this name to the salvation of a brother, and adding greatly to the fears, and showing that he is doing the opposite of that he desires.† For thou, he says, art so far from building up as thou intendest, that thou dost even destroy, and that a building too not of man but of God, and not for any great end either, but for a trivial thing. For it was "for meat," he says. Then lest so many indulgences should confirm the weaker brother in his misconception, he again becomes doctrinal, as follows,

"All things indeed are pure, but it is evil for that man who eateth with offence."

Who does it, that is, with a bad conscience. And so if you should force him, and he should eat, there would be nothing gained. For it is not the eating that maketh unclean, but the intention with which a man eats. If then thou dost not set that aright, thou hast done all to no purpose, and hast made things worse: for thinking a thing unclean is not so bad as tasting it when one thinks it unclean. Here then you are committing two errors, one by increasing his prejudice through your quarrelsomeness, and another by getting him to taste of what is unclean. And so, as long as you do not persuade him, do not force him.

Ver. 21. "It is good neither to eat flesh, nor to drink wine, nor anything whereby thy brother stumbleth, or is offended, or is made weak."

Again, he requires the greater alternative, that they should not only not force him, but

* In addition to the three possible meanings of "your good" which Chrys. mentions, two other interpretations may be noted: (1) "The good you enjoy," i. e. your Christian liberty (Godet); (2) "The kingdom of God" (v. 17) (Meyer). The connection favors the view that τὸ ἀγαθόν is a general reference to the same source of blessing which is more specifically designated as ἡ βασιλεία τοῦ θεοῦ (17).—G. B. S.
¹ 1 Cor. viii. 8, speaking of things offered to idols.

† "The work of God" is much more naturally taken as designating the Christian himself—his personality, than as designating his salvation (Chrys.).—G. B. S.

even condescend to him. For he often did this himself also, as when he circumcised (Acts xvi. 3), when he was shorn (ib. xviii. 18), when he sacrificed that Jewish sacrifice. (ib. xxi. 26, see p. 126). And he does not say to the man "do so," but he states it in the form of a sentiment to prevent again making the other, the weaker man, too listless. And what are his words? "It is good not to eat flesh." And why do I say flesh? if it be wine, or any other thing of the sort besides, which gives offence, refrain. For nothing is so important as thy brother's salvation. And this Christ shows us, since He came from Heaven, and suffered all that He went through, for our sakes. And let me beg you to observe, how he also drives it home upon the other, by the words "stumbleth, or is offended, or is made weak." And do not tell me (he means) that he is so without reason, but, that thou hast power to set it right. For the other has a sufficient claim to be helped in his weakness, and to thee this were no loss, not being a case of hypocrisy (Gal. ii. 13), but of edification and economy. For if thou force him, he is at once destroyed, and will condemn thee, and fortify himself the more in not eating. But if thou condescend to him, then he will love thee, and will not suspect thee as a teacher, and thou wilt afterwards gain the power of sowing imperceptibly in him the right views. But if he once hate thee, then thou hast closed the entrance for thy reasoning. Do not then compel him, but even thyself refrain for his sake, not refraining from it as unclean, but because he is offended, and he will love thee the more. So Paul also advises when he says, "It is good not to eat flesh," not because it was unclean, but because the brother is offended and is weak.

Ver. 22. "Hast thou faith? have it to thyself."

Here he seems to me to be giving a gentle warning to the more advanced on the score of vanity. And what he says is this, Dost thou wish to show me that thou art perfect, and fully furnished? Do not show it to me, but let thy conscience suffice. And by faith, he here means that concerned not with doctrines, but with the subject in hand. For of the former it says, "With the mouth confession is made unto salvation" (Rom. x. 10); and, "Whosoever shall deny Me before men, him will I also deny."[1] (Luke ix. 26.) For the former by not being confessed, ruins us; and so does this by being confessed unseasonably. "Happy is he that condemneth not himself in

the thing which he alloweth."* Again he strikes at the weaker one, and gives him (i. e. the stronger) a sufficient crown, in that of his conscience. Even if no man see, that is, thou art able to be happy in thyself. For after saying, "Have it to thyself," to prevent his thinking this a contemptible tribunal, he tells him this is better to thee than the world.[2] And if all accuse thee, and thou condemn not thyself, and thy conscience lay no charge against thee, thou art happy. But this is a statement he did not make to apply to any person whatever. For there are many that condemn not themselves, and yet are great transgressors: and these are the most miserable of men. But he still keeps to the subject in hand.

Ver. 23. "And he that doubteth is condemned if he eat."

Again, it is to exhort him to spare the weaker, that he says this. For what good is it if he eat in doubt, and condemn himself? For I approve of him, who both eateth, and doeth it not with doubting. See how he induces him not to eating only, but to eating with a good conscience too. Then he mentions likewise the reason why he is condemned. continuing in these words,

"Because he eateth not of faith." Not because it is unclean, but because it is not of faith. For he did not believe that it is clean, but though unclean he touched it. But by this he shows them also what great harm they do by compelling men, and not persuading them, to touch things which had hitherto appeared unclean to them, that for this at all events they might leave rebuking. "For whatsoever is not of faith is sin." For when a person does not feel sure, nor believe that a thing is clean, how can he do else than sin? Now all these things have been spoken by Paul of the subject in hand, not of everything. And observe what care he takes not to offend any; and he had said before, "If thy brother be grieved with thy meat, now walkest thou not charitably." But if one should not grieve him, much less ought one to give him offence. And again, "For meat destroy not the work of God." For if it were a grievous act of iniquity to throw down a Church, much more so is it to do so to the spiritual Temple. Since a man is more dig-

---

[1] Compare St. Ephrem. *Serm.* xx. vol. iii. adv. *Scrutatores.* pp. 172, 173, Oxf. Tr.

* Κρίνων should not be rendered "condemning" as if it were κατακρίνων (as Chrys. and many mod. interpreters). The meaning is: Happy is he who does not pass judgment upon himself, i. e. who is so confident of the rightness of his course that he has no anxiety or scruple regarding the course of action in such disputed points which he approves and has resolved upon.—G. B. S.
[2] *Nullum Theatrum virtuti conscientia majus.* Cicero, *Tusc.* ii. 26. Virtue has no field for display more ample than conscience.

nified than a Church : for it was not for walls that Christ died, but for these temples.

Let us then watch our own conduct on all sides, and afford to no one ever so little handle. For this life present is a race-course, and we ought to have thousands of eyes (Hilary in Ps. cxix.) on every side, and not even to fancy that ignorance will be an adequate excuse. For there is such a thing, there certainly is, as being punished for ignorance, when the ignorance is inexcusable. Since the Jews too were ignorant, yet not ignorant in an excusable way. And the Gentiles were ignorant, but they are without excuse. (Rom. i. 20.) For when thou art ignorant of those things which it is not possible to know, thou wilt not be subject to any charge for it : but when of things easy and possible, thou wilt be punished with the utmost rigor. Else if we be not excessively supine, but contribute our own share to its full amount, God will also reach forth His hand unto us in those things which we are ignorant of. And this is what Paul said to the Philippians likewise. "If in anything ye be otherwise minded, God shall reveal even this unto you." (Phil. iii. 15.) But when we are not willing to do even what we are masters of, we shall not have the benefit of His assistance in this either. And this was the case with the Jews too. "For this cause," He says, "speak I unto them in parables, because seeing they see not." (Matt. xiii. 13.) In what sense was it that seeing they saw not ? They saw devils cast out, and they said, He hath a devil. They saw the dead raised, and they worshipped not, but attempted to kill Him. But not of this character was Cornelius. (ib. xii. 24.) For this reason then, when he was doing the whole of his duty with sincerity, God added unto him that which was lacking also. Say not then, how came God to neglect such and such a one who was no formalist (ἄπλαστος) and a good man, though a Gentile ? For in the first place no man can possibly know for certain whether a person is no formalist,[1] but He only who "formed (πλάσαντι) the hearts severally." (Ps. xxxiii. (xxxii.) 15, LXX.) And then there is this to be said too, that perchance (πολλάκις) such an one was neither thoughtful nor earnest. And how, it may be said, could he, as being very uninformed ? (ἄπλαστος.) Let me beg you to consider then this simple and single-hearted man, and take notice of him in the affairs of life, and you will see him a pattern of the utmost scrupulousness, such that if he would have shown it in spiritual matters he would not have been

overlooked : for the facts of the truth are clearer than the sun. And wherever a man may go, he might easily lay hold of his own salvation, if he were minded, that is, to be heedful, and not to look on this as a by-work. For were the doings shut up into Palestine, or in a little corner of the world ? Hast thou not heard the prophet say, "All shall know Me from the least even to the greatest ? " (Jer. xxxi. 34; Heb. viii. 11.) Do not you see the things themselves uttering the truth ? How then are these to be excused, seeing as they do the doctrine of the truth spread far and wide, and not troubling themselves, or caring to learn it ? And dost thou require all this, it is asked, of a rude savage ? Nay not of a rude savage only, but of any who is more savage than men of the present day. For why is it, pray, that in matters of this world he knows how to answer when he is wronged, and to resist when he has violence done him, and do and devise everything to prevent his ever having his will thwarted even in the slightest degree ; but in spiritual concerns he has not used this same judgment ? And when a man worships a stone, and thinks it a god, he both keeps feasts to it, and spends money on it, and shows much fear towards it, and in no case becomes listless from his simpleness. But when he has to seek to the very and true God, do you then mention singleness and simpleness to me ? These things are not so, assuredly they are not ! For the complaints are those of mere listlessness. For which do you think the most simple and rude, those in Abraham's day or those now ? (Josh. xxiv. 2.) Clearly the former. And when that it was easiest to find religion out now or then ? Clearly now. For now the Name of God is proclaimed even by all men, and the Prophets have preached, the things come to pass, the Gentiles been convinced.[2] (Gen. xxxii. 29 ; Judges xiii. 18.) But at that day the majority were still in an uninstructed state, and sin was dominant. And there was no law to instruct, nor prophets, nor miracles, nor doctrine, nor multitude of men acquainted with it, nor aught else of the kind, but all things then lay as it were in a deep darkness, and a night moonless and stormy. And yet even then that wondrous and noble man, though the obstacles were so great, still knew God and practised virtue, and led many to the same zeal ; and this though he had not even the wisdom of those without.[3] For how should he, when

---

[1] So rendered. to keep up the play upon the words : it means, not framing himself to a false show.

[2] Or, "the systems of the Gentiles been confuted," τὰ Ἑλλήνων ἐλήλεγκται.

[3] Philo, however, makes Abraham learned in all Chaldæan wisdom. De Nob. § 5, also Joseph, Ant. i. c. 8, § 2. It is now certain that the art of writing was older than his time, in Mesopotamia as well as Egypt.

there were no letters even yet invented? Yet still he brought his own share in, and God joined to bring in what was lacking to him. For you cannot say even this, that Abraham received his religion from his fathers, because he (Terah, see Josh. xxiv. 2.) was an idolater. But still, though he was from such forefathers and was uncivilized, and lived among uncivilized people, and had no instructor in religion, yet he attained to a knowledge of God, and in comparison with all his descendants, who had the advantage both of the Law and the Prophets, he was so much more illustrious as no words can express. Why was it then? It was because in things of this world he did not give himself any great anxiety, but in things of the spirit he applied his whole attention. (In Gen. Hom. 33, etc.) And what of Melchizedek? was not he also born about those times, and was so bright as to be called even a priest of God? (In Gen. Hom. 35, 36.) For it is impossible in the extreme, that the sober-minded (νήφοντα) should ever be overlooked. And let not these things be a trouble to us, but knowing that it is the mind with which in each case the power lies, let us look to our own duties, that we may grow better. Let us not be demanding an account of God or enquire why He let such an one alone, but called such an one. For we are doing the same as if a servant that had given offence were to pry into his master's housekeeping. Wretched and miserable man, when thou oughtest to be thoughtful about the account thou hast to give, and how thou wilt reconcile thy master, dost thou call him to account for things that thou art not to give an account of, passing over those things of which thou art to give a reckoning?[1]   What am I to say to the Gentile? he asks.   Why, the same that I have been saying.   And look not merely to what thou shalt say to the Gentile, but also to the means of amending thyself.[2]   When he is offended by examining into thy life, then consider what thou wilt say.   For if he be offended, thou wilt not be called to a reckoning for him, but if it be thy way of life by which he is injured, thou wilt have to undergo the greatest danger.   When he seeth thee philosophizing about the kingdom, and fluttering at the things of this life, and at once afraid about hell, and trembling at the calamities of this life, then lay it to mind.   When he sees this, and accuses thee, and says, If thou art in love with the Kingdom, how is it thou dost not look down upon the things of this life? If thou art expecting the awful judgment, why

dost thou not despise the terrors of this world? If thou hopest for immortality, why dost thou not think scorn of death?   When he says this, be thou anxious what defence thou wilt make. When he sees thee trembling at the thought of losing thy money, thee that expectest the heavens, and exceedingly glad about a single penny, and selling thy soul again for a little money, then lay it to mind.   For these are the things, just these, that make the Gentiles stumble.   And so, if thou art thoughtful about his salvation, make thy defence on these heads, not by words, but by actions.   For it is not through that question that anybody ever blasphemed God, but through men's bad lives it is, that there are thousands of blasphemies in all quarters.   Set him right then.   For the Gentile will next ask thee, How am I to know that God's commands are feasible?   For thou that art of Christian extraction, and hast been brought up in this fine religion, dost not do anything of the kind.   And what will you tell him?   You will be sure to say, I will show you others that do; monks that dwell in the deserts.   And art thou not ashamed to confess to being a Christian, and yet to send to others, as unable to show that you display the temper of a Christian?   For he also will say directly, What need have I to go to the mountains, and to hunt up the deserts?   For if there is no possibility for a person who is living in the midst of cities to be a disciple, this is a sad imputation on this rule of conduct, that we are to leave the cities, and run to the deserts. But show me a man who has a wife, and children, and family, and yet pursueth wisdom. What are we then to say to all this?   Must we not hang down our heads, and be ashamed? For Christ gave us no such commandment; but what?   "Let your light shine before men" (Matt. v. 16), not mountains, and deserts, and wildernesses, and out-of-the-way places.   And this I say, not as abusing those who have taken up with the mountains, but as bewailing those that dwell in cities, because they have banished virtue from thence. Wherefore I beseech you let us introduce the discipline they have there here also, that the cities may become cities indeed.   This will improve the Gentile.   This will free him from countless offences.   And so if thou wouldest set him free from scandal, and thyself enjoy rewards without number, set thy own life in order, and make it shine forth upon all sides, "that men may see your good works, and glorify your Father which is in heaven."   For so we also shall enjoy that unutterable and great glory, which God grant that we may all attain to, by the grace and love toward man, etc.

---

[1] So Field with most Mss. Vulg. "for which thou art to be punished."
[2] So Field αὐτὸν for αὑτόν.

HOMILY XXVII.

ROM. XVI. 25-27.

" Now to Him that is of power to stablish you according to my Gospel, and the preaching of Jesus Christ, according to the revelation of the mystery, which was kept secret since the world began, but now is made manifest, and (Mss. τε which Sav. omits) by the Scriptures of the Prophets, according to the commandment of the everlasting God, made known to all nations for the obedience of faith : to God only wise, to Him be glory through Jesus Christ our Lord. Amen."[1]

IT is always a custom with Paul to conclude his exhortation with prayers and doxologies. For he knows that the thing is one of no slight importance. And it is out of affectionateness and caution that he is in the habit of doing this. For it is the character of a teacher devoted to his children, and to God, not to instruct them in words only, but by prayer too to bring upon his teaching the assistance which is from God. And this he does here also. But the connection is as follows : "To Him that is of power to stablish you, be glory for ever. Amen." For he again clings to those weak brethren, and to them he directs his discourse. For when he was rebuking, he made all share his rebuke ; but now, when he is praying, it is for these that he wears the attitude of a suppliant. And after saying, "to stablish," he proceeds to give the mode of it, "according to my Gospel ; " and this was what one would do to show that as yet they were not firmly fixed, but stood, though with wavering. Then to give a trustworthiness to what he says, he proceeds, "and the preaching of Jesus Christ ; " that is, which He Himself preached. But if He preached it, the doctrines are not ours, but the laws are of Him. And afterwards, in discussing the nature of the preaching, He shows that this gift is one of much benefit, and of much honor ; and this he first proves from the person of the declarer thereof, and

then likewise from the things declared. For it was glad tidings. Besides, from His not having made aught of them known to any before us. And this he intimates in the words, "according to the revelation of the mystery." And this is a sign of the greatest friendliness, to make us share in the mysteries, and no one before us. "Which was kept secret since the world began, but now is made manifest." For it had been determined long ago, but was only manifested now. How was it made manifest? "By the Scriptures of the Prophets." Here again he is releasing the weak person from fear. For what dost thou fear? is it lest[2] thou depart from the Law? This the Law wishes, this it foretold from of old. But if thou pryest into the cause of its being made manifest now, thou art doing a thing not safe to do, in being curious about the mysteries of God, and calling Him to account. For we ought not with things of this nature to act as busybodies, but to be well pleased and content with them. Wherefore that he might himself put a check upon a spirit of this sort, he adds, "according to the commandment of the everlasting God, for the obedience of faith." For faith requires obedience, and not curiosity. And when God commands, one ought to be obedient, not curious. Then he uses another argument to encourage them, saying "made known to all nations." That is, it is not thou alone but the whole world that is of this Creed, as having had not man, but God for a Teacher. Wherefore also he adds, "through Jesus Christ." But it was not only made known, but also confirmed. Now both are His work. And on this ground too the way it is to be read is,[3] "Now to Him that is of power to stablish you through Jesus Christ ; " and, as I was saying, he ascribes them both to Him ; or rather, not both of these only, but the glory belonging (or ascribed, Gr. τὴν εἰς) to the Father also. And this too is why he said, "to Whom be glory forever, Amen." And he uses a doxology again through awe at the

---

[1] These three verses are placed here by Theodoret, St. Cyr. Alex., St. John Dam. and some 200 cursive Mss. Of the few uncial Mss. which have come down to us, the *Codex Sinaiticus* the *Codex Vaticanus* and the very ancient C. D. with the chief versions of the New Testament, including the two first made, the Old Latin and the Peschito-syriac, Origen put them where we do, at the end of the Epistle. The fifth century Alexandrian Ms. in the British Museum and two or three other Mss. have the passage twice over. (For an elaborate defence both of the genuineness of this doxology and of the view that it belongs at the end of chap. xvi. see Meyer's critical note prefixed to his comments on chap. xvi.—G. B. S.)

[2] Μὴ ἀποστῇς, one Ms. οὐ μὴ, which seems to determine the construction.

[3] v. 27. in the Greek reads thus : " To God only wise through Jesus Christ, to Him (or to Whom) be glory," etc.

incomprehensibleness of these mysteries. For even now they have appeared, there is no such thing as comprehending them by reasonings, but it is by faith we must come to a knowledge of them, for in no other way can we. He well says, "To the only wise God." For if you will only reflect how He brought the nations in, and blended them with those who in olden time had wrought well, how He saved those who were desperate, how He brought men not worthy of the earth up to heaven, and brought those who had fallen from the present life into that undying and unalterable life, and made those who were trampled down by devils to vie with Angels, and opened Paradise, and put a stop to all the old evils, and this too in a short time, and by an easy and compendious way, then wilt thou learn His wisdom;—when thou seest that that which neither Angels nor Archangels knew, they of the Gentiles learnt on a sudden through Jesus. (2 Mss. add, "then wilt thou know His power.") Right then is it to admire His wisdom, and to give Him glory! But thou keepest dwelling over little things, still sitting under the shadow. And this is not much like one that giveth glory. For he who has no confidence in Him, and no trust in the faith, does not bear testimony to the grandeur of His doings. But he himself offers glory up in their behalf, in order to bring them also to the same zeal. But when you hear him say, "to the only wise God," think not that this is said in disparagement of the Son. For if all these things whereby His wisdom is made apparent were done (or made, see John i. 3) by Christ, and without Him no single one, it is quite plain that he is equal in wisdom also. What then is the reason of his saying "only?" To set Him in contrast with every created being. After giving the doxology* then, he again goes from prayer to exhortation, directing his discourse against the stronger, and saying as follows:

Chap. xv. ver. 1. "We then that are strong, ought"—it is "we ought," not "we are so kind as to." What is it we ought to do?—"to bear the infirmities of the weak."

See how he has roused their attention by his praises, not only by calling them powerful, but also by putting them alongside of himself. And not by this only, but by the advantage of the thing he again allures them, and by its not being burdensome. For thou,

he says, art powerful, and art no whit the worse for condescending. But to him the hazard is of the last consequence, if he is not borne with. And he does not say the infirm, but the "infirmities of the weak," so drawing him and bending him to mercy. As in another place too he says, "Ye that are spiritual restore such an one." (Gal. vi. 1.) Art thou become powerful? Render a return to God for making thee so. But render it thou wilt if thou settest the weakness of the sickly right. For we too were weak, but by grace we have become powerful. And this we are to do not in this case only, but also in the case of those who are weak in other respects. As, for instance, if any be passionate, or insolent, or has any such like failing bear with him. And how is this to be? Listen to what comes next. For after saying "we ought to bear," he adds, "and not to please ourselves."†

Ver. 2. "Let every one of us please his neighbor for his good to edification."

But what he says is this. Art thou powerful? Let the weak have trial of thy power. Let him come to know thy strength; please him. And he does not barely say please, but for his good, and not barely for his good, lest the advanced person should say, See I am drawing him to his good! but he adds, "to edification." And so if thou be rich or be in power, please not thyself, but the poor and the needy, because in this way thou wilt at once have true glory to enjoy, and be doing much service. For glory from things of the world soon flies away, but that from things of the Spirit is abiding, if thou do it to edification. Wherefore of all men he requires this. For it is not this and that person that is to do it, but "each of you." Then since it was a great thing he had commanded them, and had bidden them even relax their own perfectness in order to set right the other's weakness; he again introduces Christ, in the following words:

Ver. 3. "For even Christ pleased not Himself."

And this he always does. For when he was upon the subject of alms, he brought Him forward and said, "Ye know the grace of the Lord, that though He was rich, yet for our sakes he became poor." (2 Cor. viii. 9.) And when he was exhorting to charity, it was from Him that he exhorted in the words "As Christ also loved us." (Eph. v. 25.) And

---

* The grammatical form of the doxology presents a noticeable anacoluthon. The dative τῷ δυναμένῳ is resumed in μόνῳ σοφῷ θεῷ and again in the relative ᾧ *as if* the proposition begun with the dative had been completed. Thus the previous datives are left without grammatical government. ᾧ, if read (many texts omit it) is to be understood as referring to θεῷ.—G. B. S.

† Chap. xv. contains conclusions and applications drawn from the principles laid down in regard to the treatment which should be accorded to the weak in chap. xiv. The crowning consideration is that Christ pleased not himself, but bore the burdens of the weak. This is presented as the type of all Christian duty. In v. 6 the construction usually preferred is (as in R. V.) "the God and Father of our Lord Jesus Christ" (cf. Eph. i. 3, 17).—G. B. S.

when he was giving advice about bearing shame and dangers, he took refuge in Him, and said, "Who for the joy that was set before Him endured the Cross, despising the shame." (Heb. xii. 2). So in this passage too he shows how He also did this, and how the prophet proclaimed it from of old. Wherefore also he proceeds:

"The reproaches of them that reproached Thee fell upon Me." (Ps. lxix. 9.) But what is the import of, "He pleased not Himself?" He had power not to have been reproached, power not to have suffered what He did suffer, had He been minded to look to His own things. But yet He was not so minded. But through looking to our good He neglected His own. And why did he not say, "He emptied Himself?" (Phil. ii. 7.) It is because this was not the only thing he wished to point out, that He became man, but that He was also ill-treated, and obtained a bad reputation with many, being looked upon as weak. For it says, "If Thou be the Son of God, come down from the Cross." (Matt. xxvii. 40). And, "He saved others, Himself He cannot save." (ib. 42). Hence he mentions a circumstance which was available for his present subject, and proves much more than he undertook to do; for he shows that it was not Christ alone that was reproached, but the Father also. "For the reproaches of them that reproached Thee fell," he says, "upon Me." But what he says is nearly this, What has happened is no new or strange thing. For they in the Old Testament who came to have a habit of reproaching Him, they also raved against His Son. But these things were written that we should not imitate them. And then he supplies (Gr. anoints) them for a patient endurance of temptations.

Ver. 4. "For whatsoever things were written aforetime," he says, "were written for our learning, that we, through patience and comfort of the Scriptures, might have hope."

That is, that we might not fall away, (for there are sundry conflicts within and without), that being nerved and comforted by the Scriptures, we might exhibit patience, that by living in patience we might abide in hope. For these things are productive of each other, patience of hope, and hope of patience. And both of them are brought about by the Scriptures. Then he again brings his discourse into the form of prayer, and says,

Ver. 5. "Now the God of patience and consolation grant you to be like-minded one towards another, according to Christ Jesus."

For since he had given his own advice, and had also urged the example of Christ, he added the testimony of the Scriptures also, to show that with the Scripture Himself giveth patience also. And this is why he said, "Now the God of patience and consolation grant you to be like-minded one towards another, according to Christ Jesus." For this is what love would do, be minded toward another even as toward himself. Then to show again that it is not mere love that he requires, he adds, "according to Christ Jesus." And this he does, in all places, because there is also another sort of love. And what is the advantage of their agreeing?

Ver. 6. "That ye may with one mind," he says, "and one mouth, glorify God, even the Father of our Lord Jesus Christ."

He does not say merely with one mouth, but bids us do it with one will also. See how he has united the whole body into one, and how he concludes his address again with a doxology, whereby he gives the utmost inducement to unanimity and concord. Then again from this point he keeps to the same exhortation as before, and says,

Ver. 7. "Wherefore receive ye one another, as Christ also received us, to the glory of God."

The example again is as before, and the gain unspeakable. For this is a thing that doth God especial glory, the being closely united. And so if even against thy will (Field "being grieved for His sake," after Savile, but against Mss.) and for His sake, thou be at variance with thy brother, consider that by putting an end to thine anger thou art glorifying thy Master, and if not on thy brother's account, for this at all events be reconciled to him: or rather for this first. For Christ also insists upon this upon all possible grounds,[1] and when addressing His Father he said, "By this shall all men know that Thou hast sent Me, if they be one." (John xvii. 21.)

Let us obey then, and knit ourselves to one another. For in this place it is not any longer the weak, but all that he is rousing. And were a man minded to break with thee, do not thou break also. Nor give utterance to that cold saying, "Him I love that loveth me; if my right eye does not love me, I tear it out." For these are satanical sayings, and fit for publicans, and the little spirit of the Gentiles. But thou that art called to a greater citizenship, and are enrolled in the books of Heaven, art liable to greater laws. Do not speak in this way, but when he is not minded to love thee, then display the more love, that thou mayest draw him to thee. For

---

[1] ἄνω καὶ κάτω στρέφει, see Ast. *ad Platon. Phædr.* 127.

he is a member; and when by any force a member is sundered from the body, we do everything to unite it again, and then pay more attention to it. For the reward is the greater then, when one draws to one a person not minded to love. For if He bids us invite to supper those that cannot make us any recompense, that what goes for recompense may be the greater, much more ought we to do this in regard to friendship. Now he that is loved and loveth, does pay thee a recompense. But he that is loved and loveth not, hath made God a debtor to thee in his own room. And besides, when he loves thee he needs not much pains; but when he loves thee not, then he stands in need of thy assistance. Make not then the cause for painstaking a cause for listlessness; and say not, because he is sick, that is the reason I take no care of him (for a sickness indeed the dulling of love is), but do thou warm again that which hath become chilled. But suppose he will not be warmed, "what then?" is the reply. Continue to do thy own part. "What if he grow more perverse?" He is but procuring to thee so much greater return, and shows thee so much the greater imitator of Christ. For if the loving one another was to be the characteristic of disciples ("For hereby," He says, "shall all men know that ye are My disciples, if ye love one another), (ib. xiii. 35) consider how great an one loving one that hates us must be. For thy Master loved those that hated Him, and called them to Him; and the weaker they were, the greater the care He showed them; and He cried and said, "They that are whole need not a physician, but they that are sick." (Matt. ix. 12.) And He deemed publicans and sinners worthy of the same table with Him. And as great as was the dishonor wherewith the Jewish people treated Him, so great was the honor and concern He showed for them, yea, and much greater. Him do thou also emulate: for this good work is no light one, but one without which not even he that is a martyr can please God much, as Paul says.[1] Say not then, I get hated, and that is why I do not love. For this is why thou oughtest to love most. And besides, it is not in the nature of things for a man who loves to be soon hated, but brute as a person may be, he loves them that love him. For this He says the heathens and the publicans do. (Matt. v. 46.) But if every one loves those that love him, who is there that would

not love those who love while they are hated? Display then this conduct, and cease not to to use this word, "Hate me as much as you may, I will not leave off loving thee," and then thou wilt humble his quarrelsomeness, and cast out all coldness.[2] For this disorder comes either from excessive heat (φλεγμονῆς, inflammation), or from coldness; but both of these is the might of love wont to correct by its warmth. Did you never see those who indulge a base love beaten, spit upon, called names, ill-treated in a thousand ways by those fornicatresses? What then? Do the insults break off this love? In no wise: they even kindle it the more. And yet they who do these things, besides being harlots, are of a disreputable and low grade. But they who submit to it, have often illustrious ancestors to count up, and much other nobility to boast of. Yet still none of these things break the tie, nor keep them aloof from her whom they love. And are we not ashamed then to find what great power the love of the devil (v. p. 520) and the demons hath, and not to be able to display as much in the love according to God? Dost thou not perceive that this is a very great weapon against the devil? Do you not see, that that wicked demon stands by, dragging to himself the man thou hatest, and desiring to snatch away the member? And dost thou run by, and give up the prize of the conflict? For thy brother, lying between you, is the prize. And if thou get the better, thou receivest a crown; but if thou art listless, thou goest away without a crown. Cease then to give utterance to that satanical saying, "if my eye hates me, I cannot see it."[3] For nothing is more shameful than this saying, and yet the generality lay it down for a sign of a noble spirit. But nothing is more ignoble than all this, nothing more senseless, nothing more foolish.[4] Therefore I am indeed quite grieved that the doings of vice are held to be those of virtue, that looking down on men, and despising them, should seem to be honorable and dignified. And this is the devil's greatest snare, to invest iniquity with a good repute, whereby it becomes hard to blot out. For I have often heard men taking credit to themselves at their not going near those who are averse to them. And yet thy Master found a glory in this. How often do not men despise (διέπτυσαν) Him? how often show aversion to

---

[1] See St. Chrys. ad loc. Hom. 32, on 1 Cor p. 446 O.T. in some places he seems to speak exclusively of love to one's neighbor in quoting this passage, but he always views this as the carrying out of love toward God, see p. 515.

[2] Mss. ψύξιν ἐξέβαλες. Sav. ψυχὴν ἐμάλαξας, soften any soul.
[3] So Field from Mss.: old edd. "If my brother hates me, I do not even wish to see him." Perhaps the true reading is, "If my eye hates me, I do not even wish to see," ἐὰν ὁ ὀφθαλμός μου μισῇ με, οὐδὲ ἰδεῖν αὐτὸν βούλομαι, which seems more proverbial, (if the aorist will bear this construction as Matt. xiii. 14), and agrees with p. 537.
[4] So all Mss. Sav. "more cruel."

Him? Yet He ceaseth not to run unto them. Say not then that "I cannot bear to come near those that hate me," but say, that "I cannot bear to despise (διαπτύσαι) those that despise me." This is the language of Christ's disciple, as the other is of the devil's. This makes men honorable and glorious, as the other doth shameful and ridiculous. It is on this ground we feel admiration for Moses, because even when God said, "Let Me alone, that I may destroy them in Mine anger," (Exod. xxxii. 10) he could not bear to despise those who had so often shown aversion to him, but said, "If thou wilt forgive them their trespass, forgive it; else blot out me also." (ibid. 32.) This was owing to his being a friend of God, and a copyer of Him. And let us not pride ourselves in things for which we ought to hide our faces. Nor let us use the language of these lewd fellows, that are the scum of men, I know how to scorn (καταπτύσαι, spit at) thousands. But even if another use it, let us laugh him down, and stop his mouth for taking a delight in what he ought to feel ashamed of. What say you, pray, do you scorn a man that believes, whom when unbe-lieving Christ scorned not? Why do I say scorned not? Why He had such love towards him, when he was vile and unsightly, as even to die for him. He then so loved, and that such a person, and do you now, when he has been made fair and admirable, scorn him; now he is made a member of Christ, and hath been made thy Master's body? Dost thou not consider what thou art uttering, nor perceive what thou art venturing to do? He hath Christ as a Head, and a Table, and a Garment, and Life, and Light, and a Bridegroom, and He is everything to him, and dost thou dare to say, "this fellow I despise?" and not this only, but thousands of others along with him? Stay thee, O man, and cease from thy madness; get to know thy brother. Learn that these be words of unreasonableness, and frenzy, and say on the contrary, though he despise me ten thousand times, yet will I never stand aloof from him. In this way thou wilt both gain thy brother, and wilt live to the glory of God, and wilt share the good things to come. To which God grant that we may all attain, by the grace and love toward man, etc.

HOMILY XXVIII.

ROM. XV. 8.

"Now I say that Jesus Christ was a minister of the circumcision for the truth of God, to confirm the promises made unto the fathers."

AGAIN, he is speaking of Christ's concern for us, still holding to the same topic, and showing what great things He hath done for us, and how "He pleased not Himself." (Rom. xv. 3.) And besides this, there is another point which he makes good, that those of the Gentiles are debtors to a larger amount unto God. And if to a larger amount, then they ought to bear with the weak among the Jews. For since he had spoken very sharply to such, lest this should make these elated, he humbles their unreasonableness, by showing that it was by "promise made to the fathers" that they had the good things given them, while they of the Gentiles had them out of pity and love toward man only. And this is the reason of his saying, "And that the Gentiles might glorify God for his mercy." But that what is said may be made plainer, it is well to listen once more to the words themselves, that you may see what Christ's having been made "a Minister of the circumcision for the truth of God, to confirm the promises made unto the fathers," means. What then is that which is stated? There had been a promise made to Abraham, saying, "Unto thee will I give the earth, and to thy seed, and in thy seed shall all the nations be blessed." (Gen. xii. 7; xxii. 18.) But after this, they of the seed of Abraham all became subject to punishment. For the Law wrought wrath unto them by being transgressed, and thenceforward deprived them of that promise made unto the fathers. Therefore the Son came and wrought with the Father, in order that those promises might come true, and have their issue. For having fulfilled the whole Law in which He also fulfilled the circumcision, and having by it, and by the Cross, freed them from the curse of the transgression, He suffered not this promise to fall to the ground. When then he calls Him "a Minister of the circumcision," he means this, that by having come and fulfilled the Law, and been circumcised, and born of the seed of Abraham, He undid the curse, stayed the anger of God, made also those that were to

receive the promises fit for them, as being
once for all freed from their alienation. To
prevent then these accused persons from saying, How then came Christ to be circumcised,
and to keep the whole Law? he turns their
argument to the opposite conclusion. For it
was not that the Law might continue, but that
He might put an end to it, and free thee from
the curse thereof, and set thee entirely at
liberty from the dominion of that Law. For
it was because thou hadst transgressed the
Law, that He fulfilled it, not that thou mightest fulfil it,[1] but that He might confirm to thee
the promises made unto the fathers, which the
Law had caused to be suspended, by showing
thee to have offended,[2] and to be unworthy of
the inheritance. And so thou also art saved
by grace, since thou wast cast off. Do not
thou then bicker, nor perversely cling to the
Law at this unsuitable time, since it would
have cast thee also out of the promise, unless
Christ had suffered so many things for thee.
And He did suffer these, not because thou
wast deserving of salvation, but that God
might be true. And then that this might not
puff up him of the Gentiles, he says.

Ver. 9. "And that the Gentiles might
glorify God for His mercy."

But what he means is this. Those of the
Jews would have had promises, even though
they were unworthy. But thou hadst not this
even, but wast saved from love towards man
alone, even if, to put it at the lowest, they too
would not have been the better for the promises, unless Christ had come. But yet that
he might amalgamate (or temper, κεράσῃ)
them and not allow them to rise up against
the weak, he makes mention of the promises.
But of these he says that it was by mercy
alone that they were saved. Hence they are
the most bound to glorify God. And a glory
it is to God that they be blended together, be
united, praise with one mind, bear the weaker,
neglect not the member that is broken off.
Then he adds testimonies, in which he shows
that the man of the Jews ought to blend himself with those of the Gentiles; and so he says,
"As it is written, For this cause I will confess to Thee among the Gentiles, O Lord, and
will sing unto Thy Name." * (Ps. xviii. 46.)

Ver. 10–12. "And, rejoice, ye Gentiles,
with His people. And, Praise the Lord, all
ye Gentiles" (Deut. xxxii. 43); "and let all
people laud Him." (Ps. cxvii. 1.) "And,
There shall be a root of Jesse, and He that
shall rise to reign over the Gentiles, in Him
shall the Gentiles trust." (Is. xi. 1, 10.)

Now all these quotations he has given to
show that we ought to be united, and to glorify God; and also, to humble the Jew, that he
may not lift himself up over these, since all
the prophets called these, as well as to persuade the man of the Gentiles to be lowly, by
showing him that he had a larger grace to
answer for. Then he concludes his argument
with a prayer again.

Ver. 13. "Now the God of hope fill you
with all joy and peace in believing, that ye
may abound in hope, through the power of the
Holy Ghost."

That is, that ye may get clear of that heart-
lessness (ἀθυμίας) towards one another, and
may never be cast down by temptations. And
this will be by your abounding in hope. Now
this is the cause of all good things, and it
comes from the Holy Ghost. But it is not
simply from the Spirit, but on condition of
our contributing our part also. This is why
he says, "in believing." For this is the way
for you to be filled with joy, if ye believe, if
ye hope. Yet he does not say if ye hope, but,
"if ye abound in hope," so as not to find
comfort in troubles only, but even to have joy
through the abundance of faith and hope.
And in this way, ye will also draw the Spirit
to you. In this way, when He is come ye will
continually keep to all good things. For just
as food maintaineth our life, and by this
ruleth the body,[3] so if we have good works,
we shall have the Spirit; and if we have the
Spirit, we shall also have good works. As
also, on the other hand, if we have no works,
the Spirit flieth away. But if we be deserted
by the Spirit, we shall also halt in our works.
For when this hath gone, the unclean one
cometh: this is plain from Saul. For what if
he doth not choke[4] us as he did him, still he
strangles us in some other way by wicked
works. We have need then of the harp of
David, that we may charm our souls with the
divine songs, both these, and those from good
actions. Since if we do the one only, and

---

[1] See on Rom. viii. 4, *supra* p. 433.

[2] προσκεκρουκέναι, not "stumbled," but "struck against" a
person, same word as "alienation" just before.

* The quotations in the passage on which this homily is
based are all taken from the LXX. with a few trifling verbal
changes. They are designed to show that the prophetic
conception of the Messiah's work contemplated salvation for
the Gentiles, so that Christ was not to be merely a "minister
of the circumcision," but that he is to bring through the Jews
salvation to the Gentiles so that they shall "glorify God for
his mercy" (9). The passages in the O. T. relate primarily
either to the Psalmist himself (v. 9. cf. Ps. xviii. 50) or to the
King of Israel (v. 12. cf. Is. xi. 10), or to the relations of the
people of Israel to the nations (vv. 10, 11, cf. Deut. xxxii. 43; Ps.

cxvii. 1), but are applied to the relations of Christ to the nations
in accordance with the prophetico-typical exegesis which
regarded the prophets, kings and the history and people of
Israel as having their chief significance in the fact that they
embodied hopes and ideals which pointed forward to the
Messiah and were realized only in the work and principles of
His kingdom.—G. B. S.

[3] So Field with two or three Mss.: others, "and this ruleth:"
Vulg. "and life ruleth."

[4] 2 Sam. xvi. 14, LXX. ἐπνιγεν, A. V. troubled: see Matt.
viii. 32.

while we listen to the charm, war with the
charmer by our actions, as he did of old (1
Sam. xix. 10); the remedy will even turn to
judgment to us, and the madness become the
more furious.   For before we heard, the
wicked demon was afraid lest we should hear
it and recover.   But when after hearing it
even, we continue the same as we were, this
is the very thing to rid him of his fear.   Let
us sing then the Psalm of good deeds, that we
may cast out the sin that is worse than the
demon.   For a demon certainly will not deprive us of heaven, but doth in some cases[1]
even work with the sober-minded.   But sin
will assuredly cast us out.   For this is a demon we willingly receive, a self-chosen madness.   Wherefore also it hath none to pity it
or to pardon it.   Let us then sing charms
over a soul in this plight, as well from the
other Scriptures, as also from the blessed
David.   And let the mouth sing, and the
mind be instructed.   Even this is no small
thing.   For if we once teach the tongue to
sing, the soul will be ashamed to be devising
the opposite of what this singeth.   Nor is this
the only good thing that we shall gain, for we
shall also come to know many things which
are our interest.   For he discourseth to
thee both of things present, and things to
come, and of things seen, and of the invisible
Creation.   And if thou wouldest learn about
the Heaven, whether it abideth as it is or
shall be changed, he gives thee a clear answer, and will say, "The heavens shall wax
old as doth a garment, and as a vesture shalt
thou fold them up, O God, and they shall be
changed." (Ps. cii. 26.)   And if thou wishest to hear of the form of them again, thou
shalt hear, "That spreadeth forth the Heaven
like a curtain" ($\delta \epsilon \rho \rho \iota \nu$).   And if thou be
minded to know further about the back of
them, he will tell thee again, "that covereth
His upper chambers with waters." (Ps. civ.
2, 3.)   And even here he does not pause, but
will likewise discourse with thee on the
breadth and height, and show thee that these
are of equal measure.   For, "As far as the
east," he says, "is from the west, so far hath
He set our iniquities from us.   Like as the
heaven's height above the earth, so is the
Lord's mercy upon them that fear Him." (ib.
ciii. 12, 11.)   But if thou wouldest busy thyself with the foundation of the earth, even this
he will not hide from thee, but thou shalt hear
him singing and saying, "He hath founded it

upon the seas." (ib. xxiv. 2.)   And if of
earthquakes thou art desirous to know, whence
they come, he will free thee from this difficulty also, by saying, "That looketh upon the
earth, and maketh it tremble." (ib. civ. 32.)
And if thou enquire the use of the night, this
too mayest thou learn, and know from him.
For "therein all the beasts of the forest do
move." (ib. 20.)   And in what way the
mountains are for use, he will tell thee, "The
high mountains are for the stags."   And why
there are rocks, "The rocks are a refuge for
the porcupines." (ib. 18.)   Why are there
trees yielding no fruit? learn from him, for
"there the sparrows build their nests." (ib.
17.)   Why are there fountains in the wildernesses? hear, "that by them the fowls of the
heaven dwell, and the wild beasts." (ib. 12.)
Why is there wine? not that thou mayest
drink only (for water is of a nature to suffice
for this), but that thou mayest be gladdened
also, "For wine maketh glad the heart of
man." (ib. 15.)   And by knowing this you
will know how far the use of wine is allow-
able.   Whence are the fowls and the wild
beasts nourished? thou wilt hear from his
words, "All these wait upon Thee, to give
them their meat in due season." (ib. 27.)
If thou sayest, For what purpose are the
cattle? he will answer thee, that these also
are for thee, "That causeth the grass," he
says, "to grow for the cattle, and the green
herb for the service (or retinue) of men."
(ib. 14.)   What is the use of the moon? hear
him saying, "He made the moon for seasons."
(Ps. civ. 19.)   And that all things seen and
those not seen are made, is a thing that he
has also clearly taught us by saying, "Himself spake, and they were made, He commanded, and they were created." (ib. xxxiii.
9.)   And that there is an end of death, this
he also teaches when he says, "God shall deliver my soul from the hand of hell when He
shall receive me." (ib. xlix. 15.)   Whence
was our body made? he also tells us; "He
remembereth that we are dust" (ib. ciii. 14);
and again, whither goeth it away?   "It shall
return to its dust." (ib. civ. 29.)   Why was
this universe made?   For thee: "For thou
crownest him with glory and honor, and
settest him over the works of Thy hands."
(ib. viii. 5, 6.)   Have we men any community
with the Angels?   This he also tells us, saying as follows, "Thou hast made him a little
lower than the Angels."   Of the love of God,
"Like as a father pitieth his own children,
even so is the Lord merciful to them that fear
Him." (ib. ciii. 13.)   And of the things that
are to meet us after our present life, and of
that undisturbed condition, he teacheth, "Re-

[1] Such was the case of Stagirius, *vit. Chrys. Montf.* p. 97.
See St. Chrysostom's Exhortation to him, t. 1. Ben. t. vi. Sav.
Bingham, art, Energumens. . . St. Aug. *de Civ. Dei.* 19, 4.
§ 2 and 21, 14.   "A messenger of Satan" was given to St.
Paul Himself, 2 Cor. xii. 7, and it was in hope of their salvation he delivered Hymeneus and Alexander to Satan. 1 Tim.
i. 20, and another, 1 Cor. v. 5.

turn unto thy rest, O my soul." (ib. cxvi. 7.) Why the Heaven is so great, this he will also say. For it is because "the heavens declare the glory of God." (ib. xix. 1.) Why day and night were made,—not that they may shine and give us rest only, but also that they may instruct us. "For there are no speeches nor words, the sounds of which (i. e. day and night) are not heard." (ib. 3.) How the sea lies round about the earth, this too thou wilt learn from hence. "The deep as a garment is the envelopment thereof." [1] For so the Hebrew has it. But having a sample in what I have mentioned, ye will have a notion of all the rest besides, the things about Christ, about the resurrection, about the life to come, about the resting, about punishment, about moral matters, all that concerns doctrines, and you will find the book filled with countless blessings. And if you fall into temptations, you will gain much comfort from hence. If you fall into sins even, you will find countless remedies stored up here, or if into poverty or tribulation, you will see many havens. And if thou be righteous thou wilt gain much security hence, and if a sinner much relief. For if thou be just and art ill-treated, thou wilt hear him say, "For Thy sake are we killed all the day long, we are counted as sheep for the slaughter." (Ps. xliv. 22.) "All these things have come upon us, and yet have we not forgotten Thee." (ib. 17.) And if thy well-doings make thee high, thou wilt hear him say, "Enter not into judgment with Thy servant, for in Thy sight shall no man living be justified" (ib. cxliii. 2), and thou wilt be straightway made lowly. And if thou be a sinner, and hast despaired of thyself, thou wilt hear him continually singing, "To-day, if ye will hear His voice, harden not your hearts, as in the provocation" (ib. xcv. 7, 8), and thou wilt be stayed up speedily. And if thou have a crown even on thy head, and art high-minded, thou wilt learn that "a king is not saved by a great host, neither shall a giant be saved by the greatness of his might" (ib. xxxiii. 16): and thou wilt find thyself able to be reasonable. If thou be rich, and in reputation, again thou wilt hear him singing, "Woe to them that trust in their own might, and boast themselves in the mul-

titude of their riches." (ib. xlix. 6.) And, "As for man, his days are as grass" (ib. ciii. 15), And, "His glory shall not go down with him, after him" (ib. xlix. 17): and thou wilt not think any of the things upon the earth are great. For when what is more splendid than all, even glory and power, is so worthless, what else of things on earth is worth accounting of? But art thou in despondency? Hear him saying, "Why art thou so sorrowful, O my soul, and why dost thou so disturb me? Trust in God, for I will confess unto Him." (ib. xlii. 5.) Or dost thou see men in honor who deserve it not? [2] "Fret not thyself at them that do wickedly. For as the grass shall they be dried up, and as the green herb shall they soon fall away." (ib. xxxvii. 1, 2.) Dost thou see both righteous and sinners punished? be told that the cause is not the same. For "many" he says, "are the plagues of sinners." (ib. xxxii. 10.) But in the case of the righteous, he does not say plagues,[3] but, "Many are the troubles of the righteous, but the Lord delivereth them out of them all." (ib. xxxiv. 19.) And again, "The death of the sinner is evil." (ib. 21.) And, "Precious in the sight of the Lord is the death of His saints." (ib. cxvi. 15.) These things do thou say continually: by these be instructed. For every single word of this has in it an indiscoverable ocean of meaning. For we have been just running over them only: but if you were minded to give these passages accurate investigation, you will see the riches to be great. But at present it is possible even by what I have given, to get cleared of the passions that lie on you. For since he forbids our envying, or being grieved, or despondent out of season, or thinking that riches are anything, or tribulation, or poverty, or fancying life itself to be anything, he frees thee from all passions. So for this let us give thanks to God, and let us have our treasure always in hand, "that by patience and comfort of the Scriptures we may have hope" (Rom. xv. 4), and enjoy the good things to come. Which God grant that we may all attain, by the grace and love toward man of our Lord Jesus Christ. By Whom and with Whom, etc.

---

[1] Ps. civ. 6. Where Aquila and Theodotion have the feminine, which would be expected in speaking of the sea. See Theodoret on the Psalm.

[2] 2 Mss. "Receive a cure for even this."

[3] Orig. in Rom. v. 4. *Tribulatio proprie sanctorum est. impiorum autem. . . flagella appellantur.* "Tribulation properly belongs to the saints, the things the wicked suffer are called scourges."

HOMILY XXIX.

ROM. XV. 14.

"And I myself also am persuaded of you, my brethren, that ye also are full of goodness, filled with all knowledge, able also to admonish one another." (So most: S. Chrys. "others.")

HE had said, "Inasmuch as I am the Apostle of the Gentiles, I magnify mine office." (Rom. xi. 13.) He had said, "Take heed lest He also spare not thee." (ib. 21.) He had said, "Be not wise in your own conceits" (ib. xii. 16); and again, "Why dost thou judge thy brother?" (ib. xiv. 10) And, "Who art thou that judgest another man's servant?" (ib. 4.) And several other like things besides. Since then he had often made his language somewhat harsh, he now speaks kindly (θεραπεύει). And what he said in the beginning, that he doth in the end also. At the beginning he said, "I thank my God for you all, that your faith is spoken of throughout the whole world." (ib. i. 8.) But here he says, "I am persuaded that ye also are full of goodness, being able also to admonish others;" and this is more than the former. And he does not say, I have heard, but, "I am persuaded," and have no need to hear, from others. And, "I myself," that is, I that rebuke, that accuse you. That "ye are full of goodness," this applies to the exhortation lately given. As if he said, It was not as if you were cruel, or haters of your brethren, that I gave you that exhortation, to receive, and not to neglect, and not to destroy "the work of God." For I am aware that "ye are full of goodness." But he seems to me here to be calling their virtue perfect. And he does not say ye have, but "ye are full of." And the sequel is with the same intensitives: "filled with all knowledge." For suppose they had been affectionate, but yet did not know how to treat those they loved properly. This was why he added, "all knowledge. Able to admonish others," not to learn only, but also to teach.

Ver. 15. "Nevertheless, I have written the more boldly unto you in some sort."

Observe the lowly-mindedness of Paul, observe his wisdom, how he gave a deep cut in the former part, and then when he had succeeded in what he wished, how he uses much kindliness next. For even without what he has said, this very confession of his having been bold were enough to unstring their vehemency. And this he does in writing to the Hebrews also, speaking as follows, "But, beloved, I am persuaded better things of you, and things which belong unto salvation, though we thus speak." (Heb. vi. 9.) And to the Corinthians again, "Now I praise you, brethren, that ye remember me in all things, and keep the ordinances, as I delivered them to you." (1 Cor. xi. 2.) And in writing to the Galatians he says, "I have confidence in you, that ye will be none otherwise minded." (Gal. v. 10.) And in all parts of his Epistles one may find this to be frequently observed. But here even in a greater degree. For they were in a higher rank, and there was need to bring down their fastidious spirit, not by astringents only, but by laxatives also. For he does this in different ways. Wherefore he says in this place too, "I have written the more boldly unto you," and with this even he is not satisfied, but has added, "in some sort," that is, gently; and even here he does not pause, but what does he say? "As putting you in mind."* And he does not say as teaching, nor simply putting in mind, (ἀναμιμνήσκων) but he uses a word (ἐπαναμιμνήσκων) which means putting you in mind in a quiet way. Observe the end falling in with the introduction. For as in that passage he said, "that your faith is made known in all the world." (Rom. i. 8.) So in the end of the Epistle also, "For your obedience hath reached unto all." (ib. xvi. 19.) And as in the beginning he wrote, "For I long to see you, that I may impart unto you some spiritual gift, to the end that ye may be established; that is, that I may be comforted together with you" (ib. i. 11, 12); so here also he said, "As putting you in mind." And having come down from the seat of the master, both there

---

* Besides the interpretation adopted by Chrys. which joins ἀπὸ μέρους closely with ἀναμιμνήσκων and understands it to mean, *in a sort—gently*, two other views deserve notice (1) that which joins it to τολμηρότερον—*in part*, or *somewhat more boldly* (Hodge) and (2) that which joins it to ἔγραψα—I have written more boldly *in parts* of the epistle (De Wette, Meyer, Alford). Both our Eng. vss. seem to understand it as Chrys. viz.: as a conciliatory modification of "more boldly," and connecting with it the explanatory statement that the reason of his more bold writing was the kindly one of putting them in remembrance.—G. B. S.

and here, he speaks to them as brethren and friends of equal rank. And this is quite a Teacher's duty, to give his address that variety which is profitable to the hearers. See then how after saying, "I have written the more boldly," and, "in some sort," and, "as putting you in mind," he was not satisfied even with these, but making his language still more lowly, he proceeds :

"Because of the grace that is given me of God." As he said at the beginning, "I am a debtor." (Rom. i. 14.) As if he had said, I have not snatched at the honor for myself, neither was I first to leap forward to it, but God commanded this, and this too according unto grace, not as if He had separated me for this office because I deserved it. Do not ye then be exasperated, since it is not I that raise myself up, but it is God that enjoins it. And as he there says, "whom I serve in the Gospel of His Son" (ib. 9), so also here, after saying, "because of the grace given unto me by God," he adds,

Ver. 16. "That I should be the minister of Jesus Christ to the Gentiles, ministering (ἱερουργοῦντα) the Gospel of God."

For after his abundant proof of his statements, he draws his discourse to a more lofty tone, not speaking of mere service, as in the beginning, but of service and priestly ministering (λειτουργίαν καὶ ἱερουργίαν). For to me this is a priesthood, this preaching and declaring. This is the sacrifice I bring. Now no one will find fault with a priest, for being anxious to offer the sacrifice without blemish. And he says this at once to elevate (πτερῶν) their thoughts, and show them that they are a sacrifice, and in apology for his own part in the matter, because he was appointed to this office. For my knife, he says, is the Gospel, the word of the preaching. And the cause is not that I may be glorified, not that I may appear conspicuous, but that the "offering up (προσφορὰ) of the Gentiles may be acceptable, being sanctified by the Holy Ghost."

That is, that the souls of those that are taught by me, may be accepted. For it was not so much to honor me, that God led me to this pitch, as out of a concern for you. And how are they to become acceptable ? In the Holy Ghost. For there is need not only of faith, but also of a spiritual way of life, that we may keep the Spirit that was given once for all. For it is not wood and fire, nor altar and knife, but the Spirit that is all in us.[1] For this cause, I take all means to prevent that Fire from being extinguished, as I have

been also enjoined to do. Why then do you speak to those that need it not ? This is just the reason why I do not teach you, but put you in mind, he replies. As the priest stands by stirring up the fire, so I do, rousing up your ready-mindedness. And observe, he does not say, "that the offering up of" you "may be" etc. but "of the Gentiles." But when he says of the Gentiles, he means the whole world, the land, and the whole sea, to take down their haughtiness, that they might not disdain to have him for a teacher, who was putting himself forth (τεινόμενον) to the very end of the world. As he said in the beginning, "as among the other Gentiles also, I am a debtor to Greeks, and also to barbarians, to wise, and to foolish." (Rom. i. 13, 14, see p. 347.)

Ver. 17. "I have therefore whereof I may glory, through Jesus Christ, in those things which pertain to God."

Inasmuch as he had humbled himself exceedingly, he again raised his style, doing this also for their sakes, lest he should seem to become readily an object of contempt. And while he raises himself, he remembers his own proper temper, and says, "I have therefore whereof to glory." I glory, he means, not in myself, not in our zeal, but in the "grace of God."

Ver. 18. "For I will not dare to speak of any of those things which Christ hath not wrought by me, to make Gentiles obedient by word and deed, through mighty signs and wonders, by the power of the Spirit of God."*

And none, he means, can say that my words are a mere boast. For of this priestly ministry of mine, the signs that I have, and the proofs of the appointment too, are many. Not the long garment (ποδήρης) and the bells as they of old, nor the mitre and the turban (κίδαρις), but signs and wonders, far more awful than these. Nor can it be said that I have been entrusted indeed with the charge, but yet have not executed it. Or rather, it is not I that have executed, but Christ. Wherefore also it is in Him that I boast, not about common things, but about spiritual. And this is the force of, "in things which pertain

---

[1] Some Mss. "all is spiritual with us" (πνευματικὰ). Savile's marginal reading is unintelligible, but might suggest conjectures.

* Verse 18 may yield three different meanings according to the word which receives the main emphasis. If it is placed on *through me* the meaning is: I shall not mention or lay claim to results wrought by others, but only to those secured by *my own* labors. The desire of the apostle (20) not to build upon another man's foundation favors this view. (So Alford, Hodge). If the stress is placed on the word *wrought* the sense is: I shall not dare to mention any of those things which Christ did not *actually work*, i. e., I shall make no claim to success not actually achieved (Meyer). The emphasis may be placed on *Christ*. If so, it means: I will mention only what Christ (he and he alone) wrought through me for the extension of his kingdom. Chrys. understands the passage thus and, we think, rightly. (So Tholuck, Olshausen, Boise).—G. B. S.

to God." For that I have accomplished the purpose for which I was sent, and that my words are not mere boast, the miracles, and the obedience of the Gentiles show. "For I will not dare to speak of any of those things which Christ hath not wrought by me, to make the Gentiles obedient by word and deed, through signs and wonders, by the power of the Spirit of God." See how violently he tries to show that the whole is God's doing, and nothing his own. For whether I speak anything, or do anything, or work miracles, He doth all of them, the Holy Spirit all. And this he says to show the dignity of the Holy Spirit also. See how these things are more wondrous and more awful than those of old, the sacrifice, the offering, the symbols. For when he says, "in word and deed, through mighty signs and wonders," he means this, the doctrine, the system (φιλοσοφίαν) relating to the Kingdom, the exhibition of actions and conversation, the dead that were raised, the devils that were cast out, and the blind that were healed, and the lame that leaped, and the other .marvellous acts, all whereof the Holy Spirit wrought in us. Then the proof of these things (since all this is yet but an assertion) is the multitude of the disciples. Wherefore he adds, "So that from Jerusalem, and round about unto Illyricum, I have fully preached the Gospel of Christ." Count up then cities, and places, and nations, and peoples, not those under the Romans only, but those also under barbarians. For I would not have you go the whole way through Phœnicia, and Syria, and the Cilicians, and Cappadocians, but reckon up also the parts behind,[1] the country of the Saracens, and Persians, and Armenians, and that of the other savage nations. For this is why he said, "round about," that you might not only go through the direct high road, but that you should run over the whole, even the southern part of Asia in your mind. And as he ran over miracles thick as snow, in a single word, by saying, "through mighty signs and wonders," so he has comprehended again endless cities, and nations, and peoples, and places, in this one word "round about." For he was for removed from all boasting. And this he said on their account, so that they should not be conceited about themselves. And at. the beginning he said, that "I might have some fruit amongst you also, even as among .other Gentiles." But here he states the compulsion of his priesthood. For as he had spoken in a sharper tone, he shows also by it his power more

clearly. This is why he there only says, "even as among other Gentiles." But here he insists on the topic fully, so that the conceit may be pruned away on all grounds. And he does not merely say, preached the Gospel, but "have fully preached the Gospel of Christ."[2]

Ver. 20. "Yea, so have I strived to preach the Gospel, not where Christ was named."

See here another preëminence; that he had not only preached the Gospel to so many, and persuaded them, but he did not even go to those who had become disciples. So far was he from thrusting himself upon other men's disciples, and from doing this for glory's sake, that he even made it a point to teach those who had not heard. For neither does he say where they were not persuaded, but "where Christ was. not even named," which is more. And what was the reason why he had this ambition? "Lest I should build," he says, "upon another man's foundation."

This he says to show himself a stranger to vanity, and to instruct them that it was not from any love of glory, or of honor from them, that he came to write, but as fulfilling his ministry, as perfecting his priestly duty, as loving their salvation. But he calls the foundation of the Apostles "another man's," not in regard to the quality of the person, or the nature of preaching, but in regard to the question of reward. For it was not that the preaching was that of another man,[3] but so far as it went to another man's reward. For the reward of the labors of others was, to this man, another man's. Then he shows that a prophecy was fulfilled also saying,

Ver. 21. "As it is written, To whom He was not spoken of, they shall see, and they that have not heard shall understand." (Is. iii. 15. LXX.)

You see he runs to where the labor is more, the toil greater.

Ver. 22. "For which cause also I have been much hindered from coming to you."

Observe again, how he makes the end of the like texture with the introduction. For while he was quite at the beginning of the Epistle, he said, "Oftentimes I purpose to come unto you, but was let hitherto." (Rom. i. 13.)

---

[1] This is scarcely historical, except with reference to Arabia. Even St. Jerome on Amos v. 8, implies less.

[2] 2 Mss. add ὥστε δεῖξαι φιλοτιμίας τὸ κατόρθωμα ὄν. The φιλοτιμία, "zealous striving," is here opposed to mere necessity of duty, "the compulsion of his priesthood." The words thus are a gloss on those next cited, not a proper part of the text.

[3] ἀλλότριον, which means either "alien," or "another man's."

But here he gives the cause also by which he was let, and that not once, but twice even, aye, and many times. For as he says there, "oftentimes I purposed to come to you," so here too, "I have been much (or often, τὰ πολλὰ) hindered from coming to you." Now it is a thing which proves a very strong desire, that he attempted it so often.

Ver. 23. "But now having no more place in these parts."

See how he shows that it was not from any coveting of glory from them, that he both wrote and was also coming. "And having a great desire to come to you these many years,"

Ver. 24. "Whensoever I take my journey into Spain, I trust to see you in my journey; and to be brought on my way thitherward by you, if first I be somewhat filled with your company,"

For that he might not seem to be holding them very cheap, by saying, Since I have not anything to do, therefore I am coming to you, he again touches on the point of love by saying, "I have a great desire, these many years, to come unto you." For the reason why I desire to come, is not because I am disengaged, but that I may give birth to that desire wherewith I am travailing so long. Then that this again should not puff them up, consider how he lowers them by saying, "Whensoever I take my journey into Spain, I trust to see you in my journey." For this was why he stated this, that they should not be high-minded. For what he wants is to show his love, and at the same time to prevent them from being dainty. And so he places this close on the other, and uses things confirmative of either alternately. For this reason again that they might not say, Do you make us a by-object of your journey? he adds, "and to be brought on my way thitherward by you: that is, that you may be my witnesses that it is not through any slight of you, but by force of necessity, that I run by you. But as this is still distressing, he heals it over more carefully, by saying, "If I be first somewhat filled with your company." For by his saying, "in my journey," he shows that he did not covet their good opinion. But by saying "be filled," that he was eager for their love, and not only was eager for it, but exceedingly so; and this is why he does not say "be filled," but be "somewhat" so. That is, no length of time can fill me or create in me a satiety of your company. See how he shows his love, when even though in haste he doth not rise up until he be filled. And this is a sign of his great affectionate-

35

ness, that he uses his words in so warm a way. For he does not say even I will see, but "shall be filled," imitating thus the language of parents. And at the beginning he said, "that I might have some fruit." (Rom. i. 13.) But here that I may be "filled." And both these are like a person who is drawing others to him. For the one was a very great commendation of them, if they were likely to yield him fruit from their obedience; and the other, a genuine proof of his own friendship. And in writing to the Corinthians he thus says, "That ye may bring me on my journey whithersoever I go" (1 Cor. xvi. 6), so in all ways exhibiting an unrivalled love to his disciples. And so at the beginning of all his Epistles it is with this he starts, and at the end in this he concludes again. For as an indulgent father doth an only and true born son, so did he love all the faithful. Whence it was that he said, "Who is weak, and I am not weak? who is offended, and I burn not?" (2 Cor. xi. 29.)

For before everything else this is what the teacher ought to have. Wherefore also to Peter Christ saith, "If thou lovest Me, feed My sheep." (John xxi. 16.) For he who loveth Christ loveth also His flock. And Moses too did He then set over the people of the Jews, when he had shown a kindly feeling towards them. And David in this way came to be king, having been first seen to be affectionately-minded towards them; so much indeed, though yet young, did he grieve for the people, as to risk his life for them, when he killed that barbarian. But if he said, "What shall be done to the man that killeth this Philistine?" (1 Sam. xix. 5; ib. xvii. 26) he said it not in order to demand a reward, but out of a wish to have confidence placed in himself, and to have the battle with him delivered to his charge. And therefore, when he came to the king after the victory, he said nothing of these things. And Samuel too was very affectionate; whence it was that he said, "But God forbid that I should sin in ceasing to pray unto the Lord for you." (1 Sam. xii. 23.) In like way Paul also, or rather not in like way, but even in a far greater degree, burned towards all his subjects (τῶν ἀρχομένων). Wherefore he made his disciples of such affection towards himself, that he said, "If were possible, ye would have pulled out your eyes and given them to me." (Gal. iv. 15.) On this ground too it is, that God charges the teachers of the Jews above all things with this, saying, "Oh shepherds of Israel, do shepherds feed themselves? do they not feed the flock?" (Ezek. xxxiv. 2, 3.) But they did the reverse. For he says, "Ye eat the milk, and clothe you with the wool, and ye kill them that are fed, but ye feed not the flock." And Christ, in bringing out the rule for the fittest Pastor, said, "The good shepherd layeth down his life for his sheep." (John x. 11.) This David did also, both on sundry other occasions, and also when that fearful wrath from above came down upon the whole people. For while all were being slain he said, "I the shepherd[1] have sinned, I the shepherd have done amiss, and these the flock what have they done?" (2 Sam. xxiv. 17.) And so in the choice of those punishments also, he chose not famine, nor flight before enemies, but the pestilence sent by God, whereby he hoped to place all the others in safety, but that he should himself in preference to all the rest be carried off. But since this was not so, he bewails, and says, "On me be Thy Hand:" or if this be not enough, "on my father's house" also. "For I," he says, "the shepherd have sinned." As though he had said, that if they also sinned, I was the person who should suffer the vengeance, as I corrected them not. But since the sin is mine also, it is I who deserve to suffer the vengeance. For wishing to increase the crime he used the name of "Shepherd." Thus then he stayed the wrath, thus he got the sentence revoked! So great is the power of confession. "For the righteous is his own accuser first.[2] So great is the concern and sympathy of a good Pastor. For his bowels were writhed at their falling, as when one's own children are killed. And on this ground he begged that the wrath might come upon himself. And in the beginning of the slaughter he would have done this, unless he had seen it advancing and expected that it would come to himself. When therefore he saw that this did not happen, but that the calamity was raging among them, he no longer forebore, but was touched more than for Amnon his first-born. For then he did not ask for death, but now he begs to fall in preference to the others. Such ought a ruler to be and to grieve rather at the calamities of others than his own.[3] Some such thing he suffered in his son's case likewise, that you might see that he did not love his son more

than his subjects, and yet the youth was unchaste, and an ill-user of his father (πατρα-λοίας), and still he said, "Would that I might have died for thee!" (2 Sam. xviii. 33.) What sayest thou, thou blessed one, thou meekest of all men? Thy son was set upon killing thee, and compassed thee about with ills unnumbered. And when he had been removed, and the trophy was raised, dost thou then pray to be slain? Yea, he says, for it is not for me that the army has been victorious, but I am warred against more violently than before, and my bowels are now more torn than before. These however were all thoughtful for those committed to their charge, but the blessed Abraham concerned himself much even for those that were not entrusted to him, and so much so as even to throw himself amongst alarming dangers. For when he did what he did, not for his nephew only, but for the people of Sodom also, he did not leave driving those Persians before him until he had set them all free: and yet he might have departed after he had taken him, yet he did not choose it. For he had the like concern for all, and this he showed likewise by his subsequent conduct. When then it was not a host of barbarians that was on the point of laying siege to them, but the wrath of God that was plucking their cities up from the foundations, and it was no longer the time for arms, and battle, and array, but for supplication; so great was the zeal he showed for them, as, if he himself had been on the point of perishing. For this reason he comes once, twice, thrice, aye and many times to God, and finds a refuge (i. e. an excuse) in his nature by saying, "I am dust and ashes" (Gen. xviii. 27): and since he saw that they were traitors to themselves, he begs that they may be saved for others. Wherefore also God said, "I will hide not from Abraham My servant that thing which I am about to do" (ib. 17), that we might learn how loving to man the righteous is. And he would not have left off beseeching, unless God had left off first (so he takes v. 33). And he seems indeed to be praying for the just, but is doing the whole for them. For the souls of the Saints are very gentle and loving unto man, both in regard to their own, and to strangers. And even to the unreasoning creatures they extend their gentleness. Wherefore also a certain wise man said, "The righteous pitieth the souls of his cattle."[4] But if he doth those of cattle, how much more those of men. But since I

---

[1] So LXX. Cod. Alex. Theodoret *in loc.* makes David herein a type of Christ.

[2] Prov. xviii. 17, LXX. and Vulg. Our version is, "He that is first in his own cause seemeth just." The text is much quoted by the Fathers, as Hil. in Ps. cxxxv.

[3] See a remarkable form in use in China on the occasion of such calamities, *Windischman, Philos. im fortgang der Weltgeschichte,* i. p. 29.

[4] Prov. xii. 10. LXX. Know occurs in Exod. xxiii. 9, for "enter into the feelings of."

have mentioned cattle, let us just consider the shepherds of the sheep who are in the Cappadocian land, and what they suffer in kind and degree in their guardianship of unreasoning creatures. They often stay for three days together buried down under the snows. And those in Libya are said to undergo no less hardships than these, ranging about for whole months through that wilderness, dreary as it is, and filled with the direst wild beasts (θηρία may include serpents). Now if for unreasonable things there be so much zeal, what defense are we to set up, who are entrusted with reasonable souls, and yet slumber on in this deep sleep? For is it right to be at rest, and in quiet, and not to be running about everywhere, and giving one's self up to endless deaths in behalf of these sheep? Or know ye not the dignity of this flock Was it not for this that thy Master took endless pains, and afterwards poured forth His blood? And dost thou seek for rest? Now what can be worse than these Shepherds? Dost thou not perceive, that there stand round about these sheep wolves much more fierce and savage than those of this world? Dost thou not think with thyself, what a soul he ought to have who is to take in hand this office? Now men that lead the populace, if they have but common matters to deliberate on, add days to nights in watching. And we that are struggling in heaven's behalf sleep even in the daytime. And who is now to deliver us from the punishment for these things? For if the body were to be cut in pieces, if to undergo ten thousand deaths, ought one not to run to it as to a feast? And let not the shepherds only, but the sheep also hear this; that they may make the shepherds the more active minded, that they may the more encourage their good-will: I do not mean by anything else but by yielding all compliance and obedience. Thus Paul also bade them, saying, " Obey them which have the rule over you, and submit yourselves : for they watch for your souls as they that must give account." (Heb. xiii. 17.) And when he says, " watch," he means thousands of labors, cares and dangers. For the good Shepherd, who is such as Christ wisheth for, is contending, before countless witnesses. For He died once for him ; but this man ten thousand times for the flock, if, that is, he be such a shepherd as he ought to be ; for such an one can die every day. (See on Rom. viii. 36. p. 456.) And therefore do ye, as being acquainted with what the labor is, coöperate with them, with prayers, with zeal, with readiness, with affection, that both we may have to boast of you, and you of us. For on this gound He entrusted this to the chief[1] of the Apostles, who also loved Him more than the rest ; after first asking him if He was loved by him, that thou mayest learn that this before other things, is held as a proof of love to Him. For this requireth a vigorous soul. This I have said of the best shepherds ; not of myself and those of our days, but of any one that may be such as Paul was, such as Peter, such as Moses. These then let us imitate, both the rulers of us and the ruled. For the ruled may be in the place of a shepherd to his family, to his friends, to his servants, to his wife, to his children : and if we so order our affairs we shall attain to all manner of good things. Which God grant that we may all attain unto, by the grace and love toward man, etc.

HOMILY XXX.

ROM. XV. 25-27.

" But now I go unto Jerusalem to minister unto the saints. For it has pleased them of Macedonia and Achaia to make a certain contribution for the poor saints which are at Jerusalem. It hath pleased them verily, and their debtors they are."

Since he had said that I have no longer " more place in these parts," and, " I have a great desire, these many years, to come unto you," but he still intended to delay; lest it should be thought that he was making a jest of them, he mentions the cause also why he still puts it off, and he says, that " I am going unto Jerusalem," and is apparently giving the excuse for the delay. But by means of this he also makes good another object, which is the exhorting of them to alms, and making them more in earnest about it. Since if he had not been minded to effect this, it had sufficed to say, " I am going unto Jerusalem." But now he adds the reason of his journey. " For I go," says he, " to minister to the saints." And he dwells over the subject, and

---

[1] κορυφαίῳ. The common title of St. Peter among the Fathers.

enters into reasonings, and says that they "are debtors," and that, "if the Gentiles have been made partakers of their spiritual things, their duty is also to minister unto them in carnal things," that they might learn to imitate these. Wherefore also there is much reason to admire his wisdom for devising this way of giving the advice. For they were more likely to bear it in this way than if he had said it in the form of exhortation; as then he would have seemed to be insulting them, if, with a view to incite them, he had brought before them Corinthians and Macedonians.* Indeed, this is the ground on which he does incite the others as follows, saying, "Moreover, brethren, we do you to wit of the grace of God bestowed on the Churches in Macedonia." (2 Cor. viii. 1.) And again he incites the Macedonians by these. "For your zeal," he says, "hath provoked very many." (ib. ix. 2.) And by the Galatians in like manner he does this, as when he says, "As I have given order to the Churches of Galatia, even so do ye." (1 Cor. xvi. 1.) But in the case of the Romans he does not do so, but in a more covert way. And he does this also in regard to the preaching, as when he says, "What? came the word of God out from you? or came it unto you only?" (ib. xiv. 36.) For there is nothing so powerful as emulation. And so he often employs it. For elsewhere too he says," "And so ordain I in all the Churches;" (ib. vii. 17); and again, "As I teach everywhere in every Church." (ib. iv. 17.) And to the Colossians he says, "that the Gospel increaseth and bringeth forth fruit in all the world." (Col. i. 6.) This then he does here also in the case of alms. And consider what dignity there is in his expressions. For he does not say, I go to carry alms, but "to minister" (διακονῶν). But if Paul ministers, just consider how great a thing is doing, when the Teacher of the world undertakes to be the bearer, and when on the point of travelling to Rome, and so greatly desiring them too, he yet prefers this to that. "For it hath pleased them of Macedonia and Achaia, that is, it meets their approbation, their desire. "A certain contribution." And, he does not say alms, but "contribution" (κοινωνίαν). And the "certain" is not used without a meaning, but to prevent his seeming to reproach these. And he does not say the poor, merely, but the "poor saints," so making his recommendation twofold, both that from their virtue and that from their poverty. And even with this alone he was not satisfied, but he adds, "they are their debtors." Then he shows how they are debtors. For if, he says, "the Gentiles have been made partakers of their spiritual things, their debt (A. V. duty) is also to minister unto them in carnal things." But what he means is this. It was for their sakes that Christ came. To them it was that all the promises were made, to them of the Jews. Of them Christ came. (Wherefore also it said, "Salvation is of the Jews.") (John iv. 22.) From them were the Apostles, from them the Prophets, from them all good things. In all these things then the world was made a partaker. If then, he says, ye have been made partakers in that which is greater, and when it was for them that the banquet was prepared, ye have been brought in to enjoy the feast that was spread (Matt. xxii. 9), according to the Parable of the Gospel, ye are debtors also to share your carnal things with them, and to impart to them. But he does not say to share, but "to minister" (λειτουργῆσαι), so ranking them with ministers (διακόνων), and those that pay the tribute[1] to kings. And he does not say in your carnal things, as he did in "their spiritual things." For the spiritual things were theirs. But the carnal belonged not to these alone, but were the common property of all. For he bade money to be held to belong to all,[2] not to those who were its possessors only.

"Ver. 28. "When therefore I have performed this, and have sealed unto them this fruit."

That is, when I have laid it up as it were in the royal treasuries, as in a place secure from robbers and danger. And he does not say alms, but "fruit" again, to show that those who gave it were gainers by it. "I will come by you into Spain." He again mentions Spain to show his forwardness (ἄοκνον) and warmth towards them.

Ver. 29. "And I am sure that, when I come unto you, I shall come in the fulness of the blessing of the Gospel of Christ."

What is the force of, "In the fulness of the blessing? Either he speaks of alms (Gr. money), or generally of good deeds. For blessing is a name he very commonly gives to alms. As when he says, "As a blessing[3] and

---

* "That, as Chrys., Calvin, Grotius, and many, including Rückert and Olshausen assume, Paul intended 'courteously and gently' (Luther) to suggest to the Romans that they should likewise bestow alms on those at Jerusalem, is very improbable, inasmuch as no reason is perceivable why he should not have ventured on a direct summons, and seeing, moreover, that he looked upon the work of collection as concluded, ver. 25," Meyer.—G. B. S.

[1] λειτουργία, in Classical Greek, is performing a public service at one's own expense.
[2] 2 Cor. ix. 5. Mosheim de Rebus Christianorum ante Const. p. 118, also Diss. ad Hist. Eccl. pert. vol. 2, 1. St. Chrys. speaks at length of wealth on 1 Cor. xiv. 19, Hom. 35, p 499, O. T. He thinks it lawful, but dangerous, and recommends alms almost without limitation.
[3] A. V. bounty, but margin, blessing.

not as covetousness." (2 Cor. ix. 5.) And it was customary of old for the thing to be so called. But as he has here added " of the Gospel," on this ground we assert that he speaks not of money only, but of all other things. As if he had said, I know that when I come I shall find you with the honor and freshness of all good deeds about you, and worthy of countless praises in the Gospel.* And this is a very striking mode of advice, I mean this way of forestalling their attention by encomiums. For when he entreats them in the way of advice, this is the mode of setting them right that he adopts.

Ver. 30. " Now I beseech you, brethren, for the Lord Jesus Christ's sake, and for the love of the Spirit."

Here he again puts forward Christ and the Spirit, and makes no mention whatever of the Father. And I say this, that when you find him mentioning the Father and the Son, or the Father only, you may not despise either the Son or the Spirit. And he does not say the Spirit, but " the love of the Spirit." For as Christ loved the world, and as the Father doth, so doth the Spirit also. And what is it that thou beseechest us, let me hear ? " To strive together with me in your prayers to God for me,"

Ver. 31. " That I may be delivered from them that do not believe in Judea."

A great struggle then lies before him. And this too is why he calls for their prayers. And he does not say that I may be engaged in it, but " I may be delivered," as Christ commanded, to " pray that we enter not into temptation."[1] (Matt. xxvi. 41.) And in saying this he showed, that certain evil wolves would attack them, and those who were wild

beasts rather than men. And out of this he also found grounds for another thing, namely, for showing that he with good reason took the office of ministering to the Saints, if, that is, the unbelievers were in such force that he even prayed to be delivered from them. For they who were amongst so many enemies, were in danger of perishing by famine also. And therefore there was absolute need of aid coming (or " of his going ") from other quarters to them. " And that my service which I have for Jerusalem may be accepted of the Saints."

That is, that my sacrifice may be accepted, that with cheerfulness they may receive what is given them. See how he again exalts the dignity of those who were to receive it. Then he asks for the prayer of so great a people in order to what was sent being received. And by this he shows another point also, that to have given alms does not secure its being accepted. For when any one gives it constrainedly, or out of unjust gains, or for vanity, the fruit of it is gone.

Ver. 32. " That I may come unto you with joy by the will of God."

As he had said at the beginning, " If by any means now at length I might have a prosperous journey, by the will of God, to come unto you " (Rom. i. 10) ; so here again he takes refuge in the same Will, and says that this is why I press on and wish to be delivered from them, that I may see you shortly, and that with pleasure, without bringing any load of heaviness from thence. " And may with you be refreshed."

See how he again shows unassumingness. For he does not say, I may teach you, and give you a lesson, but that, " I may with you be refreshed." And yet he was the very man engaged in the striving and conflict. In what sense then does he say " that I may be refreshed with you (συναναπαύσωμαι) ? " It is to gratify them on this point too, and to make them the more cheerful by making them sharers of his crown, and to show that they too struggle and labor. Then, as was always his custom to do, he adds prayer after the exhortation, and says,

Ver. 33. " Now the God of peace be with you all. Amen."

Chap. xvi. ver. 1. " I commend unto you Phebe our sister, which is a deaconess (A. V. servant) of the church which is at Cenchrea."

See how many ways he takes to give her dignity. For he has both mentioned her before all the rest, and called her sister. And it is no slight thing to be called the sister of Paul. Moreover he has added her

---

* It is certain that Chrys. is incorrect in his interpretation of the statement: " When I come unto you I shall come in the fulness of the blessing of the Gospel of Christ." (29.) The meaning is not that he shall find them abounding in this blessing, but that he (Paul) will come to them furnished with the fulness of this blessing. The joyful hopes of Paul respecting his journey to Rome and labors there, were not, indeed, wholly thwarted, but how different were the experiences of his journey and life there from what he had expected. He went thither a prisoner and such missionary labors as he was permitted to perform were accomplished while he was kept in ward by the civil authorities of Rome. And, yet, notwithstanding these hardships, who can doubt that his prayer was answered? He found joy in the saints at Rome who came out from the city as far as Appii Forum and the Three Taverns to welcome him (Acts xxviii. 15); he was permitted for two years, at least, to occupy his own hired house and freely to " preach the kingdom of God and teach the things concerning the Lord Jesus Christ with all boldness, none forbidding him " (Acts xxviii. 30, 31); this preaching was crowned with signal success extending to the conversion of some of the members of Cæsar's household (Phil. iv. 22). It is propable that we owe to this same period of imprisonment at Rome the four epistles to the Colossians, Ephesians, Philemon, and Philippians ; if so, we have in them a reflection of the manifold activities and profound spiritual experiences of the apostle during his stay in Rome which constitute a genuine providential fulfilment of his desires, although it proved that as in the case of an earlier visit to Jerusalem, he went not knowing the things that should befall him there (Acts xx. 22).—G. B. S.

[1] 2 Mss. add, So directing them to do this.

rank, by mentioning her being "deaconess."[1]

Ver. 2. "That ye receive her in the Lord, as becometh saints. (Gr. "the saints.")

That is, for the Lord's sake, that she may enjoy honor among you. For he that receives a person for the Lord's sake, though it be no great one that he receives, yet receives him with attention. But when it is a saint, consider what attention he ought to have shown him. And this is why he adds, "as becometh saints," as such persons ought to be received. For she has two grounds for her having attention shown her by you, both that of her being received for the Lord's sake, and that of her being a saint herself. And "that ye assist her in whatsoever business she hath need (or "asks," χρήζῃ) of you." You see how little he burdens them. For he does not say, That ye despatch, but that ye contribute your own part, and reach out a hand to her: and that "in whatsoever business she hath need." Not in whatsoever business she may be, but in such as she may ask of you. But she will ask in such things as lie in your power. Then again there comes a very great praise of her. "For she hath been a succorer of many and of myself also."

See his judgment. First come the ecomiums, then he makes an exhortation intervene, and then again gives encomiums, so placing on each side of the needs of this blessed woman her praises. For how can the woman be else than blessed who has the blessing of so favorable a testimony from Paul, who had also the power to render assistance to him who had righted the whole world? For this was the summit of her good deeds, and so he placed it the last, as he says, "and of "myself also." But what does the phrase of myself also" convey? Of the herald of the world, of him who hath suffered so much, of him who is equal to assisting tens of thousands (μυρίοις ἀρκοῦντος). Let us then imitate, both men and women, this holy woman and her that followeth, with her husband also. And who are they?

Ver. 2. "Greet," he says, "Priscilla and Aquila, my helpers in Christ Jesus."

To the excellence of these St. Luke also bears witness. Partly when he says that Paul "abode with them, for by their occupation they were tent-makers" (Acts xviii. 3); and partly when he points out the woman as receiving Apollos, and instructing him in the way of the Lord. (ib. 26.) Now these are great things, but what Paul mentions are greater. And what does he mention? In the first place he calls them "helpers," [2] to point out that they had been sharers of his very great labors and dangers. Then he says,

Ver. 4. "Who for my life have laid down their own necks."

You see they are thoroughly furnished martyrs. For in Nero's time it is probable that there were thousands of dangers, at the time as he even commanded all Jews to be removed from Rome." (Acts viii. 2).

"Unto whom not only I give thanks, but also all the Churches of the Gentiles."

Here he hints at their hospitality, and pecuniary assistance, holding them in admiration because they had both poured forth their blood, and had made their whole property open to all. You see these were noble women, hindered no way by their sex in the course of virtue. And this is as might be expected. "For in Christ Jesus there is neither male nor female." (Gal. iii. 28.) And what he had said of the former, that he said also of this. For of her also he had said, "she hath been a succorer of many, and of myself also." So too of this woman "not only I give thanks, but also all the Churches of the Gentiles." Now that in this he might not seem to be a flatterer, he also adduces a good many more witnesses to these women.

Ver. 5. "Likewise greet the Church that is in their house."

For she had been so estimable as even to make their house a Church, both by making all in it believers, and because they opened it to all strangers. For he was not in the habit of calling any houses Churches, save where there was much piety, and much fear of God deeply rooted in them.* And on this ground he said to the Corinthians also, "Salute Aquila and Priscilla, with the Church that is in their house." (1 Cor. xvi. 19.) And when writing about Onesimus, "Paul unto Philemon, and to the beloved Apphia, and to the Church that is in their house." (Philem. 1, 2.) For it is possible for a man even in the married state to be worthy of being looked up to, and noble. See then how these were in that

---

[1] See Bingham, b. ii. c. 22, for a full account of the office of the widows, deaconesses, etc., also Cave, Prim. Christ. part i. c. 8. Theodoret thinks it a sign of there being a considerable Church at Cenchrea, that they had a deaconess there.

[2] συλλειτουργούς. Afterwards the common term by which Bishops spoke of each other. As the Nicene Fathers of Alexander. Ep. Synod. v. fin. Theod. i. 9.
* By "the church in the house" of Priscilla and Aquila, Chrys. understands the pious family which constituted the household. Such was the view of many of the older interpreters. The more probable view is that the "churches in the houses" (cf. 1 Cor. xvi. 19; Col. iv. 15; Philem. 2) were assemblies of a part of the collective church of the city, formed for the sake of convenience of meeting, especially in the largest towns. There is no reason to believe that all the persons named below were members of the household—church of Priscilla and Aquila.—G. B. S.

state and became very honorable, and yet their occupation was far from being honorable; for they were "tent-makers." Still their virtue covered all this, and made them more conspicuous than the sun. And neither their trade nor their marriage (συζυγία cf. Phil. iv. 3) was any hurt to them, but the love which Christ required of them, that they exhibited. "For greater love hath no man than this, He says, that a man lay down his life for his friends." (John xv. 13.) And that which is a proof of being a disciple, they achieve, since they took up the Cross and followed Him. For they who did this for Paul, would much rather have displayed their fortitude in Christ's behalf.

Let rich and poor both hear all this. For if they who lived from their labor, and were managers of a workshop, exhibited such profuseness as to be of service to many Churches; what pardon can they expect, who are rich, and yet neglect the poor? For they were not sparing even of their blood for the sake of God's will, but thou art sparing even of scanty sums, and many times sparest not thine own soul. But in regard to the teacher were they so, and not so with regard to the disciples? Nay even this cannot be said. For "the churches of the Gentiles," he says, "thank them." And yet they were of the Jews. But still they had such a clear (εἰλικρινῶς) faith, as to minister unto them also with all willingness. Such ought women to be, not adorning themselves with "broidered hair, or gold, or costly array" (1 Tim. ii. 9), but in these good deeds. For what empress pray, was so conspicuous or so celebrated as this wife of the tent-maker? she is in everybody's mouth, not for ten or twenty years, but until the coming of Christ, and all proclaim her fame for things such as adorn far more than any royal diadem. For what is greater or so great, as to have been a succorer of Paul? at her own peril to have saved the teacher of the world? And consider: how many empresses there are that no one speaks of. But the wife of the tent-maker is everywhere reported of with the tent-maker (meaning perhaps St. Paul); and the width that the sun sees over, is no more of the world than what the glory of this woman runneth unto. Persians, and Scythians, and Thracians, and they who dwell in the uttermost parts of the earth, sing of the Christian spirit of this woman, and bless it.[1] How much wealth, how many diadems and purples would you not be glad to venture upon obtaining such a testimony? For no one can say either, that

in dangers they were of this character, and lavish with their money, and yet neglected the preaching. For he calls them "fellow-workers and helpers" on this ground. And this "chosen vessel" (Acts ix. 15) does not feel ashamed to call a woman his helper but even finds an honor in doing so. For it is not the sex (φύσει) that he minds, but the will is what he honors. What is equal to this ornament? Where now is wealth overflowing on every side? and where the adorning of the person? and where is vainglory? Learn that the dress of woman is not that put about the body, but that which decorates the soul, which is never put off, which does not lie in a chest, but is laid up in the heavens. Look at their labor for the preaching, the crown in martyrdom, the munificence in money, the love of Paul, the charm (φίλτρον) they found in Christ. Compare with this thine own estate, thy anxiety about money, thy vying with harlots (i. e. in dress), thy emulating of the grass,[2] and then thou wilt see who they were and who thou art. Or rather do not compare only, but vie with this woman, and after laying aside the burdens of grass (χλόης), (for this is what thy costly dressing is), take thou the dress from heaven, and learn whence Priscilla became such as she was. How then did they become so? For two years they entertained Paul as a guest: (Probably Acts xix. 10) and what is there that these two years may not have done for their souls? What am I to do then, you will say because I have not Paul? If thou be minded thou mayest have him in a truer sense than they. For even with them the sight of Paul was not what made them of such a character, but the words of Paul. And so, if thou be so minded, thou shalt have both Paul, and Peter, and John, and the whole choir of the Prophets, with the Apostles, associating with thee continually. For take the books of these blessed ones, and hold a continual intercourse with their writings, and they will be able to make thee like the tent-maker's wife. And why speak I of Paul? For if thou wilt, thou mayest have Paul's Master Himself. For through Paul's tongue even He will discourse with thee. And in another way again thou wilt be able to receive this Person, when thou receivest the saints, even when thou tendest those that believe on Him. And so even after their departure thou wilt have many memorials of piety. For even the table at which the saint ate, and a seat on which he sat, and the couch on which he lay

---

[1] Omitted by most Mss.

[2] τὴν πρὸς τὸν χόρτον φιλονεικίαν. See Matt. vi. 30; Luke xii. 28; Clem. Al. (Pott.) p. 232.

knoweth how to pierce[1] him that received him; even after his departure. How then, think you, was that Shunamite pierced at entering the upper chamber where Elisha abode, when she saw the table, the couch on which the holy man slept; and what religiousness must she have felt come from it?[2] For had this not been so, she would not have cast the child there when dead, if she had not reaped great benefit from thence. For if so long time after upon entering in where Paul abode, where he was bound, where he sat and discoursed,[3] we are elevated, and find ourselves starting off from the places to that memory (so Field: Vulg. "the memory of that day"); when the circumstances were still fresher, what must those have been likely to feel, who had religiously entertained him? Knowing all this then, let us receive the Saints, that the house may shine, that it may be freed from choking thorns, that the bedchamber may become a haven. And let us receive them, and wash their feet. Thou art not better than Sarah, nor more noble, nor more wealthy, though thou be an empress. For she had three hundred and eighteen home-born servants, at a time when to have two servants even was to be wealthy. And why do I mention the three hundred and eighteen servants? She had become possessed of the whole world in her seed and in the promises, she had the "friend of God" (Is. xli. 8; James ii. 23) for her husband, God Himself as a Patron, a thing greater than any kingdom. And yet, though she was in so illustrious and honorable estate, this woman kneaded the flour, and did all the other servant's offices, and stood by them as they banqueted too in the rank of a servant. Thou art not of nobler birth than Abraham, who yet did the part of domestics after his exploits after his victories, after the honor paid him by the king of Egypt, after driving out the kings of the Persians, and raising the glorious trophies. And look not to this; that in appearance the Saints that lodge with thee are but poor, and as beggars, and in rags many times, but be mindful of that voice which says, "Inasmuch as ye have done it to the least of these, ye have done it unto me." (Matt. xxv. 40.) And, "Despise not one of these little ones, because their angels do always behold the face of My Father which is in heaven." (Matt. xviii. 10.) Re-

ceive them then with readiness of mind, bringing as they do ten thousand blessings to thee, through the greeting of peace. (ib. x. 12, 13.) And after Sarah, reflect upon Rebecca also, who both drew water and gave to drink, and called the stranger in, trampling down all haughtiness. However, through this, great were the rewards of hospitality she received! And thou, if thou be so minded, wilt receive even greater than those. For it will not be the fruit of children only that God will give thee, but the heaven, and the blessings there, and a freedom from hell, and a remission of sins. For great, yea, very great, is the fruit of hospitality. (Luke xi. 41.) Thus too Jethro, and that though he was a foreigner, gained for a relation him who with so great power commanded the sea. (Dan. iv. 27; Ex. iii. 1.) For his daughters too drew into his net this honorable prey. (Num. x. 29.) Setting then thy thoughts upon these things, and reflecting upon the manly and heroic[4] temper of those women, trample upon the gorgeousness of this day, the adornments of dress, the costly jewelry, the anointing with perfumes. And have done with those wanton[5] and delicate airs, and that mincing walk, and turn all this attentiveness unto the soul, and kindle up in thy mind a longing for the heavens. For should but his love take hold of thee, thou wilt discern the mire and the clay, and ridicule the things now so admired. For it is not even possible for a woman adorned with spiritual attainments to be seeking after this ridiculousness. Having then cast this aside, which wives of the lewder sort of men, and actresses, and singers, have so much ambition in, clothe thee with the love of wisdom, with hospitality, with the succoring of the Saints, with compunction, with continual prayer. These be better than cloth of gold, these more stately than jewels and[6] than necklaces,[7] these both make thee of good repute among men, and bring thee great reward with God. This is the dress of the Church, that of the playhouses. This is worthy of the heaven, that, of horses and mules; that is put even round dead corpses, this shineth in a good soul alone wherein Christ dwelleth. Let this then be the dress for us to acquire, that we also may have our praise sung everywhere, and be well-pleasing to Christ, by Whom and with Whom, etc. Amen.

---

[1] κατανύξαι, see p. 487, and p. 448.
[2] See the use made of such recollections at the close of the 32d Homily.
[3] He seems to have some place at Antioch in his mind, but we do not know that St. Paul was ever bound there.

[4] φιλοσοφίαν, he means their simple habits; as in keeping sheep, and the character perhaps implied in Moses' choice.
[5] κατακλᾶν, Phryn. ap Bek. Anec. p. 45.
[6] The remaining leaves of the Bodl. Ms. are lost.
[7] περιδερραίων thus spelt. Jul. Poll. 5, 56.

HOMILY XXXI.

ROM. XVI. 5.

"Salute my well-beloved Epenetus, who is the first-fruits of Achaia unto Christ."

I THINK that many even of those who have the appearance of being extremely good men, hasten over this part of the Epistle[1] as superfluous, and having no great weight in it. And I think that the same befalls them in regard to the genealogy that is in the Gospel. For because it is a catalogue of names, they think they cannot get any great good from it. Yet the gold founders' people[2] are careful even about the little fragments;[3] while these pass over even such great cakes of gold. That this then may not befall them, what I have already said were enough to lead them off from their listlessness. For that the gain even from this is no contemptible one, we have shown even from what was said on a former occasion, when we lifted up your soul by means of these addresses. We will endeavor then to-day also to mine in this same place. For it is possible even from bare names to find a great treasure. If, for instance, you were shown why Abraham was so called, why Sarah, why Israel, why Samuel, you would find even from this a great many real subjects of research. And from times too, and from places, you may gather the same advantage. For the good man waxes rich even from these; but he that is slothful, does not gain even from the most evident things. Thus the very name of Adam teaches us no small wisdom, and that of his son, and of his wife, and most of the others. For names serve to remind us of several circumstances. They show at once God's benefits and women's thankfulness. For when they conceived by the gift of God, it was they who gave these names to the children. But why are we now philosophizing about names, while meanings so important are neglected, and many do not so much as know the very names of the sacred books? Still even then we ought not to recede from an attention to things of this sort. For "thou oughtest," He

says, "to have put My money to the exchangers." (Matt. xxv. 27.) And therefore though there be nobody that listens to it, let us do our part, and show that there is nothing superfluous, nothing added at random in the Scriptures. For if these names had no use, they would not then have been added to the Epistle, nor would Paul have written what he has written. But there are some even so low-minded, and empty, and unworthy of Heaven, as not to think that names only, but whole books of the Bible are of no use, as Leviticus, Joshua, and more besides. And in this way many of the simple ones have been for rejecting the Old Testament, and advancing on in the way, that results from this evil habit of mind, have likewise pruned away many parts of the New Testament also. But of these men,[4] as intoxicated and living to the flesh, we do not make much account. But if any be a lover of wisdom, and a friend to spiritual entertainments, let him be told that even the things which seem to be unimportant in Scripture, are not placed there at random and to no purpose, and that even the old laws have much to profit us. For it says, "All these things are types (A. V. ensamples) and are written for our instruction." (1 Cor. x. 11.) Wherefore to Timothy too he says, "Give heed to reading, to exhortation" (1 Tim. iv. 13), so urging him to the reading of the old books, though he was a man with so great a spirit in him, as to be able to drive out devils,[5] and to raise the dead. Let us now keep on with the subject in hand. "Salute my well-beloved Epenetus." It is worth learning from this how he distributes to each the different praises. For this praise is no slight one, but even very great, and a proof of great excellence in him, that Paul should hold him beloved, Paul who had no idea of loving by favor, and not by cool judgment. Then another encomium comes, "Who is the first-fruits of Achaia." For what he means is, either that he leaped forward before any one else, and became a

---

[1] So Mss. Ben. Sav. ἐντολῆς.
[2] Stallbaum ad Plat. *Phileb.* 74.
[3] See the Introduction to Boyle's *Reflections*, where this is beautifully applied to the improvement of all fragments of time by meditation.

[4] Such as the Manichees, see St. Aug. *Conf.* p. 340, O. T. note at the end, and Marcion. Tert. adv. M. lib. 4.
[5] This was done by his relics. St. Chrys. Hom. 1 *ad Pop. Ant.* § 2, *on the Statues*, p. 4, O. T.

believer (and this were no slight praise), or that he displayed more religious behavior than any other. And on this account after saying, "who is the first-fruits of Achaia," he does not hold his peace, but to prevent your suspecting it to be a glory of the world's, he added, "unto Christ." Now if in civil matters, he that is first seemeth to be great and honorable, much more so in these. As then it was likely that they were of low extraction, he speaks of the true noble birth and preëminency, and gives him his honors from this. And he says, that he "is the first-fruits," not of Corinth only, but of the whole nation, as having become as it were a door, and an entrance to the rest. And to such, the reward is no small one. For such an one will reap much recompense also from the achievements of others, in that he too contributed much toward them by beginning.

Ver. 6. "Greet Mary, who bestowed much labor on us."

How is this? a woman again is honored and proclaimed victorious! Again are we men put to shame. Or rather, we are not put to shame only, but have even an honor conferred upon us. For an honor we have, in that there are such women amongst us, but we are put to shame, in that we men are left so far behind by them. But if we come to know whence it comes, that they are so adorned, we too shall speedily overtake them. Whence then is their adorning? Let both men and women listen. It is not from bracelets, or from necklaces, nor from their eunuchs either, and their maid-servants, and gold-broidered dresses, but from their toils in behalf of the truth. For he says, "who bestowed much labor on us," that is, not on herself only, nor upon her own advancement, (see p. 520) (for this many women of the present day do, by fasting, and sleeping on the floor), but upon others also, so carrying on the race Apostles and Evangelists ran. In what sense then does he say, "I suffer not a woman to teach?" (1 Tim. ii. 12.) He means to hinder her from publicly coming forward (1 Cor. xiv. 35), and from the seat on the bema,[1] not from the word of teaching.[2] Since if this were the case, how would he have said to the woman that had an unbelieving husband, "How knowest thou, O woman, if thou shalt save thy husband?" (ib. vii. 16.) Or how came he to suffer her to admonish children, when he says, but "she

shall be saved by child-bearing[3] if they continue in faith, and charity, and holiness, with sobriety?" (1 Tim. ii. 15.) How came Priscilla to instruct even Apollos? It was not then to cut in sunder private conversing for advantage that he said this, but that before all, and which it was the teacher's duty to give in the public assembly; or again, in case the husband be believing and thoroughly furnished, able also to instruct her. When she is the wiser, then he does not forbid her teaching and improving him. And he does not say, who taught much, but "who bestowed much labor," because along with teaching (τοῦ λόγου) she performs other ministries besides, those in the way of dangers, in the way of money, in the way of travels. For the women of those days were more spirited than lions, sharing with the Apostles their labors for the Gospel's sake. In this way they went travelling with them, and also performed all other ministries. And even in Christ's day there followed Him women, "which ministered unto Him of their substance" (Luke viii. 3), and waited upon the Teacher.

Ver. 7. "Salute Andronicus and Junia my kinsmen."

This also looks like an encomium. And what follows is much more so. And what sort is this of? "And my fellow-prisoners." For this is the greatest honor, the noble proclamation. And where was Paul a prisoner, that he should call them "my fellow-prisoners?" A prisoner indeed he had[4] not been, but he had suffered things worse[5] than prisoners, in being not an alien only to his country and his family, but in wrestling with famine and continual death, and thousands of other things. For of a prisoner the only misfortune is this, that he is separated from his relations, and often has to be a slave instead of being free. But in this case one may mention temptations thick as snow-flakes, which this blessed person underwent by being carried and taken about, scourged, fettered, stoned, shipwrecked, with countless people plotting against him. And captives indeed

---

[1] A raised place in which the Clergy were, v. Suicer, and Bingham, b. viii. c. 6, § 1, and 9-12.

[2] Or "Teaching of the word." τοῦ λόγου τῆς διδασκαλίας, but we have τοῦ λόγου τῆς παρακλήσεως, Heb. xiii. 22. The word of Exhortation.

[3] St. C. does not seem to be here alluding to the former, but to the latter part of this very difficult passage. The most comprehensive view of it, on this interpretation, seems to be, that Christ has so hallowed all pain, that it has a saving influence in it: yet not in such wise saving, that the bearing of the great pain and peril of childbearing will atone for the neglect of the after labors of education. See Marlorate and Corn. *a Lapide. in loc.* The whole interpretation is questionable. Theoph. mentions some who take the words "the childbearing" of the birth of our Lord, which he rejects as not agreeing with what follows. But Estius justly observes, that the "abiding," etc. may be better applied to the man and wife.

[4] St Chrys. takes the word in its literal sense of a captive in war. If so meant it might be figurative, but it most likely refers either to an imprisonment, or to what he speaks of 2 Cor. xi. 26, as perils from robbers.

[5] Lit. "far more like a prisoner"—for Field reads αἰχμαλωτότερα for χαλεπώτερα.

have no further foe after they are led away, but they even experience great care from those who have taken them. But this man was continually in the midst of enemies, and saw spears on every side, and sharpened swords, and arrays, and battles. Since then it was likely that these shared many dangers with him, he calls them fellow-captives. As in another passage also, "Aristarchus my fellow-prisoner." (Col. iv. 10.) Then another praise besides. "Who are of note among the Apostles." And indeed to be apostles[1] at all is a great thing. But to be even amongst these of note, just consider what a great encomium this is! But they were of note owing to their works, to their achievements. Oh! how great is the devotion (φιλοσοφία) of this woman,[2] that she should be even counted worthy of the appellation of apostle![*] But even here he does not stop, but adds another encomium besides, and says, "Who were also in Christ before me."

For this too is a very great praise, that they sprang forth and came before others. But let me draw your attention to the holy soul, how untainted it is by vanity. For after glory such as his in kind and degree, he sets others before himself, and does not hide from us the fact of his having come after them, nor is ashamed of confessing this. And why art thou surprised at his not being ashamed of this, when he shunneth not even to parade before men his former life, calling himself "a blasphemer, and a persecutor?" (1 Tim. i. 13.) Since then he was not able to set them before others on this score, he looked out himself, who had come in after others, and from this he did find means of bestowing a praise upon them by saying, "Who were in Christ before me."

Ver. 8. "Greet Amplias my beloved."

Here again he passes encomiums upon his person by his love. For the love of Paul was for God, carrying countless blessings with it.

For if being loved by the king is a great thing, what a great encomium must it be to be beloved by Paul? For if he had not acquired great virtue, he would not have attracted his love? Since as for those who live in vice and transgressions he is accustomed (οἶδε) not only to abstain from loving them, but even to anathematize them. As when he says, "If any man love not the Lord Jesus, let him be accursed" (1 Cor. xvi. 22); and, "If any man preach any other gospel unto you than that ye have received, let him be accursed." (Gal. i. 8.)

Ver. 9. "Salute Urbane, my helper in the Lord."

This is a greater encomium than the other. For this even comprehends that. "And Stachys, my beloved." This again is an honor of the same kind.

Ver. 10. "Salute Apelles, approved in Christ."

There is no praise like this, being unblamable, and giving no handle in the things of God. For when he says, "approved in Christ," he includes the whole list of virtues. And on what ground does he nowhere say my Lord such an one, my Master this? It is because these encomiums were greater than those. For those are mere titles of rank (τιμῆς), but these are of virtue. And this same honor he paid them not at random, or as addressing several of inferior virtue with the high and great characters. For so far as he is addressing, and that too one along with another, and in the same letter, he honors them all alike. But by stating the praises particularly to each, he sets before us the virtue peculiar to each; so as neither to give birth to envy by honoring one and dishonoring another, nor to work in them listlessness and confusion, by giving them all the same dignity, though they did not deserve the same. See now how he again comes to the admirable women. For after saying, "Salute them which are of Aristobulus' household,"

Ver. 11. "Salute Herodion my kinsman; greet them which be of the household of Narcissus;"

Who, it is likely, were not so worthy as the afore-mentioned, on which account also he does not mention them all by name even, and after giving them the encomium which was suited to them, that of being faithful, (and this the meaning of,

"Which are in the Lord."

He again reverts to the women, and says,

Ver. 12. "Salute Tryphena and Tryphosa, who labor in the Lord."

And in regard to the former woman, he says that "she bestowed labor upon you," but

---

[1] St. Chrys. on 2 Cor. viii. 23, p. 215 O. T. and Phil. ii. 25, p. 104 O. T. takes this word to mean messengers of the Churches. Theodoret, on Phil. ii. 25, takes it to mean "Bishop," as on 1 Tim. ii. 8, he says, "they then called the same persons Bishops and Elders, but those who are now called Bishops they named Apostles." St. Chrys. Hom. *in St. Ignat.* call him an Apostle.

[2] Hammond reads the name Junias, and supposes a man to be intended.

[*] It is impossible to determine with certainty whether ἐπισήμοι ἐν τοῖς ἀποστόλοις (7) means that the persons referred to were themselves apostles, or merely that they were held in high esteem by the apostles. The interpretation of Chrys. (the former) is possible both in point of language and in view of the fact that ἀπόστολοι embraced more than the twelve in N. T. usage, e. g. Paul, Barnabas, and probably, James, the Lord's Brother (Gal. i. 19) (so Tholuck, Rückert, Ewald). The more probable view is that Andronicus and Junias [not Junia as Chrys., certainly not if his interpretation is correct; that a woman should have been an apostle is out of the question] are designated as distinguished, honorably known among (by) the apostles. (So De Wette, Philippi, Hofmann, Meyer). —G. B. S.

of these that they are still laboring. And this is no small encomium, that they should be in work throughout, and should not only work, but labor even. But Persis he calls beloved too, to show that she is greater than these.

For he says, " Salute my beloved Persis."

And of her great laborings he likewise bears testimony, and says, "which labored much in the Lord."

So well does he know how to name each after his deserts, so making these more eager by not depriving them of any of their dues, but commending even the slightest preëminence, and making the others more virtuous, and inciting them to the same zeal, by his encomiums upon these.

Ver. 12. " Salute Rufus, chosen in the Lord, and his mother and mine."

Here again the good things are without any drawback, since the son and the mother are each of such a character, and the house is full of blessing, and the root agreeth with the fruit ; for he would not have simply said, " his mother and mine," unless he had been bearing testimony to the woman for great virtue.

Ver. 14. "Salute Asyncritus, Phlegon, Hermas, Patrobas, Hermes, and the brethren which are with them."

Here do not be looking to how he starts them without any encomium, but how he did not reckon them, though far inferior, as it seems, to all, unworthy of being addressed by him. Or rather even this is no slight praise that he even calls them brethren, as also those that are after them he calls saints. For he says,

Ver. 15. " Salute Philologus, and Julius, and Nereus, and his sister, and Olympas, and all the saints which are with them ; "

Which was the greatest dignity, and unspeakable height of honor. Then to prevent any jealousy rising from his addressing one in one way and another in another, and some by name and some with no distinction, and some with more points of praise, and some with fewer, he again mingles them in the equality of charity, and in the holy kiss, saying,

Ver. 16. " Salute one another with an holy kiss."

To cast out of them, by this salutation, all arguing that confused them, and all grounds for little pride ; that neither the great might despise the little, nor the little grudge at the greater, but that haughtiness and envy might be more driven away, when this kiss soothed down and levelled every one. And therefore he not only bids them salute in this way, but sends in like manner to them the greeting from the Churches. For "there salute you,"

he says, not this or that person individually, but all of you in common,

" The Churches of Christ."

You see that they are no small gains that we earn from these addresses, and what treasures we should have passed hastily over, unless in this part of the Epistle also we had examined it with accuracy, such, I mean, as was in our power. So if there be found any man of wisdom and spiritual, he will dive even deeper, and find a greater number of pearls.[1]   But since some have often made it a question wherefore it was that in this Epistle he addressed so many, which thing he has not done in any other Epistle, we might say that it is owing to his never having seen the Romans yet, that he does this. And yet one may say, "Well, he had not seen the Colossians either, and yet he did not do anything of the kind." But these were more honorable than others, and had come thither from other cities, as to a safer and more royal city. Since then they were living in a foreign country, and they needed much provision for security,[2] and some of them were of his acquaintance, but some too were there who had rendered him many important services, he with reason commends them by letters ; for the glory of Paul was then not little, but so great, that even from his sending them letters, those who had the happiness to have an Epistle to them, gained much protection. For men not only reverenced him, but were even afraid of him. Had this not been so,[3] he would not have said, who had been " a succorer of many, and of myself also."[4] (v. 2.) And again, " I could wish that myself were accursed." (Rom. ix. 3.) And to Philemon he wrote and said, " as Paul the aged, and a prisoner of Jesus Christ." (Phil. 9.) And to the Galatians, " Behold, I Paul say unto you." (Gal. v. 2.) And, " Ye received me even as Jesus Christ." (ib. iv. 14.) And writing to the Corinthians he said, " Now some are puffed up, as though I would not come unto you." (1 Cor. iv. 18.) And again, " These things I have in a figure transferred to myself and to Apollos, that ye might learn in us not to think of men above that which is written." (ib. 6.)   Now from all these passages it is clear that all had a great opinion of him. Wishing then that they should feel on easy terms, and be in honor, he addressed each of

---

[1] He perhaps means something in the names, as well as in the facts implied ; most of them are significant. In several places, as where he refers to Ps. xix. and in his metaphors, he shows that he knew and valued allegorical interpretation, but he makes little public use of it.
[2] This is rather an unusual way of taking " πολλῆς ἀσφαλείας ἔδει ἀπολαύειν αὐτοῖς," but the sequel allows no other.
[3] i. e. had he not been so greatly esteemed.
[4] αὐτοῦ ἐμοῦ, even of myself.

them, setting forth their praise to the best advantage he might. For one he calls beloved, another kinsman, another both, another fellow-prisoner, another fellow-worker, another approved, another elect. And of the women, one he addresses by her title, for he does not call her servant of the Church in an undefined way (because if this were so he would have given Tryphena and Persis this name too), but this one as having the office of deaconess, and another as helper and assistant, another as mother, another from the labors she underwent, and some he addresses from the house they belonged to, some by the name of Brethren, some by the appellation of Saints. And some he honors by the mere fact of addressing them, and some by addressing them by name, and some by calling them first-fruits, and some by their precedence in time, but more than all, Priscilla and Aquila. (τοὺς περὶ Πρ. κ. Ἀ.) For even if all were believers, still all were not alike, but were different in their merits. Wherefore to lead them all to greater emulation, he keeps no man's encomiums concealed. For when they who labor[1] more, do not receive the greater reward also, many[2] become more listless. On this ground even in the kingdom, the honors, are not equal, nor among the disciples were all alike, but the three[3] were preëminent above the rest. And among these three again there was a great difference. For this is a very exact method observed by God even to the last. Hence, "one star differeth from another star in glory," (1 Cor. xv. 41), it says. And yet all were Apostles and all are to sit on twelve thrones,[4] and all left their goods, and all companied with Him; still it was the three He took. And again, to these very three, He said it was possible (ἐγχωρεῖν) that some might even be superior. "For to sit," He says, " on My right hand and on My left, is not mine to give, save to those for whom it is prepared." (Mark x. 40.) And He sets Peter before them, when He says, "Lovest thou Me more than these ? " (John xxi. 15.) And John too was loved even above the rest. For there shall be a strict examination of all, and if thou be but little better than thy neighbor, if it be even an atom, or anything ever so little, God will not overlook even this. And this even from of old one might see coming out. For even Lot was a righteous man, yet not so, as was

Abraham ; and Hezekiah again, yet not so as was David : and all the prophets, yet not so as was John.

Where then are they who with all this great exactness in view, yet will not allow that there is a hell ? For if all the righteous are not to enjoy the same lot, if they exceed others even a little ("for one star," it says, "differeth from another star in glory,") (1 Cor. xv. 41), how are sinners to be in the same lot with the righteous? Such a confusion as this even man would not make, much less God ! But if ye will, I will show you that even in the case of sinners, arguing from existing facts, there is this distinction, and exact just judgment. Now consider; Adam sinned, and Eve sinned, and both transgressed, yet they were not equally sinful. And therefore neither were they equally punished. For the difference was so great that Paul said, " Adam was not deceived but the woman being deceived was in the transgression."[5] And yet the deceit was one. But still God's searching examination pointed out a difference so great, as that Paul should make this assertion. Again, Cain was punished, but Lamech, who committed a murder after him, did not suffer near so great a punishment. And yet this was a murder, and that was a murder, and that so much the worse, because even by the example he had not become the better. But since the one neither killed his brother after exhortation, nor needed an accuser, nor shrunk from answering when God questioned him, but even without any accuser both pleaded again himself, and condemned himself more severely, he obtained pardon. But the other as having done the opposite was punished. See with what exactness God sifteth the facts. For this reason He punished those in the flood in one way, and those in Sodom in another; and the Israelites again, both those in Babylon, and those in Antiochus' time, in different ways: so showing that He keeps a strict account of our doings. And these were slaves for seventy years, and those for four hundred, but others again ate their children, and underwent countless other more grievous calamities, and even in this way were not freed, either they or those that were burnt alive in Sodom. "For it shall be more tolerable," He says, " for the land of Sodom and Gomorrha, than for that city." (Matt. x. 15.) For if He hath no care for us, either when we sin or when we do aright, perhaps there will be some reason in saying that there is no

---

[1] So Field with 4 Mss. Vulg. "do,"
[2] πολλοὶ would bear to be rendered " they often."
[3] i. e. Peter, James, and John.
[4] See Macarius, Hom. vi. v. fin. " So then many that were taught by Peter, came to repentance, and formed a new world, elect of God. You see how a beginning of judgment was manifested. For then a new world was made manifest. For then was power given them to sit and judge in this world. However, they will sit and give judgment at the coming of the Lord, in the resurrection of the dead."

[5] 1 Tim. ii. 14, whence it appears that St. C. looked upon the pains of childbirth as a punishment, though they were capable of being turned to good: see Gen. iii. 16.

punishment. But since He is so exceedingly urgent about our not sinning, and adopts so many means to keep us in the right, it is very plain that He punisheth the wicked, and also crowneth those that do right. But let me beg you to consider the unfairness of the generality. For they find fault with God because He so often long-suffering, overlooks so many that are impious, impure, or violent, without now suffering punishment. Again, if He threaten to punish them in the other world, they are vehement and pressing in their accusations. And yet if this be painful, they ought to accept and admire the other. But alas the folly! the unreasonable and asinine spirit! alas the sin-loving[1] soul, that gazes after vice! For it is from this that all these opinions have their birth. And so if they who utter these things should be minded to lay hold upon virtue, they will presently find themselves satisfied concerning hell also, and will not doubt. And where (it is said) and in what place is this hell? For some fablers say that it is in the valley of Josaphat, thus drawing that which was said about a certain by-gone war, to apply to hell.[2] But the Scripture does not say this. But in what place, pray, will it be? Somwhere as I think at least quite out of the pale of this world. For as the prisons and mines are at a great distance from royal residences,[3] so will hell be somewhere out of this world. Seek we not then to know where it is, but how we may escape it. Neither yet because God doth not punish all here, therefore disbelieve things to come. For merciful and long-suffering He is: that is why he threatens, and does not cast us into it forthwith. For "I desire not," He says, "the death of a sinner." (Ez. xviii. 32.) But if there is no death of a sinner, the words are but idle. And I know indeed that there is nothing less pleasant to you than these words. But to me nothing is pleasanter. And would it were possible at our dinner, and our supper, and our baths, and everywhere, to be discoursing about hell. For we should not then feel the pain at the evils in this world, nor the pleasure of its good things. For what would you tell me was an evil? poverty? disease? captivity? maiming of the body? Why all these things are sport compared to the punishment there, even should you speak of those who are tormented with famine all their life long; or those who are maimed from their earliest days, and beg,

even this is luxury compared to those other evils. Let us then continually employ ourselves with talking about these things.[4] For to remember hell prevents our falling into hell. Dost thou not hear St. Paul saying, "Who shall suffer everlasting punishment from the face of the Lord?" (2 Thess. i. 9.) Dost thou not hear what Nero's character was, whom Paul even calls the Mystery of Antichrist? For "the mystery of iniquity," he says, "already worketh." (ib. ii. 7.) What then? Is Nero to suffer nothing? Is Antichrist to suffer nothing? or the Devil nothing? Then he will always be Antichrist, and so the Devil. For from mischief they will not leave off, unless they be punished. "Yea," you say, "but that there is a hell everybody sees. But the unbelievers only are to fall into it." What is the reason, pray? It is because the believers acknowledge their Master. And what is this to the purpose? when their life is impure, they will on this ground be punished more severely than the unbelievers. "For as many as have sinned without law shall also perish without law: but as many as have sinned in the law shall be judged by the law." (Rom. ii. 12.) And, "The servant that knew his master's will, and did it not, shall be beaten with many stripes." (Luke xii. 47.) But if there is no such thing as giving an account of one's life, and all this is said in a loose way then neither will the Devil have vengeance taken upon him. For he too knows God, and far more than[5] men too, and all the demons know Him, and tremble, and own He is their Judge. If then there is no giving an account of our life, nor of evil deeds, then will they also clean escape. These things are not so, surely they are not! Deceive not yourselves, beloved. For if there is no hell, how are the Apostles to judge the twelve tribes of Israel? How cometh Paul to say, "Know ye not that we shall judge Angels? how much more things of this life?" (1 Cor. vi. 3.) How came Christ to say, "The men of Nineveh shall arise and condemn this generation" (Matt. xii. 41); and, "It shall be more tolerable for the land of Sodom in the day of judgment?" ib. xi. 24.) Why then make merry with things that are no subjects for merriment? Why deceive thyself and put cheats upon thy reason (παραλογίζῃ, om. τὴν ψυχήνσου)? Why fight with the love of God toward man? For it was through this that He prepared it, and threatened, that we might not be cast into it, as

[1] Mss. omit "pleasure-loving" and "love of pleasure" in the next line.
[2] Joel iii. 2, which is however a type of the last judgment. Isaiah xxx. 33. can hardly be meant, as the LXX. there has not the name Tophet.
[3] Ben. and 3 Mss. βασιλειων.
[4] This whole argument is nearly that of the close of Hom. 25. The object of it is clearly to keep their minds to the subject, as well as to convince gainsayers.
[5] So Field; others: "more than many."

having by this fear become better. And thus he that does away with speaking on these subjects doth nothing else than thrust us into it, and drive us thither by this deceit. Slacken not the hands of them then that labor for virtue, nor make the listlessness of them that sleep greater. For if the many be persuaded that there is no hell, when will they leave off vice? Or when will right be seen? I do not say between sinners and righteous men, but between sinners and sinners? For why is it that one is punished here, and another not punished, though he does the same sins, or even far worse? For if there be no hell, you will having nothing to say in defence of this to those who make it an objection. Wherefore my advice is, that we leave off this trifling, and stop the mouths of those that are gainsayers upon these subjects. For there will be an exact searching into the smallest things, both in the way of sins and in the way of good deeds, and we shall be punished for unchaste looks, and for idle words, and for mere reproachful words, and for drunkenness we shall render an account, as even for a

cup of cold water we shall receive a reward, and a sigh only. (Eccl. xii. 14.) For it says, "Set a mark upon the foreheads of the men that sigh and that cry." (Ez. ix. 4.) How then darest thou to say that He, who with so great exactness will search into our doings, threatened hell in bare words, and lightly? Do not, I beseech you, do not with these vain hopes destroy thyself and those that are persuaded by thee! For if thou disbelievest our words, make enquiry of Jews and Gentiles,[1] and all heretics. And all of them as with one mouth will answer that a judgment there shall be, and a retribution. And are men not enough? Ask the devils themselves, and thou wilt hear them cry, "Why hast thou come thither to torment us before the time." (Matt. viii. 29.) And putting all this together persuade thy soul not to trifle idly, lest by experience thou come to know there is a hell, but from this thou mayest be sobered, and so able to escape those tortures, and attain to the good things to come; whereof may we all partake by the grace and love towards man, etc.

HOMILY XXXII.

ROM. XVI. 17, 18.

"Now I beseech you, brethren, mark them which cause divisions and offences contrary to the doctrine which ye have learned, and avoid them. For they that are such serve not our Lord Jesus Christ, but their own belly; and by good words and fair speeches deceive the hearts of the simple."

AGAIN an exhortation, and prayer after the exhortation. For after telling them to "mark them which cause[2] divisions," and not to listen to them, he proceeds, "And the God of peace shall bruise Satan under your feet shortly:" and, "The grace of our Lord be with you." And notice how gently too he exhorts them: doing it not in the character of a counsellor, but that of a servant, and with much respect. For he calls them brethren, and supplicates them likewise. For, "I beseech you, brethren," (he says). Then he also puts them on the defensive by showing the deceitfulness of those who abused them. For as though they were not at once to be discerned, he says, "I beseech you to mark," that is, to be exceed-

ingly particular about, and to get acquainted with, and to search out thoroughly—whom, pray? why, "those that cause divisions and offences, contrary to the doctrine which ye have learned." * For this is, if anything the subversion of the Church, the being in divisions. This is the devil's weapon, this turneth all things upside-down. For so long as the body is joined into one, he has no power

* At Rome also there were, as in so many other places, those who, either within or in contact with the church, made divisions and perverted the true Christian teaching. The Epistle to the Romans deals but to a small extent directly with these persons. It is, in the main, constructive. Galatians is a letter on similar lines of teaching but more polemic in character. In the case of how few of the churches to which the apostle wrote could he spare himself the unpleasant task of warning them against heretics or immoral tendencies of life. In Corinth the abuses were chiefly of a moral and practical character. In Colossæ and perhaps in Ephesus, there was a Judeo-Gnostic theosophy which threatened the Christian faith of the people. The Roman church was, probably, predominantly Gentile and was a Pauline church, in the sense, that, though not founded by Paul, it had been trained in the Pauline "gospel," the type of doctrine more or less peculiar to that apostle. The extended refutation of Jewish claims to special divine favor in chaps. ii. and iii. as well as the consideration of the problem offered by the lapse of the Jews in chaps. ix., x., and xi., shows that there was an important Jewish element in the church, while these concluding warnings (17, 18) intimate the presence of Judaizing heretics who sought to conceal their real wickedness by smooth and plausible language and thus to lead innocent and unsuspecting Christians astray.—G. B. S.

[1] See Bp. Taplor, *Serm.* on Sir G. Dalston; and Bp. Butler, *Anal.* 1, 2, note n.
[2] Field with most Mss. omits ποιοῦντας; of course it is to be supplied from the context.

to get an entrance, but it is from division that the offence cometh. And whence is division? From opinions contrary to the teaching of the Apostles. And whence come opinions of this sort? From men's being slaves to the belly, and the other passions. For "such," he says, "serve not the Lord, but their own belly." And so there would be no offence, there would be no division, unless some opinion were thought of contrary to the doctrine of the Apostles. And this he here points out by saying, "contrary to the doctrine." And he does not say which we have taught, but "which ye have learned," so anticipating them, and showing that they were persuaded of and had heard them and received them. And what are we to do to those who make mischief in this way? He does not say have a meeting and come to blows, but "avoid them." For if it was from ignorance or error that they did this, one ought to set them right. But if they sin willingly, spring away from them. And in another place too he says this. For he says, "Withdraw from every brother that walketh disorderly" (2 Thess. iii. 6): and in speaking to Timothy about the copper-smith, he gives him the like advice, and says, "Of whom be thou ware also." (2 Tim. iv. 15.) Then also to lash (κωμῳδῶν) those who dare to do such things, he mentions also the reason of their devising this division. "For they that are such," he says, "serve not our Lord Christ, but their own belly." And this he said too when he wrote to the Philippians, "Whose god is their belly." (Phil. iii. 19.) But here he appears to me to intimate those of the Jews, whom he ever uses particularly to find fault with as gluttonous. For in writing to Titus too, he said of them, "Evil beasts, slow bellies." (Tit. i. 12, see v. 10.) And Christ also blames them on this head: "Ye devour widows' houses" (Matt. xxiii. 14), He says. And the Prophets accuse them of things of the kind. For, "My beloved," He says, "hath waxen fat and gross, and hath kicked" (Deut. xxxii. 15). Wherefore also Moses exhorted them, and said, "When thou hast eaten and drunken and art full, remember the Lord thy God." (ib. vi. 11, 12.) And in the Gospels, they who say to Christ, "What sign showest thou unto us?" (John vi. 30) pass over everything else, and remember the manna. So do they everywhere appear to be possessed with this affection. How then comest thou not to be ashamed at having slaves of the belly for thy teachers, when thou art a brother of Christ? Now the ground of the error is this, but the mode of attack is again a different disorder, viz. flattery. For it is by "fair speeches," he says, "that they

deceive the hearts of the simple." For their attention reaches only to words; but their meaning is not such, for it is full of fraud. And he does not say that they deceive you, but "the hearts of the simple." And even with this he was not satisfied, but with a view to making this statement less grating, he says,

Ver. 19. "For your obedience is come abroad unto all men."

This he does, not to leave them free to be shameless, but to win them beforehand with encomiums, and the number of his witnesses, to arrest their attention. For neither is it I alone that am the witness, but the whole world. And he does not say for your understanding, but, "your obedience:" that is, their compliance, which was evidence of much meekness in them. "I am glad therefore on your behalf." And this is no small encomium too. Then, after the praise, admonition. For lest, after liberating them from any charges against them, he should make them the more listless, as not being observed; he gives them another hint in the words,

"I would have you wise unto that which is good, and simple concerning evil."

You see then how he attacks them again, and that without their suspecting it. For this looks like intimating that some of them were apt to be led astray.

Ver. 20. "And the God of peace shall bruise Satan under your feet shortly."

For since he had spoken of those who "caused divisions and offences among them," he has mentioned "the God of peace" also, that they might feel hopeful about the riddance of these evils. For he that rejoiceth in this (i. e., peace) will put an end to that which makes havoc of it. And he does not say, will subject, but "will bruise" (Gen. iii. 19), which is a stronger expression. And not those people only, but also him who was the general over them herein, Satan. And not "will bruise" merely, but "under your feet," so that they may obtain the victory themselves, and become noble by the trophy. And the time again is made a ground of comfort. For he adds, "shortly." And this was prayer and prophecy as well at once. "The grace of our Lord Jesus Christ be with you."

That greatest weapon; that impregnable wall; that tower unshaken! For he reminds them of the grace, that he may give them the more alacrity. Because if ye have been freed from the ills more grievous by far, and freed by grace only, much more will ye be freed from the lesser, now ye have become friends too, and contribute your own share likewise. You see how he neither puts prayer without works, nor works without prayer. For after giving them credit for their obedience, than he prays ; to show that we need both, our own part as well as God's part, if we are to be duly saved. For it was not before only, but now too, even though we be great and in high esteem, we need grace from Him.

Ver. 21. "Timotheus my work-fellow saluteth you."

Observe the customary encomiums again. "And Lucius, and Jason, and Sosipater my kinsmen."

This Jason Luke also mentions, and sets before us his manliness also, when he says, that "they drew" him "to the rulers of the city, crying," etc. (Acts xvii. 5.) And it is likely that the others too were men of note. For he does not mention relations barely, unless they were also like him in religiousness.

Ver. 22. "I Tertius, who wrote this Epistle, salute you."

This too is no small encomium, to be Paul's amanuensis. Still it is not to pass encomiums on himself that he says this, but that he might attach a warm love to him on their part, for this ministration.

Ver. 23. "Gaius mine host (ξένος), and of the whole Church, saluteth you."

See what a crown he has framed for him, by bearing witness to such great hospitality in him, and brought in the entire Church into this man's house ! For by the word ξένον, used here, he means a host, not a guest. But when you hear that he was Paul's host, do not admire him for his munificence only, but also for his strictness of life. For except he were worthy of Paul's excellency, he would never have lodged there, since he, who took pains to go beyond[1] many of Christ's commands, would never have trespassed against that law, which bids us be very particular about who receive us, and about lodging with "worthy" persons. (Matt. x. 11.) "Erastus, the chamberlain of the city, salutes you, and Quartus a brother." There is a purpose in his adding "the chamberlain of the city," for as he wrote to the Philippians, "They of Cæsar's household salute you" (Phil. iv. 22), that he might show that the Gospel had taken a hold upon great folk, so here too he mentions the title with a view to the same object, and to show that, to the man who gives heed, neither riches are a hindrance, nor the cares of government, nor anything else of the kind.

Ver. 24. "The grace of our Lord Jesus Christ be with you all. Amen."*

See what we ought to begin and to end with everywhere ! For in this he laid the foundation of the Epistle, and in this he putteth on the roof, at once praying for the mother of all good things for them, and calling the whole of his loving-kindness to their mind. For this is the best proof of a generous teacher, to benefit his learners not by 'word only, but likewise by prayer, for which cause also one said, "But let us give ourselves contiually to prayers, and to the ministry of the word." (Acts vi. 4.)

Who is there then to pray over us, since Paul hath departed? These who[2] are the imitators of Paul. Only let us yield ourselves worthy of such intercession (συνηγορίας), that it may not be that we hear Paul's voice here only, but that hereafter, when we are departed, we may be counted worthy to see the wrestler of Christ.[3] Or rather, if we hear him here, we shall certainly see him hereafter, if not as standing near him, yet see him we certainly shall, glistening near the Throne of the king.[4] Where the Cherubim sing the glory, where the Seraphim are flying, there shall we see Paul, with Peter, and as a chief[5] and leader

---

* The Mss. authorities and vss. strongly favor the omission of v. 24 (as, A, B, C, ℵ, Copt., Eth., Vulg.) It appears to be a repetition of the benediction in v. 20 and is omitted by most critics.—G. B. S.

[2] Field thinks he points to the Bishop and clergy present.

[3] The following passage strongly illustrates what St. Chrysostom says, in the first page of the Introduction, of his affectionate intimacy with the Apostle, through meditation on his writings.

[4] The Martyrs were thought to be admitted to the Beatific Vision at once. See Tertullian de Anima, 55, but this is a subject on which the Fathers speak with caution.

[5] κορυφαῖον, not of the Apostles, but of the Saints in general. The manner in which St. Paul is coupled with St. Peter, is remarkable, as in the Roman Breviary, Vesp. et Laud. Commem. Com. de Apost. "Peter the Apostle, and Paul the Teacher of the Gentiles, these taught us Thy Law, O Lord. R. Thou shalt make them princes over all the earth." In the York Breviary, F. SS. App. Petr. et Paul, ad Vesp. Hymn, St. 2. "These are the two olive trees before the Lord (Zech. iv. 3), and the candlesticks beaming with light, the two bright luminaries of Heaven." And again, non impar Paulus huic. St. Augustin observes, ad Bonif. cont. du. Ep. Pelag. 1, 3, c. 3, Ben. t. 10. "When one says, 'The Apostle,' without saying what Apostle, no one understands any but Paul, because he is best known from the number of his Epistles, and because he labored most." St. Maximus, Hom. 5, de Nat. Petr. et Paul, "Therefore the blessed Peter and Paul are eminent among all, and have a kind of peculiar precedency, but between themselves, which is to be preferred to the other, is uncertain. For I think they are equal in merits because they are equal in suffering." He also says in the same Homily, " To Peter, as to a good Steward, He gave the key of the Kingdom of Heaven. On Paul, as on an able Teacher, He enjoined the mastership in the teaching of the Church ; that is, that whom the one has instructed unto salvation, the other may receive into rest ; that whose hearts Paul hath opened by the teaching of his words, to their souls Peter may open the Kingdom of Heaven. For Paul too did also in a manner receive the key of knowledge from Christ." And St. Gregory, 1, 1 Dial. c. 12. "The Apostle Paul is brother in Apostolical preëminence (principatu) to Peter, the first of the Apostles." See also St. Chrys. on Gal. i. 18, p. 25 O. T. where he says, " equal in dignity with him, for at present I will say no more," and Gal. ii. 8, p. 34 O. T. ; Tertull. adv. Marcion. 1, 5, and others, consider him especially intended in Jacob's blessing of Benjamin. St. Cyr. Hier. Cat. vi. p. 68, O. T. speaks of " That goodly pair, Peter and Paul, the Rulers of the Church." Many more passages might be cited, but these may suffice to show in what

---

of the choir of the Saints, and shall enjoy his generous love. For if when here he loved men so, that when he had the choice of departing and being with Christ, he chose to be here, much more will he there display a warmer affection. I love Rome even for this, although indeed one has other grounds for praising it, both for its greatness, and its antiquity, and its beauty, and its populousness, and for its power, and its wealth, and for its successes in war. But I let all this pass, and esteem it blessed on this account, that both in his lifetime he wrote to them, and loved them so, and talked with them whiles he was with us, and brought his life to a close there.[1] Wherefore the city is more notable upon this ground, than upon all others together. And as a body great and strong, it hath as two glistening eyes the bodies of these Saints. Not so bright is the heaven, when the sun sends forth his rays, as is the city of Rome, sending out these two lights into all parts of the world. From thence will Paul be caught up, from thence Peter. Just bethink you, and shudder (φρίξατε) at the thought of what a sight Rome will see, when Paul ariseth suddenly from that deposit, together with Peter, and is lifted up to meet the Lord. (1 Thess. iv. 17.) What a rose will Rome send up to Christ! (Is. xxxv. 1) what two crowns will the city have about it! what golden chains will she be girded with! what fountains possess! Therefore I admire the city, not for the much gold, not for the columns, not for the other display there, but for these pillars of the Church. (1 Cor. xv. 38.) Would that it were now given me to throw myself round (περιχυθῆναι) the body of Paul, and be riveted to the tomb, and to see the dust of that body that "filled up that which was lacking" after "Christ" Col. i. 24), that bore "the marks" (στίγματα,) (Gal. vi. 17) that sowed the Gospel everywhere yea, the dust of that body through which he ran to and fro everywhere! the dust of that body through which Christ spoke, and the Light shone forth more brilliant than any lightning, and the voice started out, more awful than any thunder to the devils! through which he uttered that blessed voice, saying, "I could wish that myself were accursed, for my brethren" (Rom. ix. 3), through which he spake "before kings, and was not ashamed!" (Ps. cxix. 46) through which we come to know Paul through which also Paul's Master! Not so

awful to us is the thunder, as was that voice to the demons! For if they shuddered at his clothes (Acts xix. 12), much more did they at his voice. This led them away captive, this cleansed out the world, this put a stop to diseases, cast out vice, lifted the truth on high, had Christ riding[2] upon it, and everywhere went about with Him; and what the Cherubim were, this was Paul's voice, for as He was seated upon those Powers, so was He upon Paul's tongue. For it had become worthy of receiving Christ, by speaking those things only which were acceptable to Christ, and flying as the Seraphim to height unspeakable! for what more lofty than that voice which says, "For I am persuaded that neither Angels, nor Principalities, nor Powers, nor things present, nor things to come, nor height, nor depth, nor any other creature, shall be able to separate us from the love of God, which is in Christ Jesus?" (Rom. viii. 38, 39.) What pinions doth not this discourse seem to thee to have? what eyes? (Ez. x. 12.) It was owing to this that he said, "for we are not ignorant of his devices." (2 Cor. ii. 11.) Owing to this did the devils flee not only at hearing him speak, but even at seeing his garments. This is the mouth, the dust whereof I would fain see, through which Christ spake the great and secret things, and greater than in His own person, (for as He wrought, so He also spake greater things by the disciples,[3]) through which the Spirit gave those wondrous oracles to the world! For what good thing did not that mouth effect? Devils it drave out, sins it loosed, tyrants it muzzled, philosophers' mouths it stopped, the world it brought over to God, savages it persuaded to learn wisdom, all the whole order of the earth it altered. Things in Heaven too it disposed what way it listed (1 Cor. v. 3, 4), binding whom it would, and loosing in the other world, "according unto the power given unto it." (2 Cor. xiii. 10.) Nor is it that mouth only, but the heart too I would fain see the dust of, which a man would not do wrong to call the heart of the world, and a fountain of countless blessings, and a beginning and element of our life. For the spirit of life was furnished out of it all, and was distributed through the members of Christ, not as being sent forth by arteries, but

---

esteem St. Paul was held among the Fathers, and at the same time that this did not interfere with their view of the prerogatives of St. Peter.

[1] Some Mss. add, "and they still possess his sacred body."

[2] See Macarius, Hom. 1. and 7, also Schaare *Orah. ap. Knorrium, Kabbala Denudata*, t. l. p. 507, where this interpretation is carried farther.
[3] Alluding to John xiv. 12 ; xvi. 12.

by a free choice of good deeds. This heart was so large, as to take in entire cities, and peoples, and nations. "For my heart" he says, "is enlarged." (ib. vi. 11.) Yet even a heart thus large, did this very charity that enlarged it many a time straiten and oppress. For he says, "Out of much affliction (θλίψεως) and anguish (συνοχῆς) of heart I wrote unto you." (ib. ii. 4.) I were desirous to see that heart even after its dissolution, which burned at each one that was lost, which travailed a second time with the children that had proved abortions (Gal. iv. 19), which saw God,[1] ("for the pure in heart," He says, "shall see God,") (Matt. v. 8) which became a Sacrifice, ("for a sacrifice to God is a contrite heart,") (Ps. li. 17) which was loftier than the heavens, which was wider than the world, which was brighter than the sun's beam, which was warmer than fire, which was stronger than adamant, which sent forth rivers, ("for rivers," it says, "of living water shall flow out of his belly,") (John vii. 38) wherein was a fountain springing up, and watering, not the face of the earth, but the souls of men, whence not rivers only, but even fountains of[2] tears, issued day and night, which lived the new life, not this of ours, (for "I live," he says, "yet not I, but Christ liveth in me," (Gal. ii. 20) so Paul's heart was His heart, and a tablet of the Holy Spirit, and a book of grace); which trembled for the sins of others, (for I fear, he says, lest by any means "I have bestowed labor upon you in vain; (ib. iv. 11) lest as the serpent beguiled Eve; (2 Cor. xi. 3) lest when I come I should find you not such as I would;") (ib. xii. 20) which both feared for itself, and was confiding too, (for I fear, he says, "lest by any means after having preached to others I myself should be a castaway," (1 Cor. ix. 27) And, "I am persuaded that neither angels nor powers shall be able to separate us;") (alluding to Rom. ix. 3) which was counted worthy to love Christ as no other man loved Him; which despised death and hell, yet was broken down by brothers' tears, (for he says, "what mean ye to weep and to break mine heart?") (Acts xxi. 13) which was most enduring, and yet could not bear to be absent from the Thessalonians by the space of an hour! (1 Thess. ii. 17; iii. 10.) Fain would I see the dust of hands that were in a chain, through the imposition of which the Spirit was furnished, through which the divine writings were written, (for "behold how large a letter I have written unto you with mine own hand:" (Gal. vi. 11) and again, "The salutation of me Paul with mine own hand,") (1 Cor. xvi. 21) of those hands at the sight of which the serpent "fell off into the fire." (Acts xxviii. 5.) Fain would I see the dust of those eyes which were blinded gloriously, which recovered their sight again for the salvation of the world; which even in the body were counted worthy to see Christ, which saw earthly things, yet saw them not, which saw the things which are not seen, which saw not sleep, which were watchful at midnight, which were not effected as eyes are.[3] I would also see the dust of those feet, which ran through the world and were not weary; which were bound in the stocks when the prison shook, which went through parts habitable or uninhabited, which walked on so many journeys. And why need I speak of single parts? Fain would I see the tomb, where the armor of righteousness is laid up, the armor of light, the limbs which now live, but which in life were made dead; and in all whereof Christ lived, which were crucified to the world, which were Christ's members, which were clad in Christ, were a temple of the Spirit, an holy building, "bound in the Spirit," (Acts xx. 22) riveted to the fear of God, which had the marks of Christ. This body is a wall to that City, which is safer than all towers, and than thousands of battlements. And with it is that of Peter. For he honored him while alive. For he "went up to see Peter." (Gal. i. 18) and therefore even when departed grace deigned to give him the same abode with him. Fain would I see the spiritual Lion. For as a lion breathing (Gr. sending,) (Cant. ii. 15) forth fire (πῦρ ἀφιεὶς) upon the herds of foxes, so rushed he upon the clan of demons and philosophers, and as the burst of some thunderbolt, was borne down into the host of the devil. (Luke xiii. 32.) For he did not even come to set the battle in array against him, since he feared so and trembled at him, as that if he saw his shadow, and heard his voice, he fled even at a distance. And so did he deliver over to him the fornicator, though at a distance, and again snatched him out of his hands (1 Cor. v. 5, 2 Cor. ii. 7, 11); and so others also, that they might be taught "not to blas-

---

[1] St. Augustin *de Gen. ad Lit.* xii. 35. He has many passages on "seeing God."
[2] Acts xx. 19; 2 Cor. ii. 4 cf. Luke xviii. 7; Ps. cxxxiv. 2.

[3] So all Mss. Sav. τῶν ὀφθαλμιώντων, and so Ben. translating it "as the envious," which must be the meaning if it is the true reading.

pheme." (1 Tim. i. 20.) And consider how he sent forth his own liegemen against him, rousing them, suppling them. And at one time he says to the Ephesians, "We wrestle not against flesh and blood, but against principalities and powers." (Eph. vi. 12.) Then too he puts our prize in heavenly places. For we struggle not for things of the earth, he says, but for Heaven, and the things in the Heavens. And to others, he says, "Know ye not that we shall judge Angels? how much more the things of this life?" (1 Cor. vi. 3.) Let us then, laying all this to heart, stand nobly; for Paul was a man, partaking of the same nature with us, and having everything else in common with us. But because he showed such great love toward Christ, he went up above the Heavens, and stood with the Angels. And so if we too would rouse ourselves up some little, and kindle in ourselves that fire, we shall be able to emulate that holy man. For were this impossible, he would never have cried aloud, and said, "Be ye imitators of me, as I am of Christ." (1 Cor. xi. 1.) Let us not then admire him only, or be struck with him only, but imitate him, that we too may, when we depart hence, be counted worthy to see him, and to share the glory unutterable, which God grant that we may all attain to by the grace and love toward man of our Lord Jesus Christ, through Whom, and with Whom, be glory to the Father, with the Holy Ghost, now and evermore. Amen.

INDEXES

INDEX OF SUBJECTS

ABRAHAM, his history a reproof to Jewish pride, 97; a pattern of hospitality, 276; his faith, 349, 385, 391, 395; his justification, 388; why circumcised, 389; his true children, 389, 391; his hospitality, 504; zeal for truth, 504; prayer for Sodom, 546.

Abuse, the best answer to, 242; disgraceful, 244; its reaction, 510; see *Reviling*.

Acts of the Apostles, little known in Chrysostom's time, 1; how profitable as sequel to the Gospels, 1; an inspired book, 2; important for doctrine, 3; written by St. Luke, 2; hence gives most fully the acts of St. Paul, ib.; may be called, "Demonstration of the Resurrection," 3, 5; "Polity of Holy Spirit," 18; Gospels, history of Christ, Acts of the Holy Ghost, 7.

Adam, fell by means of the Tempter, 322; a type of Christ, 402; his sin, 464; not equally punished with Eve, 557.

Adoption, spirit of, 442; incomplete until the redemption of the body, 446.

Advent, first, why delayed, 379; second, 451.

Affliction, uses of, 104; our schoolmaster, 262; see *Tribulation*.

Allegory, examples and use of, 480, 497.

Almsgiving, efficacy of, 147, 382; twice blessed to giver and receiver, 165, 485; a means of putting away sin, 166, 495; may be done without money, 166; a ministry, 89; needs much wisdom, 91, 549; encouragement to, 137.

Analogies, between things visible and invisible, 367, 372, 379, 382, sq., 393, 403, 465.

Angels, ever attendant on Christ's acts, 14; their joy, 393; their glory, 399; how employed for the Gospel, 121; Angel, the, in the burning bush, the Son of God, 103.

Anger, the passion of, 300; like a sword, to be kept for its right use, 98; against resentment of insults, 98, 198, 204; to con-

quer, is true greatness, 300; implanted in us as a safeguard to virtue, 111; virtuous anger how shown, ib.; a blind, reckless, passion, 43, 243; its ill effects on the body, 43.

Apostles, how changed after the Resurrection, 1; their discourses, 2; dwell most on Christ as man, ib.; above all on the Resurrection, ib.; rest assertions on testimony, 3; taught by deeds, 4; why they did not receive the Holy Ghost while Christ was with them, nor until ten days after the Ascension, 6; why ordered to tarry in Jerusalem, ib.; why they did not ask Christ to appoint one in place of Judas, 18; the new apostle must be an eye-witness, 21; they overcame the world, 29; their forbearance and gentleness, 183; their suffering, 455; accusations against, 512; severe to their own, gentle to those without, 78; not always under preternatural direction, 133; Christ's Code of Laws, written on Twelve Souls, 37; their miracles greater even than Christ's, 77; their holiness not caused by miracles, 83; their prerogative to impart the Spirit, 115; their proper work, preaching and prayer, 90; why they continued to resort to the temple, 50; and the synagogues, 179.

Applause in Church, reproved, 190, 458.

Arian arguments refuted, 12, note 2; 137, note 3; 72, 112, note 4.

Arrogance, source of, 204.

Asceticism, examples of, 381, 437.

BAPTISM, grace of, 152; in it we receive the substance of all good, 248; its more essential part the Spirit, 7; makes men dead to sin, 405; represents the cross, 409; relation to Christ's resurrection, 409; not to be repeated, 410; with us, the baptism with water and with the Spirit is one act; with the Apostles two, ib.; why not administered at Pentecost (in preference to

Easter Eve), ib., and note 3; sins after, doubly heinous, 8; but there are means of remission, 9; and recovery, 158; delay of, excuses for, 8, 152, sq; many delay it till their last moments, 9; *Traditio Symboli* in, 45, note 1; teaching after, 46; form of renunciation in, 9; followed by Holy Communion, 10; baptized, evil lives of the, a reproach to God, 152; the case of Apollos and the twelve disciples of John considered, 246, sq. and notes.

Baptism of John, 247.

Bible, neglect of, 553; order of its books, 336.

Bishop, his proper work, preaching and prayer, 90; ought not to have his time taken up with secular matters, ib.; the office coveted for dignity and honor, 22 sq.; its arduousness, ib.; simony of preferment-seeking, 24 sq.; bond of unity in the church, 393.

Body, all the members need each other, 231; not in itself evil, 411; why called "of death," 431; duties toward, 440; may become spiritual, 435, 440.

Boldness for the truth, with gentleness, 111; not forwardness, 290.

CALLING, not compulsory, 453.

Celibacy, optional, 420; its frequency, 434.

Charity, the perfection of, 41; necessity of, 380; nature of, 382; rarity of, 393.

Christ, equality with the Father, 2; the Apostles insist chiefly on his Resurrection, ib.; His deeds exemplify His words, 4; meaning of the name, 338; His twofold generation, 340; power of His name, 341; His humble birth, and estate, 348; His Cross a stumbling-block, 343, 348; begs in His members, 384 sq., 452, 457, 485; the Victim on His Table, 394; His Resurrection a proof of His sinlessness, 395; the love shown in His Death, 398; its effects, 410 so.; atoned for actual sins

THE END.

INDEX OF TEXTS

573

INDEX OF TEXTS.